AUSTRALIAN DICTIONARY

OF BIOGRAPHY

General Editor
JOHN RITCHIE

AUSTRALIAN
DICTIONARY
OF BIOGRAPHY

VOLUME 14 : 1940-1980

Di - Kel

General Editor
JOHN RITCHIE

Deputy General Editor
CHRISTOPHER CUNNEEN

MELBOURNE UNIVERSITY PRESS

Melbourne University Press
PO Box 278, Carlton South, Victoria 3053, Australia

First published 1996

Typeset by Supagraphics, Collingwood, Victoria
Printed in Australia by Brown Prior Anderson Pty Ltd

National Library of Australia Cataloguing-in-Publication entry

Australian dictionary of biography. Volume 14, 1940–1980,
Di-Kel.
ISBN 0 522 84236 4 (set).
ISBN 0 522 84717 X.

1. Australia—Biography—Dictionaries. 2. Australia—
History—1945- —Biography. I. Ritchie, John, 1941-. II.
Cunneen, Christopher, 1940-.

920.094

PREFACE

In 1940 Alex Gurney's comic strip, 'Bluey and Curley', centred on two larrikin Australian soldiers, first appeared in the pages of Melbourne's *Sun-News Pictorial*. In 1980 Special Broadcasting Services (S.B.S.) commenced television transmission in Sydney on channel VHF-0 and included an Italian variety programme. Many of the events that occurred and the people who rose to prominence in the intervening years provide the subject matter for volume 14 of the *Australian Dictionary of Biography*. It contains 666 entries by 572 authors and is the second of four in the 1940-1980 section which will include some 2700 lives.

Spanning the years from 1940 to 1980, volumes 13 to 16 illustrate such themes as immigration, accelerating industrialism, urbanization and suburbanization, and war (World War ll, Korea, Malaya and Vietnam). While other themes are also illuminated —material progress, increasing cultural maturity, conservative and radical politics, conflict and harmony, loss of isolation and innocence—the emphasis of the biographies is on the individuals. The entries throw light on the complexity of the human situation, and on the greatness and the littleness of moral response and actual behaviour which this can evoke. In volume 14 the subjects range from John Fraser, a national serviceman who died at the age of 23, to the temperance worker Cecelia Downing who lived until she was 94 years old. Although the majority of the men and women included in this volume flourished in the 1940-1980 period, a minority of the lives, like that of the anthropologist Alfred Haddon, who was born in 1855, reveal facets of Australian history long before 1940.

The two volumes of the 1788-1850 section, the four of the 1851-1890 section and the six of the 1891-1939 section were published from 1966 to 1990. Volume 13, the first of the 1940-1980 section, was published in 1993. The late Douglas Pike was general editor for volumes 1 to 5, Bede Nairn for volume 6, Nairn and Geoffrey Serle for volumes 7 to 10, Serle for volume 11 and John Ritchie for volumes 12 to 14. An index to volumes 1-12 was published in 1991 and the *A.D.B.* was produced on CD-ROM in 1996. The chronological division was designed to simplify production, for 7211 entries have been included in volumes 1-12 (volumes 1-2, for 1788-1850, had 1116 entries; volumes 3-6, for 1851-1890, 2053; volumes 6-12, for 1891-1939, 4042). For the period from 1788 to 1939, the placing of each individual's name in the appropriate section was determined by when he/she did his/her most important work (*floruit*). By contrast, the 1940-1980 section only includes individuals who died in this period. Volume 13 thus marked a change from the *floruit* to the 'date of death' principle. When volumes 15-16 have been completed, the *A.D.B.* will begin work on the period 1981-1990.

The choice of names for inclusion required prolonged consultation. After quotas were estimated, working parties in each State, and the Armed Services and Commonwealth working parties, prepared provisional lists which were widely circulated and carefully amended. Many of the names were obviously significant and worthy of inclusion as leaders in politics, business, the armed services, the church, the professions, the arts and the labour movement. Some have been included as representatives of ethnic and social minorities, and of a wide range of occupations; others have found a place as innovators, notorieties or eccentrics. A number had to be omitted through pressure of space or lack of material, and thereby joined the great mass whose members richly deserve a more honoured place, but thousands of these names, and information about them, have been accumulated in the biographical register at the A.D.B.'s offices in the Australian National University.

Most authors were nominated by working parties. The burden of writing has been shared almost equally by the staff of universities and by a variety of other specialists.

The A.D.B. is a project based on consultation and co-operation. The Research School of Social Sciences at the A.N.U. has borne the cost of the headquarters staff, of much research and of occasional special contingencies, while other Australian universities have supported the project in numerous ways. The A.D.B.'s policies were originally determined by a national committee composed mainly of representatives from the departments of history in each Australian university. In Canberra the editorial board has kept in touch with these representatives, and with working parties, librarians, archivists and other local experts, as well as with research assistants in each Australian capital city and correspondents overseas. With such varied support, the A.D.B. is truly a national project.

ACKNOWLEDGMENTS

The Australian Dictionary of Biography is a programme fully supported by the Research School of Social Sciences at the Australian National University. Special thanks are due to Professor K. S. Inglis for guidance as chairman of the editorial board, and to Professor H. G. Brennan, director of the R.S.S.S., and Mrs Pauline Hore, the school's business manager. Those who helped in planning the shape of the work have been mentioned in earlier volumes.

Within Australia the A.D.B. is indebted to many librarians and archivists, schools, colleges, universities, institutes, historical and genealogical societies, and numerous other organizations; to the editors of the *Northern Territory Dictionary of Biography*; to the Australian War Memorial, the Commonwealth Scientific and Industrial Research Organization, the Australian Institute of Aboriginal and Torres Strait Islander Studies and the Australian Archives; to the archives and public records offices in the various States and Territories, and to registrars of probates and of the Supreme and Family courts, whose co-operation has solved many problems; to various town and shire clerks; to the Returned & Services League of Australia, the Australian Department of Defence and the Australian Red Cross Society; to the Royal Society of New South Wales, the Royal Australasian College of Physicians, the Royal Australasian College of Radiologists, the Royal Australian College of General Practitioners, the New South Wales Medical Board, the Dental Board of New South Wales, the Royal Humane Society of New South Wales, the Medical Women's Society of New South Wales, the Institution of Radio and Electronic Engineers, the New South Wales Police Service, the Australian Federation of Business and Professional Women, the Institute of Chartered Accountants, the Chartered Institute of Transport in Australia, the Chartered Institute of Company Secretaries in Australia, the Combined Pensioners and Superannuants Association of New South Wales, the State Chamber of Commerce, the Chamber of Automotive Industries of New South Wales, the Chamber of Manufactures of New South Wales, the Motor Traders Association of New South Wales, the National Australia Bank, the Westpac Banking Corporation, the Australasian Performing Right Association, the Australian Music Examinations Board, International P.E.N. Australia, the Australian Club, the United Grand Lodge of New South Wales, the Loyal Orange Institution of New South Wales, the Royal Sydney Golf Club, the Australian Golf Club, the New South Wales Ladies' Golf Union, the Australian Jockey Club, Hockey New South Wales, the Surf Life Saving Association of Australia, the South Sydney District Rugby League Football Club, the Salvation Army, and Relationships Australia, all in Sydney; to the Royal Melbourne Institute of Technology, the Royal Australasian College of Surgeons, the Royal Australian Chemical Institute, the Royal Australian College of Ophthalmologists, the Australian Institute of Radiographers, the Baker Medical Research Institute, the Dental Board of Australia, the Australian Institute of Physics, the Australian Academy of Technological Sciences and Engineering, the Society of Automotive Engineers, the Australian Institute of Mining and Metallurgy, the Institute of Patent Attorneys of Australia, the Churches of Christ in Australia, the Mercy Public Hospitals Inc., the Villa Maria Society for the Blind, the Victorian Artists Society, the Education History Research Service and the Australian Hockey Association, all in Melbourne; and to the Royal Australian Institute of Architects, the Australian Academy of Science, the

Institution of Engineers, Australia, the National Heart Foundation of Australia and the Air Power Studies Centre, all in Canberra. Warm thanks for the free gift of their time and talents are due to contributors, to members of the editorial board and to the working parties.

For particular advice the A.D.B. owes much to Stuart W. Alldritt, Cecily Close, Chris Coulthard-Clark, Denis Darmanin, Don Fairweather, Stephen Foster, Bill Gammage, Bryan Gandevia, Elena Govor, David Horner, Tom Lawrence, Norm Neill, Hank Nelson, Marianne Pikler, Caroline Simpson, Kenneth Smith, F. B. Smith, R. J. M. Tolhurst, Peter Yeend, Norbert Zmijewski, and to the staff of the National Library of Australia.

Essential assistance with birth, death and marriage certificates has been provided by the co-operation of registrars in New South Wales, Queensland, South Australia, Tasmania, Victoria, Western Australia, the Northern Territory and the Australian Capital Territory; by the General Register offices in London and Edinburgh; by the registrars-general in Fiji and Papua New Guinea; by the Department of Home Affairs, South Africa, and the registrar of births and deaths in Hong Kong; by the bureaus of vital statistics in the State Health departments in California, Iowa, Maryland, Michigan, New Jersey and New York; by the Immigration and Naturalization Service, Washington, the State Board of Health, Indianopolis, the county clerks' offices in Cook and Crawford counties, Ohio, and Youngstown County, Illinois, United States of America; by the National Archives of Canada, Ottawa, and the registrars-general, Toronto and Ontario; by the Public Registry, Valetta, Malta; by the City Archives, Oslo and Kristiansand, Norway, and Stockholm, Sweden; by the mayors of Auteuil, Chantilly, Dijon, Neuilly-sur-Seine, Nice, and 1e, 7e and 14e arrondissements, Paris, France; by civil status offices in Rome and Milan, Italy; by the registry offices at Aachen, Frankfurt-am-Main, Freiburg, Kreuzberg von Berlin and Munich, and the district court of Lubeck, Germany; by the city archives at Basel, Switzerland; by the civil registration offices at Antwerp, Belgium; by the National Archives in Warsaw, Poland; by the National Archives and the Central Statistical Office, Budapest, Hungary; by the Lithuanian State Archives; by St Nicholas Church, Svendborg, Denmark; by the consuls-general for the Czech Republic, Latvia and Poland, in Sydney; by the Belgian, Croatian, Danish, Mexican, Slovak and Spanish embassies, and by the South African High Commission, Canberra.

For other assistance overseas, thanks are due to Pauric Dempsey and Oonagh Walsh, Dublin, and Betty Iggo, Edinburgh; to Susan Luensmann of Remote Control, Virginia, U.S.A.; to the universities of Bristol, Cambridge, Durham, London, Oxford and Sheffield, Imperial College, London, the London School of Economics and Political Science, University College and King's College, London, St John's College, Cambridge, Oriel College, Keble College and St Edmund Hall, Oxford, and Winchester College, Winchester; to the University of Edinburgh, George Watson's College, Edinburgh, the Edinburgh College of Art, and the universities of Aberdeen, Glasgow and St Andrew's, Scotland; to the National University of Ireland, the University of Dublin and Trinity College, Dublin; to the University of Wales, Aberystwyth; to Humboldt-Universität and the Freie Universität, Berlin, Albert-Ludwigs-Universität, Freiburg, Ludwig-Maximilians-Universität, Munich, Georg-August Universität, Göttingen, and the Technische Universität, Dresden, Germany; to the Université Stendhal, Grenoble, France, the Karolinska Institute, Stockholm, the Pontificio Collegio Urbano 'de Propaganda Fide', Rome, and Charles University, Prague; to Columbia University, New York, Harvard University, the Colorado School of Mines, Clark University, Massachusetts, Renselaar Polytechnic Institute, Troy, New York, Cape Western University, Cleveland, Ohio, and the universities of California, Chicago, Miami, Michigan, Minnesota and Pennysylvania, U.S.A.; and to the

University of Malaya, the Victoria University of Wellington, the University of Otago and Otago Girls' School, Dunedin, New Zealand.

Gratitude is also due to the Royal Anthropological Institute, the Royal College of Music, the Royal Academy of Music, the Royal College of Organists, the Royal Academy of Dramatic Art, the Royal College of Physicians, the Royal College of Surgeons of England, the Royal College of Obstetricians and Gynaecologists, the Royal Veterinary College, the Royal Geographical Society, the Royal Institute of British Architects, the Institute of Physics, the Society of Radiographers, the Institution of Civil Engineers, the Institution of Mechanical Engineers, the Institute of Marine Engineers, Trinity College of Music, the Associated Board of the Royal Schools of Music, the Guild Hall, the British Academy, the Commonwealth Institute, the Inner Temple, the College of Arms, the Wellcome Trust, the Central Chancery of the Orders of Knighthood, Lambeth Palace Library, the Royal Air Force Museum, the Air Historical Branch, R.A.F., and the British Architectural Library, all in London; to the Royal Society of Chemistry, Cambridge, the Royal Northern College of Music, Manchester, the Guild of Church Musicians, Surrey, the Military History Society, Berkshire, and the Ministry of Defence, Gosport, Hayes, Innsworth and London, England; to the Royal College of Physicians and the Royal College of Surgeons of Edinburgh, the Royal College of Physicians and Surgeons of Glasgow, and the Royal Highland and Agricultural Society of Scotland, to the staffs of the *Österreichisches Biographisches Lexikon*, Vienna, *Dictionary of Canadian Biography*, Toronto, and *Dictionary of New Zealand Biography*, Wellington, to the reference librarian, Alexander Turnbull Library, Wellington, the New Zealand Defence Force, Wellington, and the New Zealand Institute of Forestry; to the Society of American Foresters, Maryland, and the Institute of Electrical and Electronics Engineers, Inc., New Jersey, U.S.A.; and to other individuals and institutions who have co-operated with the A.D.B.

The A.D.B. deeply regrets the deaths of such notable contributors as J. I. Ackroyd, Harold E. Albiston, R. R. Andrew, Jean F. Arnot, C. R. Badger, B. D. Beddie, Jean Caswell Benson, Catherine Berndt, Rupert J. Best, L. J. Blake, D. G. Bowd, W. S. Bracegirdle, J. J. Bray, Greg Brown, C. A. Burmester, Ian Burn, Ivan Chapman, Michael J. Cigler, Margaret Bridson Cribb, Frances A. M. L. Derham, George Dicker, Nicholas Draffin, E. W. Dunlop, Jill Eastwood, K. T. H. Farrer, Jim Faull, L. F. Fitzhardinge, Harley W. Forster, Lyndsay Gardiner, G. H. Gellie, M. Gibson, W. D. H. Graham, Nancy Gray, F. C. Green, Patsy Hardy, Alexandra Hasluck, L. M. Heath, John Horan, R. A. Howell, L. J. Hume, S. H. Hume, F. Jacka, G. F. James, Donald H. Johnson, Nancy Keesing, Mary Lazarus, G. L. Lockley, Margeurite Mahood, K. S. Millingen, E. J. Minchin, Christopher Morris, Fred Morton, Leonard J. T. Murphy, F. M. Neasey, W. A. Neilson, Neville Parker, John E. Price, John H. Reeves, E. L. Richard, J. E. L. Rutherford, C. E. Sayers, Michael Shepherd, Bertha M. Smith, Monica Starke, H. J. Summers, T. G. Vallance, Russel Ward, Alan Warden and A. O. Watson.

Grateful acknowledgment is due to the director and staff of Melbourne University Press, and to Sheila Tilse, Anne-Marie Gaudry, Daniel Campbell, Heather Robinson and Julie Inder who worked for the A.D.B. while Volume 14 was being produced.

WORKING PARTIES

Armed Services
P. J. Burness, H. J. Coates, C. D. Coulthard-Clark, A. J. Hill, D. M. Horner (chair), J. M. McCarthy, Perditta McCarthy, P. M. Mulcare, A. Staunton, A. W. Stephens, A. J. Sweeting.

Commonwealth
N. Brown, Patricia Clarke, G. Gilmore, I. R. Hancock, Cameron Hazlehurst (chair), Anthea Hyslop, R. Hyslop, Margot Kerley, C. J. Lloyd, G. Powell, J. Thompson.

New South Wales
Margy Burn, J. J. Carmody, C. Cunneen, R. Curnow, F. Farrell, S. Garton, E. M. Goot, Beverley Kingston (chair), J. K. McLaughlin, A. J. Moore, N. B. Nairn, Heather Radi, Jill Roe, G. Souter, G. P. Walsh.

Queensland
Ysola Best, Pat Buckridge, M. D. Cross, Lyn Finch, M. W. French, J. C. H. Gill, Helen Gregory, I. F. Jobling, W. R. Johnston (chair), Lorna McDonald, Dawn May, S. J. Routh, C. G. Sheehan, V. T. Vallis.

South Australia
W. L. Gammage, Joyce Gibberd, R. M. Gibbs, P. A. Howell, Helen Jones, J. H. Love, J. D. Playford (chair), Judith Raftery, Jenny Tilby Stock, Patricia Stretton, R. E. Thornton.

Tasmania
G. P. R. Chapman, Shirley Eldershaw, R. A. Ferrall, Margaret Glover, Elizabeth McLeod, S. Petrow, Anne Rand, O. M. Roe (chair), G. T. Stilwell.

Victoria
W. A. Bate, G. R. Browne, Mimi Colligan, B. J. Costar, G. J. Davison, F. J. Kendall, J. F. Lack, Marilyn Lake, R. A. Murray, J. R. Poynter (chair), J. D. Rickard, A. G. Serle, Judith Smart, F. Strahan.

Western Australia
Wendy Birman (chair), D. Black, G. C. Bolton, Michal Bosworth, P. J. Boyce, Dorothy Erickson, Jenny Gregory, Lenore Layman, Margaret Medcalf, C. Mulcahy, K. Spillman, A. C. Staples.

AUTHORS

AKERS, David:
Kavanagh.
ALLEN, Maree G.:
Hanigan.
ALLEY, Diane B.:
Harris, R.
ANDERSON, Grant:
Dixon, Sir O.
ANDERSON, Hugh:
Harrington, E.
ANDRÉ, Roger:
Haigh.
ANTHONY, Delyse:
Haenke.
ARNDT, H. W.
Downing, R.
ATCHISON, John:
Foxall.
ATKINSON, Anne:
Fong.
AUDLEY, R. M.:
Garside; Hartigan.

BACKHOUSE, Sue:
Holmes, E.
BAKER, Jean:
Ibbott.
BARLOW, Leila:
Honner.
BARLOW, Lorraine:
Eddy, W.
BARTER, Margaret:
Green, C.
BASSETT, Jan:
Irving.
BATE, Weston:
Fisher, C.; Hone.
BATT, Chris:
Dwyer, J. J.
BECKETT, Jeremy:
Dutton, G.
BEECHEY, Norman:
Drysdale.
BELLAMY, Suzanne:
Guthrie,
BELLIS, Clare:
Innes.
BELTON, Hilery:
Hill, A.
BENJAMIN, Rodney L.:
Fink, L.
BENNET, Darryl:
Hill, C.; Howden.
BENNETT, Gwen:
Hedditch.
BENNETT, Scott:
Guy.

BERGSTRUM, Lynette A.:
Fallon.
BERNDT, Catherine*:
Karloan.
BEST, Ysola:
Fraser, S.
BIDDINGTON, Judith:
Hutton.
BIRMAN, Jeremy:
Dwyer, Sir J. P.
BIRMAN, Wendy:
Ferguson, J. E.; Genders; Geneff; Gooch;
Juan.
BLAAZER, D. P.:
Holloway.
BLACK, David:
Hutchison.
BLACK, Margaret L.:
Issachsen.
BLACKMUR, Douglas:
Hanlon.
BOLAND, T. P.:
Gilroy.
BOLTON, Barbara:
Geddes.
BOLTON, G. C.:
Durack; Evatt, H.; Hughes, T. J.; Hunt,
B.; Johnson, H.
BOND, Jennifer:
Hamilton, J.
BONGIORNO, Frank:
Drakeford.
BONNIN, Margriet R.:
Hill, M.
BONNIN, Nancy:
Hill, M.
BOOTH, Douglas:
Evans, H.
BOSWORTH, Michal:
Hooton, H.
BOXALL, Helen:
Hateley.
BOYCE, Peter:
Frewer, Jenkins.
BOYLE, Michael:
Fraser, J.
BRADBURY, Keith:
Grant.
BRICE, Ian D.:
Gordon, C.
BRIGNELL, Lyn:
Farquharson.
BRITAIN, I. M.:
Finch.
BROOME, Richard:
Jerome.
* deceased

xiii

BROOMHAM, Rosemary:
Gallop; Hook.
BROUN, Malcolm D.:
Dovey.
BROWN, D. J.:
Earl.
BROWN, Elaine:
Foll; Gray, G.
BROWN, N. A.:
Greenwood, I.
BROWN, Nicholas:
Downing, R.
BROWNE, Geoff:
Farran-Ridge; Fisken; Joshua.
BRUNE, Peter:
Gurney, A. S.
BURDEN, Rosemary:
Hardy, K.
BURKE, Janine:
Hester.
BURNESS, Peter:
Hunt, J.
BURROWS, G. H.:
Fitzgerald.
BUTLER, Roger:
Feint.
CABLE, K. J.:
Hammond; Hope, J.; Hulme-Moir.
CAIN, Frank:
Ellis, C.
CALLAWAY, Frank:
Ford, C.
CAMPION, Edmund:
Dunlea.
CANTRELL, Carol:
Finckh.
CAPLAN, Sophie:
Gottshall.
CAPPER, Betty:
Hall, I.
CAREY, Hilary M.:
Egan, K. R.
CARMODY, John:
English.
CARNELL, Ian:
Fry, T.; Garrett, T.
CARR, Robert:
Heffron.
CARRON, L. T.:
Jacobs, M.
CASHMAN, R. I.:
Hynes.
CASTLES, Ian:
Jackson, L.
CHAPMAN, Christopher:
Downing, D.
CHAPMAN, R. J. K.:
Frost, C. W.; Henty.
CHAPPELL, Louise:
Ford, A.
CHARLESWORTH, Max:
Gibson, A. B.
CHEATER, Christine:
Kaberry.

CHRISTESEN, Nina:
Goldman; Grishin.
CLARK, Sebastian:
Harris, N.
CLARK, W. R.:
Herington.
CLEMENT, Cathie:
Greene, A.
CLEMENTS, Graham:
Donoghue.
CLIFFORD, H. Trevor:
Hebert, A.
CLUNE, David:
Enticknap.
COBB, Joan E.:
Gough.
COBCROFT, M. D.:
Jamieson, K.
COCKBURN, S.:
Dumas, Sir F.
COHEN, Alex:
Hunt, B.
COLE, Anna:
Fisher, B.
COLE, David R.:
Jarman.
COLEMAN, James H.:
Hauslaib.
COLLIGAN, Mimi:
Forbes, A.
COLLINS PERSSE, Michael D. de B.:
Hake.
COLLINS, Diane:
Doyle.
COLLIS, Brad:
Diesendorf.
COLTHEART, Lenore:
Farrar.
COLYER, Ian G.:
Harvey, H. H.
CONSANDINE, Marion:
John.
COSSART, Yvonne:
Inglis.
COSTAR, B. J.:
Dodgshun; Gair; Hocking; Hyland.
COULTHARD-CLARK, C. D.:
Eaton; Hannah; Hosking, R.
COWAN, Peter:
Drake-Brockman.
COX, Don:
Hinton.
CRAIG, Terry:
Edgley.
CRANSTON, Frank:
Dunbar.
CRAWFORD, I. McL.:
Gosse, G.
CRESWELL, C. C.:
Garran.
CRIBB, Margaret Bridson*:
Fadden.

* deceased

xiv

CROFT, Julian:
Jones, T. H.
CROSS, Manfred:
Jones, A.
CRUX, Narelle:
Jones, N.
CUNNEEN, Chris:
Gloucester; Greenhalgh; Greenwood, E.;
Jensen, L.
CURNOW, Ross:
Glasheen.
CURRY, N. G.:
Frederick.
CURTAIN, John:
Fabinyi.

DABSCHECK, Braham:
Kelly, Sir W.
DALE, Barbara:
Evatt, M.
DALLY, John:
Ingamells.
DARE, Anthony:
Ellis, F.
DARRAGH, Thomas A.:
Keble.
DAVIES, L. W.:
Hooke.
DAVIS, R. P.:
Hytten.
DAW, E. D.:
Griffith.
DAWSON, Daryl:
Dixon, Sir O.
DENHOLM, Decie:
Dutton, E.
DERKENNE, Warren:
Helmore.
DERMODY, Kathleen:
Duncan, J. S.; Gollan, R.; Jamieson, S.
DEVER, Maryanne:
Eldershaw, F.
DICKSON, D. J.:
Groves, W.
DOBREZ, Patricia:
Dransfield.
DOLLING, Alison M.:
Dolling.
DONALDSON, Tamsin:
Johnson, J.
DORLING, Philip:
Gollan, H.
DOWNS, Ian:
Fenbury.
DREYFUS, Kay:
Harrhy.
DUNCAN, Alan T.:
Groves, H.
DUNSTAN, David:
Disney.
DURDIN, Joan:
Hanton.
DURRANT, L. L.:
Frank.

DUWELL, Martin:
Haley.
DUYKER, Edward:
Fink, E.

EAGLE, Mary:
Dobell.
EATON, Brian*:
Headlam; Hely.
EDDY, J.:
Forro; Kelly, A.
EDGAR, Suzanne:
Fabro; James, J.
EDGELOE, V. A.:
Horner.
EDWARDS, John:
Dunshea.
EDWARDS, W. H.:
Dodd, T.
EGAN, Bryan:
Disher; Hayden.
ELSE-MITCHELL, R.:
Ferguson, Sir J. A.
ELY, Richard:
Drysdale.
EMILSEN, Susan:
Fuller.
ENNIS, Helen:
Jerrems.
ERICKSON, Dorothy:
Heap; Holdsworth.
EVANS, H. D.:
Fry, A.
EVANS, Kate:
Dunckley.

FAHEY, Charles:
Galvin.
FAHY, Kevin:
Joris.
FAIRWEATHER, D. F.:
Fairweather, A.; Keast.
FENNER, Frank:
Fairley; Florey; Gottschalk.
FERRALL, R. A.:
Dollery; Harris, L.
FINN, Rosslyn:
Ford, L.
FIRTH, Beverley:
Hutchens.
FISCHER, G. L.:
Finnis, H.
FISHER, Tim:
Hirschfeld-Mack.
FLANNERY, Nancy Robinson:
Hume.
FLETCHER, B. H.:
Ellis, M. H.; Hall, H.
FLETCHER, Philippa L.:
Gibson, G.
FLOREANI, Carmel:
Fabro.

* deceased

LAIRD, J. T.:
Glassop.
LANCASTER, Paul A. L.:
Gregg.
LANGMORE, Diane:
Duncan, A. C.; Hunt, R.; Hurley.
LARACY, Hugh:
Hannan, J.
LAURENT, John:
Fowler, S.
LAURIE, Godfrey:
Harrison, H.
LAWRIE, Margaret:
Frith.
LAWSON, Valerie:
Fenston; Goldberg.
LAX, Mark:
Goldsmith, A.
LAYMAN, Lenore:
Dumas, Sir R.; Embry.
LEE, Andrew:
Fraser, J. McI.
LEE, David:
Fletcher, J.
LEE, Stuart:
Howarth.
LEMON, Andrew:
Grey-Smith; Johnstone, W.
LEONG, Roger:
Findlay.
LEVER, Susan:
Flower.
LEWIS, D. C.:
Hayes, H.; Humphries.
LEWIS, Julie:
Dicks.
LEWIS, Miles:
Gawler.
LEWIS, Wendy:
Fisher, B.
LIVINGSTONE, Stanley E.:
Dwyer, F.
LLOYD, C. J.:
Finnan; Fraser, A. D. & J.; Gabb.
LOEWALD, Klaus:
Dullo; Halpern, B.
LOMAS, L.:
Howey.
LONDEY, Peter:
Field, J.
LONERGAN, John P.:
Ennor.
LONGHURST, Robert I.:
Henderson, T. M.

MCCARTHY, John:
Drummond, Sir P.
MCDONALD, G. L.:
Flynn.
MCDONALD, Jan:
Gourgaud; Hanslow; Henderson, J.
MCDONALD, Lorna:
Fraser, D. L.; Fraser, H.; Kelley.

MCGUIRE, John:
Julius.
MCHUGH, Mary:
Gibson, F.
MCINTYRE, Darryl:
Hennessy.
MACINTYRE, Stuart:
Harrison, Sir E.
MCKAY, K. J.:
Hunt, H.
MACKINNON, Alison:
Dorsch.
MACKINOLTY, Judy:
Hay, M.
MCLAREN, John:
Elder.
MCLAUGHLIN, John Kennedy:
Holmes, J. D.
MCPHEE, John:
Grieve; Hardess (Hardress); Harris, J.
MCPHERSON, B. H.:
Douglas, E. & R.
MAHER, Brian:
Haydon.
MAIDMENT, Ewan:
Duncan, J. C.
MALTBY, George F.:
Housley.
MANDLE, W. F.:
Fleetwood-Smith.
MANSFIELD, Joan:
Flockhart.
MARCHANT, N. G.:
Gardner.
MARCHANT, Sylvia:
Hoinville.
MARKEY, Ray:
Healy, J.
MARKUS, Andrew:
Heyes.
MARSDEN, Susan:
Hogben.
MARTIN, Pamela:
Fowell.
MASLEN, Joan:
Everett, M.
MAUNDERS, David:
Fairbairn.
MAYNARD, Margaret:
Jenyns.
MEABANK, Julann:
Hoy.
MELLEUISH, Gregory:
Hughes, R.
MELLOR, Elizabeth J.:
Gutteridge; Heinig.
MERCER, Peter:
Fidler.
MILLINGEN, K. S.*:
Goddard.
MINCHAM, Hans:
Ding.

* deceased

MITCHELL, Bruce:
Harris, H.
MOORE, Andrew:
Fitzpatrick, R.
MOORE, Clive R.:
Fatnowna.
MORAN, Rod:
Gray, T.
MORGAN, F. J.:
Edman.
MORGAN, Marjorie:
Green, H. G.
MORONEY, Tim:
Foley, T.; Harvey, H. J.
MORRIS, Deirdre:
Joyce, D.
MORRIS, Richard:
Fowler, J. R.; Hannam.
MOXHAM, Gwenyth C.:
Gibb.
MOYAL, Ann:
Gibson, R. B.
MULLINS, P. J.:
Grout; Hutcheon.
MULLINS, Steve:
Haddon.
MURPHY, Lynne:
Hollinworth.
MURPHY, Paul:
Joyce, A.
MURRAY-SMITH, Nita:
Gibson, D.

NASH, Heather:
Hicks.
NAYUTAH, Jolanda:
Kay.
NELSON, George E.:
James, T. & S.
NELSON, H. N.:
Grahamslaw.
NELSON, Judy:
Howell.
NETHERCOTE, J. R.:
Heydon.
NEWELL, Jenny:
Kellway.
NEWTON, Dennis:
Drummond, V.; Hughes, P.
NORTHEY, R. E.:
Haylen.
NOSCOV, Gordon:
Evans, E.

O'BRIEN, Anne:
Egan, K. M.
O'BRIEN, E. J.:
Jewell.
O'CARRIGAN, Catherine:
Healy, M.
O'CONNOR, Patrick:
Hayes, R.
O'DONOGHUE, Frances:
Duncombe.

O'NEILL, Brian:
Hodge.
O'NEILL, Frances:
Everett, P.
O'NEILL, Sally:
Fielding.
O'SHAUGHNESSY, Peter:
Fowler, J. B.
OAKES, Gerard:
Kavanaugh.
OPPENHEIMER, Jillian:
Ervin.
OPPENHEIMER, Melanie:
Keighley.

PANOZZO, Steve:
Gurney, A. G.
PANTON, Jean:
Hamilton, J.
PARBERY, D. G.:
Harrison, T.
PARKER, Neville*:
Hill, C.
PARNABY, Owen:
Foster, J.
PATERSON, M. S.:
Jaeger.
PATMORE, Greg:
Dougherty.
PATRICK, Alison:
Joske.
PATRICK, Ross:
Hirschfeld.
PEARCE, Barry:
Jackson, J. R.
PEARN, John H.:
Flecker.
PEEL, Victoria:
Fowler, J.
PEERS, Juliet:
Dyring.
PEOPLES, Jo:
Hackett.
PERKINS, John:
Ferrier.
PESMAN, Ros:
Gentile.
PICKLES, John:
Fargher.
PIERCE, Peter:
Dunn, M.; Fullarton; Hoysted; Iverson.
PIKE, A. F.:
Goffage.
PILGER, Alison:
Down; Gates; Greenwood, E.
PLAYFORD, John:
Hannan, A.
POYNTER, J. R.:
Grimwade.
PRESLAND, Gary:
Dunn, R.
PRESTON, A. N.:
Fanning.
* deceased

xix

PROUST, Anthony:
James, J. A.

RADFORD, Robin:
Helbig.
RADI, Heather:
Evans, E. P.; Jackson, A.
RADIC, Maureen Thérèse:
Johnson, G.
RAHEMTULA, Aladin:
Hart.
RALPH, Gilbert M.:
Espie.
RAMSON, W. S.:
Johnston, G. K.
RAND, A.:
Elliott, A.
RASMUSSEN, Carolyn:
Jessop.
RAWSON, Don:
Keane, R.
RAYNER, K.:
Halse.
REES, Jacqueline:
Francis; Holland.
REEVES, Tim:
Duncan, G.
REGAN, Kerry:
Fitzpatrick, A.
REID, Richard E.:
Kelliher.
REIGER, Kerreen M.:
Frame.
REYNOLDS, Peter:
Fowell.
RICH, Jenny:
Gagai.
RICH, Joe:
French, H.
RICKARD, John:
Elliott, L.
RICKWOOD, Frank K.:
Gray, K.
RIDDEL, R. J.:
Gargett.
RITCHIE, John:
Eastwood; Edmonds; Evans, I.
ROBERTS, G. W.:
Heading.
ROBERTS, Jan:
Ewart.
ROBIN, Libby:
Isaac.
ROBINSON, Margaret:
Keldie.
ROE, J. I.:
Drummond, R.
ROE, Michael:
Higgins.
RUTLEDGE, Martha:
Ellis, M. J.; Fraser, K. A.; Galea; Gerald; Greig; Griffiths; Gunn, M.; Herron; Kater.
RYAN, Jan:
Giles.

ST LEON, Mark Valentine:
Honey.
SALSBURY, Stephen:
Gandon.
SALTER, David:
Goossens.
SAMPSON, Margaret:
Kavanagh.
SCHREUDER, D. M.:
Flakelar.
SCULLY, P. J.:
Foskett.
SEARS, J. S.:
Field, T. & H.
SEKULESS, Peter:
Holland.
SENYARD, J. E.:
Hillgrove.
SERLE, Geoffrey:
Fitzpatrick, B.; Gilray.
SHANAHAN, Martin:
Garland.
SHARMAN, R. C.:
Eldershaw, P.
SHARP, Martin:
Godson.
SHARWOOD, R. L.:
Fullagar.
SHAW, George P.:
Halford.
SHAW, J. W.:
Falstein.
SHEPHERD, Rebecca:
Ewers.
SIMPSON, Caroline:
Fairfax, M.; Hordern, S.; Hordern, U.
SMART, Judith:
Downing, C.; Hopman.
SMITH, Colin:
Fowler, R.
SMITH, David I.:
Dunrossil.
SMITH, James:
Du Rieu.
SMITH, Neil:
Ferres.
SNOOKS, G. D.:
Hunter, A.
SOLDATOW, Sasha:
Hooton, H. A.
SOUTER, Gavin:
Fairfax, J.; Gellert.
SPARKE, Eric:
Hudson, Sir W.
SPAULL, Andrew:
Ellwood; Eltham.
SPEARRITT, Peter:
Gregory; Hooker.
SPEER, Albert:
Haszler.
SPURLING, T. H.:
Heymann.
STATHAM, Pamela:
Jacoby.

STAUNTON, Anthony:
French, J.
STEELE, Peter:
Gleeson.
STELL, Marion K.:
Hamilton, M.
STEPHENS, Alan:
Holmwood.
STEVEN, Margaret:
Jensen, Sir J.; Keir.
STEVENSON, Brian F.:
Dittmer.
STEWART, E. D. J.:
Gartrell.
STOCK, Jenny Tilby:
Duncan, Sir W.; Hincks.
STRAHAN, Frank:
Gibson, A. H.; Holyman.
STURMA, Michael:
Gordon, L.
SUTCLIFFE, Harold J.:
Henderson, T.
SUTTON, R.:
Edgar.
SVENSEN, Stuart:
Healy, J.
SWAIN, Peter L.:
Hosking, E.
SWAN, Doris H.:
Gilbert.
SWANTON, Bruce:
Hanson, F.

TATE, Audrey:
Dreyer; Hallstrom; Kaylock.
TAYLOR, Helen:
Fitzgibbons.
TAYLOR, Jack:
Goodwin.
TAYLOR, Robert I.:
Gunn, R.; Henry.
TEALE, Ruth:
Everett, G.
TEICHMANN, Max:
Jorgensen.
THEARLE, M. John:
Earnshaw.
THOMAS, Daniel:
Hawkins, H.
THOMPSON, L. H. S.:
Fraser, A. J.
THOMPSON, Roger C.:
Halligan.
TILSE, Sheila:
Keane, F.
TIMMS, Peter:
Halpern, S.
TOLLEY, Michael J.:
Gask.
TOWNSLEY, W. A.:
Green, F.
TRAPEZNIK, Alexander:
Grenda.

TRAVERS, Richard:
Kelly, M.
TREGEAR, Peter John:
Hanson, R.
TRIGELLIS-SMITH, Syd:
Dunkley.
TROWER, Ursula:
Healy, M. G.
TUCK, Ruth:
Harris, M.
TURNBULL, Sue:
Dyer.
TURTLE, Alison M.:
Hodgkinson.

UTTING, Muriel:
Harris, B.

VALLANCE, T. G.*:
Edwards, A.
VAN DISSEL, Dirk:
Hawker.
VAN DISSEL, Mary E. B.:
Hawker.

WADE, George C.:
Jackson, W.
WALKER, J. D.:
Fraser, K. A.
WALL, Barbara:
Jury.
WALL, Leonard:
Fletcher, J. A.
WALLAM, Dawn:
Dinah.
WALLER, Ken:
Green[e], A. J. & A. E.
WALSH, G. P.:
Falkiner; Gaffney; Hall, W.; Hardwick;
Holmes, J. M.; Jeffery.
WARD, H. A.:
Fantl.
WATERHOUSE, Richard:
Howard.
WATERS, Jill:
Grandi.
WATSON, David:
Forbes, Sir D.
WATSON, Jack:
Haviland.
WATSON, Tom:
Hanger, T.
WATTS, Owen F.:
Glew.
WEBB, Martyn:
Green, W.
WEBBER, Caroline:
Edmunds.
WEEKS, Phillipa:
Eggleston.
WEICKHARDT, L. W.:
Hartung.

* deceased

WEST, Janet:
Hilliard.
WHITE, M. W. D.:
Hanger, Sir M.
WHITE, Richard:
Flick.
WHITE, Sally A.:
Hetherington; Isaacson.
WHITE, Shirley J.:
Felan.
WHITMORE, Raymond L.:
Hornibrook.
WICKS, B. M.:
Fouché.
WILLIAMS, Jennifer:
Hughes-Jones.
WILSON, David:
Douglas, G.; Jackson, J. F. & L. D.
WILSON, Helen J.:
Haritos.
WILSON, Jan:
Jacobs, A.
WISE, Tigger:
Elkin.

WOOD, James:
Godfrey.
WORRALL, Airlie:
Foletta.
WRIGHT, Andrée:
Hansen.
WRIGHT, R.:
Horsfall.

YARWOOD, A. T.:
Flinn.
YOUNGER, Coralie:
Fink, E.

ZAINU'DDIN, A. G. Thomson:
Dodd, B.; Hay, O.
ZAMMIT, Alan:
Farncomb.
ZANADVOROFF, J. A.*:
Goloubev.
ZERNER, Burt:
Jones, T. G.

* deceased

A NOTE ON SOME PROCEDURES

Differences of opinion exist among our authors, readers and the editorial board as to whether certain information should normally be included—such as cause of death, burial or cremation details, and value of estate. In this volume our practices have been as follows:

Cause of death: usually included, except in the case of those aged over 70.

Burial/cremation: included when details available.

Value of estate: included where possible for categories such as businessmen, and if the amount is unusually high or low. In recent years, when the practice developed of distributing assets early in order to avoid estate and probate duties, the sum is not always meaningful; moreover, at times it is impossible to ascertain full details. Hence we have resorted to discretionary use.

Some other procedures require explanation:

Measurements: as the least unsatisfactory solution we have used imperial system measurements (as historically appropriate), followed by the metric equivalent in brackets.

Money: we have retained £ for pounds for references prior to 14 February 1966 (when the conversion rate was A£1 = A$2).

Religion: stated whenever information is available, but there is often no good evidence of actual practice, e.g. the information is confined to marriage and funeral rites.

[q.v.]: the particular volume is given for those included in volumes 1-13, but not for those in this volume. Note that the cross-reference [q.v.] now accompanies the names of all who have separate articles in the *A.D.B.* In volumes 1-6 it was not shown for royal visitors, governors, lieutenant-governors and those Colonial Office officials who were included.

Small capitals: used for relations and others when they are of substantial importance, though not included in their own right; these people are also q.v.'d.

Floruit and 'date of death': for the period 1788 to 1939, the placing of subjects in volumes 1 to 12 was determined by when they flourished; in contrast, volumes 13 to 16 (for the period 1940 to 1980) only include people who died in those years.

CORRIGENDA

Every effort is made to check every detail in every article, but a work of the *A.D.B.*'s size and complexity is bound to contain some errors.

Corrigenda have been published with each volume. A consolidated list, including corrections made after the publication of volume 12 (1990), forms part of the *Index* (1991). A list of corrigenda compiled since 1993 accompanies volume 14.

Only corrections are shown; additional information is not included; nor is any reinterpretation attempted. The exception to this procedure occurs when new details about parents, births, marriages and deaths become available.

Documented corrections are welcomed. Additional information, with sources, is also invited, and will be placed in the appropriate files for future use. In both cases, readers should write to:

> The General Editor
> Australian Dictionary of Biography
> Research School of Social Sciences
> Australian National University
> CANBERRA ACT 0200
> Australia.

REFERENCES

The following and other standard works of reference have been widely used, though not usually acknowledged in individual biographies:

Australian Encyclopaedia, 1-2 (Syd, 1925), 1-10 (1958), 1-12 (1983)

Biographical register for various Australian parliaments: (A. W. Martin & P. Wardle *and*

H. Radi, P. Spearritt & E. Hinton *and* C. N. Connolly—New South Wales; D. Black & G. Bolton—Western Australia; K. Thomson & G. Serle *and* G. Browne—Victoria; D. B. Waterson *and* D. B. Waterson & J. Arnold—Queensland; H. Coxon, J. Playford & R. Reid—South Australia; S. & B. Bennett—Tasmania; and J. Rydon—Commonwealth)

O'M. Creagh and E. M. Humphris (eds), *The V.C. and D.S.O.: a complete record*... 1-3 (Lond, 1934)

Dictionary of National Biography (Lond, 1885-1986)

H. M. Green, *A History of Australian Literature*, 1-2 (Syd, 1961, 2nd edn 1971), revised by D. Green (Syd, 1984-85)

C. A. Hughes and B. D. Graham, *A Handbook of Australian Government and Politics 1890-1964* (Canb, 1968) and *1965-1974* (1977); *Voting for the Australian House of Representatives 1901-1964*, with corrigenda (Canb, 1975), for *Queensland Legislative Assembly 1890-1964* (Canb, 1974), for *New South Wales*... (1975), *Victoria*... (1975), and *South Australian, Western Australian and Tasmanian Lower Houses*... (1976), D. Black, *An Index to Parliamentary Candidates in Western Australian Elections 1890-1989* (Perth, 1989)

F. Johns, *Johns's Notable Australians* (Melb, 1906), *Fred Johns's Annual* (Lond, 1914); *An Australian Biographical Dictionary* (Melb, 1934)

A. McCulloch, *Encyclopedia of Australian Art* (Lond, 1968), 1-2 (Melb, 1984), revised

S. McCulloch (Syd, 1994)

E. M. Miller, *Australian Literature*... *to 1935* (Melb, 1940), extended to 1950 by F. T. Macartney (Syd, 1956)

W. Moore, *The Story of Australian Art*, 1-2 (Syd, 1934), (Syd, 1980)

P. Serle, *Dictionary of Australian Biography*, 1-2 (Syd, 1949)

Who's Who (Lond), and *Who's Who in Australia* (Syd, Melb, present and past edns)

W. H. Wilde, J. Hooton & B. Andrews, *The Oxford Companion to Australian Literature* (Melb, 1985), 2nd ed (1994)

ABBREVIATIONS USED IN BIBLIOGRAPHIES

AA	Australian Archives	Dept	Department
AAA	Amateur Athletic Association	*DNB*	*Dictionary of National Biography*
ABC	Australian Broadcasting Commission/Corporation		
ACT	Australian Capital Territory	ed	editor
ADB	Australian Dictionary of Biography, Canb	edn	edition
		Edinb	Edinburgh
Adel	Adelaide	Eng	England
ADFA	Australian Defence Force Academy, Canb		
		Fr	Father (priest)
Agr	Agriculture, Agricultural		
AIF	Australian Imperial Force	Geog	Geographical
AJCP	Australian Joint Copying Project	Govt	Government
ALP	Australian Labor Party	HA	House of Assembly
AMPA (SLV)	Arts, Music and Performing Library, State Library of Victoria	Hist	History, Historical
		Hob	Hobart
ANU	Australian National University, Canberra	HR	House of Representatives
		HSSA	Historical Society of South Australia
ANUABL	ANU Archives of Business and Labour		
ANZAAS	Australian and New Zealand Association for the Advancement of Science	Inc	Incorporated
		Inst	Institute, Institution
		intro	introduction, introduced by
A'sia/n	Australasia/n		
Assn	Association	*J*	*Journal*
Aust	Australia/n	JCU	James Cook University of North Queensland, Townsville
AWM	Australian War Memorial, Canberra		
		LA	Legislative Assembly
Bass L	Adolph Basser Library, Australian Academy of Science, Canberra	LaTL	La Trobe Library, Melbourne
		Launc	Launceston
		LC	Legislative Council
Bd	Board	L	Library
BHP	Broken Hill Proprietary Co. Ltd	Lond	London
bib	bibliography	*Mag*	*Magazine*
biog	biography, biographical	Melb	Melbourne
BL	J. S. Battye Library of West Australian History, Perth	MDHC	Melbourne Diocesan Historical Commission (Catholic), Fitzroy
Brisb	Brisbane	mf	microfilm/s
		MJA	*Medical Journal of Australia*
c	circa	ML	Mitchell Library, Sydney
CAE	College of Advanced Education	Mort L	Mortlock Library of South Australiana
Canb	Canberra		
cat	catalogue	ms/s	manuscript/s
CO	Colonial Office, London	mthly	monthly
co	company		
C of E	Church of England	nd	date of publication unknown
Com	Commission/er	NFSA	National Film and Sound Archive, Canberra
comp	compiler		
Corp	Corporation/s	NL	National Library of Australia, Canberra
CSIRO	CommonwealthScientific and Industrial Research Organization		
		no	number
cte	committee	np	place of publication unknown
Cwlth	Commonwealth	NSW	New South Wales

NSWA	The Archives Authority of New South Wales, Sydney
NT	Northern Territory
NY	New York
NZ	New Zealand
OL	John Oxley Library, Brisbane
p, pp	page, pages
pc	photocopy
PD	*Parliamentary Debates*
PIM	*Pacific Islands Monthly*
PNG	Papua New Guinea
PP	*Parliamentary Papers*
PRGSSA	*Proceedings of the Royal Geographical Society of Australasia (South Australian Branch)*
priv pub	private publication
PRO	Public Record Office
Procs	*Proceedings*
pt	part/s
PTHRA	*Papers and Proceedings of the Tasmanian Historical Research Association*
pub	publication, publication number
Q	*Quarterly*
QA	Queensland State Archives, Brisbane
Qld	Queensland
RAHS	Royal Australian Historical Society (Sydney)
RG	Registrar General's Office
RGS	Royal Geographical Society
RHSQ	Royal Historical Society of Queensland (Brisbane)
RHSV	Royal Historical Society of Victoria (Melbourne)
RMIT	Royal Melbourne Institute of Technology
Roy	Royal
RWAHS	Royal Western Australian Historical Society (Perth)
1st S	First Session

2nd S	Second Session
SA	South Australia/n
Sel	Select
SLNSW	State Library of New South Wales
SLSA	State Library of South Australia
SLT	State Library of Tasmania
SLV	State Library of Victoria
SMH	*Sydney Morning Herald*
Soc	Society
SRSA	State Records Office, South Australia
supp	supplement
Syd	Sydney
TA	Tasmanian State Archives, Hobart
Tas	Tasmania/n
T&CJ	*Australian Town and Country Journal*
Trans	*Transactions*
ts	typescript or transcript
UK	United Kingdom
UNSW	University of New South Wales
UNE	University of New England, Armidale
Univ	University
UPNG	University of Papua New Guinea
US	United States of America
V&P	*Votes and Proceedings*
VHM(J)	*Victorian Historical Magazine (Journal)*
v, vol	volume
Vic	Victoria/n
WA	Western Australia/n
WAA	Western Australian State Archives
*	deceased

D

DICKS, ROBIN ELIZABETH (1940-1975), nurse and aviatrix, was born on 8 September 1940 at Subiaco, Perth, second daughter of Horace (Horatio) Clive Miller [q.v.10], an aeronautical engineer from Victoria, and his Adelaide-born wife (Dame) Mary Gertrude, daughter of M. P. Durack [q.v.8]. Educated at Loreto Convent, Nedlands, Robin trained at Royal Perth Hospital and graduated in 1962 with the State nurses' medical prize. By 1964 she was a triple-certificated nurse at St Anne's Hospital, Mount Lawley. With the encouragement of Dr Harold Dicks (d.1987), honorary president of the Western Australia branch of the Royal Flying Doctor Service of Australia, in 1966 she upgraded her private pilot's licence (1962) to a commercial one.

In 1967 Sabin oral vaccine replaced the Salk vaccine for immunization against poliomyelitis in Western Australia. Sister Miller obtained permission from the Department of Health to carry out a programme in the North and North-West. She borrowed money to buy a Cessna 182 and, on 22 May 1967, began a series of flights which took her to remote areas, many of them occupied by Aboriginal communities. Because the Sabin vaccine was administered on sugar cubes by a woman emerging alone from a small aircraft, Aboriginal children called her 'the tchooger bird lady'. In November 1967 Dicks asked Miller to co-pilot a Beechcraft Baron from Oakland, California, United States of America, to Perth for the R.F.D.S. Granted temporary leave from the immunization project, she undertook what was to be the first of nine ferry-trips during her career. In 1968, flying solo, she brought a single-engined Horizon from Paris to Perth. She completed the immunization programme in October 1969, after administering over 37 000 doses of vaccine and flying 43 000 miles (69 200 km).

That year Miller was awarded a diploma of merit by the Associazione Nazionale Infermieri, Mantova, Italy; in 1970 she received the Nancy Bird (Walton) award as Australia's woman pilot of the year. Replacing her Cessna with a Mooney Mark 21 and obtaining a first-class instrument rating, she regularly flew aircraft for the R.F.D.S., despite the initial hostility of male doctors. She was always on call and flew in all types of weather, responding to a range of emergencies and coping with difficult or frightened patients. Tall, fair and elegant, she was conscientious, cheerful and popular. Reacting to those who expected her to don men's clothing, she wore skirts rather than trousers on her flights. Her book, *Flying Nurse* (1971), provided a lively account of her career.

Robin Miller married the recently divorced Harold Dicks on 4 April 1973 in the registrar's office, Canberra. That year she and Rosemary de Pierres competed in the Powder Puff 'Derby', a trans-America race for female pilots. In May 1974 Robin had a melanoma removed from her thigh. She died of cancer on 7 December 1975 in South Perth and was buried with Catholic rites in Broome cemetery; she had no children. In 1976 she was posthumously awarded the Paul Tissandier diploma by the Fédération Aeronautique Internationale and the Brabazon cup by the Women Pilots' Association of Great Britain. A representation of her Mooney aircraft was unveiled at Jandakot airport, Perth, on 20 May 1978. Harold compiled *Sugarbird Lady* (1979) from Robin's manuscript and diaries.

D. Popham (ed), *Reflections* (Perth, 1978); Aust Medical Assn (WA), *AMA Branch News*, Nov 1987; Skywest Airlines Pty Ltd, *Destinations*, May-June 1991; *Age* (Melb), 5 Mar 1966, 10 Oct 1969; *Herald* (Melb), 18 Apr, 13 Dec 1968, 9 Apr, 18 July 1973; *Sun News-Pictorial* and *West Australian*, 8 Dec 1975; R. Miller [Dicks] diaries *and* Mary Durack diaries (held by the executors of Dame Mary Durack's estate, Perth); family information.

JULIE LEWIS

DIESENDORF, WALTER (1906-1975), electrical engineer, was born on 14 December 1906 in Vienna, son of Eljukim Wolf Diesendorf, travelling salesman, and his wife Henie, née Thau. At the Technische Hochschule (later Technical University of Vienna) Walter qualified in engineering (1929) and obtained a doctorate of technical sciences (1934). Fluent in English, French and German, he worked with a leading electrical manufacturer. When Germany annexed Austria in 1938, he fled his country and emigrated to Australia.

In February 1939 Diesendorf was employed by the Sydney County Council as an assistant-engineer (3rd class). The selection of an 'alien Austrian Jew' over Australian engineers created a public outcry which only ended when the council stated that it had appointed Diesendorf to perform 'abstruse technical calculations for high voltage transmission systems which could not be done by an ordinary engineer in Australia or anywhere else'. On 22 December that year he married a schoolteacher Dr Margaretha

1

Amalia Gisela Máté at the district registrar's office, Paddington; a Viennese Catholic, she had followed him to Australia. Walter and Margaretha were naturalized in 1944. Diesendorf quickly established himself in the local engineering community. In World War II he planned the development of Sydney's 33 000-volt underground-cable network. He subsequently designed transmission works for a major expansion of power output from the New South Wales coalfields. A 'sleeves-up' man, 'he stoked boilers and drove bulldozers at Bunnerong Power Station' to keep city lights burning during postwar strikes.

Disillusioned by changes to the administration of the State's electricity supply, in August 1950 Diesendorf joined the Snowy Mountains Hydro-electric Authority as system design engineer. His first task was 'to determine the transmission voltage for the interconnections' to the New South Wales and Victorian 'load centres'. At that time 220 000 volts was the highest level in general use worldwide. Diesendorf's investigations led to the adoption of a 330 000-volt system.

His joint-paper, 'The 330kV Transmission System in New South Wales', published in the *Journal of the Institution of Engineers, Australia*, in 1955, was awarded the institution's electrical engineering prize. He was to win the prize again in 1962. Leaving his family in Sydney, Diesendorf moved to Cooma in 1957. Next year he was appointed senior executive engineer for electrical and mechanical activities: his design work helped to ensure the success of these aspects of the Snowy Mountains power and irrigation project.

A member of the Institution of Engineers, Australia (fellow 1957), the Société des Ingénieurs de France and the Conférence Internationale des Grands Réseaux Electriques à Haut Tension, Diesendorf retired from the authority in 1967 and accepted a senior lectureship in electrical engineering at the University of Sydney. In the 1970-71 winter semester he was visiting professor at the Rensselaer Polytechnic Institute, Troy, New York State, United States of America. His *Overvoltages on High Voltage Systems* (Troy, 1971) became a standard text. Survived by his wife and two sons, he died of cancer on 29 December 1975 at Camperdown and was buried with Catholic rites in Northern Suburbs cemetery.

K. Bittman (ed), *Strauss to Matilda* (Syd, 1988); Archives, Snowy Mountains Hydro-electric Authority, Cooma, NSW.   BRAD COLLIS

DINAH, ROBERT BEAUFORT (c.1898-1962), Aboriginal leader and boxer, was born about 1898 at Wagin, Western Australia, son of 'King' George Jerong Dinah and his wife who was named on Beaufort's marriage certificate as Caroline Dooran. Like many Nyungars in the early 1900s, the family undertook contract clearing for farmers in the Arthur River and Wagin district of the State. George had a homestead farm with a river frontage at Kunalling. In 1906 he was reported to the Lands Department for not improving his property, and thus faced a resumption order. He received support from a neighbour Nicholas Donnelly who, in the following year, wrote to the chief protector of Aborigines: he claimed that local farmers wanted to see the block handed to Dinah and his family 'for all time', and that George had cleared much of his land and fenced some of it. By 1915 the Dinahs were living in a hessian-and-tin camp on the Wagin Aboriginal Reserve.

Beaufort attended the convent school at Wagin and left with his family whenever work arose. In 1922 his father was forced to enter Moore River Native Settlement, but escaped and returned to Wagin; thereafter he lived in fear of removal. When George died in 1926 at Boyalling Estate, near Wagin, Beaufort took the title given to his father by the colonial authorities, 'King' of the Nyungar people of south-west Western Australia. The *Wagin Argus* reported that six hundred Whites, accompanied by a brass band, attended a corroboree at the camp; the mayor presented Dinah with a chain and a document in recognition of his succession.

As his father had done, Dinah attempted to mediate between police, Whites and his own people with the object of enabling his family and relations to remain in their country, away from government institutions. By 1928, with about 180 Nyungars, he was based at Geeralying, between Williams and Narrogin. With other adults, he asked for a school to be opened at the reserve because the local bus would not collect Aboriginal children to take them to a nearby school. The request was refused. At St Joseph's Catholic Church, Wagin, on 14 December 1929 Dinah married Alice Bertha Khan; they were to have twelve children.

Although he held no official boxing crown and did not compete in the major rings, Dinah was generally known as the South-West's heavyweight champion during the 1930s. His prowess became legendary among the Nyungar. Large and strong, he appeared in boxing troupes at agricultural shows and won hundreds of fights between the early 1920s and 1956. Wins in the tents meant quick money, but A. O. Neville [q.v.11], the chief protector and commissioner for native affairs, placed restrictions on Aborigines in Western Australia that virtually disqualified them from participating in title-events at White City, Perth.

Dinah was issued a certificate of citizenship in 1960. He died of myocardial infarction on 15 July 1962 at Royal Perth Hospital and was buried in Wagin cemetery; his wife, one son and six daughters survived him.

L. Tilbrook, *Nyungar Tradition* (Perth, 1983); A. Haebich, *For Their Own Good* (Perth, 1988); *Wagin Argus*, 9 July 1926; *West Australian*, 11 Aug 1958, 19 July 1962; *Daily News* (Perth), 19 July 1962; C. Tatz, Obstacle Race: Aborigines in Sport (ms, held by its author, Dept of Hist, Philosophy and Politics, Macquarie Univ); Aborigines Dept files 35/07, 1782/14, 698/15, 1087/15, 162/28 (WAA).

MARY ANNE JEBB
DAWN WALLAM

DING, HENRY (HARRY) EDGAR (1907-1976), trucker, was born on 23 April 1907 at Petersburg, South Australia, eldest of four children of Edgar Ellis Ding, railway pumper, and his wife Edith Louise, née Richards. Educated at Olary, where his mother ran a post-office store, and for two years at Peterborough High School, in 1921 Harry began carrying supplies to sheep-stations by horse and cart. He also took Sir Douglas Mawson [q.v.10] and his students to geological sites. In 1922 Edgar Ding bought a roofless Model-T Ford buckboard with which Harry continued transporting supplies and passengers. Having opened a motor works at Olary as a Ford dealer, in 1926 the tall, rangy, softly-spoken lad started a trucking business with an old 2-ton Chevrolet.

An accident wrecked it and he bought a Dodge. With the purchase in 1932 of a 4½-ton Leyland, Ding's business flourished. Two years later he bought a garage-store at Yunta for his base. By 1935 his trucks at Cockburn, Olary and Yunta on the Port Pirie-Broken Hill railway line, and at Hawker and Lyndhurst siding on the Central Australian line, ran mail and supplies to pastoral properties, and transported wool from them. He secured the fortnightly Marree-Birdsville mail contract and Tom Kruse inaugurated this service in 1936, thereby ending the era of camel transport. Passengers were welcome on the 330-mile (530 km) route along the notorious Birdsville Track.

After an engine failure had alerted Ding to the need for radio communication, in the mid-1930s Alfred Traeger [q.v.12] installed a wireless-base for him at Yunta and his drivers were provided with transceivers. His station VHU9 used three wave-lengths, working at long or short distances by day and night. Many pastoral properties, including four in Queensland owned by Sir Sidney Kidman's [q.v.9] company, joined the busy Yunta network which also assisted Rev. John Flynn's [q.v.8] Australian Aerial Medical Service.

With Flynn officiating, on 5 October 1938 at the Presbyterian Church, Gladesville, Sydney, Harry married a nurse Catherine Alice Anderson; they were to be divorced in 1954. Cecil Madigan [q.v.10] engaged Ding in 1939 to transport equipment to Andado station, Northern Territory, the starting point for Madigan's camel trek across the Simpson Desert. At Yunta, Ding received and transmitted Madigan's messages and national broadcasts.

Ding's fleet pioneered the road transport of livestock by carting fat lambs to railway sidings and by carrying South Australian stud rams and bulls to Central Queensland. Three men kept a truck constantly travelling. A Mammoth Major, too wide to be legally driven through most towns, was used on long hauls, with Harry's brother George as senior driver. Business peaked in the early 1940s, with twenty trucks, nine mail runs and depots at Marree, Lyndhurst, Hawker, Olary and Yunta. World War II made maintenance difficult. In 1944 Harry moved to Wilcannia, New South Wales, and gradually sold the depots. From 1950 he operated a garage at Walcha.

At Norman Park, Brisbane, on 15 April 1954 Ding married with Presbyterian forms 23-year-old Phyllis Mary Bonser of Wilcannia. In 1960 he revisited the outback; in 1973 he flew to the United States of America; he frequently travelled to Fiji and he wrote an autobiography, *Thirty Years With Men* (Walcha, 1988). Survived by his wife, their daughter and two sons, and by the daughter of his first marriage, Ding died of cancer on 13 April 1976 at Tamworth, New South Wales, and was buried in Beam cemetery, Walcha.

C. T. Madigan, *Crossing the Dead Heart* (Melb, 1946); J. Maddock, *Mail for the Back of Beyond* (Syd, 1986); S. Baldwin (ed), *Unsung Heroes and Heroines of Australia* (Melb, 1988); J. S. Turner et al, *Scholz of Tarnma and Beyond 1821-1990* (Adel, 1990); *Advertiser* (Adel), 3 May 1976; information from Mr and Mrs E. Ding, Walcha, NSW, Mr T. Kruse, Adel, and Mr F. Teague, Hawker, SA.

HANS MINCHAM

DINHAM, DORIS MAY; *see* GENTILE

DISHER, HAROLD CLIVE (1891-1976), medical practitioner, army officer and pastoralist, was born on 15 October 1891 at Rosedale, Victoria, third and youngest child of Henry Robert Disher, grazier, and his wife Mary Louise, née Hagenauer, both Victorian born. Educated at Rosedale State School, Gippsland College, Sale, and Scotch College, East Melbourne, Clive entered Ormond

College, University of Melbourne (M.B., B.S., 1916; M.D., 1921). He had rowed in Scotch's 1910 and 1911 Head-of-the-River crews and became an exceptional oarsman at university.

On 17 May 1917 Disher was appointed captain, Australian Army Medical Corps, Australian Imperial Force. By November he was in France with the 5th Field Ambulance. As regimental medical officer of the 4th Field Artillery Brigade from March 1918, he achieved a reputation for efficiency and bravery, and was recommended for the Military Cross. In 1919 he moved to England and stroked the A.I.F. VIII which won the King's Cup at the Royal Henley Peace Regatta; his name was later inscribed on the Helms trophy as Australasia's outstanding amateur athlete for that year.

Returning to Victoria in November 1919, Disher served part time in the Militia. He rose to major (1924) and lieutenant colonel (1930), and from 1928 to 1936 commanded the 5th Cavalry Field Ambulance. A keen and efficient officer, in 1938 he was promoted temporary (substantive 1939) colonel and appointed assistant-director of medical services, 2nd Cavalry Division. On 6 November 1926 at St John's Anglican Church, East Malvern, he had married a nurse Doris Parks Kitson. Disher pursued his medical career mainly as an anaesthetist. In 1936 he obtained a Diploma in Anaesthetics issued jointly by the Royal College of Physicians, London, and the Royal College of Surgeons, England. He was an honorary anaesthetist (1928) and senior honorary anaesthetist (from 1938) at Royal Melbourne Hospital.

On 8 December 1939 Disher joined the A.I.F. and that month embarked for the Middle East as assistant-director of medical services, Australian Overseas Base. Appointed A.D.M.S., 6th Division, on 16 April 1940, he had responsibility for medical services in the Australian operations in North Africa in early 1941. His 'skilful dispositions of dressing stations', 'attention to detail and inspiring influence' ensured that 'casualties were collected and received attention at the earliest possible moment'. He was appointed C.B.E. (1941). In April he took part in the Greek campaign, experiencing the dangers of the retreat and subsequent voyages to Crete and Egypt.

Back in Australia in August, Disher was A.D.M.S., 1st Armoured Division, until April 1942 when he was promoted temporary brigadier and made deputy-director of medical services, II Corps. In November he was sent to Port Moresby as D.D.M.S., New Guinea Force. His final post was D.D.M.S., First Army, which he assumed in Brisbane in July 1943. Given leave without pay from October 1944, he transferred to the Reserve of Officers on 22 June 1945 as honorary brigadier.

Retiring from medicine after the war, Disher lived at Strathfieldsaye, a sheep- and cattle-station on the banks of Lake Wellington, near Stratford, Gippsland. His grandfather had acquired the property in 1869 and Clive became sole owner in 1944. He found life on the land more attractive than resuming his civilian medical career. Family ties meant much to him; he and Doris were childless and she died in 1946. At Strathfieldsaye he helped youth organizations and institutions such as the Kyndalyn Retarded Children's Home; a fête for charity was held each year in the grounds.

Disher died on 13 March 1976 at Sale and was cremated with Presbyterian forms. His estate was sworn for probate at $919 888. He bequeathed Strathfieldsaye, valued at about $588 500, and its records, to the University of Melbourne which established the Strathfieldsaye Institute of Teaching and Research in Agriculture and Allied Sciences. Sir William Dargie's posthumous portrait of Disher is held by Melbourne University Boat Club.

A. S. Walker, *Middle East and Far East* (Canb, 1953); M. Fletcher, *Strathfieldsaye* (Churchill, Vic, 1992); *Great Scot*, May 1976, p 3; *Gippsland Writer*, 1, no 1, Winter 1986, p 27; *Herald* (Melb), 16 Mar, 14 May 1976; F. Strahan, Historical notes, Strathfieldsaye Estate (ts, May 1978, held by Sale District Hist Soc); Disher papers (Univ Melb Archives). BRYAN EGAN

DISNEY, SIR JAMES STANLEY (1896-1952), businessman, lord mayor and politician, was born on 17 June 1896 at Ballarat, Victoria, fifth child of Victorian-born parents James Herbert Disney (1864-1943), van proprietor, and his wife Isabella, née Hill. James Herbert, who subsequently worked in Melbourne as a boilerman, fruiterer and second-hand clothes and furniture dealer, served on the South Melbourne City Council in 1908-18 and was mayor in 1915-16.

Educated at Albert Park State School, young James enlisted in the Australian Imperial Force on 9 September 1914 and next month embarked for Egypt with the 8th Battalion. He saw action at Gallipoli and, from June 1916, on the Western Front where he was a motor-transport driver until selected for flying training. Commissioned in the Australian Flying Corps on 28 April 1918, he was posted to No.2 Squadron and promoted lieutenant in July. His A.I.F. appointment terminated in Australia on 28 March 1919. He married a divorcee Ruby Bruce, née Chapman, on 21 July 1922 with Anglican rites at Zeehan, Tasmania.

4

Although Disney gained a commercial pilot's licence after the war, he made a name as a motorcycle racer. He won the Phillip Island 200-mile (322-km) 250-cc motorcycle road race in 1928, and many solo and sidecar events on grass tracks and at the Melbourne Motordrome. A motorcycle shop, purchased for £250, became a car and cycle business, J. S. Disney Pty Ltd. He chaired the Melbourne Used Car Traders' Association and was a member of the Australian Association of British Manufacturers.

In November 1935 Disney was elected to the Melbourne City Council. He chaired its public works committee, was a member (1937) of the Melbourne and Metropolitan Board of Works, and sponsored and chaired (1939) the council's special carnival committee. In 1948 he was elected lord mayor, narrowly defeating O. J. Nilsen as the non-Labor councillors' candidate and succeeding Sir Raymond Connelly [q.v.13]. Disney was lord mayor for three successive terms (1948-49 to 1950-51) and received the customary knighthood on their completion. Major issues of his mayoralty included postwar reconstruction and Melbourne's preparations for the 1956 Olympic Games. As lord mayor, Disney had led the 1949 delegation which pressed his city's bid before the International Olympic Committee in Rome. He continued the lord mayor's holiday camp for children at Portsea which had been established by his predecessor.

In 1940 Disney had been elected to the Victorian Legislative Council as the United Australia Party's candidate for Higinbotham. He was minister of transport and of mines in Ian Macfarlan's [q.v.] short-lived Liberal ministry in 1945 and chairman (1943-46) of the public works committee, but was defeated in 1946 when (Sir) Arthur Warner [q.v.] contested Higinbotham against him. Disney's father, the Labor member for Melbourne West Province (1916-43) and a former minister without portfolio in the Prendergast and Hogan [qq.v.11,9] governments, had served opposite him in the same House.

A foundation member (1945) of the Liberal Party of Australia, Disney hoped to return to the wider political sphere, but his health failed him. In February 1950 he suffered a severe haemorrhage. Survived by his wife and stepson, he died of Hodgkin's disease on 20 January 1952 at his Auburn home and was cremated. His estate was sworn for probate at £136 918.

Sun News-Pictorial, 25 Apr 1947; *Herald* (Melb), 29 July 1943, 15 Oct 1948, 27 Sept 1952; *Age* (Melb), 30 July 1943, 28 Aug, 11 Feb 1950, 21 Jan 1952; *Argus*, 31 Aug, 19 Nov 1948, 14 Feb 1951, 21 Jan 1952.   DAVID DUNSTAN

DITTMER, FELIX CYRIL SIGISMUND (1904-1977), medical practitioner and politician, was born on 27 June 1904 at Dugandan, near Boonah, Queensland, son of Gustav Dittmer, a chemist from Germany, and his native-born wife Marie Farris, née Massie. Felix was educated at a convent school at Bowen, Childers Primary School, St Joseph's College, Nudgee, and the University of Queensland (B.Sc., 1925; B.A., 1927). On 29 October 1927 he married Minnie Elizabeth Crow (d.1975) at St James's Catholic Church, Forest Lodge, Sydney. After studying medicine at the University of Sydney (M.B., B.S., 1930), he practised at Proserpine, Queensland. From 1937 he was chairman of Kelsey Creek Gold Mines Pty Ltd (later Dittmer Gold Mines Pty Ltd), near Proserpine, and subsequently claimed that his miners were among the first to work a 40-hour week. In 1940 he moved to Brisbane to specialize in ear, nose and throat surgery, becoming an honorary surgeon to the Mater Public and Mater Children's hospitals.

Appointed captain in the Australian Army Medical Corps on 12 July 1943, Dittmer served in hospitals at Katherine, Northern Territory, and in Brisbane before transferring to the Reserve of Officers on 26 February 1946. As Labor's candidate he had unsuccessfully contested the Legislative Assembly seat of Oxley in a 1943 by-election; he also failed as mayoral candidate for Brisbane in 1949, despite a lively canvassing for health, water and sewerage services. In 1950 he was returned to the assembly as the member for Mount Gravatt. At the 1953 Labor Party convention Dittmer introduced a motion to provide three weeks annual leave under State awards, a motion which was reaffirmed at the 1956 convention and which divided the party. He became convinced that his stand had cost him a place in Vincent Gair's [q.v.] cabinet. When Gair and most of his ministers were expelled in the split, Dittmer became deputy-leader of the party rump in April 1957. In August he narrowly lost his seat. Elected to the Senate next year, he sat (1963-71) on the standing committee on public works. He was attracted by foreign affairs, and was a member of the Australian delegation to the General Assembly of the United Nations in 1962 and a parliamentary delegate to South America in 1965. As chairman of the Federal Parliamentary Labor Party committee on social services, health and repatriation, he was an early critic of phenacetin, a drug which was eventually banned.

In 1969 Dittmer lost his Senate endorsement in what he termed a 'bloody organised assassination' by his enemies at Trades Hall. He returned to his medical practice and began to study for a commerce degree at the University of Queensland where he had been a member (1950-56) of the senate. Unostentatious in his habits, he was described in his later years as 'a little man, with a kind of hurried, slightly limping gait'. Although some found him logical, sincere and approachable, others perceived him to be wily, irascible and over-confident. His friend but political enemy Gair thought that Dittmer had made a mistake in entering politics and that he 'would have left a greater mark if he hadn't'. Survived by his two sons and four of his five daughters, Dittmer died on 29 August 1977 at Oxley and was buried in Mount Gravatt cemetery.

PD (Qld), 1 Sept 1977, p 327; *Courier-Mail*, 31 Mar 1949, 30 Aug 1977; *Herald* (Melb), 10 Aug 1957, 4 June 1966, 1 Sept 1969; *Sun News-Pictorial*, 28 Aug 1959, 22 July 1967; *Australian*, 19 July 1966; *Telegraph* (Brisb), 1 Sept 1969; *SMH*, 30 Aug 1977; family information.

BRIAN F. STEVENSON

DIXON, LORNA ROSE (1917 ?-1976), Aboriginal linguist and cultural preserver, was born probably in 1917 at Tibooburra, New South Wales, daughter of Queensland-born parents Albert Ebsworth, a stockman from the Galali language group of Aborigines, and his wife Rosie, née Jones. Lorna's maternal grandfather was George Dutton [q.v.]. Her early years were mainly spent in the north-west corner of the State with her mother's Wangkumara-speaking parents and grandparents. Albert and Rosie worked on the cattle station, Naryilco, in south-west Queensland, where there was a large, permanent camp of Wangkumaras. In the 1910s they settled at Tibooburra and rented a house in the town. Lorna and her siblings attended the public school; they spent much of their time (before and after lessons) in the surrounding bush, learning from their grandparents about the sources of bush food and the stories associated with the significant sites in the area. Lorna later worked at the local hospital.

Albert took regular breaks from droving to attend ceremonial gatherings, sometimes taking his family who attended the major initiation held at Innaminka in the early 1920s. Although they were Catholics, the Ebsworths maintained close contact with Aboriginal ceremonial and social customs, teaching the children many aspects of Wangkumara philosophy and ethics which were to remain with them all their lives. They regularly travelled over their traditional country, visiting areas such as Coopers Creek and following the *marra* tracks, routes which traditional mythological figures had taken across the land.

Forced by the Depression and mounting White intolerance, the Aborigines Protection Board changed its policy of dispersal to one that concentrated the State's Aboriginal population on a few tightly controlled 'stations'. The Ebsworth family's life was brutally interrupted in 1938. Without warning, officials and police compelled the 120 Wangkumara people of Tibooburra—at gunpoint and under threat of removal of their children—to take a few belongings and leave their homes. They were herded into trucks and driven over two hundred miles (320 km) to the board's station at Brewarrina, where James Barker [q.v.13] was handyman. Over five hundred people were crammed into accommodation that had been barely adequate for the one hundred Murawari already there. The Wangkumara, culturally very different from the more easterly language groups already 'concentrated' on Brewarrina, felt isolated and were constantly intimidated by the armed manager. Lorna's family suffered deaths, including that of her sister. In desperation the remaining eighty Wangkumara people walked off the station in 1941. Most eventually settled at Bourke. There, at the district registry office, on 3 May 1943 Lorna married Eric Dixon, a stationhand.

The bitter legacy of three years of repression at Brewarrina made Lorna conceal her extensive knowledge of her language and culture, though she was determined to preserve it. At Bourke she spoke only English, even with her own children. She devised a spelling system for Wangkumara which she imparted to a cousin at Broken Hill. They secretly corresponded over three decades, sharing memories and confidences in their own language because, Lorna said, it enabled them to express their feelings better.

By the late 1960s a cultural revival had begun among Aboriginal people, and a more liberal attitude among White Australians made it easier for people like Lorna to share their knowledge. When Janet Mathews began to study the languages of north-west New South Wales at Bourke in 1970, Lorna recorded the Wangkumara language with her, and in the process began to talk about the cultural education of her childhood in the 'Corner Country'.

Her humour, warmth, enthusiasm and dedication to the task fostered affection and respect among White colleagues and pride among her family and the Aboriginal community. In 1974 Dixon was one of the first Aborigines to become a full member of the Australian Institute of Aboriginal Studies. She continued to record language and history, and also began to revisit the sites of her childhood at Tibooburra, Naryilco and Coopers Creek. Despite ill health, she planned further work. She died of a cerebral haemorrhage on 21 December 1976 at Bourke and was buried with Catholic rites in the local cemetery. Her husband survived her, as did five sons and three daughters of their twelve children.

Lorna Dixon's strategy for conserving the Wangkumara language and culture became widely known throughout the region as a symbol of and an inspiration for the Aborigines' determination to survive culturally as well as physically.

I. White et al (eds), *Fighters and Singers* (Syd, 1985); J. J. Fletcher, *Clean, Clad and Courteous* (Syd, 1989); *Aust Inst of Aboriginal Studies Newsletter*, no 7, Jan 1977, p 27; *Aboriginal Human Relations Newsletter*, no 55, Apr-May 1977, p 11; *Aboriginal Hist*, 2, no 1, 1978, p 2.

HEATHER GOODALL

DIXON, SIR OWEN (1886-1972), judge, was born on 28 April 1886 at Hawthorn, Melbourne, only son of Joseph William Dixon, barrister, and his wife Edith Annie, née Owen, both from Yorkshire, England. Because of deafness Joseph left the Bar and formed a partnership as a solicitor with one of his brothers. Owen was later to say that it 'was not easy' being brought up in a deaf man's house. He was, nevertheless, fond of his father and as a young barrister would discuss cases with him, standing face to face, his arms around his father's shoulders, his legs slightly apart and his mouth close to his father's ear, both men rocking from side to side as they talked.

The family had little money to spare, largely as a result of Joseph's ill health and some unsuccessful investments. Educated principally at Hawthorn College, Owen won a number of prizes and did well in his matriculation examinations. While the other boys admired him for his academic attainments, he was not popular as games-players were; his main sporting achievement was in rifle-shooting.

Dixon attended the University of Melbourne (B.A., 1906; LL.B., 1908; M.A., 1909) where he did not distinguish himself as a scholar, perhaps because he was interested in learning for learning's sake rather than for passing exams. He was influenced by professors (Sir) Harrison Moore and Thomas George Tucker [qq.v.10,12]: he obtained from Moore 'a complete grasp of legal principle . . . and a lively interest in constitutional and legal development'; from Tucker he acquired 'a love of classical literature and a sympathy with classical thought that affected the cast of his mind'.

It was due to Dixon's schooling in the classics that his 'passion for exactness in thought and expression was accompanied by a consciousness of fallibility'. These studies constituted the grounding of his later style of writing which displayed elegance and a mastery of the English language and the law. Of Dixon in his university days, a contemporary said that 'he possessed a soundness of judgement that was surprising . . . My own recollection of him is one of laughing indolence, which did not preclude an almost uncanny exactness of knowledge. I believe that what he once read he never forgot'.

Admitted to the Bar on 1 March 1910, Dixon took rooms in Selborne Chambers. He was unable to read with anyone because of his family's poor financial circumstances. In his early years he was one of the barristers commissioned by (Sir) Leo Cussen [q.v.8] to work on the consolidation of Victorian statutes. While a junior, Dixon took three pupils—(Sir) Robert Menzies [q.v.], (Sir) Henry Baker [q.v.13] and (Sir) James Tait.

On 8 January 1920 at St Paul's Anglican Cathedral, Melbourne, Dixon married Alice Crossland Brooksbank (d.1971). He was greatly attached to his wife and kept in constant contact with her when they were apart. They had four children: Franklin Owen ('Bruv'), born in 1922, who suffered from conical cornea; Edward Owen ('Ted'), Elizabeth Brooksbank Owen ('Bett') and Anne Helen Owen, born in 1934. Dixon led a relatively simple life. He enjoyed horse-riding and —especially with his family—cycling and walking; he was a member of the Wallaby Club (president 1936). He also read avidly and widely. In keeping with his style of life, he disapproved of divorce, and was a teetotaller which stemmed from a promise he had made to his mother because of his father's heavy drinking.

Appointed K.C. in 1922, Dixon came to exercise 'absolute dominance' over the Bar. He was its 'acknowledged leader', 'its outstanding lawyer and its greatest advocate'. A tall, loose-jointed figure with somewhat stooped shoulders, he had a reputation for advocacy of 'calculated flippancy'. He was immensely effective, particularly in the High Court of Australia where he frequently appeared in both constitutional and non-constitutional matters; he 'set one judge against another', skilfully isolating a minority opposed to his point of view and 'persuading a majority to decide in his favour'. Before a jury, however, he was 'too intellectual' and did not shine at cross-examination.

Dixon worked prodigiously hard at the Bar, but enjoyed it enormously. He appeared on a number of occasions before the Privy Council. Sir John (Viscount) Simon, K.C., was so impressed with him that he 'suggested that he should take chambers in London and practise at the English Bar'. In 1928 Dixon was one of three barristers appointed by the committee of counsel for Victoria to present its submissions to the royal commission on the Constitution.

In July-December 1926 he had served as an acting-judge of the Supreme Court of Victoria. He refused to take a permanent post, possibly due to his opposition to hanging, a punishment which he regarded as barbaric. That year the Federal attorney-general (Sir) John Latham [q.v.10] offered him the position of chief judge on the Commonwealth Court of Conciliation and Arbitration, but he declined. On 4 February 1929 Dixon was appointed to the High Court. At 42, he was the youngest member of the bench. He later said that he had accepted the post 'because I was told I ought'.

Throughout his career on the bench Dixon was to maintain that he disliked judicial work, saying that no one could get any pleasure out of it, and that it was hard and unrewarding. Part of his unhappiness arose from relationships between members of the High Court which were initially far from harmonious. Antagonism was eased in 1950 with the appointments of (Sir) Frank Kitto and (Sir) Wilfred Fullagar [q.v.]. Dixon liked both of them and particularly respected Fullagar. The court became a more congenial place in which to work.

Dixon had been on board a ship, returning from an overseas visit to seek treatment for Franklin's eyes, when war was declared in September 1939. On arriving in Australia, he told Prime Minister Menzies that he was 'anxious to do anything [he] could for the war', although he was to say in retrospect that he was not sure it was appropriate for a judge to do other work while holding office. Dixon chaired the Central Wool Committee (1940-42), the Shipping Control Board (1941-42), the Commonwealth Marine War Risks Insurance Board (1941-42), the Salvage Board (1942) and the Allied Consultative Shipping Council (1942). He displayed marked skill as an administrator and, after he had resigned from these bodies, was still consulted informally about their work. While engaged in this extrajudicial activity, he continued to sit on the bench, though he did less court work than previously. He had been appointed K.C.M.G. in 1941.

In April 1942 Sir Owen was chosen to succeed R. G. (Baron) Casey [q.v.13] as Australian minister in Washington. Dixon accepted the position only after pressure exerted by Prime Minister Curtin [q.v.13] who argued that he could thereby make a more significant contribution to winning the war. As minister, Dixon was required to carry out the normal duties of the head of a diplomatic mission, but his major task was to ensure that the United States of America did not lose sight of the war in the Pacific and that Australia's interests were not neglected. He

also represented Australia on the Pacific War Council and, later, on the council of the United Nations Relief and Rehabilitation Administration.

Although Dixon was somewhat Anglophile and disliked many things American, he was able slowly to increase his influence in the U.S.A. and to earn respect. He came to admire individual Americans, such as General George C. Marshall, the army chief of staff, Dean Acheson, the assistant-secretary of state, and Justice Felix Frankfurter. On Dixon's departure from Washington, Marshall and Acheson were to speak warmly of him. Acheson described him as a person who would 'adorn' the Supreme Court of the United States 'if it were possible to appoint him to it'. He added that Dixon 'would be greatly missed in Washington where he had made himself "beloved"'.

Dixon's job in Washington was made much harder by the minister for external affairs H. V. Evatt [q.v.] who had sat with him on the High Court. Dixon disliked Evatt whom he regarded as politically motivated and a poor judge; he had no wish to work again with him. For his part, Evatt had not supported Dixon's appointment to Washington. Accordingly, Dixon had made it a condition of his accepting the post that he would be responsible not to Evatt but directly to the prime minister. Dixon confirmed the arrangement with Curtin on a visit to Australia in 1943. At his own request Dixon was relieved of his post in September 1944. The ostensible reason given was that victory for the Allies was certain and it was therefore proper for him to resume his judicial duties. In fact, the main cause of his wanting to return to Australia was the frustration he felt at Evatt's persistent interference and general conduct.

In 1950 Dixon was nominated as United Nations representative to mediate in the dispute between India and Pakistan over the State of Jammu and Kashmir. Later, he said that he had agreed to the appointment on the misunderstanding that it was to be a Commonwealth, rather than a U.N., operation. He considered the U.N. to be at best of no use, and at worst a danger, to British interests.

Reaching New Delhi in May 1950, Dixon travelled through the disputed territory to collect information, and on 20 July met jointly with prime ministers Jawaharlal Nehru of India and Liaqat Ali Khan of Pakistan. Dixon believed that the problem could only be solved by partitioning the region, but he was hampered by a U.N. Security Council decision to adhere to a plebiscite as the solution. At a series of meetings he advanced proposals to resolve the conflict, the last of which was that a plebiscite should be held in a limited area including the Kashmir Valley and that the rest of the State should be partitioned. India would not agree to take the preliminary steps necessary to ensure that the plebiscite would be a free and fair one. Dixon blamed Nehru for the impasse, observing that his 'strained arguments ... are characteristic of a man instinctively aware that he is taking up an untenable position and not very proud of it'. None the less, in his report to the Security Council on 15 September Dixon reproached both sides for not reaching agreement.

Despite the failure of his mission, Dixon earned praise from the parties for his efforts. It was said that the qualities he brought to his role as mediator were 'his superb intellectual penetration and his capacity, strengthened over the years at the Bar and on the Bench, to seize on the heart of a complicated issue. Combined with that was his judicious spirit (some of his critics thought too judicious)'. By October he was back on the High Court bench.

Dixon employed the common law method in his judgements with rare skill and with faith in the capacity of its reasoning processes to reach just and correct solutions to legal problems. He took the view that there was 'no other safe guide to judicial decisions in great conflicts than a strict and complete legalism'. It is legalism, in the sense of the 'strict logic and high technique' of the common law, which permeates his judgements. In particular, he considered it essential that the common law method should be applied to the construction of the Commonwealth Constitution in order to maintain public confidence in the court's judgements as apolitical.

Consistent with his endorsement of the common law method, Dixon believed that the doctrine of precedent was of paramount importance. He remained committed to the principle that in general judges should proceed upon the basis that they inherit and develop the *corpus juris*, but do not make it afresh. He deplored 'the conscious judicial innovator' who 'is bound under the doctrine of precedents by no authority except the error he committed yesterday'. His adherence to precedent is to be seen most clearly in the transport cases decided under section 92 of the Constitution over a period of some twenty years. In the course of this line of cases he bowed to the view of the majority from which he had initially dissented. He was subsequently able to dissent again in *McCarter v. Brodie* (1950) on the basis of the Privy Council's decision in the Banking case (1949), but followed the majority in *McCarter v. Brodie* when he passed judgement on *Hughes & Vale Pty Ltd v. State of New South Wales* (1953). On appeal, the Privy Council adopted the reasons Dixon had given in dissent, principally in *McCarter v. Brodie,* and expressed much of its judgement in Dixon's own language.

Yet, Dixon's regard for the doctrine of pre-cedent did not prevent him from refining, confining or extending the law in accordance with the common law method. While he accepted the decision of the court in the Engineers' case (1920), his dissatisfaction with the theoretical basis of that decision was shown in the way in which he applied the case more narrowly than others. He admitted that the Engineers' case 'is one that I have always applied with restraint'.

Further, Dixon held that the High Court, as a court of final resort, had a duty to expound the law correctly. The court was not compelled to follow decisions of the House of Lords or of itself where they were manifestly incorrect. Moreover, he never shirked a decision which reason or principle required, as is demonstrated by the Communist Party case (1951) which involved the validity of the Communist Party Dissolution Act (1950). Dixon was strongly anti-communist and devoted a great deal of time to considering the case, 'much of it ... in vain attempts to construct arguments in favour of [the] validity [of the Act] which would hold water'. For all that, he decided with the majority that the Act was invalid. Latham dissented and showed Dixon a draft of his judgement; Dixon wrote '[i]t sickened me with its abnegation of the function of the Court and I said so'.

Appointed chief justice on 18 April 1952, Dixon was sworn in three days later. He was 66 and was to hold office for twelve years. His appointment was universally acclaimed. Many thought that he was the greatest judicial lawyer in the English-speaking world; others regarded him as the most distinguished living exponent of the common law. His judgements carried persuasive effect wherever the common law was applied. An English judge, Baron Wilberforce, wrote: 'There is no such thing as substandard Dixon, but from time to time there is Dixon at his superb best'. Dixon's pre-eminence had been recognized by his appointment to the Privy Council in 1951 (although he chose not to sit on it) and by his numerous honours and awards. He was elevated to G.C.M.G. in 1954 and was appointed to the Order of Merit in 1963. Honorary degrees were conferred upon him by the universities of Oxford (D.C.L., 1958), Harvard (LL.D., 1958), Melbourne (LL.D., 1959) and the Australian National University (LL.D., 1964). In 1955 Yale University had awarded him the Harry E. Howland memorial prize 'for services to mankind' and in 1970 he became a corresponding fellow of the British Academy. The degrees from Oxford and Harvard gave him particular pleasure.

Dixon was a witty and engaging conversationalist. He tended to speak unconsciously in epigrams and his descriptions of his contemporaries could be telling. Renowned for his sense of humour, he could handle the most serious matters with an extraordinarily light touch. Working with him was likely to be punctuated by his peals of laughter, often provoked by the revelation of some human foible that delighted him. In court his sense of humour was restrained, but in conversation he took pleasure in the intellectual joke; he found in the law and lawyers an inexhaustible source of enjoyment. Dixon did have faults. He was rather vain, although he did not wear his vanity openly. In addition, he could be a little pretentious, parading his learning in languages before others who were not so knowledgeable. On the other hand, it has been said of him that he had the 'knowledge and urbanity to be able to talk without any thought of showing off and the grace to assume that others would naturally converse in the same way'. He liked gossip, but in relating the failings of others he showed amusement, not malice.

As chief justice, Dixon defended the integrity and independence of the High Court with vigour. He staunchly opposed suggestions that it should move to Canberra. Indeed, he opposed the court having a permanent seat anywhere because he thought it should not be removed from the people, the judges or the legal profession; he considered that it should be 'an all-Australian Court, going to the people rather than requiring the people to come to it'.

In the early 1960s Dixon's health deteriorated and there was a reduction in both the number of judgements that he wrote and the number of cases on which he sat. On 13 April 1964 he retired. He said that he was doing so 'because I believe I ought', and went on to observe: 'I am not one of those who subscribe to the view that the older you get the better you get . . . I believe in young everything. I thought that I had got too old and was deeply conscious of the fact that I was not doing my work adequately'. Following his retirement he took no part in public life. Asked whether he would allow himself to be nominated for the office of governor-general, he refused, and Casey was appointed. S. H. Z. Woinarski's collection of Dixon's papers and addresses, *Jesting Pilate* (Sydney), was published in 1965.

Dixon's poor health persisted and he was confined for most of his remaining life to his home at Hawthorn, for some considerable part of that time to his chair. As Sir Owen's eyesight failed, his son Franklin read aloud to him. Survived by his children, Dixon died on 7 July 1972 at his home and was buried in Boroondara cemetery. His portrait by A. D. Colquhoun is in the High Court, Canberra.

Cwlth of Aust, *Report of the Royal Commission on the Constitution*, incl Minutes of Evidence (Canb, 1929); R. G. Menzies, *The Measure of the Years* (Melb, 1970); A. Watt, *Australian Diplomat* (Syd, 1972); P. Hasluck, *Diplomatic Witness* (Melb, 1980); *Aust Law J*, 29, no 4, 19 Aug 1955, p 272, 38, no 1, 29 May 1964, p 3, 46, no 9, Sept 1972, p 429; *Cwlth Law Reports*, 28, 1920-21, p 129, 63, 1940, p 691, 79, 1949, p 497, 80, 1949-50, p 432, 83, 1950-51, p 1, 85, 1951-52, p xi, 87, 1952-53, p 49, 93, 1954-56, p 1, 108, 1962-63, p 620, 126, 1971-72, p v; *Melb Univ Law Review*, 9, no 1, May 1973, p 1, 15, no 4, Dec 1986, pp 577, 579; *Punch* (Melb), 18 Sept 1924; Dixon papers (on loan to Mr J. D. Merralls, Mont Albert, Melb); miscellaneous unpublished records, including letters and material from interviews, held by Mr J. D. Merralls.

DARYL DAWSON
GRANT ANDERSON

DIXON, RETTA; *see* LONG, MARGARET JANE

DIXON, RICHARD; *see* WALKER, CLIFTON REGINALD

DOBELL, SIR WILLIAM (1899-1970), painter, was born on 24 September 1899, at Newcastle, New South Wales, sixth surviving and youngest child of native-born parents Robert Dobell, bricklayer, and his wife Margaret Emma, née Wrightson. Educated at Cooks Hill Commercial Public School, where his teacher John Walker encouraged him to draw, in 1916 Bill became a draughtsman for the local architect, Wallace Lintott Porter. After Porter fell ill in 1923, Dobell found temporary employment for eight weeks at Narrandera before moving to Sydney to work for Wunderlich [q.v.12] Ltd, manufacturers of building materials. In 1924 he enrolled at Julian Ashton's [q.v.7] Sydney Art School, increasing his attendance at classes from three nights a week to include Saturday afternoons and then Sundays; he worked hard, as he later said, to impress his teacher Henry Gibbons.

Through the school Dobell met students who were to be his friends in London in the 1930s. Having been awarded third place in 1927, he won the Society of Artists' travelling scholarship in April 1929—£250 a year for two years; the committee for the Artists' Ball and Wunderlich Ltd each donated a further £50 a year. His scholarship pictures (illustrated in *Undergrowth*, March-April 1929) showed the influence of Gibbons and George Lambert [q.v.9]. In May he shared third prize of one hundred guineas in the State Theatre's 'Australian Art Quest' (Mary Edwards received second prize).

Dobell sailed for London and on 7 October

1929 enrolled for the winter term at the Slade School of Fine Art. His elderly teachers Henry Tonks (drawing) and Philip Wilson Steer (painting) were on the verge of retirement. On Lambert's advice, he took private lessons from William Orpen, to whom he had been given an introduction by Sir Granville Ryrie [q.v.11], the Australian high commissioner and a friend of Lambert. In England, Dobell was influenced by Augustus John, another of Lambert's friends, whose style was pervasive at the Slade. In 1930 Dobell won the school's first prize for figure painting with his 'Nude study' (Newcastle Region Art Gallery) and shared the second prize for drawing.

From late 1930, when he left the Slade, Dobell lived in a series of boarding-houses at Bayswater and Pimlico. From 1933 he was back at Bayswater, at 34 Alexander Street, where he was present at the laying-out of his dead landlord in 1936. He indulged his occasional delight 'in the macabre and vulgar' by painting his landlady Mrs Kernan brushing her hair by the bedside of her late husband in 'The Dead Landlord' (private collection). Late that year Dobell lived in basement 'digs' off Edgeware Road before shifting in February 1937 to an attic flat at 31 Gloucester Street, Pimlico, where he remained until he left for Australia.

His closest contacts were with Australian artists and the association was for mutual benefit: stylistically, through comparisons and discussions; thematically, through modelling for each other and going on sketching trips together; financially, through sharing lodgings and finding each other commercial-art work. In 1929 Dobell had mixed with Sydney students Edgar Ritchard, 'Rah' Fizelle [q.v.8] and Fred Coventry, and with Godfrey Miller [q.v.]. For a time in 1932 he looked after Coventry's Bayswater studio-flat in Westbourne Grove, whence he began a practice of drawing and painting quick studies of life in the street below. Other Australian friends in London included John Passmore, Arthur Murch, Jack and Nancy Kilgour, Vera Blackburn, Jean Appleton, Wallace Thornton, Arthur Freeman and Jack Carington Smith [q.v.13]. Among non-Australian friends were the Bertwistle sisters, Delia and Florence (whom Dobell had met in the ship from Australia), Neville Bunning (a Canadian), James and Ruth Cook (from New Zealand), and Dorothy and Edie Longdons whom he visited regularly at Clendon, Surrey.

Dobell made a serious study of such painters as Rembrandt, Renoir, Goya, Turner, Constable, Van Gogh, Soutine, Tintoretto and Ingres, whose work he saw in museums in London and during his trips on the Continent. He transformed their influences 'into a highly personal vision of hu-manity'. His colleagues saw a resemblance between his small oil sketches, dashed off in a 'personal style', and the work of Daumier. Dobell visited The Hague in the summer of 1930; in the summer of 1931 he went to Belgium, stayed at Bruges for a month and returned via Paris to London. In 1933 'Boy at the Basin' (Art Gallery of New South Wales) was one of two works by Dobell exhibited at the Royal Academy of Arts and favourably reviewed. He submitted small paintings of a street singer and a chambermaid at a window to the London Group exhibition in November 1938.

After mid-1931 Dobell no longer had the support of his scholarship. To maintain himself, he produced posters and advertisements, illustrations for magazines like the *Passing Show* and *Night and Day* (he was slightly influenced by the style of Feliks Topoloski, an illustrator for the latter journal), and even made illustrations for Sunday School cards. In 1934 he had a glamorous portrait photograph taken of himself for filmwork and was an extra in *Chu Chin Chow* and *The Man Who Knew Too Much*. From mid-1936 until September 1938 Donald Friend was based in London; he and Dobell were both homosexual and otherwise had similar tastes; they became close friends, lived near each other at Pimlico, visited restaurants and pubs together, listened to 'Negro' jazz and boogie-woogie, visited museums and art exhibitions, among them the International Surrealist Exhibition (1936), and shopped in the Caledonian Road market—one vendor became the subject of Dobell's 'The Red Lady' (1938, National Gallery of Australia). The shy and strait-laced Eric Wilson was an art student who lodged with Dobell following his arrival in London in 1937.

The only time that Dobell was financially secure in this period was from December 1937 when Murch, who had charge of decorations for the Australian wool pavilion at the Empire Exhibition, Glasgow, employed him and other Australians for six months at £10 per week. To economize, Dobell had lodgers, shared travelling expenses—his visits to the seaside and country were in company—and saved drastically on clothes. Wilson described him going out in the evening, 'holding a newspaper under his right arm to cover the tear in his overcoat. Whenever his socks have holes . . . he simply paints his leg to match'. According to Wilson's diary-entry of 12 January 1939, Dobell decided to return to Australia because 'his father sent him the fare as he wanted to see Bill before he dies'. Accompanied by Wilson, Dobell revisited Paris in February on his way home. His father died on 8 February.

Back in Sydney, Dobell initially lived with one of his sisters. In June he found an apartment with a balcony above a bank in Darlinghurst Road, Kings Cross. There he reworked various London subjects and treated local subjects in the racy, Dickensian style which he had established in London, producing 'a gallery of Australian types'. The one perceptible change in his style was a greater luminosity of colour: the paintings 'almost dissolve in the peacock light'. From 25 May 1939 until the end of first term, 1941, he taught part time at East Sydney Technical College. He left to work as a camouflage artist at various aerodromes before becoming an official war artist (1942-44) with the Allied Works Council. His wartime themes included construction workers and lumpers, as in 'The Billy Boy' and 'Cement worker, Sydney Graving Dock' (1943, 1944, Australian War Memorial, Canberra).

In March 1942, at the National Art Gallery of New South Wales, Dobell shared a loan exhibition with Margaret Preston [q.v.11]. He won the 1943 Archibald [q.v.3] prize with a portrait of Joshua Smith in January 1944. The morning after the award was announced, Smith's parents pleaded with Dobell to withdraw the portrait from exhibition; Joshua Smith refused to speak to him. Public opinion was vociferous. On 19 February 1944 the *A.B.C. Weekly* published the transcript of a radio talk by Dobell: 'To me, a sincere artist is not one who makes a faithful attempt to put on canvas what is in front of him, but who tries to create something which is a living thing in itself, regardless of its subject . . . I have been trying to develop a style of my own derived from the Old Masters. The leaders of the so-called "modern" movements have done the same—although they have developed in different directions'. Two unsuccessful artists, Mary Edwards and Joseph Wolinski, brought an action to overturn the award, claiming that 'Joshua Smith' was 'not a portrait but a caricature'. In the Supreme Court hearing of 23-26 October 1944 their main witness was J. S. MacDonald [q.v.10], who argued that portraiture was a specific genre bound by rules and, like a sonnet, had to subscribe to a correct form: 'it has to be a balanced likeness of an actual person'. The painting 'Joshua Smith', he went on, was not a portrait as it was 'very unbalanced, a caricature', and he added that the word came from '*caricare*' which meant 'to overload'.

Dobell argued in defence that he was an artist of sound training, whose experience overseas had been supported by winning the travelling scholarship. Knowing his fellow painter reasonably well, he had a considered concept of his character and body language. Joshua did have long arms, habitually held his hands clasped, and when 'very determined to gain his point' he 'naturally sits in a chair that way'. Dobell was prepared to 'admit a slight exaggeration' in the portrait. On 8 November Justice Roper [q.v.] dismissed the suit against Dobell. Edwards's and Wolinksi's appeal also failed. In April 1944 Dobell had been appointed a trustee of the Art Gallery for a four-year term.

Scarified by the court case, by the publicity and by abusive letters from total strangers, Dobell suffered an acute attack of dermatitis, followed by a nervous breakdown; he refused to leave the house, to think, to paint or do anything at all. In 1945 he retreated to Wangi Wangi, on the shores of Lake Macquarie, to live with his sister Alice in the holiday home that had been built by his father. 'Lord Wakehurst' [q.v.] (1944, private collection), the first portrait he produced after that of Smith, was markedly conventional. Some of his later works such as 'Mathias' and 'Frandam' (1953, private collections) were reminiscent of portraits by his rival Mary Edwards. In January 1949 Dobell was awarded the Archibald prize for a portrait, 'Margaret Olley' (A.G.N.S.W.), and also the Wynne landscape prize for 'Storm approaching Wangi' (private collection).

Artistically there were two highlights in his later career, a series of paintings of New Guinea in the early 1950s, and a series of major portraits in the late 1950s and early 1960s. He visited New Guinea for three months after Easter 1949 as a guest of (Sir) Edward Hallstrom [q.v.] who had chartered a plane to fly guests to his experimental sheep-station in the central highlands. Dobell destroyed his first drawings—for being too much like tourist fare—and began seriously to sketch. He revisited the Territory next year and worked on New Guinean subjects almost exclusively until 1954. He was a notable miniaturist, but his 'tiny masterpieces' were publicly criticized for being too small in scale. He took the criticism badly, and ceased to paint New Guinean subjects.

In 1957 Dobell completed a portrait of Dame Mary Gilmore [q.v.9] (A.G.N.S.W.) and painted the first of eight portraits of the cosmetician Helena Rubinstein [q.v.11] (private collection). These works were recognized as among his highest achievements. By then, he was able to pick and choose from many offers of commissions. In 1958 he underwent an operation for cancer; after convalescing, he learned to drive a motorcar and bought a 3.8-litre Jaguar. He won his third Archibald prize in January 1960 for a portrait of his surgeon E. G. MacMahon. That year he painted the first of four portraits commissioned by *Time* magazine for cover illustrations: 'Prime Minister Menzies' [q.v.] (A.G.N.S.W.) appeared on 4 April 1960, and was followed by portraits of Ngo Dinh Diem, president of South Vietnam (4 August 1961), Frederick G. Donner, chairman of General Motors Corporation (18

May 1962), and Tunku Abdul Rahman, prime minister of Malaysia (N.R.A.G.), (12 April 1963).

Dobell was a reserved and gentle man, with dark hair turning grey by 1961. John Hetherington [q.v.] wrote that, when he smiled, 'his grey-blue eyes are all but lost in nests of fine wrinkles, and the normally rather serious expression of his oval face becomes irresistibly quizzical'. In 1964 the Art Gallery of New South Wales held a retrospective exhibition of Dobell's works; James Gleeson's biography, *William Dobell*, was published; and Dobell received a £5000 Britannica-Australia award which enabled him to buy 'a few antiques' for his house. Appointed O.B.E. (1965), he was knighted in 1966. He died of hypertensive heart disease on 13 May 1970 at Wangi and was cremated with Anglican rites; according to his wish, his estate was used to establish the Sir William Dobell Art Foundation. Walter Pidgeon's portrait of Dobell is in the Art Gallery of New South Wales.

Gleeson has suggested that Dobell's one truly creative period was the ten years in London. Most of his major paintings of the 1940s depended on the work he had done in those years, either directly through using studies, or indirectly through reference to stylistic ideas he then encountered. To look to Europe was necessary, given his conventional belief that Australia could not offer the nourishment necessary for great art; but, while his attention was given to preserving styles and genre themes of European art, he responded to his own, immediate, expatriate Australian culture. He acquired 'a complete mastery of traditional techniques' and a noticeably 'democratically egalitarian handling' of a wide range of subjects. Dobell shared with writers of his generation, Patrick White and Hal Porter, and the painters, Russell Drysdale and Albert Tucker, a singularly sharp perception of social manners. Their art focussed upon the articulate and telling moment, and described only the salient aspects of a situation. Each at times was accused of caricature. It may be significant that these artists were tardy in deciding on a career, slow to mature, and, conversely, spectacular and controversial in their fame. Comparisons outside Australia may be made with the British painter Francis Bacon and the French photographer Henri Cartier-Bresson whose art was to choose 'the decisive moment'.

B. Penton, *The Art of William Dobell* (Syd, 1946); J. Gleeson, *William Dobell* (Lond, 1964, Syd, 1981) and *The Drawings of William Dobell in the Australian National Gallery* (Canb, 1992); V. Freeman, *Dobell on Dobell* (Syd, 1970); G. Serle, *From Deserts the Prophets Come* (Melb, 1973); B. Adams, *Portrait of an Artist* (Melb, 1983); *Age* (Melb), 11 Nov 1961; Dobell's sketch-books *and* J. Gleeson, research papers on Dobell, *and* E. Wilson papers (National Gallery of Aust L, Canb); information from the Sir William Dobell Art Foundation, Syd.
                                                        MARY EAGLE

DODD, BEATRICE OLIVE VICTORIA (1897-1968), social worker, was born on 10 June 1897 at Kew, Melbourne, second child of English-born parents Harry Dodd, manager, and his wife Rose Isabella, née Hoadley. Olive was educated (1911-15) at Methodist Ladies' College, Kew, and was an active member of the Old Collegians' Club for the remainder of her life, serving as editor (1922) of its magazine, secretary (1923-27) and president (1932). A non-resident member of Queen's College, University of Melbourne (B.A., 1919; Dip.Ed., 1920; M.A., 1921), she was foundation secretary (1920) of the 16 Club which was formed by women graduates who had entered the university in 1916; she was an active member of the club from 1920 to 1935 and, after leave of absence, from 1952 to 1968.

Having taught briefly at a small private girls' school, in 1929-30 Dodd visited Britain and the Netherlands. In 1933-34 she was one of the earliest students to take the new diploma of social studies course at the University of Melbourne. The Free Kindergarten Union appointed her in 1936 as its first social worker; she was employed part time that year and full time in 1937-40. At the inaugural biennial conference of the Australian Association for Pre-School Child Development in 1939, she presented 'a masterly survey' of the duties and opportunities of the social worker in the kindergarten.

In 1940 Dodd completed a transport course, including vehicle maintenance, and drove the Myer [q.v.10] delivery van around the city and its suburbs. After taking a position as a social worker at the Lady Gowrie [q.v.9] Child Centre, she enlisted in the Australian Women's Army Service on 5 September 1942. Commissioned lieutenant in April next year, she served in No.5 A.W.A.S. Administrative Cadre, then, as welfare officer for Victoria, interviewed army servicewomen at the time of their discharge and supervised their return to civilian life. She was promoted captain in November 1944 and transferred to the Reserve of Officers on 26 June 1946.

Resuming civilian life, Dodd worked each Wednesday at the Mews, Government House, with the Women of the University Save the Children Fund, and continued her interest and involvement in the F.K.U. as a member of its executive from 1951 until her death. As president (1955-59), she dealt capably with ministers, heads of departments and increasingly complex financial affairs. It was 'her anxious task to contemplate the possible disbandment of the Union and her triumph to have so led her executive and the local committees that together they faced and overcame the financial crisis and enabled the Union to carry on' as an independent body.

Miss Dodd died on 2 May 1968 at Kew and was cremated. In the words of an obituary, 'she was a very good friend to many people and was always ready to give her time, her knowledge and her help to anyone who wanted it'.

L. Gardiner, *The Free Kindergarten Union of Victoria 1908-80* (Melb, 1982); *Hist of Education Review*, 19 no 2, 1990; MLC, *Old Collegian*, 1922, 1923, Oct 1929, Apr 1930, Dec 1940; *Age* (Melb), 10 Apr 1929; *Argus*, 13 July 1943; *Herald* (Melb), 30 Mar 1955.   A. G. THOMSON ZAINU'DDIN

DODD, TOMMY (c.1890-1975), stockman and cameleer, was born about 1890 at Running Waters on Henbury station, by the Finke River in the Northern Territory, about 75 miles (120 km) south-west of Alice Springs. He was one of several men of shared Aboriginal and non-Aboriginal ancestry who bore this name in that era, and his life was typical of many of his people. His father was of Afghan and European descent, and came from the Hergott Springs (Marree) region of South Australia. His mother was a Pitjantjatjara woman from a group which, in the early 1900s, had been absorbed by their north-east neighbours, the Matutjara. Tommy was born in a bush camp and raised among the Yankuntjatjara in the Everard Ranges.

A competent horseman by the age of 10, Dodd was taken by a station-owner to ride in bush meetings. He gained a reputation throughout Central Australia as a horse-breaker and broke remounts for the Indian Army. He was short and wiry, and his gait in later life reflected his years in the saddle: bowed legs and a limp resulting from the many fractures he had received. In remote areas in the north of South Australia he worked at mustering, horse-breaking, yard-building and fencing on stations such as Todmorden, Mount Barry, Granite Downs, Wallatina and Everard Park. He drove supply-carrying teams of camels from Oodnadatta to Alice Springs, then travelled west into the Aboriginal reserve to trade food for dingo scalps—obtained by the Pitjantjatjara and Yankuntjatjara people—on which the government paid a bounty. During these expeditions he gained knowledge of a vast area of the country and learned much about the mythological and ritual life of the Aborigines. A Pitjantjatjara woman recounted that, as a girl, she had been surprised to see him dancing with the men in a ceremony.

His first wife Rosie was an Arrernte woman. Their four sons were sent as youngsters to the Colebrook Home for Aboriginal Children at Quorn, South Australia, and their parents had limited contact with them. Dodd had two other wives from Pitjantjatjara-Yankuntjatjara country, Katie Tjungura and Tjunyun, as well as another son and daughter. He spent periods at Ernabella mission (established 1937) in the Musgrave Ranges where he assisted the staff as an interpreter. In the 1950s he lived at Ernabella, before moving west to the Amata government settlement after 1961. In his old age he received a state pension.

Dodd's familiarity with Aboriginal life prepared him for his role as guide, informant and interpreter for government officials, patrol officers and researchers. In 1963 and 1966 he acted as a translator for the ethnologist Norman Tindale when he recorded Pitjantjatjara ceremonies. Dodd accompanied officers on their patrols to protect Aborigines in the area of the Woomera Rocket Range; for this work he was awarded the British Empire Medal in 1970. The *Advertiser* described him as 'a quiet, decent fellow who knows the North-West better than any other man'. Survived by at least two of his sons, he died at Amata Hospital on 22 January 1975 and was buried in the local cemetery. His gravestone is inscribed: 'A man of two worlds—stockman, camelman, guide and friend'.

N. B. Tindale, *Aboriginal Tribes of Australia* (Canb, 1974); W. M. Hilliard, *The People in Between* (Adel, 1976); *Advertiser* (Adel), 13 June 1970, 4 June 1971; information from Messrs B. Evans, Plympton Sth, Adel, M. Dodd, Coober Pedy, R. Trudinger, Ernabella, SA, R. Verburgt, Kuranda, Qld, and Mrs A. Elliott, Teesdale, Vic.
                                                    W. H. EDWARDS

DODGE, ETTIE (1885-1973), vigoro administrator, was born on 29 September 1885 in South Melbourne, fifth of six children of Joseph Terrill Crowl, a Victorian-born bank clerk, and his wife Matilda Orr, née Forbes, from Ireland. Ettie attended schools at Geelong and Jung where her father worked for the National Bank of Australasia. On 25 April 1905 at the National Bank, Geelong, she married with Congregational forms Leonard William Dodge (d.1960), a clerk fourteen years her senior who mixed in cricketing circles.

Moving to Sydney, by 1909 Leonard was probably a partner in Victor Trumper's [q.v.12] sports store; from 1911 the firm traded as Victor Trumper & Dodge Ltd at 317 George Street. In 1914 L. W. Dodge & Co., Sydney Sports Stores, opened in Hunter Street. The business succumbed during the Depression. Ettie joined W. S. Friend & Co., wholesale hardware merchants, as a book-keeper and remained with that company until the mid-1940s.

She devoted her leisure to promoting vigoro, a game invented by John George Grant whom her husband had met in England. Similar to cricket and played with eleven in a team, vigoro uses paddle-shaped bats and two different coloured balls which are bowled alternately. When the game was introduced to New South Wales schools in the 1920s, Dodge & Co. began selling vigoro equipment. Grant died in 1927 and bequeathed the trademark and copyright of the game to Ettie.

President (1919-66) of the New South Wales Women's Vigoro Association and foundation president (1932-66) of the All Australian [Vigoro] Association, Ettie organized State competitions and interstate carnivals each year. She took a special interest in instructing and encouraging junior players, and in the mid-1950s guided the formation of the Australian [Vigoro] Umpires' Association. On her retirement in March 1966, she was appointed patron and a life member of the N.S.W.W.V.A. Like other women's team sports, such as hockey, basketball and cricko, vigoro enjoyed great popularity in the 1920s and 1930s, particularly in Queensland, New South Wales and Tasmania. Played in a competitive spirit, the game provided thousands of girls with a sport at school and gave women a break from domestic responsibilities. Teams trained to improve their batting, bowling and fielding skills.

An able speaker and conscientious administrator, Mrs Dodge was respected and well liked by players and officials. Although modest and reserved in manner, she had a good sense of humour, but could be strict when necessary. Five ft 5 ins (165 cm) tall and of medium build, she wore glasses and was rarely seen without a hat. Survived by her daughter, Ettie Dodge died on 3 January 1973 at Mosman and was cremated with Anglican rites. Her legacy, the Dodge Cup, in which are preserved the ashes of the stumps and bails used in the first interstate match of 1931, is the trophy for an annual competition.

L. W. Dodge, *The History of Vigoro* (Syd, nd); M. K. Stell, *Half the Race* (Syd, 1991); *SMH*, 23 Mar 1931; *Sun-Herald* (Syd), 20 Mar 1966; information from Mr G. I. Conen, Mosman, Mrs E. Butters, Carlton, and Mrs M. Slowgrove, Sans Souci, Syd.

ANNE-MARIE GAUDRY

DODGSHUN, KEITH (1893-1971), farmer and politician, was born on 31 July 1893 at Hawthorn, Melbourne, son of Frederick William Dodgshun, a Victorian-born warehouse proprietor, and his wife Rosa May, née Russell, from London. Keith's grandfather, Yorkshire-born James Dodgshun

(1833-1904), had been lord mayor of Melbourne in 1882-83. Educated at Camberwell Grammar School and Burnley School of Horticulture (where he was dux), Keith farmed and managed the family property at Egerton, near Ballan. On 7 November 1917 he joined the Australian Imperial Force. He served briefly in France as a gunner in the 1st Field Artillery Brigade. Discharged on 6 June 1919, Dodgshun took up a soldier-settlement block at Hopetoun, Victoria, where on 15 September 1925 he married Dorothy Lilian Gulliver in St Luke's Anglican Church.

A Baptist and a Freemason, Dodgshun was active in returned servicemen's and wheatgrowers' associations, and played cricket and football. He joined the Victorian Farmers' Union in 1922 and was elected to the Karkarooc Shire Council in 1933. President of the Hopetoun branch of the Victorian United Country Party, he chaired its Ouyen electorate council and (Sir) Albert Bussau's [q.v.7] campaign committee during the 1930s. As chairman of the Wimmera electorate council, Dodgshun was opposed to the Country Party forming coalition ministries. In 1934 he clashed with a Federal member Hugh McClelland [q.v.10] who refused to sign a pledge not to join a coalition government without the permission of the V.U.C.P.'s central council. When Bussau was appointed Victorian agent-general to London, Dodgshun won the keenly contested pre-selection for Ouyen and was elected unopposed to the Legislative Assembly at the by-election on 5 May 1938.

At the State level, internal Country Party politics in the late 1930s were both complex and spiteful. (Sir) John McEwen's [q.v.] expulsion from the party in 1937 for joining the Lyons-Page [qq.v.10,11] ministry occasioned the formation of the breakaway Liberal Country Party, against which Dodgshun campaigned vigorously. In 1939 Premier (Sir) Albert Dunstan [q.v.8] and A. E. Hocking [q.v.] fell out over the central council's refusal to endorse Dunstan's son as the candidate for Bulla-Dalhousie; Dunstan subsequently removed Hocking from the board of the State Savings Bank of Victoria. Because Dodgshun supported Hocking, Dunstan excluded him from his cabinets. Dodgshun regularly voted against the government and assisted in its downfall in 1945. From that year, following a redistribution, he represented the electorate of Rainbow.

Although Dodgshun had differences with Dunstan's successor (Sir) John McDonald [q.v.], he served him loyally as deputy-leader in 1945-55. On the formation of the Hollway [q.v.]-McDonald coalition in November 1947, Dodgshun was appointed chief secretary. He later complained—rather than the coveted agriculture portfolio which went to a Liberal—to prevent the Country Party from attaining greater prominence on rural issues. The coalition proved unstable. In November 1948 Hollway settled an industrial dispute in a manner which McDonald regarded as disloyal. Having complained that he had been called off the Hopetoun bowling green to be informed of Hollway's action, Dodgshun was nicknamed 'Sir Francis'. On 3 December the Country Party withdrew from the coalition.

Hollway's new Liberal ministry collapsed on 27 June 1950. In McDonald's Country Party government (1950-52) Dodgshun was again chief secretary, with the added portfolios of electoral undertakings and immigration. His significant legislative achievement was the introduction in 1950 of full adult suffrage for Legislative Council elections, agreed upon in an Australian Labor Party-Country Party deal. A colleague T. W. Mitchell, however, recalled that Dodgshun's major contribution was to act as a calming and moderating influence in a turbulent and sometimes fiery cabinet.

The A.L.P.'s support for the McDonald government waned as the ministry consistently resisted pressure for electoral reform. With A.L.P. backing, Hollway moved a want of confidence motion on 17 September 1952 and 'Dodger Dodgshun' was denounced for allegedly reneging on an agreement to moderate the high weighting given to rural electorates. The A.L.P. won an absolute majority of assembly seats at the 1952 election. Dodgshun continued as deputy-leader of the Country Party, but, conscious of a worsening heart condition, retired reluctantly in 1955 after his seat had been abolished in the 1953 redistribution.

In retirement at Hopetoun, Dodgshun was chairman of directors (1965-71) of the Phosphate Co-operative Co. of Australia Ltd, of which he had been an original shareholder in 1919. He campaigned for the extension of electricity to remote areas. Survived by his wife and son, he died on 12 May 1971 at Hopetoun; he was accorded a state funeral and buried in the local cemetery.

E. Barbor, *They Went Their Way* (Traralgon, Vic, 1960); *PD* (LA Vic), 7 Dec 1948, 9 Aug 1950, 31 Aug 1971; *Countryman* (Melb), 25 Feb, 14 Apr, 29 Apr 1938, 30 Sept 1955, 3 June 1971; *Age* (Melb), 27 Apr 1938; *Sun News-Pictorial*, 6 May 1938; *Argus*, 18 Sept 1954; J. B. Paul, The Premiership of Sir Albert Dunstan (M.A. thesis, Univ Melb, 1961).   B. J. COSTAR

DOLLERY, EDWIN MAXWELL (1897-1973), army officer and administrator, was born on 21 April 1897 in Hobart, son of Elias Mark Dollery, civil servant, and his wife Emma Ann, née Byfield. Max was educated at Queen's College (1906-12) and The Hutchins School (1913-14) where he excelled as an all-round sportsman. Having served in the cadets and as an officer in the 93rd (Derwent) Infantry, Militia, on 3 June 1916 he enlisted in the Australian Imperial Force. He sailed for Britain in August, joined the 12th Battalion on the Western Front in July 1917 and was commissioned in October. Wounded in action in May 1918, he convalesced in England and returned to his battalion in August. At Proyart, France, later that month he led a party of six across open country in the face of enemy fire and silenced two machine-guns. He was awarded the Military Cross. His A.I.F. appointment terminated in Australia on 21 April 1919.

Entering the Royal Military College, Duntroon, Federal Capital Territory, in February 1920, Dollery graduated next year. On 4 January 1922 at Holy Trinity Church, Hobart, he married with Anglican rites Norma Agnes Best. He held a succession of posts as adjutant and quartermaster before being sent in 1926 to British Army units in India to study mechanical transport, a subject that was to become his specialization. Back home in 1927, he was promoted captain in 1929 and major in 1938; he spent most of the intervening years on staff and instructional duties connected with motor transport. In 1938 he was posted as assistant-director, mechanization, Army Headquarters, Melbourne.

Seconded to the A.I.F. in April 1940 as lieutenant colonel and posted to Headquarters, he embarked for the Middle East in August. As assistant-director, then deputy-director, of ordnance services, he was responsible for managing the force's motor transport requirements. He was appointed O.B.E. in 1942 and arrived home in February 1943. Brigadier-in-charge of administration at headquarters, Northern Territory Force (1943-45), and at headquarters, Queensland Lines of Communication Area (1945-46), he subsequently spent a term in Melbourne as deputy quartermaster general. In September 1947 Dollery went to Hobart as commandant, 6th Military District, where he did much to restore and maintain the city's historic barracks. He was promoted substantive brigadier in 1950 and retired on 21 April 1952.

Dollery's interest in military matters never flagged. He began a collection of military uniforms and artefacts (now the Tasmanian Command Collection, Tasmanian Museum and Art Gallery) and promoted the Australian Cadet Corps of which he was honorary colonel (Tasmania) in 1962-67. Devoted to The Hutchins School, he was a member (1950-60) and chairman (1951-54 and 1956-58) of its board of management, president (1948-50) of the old boys' association and worshipful master of their Masonic lodge. He was chairman of the

Kingborough Commission (1960-71), the Ambulance Board of Southern Tasmania (1966-71) and the Southern Metropolitan Master Planning Authority (1971); he was also a foundation member (1951) of the Tasmanian Historical Research Association and a contributor to the *Australian Dictionary of Biography*. In 1967 he used his organizational skills to help victims of the State's bushfires.

Survived by one of his two daughters, Dollery died on 17 July 1973 at Ashburton, Melbourne, and was cremated.

L. M. Newton, *The Story of the Twelfth* (Hob, 1925); G. H. Stephens, *The Hutchins School, Macquarie Street Years, 1846-1965* (Hob, 1979); *Church News* (Hob), Aug 1973; *Mercury* (Hob), 29 Aug 1968, 18 July 1973; information from Bishop R. E. Davies, Hob, and the late Mr Justice Neasey; personal information.   R. A. FERRALL

DOLLING, DOROTHY ELEANOR ETHEL VICTORIA GEORGINA BARBER (1897-1967), community worker and journalist, was born on 9 June 1897 at Woodhaugh, Dunedin, New Zealand, only daughter and youngest child of Edgar Scott Clarke, produce merchant, and his wife Alice Jane, née Barber, both from Yorkshire, England. Educated at Otago Girls' High School on a scholarship and at the University of Otago (B.Sc., N.Z., 1918; M.Sc., 1919), Dorothy taught mathematics and physics at the University of Leeds, England, in 1920-21 before returning to Otago and studying advanced mathematics. On 13 February 1923 at St Paul's Anglican Church, Adelaide, she married a medical practitioner Charles Edward Dolling (d.1936); they shared a love of cricket and in 1928 he became an Australian Test selector.

In 1929-34 Mrs Dolling was treasurer of the South Australian Country Women's Association. She organized handicraft classes, tree-planting, bushfire and flood relief, a toy fund, a kiosk at the Adelaide Royal Show and holiday cottages at the seaside for country women. During the Depression she and her fellow workers visited many families in remote rural areas, distributing 10 000 blankets and other necessities. Accompanying her husband to Europe in 1934, she represented the C.W.A. on the executive-council of the Associated Country Women of the World. State secretary (1935-47), deputy State president (1947-50) and a life member (from 1945) of the C.W.A., Dolling drafted constitutions for the South Australian branch and the C.W.A. of Australia.

The Women's Centenary Council of South Australia, of which Dolling was a committee-member, raised money in 1936 to found a base of the Australian Aerial Medical service at Alice Springs, Northern Territory, and to establish the Pioneer Women's Memorial Garden on lawns adjacent to the Torrens Parade Ground, Adelaide. That year she returned to work. As 'Marian March' she edited the women's pages of the *Advertiser* and as 'Eleanor Barbour' its rural weekly, the *Chronicle*; she retired from the latter newspaper in 1966.

During World War II Dolling initiated a volunteer personnel register and organized five of the State's wartime committees. Among their numerous achievements, they sent twenty tons of soap to Britain and set up the All Service Library Fund which distributed books to servicemen. She was also an executive-member of the Allied Forces Information Bureau, an officer of the Women's Air Training Corps and chaired (from 1943) the central welfare committee of the Women's Land Army (South Australia). In 1944 she was appointed O.B.E. Two years later, to accommodate country people visiting their relations in Daw Park Repatriation Hospital, the C.W.A. bought a house and named it Dolling Court.

Interested in people and in their development through education, in 1948 Dolling began leadership schools for C.W.A. officers, an initiative later adopted by the Victorian branch. In addition to being the sole woman on the South Australian Documentary Films Committee, she was president of the State section of the Royal Flying Doctor Service of Australia, of the Adelaide University Graduates' Union and of the Bowden Free Kindergarten; she also served on the South Australian Broadcasting Advisory Committee and was a committee-member of St Margaret's Convalescent Hospital, Semaphore. She belonged to the Lyceum Club.

Dolling was noted for her exuberant energy, her industry and her ability to enthuse others; she won the devoted support of her colleagues, especially those in the country. She was without pretension and mixed easily with men and women from all walks of life. When she entered a room, everyone noticed her tall, commanding presence: her dark hair was usually offset by earrings, and she had observant, flashing eyes and a roguish smile. With a penchant for toques and broad-brimmed hats, she wore clothes with panache. Nothing defeated her and she allowed 'no regrets'. She enjoyed cooking, gardening and playing bridge. On outback camping trips she added to her photographic collection of native trees and to her knowledge of local history. Her fund of experience enriched the pages of the *Chronicle*.

Survived by her daughter and son, Dolling died of hypertensive heart disease on 27 June 1967 at Anaster Private Hospital, Parkside, and was cremated. One reader wrote: 'I have lost a friend, though I never met her'. Dolling's estate was sworn for probate in Victoria and South Australia at $64 521. Her son founded the Dorothy Dolling memorial trust to assist country women and their children to obtain further education. A portrait and a miniature are held by the family.

J. Britton et al, *The Royal Flying Doctor Service of Australia* (Syd, 1961); *The First Fifty Years* (Adel, 1979); *Greater than their Knowing* (Adel, 1986); SA Country Women's Assn, *SA Countrywoman*, 30 June, 15 Dec 1967, and *Farmer & Grazier*, 22 June 1972; *Advertiser* (Adel), 12 June 1936, 27 June 1967; *Otago Daily Times*, 9 Jan 1948; *Chronicle* (Adel), 6 July 1967, 24 Sept 1971; Dolling papers (held by CWA Headquarters, Adel, *and* Mr C. H. S. Dolling, McLaren Vale, SA).

ALISON M. DOLLING

DONOGHUE, RAYMOND TASMAN (1920-1960), tram conductor, was born on 10 December 1920 in Hobart, seventh of twelve children of Percy Donoghue, fisherman, and his wife Elsie Ruby Myrtle, née Guppy, both Tasmanian born. Raymond was educated at Macquarie Street School, South Hobart, and Albuera Street State School (1930-34). On 14 March 1940 he enlisted in the Australian Imperial Force. He served with the 2nd/12th Battalion in Britain and the Middle East before being sent to Greece where he was captured by the Germans on 28 April 1941. Freed on 8 May 1945, he returned to Tasmania and was discharged from the A.I.F. on 7 November. At Holy Trinity Church, Hobart, on 12 July 1947 he married with Anglican rites Eileen Patricia Morris, a biscuit-packer. Donoghue worked in turn as a racking cellarhand, mariner, wood carter, tradesman's assistant and lorry driver. Nicknamed 'Puddin', on 25 September 1959 he joined the Metropolitan Transport Trust as a car cleaner, but hoped to become a driver. Within seven months he qualified as a tram conductor.

On Friday 29 April 1960 Donoghue was the conductor of tram 131 as it left the city, bound for Springfield (Moonah). About 4.45 p.m. it collided with a lorry in Elizabeth Street, near Warwick Street, leaving the driver dazed in his damaged cab. The tram, with air-brake pipes fractured and emergency electric brakes ineffective, began rolling downhill, gaining speed towards the city. Assisted by passengers, Donoghue tried to apply the handbrake, but without effect. He then moved the passengers as far back into the car as possible, doing his best to calm them. As the tram rushed backwards at 40 to 50 miles (64 to 80 km) per hour along Hobart's main street in peak-hour traffic, he occupied the cab, sounding the warning gong and struggling to apply the handbrake. Neglecting ample opportunity to save himself by retreating into the passenger compartment or jumping clear, he continued to warn traffic until his tram struck tram 137 at the foot of the Elizabeth Street hill. Partly telescoped, both were projected almost the length of a city block before stopping near Bathurst Street. Donoghue was killed instantly and forty-three passengers were injured, four seriously. It was the Hobart tramways most serious accident.

Donoghue was buried in Cornelian Bay cemetery. The Returned Sailors', Soldiers' and Airmen's Imperial League of Australia conducted the service at which fifty tramwaymen marched ahead of the cortège to join a police guard of honour at the graveside. At the time of the accident the Donoghues had four sons and two daughters; a third daughter was born three weeks later. An appeal to assist the family confirmed the remarkable depth of public feeling by collecting over £7000. Praised in the coroner's report for 'great fortitude in the face of imminent danger . . . doing all in his power to save the lives of numerous passengers', Donoghue was posthumously awarded the George Cross on 11 October 1960. The medal and citation are displayed in the Tasmanian Museum and Art Gallery, Hobart. A memorial plaque was placed in the Metropolitan Transport Trust's depot at Moonah in June 1961.

Mercury (Hob), 30 Apr, 5, 31 May, 3 Aug 1960; *SMH*, 11 Oct 1960; Premier's and Chief Secretary's Dept records, PCS 19/3/44 (TA); Metropolitan Transport Trust records; information from Mrs P. Dixon, Seven Mile Beach, Tas, and Mr G. Donoghue, Mornington, Hob.

GRAHAM CLEMENTS

DORRON, VICTOR HENRY (1903-1969), instructor in woolclassing, was born on 24 July 1903 at Ellensvale, Genoa, Victoria, second son of Thomas Henry Dorron, a farmer from New South Wales, and his South African-born wife Eileen May, née Bucknall. In 1882 Victor's paternal grandfather, John Augustus Dorron, had selected land to the east of Mallacoota and built the Lakeview Hotel which remained the local centre of social activity until the end of World War I. Victor's maternal grandfather Henry Bucknall was the original selector at Gipsy Point. In 1901 Thomas and Eileen settled at Ellensvale on the Wallagaraugh River, four miles upstream from Gipsy Point. Seven years later, when Victor and his brother were of school age, the family shifted to grandfather Bucknall's Amberlee, near Gipsy Point, and the boys rowed four miles to the nearest school at Genoa.

Like most children reared in the country, they made their own pleasures, mostly in the bush or on the rivers: they went hunting, shooting, snaring or fishing, and sometimes put the proceeds from their exploits towards their school expenses. Skins were worth around three shillings each; dingo scalps earned £5 from the shire and wombat scalps five shillings. Victor sold fresh fish for three shillings per lb. As he grew older, he assisted his father in such enterprises as wattle-bark harvesting and road construction.

In 1921 Victor joined the Gordon Institute of Technology at Geelong to learn woolclassing, rapidly reaching a degree of proficiency which enabled him to win the Geelong Woolbrokers' Association's scholarship, worth £400. Having gained practical experience in the shearing sheds of Victoria, New South Wales and Queensland, he became assistant to the head of the woolclassing section of the G.I.T. in 1925 and was subsequently appointed senior instructor in woolclassing. During 1929 he had charge of the sheep and wool section on the Better Farming Train which toured most Victorian country centres. In 1931 Dorron travelled to Britain and took a textile course at the University of Leeds; he also visited textile centres in Germany, Switzerland, France and Belgium, as well as colleges in England and Scotland. He returned to Geelong where he married a saleswoman Jessie Isobel Gordon on 23 December 1933 at St Paul's Anglican Church.

Dorron supervised (1926-56) weekend wool classes at the Ballarat School of Mines, and gave instruction in shearing and woolclassing at Dookie and Longerenong agricultural colleges. In 1956 he was appointed head of the wool school at the G.I.T. He was in demand as a judge at the Geelong Agricultural Show, and at the Geelong and the Hamilton legacy shows. In 1966 he helped to introduce recognized woolclassing courses into country technical and high schools. He retired in 1968. Still fit and active, Dorron boasted that he had never been ill in his life and attributed his health to a 'tough' upbringing in a bush environment. He looked forward to enjoying his favourite pastimes of boating and fishing, but died of acute myeloid leukaemia on 7 October 1969 at Geelong. Survived by his wife, son and daughter, he was buried in Western cemetery.

K. R. Howe and J. G. Browne (eds), *Mallacoota Reflections* (Mallacoota, Vic, 1990); *Snowy River Mail*, 27 Nov 1968; information from the late Mrs J. Dorron.   K. R. HOWE

DORSCH, AGNES MARIE JOHANNA (1871-1958), teacher, was born on 18 December 1871 in Adelaide, eldest of four surviving children of Ernst Bernhard Heyne (d.1881), a florist and seedsman from Saxony, and his wife Wilhilmina Maria Laura, née Hankel. Ernst had studied at the University of Leipzig and assisted Baron von Mueller [q.v.5] in Melbourne. Educated at a Unitarian Sunday School and Norwood Public School, Agnes was identified by J. A. Hartley [q.v.4] as particularly gifted and given extra coaching in Latin and Greek. She won scholarships to the Advanced School for Girls and the University of Adelaide (B.A., 1891). The second woman to graduate in arts from that university, and one of the first to use state-provided bursaries to higher education, she gained first-class honours in classics and mathematics. On 5 April 1893 at her mother's Norwood home she married Caspar Dorsch (d.1916), a Bavarian-born, Lutheran clergyman who had studied in the United States of America; thirteen years her senior, he was a widower with three children. Agnes bore him four sons and four daughters, all of whom she was proud to have breast-fed.

The Rev. Dorsch forbade dancing, picture theatres and card games, seeing them as signs of the devil; his constraints cast a heavy shadow over the growing family. When he suffered a breakdown, he was sent to his people in America to recuperate for two years, but remained a semi-invalid. His subsequent inability to maintain a parish necessitated Agnes's involvement in teaching—at Tormore House School under the redoubtable Caroline Jacob [q.v.9], then at Presbyterian Girls' College and later (for about twenty years) at a Lutheran school, Concordia College. During this time Mrs Dorsch also gave classes at the Young Women's Christian Association and coached private pupils in the evenings. Apart from her daughters she had no domestic help. She was regarded as 'a saint' by her children and fondly remembered for her brilliance as a teacher by several generations of Adelaide students, especially those who went on to do degrees in classics. To be taught by Mrs Dorsch was 'to enter a different world . . . She was big intellectually and culturally'. Many German South Australians had their sense of culture enriched by 'lessons from any of the Heyne family'. Agnes Dorsch 'could read Greek poetry so that it really sounded like poetry'. Her skill in teaching was shared by her younger sisters Laura and Ida, both graduates in arts.

While Mrs Dorsch had little time for the domestic concerns of her large household, she did not neglect to provide books for her children, six of whom obtained university degrees and distinguished themselves with prizes and scholarships. Following her retirement from Concordia in 1942, she continued coaching for many years, even after a stroke at the age of 74. She felt honoured to have taught the children of five governors, including grandchildren of Alfred, Lord Tennyson. Survived by three daughters and three sons, she died on 13 October 1958 at Fullarton and was buried in West Terrace cemetery.

A. Mackinnon, *The New Woman* (Adel, 1986); information from the late Mrs I. Kearney.

ALISON MACKINNON

DOUGHERTY, TOM NICHOLSON PEARCE (1902-1972), trade unionist, was born on 2 March 1902 at Bollon, Queensland, sixth child of native-born parents Robert Alexander Dougherty, telegraph linesman, and his wife Louisa Sarah, née Gibson, schoolteacher and postmistress. Leaving Goondiwindi State School at 13, Tom had a variety of jobs—dairying, clearing timber, road and stock work, and tramway construction; he was also employed on a rubber plantation in New Guinea. He gave his occupation as salesman when he married Ruby McArthur, a waitress, on 14 July 1924 at the Presbyterian manse, South Brisbane; they were to have two sons and a daughter.

Working as a canecutter in the Mackay district until 1932, Dougherty rose through the dominant Queensland branch of the Australian Workers' Union: he was a job representative (from 1924), a paid organizer around Mackay (1932-38), northern district secretary at Townsville (1938-43) and the branch president (1943-45). In addition, he was a delegate to the A.W.U.'s State and federal conventions, and represented the union on the central executive of the Queensland Labor Party. Dougherty became a fervent anti-communist, accusing the 'Reds' of disrupting and undermining the A.W.U.

Elected in 1942 to the federal executive of the A.W.U., in January 1944 he was appointed general secretary in Sydney, following the removal of W. B. Hay. Dougherty was to maintain tight control over the union until his death. He fought with Clarrie Fallon [q.v.] for federal control of union assets and defeated Fallon's efforts to replace him as general secretary. In 1944 Dougherty intervened in the New South Wales branch, removing officials he perceived as hostile, and maintaining federal control until elections in December 1952. His domination of the A.W.U. led to a long-running feud with Clyde Cameron, Federal Labor parliamentarian and former Adelaide branch secretary, who launched a successful legal challenge against certain A.W.U. rules in 1959. Dougherty was once (in 1960) sued for having 'terrorised' branch secretaries. In 1971 he was to be awarded $150 000 damages after he had been accused in the *Australian* of being a 'ballot-rigger and of crushing anyone who refused to be subservient to him'.

Despite all his political manoeuvring, Dougherty gained a reputation as an extremely competent industrial advocate and bargainer on behalf of his 180 000 members. He won good awards for Snowy River workers and helped to make Australian shearers the highest paid in the world. A shrewd, hard-headed businessman, he built up the union's assets and in 1960 the once ramshackle Macdonell [q.v.10] House brought in over £40 000 in rents.

As general secretary, Dougherty continued the A.W.U.'s hostility to the Australian Council of Trade Unions which he claimed was communist influenced. In 1959 he flirted with the idea of forming an anti-communist confederation of trade unions to challenge the A.C.T.U. Eventually, in 1967, he supported the affiliation of the A.W.U. with the A.C.T.U., claiming that communist influence had become negligible. A friend of Professor Harry Messel, in 1957 Dougherty had persuaded the A.W.U. to affiliate with the Nuclear Research Foundation within the University of Sydney and to contribute funding. He opposed the nuclear arms race, particularly British nuclear testing in Australia, but believed that the benefits of peaceful nuclear research would help to weaken the communist threat to the West.

Dougherty represented (1945-53) the A.W.U. on the Wool Consultative Council, served on the boards of the People's Printing & Publishing Co. (later Westland Broadcasting Co.) and Labor Papers Ltd (managing director from 1950), and was secretary of the board of control of the *Australian Worker.* At the invitation of the American Federation of Labor, he visited the United States of America in September-October 1950 and addressed its convention at Houston, calling for the end of all trade with the Soviet Union. In Sydney in October 1953 he and Laurie Short, federal secretary of the Federated Ironworkers' Association, briefed Vice-President Richard Nixon on the continuing strength of communism in Australian unionism.

A member (1950-54) of the New South Wales Labor Party executive and a delegate to A.L.P. federal conferences, Dougherty was committed to the abolition of the Legislative Council. In January 1952 he criticized the New South Wales party for failing to honour its abolitionist policy and claimed that a number of those on the State executive supported retention of the council because they enjoyed the perquisites of membership. At the party conference in June he successfully moved a resolution excluding parliamentarians from the State executive, thereby assisting the anti-communist 'groupers' to gain control of the executive. His support for the 'groupers' evaporated when he suspected that they were trying to seize control of the A.W.U. In September 1957 the Labor Party chose Dougherty to fill a casual vacancy in the Legislative

Council. He promised to resign if he failed to abolish the council and did so in May 1961, following the defeat of the abolition referendum.

'Big Tom' was over 6 ft (183 cm) tall and weighed 14 stone (89 kg). Physically and mentally tough, he had a racy vocabulary, 'interlarded with homely bush sayings'. He continued to show 'traces of his old arrogance and impatience of restraint', dressed in 'well-cut suits, smart ties' and in summer a stylish straw hat, and enjoyed fishing and playing golf. A widower, Dougherty married a 33-year-old divorcee Gwendoline Gertrude Church (d.1956), née Farrow, at the Presbyterian Church, Kogarah, on 25 July 1951; they were to have one son. On 14 November 1959 at the Presbyterian manse, Randwick, he married another divorcee, 39-year-old Elaine Mary Reynolds, née Daley. Survived by his wife and their daughter, and by the children of his previous marriages, he died of coronary thrombosis on 14 October 1972 at his Laurieton home and was cremated.

S. Short, *Laurie Short* (Syd, 1992); D. Connell, *The Confessions of Clyde Cameron 1913-1990* (Syd, 1990); R. Murray, *The Split* (Melb, 1972); *People* (Syd), 28 Feb 1951, p 48; *Bulletin*, 24 Mar 1962; *Australian*, 16, 20 Oct 1967; *Sun-Herald* (Syd), 15 Oct 1972; M. Dodkin, Charlie Oliver—A Political Biography (M.A. thesis, Univ Syd, 1990); K. I. Turner, The New South Wales Legislative Council: An Evaluation with Special Reference to the 1961 Attempt at its Abolition (M.Ec. thesis, Univ Syd, 1965); AWU records (ANUABL); information from Mr R. J. Hawke, Prof H. Messel, and Ms W. Pymont, Syd.   GREG PATMORE

DOUGLAS, CLIVE MARTIN (1903-1977), musician, conductor and composer, was born on 27 July 1903 at Rushworth, Victoria, only child of Rolland Edward Ellerman Douglas, police constable, and his wife Annie Amelia Ellen, née Martin, both Victorian born. Rolland died in the course of duty in 1906. Clive's early childhood was unsettled: he lived for some time with his grandparents at Ballarat and Geelong, and later with his mother and stepfather. Educated at Rushworth State and Coburg High schools, in 1918 he joined the State Savings Bank of Victoria with which he worked for the next eighteen years. He married a 19-year-old typist Isabel Knox on 11 September 1926 with Presbyterian forms at Scots Church, Melbourne; they were to be divorced on 11 September 1935.

Douglas's earliest musical education came from his mother, a pianist. He studied violin with Franz Schieblich, and later theory and orchestration with Alberto Zelman [q.v.12]. As a young man he was active in theatre and community orchestras as violinist and con-

ductor. His first compositional exercises (dating from 1927) led in 1929 to his entry on an Ormond [q.v.5] exhibition to the University Conservatorium of Music (Mus.B., 1934) where he studied composition with A. E. H. Nickson [q.v.]. Works from this period, *Symphony in D* and a symphonic poem, *The Hound of Heaven*, won special prizes in a competition sponsored by the Australian Broadcasting Commission in 1933, and his opera, *Ashmadai*, won first prize in 1935. Through its performance, Douglas met the soprano Marjorie Eloise Ellis whom he married on 15 August 1936 at the Methodist Church, Malvern.

That year Douglas began his professional association with the A.B.C. as conductor of its new Tasmanian orchestra. He developed a deep and lasting interest in Aboriginal folklore and in the Australian landscape which informed his *Bush Legend* (1938, subsequently reworked as *Kaditcha* and submitted for a Mus.D., University of Melbourne, 1958), the ballet scene, *Corroboree* (1939), and the tone poem, *Carwoola* (1939). In 1941-47 he was conductor of the A.B.C.'s Brisbane orchestra, was active with the Army Education Service and completed the opera, *Eleanor* (inspired by the Battle of Britain), in various performances of which his wife sang the principal role. Other appointments included associate-conductorships of the Sydney Symphony Orchestra (1947-53) under (Sir) Eugene Goossens [q.v.] and of the Melbourne Symphony Orchestra (1953-66). Douglas produced scores for documentary films in these years, as well as concert music, and taught at the university conservatorium, Melbourne, in 1959-68.

His extensive travel as staff conductor on country tours inspired works in which he sought to capture the quality of the landscape and to find a musical idiom 'so entirely Australian that no other influence can be felt'. *Wongadilla*, *Namatjira* and *Sturt 1829*, among other compositions, reflected this interest. Douglas's incorporation of melodic materials derived from Aboriginal song was another distinctive feature of his output. These two characteristic elements led some writers to associate his work with Jindyworobakism, but nowhere did Douglas suggest any such connexion, and the application of this term to music is problematical.

Douglas's style was colouristically tonal, although influenced by modalism, exoticism and a slightly dissonant harmonic palette. His music is structured by means of conventional thematic and contrapuntal devices, and occasionally possesses an episodic character. He was little interested in the more progressive musical developments of his time, although he experimented with a modified serialism in such works as the *Divertimento*

No.2 for Orchestra and *Three Frescoes*. In the late 1960s, after retiring from the A.B.C., Douglas visited Europe where he promoted Australian music and absorbed current influences. In his later life his music received only moderate attention at home and abroad, and, with the emergence of new generations of progressive Australian composers, it has been substantially eclipsed, yet Douglas was one of the country's most consistent and committed composers in a period when a creative musical life was struggling to assert itself.

Throughout his career Douglas continued to win awards, including first prize in the Commonwealth Jubilee Competition (1951) and in the A.B.C.-Australasian Performing Right Association competition (1955). In 1963 he was elected a life fellow of the International Institute of Arts and Letters. He died on 29 April 1977 at East Brighton, Melbourne, and was cremated. His wife, their daughter and the daughter of his first marriage survived him. Two portraits are held by the family.

R. Covell, *Australia's Music* (Melb, 1967); J. Murdoch, *Australia's Contemporary Composers* (Melb, 1972); G. Howard, 'Clive Douglas', in F. Callaway and D. Tunley (eds), *Australian Composition in the Twentieth Century* (Melb, 1978); *Aust Musical News*, Oct 1933; *Sounds Aust*, 30, 1991, p 32; N. Saintilan, The Myth of the Musical Jindyworobak: Some Aspects of the Appropriation of Aboriginal Culture in the Music of Clive Douglas and Other Arts in Australia (B. Creative Arts Hons thesis, Univ Wollongong, 1990); Composer Profile: Clive Douglas (interview by C. Southwood, ABC radio, tape held ABC Federal Music L, Syd); Douglas papers (LaTL, Hince collection in NL, Aust Music Centre, Syd).   G. W. HOWARD

DOUGLAS, EDWARD ARCHIBALD (1877-1947) and ROBERT JOHNSTONE (1883-1972), judges, were born on 2 November 1877 at Fortitude Valley, Brisbane, and on 13 April 1883 at Sandgate, first and fourth sons of London-born John Douglas [q.v.4], premier (1877-79) of Queensland, and his second wife Sarah, née Hickey, from Ireland. Educated at various Queensland schools, in 1892 Edward and Robert journeyed with their brothers to Scotland to attend St Benedict's College, Fort Augustus. On his return in 1895, Edward entered the pearling industry based on Thursday Island where his father was government resident. In December 1901 Edward was admitted to the Queensland Bar, having been an associate from 1897 to Sir Samuel Griffith [q.v.9] and then to Justice Virgil Power whose daughter Annette Eileen he married on 9 January 1907 at St Joseph's Catholic Church, Rockhampton. In Brisbane his practice grew steadily. Specializing in taxation and company law, he appeared as coun-

sel in leading commercial, revenue and constitutional cases.

After returning from Scotland, Robert completed his schooling at St Ignatius' College, Riverview, and graduated from the University of Sydney (B.A., 1905). Admitted to the Queensland Bar in September 1906, he served briefly as an associate of Justice Real [q.v.11], commenced practice in 1907 at Townsville, and soon acquired a reputation as a persuasive and successful advocate. On 15 January 1912 he married Annie Alice May Ball (d.1952) at St Joseph's Catholic Church, Townsville. He made a special study of arbitration and in 1915 T. J. Ryan's [q.v.11] Labor government appointed him a judge of the Industrial Court of Queensland. His duties entailed extensive travel in the north where he sometimes worked in shanties. Prominent in civic and social activities, he was also an alderman (1907) of the City of Townsville. He was tall and upright, with a resonant voice, and precise, factual and direct in the courtroom. In 1923, when 'R.J.' became a judge of the Supreme Court, sitting at Townsville, northerners hailed his elevation as a triumph for the region. His reciprocated loyalty later led him to decline an invitation to join the court in Brisbane.

In 1929 Edward was appointed to the Supreme Court in Brisbane. A hard-working, scholarly and erudite judge, with an 'impressively austere' manner, he attracted little public attention until 1938. That year a campaign for the seat of Ithaca was marred on both sides by sectarian bitterness. Sitting as Elections Tribunal judge, Edward found irregularities sufficient to justify setting aside the return of Labor minister E. M. Hanlon [q.v.] to the Legislative Assembly. The decision against Hanlon (who did not give evidence at the hearing) was reversed on appeal by a majority of the Full Court—one of whom was Edward's brother Robert.

Following the resolution of the Ithaca case, 'E.A.' found himself being passed over for offices or honours which he might reasonably have expected. In 1944 another disagreement between Edward and the government over failure to restore judicial pensions, abolished in 1921, attracted further publicity in the press and parliament. Survived by his wife, two of his three daughters and five of his eight sons, Edward Douglas died of a coronary occlusion on 27 August 1947 at Ascot and was buried in Toowong cemetery after a requiem Mass presided over by Archbishop (Sir) James Duhig [q.v.8]. Speaking on behalf of the profession, A. D. McGill [q.v.10]—who had represented Hanlon in the Ithaca case—stressed the esteem and admiration which the judge's conduct in that matter had earned for him among all those who 'look for a fearless and independent Judiciary'. Two of Edward's sons, (Sir) Edward Sholto and Andrew Brice, became active members of the Queensland Law Society.

Robert Douglas retired in 1953. Survived by his three sons and two daughters, he died on 24 December 1972 at Townsville and was buried in Belgian Gardens cemetery. One son, James Archibald, was also a Supreme Court judge.

R. Johnston, *History of the Queensland Bar* (Brisb, 1979); B. H. McPherson, *The Supreme Court of Queensland 1859-1960* (Brisb, 1989); *PD* (Qld), 1944, p 1058; *Qld State Reports*, 1939, p 90, 1947, p ii; *Cwlth Law Reports*, 1938-39, p 313; *Aust Bar Review*, 22 July 1940, p 183; *Daily Mail* (Brisb), 24 Jan 1923; *Brisb Courier*, 24 Jan 1923, 6, 22 Mar 1929; *Telegraph* (Brisb), 6 March 1929, 26-30 Sept, 3, 4, 12 Oct 1938; *Courier-Mail*, 20 Oct 1944, 28 Aug 1947, 26 Dec 1972; *Truth* (Brisb), 22 Oct 1944; *Townsville Daily Bulletin*, 10, 11 Apr 1953.
           B. H. McPHERSON

DOUGLAS, GILBERT ERIC (1902-1970), air force officer, was born on 6 December 1902 at Parkville, Melbourne, second son of Gilbert Douglas, watchman, and his wife Bessie, née Thompson, both Victorian born. Educated at Swinburne Technical College, Eric served three years in the senior cadets before joining the Australian Air Corps in November 1920. He enlisted in the (Royal) Australian Air Force on 31 March 1921 as an aircraftman class 2, fitter aero, and gave his religion as Methodist. Douglas's early postings were to No.1 Flying Training School, Point Cook (1921 and 1922-29), and No.1 Aircraft Depot, Laverton (1921-22). He graduated as airman pilot on 1 December 1927 and was promoted substantive sergeant in October next year.

On 22 November 1922 Douglas had been front-seat passenger in an Avro 504K which attempted to land at Mascot, Sydney. Realizing that the aircraft was about to hit a fence, he stood up: the crash 'propelled him forward' and he was found 'squatted astride the crankshaft, unconscious and bleeding', when the plane came to rest. His quick reaction had saved his life. In 1928, while he was passenger in a test-flight of the Warrigal I, the pilot was unable to recover from a spin. Ordered to abandon the aircraft, Douglas got to his feet: his tall, spare frame 'apparently varied the air flow over the tail', enabling the pilot to regain control and Douglas to resume his seat.

In April 1929 he flew a D.H.9A to the Northern Territory to join Charles Eaton's [q.v.] team in the search for the ill-fated crew of the *Kookaburra*, Keith Anderson and Bob Hitchcock. Douglas was one of the ground party which left Wave Hill on the 24th and reached the *Kookaburra*'s forced-landing site in the Tanami Desert. He helped to bury Anderson and Hitchcock, and was recommended for the Air Force Medal for his part in the mission. On 1 August he was promoted pilot officer.

Following the decision to equip the British, Australian and New Zealand Antarctic Research Expedition with a Gipsy Moth seaplane, Douglas and Flying Officer Stuart Campbell were selected to accompany the explorers on their polar voyage in the summer of 1929-30. The pilots made reconnaissance flights and guided the ship, *Discovery*, through the ice. Because of his mechanical knowledge, Douglas had prime responsibility for maintenance of the aircraft. The expedition's leader Sir Douglas Mawson [q.v.10] also took the Moth and its pilots on the second B.A.N.Z.A.R.E. (1930-31). A flight by Douglas and Mawson on 27 January 1931 almost ended fatally due to a mishap when the plane was being hoisted on board *Discovery*. In 1934 Douglas was awarded the Polar Medal.

From May 1931 Douglas performed instructional duties at No.1 Flying Training School. On 6 January 1934 he married Ella Sevior at Christ Church, South Yarra, with Anglican rites. Promoted flight lieutenant in July, he commanded the R.A.A.F. contingent in *Discovery II* which sailed in December 1935 for the Bay of Wales, Antarctica, to search for the American explorer Lincoln Ellsworth and his pilot Herbert Hollick-Kenyon. On 15 January 1936 Douglas flew over the United States' base, Little America, and sighted Hollick-Kenyon. Both men were safe and Ellsworth made the return trip to Melbourne in *Discovery II*. He and Douglas became close friends; Douglas named his first son Ian Ellsworth.

Transferring to engineering duties in June 1937, Douglas returned to No.1 Aircraft Depot in command of the Technical Squadron's aircraft repair section. By July next year he was back at No.1 F.T.S. as engineer officer. He introduced sailing as a recreational activity for cadets and test-flew aircraft when required. Promoted temporary wing commander, in June 1940 he assumed command of No.1 A.D. In June 1942 he moved to Queensland to command No.3 A.D. at Amberley where he was responsible for servicing aircraft of the Australian and U.S. air forces. On 1 December 1943 he was promoted temporary group captain and in August 1947 became commanding officer of R.A.A.F. Station, Amberley. He retired on 1 July 1948 as honorary group captain.

In 1949-60 Douglas was a civilian technician with the navy's Aircraft Maintenance and Repair Division, Melbourne. Survived by his wife, daughter and two sons, he died of cardiac disease on 4 August 1970 at Heidelberg and was cremated.

C. D. Coulthard-Clark, *The Third Brother* (Syd, 1991); D. Wilson, *Alfresco Flight* (Melb, 1991); *Age* (Melb), 8 Aug 1970; unit history records of No 1 Flying Training School, Point Cook, Vic, No 1 Aircraft Depot, Laverton, Vic, No 3 Aircraft Depot, Amberley, Qld, and RAAF Base, Amberley, Qld, all held by Dept of Defence (Air Force Office), Canb.   DAVID WILSON

DOVEY, WILFRED ROBERT (1894-1969), judge, was born on 10 April 1894 at Bathurst, New South Wales, son of Robert Dovey, a native-born farmer who had been an assistant to William Farrer [q.v.8], and his wife Winifred Isabel Agnes, née Adams, born in China. 'Bill' was educated on scholarships at Sydney Grammar School and the University of Sydney (B.A., 1916). On 11 August 1914 he enlisted in the Australian Naval and Military Expeditionary Force; on 15 August at St John's Anglican Church, Glebe, he married a teacher Mary Dorothy Duncan; and on 19 August he embarked for Rabaul where he served as a sergeant. He was discharged on 4 March 1915. While teaching at Brisbane Grammar School, Dovey studied law at the University of Queensland. An associate successively (1918-21) to chief justices Sir Samuel Griffith and (Sir) Adrian Knox [qq.v.9], he was admitted to the New South Wales Bar on 1 June 1922.

His fine presence, which was enhanced by a monocle, and his rich voice, which conveyed a Shakespearian vocabulary, brought Dovey success at the Bar and he was appointed K.C. in 1935. He was involved professionally in many highly publicized Federal and State royal commissions and inquiries, including those on doctors' remuneration for national insurance (1938), on the detention of members of the Australia First Movement (1944) and on the liquor laws (1951-52). He appeared as prosecutor against Sydney newspapers (1944), C. H. Cousens [q.v.13] (1946), General H. G. Bennett [q.v.13] (1946), S. M. Falstein [q.v.] (1947), L. L. Sharkey [q.v.] (1949) and miners' officials (1949).

Dovey was an alderman (1935-36) on Waverley Municipal Council, and served on the Aliens Classification and Advisory Committee (1941-45) and the Commonwealth Immigration Advisory Council (1945-65). He leased successful racehorses and was a foundation member (vice-chairman) of the Sydney Turf Club in 1943. One year later he was elected to the committee of the Australian Jockey Club (vice-chairman 1953-61).

Appointed a judge of the Supreme Court of New South Wales in 1953, in the following year Dovey became judge in divorce and matrimonial causes. His career on the bench was marred by public criticism. As royal commissioner inquiring into D. E. Studley-Ruxton's allegations of police brutality in 1954, he was censured by the Bar Association of New South Wales for lacking tolerance and judicial calm, and also by the Incorporated Law Institute for departing 'from accepted standards of courtesy, fairness and patience'. He was attacked by State politicians in 1953 for continuing on the A.J.C. committee and in August 1960 for allegedly attending to A.J.C. business to the neglect of his judicial duties. On the bench he was often irascible and his judgements were liberally dosed with sharp criticism.

Retiring in April 1964, Dovey belonged to Vaucluse Bowling Club. He died 12 December 1969 in St Vincent's Hospital, Darlinghurst, and was cremated. His wife survived him, as did their son William who was to become a judge of the Family Court of Australia and their daughter Margaret who married Edward Gough Whitlam.

G. E. Hall and A. Cousins (eds), *Book of Remembrance of the University of Sydney in the War 1914-1918* (Syd, 1939); *SMH*, 29 Oct 1947, 27 Aug 1953, 5 May, 31 July, 6 Aug 1954, 17, 19 Dec 1957, 27 Aug 1959, 13 Dec 1969; *Daily Mirror*, (Syd), 23, 25-27, 30, 31 Oct, 1-3 Nov 1967; information from Hon E. G. Whitlam, Syd; personal information.   MALCOLM D. BROUN

DOWLING, SIR ROY RUSSELL (1901-1969), naval officer, was born on 28 May 1901 at Condong, on the Tweed River, New South Wales, sixth child of native-born parents Russell Dowling, sugar-cane inspector, and his wife Lily Jane, née Ingram. J. S. Dowling [q.v.4] was Roy's grandfather. In 1915 young Dowling entered the Royal Australian Naval College, Jervis Bay, Federal Capital Territory. Although his academic performance was undistinguished, he was a natural sportsman; he was made chief cadet captain and graduated as King's medallist in 1918.

Sent to Britain in 1919 for training with the Royal Navy, Midshipman Dowling was present at the scuttling of the German High Seas Fleet on 21 June in Scapa Flow, Orkney Islands. Next year he participated in operations in the Bosporus and the Sea of Marmara against Turkish nationalists. Having completed courses at Greenwich and Portsmouth, he returned to Australia in 1922, joined the cruiser, H.M.A.S. *Adelaide*, and was promoted lieutenant in March 1923. The ship accompanied the R.N.'s Special Service Squadron from Australia to England in 1924.

With a growing reputation as a competent young officer, Dowling left *Adelaide* in October 1924 and completed the specialist gunnery course at Portsmouth. He came home in

December 1926 and served in the destroyer depot ship, *Platypus*, and the destroyer, *Anzac*, as flotilla gunnery officer. In July 1928 he was posted to the gunnery school at Flinders Naval Depot (H.M.A.S. *Cerberus*), Westernport, Victoria, where he had a busy teaching schedule. On 8 May 1930 in the chapel of Melbourne Church of England Grammar School he married Jessie Spencer, younger daughter of G. E. Blanch [q.v.7]; they were to have five children, including two sets of twins.

In December Lieutenant Commander Dowling embarked with his wife for England. From May 1931 he was gunnery officer of the light cruiser, *Colombo*, on the Mediterranean Station; the vessel spent six months as flagship of the Third Cruiser Squadron. Back home, in 1933-35 Dowling was squadron gunnery officer in the cruiser, *Canberra*. Rear Admiral (Sir) Wilbraham Ford considered him an 'officer of outstanding ability'. On 10 July 1935 Dowling took charge of the gunnery school, but his prospects were tempered by the continuing effects of the Depression. Despite further good service and more golden opinions from his seniors, he had to wait until 31 December 1936 for promotion to commander.

Next month Dowling assumed command of the new sloop, *Swan*, which performed squadron work and conducted independent cruises. Baron (Earl) Gowrie [q.v.9] and Lady Gowrie travelled with him in 1937 during part of their tour of Papua and the mandated Territory of New Guinea. Although Dowling probably enjoyed his time in *Swan*, he had some difficult moments and clashed on at least one occasion with Rear Admiral (Sir) Richard Lane-Poole, the commander of the Australian Squadron. Lane-Poole recommended that Dowling gain experience as executive officer of a major vessel. By October 1939 he was standing by the anti-aircraft cruiser, *Naiad*, under construction in Britain.

Completed in mid-1940, *Naiad* served in the British Home Fleet. A pressing need for anti-aircraft units in the Mediterranean led to her transfer there in May 1941. During operations off Crete that month, the cruiser was bombed and badly damaged. Dowling played a leading part in work which enabled her to reach harbour. Following five weeks of repairs, *Naiad* escorted convoys to Malta and protected the fleet from air attacks. In November she hoisted the flag of Rear Admiral (Admiral of the Fleet Sir) Philip Vian and next month took part in the first battle of Sirte in which British cruisers and destroyers drove off a more powerful Italian force. On 11 March 1942 *Naiad* was torpedoed by U-565 about 50 nautical miles (93 km) off the coast of Egypt. She sank in little over twenty minutes with the loss of eighty-two men.

A survivor of the sinking, in July 1942 Dowling became director of plans at Navy Office, Melbourne. The R.A.N.'s heavy losses continued until August and he was involved in efforts to restore the service's strength. In September 1943 he was made acting (substantive June 1944) captain and deputy chief of Naval Staff. As such, he played a key role in initial planning for the postwar navy: a carrier force was envisaged as part of the measures to give the R.A.N. greater ability to operate independently in the Pacific and Indian oceans.

In November 1944 Dowling took command of the cruiser, *Hobart*, as she emerged from a prolonged refit. Strikes and an erratic supply system hampered his efforts to make the ship fully operational, but he eventually ensured that she acquitted herself well in action. Next year *Hobart* supported the invasions of Cebu Island, Philippines (March), Tarakan Island, Borneo (April-May), Wewak, New Guinea (May), and Brunei (June) and Balikpapan (July), Borneo. For 'outstanding courage, skill and initiative' in these operations, Dowling was awarded the Distinguished Service Order.

Present at the Japanese surrender in Tokyo Bay on 2 September 1945, *Hobart* became the flagship of the Australian Squadron. Until February 1946 Dowling acted as flag captain and chief of staff to Commodore (Vice Admiral Sir) John Collins. Although ill as a result of wartime strain, Dowling impressed Collins as a capable officer. A period of leave restored Dowling's health and in May he was appointed director of naval ordnance, torpedoes and mines, at Navy Office. While this post did not have the broad responsibilities of D.C.N.S., he had to plan for the acquisition of modern weapons and the development of manufacturing facilities to produce them in Australia.

Dowling was only tangentially involved in preparations for the Fleet Air Arm, but the purchase of the first of the new carriers offered him a great opportunity. Four R.A.N. captains senior to him had been killed in the war; of those surviving, only J. M. Armstrong was in the running for carrier command. When Armstrong became medically unfit for sea service, Dowling went to England in his stead and in December 1948 commissioned H.M.A.S. *Sydney*. Provided he were successful in the ship, he was certain to be selected for flag rank. *Sydney* and her air group soon established a high level of efficiency.

In April 1950 Dowling left *Sydney* with great regret and in need of rest. He was given leave before his appointment in June as chief of naval personnel. Elevated at the same time to commodore, first class, he had much of the status of a rear admiral. It is likely that Dowling would have later received an exchange posting with the R.N., had not Rear Admiral H. B. Farncomb [q.v.]—who was in line to succeed Collins as chief of Naval Staff—been retired in 1951. Farncomb's departure made Dowling the heir apparent.

Dowling's term in charge of personnel reinforced his interest in sailors' welfare and pay. The demands of the Korean War and the expansion of the R.A.N. in a period of low unemployment occasioned considerable manpower problems. Dowling did his best to make the navy an attractive career, recruited former R.N. personnel and expanded the women's service. Appointed C.B.E. in 1953, he attended the Imperial Defence College, London, that year. On 8 July he was promoted rear admiral and in December assumed command of H.M.A. Fleet. The Federal government introduced economies after hostilities ceased in Korea, and he was obliged to oversee a reduction in operations. Contrariwise, he had the pleasure of escorting the royal yacht, *Gothic*, during Queen Elizabeth II's tour of Australia in 1954.

Superseding Collins as chief of Naval Staff on 24 February 1955, Dowling was promoted vice admiral and appointed C.B. in June. His term of office was marked by continuous pressure on the R.A.N. as the government curbed defence spending and accorded the navy the lowest priority of the three services. Collins had reluctantly decided to cancel new construction. Dowling struggled to retain the Fleet Air Arm and the aircraft carrier, *Melbourne*.

With a limited capacity in the Naval Staff for assessing technological developments, Dowling came to rely on the advice of the British first sea lord, Earl Mountbatten, whom he admired and whose friendship he valued. The years 1955-59 marked the last flourish of the client relationship of the R.A.N. with the R.N., even though Britain was no longer able to help in maintaining those capabilities which Australians thought essential in their service. Alarmed by the expansion of the Soviet and Indonesian navies, Dowling canvassed the purchase of tactical nuclear weapons to provide some means of destroying large warships.

The need for an offensive capacity of this nature and for protection against modern aircraft increasingly concerned the Naval Staff. Much of the groundwork was laid in Dowling's time for the later decision to buy American guided-missile destroyers, though he held that the R.A.N.'s primary contribution to the Western alliance should remain in anti-submarine warfare. He was one of the first to propose that the R.A.N. be equipped with submarines and believed that they would be essential if the Fleet Air Arm could not be sustained. His long-held wish to return the R.A.N.C. from Flinders Naval Depot to Jervis Bay was realized in 1958. He moved his office to Canberra in 1959.

Elevated to K.B.E. in 1957, Sir Roy anticipated retirement at the end of his term in 1959, but was unexpectedly offered the chairmanship of the Chiefs of Staff committee. Despite the position's lack of executive authority, Dowling accepted with enthusiasm. He was relieved as C.N.S. on 22 March and took up the chairmanship next day. The office proved largely frustrating for him. Advised by Mountbatten, who was then chief of the Defence Staff in Britain, he attempted to achieve similar status and title, but the prospect of an executive head did not appeal to the services, nor to the Department of Defence, and Dowling's suggestion made little progress. He also had to preside over the decision to abandon the Fleet Air Arm—a move reversed after his retirement—and other defence cuts.

Convinced that Australia should be prominently involved in the South-East Asia Treaty Organization, in March 1961 Dowling addressed a press conference in Bangkok and affirmed his country's readiness to send troops to Laos in an emergency. Under Opposition pressure, the Federal government declined to endorse his remarks.

Dowling retired on 28 May 1961, but wanted other employment. Eschewing commerce, he had hoped that Prime Minister (Sir) Robert Menzies [q.v.] would find him a diplomatic posting and was disappointed that nothing eventuated. He remained in Canberra where he pursued an active role in the Anglican Church, of which he was a devout member, and served as chairman (1962-67) of the local division of the Australian Red Cross Society.

In July 1962 Dowling was chosen to plan the forthcoming royal tour of Australia. He threw himself into the work and in March 1963 Queen Elizabeth II invested him as K.C.V.O. In November he was appointed permanent Australian secretary to the Queen. Survived by his wife, two sons and three daughters, he died of a coronary occlusion on 15 April 1969 in Canberra Hospital and was cremated.

A physically robust man who considered himself primarily a sea-going officer, Dowling possessed fine powers of leadership and a sound rather than penetrating intellect. He was thrust into the highest positions of the R.A.N. largely as a result of the heavy casualties of World War II. That his terms as C.N.S. and chairman of the Chiefs of Staff committee were marked by few innovations was as much due to the limited priority given to defence as to any lack of effort on his part. His task had been to hold the line.

F. M. and P. McGuire, *The Price of Admiralty* (Melb, 1944); F. B. Eldridge, *A History of the Royal*

Australian Naval College (Melb, 1949); J. Collins, *As Luck Would Have It* (Syd, 1965); H. Burrell, *Mermaids Do Exist* (Melb, 1986); R. Hyslop, *Aye Aye, Minister* (Canb, 1990); L. Le Bailly, *The Man Behind the Engine* (Lond, 1990); A. Cooper, Anglo-Australian Naval Relations in 1945-1960 (B.A. Hons thesis, Univ NSW (ADFA), 1991); Dowling papers (held by Mr A. Dowling, Mornington, Vic); Captain J. B. Foley papers (held by the author, Warfare School, HMAS *Watson*, Watsons Bay, Syd); Earl Mountbatten of Burma papers (Hartley L. Univ Southampton, Eng); A3978/8, item Dowling, R. R. *and* Aust Naval Bd, Minutes, 1952-58 (AA, Canb); ADM 205/76, 101, 105, 110, 169, 173 (PRO, Lond); information from Mr A. Dowling, Mornington, Cdr A. W. Grazebrook, Mansfield, Vic, and the late Rear-Admiral W. D. H. Graham.

J. V. P. GOLDRICK

DOWN, JOHN EGBERT (1885-1963), dentist and army officer, was born on 29 July 1885 at Ascot Vale, Melbourne, third child of Victorian-born parents Fred Adolphus Down, dentist, and his wife Fanny Mary, née Gardener. Educated at Scotch College and the University of Melbourne (L.D.S., 1906; B.D.Sc., 1920), John practised at Casterton where, on 16 April 1913 in Christ Church, he married with Anglican rites Ethel Ruth Jackson (d.1940).

After serving with the cadets, by 1914 Down was a lieutenant in the 20th Light Horse Regiment, Militia. On 14 July 1915 he joined the Australian Imperial Force as an honorary lieutenant, Dental Corps. Three days later he sailed for Egypt. He was sent to France in November and spent one year at the Divisional Base Depots, Etaples, before being attached to units in England. From November 1917 to October 1918 he was staff officer, dental services, A.I.F. Depots in Britain; from October to December 1918 he held a similar post in France. In 1917 he had been promoted captain (April) and major (December). He was appointed O.B.E. in 1919.

Down's A.I.F. appointment terminated on 21 April 1919 and he took over his father's Melbourne practice. He resumed his Militia career in 1924 as senior dental officer, 3rd District Base. In 1928 he was appointed inspector of dental services, Army Headquarters, Melbourne, and promoted lieutenant colonel; his posting marked the beginning of an established dental service in the Australian Military Forces.

As president (1928) of the State Dental Society of Victoria, Down had seen it become a branch of the Australian Dental Association: the change to a national body was intended to secure for the profession something of the power and status which the British Medical Association had brought to medicine. He was a member (1924-31) and president (1929-31) of the Dental Board of Victoria.

Appointed assistant director-general medical services (dental) in October 1939, Down was seconded to the A.I.F. on 30 June 1940 as senior officer, dental services, administrative headquarters. On 19 September that year at St James's Old Cathedral, West Melbourne, he married Jetta Crystal Bowman, a 23-year-old nurse. He embarked for the Middle East in October. Promoted colonel in January 1941, he was assistant-director of medical services (dental), A.I.F. in the Middle East, until January 1942. Down returned to Melbourne in February as A.D.G.M.S.(D.), Land Headquarters. He was mentioned in dispatches in June.

Rejecting the notion that dentistry was merely a branch of medicine, Down insisted that military dentists should have autonomy in professional matters. His Middle East experience revealed that the dental health of Australian soldiers was as poor as it had been in World War I. He was convinced that the provision of dental personnel, equipment and supplies received low priority because medical officers did not recognize the importance of dental treatment in maintaining the efficiency of troops in the field.

Down worked long and effectively to have the dental service separated from the medical corps, even using his friendship with General Sir Thomas Blamey [q.v.13]. On 23 April 1943 the (Royal) Australian Army Dental Corps was formed; as director, Down was promoted temporary brigadier in August. In 1945 he was appointed C.B.E. Relinquishing his A.I.F. appointment in August 1946, he continued as part-time director, served in the Citizen Military Forces and grew fruit on his farm at Mitcham. He was placed on the Retired List on 4 May 1951.

Down brought military dentistry out of the shadow of medicine at a personal cost. By encouraging his subordinates to resist encroachments on their professional field, he aroused resentment among a number of senior medical officers. Forthright and uncompromising, even abrupt and abrasive on occasions, he made as many enemies as friends among civilian and army colleagues alike. Never the academic nor technical expert, Down was remembered more in admiration than affection as very much the military leader. He died on 30 November 1963 at Mornington and was cremated. His wife survived him, as did the three daughters of his first marriage. The J. E. Down Dental Training Centre, School of Army Health, Portsea, commemorates him.

A. S. Walker, *Clinical Problems of War* (Canb, 1952) and *Middle East and Far East* (Canb, 1953); *Aust J of Dentistry*, 1 Dec 1928, 1 Oct, 1 Nov 1930,

1 Feb, 1 Mar, 1 Nov 1931, Nov 1946; *Aust Dental J*, June 1977; Roy Aust Army Dental Corps, *Cadmus*, 7, 1988, 11, 1992; *Age* and *SMH*, 1 Jan 1945; J. W. Skinner, The Origin of the Dental Service in the Australian Army (ts, held by director of Dental Services—Army, Dept of Defence, Canb).

ALISON PILGER

DOWNIE, EWEN THOMAS TAYLOR (1902-1977), medical practitioner, was born on 22 April 1902 at Fitzroy, Melbourne, son of Thomas Taylor Downie, a doctor from Scotland, and his wife Katherine, née Smith, who was born in the Philippines. Educated at Scotch College and the University of Melbourne (M.B., B.S., 1925; M.D., 1929), Ewen spent two years as a resident and registrar at the Alfred Hospital. He made the conventional pilgrimage to London where he worked with (Sir) Francis Fraser at St Barthomolew's Hospital and qualified M.R.C.P. (1928).

Returning to Melbourne, Downie was appointed assistant to the asthma clinic at the Alfred. He developed a particular interest in diabetes and, with A. B. Corkill [q.v.13], launched an educational programme on the treatment of diabetes mellitus with diet and insulin. In 1929 he succeeded Corkill as physician in charge of the hospital's diabetic clinic. He also worked at the Baker [q.v.7] Medical Research Institute on aspects of carbohydrate metabolism and in 1932 was awarded the Bertram Armytage prize for medical research. On 10 March that year at Scots Church, Melbourne, he married with Presbyterian forms a nursing sister Muriel Mary Cumming. Physician to out-patients (1932-41) and honorary physician to in-patients (1941-56) at the Alfred Hospital, he was subdean (1932-45) of the clinical school and a foundation fellow (1938) of the Royal Australasian College of Physicians.

On 1 February 1941 Downie was appointed major, Australian Army Medical Corps, Australian Imperial Force. He served in general hospitals in the Middle East (1941-42) and in Australia (1942-44). Promoted temporary colonel, he was sent to Washington in 1944 where he became assistant director general, medical services, with the Australian Military Mission. Back home, he transferred to the Reserve of Officers as lieutenant colonel on 13 December 1945.

Elevated F.R.C.P. (1945), in 1948 Downie was Stewart lecturer in medicine at the university. As dean (1946-57) of the clinical school, he succeeded (Sir) Wilberforce Newton [q.v.] and dominated the hospital's medical education policy. He also ran the diabetic and metabolic unit until 1962. Six years later it was named after him. Downie's contributions to the fields of metabolism, nutrition and diabetes had earned him a reputation outside Australia. In 1955 he lectured at the University of Toronto, Canada, and in 1950 and 1957 to the American College of Physicians at Philadelphia. His interest in diabetes and metabolism led to the recognition of endocrinology as a sectional specialty in internal medicine and to the formation of the Endocrine Society of Australia, of which he was first president (1958-60).

After his retirement in 1962, Downie retained an association with the Alfred through its board of management (vice-president 1960-67) and as honorary consultant physician to the diabetic clinic. Despite a laryngectomy, he continued to practise and to participate in public meetings almost until his death. Friends and critics admired his fortitude during these latter years. While he could be acerbic with colleagues who had not gained his respect and was intolerant of anyone who created disorder, he was intensely loyal to those who served him well, and spared no effort to help younger people in their careers. He belonged to the Metropolitan Golf and Melbourne clubs. Survived by his wife, son and daughter, he died on 1 August 1977 at Kew and was cremated; his estate was sworn for probate at $162 649.

T. E. Lowe, *The Thomas Baker, Alice Baker and Eleanor Shaw Medical Research Institute* (Melb, c1974); A. M. Mitchell, *The Hospital South of the Yarra* (Melb, 1977); *SMH*, 17 June 1953, 20 May 1956.

BRYAN HUDSON

DOWNING, CECILIA (1858-1952), temperance worker, community activist and political organizer, was born on 13 January 1858 at Islington, London, second child of Isaac Hopkins, plasterer, and his wife Mary, née Morgan. That year the family emigrated to Melbourne where Isaac set up as a contracting plasterer. Cecilia was educated at Trinity Girls' School, Williamstown, and the Training Institution, Carlton. On receiving her primary teacher's certificate, she was posted to Portarlington, but continued to play the organ and teach Sunday School at Williamstown Baptist Church. On 12 February 1885 at her parents' Williamstown home she married a pastor, John Downing (d.1939). After serving a further six years (at Williamstown and Kyneton), John retired from the ministry and was employed by the State Savings Bank of Victoria as a branch manager at Portland, Horsham and Sale. The Downings returned to Melbourne in 1901.

Despite the demands of her seven children, Cecilia involved herself in church, temperance and philanthropic work. A founding member of the Kyneton branch of the

Woman's Christian Temperance Union, she became Victorian recording secretary (1909) and president (1912), and founding superintendent (1911) of the W.C.T.U.'s immigration department. She was also one of the government's first child-probation officers (1907). Having joined the Collins Street Baptist Church in 1906, she expanded her interests to include the Women's Guild, which she helped to establish in 1910, the Melbourne Ladies' Benevolent Society and a 'school for mothers' at Richmond. She also joined the Australian Women's National League.

Mrs Downing's political principles reflected both the Baptist stress on individual conscience, initiative and responsibility, and Free Church suspicion of government regulation. Her fundamentalist evangelical faith channelled her intelligence into applied knowledge rather than reflective or critical thinking. The emphasis of her early career was on moral reform. While she never forsook her commitment to temperance and rescue work, her subsequent activities were grounded in equally fundamentalist free-market doctrines. To her, government interference in the relationship between producer and consumer was analogous to interference between the individual Christian and God.

A pacifist at the outbreak of World War I, by the end of 1914 Downing was unqualified in her support of the war effort. Until November 1915, she devoted her energies to the battle against drink. Under her leadership the W.C.T.U.'s Victorian branch expanded more rapidly than any other and galvanized nearly all women's organizations in the State to demand 'dry' canteens in military camps and the early closing of hotels. With three sons serving in the Australian forces, she supported conscription for overseas service.

War confirmed Downing's transition from the local realms of church and community to the spheres of economy, state and nation. An early member and vice-president (1917) of the Housewives' Co-operative Association (later the Housewives' Association of Victoria), she served on the executive during the period of heightened activity in the 1920s when membership grew to 29 000. In 1930 she took part in a revolt of the Housewives' Association's Victorian executive against its autocratic president Delia Russell [q.v.11 P.J. Russell]. From 1920 Downing had reduced her involvement in the A.W.N.L., though she later represented that body on the executive of the Australian Association for Fighting Venereal Disease.

In 1925 she founded and became publicity-agent for the Victorian Baptist Women's Association which affiliated with the National Council of Women in 1926 and began to press for places on the Baptist Union's council and committees. The Downings visited North America, Switzerland and Britain in 1928 where Cecilia represented Australian Baptist women and the Australian W.C.T.U. at international conferences. Secretary to the Victorian Baptist Women's Association from 1932, she made a proposal (approved next year) that women should sit on the executive and standing committees of the Baptist World Alliance. When interstate agreement for a federal organization was achieved in 1933, she drafted a constitution and on 6 September 1935 was elected foundation president of the Women's Board of the Baptist Union of Australia.

In 1928 Downing had been appointed honorary secretary of the National Council of Women in Victoria; in 1934 she joined its Centenary Council executive-committee. On resigning as secretary in 1936, she was awarded the council's gold badge for distinguished service. In the Depression her welfare work focussed on the Travellers' Aid Society of Victoria, of which she had been an executive-member since 1920. She was elected junior vice-president in 1932.

During World War II Downing was actively involved in the Australian Comforts Fund, the Victorian Council of Women's Emergency Service, and the War Loan and War Savings Certificates committee. In June 1940 she was elected national president of the Federated Association of Australian Housewives, a position she held throughout the war years in addition to the State presidency which she had assumed in 1938. Under her leadership the F.A.A.H. increased its membership to 130 000—the largest women's organization in Australia. Her most important wartime achievement was to secure legislation which provided home help for women with large families.

After initiating the establishment of the Victorian Women's Inter-Church Council, Downing became a Baptist delegate on that organization in 1940. She resigned her secretaryship of the V.B.W.A. in 1942, but continued as publicity-officer and was elected vice-president (1944) of the Women's Board of the B.U.A. President of Travellers' Aid in 1941, she accepted the vice-presidency in 1943 and was re-elected president in 1945. When the National Travellers' Aid Society was established in 1944, she was elected president and established an effective working relationship between Travellers' Aid and the minister for immigration Arthur Calwell [q.v.13].

Relinquishing her federal presidency of the Housewives' Association in 1945, Downing remained State president until her death. Her campaign for freedom from the economic restrictions of wartime was criticized by those who saw them as a means of ensuring equality of sacrifice; her continuing attacks on strikers and her opposition to a reduction in the working week also alienated some working-class branches. Despite persistent efforts to maintain a non-party stance, Downing was accused of anti-Labor bias. She openly supported attempts to ban the Communist Party of Australia in 1950-51.

Ignoring medical advice to restrain her activities, Downing was re-elected national president of Travellers' Aid in 1947. She was appointed a life officer (1945) of the V.B.W.A., co-opted to the Victorian Baptist Union's executive-council in 1946 and made a life member (1948) of the Women's Board. In 1949-51 she again served as federal president of the Housewives' Association. She was appointed M.B.E. in 1950. Survived by her three daughters and two of her four sons, Cecilia Downing died on 30 August 1952 at Ivanhoe and was buried in Kyneton cemetery.

Her fifth child WALTER HUBERT DOWNING (1893-1965), was born on 10 December 1893 at Portland, Victoria. Educated at Tooronga Road and Fairfield state schools, Scotch College and the University of Melbourne (LL.B., 1921), he enlisted in the Australian Imperial Force on 30 September 1915 and served with the 57th Battalion in Egypt and on the Western Front. He was awarded the Military Medal for bravery near Glencorse Wood, Belgium, in September 1917, and was promoted sergeant next year, but his real talent lay in the observation of his fellows.

Discharged in Melbourne on 29 May 1919, Walter Downing completed the two books on which his reputation rests: *Digger Dialects* (1919), a lexicon of Australian idiom in World War I, and *To the Last Ridge* (1920), a series of vignettes of life in the trenches and behind the lines. He edited *Melbourne University Magazine* and was awarded the university's Dublin prize in 1921. A keen sportsman, he won a Blue in lacrosse and gained Ormond [q.v.5] College cricket colours; in the mid-1920s he took up skiing.

Admitted to the Bar on 3 October 1921, he formed a partnership with H. E. Elliott [q.v.8]. In 1924-35 Downing was a legal officer in the Militia and rose to lieutenant-colonel. While experience of war had softened his intolerance of drink and gambling, his Baptist convictions remained firm and were reflected in his work for Legacy and, as acting-consul for Yugoslavia, his services to travellers and refugees. Duty sometimes forced him into public life, though he shared his father's quiet temperament and preference for privacy. On 11 May 1929 he had married Dorothy Louise Hambleton with Methodist forms at Queen's College chapel, Carlton. Survived by his wife and four sons, he died on 30 October 1965 at Heidelberg and was cremated.

B. S. Brown, *Baptised into One Body* (Melb, nd); F. Fraser and N. Palmer (eds), *Centenary Gift Book* (Melb, 1934); I. McCorkindale (ed), *Pioneer Pathways* (Melb, 1948); A. Norris, *Champions of the Impossible* (Melb, 1978), *White Ribbon Signal*, Dec 1914, Aug 1915, Oct 1916; *Housewife* (Melb), June 1937, Jan, Mar, Apr, June, Nov 1939, June-Aug 1940, Mar, June, Dec 1947; *Herald* (Melb), 8 Nov 1947, 3 Aug 1952; *Argus*, 3, 4 May 1949, 8 June 1950, 31 Aug 1951; Travellers' Aid Soc (Vic), Annual Report, 1917-53, *and* Housewives' Assn of Vic, Minute-books, 1915-17, 1952 (SLV); Baptist Union of Vic Archives, Melb; information from Miss G. Downing, Karara Baptist Home, Kew, Melb.

JUDITH SMART

DOWNING, DESMONDE FLORENCE (1920-1975), stage designer, was born on 26 November 1920 at Neutral Bay, Sydney, eldest of five children of Frank Hammersley Downing, a Victorian-born engineer, and his wife Violet Hester, née Sadler, from Tasmania. Des won a scholarship to Meriden Church of England Grammar School, Strathfield, studied art at East Sydney Technical College from 1937 and was taught singing with her three talented sisters. Employed as a solicitor's clerk with Allen, Allen [qq.v.3,13] & Hemsley, on 3 December 1942 she enlisted in the Citizen Military Forces and trained as a voluntary aid. On 3 March 1943 she transferred to the Australian Imperial Force and served in hospitals in Australia before embarking for Bougainville in February 1945. From October that year until February 1946 she was based at Lae, New Guinea. Discharged in Sydney on 11 November, she was mentioned in dispatches.

Under the Commonwealth Reconstruction Training Scheme, Downing studied painting at the Julian Ashton [q.v.7] School and dramatic art with (Dame) Doris Fitton. She appeared in plays at the Independent Theatre, and from 1947 designed decor and costumes, including 'provocative and amusing' surrealist sets for *The Melody That Got Lost* (1949). In 1950 Downing designed the scenery for Fitton's production of *Dark of the Moon* at the Independent and at the Comedy Theatre, Melbourne. Her work for Gertrud Bodenwieser [q.v.13] included the ballet, *Test of Strength*, which toured India in 1952. When she encountered difficulties with mechanical aspects, she studied electronics and architectural drawing.

Distinguished for the originality of her work, Downing designed sets for Gertrude Johnson's [q.v.] National Theatre Arts Festival (*Lohengrin* and *Cavalleria Rusticana*, 1952) and for the Australian Elizabethan Theatre Trust's *The Magic Flute* (1956-57, revived 1968), employing imagery projected from painted 7 x 5 ins (18 x 13 cm) glass slides onto a broad gauze screen. As soon as the costumes for Douglas Stewart's *Ned Kelly* at the Elizabethan Theatre were made to her specifications, she pulled off buttons, split seams and smeared them with paint to ensure authenticity. Her sets complemented the backcloths produced by (Sir) Sidney Nolan.

Working in her studio at a rapid pace, Downing made miniature sets before transferring the scenes to canvas and painting the huge flats herself. She adored the theatre and spent time on research to ensure period authenticity; she also appreciated that decor for ballet was more than a backdrop for the dancers and that designing for television required even greater accuracy. From the early 1950s her drawings for stage productions were included in exhibitions at the Macquarie and Woolloomooloo galleries, Sydney, and at the National Gallery of Victoria.

Having helped with *Long John Silver* (1954), a feature film and twenty-six part television series, in 1957 Downing joined the Australian Broadcasting Commission as a full-time designer at Channel 2 in Sydney, working on such productions as 'G'day Digger' (1958)—a ballet created expressly for television—and designing lavish costumes for the live telecast of *Richard II* (1960). While travelling abroad in 1962-63, she produced fibreglass and steel sets for 'The Beatles' ballet, *Mods and Rockers* (1963), in London; she was particularly interested in lighting and in the experimental theatre in Prague. Back in Sydney, her projects included the decor for Tennessee Williams's *Night of the Iguana* (Independent Theatre, 1964), the costumes for *Kukaitcha*, the Australian segment of the *Ballet of Five Continents* danced by the Ballet Folklorico de Mexico in conjunction with the 1968 Olympic Games in Mexico City, and Norman Lindsay's [q.v.10] *Cousin from Fiji* (A.B.C., 1972).

With blue eyes and dark curly hair, Downing was 5 ft 5 ins (165 cm) tall, 'charming, slow-spoken', gentle and considerate. She continued to live at the family home at Balgowlah and was a great friend of her cousin Richard Downing [q.v.]. Her only brother had been killed while serving with the Royal Australian Air Force. In 1975 Downing completed work for the epic A.B.C.-British Broadcasting Corporation television series, *Ben Hall*. She died of cancer on 11 July 1975 at Manly and was cremated. Her decor and costumes, influential in establishing the arts on Australian television, are represented in the Performing Arts Museum, Melbourne.

Listener In, 12-18 Aug 1950; *TV News*, July 1958; *Radio Active*, June 1968; *TV Times*, July 1975; *Sun-Herald*, 26 June 1949, 20 Apr 1952, 23 Sept 1956, 11 Oct 1959, 5 Jan 1964, 9 Apr 1978; *SMH*, 17 Oct 1951, 5 Jan 1957, 30 Apr 1964; *Sun News-Pictorial*, 12 Jan 1952; *Christian Science Monitor* (Boston), 24 Mar 1953; *Canb Times*, 28 Feb 1968; D. Downing, designs and papers (Sydney Opera House archives); information from Miss S. Downing, Balgowlah, NSW.

CHRISTOPHER CHAPMAN

DOWNING, RICHARD IVAN (1915-1975), economist, was born on 13 March 1915 at Caulfield, Melbourne, second child of Horace Gleadow Downing, public servant, and his wife Blanche Pauline, née Domec-Carré, both Victorian born. When his father was transferred to Canberra with the Bureau of Census and Statistics in 1927, Dick remained in Melbourne with his mother, brother and sister. Educated at state schools and (from 1928) at Scotch College, Hawthorn, in 1932 he won a scholarship to the University of Melbourne (B.A. Hons, 1935). His studies ranged across history, commerce and law, but centred on economics, an interest he 'accidentally stumbled into' in 1929 and had confirmed for him by his awareness of the Depression.

The study of economics in Melbourne was enlivened by senior academics, most prominently (Sir) Douglas Copland and L. F. Giblin [qq.v.13,8], who participated in policy advice and public debate. In this environment Downing developed a lasting sense of the duty of economists to improve the world around them. At the end of his second year he became a part-time research-assistant to Giblin; following his graduation with first-class honours in economics, the position was made full time. Giblin encouraged Downing in the collection and analysis of statistics for understanding current problems and policy options. This emphasis shaped Downing's enduring fields of professional interest: macroeconomic policy, public finance, social welfare and wage policy, and demography. The last-mentioned area yielded his first publication, 'Forecasting the Age Distribution of Future Population', which appeared in the *Economic Record* in 1936. That year Downing encouraged W. B. Reddaway, who had arrived from Cambridge with page-proofs of J. M. (Baron) Keynes's *The General Theory of Employment, Interest and Money* (1936), to give the talk that reputedly began the 'Keynesian revolution' in Australia.

During his years at university, and intermittently afterwards, Downing resided at Ormond [q.v.5] College. He cut a striking figure there, already possessing those qualities which characterized him throughout his life: a deep, sonorous, modulated voice, fine and expressive features, a distinctive style and wit, but above all an earnest desire to convey intellectual understanding and moral concern. At Ormond he combined interest in music and theatre with study, and continued to do so at King's College, Cambridge, in 1938-39. Although Keynes was not giving regular lectures, Downing did attend his 'Monday Club'. Downing was more familiar with Michal Kalecki and met A. C. Pigou. At Cambridge he completed a diploma in economics and wrote a sub-thesis, 'The control of wages in Australia'. Before returning home in June 1939, he toured extensively in Europe with Dorian Le Gallienne [q.v.], a friend from Melbourne who was studying music in London.

After a term as temporary lecturer in economics at the University of Western Australia, Downing was appointed lecturer at the University of Melbourne in 1940. Resuming old contacts, he was influential in persuading Sir George Beeby [q.v.7] of the Commonwealth Court of Conciliation and Arbitration to defer a basic-wage increase on condition that the Federal government introduce a child endowment scheme paid for by a payroll tax. In July 1941 Downing was summoned to Canberra to work as an assistant to Copland who had been appointed economic consultant to Prime Minister John Curtin [q.v.13]. With Copland, he prepared drafts on wartime economic policy and price stabilization. Convinced that the war effort provided unprecedented opportunities to secure a wider conception of the 'national interest' and for 'giving justice to the people', Downing was also a member of the small group which drafted and revised sections of the white paper on full employment, published in 1945. Later that year, on Copland's recommendation, he joined the International Labour Organization at Montreal, Canada. The main product of this period with the I.L.O. was a report, *Housing and Employment* (1948).

Downing returned to Melbourne in 1947. After a short interlude in Canberra on secondment as acting chief economist to the Department of Post-war Reconstruction, he resumed lecturing in Melbourne on public finance, social accounts and statistical method. In 1950 he again joined the I.L.O., in Geneva, as assistant economic adviser. There he was involved in a diverse range of inquiries, including programmes of technical assistance in South East Asia and studies of international wages. He also completed a short textbook, *National Income and Social Accounts* (1951), which was to run to numerous editions. In 1954 Downing went back to Melbourne as Ritchie professor of economic research (Giblin's old chair).

For the next twenty-one years he adapted Giblin's legacy from times of uncertainty and restraint to the circumstances of affluence. In addition to his own research, Downing's activities encompassed some teaching and bouts of university administration (as chairman of the professorial board, 1968-70, and assistant vice-chancellor, 1969-74), the edi-

torship of the *Economic Record* (1954-73), public comment on many issues, and advice to business and government. His central interest lay in promoting social welfare primarily through public policy, whether through the tax system (*Taxation in Australia*, 1964, with others), the reform of pensions (*Raising Age Pensions*, 1957), superannuation (*National Superannuation*, Adelaide, 1958) and medical and hospital benefits, or through public works and services, from transport to education. From 1962 the Institute of Applied Economic Research, which Downing had been instrumental in founding at the university, extended the tenor of these inquiries, particularly in relation to poverty. The dilemma faced by Downing in each of these areas was to frame policies which would secure specific equity objectives while advancing economic growth and without exacerbating inflation. He was concerned with balanced development, not only in the domestic context but also in relation to the Asian region.

Downing was always aware of the claims of conflicting sectional interests and of the need to mediate between them through public advocacy. Economists, he wrote, were trained to 'identify what we have to give up, and how much, in order to get a little more of something we want'. He admitted candidly that economics, as an 'instrument of human progress', relied on value judgements, and described himself as a 'poetic' or 'literary' economist; he was alarmed by what he saw as an increasing reliance on jargon in the discipline. To assist informed debate, in 1956 the *Economic Record* commenced publishing regular surveys of the Australian economy, the first written by Downing. Earlier that year he joined seven other senior economists in a public 'manifesto', recommending taxation and interest-rate increases to redress 'spendthrift prosperity'. Elected chairman of the Social Science Research Council of Australia in 1969 and president (1971-73) of its successor, the Academy of the Social Sciences in Australia, he also adapted this platform to foster greater co-ordination and public awareness of research. He wrote frequently for (and to) the press, as well as for economic journals; conferences, lectures and addresses were some of his routine engagements.

While advocating substantial reforms in the 1950s and 1960s, Downing praised the 'real social advance' that had occurred since the 1930s, and was essentially an optimistic commentator on Australia's economic prospects. He described himself as 'not political'; he had 'little respect' for the Menzies [q.v.] governments and was wary of Labor's narrowness and inexperience. In 1949, however, following an approach from R. G. (Baron) Casey [q.v.13], he drafted with Benjamin Higgins (then Ritchie professor) the economic platform of the Liberal Party of Australia—as much out of a sense of the need for broader policy debate as in direct support of the party. Similarly, and more openly, in 1972 he signed, with sixteen others, a letter to the national press urging a vote for E. G. Whitlam. Again, he confided that he signed on 'democratic principle' rather than 'relative merits'. The election of Whitlam's Labor government brought Downing further opportunities to pursue his interest in Australian culture and the arts. Having served on the boards of the Melbourne Theatre Company, the National Gallery of Victoria and the Australian Ballet School, early in 1973 he joined the Australian Council for the Arts.

In June that year Downing was appointed chairman of the Australian Broadcasting Commission. He took to this position with vigour and was soon embroiled in controversy as the A.B.C. itself was adjusting to social change. If he was 'instinctively opposed' to artistic novelty for its own sake, Downing had little tolerance of censorship. He sought instead an 'adventurous, innovative and informing' broadcasting service which would correspond to the diversity of contemporary society. By upholding the broadcasting of material dealing directly and realistically with sexuality, violence and obscene language, he generated considerable criticism both within the A.B.C. and publicly. Yet, at the same time as he was encouraging cultural tolerance, he expressed concern as an economist that a lack of 'self-restraint' evident in the inflationary pressures of 1974-75 might lead to 'a breakdown of the very real achievements on which continued economic growth depends', threatening democracy itself.

Outwardly gregarious, Downing also valued his privacy. In 1948 he and Le Gallienne had jointly bought 300 acres (120 ha) of bushland at Eltham with the intention of building a weekend retreat. Such was their attraction to the area that they lived there in a mud-brick house designed for them by Alistair Knox. Over the years more land was acquired to secure it from developers. During extensive international travels, Downing maintained broad interest in theatre, music, film and opera, yet he delighted in the bush and proclaimed himself to be 'fiercely—not proud, just pleased to be Australian'. Following Le Gallienne's death in 1963, Downing lived alone. On 15 February 1965 at Littlejohn [q.v.10] Memorial Chapel, Scotch College, he married Jean Olive Norman, née McGregor, a widow and mother of six children. They joined him at Eltham. A daughter was born in 1967.

Chairing the A.B.C. was a stimulating experience for Downing, but it was demanding and allegations of political partiality dis-

tressed him. Added to other commitments, among them the chairmanship (1972-75) of the Ormond College council and a directorship (1971-75) of the Gas and Fuel Corporation of Victoria, it sometimes left him 'past exhaustion'. After attending an A.B.C. concert in Canberra, Downing died of a coronary occlusion on 10 November 1975 at Acton and was cremated. His wife and daughter survived him, as did his four stepsons and two stepdaughters. Tributes were legion: they referred to him as one of the founders of the welfare state in Australia and to 'the singular warmth and force of his personality'. A fellowship in his memory was established at the University of Melbourne to bring international scholars in social economics to Australia.

K. S. Inglis, *This is the ABC* (Melb, 1983); A. G. L. Shaw (ed), *Victoria's Heritage* (Syd, 1986); R. Watts, *The Foundation of the National Welfare State* (Syd, 1987); B. Higgins, *The Road Less Travelled* (Canb, 1989); H. W. Arndt, 'R. I. Downing: Economic and Social Reformer', *Economic Record*, 52, no 2, 1976, p 281; *Australian*, 23 Aug 1975; H. W. Arndt papers (NL); Downing papers (Univ Melb Archives).
NICHOLAS BROWN
H. W. ARNDT

DOYLE, RALPH RAYMOND (1894-1955), film company manager, was born on 7 April 1894 at Leichhardt, Sydney, third son of English-born parents Frank Doyle, draper, and his wife Jane Grinsell, née Robinson. Educated at public schools, in May 1910 Ralph joined the Commercial Banking Co. of Sydney and was sent to Cooma in 1911. He enlisted in the Australian Imperial Force on 1 August 1916 and served on the Western Front with the 1st Light Trench Mortar Battery and the 2nd Battalion. Commissioned on 1 August 1918, he was promoted lieutenant in January 1919. His appointment terminated on 20 July in Sydney.

Returning to the bank (at Neutral Bay), Doyle resigned in March 1922 to establish his own practice as a public accountant. At St Philip's Anglican Church, Sydney, on 5 April that year he married Mary Isabel Body (d.1931); they were to have two sons and a daughter. Encouraged by his brother Stuart Doyle [q.v.8], in 1922 Ralph became Victorian sales manager for United Artists (Australasia) Ltd, the only local distributor of American films to operate outside the controversial block-booking system. Within nine months he was appointed general sales manager and in 1924 general manager in Australasia. He was a foundation member of Motion Picture Distributors (Association) of Australia, an influential trade lobby founded that year. Although he publicly expressed sympathy for the plight of struggling Australian film-makers, he offered them no significant support.

An associate of the Commonwealth Institute of Accountants, in 1933 Doyle resigned from United Artists, allegedly to pursue other business interests (he was a director of the British and Mercantile Insurance Co. Ltd), but in May he was appointed managing director for Australasia of the American production-distribution company, R.K.O. Radio Pictures Inc. On 9 January 1935 at Christ Church, Kilmore, Victoria, he married a 24-year-old actress (Helen) Patricia Minchin with the rites of the Church of Ireland; they had a son and a daughter before being divorced. For twenty years Doyle brought Hollywood culture to Australian audiences; he also assisted in the distribution of a few local feature films, most notably Charles Chauvel's [q.v.7] *The Rats of Tobruk* (1944), which R.K.O. also helped to finance.

In a new trend, Doyle was one of the earliest finance professionals to take control of the moving-picture industry from people with direct experience in film-making. He was loyal to his employers and remarkably successful at a time when American companies usually appointed their own nationals to run branch operations abroad. A member of Tattersalls and the Millions clubs, he was vice-president of the British-American Co-operation Movement (Australian-American Association from 1947).

Doyle was 5 ft 8 ins (173 cm) tall, with deep-set, penetrating eyes. He enjoyed playing golf and belonged to the New South Wales Golf and Elanora Country clubs. On 14 November 1947 at the Australia Hotel, Sydney, he married with Presbyterian forms a 36-year-old divorcee Edna Lillian Penn, née Reynolds. After resigning from R.K.O. in 1953, he pursued various business interests and undertook considerable charitable work within the film industry. On 20 March 1955 at Rose Bay he committed suicide by shooting himself in the head; survived by his wife and the children of his previous marriages, he was cremated with Anglican rites.

Cwlth of Aust, *Royal Commission on the Moving Picture Industry in Australia: Minutes of Evidence* (Canb, 1928); *Everyone's*, 8 Nov 1922, 5 Apr 1933; *A'sian Exhibitor*, 1 Oct 1953; *SMH*, 11 Aug 1936, 4 Oct 1944, 13 Aug 1947, 21 June 1954, 21 Mar 1955; information from National Aust Bank, Springvale, Vic.   DIANE COLLINS

DRAKE-BROCKMAN,   GEOFFREY (1885-1977), civil engineer and army officer, and HENRIETTA FRANCES YORK (1901-1968), author, were husband and wife. Geoffrey was born on 2 November 1885 at Guildford, Perth, fourth of seven children of Frederick Slade [Drake-] Brockman [q.v.8], surveyor, and his wife Grace Vernon, née Bussell, both Western Australian born. E. A. Drake-Brockman [q.v.8] and (Lady) Hackett [q.v.9] were Geoffrey's brother and sister. Educated at Guildford Grammar School, in 1903 he was employed as a cadet in the engineering branch of the Public Works Department and studied part time at Perth Technical College. He worked on railway survey and construction, and was seconded to the Commonwealth in 1908 to map a rail route from Kalgoorlie to Port Augusta, South Australia.

Five ft 11¼ ins (181 cm) tall, with grey eyes and dark hair, Drake-Brockman enlisted in the Australian Imperial Force on 5 October 1914 and was posted to the 10th Light Horse Regiment. He sailed to Egypt and in May 1915 embarked for Gallipoli where he was commissioned in August and attached to the 2nd Field Company, Engineers. Wounded next month, he recuperated in England before rejoining his unit in Egypt. In May he arrived in France. He was awarded the Military Cross for his devotion to duty at the front between December 1916 and January 1917, and was promoted major in March. On 17 May 1917 at St Augustine's Presbyterian Church, New Barnet, Hertfordshire, England, he married Alice Annie Wardlaw Milne (d.1918). He performed training and staff duties, and commanded the 9th Field Company in 1917-18. His A.I.F. appointment terminated on 8 May 1920, but he remained on the Reserve of Officers in Western Australia.

Employed in the Forests Department, Geoffrey was sent to China to investigate the marketing of sandalwood. On 1 August 1921 he was appointed commissioner of the newly formed Department of the North-West. Two days later he married 20-year-old Henrietta in the Anglican Chapel of St Mary and St George, Guildford.

Born on 27 July 1901 in Perth, Henrietta was the only child of English-born Martin Edward Jull, public servant, and his wife Roberta Henrietta Margaritta, née Stewart [qq.v.9], a medical practitioner from Scotland. Henrietta was educated at a boarding-school in Scotland and at Frensham, Mittagong, New South Wales, and studied literature at the University of Western Australia and art in Henri Van Raalte's [q.v.12] Perth studio. After their marriage, Geoffrey and Henrietta left for their base at Broome. A gifted and independent young woman, she welcomed the prospect of life on the frontier. She accompanied her husband on his workrounds and began to publish her observations for the *Western Australian* under the pseudonym 'Henry Drake'. As commissioner, Geoffrey recommended a survey of agricultural land at the Ord River, the planting of cotton and the development of the Kimberley region. The Drake-Brockmans returned to Perth when the Department of the North-West was abolished in 1926.

Geoffrey became principal assistant engineer (1926) and engineer for the North-West (1931) in the Public Works Department. On 28 April 1941 he was called up for full-time service and posted to Army Headquarters, Melbourne. As temporary colonel, then temporary brigadier, he occupied senior engineering staff posts before transferring to the Retired List on 16 June 1944. In their South Yarra home the Drake-Brockmans entertained numerous literary acquaintances. Back in Perth, Geoffrey was successively assistant-director of public works (1946-49) and chairman (1949-52) of the Western Australian Transport Board. A friend described him as 'a bit of a Showman', essentially friendly, very interested in other people and 'a stickler for historical accuracy'. In his retirement Geoffrey wrote an autobiography, *The Turning Wheel* (1960).

Meantime Henrietta's reputation as a writer had become established. From her experiences of the little-known region of the North-West, she had written sketches and stories, and in the early 1930s published a serial, *The Disquieting Sex. Blue North*, an historical novel about life in the 1870s, was serialized in the *Bulletin* and published in 1934, while *Sheba Lane* (1936) used contemporary Broome as its setting. *Younger Sons* (1937) was a carefully documented novel of Western Australian settlement and *The Fatal Days* (1947) focussed on Ballarat, Victoria, during World War II. Her last novel, *The Wicked and The Fair* (1957), centred on the voyage of the *Batavia* in 1629; her final book, *Voyage To Disaster* (1963), was largely a biography of the *Batavia's* captain Francisco Pelsaert [q.v.2]. Her extensive research entailed the use of material from Dutch archives and of E. D. Drok's translations of Pelsaert's journals, as well as trips by sea and air to the probable site of the wreck. In an article in *Walkabout* in January 1955 Henrietta had diverged from general opinion and closely estimated the *Batavia's* correct resting-place. Eight years later she used an aqualung to inspect the vessel's wreckage off the Albrolhos Islands.

Claiming that she would rather have been a playwright than a novelist, and that there were almost no opportunities for Australian plays when she had begun to write, Henrietta did manage to have some of her plays staged. *The Man from the Bush* was produced in Perth in 1932 (and later in Melbourne), *Dampier's Ghost* was performed in 1934 and *The Blister* in 1937. In *Men Without Wives*, her best-known play, she extended her work beyond the one-act genre and won a sesquicentenary drama prize in 1938. *Men Without Wives and Other Plays* was published in 1955. Her plays, for the most part, depicted the people and isolated places of her earlier fiction. She admired and wrote on the work of Katharine Susannah Prichard [q.v.11].

A tall and elegant woman, Henrietta was a foundation member (1938) and president of the Fellowship of Australian Writers, Western Australia branch, and a committee-member of *Westerly*. She edited several collections of short stories and her own were compiled in *Sydney or the Bush* (1948). In 1967 she was appointed O.B.E. Henrietta died of a cerebral haemorrhage on 8 March 1968 and was buried in Karrakatta cemetery. Survived by their daughter and son, Geoffrey died on 27 December 1977 at Victoria Park and was cremated with Anglican rites.

J. A. Hetherington, *Forty-Two Faces* (Melb, 1962); A. Hasluck, *Of Ladies Dead* (Syd, 1970); D. Popham (ed), *Reflections* (Melb, 1978); B. Bennett (ed), *The Literature of Western Australia* (Perth, 1979); *Winthrop Review*, 3, 1953-54; *Westerly*, 2 July 1968; *Western Mail* (Perth), 21 July, 11 Aug 1921; *Herald* (Melb), 12 Mar 1938; *Sun News-Pictorial*, 17 June 1944; *West Australian*, 11 Mar 1968, 31 Dec 1977; *Age* (Melb), 23 Mar 1968; H. Drake-Brockman papers (BL).   PETER COWAN

DRAKEFORD, ARTHUR SAMUEL (1878-1957), engine driver, trade unionist and politician, was born on 26 April 1878 at Fitzroy, Melbourne, second son of Samuel Finch Drakeford, a jeweller from England, and his Victorian-born wife Elizabeth Margaret, née Josephs. On leaving school, Arthur found work as a railway-engine cleaner at Benalla. At the local Presbyterian manse on 9 May 1902 he married a widow Ellen Tyrie, née Warrington (d.1906). In 1903 he participated in the Victorian railway strike and became secretary of the Benalla branch of the Locomotive Engine Drivers' and Firemen's Association. He also joined the Labor Party.

Having qualified as an engine driver, in 1908 Drakeford transferred to Melbourne. On 19 April 1911 he married Ellen Unger at the office of the government statist, Queen Street. Elected to the State executive of the L.E.D.F.A., he was its vice-president (1914-15), president (1916-17) and general secretary (from 1918). On the formation of the Australian Federated Union of Locomotive Enginemen in 1920, he was chosen as federal secretary. He made arrangements for the union's registration with the Commonwealth Court of Conciliation and Arbitration, and expertly argued its case for a Federal award in 1924-25. An energetic organizer, he was national president (1929-48) and a life-member (from 1929) of the A.F.U.L.E. Drakeford had been a founder of the Commonwealth

Council of Federated Unions in 1923 and was senior vice-president when it was superseded by the Australasian Council of Trade Unions in 1927. He was a consistent advocate of the standard railway gauge.

After his union affiliated with the Australian Labor Party, Drakeford became senior vice-president (1928) and president (1929) of the party's Victorian central executive. He represented Essendon in the Legislative Assembly from 1927 until he was defeated in 1932, mainly as a result of his opposition to the Premiers' Plan. In 1934 he won the Federal seat of Maribyrnong from the Labor renegade J. E. Fenton [q.v.8]. Maurice Blackburn's [q.v.7] decision to give Drakeford his proxy secured John Curtin's [q.v.13] election to the party leadership next year. The Menzies [q.v.] government made Drakeford a member of the Manpower and Resources Survey Committee in 1941.

In October Drakeford was appointed minister for air and for civil aviation in the new Labor government; he was to hold both portfolios until 1949. Initially, he relied on the guidance of senior departmental and Royal Australian Air Force officers. He endeavoured to resolve the R.A.A.F.'s higher command problems, did not feign expertise on air strategy, and generally confined his attention to budgetary matters and to the allocation of manpower and resources. Airmen admired him for advancing their interests. A member of the War Cabinet in 1941-46, he was briefly minister for the navy in 1946. He stood unsuccessfully for the deputy-leadership of the Labor Party that year.

Drakeford's most enduring achievement was in laying the foundation for the expansion of Australian civil aviation after the war. He had long favoured the nationalization of the domestic airline industry. In 1945 he introduced the Australian national airlines bill which, when enacted, empowered the Australian National Airlines Commission to take over interstate services. Next year the commission established Trans-Australia Airlines. A decision by the High Court of Australia invalidated Drakeford's attempt to create a government monopoly and T.A.A. was forced to compete against private companies. In 1946-47 he oversaw the government's purchase of Qantas Empire Airways Ltd, Australia's major overseas carrier. Vice-president (1946) of the Provisional International Civil Aviation Organization's conference at Montreal, Canada, he was president of the first assembly of the permanent body in 1947.

Although he was a moderate socialist, Drakeford campaigned vigorously against the 1951 referendum proposal to ban the Communist Party of Australia. He narrowly lost his seat in 1955, a casualty of Labor's split.

Small and bespectacled, he was an energetic man who carried into political life the qualities of honesty and loyalty which had characterized his trade-union career. He was clear minded rather than brilliant, and won respect for his 'obvious personal integrity'. Devoted to his family, Drakeford read widely and loved sport, especially horse-racing and Australian Rules football. His support aided Melbourne's successful bid for the 1956 Olympic Games.

Drakeford died on 9 June 1957 at his Moonee Ponds home; following a state funeral, he was cremated. His wife and their four daughters survived him, as did the son of his first marriage, Arthur Harold Finch Drakeford, who represented Essendon (1945-47) and Pascoe Vale (1955-58) in the Legislative Assembly.

D. Gillison, *Royal Australian Air Force 1939-1942* (Canb, 1962); S. Brogden, *Australia's Two-Airline Policy* (Melb, 1968); N. W. de Pomeroy and R. Gilbert (eds), *Men of the Footplate* (Melb, 1992); *Locomotive J*, 8 Nov 1941, p 30, 11 July 1957, p 2; *Essendon Gazette*, 5 May 1932; *Labor Call*, 15 Jan 1942; ALP (Vic Branch), Minutes, 1924-29 (LaTL); Drakeford papers (NL); information from Mrs D. Robertson and Mrs G. Leversha, Durack, Brisb, and the late F. M. Daly.   FRANK BONGIORNO

DRANSFIELD, MICHAEL JOHN PENDER (1948-1973), poet, was born on 12 September 1948 at Camperdown, Sydney, second child of native-born parents John Francis Dransfield, clerk, and his wife Elspeth Gladys, née Pender. Michael was educated at Brighton-le-Sands Public and Sydney Grammar schools. After 'dropping out' of the universities of New South Wales and Sydney, he worked intermittently on newspapers and as a government clerk.

For Dransfield, 1968 was a significant year, marked by an addiction to morphine, the severance of his relationship with Kathy Rees (to whom many of the early poems were dedicated) and the challenge of being balloted for national service. A protester against Australia's involvement in the Vietnam War, he was eventually excused from service, possibly for health reasons. While living at Casino he wrote of his preoccupations: love, pain, addiction and an inhospitable society; a major poetic symbol was the decaying country house, Courland Penders, into which he built his nostalgia for an older civilization. His work was accepted by Rodney Hall, poetry editor of the *Australian*.

Next year Dransfield grew his hair longer, joined Sydney's counter-culture and, until early 1972, lived with the Sydney artist Hilary Burns. He was of tall and slender build, with stooping shoulders. Hall discerned that 'there was a grace about him', and was struck by his charm, generosity and talent for friendship. At intervals, when either hitchhiking or riding his motorcycle, Dransfield established 'a circuit of friends from Melbourne to Brisbane'.

Celebrated by the editor Thomas Shapcott as being 'terrifyingly close to genius', Dransfield joined such members of the 'Generation of '68' as Robert Adamson, John Tranter and Nigel Roberts in a rebellion against older, conservative poets, like James McAuley [q.v.] and A. D. Hope. His work appeared in *Meanjin Quarterly*, *Southerly*, *Poetry Australia*, *Poetry Magazine* (*New Poetry* from 1971) and ephemeral magazines. University of Queensland Press was to publish all Dransfield's books: the first, *Streets of the Long Voyage* (1970), won a University of Newcastle award; it was followed in 1972 by *The Inspector of Tides*, and by *Drug Poems* which explored states of mind through drug consciousness and served his aim of social protest.

In the 'Nimbin spirit', Dransfield quitted the city and moved with Hilary to Cobargo where he began to circulate the manuscript of *Memoirs of a Velvet Urinal* (published posthumously, 1975). He suffered a motorcycle accident in April 1972. In October he received a $2500 grant from the Commonwealth Literary Fund to work on a book of prose. After many desperate months in and out of Canberra Community Hospital, trying to shed his addiction to heroin, he returned to Sydney. Dransfield died in a coma on 20 April 1973 in the Mater Misericordiae Hospital, North Sydney, and was cremated with Presbyterian forms. The coroner found that his death followed a self-administered injection of an unknown substance. During the last months of his life Dransfield had met (in Canberra hospital) a soul mate Paula Keogh and experienced a last rush of creative energy which resulted in *The Second Month of Spring* (1980). The manuscript was edited by Hall who also brought out selections of Dransfield's unpublished work, *Voyage into Solitude* (1978) and *Michael Dransfield* (1987).

T. W. Shapcott (ed), *Australian Poetry Now* (Melb, 1970); P. K. Elkin (ed), *Australian Poems in Perspective* (Brisb, 1978); R. Hall's introductions to M. Dransfield, *Voyage into Solitude* (Brisb, 1978), and *The Second Month of Spring* (Brisb, 1980), and *Michael Dransfield: Collected Poems* (Brisb, 1987); L. Dobrez, *Parnassus Mad World* (Brisb, 1990); *SMH*, 30 Oct 1972, 10 May, 25 June 1973.

PATRICIA DOBREZ

DREYER, MARIEN OULTON (1911-1980), writer and journalist, was born on 24 September 1911 at Mornington, Victoria, daughter of Joseph Dreyer, a journalist from New Zealand, and his second wife Mary Oulton, née Rosson, a fourth-generation Australian. The loss of a leg during childhood turned Marien into 'something of a battler'. She left her convent school in Melbourne at the age of 14 and worked as a stenographer. Bright and smiling, with 'grey-green eyes' and curly black hair, she dreamed of going on the stage and, as 'Gallery Girl', wrote theatre pieces for women's magazines. In Sydney she frequented Pakies [q.v. Macdougall] Club and had sixteen jobs between 1937 and 1939. Back in Melbourne in 1940, she was a telephonist at 6th Division headquarters, Australian Imperial Force.

In the early 1940s Dreyer settled in Sydney with her husband Rodney Beaumont Lovell Cooper, a journalist; they lived with their young son near Kings Cross. She maintained a prodigious output of stories, serials and plays for magazines and radio: 'The Windows of Heaven' and 'The Big Wind' were included respectively in *The Man Gift Book* (1946) and Kylie Tennant's *Summer's Tales 1* (Melbourne, 1964). Soon after the birth of her second son, Dreyer began writing a popular column for *New Idea*, 'This Week with Marien Dreyer' (1955-62).

Her scripts for the Australian Broadcasting Commission included 'Story of a Lame Duck' (31 March 1951) which concentrated on the problems of the disabled and was largely autobiographical. In 1953 the Commonwealth Department of Health refused permission for the broadcast of 'The Hard Way Back', Dreyer's factual account of a patient's struggle to rehabilitate himself after suffering from tuberculosis; the department claimed that she had over-emphasized the difficulties. Dreyer regarded the dismissal of her appeal under the Australian Broadcasting Act (1942) as 'a slur on her reputation and contrary to free speech'. In 1959 she shared the Walkley award for a non-fiction magazine article with 'The Day I Wiggled My Big Toe' (*New Idea*, February 1959). Three of Dreyer's 'charming but slight' one-act plays were produced at the Pocket Playhouse Theatre in November. Her adult fairy tale, 'Wish No More', had a cast of twenty-four—too many for a viable production. Conversely, her satire on city life, *Bandicoot on a Burnt Ridge* (winner of the Journalists' Club £1000 award for 1962-63), was criticized for having a cast of only two!

Publicity officer for the King's Cross Protection Association, Dreyer bitterly opposed the construction of the tunnel at the top of William Street. The *Sydney Morning Herald* was flooded with her letters on a miscellany of topics: too much cricket on the wireless, sewing-cotton that snapped, the poor quality of jam, the stench of circus animals, and the noise of flying boats and motor horns. She assisted the stipendiary magistrate Arthur

Debenham to write his memoirs, *Without Fear or Favour* (1966), as well as two books dealing with social problems.

Although she dressed 'carelessly in skirts and sweaters', Dreyer had 'a passion for ornate drop earrings and exotic perfumes'. Humorous and warm hearted, she gave an annual party for 'Annabella', her wooden leg. She was an active member of the Australian Journalists' Association, spoke her mind 'sometimes with devastating frankness' and sympathized with the underprivileged. Survived by her husband and two sons, she died of coronary vascular disease on 16 January 1980 at her Darlinghurst flat and was cremated.

Women's Weekly, 17 Feb 1940, p 30; *ABC Weekly*, 31 Mar 1951; *People*, 26 Sept 1951, p 14; *Voice*, 2, Aug 1953, p 13; *Aust Mag* (Syd), 11 Aug 1953, p 26; *Overland*, no 37, Oct 1967; *New Idea*, 13 Jan 1960; *Aust Q*, 32, no 1, Mar 1960, p 123; *Theatregoer*, 2, nos 2-3, Dec-Jan 1961-62, p 40; *SMH*, 3 Mar, 13 June 1953, 19 Jan 1954, 2 Nov 1955, 5 Mar, 10 May 1956, 8 Nov 1957, 27 May 1958, 30 Nov 1959, 11 Feb 1961, 16 June 1963, 4 May, 6 June 1964, 12 May 1965, 21 Apr, 5 May 1969, 18 Jan 1980; *Herald* (Melb), 6, 31 May 1965; *Age* (Melb), 11 May 1965; *Sun News-Pictorial*, 22 May 1965.   AUDREY TATE

DRUMMOND, IRENE MELVILLE (1905-1942), army matron, was born on 26 July 1905 at Ashfield, Sydney, daughter of Cedric Drummond, marine engineer, and his wife Katherine, née Melville, both Queensland born. Educated at Catholic schools in Adelaide and at Broken Hill, New South Wales, Irene returned to Adelaide, trained as a nurse at Miss Laurence's Private Hospital, qualified in obstetrics at the Queen's Home and worked at Angaston Hospital. In 1933 she moved to the Broken Hill and District Hospital where she proved to be a compassionate and extremely competent nurse, well liked and respected by her superiors and colleagues. She served as a surgical sister, assistant-matron and acting-matron.

Appointed sister in the Australian Army Nursing Service, Australian Imperial Force, on 8 November 1940, Drummond was called up for full-time duty with the 2nd/4th Casualty Clearing Station in January 1941. Next month she sailed for Singapore to join the 2nd/9th Field Ambulance. Briefly back with the 2nd/4th C.C.S., she was promoted matron on 5 August and posted to the 2nd/13th Australian General Hospital in September. When the Japanese invaded Malaya on 8 December, the hospital was situated near Johore Bahru. In January 1942 it was hurriedly moved to St Patrick's School, Singapore. Despite chaotic conditions—brought on by the hasty retreat, enemy air-raids and increasing admissions

of battle casualties—Drummond's quiet efficiency helped to ensure that the wards were operational within 48 hours.

By early February 1942 surrender to the Japanese appeared likely. Throughout January, Major General Gordon Bennett [q.v.13] had repeatedly refused to allow the evacuation of A.A.N.S. personnel. It was not until 10 February that they began leaving, five days before the capitulation. On the 12th only Drummond, Matron Olive Paschke [q.v.] of the 2nd/10th A.G.H. and sixty-three members of their staffs remained in Singapore. Although the nurses had begged to be allowed to stay with their patients, they were put on board the steamer, *Vyner Brooke*, that day for the perilous voyage to Australia. On the 14th in Banka Strait the vessel was hit by bombs. The nurses helped other passengers to abandon ship. Scooping up a small Chinese boy as the *Vyner Brooke* sank, Drummond escaped in a lifeboat.

A group of survivors, including Drummond and twenty-one fellow nurses, came ashore at Radji Beach, Banka Island. They were joined by some twenty British servicemen from another sunken ship. Having discovered that the island was already in the hands of the Japanese and that no help could be expected from the local population, on 16 February the party resolved to surrender. One of the *Vyner Brooke*'s officers was sent to Muntok to negotiate with the Japanese. While he was away Drummond suggested that the civilian women and children should leave for Muntok. Shortly after the civilians departed, a Japanese officer and twenty soldiers arrived at the beach.

Ignoring pleas that the remaining group was surrendering, the Japanese separated the men from the women. The men were marched around a small bluff to another cove; there they were shot and bayoneted. The Japanese returned to the nurses who had been left sitting on the beach and ordered them to walk into the sea. All knew their fate as they entered the water in silence. The Japanese soldiers opened fire with a machine-gun. Irene Drummond was one of the first to die.

She was mentioned in dispatches in 1946. The Sister Drummond Memorial Park, opened at Broken Hill hospital in 1949, commemorates her.

A. S. Walker, *Middle East and Far East* (Canb, 1953) and *Medical Services of the R.A.N. and R.A.A.F.* (Canb, 1961); L. Wigmore, *The Japanese Thrust* (Canb, 1957); *Barrier Miner*, 10 Oct 1949; AWM 52, item 11/2/13, AWM 54, item 1010/4/23, AWM 76, item B150, PR87/187 (AWM); information from Mrs E. Hannan, Weetangera, Canb, and Mrs V. Statham, Nedlands, Perth.

JULIE GORRELL

DRUMMOND, SIR PETER ROY MAXWELL (1894-1945), air force officer, was born on 2 June 1894 in Perth and registered as Roy Maxwell, son of John Maxwell Drummond, merchant, and his wife Caroline, née Lockhart. Educated at Scotch College, Perth, young Drummond served in the cadets and passed the senior and higher public examinations set by the University of Adelaide. On 10 September 1914 he enlisted in the Australian Imperial Force, giving his occupation as bank clerk. His slight build was deemed to preclude active service and in November he was posted to the 2nd Australian Stationary Hospital as a medical orderly. In December he embarked for the Middle East and by April 1915 was in a hospital ship off Gallipoli. He assisted surgeons who operated by candlelight in primitive conditions, and was struck by 'the ghastly sight' of the wounded. Suffering from dysentery and debility, he was evacuated to England where he was hospitalized.

In December Drummond applied for a commission in the Royal Flying Corps. He had 'mixed feelings' when he was discharged from the A.I.F. on 14 April 1916 and appointed temporary second lieutenant. After flying-training at Shoreham-by-Sea, Sussex, in September he was attached as a pilot to No.1 Squadron, Australian Flying Corps, based in Egypt. While serving with this unit, he won the Military Cross for an action in which he was engaged against six enemy aircraft; the citation noted his 'skill and courage on all occasions'.

Promoted temporary captain, in October 1917 Drummond joined No.111 Squadron, R.F.C., which was equipped with Nieuports and S.E.5a's. In December he and his observer engaged three German fighters over Tul Keram, Palestine, and destroyed them all. Drummond was awarded the Distinguished Service Order. His single-handed fight against six enemy scouts in March 1918 resulted in the destruction of two and the award of a Bar to his D.S.O. From July he commanded No.145 Squadron, Royal Air Force. He was promoted acting major in September and mentioned in dispatches for the attacks he made on Turkish infantry next month. His seven-and-a-half confirmed 'kills' included six of the Albatros DV type. In August 1919 he received a permanent commission in the R.A.F.

As acting squadron leader, in 1920 Drummond commanded 'H' Unit which accompanied a punitive expedition against the Garjak Nuers in south-eastern Sudan. Following four weeks of bombing and machine-gunning, the rebels capitulated. Drummond returned to England and was appointed O.B.E. (1921). He graduated from the R.A.F. Staff College, Andover, in 1923, then worked directly to Air Chief Marshal Sir Hugh (Viscount) Trenchard at the Air Ministry. Between 1925 and 1929 Drummond was on loan to the Royal Australian Air Force, and was director of operations and intelligence at Headquarters in Melbourne. He acted as aide to Air Marshal Sir John Salmond who visited Australia in 1928 to report on the R.A.A.F. On 17 July 1929 Drummond married Isabel Rachael Mary Drake-Brockman at St John's Anglican Church, Toorak; they were to have a son and two daughters.

Back in England, in 1930 Drummond attended the Imperial Defence College, London. Next year he was promoted wing commander and given command of Tangmere, Sussex, an important fighter station in Britain's air-defence system. In 1933-36 he was again at the Air Ministry. While commanding R.A.F. Station, Northolt, Middlesex, in January 1937 he was promoted group captain.

He returned to the Middle East in November as senior air staff officer in the R.A.F. Middle East Command. There, he built the infrastructure for a modern air force. The task was almost completed when Italy entered the war (10 June 1940) and the region became an operational theatre. Drummond had risen to air commodore and in January 1941 was promoted air vice marshal. On 1 June Air Chief Marshal (Sir) Arthur (Baron) Tedder took over as air commander-in-chief, Middle East, and Drummond was appointed his deputy, as acting (temporary June 1943) air marshal. Together they developed the concept of a mobile strike-force capable of co-operating fully with the other two services.

In 1942 Drummond rejected the post of chief of the Air Staff, R.A.A.F. which had been offered to him in an attempt to solve the crisis in the service's higher command arrangements in the South-West Pacific Area. The Australian government raised the matter once more in April 1943, but the Air Ministry refused to release Drummond who had been selected to become air member for training on the Air Council. In Tedder's opinion, the Air Ministry's decision was wise; he later referred to Drummond's ability and support as important factors in winning the war in North Africa.

Drummond was responsible for managing part of the Empire Air Training Scheme. He contributed to the bungling which led to a massive surplus of aircrew receiving instruction. By May 1944 he thought that only high casualty rates in the planned invasion of Europe would take up the over-supply. Appointed C.B. in 1941, he was elevated to K.C.B. in 1943. He then formally took his nickname Peter—which he had acquired at Scotch College—as an additional Christian name.

Five ft 7¼ ins (171 cm) tall, with a fair complexion, brown eyes and brown hair, Drummond had a pleasant, unaffected manner which made him popular among all ranks. On 27 March 1945, *en route* to Canada, the Liberator in which he was travelling was lost near the Azores. The aircraft was never found: Drummond and its other occupants were presumed to have died that day. The Imperial War Museum holds a portrait of Sir Peter by Eric Kennington and the Air Ministry another by Cuthbert Orde.

DNB, 1941-1950; P. Firkins, *The Golden Eagles* (Perth, 1980); *The Times*, 17 Aug 1917, 27 Mar, 27 July, 26 Aug 1918; PRO Air 2/5943 (PRO, Lond); AWM records; papers held by author (Aust Defence Force Academy, Campbell, Canb).

JOHN MCCARTHY

DRUMMOND, RUTH JANET ('LUTE') (1879-1949), operatic coach, was born on 6 September 1879 at Ulmarra, New South Wales, eighth of nine children of James Drummond, a blacksmith from Scotland, and his native-born wife Annie, née Cameron. Known as 'Lute', she was bred on Shakespeare and the Bible; her education was more a matter of strong home influences than formal schooling. The family moved to Ballina by 1893 and Lute subsequently went to Perth with her younger sister Jean.

About 1907 Clark Irving's [q.v.4] daughter Florence took them to Berlin where Lute had piano lessons from Edwin Fischer, and also studied German literature and Italian. She was Jean's accompanist during her five years training as a dramatic soprano. They heard Richard Strauss conduct *Der Rosenkavalier* in 1911 and later attended a performance of *Eugene Onegin* at Petrograd, Soviet Union. The sisters had spent World War I in Germany under the protection of the American embassy and were among the first British women to be exchanged in 1918. Lute assisted with auditions at Covent Garden, London. Having learned an appropriate repertoire, Jean obtained operatic engagements in Italy; there Lute translated Puccini's opera *Il Trittico*. Family concern about the postwar influenza pandemic brought them home.

Back in Sydney they stayed with the Ainsworth family at Warrawee and in 1921 joined Count Ercole Filippini's Italian opera company which toured Queensland. Next year Lute organized opera recitals at the New South Wales State Conservatorium of Music to raise funds for a 'National Opera House', a cause she constantly advocated: after Jean's death in 1935, Lute used the proceeds to buy opera scores which she donated to the Sydney Municipal Library.

In 1921 Lute had established a circle in Sydney to study the works of Rudolf Steiner. During a tour (1922-24) of Europe with her nieces Fay and Ruth Ainsworth, she heard Steiner lecture in Wales and on 1 January 1924 visited the Anthroposophical Society at Dornach, Switzerland, for her admission as one of its initial Australian members. She was general secretary (1935-48) of the Anthroposophical Society in Australia.

Returning to Sydney in late 1930, Lute Drummond was an accomplished linguist with an encyclopaedic musical knowledge, especially of opera. She taught and lectured from her tiny roof-top studio in Bond Street until 1947; her pupils included (Dame) Joan Hammond and Kenneth Neate. Following Steiner's lead, in the mid-1930s—with Marion Mahony Griffin [q.v.9]—she successfully directed classical and sacred drama in an open-air theatre at Castlecrag as part of seasonal anthroposophical festivals. In 1936 she produced the first of several opera series for the Australian Broadcasting Commission; in the late 1930s she was active in the free libraries movement; and in World War II she arranged musical programmes for army camps and hospitals.

When she fell ill with cancer, a gala concert at the Theatre Royal on 5 August 1948 raised £1000. Lute Drummond died on 27 May 1949 in hospital at Lindfield and was cremated; a memorial service was held at Christ Church St Laurence. Recalled by her associates as 'a radiant soul', she had exercised a significant cultural influence in Sydney. The high school building of the Glenaeon Rudolf Steiner School, Middle Cove, is named in her memory.

NSW State Conservatorium of Music, *Six Stories of the Opera*, concert programme (Syd, nd, 1922?); *Aust Musical News*, 1 June 1948, 1 July 1949; *Glenaeon Mag*, 1985; *Daily Examiner* (Grafton), 22 Mar 1935; *SMH*, 19 Aug, 22, 30 Sept 1933, 23 Oct 1940; M. M. Griffin, The Magic of America (microfilm NL); Syd Municipal Council records, 1935 (Archives, Town Hall, Syd); information from Miss R. Ainsworth, Epping, Syd.   J. I. ROE

DRUMMOND, VANCE (1927-1967), air force officer, was born on 22 February 1927 at Hamilton, New Zealand, third of six children of Leonard Henry Vance Drummond, office manager, and his wife Dorothy Josephine May, née McKnight, both New Zealand born. Educated at Hamilton West Public and Te Awamutu District High schools, Vance left early to help his father farm. Leonard's four sons were all interested in flying; Fred, the eldest, was killed in 1941 while serving in the Royal Australian Air Force. In May 1944 Vance joined the Royal New Zealand Air

Force. His training ended in September 1945 and in October he was demobilized as sergeant navigator.

In March 1946 Drummond enlisted in the New Zealand Military Forces. He was sent to Japan in July with 'J' Force and qualified as an interpreter. Back in New Zealand in October 1948, he left the army and applied to rejoin the R.N.Z.A.F., hoping to train as a fighter pilot. When he was rejected as being too old, he moved to Australia and was accepted by the R.A.A.F. on 29 August 1949.

Graduating top of his course as sergeant pilot in February 1951, Drummond was posted to No.78 Wing at Williamtown, New South Wales, and in August to No.77 Squadron in Korea with which he flew Gloster Meteor jets against superior Soviet-built MiG-15s. He was recommended for the American Air Medal (gazetted 1953) and commissioned on 30 November 1951. Next day his aircraft was shot down and he was captured by the North Koreans. On Good Friday, 1952, he and four companions escaped from Pinchon-ni prisoner-of-war camp, but all were recaptured and punished. Drummond was repatriated in September 1953.

After completing courses in advanced navigation and fighter-combat instruction, in 1954 Drummond became an initial member of the R.A.A.F.'s Sabre Trials Flight at Williamtown. In St Peter's Anglican Church, Hamilton, Newcastle, on 9 September 1955 he married a law clerk Margaret Hope Buckham. He was posted to headquarters, Home (Operational) Command, Penrith, in 1959 and attended the R.A.A.F. Staff College, Canberra, in 1961.

By December Drummond was a flight commander in No.75 Squadron. He was promoted squadron leader in January 1962 and in October took charge of the unit's 'Black Diamonds' aerobatic team, the official R.A.A.F. squad. The team's Sabres became a familiar sight at functions around Australia. They gave displays at the Seventh British Empire and Commonwealth Games in Perth in November, the Royal Hobart Regatta, attended by Queen Elizabeth II, in February 1963 and in Port Moresby in June 1964 to celebrate the opening of Papua New Guinea's House of Assembly. Drummond was awarded the Air Force Cross (1965) for his work in No.75 Squadron and his leadership of the 'Black Diamonds'.

From December 1964 he carried out staff duties at the Department of Air, Canberra. Twelve months later he was promoted acting wing commander (substantive January 1967) and sent to the Republic of Vietnam (South Vietnam) where he was attached to the United States Air Force. On 8 July 1966 he joined the 19th Tactical Air Support Squadron as a forward air controller. He flew in a Cessna 0-1 'Bird Dog', a two-seat observation aircraft, nicknamed 'Snoopy'.

On the night of 24-25 July Drummond and his American pilot went to the aid of an army company which was surrounded by troops of the People's Liberation Armed Forces (Viet Cong). Despite heavy anti-aircraft fire, they kept low, dropping flares, illuminating enemy positions, and calling up support from fighter-bombers and helicopter-gunships. They flew for a total of eleven hours in four sorties, in addition to the five hours which they had flown in daylight on the 24th. By dawn on the 25th the soldiers had been saved. Drummond was to be awarded the Distinguished Flying Cross. For similar work on 27 October, he won the Republic of Vietnam's Cross of Gallantry with Silver Star. He flew a total of 381 operational missions and set a high standard for Australian F.A.C.s who followed him.

Returning home, on 20 February 1967 Drummond assumed command of No.3 Squadron at Williamtown. On 17 May that year he and three other pilots were engaged in training exercises off the New South Wales coast. At 4.20 p.m., about 50 miles (80 km) north-east of Newcastle, his Mirage went into a dive and plummeted into the sea. Neither his body nor the aircraft was recovered. Margaret took their only child, 9-year-old David, to Government House, Canberra, to receive Vance's D.F.C. on 5 April 1968.

G. Odgers, *Across the Parallel* (Melb, 1952) and *Mission Vietnam* (Canb, 1974); *Mirage*, June 1967; D. Newton, 'Black Diamond Leader', *Aust Aviation*, Dec 1982; *Age* (Melb) and *Courier-Mail*, 13 Sept 1967; *SMH*, 18, 19, 23 May 1967; *NZ Herald*, 23 Sept 1967; information held by author from Mrs M. H. Drummond.   DENNIS NEWTON

DRYSDALE, ARTHUR JAMES (1887-1971), financier and pastoralist, was born on 23 April 1887 at Battery Point, Hobart, tenth child of John Drysdale, a mill-owner and storekeeper at Dover, Port Esperance, and his wife Jane, née Inches. Influenced by the Open Brethren, John was strongly religious. As a boy, Arthur showed uncommon determination when his right arm and shoulder were crippled by poliomyelitis: persistent manipulation exercise restored their use. As a young man at Dover, he began what became a successful pattern of entrepreneurial activity, borrowing, buying, improving, selling; he also aimed at eliminating the middleman. His first commercial venture was to buy calves, fatten them and sell them for a profit. He soon learned butchering and travelled the district with a 'cutting cart'. After disposing of this concern, he bought and built up a run-down butcher's shop at Dover which he again sold advantageously. On 26 April 1910 at Holy

Trinity Church, Hobart, he married Charlotte Rebecca Lewis (d.1969) with Anglican rites; they had no children.

In 1919 Drysdale launched himself upon the Hobart business world. His butchers' shops in the city were eventually supplied from his own farms. Diversifying, he established meatworks and processed smallgoods to supply his retail outlets. At various times he owned Belgrove, Mount Vernon, Kelvin Grove, Meadowbank and some half-dozen other pastoral properties, and applied the buy, improve and sell principle to them. Obtaining the agency for Ford motorcars in 1928, he sold out at a profit five years later. In 1937 he embarked on the first of several large ventures in the hospitality industry by building the lavishly appointed Wrest Point Hotel which was completed in 1939. Wartime seemed a distinctly bad time to open, but good management helped the hotel to prosper, aided by the patronage of American servicemen. Drysdale sold out for a profit in 1947. Five years later he bought the historic Hadley's Hotel, and began extensive renovations.

His most ambitious venture arose in the wake of the transfer of George Adams's [q.v.3] Tattersall's lotteries from Tasmania to Victoria in 1954. Following lengthy negotiation with the Cosgrove [q.v.13] government, Drysdale became sole licensee and proprietor of Tasmanian Lotteries. Popular on the mainland and in New Zealand, in 1955-56 the lottery and sweepstakes grossed about £3 750 000. The government received almost 30 per cent; Drysdale received 10 per cent, from which he paid salaries and expenses; the balance provided his profit. Ticket sales rapidly declined from 1958 and he surrendered the licence in 1961. Known to close associates as 'A.J.', he was often called 'Tasmania's self-made millionaire', the 'Lottery Czar' and 'the man with the Midas touch'. From the late 1950s he was considerably assisted in business by his natural daughter Nora (b.1919). A member of the Hobart Racing Club and a Freemason, he was an affable but private man. Drysdale died on 21 May 1971 in Hobart and was buried in Cornelian Bay cemetery; he was survived by his daughter to whom he left most of his Tasmanian estate, sworn for probate at $754 513.

J&PP(Tas), 1962, vol 167, *for* Auditor General's Report (28), p 16, *and* Budget Speech and Financial Statement (21), p 4; *Rydge's Business J*, 1 May 1956; *Saturday Evening Mercury*, 13 Nov 1954, 1 Feb 1975; *Mercury* (Hob), 12 Nov 1973; General Law Deeds, vol 20/6877, vol 23/2796 (Lands Titles Office, Hob); information from Mrs N. Drysdale Bates, Margate, Tas.   RICHARD ELY
                                  NORMAN BEECHEY

DUFF, VICTOR CLARK-; *see* CLARK-DUFF, VICTOR

DUGAN, WINSTON JOSEPH, BARON DUGAN OF VICTORIA AND OF LURGAN (1876-1951), soldier and governor, was born on 3 September 1876 at Parsonstown, King's County, Ireland, son of Charles Winston Dugan, inspector of schools, and his wife Esther Elizabeth, née Rogers. Educated at Lurgan College, County Armagh, Dugan (pronounced Duggan) enlisted in the British Army in 1896 and was commissioned on 24 January 1900 in the Lincolnshire Regiment. In 1899-1902 he saw active service in South Africa. He was appointed captain in the Worcestershire Regiment in 1904 and was garrison adjutant, Irish Command, in 1910-14. At the register office, Kensington, London, on 2 December 1911 he married Ruby Lilian (Applewhaite-) Abbott.

In World War I Dugan served ably and gallantly on the Western Front. While commanding the 2nd Battalion, Royal Irish Regiment, he was awarded the Distinguished Service Order (1915). Promoted temporary brigadier general in July 1916, he commanded the 184th Infantry Brigade until he was severely wounded in September. He led the 73rd Brigade from December 1916 to July 1918, was appointed C.M.G. (1918) and was mentioned in dispatches six times.

After commanding the 10th Brigade in 1919-23, Dugan was placed on half-pay in 1924. He returned to duty as assistant adjutant-general, Southern Command (1926-30), and commanded the 56th (1st London) Division, Territorial Army (1931-34). Appointed aide-de-camp to King George V in 1928 and C.B. in 1929, he was promoted major general on 13 April 1930. In 1933 he presided at the court martial of Lieutenant Norman Baillie-Stewart for offences against the Official Secrets Act and was commended for his efforts to ensure the accused a fair hearing. He drew further press notice that year when he allowed himself to be 'kidnapped' to shake his subordinates out of the rut of peacetime routines.

Early in 1934 Dugan was chosen to succeed Sir Alexander Hore-Ruthven (later Lord Gowrie [q.v.9]) as governor of South Australia. Appointed K.C.M.G., Dugan retired from the army and arrived in Adelaide with his wife on 28 July. The most handsome couple ever to occupy Government House, they were effective and witty public speakers, and good listeners; they dedicated themselves to the service of the people, travelling widely, identifying problems and bringing them to the attention of ministers. They gave financial as well as moral support to all manner of good causes and to needy individuals. Labor, Independent and government members of parliament wanted Dugan to remain for a second term, but he had agreed to succeed Lord Huntingfield [q.v.9] as governor of Victoria.

The Dugans reached Melbourne on 17 July 1939. To the chagrin of the Dominions Office in London, Sir Winston still regarded meeting people as more important than writing reports. He provoked controversy by telling members of the Victorian Chamber of Manufactures that they looked well fed and ought to be taking more initiatives to reduce unemployment. His wife denounced the conditions she found in some country hospitals. Meanwhile, she had converted the ballroom at Government House into a wartime workroom for the Australian Red Cross Society, of which she was national president. The Dugans 'contrived uncomplainingly' to conceal the shabby and dilapidated state of their residence by 'an ingenious deployment of their own possessions'.

Sir Winston played an active role in stabilizing Victorian politics in the 1940s. When the Dunstan [q.v.8] Country Party government disintegrated in September 1943, he commissioned the Labor leader John Cain [q.v.13] as premier; four days later Dunstan cemented a coalition with the United Australia Party. On the collapse of that ministry in September 1945, Dugan invited in turn Dunstan, T. T. Hollway [q.v.] and Cain to form a stopgap ministry until elections could be held, but none of them was able to guarantee supply. Dugan then sent for the Liberals' deputy-leader, Ian Macfarlan [q.v.]. As soon as a supply bill was passed, Dugan dissolved parliament. After a general election in November left the Independents holding the balance of power, he commissioned Cain to form a ministry.

At the request of governments of all hues, Dugan's term in Victoria was extended five times. He had been appointed a knight of the Order of St John (1935) and elevated to G.C.M.G. (1944); and he had served (6 September 1944 to 29 January 1945 and 19 January to 10 March 1947) as administrator of the Commonwealth. He was raised to the peerage in January 1949 and retired to England in February.

Tall, with an aquiline nose above a well-trimmed white moustache, always immaculately dressed, and a chain-smoker, Dugan had turned to golf in 1918 when his war injuries compelled him to give up hunting and polo. He occasionally rode a police horse in the Adelaide or Melbourne parklands until one reared and threw him in 1941. In later life he wore a monocle, but spurned comparisons with Colonel Blimp, saying that, when only one eye needed correction, a single lens was cheaper than spectacles. An Anglican in the Irish Protestant tradition, he read a chapter or two of the Bible every day and supported foreign missions. Lord Dugan died without issue on 17 August 1951 at Marylebone, London, and was buried in the Applewhaite family vault at Pickenham Hall, Swaffham, Norfolk. His widow died in 1985, leaving nearly all her estate, valued at £813 929, to charity.

S. Sayers, *Ned Herring* (Melb, 1980); *SMH*, 4, 7 June 1934, 30 Aug 1939; *Advertiser* (Adel), 23 Feb 1939; *Age* (Melb), 30 Mar 1939, 4 Aug 1947, 22, 24 May 1948, 20 Aug 1951; *Argus*, 5 July 1939, 22 May 1948, 1 Feb 1949, 20 Aug 1951; *The Times*, 20 Aug 1951; DO 35/582, 584, 592, 594, 1120 (AJCP, microfilm, NL); GRG 2/5/41-43, 11/20-22 (SRSA); Dispatches 1937-39 (Government House, Adel); VPRS 7582/P1/2, 8299/P1/10-11 (PRO, Vic).

P. A. HOWELL

DULLO, WALTER ANDREAS (1902-1978), chocolate-maker and musicologist, was born on 26 November 1902 at Königsberg, East Prussia, Germany, son of Andreas Franz Wilhelm Dullo, an administrator and mayor, and his Jewish wife Clara Alice, née Japha. Raised as a Lutheran, Andreas attended the *gymnasium* at Offenbach before reading mathematics (1921-24) and law (1929-33) at the Humboldt University of Berlin. In the intervening years he studied music at the University of Heidelberg. Prevented by the Nazi administration from practising law, he first learned massage and then Swiss chocolate-making. On 9 June 1937 at Berlin-Friedenau he married Annemarie Deutsch of Berlin; they were to remain childless. The couple reached Sydney in the *Rendsburg* on 11 September, bringing with them second-hand, chocolate-manufacturing machinery.

After attempting to make chocolate in their flat at Double Bay and working as a married couple in domestic service, in 1939 they opened a small shop in New South Head Road. In their one-roomed premises the Dullos—eventually assisted by Walter's two younger sisters—made the chocolates by hand; a curtain screened them from a minuscule sales area. To attract his first customers, Dullo sold small packages door-to-door. As the fame of the product spread, wartime rationing of ingredients posed difficulties and customers had to be content with ¼-lb. purchases. Classified as a refugee alien, in 1943-44 Walter served with the Allied Works Council as a labourer at Alice Springs, Northern Territory. He was naturalized in 1944.

In time the quality and novelty of the Dullos' chocolates and truffles attracted customers from many parts of eastern Australia; foreign consuls and ambassadors were among the earliest enthusiasts; and children loved the surprise Easter eggs and rabbits. Despite growing prosperity, cautious Mr Dullo never expanded the business, preferring to devote his leisure hours to music, his dominating passion. He retired in 1970.

With Richard Goldner, Dullo had founded the Musica Viva Society of Australia in 1945; he was also vice-president of the Sydney Mozart Society and correspondent of the Mozarteum at Salzburg, Austria. Dullo came to know soloists and conductors who relied on his advice, listened to his collection of recordings, and acquired scores and sheet music that he obtained for them from Berlin. He completed two unfinished piano sonatas by Schubert (later recorded by the Australian pianist Romola Costantino), composed cadenzas for several Mozart piano concertos, wrote 'Schubert and the Twin Brothers' (*24 Hours*, July 1977), and prepared programme notes for the Australian Broadcasting Commission, Musica Viva and the Mozart Society. As patron of the Music Broadcasting Society of New South Wales Co-operative Ltd, he arranged classical programmes for radio 2MBS-FM.

Appointed to the Order of Merit of the Federal Republic of Germany in 1977, Dullo had an extensive knowledge of the history of art, the German classics and European religious sculpture. His hobby was to expose, in marginalia, errors in logic made by writers of detective stories. A powerfully built and gentle man, he combined his wide learning with a dry wit, an encyclopaedic knowledge of classical and romantic music, and unending devotion and loyalty to friends. Dullo died on 22 August 1978 in Royal North Shore Hospital and was cremated; his wife survived him.

J. Wilton and R. Bosworth, *Old Worlds and New Australia* (Melb, 1984); *SMH*, 11 Apr, 21 Dec 1976, 11 Feb, 23 Aug, 18 Dec 1978; Naturalization file, A435/1 item 44/4/3968 (AA, Canb); information from Mrs A. Dullo, Clovelly, Syd; personal information.   KLAUS LOEWALD

DUMAS, SIR FREDERICK LLOYD (1891-1973), journalist and newspaper executive, was born on 15 July 1891 at Mount Barker, South Australia, one of five children of native-born parents Charles Morris Russell Dumas, printer, and his wife Amelia, née Paltridge. Lloyd's grandfather Victor Dumas had emigrated from Britain in the mid-nineteenth century. The family was Huguenot in origin: speculation that they were descended from the French novelist Alexandre Dumas remains unconfirmed. From 1880 Charles Dumas had been founding editor and sole proprietor of the *Mount Barker Courier*; he was also a member of the House of Assembly in 1898-1902.

Lloyd was educated at public schools in Adelaide and Victor Harbor. He and his eldest brother (Sir) Russell [q.v.] were among the top state scholarship schoolboys of their day. Leaving Teachers' Training College at 15, Lloyd began a cadetship on Adelaide's morning newspaper, the *Advertiser*. In 1911 he was one of the founders of the State branch of the Australian Journalists' Association. After achieving recognition as a sports and parliamentary reporter, he joined the Melbourne *Argus* in 1915 and rapidly rose to be its Federal political roundsman. On 23 November 1915 at St Oswald's Anglican Church, Parkside, Adelaide, he married a stenographer Daisy Minna Hall (d.1962), daughter of a bank-manager and great-granddaughter of Edward Smith Hall [q.v.1].

During the second conscription campaign (1917) Prime Minister W. M. Hughes [q.v.9] invited Dumas to join his staff. Next year he accompanied Hughes to the Imperial Conference in London. In 1919 Dumas rejoined the *Argus* and in 1921 became its youngest ever chief of staff. Three years later he was appointed editor of the *Sun News-Pictorial*. In 1927-29 he worked in Fleet Street, London, as editor and manager of the Sydney *Sun's* and Melbourne *Herald's* United Cable Service. By this time he had attracted the admiration and friendship of many of the newspaper industry's leaders throughout Australia, not so much for his literary gifts as for his administrative talents, energy, clear mind, reporting flair and news sense, and for his capacity as a mediator.

In 1929 a syndicate headed by (Sir) Keith Murdoch [q.v.10], managing director of the Melbourne *Herald*, acquired the *Advertiser* for £1 387 000 and invited Dumas to be its managing editor. The paper's issued capital was £475 000, its circulation 85 000, and it had three hundred employees. When Dumas retired as chairman of Advertiser Newspapers Ltd in 1967, the issued capital had risen to £12 million, circulation to 208 000 and the staff totalled 1500. From the outset, he was widely regarded as a shrewd but decent man, sensitive to the feelings of others, anxious to be a good employer and equally anxious to run a newspaper which supported 'sound' government and which would be recognized as giving genuine public service to the community. With the paper's major owners and shareholders in Melbourne, Dumas' power was considerable, and he was soon handling it comfortably and confidently, with little interference from his Melbourne principals. In 1930 he joined the Adelaide Club. Although the Depression coincided with Dumas taking the managing editorship, he was fortunate in the political and social circumstances in which his career prospered.

With Murdoch's agreement, he at first

swung the *Advertiser* behind Lionel Hill's [q.v.9] government and continued to back Hill and his followers after their expulsion (August 1931) from the Australian Labor Party for implementing the Premiers' Plan. The paper's support, coupled with that of prominent Liberals, enabled Hill's Parliamentary Labor Party minority government to survive. Dumas justified his actions by the need to rescue the State from the Depression. In 1932 he arranged key meetings in Adelaide and interstate, designed to form a National Party by uniting the P.L.P. with the Liberal Federation. Led by (Sir) Richard Layton Butler [q.v.7], the Liberals refused to co-operate. They united with the Country Party and won the election in April 1933. Dumas and Murdoch promoted Hill's appointment as agent-general in London and gave him financial help each year until his death.

In November 1938 (Sir) Thomas Playford came to office as leader of the Liberal and Country League government. He and Dumas met privately soon afterwards. The premier outlined his plans to industrialize South Australia and to restore prosperity: the Depression had battered the State, with unemployment peaking at over 30 per cent of all trade unionists. Dumas believed that, if Playford were successful, the entire community would benefit and population would increase, lifting the circulation of the *Advertiser* which then enjoyed a metropolitan morning monopoly. He promised Playford that the paper would back his policies vigorously.

World War II stabilized and unified South Australia. When the war ended a malapportioned electoral system—coupled with Playford's intelligent leadership—gave premier and editor the opportunities they needed. A weak Labor Opposition attacked what it saw as an unholy alliance between Playford and the State's dominant news medium. They dubbed the paper 'the L.C.L. House Journal'. Although neither Playford nor Dumas was a rigid conservative, 'sound government' did not, in the eyes of either, embrace the ideal of a modern welfare state. Their common priorities were the needs of business and industry. During what was to be a record term of nearly twenty-seven years, successive Playford governments were vulnerable to charges that they starved hospitals, schools, libraries and other social services of appropriate funding.

The two men never became close friends, but Dumas used his newspaper to praise Playford's initiatives, with little challenge or dissent, especially during elections. The *Advertiser* upheld the traditional structures of the day—the government, the courts, the police, the churches, the family, and the Returned Services League of Australia. Both men saw the proper place of women as in the home, or

in giving voluntary service to good causes. A mocking profile of the *Advertiser* came from the pen of the jurist and poet, Dr John Bray, in the *Current Affairs Bulletin* (May 1965): 'It reflects in so many ways the tone of South Australian life. A comparison with one of the great dailies of the eastern States is instructive. The *Advertiser* is more restrained; the editorials are heavier, the headlines less exciting; the social columns more extensive; the preference to and the reverence for the local institutions and the local dignitaries more prominent. Those parts of it which are addressed to a popular audience are less vulgar; and those parts of it which are addressed to a quasi-intellectual or quasi-aesthetic audience more inadequate. There lingers about it still the aura of the nineteenth century provincial organ, the note of ponderous respectability, but also of ponderous responsibility'.

The power, influence and goodwill of Dumas and his newspaper were prime factors in helping the Playford government to retain office for so long. Under their joint benevolent despotism, however, South Australia was transformed from its mendicant status during the Depression. The population almost doubled, from 600 000 to more than one million; general prosperity increased dramatically; and unemployment was virtually eliminated. Meanwhile the State remained almost free from public scandal and corruption. The Dumas era at the *Advertiser* also saw the advent of commercial radio and television. The newspaper established radio 5AD and several rural subsidiaries, as well as the television station ADS-7 (1959); the small job-printing office at the *Advertiser* developed into the Griffin Press, one of Australia's largest printing-houses.

In his autobiography, *The Story of a Full Life* (Melbourne, 1969), Dumas wrote in a surprisingly folksy and unsophisticated style. He reviewed his experiences on the national and world stages, including a three-month visit to overseas war zones in 1943 as leader of a party of Australian editors who reported to Prime Minister John Curtin [q.v.13] on the British war effort. They interviewed General Douglas MacArthur [q.v.], President Franklin Delano Roosevelt, (Sir) Winston Churchill, King George VI and Queen Elizabeth. The book artlessly revealed his immense pride in his many achievements: helping to resolve the 'bodyline' crisis in Test cricket between England and Australia in the 1930s; his mediation between Playford and the Adelaide Electric Supply Co. which Playford nationalized in 1946, the year in which Dumas was knighted; and his crucial role in establishing, and securing financial backing for, the first Adelaide Festival of Arts in 1960. He ended his book with the words, 'I must sign myself "The Luckiest Man in the World"'.

Dumas was a foundation director (1938-67) of Australian Newsprint Mills Pty Ltd at Boyer, Tasmania, a board-member (1946-67) of the Herald and Weekly Times Ltd and chairman of directors (1950-53) of Reuters News Agency, London. He was also a governor of the National Gallery of South Australia from 1945 and chairman of its board in 1955-63; an extension to the main building has been named the Sir Lloyd Dumas Gallery. In addition, he sat on the board of directors of Elder, Smith [qq.v.4,6] & Co. Ltd in 1941-67 and was a governor (1942-67) of the Wyatt [q.v.2] Benevolent Institution which gave financial support to people 'above the labouring class' who were in reduced circumstances.

Although Dumas had been obliged to resign from the A.J.A. when he became chief of staff of the *Argus*, he never treated his employees as ruthlessly as did some other Australian newspaper managers. Arbitration awards provided for most employees to receive their full salaries for up to three months when ill, but the *Advertiser* overlooked these limits and, in some cases, carried sick workers of all ranks and status on full pay for six months. On his retirement, the A.J.A. gave a dinner in his honour and readmitted him to life membership. The State president recognized that Sir Lloyd had 'always been a journalist at heart and an unwavering friend of the AJA'. These sentiments lent point to a comment by (Sir) Robert Menzies [q.v.] in 1952: 'Dumas is one of the least bloody-minded of his breed'.

Sir Lloyd was a lover of good food and fine wine, and a genial host; during the latter part of his life he failed to control his weight. He had been raised as an Anglican, but was not a regular churchgoer. Yet, he defended those who were: 'those who have faith draw comfort and encouragement and hope from their religion, whether it be Christianity, Mohammedanism, Buddhism, or some other, and academics should respect that faith and not sneer at it'. Survived by his three daughters, he died on 24 June 1973 at Calvary Hospital, North Adelaide, and was cremated. His estate was sworn for probate at $223 332. A portrait by (Sir) Ivor Hele is held by Dumas' daughter Mrs H. De Pledge Sykes.

D. Whitelock, *Festival!* (Adel, 1980); S. Cockburn, *Playford* (Adel, 1991); *Advertiser Pi*, May-June 1973; *Current Affairs Bulletin*, 24 May 1965; *Labour Hist*, no 31, Nov 1976, p 14; *Advertiser* (Adel), 9 Mar 1967, 18 Oct 1969, 26 June 1973; *Mount Barker Courier*, 1 Oct 1880, 1 Oct 1980 (centenary souvenir); Dumas papers (NL); personal information.   S. COCKBURN

DUMAS, SIR RUSSELL JOHN (1887-1975), engineer, was born on 17 January 1887 at Mount Barker, South Australia, one of five children of Charles Morris Russell Dumas, printer, and his wife Amelia, née Paltridge. (Sir) Lloyd [q.v.] was his younger brother. After winning a bursary to complete his schooling at Prince Alfred College, Russell studied engineering at the University of Adelaide (B.Sc., 1909; Dip.Elec.E., 1910; B.E., 1913; M.E., 1931). On 11 April 1910 he began work as a draughtsman in the South Australian Engineer-in-Chief's Department and from July 1912 was employed designing drainage-works at Naracoorte.

Enlisting in the Australian Imperial Force on 26 January 1916, Dumas was commissioned in June. He served on the Western Front in 1917-18, mainly with the 5th Field Company, Engineers, rose to lieutenant and was twice wounded. His A.I.F. appointment terminated in Australia on 16 November 1919. Next day he resumed his former job. As assistant resident engineer (from 1923 resident engineer), he helped to build locks on the Murray River.

At St Paul's Anglican Church, Naracoorte, on 2 November 1920 Dumas had married Muriel Elsie Rogers (d.1960), a nurse. With their two children, in 1925 they moved to Western Australia where he took up an appointment with the Metropolitan Water Supply, Sewerage and Drainage Department as resident engineer on the construction of Churchman Brook Reservoir, the first of several proposed dams in the hills that were designed to supply Perth's demand for water. A number of similar projects followed its completion in 1928. Between 1929 and 1933 he directed construction of Drakesbrook and Wellington dams, the raising of Harvey Weir, and the extension of the Collie and Harvey irrigation areas, all carried out by sustenance labour. Dumas' own employment was precarious in these Depression years. In 1930 he was placed on the temporary staff at a reduced salary and was not reclassified until 1933. Meantime, he chaired (1932) the Perth division of the Institution of Engineers, Australia. Appointed chief engineer in the department in 1934, he directed the design and construction of the Canning, Samson Brook and Stirling dams, and established his reputation. He had gained his master's degree with a thesis on the design of high masonry dams. Stirling Dam, at 148 ft (45 m), was the highest earthen dam in Australia. Proud of these engineering achievements, Dumas was none the less critical of the State's development process: 'no time or money for preparation, and the designs and plans barely a nose ahead of construction if they are so much as that'. 'Planning ahead' was needed. It was a tenet he practised as he forged his career.

Made director of works and buildings in 1941, Dumas became engineering head of the

Public Works Department. He had great faith in his profession. 'Engineering is the basis of civilisation', he declared, and its greatest work the storage and distribution of water. Water shortage was Western Australia's most immediate agricultural problem. The Depression had highlighted the wheat-belt's need for a comprehensive water-supply to enable farmers to carry sheep as an alternative source of income. Engineers, among them Dumas, had put various proposals to provide this service. The preferred scheme—to raise Mundaring Weir and Wellington Dam—was to become Western Australia's major, post-war public-works project, involving both the State and Federal governments. The commitment of Commonwealth funds, finally negotiated in 1947, was primarily Dumas' achievement.

Having been requested in 1941 to investigate the North-West's potential for 'increased settlement and greater productiveness', Dumas concluded that closer settlement, through irrigation, was the answer and identified the Ord River as the most promising site. He promoted the Ord River Scheme and facilitated the first stages of its development, seeing it as a forerunner of many similar settlements. His visits to the North in 1941 and 1942 fostered an interest in that region of the State which strengthened after World War II through his appointments as chairman of the North-West Development Committee and member of the Commonwealth Northern Australia Development Committee. From 1949 he was a powerful supporter of government assistance for I. H. Grabowsky (of Australian National Airways Pty Ltd) to trial the Glenroy Air Beef project, but, as a member of the 1954-55 Commonwealth Air Beef Panel, he agreed that air transport of beef was 'not economically sound' at that time.

Dumas believed that bold initiative, basic planning and large-scale development were essential to lift Western Australia from its status as a claimant State. As chairman (1946-53) of the Albany Zone Development Committee, he drove the extensive land development in that district. Industry had to be attracted, too, and in 1951-52 he had his greatest success. With Premier (Sir) David Brand's [q.v.13] support, Dumas negotiated the establishment at Kwinana of the £40 million Anglo-Iranian Oil Co.'s refinery, Broken Hill Pty Ltd's £4 million steel-rolling-mill and Rugby Portland Cement Co.'s £2.2 million works (through its subsidiary Cockburn Cement Pty Ltd). His role in attracting this capital was so crucial that the government extended his employment beyond normal retirement age, giving him additional power and status as co-ordinator of works and industrial development to ensure co-oper-ation from all public service departments in the Kwinana initiatives. Dumas finally retired in December 1953.

He then joined the Weld Club and became a director of several companies, including Cockburn Cement and Freney Kimberley Oil Co. In the early 1960s, in an unusual display of public activism, he participated in the campaign to save Perth's Barracks Arch. He remained influential in shaping economic development policies through his advisory role to (Sir) Charles Court who, when he became minister for industrial development in 1959, made Dumas chairman of the newly formed Industries Advisory Committee.

One of Western Australia's most powerful public servants, Dumas transformed the State's approach to development. He named Robert Chapman [q.v.7], his university engineering teacher, as 'possibly the greatest influence' on his life, and Essington Lewis [q.v.10] as the Australian who had contributed most to the country's 'real advancement'. A man of great energy, prodigious hard work and determination, Dumas seemed to those around him to be able to 'see far ahead' and 'make things happen'—a 'visionary' and a 'bulldozer'. His achievements were well acknowledged: a series of awards culminated in the Peter Nicol Russell [q.v.6] medal (1952); he was appointed C.M.G. (1950), K.B. (1959) and K.B.E. (1964); and, prominent in Perth's landscape, the new multi-storey headquarters of the Public Works Department was named Dumas House. Survived by his daughter and son, Sir Russell died on 10 August 1975 at Albany and was buried in Allambie Park cemetery.

J. S. H. Le Page, *Building a State* (Perth, 1986); B. Moore, *From the Ground Up* (Perth, 1987); *Public Service Review* (SA), Oct 1914, p 184, Feb 1917, p 117; L. Layman, 'Development Ideology in Western Australia', *Hist Studies*, no 79, Oct 1982; *West Australian*, 17, 22 Jan 1953, 1 Jan 1959, 30 Apr 1960, 13 June, 31 Dec 1964, 11, 12 Aug 1975; *Albany Advertiser*, 3 May 1960; Dumas papers (WAA); Public Works Dept, Dumas file (WAA); R. G. Hartley, Norman Fernie—Engineer, 1898-1977 (1991, ts, BL).   LENORE LAYMAN

DUNBAR, WILLIAM JOHN HANLEY (1903-1972), publisher, publicist and journalist, was born on 30 April 1903 at Scone, New South Wales, eldest of four children of John James Dunbar, farmer, and his wife Clara Kathleen, née Hanley, both native-born. Bill attended primary school at Red Range, near Glen Innes, and was privately tutored before entering St John's College, Armidale, in 1922 to study for the Anglican priesthood. He left in 1925, returned to the college (by then relocated at Morpeth) in 1927, but was not ordained.

Encouraged by the warden (Bishop) E. H. Burgmann [q.v.13], in late 1927 Dunbar established St John's College Press. Burgmann envisaged a Church press, which would also nurture and advance Australian letters, and which would operate a printery able to produce material of technical excellence. From 1927 to 1934 the press published and printed the quarterly magazine, the *Morpeth Review*, 'bringing together much of the richest scholarship of our day and nation', as Dunbar later noted. In addition, it published works of theology, literary criticism, social research and biography, and undertook general printing. On 10 January 1930 at St James's Anglican Church, Sydney, Dunbar married a kindergarten teacher Helen May Longfield.

After the press closed in September 1935, Dunbar was employed by the West Maitland printers and stationers, Thomas Dimmock Ltd, and became the firm's travelling representative based at Newcastle. His interest in high-quality printing led him to collect the best examples of tourism advertising from around the world. In April 1937 he was appointed secretary (subsequently director) of the Canberra Tourist Bureau which was jointly administered by the Commonwealth government and the Canberra Chamber of Commerce. Within months Dunbar announced that tourism had become the city's biggest industry. In the first year of the bureau's operations, he and one staff member handled more than ten thousand inquiries. They made accommodation bookings, arranged means of travel and distributed brochures publicizing the national capital. The number of visitors to Canberra rose annually, reaching approximately 170 000 in 1949-50.

Involved in community affairs, Dunbar was a foundation member (1950) and sometime chairman of the Good Neighbour Council of the Australian Capital Territory; he was its delegate to Australian citizenship conventions in 1957-59. He was also an office-bearer in the Church of England Men's Society in Australia, the Canberra Film Centre (later Society), the local alpine and aero clubs, and the Rotary Club of Canberra (president 1949-50).

In 1960 Dunbar retired from the bureau and began a four-year government contract to lecture in Britain promoting Australia's immigration programme. He joined the editorial staff of the *Canberra Times* in 1964 and was variously bowls correspondent, community roundsman and the newspaper's librarian. Survived by his wife, son and daughter, he died of cancer on 7 March 1972 in Canberra Hospital and was cremated.

Canb Times, 8 Mar 1972; A431, item 1946/1036, 1950/415 *and* A601, item 175/1/37 (AA, Canb); Dunbar's application to Canb Tourist Bureau and Dunbar family papers (held by Mrs H. Kelman, Dickson, Canb).   FRANK CRANSTON

DUNCAN, ADA CONSTANCE (1896-1970), welfare activist and international affairs specialist, was born on 26 October 1896 at Canterbury, Melbourne, third daughter of Australian-born parents Andrew William Bartlett Duncan, agent, and his wife Alice Dalby, née Bellin. She was educated at Hessle College (a local Baptist school) and at the University of Melbourne (B.A. Hons, 1917; M.A., 1922) where she was one of the first women to own a motorcycle: during World War I she offered rides to raise funds for the Australian Red Cross Society. After graduating, she worked for two years as a travelling secretary for the Australian Student Christian Movement.

In 1922 Constance Duncan was appointed an Australian secretary of the Young Women's Christian Association, on loan to the association in Japan. She learned Japanese and worked for the Y.W.C.A. in Tokyo and at Kyoto as a secretary and teacher of English. On furlough in 1928-29, she visited Australia and also studied at the London School of Economics.

Returning to Australia in 1932 when her father fell ill, Duncan joined the Lyceum Club and, in 1934-41, was employed as secretary of the Victorian branch of the Australian League of Nations Union and of the Bureau of Social and International Affairs. In 1936 she was a Victorian delegate to the Institute of Pacific Relations conference at Yosemite, California, United States of America. On her way home, she toured China and Japan for the Australian Broadcasting Commission, inquiring into the reception of short-wave programmes.

Her wide experience with international affairs led to her commitment to the peace movement, and, with Dorothy Gibson [q.v.], she served on the executive of the United Peace Council. In 1937 Duncan became secretary of the International Peace Campaign. She was valued not only for her administrative capability, but also because, essentially more conservative than most of its members, she helped broaden public support, especially from women's organizations. Duncan resigned after the Munich agreement and was replaced by Doris Blackburn [q.v.13]. At the same time she continued her association with the Y.W.C.A., serving as president (1938-42) of the Melbourne branch.

In December 1938 the Victorian International Refugee Emergency Council, sponsored by the L.N.U. and the churches, was formed to assist in selecting European refugees and helping them adapt to Australian life. Duncan was appointed director. She fought to dispel community prejudice against refugees, publicly condemning, for instance, the reference by Sir Frank Clarke [q.v.8], president of the Legislative Council, to 'slinking, rat-faced men' who provided sweated labour for 'backyard factories'. She asserted that stringent selection criteria ensured high-calibre immigrants, and reminded Australians that it was their responsibility to acquaint new arrivals with the language and labour laws.

Early in September 1940 Duncan learned through British Quakers that internees deported from Britain in the *Dunera* were headed for Australia. According to her friend the composer Margaret Sutherland, 'Con, being a practical and compassionate person, got immediately busy. She found clothes, cases, rugs' and met the ship at Port Melbourne. Following initial refusal, she was later permitted to visit the refugees in camps at Tatura, Victoria, and Hay, New South Wales. She informed the British Society of Friends that conditions on the ship had been 'deplorable', and that the men had arrived in 'a destitute condition and did not possess a razor blade, much less a change of underwear'. As a result of her letter, she was summoned to Victoria Barracks. Profiting by the experience of two colleagues who had been interrogated, she insisted on having her lawyer present. She was treated courteously, but conflict with officials persisted as she tried to ameliorate conditions for the refugees. In February 1941 she reported that new restrictions had been imposed on contacts with them, but these were eased from May.

Throughout 1941 Duncan continued to spearhead V.I.R.E.C.'s activities. She maintained her campaigns to remove the perception of refugees as 'enemy aliens', and to gain an impartial tribunal to assess their loyalty and suitability to serve with the Australian forces. In December she resigned from V.I.R.E.C. and joined the Department of Labour and National Service to investigate the welfare of children whose mothers were in the workforce. She produced a report in 1944 for the National Health and Medical Research Council which advocated a national programme of maternal and child welfare, further support services for mothers, better pay for domestic workers, crèches, subsidized kindergarten training colleges and uniform divorce laws. In 1943 she had stood unsuccessfully as an Independent candidate for the Federal seat of Balaclava.

Appointed in 1945 to the United Nations Relief and Rehabilitation Administration as welfare officer for the South-West Pacific, Duncan visited Korea next year as a member of an U.N.R.R.A. special mission and stayed on as liaison officer to the commanding generals of the United States and Soviet armies. When she returned to Australia she continued to use her expertise as a university extension lecturer in international affairs. In 1948 she helped organize the first United Nations appeal for children.

After spending a year abroad with Sutherland, in 1953 Duncan was invited by (Sir) Ian Clunies Ross [q.v.13] to be city organizer for the university's International House building appeal; she later became a foundation member (1955-66) of the International House council. Her fund-raising task completed, she diverted her still considerable energies to the Australian Council of Churches. She belonged to its resettlement committee and was employed from 1955 as agency sponsorship officer.

Throughout her varied career, Duncan's commitment to international peace and to justice for those whose lives were dislocated by war remained firm. Some remembered her as a 'large and imposing' woman, although the impression may have been 'due more to personality than to cubic capacity'. Others were intimidated by her 'big, booming voice' and her tendency to give short shrift to those—especially men—who did not match her energy and dedication. (She referred to one unfortunate as a 'milksop'.) Despite her 'almost masculine forcefulness', most colleagues were disarmed by her warmth, compassion, humour and thoughtfulness. Friends relaxed with her at her weekend cottage at Olinda where she enjoyed gardening and woodwork. Having shared a house at Kew with Sutherland for many years, Miss Duncan retired to a Baptist hostel at Canterbury. She died on 13 September 1970 at Kew and was cremated. In 1972 the private dining-room at International House was named after her.

R. Gibson, *One Woman's Life* (Syd, 1980); C. Pearl, *The Dunera Scandal* (Syd, 1983); *SMH*, 23 May 1928, 3 Dec 1936, 9 Mar, 20 Aug 1938, 19 July 1943, 9 Dec 1944, 2 May 1945, 2 Jan, 5 Mar 1946; *Age* (Melb), 9 May 1939; *Argus*, 4 Nov 1940, 14 Aug 1943, 30 Oct 1952; *Herald* (Melb), 12 May 1955; Vic Immigration Refugee Emergency Council minutes (Aust Council of Churches, Melb); Aust Refugee Immigration Cte policy file, A434, item 49/3/7286 (AA, Canb); Brookes *and* Eggleston papers (NL); information from Miss J. Leigh and Miss M. Crump, Hawthorn, Dr L. Benyei, Kew, the Lyceum Club, Melb, and Mr A. Clunies Ross, Kinbuck, Scotland.   DIANE LANGMORE

DUNCAN, ALEXANDER MITCHELL (1888-1965), policeman, was born on 25 September 1888 at Mortlach, Banffshire, Scotland, son of John Duncan, farmer, and his wife Elizabeth, née Mitchell. Educated at nearby Dufftown, Alexander joined the London Metropolitan Police Force on 19 December

1910. He married Elizabeth Ann MacDonald on 1 September 1917 at Trinity Presbyterian Church, Lambeth. For twenty-six years Duncan served in the force, rising from constable to chief inspector (1934). Most of his work was in the Criminal Investigation Department and he headed (from 1935) Scotland Yard's 'Flying Squad'. Described by his peers as a 'strong silent type', he received forty-five commissioner's commendations for solving murders and other major crimes, and taught at the Scotland Yard School for Detectives.

In 1936, on the recommendation of his commissioner Sir Philip Game [q.v.8], Duncan was seconded to Melbourne in response to Premier (Sir) Albert Dunstan's [q.v.8] request for a senior officer from Scotland Yard to inspect and report on the Victoria Police Force. The force had been rocked that year by the bizarre shooting of Superintendent John O'Connell Brophy, head of the Criminal Investigation Branch, and by the controversial resignation of the chief commissioner Sir Thomas Blamey [q.v.13]. Under the temporary command of Superintendent W. W. Mooney, the force was beset by public allegations of inefficiency and corruption.

Reaching Melbourne on 12 October, Duncan was described by the Argus as a 'genial, but quiet man, with broad shoulders and thick grey hair'. He was of middle height and thickset, and spoke with a trace of a Scottish accent. Within months of his arrival, Duncan had completed his inspection of the force. He presented his interim report on 16 December 1936 and his final report on 22 January 1937. The first report, focussing on the wireless patrol, C.I.B. and plain-clothes branch, made sixteen recommendations, including proposals for detective training and the use of forensic science. His second report contained a further twenty-five recommendations, addressing such issues as traffic control, police transport, the promotion system and deployment of personnel. Both reports were blueprints for change. The Dunstan government gave them full effect when it appointed Duncan chief commissioner on 7 February 1937, with a mandate to implement his reforms.

Although the Australian Labor Party and others criticized the appointment of an 'outsider', Duncan moved quickly to improve the force. Despite the added pressures of World War II and his role as chief air-raid warden for the State, he became one of Victoria's most successful and its longest serving chief commissioner in the twentieth century. Appointed C.M.G. in 1946, he retired from the force in 1954, but remained active as a member of the Boy Scouts' Association, Melbourne Rotary, the Young Men's Christian Association, the Royal Humane Society, the National Fitness Council and the State Relief Committee. He died on 1 September 1965 at Brighton and was cremated; his daughter survived him.

R. Haldane, The People's Force (Melb, 1986); People, 16 Dec 1953; Police Life, Sept 1965, p 9, Mar 1981, p 14; Herald (Melb), 14, 27 Jan, 6 Feb, 29 July 1937, 8 June 1949, 2 Sept 1965; Argus, 13 Oct 1936, 14, 27 Jan 1937; Age (Melb) and Sun News-Pictorial, 3 Sept 1965; information from Comr of Police, New Scotland Yard, Lond, and Vic Police Hist Unit, Melb.   ROBERT HALDANE

DUNCAN, ALISON BAILY; see REHFISCH

DUNCAN, GEORGE BERNARD; see REHFISCH, ALISON

DUNCAN, GEORGE IAN OGILVIE (1930-1972), university lecturer, was born on 20 July 1930 at Golders Green, London, only child of New Zealand-born parents Ronald Ogilvie Duncan (d.1952), company manager, and his second wife Hazel Kerr, née Martell (d.1944). Ronald had a daughter from his first marriage. The family came to Victoria in 1937. Ian attended Melbourne Church of England Grammar School where he won prizes and scholarships, and was dux in 1947. His study towards an honours degree in classical philology at the University of Melbourne was interrupted in 1950 by a prolonged bout of tuberculosis.

Seven years later Duncan entered St John's College, Cambridge (B.A., 1960; LL.B., 1961; M.A., 1963; Ph.D., 1964). In 1966-71 he taught law part time at the University of Bristol where his colleagues described him as 'a mystery'. Tall and slim, with fair hair and blue eyes, he wore thick-framed glasses and possessed the demeanour of a dedicated, self-effacing scholar, but he was intensely shy and taciturn, and found it difficult to communicate with students and fellow academics. He was a devout Anglican and a regular churchgoer. About 1970 he joined the Gaytime Friendship Society, a London club.

In 1971 Duncan's doctoral thesis was published as The High Court of Delegates (London). The book was generally well received and he continued his research in legal history, preparing an edition of the notebook of a seventeenth-century lawyer. The deaths of his parents and half-sister (1970) had left him relatively wealthy. He returned to Australia on 25 March 1972 to take up a lectureship in law at the University of Adelaide and moved into Lincoln College, North Adelaide. About 11.00 p.m. on 10 May that year he was thrown into the River Torrens from the southern bank, near Kintore Avenue, and drowned. The area was a known meeting-place for homosexuals and rumours spread that Duncan had been killed by police engaged in 'poofter-bashing'. Following a service at St George's Church, Goodwood, he was buried in Centennial Park cemetery.

An inquest began on 7 June. Based on questionable evidence, Dr C. H. Manock testified that his autopsy had indicated that Duncan had been a practising homosexual. On 29 June two members of the vice squad refused to answer questions put to them. Three officers were suspended from the police force and eventually resigned. When the coroner returned an open finding on 5 July, public concern was so great that Premier D. A. Dunstan permitted his police commissioner, Harold Salisbury, to call in detectives from the Metropolitan Police, New Scotland Yard, London. On the basis of their report, which has never been made public, it was announced on 24 October that the crown solicitor had decided against proceeding with any prosecution.

The case gained nationwide publicity because it involved 'the broader issue of homosexuality and attitudes towards it'. On 26 July 1972 Murray Hill introduced a bill in the Legislative Council to decriminalize homosexual acts between consenting males over the age of 21; after two months of debate the bill was passed, but with an amendment that weakened its original intentions. In 1975 South Australia became the first State in Australia to legislate for full decriminalization. To members of the gay movement in Adelaide, Duncan was a symbol of the persecution of a sexual minority by an intolerant society; they called for a memorial to be erected near his place of death.

On 30 September 1988 two ex-members of the vice squad were acquitted of Duncan's manslaughter. A police task force interviewed eighty-one people and reported to parliament in April 1990 that there was 'insufficient evidence to charge any other person'.

T. Reeves, 'The 1972 Debate on Male Homosexuality in South Australia', in R. Aldrich (ed), *Gay Perspectives II* (Syd, 1993); *Advertiser* (Adel), 12, 29 May, 5, 8, 13, 30 June, 6, 7, 28 July, 25 Oct 1972, 6 Feb 1986, 1 Oct 1988, 4 Apr 1990; *News* (Adel), 20 May 1972; *Review* (Melb), 27 May-2 June 1972; *The Times*, 7 July 1972; *Age* (Melb), 22 Feb 1986, 7 Apr 1990; R. G. Lean et al, Duncan Task Force Final Report (ts, 1990, Parliamentary L, Adel); Coroner's Report on G. I. O. Duncan *and* coronial inquiry re Duncan *and* inquest (GRG 1/44/1972/841, SRSA); information from Coroner's Office, Adel.   TIM REEVES

DUNCAN, JOHN COWAN (1901-1955), company manager, was born on 8 September 1901 at Collingwood, Melbourne, son of Victorian-born parents Frederick Augustus Lowick Duncan, picture-framer, and his wife Louisa Maria, née Renos. Educated at Hawthorn (Manningtree Road) State School, John rowed in 'many winning Hawthorn pairs and fours'; he was to maintain his connexion with the sport as a member of the Old Oarsmen's Association and the Henley Masonic Lodge, St Kilda, which was 'composed entirely of rowing men'. He received his early training in the oil industry as a territorial representative in Victoria and Tasmania for C. C. Wakefield & Co. Ltd, and rose to the position of South Australian sales manager, based in Adelaide.

On 20 November 1929 at St John's Anglican Church, Camberwell, Melbourne, Duncan married Dorothy May Wynne. After holding an executive position under S. A. Cheney [q.v.7], in 1935 he was appointed Melbourne manager of the Alba Petroleum Co. of Australia Pty Ltd, an independent distributor formed in 1933. Duncan played a major role in the firm's development. By 1936-37 it had annual sales of over six million gallons of motor spirit from nine hundred outlets in Victoria, South Australia, Tasmania and the Riverina district of New South Wales.

An amalgamation between Alba and the Australian Motorists Petrol Co. Ltd (Ampol Petroleum Ltd 1948) was completed in September 1945. As the new company's general manager for Victoria—with responsibility for South Australian and Tasmanian operations as well—Duncan was an outstanding promoter of its products. In 1946 he served on the management-committee at head office whose members were authorized by (Sir) William Walkley [q.v.] to implement managerial and other changes stemming from the merger. From 1947 until his death Duncan was an associate-director and attended the company's board-of-management meetings. He was also president of the Ampol Social Club.

A skilled negotiator, in 1949 Duncan went via the United States of America to Europe, aiming to buy petroleum products with sterling. In October he arranged to purchase petrol from La Compagnie Française de Raffinage. Ampol gave wide publicity to his successful search for non-dollar petrol as part of the firm's campaign against the postwar rationing that restricted its share of the market. The crusade was taken up by the Liberal and Country parties, and was a significant factor in their victory at the Federal elections that year. Although the first supplies of Duncan's petrol reached Australia in early 1950, further shipments were withdrawn by the French under pressure from United States oil interests.

The knowledge Duncan had acquired

abroad led to innovations in a number of Ampol's practices, including improved merchandising and marketing, and the introduction of an American scheme of regular reports on employee performance. An approachable, solidly built man, with a 'million dollar smile' and an 'easy manner most evident in times of stress', Duncan was well liked and respected for his business methods. He died suddenly of heart disease on 7 May 1955 at South Yarra and was cremated; his wife, daughter and son survived him.

C. Simpson, *Show Me a Mountain* (Syd, 1961); *Ampol Staff News*, June 1955; *Herald* (Melb), 9 May 1955; Ampol (Alba) Petroleum Pty Ltd (Ampol Petroleum Vic Pty Ltd), Bd of Directors minutes, 1945-91, *and* Aust Motorists Petrol Co Ltd (Ampol Petroleum Ltd), Bd of Directors minutes, 1939-58, Head Office Management Cte minutes, 1946, *and* Associate Directors minutes, 1947-50 (held at Ampol Head Office, Syd); Cwlth Treasury, Importation of Petrol and Oils, A571, file 52/1891, pts 12, 13 (AA, Canb).   EWAN MAIDMENT

DUNCAN, JOHN SHIELS (1886-1949), public servant and diplomat, was born on 19 August 1886 at Hamilton, New South Wales, and registered as John Shields, son of Scottish-born parents William Duncan, tailor, and his wife Annie, née Shields. Educated locally, at the age of 17 John entered the New South Wales Public Service as a clerk in the coalfields branch of the Department of Mines. He gave Shiels as his second Christian name when he married Christina ('Jean') Chalmers with Presbyterian forms on 20 April 1911 at Boolaroo; they were to have two children.

Determined, hard working and conscientious, Duncan progressed steadily. He moved to Sydney in 1912 to take a position as shorthand writer with the Public Service Board. By 1920 he was industrial arbitration officer and senior inspector, and conducted cases for the Crown before the arbitration courts. In 1923 he transferred to the Commonwealth as public service inspector for New South Wales and on 14 December 1925 was admitted to the Bar. As chief administrative officer he assisted the 1929-30 royal commission on the coal industry. The Newnes investigation committee (1933-34) sought his advice on industrial relations in a proposed shale-oil undertaking to the north of Lithgow. He also helped to prepare, collate and present evidence to the royal commission (1934-36) on the wheat, flour and bread industries.

His professional associates esteemed his zeal, co-operation, competence and commitment. Similar dedication characterized his activities beyond the public service. Duncan had joined the Rotary Club of Sydney in 1926 and was its president in 1933. Two years later he became governor of the 76th District

of Rotary International and attended the world convention in Mexico City. In August 1935 he was promoted deputy-director of posts and telegraphs in New South Wales. Appointed C.B.E. in 1938, he was sent to London that year as official secretary under the Australian high commissioner. His family accompanied him; suffering poor health, his son was to die in 1942.

Duncan proved his worth in London, especially during World War II. S. M. (Viscount) Bruce [q.v.7] described him as a man of 'marked ability' who handled 'the many and complicated problems' involved in the negotiation of financial arrangements and the supply of munitions and machinery. Duncan was deputy high commissioner from 1942 and occasionally acted as high commissioner. In 1946 he was appointed Australian minister to Chile. He arrived in Santiago on 8 August and was accredited as special minister to attend the inauguration of Gabriel Gonzáles Videla's presidency in November. Duncan worked to establish and strengthen diplomatic, commercial, cultural and social ties between Chile and Australia, and continued his involvement in Rotary.

During a visit to Argentina in June 1947 he fell gravely ill. Although in pain, he resumed his duties, but left Chile in January 1948 to enter a clinic in London. Returning to Sydney, he died of cancer on 8 March 1949 at Elizabeth Bay and was cremated. His wife and daughter survived him.

A. Stirling, *Lord Bruce* (Melb, 1974); CP268/1/1 A1/960 Box B2 *and* A1066/1 IC45/64/9/1, A1067/1 T46/248, A6348/1 S25/50 pt 1 *and* A3318/1 L48/1/2/1/3 (AA, Canb).
                                      KATHLEEN DERMODY

DUNCAN, SIR WALTER GORDON (1885-1963), pastoralist and politician, was born on 10 March 1885 at Hughes Park, near Watervale, South Australia, third of six children of (Sir) John James Duncan [q.v.4], a Scottish-born pastoralist and politician, and his second wife Jean Gordon, née Grant, from England. The family derived its considerable wealth from the pastoral and mining activities of John's father Captain John Duncan and maternal uncle Sir Walter Watson Hughes [q.v.4]. Young Walter was educated at Cheltenham College, Gloucester, England (1897-98), and at the Collegiate School of St Peter, Adelaide. Athletically rather than academically inclined, he captained the school cricket team in his final year and maintained a passion for the game, along with riding, racing and golf.

Leaving school in 1903, Duncan worked at Hughes Park, and on other family properties —Gum Creek, near Burra, and Manunda in the saltbush country near Yunta. On 20 October 1909 at Chalmers Church, North Terrace, Adelaide, he married with Presbyterian forms Bessie Graham Fotheringham; they lived at Parkside and were to have three children. He became part-owner of several properties, a director of the Milo and Bon-Bon pastoral companies, and chairman of directors of Manunda Pastoral Co. Ltd. As the result of a family decision in 1914, Walter—the only son with young children—remained in South Australia in charge of the Duncan concerns while his mother accompanied her three other sons to England where they joined the British armed services. In 1918, as a Coalitionist, Walter was returned to the Legislative Council as a member for Midland, the district which his father had represented in 1900-13. Ability, and an electoral system that favoured rural property owners, kept him there for forty-four years.

An astute, practical and likeable man, Duncan emerged as a major figure in the State's commercial, agricultural and political life. He was a director (1922-62) of Broken Hill Proprietary Co. Ltd and, with Harold Darling [q.v.8], was one of Essington Lewis's [q.v.10] closest friends; all three crossed the continent from Adelaide to Darwin by train and car in 1924. Duncan also enjoyed overseas travel: he visited Britain and Europe with his wife in 1926, and inspected steel-mills in India with Lewis in 1938-39. South Australia's industrial development at Whyalla owed much to Duncan's influence in B.H.P. and Australian Iron & Steel Pty Ltd. He chaired the board of Bagot's Executor & Trustee Co. Ltd (1921-54), and the Adelaide boards of the Australian Mutual Provident Society and Goldsbrough Mort [qq.v.4,5] & Co. Ltd, and was a director of the Adelaide Steamship Co. Ltd (1932-60) and of Wallaroo-Mount Lyell Fertilisers Ltd. During World War II he was chairman of the State's Business Administration Committee, which was established to investigate allegations of wastage and which reported to the Department of Defence Co-ordination, Melbourne.

A source of personal and professional satisfaction to Duncan was his long association with the Royal Agricultural and Horticultural Society of South Australia. As president in 1924-25 (and also in 1932-50) he oversaw the move from North Terrace to the Wayville showgrounds; much of the new venture's success was due to his efforts. In 1939 he was knighted. He was president of the Stockowners' Association of South Australia and an honorary member (1943) of the Royal Agricultural Society of England. An exhibition hall bearing his name was opened at the Wayville showgrounds in 1962.

For four decades Duncan influenced non-Labor politics. Heeding his father's advice that more power could be exercised 'as an outside member' of the council, he did not seek ministerial office or a seat in the House of Assembly. While Liberal Federation president (1930-32), he kept the Hill [q.v.9] Labor government in office to implement the Premiers' Plan. Duncan also helped to recruit (Sir) Archibald Grenfell Price [q.v.] as organizer of the 'non-party' Emergency Committee of South Australia which neutralized the Citizens' League and delivered a united conservative vote (and six of South Australia's seven Federal seats) to the Lyons [q.v.10] government in 1932. Duncan was one of the Liberals who ended fourteen years of feuding with the State Country Party by negotiating a merger which formed the Liberal and Country League in June.

A member of the South Australian gentry, and of the Adelaide (from 1914) and Australian clubs, Sir Walter led the council in 1932-44, defended States rights and was deeply suspicious of any suggestion of socialism. He fought Lyons's 1937 referendum on marketing, and favoured big merchants over small farmers in the protracted debates on bulk-handling and wheat-pooling. His opposition spelt defeat in 1938 for Premier (Sir) Richard Layton Butler's [q.v.7] voluntary equalization scheme for the depressed dairy industry. Yet, Duncan was not averse to government assistance for projects endorsed by trusted business associates or deemed to be for the greater good, like Whyalla, Cellulose (Australia) Ltd and the South Australian Housing Trust. He and his friend the premier (Sir) Thomas Playford each valued the other's common sense and pragmatism.

As president (1944-62) of the Legislative Council Duncan was fair minded, good humoured and prepared to bend the rules to expedite proceedings. He won both popularity and respect. With severely parted grey hair and eyes that twinkled behind heavy horn-rimmed glasses, he wore a spotted bow-tie and smoked a large-bowled pipe. He retired due to age and increasing deafness in 1962. His last years were shadowed by the death of a daughter, Bessie's ill health and his own battle with cancer. Survived by his wife, son and a daughter, he died on 27 August 1963 at Parkside and was cremated. His estate was sworn for probate at £125 617. G. A. Thorley's portrait of Duncan is held by the Legislative Council.

G. Blainey, *The Steel Master* (Melb, 1971); C. and M. Kerr, *Royal Show* (Adel, 1983); *Sth Australiana*, 17, no 1, Mar 1978, p 5; *Observer* (Adel), 23 Mar, 27 Apr 1918; *News* (Adel), 1 Oct 1928; *Advertiser* (Adel), 2 Jan 1939, 3 Nov 1961, 3 Nov 1962, 28 Aug 1963; R. F. I. Smith, The Butler Government in South Australia, 1933-1938 (M.A. thesis, Univ Adel, 1964).   JENNY TILBY STOCK

DUNCKLEY, DOROTHY HARRIETTE (1890-1972), actress and make-up artist, was born on 27 February 1890 at Bacchus Marsh, Victoria, daughter of John Fraser, a bank clerk from Scotland, and his Victorian-born wife Mary Charlotte, née Crook, late Francis. The family moved to Perth where Dorothy attended Mrs Elizabeth Messer's school and passed the senior public examination in 1906. Having studied (1909-10) at the Royal Academy of Dramatic Art, London, she returned to Perth and worked as a typist. On 19 October 1919 at St John's Anglican Church, Fremantle, she married Major Charles Gilmour Dunckley, a farmer. They lived on a station at Bruce Rock; their only child was stillborn. After her husband died in 1924, she was secretary of the Perth Repertory Club.

Dorothy Dunckley appeared in two films made in Sydney for Ken Hall's Cinesound Productions in 1932-33, *On Our Selection* and *The Squatter's Daughter*, as well as in Paulette McDonagh's [q.v.10] film, *Two Minutes Silence* (1933). She spent eighteen months in 1933-34 in the United States of America, mainly at Hollywood, investigating make-up, interior decoration, lighting and clothes for Cinesound. Back in Sydney, she skirmished on stage with Cecil Kellaway [q.v.9] in *Wild Violets* (1936). In May 1939 she appeared in Robert Sherwood's satire, *Idiot's Delight*, the opening production at D. N. Martin's [q.v.] new Minerva Theatre, Kings Cross. Kathleen Robinson acquired the Minerva in 1941 and began Whitehall Productions; Dunckley was a regular player—from Mrs Eynsford Hill in *Pygmalion* to Amanda Wingfield in *The Glass Menagerie*. As an older woman, she worked consistently in character roles and in radio farce, but she was fast acquiring a reputation for her skills as a make-up artist.

While they were playing in *Roberta* in 1934, she had persuaded Madge Elliott [q.v.] to give up her pink-and-white make-up and concocted the honey-coloured base which she used thereafter. In the 1940s Dunckley gave Aileen Britten false eyelashes for her opening night in *French Without Tears*. Dunckley advertised 'Glamour by appointment ... Creative makeup for—Social engagements, day or night, screen tests, stage, still photography, hairstyling, manicure', and virtually quit the stage in 1949 to concentrate on her business.

Aware of the discomfort of using commercially available greasepaint, Dunckley made (and marketed) her own creams, rouges, eyeshadows and eye-lashes in her Macleay Street home. It was 'more like an alchemist's den than a flat', and generally in turmoil, the telephone ringing constantly. Her advice ranged from the impact of lighting on body-paint to the best way of changing hair colour. In 1952 she devised body make-up for (Sir) Anthony Quayle (then touring as Othello with the Shakespeare Memorial Theatre company), visited Fiji as part of the make-up team for the Warner Bros' film, *His Majesty O'Keefe*, and had to limit her appearances in radio serials because of her commitments to the New South Wales National Opera. She spent two months in 1955 at Columbia Broadcasting System, New York, studying television make-up for Hall. In 1962 she had the role of an elderly vagrant in the Australian Broadcasting Commission's television play, *Fly By Night*.

A warm and lovable eccentric, Dunckley was said to walk down Macleay Street—fair-haired, blue-eyed, often wearing a beret-style hat—with her mind preoccupied by her cosmetic business. When she received greeting cards, she returned them unopened and endorsed 'And the same to you'. She died on 7 March 1972 in the Sacred Heart Hospice, Darlinghurst; her body was bequeathed to the University of Sydney for medical research.

G. Laurie, *The Australian Theatre Story* (Syd, 1960); A. Simmonds, *Plumb Crazy/Gwen Plumb* (Syd, 1994); *Woman's World*, 1 June 1934, p 74; *Bulletin*, 30 Dec 1936; *J. C. Williamson Ltd Mag*, 13 May 1939, pp 13, 15; *Stages*, 1, no 4, 1947; *Theatre Review*, 1, no 1, Aug 1952, p 2, Sept-Oct 1952, pp 13, 35; *Aust Women's Weekly*, 13 July 1955, p 23; *Theatreland*, 1, no 1, Sept 1955, p 3; *SMH*, 24 Apr 1934, 1, 6 July, 3 Aug 1952, 25 Aug, 4 Dec 1955, 18 June 1962, 9 Mar 1972; Metropolitan Theatre scrap-book, 1947, *and* Minerva Theatre programmes, 1939-46 (Dennis Wolanski L and Archive of the Performing Arts, Syd Opera House); J. Lewis papers, 1947-50 (ML).

KATE EVANS

DUNCOMBE, MARY ELIZABETH (1899-1980), Sister of Mercy, was born on 6 September 1899 at Hughenden, Queensland, eldest of three children of Horace Henry Duncombe (d.1907), a native-born hotel-keeper and grazier, and his wife Kate, née O'Keefe, from Ireland. Educated at primary level as a boarder at St Mary's convent school, Ipswich, Molly visited Ireland with her mother before attending All Hallows School, Brisbane. She was awarded a licentiate in pianoforte (1915) by Trinity College of Music, London, with a gold medal for the highest pass in the State. Having rejected the offer of a teacher's scholarship to the University of Queensland, she helped her mother on the family property at Winton where she learned much about land management and sheep-farming. She made frequent sallies to Melbourne and Sydney, returning in the latest expensive fashions, and declined offers of marriage. Secretly she felt called to the religious life. Following her mother's remarriage, Molly sought counsel from former teachers. Despite an unsympathetic response from home, she began her novitiate with the Sisters of Mercy at All Hallows Convent on 24 September 1927 and was professed in 1930, taking the religious name Damian.

After teaching for sixteen years, Sister Damian turned to administration and remained pastoral in her relationship with the Sisters and staff of the various institutions that came under her care—schools, hospitals, and homes for children and the handicapped. Within the order, former school companions remembered her as a warm and loving friend who frequented plays and concerts; but younger novices could be intimidated by her deportment, large frame and air of self-sufficiency, as well as by her incapacity to make small talk. In 1944 she was appointed superior of the Mater Misericordiae hospitals, Brisbane, and from 1951 supervised the planning and completion of the Mater Mothers' Hospital which opened in 1960. By that time she was administrator of the largest denominational hospital-system in Australia.

In 1954 the Sisters had elected her Reverend Mother and in 1956 she became mother general of All Hallows Congregation. Perceiving advantages from combining with other Mercy Sisters, she patiently negotiated her proposal for union and in 1958 was elected mother president of the Australian Federation of Sisters of Mercy. When the call for 'aggiornamento'—Pope John XXIII's word for religious renewal—encountered resistance, Mother Damian advanced courageously over the middle ground by inviting theologians and sociologists to enlarge the Sisters' spiritual and mental horizons.

A keen educationist, she had been involved in establishing a teachers' training college (later Damian House) which was opened in November 1958 at All Hallows. Sisters were sent abroad for further studies, and two teams extended teaching services to the Territory of Papua and New Guinea. Mother Damian also promoted secondary education, but her wish to include Aboriginal children in Mercy schools by means of scholarships was thwarted by opponents of integration. Besides providing responsibly for her various undertakings, she progressively modernized buildings and facilities in homes for the handicapped and disadvantaged. In 1962 she was appointed O.B.E.

Although it took discretion and discernment for her to attain a high degree of consensus among seven hundred Mercy Sisters, Mother Damian depended largely on the force of her personality. A woman of humanity, integrity and honour, she never sought acclaim or popularity, and often appeared preoccupied with her own thoughts and projects. She could be obstinate in the face of contrary ideas. To make a point, she talked around a subject for hours on end, especially with her group of four councillors. She was torn between her personal need for the support of friends and her ethical view that she must prove even-handed to all ('a Superior . . . can have no friends'). This conflict may have been a factor in the breakdown in health that occurred in 1973 during her last of many visits to the Sisters in Papua New Guinea.

Lonely, inward looking and contemplative, in 1978 she retired to Emmaus, the home at Nudgee which she had built for those Sisters no longer engaged in active service. She died there on 30 July 1980 and was buried in the local cemetery.

M. X. O'Donoghue, *Beyond Our Dreams* (Brisb, 1961); J.-M. Mahoney, *Dieu et Devoir* (Brisb, 1985); *Courier-Mail*, 2 June 1962, 3 July 1980; Sisters of Mercy Archives, Brisb.   FRANCES O'DONOGHUE

DUNKLEY, HARRY LESLIE EWEN (1911-1979), army officer and schoolmaster, was born on 22 December 1911 at Creswick, Victoria, third child of Edwin Ewen Dunkley, mounted policeman, and his wife Priscilla, née Williams, both native-born. Edwin had numerous postings and Harry spent much of his childhood with his mother at her parents' home. After attending North Creswick State and Ballarat High schools, he went to Sebastopol Primary School as a student-teacher, trained at Melbourne Teachers' College in 1933-34 and studied part time at the University of Melbourne (B.A., 1947). In 1935 he gained a position at Geelong College as a boarding-house master; his manner and bearing transmitted confidence to the boys.

Having served (1927-33) in the 8th Battalion, Militia, and risen to corporal, in 1937 Dunkley was appointed lieutenant in the senior cadets. On 18 November 1939 he enlisted in the Australian Imperial Force. Posted to the 2nd/6th Battalion, he was commissioned lieutenant on 27 November and selected as battalion intelligence officer. In April next year he embarked for the Middle East. At Bardia, Libya, between 28 December 1940 and 2 January 1941 he made frequent reconnaissances of the forward area and repeatedly obtained information under enemy fire during the attack on 3 January. He was awarded the Military Cross.

In April Dunkley took part in the Greek campaign and in July transferred to the 2nd/7th Battalion as adjutant. Promoted captain in February 1942, he was based in Ceylon from March to July, then returned to Australia and was sent to Milne Bay, Papua, in October. Next month he was promoted major and seconded to 17th Brigade headquarters as brigade major (learner). By early 1943 he was in New Guinea for the Wau-Salamaua operations. Rejoining his battalion in May, he commanded 'B' Company and was severely wounded in the chest on 11 September.

Dunkley was intermittently hospitalized until January 1944 and between June and October. He was mentioned in dispatches for his New Guinea service. On 28 December 1943 at the office of the government statist, Melbourne, he had married a clerk and friend from his days at teachers' college, Grace Stuart McCutchan. In October 1944 he was promoted lieutenant colonel and given command of the 7th Battalion, then in the Solomon Islands. From April to August 1945 he led the unit in the Bougainville campaign; for his relentless aggression against the enemy and tactical skill in minimizing casualties among his men, he was awarded the Distinguished Service Order.

Relinquishing his command in November, Dunkley returned to Melbourne and transferred to the Reserve of Officers on 16 January 1946. He lived at Brighton and completed his degree before rejoining Geelong College in 1947 as master-in-charge of social studies in the senior school. In 1948-68 he commanded the school's cadet unit. He was a gifted organizer and an enthusiastic teacher. War-related ill health caused him to retire in December 1970. Survived by his wife and daughter, he died of myocardial infarction on 21 October 1979 at Geelong West and was buried in Highton cemetery.

W. P. Bolger and J. G. Littlewood, *The Fiery Phoenix* (Melb, 1983?); D. Hay, *Nothing Over Us* (Canb, 1984); A. Pedder, *The Seventh Battalion 1936-1946* (Melb, 1989); Geelong College, *Pegasus*, June 1971, p 14; information from Mrs A. W. Jones, Sth Yarra, Mr P. W. Grutzner, Middle Park, and Dr P. G. Law, Canterbury, Melb.

SYD TRIGELLIS-SMITH

DUNLEA, THOMAS VINCENT (1894-1970), Catholic priest, was born on 19 April 1894 at Ballina, County Tipperary, Ireland, son of Thomas Dunlea, farmer, and his wife Bridget, née Minogue. Educated at Roscrea college, Mount Melleray monastery and St Peter's College, Wexford, he was ordained priest on 20 June 1920. He took up duties in the archdiocese of Sydney at the end of the year. Three sons of the thirteen Dunlea children emigrated and became a paradigm of Irish-Australian experience—one was a publican, another a policeman, the third a priest.

As curate in inner-city parishes, Dunlea got close to people in distress. All his life he remembered hearing a boy at the Albion Street children's shelter singing, 'I wish I had someone to love me'. When he was appointed parish priest of Sutherland in 1934, he found some of his Depression-hit parishioners living in caves and humpies. Riding a white horse, he brought them food and hope. At the presbytery he collected homeless boys and moved into a larger house when numbers grew. After Sutherland Shire Council forced them onto the road, they set up tents in nearby (Royal) National Park.

Publicity led to a gift of seven acres (3 ha) at Engadine, where 'Boys' Town' started in August 1940. It was to be partly self-supporting and to be run by the boys themselves—with the priest's oversight—on the lines of a similar settlement in Nebraska, United States of America, made famous by a Hollywood movie. Dunlea won support for the town from sporting and journalistic circles: the Jewish bookmaker George Nathan each Sunday organized a fund-raising carnival, with trotting, cycling and midget-car racing that packed the Sydney Sports Ground. In 1942, at Archbishop (Cardinal Sir Norman) Gilroy's [q.v.] request, the De La Salle Brothers came to Boys' Town; having visited the U.S.A. and resigned his parish, Dunlea moved there in 1947.

In the late 1940s he was working among alcoholics with Dr Sylvester Minogue and Archibald McKinnon of the Darlinghurst reception house. For a time the pioneer Alcoholics Anonymous group met in the Boys' Town city office and at other locations found by Dunlea. He was a good facilitator, but some of his swans turned into geese. A bush camp for alcoholics and a residential 'Christmas House' both collapsed, which seemed to prove that a controlled environment was not the answer to alcoholism. Boys' Town fund-raising functions had sharpened Dunlea's own drinking problems and he came to recognize that he himself was an alcoholic. In 1950 he took a years leave of absence to wander around Australia.

On his return, Dunlea became chaplain to the Matthew Talbot Hostel for destitute men. There his listening kindness was given full stretch. In 1952 he went to Hurstville as parish priest, devoting his time to A.A., to a new organization for people with psychiatric problems, Recovery Group, as well as to a menagerie of odd animals. 'When Tom Dunlea doesn't take an interest in stray dogs any longer', he said, 'you'll know that he's had it'. In 1965 he was appointed O.B.E. He died on 22 August 1970 in Lewisham Hospital and was buried in Woronora cemetery. The congregation which attended his reburial at Boys' Town on 7 September included a pet sheep and a stray dog.

A. McKinnon, *They Chose Freedom* (Bonnell's Bay, NSW, c1985); D. Halliday, *Father Dunlea's Approach to Dealing with Young People in Difficulties* (Engadine, NSW, 1987); D. Coleman, *Priest of the Highway* (Syd, 1973); M. Austen and M. Richardson, *Father Dunlea and Those with a Drinking Problem* (Engadine, NSW, 1987); *Voice of Boys' Town*, 1941-48; *Sunday Telegraph* (Syd), 10 Dec 1939; *Daily Telegraph* (Syd), 25 Nov 1960; *Daily Mirror* (Syd), 19 June 1970; *Sun-Herald*, 27 Nov 1960; *SMH*, 16 Aug, 27 Dec 1939, 25 Jan 1947, 12 June 1965, 24 Aug 1970.   EDMUND CAMPION

DUNN, MAXWELL WALTER DUMONT (1895?-1963), poet and Buddhist, was born probably in 1895 in Dublin, reputed son of Richard Laurence Dunn, barrister, and his wife Helen Eloise, née Hunyady-Dumont. Max's versions of his early life were sufficiently various to provoke friends to scepticism. Privately educated in his youth, he claimed to have passed through the medical faculty at the University of Edinburgh and to have served in the Royal Flying Corps in World War I; there is no evidence that he did either. Following a trip to the United States of America, he arrived in Australia in 1924 as a remittance man and settled in Melbourne.

When his allowance diminished in the Depression, Dunn 'began his adventures in various vocations', which included running an art gallery, translating and freelance writing. He won first prize in the International Play Competition in 1938 and in the All-Australian Competition in 1939. During World War II he was aviation correspondent for the *Argus* and published the first of numerous books, *War in the Sky* (1940).

Thenceforward, Dunn's energies were increasingly occupied with poetry, self-published in volumes as fine as wartime restrictions allowed. First was *Random Elements* (1943), from Dunn's Anvil Press. His most substantial volumes, published after he had abandoned journalism for poetry, were *Time of Arrival* (1947), *Portrait of a Country* (1951) and *The Mirror and the Rose* (1954). An association with Jack Kirtley led to an edition, limited to 14 copies, of Dunn's *The Journey of John Donne* (1952). He wrote of one with whom he almost shared a name, and with whose journey he empathized:

Mapping his darkened hemispheres,
He found love's paradigm
Nailed as the answer to his grief
On one green branch of time.

Poems translated from the Chinese (one of numerous languages with which he claimed acquaintance), *The City of Wide Streets by the Friendly River*, appeared in 1952.

While Dunn was once mistakenly regarded as an antipodean Blake, the influence of Yeats is audible:

My father gave me a branch of bells ...
My mother gave me a crystal quill.

Elsewhere he sounds like Ern Malley:

On the I, the upright pin of me
Ardent, my haloed coil revolves ...

Some of Dunn's most lucid and accomplished work was published in *Eight by Eight* (1963), to which he contributed with other Melbourne poets.

In the 1950s, an epileptic living behind a shop in South Yarra 'surrounded with the vestigial remains of better days', he was helped by J. K. Moir [q.v.], president of the Bread and Cheese Club, who on Sundays 'kept open house for undernourished poets'. In 1955 Dunn was converted to Buddhism. He adopted the title Reverend, but refused to teach at a Buddhist university in Thailand, arguing that 'where there is no frost there is no thought'. President and a life member of the Buddhist Society of Victoria, he was Buddhist chaplain at the 1956 Olympic Games. On 11 October that year in Melbourne he married with Unitarian forms Joan Thorpe, a 25-year-old nurse whom he had met at a Buddhist meeting. Survived by his wife, he died of cancer on 4 September 1963 at South Yarra and was cremated.

R. A. Simpson owned that he had heard Dunn called 'a sham', but judged him as 'intrinsically a true innocent'. For Leigh Cook, he was a 'cultivated sophisticate'; for David Martin, simply 'our austere Buddhist'. An accounting of the shifts and fabrications of Dunn's life must admit his dedication to poetry and printing, his affinity with languages, and his determination to live a literary life within a culture that incompletely supported him.

H. W. Malloch, *Fellows All* (Melb, 1943); D. Martin, *My Strange Friend* (Syd, 1991); *Southerly*, 11, no 3, 1950; *Quadrant*, Oct-Nov 1964; *Westerly*, May 1966 (issues 3-4 of 1965); *Age* (Melb), 6 Sept 1963.
                                                      PETER PIERCE

DUNN, RAYMOND HUDSON (1910-1971), lawyer and football administrator, was born on 21 June 1910 at Geelong, Victoria, second son of THOMAS DUNN (1884-1953), constable, and his wife Mary Ellen, née Hudson, both Victorian born. A member (from 1906) of the Victoria Police Force, Tom was then serving at his first station. Impressed with his intelligence and efficiency, his superiors transferred him in 1924 to headquarters at Russell Street, Melbourne. In 1927-37 he successively worked as a special adviser and assistant to (Sir) Thomas Blamey [q.v.13] and to Alexander Duncan [q.v.]. Dunn was awarded the Royal Victorian medal in 1934 and retired as superintendent—second in rank only to the chief commissioner—on 15 June 1944.

Ray Dunn attended schools at Geelong and Essendon, and gained a scholarship to the University of Melbourne (LL.B., 1930; LL.M., 1932) where, in his final year, he won the Supreme Court judges' prize. On 2 June 1934 at St Teresa's Catholic Church, Essendon, he married a milliner Marie Ellen Whelan; they were to have two daughters before being divorced. At St Philip's Anglican Church, Sydney, on 3 November 1951 he married a hairdresser Kathleen Monica Patricia Foster-Wightman; they had a son and were later divorced.

Short, balding, bespectacled and plump, with a deep, gravelly voice, Dunn pursued his legal career in the magistrates' courts. He chose to work as a solicitor and declined subsequent inducements to become a barrister. None the less, he achieved a reputation as an outstanding defence lawyer of stunning mental agility. He acted for his clients against police prosecutions of any type, but his speciality was legislation relating to gaming. In 1967 his successful defence of a truck driver charged with exceeding the .05 blood-alcohol reading was brilliant in its simplicity and resulted in an amendment that year to the Motor Car Act (1958).

Dunn's close association with the police force was continual, both in the courtroom and elsewhere. From 1956 he had lectured on prosecution and criminal law in courses at the Detective Training School and the Victoria Police College. He acted as legal counsel for police on numerous occasions. About 1966 he was engaged by the Victoria Police Association to defend members of the force who had been counter-summonsed by people they had arrested: in more than eighty such cases, his defence failed in only two. A part-time lecturer in criminal procedure at the university in 1952-65, he was also an outstanding after-dinner speaker.

Passionately interested in Australian Rules, Dunn had joined the Richmond Football Club through his friendship with Martin Bolger, a policeman and back-pocket player for the 'Tigers'. Dunn was a vice-president (from 1940) and president (1964-71). He successfully negotiated the right for Richmond to play their home games at the Melbourne Cricket Ground from 1965. Whereas Richmond had not won a premiership since 1943, under his administration the club took the flag in 1967 and 1969. After suffering from diabetes for a decade, Dunn died of a coronary occlusion on 26 August 1971 at his Metung holiday home and was buried in St Kilda cemetery. He was survived by the children of his two marriages. His estate was sworn for probate at $239 264.

J. A. Hetherington, *Blamey* (Melb, 1954); *Vic Police J*, 39, no 12, May 1970, p 303, 41, no 5, Oct 1971, p 125; *Argus*, 16 June 1944; *Herald* (Melb), 1 June 1967, 26 Sept 1969, 26 Aug 1971; *Age* (Melb), *Australian* and *Sun News-Pictorial*, 27 Aug 1971; Dunn file (Law Inst of Vic records).

GARY PRESLAND

DUNROSSIL, WILLIAM SHEPHERD MORRISON, 1ST VISCOUNT (1893-1961), governor-general, was born on 10 August 1893 at Torinturk, near Oban, Argyllshire, Scotland, sixth of eight sons of John Morrison, farmer, and his wife Marion, née McVicar. John had worked in the South African diamond fields before selling out to De Beers and settling at Torinturk. Educated at George Watson's College, Edinburgh, in 1912 William entered the University of Edinburgh (M.A., 1920) to study arts and law. His initials W. S., and his love of Shakespeare, earned him the nickname 'Shakes' which stuck to him. In August 1914 he was commissioned in the Royal Field Artillery (Special Reserve). At Neuve-Chapelle, France, in March 1915, he maintained communications with his battery, despite being wounded, and was awarded the Military Cross. He rose to captain, was thrice mentioned in dispatches and resigned his commission in August 1919.

Called to the English Bar at the Inner Temple on 19 November 1923, Morrison was private secretary (1922-29) to Sir Thomas Inskip (Viscount Caldecote) who was successively solicitor-general and attorney-general. At South Leith parish church, Scotland, on 22 April 1924 Morrison married Katharine Allison Swan; she, too, was an Edinburgh graduate and was reading for the Bar. Following two unsuccessful attempts (1923 and 1924) to enter the House of Commons as Unionist candidate for the Western Isles, he was elected in 1929 as Conservative member for the Cirencester and Tewkesbury division, Gloucestershire; he was to retain the seat for thirty years.

Morrison took silk in 1934. Appointed recorder of Walsall, Staffordshire, in 1935, he became financial secretary to the Treasury later that year. In 1936 he was appointed minister of agriculture and fisheries, and was sworn of the Privy Council. He was chancellor of the Duchy of Lancaster and minister of food in 1939-40, postmaster-general in 1940-42, and minister of town and country planning from 1943 until 1945 when his party went into Opposition.

On the Conservatives' return to power in 1951, Morrison was elected Speaker. He presided over debates on the Suez crisis in 1956 'when feelings rose so high as seriously to threaten the preservation of parliamentary order and the cohesion of the Conservative Party'. That the standing of the institution of parliament remained undamaged was largely due to the personal characteristics and talents which he displayed as Speaker. These skills stemmed from his years at university where he chaired debates and was senior president of the Students' Representative Council.

In 1959 he announced his retirement for reasons of health. There was therefore some surprise when it was announced soon afterwards that he had been chosen to succeed Sir William (Viscount) Slim [q.v.] as governor-general of Australia. Morrison was created Viscount Dunrossil of Vallaquie (on the island of North Uist, Outer Hebrides) and appointed G.C.M.G. that year. He was sworn in as governor-general on 2 February 1960 in Canberra.

The way he approached Australia and Australians in his year of office was shaped by his relatively humble Scottish origins, his non-Establishment education, the egalitarian nature of Hebridean society, and his long-standing friendship with Prime Minister (Sir) Robert Menzies [q.v.] who had recommended his appointment. Lacking an appreciation of the large amount of work involved in vice-regal office, he plunged into his duties with energy and enthusiasm, but at great cost to his health. He and his wife travelled widely throughout Australia and its territories. Lady Dunrossil accepted her own heavy responsibilities, as well as quietly and efficiently assuming additional public duties whenever her husband's illness prevented him from discharging them.

Dunrossil's appearance was impressive, even forbidding, but his personal staff found him warm and friendly. Journalists described him as a very human person with a rich sense of humour. All who met him were struck by his simple sincerity. Survived by his wife and four sons, he died of pulmonary embolism on 3 February 1961 at Government House, Canberra; after a state funeral, he was buried at his family's request in the graveyard of the Church of St John the Baptist, Reid. His eldest son John succeeded to the viscountcy. Lady Dunrossil died in England in 1983; her ashes were interred in a niche in the cover of her husband's grave. Rex Bramleigh's portrait of Dunrossil is held by Parliament House, Canberra.

University of Edinburgh Roll of Honour 1914-1919 (Edinburgh, 1921); *DNB*, 1961-70; *PD* (Cwlth, both Houses), 7 Mar 1961; *Univ Edinburgh J*, 20, no 2, 1961-62, 31, no 1, June 1983; *Daily Telegraph* (Syd), 13 Apr 1960; *The Times*, 3 Feb 1961; *Canb Times*, 4 Feb 1961, 22 July 1983; *SMH*, 4, 5, 7 Feb 1961; family papers held by the 2nd Viscount Dunrossil (North Uist, Scotland); information from Miss J. Lester, Griffith, ACT, and Mr C. Campbell, Queanbeyan, NSW; personal information.   DAVID I. SMITH

DUNSHEA, ERIC ERNEST (1906-1972), businessman, was born on 8 April 1906 at Petersham, Sydney, sixth child of Frederick Albert Dunshea, an advertising agent from New Zealand, and his native-born wife Emma, née Gazzard. Eric later recalled of his childhood at Summer Hill: 'We were not what you would call a wealthy family, rather you could say we were a little below average'. He attributed his ambition, persistence, ethical outlook and energy to three influences. One was his mother, 'a wonderful person with a strong sense of responsibility'. Another was the businessman (Sir) Hugh Dixson [q.v.8] who told young Dunshea: 'You should never be satisfied with the second best'. The third was Joshua 1:9 ('Be strong and of a good courage; be not afraid, neither be thou dismayed: for the Lord thy God *is* with thee whithersoever thou goest'), a text which he first saw in a dentist's waiting-room as a child and which he still carried folded in his wallet half a century later. Completing his education at Katoomba High School, at age 17 he joined the Perdriau [q.v.11] Rubber Co. Ltd as a junior clerk, and studied accounting and finance at night. On 5 October 1929 he married a stenographer Ursula Harbron Mill at the Baptist Church, Chatswood, where her father was minister.

In 1929 Perdriau was acquired by the Dunlop Rubber Co. of Australasia Ltd. Dunshea, who had headed the statistical department in Sydney, was sent next year to the Melbourne head office of Dunlop-Perdriau Rubber Co. Ltd to direct the introduction of punched-card accounting, sales analysis and budgetary control; six years later he was promoted again to head a suppliers' department and in 1944 he was made company secretary. In 1951 he became a director of the group and by 1960 was 'right hand man' to the general manager, (Sir) Robert Blackwood. When Blackwood stepped down in 1966, Dunshea was appointed chief general manager and chief executive of Dunlop Rubber Australia Ltd, one of the country's five biggest manufacturing firms. In 1968 he replaced Sir Daniel McVey [q.v.] as chairman of the board and ruled the company as a benevolent despot.

With his appointment as general manager, Dunshea began a remarkable business transformation. Almost immediately he commenced a programme of company takeovers which surprised, then astonished and finally frightened his own board of directors, and which in a few years doubled Dunlop's turnover and capital, increased the number of employees to 20 000 and diversified the tyre company into textiles, footwear and industrial products. The peak of his success was March 1970 when he was able to report that new acquisitions were earning 9.5 per cent on their gross assets, compared with half that rate on the old lines of tyres, conveyor belts and sporting goods. By late 1971, however, general economic growth had declined and Dunlop found itself with very large debts. In later years some of Dunshea's takeover decisions and the pace of his expansion were criticized, but the combination of high debt, layoffs and corporate reconstruction which followed him in the early 1970s was on a minor scale compared with the miscalculations in other corporations in the 1980s.

Solidly built, with a reddish-tinged complexion, soft skin, grey eyelashes and a fringe of white hair, Dunshea spoke with a rasping voice. During his long career he was president of the Productivity Promotion Council of Australia, foundation chairman of the Australian Rubber Manufacturers' Association, and a councillor of the Australian Institute of Management and of the Australian Industries Development Association. Apart from business, his interests included classical music and photography. He was chairman (1952-72) of the council of Carey Baptist Grammar School, Kew, where enrolments expanded from 500 to 1200. Although a religious man, Dunshea was neither sanctimonious nor a regular churchgoer, and was liberal in his outlook. Active in welfare, he was director of the Australian Neurological Foundation and of the Karana home for the aged, and a trustee of the National Youth Council.

After completing forty-eight years with Perdriau and Dunlop, Dunshea died of cancer on 16 April 1972 in Melbourne and was cremated. He was survived by his wife, daughter, and three of his four sons. His estate was sworn for probate at $295 329.

S. Sayers, *By Courage and Faith* (Melb, 1973); G. Blainey, *Jumping Over the Wheel* (Syd, 1993); *Aust Financial Review*, 29 Apr 1971; *Age* (Melb), *Canb Times* and *SMH*, 17 Apr 1972; biog notes supplied by Mr J. McClean, archivist for Pacific Dunlop Ltd, Melb; family information collected by Mr J. Dunshea, Nth Balwyn, Melb.   JOHN EDWARDS

DURACK, KIMBERLEY MICHAEL (1917-1968), agricultural scientist, was born on 17 May 1917 at Claremont, Perth, fourth of six children of Michael Patrick Durack [q.v.8], pastoralist, and his wife Bessie Ida Muriel, née Johnstone. Kim's sisters (Dame) Mary Durack Miller and Elizabeth Durack became a noted author and artist respectively. Educated at Christian Brothers' College, Perth, and Muresk Agricultural College, Northam, he moved in 1936 to the family's cattle-stations on the Western Australia-Northern Territory border. The properties were heavily indebted and, after fifty years of open-range grazing, new approaches were needed. Durack, who brought the first plough into East Kimberley, advocated the introduc-

tion of irrigation for pasture management, complemented by agricultural crops. His ideas were sharpened by the abortive scheme to establish a Jewish homeland on the Durack properties in 1938-39. He experimented with lucerne at Argyle before establishing an experimental plot at Ivanhoe on the Ord River.

In 1941 the Western Australian government sent the experienced engineer-administrator (Sir) Russell Dumas [q.v.] to accompany Durack in selecting the site for an Ord River dam. Between 1942 and 1945 Kim and his brother William grew successful trials of sorghum and millet at Carlton Reach, publishing their findings in the journal of the Department of Agriculture. Impatient for progress, in March 1947 Kim Durack stood as an Independent for the Legislative Assembly seat of Kimberley, his manifesto, 'A New Deal for Kimberley', urging an integrated irrigation programme for the entire district. Although polling respectably, he failed to shift Labor's hold. About 1948 he visited Rhodesia and was impressed with cattle husbandry there.

To his consternation, in 1949 his father decided to sell the family properties. Kim reacted by accepting overtures from M. E. ('Peter') Farley, a rice-grower from the Murrumbidgee, New South Wales, who was interested in Kimberley potential. Next year the new firm began experiments in rice-growing at Camballin, near Liveringa on the Fitzroy River. Following success with Magnolia and Zenith varieties, Farley wanted to press ahead with commercial rice-growing. Durack thought this intention premature and in 1958 was ousted from the company, Northern Development Ltd, of which he was a director and field-manager. After several months of pamphleteering for planned development of northern irrigation, Durack initially welcomed the return in 1959 of a State Liberal-Country Party government with a dynamic minister for the North-West, (Sir) Charles Court.

Court's zeal to push forward with an Ord River dam dismayed Durack, who considered the project needed further research. Rebuffed by Court, he went to Canberra to put his ideas to (Sir) Robert Menzies' [q.v.] cabinet. Menzies listened sympathetically, others uncomprehendingly, but nothing resulted, except that the Federal government committed no funds to the Ord dam while he remained prime minister. Near the end of his resources, Durack took employment as a government stores clerk, lived simply and devoted himself to the study of philosophy, writing an unpublished refutation of Immanuel Kant's *Critique of Pure Reason*. Durack died of staphylococcal pneumonia on 21 May 1968 at Canberra Community Hospital and was buried with Catholic rites in Canberra cemetery. He was unmarried. His estate was sworn for probate at $5209.

One of the 'sandy' Duracks, Kim was tall, with memorably bright blue eyes and a laconic wit. He was widely considered a visionary, but met opposition largely through his caution in insisting—against 'practical' entrepreneurs —that schemes of lavish expenditure on irrigation should follow only the most thorough-going research. The failure of several companies at Camballin and the chequered fortunes of the Ord River scheme suggest considerable merit in his attitude.

Chronical (Adel), 1 Aug 1957; *West Australian*, 30, 31 May 1968; K. M. Durack papers (held by the executors of Dame Mary Durack's estate and by Miss E. Durack, Dalkeith, Perth); personal information.   G. C. BOLTON

DURAS, FRITZ (1896-1965), physical educationist, was born on 19 April 1896 at Bonn, Germany, son of Markus Levi, barrister and councillor-at-law, and his wife Maria Catharina, née Duras. When his father died and his mother remarried, Fritz took her maiden name as his surname in 1914. After receiving a classical education at the Royal Gymnasium, he enlisted in the German Army in 1915; he served with the infantry, was awarded the Iron Cross and was promoted lieutenant (1918).

On returning to civilian life, Duras enrolled at the University of Freiburg-im-Breisgau to study medicine; he graduated M.B. in 1922 and subsequently took his M.D. He worked as house physician (1923-27) in the wards of the university hospital, and as clinical assistant (1927-28) at the associated Institute for Sports Medicine where in 1929-33 he was director and senior physician. On 19 June 1933 he married Betty von Klufer, an assistant at the university dental hospital. Shortly afterwards, Duras—whose father was Jewish —was forced to resign his position. The young couple moved to Todtnuauberg, in the Black Forest, before Quaker contacts arranged for him to go to England to improve his competence in English.

In London, Duras was introduced to the Academic Assistance Council which helped German exiles to find suitable posts. Meanwhile educationists in Victoria, led by Professor G. S. Browne [q.v.13], had persuaded the council of the University of Melbourne to establish a one-year course in the faculty of education to train teachers of physical education. Following interviews with (Sir) Keith Hancock and (Sir) Raymond Priestley [q.v.11], and a successful application to the Carnegie Corporation of New York for funding, Duras was appointed director of physical education. He was to offer the first, and, for many years, the only such course in Australia.

Accompanied by his family, Duras arrived in Melbourne on 1 March 1937. The curriculum he offered required students to study the history, principles and methods of physical education, its anatomical and physiological bases, body mechanics, hygiene, diet and first aid. Within seven months the university council approved an extension of the course to two years (as suggested by its director); by 1939 Duras's appointment was renewed with the status of senior lecturer. In 1945 he was granted special admission to the degree of master of education; in 1954 he was promoted associate professor. Professor Alexander Boyce Gibson [q.v.] wrote: 'He is an outstanding human being, vital, energetic, keen, self-sacrificing, disciplined, cultivated and filled with the deepest sense of public duty'.

In 1956, before the Olympic Games were held in Melbourne, Duras directed a World Congress in Physical Education for three hundred and fifty participants from thirty countries. In November an amendment to the Medical Act (1928) enabled persons with acceptable foreign qualifications to practise in Victoria: Duras was among the earliest admitted. He was also prominent in having the Beaurepaire [q.v.7] Centre for sport and physical education built at the university that year.

A pioneer in his field, Duras had a career studded with 'firsts'. He was a foundation member and first vice-president of the Australian Sports Medicine Association, the first Australian to be elected a fellow of the American Academy of Physical Education, the first president (1954-59) of the Australian Physical Education Association and later of the International Council for Physical Education and Sport. Other organizations with which he was associated included the National Fitness Council, the Marriage Guidance Council, the Playgrounds and Recreation Association of Victoria, the Youth Advisory Council and the Victorian Association of Youth Clubs.

Duras was 'an extremely kind man, deeply interested in people and their problems, never too busy, never too tired to be at the disposal of anyone who sought his help'. He retired in December 1962. Revisiting Europe with Betty, he died on 19 March 1965 while travelling by train to Genoa, Italy, and was buried at Freiburg, Germany. His wife, two daughters and two sons survived him.

G. F. Kentish, *Fritz Duras* (Adel, 1984); *Aust J of Physical Education*, no 27, Feb-Mar 1963, no 34, June-July 1965; *Age* and *Herald* (Melb), 20 Mar 1965; Duras papers (Univ Melb Archives).

GERTRUDE F. KENTISH

DU RIEU, DESMOND THEODORE (1890-1969), winemaker, was born on 20 November 1890 at Broken Hill, New South Wales, second of three children of Adolph Theodore Du Rieu, an electrician who became a hotelkeeper, and his wife Lillie Mary, née Crabb, both South Australian born. Desmond was educated at Largs Bay College, Adelaide, and later represented South Australia in lacrosse. Enlisting in the Australian Imperial Force on 19 August 1914, he sailed with the 10th Battalion for the Middle East. He was shot in the neck at Gallipoli in April 1915. After transferring to the military police, in March 1916 he was sent to the Western Front. Du Rieu was commissioned in August 1917, rejoined his old battalion and was promoted lieutenant in January 1918. Within three months he was again wounded, this time in the thigh and groin. He was invalided to Australia where his A.I.F. appointment terminated in Adelaide on 6 December.

As a soldier settler, Du Rieu took up land at Renmark in the Murray Valley region of South Australia. He described himself as a horticulturist when he married Kathleen Robertson on 4 March 1924 in St Peter's Anglican Cathedral, North Adelaide. Her father Robert had founded Chowilla station, of which Du Rieu was subsequently appointed a director and chairman (1958-68). He became president of the Renmark branch of the Returned Sailors', Soldiers' and Airmen's Imperial League of Australia, and chaired the River Murray Districts Arbitration Committee, the Renmark Homes Trust and the local racing club.

'Skee', as he was known, was 5 ft 9¼ ins (176 cm) tall, with receding brown hair and heavy jowls. Although he seemed gruff on occasions, he was a talented raconteur with a genial wit. Chairman (1928-58) of the Renmark Grower's Distillery Ltd, he served for twenty-three years as its managing director and sales manager, developing the company into one of the largest of its kind in Australia. He was also a foundation member (1929-33) of the Australian Wine Board and was chairman for several years of the Co-operative Winemakers' Association. During the 1930s he twice visited Britain to promote Australian wines and brandies. To enhance the public image of the industry, in the late 1940s he appointed a federal public-relations agent who encouraged the national press to present news about wine in a favourable light.

A life member of the Wine and Brandy Producers' Association of South Australia, Du Rieu was chairman (1939-44 and 1949-50) of the Federal Viticultural Council (later the Federal Wine and Brandy Producers' Council of Australia). He was the council's longest serving delegate, and an effective negotiator with politicians and government agencies. In 1954 he was appointed O.B.E. His final appointment was to the State royal commission (1965-66) on the grape-growing industry. Du Rieu's administrative skills guided the internal and external politics of the wine and brandy industry, and its domestic and foreign marketing. Survived by his wife, daughter and son, he died on 8 June 1969 at Renmark and was buried in the local cemetery.

Aust Wine, Brewing and Spirit Review, 28 June 1969; *Advertiser* (Adel), 10 June 1969; *Murray Pioneer*, 12 June 1969.   JAMES SMITH

DUTTON, EMILY (1884-1962), musician, artist and Red Cross worker, was born on 13 November 1884 at Gawler, South Australia, one of four children of John Felix Martin, manufacturer, and his wife Christina, née McNeil. Emily was privately educated. On 29 November 1905 in the garden at Martindale, her parents' Gawler home, she married Henry Hampden Dutton, of Anlaby, Kapunda, grandson of W. H. Dutton [q.v.1]. The couple honeymooned in Britain and Europe, and were to have four children. When Henry and Emily revisited London in 1910, George Lambert [q.v.9] painted her portrait. Tall and strikingly beautiful, she rarely ventured outdoors without a hat and preserved her delicate complexion. She was an accomplished pianist and violinist who gave public concerts for various charities and became a foundation member (1920) of the South Australian Orchestra; she was also a talented artist and an exhibiting member of the (Royal) South Australian Society of Arts.

At Anlaby, Emily was hostess to many musicians, actors, artists and public figures; the entertaining was always formal. A library was built to house the Duttons' collection of Australiana. She reorganized the grounds in a romantic style, planting native trees, shrubs and flowers. The Duttons owned three other homes—in Adelaide, at Victor Harbor and on Kangaroo Island. Like her husband, Mrs Dutton enjoyed motoring, and in 1921 drove a Dodge nearly 2100 miles (3380 km) from Adelaide to Darwin. In 1927 she helped to establish a division of the Girl Guides' Association in the mid-north of the State. Next year Emily and Henry embarked on a tour of Britain and Europe. While staying at Claridge's in London, she seldom retired before 3.30 a.m. and spent £230 on clothes at Maison Alexander. She was again abroad when her husband died at home in 1932. For several years his widow triumphed in London. King George II of Greece was an admirer; each year she received gifts and telegrams from Athens on her birthday and at Christmas. She became, in part, the model for Mrs

Polkinghorn in Patrick White's story, 'The Letters'.

In 1938-55 she belonged to the South Australian divisional council of the Australian Red Cross Society. An emergency services committee was formed in 1939 to organize women during World War II. For the next six years Mrs Dutton served as a country supervisor of the Voluntary Services Detachment, an assistant controller (country districts) of the Voluntary Aid Detachments and a district officer of the St John Ambulance Brigade. In October 1940 she organized a weekend camp for 114 officers at Anlaby to co-ordinate training for country V.A.D.s and V.S.D.s, the Red Cross transport service and transport auxiliaries. Lectures took place in the library. A mock battle was held to provide training in first aid, with an ambulance, stretchers, casualty clearing stations and a base hospital. In 1946 Mrs Dutton was awarded the Red Cross Society's commandant-in-chief's card.

Survived by her daughter and two of her three sons, she died at Anlaby on 11 May 1962 and was buried in the graveyard of St Matthew's Church, Hamilton, the church where she had been organist. Her son Geoffrey became a noted writer.

National Council of Women of SA Inc, *Greater than their Knowing* (Adel, 1986); D. Marr, *Patrick White* (Syd, 1991); Red Cross Soc (SA), *Annual Report*, 1938-55, *and* newspaper cuttings; NL, *Voices*, Summer, 1993-94; *Adel Chronicle*, 23 Aug 1924; *Advertiser* (Adel), 12 May 1962; family papers (held by Mr G. Dutton, Glasshouse Mountains, Qld).   DECIE DENHOLM

DUTTON, GEORGE (c.1886-1968), drover and Aboriginal elder, was born about 1886 at Yancannia station, north of Broken Hill, New South Wales, son of an English-born drover George Vicars Dutton (d.1890) and an Aboriginal woman. He called himself a Banjigali as he was born in that country, but his mother belonged to the neighbouring Wangkumara people; his Aboriginal stepfather was a Maljangaba who saw him through the *milia* initiation during which he was circumcised.

Young George embarked on what became a successful career in the pastoral industry. He worked mostly as a drover and mainly in the region where the borders of New South Wales, Queensland and South Australia abut. Unlike most of his contemporaries, however, he ranged as far afield as Adelaide, Maree, Birdsville and Windorah. On his travels he contacted local Aborigines and took part in their ceremonial life. While he was at Finniss Springs, some Arabana friends put him through the *wilyaru*, a form of which had also been practised in his home country. This rite made him an Aboriginal man of 'high degree' and his own people believed him to be 'clever'.

By three Aboriginal women, Ruby Ebsworth, Charlotte, and Alice Bates from Yandama station, Dutton had at least nine children. He had based himself at Tibooburra by 1914. The Aborigines Protection Board forced him to move with his family to its settlement at Brewarrina in 1938. Unable to find work there, he soon left; after moving around pastoral stations for a while, he settled at Wilcannia, on the Darling River, which became home for himself and his family until he died. He confined his travelling essentially to western New South Wales. In 1958 the Australian Aboriginal Affairs Council arranged for him to visit Melbourne (with his youngest son Charlie) to teach the rituals, dances and songs of corroborees to Victorian Aborigines; he also visited Coopers Creek in 1965.

In the places where Dutton lived there was little ritual activity after the 1920s. He retained his commitment to Aboriginal culture, and tried to pass on to the younger generation —including his grand-daughter Lorna Ebsworth [q.v. Dixon]—his extensive knowledge of languages, songs, stories and rituals, and of the country which he had travelled as a drover. From the 1930s he helped anthropologists and linguists to record his knowledge and life story, and revealed his rare combination of pride and humour. He delighted in the drama and the comedy of Aboriginal stories, but also communicated the solemnity of important rituals.

Dutton interested himself in the ways of other peoples, among them the Afghans, Indians, Greeks and Eastern Europeans whom he met. He took pride in his skill as a drover and horseman. Despite the climate of racial exclusion that clouded his later years, he claimed the right to be treated as an equal. Survived by his wife Alice, and by two of their three sons and three of their five daughters, Dutton died on 29 October 1968 at Wilcannia and was buried with Catholic rites in the local cemetery.

K. Gilbert, *Living Black* (Melb, 1977); *Aboriginal Hist*, 2, pt 1, 1978, p 2; *Oceania*, 29, no 2, 1958, p 91; *Age* (Melb) and *Herald* (Melb), 12 Sept 1958.   JEREMY BECKETT

DWYER, FRANCIS PATRICK JOHN (1910-1962), professor of chemistry, was born on 3 December 1910 at Nelsons Plains, near Raymond Terrace, New South Wales, eldest of five children of William John Dwyer, farmer, and his wife Susan, née O'Loughlin, both native-born. Frank was educated at Marist Brothers' High School, West Maitland, and the University of Sydney (B.Sc., 1931; M.Sc., 1933; D.Sc., 1946). As an undergraduate he developed an improved method for preparing pure diazoaminobenzene. Although he was interested in organic chemistry, his only opportunity to do research was in X-ray crystallography under David Mellor [q.v.]; for his master's degree he examined the crystal structure of indium and the occurrence of β-cristobalite in opal. Dwyer's interest in coordination chemistry was aroused by Mellor and strengthened by Francis Lions's [q.v.] encouragement.

Appointed head teacher of inorganic chemistry at Sydney Technical College in 1934, Dwyer began an investigation of the reaction of diazoamino compounds with metal salts in producing highly coloured 'lakes'—loose coordination complexes adsorbed at the surface of metal hydroxides. Using these reactions, he devised micro-analytical tests for various metal ions. This work was reported in eighteen papers in the journals of the Society of Chemical Industry and the Royal Australian Chemical Institute. On 12 January 1938 at St Paul's Catholic Church, Dulwich Hill, he married Lola Mary Bosworth, a stenographer.

(Sir) Ronald Nyholm [q.v.] joined the staff in 1940. He and Dwyer collaborated in their research and formed a close personal friendship. Despite heavy teaching loads, between 1942 and 1947 they reported complexes of rhodium, iridium and osmium in seventeen papers in the *Journal and Proceedings of the Royal Society of New South Wales*. Dwyer had joined the society in 1934 and was a councillor (1942-45 and 1948-49). He was awarded the R.A.C.I.'s 1940 Rennie and 1943 H. G. Smith [qq.v.11] medals.

Dwyer was appointed senior lecturer in chemistry at the University of Sydney in December 1945. While continuing his research on metal coordination compounds, he began to study the optical activity of metal complexes—which eventually led him into biological chemistry—and also started work on configurational activity, stereochemistry of sexadentate complexes, and electron-transfer reactions. He shared the University of Melbourne's 1953 David Syme [q.v.6] research prize.

In the United States of America in 1953-54, Dwyer was visiting professor at Northwestern University, Illinois, and George Fisher Baker lecturer at Cornell University, New York. In 1957 he was offered a chair at Pennsylvania State University. K. L. Sutherland, (Sir) Hugh Ennor [qq.v.] and others, with help from the Commonwealth Scientific and Industrial Research Organization, persuaded Dwyer to accept a readership in biological inorganic chemistry at the John Curtin School of Medical Research, Australian National University. He was given a personal chair in 1960 and elected a fellow (1961) of the Australian Academy of Science. In Can-

berra he investigated the effect of metal complexes on biological activity. He published 160 research papers. With Mellor, he commenced editing the book, *Chelating Agents and Metal Chelates* (New York, 1964).

Considered by his students to be an excellent teacher, Dwyer was quietly spoken, with expressive eyes which lit up when he smiled; he had friendliness, modesty, unfailing cheerfulness and enthusiasm for everything he did. He enjoyed golf and fishing. Survived by his wife, daughter and two sons, he died of a coronary occlusion on 22 June 1962 at his Griffith home and was buried in Canberra cemetery. His friends and former students established a fund to endow the Dwyer memorial lecture and medal of the University of New South Wales Chemical Society; the first lecture (1963) was given by his old friend Nyholm.

Aust J of Science, 25, 21 Nov 1962, p 215; *Chemistry and Industry*, 15 June 1963, p 980; Aust Academy of Science, *Year Book*, 1963, p 32, *and* for his publications; Roy Soc NSW, *J and Procs*, 97, 1964, p 126; *ANU News*, 5, Nov 1970, p 13; Roy Aust Chemical Inst, *Procs*, 37, no 8, Aug 1970, p 199; A. T. Baker and S. E. Livingstone, 'The early history of coordination chemistry in Australia', *Polyhedron* (Oxford), 4, 1985, p 1337; *SMH*, 23 June 1962.

STANLEY E. LIVINGSTONE

DWYER, JOHN JAMES (1890-1962), politician and soldier, was born on 9 March 1890 at Port Cygnet, Tasmania, son of Charles Dwyer, farmer, and his wife Mary, née Scanlon. Jack was educated at Mills Reef State School until the age of 12. From 1910 he cut cane and timber in Queensland before returning to Tasmania in 1913 to work on the Lake Margaret Hydro-electric Power Scheme.

Enlisting in the Australian Imperial Force on 4 February 1915, Dwyer sailed for the Middle East and joined the 15th Battalion on Gallipoli in August. Following the evacuation in December, he was sent to Egypt and transferred to the 4th Machine-Gun Company. He moved to France where he was wounded in action on 9 June 1916. Two months later he was promoted sergeant. Near Zonnebeke, Belgium, on 26 September 1917 Dwyer had charge of a Vickers machine-gun during an attack. When an enemy machine-gun began to inflict casualties among his comrades, he rushed his Vickers forward, fired at point-blank range, killed the German crew and carried their gun back to his lines. Commanding both weapons, he helped to repulse a counter-attack. Next day he fought with equal determination and inspired his sector. He was awarded the Victoria Cross. Commissioned in May 1918, he was promoted lieutenant in

August and returned home in October. His A.I.F. appointment terminated on 15 December.

Under the soldier-settlement scheme, Dwyer established an orchard on Bruny Island. On 24 September 1919 at St Brendan's Catholic Church, Alonnah, he married Myrtle Mary Dillon. The irregularity of income from his farm led him to join J. J. Dillon & Sons, his father-in-law's sawmilling enterprise near Alonnah. Dwyer served as a Bruny Island councillor (from 1924) until he moved to New Norfolk in 1928. He set up his own sawmill at Moogara.

Encouraged by Dillon to enter parliament, in May 1931 Dwyer was elected to the House of Assembly as a Labor member for Franklin. He was to retain the seat until his death. As Speaker (1942-48) of the House, he was renowned for his fairness and his insistence on 'a fair go for all', particularly new members. He was appointed minister for agriculture on 29 June 1948 in (Sir) Robert Cosgrove's [q.v.13] cabinet. Following an electoral redistribution, in 1949 Dwyer sold his sawmill and moved to Glenorchy within the redrawn boundaries of Franklin. From 26 August 1958 to 12 May 1959 he served as deputy-premier. Respected as a competent minister, he developed a network among rural interests, especially in the Huon and Derwent valleys, but was forced by illness to resign his portfolio on 19 September 1961.

Dwyer was a 'grassroots' politician who believed in maintaining personal contact with his constituents: he was returned to parliament in ten successive elections. Jovial and kindly, he enjoyed a beer with his friends, but, perhaps because of his impoverished upbringing, he had a stern sense of propriety and a strong work ethic. He seldom discussed his war experiences. Eric Reece recalled that, when asked about his exploits in Belgium in 1917, Jack modestly replied that he 'was drunk at the time'. Keenly interested in community and social life, Dwyer was a justice of the peace (from 1924), a member of the New Norfolk licensing court and the fire brigade board, and an official visitor to Lachlan Park Mental Hospital. He belonged to the New Norfolk Golf Club, and the Buckingham and Claremont bowling clubs.

In 1961 Dwyer spent time in hospital with dermatitis, which his family attributed to exposure to mustard gas during World War I. Survived by his wife, son and five daughters, he died on 17 January 1962 on Bruny Island; he was accorded a state funeral with military honours and buried in Cornelian Bay cemetery.

L. Wigmore (ed), *They Dared Mightily* (Canb, 1963); Returned Services League of Aust (Tas), *On Service*, Apr 1986; *Mercury* (Hob), 18, 19 Jan 1962; information from Messrs E. Reece, Claremont, and J. J. Dwyer, Moonah, Hob.

CHRIS BATT

DWYER, SIR JOHN PATRICK (1879-1966), chief justice, was born on 24 June 1879 at Aberfeldy, Victoria, son of Thomas Dwyer, a butcher from Ireland, and his Melbourne-born wife Elizabeth, née Donaldson. John was educated at Geelong College (dux 1893) where he played football for the first XVIII and cricket for the first XI. In 1897 he began an articled clerks' course through the University of Melbourne. Called to the Victorian Bar on 1 August 1902 and to the Western Australian Bar on 19 December 1904, he practised with M. L. Moss at Fremantle. On 28 December 1908 at St John's Anglican Church, Fremantle, he married Emily Louise Munro (Irgens) (d.1950). He was employed by Haynes & Robinson at Albany from 1908, before forming a partnership with Moss in 1911.

Five ft 9½ ins (177 cm) tall, slightly built, with blue eyes and a fair complexion, Dwyer enlisted in the Australian Imperial Force on 30 May 1916 and was commissioned on 16 May 1917. He arrived in France in August 1918, served with the 44th Battalion and rose to lieutenant. His A.I.F. appointment terminated in Australia on 23 July 1919. A senior partner (1918-22) in Moss, Dwyer, Unmack & Thomas, in 1922 he was one of three representatives from the Barristers' Board who sat on a committee which considered the establishment of a law school at the University of Western Australia. He became a foundation lecturer of the newly created law faculty in 1928. Next year Dwyer succeeded R. B. Burnside [q.v.7] as a puisne judge of the Supreme Court; he was appointed chief justice on 1 January 1946, following the retirement of Sir John Northmore [q.v.11]. Dwyer was knighted that year and elevated to K.C.M.G. in 1949.

Highly regarded as a classical lawyer, he had 'one of the finest, most incisive minds' the State had known. He was more concerned with applying legal principles rigorously and impartially than with interpreting them to achieve social or legislative objectives. Dwyer abhorred verbosity. As an advocate, he once told a jury that he would not insult their intelligence with the customary closing address supporting his client's case. As a judge, he was intolerant of obfuscating witnesses and also of ill-prepared barristers, some of whom reputedly abandoned advocacy as a career because of his attacks.

Dwyer was administrator of the State from 1 July to 6 August and from 28 August to 5 November 1951. Next year he was appointed honorary lieutenant-governor for life, the last such life appointment in Western Australia. He retired as chief justice on 28 February 1959. Taking his civic duties seriously, on one occasion he presided over an Executive Council meeting from his hospital bed. He was chief scout (1942) of Western Australia and knight commander (1947) of the commandery of the Order of St John; he was also chairman of trustees (1947-54) of the public library, museum and art gallery, and chairman (1948) of the State electoral commission. In private he was pleasant, even charming. A member of Royal Perth Golf and the Weld [q.v.6] clubs, he played golf until he was 78 and lawn bowls until he was 82. Sir John died on 25 August 1966 at Shenton Park. Accorded a state funeral, he was buried in Karrakatta cemetery; his estate was sworn for probate at $106 023; he had no children.

F. Alexander, *Campus at Crawley* (Melb, 1963); *West Australian*, 6 Dec 1945, 6 Mar, 1 June 1946, 1 Jan, 21 Sept 1949, 12, 13 Feb 1959, 26, 29, 30 Aug, 27, 28 Oct 1966; information from Univ Melb, Geelong College, Vic, and Hon I. G. Medcalf, Nedlands, Perth.   JEREMY BIRMAN

DYER, MICHAEL DAVID (1932-1978), radio announcer and television producer, was born on 2 October 1932 in London, son of Carleton Leroy Dyer, businessman, and his wife Dorothy Bernice, née Wemp, both from Canada. In 1940 Michael accompanied his mother, sister and brother to Ontario where he attended Lakefield Naval Boarding College and Oakville High School.

In 1951-52 Dyer undertook a professional training course in radio and television arts at Ryerson Institute of Technology, Toronto. Although he was offered an appointment with the National Broadcasting Corporation of Canada, he decided to travel, and sent home regular features to a newspaper syndicate. He worked briefly as an English-speaking announcer for the international service of Radio Nederlands and was based at Hilversum. After exploring Europe, he travelled to South Africa to be reunited with his father who encouraged him to visit Australia.

Dyer arrived in Melbourne on 19 May 1954, and stayed. He was first employed at nights as an announcer on radio station 3DB and later produced 'The Happy Gang'. A jazz enthusiast since his high school days, he instituted a late-night jazz show, 'Sound Study', which ran for seven years on 3DB, 3XY and 3AK; his closing tag, 'Stay gay', then carried no sexual connotations. He compered jazz concerts, lectured on the history of jazz at such diverse establishments as the Royal Melbourne Institute of Technology and Pentridge prison, corresponded with many American performers and entertained them on their visits to Australia. On 17 October 1956 at Ewing Memorial Church, East Malvern, he married with Presbyterian forms Judith Elizabeth Tilton.

In August that year Myke had moved to Australian Radio and Television productions; in 1958 he moved again, to the television station GTV-9. There, between 1961 and 1969, he produced the Logie award-winning show, 'It Could Be You', hosted by Tommy Hanlon. Through that programme, Dyer relished opportunities to make people's dreams come true. From 1963 to 1977 he was a regular panellist on Bert Newton's 'New Faces', and Graham Kennedy was godfather to his first child. After two years as publicity manager for Channel 9, Dyer left in 1976 (following Kerry Packer's takeover) and set up an independent production house which enjoyed only modest success. A slim, handsome man, who sported a moustache or beard on holidays, but was usually clean shaven for work and public appearances, he loved the media in which he worked, was a skilled and amusing communicator, and gave generously of his time to many charitable causes.

Two days before he was due to take up a new appointment with Armstrong Audio Video Pty Ltd, on 7 January 1978 Dyer went swimming in the surf at Mullaway Beach, New South Wales. He was swept out to sea by a strong rip and drowned. Survived by his wife, daughter and son, he was cremated.

P. Beilby (ed), *Australian TV* (Melb, 1981); B. McLaughlin, *From Wireless to Radio* (Melb, 1986?); *Herald* (Melb), 19 May 1954, 9 Jan 1978; *Age* (Melb), *Sun News-Pictorial*, and *Advertiser* (Adel), 9 Jan 1978; personal information *and* memorabilia (held by Mrs J. Dyer, Brighton, Melb).
                                                    SUE TURNBULL

DYNON, MOIRA LENORE (1920-1976), welfare worker and scientist, was born on 4 September 1920 at Elsternwick, Melbourne, eldest of five children of Percy Gerald Shelton, medical practitioner, and his wife Lily Eliza, née Johnston, both Victorian born. Educated at O'Neill College, Elsternwick, and Loreto Convent, Toorak, Moira studied science at the University of Melbourne (B.Sc., 1941). On 10 October 1942 she was commissioned in the Women's Australian Auxiliary Air Force and was posted to the Directorate of Armament on 29 March 1943. She was responsible for 'inspection of R.A.A.F. offensive and defensive chemical warfare munitions and Storage Depots throughout Australia, the disposal of leaking bombs, the unloading of cargoes of chemical warfare stores from ships, the chemical analysis of different charges and the training of persons in both offensive and defensive chemical warfare measures'. Usually the only female officer training or inspecting all-male units, she was the sole female participant in trials. She was burnt several times on the skin, eyes, throat and lungs. On 10 April 1943 she was promoted section officer and on 1 July 1944 flight officer.

After being demobilized on 8 February 1946, Moira became a research officer (antibiotics) with the Commonwealth Serum Laboratories in Victoria. Appointed female officer on the staff council, Council for Scientific and Industrial Research, in 1948, she worked with Dr H. C. Forster and (Sir) Ian Clunies Ross [q.v.13]. A slight, softly spoken, dark-haired woman, she united her scientific knowledge with sound common sense and organizing ability, and possessed sincerity, warmth and charm. On 2 December 1950 at Xavier College, Kew, she married John Francis Dynon, a barrister and solicitor. They lived at Malvern where they raised five children.

Mrs Dynon worked to establish the Federation of Loreto Old Girls' Associations, of which she was foundation president (1954-55). She was also active in other Catholic women's organizations, particularly as vice-president of the Catholic Mothers' Clubs' Federation (1958-59), the Catholic Women's Social Guild (1966-68) and the Australian Council of Catholic Women (1968). These bodies supported her international welfare campaigns.

From 1952 she belonged to the Stonnington (Malvern) branch of the Liberal and Country Party, but resigned in 1959 over the matrimonial causes bill which she found 'objectionable on religious, moral and sociological grounds'. Four years later she joined the Hawthorn branch of the Australian Labor Party in gratitude to Dr Jim Cairns for assisting her philanthropic causes. In 1952 the Dynons had established the Malvern branch of the United Nations Australia Association, Victorian division. Working with Sir Charles Lowe [q.v.], (Sir) Edward Dunlop and Sir Albert Coates [q.v.13] on the executive of the Australian-Asian Association, in 1960 Moira initiated and ran an appeal to provide secondary education for Japanese children of returned Australian servicemen. She involved international and Japanese welfare agencies; although the appeal met political opposition, an estimated $150 000 was raised by 1969.

Through her chairmanship (1964-67) of Aid for India, Dynon organized the shipment of 2600 tins of powdered milk in 1964. As president (1967-72) of its successor, Aid India, she saw twenty-five million pints of milk dispatched by 1970. In addition, she assisted famine-relief campaigns in Bengal, Bangladesh and Pakistan. Concurrently, she was president (1961-67) of the Italo-Australian Welfare Association, women's division, which had been founded to raise funds for unemployed Italian immigrants. In 1968 she was appointed to the order of Stella della Solidàrieta Italiano.

A committed Christian and an ecumenist, Dynon saw herself as an ordinary citizen of the world whose duty was to work for humanitarian ends. She read extensively in international affairs. Honest in her beliefs and courageous in stating her views, she was able to identify specific areas where practical help could be given, and she acted as a catalyst for international assistance. She died of cancer on 23 October 1976 at Malvern and was buried in Melbourne general cemetery; her husband, two daughters and three sons survived her.

J. Thomson, *The WAAAF in Wartime Australia* (Melb, 1991); *PD* (Cwlth), 29 Sept 1961, 21 Oct 1964; *Argus*, 5 Mar 1945; *Sun News-Pictorial*, 15 July 1947, 16 Nov, 26 Dec 1959, 18 Dec 1964, 17 Apr 1965; *Advocate* (Melb), 2 Nov 1967, 1 Feb 1968, 28 Oct 1971, 23 Sept 1972, 4 Nov 1976; *Age* (Melb), 11 Oct 1967; family papers (closed access).
                                    M. R. HUMPHRIS

DYRING, MOYA CLAIRE (1909-1967), artist, was born on 10 February 1909 at Coburg, Melbourne, third child of Carl Peter Wilhelm Dyring, medical practitioner, and his second wife Dagmar Alexandra Esther, née Cohn, both Victorian born. Moya was educated (1917-27) at Firbank Church of England Girls' Grammar School, Brighton. After visiting Paris in 1928, she studied (1929-32) at the National Gallery schools, Melbourne, and shared fellow student Sam Atyeo's interest in artistic innovation.

Classical modernism engaged her attention in the early 1930s. She painted at the George Bell [q.v.7] school and studied under Rah Fizelle [q.v.8] in Sydney; Mary Alice Evatt [q.v.] and Cynthia Reed [q.v. Nolan] were her colleagues. For several months in 1937 she took charge of Heide, the home and garden of John and Sunday Reed, at Bulleen, Melbourne. The Reeds were pivotal both to her sympathy for modernism and her belief in congenial fellowship. She enjoyed something of the intense relationship with Sunday Reed that the latter would subsequently extend to Joy Hester [q.v.]. In June Dyring held an exhibition, opened by H. V. Evatt [q.v.], at the Riddell Gallery, Melbourne. Less enthusiastic than the Reeds and the Evatts about her art, Basil Burdett [q.v.7] wrote of her 'somewhat incoherent interpretation of modern ideas', although he did acknowledge that her work had 'audacity of colour and a certain monumental feeling for form ... qualities rare enough in Australian painting'.

In August Dyring embarked for Panama

whence she travelled by bus to New York, breaking her journey to view major galleries. She had intended to paint in the United States of America, but disliked the work of contemporary American artists and sailed for France. In 1938 she was based in Paris, taking advantage of Atyeo's contacts within the *avant-garde*. She studied at the Académie Colarossi, the Académie de la Grande Chaumière and with Andre Lhote, although by October she denounced him as a 'racketeer'.

In 1939 Dyring and Atyeo settled on a farm at Vence, France; inspired by memories of Heide, they grew fruit and flowers. Sam accepted a commission to decorate a house in Dominica, West Indies, leaving Moya at Vence. Evacuated to Australia via South Africa, where she painted and searched for tribal art, she then journeyed to Dominica and married Atyeo. They were not happy, neither painted and Dyring was ill. Evatt offered Atyeo work and Dyring accompanied him to the U.S.A. She viewed art, painted occasionally and claimed to have exhibited in Washington in 1943. After World War II Evatt found Sam various postings, while Moya returned to Paris to pursue a full-time career in art. They were to be divorced in 1950.

From about 1946 Dyring's art was more personal than innovative. She gained a considerable reputation among French regionalist and nationalist artists for her sympathetic appreciation of provincial scenes and life. Bernard Smith placed her in the French tradition of *intimiste* painters. In 1948 she leased and renovated an apartment on the Ile St Louis, which, as Chez Moya, became a centre for Australians who enjoyed her hospitality, cooking and practical assistance. She revisited Australia and exhibited in various cities in 1950, 1953, 1956, 1960 and 1963; the press carried her reports of Parisian cultural life.

Dyring held a solo exhibition in London in December 1949 and was in close contact with expatriate Australians, among them Loudon Sainthill [q.v.], Donald Friend, David Strachan [q.v.], Alannah Coleman and Margaret Olley. In 1961 she curated the Australian section of the Paris Biennale. She died of cancer on 4 January 1967 at Wimbledon, London. An apartment for visiting Australian artists was established in her memory at the Cité Internationale des Arts, Paris.

B. Reid (ed), *Modern Australian Art* (Melb, 1958); C. France, *Margaret Olley* (Syd, 1990); *People* (Syd), 3 June 1953; *Art and Aust*, 4, no 4, Mar 1967; *Herald* (Melb), 24 May 1937, 18 Oct 1963; *Argus*, 4 June 1937; *Bulletin*, 9 June 1937; *SMH*, 3 July 1950; Moya Dyring studio, Art Gallery of NSW files; Reed papers (LaTL); papers held by author (Glen Iris, Melb); personal information.

JULIET PEERS

E

EADY, MARSHALL THOMAS WILTON (1882-1947), engineer, was born on 18 November 1882 at Summer Hill, Sydney, eldest child of William Wilton Eady, a native-born ironmonger, and his wife Barbara Rose, née McPherson, from Scotland. When William died in 1892, the family moved to Melbourne where Marshall's uncle (Sir) William McPherson [q.v.10] took responsibility for them. Educated at Scotch College, Eady was apprenticed to the Austral Otis Engineering Co. Ltd before joining his uncle's firm. In 1903 he was sent to Ruston & Hornsby Ltd in Lincolnshire, England, to gain experience as an engineer.

Returning in 1907 to McPherson's (McPherson's Pty Ltd from 1913), Eady was given responsibility for establishing a department to import agricultural machinery and machine tools. He was made a director of the firm in 1913. Having visited England to investigate supply, in 1914 he recommended that local production should immediately commence: under his supervision, McPherson's Machine Tool Works was established at Kensington. On 30 November 1915 at the Methodist Church, Auburn, Eady married Sheila Lydia Whitehead.

After World War I Eady gradually became involved in the wider aspects of industry. In 1931 he represented employers at an International Labour Office conference in Geneva. A member (1928-44) of the Victorian Apprenticeship Commission, he was especially interested in training for industry. In 1938, while sitting on Melbourne Technical College's advisory committee, he helped E. P. Eltham [q.v.] to introduce classes in foremanship which, in turn, led to the formation of the Institute of Industrial Management, of which Eady was foundation vice-president and later president. Because of his expertise, he was appointed to the Federal government's advisory panels on industrial organization (1938) and technical training (1939). His work with the Associated Chamber of Manufactures of Australia was perhaps his greatest interest. He was president of the Victorian chamber in 1935-43 and of the national body in 1937-38. At Imperial trade negotiations held in London in 1938 to review the Ottawa Agreement, he served as an official consultant to the Australian ministerial delegation.

In that year Eady had accompanied W. E. McPherson [q.v.] to Britain, Germany and the United States of America, seeking ways to develop defence production. During World War II Eady continued his activity in industrial relations. His work on labour recruit-

ment, and the dilution scheme in particular, was acknowledged by (Sir) John Jensen [q.v.], secretary to the Department of Munitions.

Described in 1939 as 'rather bald, bespectacled and mild-mannered', with 'cherubic' features, Eady was a council-member (1942-47) of the University of Melbourne and a co-opted member of the Council for Scientific and Industrial Research. He served as trustee for the Burke Road Methodist Church, Glen Iris, and on the employment committee of the Victorian Society for Crippled Children. In 1947 he was appointed managing director of McPherson's Ltd (a public company from 1944) and was elected chairman of the Institution of Production Engineers. He died of a coronary occlusion on 8 December 1947 at the wheel of his car in Collins Street, Melbourne. Survived by his wife, daughter and two sons, he was cremated; his estate was sworn for probate at £50 685.

C. R. Hill, *The Manufacturers* (Syd, 1971); B. Carroll, *Australian Made* (Melb, 1987); S. Murray-Smith and A. J. Dare, *The Tech* (Melb, 1987); *A'sian Manufacturer*, 27 Dec 1947, p 10; *Univ Melb Gazette*, Dec 1947, p 102; *AIM Management Review*, 6, no 4, 1981, p 3; *SMH*, 15 Apr 1931, 25 Feb 1932, 3, 10 Mar, 25 Oct 1938, 28 Sept 1939, 27 Dec 1947; *Smith's Weekly* (Syd), 16 Dec 1939; *Age*, *Argus* and *Sun News-Pictorial*, 9 Dec 1947; information from Mr W. Eady, Camberwell, Melb, and miscellaneous letters supplied by him (held by author).

BARBARA HAMER

EAGER, SIR CLIFDEN HENRY ANDREWS (1882-1969), politician and barrister, was born on 14 June 1882 at Sorrento, Victoria, third child of Irish-born Clifden Henry Eager, Church of England reader (and subsequently Congregational minister), and his wife Kate Amelia, née Andrews, from New South Wales. Educated at state schools and the Melbourne Educational Institute, in 1905 young Clifden began work as an accountant before studying at the University of Melbourne (LL.B., 1910; LL.M., 1912). He was admitted to the Bar in Victoria on 8 March 1911 and in New South Wales on 19 June 1939.

At the Congregational Church, South Melbourne, on 24 December 1909 Eager had married Ernestine Isabella May Campton (d.1964); they were to have four sons and a daughter. After building a practice in commercial law, taxation and local government, and holding several directorships, in 1930 he succeeded (Sir) Robert Menzies [q.v.] as a Nationalist—later United Australia Party and then Liberal—member of the Legislative Council for the Province of East Yarra. In March-April 1935 he was a minister without portfolio for a fortnight in the government of Sir Stanley Argyle [q.v.7] and in November was appointed K.C. He succeeded H. I. Cohen [q.v.8] as unofficial leader (1937-43) of the Legislative Council and was a member (1940-45) of the State War Advisory Council.

On the retirement of Sir Frank Clarke [q.v.8], Eager was elected president of the Legislative Council on 29 June 1943 and was to retain office until June 1958. Elected to the joint library committee in 1940, he served as chairman in 1947-58. He was knighted in 1945 and elevated to K.B.E. in 1952.

During the Country Party government of (Sir) John McDonald [q.v.], which had Labor backing, Eager lost party endorsement in 1952 after he resisted Liberal pressure to leave the chair and vote on the floor against the Greater Melbourne Council bill. In the June elections, which resulted in sweeping victories for the Australian Labor Party, Eager contested East Yarra as an Independent Liberal, received Labor Party support, and won. He was nominated for re-election as president by Labor. In 1958 he contested East Yarra again, as an Independent Liberal with Labor support, but was defeated by (Sir) Rupert Hamer. Eager remained active in public life as chairman of Equity Trustees Executors & Agency Co. Ltd, Mutual Store Ltd, Pearl Assurance Co. Ltd, Australian Cement Ltd and the Sir William Angliss [q.v.7] Charitable Fund.

Of somewhat 'forbidding exterior', Sir Clifden possessed great dignity and became a firm, deeply respected council president. He was widely read in many subjects, including the classics and the fine arts. Earlier in his career he had been president of the Royal Society of St George (1940-42 and 1959-61) and of the Trinity Grammar School council (1946-52). Survived by his sons, he died on 11 August 1969 at Corowa, New South Wales, and was buried in Melbourne general cemetery.

P. Aimer, *Politics, Power and Persuasion* (Syd, 1974); *PD* (LC Vic), 9 Sept 1969, p 5; *Argus*, 5 Nov 1935, 18 Nov 1937, 14 June 1945, 3 July 1946; *Age* (Melb), 24, 26 Apr 1952, 14 Aug 1969; *Sun News-Pictorial*, 14 Aug 1969.   BARRY O. JONES

EARL, JOHN CAMPBELL (1890-1978), chemist, was born on 18 May 1890 in North Adelaide, son of Robert Campbell Earl (d.1895), civil servant, and his wife Elizabeth Mortlock, née Lucas (d.1901). John attended primary school in Adelaide. When his parents died, he was sent to England for further education at Great Yarmouth Grammar School.

After studying chemistry at the City and Guilds Technical College, Finsbury, London, he was employed from 1911 at the Imperial Institute, South Kensington. In 1913 he returned to South Australia where he was assistant government analyst (1915-17) and entered the University of Adelaide (B.Sc., 1921; D.Sc., 1926). Answering a call in 1917 for qualified chemists to staff explosive factories in Britain, he was stationed at Gretna, Scotland, before transferring to a research unit at the University of St Andrews (Ph.D., 1920; D.Sc., 1949). In 1922 he accepted a lectureship at the University of Sydney; six years later he was appointed to the chair of organic chemistry.

During the 1930s Earl investigated aliphatic nitroso compounds and discovered a new class of cyclic compounds which he named *sydnones*. In 1935 he published his findings in the *Journal of the Chemical Society* and was awarded the H. G. Smith [q.v.11] medal by the Royal Australian Chemical Institute. At St Augustine's Anglican Church, Neutral Bay, on 8 September 1938 he married Winifred Kate Vincent Jones; they were to remain childless. That year he was elected president of the Royal Society of New South Wales.

Late in 1939 Earl began to focus his department's research on government-assisted projects related to defence. He undertook urgent investigations as diverse as the pilot-scale preparation of the antiseptic, proflavine, for war wounds, the large-scale preparation of British Anti-Lewisite (the only effective antidote for the chemical warfare agent, lewisite), the formulation of coloured smokes for effective signalling under jungle conditions, the industrial production of dimethylaniline for conversion into the essential explosive, tetryl, and the development of a practical dyeline process for the rapid reproduction of maps and machine drawings. In recognition of his work he was appointed a life member of the Society of Chemical Industry, London.

Earl was a highly effective supervisor of honours students, in whom he instilled habits of clear thinking, hard work and persistence. Although he was invariably considerate and helpful to co-workers, he held unusually firm and unconventional ideas on how to run a university. Recurrent disagreements with successive vice-chancellors and even with many of his colleagues in other science departments induced him to take early retirement in 1947. With his wife, he settled at Thurlton, Norfolk, England. Earl maintained his scientific interests at City College, Norwich, as a consultant to a local malting establishment and as a specialist editor for *British Chemical Abstracts*.

A small, kindly and basically cheerful man, with exceptionally bright eyes and a nice sense of humour, Earl was a good conversationalist on almost any subject. He was particularly fond of Gilbert and Sullivan operas and of the works of C. J. Dennis [q.v.8]. Reasonably proficient in German, he assisted some scientists who had come to Australia as refugees from Hitler's regime. When Winifred died in 1967, Earl returned to Adelaide. He spent much of his time at the university, was acting-master (1969-70) of Kathleen Lumley College, attended symposia and published occasional papers. He died on Christmas Day 1978 in Royal Adelaide Hospital and was cremated.

Industrial Aust and Mining Standard, 15 Mar 1928, p 270; *Chemistry and Industry* (Lond), 7 Mar 1953, p 204; *Chemistry in Aust*, 45, no 4, Apr 1978, p 92, 46, no 5, May 1979, p 219; *Chemistry in Britain*, 17, no 1, Jan 1981, p 30; *SMH*, 7 Mar 1928, 23 Dec 1933, 21 Nov 1935, 14 May 1938; John Campbell Earl's talk on ABC radio station 2FC, 11 Feb 1945 (held ABC Archives, Syd).

D. J. BROWN

EARNSHAW, PERCY ALAN (1893-1980), paediatrician, was born on 17 October 1893 in Brisbane, eldest son of English-born parents William Earnshaw, schoolmaster, and his wife Kate Louise, née Gaylard. Educated at Maryborough and Brisbane grammar schools, and at the University of Sydney (M.B., Ch.M., 1916), Percy was a house surgeon (1916) at Sydney Hospital and resident medical officer (1917) at Brisbane General Hospital. On 13 July 1917 he was appointed captain, Australian Army Medical Corps, Australian Imperial Force. Reaching the Western Front in October, he served in the 8th and 14th field ambulances, and as regimental medical officer of several units of the 5th Division. In March 1918 he was gassed. He recuperated in England before resuming duty in France in June. Returning to England in April 1919, he resigned his A.I.F. appointment on 29 May 1920. Earnshaw was a house physician (1919-21) at the Hospital for Sick Children, London, then gained postgraduate experience in paediatrics at the West London Hospital and in Edinburgh. On 27 April 1923 at the parish church of St Martin-in-the-Fields, Westminster, London, he married a nurse Marian Eileen Blandford.

The couple returned to Brisbane. Earnshaw entered general practice, but essentially confined his work to children. He was honorary physician (1923-31) at the Hospital for Sick Children and honorary medical officer (1923-38) to the State government's Infant Welfare Service. At the Mater Children's Hospital, where he was senior honorary physician (1931-61), the unassuming but methodical 'P.A.' established a reputation as an outstanding clinician; during World War II he was senior paediatrician at the hospital. He was a major on the Reserve of Officers, attached to the Queensland Lines of Communication Area in 1942-44. A member (1946-59) of the advisory board of the Mater Misericordiae hospitals, he was chairman (1958-78) and president (1959-62) of the medical committee of the Queensland section of the Royal Flying Doctor Service of Australia, and an honorary life member of that institution. From 1951 until 1959 he was clinical lecturer in child health and a member of the board of the faculty of medicine at the University of Queensland.

Earnshaw was a member (1922-77), councillor (1937-38 and 1960-64), president (1961-62), fellow (1966) and honorary life member (1971) of the Queensland branch of the British Medical Association. He was founding president (1949) of its paediatric section and vice-president (1937, 1950 and 1952) of the paediatric section of the Australasian Medical Congress. A member (1931-47) of the University of Queensland's postgraduate medical education committee, he was also a member (1963-75) and chairman (1965-66) of the B.M.A.'s medical fees tribunal. In addition, he was president (1953-54) of the Australian Paediatric Association, a foundation fellow (1938) of the Royal Australasian College of Physicians and chairman (1962-66) of its State committee. In 1965 he delivered the (E. S.) Jackson [q.v.9] lecture to the Queensland branch of the Australian Medical Association.

Widely esteemed as a pioneer of paediatrics in Queensland, Earnshaw retired from practice in 1961 and was appointed C.B.E. in 1964. He died on 13 January 1980 at Clayfield and was cremated; his wife, son and four daughters survived him.

J. H. Pearn, *Focus and Innovation* (Brisb, 1986); Mater Misericordiae Public Hospital, Sth Brisb, *Annual Report*, 1960-61, 1979-80; *Aust Paediatric J*, 9, Apr 1973, p 72; *AMJ*, 28 June 1980, p 678; P. A. Earnshaw diary, 30 July 1917-18 May 1919 (ts, OL *and* AWM).

M. JOHN THEARLE

EASTWOOD, MILLICENT (1872-1947), landlady, was born on 18 January 1872 at Wahring, Victoria, eldest child of Hardy Hill (1828-1908), a farmer from Lincolnshire, England, and his Irish-born wife Mary, née Gallagher (1848-1934). Raised in her mother's Catholic faith, Milly was educated at home by a Presbyterian governess and at the nearby state school until the age of 14. As she grew up, she helped Mary with the housework and in caring for four sisters and four brothers, the last of whom was born in 1889. Her high spirits gradually led her to bridle against the restricting patterns of rural life and to yearn for something better, or, at least, for change. Millicent never liked cows and regarded herself as 'a bit of a rebel' long before she read Miles Franklin's [q.v.8] *My Brilliant Career*. The book 'put into words so much of what she felt'. Resolute yet by no means arrogant, hopeful without being assured, she journeyed to Melbourne in the early 1900s and was apprenticed to a dressmaker.

On 16 August 1907 at 448 Queen Street she married with Congregational forms 43-year-old Francis Eastwood, a hatter like his father before him. They had three daughters, Isabel, Evelyn and Amy, before Frank went alone to Western Australia in 1913. He and Millicent were never reunited. To support her young children, Mrs Eastwood leased a boarding-house at South Melbourne, but soon moved to Carlton where she earned a living as a landlady in charge of a succession of apartment-houses—47 Victoria Street, 3 Lincoln Square, and numbers 37, 51 and 201 Drummond Street. As lessee, she lived on the premises, paid a sum each week to the owner, cleaned the house, had responsibility for its order and maintenance, and received the tenants' rent. She and her daughters shared the advantages of being together, and, after school and at weekends, the children could also visit the fire-brigade station or the museum, and play in the gardens of the Exhibition Building or by the lake at the University of Melbourne. Contrariwise, a number of the apartment-houses were poorly drained, there was a lurking danger of diphtheria, Millicent's own rent could be raised without notice, and the repeated walk up and down two or three flights of stairs each day proved tiring as she aged.

Reverting from landlady to tenant in 1924, Mrs Eastwood became the proprietress in turn of two sandwich shops in the city—in Little Collins Street and at the Eastern Market. She began early and worked five days a week until 8 p.m., and on Saturday mornings. Having moved six times in thirteen years, in 1926 she again shifted with her daughters, this time to 65 (now 19) Queensberry Street, Carlton. Her mother gave her £300 to buy into the apartment-house as landlady. Built of brick in 1889 and named Cavazzi, it had two storeys, ten rooms (including former servants' quarters), stables at the rear, a cast-iron balcony on the first floor, iron railings at the entrance to the front porch and a grapevine along the seven-foot-high side fence. Millicent and her daughters occupied two bedrooms upstairs, and had a living-room and kitchenette downstairs. The other lodgers were Australians. During World War II the first Greek tenant arrived; eventually seven of the tenants came from Greece. Mrs East-

wood made of this home a sanctuary, for herself, for her daughters and for those members of the extended Hill family who visited.

A woman of strong character who believed that there was no middle course between right and wrong, Millicent sent her daughters to Catholic schools and attended Mass with them every Sunday. She was a devoted mother, and a firm but considerate landlady, with a clear mind, a gracious manner, a generous nature and a hearty laugh. While she had a few close friends, for the most part she kept to herself. Fond of the cinema, the theatre and the opera (she sat in the gods and her favourite was *Madama Butterfly*), she also enjoyed 'a day in town' (usually Fridays) when she had afternoon tea at the Myer [q.v.10] Emporium in Bourke Street. She bought shrewdly with very little, and dressed well in her brown suit, cream blouse, and matching hat and shoes. Tall, spare and bespectacled, she liked reading, took the *Age* newspaper each morning and voted Labor.

In 1946 Mrs Eastwood was diagnosed as having cancer. She died on 6 March 1947 in the home of her married daughter Evelyn at Regent and was buried in Preston cemetery. Isabel worked as a librarian with the Australian Broadcasting Control Board and Amy as an administrative assistant at the university; they remained single; in 1959 they jointly bought No.65. Within a generation Australia Post built a high-rise centre next door, a large motel was erected at the rear, and lawyers and businessmen converted the adjacent terrace-houses to suites of offices.

M. Kelly, *Faces in the Street* (Syd, 1982); A. Eastwood, I. Eastwood and H. Merlo, *Uphill After Lunch* (Melb, 1986); *Nagambie Times*, 20 Nov 1908; Hill *and* Eastwood papers (on file at ADB); information from Mr V. H. V. Hill, Drysdale, Vic; family information.
         JOHN RITCHIE

EATON, CHARLES (1895-1979), air force officer and diplomat, was born on 21 December 1895 at Lambeth, London, son of William Walpole Eaton, master butcher, and his wife Grace Maude, née Martin. Educated at Wandsworth, in August 1914 Charles enlisted in the London Regiment and fought in France before being commissioned in the Royal Flying Corps on 2 August 1917. He qualified as a pilot in October, helped to defend London against zeppelins and in early 1918 returned to France where he flew bombers. In April Eaton was promoted flying officer in the Royal Air Force. Shot down on 29 June near the Nieppe Forest, he became a prisoner of war at Holzminden, Germany. After his first escape he was recaptured, court-martialled and held in solitary confinement; his second escape was successful and he rejoined his unit. On 11 January 1919 he married Beatrice Rose Elizabeth Godfrey at St Thomas's parish church, Shepherds Bush, London.

Serving with No.1 Squadron, in 1919 Eaton flew politicians between London and Paris for the peace conference at Versailles. In December he moved to India where he was involved in aerial surveying. Leaving the R.A.F. on 23 July 1920, he joined the Indian forestry service. He came to Australia in 1923 and was employed as a forester in Queensland. On 14 August 1925 he was appointed flying officer in the Royal Australian Air Force and posted to No.1 Flying Training School at Point Cook, Victoria. Tall and lean, with an easy smile, Eaton was nicknamed 'Moth' partly because of his association with the R.A.A.F.'s primary trainer, the D.H.60 Moth. He was promoted flight lieutenant in February 1928.

In April 1929 Eaton led the R.A.A.F.'s search for a civilian plane, *Kookaburra*, missing in Central Australia. When the aircraft was found in the Tanami Desert, he headed a ground party which made an arduous journey to locate and bury the remains of the two-man crew. For this work he was awarded the Air Force Cross (1931). In August 1929 he was posted as director of manning at R.A.A.F. Headquarters, Melbourne. Next month he took leave to compete in the Sydney to Perth air race. Regarded as the air force's outstanding cross-country pilot, he had charge of two more missions to the Northern Territory (November 1930 and January 1931) which searched for downed aviators.

Returning to Point Cook in January 1931, Eaton transferred in December to No.1 Aircraft Depot, Laverton: he performed flying and administrative duties, and rose to squadron leader (1936). In May 1937 he took command of No.21 Squadron of the Citizen Air Force and immediately participated in another search in Central Australia. No.12 Squadron was formed at Laverton in February 1939, with Eaton as commanding officer. He was promoted wing commander next month and in July-August moved his unit to Darwin. On 1 September 1940 he was promoted temporary group captain.

As local air commander, he was a member of the Darwin defence co-ordination committee, along with his naval and army counterparts. His relations with the senior naval officer, Captain E. P. Thomas, were less than cordial, and Eaton also alienated unionists by placing his airmen on the docks to unload stores. As an apparent outcome, he was transferred in October 1941 to command No.2 Service Flying Training School at Wagga Wagga, New South Wales. Despite the circumstances of his departure from Darwin, he was appointed O.B.E. in 1942 for his 'marked success' there, and for his 'example',

'untiring energy', 'cheerful outlook and tact in handling men'.

Posted to Ascot Vale, Victoria, in April 1942, Eaton commanded No.1 Engineering School. One year later he was sent to Townsville, Queensland, to form No.72 Wing, a formation he took to Merauke, Netherlands New Guinea. His command was subordinate to area combined headquarters, Townsville, and he was to write that 'the problems of Merauki were not understood from there . . . difficulties arose, mountains were made out of molehills' and, after 'one or two fairly cryptic signals', he was posted in July as commanding officer of No.2 Bombing and Gunnery School, Port Pirie, South Australia.

In November 1943 Eaton accepted his 'finest appointment'. At Batchelor, Northern Territory, he commanded No.79 Wing, consisting of four squadrons—two of Beauforts, one of Beaufighters and one of Mitchells operated by the Dutch. His aircraft attacked targets in the Netherlands East Indies. In 1944 he was mentioned in dispatches and next year the Dutch awarded him the cross of a commander of the Order of Oranje-Nassau.

Having spent eleven months as air officer commanding, Southern Area, Melbourne, Eaton retired from the R.A.A.F. in December 1945. Next month he was appointed Australian consul at Dili, Portuguese Timor; he commenced duty in April 1946 and moved to Batavia (Jakarta) in August 1947. He was consul-general and Australian representative on the United Nations Security Council's consular commission during much of the period when the Dutch attempted to reimpose colonial rule on Indonesia. Eaton clashed with Dutch administrators who subsequently complained of his 'impropriety', but the allegation was firmly rejected in Canberra. Following the transfer of sovereignty to the Republic of the United States of Indonesia in December 1949, he became first secretary and chargé d'affaires.

Back in Australia, Eaton worked (1950-51) in the Department of External Affairs, Canberra; he then farmed at Metung, Victoria; he later shifted to Frankston and set up as a company promoter. Survived by his wife and two sons, he died on 12 November 1979 at Frankston and was cremated. His daughter Aileen, who had served (1944-57) as a nurse in the R.A.A.F., predeceased him.

E. Coote, *Hell's Airport* (Syd, 1934); G. Odgers, *Air War Against Japan 1943-1945* (Canb, 1957); D. Gillison, *Royal Air Force 1939-1942* (Canb, 1962); M. George, *Australia and the Indonesian Revolution* (Melb, 1980); D. Smith and P. Davis, *Kookaburra* (Syd, 1980); W. H. Brook, *Demon to Vampire* (Melb, 1986); A. Powell, *The Shadow's Edge* (Melb, 1988); C. D. Coulthard-Clark, *The Third Brother* (Syd, 1991); *Age* (Melb), 14, 15 Nov 1979; *Argus*,

11 Mar 1931, 26 Jan 1946; private papers (held by Mr C. S. Eaton, Perth).

C. D. COULTHARD-CLARK

ECUYER, JEAN CLAUDE (1932-1970), ski instructor, was born on 11 January 1932 at Lausanne, Switzerland, second child of Emile Henri Ecuyer, railway supervisor, and his wife Anna, née Haller. Jean grew up in the alpine village of Chernex where he was known as 'Cui Cui' (pronounced 'Qui Qui'). Educated at the local school and at Montreux, from the age of 16 he trained as a mechanic at the École des Métiers, Lausanne, then worked for Swissair at Geneva airport.

Like many people raised in the alpine region of Switzerland, Ecuyer loved skiing. He was 'Champion Romand Junior' in 1949 and joined the Swiss National Ski Team next year. Hoping to train as a pilot, he travelled to Australia in 1954. After working for the Snowy Mountains Hydro-electric Authority, he returned to Switzerland to obtain a ski-instructor's licence. He arrived permanently in New South Wales on 22 March 1956 and stayed at Snow Revellers Lodge and the Cooma Ski Club, Perisher Valley, instructing, doing odd jobs and racing for the clubs.

Through his entrepreneurial spirit, love of life and much hard work, Ecuyer developed several enterprises. With Jake Zweifel and Eric Mawson, he set up camp under a tarpaulin between two rocks and used second-hand materials from the authority's old depot at Island Bend to build Perisher View Motel (opened July 1960). A group of freelance instructors, who believed that a more professional approach to skiing should be taken, chose him as the first head of the Sun Deck (later Perisher) Ski School. He later joined the Dowling family in building a second lodge, Chalet Chez Jean, named after him.

Tall and of medium build, with an olive complexion and dark brown hair, Ecuyer retained his strong French accent and was proud of his Swiss-French heritage. He was an accomplished guitarist, could yodel and sing well, and was popular socially. Fly-fishing became his much-loved summer sport. His friend, the ski-lodge proprietor Tony Sponar, described him 'as a legend, a rare mountain specimen, now almost extinct'. In July 1960 Ecuyer appeared on the cover of the *Australian Women's Weekly*. He was naturalized on 18 October 1961. Two days earlier he had married Jennifer Dayrell Canning McCreadie at St Swithin's Anglican Church, Pymble; they were to be divorced in 1965. He married a 25-year-old secretary Elma (Ellie) Joan Bunt on 22 March 1969 with Methodist forms at the Wayside Chapel, Potts Point. Jean built for her one of the early over-snow transport-

ers, the 'Pink Panther', which was a familiar sight in Perisher Valley.

Having recently returned from Switzerland, on 22 January 1970 Ecuyer went to catch trout (for the visit of his parents-in-law) in the Snowy River below Guthega dam. That day water was suddenly released into the river and he died from the 'effects of immersion as a consequence of head injuries accidentally received'. Survived by his wife and the daughter of his first marriage, he was cremated with Anglican rites. Some of his ashes were placed under a tree outside Perisher View Motel and the remainder were sent to his sister Yvette in Switzerland.

Aust Women's Weekly, 20 July 1960; *Ski Australia*, 2, no 1, Apr-May 1970, p 12; information from Mr M. Genasci, Vevey, Switzerland, Ms G. Pinkas, Farrer, Mrs J. Dowling, Curtin, and Mr F. Michel, Hughes, Canb, Messrs B. Hasligten, Cooma, T. Sponar, Jindabyne, and Mrs S. Litchfield, Nimmitabel, NSW, Mr L. Harrison, Terry Hills, Syd, and Mrs E. Saw, Sunshine Beach, Qld.

PETER R. KOBOLD

EDDY, CECIL ERNEST (1900-1956), radiological physicist, was born on 21 June 1900 at Albury, New South Wales, son of native-born parents Alfred Eddy, a primary schoolteacher, and his wife Samuelina, née Evans. The family moved several times in Cecil's childhood as Alfred was transferred from one Victorian country school to another. Cecil boarded at Colac and attended high school there before joining the Victorian Education Department in 1918 as a junior teacher.

After a year at Wangaratta High School, Eddy entered the University of Melbourne (B.Sc., Dip.Ed., 1923). Instead of returning to the classroom, he was granted leave in 1923 to undertake research on X-ray emission spectra for his M.Sc. (1925) under T. H. Laby [q.v.9]. Eddy spent 1924-25 investigating the spectra of several rare earth-elements. Although his undergraduate degree had been relatively undistinguished, he had been marked out by Laby for a career in research, and he eventually resigned from the Education Department and paid out his bond.

Eddy spent 1926 as senior science master at Geelong College. Appointed research physicist at the university next year, he investigated the possibility of doing chemical analyses by X-ray emission spectroscopy; he then obtained a Rockefeller Foundation fellowship and leave to work under Sir Ernest (Baron) Rutherford at the Cavendish Laboratory, Cambridge.

At the registrar's office, Collins Street, Melbourne, on 19 August 1927 Eddy married Letitia Isabella Reid who later joined him in

England. He matriculated as a research student of Trinity College, Cambridge, implying an intention to do a Ph.D., but he did not enjoy Cambridge and stayed only one year before returning to his earlier project in Melbourne. Several publications followed in which he and Laby announced promising results for the X-ray method in detecting minute quantities of impurities in metals. For this (now classical) work Eddy was awarded a D.Sc. in 1930 and shared the David Syme [q.v.6] research prize in 1931.

Eddy's knowledge of X-rays qualified him to advise those using them for medical purposes, and also to judge the research of his peers. In the 1930s his annual review of the latest developments in X-ray physics became an eagerly awaited feature of the Australian Cancer Conference. When he published damning criticism in 1935 of the X-ray techniques pivotal to the research programme of the University of Sydney's cancer research committee, his opinion carried weight.

In that year the Commonwealth Radium Laboratory, a small unit housed at the University of Melbourne, was given new responsibilities in relation to X-rays and renamed the Commonwealth X-ray and Radium Laboratory. On 8 August Eddy was appointed physicist-in-charge (director), a position he was to retain until his death. The laboratory continued to house the Commonwealth's stock of radium and to prepare from it radon applicators for the treatment of cancer. It was additionally charged with establishing a system of national standards for radiation dosimetry, with carrying out research on all physical aspects of radiotherapeutics (including questions of safety), and with advising cancer-treatment centres on these matters. Eddy was almost at once transformed into a full-time science administrator, responsible, in effect, for overseeing the provision of medical-physical services in hospitals throughout Australia. He travelled widely, advising and giving lectures that were renowned for their 'lucid and critical style'.

World War II brought further demands, especially in relation to the use of radiographic techniques for quality control of munitions, and of chest X-rays to screen members of the armed services and munitions workers for tuberculosis. Eddy also advised the armed forces on X-rays and medical X-ray equipment. When chest X-ray surveys were initiated *en masse* after the war, his laboratory drew up specifications for the equipment. The laboratory also became the sole authority for the procurement and distribution of radioisotopes in Australia.

Because of the laboratory's responsibilities for dosimetry standards, Eddy was a government nominee on the council of the National Association of Testing Authorities from its formation in 1946. Chairman of the National Health and Medical Research Council's standing committee on X-rays, he was a member of its standing committee on industrial hygiene and chaired (from 1947) its standing committee on radioactive isotopes. He represented Australia at several international conferences on radiation physics and in 1956 was elected chairman of the United Nations scientific committee on the effects of atomic radiation.

In the absence of a local professional organization for physicists, Eddy had joined the (British) Institute of Physics as a fellow in 1931 and was president of its Australian branch in 1948-49. He presided over section A at the congress of the Australian and New Zealand Association for the Advancement of Science, held in Hobart in 1949. The (British) Society of Radiographers made him an honorary member (1945) and he was a founding fellow (1950) of the Australasian Institute of Radiography. His medical colleagues elected him an honorary member (1950) and honorary fellow (1953) of the College of Radiologists (Australia and New Zealand), and an honorary member (1952) of the Faculty of Radiologists, London.

A large man, widely liked and trusted, Eddy was good company and enjoyed a beer with friends. From 1954 he was president of Kingswood Golf Club, Melbourne. He and his wife were staunch supporters of the Yooralla Society of Victoria. As a member of the Federal government's safety committee for atomic weapons tests, in mid-June 1956 he observed tests conducted at the Monte Bello Islands, off Western Australia. While there he fell ill. He died of lobar pneumonia with myocarditis and septicaemia on 27 June 1956 at Subiaco, Perth, and was cremated; his wife and two sons survived him.

J. F. Richardson, *The Australian Radiation Laboratory* (Canb, 1981); R. W. Home, *Physics in Australia to 1945* (Melb, 1990); *Aust J of Science*, Oct 1956, p 63; *British J of Radiology*, 29, 1956, p 535; *Radiographer*, 6, no 4, July 1958, p 6, 11, no 2, June 1964, p 6; H. Hamersley, Radiation Science and Australian Medicine, 1896-1940 (M.A. thesis, Univ Melb, 1984); Cwlth Dept of Health, Eddy staff file, A 1928/1, item 1036/1 (AA, ACT); MP 81/1 (AA, Vic).

R. W. HOME

EDDY, WILLIAM HENRY CHARLES (1913-1973), educationist, was born on 15 September 1913 at Maryborough, Queensland, son of native-born parents William Eddy, blacksmith, and his wife Dorothy, née Bower. Harry moved with his family to Newcastle when he was 6 and remained proud of being a Novocastrian. Educated at Newcastle (Boys') High School, he entered Moore Theological

College and the University of Sydney (B.A., 1934; M.A., 1936) with the intention of becoming a priest of the Church of England. While studying philosophy—'to discover proofs of God's existence'—he was deeply influenced by Professor John Anderson [q.v.7]. After an intense personal struggle, Eddy abandoned his religious vocation and adopted Anderson's atheistic philosophy. Graduating during the Depression with first-class honours in philosophy, he found work tutoring in the Newcastle district.

In 1936 Eddy took up a scholarship at Teachers' College, Sydney (Dip.Ed., 1938). At the district registrar's office, North Sydney, on 14 May 1938 he married Madge Leonie Chick, a fellow schoolteacher. Eddy taught at high schools at Liverpool and Randwick until 1945 when he was appointed senior staff tutor of the university's Department of Tutorial Classes at Newcastle. His dual role of adult education teacher and council-member of the Workers' Educational Association of New South Wales continued until his death. For ten years Eddy was active in the intellectual and cultural life of the Newcastle district. He reinvigorated the adult education movement, helped to ensure some measure of financial independence for the W.E.A., founded the Newcastle branch of the Australasian Association of Psychology and Philosophy (later State president), worked for the establishment of the city's cultural centre and headed a campaign for an autonomous university of Newcastle.

Elected president of the W.E.A. in 1954, Eddy moved to Sydney next year as senior lecturer in philosophy with the Department of Tutorial Classes at the University of Sydney. He was co-founder and first president of the Sydney Philosophy Club, and a member of the editorial committee of the *Current Affairs Bulletin* for twenty years. A staunch anticommunist, he studied Marxist theory and practice in order to refute them, and wrote several lengthy articles on the 1956 Hungarian uprising.

While Eddy published many articles on adult education, current affairs and politics, his major and most widely known work, *Orr* (1961), was a long and detailed analysis of Sydney Sparkes Orr's [q.v.] dismissal from the chair of philosophy at the University of Tasmania. Eddy's involvement stemmed from his belief that Orr's sacking posed a threat to the freedom of academic institutions. He soon became personally acquainted with Orr who, in 1961, took refuge with Eddy in his family home at Henley. The book, written in close collaboration with Orr, made the issue a *cause célèbre.* Angus (Lord) Maude, editor of the *Sydney Morning Herald,* commented: 'Mr Eddy says that he has tried hard to set down facts objectively and dispassionately. It must be said that he has not succeeded'. Yet Eddy's version became commonly accepted. Thirty-two years were to pass before a revisionist account of the case was published.

Eddy was content to remain an orthodox Andersonian. A scholar and activist, he had a temperament which required a system of beliefs that satisfied his intellect and enabled him to work for the improvement of society. Throughout his career at the university he fought to preserve classical liberal studies as the focus of adult education. He had an excellent reputation as a tutor and devised methods for encouraging students to do written work. Eddy was a dominating figure in adult education for almost three decades. His Andersonian ideas on the character and requirements of liberal education had a profound influence on the W.E.A. which provided the organizational structure through which he channelled his missionary zeal for liberal democracy.

Physically a big man, with a forceful mind and personality to match, Eddy made an impact on all who met him. Although his vigorous intellectual style antagonized many, his friends found him warm, courteous and loyal, with a sense of fun. Driven by a concept of duty, he worked excessively and rarely took holidays. His main form of relaxation was canoeing on the Parramatta River near his home. Survived by his wife, son and two daughters, he died of hypertensive cardiovascular disease on 9 December 1973 and was cremated with Anglican rites.

O. Harries (ed), *Liberty and Politics* (Syd, 1976); C. Pybus, *Gross Moral Turpitude* (Melb, 1993); *Quadrant,* Feb 1974, p 72; *WEA News,* Mar 1974, p 1; *Newcastle Morning Herald,* 24 Apr 1950, 16 July 1954; *SMH,* 19 May 1961; C. F. Bentley and W. H. C. Eddy, International Biography on Adult Education (ts held by Mrs M. Eddy, Henley, Syd, who also holds priv print obituaries); information from Miss B. Anderson, Henley, Syd.

LORRAINE BARLOW

EDGAR, CEDRIC RUPERT VAUGHAN (1901-1967), soldier and bank manager, was born on 9 July 1901 at Wedderburn, Victoria, son of native-born parents Thomas George Edgar, farm-manager, and his second wife Bessie, née Trotman. In 1918 Cedric joined the Commonwealth Bank of Australia in Melbourne. Having served in the senior cadets, he enlisted in the Australian Field Artillery, Militia, and was commissioned on 10 April 1922. Over the next seventeen years he held regimental and staff posts—in the infantry as well as the artillery—and rose to major. Meanwhile, pursuing his career with the bank, he worked at Hamilton (1924), Tamworth, New South Wales (1928), and in Sydney (1934). At the Presbyterian Church, St Kilda, Melbourne, on 6 September 1930 he married a saleswoman Ruby Pearl Haworth.

On 13 October 1939 Edgar was appointed major in the Australian Imperial Force and posted to the 2nd/2nd Battalion. The unit sailed for the Middle East in January 1940 and trained in Palestine. As officer commanding the Headquarter Company, Edgar acted firmly to quell a threatened strike by the battalion's cooks. He was second-in-command in January 1941 when the 2nd/2nd took part in successful attacks on Bardia and Tobruk, Libya. In March the battalion was sent to Greece. After the delaying action at Piniós Gorge on 18 April, next morning Edgar established a 'straggler post' south of Lamia, collected over three hundred men from the 2nd/2nd and escorted them to the port of Kalámai (Kalamáta) whence they sailed for Egypt.

Returning to Palestine, from June he reformed the depleted 2nd/1st Battalion. By October the 2nd/2nd was helping to fortify Qatana, Syria; Edgar was promoted lieutenant colonel and assumed command on 16 November. Leaving the Middle East in February 1942, he and his men spent nearly four months in Ceylon (Sri Lanka) preparing defences against a possible Japanese landing; the battalion eventually reached Australia in August.

In September the 2nd/2nd embarked for Port Moresby and in the following month fought at Templeton's Crossing and Eora Creek. At Oivi, in November, Edgar pioneered the tactic of immediate company (as opposed to platoon) deployment on contact with the enemy. Suffering from malaria, he was hospitalized on 11 November. By the time he resumed the leadership in December, the battalion had been relieved on the Sanananda Track and he returned to Australia in January 1943. For his part in the Papuan campaign he was awarded the Distinguished Service Order.

Promoted temporary brigadier on 16 June 1943, he assumed command that month of the 4th (Militia) Brigade at Milne Bay, Papua. The brigade moved to New Guinea and in December advanced north from Finschhafen, destroying the Japanese rearguard and capturing Fortification Point. After leave in Australia, in January 1945 the 4th was sent to New Britain where it was involved in operations from April to August. In December Edgar took over the 13th Brigade. Back home in January 1946, he transferred to the Reserve of Officers on 3 July as honorary brigadier. He was twice mentioned in dispatches, and appointed C.B.E. in 1947.

'Boss' Edgar was 5 ft 11 ins (180 cm) tall, with a fair complexion, blue eyes, brown hair,

a commanding presence and a reputation for his colourful language. His military knowledge, experience, understanding of the enemy, appreciation of terrain, and balanced judgement were noteworthy. He planned in detail and successfully undertook aggressive and innovative operations. 'Magnificently loyal', calm and cheerful, he was highly regarded by his officers and men.

On 6 August 1946 Edgar had resumed his civilian career as the bank's relieving manager in Sydney; he was appointed manager at Yass (1948), Sale, Victoria (1950), and Summer Hill, Sydney (1957); he retired on 3 January 1964. Survived by his wife and two daughters, he died of myocardial infarction on 2 September 1967 at the Repatriation General Hospital, Concord, and was cremated with Anglican rites. Lieutenant General Hector Geoffrey Edgar (1903-1978) was his brother.

A. J. Marshall (ed), *Nulli Secundus Log* (Syd, 1946); G. Long, *Greece, Crete and Syria* (Canb, 1953); D. McCarthy, *South-West Pacific Area—First Year* (Canb, 1959); D. Dexter, *The New Guinea Offensives* (Canb, 1961); S. Wick, *Purple Over Green* (Syd, 1977); E. C. Givney (ed), *The First At War* (Syd, 1987); *SMH*, 4 Sept 1967; War diaries, 2nd/1st *and* 2nd/2nd Aust Infantry Battalions, AIF, and Headquarters 4th *and* 13th Aust Infantry Brigades (AWM); Cwlth Bank of Aust (Syd) records; information from Major General Sir Ivan Dougherty, Cronulla, Syd, and Brigadier Sir Frederick Chilton, Clareville Beach, NSW.   R. SUTTON

EDGEWORTH DAVID, CAROLINE MARTHA; *see* DAVID, CAROLINE MARTHA

EDGLEY, ERIC (1899-1967), theatre performer and impresario, was born on 1 August 1899 at Deritend, Warwickshire, England, son of Richard White, musician, and his wife Lizzie, née Warton, a dancer. Because the family was constantly on the move, Eric's education was spasmodic. At 9 he appeared with his younger brother Clement Edward as a tap-dancer in *The Eight Lancashire Lads*. Following the outbreak of World War I the family's group broke up. Eric and Clem changed their stage-names to 'Edgley' and 'Dawe' (allegedly the names of London streets), developed a song-and-dance routine and went on the vaudeville circuit. They cleaned theatres between engagements.

In 1920 they came to Melbourne to perform at the King's Theatre in a twenty-week pantomime season of *Sinbad the Sailor* for J. & N. Tait [qq.v.12]. They subsequently toured Australasia for J. C. Williamson [q.v.6] Ltd in shows which included *Robinson Crusoe*, *Love Lies* and *So This Is Love*. On 22 July 1925 Eric married an actress Phyllis Edith Amery with Anglican rites at Christ Church Cathedral, Newcastle, New South Wales; she was to die in childbirth on 8 January 1930. Forming their own troupe, 'The Midnight Frolics', Edgley and Dawe again toured Australasia in 1930-35. In September 1935 they took fourteen Australians to England in a revue, *Seeing the World*. Eric married a dancer Edna Theresa Luscombe on 16 February 1940 at the register office, Hampstead, London.

After a three-month engagement at Cape Town, South Africa, the three performers arrived in Australia in August. In December they appeared in the pantomime, *The Sleeping Beauty*, for Williamson's and Eric directed the revue, *Thumbs Up*. For the next three years they toured Australia on the Tivoli and Fuller [qq.v.8] circuits. Eric and Clem also starred for two years in 'Keep It Clean', a weekly revue sponsored by Gouge Dry Cleaning Co. on 3DB radio station, Melbourne. In 1948 they took 'The Midnight Frolics' to the Theatre Royal, Hobart, where it played for two years.

Edgley and Dawe moved to Perth in 1951 to manage His Majesty's Theatre. They staged *Kiss Me Kate* and *Oklahoma*, presented their own and other variety shows, and brought opera, ballet, drama and musical comedy to Perth. In March 1954 they bought a seven-year lease of the theatre. Clem's death in 1955 obliged Eric to concentrate on management, but the advent of television caused a slump in theatre attendances. Visiting the Soviet Union at the height of the Cold War, Edgley eventually succeeded in arranging Australasian tours between 1962 and 1966 by the Bolshoi Ballet, the Georgian State Dance Company and stars of the Moscow State Variety Theatre. Each venture was elaborate, expensive, extremely risky, but very successful.

An avid cricket enthusiast, and a warm, friendly and generous man, Edgley encouraged and subsidized amateur groups and struggling theatre companies. Reflecting on the theatrical profession in 1958, he had remarked: 'You are born into it; you die in it. One life in show business is not enough'. He died of cancer on 3 February 1967 at Subiaco and was buried with Anglican rites in Karrakatta cemetery; his wife and their daughter and son Michael (who carried on the entrepreneurial business) survived him, as did the son of his first marriage. His estate was sworn for probate at $111 560.

J. West, *Theatre in Australia* (Syd, 1978); S. Mitchell, *The Matriarchs* (Melb, 1987); Aust National Airlines, *Aust Way*, Nov 1991; *Sunday Mail* (Adel), 26 June 1954; *West Australian*, 4, 6 Feb, 13 Oct 1967; programmes and news-cuttings (His Majesty's Theatre Archives, Perth); oral history project (TRC 1893/1, NL); information from Mrs E. Edgley, Sth Yarra, Melb, and Ms C. Edgley, Claremont, Perth.   TERRY CRAIG

EDMAN, PEHR VICTOR (1916-1977), biochemist and medical researcher, was born on 14 April 1916 in Stockholm, Sweden, son of Victor Pontus Edman, judge, and his wife Alba Edvina Fredrika, née Nordström. In 1935 Pehr entered the Karolinska Institute (M.B., 1938; Med.Lic., M.D., 1946) to study medicine. Interested in research, he joined the laboratory of Professor Erik Jorpes, spent a year at the Rockefeller Institute, Princeton, United States of America, and in 1947 accepted an associate-professorship at the University of Lund, Sweden. On 16 August 1944 at Kungsholm he had married Siri Barbro Theresia Bergström; they had a son and daughter, separated in 1957 and were later divorced.

In 1957 Edman came to Melbourne as the first John Holt [q.v.9 Michael Holt] director of research at St Vincent's School of Medical Research, an institution specializing in biochemistry. He remained there for fifteen years. At the office of the government statist, Melbourne, on 5 April 1968 he married his colleague Agnes Helena Cecilia Leux Henschen, a doctor and biochemist, who had also studied at the Karolinska Institute (M.B., 1954; Med.Lic., 1958; M.D., 1964). Associate-professor in medical chemistry at the Karolinska in 1965, she had been invited to join the research team at St Vincent's where she worked on unravelling the chemical structure of the blood protein fibrinogen. She was also an accomplished violinist.

A pioneer and major figure in the field of protein chemistry, in the mid-1940s Edman had become interested in determining the detailed structure of proteins and providing a structural explanation of their varied biological activities. Swedish physical chemists had only recently discovered that different proteins had specific molecular sizes and probably individual chemical structures. For his doctorate, Edman had isolated (from blood) and analysed the small protein hormone angiotensin which regulates blood pressure, but he realized that—as all proteins are made up of combinations of only eighteen amino acid 'building blocks'—it was essential to identify the order in which the amino acids were joined.

Edman conceived the idea of a series of three reactions based on the coupling of the organic reagent phenylisothiocyanate (PITC) with a purified protein. This reaction series would enable him to analyse any protein sequentially, amino acid by amino acid, and thus preserve the linear structural information necessary to interpret biological activity. At the University of Lund he had devised reaction conditions which were suitable for all amino acids and most classes of proteins, and which minimized side reactions. The method for protein structural determination was named the 'Edman degradation' by the Danish biochemist Kai Linderstrøm-Lang. Assisted by G. S. Begg, in 1961 Edman designed and built an automated instrument called a 'protein sequenator' to determine the structure of proteins by analysing the sequence of amino acids. The reaction scheme is still widely used.

Shy and somewhat aloof, with a single-mindedness that could look like stubbornness, Edman was not involved in scientific or academic politics in Australia; nor did he build up a large research group, although overseas scientists frequently visited his laboratory to learn his techniques. Close friends and colleagues appreciated his integrity, his humanism, his cultural interests, especially music, and his hospitality.

In 1965 Edman was granted Australian citizenship. Three years later he was elected a fellow of the Australian Academy of Science and awarded the Britannica Australia science prize. He won the gold medal of the Swedish Society of Physicians and Surgeons in 1971. Next year he moved to Germany, having been appointed professor at the Max Planck Institute for Biochemistry at Martinsreid. In 1974 be became a fellow of the Royal Society, London. He died of a cerebral tumour on 19 March 1977 in Munich; his wife and their son and daughter survived him, as did the children of his first marriage.

B. Egan, *Ways of a Hospital* (Syd, 1993); St Vincent's School of Medical Research, Melb, *St Vincent's Researcher*, Apr, June 1971; *MJA*, 14 Jan 1978; *Biog Memoirs of Fellows of Roy Soc* (Lond), 25, 1979, p 241; *Hist Records of Aust Science*, 8, no 2, June 1990, p 85; *Age* (Melb), 18 May 1957, 2 July, 3 Oct 1970, 13 Nov 1971, 5 Apr 1977; *Herald* (Melb), 15 June 1963, 1 Nov 1969.

F. J. MORGAN

EDMONDS, CATHERINE BEATRICE (1900-1960), barmaid, was born on 11 November 1900 at Penrith, New South Wales, second daughter and fifth of eleven children of Hugh Edmonds, a labourer from Ireland, and his Scottish-born wife Maggie Elizabeth, née Helme (d.1945). Raised in poverty, Cathy received her elementary schooling locally and at Glenbrook where Hugh took a job as a railway fettler. His family camped in tents and reputedly suffered his drunkenness, temper and brutality. Catherine fled to Sydney and found work as a shop assistant. On 25 January 1919 at St Stephen's Anglican Church, Newtown, she married 23-year old Frederick George Holloway, a clerk who became a commercial traveller. His widowed mother and his sister allowed them to share their home at Tupper Street, Marrickville. Catherine bore him a son (1920) and a daughter (1923) before obtaining a divorce on 20 December 1929.

From 1924 she was employed as a barmaid in tough, working-class pubs in Sydney, and in time handled starting-price betting on the side. She is alleged to have had an illegitimate daughter by a man who gave her the nickname 'Caddie', after 'the sleek body and class of his Cadillac' motorcar. In 1943, while at Stanmore and calling herself 'Serrenne', she met Harry Joseph Elliott, a labourer and ganger, with whom she formed a de facto relationship. He claimed to be her third 'husband' in a month. They lived at Glebe before moving to Hazelbrook (about 1944) and to Regentville (by 1955). She successively styled her surname as Elliott, Mackay-Elliott and Elliott-Mackay (by deed poll). Although Harry described his wife as being 'affectionate', he later callously told a reporter that she weighed 14 stone (89 kg) and was 'a born liar, unfaithful, and at times wicked'.

In March 1945 'Caddie' was hired as a charwoman by two authors, Dymphna Cusack and Florence James, who occupied a cottage in the Blue Mountains. Fascinated by her account of how, as a lone mother, she had raised her children through the worst years of the Depression, they encouraged her to write. She taught herself to type and by 1952 had finished the seventh draft of an autobiography. Set in the years 1924-39, edited and introduced by Cusack, and entitled *Caddie, A Sydney Barmaid*, the book was released by Constable & Co. Ltd in London in May 1953 to glowing reviews. By September it had been reprinted three times, although, at this stage, it was not a best seller. Catherine wrote under a pseudonym and shrank from publicity. Plump and round faced, she had narrow, grey-blue eyes, 'wavy, light brown hair streaked with grey', and deeply-graven lines at the corners of her mouth. She died of a coronary occlusion on 16 April 1960 at her Regentville home and was buried in Penrith cemetery; her son and daughter survived her.

To some degree, *Caddie* embellished the truth and fabricated a legend. Cusack regarded its factual discrepancies as relatively unimportant: she saw her late protégé as an archetypal battler, a woman imbued with resilience and humanity 'who never asked for pity'. Eventually published in Australia in 1966, the book was reprinted in 1975 and 1976 (seven times). That year *Caddie* was adapted as a feature film. Produced by Anthony Buckley and supported by, among other organizations, the International Women's Year Secretariat, it starred the ethereal Helen Morse in the title role. In less than a year it won international acclaim and grossed over $2 million.

Caddie, A Sydney Barmaid, D. Cusack introd (Melb, 1977); A. Pike and R. Cooper, *Australian Film, 1900-1977* (Melb, 1980); *Labour Hist*, no 61, Nov 1991, p 3; *Nepean Times*, 21 Apr 1960; *Herald* (Melb), 17 Feb 1976; *West Australian*, 9 July 1976; *Sun* (Syd), 4 Aug 1976.   JOHN RITCHIE

EDMONDSON, JOHN HURST (1914-1941), soldier, was born on 8 October 1914 at Wagga Wagga, New South Wales, only child of native-born parents Joseph William Edmondson, farmer, and his wife Maude Elizabeth, née Hurst. The family moved to a farm near Liverpool when Jack was a child. Educated at Hurlstone Agricultural High School, he worked with his father and became a champion rifle-shooter. He was a council-member of the Liverpool Agricultural Society and acted as a steward at its shows. Having served (from March 1939) in the 4th Battalion, Militia, he enlisted in the Australian Imperial Force on 20 May 1940 and was posted to the 2nd/17th Battalion. Later that month he was promoted acting corporal (substantive in November). Well built and about 5 ft 9 ins (175 cm) tall, Edmondson settled easily into army life and was known as a quiet but efficient soldier.

His battalion embarked for the Middle East in October and trained in Palestine. In March 1941 the 2nd/17th moved with other components of the 9th Division to Libya and reached Marsa Brega before an Axis counterattack forced them to retreat to Tobruk. The siege of the fortress began on 11 April. Two days later the Germans probed the perimeter, targeting a section of the line west of the El Adem Road near Post R33. This strong-point was garrisoned by the 2nd/17th's No.16 Platoon in which Edmondson was a section leader. The enemy intended to clear the post as a bridgehead for an armoured assault on Tobruk.

Under cover of darkness thirty Germans infiltrated the barbed wire defences, bringing machine-guns, mortars and two light fieldguns. Lieutenant Austin Mackell, commanding No.16 Platoon, led Edmondson's five-man section in an attempt to repel the intruders. Armed with rifles, fixed bayonets and grenades, the party of seven tried to outflank the Germans, but were spotted by the enemy who turned their machine-guns on them. Unknown to his mates, Edmondson was severely wounded in the neck and stomach. Covering fire from R33 ceased at the pre-arranged time of 11.45 p.m. and Mackell ordered his men to charge. Despite his wounds, Edmondson accounted for several enemy soldiers and saved Mackell's life. When the remaining Germans fled, the Australians returned to their lines. Although Edmondson was treated for his wounds, he died before dawn on 14 April 1941. The Germans' armoured attack that morning was thwarted, partly due to the earlier disruption of their plans. Edmondson was buried in Tobruk war cemetery. He had not married.

His Victoria Cross, gazetted on 4 July, was the first awarded to a member of Australia's armed forces in World War II. In April 1960 Mrs Edmondson gave her son's medals to the Australian War Memorial, Canberra, where they are displayed alongside his portrait (1958) by Joshua Smith. At Liverpool a public clock commemorates Edmondson, as do the clubrooms used by the sub-branch of the Returned Services League of Australia.

W. L. Havard (comp), *Souvenir . . . to commemorate the opening of the . . . John Edmondson, V.C., Memorial Club Rooms* (Syd, 1961); L. Wigmore (ed), *They Dared Mightily* (Canb, 1963); B. Maughan, *Tobruk and El Alamein* (Canb, 1966); *"What We Have—We Hold!"* (Syd, 1990?); AWM records.   IAN GRANT

EDMUNDS, ROSINA (ROSETTE) MARY (1900-1956), architect and town planner, was born on 31 May 1900 at Strathfield, Sydney, second of six children of native-born parents Walter Edmunds [q.v.8], barrister, and his wife Monica Victoria May, née McGrath. Educated at the Dominican Convent School, Strathfield, and the University of Sydney (B.A., 1921; B.Arch., 1924), Rosette—as she then styled herself—began working for the Sydney architect Clement Glancey. She was responsible for drawing plans for numerous churches and schools in Sydney, and in the country districts of New South Wales.

Having designed naval installations in the early years of World War II, in 1944 Edmunds became a field-officer for community activities with the Commonwealth Department of Post-war Reconstruction. In 1946 the Cumberland County Council appointed her as civic survey officer to assist in the preparation of a master plan for Sydney. Her job was 'to study social aspects of the scheme, including the demolition of slum areas'. Believing that 'cities are for the people, not people for the cities', and that slums were the product of 'a wrong sense of human values', she considered that it was indefensible on both moral and economic grounds to compel persons on low incomes to live in conditions which gave them 'no opportunity for maintaining dignity and self-respect'.

In the early 1950s Edmunds designed

extensions to the Catholic presbytery (later Archbishop's House), Parkes, Australian Capital Territory. Through this work she came to love Canberra and moved there in 1952. In addition to her private practice, she acted as a consultant to government architects on planning matters. An associate (1934) and fellow (1950) of the Royal Australian Institute of Architects, she helped to establish its Canberra area committee of which she became president (1956); she also served on the institute's federal board of architectural education. She was an associate (1931) of the Royal Institute of British Architects and a member of the Town and Country Planning Institute of Australia.

Edmunds had published *Architecture: An Introductory Survey* (Sydney, 1938) in which she endeavoured to 'dispel the idea that architecture is merely a mass of academic formulae relating to ornament' and to present it 'in its right relation with the life we lead—as something vital that plays a formative part in everyday life'. While she appreciated the romance of her profession, she also recognized its realities. She contributed articles on the poet Christopher Brennan [q.v.7], and on town and country planning, to the journal, *Twentieth Century*. Her idealism, ability to offer an opinion on a range of subjects, quiet manner and appreciation of the work of others made her 'a sympathetic and stimulating colleague'. She never married. Hypertensive, she died of a coronary occlusion on 23 April 1956 at her Griffith home and was buried in Canberra cemetery with Catholic rites.

Architecture in Aust, 45, no 2, Apr-June 1956, p 69; *SMH*, 28 Jan 1918, 16 Nov 1937, 25 Apr, 1 May 1946; *Canb Times*, 26 Apr 1956.

CAROLINE WEBBER

EDWARDS, AUSTIN BURTON (1909-1960), geologist, was born on 15 August 1909 at Caulfield, Melbourne, third son of William Burton Edwards, public service inspector, and his second wife Mabel, née Mueller, both Australian born. Austin was educated at Caulfield Grammar School where he was dux and captain. At the University of Melbourne (B.Sc., 1930; D.Sc., 1942) he graduated with first-class honours in geology. A scholarship then enabled him to study the geology and petrology of the Healesville and Warburton districts: his account of the work was published in 1932. In that year he won an 1851 Exhibition scholarship to the Royal College of Science, University of London (Ph.D., 1934), where he wrote his thesis on the tertiary volcanic rocks of Victoria.

On 22 April 1935 in the chapel of the Collegiate School of St Peter, Adelaide, Edwards married with Anglican rites Eileen Mary McDonnell, a psychologist. Six months earlier he had joined F. L. Stillwell [q.v.12] in the mineragraphic section of the Council for Scientific and Industrial Research, Melbourne. There Edwards learned the techniques of ore microscopy and mineralogy from Australia's leading expert. When Stillwell retired in 1953, Edwards succeeded him as officer-in-charge of what had become a section of the Commonwealth Scientific and Industrial Research Organization. He was a councillor (1953-60) of the Australasian Institute of Mining and Metallurgy.

A major paper (1936) on the mineragraphy of the iron ores of the Middleback Ranges, South Australia, had reported Edwards's first research for the C.S.I.R. It was followed by other detailed studies, for instance on the iron ores of Yampi Sound, Western Australia, and the copper deposits of Mount Lyell, Tasmania. Few Australian ore deposits escaped his attention. His own contributions to *Geology of Australian Ore Deposits*—the volume he edited for the Fifth Empire Mining and Metallurgical Congress (1953)—no more than hint at the range of his experience.

Like Stillwell, Edwards sought to understand the significance of textural relations between mineral phases in ore deposits, a subject of practical value in the treatment of ores but more particularly important in elucidating the genesis of ore assemblages. *Textures of the Ore Minerals and their Significance* (1947) revealed not only Edwards's mastery of mineragraphy but also his grasp of structural crystallography and experimental phase chemistry. In 1952 he delivered the (W. B.) Clarke [q.v.3] lecture to the Royal Society of New South Wales and in 1960 was awarded its Clarke medal for outstanding work in geology.

Edwards undertook research covering geological inquiries outside mineragraphy and ore deposits. Some, like the detailed study of coal made for the State Electricity Commission of Victoria, had economic interest. Many others simply added to knowledge in fields as diverse as the development of landforms, the nature of meteorites and various aspects of petrology, his first scientific love. He published several useful papers on both sedimentary and metamorphic petrology, but igneous rocks dominated his petrological interest. His numerous contributions on the nature of basalts and basaltic differentiation, in particular, won him an international reputation. He was a fellow of the Mineralogical Society of America, a corresponding fellow of the Edinburgh Geological Society and an honorary member of the Mineralogical Society of India.

A talented teacher, Edwards never allowed himself to be isolated in his research position. In 1941-55 he lectured part time in geology at the University of Melbourne and occasionally offered postgraduate lectures. Although at times impatient with those he thought undeserving of his interest, he supported his staff and they in turn gave him impressive loyalty. Authorship of many of his papers he shared with colleagues. As a student, Edwards had excelled at sport, winning a half-Blue for football at Melbourne and colours for athletics at Imperial College. Latterly, he coached the university third XVIII football team. Among other outside interests, he served on the council of his old school. He travelled widely, in Australia and abroad.

While on a working visit to Europe, Edwards collapsed and died on 8 October 1960 in Rome; he was buried in the Protestant cemetery of that city. His wife, son and three daughters survived him.

Dictionary of Scientific Biography, 17, supp 2 (NY, 1990); A'sian Inst of Mining and Metallurgy, *Procs*, no 196, 1960; *Aust J of Science*, 23, 1961, p 260; *American Mineralogist*, 45, Mar-Apr 1961, p 488 *and* for bibliog; personal information.

                                T. G. VALLANCE*

EDWARDS, WILLIAM JOHN (1891-1967), Anglican clergyman and headmaster, was born on 9 December 1891 at Riverstone, New South Wales, son of native-born parents John Edwards, butcher, and his wife Ida, née Drayton. Educated at Fort Street Model School, Moore Theological College and the University of Sydney (B.A., 1916), William enlisted in the Australian Imperial Force in January 1916, but was discharged in July to become a field secretary for the Young Men's Christian Association of Australia. On 29 April that year he had married Amy Stephenson (d.1963) at St Anne's Church, Ryde.

Embarking for England in October 1916, Edwards served on the Western Front as a Y.M.C.A. representative and was appointed honorary second lieutenant, A.I.F., in May 1918. Next year he gained a certificate from Cambridge University Training College for Schoolmasters and completed his studies at Ridley Hall for the Anglican priesthood. Returning to Sydney, he was made deacon on 14 March 1920 and ordained priest on 21 December. He taught at Trinity Grammar School while a curate (1920-22) at Dulwich Hill and from 1923 was rector of the parish of Bulli.

In 1926 Edwards was appointed headmaster of Monaro Grammar School, Cooma. Three years later he took charge of its successor, relocated as Canberra Grammar School. Overcoming funding difficulties during the Depression and staff shortages in World War II, he saw the school through its formative years, laying a foundation based on sound learning, effort and application, and setting a discipline characterized by firmness, fairness and gentleness. After clashing with Bishop E. H. Burgmann [q.v.13], especially over control of the school, Edwards resigned in 1947. He was a member (1930-47) and acting-chairman (1937) of the council of Canberra University College and a canon (1935-56) of St Saviour's Cathedral, Goulburn.

Edwards had been a delegate to the British Commonwealth Relations Conference, Lapstone, New South Wales (1938), and to the Institute of Pacific Relations Conference, Hot Springs, Virginia, United States of America (1945). He was chief of the United Nations Children's Relief Mission to Greece in 1947-52 and also worked in Italy and Malta in 1951-52. Despite the lack of interest by officials and the opposition of black marketeers, he succeeded in establishing an aid organization. The National and Capodistrian University of Athens awarded him an honorary Ph.D. in 1951. Back in Australia, in 1952-53 he was senior welfare adviser to the Department of External Affairs. As rector (1956-62) of St James's Church, King Street, Sydney, he developed its property to provide a permanent income for the parish.

His face conveyed strength and authority, emphasized by impressive eyebrows, but his gaze was often kindly and compassionate, and betrayed a keen sense of humour. Edwards's Anglicanism was representative, upholding the best of the Church's traditions while combining progressive thought with action for human welfare and dignity. He kindled faith in many, and restored and strengthened it in others. Possessing a clear vision of what was attainable, once his goals were set he gave of himself unstintingly. He died on 24 September 1967 at Bellevue Hill, Sydney, and was cremated; his three daughters and one of his two sons survived him.

P. J. McKeown (ed), *Deo, Ecclesiae, Patriae* (Canb, 1979); *SMH*, 18 Nov 1947, 8 July 1962; information from Dr K. Cable, Randwick, and Mrs J. Pulford, Bellevue Hill, Syd.

                                GEORGE GARNSEY

EGAN, KATHERINE ROSE (1861-1951), charity worker, was born on 4 September 1861 at Walmer, Kent, England, daughter of Thomas Henry Charles Egan, barrack sergeant, and his wife Mary Ann, née Santry. Kate was educated at Catholic schools in France. About 1900 she came to Sydney to join her elder sister Annie Mary (d.1928) who had married John Thomas Toohey [q.v.6]. A keen golfer (with a handicap of ten in 1907), Miss Egan had become an associate member (1902) of Royal Sydney Golf Club and was to be associate president (1926-42); she was also an associate (from 1904) of the Australian Golf Club and secretary (by 1906) of the New South Wales Ladies' Golf Union. In 1912 Egan was an original shareholder in the Queen's Club.

A foundation member (1913) of the New South Wales division of the Australian branch of the British Red Cross Society, Egan served on its executive until her death. In World War I she was a member of the finance, clothing and convalescent homes sub-committees, director of the receiving and packing depot, and a delegate (1914-38 and 1940) to the central council. In 1918 she was appointed M.B.E. She had charge of the Red Cross clothing depot in the 1920s, served on the finance committee in the 1930s and was the Red Cross representative (1933-51) on the council of the New South Wales Bush Nursing Association. An honorary life member of Red Cross from 1934, she was a vice-president (1948-51) of the State division.

Egan's affluence and English background distinguished her from the predominantly working-class, Irish Catholics in Sydney. One of the most influential women in the archdiocese, she and Lady Sheldon led the committee which raised funds for an independent college for Catholic women within the University of Sydney; Egan was an original member of the Sancta Sophia College council from 1929. She received a Papal diploma and 'Benemerenti' medal that year.

Following the death of her friend Mary Barlow [q.v.7] in 1934, Egan was recommended to Archbishop Kelly [q.v.9] to be president of the Catholic Women's Association. She used the association to further projects and supported them with her own money. In 1936 she established the Catholic Women's Club, as well as auxiliaries to work for the blind, the deaf and the sick. Interested in setting up a Catholic mission and facilities for religious instruction in the Aboriginal settlement at La Perouse, she organized members to fund and staff mission work, and gave £1000 for a brick hall at Yarra to which she refused the state schoolmaster access. A subsidy from the association later allowed the Sisters of Our Lady of the Sacred Heart to run a convent school at Yarra. When Archbishop (Cardinal Sir Norman) Gilroy [q.v.] assumed tighter control of Catholic laywomen's affairs, Egan resigned as president of the Catholic Women's Association in 1941, but became a vice-president of its successor, the Legion of Catholic Women.

During World War II, as well as working for the Red Cross as honorary director (1941-48) of branch material supply, Egan was foundation president (1939) of the Catholic United Services Auxiliary which in 1940 opened and staffed a recreational hut in St Marys Road, Sydney, for service personnel.

She chaired the R.S.G.C.'s comforts fund and in 1943 provided afternoon teas at the club which raised over £1000 for war charities. In addition, she worked for Lewisham and St Vincent's hospitals, and for the Waitara Foundling Home. Kate Egan died on 9 September 1951 in Lewisham Hospital and was buried in South Head cemetery. Her estate was sworn for probate at £31 123; part of her income had derived from Toohey's will.

S. Kennedy, *Faith and Feminism* (Syd, 1985); H. Carey, *Truly Feminine, Truly Catholic* (Syd, 1987); C. Tatz and B. Stoddart, *The Royal Sydney Golf Club* (Syd, 1993); Aust Red Cross Soc (NSW), *Annual Report*, 1913-1951; *Syd Mail*, 23 Aug 1902, 12 Aug 1903, 17 Aug 1904, 16 Aug 1905, 22 Aug 1906, 21 Aug 1907; *SMH*, 18 Mar 1918, 18 Feb 1925, 24 May 1929, 4 July 1934, 6 Aug 1940; *Catholic Weekly* (Syd), 13 Sept 1951.

HILARY M. CAREY

EGAN, KATHLEEN MARY (1890-1977), Dominican Sister and educationist, was born on 16 December 1890 at The Rock, near Wagga Wagga, New South Wales, third child of Richard Egan, a railway stationmaster from Ireland, and his native-born wife Catherine, née Connors. Educated from the age of 15 by the Dominican nuns at Maitland, Kathleen entered the order's novitiate in 1910 and was professed on 14 November 1912, taking the religious name Mary Madeleine Thérèse.

Sr Madeleine taught mathematics and also served as mother superior at Tamworth (1924-26 and 1930) and Mayfield (1927-29). In 1931 she was appointed to the Institution for the Deaf and Dumb at Waratah, Newcastle; as superior (1933-41) she made many innovations based on her previous classroom experience. Believing that 'the deaf child has tastes, dislikes, ambitions similar to those of her unhandicapped sister', she introduced the State curriculum (using conventional textbooks where possible), drama, art, physical culture, eurhythmics and current affairs. She encouraged pupil participation and oversaw the change of the institution's name to School for Deaf Girls. In 1938 Sr Madeleine invited Fr L. Page, director of the Deaf and Dumb Institute at Montreal, Canada, to teach the nuns the latest 'oral' techniques—speech, lip-reading and the use of modern equipment to amplify sound. Considerable debate emerged within the order in the 1930s between those who advocated 'oralism' and those who favoured sign language.

From 1942 to 1947 Sr Madeleine taught at Dominican convents at Maitland and Mayfield, and was superior (1945-47) at Tamworth. Early in 1948 she was appointed superior of the new St Mary's School for Deaf Children at Delgany, Portsea, Victoria. In

May, with a group of Catholic educationists, she visited New Zealand where by law all schools for the deaf used oralism. At Delgany oralism was used exclusively. A. W. G. and I. R. Ewing's 1950 report to the Commonwealth government praised the 'impressively high' standard of speech at Portsea. Sr Madeleine remained as principal for nine years.

An honorary foundation fellow (1935) of the Australian Association of Teachers of the Deaf, Sr Madeleine had presented a paper (1938) at its second conference: 'The Residential Deaf Girl in the World of Sport and Leisure'. She produced ephemeral magazines, including *Ephpheta*, published a *Prayer Book for the Catholic Deaf* (1938), compiled a *History of Deaf Education in Australia, 1927-1950* (n.d.), and—in retirement at the Rosary Convent, Waratah, New South Wales—completed a companion volume, *Pictorial Centenary Souvenir* (1975). A woman of great strength, she led reforms in the education of the deaf within Dominican schools which were at the forefront of change in the wider community. She eventually concluded that oralism by itself was insufficient and suggested (behind the scenes) that Sisters should also be trained in sign language. Known among the nuns as 'Madeleine the Builder', she was responsible for enlarging the various schools of which she was superior. She was tall and 'lady-like', generous and kindly, trusting of the younger Sisters in her charge. Sr Madeleine died on 17 June 1977 at Waratah and was buried in Sandgate cemetery, Newcastle.

A. Dooley, *To Be Fully Alive* (Syd, nd); A. O'Hanlon, *Dominican Pioneers in New South Wales* (Syd, 1949); B. L. Crickman, *Education for the Deaf and Hearing Impaired* (Mayfield, NSW, 1990); Inst for the Deaf and Dumb (Waratah, NSW), *Annual Report*, 1913-18, 1927-28, 1933-39; *Newcastle Morning Herald*, 21 June 1977; J. Burke, The History of Catholic Schooling for Deaf and Dumb Children in the Hunter Valley (M.A. thesis, Univ Newcastle, 1974); Dominican Archives, Santa Sabina, Strathfield, Syd; information from Sr Henrietta, St Martin de Pores Hostel, Waratah, NSW, and Sr Ann Walsh, Lidcombe, Syd.   ANNE O'BRIEN

EGGLESTON, ELIZABETH MOULTON (1934-1976), academic lawyer and activist, was born on 6 November 1934 at Armadale, Melbourne, eldest child of Victorian-born parents (Sir) Richard Moulton Eggleston (d.1991), a barrister who became a judge and chancellor of Monash University, and his wife Isabel Marjorie, née Thom, a mathematics teacher. Educated at Presbyterian Ladies' College and Tintern Church of England Girls' Grammar School, Elizabeth studied at the University of Melbourne and was active in the Australian Student Christian Movement,

the Students' Representative Council, a voluntary legal-aid service and the editorial board of the legal journal, *Res Judicatae*. She graduated (LL.B., 1956) with second-class honours (division B).

After briefly practising law in Melbourne, Eggleston studied at the University of California at Berkeley (LL.M., 1958), United States of America, then worked and travelled in Britain and Europe. She returned to Melbourne in early 1961, practised as a solicitor for three years and in 1964 completed an arts degree at the University of Melbourne. In the following year she became the first doctoral candidate in the faculty of law at Monash University (Ph.D., 1970). Inspired by her earlier visit to Navajo Indian country in America, she wrote her thesis on Aborigines and the administration of justice, conducting extensive field-work in Victoria, Western Australia and South Australia.

In 1969 Eggleston was appointed lecturer in the faculty of law at Monash. Two years later she was promoted to senior lecturer. She established new courses in industrial law, legal aid and poverty law, and co-authored *Cases and Materials on Industrial Law in Australia* (Sydney, 1973). From 1971 she was also director (part time) of the university's Centre for Research into Aboriginal Affairs. Under her leadership the centre generated and co-ordinated research, organized seminars and national conferences, established a course in Black Australian Studies, provided resources for Aboriginal groups and individuals, and liaised with government and overseas bodies.

A founder (1972) of the Victorian Aboriginal Legal Service, Eggleston conducted a discussion group with Aborigines in Pentridge gaol and advised Aboriginal communities. She addressed conferences throughout the country, published articles, and made submissions to government inquiries and parliamentary committees on discrimination, Aboriginal legal services, and the recognition of Aboriginal land rights and cultural heritage. Study leave in North America in 1972-73, where she undertook research in Indian communities, gave a comparative dimension to her work. Her major publication, *Fear, Favour or Affection* (Canberra, 1976), which was based on her doctoral thesis, was published two months before her death. Reviewers acclaimed her contribution to Australian scholarship and policy-making in revealing systemic discrimination against Aborigines in the administration of criminal justice.

Eggleston was 'gentle and unassuming', but was moved to exploit her lawyer's skills by a deep-rooted and burning sense of injustice. Five ft 7 ins (170 cm) tall, with blue eyes, and wavy brown hair cut short, she wore glasses and, from her early thirties, took daily medication for asthma. She died of cancer on 24 March 1976 in East Melbourne and was buried in Brighton cemetery; Aboriginal friends sang and played traditional music at a memorial service at Monash.

Legal Service Bulletin, 1, no 13, Mar 1976, p 350; *Nation Review*, 6, no 25, Apr 1976, p 620; *Politics*, 11, no 2, Nov 1976, p 235; *Monash Univ Law Review*, 3, Nov 1976, p 1, p 5, p 173; *Australian*, 6 Apr 1974, 7 Feb 1976; *Age* (Melb), 21 Feb, 25 Mar, 2 Apr 1976, 19 Jan 1978; *Sun News-Pictorial*, 25 Mar 1976; *Herald* (Melb), 30 Mar 1976; Sir R. and Dr E. Eggleston papers (Monash Univ Archives); student, staff *and* research files of E. Eggleston (Monash Univ Archives); information from Mrs S. James, East Hawthorn, Melb. PHILLIPA WEEKS

ELDER, ANNE JOSEPHINE CHLOE (1918-1976), ballet dancer and poet, was born on 4 January 1918 at Remuera, Auckland, New Zealand, elder daughter of Norman Robert Mackintosh, an insurance-manager from Victoria, and his New Zealand-born wife Rena Dillon, née Bell. Anne came to Melbourne with her parents in 1921. Educated at home by a governess and at St Margaret's School, Berwick, she travelled with her family to Norfolk Island and New Zealand, and at the age of 15 to England and Scotland.

At St Catherine's School for Girls, Toorak (1934-36), she edited the school magazine, and was a prefect and dux. Inspired by Anna Pavlova, she commenced ballet lessons with Laurel Martyn. From 1938 Anne Mackintosh danced with Colonel de Basil's Ballet Russe de Monte Carlo and then as a soloist (1940-44) with the Borovansky [q.v.13] Australian Ballet Company. Having learned typing and shorthand, she took a clerical job with the Australian Military Forces. On 30 April 1940 at Christ Church, South Yarra, she married with Anglican rites John Stanley Elder, a solicitor serving in the 2nd/8th Field Regiment, Australian Imperial Force. Their son was born in 1945, their daughter in 1947.

Illness troubled Elder throughout her life. Slightly built, with dark hair and eyes, and a fiery temper, she turned her creative energies to painting, poetry-writing, gardening and her house, which she filled with light and beauty. In 1960 she and her husband visited England and Europe. She 'read poetry like eating sweets', but, hurt by rejections, published little. Her strong Anglican faith was revealed in her *Short History of St John's Church of England, Heidelberg* (1961), and in several unpublished hymns. Encouraged by Bruce Dawe and Philip Martin, in the mid-1960s she began to publish regularly in newspapers and periodicals, including the *Australian, Quadrant, Meanjin, Overland* and *Southern Review*.

Elder's first collection, *For the Record* (1972), was wintry in tone, but charged with a music that affirmed the power of the ordinary moment against the bleakness of decay and death. Of conservative temperament, though an iconoclast, she refused to be classified as a feminist and objected to the use of poetry for political purposes: when three of her poems appeared in the collection, *Mother I'm Rooted* (1975), she was appalled by the polemical tone of the introduction. Yet her poetry was defiantly feminine, in its celebration of the domestic and in its implicit protest against the exclusion of the feminine from the public sphere. She saw the female not as equal, but as centre.

After suffering a heart attack about 1968, Elder declined in health and spirits. Passionately attached to natural beauty, she felt the encroachment of suburbia on her home at Eaglemont until—in 1972—she and John moved to Parkville while awaiting the completion of Ballindean, their home near Romsey. She died of cardiopulmonary disease complicating scleroderma on 23 October 1976 in Royal Melbourne Hospital and was cremated. Her husband and children survived her. Administered by the Victorian Fellowship of Australian Writers, the Anne Elder award for a first book of poetry was initially presented in 1977.

A second collection of Elder's poems, *Crazy Woman* (1976), was published posthumously. In its personal lyrics and elegiacs, and its witty observation of social absurdities, she continued her defiance of death and her search for the universal as a means of overcoming individual loneliness. The poems, none the less, remain sociable: the sudden delights of a morning drive and the mysteries of family are never entirely cancelled by life's inexplicable horrors. A commemorative volume, *Small Clay Birds*, was published by Monash University in 1988.

F. Salter, *Borovansky* (Syd, 1980); D. Brooks and B. Walker (eds), *Poetry and Gender* (Brisb, 1989); *Overland*, no 68, 1977, p 20; *SMH*, 22 July 1972, 10 Mar 1979; P. Martin, 'Introduction' to Collected Poems of Anne Elder (ms, held by Ms C. Elder, Linguistics and Language Dept, Univ Melb, who also holds other papers and provided information). JOHN MCLAREN

ELDERSHAW, FLORA SYDNEY (1897-1956), author and critic, was born on 16 March 1897 at Darlinghurst, Sydney, fifth of eight children of native-born parents Henry Sirdefield Eldershaw, station-manager, and his wife Margaret, née McCarroll. Flora was a grand-daughter of Finney Eldershaw, author of *Australia as it Really Is* (London, 1854), and a cousin of the water-colourist John Ray Eldershaw. She grew up in the Riverina district and boarded at Mount Erin Convent, Wagga Wagga.

At the University of Sydney (B.A., 1918), Eldershaw studied history under G. A. Wood and Latin under T. J. Butler [qq.v.12,7]. In 1916 she met Marjorie Barnard, a fellow student. To the shy Barnard, Flora appeared a 'dark-haired, vivacious girl, a fountain of energy, ideas and laughter'. Eldershaw served (1917-20) as secretary and treasurer of the university women's union, then accepted a post at Cremorne Church of England Grammar School for Girls. In 1923 she moved to Presbyterian Ladies' College, Croydon, where she rose to senior English mistress and head of the boarding school. Her Catholic upbringing precluded her promotion to headmistress.

Using the pseudonym 'M. Barnard Eldershaw', Flora and Marjorie collaborated on their first novel, *A House Is Built* (London, 1929), which shared first prize in the *Bulletin* novel competition with Katharine Susannah Prichard's [q.v.11] *Coonardoo* (London, 1929). On occasions, Barnard and Eldershaw together drafted an outline before each worked on sections which the other revised. They wrote *Green Memory* (London, 1931), *The Glasshouse* (London, 1936) and *Plaque With Laurel* (London, 1937). Under her own name, Eldershaw published *Contemporary Australian Women Writers* (1931, an address to the Australian English Association, Sydney) and several articles in the *Journal of the Royal Australian Historical Society*; she also edited *The Australian Writers' Annual* (1936) and *The Peaceful Army* (1938). In 1938 Eldershaw and Barnard produced a critical study of Australian literature, *Essays in Australian Fiction* (Melbourne); an historical work, *Phillip of Australia* (London), was followed by *My Australia* (London, 1939) and *The Life and Times of Captain John Piper* (1939) which was commissioned by the Australian Limited Editions Society.

A leading figure in Sydney literary circles, in 1935 Eldershaw had become the first woman president of the Fellowship of Australian Writers, an office she was again to hold in 1943. With Barnard and Frank Dalby Davison [q.v.13], she developed policies on political and cultural issues, and helped to transform the F.A.W. into a vocal and sometimes controversial lobby group. Her literary friends included Jean Devanny, Vance and Nettie Palmer [qq.v.8,11], Tom Inglis Moore [q.v.], Prichard and Judah Waten. In 1938 Eldershaw helped to persuade the Federal government to expand the Commonwealth Literary Fund to include grants (as well as pensions) for writers and funding for university lectures on Australian literature. She was a member (1939-53) of the C.L.F.'s advisory board. Vance Palmer described her as being 'passionately devoted' to the interests of the fund and the board's 'most valuable member'.

Tired of teaching, in 1941 Eldershaw joined the Department of Labour and National Service; she worked for the division of postwar reconstruction in Canberra and later transferred to the division of industrial welfare in Melbourne. She gave advice on women's legal rights, working conditions and equal pay, and extended her interests to the welfare of Aboriginal and migrant women.

Despite the exigencies of her job, Eldershaw remained active in literary matters throughout World War II and delivered C.L.F. lectures on Australian literature at the University of Sydney in 1945. After delays due to wartime censorship and paper shortages, Eldershaw and Barnard's final novel, *Tomorrow and Tomorrow [and Tomorrow]* appeared in 1947 (the uncensored version in 1983). This book was widely considered to be the work of Barnard alone until recent scholarship established Eldershaw's contribution. Its political content was exploited by William Wentworth in 1952 to support his allegation that Eldershaw and other prominent members of the C.L.F. advisory board were communist sympathizers.

Failing on the grounds of health to gain permanent appointment in the public service, Eldershaw became a private industrial consultant in 1948 and a fellow (1950) of the Australian Institute of Management, but gradually withdrew from public affairs and by 1955 had retired to her sister Mary's property at Forest Hill. Flora died of cerebral thrombosis on 20 September 1956 in hospital at Wagga Wagga and was cremated with Anglican rites.

Women and Labour Publications Collective, *All Her Labours*, 2 (Syd, 1984); *PD* (Cwlth), 1952-53, p 723; *Aust Woman's Mirror*, 4 Sept 1928, p 12; *Labour Hist*, no 46, May 1984, p 1; *Meanjin Q*, 15, no 4, 1956, p 390; *Walkabout*, 1 Oct 1959, p 8; M. Dever, 'The Case For Flora Eldershaw', *Hecate*, 15, no 2, 1989, p 38, *and* 'Aspects of the Political Activities of Marjorie Barnard and Flora Eldershaw', *Hecate*, 17, no 2, 1991, p 9; *Age* (Melb), 30 Aug 1947; M. Barnard *and* F. Eldershaw *and* Fellowship of Aust Writers papers (ML); information from Mr J. M. Eldershaw, Mosman, and Miss M. Swain, Castle Hill, Syd.   MARYANNE DEVER

ELDERSHAW, PETER ROSS (1927-1967), archivist, was born on 5 January 1927 at West Looe, Cornwall, England, son of Australian-born parents John Roy Eldershaw, artist, and his wife Dorothea Willis, née Barclay, a sculptress. Peter spent much of his youth at the family home at Richmond, Tasmania, but fell victim to poliomyelitis in the epidemic of 1937-38. It left him with no muscular ability in his legs and doctors said that he would never walk again. He completed his primary and undertook his secondary education at Wingfield House, a hospital in Hobart, then attended the University of Tasmania (B.A., 1950) in a wheelchair.

Thanks to Eldershaw's ingenuity, splints and other apparatus were designed and built, which enabled him gradually to walk, but with great difficulty. When the State Archives was being established in Hobart as an arm of the State Library of Tasmania, the authorities were persuaded in 1951 to employ him as a temporary 'Indexer of Historical Records'. Next year he was appointed assistant-archivist. His major work for the archives was his preparation of the first three parts of the *Guide to the Public Records of Tasmania* (1957-58 and 1965), inventories of the documents of the Colonial Secretary's and the Governor's offices, and of the Convict Department.

A founder (1951) of the Tasmanian Historical Research Association, Eldershaw edited its *Papers and Proceedings* until his death. His editing was extensive, rigorous and creative. He was extremely conscious of the need for historians and other archives-users to have help at every level; he undertook a considerable amount of voluntary editorial work by assisting, for example, with N. J. B. Plomley's monumental *Friendly Mission: the Tasmanian Journals and Papers of George Augustus Robinson, 1829-1834* (1966). Eldershaw was made an honorary life member of the T.H.R.A. in 1958. A member of the *Australian Dictionary of Biography*'s Tasmanian working party, he contributed ten articles to volumes 1 and 2.

He also participated in early efforts by Australian archivists to develop an independent professional identity. His contributions to journals such as *Public Administration* and the *Bulletin for Australian Archivists* indicated both a philosophical and a practical support for archivists to have their own organization. When attempts to establish a separate association failed in 1958, Eldershaw promoted the archives section of the Library Association of Australia. He published articles in its journal, *Archives and Manuscripts*, prepared papers for conferences and was an associate-examiner for archives subjects in the registration examination. In 1963 he was made a fellow of the L.A.A.

Three years earlier Eldershaw had succeeded Robert Sharman, the first full-time archives officer, State Archives of Tasmania. On 18 April 1960 at St John's Anglican Church, New Town, Eldershaw married Shirley Margaret Franks, a librarian. A good deal of his time and talent was devoted to the rather frustrating search for misplaced or missing documents. Reports frequently reached him of Tasmanian public records

being offered for sale, and, as the Public Records Act (1943)—under which he operated—made provision for the compulsory acquisition of such items, attempts were made through the courts for this material to be repossessed for the Crown. After an effort to acquire records from a museum at Port Arthur went disastrously wrong, Eldershaw took a leading role in the preparation of new legislation for the Tasmanian Archives Act (1965). A milestone in archival legislation in Australia, it had a significant bearing on that which was subsequently passed in other States. In March 1966 Eldershaw's position was reclassified as principal archivist.

'Behind many of his quiet and dry remarks lurked both an informed irony and a keen humour which commanded respect.' Eldershaw was completely without pretentiousness or pomposity, and devoid of self-pity. He died of hypertensive coronary vascular disease on 23 July 1967 at his Kingston home and was cremated; his wife, son and two daughters survived him. In 1975 the T.H.R.A. established an annual lecture in his memory.

Archives and Manuscripts, 3, Nov 1967, p 4; R. C. Sharman, 'Peter Ross Eldershaw, 1927-1967', *Aust Library J*, Dec 1967, p 253 *and* 'Peter Ross Eldershaw', *PTHRA*, 15, no 3, Jan 1968, p ii, *and*, 'Tasmanian Archives and the Eldershaw Tradition', *PTHRA*, 22, no 2, June 1975, p 84; *Mercury* (Hob), 25 July 1967; Eldershaw file (TA); personal information.   R. C. SHARMAN

ELKIN, ADOLPHUS PETER (1891-1979), Anglican clergyman and professor of anthropology, was born on 27 March 1891 at West Maitland, New South Wales, second son of Reuben Elkin, a salesman from England, and his native-born wife Ellen Wilhelmina, née Bower, a seamstress of German stock. Reuben came from a family of Jewish intellectuals who had emigrated to New Zealand; his father was a rabbi at Auckland. Peter's only brother died as an infant in 1891. Reuben and Ellen were divorced in 1901 and Peter never saw his father again. Next year his mother died of typhoid. He was raised as an Anglican by his maternal grandparents.

Educated at Singleton and at Maitland East Boys' High School, Elkin matriculated in 1907 and worked as a clerk for the Commercial Banking Co. of Sydney. He spent the succeeding four years in country towns. Dissatisfied with banking as a career, in 1912 he won a scholarship for candidates for Holy Orders and entered St Paul's College, University of Sydney (B.A., 1915; M.A., 1922); his contemporaries included V. G. Childe [q.v.7] and H. V. Evatt [q.v.]. Elkin was appointed assistant-curate at Newcastle cathedral, ordained priest on 17 March 1916 and posted to small country parishes in the diocese. From 1919, as vice-warden, he taught full time at St John's Theological College, Armidale, under (Bishop) E. H. Burgmann [q.v.13].

Already fascinated by Darwin's [q.v.1] *On the Origin of Species* (1859), in 1918 Elkin made a chance visit to the outback near Bourke which whetted his interest in Aboriginal society. Intrigued by artefacts, deserted occupation-sites and burial grounds, he began to read widely about the Aborigines. No anthropology courses were then available in Australian universities, but he chose the religion of the Australian Aborigines as the topic for his master's thesis and lectured his students at St John's on human origins. On 7 January 1922 at St Paul's Anglican Church, Burwood, Sydney, he married Sara (Sally) Thompson, a nursing sister from Ireland whom he had met during the influenza epidemic. While rector of Wollombi in 1922-25, he taught part time for the university's Department of Tutorial Classes, offering lectures on early society and culture to the citizens of the Hunter Valley.

Having resigned his living in 1925, Elkin studied the Australian Aborigines under (Sir) Grafton Elliot Smith [q.v.11] at University College, London (Ph.D., 1927). In 1927 A. R. Radcliffe-Brown [q.v.11], foundation professor of anthropology in Sydney, helped Elkin to secure a Rockefeller grant to undertake field-work in the Kimberleys, Western Australia. He not only met traditional Aborigines, but also observed the brutality of the frontier, the clash between settlers and indigenous tribes, the ambivalent place of the missions and the apparently aimless policies of governments. That year he started campaigning for what he regarded as social justice for the Aboriginal people. He returned to New South Wales in 1928.

On the understanding that he could take time to pursue his anthropological interests, in 1929 Elkin became rector of Morpeth. He also co-edited the *Morpeth Review*, a well-regarded periodical published by St John's College (by then relocated at Morpeth). Convinced of the urgency of the Aborigines' plight, he felt that research must be carried out—and published—before it was too late. He contributed to the *Morpeth Review* and *Oceania*. In addition to publishing academic material, Elkin wrote a stream of letters and articles for the popular press on race relations and the problem of prejudice. He was an indefatigable speaker who fought throughout New South Wales for justice and citizenship for Aborigines. In 1930 he received a grant to do field-work in South Australia. By the time Elkin came home, Radcliffe-Brown had resigned and the future of the anthropology department was in doubt.

Late in 1932 Elkin was appointed lecturer-in-charge of the anthropology department for one year. Funds were eventually secured for the chair and he was promoted professor in December 1933. Virtually in total charge of anthropology in Australia, he was an adviser to governments, editor of *Oceania* and director of field-research through the Australian National Research Council (chairman of its anthropological committee, 1933-42, executive-member, 1942-55, and chairman, 1954-55). He taught all students in the discipline, trained cadets for Papua and New Guinea, administered his department increasingly autocratically and undertook field-research. His succession of female research-assistants included Phyllis Kaberry, Camilla Wedgwood, Olive Pink and Ursula McConnel [qq.v.]. Some thought him prickly and conceited: he strenuously opposed C. P. Mountford's [q.v.] leadership of the Australian-American expedition to Arnhem Land (1948) and once reviewed his own book in *Oceania* (December 1974).

The title of professor of anthropology strengthened Elkin's standing as president (1933-62) of the Association for the Protection of Native Races and vice-president of the Aborigines Protection Board of New South Wales (Aborigines Welfare Board from 1940). Following a large meeting held in Sydney in 1934 to protest against the death sentence passed on an Aborigine in the Northern Territory, Elkin and the A.P.N.R. were partly responsible for gaining a reprieve; it was followed by an appeal and the eventual release of Tuckiar, who they believed had not received a fair trial when charged with the murder of a White man. Elkin also managed to have patrol officers appointed in the Northern Territory in the mid-1930s; in 1939 he advised (Sir) John McEwen [q.v.], minister for the interior, on the organization of a new department of native affairs. Elkin spent years championing the Aboriginal cause—as he interpreted it—before State and Federal governments.

As an anthropologist, he was a meticulous observer and recorder, with a particular interest in ritual and kinship; in terms of theory, he was a functionalist, a diffusionist, a Darwinist. In his religious beliefs, he was a humanist—in the tradition of his heroes Frederick Maurice and Charles Kingsley. As a lobbyist for the rights of Aborigines, he believed in the politics of compromise, courtesy and restraint; he proved tenacious in method and optimistic in outlook. Elkin regarded protection as the basis for growth and considered that Aborigines would inevitably be assimilated by White Australia (although he did not envisage them losing their identity in the process). He was a pragmatist, a plain speaker, a conservative who believed there was no point wasting energy on battles that could not be won.

As Elkin grew older and Aboriginal activism increased, his attitudes were severely criticized. Many saw his assimilation policy as weakening Aboriginality. Many interpreted his work on the Aborigines Welfare Board as meddling interference. Others felt he should have been more confrontationist, more opposed to authority, more aggressive in dealing with White racists when championing the Aborigines of the Northern Territory and the Kimberleys. This was not his way. He believed in adaptation—that all human beings must adjust to their circumstances—White must adapt to Black, and Black to White.

Elkin wrote numerous articles, reports, reviews, books, pamphlets, introductions and chapters, and was a voluminous correspondent. His detailed and careful description of a unique way of life in *The Australian Aborigines: how to understand them* (1938) moved hundreds of students some way towards a sympathetic appreciation of Aborigines as fellow human beings. This book, with *Aboriginal Men of High Degree* (1946), in which his respect for the tribal elders is evident, and the numerous field-work reports in *Oceania* highlighted Elkin's academic contribution. The political work of which he was most proud was *Citizenship for the Aborigines* (1944). *The Diocese of Newcastle* (1955) was his historical tribute to the Church of England, and *Morpeth and I* (1937) his personal reminiscence.

Prominent in scientific circles, Elkin was president of the Anthropological (1934) and Royal (1940-41) societies of New South Wales, the Australian Anthropological Association (1941) and the Australian Institute of Sociology (1941-44); he was a fellow (from 1937) of the Australian and New Zealand Association for the Advancement of Science, Australian councillor (from 1947) on the Pacific Science Association, a fellow (from 1953) of the Social Science Research Council of Australia, a founding councillor (1961) of the Australian Institute of Aboriginal Studies and a trustee of the Australian Museum, Sydney. He enjoyed music and playing tennis, and belonged to the Royal Empire (Commonwealth) Society.

Although Elkin retired in 1956, his 'thin, bird-like figure' was seen at meetings of the university senate; he was chairman of St Paul's College council and helped to establish International House, a residence for overseas students. He remained involved in Aboriginal causes, edited *Oceania* until his death and was foundation editor (1966-79) of *Archaeology & Physical Anthropology in Oceania*. Elkin was awarded the local Royal Society's James Cook [q.v.1] medal (1956), A.N.Z.A.A.S.'s Mueller [q.v.5] medal (1957), and the Herbert E. Gregory medal (1961); he was appointed

C.M.G. in 1966 and in 1970 received an honorary doctorate of letters from the University of Sydney. In his eighties, he lived at Mowll [q.v.] Memorial Village and wrote prolifically. After collapsing at a meeting at International House, Elkin died on 9 July 1979 at the university and was cremated; his wife and two sons survived him.

T. Wise, *The Self-Made Anthropologist* (Syd, 1985); R. MacLeod (ed), *The Commonwealth of Science, ANZAAS and the Scientific Enterprise in Australasia, 1888-1988* (Melb, 1988); *Oceania*, 50, no 2, Dec 1979, p 81; *People* (Syd), 17 Jan 1951; *SMH*, 25 Oct 1928, 22 Dec 1933, 2 Oct 1941, 17 Jan 1957, 18 Aug 1961, 11 July 1979; A. P. Elkin papers (Fisher L Archives, Univ Syd).

TIGGER WISE

ELLERY, REGINALD SPENCER (1897-1955), psychiatrist and author, was born on 12 August 1897 at Rose Park, Adelaide, son of Torrington George Ellery, secretary to the city's mayor, and later town clerk in Melbourne (1914-24), and his wife Mabel Alice, née Wood. Educated at the Collegiate School of St Peter, Reg studied medicine at the University of Melbourne (M.B., B.S., 1923; M.D., 1930). Most of his energies went into writing critical articles for daily newspapers and periodicals. Arthur Phillips, a fellow student, remembered Ellery cultivating an outdated bohemian pose which, despite its elegance, was slightly ludicrous, 'nearer to Oxonian practice than to the no-nonsensicality of Melbourne'. Ellery's style was partly derived from his mentor Professor W. A. Osborne [q.v.11] whose flamboyant mix of physiology and poetry appealed to the aspiring young writer. These literary ambitions were at odds with the wishes of his domineering father who was determined to see his son enter a respectable profession. In 1921 Ellery edited the medical student's journal, *Speculum*, and sparked public outrage over the lewd material it contained.

On 26 June 1918 Ellery suspended his studies to enlist in the Australian Imperial Force. He was discharged at his own request on 20 November. Shortly after receiving his first professional appointment with the Victorian Lunacy Department as junior medical officer at Kew Hospital for the Insane, on 22 June 1923 at Holy Trinity Church, Kew, he married with Anglican rites Mancell Flo Kirby, a pianist and music teacher. Next year he was again embroiled in public controversy. In retaliation against his hastily imposed reforms to their negligent routines, the general medical staff made a series of accusations against him. The affair culminated in a royal commission (1924) which found the allegations to be unfounded. For his part in stirring up trouble, the Lunacy Department authorities transferred Ellery to Sunbury Hospital for the Insane.

Under Dr J. K. Adey's supervision at Sunbury, Ellery developed a greater understanding of psychiatry; together they were responsible in 1925 for the first successful application in Australia of Wagner-Jauregg's malarial-fever treatment for general paralysis of the insane. With this work Ellery firmly established his reputation. He became assistant to the psychiatrist at the (Royal) Melbourne Hospital's out-patient clinic, and, as such, was the first asylum officer in the State attached to a teaching hospital. Ellery began contributing to the *Medical Journal of Australia*, discussing such innovations as Sigmund Freud's *avant-garde* practices. In 1928 he was appointed medical officer of the new Mont Park mental hospital and was invited to deliver the annual (William) Beattie Smith [q.v.11] lecture.

Constrained by the Lunacy Department's regulations, Ellery resigned in 1931; he set up a Collins Street practice as a psychiatrist and was honorary consultant psychiatrist at the Alfred Hospital. He defied the department's monopoly on mental health care by opening at Malvern in 1933 'the first private psychopathic hospital in Victoria'. In 1936-37 he visited the Soviet Union and Europe, ostensibly to investigate treatments for schizophrenia, and was entertained by Freud's daughter Anna at their home in Vienna. A member of the British Psychological Society, from 1938 Ellery allied himself with a group of progressive psychiatrists led by Dr Paul Dane. In establishing the Melbourne Institute for Psycho-Analysis in October 1940, the group encountered opposition from both the Federal government and the local branch of the British Medical Association.

Although he never became a party member, Ellery was attracted to communism. During the early 1940s he published several pamphlets and books which prescribed communism as a panacea for mental and social ills. This stand led to some professional isolation and, Ellery believed, to his failure to be reappointed to the Alfred Hospital in 1946. His enthusiasm for communism waned, but he continued to advocate a radical restructuring of society based on scientific planning and a greater use of psychiatric tools. An essayist and writer of poetry, Ellery was also a peripheral figure in the Angry Penguins movement. He provided the artist (Sir) Sidney Nolan with examples of drawings by psychotic patients which influenced his work, in particular a series of 'heads' exhibited in 1943. Ellery used one of them on the cover of his book, *Psychological Aspects of Modern Warfare* (1945), published by John Reed and Max Harris.

After suffering from rheumatoid arthritis for eighteen years, Ellery died of cancer on 27 December 1955 at Prahran and was cremated. He had just completed *The Cow Jumped Over the Moon* (1956), a mannered and eccentric autobiography which, through its compassionate but uncompromising account of the care of the mentally ill, made a significant contribution to medical history. His wife, who had continued to pursue her musical career, winning recognition as a harpsichordist, survived him, as did their son.

C. Semmler and D. Whitelock (eds), *Literary Australia* (Melb, 1966); R. Haese, *Rebels and Precursors* (Melb, 1981); H. Dow (ed), *Memories of Melbourne University* (Melb, 1983); B. Head and J. Walter (eds), *Intellectual Movements and Australian Society* (Melb, 1988); *Melb Univ Mag*, 1946-47, p 20; *MJA*, 21 Apr 1956; *Quadrant*, 7, no 1, Sept 1963, p 5; *Meanjin Q*, 26, no 3, Spring 1967, p 313; S. Gold, 'The Early History of Psychoanalysis in Australia', Address to the Freud Conference, Lorne, Vic, Apr 1982 (pc held by Dr Angus McIntyre, Politics Dept, La Trobe Univ, Bundoora, Melb); Ellery collection (LaTL); information from Mrs M. Ellery (transcripts and notes held by Dr A. McIntyre).
SEBASTIAN GURCIULLO

ELLIOTT, ALICE GORDON (1886-1977), nurse and community worker, was born on 21 August 1886 in Hobart, only daughter of William Westfold King, jeweller, and his wife Mary Ann, née Fisher. Alice was educated locally at Miss D'Emden's Private School and later returned there as a teacher. She also worked as an estate-agent's clerk before training (1908-12) as a nurse at Hobart General Hospital where she stayed on as a sister. Joining the Australian Army Nursing Service in 1913, King began full-time service with the Australian Imperial Force in September 1914. Next month she sailed for the Middle East in the transport, *Geelong*.

After helping to establish hospitals in Egypt, Sister King spent twelve months in hospital ships in Mediterranean waters and was mentioned in dispatches for her work. In July 1916 she was sent to England. From April to August 1917 she had charge of the theatre ward of the 3rd Australian General Hospital in France, and was then transferred to the 1st Australian Casualty Clearing Station, Belgium. As part of the operating team, she worked long hours treating heavy casualties from engagements near Passchendaele. She was again posted to England in December.

On 20 December 1917 she married Lieutenant Colonel Charles Hazell Elliott (d.1956) [q.v.8] at the parish church, St Marylebone, London. Although she had to resign from the A.I.F. on her marriage, she continued voluntary work until she and her husband embarked for Tasmania in 1919. The Elliotts set up house at New Town. Their only child was born in 1925. Alice was a generous, serious-minded and capable woman. Foundation president (1920) of the Returned Sisters' Association and an office-bearer until 1945, she was active on the house-committee of the R.S.A.'s memorial cottage at Lindisfarne which was established in 1924 as a holiday home for working nurses. She was also a foundation member (1922), first organizing secretary and treasurer of the Nurses Club, a professional centre, agency and residence. In 1929-44 she served on the management-committee of the Girls' Industrial School, New Town. A committee-member (1945-56) of the Ladies' Harbour Lights Guild of the Tasmanian branch of the Missions to Seamen, she helped the organization's fund-raising activities. She had been appointed a justice of the peace in 1924 and from 1936 to 1952 was a special magistrate in the Children's Court, Hobart.

During World War II, as commandant of a Voluntary Aid Detachment, Elliott lectured on war-nursing and acted as liaison officer with the civil defence authorities; in addition, she trained staff and oversaw the provision of dressings for local first-aid posts. In 1956 she was appointed O.B.E. and elected a life member of the Returned Sailors', Soldiers' and Airmen's Imperial League of Australia. Elliott had joined the Field Naturalists' Club in 1918 and became a life member in 1969. She enjoyed tennis until she was over 70. Survived by her son, she died on 29 August 1977 at Lindisfarne and was cremated. The Alice Elliott Day Club at the Repatriation General Hospital, Hobart, was named in her honour in 1987.

Her brother CHARLES STANLEY KING (1889-1959) was born on 23 December 1889 in Hobart. Educated at The Hutchins School and Queen's College, University of Tasmania (B.A., 1911), he proceeded to Corpus Christi College, Oxford (M.A., 1914), as a Rhodes scholar and rowed for his college. After serving in the King Edward's Horse, he was commissioned on 5 December 1914 in the Royal Field Artillery and sent to France. On 15 December 1915 he was awarded the Military Cross for his conduct as a forward observation officer at the battle of Loos. Wounded in June 1917, he spent twelve months in hospital.

King returned to Hobart, taught briefly at his old school, and was a lecturer (1920-32) in economics and history at the university. He captained the New Town cricket team and played football for the university and Lefroy clubs. At St Columb's Anglican Church, Hawthorn, Melbourne, on 27 May 1927 he married Nancy Thurgate Hudson, a 22-year-old schoolteacher. Appointed associate-

professor of history at the University of Tasmania in 1933, he was promoted to professor two years later. He retired in 1956, having been a member (1928-33, 1947-49) of the university council and acting vice-chancellor (1948). Foundation chairman (1951-52) of the Tasmanian Historical Research Association, he also served (1942-47) on the board of The Hutchins School. King was acclaimed as one of 'nature's gentlemen' who 'represented a kind of old-world courtesy'; courteous, steady and reliable, he was shy in manner and disliked immodesty and boastfulness. He died of a coronary occlusion on 26 April 1959 in his home at Montagu Bay and was cremated; his wife, daughter and one of his two sons survived him.

A. Downie, *Our First Hundred Years* (Hob, 1975); *Hutchins School Mag*, 1945, p 56, 1947, p 40, July 1959, p 7, Dec 1959, p 21, July 1960, p 22; *Mercury* (Hob), 2 Jan 1956, 27 Apr 1959, 31 Aug 1977; Dept of Veterans' Affairs (Hob), file 87/344: RGH Alice Elliott Day Club; Nurses Club (Hob) minutes, 1922-70 (Roy Nursing Federation office, Hob); NS 1428/5 (TA); Univ Tas Archives; information from Mrs M. Wall and Mrs L. Johnstone, Hob.   A. RAND

ELLIOTT, LEAH MADELEINE (1896-1955) and **RITCHARD, CYRIL JOSEPH (1897-1977)**, dancers and actors, were known affectionately by their public as Madge and Cyril. Madge was born on 12 May 1896 at Fulham, London, daughter of Nicholas Phillipps Elliott, physician and surgeon, and his wife Frances Selina Curtis, née Heighton. The family emigrated to Australia when Madge was an infant and she was educated at a grammar school at Toowoomba, Queensland. After her father moved his practice to Randwick, Sydney, Madge took dancing classes with Minnie Hooper, ballet mistress for J. C. Williamson [q.v.6] Ltd. Hooper, herself an institution in Sydney theatre, recalled her young pupil as 'very dainty and very pretty, energetic and persevering with her work from the start'. It was said that Madge was signed up by Williamson's as a dancer at the age of 13, but, as she later lopped four years off her age, doubt must be cast on this precociousness. Her first contract was with the children's ballet of the Melba [q.v.10]-Williamson Opera Co. in 1911. Remaining with Williamson as a member of the chorus, she was soon promoted to a group called the 'Exquisite Eight'.

Cyril was born on 1 December 1897 at Surry Hills, Sydney, son of Sydney-born parents Herbert Trimnell Ritchard, grocer, and his wife Marguerite, née Collins. Educated at St Aloysius' College, he fulfilled his family's expectations by beginning medicine at the University of Sydney. His studies soon foundered, and, initially against his family's wishes, he veered towards the stage. Cyril lacked Madge's training as a dancer, but was tall and good looking; following some experience in the chorus he was picked out as a possible partner for her. 'I don't dance with beginners', is said to have been Madge's frosty comment, but in this case she did and their partnership began in 1918 with *Katinka*. In 1924 they briefly went their own ways—Cyril to the United States of America and Madge to England—though when the opportunity arose to partner her in London musicals, *Midnight Follies* and *Lady Luck*, he quickly joined her. He too was to trim a couple of years off his age, yet, in doing so, he gallantly pretended that he was older than Madge.

Madge and Cyril established themselves at the Gaiety Theatre in London as a dance act, stylish, romantic and sophisticated. By the time they returned to Australia in 1932 to star in *Blue Roses*, they had graduated to leading roles. Neither was a gifted singer, but each acquired an appropriate vocal technique to facilitate this development of their joint career. In these years it was Madge who was regarded as the star, Cyril her partner: her contract with 'the Firm' laid down a salary of £75 per week plus 5 per cent of gross receipts in excess of £1500 a week.

The success of their partnership paved the way for their wedding on 16 September 1935, a wedding which became part of Sydney folklore. The setting was a crowded St Mary's Cathedral, but the ceremony itself took place in the Archbishop's sacristy, as Madge did not share Cyril's Catholicism. Fifty police were required to control the crowd of some five thousand outside the cathedral. In earlier years Madge had vigorously denied any romantic involvement with Cyril; they were, she insisted, 'just good companions' who danced together. Cyril himself joked that they married 'after ten years of whirlwind courtship'. At the time of their marriage Madge was 39 and Cyril almost 38, so it might well have been a marriage of theatrical convenience, particularly for Cyril who was, years later, described by (Sir) Noël Coward as being 'as queer as a coot' though unable fully to accept it. They were, however, a devoted couple, and the wedding became part of their myth, the size of the crowd escalating over the years to twenty thousand. After honeymooning in Honolulu, they returned to England where they were now resident, with a flat in London and a farmhouse, Appletrees, in Kent. In 1939 Madge had a son who died soon after birth.

During World War II Madge and Cyril played in *The Merry Widow*, both in London and to troops in Egypt and Europe. In 1945 they co-starred in Coward's revue, *Sigh No More*. The experience was not an altogether happy one. Coward at first appreciated them as 'real dyed-in-the-wool pros', but, during the Manchester try-out season, tensions developed, Coward accusing Ritchard of 'raucous vulgarity'. Madge and Cyril maintained the Coward connexion when they successfully toured Australia in *Tonight at 8.30* (1946) and *Private Lives* (1951). In 1954-55 Cyril starred on Broadway as Captain Hook in the musical version of *Peter Pan*. Madge died of bone cancer on 8 August 1955 in Lenox Hill Hospital, New York. According to Cyril, they had never been separated since their marriage.

Nevertheless, their careers had significantly diverged. Even in the 1930s they had at times gone their separate ways, Madge making a name for herself as a principal boy in pantomime, and Cyril acquiring a reputation as a light comedian and straight actor. According to Cyril, 'John Gielgud made me legitimate' when he cast him as Algernon in the celebrated 1942 revival of *The Importance of Being Earnest*. Cyril also began to direct revues and plays, including their 1946 and 1951 tours. Thus the balance in their partnership tended to shift in the postwar years, as Cyril diversified his theatrical talents.

After Madge's death, Cyril pursued his career mainly in the U.S.A., appearing in musicals such as *The Roar of the Grease Paint* and *Sugar*, directing opera at the New York Metropolitan Opera House and plays ranging from Shakespeare to farce. In 1960 he toured Australia in the comedy, *The Pleasure of His Company*, by Samuel Taylor and Cornelia Otis Skinner (the latter co-starring), having earlier played it on Broadway. This was his last stage appearance in Australia. He died on 18 December 1977 at Chicago and was buried in St Mary's cemetery, Ridgefield, Connecticut.

'Madge and Cyril' were remembered as a charmed and charming couple, international stars of the popular stage who remained 'two very nice Australians'. Even as they acquired a West End sophistication, Australians were reassured that 'they are still the Madge and Cyril we used to know'. Above all, their partnership was enshrined as a 'great love story of the Australian theatre'.

H. Porter, *Stars of Australian Stage and Screen* (Adel, 1965); G. Payn and S. Morley (eds), *The Noel Coward Diaries* (Lond, 1982); *Aust Women's Weekly* and *Woman*, 22 Aug 1955; *Star* (Melb), 16, 18, 21, 22, 25 Mar 1935; *Sun News-Pictorial*, 14 Aug 1946; *Herald* (Melb), 26 Mar 1958; J. C. Williamson contracts, news-cuttings, theatre programmes and taped interviews with Cyril Ritchard (Performing Arts Museum, Vic Arts Centre, Melb).

JOHN RICKARD

ELLIS, CHARLES HOWARD (1895-1975), soldier and intelligence officer, was born on 13 February 1895 at Annandale, Sydney, second son of English-born parents William Edward Ellis, clothing manufacturer, and his wife Lillian Mary, née Hobday. After Lillian died in 1898, William took his sons to Brisbane and Launceston, Tasmania, before settling in Melbourne about 1902. Completing his education at Stott & Hoare's Business College, young Ellis worked for the booksellers, Melville & Mullen Pty Ltd, and played oboe with the Royal Melbourne Philharmonic Society. He sailed to Britain in June 1914, intending to study there.

Initially rejected as too short, on 26 July 1915 Ellis enlisted in the 100th Provisional Battalion, Territorial Force. He was promoted corporal and was thrice wounded in action on the Western Front. Commissioned in September 1917, he joined the 5th Battalion, Middlesex Regiment, and suffered further wounds before escorting troops to India where he studied Persian and Urdu. He took part in Major General (Sir) Wilfrid Malleson's military mission which entered Turkestan in August 1918. Malleson's aim was to block possible German-Turkish thrusts towards India and Afghanistan, but his soldiers became involved in fighting Bolsheviks around Merv (Mary). The force withdrew in March-April 1919. That year Ellis was appointed O.B.E. and mentioned in dispatches.

Having visited Melbourne in 1920, he began a course in Russian at St Edmund Hall, Oxford, England. In 1922-23 he was a captain, Territorial Army Reserve, based in Constantinople on intelligence work. At the British High Commission on 12 April 1923 he married a 17-year-old White Russian, Elizabeth (Lilia) Zelensky; they were to have a son before being divorced. In December Ellis became British vice-consul in Berlin: there and elsewhere he maintained surveillance on White Russians fabricating intelligence documents for the British Special (Secret) Intelligence Service (M.I.6) and probably joined the S.I.S. at this time. By 1926 he was employed by the British Chamber of Commerce in Vienna; as a journalist with the London Morning Post, he reported from Geneva on sessions of the League of Nations Assembly. He travelled to Australia and New Zealand in 1930, and from 1931 worked for the S.I.S. under his journalistic cover. On 19 April 1933 he married 21-year-old Barbara Mary Burgess Smith at St Peter's parish church, Cranley Gardens, London; they had a daughter, but their marriage ended in divorce.

Early in World War II, to attract support for Britain's cause and to monitor German activities in the United States of America, the S.I.S. opened the British Security Co-ordination office in New York. Bearing the official title of British consul, Major Ellis was sent to the B.S.C. in 1940 as assistant-director; in 1941 he became head of its Washington office. Some American officials were eager to preserve their country's neutrality and opposed the B.S.C., but the intelligence links it established bore fruit when the U.S.A. entered the war in December. Next year Ellis was in the Middle East where he worked with R. G. (Baron) Casey [q.v.13], the British minister of state who was based in Cairo. Ellis rejoined the B.S.C. in 1942 as a local colonel and returned to London in August 1944. He was appointed to the U.S. Legion of Merit and C.B.E. in 1946.

Posted that year to the S.I.S.'s Singapore office as field-officer in charge of South-East Asia and the Far East, he retained the post until his retirement in 1953 when he was appointed C.M.G. On 24 August 1954 at the register office, Kensington, London, he married a 48-year-old widow and retired schoolteacher Alexandra Wood, née Surtees (d.1970). In the 1950s he spent periods in his native-land, assisting with the establishment of the Australian Secret (Intelligence) Service. He also helped to found the journal, Hemisphere (1956), which focussed on Asian-Australian affairs. His publications included The Transcaspian Episode, 1918-1919 (London, 1963), and he frequently contributed to the Journal of the Royal Central Asia Society.

Allegations have been made that 'Dick' Ellis had passed information to German intelligence before and during World War II, and that he could have worked for Soviet intelligence while with the B.S.C. and subsequently. Experts have dismissed these claims, if only because important information held by Ellis was known not to have been transmitted to the Soviet Union. On 25 January 1973 at the register office, Eastbourne, Sussex, he married a 44-year-old widow Joyce Hatten, née Steeples. He made his final visit to Australia that year. Survived by his wife, and by the son and daughter of his previous marriages, he died on 5 July 1975 at his Eastbourne home and was cremated.

H. M. Hyde, Secret Intelligence Agent (Lond, 1982); information from Mr O. C. Ellis, Ottawa, Canada.
FRANK CAIN

ELLIS, FRANK (1886-1964), educationist, was born on 24 February 1886 in Adelaide, son of Joseph Ellis, collector, and his wife Bertha, née Tapson. Frank attended state primary schools and Prince Alfred College where he was dux; a Hartley [q.v.4] studentship (1903) took him to the South Australian School of Mines and Industries, and to the University of Adelaide (B.Sc., 1907; B.A., 1911; B.E., M.A., 1913). While he was studying, he successively worked as a junior engineer with the Municipal Tramways Trust, an assistant-lecturer at the School of Mines and an instructor in the department of mechanical engineering, School of Mines, Charters Towers, Queensland.

At Stow [q.v.2] Memorial Church, Adelaide, on 14 January 1911 Ellis married Dora Stephens with Congregational forms. After serving as head (1912-17) of the department of engineering at the Bendigo School of Mines, Victoria, he was superintendent (1918-27) of technical education in Tasmania where he did much to reorganize courses and teaching.

In 1927 Ellis was appointed principal of the Working Men's College, Melbourne (Melbourne Technical College from 1934). He presided over many changes and developments during an eventful twenty-five years. His four major achievements were the establishment (1943) of fellowship diploma courses, the expansion of the college through ten major building projects, the extension of business and management studies, and a campaign to have the college recognized as the pre-eminent technological institution in Victoria.

Ellis toured the United States of America in 1939-40 on behalf of the Commonwealth government to buy precision tool-making and gauge-making equipment. His impressions of American institutes of technology provided a catalyst to his thinking about the future status of technical education. On his return, he argued eloquently that the State's technical education system should receive greater recognition and pressed for complete autonomy from the Education Department. In 1947 he almost succeeded in having the college chosen as the nucleus of a proposed university-level institute of technology (a scheme that failed, owing partly to the defeat of the Cain [q.v.13] Labor government). He had joined Malcolm Moore and (Sir) John Storey [qq.v.] in a campaign conducted through the Institute of Industrial Management, Australia, to promote a postwar nation that would be self-sufficient in industrial production. Ellis expressed his views in an address to the institute, delivered on 5 December 1944 and published as *Education for Industry*. He retired in 1952 and was appointed M.B.E. that year. As a specialist in vocational training, he visited Egypt in 1953-54 under the auspices of the International Labour Organization's technical assistance programme.

Small and sharp featured, with an expression that sparkled with good humour, Ellis was a man of immense charm and persuasive ability. To his staff, he was 'a real gentleman' who brought a breadth of vision to the rather narrow world of machine shops, drawing offices and engineering laboratories. He belonged to the Wallaby Club, and enjoyed walking and tennis. Survived by his three daughters, he died on 29 March 1964 at Sandringham, Melbourne, and was cremated. E. P. Eltham [q.v.] referred to him as 'the outstanding figure in technical education in Victoria'.

D. P. Mellor, *The Role of Science and Industry* (Canb, 1958); A. J. Dare, 'Melbourne Technical College and the proposed institute of technology', in *Melbourne Studies in Education, 1977*, S. Murray-Smith ed (Melb, 1977); S. Murray-Smith and A. J. Dare, *The Tech* (Melb, 1987); *Age* (Melb), 31 Mar 1964; Ellis papers (Univ Melb Archives); oral hist archives and Ellis personal file (RMIT Archives).

ANTHONY DARE

ELLIS, SIR KEVIN WILLIAM COLIN (1908-1975), solicitor and politician, was born on 15 May 1908 at Grenfell, New South Wales, third son of native-born parents James Palmer Ellis, farmer, and his wife Florence Mary, née Wyse. Kevin was educated at Fort Street Boys' High School and the University of Sydney (LL.B., 1931; B.Ec., 1939), graduating in law with first-class honours and the university medal. While president of the students' representative council, he was the first to represent undergraduates (1937-39) on the university senate. Admitted as a solicitor on 4 March 1932, he practised with D. Lynton Williams (1933-45), as Kevin Ellis & Co. (1946-54) and with David Price (until 1975). At St Mark's Anglican Church, Darling Point, he married Betty Mena Maunsell on 26 June 1941. He joined the Royal Australian Air Force next year, rose to temporary flight lieutenant and served in the administrative and special duties branch until 24 February 1945.

A 'small l' Liberal, Ellis narrowly won a by-election in May 1948 for the marginal Legislative Assembly seat of Coogee which he held (save for 1953-56 and 1962-65) until his retirement in 1973. While in Opposition he focussed on routine issues, such as ensuring closer parliamentary scrutiny of public accounts. Something of a 'maverick', he regarded the Legislative Council as an 'outmoded anachronism' and 'a burlesque of democracy'. In 1960 he supported the Labor government's measures aimed at abolishing the council. In the rough and tumble of State politics Ellis was a rather austere figure who secured his colleagues' respect, though he remained aloof from the more boisterous manifestations of parliamentary camaraderie.

When the Liberal-Country Party coalition was returned to office in 1965, Ellis was appointed Speaker. He tried to restore some decorum to a parliament long marred by vit-riolic party debate and allegations of partiality against previous Speakers. As a symbol of his respect for his 'exalted' office, he reinstituted the wearing of the Speaker's wig; he empha-sized the impartiality of his office by refrain-ing from attending meetings of his own party. Over almost nine years his rulings and his ability to control the traditionally raucous proceedings of the assembly won praise from both sides. Neville Wran, leader of the Oppo-sition, acclaimed him as 'one of the most distinguished and respected Speakers in the history of the House'.

Ellis was a director of James N. Kirby [q.v.] Holdings Pty Ltd (1964-75), and a member of the council (1965-75) and deputy-chancellor (1970-75) of the University of New South Wales. A director (1960-70) of the National Heart Foundation of Australia, he sat on the boards of Prince Henry (1962-75), Eastern Suburbs (1968-75) and Prince of Wales (1961-75) hospitals, and was president (1969-75) of the Psychiatric Rehabilitation Association. In 1969 he was appointed K.B.E. He belonged to the Imperial Service Club, and enjoyed fishing and playing bowls. Survived by his wife, son and daughter, Ellis died of myocardial infarction on 22 November 1975 at his Point Piper home; he was accorded a state funeral and was cremated.

PD (NSW), 25 Nov 1975, p 3097; Univ NSW, *Uniken*, Feb 1976; *Legislative Studies*, 7, 1992, p 13; *SMH*, 17 Mar 1931, 2 Apr 1935, 3 Apr 1936, 23 July 1937, 14 Aug 1959, 4, 5 Mar 1961, 1 Jan 1969, 24 Nov 1975; *Sun* (Syd), 1 Apr 1960, 9 Mar 1961; *Daily Mirror* (Syd), 7 June 1965; personal information.　　　　　　　　　　JOHN GASCOIGNE

ELLIS, MALCOLM HENRY (1890-1969), journalist and historian, was born on 21 August 1890 at Narine station, near Dirran-bandi, Queensland, eldest of seven children of Thomas James Ellis, an Irish-born store-keeper and book-keeper, and his wife Con-stance Jane, née Ruegg, from England. In the 1890s depression the family led an itinerant existence in northern Queensland. Yet, dec-ades later, in a series of *Bulletin* articles, Malcolm wrote of his early upbringing with warmth and affection, describing ungrudg-ingly the privations he had experienced. He formed a strong attachment to outback Queensland and relished life in the bush. Else-where, he recounted his experiences with the Aborigines, referring especially to the lack of 'distinction between white and black'. He de-veloped resilience and independence, as well as a 'sense of intense curiosity' and a capacity to observe detail. In addition, he found stab-ility and happiness in a close-knit family circle.

From his father he derived a love of adven-ture and a toughness of spirit; from his mother came a regard for learning, and an appreciation of English manners and culture.

Constance's 'yearning for culture' brought the family to Mount Morgan in October 1899. Life was still harsh, but it was settled. Malcolm mixed with the miners and helped his father to prospect for gold. He attended school, initially under a cane-wielding head-master, then in a more humane atmosphere at Red Hill. In January 1904 he won a bursary to Brisbane Grammar School where he boarded and was taught by dedicated masters who, he wrote, 'might have been selected by a committee consisting of Arnold of Rugby, Rudyard Kipling and Dean Farrar'. An able student, he edited the school magazine. In 1907 he took up a cadetship with the *Brisbane Daily Mail*, partly because there was no university in Queensland, partly because he could not afford to read privately for the Bar.

Ellis excelled as a journalist and by the age of 19 had been appointed chief of the parlia-mentary staff. He transferred to the *Brisbane Courier* in 1910. At St Luke's Anglican Church, Brisbane, on 25 April 1914 he married 27-year-old Melicent Jane (Jean) Ayscough [q.v. Ellis]. Next year he returned to the *Mail* as leader-writer and commercial editor. Rejected for active service because a childhood accident had blinded him in one eye, he undertook 'special duties' before spending eighteen months travelling in the outback and New Caledonia. In 1918 he was appointed to the executive of a war propaganda com-mittee. One year earlier he had managed the National Party's Senate campaign for Queensland and over the next four years helped to spearhead the opposition to the abolition of the Legislative Council. A staunch critic of the Labor Party, he attacked it for disloyalty during the war and in 1918 pub-lished *A Handbook for Nationalists*.

By 1919 Ellis had established a reputation as a versatile writer and a man of strongly conservative views. Widely known in political circles, he included W. M. Hughes [q.v.9] among his close contacts. In December 1920 Ellis joined the *Daily Telegraph* in Sydney as chief political correspondent and a member of the editorial board, winning renown for his leaders on commerce and finance. He assisted the Australian Meat Council and was com-missioned by a number of newspapers to visit New Guinea, Papua and the Northern Terri-tory: one outcome was a series of 'sizzling articles' attacking aspects of the administra-tion in all three regions. Subsequently, Federal government officials sought his advice when preparing a constitution for the Northern Territory. Fond of adventure, Ellis led the *Daily Telegraph* expedition that made the first return crossing of Australia by car;

he recorded his adventures in *The Long Lead* (London, 1927).

Sent to London in 1926 to take charge of the *Telegraph* office, Ellis reported on the Imperial Conference and League of Nations sessions. He set out in February 1927 to drive a British car to India—in order to test it for Australian conditions—and reached Delhi where bad weather thwarted progress. Travelling by sea to Sydney and to the *Telegraph*, he wrote of his exploits in *Express to Hindustan* (London, 1929). In October 1928, disillusioned by the state of the press, he became director of the Electrical and Radio Development Association. After it folded in 1931, he engaged in freelance work until 1933 when he joined the senior staff of the *Bulletin*. There he remained until retiring in 1965.

His capacity to produce a 3000-word article on any subject within twenty-four hours enabled him to make a substantial contribution to the *Bulletin*'s columns. He refined his vigorous, hard-hitting style, and spoke out against communism, strengthening his political contacts who included (Sir) Robert Menzies [q.v.]. During World War II Ellis won acclaim for his column, 'The Service Man', which appeared under the pseudonym 'Ek Dum'. Drawing on radio reports and his knowledge of the terrains, he described military campaigns so realistically that he was assumed to have been present. In the postwar years his column became a vehicle for warnings about the spread of communism that formed the basis of his books, *Socialisation in Ten Years* (1947) and *The Garden Path* (1949). The first dealt with the issue of nationalization of the banks and the second with the growing hold of communism over the labour movement—a subject he had earlier explored in *The Red Road* (1932). A solitary and secretive man who usually wore a suit and tie, Ellis was tall and 'chubby-faced', with a 'slightly stuttery voice'. He enjoyed fishing and boating. Divorced in 1939, he married Gwendoline Mary Wheeler on 20 July 1946 at St Stephen's Presbyterian Church, Sydney.

Ellis was noted as an historian as well as a journalist. Some of his work reflected his interest in manufacturing and rural industry: *The Beef Shorthorn in Australia* (1932), *The Torch* (1957), *Metal Manufacturers Ltd* (1966) and *A Saga of Coal* (1969). It was, however, his biographies of Lachlan Macquarie [q.v.2] (1947), Francis Greenway [q.v.1] (1949) and John Macarthur [q.v.2] (1955) that brought him to the fore. In 1942 he was awarded the S. H. Prior [q.v.11] prize by the *Bulletin* for his John Murtagh Macrossan [q.v.5] lectures at the University of Queensland on Macquarie; in 1948 the University of Melbourne awarded him the Harbison-Higinbotham [q.v.4] research scholarship for *Macquarie*. He was appointed C.M.G. in

1956. From the 1920s his overall, but unfulfilled, objective was to produce a history of New South Wales to the mid-nineteenth century based on primary sources and the lives of great men. He undertook research for biographies of William Bligh and W. C. Wentworth [qq.v.1,2]: although he received a Commonwealth Literary Fund grant of £1000 in 1965, he published neither.

Bringing to history the qualities that marked his work as a journalist, Ellis was forthright, colourful and lively in his writing. He had a remarkable grasp of detail and was a meticulous researcher who assiduously combed the available material. At a time when there were few scholarly studies of Australian history his books stood out as major pieces of original research. For all that, Ellis could not avoid identifying himself too closely with his central figures. He viewed the past through their eyes, fought their battles and denigrated their opponents. His work possessed great strengths, but detachment was not among them.

Nor could one expect otherwise given his personal characteristics. He relished and sometimes created controversy. Strongwilled, assertive and principled, he could not be deflected once he had made up his mind. Inevitably, he conflicted with others, revealing a capacity to be vituperative and savagely outspoken. He accused Marjorie Barnard of having improperly read his manuscript of Macquarie before she published *Macquarie's World* (Melbourne, 1946). In 1949 he resigned from the Australian Journalists' Association when he concluded that it had come under communist influence. He also resigned his fellowship, vice-presidency and membership of the Royal Australian Historical Society in April 1954, following an acrimonious controversy centring around his attempts to infuse new blood into the council. After longstanding, unpleasant disputes, in January 1962 he ceased to be period editor of volume 1 and a member of the editorial board of the *Australian Dictionary of Biography*; he resigned from its national committee in June 1963. There were underlying clashes of personality, and differences of opinion both as to how work should proceed and the selection of authors. Two years later he severed connexions with the Australasian Pioneers' Club, to which he had given much since 1953 as historical adviser, honorary librarian and president.

Such episodes isolated Ellis from organizations to which he had a great deal to contribute. A formidable critic and reviewer, he clashed with leading historians and was severe in his strictures on anything that he thought inaccurate. Contrariwise, he could also be helpful and he commanded respect. He belonged to the Australian Club (from 1947), served on the humanities advisory panel at the University of New South Wales in the 1950s and became an honorary member (1964) of the Australian Humanities Research Council. On 21 October 1966 he was among the recipients of the first honorary doctorates conferred by the University of Newcastle. The vice-chancellor, Professor James Auchmuty, praised him for contributing more than any other historian to 'knowledge of our country in the first half century of its existence'. This comment was open to debate, but Ellis was certainly among the foremost biographers of his day in Australia. Survived by his wife and by the daughter of his first marriage, he died on 18 January 1969 at Mosman and was cremated with Anglican rites.

P. Rolfe, *The Journalistic Javelin* (Syd, 1979); Aust Humanities Research Council, *Annual Report,* 1968-69; *SMH,* 22 Jan 1929, 27 Aug 1941, 10 Aug 1948, 30 Oct 1965, 15 Aug 1966; *Bulletin,* 15, 22 June 1963, 9 Jan, 9 Oct 1965, 25 Mar 1967, 1 Feb 1969; papers of Angus & Robertson *and* M. H. Ellis (ML); papers of Aust Limited Editions Soc *and* U. Ellis *and* Sir John Latham *and* G. Mackaness *and* taped interview of H. de Berg with M. H. Ellis, 7 Nov 1967, *and* M. H. Ellis collection on communism (NL); information from Miss F. J. Ellis, Potts Point, Syd.   B. H. FLETCHER

ELLIS, MELICENT JANE (1887-1974), founder of the Penguin Club, was born on 23 March 1887 in Brisbane, seventh child of English-born parents James William Ayscough, pharmaceutical chemist, and his second wife Catherine, née Lowe. Jean attended Brisbane Girls' Grammar School in 1899-1901, then lived at home. After the death of her sister, she embroidered church vestments to earn the £50 premium to train as a nurse. Instead, on 25 April 1914 at St Luke's Anglican Church, Brisbane, she married a journalist Malcolm Henry Ellis [q.v.]; their daughter Frances was born next year. Moving to Sydney in December 1920, Jean attended tutorial classes in psychology and economics at the University of Sydney. The family spent 1926-27 in Britain. Back in Sydney, they lived at Mosman; she swam every morning before breakfast, played tennis and sailed their 22-footer (6.7 m), *Penguin.* Inspired by Zoe Benjamin [q.v.7], she joined the Woolloomooloo Free Kindergarten committee (president 1929-34).

After her divorce in 1939, Jean lived with Frances in a flat at Potts Point. To augment her small income, she lectured on public speaking, chairmanship and committee-procedure to such organizations as the New South Wales College of Nursing and the Council of Jewish Women of New South Wales. Early in 1941 she was asked to establish centres to make large, mesh camouflage nets from sisal twine for the army. She started the Central Netting Depot in the ballroom of Mark Foy's [q.v.8] Ltd, soon transferring to Anthony Hordern & Sons [qq.v.4] Ltd. By mid-1945 she was running fifty centres which had supplied thousands of nets.

In December 1937 Mrs Ellis and her diffident friend Dorothy, wife of C. T. Parkinson [q.v.11], had founded the Penguin Club to train women to speak fluently in public. Jean took over as president next year. She had 'a clear, beautifully modulated voice that carried easily' and insisted on 'the correct use of the English language'. Despite the difficulties of wartime travel, she visited Melbourne (January 1942) and Perth (June 1945) to form interstate branches. As federal president and honorary organizer of the Penguin Club of Australia from February 1945, 'Mother Penguin' forbade changes to the rules and demanded absolute obedience. She tried to attend a meeting daily in Sydney, annually visited country areas and most States and Territories, and twice flew to the Territory of Papua and New Guinea to establish groups in Port Moresby (1968) and at Mount Hagen (1969). Well-known 'Penguins' included Mary Tenison Woods [q.v.12], Gertrude Johnson [q.v.] and Margaret Whitlam.

Forceful, with an agile mind and a 'puckish sense of humour', Mrs Ellis revelled in any mental interplay. She was intolerant of fools and weaklings, abhorred carelessness and vulgarity, and stressed the importance of old-fashioned, ladylike behaviour. Although outwardly reserved and formal, she could also seem 'extraordinarily rude'. She infuriated many by her autocratic demeanour and proprietorial attitude to the club.

Having been a foundation member (1937) of the local British Drama League, she worked for the Industrial Arts Society, the Girls' Secondary Schools' Club and the Victoria League. In 1946 she joined the Australian Institute of International Affairs and served (1947-73) on its New South Wales council. Mrs Ellis was also a member of convocation (1964-74) of Macquarie University. She was appointed O.B.E. in 1963 and was invested by Queen Elizabeth II in Sydney.

Jean Ellis was small, with 'beautiful blue-grey eyes' and an 'Edwardian' appearance. An expert needlewoman, she dressed well—on a shoestring budget: in public her accessories always included a hat and immaculate white gloves. She had a fine contralto voice and enjoyed playing her cherished piano, its top covered with penguins—'big ones, little ones, cloth ones and china ones'. Survived by her daughter, she died on 6 July 1974 at Rose Bay and was cremated. Her portrait (1965) by Andrew Schlecht is held by the Mitchell [q.v.5] Library.

R. M. James, *Untamed by Time* (Perth, 1987); *SMH*, 1 Jan 1963, 10 July 1974; *Herald* (Melb), 5 May 1963; *Canb Times*, 22 Oct 1968; *Mercury* (Hob), 17 Nov 1972; *Age* (Melb), 27 June 1973; information from Miss F. J. Ellis, Potts Point, Syd.   MARTHA RUTLEDGE

ELLWOOD, WILLIAM HENRY (1889-1972), educationist, was born on 19 April 1889 at Congupna, Victoria, seventh surviving child of John Ellwood, an English-born farmer, and his wife Catherine, née Patience, from Scotland. William attended Wunghnu State School and there, in 1904, joined the Education Department of Victoria as a monitor (formerly pupil-teacher). Studying and teaching, he qualified as a primary-school teacher in 1907 and was sent to a number of schools including Strathmerton West, Hiawatha (Gippsland), St Kilda Park and Albert Park.

On 8 January 1915 Ellwood enlisted in the Australian Imperial Force. Commissioned in May, he embarked for the Middle East and in October joined the 24th Battalion at Gallipoli. By August 1916 he was a captain in France. Although severely wounded on 3 May 1917 during a charge at Bullecourt, he remained on duty and inspired his company to repel five counter-attacks; for this action he was awarded the Military Cross. In January 1918 he was promoted major and in June 1919 returned to Australia where his appointment terminated on 15 September. He served in the Militia in 1920-38 and rose to lieutenant colonel while commanding the 8th Battalion.

At Ascot Vale Presbyterian Church on 27 March 1915 Ellwood had married Elsie May Cross. On demobilization, he returned to schoolteaching and studied part time at the University of Melbourne (B.A., 1922; M.Ed., 1928; M.A., 1935). In 1922 he was appointed lecturer in primary method at Melbourne Teachers College. His lectures and exercises formed part of J. W. Elijah's *The Principles and Technique of Teaching in Elementary Schools* (1924). In 1925 Ellwood became district inspector for Ouyen-Mildura.

Next year he was appointed principal of Ballarat Teachers College where he remained until 1931 when it was closed as part of the government's economy measures. While at Ballarat, Ellwood established a reputation as a warm, generous leader who was interested in student welfare and staff development. He transferred these values to his work as district inspector (1932-35) in the Maryborough region. Sympathetic to the plight of teachers in their neglected schools, he none the less insisted that they should

practise progressive methods which would develop the interest of the individual child. His occasional demonstration lessons showed that he had lost none of his practical skills, especially in the teaching of reading and literature. During 1936 he visited Tasmania to study the progress of the new Area Schools. In 1938-45 he was chief inspector of Victorian primary schools, the last person to fill this post after commencing a departmental career as a monitor.

World War II seriously interrupted Ellwood's plans to enrich the primary school curriculum. He was obliged to keep many of the schools operating with under-trained teachers. He took pleasure in the expansion of civics education and in the publication of the second edition of the *Victorian Readers* (he had planned something brighter, but wartime restrictions resulted in a more traditional publication). His *Handbook for the Elementary School Teacher* (1943) was used as an essential text for twenty years. In 1945 he established a curriculum and research branch in the Education Department, introduced a supervisor of school libraries and began a major revision of the primary-school curriculum. Ellwood hoped that, unlike previous revisions, the process would be continuous and involve classroom teachers in its formulation.

In 1946 the Cain [q.v.13] government acceded to a campaign by the Victorian Teachers' Union to establish a teachers' tribunal for the independent determination of salaries and promotions. Ellwood was appointed its first chairman. He was able to improve teachers' employment conditions following years of indifference by governments of all persuasions. In the early determinations of the Victorian Teachers' Tribunal he reduced the salary differentials between primary and secondary teachers. The tribunal was less responsive to union claims for equal pay for women teachers: in a 1948 decision it conceded the principle of equal pay, but found that women teachers' material needs were less than those of men. Ellwood retired from the tribunal in 1954.

A trustee (1945-65) of the Public Library of Victoria, he effectively represented that body on the Documentary Film Board, at the library school of the Royal Melbourne Technical College (from 1960 Royal Melbourne Institute of Technology) and in public campaigns such as Library Week. Survived by his wife and three sons, Ellwood died on 26 June 1972 at Glen Iris and was cremated.

B. Bessant and A. D. Spaull, *Teachers in Conflict* (Melb, 1972); Education Dept (Vic), *Vision and Realisation*, 1, L. J. Blake ed (Melb, 1973); *Argus*, 21 Jan 1937; *Age* (Melb), 6 Nov 1965; *Sun News-Pictorial*, 27 June 1972.   ANDREW SPAULL

ELTHAM, ERNEST PERCY (1892-1964), educationist, was born on 15 September 1892 at Boolar(r)a, Victoria, third son of Andrew Mathew Eltham, a labourer from England, and his native-born wife Mary Virginia, née Forrest. In 1900 the family of seven moved to Bendigo where Ernest attended Violet Street State School. When his father was blinded in one eye in an accident, Ernest was obliged to work—at the age of 12—as a junior pay-clerk to a mining company. He studied at night, won a scholarship to the Bendigo School of Mines, completed a diploma of electrical engineering and was awarded the school's gold medal.

In 1912-18 Eltham was an instructor in engineering at the Working Men's College, Melbourne. He enlisted in the Australian Imperial Force in March 1917, but was discharged after two months at the request of the Victorian Education Department. Seconded to the Department of Defence in September 1918, he was sent to England to learn about machine-gun manufacturing. In 1921 he joined the Education Department as principal of Footscray Technical School. At the W.M.C. he had come to the notice of Donald Clark [q.v.8], chief inspector of technical schools, who was impressed by Eltham's enthusiasm for vocational education and his interest in new fields of engineering.

With Clark's patronage, Eltham became senior inspector of technical schools in 1922. At Scots Church, Melbourne, on 25 September 1923 he married Phyllis Elise Sydney Graham. He studied part time at the University of Melbourne (B.E.E., 1925) and won a Blue in cricket. In 1928-34 he was founding chairman of the Apprenticeship Commission of Victoria.

Eltham was appointed to succeed Clark in 1930. The director of education, Martin Hansen [q.v.9], who had never forgiven Clark and his inspectors for saving the secondary technical schools from closure, downgraded the position and insisted that Eltham's appointment be probationary. Having asked Eltham to prepare five reports on technical education administration in six months, he declared them barren of practical suggestions and relieved Eltham of his post. Next day cabinet overturned Hansen's decision and confirmed Eltham in a permanent appointment and in the presidency of the Apprenticeship Commission.

Confronting the financial stringencies of the Depression, Eltham persuaded the government to adopt emergency measures, including mergers between some technical schools and the offer of free courses. He also successfully endeavoured to obtain equipment from local manufacturers and grants from unemployment funds, but was less effective in his plans for day-training of apprentices. A study tour of Europe and North America in 1935-36 had convinced him that such a policy was fundamental to the revival of Victorian secondary industry and he published his findings in his *Report on Technical Education Systems in Other Countries* (1936).

Eltham supported the proposal of David Drummond [q.v.8], minister for education in New South Wales, that the Federal government should subsidize technical education as part of its defence arrangements. Impatient with the Commonwealth's indifference, in 1938 Eltham and (Sir) John Jensen [q.v.], controller of munitions supply, devised a scheme for the vocational training of defence workers. In November 1939 Eltham was appointed director of training in what became in June 1940 the Commonwealth Technical Training Scheme. The Federal government took over the States' technical colleges to provide under Eltham's leadership short-term, intensive training for members of the armed forces and for civilian employees in defence industries.

In 1947 Eltham resigned from the Victorian Education Department (from which he had taken leave) to remain as director of industrial training in the Department of Labour and National Service. A member of the Commonwealth Reconstruction Training Committee, he had published the *Educational Rehabilitation of Men and Women of the Services* (1945) and now took responsibility for technical training under the C.R.T. scheme. His later efforts to enhance the status of vocational education waned in the 1950s with the immigration of skilled labour. Eltham was influential in vocational-education planning overseas, especially in Malaya. Although he retired in 1958, he continued to advocate training as the key to sustained industrial growth.

Tall, silver-haired and unassuming, Eltham never forgot his humble origins. He was accessible and enthusiastic in promoting education and apprenticeship training. Farsighted and dedicated, he had a broad view of public education which he forcefully articulated on many State and Federal committees. Throughout his busy life he maintained his interest in sport and belonged to the Victoria Golf and Sandringham Bowling clubs. He died on 16 December 1964 in East Melbourne and was cremated; his wife and son survived him.

D. P. Mellor, *The Role of Science and Industry* (Canb, 1958); Education Dept (Vic), *Vision and Realisation*, L. J. Blake ed (Melb, 1973); A. D. Spaull, *Australian Education in the Second World War* (Brisb, 1982); S. Murray-Smith and A. J. Dare, *The Tech* (Melb, 1987); *Educational Mag*, May 1966; B. Parker, The Life and Contribution of Ernest Eltham: Technical Education (M.Ed., minor thesis, Monash Univ, 1982); Eltham papers (Univ Melb Archives *and* AA, Melb). ANDREW SPAULL

EMBRY, SIR BASIL EDWARD (1902-1977), air chief marshal and farmer, was born on 28 February 1902 at Longford, Gloucestershire, England, youngest of three children of Rev. James Embry, Anglican clergyman, and his wife Florence Ada, née Troughton. Educated at Bromsgrove School, from the age of 10 Basil longed to fly aeroplanes. On 29 March 1921 he was commissioned in the Royal Air Force. In 1922-27 he served in Iraq where he pioneered an airmail route across the desert, developed new techniques of 'air control' to keep the peace on the Kurdish border, worked with the air-ambulance service and won the Air Force Cross (1926). He married Australian-born Margaret Mildred Norfolk Hope Elliot on 1 August 1928 in Paris; they were to have five children. He was based in India in 1934-39 and was awarded the Distinguished Service Order (1938) for operations on the North-West Frontier.

Back home, in 1939-40 Embry commanded No.107 Bomber Squadron and became famous for his leadership, courage and exploits, including two daring escapes from the Germans after being shot down over France. He was awarded two Bars to his D.S.O. Having commanded a night-fighter wing in the Battle of Britain and served a stint in the Middle East, he performed staff duties in England. In 1943 Embry was promoted acting air vice marshal and given command of No.2 Bomber Group. Flying with his squadrons at every opportunity, he won a third Bar to his D.S.O., was awarded the Distinguished Flying Cross and was mentioned in dispatches. He was appointed C.B. and K.B.E. in 1945, and received a number of foreign honours.

Following World War II, Sir Basil was assistant chief of Air Staff (training) at the Air Ministry, then (from 1949) commander-in-chief of Fighter Command, in which post he was promoted air marshal. In 1953 he was appointed K.C.B., promoted air chief marshal and sent to France as commander-in-chief, Allied Air Forces Central Europe. On his retirement on 26 February 1956, he was appointed G.C.B. His *Mission Completed* (London, 1957) recounted his triumphs in the air, and expressed his postwar disillusionment with the higher management of the R.A.F. and of the forces assigned to the North Atlantic Treaty Organization.

In March 1956, accompanied by his wife Hope, Embry left England 'in search of a new life'. The search ended in Western Australia.

He bought a largely undeveloped farming property of 1400 acres (567 ha) at Chowerup in the south-west. The land had to be cleared before mixed farming could begin. He also acquired land at Cape Riche, east of Albany, and moved to this block in the late 1960s. The family established themselves as sheep-farmers.

Embry became active in the politics of agriculture through the Farmers' Union of Western Australia. After only a few months involvement in that organization, he was elected general president in 1971 and held office for two years. He assisted in restructuring the union and making it more professional. Embry focussed on perennial concerns of the farming sector: the burden of protective tariffs, the need for long-term rural finance, the level of farmers' returns, and, especially, the state of overseas trade. In the context of rural recession with depressed prices for wheat, wool and livestock, the need for new outlets was pressing. Convinced that farmers needed to market their own products in order to receive a greater share of their value, in 1972 he led a delegation through South East Asia and instigated the establishment of Rural Traders Co-operative (W.A.) Ltd. With Embry as first chairman (1972-75), and the involvement of the Pastoralists' and Graziers' Association of Western Australia, the co-operative sought overseas markets for rural products, in the first instance sheep, mutton and lamb. Although initial plans (to establish a co-operative-owned abattoir in Western Australia and then, in a joint venture, to build cool-rooms in the Middle East) were not realized, the company developed into an effective marketing enterprise.

Small and spare, wiry and strong, 'with extremely piercing blue eyes under fierce eyebrows', Embry had 'a puckish face' which could express 'a wide variety of emotions from demoniac rage to delight, laughter, and goodwill, often within a few seconds'. He was a forceful man of great energy and powers of persuasion, who believed in 'leading from the front'. The span of his activities in Britain and Australia made him a widely respected adviser in the public and private sectors. He worked at a punishing pace—staying high-tuned he called it—until illness intervened in 1975. Survived by his wife, daughter and three of his four sons, he died on 7 December 1977 at Boyup Brook and was buried with Catholic rites in the local cemetery.

DNB, 1971-80; *Harvey-Murray Times*, 22 Feb 1957; *West Australian*, 22 Apr 1971, 14 Feb 1973; Air Chief Marshal Sir Basil Embry (ms, R2824, Herald L, Melb, biog service); information from Mr P. Embry, Cape Riche, and Sir D. Eckersley, Harvey, WA.   LENORE LAYMAN

ENGLAND, ERNEST ROY (1896-1978), soldier and railway worker, was born on 28 July 1896 at Middle Park, Melbourne, fourth child of English-born parents Joseph Henry England, miner, and his wife Elvera, née Smith. The family moved to Boulder on the Western Australian goldfields where Joseph was later killed in an industrial accident. Ernest worked for the Western Australian Government Railways and served in the 84th Infantry (Goldfields Regiment), Militia. When he enlisted in the Australian Imperial Force on 23 May 1915 he was 5 ft 10 ins (178 cm) tall, with blue eyes and brown hair.

Sailing for Egypt in June 1915, England joined the 16th Battalion on 2 August at Gallipoli. He was evacuated sick on the 28th and did not return to the peninsula until 8 December, ten days before the general withdrawal began. The battalion moved to France in June 1916 and on 9-10 August suffered heavy losses north of Pozières. England was one of two stretcher-bearers who were praised for 'repeatedly bringing-in wounded under heavy shell-fire' within their front line and for venturing into no man's land to recover casualties from earlier fighting. He was awarded the Military Medal.

On 11-12 April 1917 at Riencourt, near Bullecourt, England and three of his comrades showed 'conspicuous bravery and determination' by carrying injured soldiers to the rear in the face of heavy shell, rifle and machine-gun fire. England won a Bar to his M.M. He was promoted corporal in June and sergeant next month. Near Hebuterne on 15 April 1918 he had charge of a small daylight-reconnaissance patrol which unexpectedly came upon an enemy machine-gun post. According to the battalion's records, he took the Germans' gun and returned with it to his own lines. Quickly gathering a larger party, he again attacked the post, killing one German and capturing five. He was awarded the Distinguished Conduct Medal. In May he was sent to Britain for officer-training and was commissioned on 18 December.

England's A.I.F. appointment terminated in Perth on 8 May 1919. He rejoined the W.A.G.R., working in the Collie-Brunswick Junction district and playing Australian Rules football with the Railways Club; in 1920 he won a best-all-round-player award. On 12 October 1921 he married a 35-year-old divorcee Bessie Williams, née James (d.1973), at the Presbyterian Church, North Perth. Ernest took up dairy-farming near Collie, where Bessie had small business interests. After they moved to Perth in the early 1930s, he drove for United Buses Ltd, then assisted her in managing two popular guesthouses in the Claremont-Cottesloe area. A quiet, unassuming man, he was involved in horse-breeding and training, and achieved modest success: one of his favourite winners was named Hebuterne.

Survived by his two sons and stepson, England died on 21 January 1978 at Subiaco and was cremated with Anglican rites. His elder son Bert was commissioned in the Royal Australian Air Force in World War II; the younger Ernie played Sheffield Shield cricket for Western and South Australia; both became medical practitioners.

C. Longmore, *The Old Sixteenth* (Perth, 1929); C. E. W. Bean, *The A.I.F. in France*, 1916-18 (Syd, 1929, 1933, 1937, 1942), and *Anzac to Amiens* (Canb, 1968); AWM records; information from Dr E. J. England, Cottesloe, Perth.

KEITH D. HOWARD

ENGLISH, GEORGE SELWYN (1912-1980), composer, was born on 16 September 1912 in Sydney, son of native-born parents George Philip John Engisch (later English)—who had a long but peripatetic career as a teacher of singing, a composer and a conductor—and his wife Marjorie Blanche, née Hodgson. Educated at Malvern Church of England Grammar and Melbourne High schools, young George learned music partly from his father and partly through his own efforts: his mother vetoed proper training as a result of an unhappy marriage and an acrimonious divorce (1929).

Living in Britain from 1935, English assiduously studied in libraries, attended concerts, worked as a music critic, and established and edited the *British Motorist* magazine. On 19 December 1936 at the register office, Hampstead, he married Clare Rosina Henkes; they were to have a son and daughter before being divorced in 1975. Returning to Sydney in 1939, he was employed by Amalgamated Wireless (Australasia) Ltd until he enlisted in the Royal Australian Air Force on 14 July 1942. He was discharged on 23 December on medical grounds.

English worked as a critic for Sydney newspapers and subsequently as chief editor for the music publishers, W. H. Paling [q.v.5] & Co. Ltd, doing a great deal of freelance composing and arranging, especially for theatre, radio and films. He assembled an extensive collection of 'mood music' while associated with the Australian Commonwealth Film Unit and with the Shell and Vacuum oil companies' production units. His experiences during the filming of *Alice through the Centre* (1950) developed his craft as a composer and led to such works as *The Australian Dingo* (1958), *Death of a Wombat* (which won a *Prix Italia* in 1959) and *The First Waratah* (for narrator, wind quintet and percussion, 1972) which were imaginative evocations in music and text of aspects of the Australian bush.

He also wrote numerous songs, including *Song for a Crowning* (1953), to a poem by Elizabeth Riddell, and won an Australian Broadcasting Commission prize for the overture for full orchestra, *For a Royal Occasion* (1952). English was not prolific, but wrote reliably to order. His serious compositions included *Sinfonia* (1967), the overture, *Botany Bay 1770* (1960), *Quintet for Wind Instruments* (1969), *Chiaroscuro* (1966) for string trio, and an undated *Symphony in A minor*. A technically skilled composer of limited imagination, he produced a tempered version of the English modernist style of the 1920s and 1930s. Only after *Chiaroscuro* did he show 'a cautious acceptance of the principles of serialism'.

Active in music politics, English was a 'writer member' (1961-68) of the board of the Australasian Performing Right Association, editor (1969-78) of its journal, and founding president (1960) of the Fellowship of Australian Composers (later secretary and a long-time councillor). In 1961 he began to campaign for a musical counterpart of the Commonwealth Literary Fund. Eventually, in 1965, he led a delegation to meet Prime Minister Harold Holt [q.v.]; the Commonwealth Assistance to Australian Composers Advisory Board was established in 1967.

On 13 June 1975 English married an advertising executive Marcia Clement Rose in a civil ceremony at Cremorne. Accounts of the nature of this tall, strongly built, bushy-browed man emphasize his tenacity and his mercurial temperament—at times charming, at times fiercely unpleasant, owing in part to alcohol. Survived by his wife and their son, English died of cancer on 8 October 1980 at Mosman and was buried in Northern Suburbs cemetery. He belonged to that generation of composers—including Roy Agnew [q.v.7] and Raymond Hanson [q.v.]—who, despite their professionalism, were overshadowed by the emergence of an Australian *avant-garde* in the 1960s.

Aust Musical News, no 50, Sept 1959, p 10; *Canon*, Mar-Apr 1961, p 136; *SMH*, 3 Sept 1950, 25 Mar 1952, 27 Apr 1953, 2 July 1971; *Sun News-Pictorial*, 25 Mar 1952; ABC Archives (Syd); Aust Music Centre L (Syd); information from Mr S. Rose, Balmain, Mrs C. English, Elizabeth Bay, Ms D. Dodd, Strathfield, and Dr E. Gross, Drummoyne, Syd.   JOHN CARMODY

ENNOR, SIR ARNOLD HUGHES (1912-1977), biochemist and administrator, was born on 10 October 1912 at Gardenvale, Melbourne, son of Arnold Martin Ennor, joiner, and his wife Charlotte Vandeluer, née Hughes, both Victorian born. Choosing to be called Hugh, young Ennor was educated at O'Neill College (Elsternwick), Melbourne Technical College and the University of Melbourne (B.Sc., 1938; M.Sc., 1939; D.Sc., 1943). In 1929 he began work as a laboratory-assistant at the Baker [q.v.7] Medical Research Institute and from 1938 continued there as a junior fellow of the National Health and Medical Research Council; his specialty was biochemistry. On 18 March 1939 at Wesley Church, Melbourne, he married a dress designer Violet Phyllis Isobel Argall.

Engaged in defence work in World War II, Ennor conducted research into chemical warfare and from 1944 had charge of scientific services at the Australian Field Experimental Station, Proserpine, Queensland. In 1946 he entered the University of Oxford, England, on a two-year Wellcome Trust fellowship. Back in Melbourne in 1948, he was appointed senior biochemist, Commonwealth Serum Laboratories. On 15 August he accepted the foundation chair of biochemistry in the John Curtin [q.v.13] School of Medical Research, Australian National University, and was initially based at the C.S.L. Ennor undertook research into carbohydrate metabolism and the distribution and turnover of phosphorous compounds in muscle and liver. He was to publish ninety papers—mostly co-authored—and he and his collaborators produced highly original work, both in their findings and experimental techniques.

Ability in research had brought Ennor to the A.N.U., but the course of his later career was to be shaped by his administrative skills. Although Sir Howard (Baron) Florey [q.v.] had planned the John Curtin school, it was Ennor who brought it into being as a thriving research centre. Moving to Canberra, he was dean of the school in 1953-67 and effectively its administrative head. His responsibilities increased after 1957 when Florey's involvement ceased. Ennor was also deputy vice-chancellor of the university in 1964-67. Appointed C.B.E. in 1963, he was knighted in 1965.

With the establishment of the Commonwealth Department of Education and Science, Sir Hugh became its permanent head on 1 February 1967. One of his early initiatives led to the formation of the educational research and development committee. Responding to calls for increased Federal funding of schools, he emphasized the need for qualitative rather than quantitative improvements, and wanted teachers to become more professional. He had been a member of Sir Leslie Martin's committee on the future of tertiary education in Australia whose report (1964) led to sweeping reforms.

In 1972 the Whitlam government separated the portfolios of science and education, and Ennor opted to head the Department of Science (Science and Consumer Affairs in

1975). Despite limited resources, he endeavoured to increase efficiency and promote sound policies. The department was unfairly blamed for the government's decision in 1975 to reduce the Australian Research Grants Committee's funds. That year Ennor publicly resisted an attempt by the royal commission on Australian government administration to have his department abolished. He oversaw the gradual development of the agreement (1968) with the United States of America for scientific and technological co-operation, and successfully pressed the government to make a budget provision in 1977-78 for building a station in Australia to receive and process 'Landsat' satellite information.

Ennor's contributions to science, medicine and administration were recognized by fellowships of the Royal Australian Chemical Institute (1951) and the Australian Academy of Science (1954), of which he was treasurer (1963-67); the University of New South Wales conferred an honorary doctorate of science on him in 1968 and Monash University an honorary doctorate of medicine in 1969. He had been prominent in establishing the Australian Biochemical Society in 1955 (president 1959-61) and the National Heart Foundation of Australia in 1959.

A tall, well-built man, with rugged features and wavy hair of fair to gingerish colour, Ennor had immense energy and drive, and did things promptly. He had the ability to assess people quickly, and had no time for stupidity, indolence, obfuscation or duplicity. Those he trusted appreciated his loyalty and kindliness; yet, in the mid-1960s a number of his colleagues at the J.C.S.M.R. thought that his style was arrogant and distant. Possessing great integrity, Ennor did what he believed to be right, irrespective of the consequences. Once he had made up his mind, he committed himself to whatever the end entailed, though he was always willing to reconsider the grounds for his actions. He expressed himself elegantly and forcefully in both the written and the spoken word. Equipped with a fund of stories which he told with gusto, he had an infectious, exuberant manner that projected confidence and optimism. He could comfortably mix with the mighty and the lowly.

After being gravely ill for several months, Ennor retired on 10 October 1977. Farewell functions planned by his friends in Australia, Japan, the U.S.A. and England were unable to be held: Ennor died of lymphoma on 14 October 1977 in Canberra Hospital and was cremated. Lady Ennor survived him, as did their daughter and son.

Records of Aust Academy of Science, 4, no 1, Nov 1978 (issued Apr 1979), p 105, *and* for publications; personal information.

JOHN P. LONERGAN

ENTICKNAP, AMBROSE GEORGE (1894-1976), orchardist and politician, was born on 19 May 1894 at St Kilda, Melbourne, fifth child of Ambrose Enticknap, painter, and his wife Alice, née Nankivell, both Victorian born. At the age of 7, George became seriously ill with osteomyelitis and had a leg amputated above the knee; he used a crutch for the rest of his life and was nicknamed 'the Ibis'. Educated at Lilliput and Rutherglen state schools, he worked as a wheat-buyer and timber-cutter in Victoria (once winning a tree-felling competition). In 1918 he moved to the Murrumbidgee Irrigation Area in New South Wales and obtained employment as a carpenter. On 18 October 1922 at Hawksburn, Melbourne, he married with Free Christian Church forms Beatrice Olive Mitchell. Next year he began to grow fruit in the M.I.A.

A founder (1925) of the Yanco fruitgrowers' association, Enticknap chaired (1927-37) its successor, the Leeton Fruitgrowers' Co-operative Society Ltd. With fellow growers, he formed the Leeton Co-operative Cannery Ltd in 1934 to purchase the Leeton works from the Stevens [q.v.12] government. He chaired the company from 1935 to 1954 and was also involved with other fruit growers' associations. A widower, on 20 May 1937 at St Barnabas's Anglican Church, Sydney, he married a nurse Rose Anne Laverty.

Having been elected to Willimbong Shire Council in 1928, Enticknap was its president in 1938, but resigned that year to be general manager (1938-41) of the Yenda Producers' Co-operative Society Ltd. He unsuccessfully contested the Legislative Assembly seat of Murrumbidgee in 1935 and 1938 for Lang [q.v.9] Labor. Ineligible to stand in 1941 for pre-selection as the official Labor candidate because of his affiliation with Lang's breakaway Australian Labor Party (Non-Communist), Enticknap won Murrumbidgee as an Independent. The 1942 annual conference readmitted him (with continuity) to the official party.

From 1941 to 1965 the State Labor governments were notable for prominent, able, long-serving rural members such as Enticknap. Chairman of caucus (1950-53), in November 1952 he was appointed minister for conservation in J. J. Cahill's [q.v.13] cabinet, with responsibility for extending the M.I.A. and creating the Coleambally Irrigation Area. On 15 March 1956 he was given the transport portfolio, partly because it was hoped that, as a rural member, he would not be vulnerable to pressure from urban trade unions. He clashed with the transport unions on numerous occasions. In 1960 he returned to conservation and was also minister for agriculture from 1962 until his retirement in 1965. A strong minister who kept on top of his department, he was associated with the dominant, right-wing group in the government.

Although Enticknap was popular and convivial, he had a tougher side: on one occasion he was involved in a brawl with a colleague in the parliamentary dining-room. He was a keen fisherman, an accomplished mouth-organ player and made toys for charity with a craftsman's skill. In retirement he ran a shoe-repair service for needy pensioners. Survived by his wife, Enticknap died on 3 January 1976 at his Hurstville home. Both his marriages were childless.

PD (NSW), 6 Nov 1951, p 4100, 26 Mar 1952, p 5764, 24 Feb 1976, p 3591; ALP, *J*, Aug 1961, p 27; *SMH*, 16 June 1941, 15 June 1942, 27, 28 Mar 1952, 7 Dec 1957, 26 May 1960, 31 Dec 1966, 5 Jan 1976; *Daily Mirror* (Syd), 25 Feb 1954; D. Clune, The N.S.W. Election of 1941 in Rural Areas (M.A. thesis, Univ Syd, 1982); information from the late Mr R. R. Downing, Mr L. A. Jeckeln, Turramurra, Hon J. R. Johnson, Parliament House, and Mr R. B. Nott, Brighton-le-Sands, Syd.

DAVID CLUNE

ERVIN, SAMUEL HENRY (1881-1977), woolbroker and benefactor, was born on 21 January 1881 at Monkland, Queensland, fourth and youngest child of Samuel Ervin (d.1881), a miner from Ireland, and his German-born wife Matilda, née Ostwald. Matilda married Ernest Theodor Henry Rohde in 1883 and the family moved to Sydney. As a schoolboy, Harry used his stepfather's surname, grew up at Mosman, attended Sydney Church of England Grammar School (Shore) and frequented the artists' camp at Sirius Cove.

On leaving school, Ervin worked in woollen mills in Europe to gain experience of all aspects of the industry. Back in Sydney, his brother-in-law Karl Lothringer arranged for Harry to buy for the Belgian firm of Hauzeur-Gerard Fils of Verviers. During World War I Ervin took over Lothringer & Co.; he established S. H. Ervin Ltd, woolbrokers, in 1927. At the district registrar's office, Mosman, on 7 April 1926 he married 38-year-old Muriel Beatrice Gray, daughter of J. G. Appel [q.v.7]; she had two daughters from her previous marriage. From 1929 the Ervins lived at Glanworth, Darling Point, until moving in 1946 to the Astor flats, Macquarie Street. Influenced by the artists of Sirius Cove, as early as 1905 Ervin had purchased works from Charles Conder, J. J. Hilder, Norman Lindsay, Sydney Long, H. S. Power, Tom Roberts and (Sir) Arthur Streeton [qq.v.3,9,10,11,12]. For most of his life he bought and sold paintings, antique furniture, porcelain, bronzes and other works of art.

In World War II Ervin was a senior appraiser under the United Kingdom Wool Purchase Arrangement. His firm benefited from the wool boom in the 1950s: because he worked on a commission basis, his personal income increased with the rise in wool prices. He retired shortly before H.G.F. collapsed due to its losses in the Belgian Congo.

When legislation was passed in the 1960s to allow taxation exemption for cultural gifts to the nation, Ervin became a substantial benefactor. In 1962 he gave his collection of paintings (later valued at about £200 000) to the Commonwealth of Australia to encourage the government to erect a national art gallery. He donated $50 000 to the New South Wales branch of the National Trust of Australia in 1971 to purchase Lindsay's home at Springwood. Influenced by his offer to donate $200 000 to restore two buildings at Observatory Hill as an art gallery and museum, in 1974 the State government made the former Fort Street Girls' High School available to the National Trust for headquarters. Ervin was deeply concerned about the protection and presentation of Australia's heritage; he bought works of art, donated them to the S. H. Ervin gallery and established a fund for future purchases.

A dapper little man with a charming smile, Ervin mostly dressed in a grey suit and bow tie. He was shy and reserved, and often walked by himself in the Royal Botanic Gardens. Predeceased by his wife and step-daughters, he died on 29 October 1977 at the Astor and was cremated. He bequeathed the residue of his estate to the National Trust, bringing his total donations to about $1.25 million. A portrait of Ervin by Sir William Dargie is in the Queensland Art Gallery and one by Reginald Campbell in the S. H. Ervin Museum and Art Gallery, Observatory Hill, Sydney.

S. H. Ervin Museum and Art Gallery *and* National Trust of Aust (NSW), *S. H. Ervin Memorial Exhibition 18 May-29 July 1979*, exhibition cat (Syd, 1991); *National Trust Q*, Oct 1992; *SMH*, 18 Dec 1962, 5 Nov 1977; *North Shore Times*, 8 Mar 1978; *Sun-Herald* (Syd), 4 June 1978; National Trust of Aust (NSW) *and* S. H. Ervin Museum and Art Gallery Archives (Syd); family papers (held by Mr H. Lothringer, Whale Beach, Syd).

JILLIAN OPPENHEIMER

ESPIE, FRANK FANCETT (1890-1962), mining engineer, was born on 3 September 1890 in East Adelaide, only son of James Espie, stockbroker, and his wife Alice Maude, née O'Rielly, who had taken the surname of her adoptive parents Fancett. Educated at the Collegiate School of St Peter, where he was a prefect, and the University of Adelaide (B.E., 1913), Frank was 'a born leader' and 'exceedingly popular with his fellow students'. In

1910 he was awarded a Blue for boats and was a member of the VIII which won the intervarsity championship. He gained a fellowship in mining (1913) from the South Australian School of Mines and Industries.

In 1914 Espie joined the Burma Corporation at Bawdwin, northern Burma. He married Laura Jean Fletcher on 6 December 1915 at Christ Church, Rangoon; they were to have three children. By 1941 he had risen to become general manager of the lead-zinc mine at Bawdwin—one of the richest in the world—which employed almost ten thousand workers.

On 24 April 1942 news arrived of the approach of Japanese forces. Espie supervised the destruction of all company property, and planned the evacuation of staff and their families. Under his direction the main party went to Nam Kham on the Chinese border. From there the women and children, and men over 45, were flown to safety. The remaining men then proceeded by road, boat and foot, over difficult mountain terrain, eventually reaching Calcutta, India, on 24 May. A company officer, R. C. (Dick) Leach, praised 52-year-old Espie's 'calm efficiency, leadership, and judgement', and noted that he 'could with every justification have also gone by air . . . but he chose to continue with us on foot'.

Back in Australia in 1943, Espie was appointed general superintendent of Western Mining Corporation Ltd at Kalgoorlie, Western Australia, and oversaw the re-establishment of the firm's operations after the war. He became a director in 1947 and deputy managing director in 1952. Six years later he transferred to the Melbourne office. He was a board-member of such companies as the Burma Corporation Ltd and Broken Hill South Ltd.

It was said of Espie that his outstanding characteristic was an ability to draw out the best in people and gently guide them to a solution to their problems. Sir Lindesay Clark described him as 'an able and considerate' manager whose 'success in the industrial and other fields was shown by his sobriquet of "Father Espie"'. Widely respected in the business community, he was a vice-president (1949-59) of the Chamber of Mines of Western Australia and president (1948) of the Australasian Institute of Mining and Metallurgy; in 1953 he was awarded the institute's medal for his professional accomplishments and for his achievement in leading his staff to safety in 1942.

Espie's presidential address to the Aus.I.M.M. in 1948 had reaffirmed his confidence in Western Australia's gold industry and in Australia's potential for further economic development. Survived by his wife, son and two daughters, he died on 9 May 1962 at Epworth Private Hospital, Richmond, Melbourne, and was cremated. His son (Sir) Frank also pursued a career in mining.

W. S. Robinson, *If I Remember Rightly*, G. Blainey ed (Melb, 1967); G. L. Clark, *Built on Gold* (Melb, 1983); G. M. Ralph, *A Pictorial History* (Melb, 1983); A'sian Inst of Mining and Metallurgy, *Procs*, nos 148-149, Jan-June 1948, *and* membership records, *and* minutes of ordinary meeting, 4 June 1954; M. Smith, Espie Family History (ms, Bowenville, Qld, copy held by Sir Frank Espie, Sth Yarra, Melb); E. D. J. Stewart, Olympian Green and Gold (ms, Melb, 1992, copy held by author); E. W. Hughes personal correspondence (1954, CRA Archives, Melb); Western Mining Corporation Archives (Melb); information from Sir Laurence Brodie-Hall, Perth, and Sir Frank Espie.

GILBERT M. RALPH

ESSEX, HARCOURT ALGERNON LEIGHTON; see ALGERANOFF

EVANS, ERNEST (1892-1965), sugarcane farmer and politician, was born on 6 March 1892 at Killarney, Queensland, eighth child of Joseph Evans, sawyer, and his wife Harriet, née Murphy, both native-born. Educated at Spring Creek and Killarney state schools, Ernest became a canecutter, timberworker and shearer in the Cairns district. On 31 October 1914 he married Winifred Ellen Cronin with Anglican rites at Christ Church, Bundaberg. Tall and heavily built, Evans was active on behalf of the Australian Workers' Union and earned the nickname 'Firestick Ernie'. In 1920 he took up a cane-farm at Little Mulgrave, near Cairns, and organized the local farmers into a company which built and operated a tramline to carry their cane to the Mulgrave Sugar Mill. Following a brief sojourn at Southport, in 1929 he returned to sugar-farming at Nindaroo, near Mackay. A member (from 1929) of the Pioneer Shire Council (chairman 1934-47 and 1955-57), he was also a director and chairman (1935-57) of the Farleigh Co-operative Sugarmilling Association Ltd.

In May 1947 Evans won the Legislative Assembly seat of Mirani for the Country Party, defeating Labor's deputy-premier and minister for transport E. J. Walsh [q.v.] in a bitter campaign. From 12 August 1957, in (Sir) George Nicklin's [q.v.] Country Party-Liberal Party coalition, Evans held the newly created portfolio for development, mines and main roads; from 9 June 1960 until 28 February 1965 he was minister for development, main roads and electricity. Previously a member of the Hillsborough Oil Syndicate, he had taken part in exploration at Cape Hillsborough. This experience aided him in introducing legislation which opened Queensland to oil prospectors, and which led to the

Moonie and Roma strikes. His efforts helped to establish Australia's oil industry. He was also responsible for enacting legislation which authorized agreement with Comalco Industries Ltd to mine bauxite reserves at Weipa, and which allowed coal deposits at Moura to be developed by Japanese interests.

Presiding over the Department of Main Roads, Evans overcame problems associated with the increase in heavy transport vehicles by providing sealed roads across large areas of the State. As a shire councillor himself, he lent a sympathetic ear to local authority representatives and his proposals, raised at an interstate conference of road ministers, contributed to moves towards uniform road charges in 1963. Queensland farmers particularly appreciated a concession that authorized them to carry primary produce on trucks of less than four tons without incurring road tax. Evans's administration changed a patchwork pattern of *ad hoc* policies into a co-ordinated programme which gave Queensland an all-weather road from Cairns to the New South Wales border. While he was minister for electricity with responsibility for the State Electricity Commission, reticulation was accelerated to meet growing demand, and, as minister for mines, he actively encouraged the discovery of new mineral deposits.

His energy could always be harnessed in the interests of the sugar industry. In 1957, when he had severed many formal links with Mackay organizations, the Farleigh mill was about to build a tramway to Wagoora. Evans was one of those who conceived and executed this undertaking which built the mill into one of the finest in the industry. He was an executive-member (1935-50) of the Australian Sugar Producers' Association and served as millers' representative on the Queensland Sugar Board's consultative committee on bulk handling. Sincere and purposeful, he was a fierce advocate and a forthright opponent. His understanding of the sugar industry was considerable; his counsel carried weight and influence among primary producers and in the political sphere.

Survived by his wife, daughter and three sons, Evans died on 28 February 1965 in Brisbane; he was accorded a state funeral and buried in Mount Bassett cemetery, Mackay. The degree to which he benefited his district was less widely known than his emphatic conviction, 'I work for Queensland'.

C. Lack (comp), *Three Decades of Queensland Political History, 1929-1960* (Brisb, 1962); *Qld Government Mining J*, Mar 1965, p 104; *Local Government* (Brisb), 25 June 1965, p 5; *Australian* and *Courier-Mail*, 1 Mar 1965; *Daily Mercury*, 1-3 Mar 1965; personal papers held by, and information from Mr B. Evans, Mirani, Qld; personal information.

GORDON NOSCOV

EVANS, EVELYN PAGET (1881-1960), administrator, was born on 11 November 1881 at Auckland, New Zealand, daughter of Welsh-born parents Lawford David Evans (d.1903), physician, and his wife Lillie Elizabeth, née Price [q.v.9 Goodisson]. By 1897 Lillie was running a private hospital at St Kilda, Melbourne. Educated nearby at The Priory, Evelyn worked as a typist and by 1913 had moved to Sydney.

In July 1917 Evans became the first paid secretary of the Australasian Trained Nurses' Association. Her duties included managing the *Australasian Nurses' Journal* and being general secretary of the Australasian Massage Association (later Australian Physiotherapy Association). When the (Royal) Australian Nursing Federation was founded in 1924 to represent nurses' interests, she also became its secretary. The three organizations for which she worked espoused dedicated, selfless professionalism for their members, an ideal she applied to herself.

Staunchly opposed to trade unionism for nurses, in 1929 Evans gave evidence to the Industrial Commission of New South Wales against an application by the Hospital Employees' Association to include nurses under its award. The formation of the New South Wales Nurses' Association in 1931 greatly upset her and in 1934, as an independent witness, she opposed a reduced working week for nurses. Her evidence reflected her employers' policy and she argued that improved working conditions would only exacerbate the over-supply of nurses. Evans's correspondence with impoverished nurses revealed her firmness and kindness. Secretary of the State branch of the Florence Nightingale Committee of Australia, she was also a foundation member (1934) of the nurses' memorial fund sub-committee which in 1946 opened A.T.N.A. House for retired and destitute nurses.

Evans gave notice as general secretary of the A.T.N.A. in 1945, but a replacement was not found until the secretary's salary was nearly doubled one year later. In appreciation of her unselfish services, she was given a £300 retiring allowance and made vice-president of A.T.N.A. House. In 1950 she retired from the A.N.F., but remained secretary of the Australian Physiotherapy Association until 1956. She revealed her firm grasp of detail in articles in the *International Nursing Review* (1938) and the *Australian Journal of Physiotherapy* (1955).

A delegate (from 1924) to the National Council of Women of New South Wales and a member (1926-46) of its executive, Evans had been active on the health and professionalism sub-committees. In 1939-45 she was involved in the Women's Voluntary Services which was founded to spearhead civilian war-work. She organized first aid for the National Emergency Services in 1940-43 and was a serving sister of the Order of St John. A member of the central council of women's auxiliaries of the New South Wales Society for Crippled Children, she was vice-president of the Business and Professional Women's Club of Sydney, and a justice of the peace. She belonged to the Lyceum Club and her major recreation was music. In 1955 she was appointed M.B.E. Although she was loyal, conscientious and self-effacing, Evans's employers consistently congratulated themselves, not her, on her ability and achievements. She died on 10 April 1960 in Rydalmere Mental Hospital and was cremated with Anglican rites.

Aust Nurses' J, July 1917, pp 231, 233, Feb 1955, p 31, May 1960, p 129; *Aust J of Physiotherapy*, 1, no 2, 1955, p 78; papers of Aust Trained Nurses' Assn (NSW) *and* Women's Voluntary Services (ML); National Council of Women (NSW), papers for 1930s *and* Minutes of General Meetings and Executive Cte Meetings, 1924-46 (ML); information from Dr B. Gandevia, Randwick, Syd.

JUDITH GODDEN
HEATHER RADI

EVANS, HAROLD CECIL (1902-1954), surfboat sweep and furrier, was born on 3 October 1902 at Enfield, Sydney, fourth child of Sydney Ernest Evans, commercial traveller, and his wife Alice Emily, née Tant, both native-born. Schoolkids gave Harold the nickname 'Rastus' (at that time a popular appellation for Black people) as a jocular play on his blond hair, fair skin and blue eyes. Although under age, he joined North Steyne Surf Life Saving Club at 15, avoiding suspicion because of his large frame. He was a member of the team that won the Surf Life Saving Association of Australia's rescue and resuscitation title in 1921.

In 1920 Dick Matheson had been persuaded to coach North Steyne's surfboat crews. He taught Evans, his star pupil, to control a boat by using the heavy 'sweep' oar in the stern. Appointed boat captain when Matheson returned to Freshwater, Evans won seven S.L.S.A.A. senior boat titles between 1921 and 1930 which remains a club record. His sea skills and uncompromising training regimes made him 'king of sweeps'; his crews were known as 'Rastus's Slaves'. With master boatbuilder W. M. Ford, in 1927 Evans designed a carvel surfboat, made from cedar, which cost £130 to build. He cajoled club members to contribute sixpence a week to pay for the boat; thinking that they were being 'stung', the secretary suggested christening her *Bluebottle*. Next year Evans

took a crew to the Queenscliff bombora and manoeuvred *Bluebottle* onto a twenty-four-foot wave that drove her under water. Club members eventually hauled the partly submerged boat ashore.

The Royal Shipwreck Relief and Humane society of New South Wales presented Evans with a certificate of merit for rescuing a drowning man at North Steyne in 1928. At the carnival at Bronte in February 1931 the surf seethed like a cauldron. 'Escalators' (strong currents) swept out the thirty-six competitors in the first event—the junior surf race. Senior swimmers and boat crews rushed to the rescue, but only *Bluebottle* breached the thunderous breakers at first try. Evans and his crew made three trips to gather the scattered swimmers. The *Evening News* reported that 'Rastus Evans upheld the prestige of the champion sweepman when he came in on a wave with his overloaded boat and landed high and dry'. The S.L.S.A.A. sent him a letter of commendation for heroism. Evans and *Bluebottle* were subsequently filmed by Fox Movietone News.

In the 1920s Evans worked as a commercial traveller. On 16 November 1929 he married Isabel Iris Wilson at St Stephen's Presbyterian Church, Sydney; they were to remain childless. A 'good-humoured fellow with his soft speech (so unmistakably borrowed from Welsh forbears)', he went to New Zealand on business in 1933 and joined the surf lifesaving club at Lyall Bay, Wellington. Back in Sydney in 1938, he set up as a manufacturing furrier in George Street. He enlisted in the Australian Imperial Force on 20 March 1942 and served as a gunner in Western Australia until 10 February 1944 when he was discharged medically unfit (peptic ulcer). In 1948 he agreed 'to desert for a time his beloved garden' to stand in as captain of North Steyne and appear for the last time at an Australian championship. Survived by his wife, he died of coronary thrombosis on 6 July 1954 at his Seaforth home and was cremated with Methodist forms.

C. B. Maxwell, *Surf* (Syd, 1949); North Steyne Surf Life Saving Club, *North Steyne Surf Life Saving Club* (Syd, 1957), and *Annual Report*, 1920-39; B. Galton, *Gladiators of the Surf* (Syd, 1984); *Daily Telegraph* (Syd), 28, 29 Jan 1929; *SMH*, 29 Jan, 4 Feb 1929, 9 Feb 1931, 10, 20 Mar 1948, 8 July 1954; *Sun* (Syd), 7, 8 Feb 1931, 9 July 1974; *Sunday Pictorial* (Syd), 8 Feb 1931; *Daily Telegraph Pictorial* (Syd), 9 Feb 1931; *Syd Mail*, 11 Feb 1931; *Daily Mirror* (Syd), 7 June 1982; information from Mr C. Walton, Manly, Syd.   DOUGLAS BOOTH

EVANS, IVOR WILLIAM (1887-1960), flag designer and canvas goods manufacturer, was born on 24 July 1887 at Carlton,

Melbourne, third son of Evan Evans (d.1927), a tentmaker from Wales, and his Tasmanian-born wife Sally Clara, née Russell. While attending Princes Hill State School, at the age of 13 Ivor entered a competition announced by the prime minister's office on 29 April 1901 to design a Federal flag. Each entrant was required to submit, under a nom de plume, two coloured sketches—'one for the merchant service, and one for naval or official use'—by 31 May. According to one reckoning, 32 823 entries were received. At 2.30 on the afternoon of 3 September a flag made to the winning design was unfurled above the dome of the Exhibition Building, Melbourne, and flapped breezily in a strong sou'-westerly.

The prize of £200 was shared by five people who had independently submitted almost identical designs—Annie Dorrington, L. J. Hawkins, E. J. Nuttall, William Stevens and Evans. Their winning entries gave place of honour (top left of the hoist) to the Union Jack; beneath it a large white star was featured, with six points (one for each State in the Commonwealth); in the fly the Southern Cross appeared (almost vertical, composed of five smaller white stars in stylized form). Evans regarded the three symbols as representing—respectively—loyalty to the British Empire, the component parts that had united under Federation, and Australia's geographical relationship to the rest of the world. King Edward VII approved the design which was gazetted on 20 February 1903 and specified a blue ground for the ensign and a red for the merchant flag.

Proceeding on a scholarship to Box Hill Grammar School in 1902, Evans was employed by the Commercial Bank of Australia from April 1904 and rose to be manager of its branch at Chillingollah. On 13 January 1913 he joined his father's firm (founded 1877, Evan Evans Pty Ltd from 1920) which manufactured canvas goods. Located at 680 Elizabeth Street, Melbourne, it employed a staff of nine. Ivor was admitted to partnership in 1914. By the end of World War I the firm had made 354 581 items for the armed services. In 1924 it acquired land at 632 Bourke Street on which to build a new factory, and in 1938 opened a bulk store at 212 Pelham Street, Carlton. Employees numbered 109 in 1952. Evan Evans held agencies for three British firms, and had outlets for its own goods in Tasmania, Queensland, South Australia and Western Australia.

On 27 January 1917 at St Michael's Anglican Church, North Carlton, Ivor had married 21-year-old Stella Coles Arthur. He was managing director (1922-56) of the company and guided it through the Depression when he rarely placed his workers on short time. In January 1944 the Commonwealth Department of Supply appointed him honorary controller of canvas goods. During World War II his firm produced flags, tents, haversacks, waterbags, troughs, baths, aprons, chairs, beds, sleeping-bags, hammocks, tarpaulins and stretchers for the Allies. As head of one of Australia's largest manufacturers of its kind, Evans felt entitled to exploit his role as a designer of the nation's flag to promote his company's business. Believing that his fellow citizens 'were not one bit flag conscious', he continued to publish new editions of his booklet, *The History of the Australian Flag* (1918). In 1952 Prime Minister (Sir) Robert Menzies [q.v.] was asked in the House of Representatives to correct any false impression that the booklet may have made as to Evans being the sole designer of the country's flag.

From his youth, Evans loved sport and the outdoors. In later life he belonged to the Commercial Travellers' Association, and the Kingston Heath Golf and Melbourne Cricket clubs. He barracked for the Carlton Football Club, drove an Austin Cambridge motorcar and was an early devotee of television. Five ft 7 ins (170 cm) tall, with a strong brow and a sparkle in his eyes, he was direct and gruff in manner, but fair minded, warm hearted and generous by nature. His family was his chief source of happiness and relaxation. Evans died on Anzac Day 1960 at his Beaumaris home and was cremated; his estate was sworn for probate at £64 761. His wife survived him, as did two of their sons; the other son Thomas Guy had been killed in action off Timor with the Royal Australian Air Force in 1945.

Evan Evans Pty Ltd, *75 Years of Service and Progress* (Melb, 1952); F. Cayley, *Beneath the Southern Cross* (Syd, 1980); *Review of Reviews for A'sia*, 20 Sept 1901; *SMH*, 24 Jan 1944; *Age* (Melb), 26 Apr 1960; *Herald* (Melb), 27 Apr 1960; CRS A1 1904/4897, A461 B336/1/1, A462 828/1/7 (AA, ACT); information from Mr and Mrs A. B. D. Evans, Black Rock, and the late Mr I. R. Evans.
JOHN RITCHIE

EVATT, HERBERT VERE (1894-1965), politician and judge, was born on 30 April 1894 at East Maitland, New South Wales, fifth of eight sons of John Ashmore Evatt, a publican from India, and his Sydney-born wife Jane 'Jeanie' Sophia, née Gray. His father, the amiable but ineffectual scion of a well-connected English family, died when Bert was 7, and his Irish-Australian mother shouldered the task of encouraging an intellectually gifted family. Bert attended East Maitland Superior Public School and from 1905 Fort Street Model (Boys' High) School, Sydney, matriculated brilliantly in 1911 and entered St Andrew's College, University of Sydney (B.A.,

1915; M.A., 1917; LL.B., 1918—each with first-class honours), where he achieved excellent results in mathematics, logic, philosophy and English, and won a swag of medals and awards.

Prodigiously energetic, he played cricket, Rugby League football, hockey and baseball, edited *Hermes*, tutored at his college and presided (1916-17) over the University Union. He was rejected for service in World War I because of astigmatism. At first he supported conscription, but grew disenchanted with the 'Yes' arguments in the referendum of 1917. His anti-conservatism was reinforced by the influence of his radical friend Gordon Childe [q.v.7]. In 1918 Evatt published *Liberalism in Australia* (a thesis on the evolution of Australian politics towards liberal democracy) and joined the Australian Labor Party. After a period as associate to Sir William Cullen [q.v.8], chief justice of New South Wales, he was admitted to the Bar on 31 October 1918.

The 1920s were golden years for Evatt. He advanced fast at the Bar and in 1924 the university awarded him an LL.D. From 1920 to 1921 he had assisted the royal commission into the victimization of the 1917 transport strikers; in 1920 he had been junior counsel for the State government in the Engineers' case and encountered the successful rivalry of (Sir) Robert Menzies [q.v.] in the High Court of Australia. At the Congregational Church, Mosman, on 27 November 1920 Evatt married Mary Alice Sheffer [q.v. Evatt]; their partnership, sometimes turbulent, was always devoted. The honeymoon was spent in Hawaii and California where Evatt conducted an inquiry for the Commonwealth government into American treatment of Asian minorities. Immigration issues occupied him for several years. Assisting Andy Watt in the High Court, he failed in 1923 to prevent the expulsion of two Irish republican 'envoys', but succeeded in 1925 in averting the deportation of the trade union militants Tom Walsh [q.v.12] and Jacob Johnson. Evatt travelled to London in 1926 to attend an international conference on labour migration, at which he strongly upheld the White Australia policy.

Elected to the Legislative Assembly in May 1925 as a Labor member for Balmain, he soon fell foul of Premier J. T. Lang [q.v.9]. Evatt rapidly became an outspoken back-bench critic of Lang's machine politics. In 1926 he provoked discord by chairing a parliamentary select committee which investigated allegations by the *Labor Daily* that the Nationalists had bribed Labor politicians. Refused endorsement in 1927, he held Balmain that year as an Independent Labor candidate and cultivated E. G. Theodore [q.v.12], but had no political future while Lang remained dominant. In 1929 Evatt was appointed K.C. He

quit State politics in October 1930 to devote himself to the law; his practice was one of the largest in the State, earning £8000 to £10 000 a year. On 19 December he was appointed a justice of the High Court of Australia.

At 36 Evatt was the youngest judge elevated to the High Court. He invited controversy not only because he had been nominated by a Labor cabinet, but also because of his secretive and disputatious working habits and his frequent dissenting judgements. Yet, his isolation can be exaggerated. Surviving correspondence suggests civility and even cordiality in his dealings with most of his brother judges, (Sir) Hayden Starke [q.v.12] excepted.

Evatt's centralist tendencies were consistent with the High Court's post-1920 trend and admitted exceptions. With Chief Justice Sir Frank Duffy [q.v.8], in 1932 he dissented from the majority view which upheld the Commonwealth's claim against the New South Wales government after the Federal government had paid that State's repudiated interest bills. During the 1930s, in a tangled series of decisions about section 92 of the Constitution (which was concerned with trade between the States), Evatt consistently construed the term 'absolutely free' as being designed to inhibit protectionist policies. He also showed growing awareness of the potential of the Commonwealth's external affairs power for strengthening the authority of the Federal government.

In two notable victories for civil liberties Evatt joined the majority in upholding appeals by the left-wing journalist Hal Devanny in 1932 against a conviction under the Crimes Act (1914-32) and by the Czech communist Egon Kisch [q.v.] in 1934 against his exclusion from Australia. Geoffrey Sawer considered that, despite Evatt's enormous learning, his law lacked 'analytical muscle', but added that his 'forte was a feeling for the social revelations of law, for moulding doctrine to developing needs and to the values of contemporary men'. Evatt's verdicts were sometimes preconceived, often pragmatic, and he sought to explore the intent of legislation; he was influenced by decisions of the Supreme Court of the United States, and by jurists such as Oliver Wendell Holmes and Felix Frankfurter. In a conservative decade Evatt's presence on the court was a useful and timely stimulus.

He contributed significantly to Australian cultural life, especially in the 1930s. A discerning and influential patron of modern art, he supported the Contemporary Art Society and collected extensively—he and his wife may have been the first Australians to own a Modigliani. In 1937-63 he was president of trustees of the Public Library of New South

Wales. He was a productive historian. *The King and His Dominion Governors* (London, 1936), a constitutional study prompted by Lang's dismissal in 1932, was consulted by partisans of both sides when Sir John Kerr dismissed the Whitlam government in 1975. *Injustice Within the Law* (1937), a dissertation on the Tolpuddle martyrs, and *Rum Rebellion* (1938), an attempted rehabilitation of Governor William Bligh [q.v.1], both used the methods of legal advocacy to redress perceived defects in earlier historiography. Unashamedly partisan in their support for the underdog, the two books have been overtaken by later scholarship, and some readers find uncanny elements of self-portrayal in Evatt's account of Bligh. *Australian Labour Leader* (1940) was probably Evatt's finest work, a perceptive and sympathetic tribute to a hero of his youth W. A. Holman [q.v.9]. The university awarded Evatt a D.Litt. in 1944.

On the outbreak of World War II he had seemed a comfortably established public figure, subject to periodic criticism, but growing in reputation. He maintained his interest in Rugby League and cricket; his knowledge of sporting statistics was, if anything, excessive. With few close friends, he held the affection of many, ranging from social critics, such as Eleanor Dark and Kylie Tennant, to the archetypal mining capitalist W. S. Robinson [q.v.11]. Evatt's family life was notably supportive; he and Mary Alice had adopted two children, Peter and Rosalind. Bert smoked seldom, drank moderately and enjoyed food. The stocky, broad-shouldered figure of earlier years was acquiring a paunch. But his restless energy was undiminished, and continuing service on the High Court no longer contented him. He sought more active means of serving his country during wartime, possibly because he had no hope of becoming chief justice ahead of (Sir) Owen Dixon [q.v.]. With Lang's overthrow in 1939, a return to politics was feasible. At the September 1940 Federal elections he secured Labor endorsement for the seat of Barton, won it and was to hold it, on occasions precariously, until 1958.

He entered a hung parliament, with the Menzies government's survival in the hands of two Independents. Impatient for office, Evatt chafed at the caution of his leader John Curtin [q.v.13] and schemed ceaselessly. In December 1940 he rushed to Western Australia in the forlorn hope of helping Labor's candidate to win the Swan by-election, and in May 1941 wrote to Menzies offering inadequately veiled support for a national government. Curtin, who had nominated Evatt to the Advisory War Council in March, admired his ability, but withheld full trust. Following Menzies' resignation in August, Evatt busied himself in courting the Independent Alex Wilson [q.v.] whose defection helped to bring

Labor into office. In the Curtin government, sworn in on 7 October, Evatt was attorney-general and minister for external affairs. He was to retain both offices until 1949.

Evatt's ministerial style soon aroused antagonism. Unsparingly hard working, and capable of mastering immense detail, he pursued the objective of the moment obsessively, though his tactics were often flexible and at times devious. To his staff he was frequently demanding, hectoring and inconsiderate, but capable of unexpected flashes of empathy. Cabinet and diplomatic colleagues respected his competence, while doubting his loyalty; he had too much ego and too little self-awareness for good teamwork. He attracted more than the average politician's share of vicious rumour.

Following Japan's entry into the war and southward thrust towards Australia, in March 1942 the government decided to send Evatt to Washington and London to state Australia's needs. Menzies and others gossiped that the Evatts were fleeing the Japanese peril. In fact, Evatt pathologically hated flying, but he readily convinced himself that only he could put his country's case forcefully enough. His six weeks in Washington accomplished little beyond the setting up of the token Pacific War Council; in reporting to Curtin, however, Evatt claimed that the Americans recognized Australia's strategic importance and political consequence. It was only in London in May, apparently at first by accident, that he discovered that Britain and America were committed to a 'beat Hitler first' strategy.

Coached by Robinson, Evatt contained his outrage. Having earlier ruffled feathers in both countries by an over-aggressive approach, he schooled himself to build bridges with the British. Prime Minister (Sir) Winston Churchill was responsive and promised to send three Spitfire squadrons to Australia—a crisis in the Middle East delayed their arrival, but the squadrons seemed a symbol that Evatt's forthrightness could reap dividends. Before leaving England, he was sworn of the Privy Council and made an honorary master of the bench of the Middle Temple, compliments which he appreciated. The need for planes for the Royal Australian Air Force continued, and in April 1943 Evatt was dispatched on another mission to the U.S.A. and Britain. He secured substantial promises of aircraft, but delivery later fell short of the promises. Evatt's journey reinforced his belief that the U.S.A. was careless of his country's national interests and strategic priorities, and convinced him that Australia's prospects were better served by the British alliance, an alliance which to him was compatible with an emphatic assertion of Australian nationalism.

For much of the war Evatt's role as attorney-general preoccupied him most. His record over civil liberties was chequered. On taking office, he had immediately secured the release from internment of the communist trade unionists Horace Ratliff and Max Thomas, yet he did not lift the ban on the Communist Party of Australia until December 1942. He moved slowly on the plight of interned aliens. Nor did he hasten the release of sixteen members of the Australia-First Movement who had been interned without trial during his absence in 1942, thus earning the obloquy of their spokesman P. R. Stephensen [q.v.12]. Evatt believed that the war effort overrode individual freedom. He was given to interfering with broadcasting policy, and chaired a parliamentary censorship committee in 1944. None the less, he usually curbed efforts to use national security for political ends.

Despite a daunting load of routine business in shaping national security regulations and drafting legislation for measures such as uniform taxation, Evatt took energetic initiatives towards constitutional change. The Statute of Westminster was adopted in 1942, with some Opposition support. Concerned for postwar reconstruction, he unsuccessfully sought from the States fourteen new powers which the Commonwealth planned to exercise for five years after hostilities ceased. In August 1944 the Federal government submitted the fourteen proposals to a referendum on an all-or-nothing basis, adding guarantees of religious toleration and freedom of speech which Evatt hoped would reconcile public opinion. Following vehement Opposition hostility, the referendum was lost. The experience nourished Evatt's belief that social change was most readily achieved through a strengthened central government.

In October 1944 the American minister to Australia Nelson F. Johnson complained of Evatt: 'when he has finished with his politicking, and his Attorney-Generaling, he has damned little time for External Affairs'. Johnson may have soon rued his remark. Evatt had already shown disrespect for Great Power leadership. Irked that Britain, the U.S.A. and the Soviet Union had made important decisions at conferences in Moscow and Cairo in 1943 without consulting their allies, in January 1944 he persuaded New Zealand to join Australia in an agreement for a regional commission for the South Pacific. American foreign policy advisers disliked this assertion of regional interests, though the British covertly sympathized. Evatt's opportunity to act with greater effect arose after the Yalta discussions of February 1945, at which the Great Powers agreed to call a United Nations conference on a proposed world organization. Scheduled to begin on 25 April at San Fran-cisco, this gathering was to make Evatt's international reputation.

The Australian delegation included Frank Forde, deputy prime minister and nominally Evatt's senior. It was uncertain whether Forde or Evatt was leader, and it may have been that the ailing Curtin wanted both men out of the way to bolster J. B. Chifley's [q.v.13] prospects as his successor. Evatt took with him an able team of advisers, among them (Sir) Kenneth Bailey [q.v.13], John Burton, (Sir) Paul Hasluck and (Sir) Alan Watt. Thus supported, Evatt gained prominence during the next two months as spokesman for Australia and for the smaller and middle-ranking nations who wished to empower the U.N. as an instrument of collective security. Evatt probably intervened on too many fronts, but his achievements were significant. Although his vigorous campaigning failed to reduce the Great Powers' right of veto in the Security Council, the role of the smaller nations was strengthened by enlarging the scope of discussion in the General Assembly.

Evatt's team also succeeded in writing into the U.N. Charter a stronger commitment to full employment than originally planned. Where Australia's domestic interests were concerned, Evatt manoeuvred shrewdly. Seeking a definition of colonial trusteeship which would facilitate Australian control of the territories of Papua and New Guinea, he accepted a lesser degree of international accountability than he had originally advocated. He also accepted a concept of domestic jurisdiction compatible with Australia's policies on immigration and towards the Aborigines.

While Evatt was returning to Australia in July 1945, Curtin died. In the ensuing leadership ballot, one or two votes, apparently unsought, went to Evatt; Chifley was elected prime minister and confirmed Evatt in his portfolios. On 15 August the war in the Pacific ended. By then Evatt had a clearly defined foreign policy strategy, though his day-to-day tactics sometimes obscured his aims. Australia's regional security was paramount. It was essential, therefore, that the country's northern neighbours were in stable and friendly hands; in the early postwar months he favoured the restoration of Dutch, British and Portuguese authority in South-East Asia. In addition, Evatt held that Australia and New Zealand should wield influence in the South-West Pacific, without too much American intervention—a policy which led to the wrangle (1945-47) between Australia and the U.S.A. over Manus Island.

For Evatt, the Americans were better occupied in ensuring that Japan was permanently pacified, and he was annoyed by their refusal to arraign Emperor Hirohito as a war criminal. The U.S. State Department came to view Evatt as a troublemaker; for his part, Evatt increasingly valued Australia's British Commonwealth connexions as a buttress against American pressure. This viewpoint did not entail presenting a united front. At San Francisco he had made it plain that Australia would speak with its own voice in the international arena. In the brief interval between the end of World War II and the onset of the Cold War many Australians found this stand attractive.

It remained questionable how far a nation of Australia's modest military-industrial strength could carry an autonomous foreign policy. Believing that international relations could become a new province for law and order, based where possible on democratic and ethical standards, Evatt argued that, in the U.N., Australia should not align itself automatically with any major power bloc, but should judge questions on their merits. By enabling the U.N. to develop in its early years as a forum whose outcomes were not always predictable, Evatt's Australia may have helped to secure legitimacy for the new organization, and perhaps allowed the U.N. to act as a force for restraint in the Cold War.

Evatt participated tirelessly. He sat on the U.N. Security Council and became first president (1946) of the Atomic Energy Commission. In January 1947 he attended a South Pacific regional conference in Canberra. At the second session of the General Assembly he chaired a special committee on Palestine; and he attained a cherished ambition with his election as president of the third session (September 1948 to May 1949). Australia's mediatory role during these years was not always fruitful: the resolution of the long-running crisis in Greece owed little to Evatt's endeavours and he failed to defuse the Berlin crisis of 1948-49. Australia's influence helped to bring about partition in Palestine, though Israel did not welcome Evatt's support for the internationalization of Jerusalem. Outside the U.N., a particularly constructive initiative was his advocacy in 1948 that Britain accept Ireland's declaration of independence from the Commonwealth without reprisals.

Nearer to home, Evatt had at first hoped to safeguard Australia's northern approaches by leasing or taking over Timor, the Netherlands New Guinea (Irian Jaya) and the New Hebrides (Vanuatu), or by at least establishing Australian bases there. Influenced to some degree by his new departmental secretary and protégé Burton, Evatt grew more alert to South-East Asian nationalism, and in August 1947 formally offered Australia's services in mediating between the Indonesian republicans and the Dutch. The Indonesians accepted, and Australia worked for an orderly transfer of power in 1949.

Australia's concern to prevent a re-surgence of Japanese power had been thwarted from 1947 by the Americans' intention to revive Japan's economy as a bulwark against communism. That year Evatt lobbied General Douglas MacArthur [q.v.], supreme commander, Allied Powers in Japan, in the hope of obtaining an assured role for Australia in any peace negotiations, but Australia's influence remained negligible, especially after the communists' victory in China in 1949.

Evatt's concentration on foreign policy cost him some of his effectiveness as postwar attorney-general. Confident of his ability to master complex issues quickly, he was apt to display a poor tactical sense in promoting the Labor government's policies. Although the High Court consistently restricted the spread of Federal power, Evatt showed an honourable, albeit a politically crippling, reluctance to influence the composition of the court. He repudiated a cabinet proposal in 1945 to appoint three new judges, made no attempt to introduce a retirement age and chose as his only nominee to the bench the lacklustre Sir William Webb [q.v.].

Having publicly supported the contentious bank nationalization legislation of 1947, Evatt chose to lead for the government when the banks took the matter to the High Court. His forensic skills were rusty and his ex-colleagues sceptical; the majority found that the legislation was invalidated by s. 92 of the Constitution. Forgetful of nationalist sentiment, Evatt appealed to the Privy Council in London. His presentation took fourteen days and his response eight, interrupted by a dash to New York to preside over the U.N. General Assembly. In July 1949 the Privy Council upheld the High Court's decision. By this time an election was imminent.

An early enthusiast for the development of atomic energy in Australia, Evatt had keenly supported (Sir) Mark Oliphant's plans to build a cyclotron at the Australian National University; he was also involved in promoting the Anglo-Australian Joint Project (1947) which established the Woomera rocket range. In 1948 the U.S.A. ceased passing classified information to Australia, ostensibly for security reasons. Chifley responded in 1949 by forming the Australian Security Intelligence Organization within the attorney-general's department. The Americans did not remove their embargo until the government changed.

Labor's enemies made much of bank nationalization and the Cold War as harbingers of creeping socialism. Evatt, who had been deputy-leader of his party from October 1946, parried these thrusts energetically. Anxious to rebut the Opposition's allegations of being soft on communism, he willingly framed legislation in June 1949 to defeat the coalminers' strike, and rejected advice from the Department of External Affairs favouring diplomatic recognition of the communist regime in China. More constructively, he approved the departmental initiatives which led in 1950 to the formulation of the Colombo Plan. But by then Evatt was out of office following Labor's defeat on 10 December 1949.

In April 1950 the Menzies government introduced a bill to outlaw the Communist Party of Australia. Slow at first to resist the measure, Evatt swung into strong opposition when it became clear that civil liberties would be jeopardized. Although Labor was obliged by its executive to support the legislation in principle, Evatt accepted a brief to appear in the High Court for the Waterside Workers' Federation in a challenge to the Act. This time his arguments persuaded the court, which, by a six to one majority, held in March 1951 that the statute was invalid. That month Menzies secured a double dissolution. His government was returned in April with a majority in both Houses. Chifley died in June and Evatt was unanimously elected to succeed him.

The Menzies government responded to its defeat in the High Court by proposing a referendum giving the Commonwealth power to deal with communism. Evatt might have chosen to proceed cautiously. Instead, he launched himself into one of his most vigorous barnstorming campaigns, stumping the country for a 'No' vote in defiance of public opinion polls which forecast majorities of between 70 and 80 per cent in favour of the proposal. It has been called his finest hour. Enough voters were persuaded to change their minds for the referendum to be defeated by a narrow margin in September 1951.

Evatt's attack on anti-communist legislation had come under fire from a right-wing section of his party, mainly Victorian Catholics sympathetic to the industrial groups who were attempting to wrest control from communists in the trade unions. Identified with the 'groupers', though separate from and not always in accord with them, was the Catholic Social Studies Movement directed by B. A. Santamaria. Evatt sought to conciliate these factions, initially with some success. In 1952-53 Labor benefited from the government's inept handling of inflation, performing well in State polls and at the half-Senate elections in May 1953. Yet, at the May 1954 Federal elections, although Labor won over 50 per cent of votes in all contested seats, the Menzies government scraped home with a 64 to 57 majority.

This outcome was partly due to the aftermath of the first visit (February to April 1954) by Queen Elizabeth II and the Duke of Edinburgh to Australia and more immediately to the rash prodigality of Evatt's campaign promises. Eager for office, he had pledged to abolish the means test on pensions without costing the scheme. To his colleagues he made contradictory commitments about the allocation of cabinet offices. Ultimately, the scales may have been tilted against Labor by the defection of Vladimir Petrov, an official from the Embassy of the Soviet Union. Menzies announced the defection on 13 April, the last night of the outgoing parliament, without managing to alert Evatt to the imminence of an important issue which might have led him to cancel a prior appointment in Sydney. Petrov's wife was subsequently removed in dramatic circumstances from a Moscow-bound aircraft. Menzies set up a royal commission to investigate the Petrovs' testimony about Soviet espionage in Australia. Evatt convinced himself that the Petrov revelations were timed for maximum effect in damaging Labor's prospects at the elections. This conviction hardened into certainty when the royal commission heard allegations that members of his personal staff had been in communication with the Soviet embassy.

To a person of Evatt's intense ambition and suspiciousness, the provocation was irresistible. He decided to appear as counsel before the royal commission to defend his staff and expose what he saw as a conspiracy orchestrated by Menzies. Despite the hostility of the three royal commissioners (all judges of lesser stature than his own), Evatt made some progress against A.S.I.O.'s witnesses, but his conduct was sufficiently unguarded to give the commissioners a pretext in September for prohibiting his further appearance before them.

Sections of the Labor caucus were also growing restive at Evatt's preoccupation with the Petrov inquiry. In August he faced a post-election challenge to his leadership from T. P. Burke [q.v.13], and, although he won easily, it was an omen of future dissension. A subtler leader might have noticed differences between Santamaria's 'Movement' and Labor's largely Catholic Victorian right wing, and used them to maintain party unity. Such was not Evatt's style. On 5 October 1954 he launched a sensational attack against 'disloyal' elements which aimed 'to deflect the Labor Movement from the pursuit of established Labor objectives and ideals'. At a caucus meeting on 20 October the party voted by 52 votes to 28 against a motion to throw all leadership positions open to contest, but Evatt's insistence on counting the names on either side added to the acrimony. He then urged the federal executive of the A.L.P. to investigate the pro-'grouper' Victorian branch. The showdown came at a special federal conference in Hobart in March 1955. By a narrow margin the conference backed Evatt and withdrew support from the industrial groups. Seven Victorian members of the House of Representatives and a Tasmanian senator quit the A.L.P. to form the Anti-Communist (later Democratic) Labor Party.

The breakaways feuded venomously with the Evatt party for much of 1955, but it was Evatt himself who most damaged his credibility as leader. In September the final report of the royal commission on espionage came before parliament. Despite all the muckraking, it had been unable to furnish the basis for a single prosecution. Its futility was overlooked when Evatt stated in the House that he had asked V. M. Molotov, the Soviet foreign minister, about the authenticity of Russian-language documents supplied by the Petrovs, and had received Molotov's denial. Evatt's defenders argue that he was simply seeking to establish a basis for an international commission into the affair. Politically, it was an extremely naive move, made without consultation and without the excuse of impulse. Menzies seized the opportunity to call elections in December 1955 and Labor was thrashed.

Evatt lasted as Labor's leader for four more years. On his good days he continued to figure as an impressive libertarian. In the spring of 1956 he trenchantly opposed Menzies' role in support of Britain and France during the Suez crisis, though without avail. His party valued his services enough to move him to the safe seat of Hunter before the 1958 Federal elections. He again invited controversy by offering—without seeking advice from his colleagues—to step down as leader if the D.L.P. (then commanding about 9 per cent of the popular vote) would direct its second preferences to the A.L.P. The offer was spurned and Labor was once more soundly beaten. In February 1959 E. J. Ward [q.v.] stood against Evatt for the leadership but lost by 32 votes to 46.

Some have argued that Evatt's tactics of confrontation and conflict in his dealings with the right-wing breakaways suggest mental instability. Contrariwise, there is testimony that his mood was mellow and serene even after the disappointment of the 1958 election campaign. By the time the New South Wales Labor government narrowly decided in January 1960 to offer him the State's chief justiceship, Evatt was gradually succumbing to a breakdown in his intellectual powers. He was suffering from cerebral thrombosis and arteriosclerosis. His memory faltered and his habits became increasingly erratic. He possibly had an epileptic tendency, though this in itself would be insufficient to account for the painful deterioration which marked his term (from 15 February) as chief justice. Largely shielded by his colleagues from open scandal, he suffered a stroke in March 1962 while *en route* to a law reform commission meeting in London. On 24 October he resigned.

Thereafter Evatt was under the devoted care of family and nurses. Survived by his wife and adopted children, he died on 2 November 1965 at Forrest, Canberra. He was accorded a state funeral and buried with Anglican rites in Canberra cemetery; Menzies was a pallbearer. Arnold Shore's [q.v.11] portrait of Evatt is held by the family and another by W. E. Pidgeon is in the Supreme Court of New South Wales.

In death as in life, controversy has surrounded Evatt's reputation. To Katharine Prichard [q.v.11] he was an unappreciated Titan, to Manning Clark 'a man who had the image of Christ in his heart'; others found him evil and a treacherous monster. Like Menzies, Evatt was an educated man who chose public life instead of enriching himself through the law. His genuine love of sport and careful cultivation of a flat, monotonous, proletarian voice bridged many gaps. It is difficult to reconcile the high principles of Evatt's international thought and his tenacious concern for justice with the self-seeking adventurism of much of his day-to-day political conduct. W. J. Hudson may well be correct in attributing Evatt's greed for publicity and suspicion of rivals to the uncertainties of a boy orphaned of his father when young and brought up by a demanding mother who grudged praise. It remains a paradox that the man who was Australia's most creative and innovative foreign minister, with an impressive, though uneven, record as a libertarian jurist, should have alienated so many through his deficiencies in personal relations and his incapacity for teamwork.

DNB, 1961-70; A. Dalziel, *Evatt the Enigma* (Melb, 1967); K. Tennant, *Evatt* (Syd, 1970); A. Curthoys and J. Merritt (eds), *Australia's First Cold War 1945-1953*, 1 (Syd, 1984); P. Crockett, *Evatt* (Melb, 1993); W. J. Hudson, *Australia and the New World Order* (Canb, 1993); K. Buckley, B. Dale and W. Reynolds, *Doc Evatt* (Melb, 1994); *Hist Studies*, 18, no 73, Oct 1979, p 546, 22, no 89, Oct 1987, p 587; *Aust J of Politics and Hist*, 38, no 3, 1992, p 316; Evatt papers (Flinders Univ L).

G. C. BOLTON

EVATT, MARY ALICE (1898-1973), art patron, was born on 15 December 1898 at Ottumwa, Iowa, United States of America, daughter of Samuel Sheffer (d.1929), manufacturing chemist, and his wife Alice Maud, née Holt. One year old when she reached Sydney with her parents, Mary Alice grew up at Mosman; her childhood was happy and carefree, her nature optimistic and gregarious. Educated at St Hilda's Grammar School, from 1918 she studied architecture (passing only in drawing) then arts at the University of Sydney where she met Herbert Vere Evatt [q.v.] (d.1965), a tutor at St Andrew's College. They were married on 27 November 1920 at the Congregational Church, Mosman, and were to adopt a son and daughter. Mrs Evatt was of middle height and medium build, with titian hair, blue eyes and a manner that charmed. A devotee of the socialist writings and ideas on art of William Morris, in 1925 she campaigned for her husband when he won the Legislative Assembly seat of Balmain for Labor. They lived in the electorate until 1930; she organized a women's co-operative in 1929 which produced cheap clothing for needy families.

Encouraged by Bert, in the early 1930s Mary Alice attended classes in modernist painting run by Grace Crowley and Rah Fizelle [qq.v.13,8]. She became a close friend of Crowley and her circle which included Ralph Balson [q.v.13] and Frank and Margel Hinder. In 1936 she attended the George Bell [q.v.7] school in Melbourne; among her fellow students were (Sir) Russell Drysdale, Sali Herman and Maie Casey. She also met John and Sunday Reed, and became friends of the experimental painters Moya Dyring [q.v.] and Sam Atyeo who was to introduce the Evatts to Picasso in Paris in 1946. To this period belong her paintings, 'Seated Figure' and 'The Footballers'. Abroad in 1938, she studied at Andre Lhote's studio in Paris; in New York the Evatts met modernist painters. At home they supported the Contemporary Art Society. Mary Alice bought pictures and drawings from struggling young artists such as Drysdale and (Sir) Sidney Nolan (often giving them away to friends and relations, local councils and art galleries). At the (Melbourne *Herald*) Exhibition of French and British Contemporary Art (1939) she acquired a portrait by Modigliani, together with works by Soutine, Leger and Vlaminck.

Her husband's entry into Federal parliament (September 1940) and cabinet office (October 1941) propelled Mary Alice into the public arena. In March 1942, at Prime Minister Curtin's [q.v.13] request, she went with Bert on his mission to Washington. On her return, Curtin praised her 'courage and patriotism' in accompanying Evatt. She proved an able public speaker, and her contacts with women's organizations and the press raised the American public's awareness of Australia. She was a good cook and keen gardener, growing her own herbs as well as Australian native plants, unfashionable at that time.

In March 1943 Mrs Evatt was the first woman to be appointed a trustee of the National Art Gallery of New South Wales. She joined forces with the moderates Sydney Ure Smith and (Sir) Charles Lloyd Jones [qq.v.11,9] against entrenched conservatives like Sir Lionel Lindsay [q.v.10]. In January 1944 she voted for awarding the 1943 Archibald [q.v.3] prize to (Sir) William Dobell [q.v.] for his controversial portrait of Joshua Smith.

On visits to the U.S.A. in 1944 and 1945 she represented the gallery in discussions with the Carnegie Trust, New York, about postwar exhibitions. She was, according to Bernard Smith, a 'very effective, outspoken and shrewd member of the [gallery] Trust', and promoted travelling art exhibitions to country areas. During overseas trips she maintained contact with developments in the art world and was a persuasive advocate for modern Australian painting. Her donations to the Art Gallery included a sculpture by Zadkine and 'The Bicycle', a painting by Leger (in memory of her husband). She continued to serve on the board until 1970.

Survived by her daughter, Mary Alice died on 16 June 1973 at McMahons Point, Sydney, and was buried with Anglican rites beside her husband in Canberra cemetery. In 1975 John Coburn gave one of his paintings, 'Facade', to the Art Gallery in her memory; in 1990 the H. V. Evatt Memorial Foundation established the annual Mary Alice Evatt art award at the University of Western Sydney.

G. Dutton, *The Innovators* (Melb, 1986); P. Timms and R. Christie (eds), *Cultivating the Country* (Melb, 1988); R. Haese, *Rebels and Precursors* (Melb, 1991); K. Buckley, B. Dale and W. Reynolds, *Doc Evatt* (Melb, 1994); *Age* (Melb), 16 Feb 1968; M. A. Evatt, taped interviews, 1973 (oral history collection, NL); Evatt papers (Flinders Univ L); Art Gallery of NSW, Minutes of meetings of Bd of Trustees *and* Annual Report, 1943-75; information from Mrs R. Carrodus, Leura, NSW, and Emeritus Prof Bernard Smith, Fitzroy, Melb.

BARBARA DALE

EVE, SYDNEY JAMES WALLACE (1899-1978), sports administrator, and RICHMOND CAVILL (1901-1970), Olympic diver and woolclasser, were born on 23 October 1899 and 19 March 1901 at Parramatta, New South Wales, eldest and second of three sons of Albert Sydney Eve, a native-born tobacconist, and his English-born wife Freda Maude, daughter of the 'professor of swimming' Frederick Cavill [q.v.7]. Jim and Dick were educated respectively at Neutral Bay and at Manly commercial public schools; they were taught to swim and dive at an early age by their mother and both belonged to Manly Amateur Swimming Club. In 1915 they accompanied their parents to San Francisco, United States of America; Jim attended Alamada High School, outclassed Dick in their early diving competitions, and won junior swimming and diving championships at the Panama Pacific International Exposition. Back in Sydney by 1917, Jim became a clerk and later a company secretary; Dick studied woolclassing through Sydney Technical College in 1921.

From 1917 Jim held various honorary

positions with the New South Wales Amateur Swimming Association and introduced marked lanes at the Domain Baths in 1924. Paying his own way, he accompanied the Australian Olympic team to Paris that year. While honorary secretary-treasurer (1924-47) of the Australian Olympic Federation, he managed the Australian team at the 1932 Olympic Games in Los Angeles, U.S.A., and organized the teams for Amsterdam (1928) and Berlin (1936). He was foundation secretary (1929-69) of the Australian British Empire (and Commonwealth) Games Association, organizing secretary for the British Empire Games held in Sydney in 1938 and a member of the organizing committee for the 1956 Olympic Games in Melbourne.

A keen golfer, Jim had founded Balgowlah Golf Club in 1926; he played regularly at Castle Hill and was full-time secretary of Oaklands Golf Club (1946-56) and of the State branch of the Professional Golfers' Association of Australia (from 1956). He was also a life member of the New South Wales Sports Club. In 1951 he was appointed M.B.E. Jim Eve remained a bachelor. He died on 24 August 1978 in Royal Prince Alfred Hospital, Camperdown, and was cremated.

In diving, Dick Eve's efforts 'were marked by extreme grace, alertness, and crispness'. Although unbeaten in springboard championships in Australia from 1921, he was not expected to gain a medal at the 1924 Olympic Games in Paris because of the lack of international competition in his own country. His perfect swallow dive won him the Olympic gold medal in the plain diving (high tower); his overall score was 13.5 points. Although he qualified for the final of the fancy diving (springboard) event, he was suffering from recurrent ear trouble and his performances were below form; he came fifth in the final round. Despite medical treatment, he had to withdraw from the fancy diving (high tower) event. He was blue eyed, 5 ft 4 ins (163 cm) tall and, like the Cavills, 'had a good, strong swimmer's physique with huge shoulders, a big chest and solid legs'.

In 1925 Dick won the Australian springboard championship for the fifth successive time. It was to be his last title. After he succeeded his father as manager of Manly Swimming Baths, his amateur status was questioned in November 1926 by the N.S.W.A.S.A. which deemed him to be a professional and not a government or council employee. The loss of his amateur status prevented him from being considered for the 1928 Olympic Games. Gravely disappointed at what he considered unfair treatment by Australia's aquatic officials, he never sought to be reinstated as an amateur, even when the ruling became less stringent.

On 12 March 1924 at St Barnabas's Angli-

can Church, Sydney, Dick Eve had married Florence Alice Maud Turner, a florist; they were to have a son and a daughter before he divorced her in 1933. He managed the Pavilion at Manly in the 1930s. At her Enfield home on 30 November 1936 he married with Presbyterian forms Iris White, a stenographer.

Enlisting in the Australian Imperial Force on 23 March 1942, Dick served as gunner in the Middle East. He returned to Sydney in February 1943 and was discharged medically unfit on 11 June. Following the war, he returned to woolclassing. He remained involved in aquatics for most of his life and reputedly taught the Olympian Murray Rose to swim. An examiner for the Royal Life Saving Society, Dick devised the 'Eve Rocker', a resuscitation device. He died of myocardial infarction on 13 March 1970 in Concord Repatriation General Hospital and was cremated; Olympic symbols adorn a plaque at Woronora cemetery commemorating him. His wife and their daughter survived him, as did the children of his first marriage.

G. Atkinson, *Australian and New Zealand Olympians* (Melb, 1984); J. Blanch and P. Jenes, *Australia at the Modern Olympic Games* (Syd, 1984); G. Lester, *Australians at the Olympics* (Syd, 1987); R. and M. Howell, *Aussie Gold* (Brisb, 1988); W. Vamplew et al (eds), *The Oxford Companion to Australian Sport* (Melb, 1992); *Referee*, 23 July 1924; *SMH*, 1 Jan 1951, 28 Jan, 1 Feb 1956; *Sun-Herald*, 10 Nov 1957; correspondence with Dr K. Moore, Univ Alberta, Canada, held by author, Univ Qld; information from Mr R. Eve, Westlake, Brisb, and Mrs J. Barron, Castle Hill, Syd.

IAN F. JOBLING

EVERETT, GLADYS GORDON (1888-1971), headmistress, was born on 6 May 1888 at Nelson, New Zealand, daughter of Albert Everett, a New Zealand-born draper, and his wife Ada, née Gordon, from Melbourne. Educated at Nelson College (Girls) and Victoria University College, Wellington (B.A., N.Z., 1912; M.A., 1916), Miss Everett taught in New Zealand before becoming foundation house mistress of Presbyterian Ladies' College, Pymble, Sydney, in 1918. Made principal in 1920, she resigned in August 1921, to the regret of the school council. She studied in France at the University of Grenoble (certificat d'études Françaises, 1922) and the Sorbonne (certificat d'études phonétiques élémentaires de Paris, 1923), then travelled in Italy and Germany. From 1925 she taught French at the Girls' Grammar School, Ashby-de-la-Zouch, England, before serving as headmistress (1930) of Katanning Church of England Girls' School, Western Australia.

Chosen from a field of twenty, in December

1930 Everett was appointed headmistress of Abbotsleigh Church of England School for Girls, Wahroonga, Sydney. Under her guidance enrolments more than doubled, reaching 660 in 1954; the waiting list, opened in 1938, has never closed. Tradition was fostered by her introduction in 1931 of a house system and by the annual celebration (since 1933) of the school's foundation day. Through judicious purchases of houses and land in 1933 and 1937, she expanded the school: in June 1939 a new classroom block was opened, containing facilities for science, and art and craft. Unlike some boarding schools in Sydney, Abbotsleigh did not close during World War II; instead, it began in 1944 an entrance examination for the junior school. One of Everett's ambitions was realized when a separate junior school was opened in 1954. It was named after her. She left bequests for a chapel and library expansion.

Among girls' church schools, Abbotsleigh became noted for its academic and cultural curriculum. Increasing numbers matriculated and undertook university studies; drama and speech training, music, art and ballet were promoted. The head's own collection of Post-Impressionist paintings was hung in the school. She herself taught French and divinity. Although rules on dress and behaviour in public were tirelessly enforced, Miss Gordon Everett (as she styled herself) maintained at school a more relaxed discipline, particularly among her senior 'gels' who referred to her as 'Ev', though not to her face. Tall and spare, with golden hair, an athletic gait and a presence reinforced by her habit of carrying her deceased fiancé's army cane, she brought to the school administrative abilities, personal charm and a belief in the virtues of a cultured womanhood.

Retiring in May 1954, Miss Everett lived close to the school. In 1960 she was appointed M.B.E. She died alone on 18 June 1971 while travelling in Russia. Her portrait by Joshua Smith is held at Abbotsleigh.

D. Burrows, *History of Abbotsleigh* (Syd, 1968); *Kobeelya, 1922-1982* (Katanning, WA, 1986); J. K. Conway, *The Road from Coorain* (Lond, 1989); *Weaver*, June 1934, June 1938, Dec 1954, Mar 1972; *SMH*, 1 Nov 1930, 6 May 1954; Abbotsleigh School archives; information from Miss H. E. Archdale, Killara, Syd.   RUTH TEALE

EVERETT, MINNIE REBECCA (1874-1956), dancer and producer, was born on 28 June 1874 at Beaufort, Victoria, twelfth (and seventh surviving) child of English-born parents George Everett, bricklayer, and his wife Eliza Ann, née Hardy. After the family moved to Melbourne, Minnie trained under Emilia Pasta, a ballet dancer from Italy. From the age of 13 Everett took casual engagements at the Alexandra Theatre, the Opera House and the Theatre Royal. For a time the dancers were required to complete their performance at the Theatre Royal and be driven by wagonette to the Princess Theatre to appear with Nellie Stewart [q.v.12] in the last act of *Dorothy*.

Having joined J. C. Williamson [q.v.6] in 1888, Everett became one of the Royal Ballerinas, a permanent ballet of trained dancers who appeared with his Royal Comic Opera Company. Promoted to soloist, she appeared in December 1893 at the Princess Theatre in the pantomime *Little Red Riding Hood*. On 28 November 1895 at St Peter's Anglican Church, Melbourne, she married William Walter Rice who played the viola in the orchestra accompanying her performances.

Minnie Everett, as she continued to be professionally known, made her debut as a choreographer in 1897. Henry Bracy [q.v.7] presented a revival of Karl Millöcker's *The Beggar Student*; it included a grand Polish mazurka, staged by Everett, in which she appeared with a troupe of dancers. Next year she created the dances for *The Geisha* and appeared as *première danseuse* of the Royal Ballerinas, of which she was made director in 1899. As ballet mistress for thirty years, she created and produced dances for most of J. C. Williamson Ltd's productions.

From the early twentieth century Everett won renown for her work not only as a ballet mistress but as a producer of comic and grand opera. In 1914 'the Firm' sent her to produce pantomime in South Africa; two years later in England she was responsible for *High Jinks* and was hailed as the first woman producer in London. Back home, her productions of Gilbert and Sullivan were full of sparkle and freshness, and, while traditional, were not rigidly so. She knew every note of the music, the full dialogue and all the stage 'business', and had the ability to turn raw beginners into polished ensembles. Among the stars she worked with were Strella Wilson, Gladys Moncrieff [q.v.10], and Cyril Ritchard and Madge Elliott [qq.v. Elliott]. With Gustave Slapoffski [q.v.11] as her musical director, she was largely responsible for J. C. Williamson's brilliant Gilbert and Sullivan seasons of 1920, 1926-27 and 1931.

For many years Everett ran her own theatrical schools in Melbourne and Sydney where she taught singing, dancing, voice production, deportment and stage technique. She employed many of her pupils in her productions. In the late 1930s she independently produced several pantomimes, using companies of her juveniles. Although she retired in 1940, Everett continued to take a keen interest in amateur theatrics and in 1955 was coaxed into producing *The Mikado* for the Victorian Council of Adult Education. Survived by her daughter, she died on 7 June 1956 at Prahran and was cremated.

V. Tait, *A Family of Brothers* (Melb, 1971); E. H. Pask, *Enter the Colonies, Dancing* (Melb, 1979); *Theatre* (Syd), 8, no 11, 1 Nov 1910; *Herald* (Melb), 12 Jan 1924, 18 Apr 1931, 24 Sept 1949, 8 June 1956; *A'sian Post*, 20 July 1950; *Age* (Melb), 8 June 1956; theatre programme collection (LaTL).   JOAN MASLEN

EVERETT, PERCY EDGAR (1888-1967), architect and headmaster, was born on 26 June 1888 at Geelong, Victoria, seventh child of Joseph Everett, a blacksmith from England, and his native-born wife Emma Mary, née Elliott. Educated locally at Ashby Public School, Percy was articled to W. H. Cleverdon, a Geelong architect, and studied at the Gordon Technical College. He was employed as architectural draftsman (1907-10) to the Geelong Harbour Trust before he joined the firm of Seeley & King and later became a partner; during this time he designed the Sailors' Rest building. In 1913 he visited Britain and Europe. When he returned to Geelong his firm was taken over by Laird & Buchan.

While retaining ties with Laird & Buchan, in 1914 Everett moved to Melbourne where the wartime shortage of architectural work led him in 1916 to take up the headmastership of Brunswick Technical School. On 11 June 1924 at Mentone he married with Presbyterian forms a widow Georgina Buchanan Arthur, née Boyd (d.1956). In 1932 he was transferred to Brighton Technical School as headmaster. Although he maintained a private practice in these years and was responsible for the development of the Victorian Education Department's architectural curriculum, his practical work was sparse.

In 1934 Everett was appointed chief architect in the Victorian Public Works Department. There he formed a strong design division—divorced from the documentation and contract administration sections—and recruited his architects from private practice. Insisting on approving every architectural drawing, he retained absolute control over the designs produced in the department. As chief architect, he was responsible for the construction and maintenance of the State's public buildings, including courthouses, police stations, prisons, mental hospitals, sanatoriums, schools and tertiary institutions, as well as residences for government employees.

Autocratic in temperament and energetic in application, Everett made his distinctive imprint on public buildings throughout Victoria. He had completed a world tour in 1930, and, in 1945, travelled to North America to study recent trends in public architecture. Although his eclecticism embraced Art Deco, American Beaux-Arts and Modernism, his additions to existing buildings were unsympathetic to the work of earlier architects. In their siting and insistently three-dimensional character, his buildings were statements of civic importance. Among his more notable achievements in design were the Ballarat Public Offices (1941), and the Russell Street Police Headquarters (1942-43), Melbourne, which exemplified the stepped skyscraper form. He retired from the department in 1953. On 26 June 1956 at Brighton he married a widow Mavis Delgany Stewart, née Richards.

Everett had been chairman of the State Building Regulations Committee, vice-president of the Town Planning Association, a fellow of the Royal Australian Institute of Architects and of the Royal Victorian Institute of Architects, and a member of the Architects' Registration Board. Survived by his wife and two stepchildren, he died on 6 May 1967 at Brighton Beach and was cremated.

Aust Builder, Apr 1952, p 225; *Argus*, 3 July 1934, 26 June 1953; *Herald* (Melb), 27 Nov 1944, 7 May 1967; *Age* (Melb) and *Sun News-Pictorial*, 8 May 1967; R. Swansson, Percy Edgar Everett: Essays and Appendices (investigation project, Faculty of Architecture, Univ Melb, 1988); Roy Aust Inst of Architects, Vic Chapter, papers MS9454, box 104/2 (LaTL).   FRANCES O'NEILL

EWART, JOYCE VERA MARY (1916-1964), artist and teacher, was born on 29 August 1916 at Murrumburrah, New South Wales, second daughter of native-born parents Archibald Charles Ewart, railway fireman, and his wife Lilian Ethel, née Harper. Joy was born with Marfan's syndrome, a congenital disorder of the connective tissues which led to the early deaths of her sister and brother. The Ewarts were Christadelphians, a fundamental Christian sect which Joy was to reject. The family moved to Maitland where she attended school and at the age of 11 began art lessons under Reginald Russom at the local technical college. In 1935 she won a scholarship to East Sydney Technical College, but found the atmosphere under Frank Medworth [q.v.] stifling. Frequently ill herself, Ewart worked for a time as a nurse's aide, and studied painting under Dattilo Rubbo [q.v.11] and Lo Schiavo. In 1939 she and her friend Enid Fisk were students of the Hungarian artist Desiderius Orban. His classes were liberating, introducing them to Zen Buddhism and to the modern art movement, seen in Sydney for the first time at the (Melbourne *Herald*) Exhibition of French and British Contemporary Art.

When she lived with her parents at Chatswood and from 1942 at Greenwich, Ewart's health improved. She taught drawing with Thea Proctor [q.v.11] and began to gain recognition. Ewart's solo exhibitions at the Macquarie Galleries in 1942, 1943, 1944, 1948 and 1953 were well reviewed; she also showed with the local Contemporary Art Society of Australia, the Encouragement of Art Movement, and in the Archibald [q.v.3] exhibitions of 1943 and 1944. In 1948 the National Art Gallery of New South Wales bought her painting 'George Street North' and her 'Onion's Point' won the Mosman art prize. Next year she went abroad.

London was hard. Too sick to do more than paint flowers on glass tumblers and too poor to pay board, Ewart lived with the family of Douglas Parnell, an Australian opera singer. Paris was better. Her French was excellent, she worked as a nanny, travelled to Spain and Italy, painted and sent canvases to Australia. Hayter's Paris studio, Atelier 17—where Miro, Picasso, Ernst and Chagall had their work printed—inspired her with the idea of starting a similar workshop in Sydney.

Back home in 1952, Ewart drove herself so hard that she sometimes fainted in front of her students. She taught at the University of Sydney, Presbyterian Ladies' College, Pymble, Church of England Grammar School for Girls, Newcastle, Maitland and Newcastle technical colleges, and at summer schools and youth camps. In 1955 she opened a painting studio at Chatswood, in a dilapidated old stable with a loft and brick courtyard. Adults, adolescents ('transitionals') and children attended her practical art classes. Lawrence Collings made a film, *Youth Creates*, which showed her teaching and which impressed gallery audiences in Melbourne and New York.

Having won a Fulbright scholarship in 1959, Ewart undertook a course in painting and printmaking at Newcomb College, Tulane University of Louisiana, United States of America, but had to leave early. She used her dying landlady as the subject of her lithograph, 'Fever': James Gleeson wrote, 'in no other work is her . . . knowledge of suffering so blazingly displayed'. In 1960 she visited Madame Lacouriere's print workshop in Paris and saw 'artists and artisans working together'. Knowing how limited her life was, Ewart threw herself into encouraging quality printmaking, especially lithography, using presses set up in her Chatswood studio. The Workshop Arts Centre was formed with Joy its honorary art director; classes commenced in February 1963 in premises at Willoughby.

Miss Ewart died of a dissecting aneurysm of the aorta on 4 July 1964 in Royal North Shore Hospital and was cremated. The fo-

cussed will of this crusading, mystic zealot had dominated those who fell under her influence. Sleeping only several hours a night, driving her frail, elongated body, she strove to release the creative spirit in herself and in others, especially children. Her arts workshop became a model for new centres which developed in the 1970s.

Aust Soc for Education through Art, *ASEA Bulletin*, 2, no 3, Oct 1966, p 12; Workshop Arts Centre (Willoughby, Syd), *Community*, no 3, Sept 1974, p 8; *SMH*, 27 Jan 1943, 12 May 1945, 18 Feb, 7 July 1948, 10 Aug 1961, 17 July 1963, 6, 12 July 1964; J. Ewart scrap-book, held by Mrs P. Lemcke, Willoughby, Syd; information from Dr A. Lee, Rozelle, and Ms E. Rooney, Lane Cove, Syd.

JAN ROBERTS

EWERS, JOHN KEITH (1904-1978), teacher and writer, was born on 13 June 1904 at Subiaco, Perth, second son of Victorian-born parents Ernest Ewers, orchardist, and his wife Annie Eliza, née Gray. After his mother died when he was 6, Keith lived with an aunt and uncle in Subiaco until his father found stable employment as a wharf labourer and remarried. In 1914 the family moved to Carlisle. Educated at James Street Intermediate and Perth Modern schools, in 1923 Ewers served as a monitor at the Thomas Street primary school, Subiaco, before attending Claremont Teachers' College. The *Australian* published (1922) his first short story, under the nom de plume, 'J. K. Waterjugs'.

In 1924 Ewers was posted to a small school at South Tammin. The surrounding wheatbelt district provided the setting and characters for much of his writing. While teaching there and at other country schools, he published more than forty pieces of work (mainly short stories) in local newspapers. From 1929 to 1939 he taught at Beaconsfield State School, south of Fremantle. He published his first book privately, a collection of poems entitled *Boy and Silver* (1929). His first novel, *Money Street* (London, 1933), a romantic story about a group of residents of inner-suburban Perth, remains the work for which Ewers is most noted. During the 1930s his literary review, 'Australiana', appeared regularly in the *West Australian*; subsequently, his column, 'Australian Bookman', was published in the *Daily News*. At St Alban's Anglican Church, Highgate, on 20 June 1936 he married Jean Grant McIntyre; their only child was born in 1939.

Ewers taught at Nedlands (1939-42) and Perth Boys' (1943-47) schools, then retired to write full time. Within twelve years he published five major works of fiction: *Tales from the Dead Heart* (Sydney, 1944), *Men Against the Earth* (Melbourne, 1946), *For Heroes to*

Live In (Melbourne, 1948), *Harvest and Other Stories* (Sydney, 1949) and *Who Rides on the River?* (Sydney, 1956). He also wrote poetry, educational texts and critical essays, and showed his talent for local history in *Bruce Rock* (1959).

As a young man, he had been actively involved in promoting an appreciation of literature in the wider community and had assisted (Sir) Walter Murdoch [q.v.10] to found the Australian Reading Circle in 1930. Later, as one of Western Australia's foremost writers, Ewers helped to establish the State branch of the Fellowship of Australian Writers (president 1938-39 and 1946-47). He co-ordinated the acquisition and preservation of Tom Collins [q.v.8 Joseph Furphy] House, Swanbourne, by the F.A.W., of which he was made a life member (1967).

Despite Ewers's Methodist and Congregational upbringing, in his twenties he rejected church-based faith and declared himself an agnostic and a sceptic. In middle age he read J. G. Bennett's *The Crisis in Human Affairs* (London, 1954). His subsequent association with Bennett led him in 1958 to become a follower of Subud, an Indonesian-based spiritual group. Ewers died on 9 March 1978 at Shenton Park and was buried in Karrakatta cemetery; his wife and daughter edited his autobiography, *Long Enough for a Joke* (1983).

J. A. Hetherington, *Forty-Two Faces* (Melb, 1962); H. Anderson (ed), *The Singing Roads* (Syd, 1965); P. Bibby (ed), *The Ultimate Honesty* (Perth, 1982); *Aust Author*, 10, no 3, July 1978, p 30; *Age* (Melb), 25 Mar 1961; *West Australian*, 11 Mar 1978; Ewers papers *and* S. Balme, taped interview with J. K. Ewers, 1975 (ts, BL); J. K. Ewers reminiscences, 30 May 1985 (Oral History Project, NL).   REBECCA SHEPHERD
                                JENNY GREGORY

F

FABINYI, ANDREW (ANDOR) (1908-1978), publisher, was born on 27 December 1908 in Budapest, son of Imre Fabinyi, lawyer, and his wife Margit, née Nagel. Andor was educated at Minta Gymnasium and Pazmany University. After graduating, he continued his studies part time and was awarded what he described as 'the equivalent of a D. Phil' for his thesis on the psychology of aesthetics. He worked at Lauffer's Bookshop, Budapest, and in 1932 established an agency for the distribution of British books in Hungary.

Concerned at the spread of Nazism, Fabinyi obtained a visa to travel to New Zealand; sailing from Italy in the *Viminale*, he reached Melbourne on 17 July 1939. There his journey ended when he was offered employment by the Melbourne bookseller F. W. Cheshire. In May 1940 he applied for permanent residence as Andrew Fabinyi. Five ft 8½ ins (174 cm) tall, with black hair and brown eyes, on 26 October that year at the Presbyterian Church, Toorak, he married a librarian Elisabeth Clare Robinson; they were to have five children.

In 1941 Fabinyi was rejected for service in the Australian Imperial Force because of his nationality. He was mobilized in the Citizen Military Forces on 28 January 1942 and posted to the 4th Labour Company at Albury, New South Wales. In October 1943 he transferred to the Army Education Service. Naturalized in December 1944, he had charge of A.A.E.S. libraries and rose to warrant officer before his discharge on 13 May 1946.

Returning to F. W. Cheshire Pty Ltd, Fabinyi developed the general bookselling side of the business and was made retail manager. When Cheshire discovered his interest in publishing, a new company—F. W. Cheshire Publishing Pty Ltd—was established and Fabinyi appointed general manager. He believed that 'a real publisher must be eclectic'. Over the next twenty-five years his list covered poetry, such future Australian classics as Robin Boyd's [q.v.13] *The Australian Ugliness* (1960) and Alan Marshall's *I Can Jump Puddles* (1955), novels by Xavier Herbert, Judah Waten, Joan Lindsay, Barry Oakley, David Martin and Kenneth Cook, non-fiction by Brian Fitzpatrick [q.v.], Wilfred Burchett, Clive Turnbull [q.v.] and C. P. FitzGerald, studies of Asia by Australian diplomats, books on sculptors and artists and on the collection of the National Gallery of Victoria, literary criticism and agricultural science. A publishing colleague and friend, John Hooker, later wrote: 'Fabinyi's publishing decisions were a mixture of shrewd commercialism (eternally successful school books most of which are still in print) and . . . wildly improbable successes and failures. But under his direction, the Cheshire list grew in all directions, as did his power and influence in the book trade and the literate society at large'. In 1960 he was appointed O.B.E.

Under the pseudonym 'Peter Pica', Fabinyi contributed an influential critical column on the design of Australian books to the *Australian Book Review*. In addition to bringing an appreciation of more sophisticated design and production than was then the antipodean norm, his European bookseller's experience in international sales made him a strong advocate for the export of Australian books and he envisaged a major place for Australian publishing in Asia.

An enthusiastic committee-man and the central switchboard for trade intelligence, Fabinyi was president of the Australian Book Publishers' Association in 1965-70. He chaired the Australian Book Trade Advisory Committee (1966-68) and the A.B.P.A. book export development committee (1971-73), and served the wider book community as president of the Australian Book Fair Committee (1955-60), and of the Victorian branch (1955, 1959, 1965-67) and public libraries division (1962) of the Library Association of Australia. In recognition of his contribution to the work of libraries, he was given the L.A.A.'s (Sir) Redmond Barry [q.v.3] award in 1974. Fabinyi further promoted the interests of the book and the book trade through articles in newspapers and journals, and in *The Development of Australian Children's Book Publishing* (1971). He also wrote *Living in Cities* and *Social and Cultural Issues of Migration*, both published in 1970.

Fabinyi was president of the Victorian branch of the Australian Institute of International Affairs in 1966-70 and of the New South Wales branch in 1971-73. He held executive positions (from 1960) on the Committee for the Economic Development of Australia and served from 1966 on the national advisory committee (chairman 1973-77) of the United Nations Educational, Scientific and Cultural Organization. In 1971-73 he was a member of U.N.E.S.C.O.'s advisory committee on documentation. He enjoyed the associations he made and regarded the contacts provided as an essential part of the business of publishing.

Remaining at Cheshire's through changes of ownership and organization, Fabinyi was a director of the various companies that became the Cheshire group, including Lansdowne Press, Jacaranda Press and Bellbird Books, and was chairman (1968-69) of the group. In 1969 he left to take the post of managing director of Pergamon Press (Australia) Pty Ltd, but, under Robert Maxwell's ownership, did not achieve the satisfaction he required of publishing. Resigning in 1975, he accepted a research fellowship at the University of New South Wales where he hoped to fulfil his often-stated ambition of writing a book on Australian publishing. He maintained his involvement in books as a director of La Trobe University Bookshop (1970-78) and Longman Cheshire (1977-78), and continued his international interests with U.N.E.S.C.O. and the A.I.I.A. Survived by his wife, three sons and two daughters, he died suddenly of cardiovascular disease on 25 July 1978 at Hornsby, Sydney, and was cremated. Max Harris had described him as 'the wiliest fox and most practical visionary in the history of modern Australian publishing'.

J. McLaren (ed), *A Nation Apart* (Melb, 1983); F. Cheshire, *Bookseller, Publisher, Friend* (Melb, 1984); *Bookseller and Publisher*, Aug 1978; *Herald* (Melb), 12 Nov 1955; *Age* (Melb), 23 Feb 1963, 15 May 1969, 26 July 1978; *Australian*, 21 June 1969; H. de Berg, Andrew Fabinyi (taped interview, 27 Feb 1974, NL); Fabinyi papers (NL); naturalization file (AA).   JOHN CURTAIN

FABRO, ALLEGRO CELSO (1902-1962), restaurateur, was born on 28 July 1902 at Treppo Piccolo, Udine, Italy, eldest of four sons of Antonio Giuseppe Fabro, bricklayer, and his wife Rosa, née Peresesano, who worked their small farm. Celso attended primary school at Treppo Grande before finding a job as a shop-assistant to a draper at nearby Tricesimo. After World War I the Friuli region was so depressed that many people were forced to emigrate. Travelling in the *Moncalieri*, Fabro disembarked at Fremantle, Western Australia, in 1926. Next year he made his way to Adelaide and was briefly secretary of the Italian club, Vittorio Veneto. He later cleared scrub and chopped wood at Mildura, Victoria, but by 1932 was living in Melbourne where his relations had settled.

From working as a kitchenhand, Fabro rose to be head waiter and manager of the Italian Society Club Restaurant, Bourke Street. Meanwhile his friend Napoleone Floreani had prospered in Adelaide; he encouraged Fabro to return there in 1945 and helped him to buy the Cabin Café, renamed Allegro's Café, at 41 Rundle Street. With his partner Henry (Harry) Albert Hopkinson as chef, and his brothers Alfredo in the kitchen and Giovanni as head waiter, he introduced South Australians to minestrone, spaghetti bolognese, veal scaloppine and whiting cooked in the Milanese way; real coffee was served from a thirty-cup percolator, another novelty. Although the café could seat 112 customers, its style was homely.

By 1950 Fabro possessed assets worth £2000 and his annual income was about £800. Fair haired and charming, he regularly travelled with Hopkinson in Europe, collecting ideas for dishes which they tried out on family and staff before expanding Allegro's menu. The café attracted students, intellectuals and overseas visitors (among them the actress Deborah Kerr and the pianist Winifred Atwell). Fabro drove imported cars. He was cultured, well read and well spoken, popular with his staff and customers. His fluent English enabled him to assist compatriots with immigration and other documents. Able to guarantee accommodation and employment, he sponsored about thirty men from his province to follow him. Two such young immigrants were Pompeo Patat and Ermanno Olivo; they worked for him and lived at his Joslin home where he grew gladioli and chrysanthemums for the café's spectacular floral arrangements. Vice-president of Norwood Football Club, he provided dinner tickets for two to the best player in Saturday's matches.

In 1955 Fabro was given notice to quit his premises. Two years later, in Gilbert Place in the city, he re-opened the more elegant Allegro's Restaurant. It adjoined the Quelltaler House of H. Buring [q.v.3] & Sobels Ltd whose wines he served. In 1958 he helped to found Fogolar Furlan, the Italian club at Payneham, through which people obtained work and where the traditions of Italy, particularly those of the Friuli region, were preserved. While sharing Christmas dinner at Renato Floreani's Hazelwood Park home on 25 December 1962, Fabro died of a coronary occlusion; he was buried with Catholic rites in Centennial Park cemetery. Most of his estate (sworn for probate at £14 224) was bequeathed to Hopkinson, to 'enjoy . . . as he pleases . . . that he may live in a sober, sensible, amicable way, in recognition of all the . . . companionship, assistance and help he has given me'. The name Allegro is commemorated by a sign on Quelltaler House and Fabro's gravestone bears a photograph.

Norwood Football Club, *Annual Report*, 1959-60; *Advertiser* (Adel), 25 June 1955, 26, 27 Dec 1962; D400, file 53/5382 (AA, Adel); information from Mrs L. Fabro, Seaton, Mr A. Fabro, St Morris, Adel, and Dr D. O'Connor, Flinders Univ of SA.
                                  SUZANNE EDGAR
                                  CARMEL FLOREANI

FADDEN, SIR ARTHUR WILLIAM (1894-1973), accountant and prime minister, was born on 13 April 1894 at Ingham, Queensland, eldest of ten children of Irish-born parents Richard John Fadden, police constable, and his wife Annie, née Moorhead. The son of a Presbyterian minister, Richard had served in the Royal Irish Lancers before emigrating to Australia; he joined the Queensland Police Force and, about 1900, took charge of the station at Walkerston, near Mackay. Educated at the local state school, at 15 Artie began work as billy-boy to a gang of cane-cutters and soon became office-boy at the Pleystowe mill.

As a young man he participated enthusiastically in social and sporting activities. He excelled at cricket, Rugby Union football, boxing and foot-racing, and performed in amateur theatricals as an original member of the Walkerston 'Nigger Minstrel Troupe'. Exhibiting a flair for figures, in April 1913 he was employed as a clerk with the Mackay Town Council. Three years later he discovered defalcations in the books kept by the town clerk; the man was dismissed and Fadden appointed in his place. He married a milliner Ilma Nita Thornber on 27 December 1916 with Presbyterian forms at her mother's Mackay home; they were to have four children.

On 20 January 1918 a cyclone hit Mackay, wrecking the town, killing more than twenty people and cutting off help from outside. Fadden and his family narrowly escaped being drowned. As a member of the cyclone relief committee, he worked tirelessly and effectively to find shelter for the homeless, and to distribute food, clothing and building materials. Having qualified in accountancy through a correspondence course, he resigned his local-government post in September and set up as a public accountant at Townsville. He became a member (1921) and fellow (1928) of the Commonwealth Institute of Accountants (Australian Society of Accountants). His business prospered and he was to establish the firms Fadden, Sutton & Co., Townsville, and A. W. Fadden & O'Shea, Brisbane.

Leading 'a non-political team' known as the 'Serviceable Six', Fadden was elected to the Townsville City Council in 1930 and held office as an alderman for three years. In 1932 he won the Legislative Assembly seat of Kennedy for the Country and Progressive National Party and rose to shadow treasurer in 1934. When a redistribution made Kennedy untenable for the C.P.N.P., Fadden unsuccessfully stood for the sugar-belt seat of Mirani in 1935.

At a conference at Toowoomba in March 1936, rural elements of the C.P.N.P. reformed a separate organization, the Queens-land Country Party, dedicated to maintaining an independent identity from the major conservative body, the United Australia Party. The death of Sir Littleton Groom [q.v.9] in November precipitated a by-election for the Federal seat of Darling Downs. Endorsed as the Q.C.P.'s candidate, Fadden emphatically supported the new party's tenets throughout his campaign and on 19 December took the seat from the U.A.P.; he was to hold it until 1949 and then to represent the neighbouring seat of McPherson in 1949-58.

In April 1939 the leader of the Country Party, Sir Earle Page [q.v.11], attacked (Sir) Robert Menzies [q.v.] in the House of Representatives, hoping to prevent him from becoming prime minister. Fadden objected vigorously and withdrew from the parliamentary wing of the party, as did B. H. Corser, T. J. Collins [qq.v.13] and A. O. Badman. Page stood down as leader in September and A. G. Cameron [q.v.13] succeeded him. In November Fadden and his group returned to the fold. Menzies included Country Party members in his cabinet in March 1940 and Fadden was named minister without portfolio, assisting the treasurer and the minister for supply and development. Following the deaths of J. V. Fairbairn, Sir Henry Gullett and G. A. Street [qq.v.8,9,12] in an aircraft accident, on 14 August Fadden received the portfolios of air and civil aviation, while retaining his assisting roles.

Cameron's leadership was challenged in the party room in October 1940. After he withdrew from the contest, Page and (Sir) John McEwen [q.v.] tied with eight votes each. To break the deadlock, Fadden was appointed acting-leader until harmony could be restored. He was confirmed as leader on 12 March 1941.

Promoted treasurer on 28 October 1940, Fadden had joined the all-party Advisory War Council that day. In November he brought down the first of his record eleven budgets. Menzies left on a four-month visit to London on 24 January 1941 and Fadden became acting prime minister. Next month he, John Curtin and J. A. Beasley [qq.v.13] issued a press statement, exhorting Australians to a greater war effort: the communiqué seemed to warn of the country's imminent danger and created a flurry of diplomatic exchanges.

Fadden's withdrawal from the Federal parliamentary Country Party in 1939 had unsettled members of the Queensland organization. They were outraged when, on 27 April 1941, he convened a secret meeting in Brisbane of Queensland Federal and State Country Party and U.A.P. parliamentarians which saw the amalgamation of the two parties as the short-lived Country National Organization. Fadden had ostensibly sought to lay the foundations for a national wartime government. When no other State Country Party branch followed his lead and the A.L.P. continued to rebuff overtures to enter a national government, the Queensland central council of the Country Party took a jaundiced view of his motives. It believed 'that Fadden had formed the C.N.O. in pursuit of his goal to eventually become Prime Minister, leading an Australia-wide anti-labor party'. L. A. G. Boyce warned that 'it may be that, as an election approaches, he will desire to give colour to his claim to be a Country Party man, but if the Queensland Country Party wishes to continue to exist on the basis on which it was formed, it appears to me that there is not room in it for Mr Fadden'. Doubts persisted as to the extent to which he was committed to the interests of country people.

Under increasing pressure from elements within the coalition, Menzies resigned the prime ministership on 28 August 1941. A joint party meeting chose Fadden as his successor and he was commissioned next day. 'The comparative tranquillity in party relations' which Fadden had achieved in his term as acting prime minister may have been a factor in his selection, and he had earned respect for his down-to-earth manner, his friendliness and his capacity for hard work. His government, however, lasted only forty days.

Previous administrations had been criticized for their lack of urgency in placing the nation on the necessary wartime footing. Fadden's government suffered similar jibes. He was irresolute in dealing with problems, and had difficulty in coping with U.A.P. colleagues too engrossed in political intrigues and personal animosities to give him the support he needed. In contrast, from Curtin, the leader of the Opposition, he received 'friendship . . . co-operation, understanding and loyalty' in difficult times. Curtin's backing was important when Fadden renewed Menzies' earlier representations to the British prime minister, (Sir) Winston Churchill, to relieve the Australian 9th Division at Tobruk, Libya, and to reassemble the Australian Imperial Force in the Middle East as one formation.

Despite Fadden's denials, some believed that he had plotted Menzies' downfall. Aware of Menzies' suspicions, Fadden thought that Joseph Winkler, a former officer in the Prime Minister's Department, had told Menzies that he was a conspirator. On 13 September 1941 Winkler gave Curtin copies of official documents which were potentially embarrassing to Fadden. Curtin declined to take political advantage of the matter and attacked Fadden's budget instead. On 3 October the government was defeated on the floor of the House by 36 votes to 33, two Independents—Alexander Wilson [q.v.] and (Sir) Arthur Coles—voting with the Labor Party. Fadden

resigned and led the conservatives into Opposition. Curtin took office on 7 October. Defeated at the 1943 elections, the coalition broke apart and Menzies became leader of the Opposition.

As Labor introduced successive measures to expand the role of government in the economy, Fadden campaigned against what he saw as the imposition of socialism. He urged electors to vote 'No' in the 'fourteen powers' referendum of 1944. After World War II he condemned J. B. Chifley's [q.v.13] government for its plans to nationalize the banks and for its alleged 'soft line on communism'. Reinvigorated, 'united, determined and loyal', the Country Party formed a cohesive force behind Fadden. By 1949 the party was prepared to make an electoral pact with the Liberals. Convinced he had 'an election winner if ever there was one', Fadden persuaded Menzies to promise that he would abolish petrol rationing. At the polls on 10 December the Liberal-Country Party coalition was returned to power, with Fadden as deputy prime minister and treasurer (from 19 December).

The immediate problem confronting the government was inflation, caused by pent-up consumer demand and exacerbated (after June 1950) by the war in Korea. Wool prices soared in 1950-51. Menzies and his supporters argued for an appreciation of the Australian pound; Fadden and the Country Party were adamantly opposed to such a course. Cabinet was so divided on the issue that, had not three Liberals sided with Fadden, the coalition may have collapsed. Nor could its members agree to alternative proposals for an export tax on wool or a special wool tax, both potentially disastrous for the Country Party. A compromise solution, embodied in the wool sales deduction scheme of 1950, provided for '20 per cent of the value of wool sold or exported [to] be paid to the Treasury . . . as a credit against woolgrowers' income tax obligations'. The legislation was repealed in the following year when wool prices began to fall, but growers were furious and a decade later Fadden's actions still rankled.

Further trouble with primary producers and the Country Party's rank and file awaited Fadden after he brought down his 1951-52 'horror' budget which entailed a 'large counter-inflationary surplus'. After the budget he was so unpopular that he ruefully remarked, 'I could have had a meeting of all my friends and supporters in a one-man telephone booth'. Rural people were particularly upset by modifications to the longstanding law permitting primary producers to average their incomes over five years for taxation purposes. Because the wool boom gave growers tax advantages not available to others, the portion of their income above £4000 was removed from the averaging scheme. Government fiscal and economic policies continued to alarm primary producers throughout Fadden's term as treasurer, but much was done on their behalf. The hated provisional tax notwithstanding, many ameliorative taxation measures were introduced, including increased depreciation rates and the abolition of Federal land tax in 1952.

In January that year Fadden went on his first official mission abroad, to attend a Commonwealth finance ministers' conference in London. The meeting had been called in response to a balance-of-payments crisis in the sterling area. Reflecting the Australian government's wish to accelerate economic development, Fadden resisted a British proposal that sterling-area countries restrict imports from the dollar area and Europe; he 'took the line that the sterling area could no longer continue as a closed and discriminatory system'. While in London he was invested with his knighthood (K.C.M.G., 1951) by King George VI and sworn of the Privy Council, an honour sponsored by Curtin in 1942. Fadden was to be elevated to G.C.M.G. in 1958.

Throughout the 1950s the private banks pressed the government to eliminate what they claimed to be unfair competition from the Commonwealth Bank of Australia. For all his readiness to placate the private banks, Fadden had no intention of reducing the commercial activities of the publicly owned system. In 1957 he introduced legislation to revise the banking structure. The reforms established the Reserve Bank of Australia to carry out central banking functions and control the note issue, and set up the Commonwealth Banking Corporation with authority over the Commonwealth Savings and Trading banks, and over the newly established Commonwealth Development Bank of Australia. Fadden regarded the Development Bank as his 'own brain child . . . designed to overcome the lack of adequate long-term borrowing finance for farm development and small industries' requirements'. He piloted the bills through the House, but they were initially rejected by the Senate and did not become law until 1959.

As treasurer, Fadden was fortunate that his tenure encompassed a period of prosperity during which there were generally good seasons and high prices for rural products. Yet his own qualities also contributed to his success. He relied heavily on the advice of Sir Roland Wilson, the head of the Treasury, but 'was quite capable of exercising his independent judgement'. Fadden was a 'shrewd assessor' who knew intuitively the quality of the advice he was given and could quickly see its political implications. His habit of cultivating 'confidence, indeed affection', with

those with whom he worked won co-operation and loyalty.

Fadden's relationship with Menzies was a curious one. 'They became friends as politicians, never as men. It was always politics which dictated their relationship'. Fadden had few intellectual pretensions and his lack of a university education kept him rather in awe of his leader. None the less, Fadden was as much the architect of their successful collaboration as was Menzies. To the warm-hearted Fadden, it was hurtful that Menzies appeared 'to take his loyal friends for granted and impose on their loyalty'. Fadden reckoned that he had spent a total of 692 days as acting prime minister during Menzies' absences abroad.

While treasurer, Fadden chaired twenty meetings of the Australian Loan Council and attended numerous conferences of the International Monetary Fund and the International Bank for Reconstruction and Development. He stood down as parliamentary leader of the Country Party on 26 March 1958, did not contest the elections that year and was succeeded as treasurer by H. E. Holt [q.v.] on 10 December. Hoping to be chairman of the new Commonwealth Banking Corporation board, Fadden was deeply wounded when a committee headed by McEwen appointed (Sir) Warren McDonald [q.v.] to the post. Fadden refused the government's subsequent offer to chair the Australian National Airlines Commission. Living in Brisbane, he accepted directorships of a wide range of companies. His memoirs, *They called me Artie*, were published in 1969.

In his declining years Fadden was aware of moves within the Country Party to change its name and to contest urban seats as well as those in its traditional heartland. Although conscious of the steady decline in Country Party representation at Federal and State levels, he saw no advantage in such changes. He steadfastly believed that the interests of primary producers and the inhabitants of country towns could be given proper attention only by a specialist party which understood them and their needs. To increase its numerical strength, he argued, his party needed to win country seats held by its opponents.

Ebullient and gregarious, Fadden had liked political campaigning, thrived on repartee with hecklers, and put his case with vehemence and fluency. While never 'marked out to be an outstanding political leader', he was an exceptionally astute operator. He had the gift of friendship, and his encouragement and kindness to colleagues on both sides of the House were legendary. He relished convivial occasions, enjoyed his drink, and had a prodigious collection of stories which he told with zest and humour.

Political cartoonists delighted in the opportunities afforded by Fadden's sharp nose, his slightly prominent teeth, and his chin which receded into a heavy jowl as he aged. Journalists viewed him with considerable affection, portraying him as the epitome of mateship. He concluded his memoirs with an anecdote about his arrival at Mackay soon after he had been knighted. An old acquaintance from his childhood, an Aborigine named Harry, greeted him warmly, only to be told by one of the entourage that he should address Fadden as 'Sir'. 'What', replied the unabashed Harry, 'you now a school teacher, Artie?'

The University of Queensland conferred an honorary LL.D. on Fadden in 1972. Survived by his wife, two daughters and a son, Sir Arthur died on 21 April 1973 in Brisbane and was cremated. A portrait (1947) by (Sir) William Dargie is held by Parliament House, Canberra; another by Dargie and one by Graeme Inson are in the family's possession.

P. Hasluck, *The Government and the People 1939-1941* (Canb, 1952); U. Ellis, *A History of the Australian Country Party* (Melb, 1963); E. Page, *Truant Surgeon*, A. Mozley ed (Syd, 1963); F. C. Green, *Servant of the House* (Melb, 1969); P. Spender, *Politics and a Man* (Syd, 1972); A. J. Campbell, *Memoirs of the Country Party in Queensland 1920-1974* (Brisb, 1975); C. W. Russell, *Country Crisis* (Brisb, 1976); H. C. Coombs, *Trial Balance* (Melb, 1981); C. B. Schedvin, *In Reserve* (Syd, 1992); *J of Imperial and Commonwealth Hist*, 22, no 3, Sept 1992, p 445; *Sun News-Pictorial*, 23 Apr 1973; T. H. Thelander, The Nature and Development of Country Party Organization in Queensland 1936-1944 (B.A. Hons thesis, Univ Qld, 1974); D. Lee, From Fear of Depression to Fear of War (Ph.D. thesis, ANU, 1991).

MARGARET BRIDSON CRIBB*

FAIRBAIRN, IRENE FLORENCE (1899-1974), Girl Guide commissioner, was born on 30 March 1899 at Stamford Hill, Hackney, London, daughter of Bishop Latimer Ridley, tailor's cutter, and his wife Florence Ada, née Edwards. Educated at Queenswood School, Eastbourne, Sussex, Rene captained the cricket team, played tennis and acquired her lifelong love of sport. In 1917-18 she worked as a volunteer aide at the Hospital for Wounded Officers, Park Lane, London. She was awarded the British Red Cross Society's service medal. In 1920 she helped to establish a Girl Guide company in Surrey. At the hospital she had met and nursed Captain Charles Osborne Fairbairn (d.1959), an Australian pastoralist serving with the Royal Air Force. He was brother of James Valentine Fairbairn [q.v.8]. Irene married Charles on 9 February 1922 at the parish church, Sutton,

Surrey, and accompanied him to his sheep-stud property, Banongill, near Skipton in western Victoria. They were to have three daughters and a son who was killed on active service with the Royal Australian Air Force on 1 February 1945. An orphaned niece was also taken into the family.

Guiding was in its infancy in Australia when Mrs Fairbairn joined the Beaufort-Skipton association in 1922. She became first secretary there in 1924 and was divisional commissioner (1925-38) for the Ballarat and Beaufort districts. In the 1930s she was asked in addition to be commissioner for Rokewood, some forty miles distant. She telegraphed headquarters: 'Delighted to accept Rokewood. Is Antarctica free also?' She sat on the Victorian executive-committee from the 1930s and served as State commissioner in 1958-63. Honorary secretary (1938-47) of the federal council of the Girl Guides' Association of Australia, Fairbairn was federal commissioner (1947-52) and chief commissioner for Australia (1952-55). In 1969 she was appointed life vice-president. To many of the women and girls of the guide movement, she was affectionately known as 'Gran'.

Fairbairn represented the Australian guide movement at six world conferences between 1926 and 1969, and was a member of the world association's sub-committee for the international centre, Sangam, in India. In appreciation of her work, the Girl Guides' Association of Australia established the Irene Fairbairn fund (1955) to assist guides with travel interstate and overseas. She was awarded the Silver Fish (guiding's highest honour) in 1948, and was appointed O.B.E. in 1953 and C.B.E. in 1969. The Indian Guide Association awarded her the Silver Elephant posthumously.

With her husband, Rene had extended the gardens of Banongill to fourteen acres (6 ha) and the three-mile (5 km) drive to their home was bordered by daffodils. From the 1920s the Fairbairns aimed to perfect pink, red and yellow varieties of these flowers by careful crossing; both were respected show judges in Australia and overseas. Rene maintained her interest in daffodils after Charles's death and opened the garden to raise money for charity.

A tall, blond, glamorous woman who retained traces of her English accent, Mrs Fairbairn had a sense of humour which was typified when she prefaced an award of the Silver Fish to an elderly guider by remarking, 'As one old trout to another . . .'. She was an active member of the Country Women's Association, the Australian Red Cross Society, the Citizens' Welfare Service and the Victoria League. A loyal worker for the Church of England, she was president (1959-70) of the rural deanery guilds of Ballarat. She played the organ on Sundays at Christ Church, Skipton, where a stained-glass window was to be installed in her memory in 1992. Survived by two of her daughters, she died on 14 March 1974 in East Melbourne and was cremated. A portrait by Graham Thorley is held by the family.

M. Coleman and H. Darling, *From a Flicker to a Flame* (Syd, 1989); Girl Guides Assn of Vic, *Matilda*, Apr 1974; *Age* (Melb), 26 Nov 1948, 5 Mar 1954, 2 June 1955, 12 Nov 1957, 4 Sept 1958, 2 Sept 1963, 19 Apr 1969; *Argus*, 9 Nov 1948, 1 Jan 1953, 5 Mar 1954, 2 June 1955; information from Miss M. W. Barr, Girl Guides Assn of Vic, Nth Balwyn, Melb, and Mrs A. Russell, Ocean Grove, Vic.   DAVID MAUNDERS

FAIRFAX, JOHN FITZGERALD (1904-1951), journalist and company director, was born on 18 April 1904 in Sydney, elder son of native-born parents Edward Wilfred Fairfax, medical practitioner, and his wife Mary Marguerite, née Lamb. John was educated at Geelong Church of England Grammar School, Victoria, and in England at Pembroke College, Oxford. Back in Sydney, he joined the Union Club in 1927 and next year entered John Fairfax & Sons [qq.v.4,8] Ltd, the family's newspaper firm. On 28 October 1930 he married Valerie Moule at St John's Anglican Church, Toorak; they were to have two daughters before being divorced in 1946.

Although he started work in the accounts and circulation departments, Fairfax soon displayed a talent for journalism, as had his elder cousin (Sir) Warwick, the company's managing director. As a mainly anonymous special writer, John produced many articles for the Fairfax weekly, *Sydney Mail*, some of which were collected in *Then and Now* (1937), a book of vignettes about the highways around Sydney. He was also an adventurous canoeist who took his kayak on the roof of a baby Morris to the Snowy gorges and other remote stretches of river. From these journeys came another book, *Run o' Waters* (1948). His *The Story of John Fairfax* was published in 1941 to commemorate the centenary of Fairfax ownership of the *Sydney Morning Herald*, which had been founded in 1831—oddly enough, on the author's own birthday.

From 1940 Fairfax served in the Militia; on 19 August 1941 he enlisted in the Australian Imperial Force. While serving at headquarters, 1st Armoured Brigade, for the next seventeen months he edited the divisional magazine, *Ack Willie* (later *Stand Easy*). He was discharged on 16 March 1943 and accredited a war correspondent for the *Sydney Morning Herald* with United States naval forces in the South Pacific. He covered the Solomon Islands campaign and accompanied

New Zealand troops who landed on Japanese-held Mono Island (October 1943).

Returning to Sydney in 1944, Fairfax resigned from the literary staff and succeeded his father as a director of the company. By 1946 the Fairfax board consisted only of the cousins Warwick, (Sir) Vincent and John—a trio once described as the company's 'head, hands and heart'. John, an unconventional man endowed with a debonair appearance and zestful manner, was popular but erratic, and therefore more vulnerable in the board-room than the intellectual Warwick and practical Vincent. In 1946 the general manager Rupert Henderson, anxious for defensive reasons to consolidate the company's widely dispersed family shareholding into fewer hands, prevailed upon John to resign from the board and sell his shares, mainly to Warwick.

At the district registrar's office, Mosman, on 24 April 1948 Fairfax married a divorcee Gwendoline Clarice Bennett, née Annabel; that year he bought into a country newspaper owned by her brother. His moods became more unstable; for a time he underwent psychiatric treatment; and on 31 October 1951 at Gocup, his property near Tumut, he used a shotgun to commit suicide. Survived by his wife and the daughters of his first marriage, he was cremated. Two collections of his writing, *Drift of Leaves* (1952) and *Laughter in the Camp* (1958), were published posthumously.

G. Souter, *Company of Heralds* (Melb, 1981); *Newspaper News* (Syd), 1 Dec 1951; *SMH*, 6 Feb, 27 Dec 1941, 11 May 1944, 6 July 1946, 1 Nov 1951; J. F. Fairfax file (John Fairfax Group Pty Ltd Archives, Syd).   GAVIN SOUTER

FAIRFAX, MARY ELIZABETH (1858-1945), philanthropist and women's leader, was born on 15 March 1858 at Macquarie Street, Sydney, eldest of seven children and only daughter of (Sir) James Reading Fairfax [q.v.8], newspaper proprietor, and his wife Lucy, née Armstrong. Upon her arrival her father exclaimed, 'only a girl'. The family moved in 1867 to Trahlee, Bellevue Hill, built by her father; after the death of her grandfather John Fairfax [q.v.4] in 1877, they moved again, to his nearby house, Ginahgulla. Mary was educated at home. The Fairfaxes spent 1881-83 abroad: with her parents, who were assiduous visitors of galleries and museums, she toured the Riviera and Italy. Back in Sydney, from 1884 they spent the summer months at Woodside, their country house at Moss Vale.

A foundation member (1887) of the executive of the Queen's Jubilee Fund, Miss Fairfax acted as honorary secretary for the ladies' committee, set up in 1887 to promote and endow a college for women at the University of Sydney; from 1893 until her death she was a councillor of Women's College. She was a State council-member of the Girl Guides' Association and was actively associated with the Boys' Brigade (founded by her father), the Royal Society for the Prevention of Cruelty to Animals, the Young Women's Christian Association, the Kindergarten Union, the (Sydney) District Nursing Association and the Bush Book Club. During World War I and II she worked for the Australian Comforts Fund and the British (Australian) Red Cross Society.

The Victoria League was very dear to her heart because it symbolized a link between Australia and the 'Old Country'. She joined the league in England, and was a founder (1917) and executive-member (1925-45) of its New South Wales branch. President (1912-19) and a vice-president (1920-45) of the Society of Arts and Crafts of New South Wales, she enjoyed contemporary exhibitions, though not as a collector. She was a foundation member (1936) of the Sydney Symphony Orchestral Ladies' Committee.

After her mother's death in 1925, Mary had inherited Ginahgulla and Woodside, as well as 2196 of her father's shares in John Fairfax & Sons Ltd, publishers of the *Sydney Morning Herald*. With an eye to the progress and reputation of the newspaper, she visited its offices periodically. She took on her large houses with her usual energy, delighted in their gardens and liked farming at Woodside; she retained the Victorian furnishings of the homes in which she had grown up. Remembered for her hospitality at Ginahgulla, she entertained all manner of people, from leading figures in literature, art and music to allied servicemen. Despite wartime difficulties and the dining-room being used to billet servicewomen, she continued all her life the custom (dating from 1858) of holding the family Christmas lunch at Ginahgulla. Children looked forward to peanut-hunts at the annual parties she held for them. Mary was a short, compact woman, with fair skin, blue eyes and white hair worn in a neat roll. A prim mien belied her lively sense of humour and her kindness. No matter the fashion, she wore light-coloured, full-length dresses with long sleeves and white gloves.

Mary Fairfax died on 20 May 1945 at Ginahgulla and was buried in the family grave in South Head cemetery, following a service at Woollahra Congregational Church where she had worshipped regularly. Her estate was sworn for probate at £428 278: substantial bequests were made to charities and employees, and the bulk was left to the Fairfax family. Ginahgulla was bought by Scots College. The Women's College council established the Mary Fairfax Memorial Library,

assisted by her legacy of £1000. A brass plaque, dedicated to her memory in 1948 at the Woollahra Congregational Church, survived the 1989 fire and is held by the Uniting Church.

The breadth of her interests was astonishing. Her eager mind, alert for new ideas, made her a valuable counsellor to the innumerable charities with which she was connected. She was broad-minded and tolerant, but positive in her views of right and wrong, and she never compromised the standards of conduct of her upbringing. Given her spontaneous generosity, the full measure of her philanthropy will never be calculated. Miss Mary, as she was known from childhood, was the quintessential maiden aunt. Inheriting ideas of public service from an earlier century, she was among the last of the great Victorians.

G. N. Griffiths, *Some Houses and People of New South Wales* (Syd, 1949); J. F. Fairfax, *Drift of Leaves* (Syd, 1952); W. V. Hole and A. H. Treweeke, *The History of the Women's College within the University of Sydney* (Syd, 1953); C. Simpson, *John Fairfax, 1804-1877* (Syd, 1977); G. Souter, *Company of Heralds* (Melb, 1981) and *Heralds and Angels* (Melb, 1991); J. O. Fairfax, *My Regards to Broadway* (Syd, 1991); *SMH*, 7 Dec 1932, 21, 22 May, 4, 8 June 1945; *Sun* (Syd), 27 Aug 1945; information from Mrs A. Biso, Roquebrune, France, Mrs A. Ogden, Cirencester, Eng, and Mrs A. Dupree, Rose Bay, Syd.   CAROLINE SIMPSON

FAIRLEY, SIR NEIL HAMILTON (1891-1966), physician, medical scientist and army officer, was born on 15 July 1891 at Inglewood, Victoria, third of six sons of native-born parents James Fairley, bank manager, and his wife Margaret Louisa, née Jones. Their four sons who survived to adulthood all took up medicine as a career. Neil was educated at Scotch College, East Melbourne, where he excelled at high-jumping. Graduating from the University of Melbourne (M.B., B.S., 1915; M.D., 1917; D.Sc., 1927) with first-class honours in 1915, he served his residency at the Melbourne Hospital and investigated an epidemic of cerebral meningitis.

On 5 September 1916 Fairley was appointed captain, Australian Army Medical Corps, Australian Imperial Force, and posted to the 14th Australian General Hospital in the Middle East. There he came under the influence of (Sir) Charles Martin [q.v.10], director of the Lister Institute of Preventive Medicine, London. In Egypt and Palestine, Fairley investigated schistosomiasis, dysentery, typhus and malaria, making significant contributions in each and kindling an enduring interest in tropical medicine. By 1918 he had become senior physician to the hospital. Promoted temporary lieutenant colonel in 1919, he was mentioned in dispatches and appointed O.B.E. On 12 February that year at the Garrison Church, Abbasiya, Cairo, he married Violet May Phillips; they were to be divorced on 21 November 1924.

After the war Fairley worked for two years with Martin at the Lister Institute and qualified as a member of the Royal College of Physicians, London. In 1920 he gained a diploma of tropical health and hygiene from the University of Cambridge and joined the Walter and Eliza Hall [qq.v.9] Institute of Research in Pathology and Medicine, Melbourne, before accepting a five-year appointment in Bombay, nominally as Tata professor of clinical tropical medicine but ultimately as medical research officer of the Bombay Bacteriological Laboratory and honorary consulting physician at two of the city's leading hospitals. Continuing his investigations of schistosomiasis, he carried out pioneering work on dracunculiasis and sprue. Fairley contracted sprue and was eventually invalided out of India. On 28 October 1925 at the Presbyterian Church, St Marylebone, London, he married Mary Evelyn Greaves. He returned to the Hall Institute in 1927 and worked there for two years, collaborating with its director Charles Kellaway [q.v.9] in studies of snake-venoms and with (Sir) Harold Dew [q.v.13] on the development of diagnostic tests for hydatid disease.

In 1929 Fairley returned to London to take up private practice in tropical medicine; he held appointments as assistant-physician and pathologist at the Hospital for Tropical Diseases, and as lecturer at the London School of Hygiene and Tropical Medicine. Although he investigated filariasis and leptospiral jaundice, his major research interest at this time was in malaria; in Salonica (Thessaloniki), Greece, he did notable work on Macedonian blackwater fever.

Appointed colonel in the A.I.F. on 15 July 1940, Fairley served as consulting physician to the Australian forces in the Middle East and also acted as honorary consultant in tropical diseases at British Army headquarters in that region. He focussed his attention on dysenteries and malaria. His earlier experience with malaria in Macedonia led to a confrontation with General Sir Archibald (Earl) Wavell over the proposed invasion of Greece in 1941, which led Wavell to change his plans, although in the event the British and Australian troops were driven from Greece before the malaria season began. Back in Australia in March 1942, next month Fairley was appointed director of medicine at Land Headquarters, Melbourne. He was to be promoted temporary brigadier in February 1944.

From the beginning of the war in the Far East and the Pacific, dysentery and malaria took a terrible toll of the allied forces. Building on his studies in Palestine of the use of sulphonamides for the treatment of bacillary dysentery, in 1942 Fairley sent all available supplies of sulphaguanidine to the front line in Papua where dysentery was threatening the effort by Australian troops to prevent the capture of Port Moresby. Early in 1943, at Fairley's instigation, General Douglas MacArthur [q.v.] established a combined advisory committee on tropical medicine, hygiene and sanitation, with Fairley as chairman.

Malaria, hyper-endemic throughout the theatre of operations, was even more threatening. In February 1942 Fairley had visited Java and succeeded in buying 120 tons of quinine, which was loaded in two ships. Neither reached Australia, and Fairley himself escaped in one of the last ships to get through. With quinine supplies in Japanese hands, Fairley went to London and Washington to urge the manufacture of atebrin (mepacrine) which was then the only other potent anti-malarial drug. In 1943 he and his colleagues E. V. Keogh [q.v.] and H. K. Ward persuaded the Australian army to establish the Land Headquarters Medical Research Unit (directed by Fairley) at Cairns, Queensland. The sole objective of this unit was to investigate malarial pathogenesis and chemoprophylaxis, using human 'guinea-pigs'. Fairley made it his own task to appeal for these people, addressing military units and explaining carefully the objectives of the work. He elaborated on the potential dangers and likely discomforts, and his convincing sincerity succeeded.

Over the period 1943 to 1945 several hundred volunteers were infected with malaria parasites—mainly with *Plasmodium falciparum*—without a single death. The results of these investigations were subsequently published and contained contributions of theoretical and practical importance. A direct transfusion of 7-18 fl. oz. (200-500 ml) of blood between human volunteers gave positive results for about seven minutes after the bite of an infected mosquito, and again after six to seven days with malignant tertian *(falciparum)* malaria and eight to nine days after benign tertian *(vivax)* malaria, foreshadowing the discovery of the exoerythrocytic cycle. Using the 'subinoculation' technique, the investigations showed that atebrin in adequate doses, when taken daily with unfailing regularity, would suppress *vivax* malaria and act as a causal prophylactic and cure for *falciparum* malaria, even under conditions of long and exhausting marches with full equipment, extremes of heat and cold, shortages of food and water, and lack of sleep. Having satisfied the immediate requirement, investigations followed into the atebrin resistance of certain strains of

Plasmodium falciparum, and a number of other drugs were examined, among them plasmoquine, paludrine and chloroquin. The findings, recorded in great detail, have never been challenged, and provide unique information, unobtainable under any conditions except those of a major war.

As an outcome of the findings with atebrin, the Australian army promulgated orders to ensure that the proper dosage was taken regularly, and that the responsibility for ensuring this procedure rested with the unit commander, not with the medical officer. The results were dramatic. Whereas early in the Papuan campaign the malaria rate had been as high as 2496 per thousand per annum, it fell to 740 per thousand in December 1943 and to 26 per thousand by November 1944. Earl Mountbatten, allied supreme commander, South-East Asia, adopted the Australian orders, with similar results among his forces. The control of malaria was a turning-point in the war in Burma and the Islands.

When World War II had ended, Fairley returned to the Hospital for Tropical Diseases, London; in 1945 he was appointed the first Wellcome professor of clinical tropical medicine at the London School of Hygiene and Tropical Medicine. On 3 July 1946 he transferred to the Reserve of Officers. In 1948, while at the height of his career, he suffered a serious illness from which he never fully recovered. He resigned his chair in 1949, but continued in practice and contributed to many committees, becoming the elder statesman of tropical medicine in Britain.

Fairley had made major contributions in several fields of tropical medicine. His publications comprised 149 scientific papers. He was thorough and meticulous in all he did, and spared no effort in exploring all possible interpretations of his results. Possessing great singleness of purpose, he threw himself into anything that he undertook, and was not to be deflected from his course. From the time of his investigations in Macedonia he showed an uncommon ability to delegate responsibility, a capacity that served him well in the supervision from Melbourne of the complex operations of the L.H.Q. Medical Research Unit at Cairns. His stature and authority in tropical medicine enabled him to persuade General Sir Thomas Blamey [q.v.13] and MacArthur of the operational importance of measures to control malaria and other disabling tropical diseases, and he was capable of making difficult and painful decisions if necessary. He had a slightly 'bulldoggish' appearance, especially in profile, which matched his attributes of intellectual and scientific courage, his tenacity, and his loyalty to colleagues.

Beneath Fairley's somewhat daunting 'working' exterior, there lay a warm personality that endeared him to many. His ability to gain enthusiastic co-operation was crucial to the success of his greatest work, the study of malaria pathogenesis and chemoprophylaxis in human volunteers. He inspired loyalty in his subordinates, and did everything he could to further their careers.

Fairley's contributions were honoured during his lifetime and commemorated after his death. He had been appointed C.B.E. (1941), a commander brother of the Order of St John (1947) and K.B.E. (1950). He became a fellow of the Royal colleges of physicians of London (1928), Australasia (1940) and Edinburgh (honorary, 1947). Elected a fellow of the Royal Society in 1942, he received honorary degrees from the universities of Adelaide (M.D., 1949), Melbourne (LL.D., 1951) and Sydney (D.Sc., 1956). He was awarded numerous medals and prizes, including the Chalmers memorial medal for research in tropical medicine (1931), the Richard Pierson Strong medal of the American Foundation of Tropical Medicine (1946), the Moxon medal of the Royal College of Physicians (1948), the Manson medal of the Royal Society of Tropical Medicine and Hygiene (1950), and the Buchanan medal of the Royal Society (1957).

Survived by his wife and their two sons, and by the son of his first marriage, Sir Neil died on 19 April 1966 at The Grove, Sonning, Berkshire, England, and was buried nearby in the graveyard of St Andrew's Church. A portrait (1943) by (Sir) William Dargie is held by the family; other portraits (by Dargie and Nora Heysen) are held at the Australian War Memorial, Canberra.

In 1968 the Royal College of Physicians, London, in association with the Royal Australasian College of Physicians, inaugurated the Neil Hamilton Fairley medal, awarded alternately by each college every five years 'to any citizen of any country of any age who has made outstanding contributions to medicine'. A memorial stone commemorating his work in the L.H.Q. Medical Research Unit was unveiled in 1972 at Cairns, near the site of the wartime laboratories. In 1980 the National Health and Medical Research Council created Neil Hamilton Fairley fellowships 'to provide training in scientific research methods which can be applied to any area of clinical or community medicine'.

DNB, 1961-70; A. S. Walker, *Clinical Problems of the War* (Canb, 1952) and *Middle East and Far East* (Canb, 1953) and *The Island Campaigns* (Canb, 1957); F. M. Burnet, *Walter and Eliza Hall Institute 1915-1965* (Melb, 1971); I. J. Wood, *Discovery and Healing in Peace and War* (Melb, 1984); G. L. McDonald (ed), *Roll of the Royal Australasian College of Physicians*, 1, 1938-75 (Syd, 1988); F. Fenner (ed), *History of Microbiology in Australia* (Canb, 1990); *Biog Memoirs of Fellows of Roy Soc* (Lond), 12, 1966, p 123; *MJA*, 2, 15 Nov 1969; Fairley's scientific papers (Basser L, Canb);

R. R. Andrew's appreciation of Fairley (ts, held by Roy A'sian College of Physicians L, Syd); information from Lady Hamilton Fairley, Reading, Berkshire, Eng, and Mrs C. J. Hackett, Lond.

FRANK FENNER

FAIRWEATHER, ANDREW

(1882-1962), mining engineer, was born on 31 May 1882 at Port Adelaide, one of four children of Andrew Abercrombie Fairweather, engineer, and his first wife Cecelia, née Russell. Young Andrew was educated at public schools, Way College (on a scholarship), the University of Adelaide (B.Sc., 1901; converted to B.E., 1913) and the School of Mines and Industries of South Australia (fellowship diploma in mining and metallurgy, 1904). He gained practical experience underground in the Sulphide Corporation Ltd's Central Mine at Broken Hill, New South Wales, and in 1904 was appointed to the underground technical staff of the South Mine of Broken Hill South Silver Mining Co. (from 1918 Broken Hill South Ltd). At the Methodist Church, Port Adelaide, on 16 October 1907 he married Emily Edna Symes, a nurse.

Promoted underground superintendent (1910) and mine superintendent (1920), Fairweather completely reorganized the system of underground management at the South Mine and achieved improved efficiency. With W. E. Wainwright's [q.v.12] backing, he engaged qualified engineers such as A. B. Black [q.v.13] whose work led to safer mining methods. In 1932 Fairweather badly underestimated the remaining potential of the ore body, believing it likely to last only fifteen years. His conservative instincts prevented him from advocating exploration for other deposits: he regarded such expenditure as too great a gamble for the shareholders. In 1937 he succeeded Wainwright as general manager of B.H.S. Ltd.

Fairweather's main contribution was in the field of industrial relations. The workers' bitterness and distrust of the companies had culminated in the 'Big Strike' of 1919-20. Fairweather studied the causes of unrest. With leading unionists, he attended Workers' Educational Association lectures on socialism to gain an insight into miners' attitudes and aspirations. 'Come the revolution, Andy', said one prominent unionist, 'when the workers get control of the mines, you'll be our mine manager'. Fairweather resented paternalism and disliked arbitration tribunals with their entourage of lawyers who encouraged argument instead of discussion and promoted division instead of harmony. As president (1935-44) of the Mine Managers' Association, he represented all the mining companies and headed delicate and critical negotiations with the unions. He was trusted by both sides and was the key figure in maintaining industrial peace in the B.H. mines.

Had his father been able to afford the cost, Fairweather would have studied medicine rather than engineering: he paid particular attention to the medical and health aspects of work in the B.H. mines. He served on the Broken Hill and District Hospital board and the local water board, and was a member of the joint committee under the Workmen's Compensation (Broken Hill) Act (1920). After retiring in 1944 to Rose Park, Adelaide, he became a director of B.H.S. Ltd (1944-54), the Electrolytic Zinc Co. of Australasia Ltd (1947-54), the Electrolytic Refining & Smelting Co. of Australia Pty Ltd (1946-54) and Western New South Wales Electric Power Pty Ltd (1944-54). He had been president (1932) of the Australasian Institute of Mining and Metallurgy, and was awarded its medal for 1945 'in recognition of his long and efficient service to the mining industry, his valuable contributions to the industrial phase of Broken Hill operations, and also to the splendid work he has done in guiding and introducing students to the profession'.

Widely read, Fairweather believed in education in the humanities as a background for all professions. His knowledge of Shakespeare's plays and characters had proved valuable, he claimed, in management and industrial relations. He welcomed retirement as an opportunity to catch up on a backlog of reading, but his sight deteriorated. A man of quiet, studious and serious nature, and an upright character with a strong sense of justice, Fairweather was firm but fair as a manager. He was a little below middle height and of average build, with hazel eyes, brown hair (which turned grey), an open countenance, a steady gaze and a firm mouth. Survived by his wife, son and two daughters, Fairweather died on 4 May 1962 at Toorak Gardens and was cremated.

G. Blainey, *The Rise of Broken Hill* (Melb, 1968); B. Carroll, *Built on Silver* (Melb, 1986); R. J. Solomon, *The Richest Lode* (Syd, 1988); *SMH*, 3 July 1937, 3 Apr 1944, 9 Mar 1946, 10 Feb 1947; A'sian Inst of Mining and Metallurgy records (held at Clunies Ross House, Parkville, Melb); family records (held by Mr F. L. Fairweather, Klemzig, Adel); personal information.

D. F. FAIRWEATHER

FAIRWEATHER, IAN (1891-1974), artist, was born on 29 September 1891 at Bridge of Allan, Stirlingshire, Scotland, youngest of nine children of James Fairweather, deputy surgeon general, Indian Medical Service, and his wife Annette Margaret Dupré, née Thorp.

From the age of six months Ian was raised by Scottish aunts until his parents returned from India in 1901. Educated in London, on Jersey (where the family lived) and at Champéry, Switzerland, he joined the British Army and was commissioned in June 1914. Two months later he was captured in France by the Germans. Between unsuccessful escapes, Fairweather read E. F. Fenollosa and Lafcadio Hearn, studied Japanese, began drawing, and illustrated prisoner-of-war magazines. While billeted at The Hague in 1918, he studied briefly at the Academy of Arts and privately with Johann Hendrik van Mastenbroek. Resigning his commission in 1919, Fairweather enrolled at the Commonwealth Forestry Institute, Oxford, before studying (1920-24) under Dr Henry Tonks at the Slade School of Fine Art, London, where he was awarded second prize for figure drawing in 1922. At nights he studied Japanese, then Chinese, at the School of Oriental and African Studies, University of London. About this time he met H. S. Ede who was to be a lifelong friend and supporter. From 1925 until 1927 Fairweather painted with a patron, though only four canvases—the only canvases he ever painted—resulted.

Having been employed as a farm labourer in Canada in 1929, he departed in May for Shanghai, China, to work, travel and paint. When he reached Bali in March 1933, he painted full time. Fairweather visited Western Australia and Colombo before arriving in Melbourne in February 1934. The exceptional quality of his work was immediately recognized by the art entrepreneur Gino Nibbi [q.v.], and by local artists such as George Bell, 'Jock' Frater and Arnold Shore [qq.v.7,8,11]. Fairweather's work was presented for sale at Cynthia Reed's [q.v. Nolan] gallery in March. After six months unfinished work on a mural for the Menzies Hotel, he left Melbourne abruptly. Travelling through Sydney and Brisbane to the Philippines, he painted at Davao for a few months before returning to China. He lived in abject poverty, away from other Westerners, and at times was reduced to working with Chinese chalks. Much of his time was spent in absorbing the methods of calligraphy. In April 1936 he left China; he visited Japan, Taiwan, Hong Kong, Borneo and the Philippines. Most of the work he did in 1937 was destroyed by a fire in his room in Manila. He suffered lead-poisoning, and part of the little finger on his right hand was removed following infection from an injury.

Meanwhile, through Ede's influence a successful exhibition of Fairweather's work was held at the Redfern Gallery, London; it was followed by exhibitions in 1937 at the Carnegie Institute's 'International', Pittsburgh, United States of America, and at the National Gallery of Victoria. In September 1938 Fairweather sailed for Australia and at Sandgate, near Brisbane, rented the Beach Theatre, a disused cinema, 'the most perfect studio I . . . ever had'. He could not afford conventional painting materials, so used a concoction of borax and water-glass, but 'mostly it fell off'. Disheartened, he went to Cairns in June 1939. He was unable to find work and initially lived with the Aborigines. His first known Australian subjects were two landscapes, 'Alligator Creek, Cairns'. Two figure studies, 'Portrait' and 'Lads Boxing', placed him among the first major Australian artists 'who felt merit in painting Aborigines or Islanders without condescension'. Because he had become allergic to oils, these paintings were his last in that medium. He turned to gouache, which encouraged his use of unstable surfaces.

In May 1940 Fairweather left Australia to support Britain's war effort. He was given a desk-job in censorship at Singapore, and another at Calcutta, India, and was appointed temporary captain in a prisoner-of-war camp for Italians, at Bombay. Following his discharge, he returned to Melbourne on 1 June 1943. His work had been exhibited in London, at the National Gallery in 1940 and the Redfern Gallery in 1942. He went north to Cooktown, Queensland, where difficulty in obtaining painting materials forced him to experiment with both soap and casein. At Sandgate, Brisbane, he applied unsuccessfully for the directorship of the National Art Gallery of New South Wales, then became a labourer in an aircraft factory. In March 1945 he embarked in an old lifeboat, landed by chance on nearby Bribie Island, and found 'the idea of the bush that haunted me in India and brought me back here against all reason'. He stayed seven months, but, after the theft of his diaries, moved to Melbourne and to Lina Bryans's Darebin studio at Heidelberg. There he lived among other artists and worked tirelessly for two years, seemingly content. Most of the gouaches he produced were irretrievably damaged before reaching the Redfern Gallery.

At the end of 1947 Fairweather went back to Cairns and later sent his work to the Macquarie Galleries, Sydney. In September 1949 the gallery organized a solo exhibition, and subsequently showed his work almost annually until 1970. In 1949 he moved off again, through Bribie and Townsville to Darwin, where he lived in an old boat during 1951-52. His relatively scarce drawings mostly date from this Cairns-Darwin period. On 29 April 1952, having carefully studied seamanship and navigation, he set out for Timor in a small raft which he had made from discarded materials. After almost perishing, he collapsed on the beach at Roti, Indonesia, sixteen days later. He was interned, shunted to Timor, Bali and Singapore, then (apparently after diplomatic intervention) placed in a home for derelicts whence he was repatriated to England. It was some five years before direct references to the raft experience appeared in his painting (including 'Lit Bateau' and 'Roti'). In England, Fairweather dug ditches to help repay his passage, but his 'strange experience going home after twenty-five years . . . wasn't a happy one'.

Eventually his relations funded his return to Australia. Reaching Sydney in August 1953, he headed straight to Bribie, 'glad to be back in the sun . . . in the friendly bush'. On a site affording him almost complete solitude, he erected two Malay-style thatched huts of local bush materials in which to live and work. 'Roi Soleil' (1956-57) began his larger works. From mid-1958 Fairweather used synthetic polymer paint, often mixed with gouache; thereafter his works were generally more stable. Thirty-six abstract paintings sent to the Macquarie Galleries in 1959-60 are among Australia's finest. 'Last Supper' (1958) was the first of his great religious subjects; 'Monastery' (1961) won the John McCaughey Prize in 1966; and his largest, 'Epiphany' (1962), Fairweather thought his best. His exhibition at the Macquarie Galleries in August 1962 remains significant in Australian art history. From early 1963 Fairweather devoted more time to translating and less to painting: he translated and illustrated *The Drunken Buddha* (1965). His painting, 'Turtle and Temple Gong', won the W. D. & H. O. Wills prize in 1965. A travelling retrospective exhibition of eighty-eight of his works, mounted by the Queensland Art Gallery that year, enabled Fairweather to see, for the first time, his paintings publicly shown. His work had also been included in the Bienal de Sao Paulo, Brazil (1963), and toured Europe with 'Australian Painting Today' (1964-65) and Asia with 'Contemporary Australian Paintings' (1967-68).

Bribie's increasing accessibility and tourist appeal—acknowledged in 'Barbecue' (1963) —together with the publicity that surrounded his exhibitions, prompted Fairweather to leave Australia on 7 August 1965. He went to Singapore and India, then returned in September. One year later he flew to London, where he contemplated establishing a studio. Realizing that he was a misfit, he came back to Bribie. He briefly resumed abstract painting in 1968, producing his last great work, 'House by the Sea'. In 1973 his fellow artists bestowed on Fairweather the International Co-operation Art Award for his outstanding contribution to art in Australia. About 1970 publicity had prompted investigations which revealed that he owed a five-figure sum to the taxation office. Fairweather's inability or unwillingness to accept his increasing income had prompted the Macquarie Galleries to establish a trust account on his behalf. The realization of his financial security came too late for his enjoyment. Plagued by arthritis and cardiac disease, from 1969 he had found it hard to stand and paint (in his customary manner) over a low, flat table. He died on 20 May 1974 in Royal Brisbane Hospital and was cremated with Presbyterian forms.

Fairweather's work is held by the National Gallery of Australia, Canberra, all State and many regional galleries, the Tate gallery, London, the Leicester art gallery and the Ulster museum, Belfast. Many influences affected him, including Turner, Cézanne, Chinese culture and Buddhism. Chinese calligraphy, Post-Impressionism, cubism, abstraction and Aboriginal art strengthened and individualized his style. The content of his work was significantly autobiographical, and mostly reflective. A master colourist, he used colour sparingly. Starting as a landscape painter, he became more interested in figures, almost exclusively in people 'generally speaking'. 'MO, PB and the Ti Tree' is a rare portrait of individuals. He worked slowly, making many alterations as ideas occurred to him, whether by day or at night. 'Painting to me is something of a tightrope act; it is between representation and the other thing—whatever that is. It is difficult to keep one's balance'. A tall, slim figure, with intense blue eyes, Fairweather had a shy, gentle and dignified manner. He resented interference with his style of life, which was reclusive, self-disciplined, austere, and determinedly unrestrained by society. His painting, an 'inner compulsion', was self-consuming—'It leaves no room for anything else'.

Qld Art Gallery, *Fairweather: A Retrospective Exhibition*, exhibition cat (Brisb, 1965); C. McGregor et al, *Australian Art and Artists in the Making* (Melb, 1969); N. Abbott-Smith, *Ian Fairweather* (Brisb, 1978); M. Bail, *Ian Fairweather* (Syd, 1981); Philip Bacon Galleries, *Ian Fairweather*, exhibition cat (Brisb, 1984); Niagara Galleries, *Ian Fairweather: Paintings & Drawings 1927-1970*, exhibition cat (Melb, 1985); Film Australia, 'Contemporary Painting, 1950-1979', video (Syd, 1989); G. Dutton (comp), *Artists' Portraits* (Canb, 1992); *Art and Aust*, 12, no 7, July-Sept 1974, p 40, 21, no 3, Autumn 1984, p 337; I. Fairweather: artist biog files *and* confidential files (Qld Art Gallery L, Brisb).

JANET HOGAN

FALKINER, GEORGE BRERETON SADLEIR (1907-1961), sheep-breeder, was born on 12 February 1907 at Royal Park, Melbourne, third child and elder son of Victorian-born parents Franc Brereton Sadleir Falkiner [q.v.8], sheep-breeder, and his wife Ethel Elizabeth, née Howat. George was educated at Geelong Church of England Grammar School and at St Paul's College, University of Sydney (B.E., 1931), where he specialized in engineering technology and was a member of the rifle team that won two intervarsity competitions and the Imperial Universities' Rifle Match in 1929. When his father died that year, Falkiner took over Haddon Rig, an 82 000-acre (33 200 ha) property near Warren. In 1930 he gained a pilot's licence. After experiencing drought, debt and the Depression—when he brought dead wool home 'at about three bob a time'—by the late 1930s he had spent £45 000 on improvements, including an airstrip, and Haddon Rig was operating profitably.

Returning from the United States of America after the outbreak of World War II, Falkiner set up and was chairman of Turner Parachute Pty Ltd which made 25 000 parachutes for dropping supplies in New Guinea. He was also chairman of York Air Conditioning and Refrigeration (Australasia) Pty Ltd which delivered defence equipment worth nearly £1 million. Twice rejected in 1941 for the Royal Australian Air Force because of deafness, he voluntarily flew for the Allied Works Council and in connection with the anti-aircraft defences of Sydney.

A ready innovator who was fascinated by technology, Falkiner took a keen, practical interest in a wide range of activities, including rain-making experiments, fire-fighting equipment, soil conservation, artificial stock-insemination and the scientific measurement of wool. He was one of the first studmasters to employ a resident veterinarian. An expert pilot and winner of numerous flying-trophies, he was a pioneer of rural air transport and from 1946 sent his rams by air to the Sydney sales. He had an office in O'Connell Street, Sydney: in addition to six company directorships, among them the clothing firm Scamp Pty Ltd, he ran an import-export business in partnership with his friend Clive Caldwell, a wartime flying-ace. On 2 June 1949 at the King's Chapel of St John the Baptist, Savoy, London, Falkiner married Pauline Arnold Weir (1922-1977), a well-known equestrienne from Bowning.

In 1954 he gave £50 000 to the University of Sydney to establish a nuclear research laboratory in memory of his father. George Falkiner was governor of the university's Nuclear Research Foundation. In 1955 he received an honorary D.Sc.

An indefatigable spokesman, writer and publicist for the wool industry, Falkiner travelled throughout the world studying the latest developments; he gave money to support wool research and promotion, strongly opposed the ban on the export of merino rams and advocated that Australian wool should be marketed abroad under a distinctive trade name. He was a council-member (from 1932), president (1958-61) and a life member of the New South Wales Sheepbreeders' Association; in 1959 he helped to found and was first president of the Australian Association of Stud Merino Breeders. That year he gave seventy stud rams to soldier settlers. Falkiner's enterprise and progressive thinking, backed by the skills of his general manager A. B. Ramsay and sheepclasser Malcolm McLeod, made Haddon Rig a cornerstone of the Australian wool industry and the most famous medium-strong wool merino stud in the world. In 1960 Haddon Rig topped the aggregate at the Sydney ram sales for the twentieth successive year and two rams, sold for £7350 and £8715, set world record prices. By the 1960s Haddon Rig blood accounted for 35 per cent of Australian merinos.

Short and stocky, outwardly serious, but with a good sense of humour, 'G.B.S.' enjoyed a flamboyant social life. In addition to the Australian Jockey, Sydney Turf and sundry picnic race clubs, he belonged to the Australian, University and Royal Sydney Golf clubs, and to the Royal Aero Club of New South Wales. Survived by his wife, two daughters and 6-year-old son, Falkiner died of cancer on 15 October 1961 in Royal Prince Alfred Hospital, Sydney; following a service at St Mark's Anglican Church, Darling Point, he was cremated and his ashes were scattered at Haddon Rig. His estate was sworn for probate at £766 629. As he willed, his pastoral interests were carried on by his executors as a company, with his wife as 'general supervisor' until their son attained the age of 23. A dispute over death duties was resolved in November 1972 when the Privy Council found against the executors.

S. Falkiner, *Haddon Rig, the First Hundred Years* (Syd, 1981); C. Massy, *The Australian Merino* (Melb, 1990); *Pastoral Review*, 16 Feb 1933, 16 Aug 1934, 17 Feb, 18 Nov 1961; *Aust Q*, 22, June 1960, p 17; *Corian*, Dec 1961, p 260; *SMH*, 23, 29 May 1936, 13 July 1939, 27 July 1940, 7, 8 Apr 1943, 6, 8 Feb 1945, 10 June 1947, 31 May 1949, 2 June 1950, 4 Dec 1953, 6, 14 Mar 1954, 6, 19, 20, 28 May, 3 June 1955, 6, 24 Jan, 10 June, 7 July 1959, 4 Jan, 2, 3, 9 Mar, 16 Apr, 30 May, 18, 23 Aug 1960, 11, 15, 22, 25 Feb, 23, 30, 31 May, 2 June, 18, 30 Sept, 16, 17 Oct 1961, 6 Mar 1969, 12, 15 July, 9 Nov 1972, 4 Sept 1977.

G. P. WALSH

FALLON, CLARENCE GEORGE (1890 ?-1950), trade unionist, was born probably in 1890 at Rockwood, near Tangorin, Central Queensland, third of seven children of James Fallon, a native-born shearer, and Florence Catherine Smith, a domestic servant from

England. Both his parents participated in the 1890 shearers' strike. Young Clarrie received little schooling, but read voraciously. Years later he was remembered as having come out of the heart of the back-country as a raw youth, 'bursting with energy, endowed with a wonderful physique'. He worked in the transport, mining and pastoral industries. Having joined the Trolley, Draymen and Carters' Union in 1908, he helped to form a sugar-workers' union in the Bundaberg district; he was also active in the Gladstone branch of the Railway Workers' Union and in the General Labourers' Union. On 11 March 1913 he married 19-year-old Lillian Matilda Sansum with Anglican rites at Christ Church, Bundaberg; they were to have five children. Fallon enlisted in the Australian Imperial Force on 18 September 1916, but was discharged in November because of defective vision. His brother Jack was killed in France in 1917.

When he joined the Australian Workers' Union in 1917, Fallon was a municipal worker. By August 1921 he was a temporary organizer for that union at Bundaberg, 'gaining his first real insight into the manipulations of certain sugar employers to hamper the worker's progress'. In charge of the A.W.U. office at Rockhampton in 1923, one year later he transferred to Mackay where he developed a friendship with William Forgan Smith [q.v.11]. Fallon rose quickly in the union hierarchy. He became northern district secretary at Townsville in April 1928 and in the following year narrowly won the presidency of the Queensland branch. From January 1933 until his death he was State secretary of the A.W.U.; in conjunction, he was managing director of the Queensland *Worker*, chairman of the *Daily Standard* and director of Labor's radio station, 4KQ. On 14 June 1938 he was elected secretary of the State branch of the Australian Labor Party. He pursued causes vigorously. After his son Jack—a pilot in the Royal Australian Air Force—died in an air crash in 1937, Fallon attacked the 'hopeless inefficiency and inadequacy' of the R.A.A.F., and demanded an official investigation into its organization. Frequent criticisms directed at improving standards of air safety also appeared in the *Worker*. He later repeatedly called on the Federal government to strengthen inadequate defences in Northern Australia.

Vice-president (from 1933) of the A.L.P.'s Queensland central executive, Fallon succeeded W. H. Demaine [q.v.8] as president in November 1938. Fallon's friendship with Premier Forgan Smith was then transformed into a political alliance that completely dominated the Q.C.E. until Forgan Smith's resignation in 1942. Good working relationships continued with successive Labor premiers,

F. A. Cooper [q.v.13] and E. M. Hanlon [q.v.]. In late 1942 Prime Minister Curtin [q.v.13] attempted to persuade the A.L.P.'s State executives to support conscription for overseas service in a limited area of the South-West Pacific. The proposal, placed before the Q.C.E. with the support of Cooper, Hanlon and Forgan Smith, was opposed 'under instruction from the Queensland Delegates'— headed by Fallon.

From June 1938 Fallon had also been president of the federal executive of the A.L.P. During his term of office the party experienced one of its most turbulent periods. In August 1939 he chaired the unity conference convened to reform the New South Wales Labor Party led by J. T. Lang [q.v.9]. In controversial circumstances surrounding the resignation of Edward Grayndler [q.v.9], Fallon was elected general secretary of the A.W.U in 1940. He intended to hold the position conjointly with his State secretaryship, and refused the salary of £2000. Eventually forced to choose between remaining in Queensland and moving to the national office in Sydney, he resigned as general secretary in February 1943 and supported W. B. Hay's candidature for the position. Tom Dougherty [q.v.] wrested the post from Hay in January 1944, weakening Fallon's power at the national level and creating a deep rift between the two. That year the Allied Works Council altered the working conditions of cooks in the Civil Construction Corps, without reference to the conciliation and arbitration process. In protest, Fallon resigned his presidency of the A.L.P.'s federal executive on 7 July. He remained convinced that Curtin's Labor government had compromised its principles and policies. As Queensland director for the 'Yes' campaign in the 1944 referendum to give the Commonwealth fourteen new powers, Fallon made statements that were detrimental to the case.

From his initial prominence in the 1929 South Johnstone sugar-workers' strike, Fallon had set an impressive record as an advocate in industrial matters. He represented the A.W.U. and many other unions in basic-wage cases, and worked long hours, often seven days a week. His commitment to A.W.U. affairs led him to refuse offers of alternative appointments, including that of industrial commissioner for Queensland, though in 1944 he agreed to become government representative on the senate of the University of Queensland. Nicknamed 'the red terror'—as much for his intense opposition to communism as for the original colour of his hair— Fallon was 5 ft 10 ins (178 cm) tall, with a fair complexion, brown eyes and a resounding voice; he attributed his poor eyesight to sandy blight (trachoma) from his days as a bush worker. He demanded absolute loyalty from members and officials. During his long stewardship the Queensland branch of the A.W.U. was noted for its cohesion. Colleagues remembered his decisiveness, and his unforgiving nature. First and foremost a Queenslander, he fiercely defended the principles of the labour movement, and tirelessly endeavoured to improve working-class wages and conditions.

Survived by his wife, two daughters and two of his three sons, Fallon died of a cerebral haemorrhage on 11 January 1950 in North Sydney, on the eve of an A.W.U. convention, and was buried in Lutwyche cemetery, Brisbane.

D. J. Murphy et al (eds), *Labor in Power* (Brisb, 1980); T. Sheridan, *Division of Labour* (Melb, 1989); C. Cameron, *The Confessions of Clyde Cameron 1913-1990*, D. Connell comp and ed (Syd, 1990); R. McMullin, *The Light on the Hill* (Melb, 1991); *Worker*, 30 Jan 1929, 16 July 1940, 16 Jan 1950, 18 Jan 1954; *Qld Industrial Gazette*, 31 Mar 1948; *Courier-Mail*, 12 Jan 1950; *Bulletin*, 11 Feb 1986; information from Mr M. D. Cross, Ashgrove, Mr C. W. E. Williams, Brisb, and the late Mr G. G. Goding.   LYNETTE A. BERGSTRUM

FALSTEIN, SYDNEY MAX (1914-1967), politician, lawyer and businessman, was born on 30 May 1914 at Coffs Harbour, New South Wales, son of Abram Max Falstein, a grazier from Russia, and his German-born wife Rosa, née Goldman. Educated at Sydney Boys' High and Sydney Grammar schools, young Max entered the University of Sydney (B.A., 1935) and later studied for a law degree. On 13 March 1937 at St John's Anglican Church, Darlinghurst, he married a nurse Ila Brenda Greig; by marrying outside the Jewish faith, he was estranged from his wealthy mother. He went to New Zealand, took several jobs and became an organizer for the Labour Party. Back home, on 23 August 1940 he was admitted to the New South Wales Bar.

As the Australian Labor Party's candidate for Watson, in September that year Falstein was elected to the House of Representatives; he was to retain the seat in 1943 and 1946. Colleagues found him blunt, impetuous and reckless. One observer noted his 'superb confidence in himself that leads either to a big success or a big crash'. In his first speech he attacked (Sir) Robert Menzies' [q.v.] government for failing to prosecute the war with vigour and for favouring the interests of employers over those of workers. He aligned himself with A. A. Calwell [q.v.13] and forces within the parliamentary Labor Party opposed to the leadership of John Curtin [q.v.13]. After the A.L.P. came to power Falstein clashed openly with Curtin in 1944 over the recruitment and employment of Royal Australian Air Force personnel.

On 18 July 1942 Falstein had enlisted in the R.A.A.F. He was court-martialled in September for using insubordinate language to a superior officer, convicted and sentenced to twenty-eight days detention. An appeal to the Air Board was dismissed, despite his flurry of telegrams to Labor politicians. Having qualified as a pilot, he was commissioned in May 1943 and completed an operational tour (1944-45) with No.42 (Catalina) Squadron in the South-West Pacific Area. His appointment terminated on 4 September 1945.

Following the war, Falstein set up in business. In September 1948 he was fined £320 for falsifying documents to understate the value of imported wristwatches. His appeal failed. Apparently as a consequence, the Labor Party refused him endorsement for Watson at the next general elections, although he had strong support from Calwell who argued that he had been convicted of merely 'technical offences'. Falstein's unsuccessful attempt to retain Watson as an Independent Labor candidate in 1949 led to his expulsion from the A.L.P. He played no further substantial role in politics, except to urge Labor support in 1950 for Menzies' Communist Party dissolution bill. Although Falstein had publicly expressed his detestation of communism, he had also advocated the socialization of industry and the recognition of Communist China.

On 12 August 1958 he was declared bankrupt, with unsecured liabilities of £34 553 and assets of £1581. Refusing to discharge him in 1962, the judge in bankruptcy Sir Thomas Clyne found that his conduct 'exhibited very little sense of business morality or of honest dealing'. Falstein had returned to the Bar in March 1961. In late 1962 he represented himself before the High Court of Australia in a challenge to Clyne's refusal to exempt from the bankruptcy order his income as a barrister. The court dismissed the appeal, along with his separate appeal to be discharged from bankruptcy.

Falstein was energetic, rebellious and hubristic. His promising career had been marred by unproductive clashes with authority and dubious business ventures. Suffering from diabetes and hypertension, he died of a cerebral thrombosis on 18 May 1967 at the Repatriation General Hospital, Concord, and was cremated with Jewish rites. His wife, daughter and three of his four sons survived him.

P. Weller (ed), *Caucus Minutes 1901-1949*, 3, 1932-49 (Melb, 1975); F. Daly, *From Curtin to Kerr* (Melb, 1977); C. Kiernan, *Calwell* (Melb, 1978); G. Souter, *Acts of Parliament* (Melb, 1988); *PD* (Cwlth), 22 Nov 1940, p 129, 19 June 1941, p 187, 20 June 1941, p 230, 7 Nov 1941, p 195, 22 June 1943, p 71, 14 Sept 1944, pp 857, 859, 4 July 1946, p 2240, 15 May 1947, p 2445, 10 Oct 1947, p 642,

16 June 1948, p 2049, 5 Oct 1949, p 972; *State Reports*(NSW), 49, 1949, p 133; *Cwlth Law Reports*, 108, 1962-63, p 523; *Aust Law J*, 36, 1962, p 267; *Smith's Weekly* (Syd), 12 Oct 1940, 30 Mar 1946, 19 Nov 1949; *SMH*, 12, 23 Sept 1942, 15 Sept 1944, 27 Sept 1947, 18 Dec 1948, 1 Oct, 16 Nov 1949, 5 May 1950, 23 Nov 1962, 19 May 1967.

J. W. SHAW

FANNING, LAWRENCE BEDE (1885-1970), public servant, was born on 18 August 1885 at Casino, New South Wales, sixth son of James Fanning, a contractor from New Zealand, and his English-born wife Harriett, née Van der Warden. Educated at Lismore, in December 1904 Bede joined the Postmaster-General's Department and worked as a telephone attendant in Sydney. On 5 June 1910 at the Sacred Heart Catholic Church, Darlinghurst, he married a barmaid Amy Edwards (d.1951) also known as Green; they were to have a daughter and a son.

Rising to managerial positions in the department's New South Wales and Queensland divisions, in 1918 Fanning was promoted to traffic officer (telephones) in the chief electrical engineer's office, central staff, Melbourne. By 1924, as head of the new telephone branch, he was directly responsible to the secretary (Sir) Harry Brown [q.v.7]. In the next fifteen years he and Fanning achieved substantial progress in developing telephone services, despite reductions in government expenditure during the Depression. The 1930s saw most manual exchanges in major cities and towns replaced by automatic apparatus. Fanning was appointed I.S.O. (1941).

After Brown's successor (Sir) Daniel McVey [q.v.] was detached from the department in 1941, Fanning became acting director-general of posts and telegraphs: his first priority was to meet wartime defence requirements. He replaced McVey as director-general on 11 June 1946 and faced the immediate challenge of meeting the accumulated demand for services at a time when equipment and materials were scarce. In 1947 Fanning visited England where he obtained supplies and encouraged British manufacturers to open factories in Australia. While abroad he also studied developments in television, and attended telecommunication and postal conferences in Europe and the United States of America. He was a member (1946-49) of the Australian National Airlines and Overseas Telecommunications commissions.

In 1949 the government established the Australian Broadcasting Control Board to supervise the provision of radio and television services, and the maintenance of technical and programming standards. Fanning retired from the public service on 14 March and next day began a three-year term as the board's chairman. On 3 June the board recommended that television should be introduced in the six State capitals, but transmission did not commence until 1956. With the Federal general elections approaching, on 8 September 1949 the board issued an order requiring political matter to be broadcast 'on an equitable basis'. The order 'received a hostile reception' in parliament and the press, and most of its conditions were withdrawn.

A short, spare, elegant figure, Fanning had an air of authority; although some people regarded him as aloof, he was unfailingly courteous and considerate. He was respected for his administrative capability and for being 'an articulate communicator'. His career was typical of those of his generation who surmounted limited education by their natural abilities. Fanning retired in 1952, joined the board of Edward H. O'Brien Pty Ltd, advertising contractors, and played golf for recreation. Survived by his son, he died on 14 August 1970 at Hawthorn and was buried in Melbourne general cemetery.

A. Moyal, *Clear Across Australia* (Melb, 1984); *PP*(Cwlth), 1945-46, 3, p 979, 1950-51, 2, p 999, 1951-53, 2, p 1095, 1954-55, 3, p 679; *Herald* (Melb), 8 Nov 1941; *SMH*, 3 Apr 1947, 3 Jan 1948, 29 Jan 1949, 28 Feb 1952; information from Miss K. E. Blackie, Toorak, Melb, Ms J. M. Fanning, Payneham, Adel, and Mr D. MacDonald, Elwood, Melb.

A. N. PRESTON

FANTL, PAUL (1900-1972), biochemist, was born on 29 August 1900 in Vienna, son of Leopold Fantl, travelling salesman, and his wife Cilli, née Weinstock. Paul studied chemistry and engineering at the Technische Hochschule in 1918-22, taking his doctorate (1923) with a thesis entitled 'Ueber einen Sesquiterpenalkohol aus dem Elemioel'. In November 1919 he had become a demonstrator at the University of Vienna and in 1921-28, as an assistant, worked and studied with the Nobel prize-winner, Hans Fischer. Fantl had also spent one semester in 1920 at the University of Graz (Styria) with another Nobel prize-winner, Fritz Pregl. On 1 August 1925 Fantl married Polish-born Irene Munz in Vienna. From 1928 to 1931 he was a scientific adviser in the perfume and essential oils industry.

In 1931 he was appointed chief biochemist at the Wilhelmina Hospital, Vienna. Being Jewish, he realized the dangers of Nazism. After the Anschluss in March 1938, Fantl left Vienna and lived for six months in Trinidad before arriving in Melbourne on 8 August 1939 to take up an appointment as organic chemist and biochemist in the Baker [q.v.7] Medical Research Institute at the Alfred

Hospital, Prahran. Having participated in the development of clinical biochemistry as a distinct profession, he contributed to routine biochemistry in the hospital. His experience in organic chemistry proved valuable in wartime projects on the feasibility of manufacturing certain drugs in Australia.

Fantl's initial research areas at the Baker Institute included carbohydrate metabolism, vitamin K and sterols, but he gradually focussed on the biochemistry of blood coagulation which remained his main research interest for the rest of his life. In the 1940s he developed an anticoagulant drug, 3,3'-ethylidene-bis-4-hydroxycoumarin (ethylidene dicoumarol, EDC), which clinicians found superior to an existing anticoagulant for treating myocardial infarction and preventing thrombosis.

Naturalized in June 1945, Fantl was appointed assistant-director of the Baker Institute that year. In 1949 he became associate-director, a post he was to occupy until 1966. He also served as consultant biochemist to the Alfred Hospital and part-time lecturer at the University of Melbourne, and was elected a fellow (1953) of the Royal Australian Chemical Institute. In 1958 he was invited to chair a session in the symposium on blood-clotting factors at the fourth International Congress of Biochemistry, held in Vienna. Although in a sense a personal triumph, it proved for him a somewhat disturbing visit because of memories of past events.

As one who delighted in Shakespeare's superb skill in the use of words, Fantl was meticulous in experimentation and in writing scientific papers. He approached problems logically and had a prodigious memory. Using simple equipment for the most part, he designed experiments with insight, made important contributions to many aspects of blood coagulation and applied his findings to clinical situations, among them the development of open-heart surgery at the Alfred Hospital. One major contribution was his discovery of the blood-clotting component now named Factor V in the terminology adopted by the International Committee for the Standardization of the Nomenclature of Blood Clotting Factors, of which he was a member. An example of his far-sightedness was his concept (1960) of using gene therapy for haemophilia, although, as a realist, he was aware of the difficulties in achieving this aim. During his career he published over one hundred papers, eighty of them on blood coagulation.

In scientific discussions Fantl was not afraid to oppose—usually with sound arguments—any orthodox views he considered wrong; although his comments and criticisms could be very frank, they were quite impersonal. He had a fine sense of humour and a compassionate nature. His concern for people was evident in his attitude to patients whose haemophilia and other blood-coagulation disorders he investigated with his colleague, Dr Ronald Sawers. Despite Fantl's lack of formal medical qualifications, his association with, and interest in, clinical matters often enabled him to give a sound opinion.

Democratic in temperament, Fantl greatly appreciated the freer attitudes of Australian society which he contrasted with those he had experienced in Europe. He said that the 'obsession with football' was one of the factors that encouraged him to settle in Melbourne: 'A people so obsessed would have no room in their hearts for anti-semitism and other nasties that scarred pre-war and war-time Europe'. His recreations spanned reading, music, theatre, gardening and golf. Following an absence on leave in 1966, he resumed his laboratory work. He died on 30 August 1972 at Prahran and was cremated; his wife and daughter survived him.

Baker Medical Research Inst, *Annual Report*, 14 to 46, 1939-72, esp. 46, 1972, p 19, and *Baker Inst News*, 3, no 1, 1990, p 9, 4, no 3, 1991, p 8, 6, no 2, 1993, p 36; *MJA*, 30 Sept 1972, p 793; BMRI Archives; personal information.   H. A. WARD

FARGHER, JOHN ADRIAN (1901-1977), engineer, was born on 13 January 1901 at North Carlton, Melbourne, fourth child of Philip Fargher, an engineer from the Isle of Man, and his Victorian-born wife Matilda Maude, née Blacker. Educated at Fairfield State School, John won scholarships to Melbourne High School and the University of Melbourne (B.C.E., 1924; M.C.E., 1926). In May 1923 he joined the construction branch of the Victorian Railways and six months later transferred to the South Australian Railways as a structural draftsman. He assisted R. H. Chapman in the design and construction of a new railway bridge at Murray Bridge and in 1924 was promoted to civil design engineer. On 27 February 1926 at the Methodist Church, Northcote, Melbourne, he married Elsie Pearl French.

Back in South Australia, Fargher designed a new jetty at Wallaroo, planned and supervised the duplication of parts of the Adelaide-Murray Bridge railway line, and was responsible for the construction of a marshalling yard at Dry Creek in 1927-29. His papers, 'Stresses in the walls of elevated cylindrical tanks of reinforced concrete' (1930) and 'Temperature stresses in welded railway track' (1933) were published in the journal of the Institution of Engineers, Australia, of which he was a member. He also belonged to the Australian Institution of Transport. Having planned works for Port Pirie's railway, he was involved with R. J. Bridgland in designing the University Foot Bridge (1937) over the River Torrens in Adelaide and the Birkenhead Bridge (1940) over the Port River at Port Adelaide.

During World War II Fargher's office was commandeered by the Department of Munitions and he was given the task of developing standardized building designs for works at Hendon, Finsbury and Penfield. Appointed State controller of air-raid shelters, he published a paper on the subject in the *Journal of the Institution of Engineers, Australia* (1940). In 1946 he was promoted assistant to Chapman, who was then S.A.R. commissioner, and succeeded him in 1953. Railways were changing from steam to diesel-electric locomotives, and Fargher was the driving force in converting the S.A.R.'s technology and system. He wrote another paper, 'Diesel railway traction in South Australia', for the *J.I.E.A.* (1955). At the same time, he made considerable efforts to forge harmonious relations with the many unions involved in railway operations. In 1957 he was appointed C.M.G. and travelled in North America studying railway developments. He retired in 1966.

An august and imposing man, Fargher was 6 ft 2 ins (188 cm) tall, with a large head, piercing blue-grey eyes and, from the age of 30, silver hair. He maintained an intellectually disciplined approach to everything he did. His incisiveness and his intolerance of weakminded or sloppy methods caused him to be held in awe by many, and in deep respect by the few who knew him well. He had played cricket before taking up golf; he enjoyed music, played the piano and was widely read; his love of learning never deserted him and his interest in the world was broad and inquiring. Survived by his wife, son and one of his two daughters, Fargher died on 16 November 1977 in St Andrew's Hospital, South Terrace, Adelaide, and was cremated.

D. A. Cumming and G. C. Moxham, *They Built South Australia* (Adel, 1986); *PP* (SA), 1966-67 (47); *Advertiser* (Adel), 25 Mar 1939, 1 Jan 1957, 18 Mar, 8 July 1957, 12 Dec 1961, 10 Jan 1966; *Mail* (Adel), 31 Mar 1956; *News* (Adel), 12 Dec 1961; information from Mr P. J. Fargher, Rose Park, Adel.   DEANE KEMP
                                            JOHN PICKLES

FARNCOMB, HAROLD BRUCE (1899-1971), naval officer and lawyer, was born on 28 February 1899 in North Sydney, second child of Frank Farncomb, a timber surveyor from England, and his Victorian-born wife Helen Louisa, née Sampson. Educated at Gordon Public and Sydney Boys' High schools, in 1913 Harold was among the first intake at the Royal Australian Naval College,

Osborne House, Geelong, Victoria (soon to be relocated at Jervis Bay, Federal Capital Territory). He did well academically, gained colours for cricket and topped his final year (1916). Promoted midshipman in January 1917, Farncomb was immediately sent to Britain for training with the Royal Navy: his first appointment was to the battleship, H.M.S. *Royal Sovereign*, in the Grand Fleet; in 1920 he was awarded the maximum of five first-class certificates for his lieutenant's courses.

Back home, in 1921-22 he was gunnery officer in the destroyer, H.M.A.S. *Stalwart*. While serving on Commodore (Sir) Percy Addison's staff in the flagship, *Melbourne*, Farncomb was commended for intelligence work during the fleet's northern cruise in 1922. Next year he sailed for England and in 1924 graduated from the R.N. Staff College, Greenwich. Returning to Australia in 1925, he performed staff duties at sea. On 31 March 1927 at Trinity Congregational Church, Strathfield, Sydney, he married Jean Ross Nott; they were to remain childless. Jean provided staunch support throughout the vicissitudes of her husband's career.

Promoted lieutenant commander (1927), Farncomb attended the Imperial Defence College, London, at the unusually young age of 31. While posted to Navy Office, Melbourne, he was promoted commander on 30 June 1932. He joined the heavy cruiser, H.M.A.S. *Australia*, as executive officer in April 1933. Strict but fair, he fostered high morale in the ship. With her midshipmen, he was curt yet considerate, usually addressing them as 'Mr Bloody . . .'; they nicknamed him 'Uncle Hal'. The commanding officer, Captain W. S. F. Macleod, R.N., was impressed by his ability and recommended him for accelerated promotion. In December 1934 the Duke of Gloucester [q.v.] embarked in *Australia* on his voyage to England, following which Farncomb was appointed M.V.O. (1935).

From August 1935 he was attached to the Naval Intelligence Division at the Admiralty. By 1937 he thought that war with Germany was inevitable, and took leave to visit that country and improve his knowledge of the language. On 30 June 1937 Farncomb was the first R.A.N.C. graduate to be promoted captain. Home again, he commanded the sloop, H.M.A.S. *Yarra* (October 1937 to November 1938), then went back to England to commission the cruiser, H.M.A.S. *Perth*, in June 1939.

The ship was in the western Atlantic *en route* to Australia at the outbreak of war in September. She interrupted her voyage, and for six months patrolled Caribbean and nearby waters. It was probably at this time that Farncomb acquired the nickname 'Fearless Frank'. Signalling instructions to a convoy in the event of an attack, he is reported to have said: 'My intention is to engage the enemy with my main armament and close him until I am in torpedo firing range. If gunfire and torpedoes are not sufficient in disabling the raider, I intend to ram the enemy ship'.

In June 1940 Farncomb transferred to the heavy cruiser, *Canberra*, which spent most of the next eighteen months in the Indian Ocean escorting convoys and hunting German raiders, among them the 'pocket-battleship', *Admiral Scheer*. On 4 March 1941, south-east of the Seychelles Islands, *Canberra* encountered two ships, reported by her aircraft to be an armed raider and a tanker. The supposed raider ignored warnings. *Canberra* opened fire from about 21 000 yards (19.2 km). Farncomb manoeuvred *Canberra* to keep the range beyond 19 000 yards (17.4 km) in case his adversary carried torpedoes; firing ceased when the merchant ship was seen to be burning.

It transpired that *Canberra* had attacked the enemy supply-ship, *Coburg*; the accompanying tanker was the *Ketty Brovig*. Both were scuttled by their crews and sank. Having interrogated his German prisoners, Farncomb warned the Admiralty of the *Admiral Scheer*'s projected movements. Papers which later circulated in Navy Office criticized him for being 'over cautious' in the action: had he approached nearer to *Coburg*, he could have saved ammunition. The adverse reaction to Farncomb's prudent conduct may have influenced the subsequent behaviour of Captain Joseph Burnett in H.M.A.S. *Sydney*. His decision in November to close with the disguised raider, *Kormoran*, resulted in the loss of his ship and all on board.

On 24 December 1941 Farncomb joined *Australia* as commanding officer and chief staff officer to Rear Admiral (Sir) John Crace [q.v.13]. At sea on 12 March 1942 a stoker John Riley was stabbed. Before he died the following day, he named fellow stokers Albert Gordon and Edward Elias who, he claimed, attacked him after he had threatened to report their homosexual activities. The men were charged with murder. It was Farncomb's unwanted duty to prosecute at their court martial, convened on 15 April at Noumea. He studied available law books and, after a 'masterly' performance, secured convictions. Gordon and Elias were sentenced to death. Reverting to the role of commanding officer, Farncomb then submitted an eloquent appeal for their lives; the sentences were subsequently commuted to imprisonment.

On 7 May 1942, in the Coral Sea, *Australia* led a force of cruisers and destroyers sent without air cover to intercept Japanese troopships headed for Port Moresby. The flagship came under heavy bombing and aerial torpedo attack. Although *Australia* was given up as lost, she emerged safely from the smothering spray. Farncomb had handled her brilliantly. He was mentioned in dispatches for his part in the battle of the Coral Sea. Extolling his qualities, Crace recommended him for promotion to flag rank.

Rear Admiral (Sir) Victor Crutchley replaced Crace in June. He and Farncomb joined officers of the United States Navy in planning the invasion of Guadalcanal. Embarked in *Australia*, Crutchley commanded the force that screened the transports. The landings took place on 7 August. Dive-bombers and torpedo-bombers harried the allied ships. On the night of 8-9 August Crutchley placed five of his heavy cruisers around Savo Island, before being summoned in the flagship to attend a conference off Lunga Point. At about 1.40 a.m. a Japanese force of seven cruisers and a destroyer caught the defenders by surprise. In the ensuing battle the Allies lost four heavy cruisers, including *Canberra*, and the Japanese none. Had *Australia*—with Farncomb and his experienced crew—been at Savo Island, the tragedy might have been averted.

For the remainder of the month *Australia* operated in the South Pacific and escorted U.S. aircraft-carriers which fought in the battle of the Eastern Solomons. Farncomb was awarded the Distinguished Service Order (1942) for his services in the Solomon Islands. He saw little action in 1943 until December when he directed the ship's bombardment that supported the landings at Cape Gloucester, New Britain.

Crutchley was less impressed with Farncomb than Crace had been. In early 1944 the Federal government decided that Captain (Sir) John Collins would be the first R.A.N.C.-trained officer to command the Australian Squadron and that Farncomb would succeed him. Farncomb left *Australia* in March, took short courses in England and was given command of the escort-carrier, H.M.S. *Attacker*, in May.

Under Farncomb, *Attacker* was senior ship of a group of escort-carriers. On 12 August 1944 she sailed from Malta to support the invasion of the south of France. Allied troops landed on the 15th and *Attacker*'s aircraft smashed railways, roads and bridges to block the enemy's escape. In October the ship was involved in operations to clear the Germans from the Aegean Sea and to liberate Greece. Farncomb was twice mentioned in dispatches for his work in *Attacker*. His immediate superior, Rear Admiral (Sir) Thomas Troubridge, thought highly of him, but observed his 'tendency to fortify himself with liquor' before important social occasions in harbour.

In October 1944 Collins was wounded in action. Farncomb flew from the Mediterranean to Manus Island and, on 9 December, assumed command of the Australian Squadron as commodore first class. The invasion of Luzon, Philippines, was imminent. H.M.A. ships *Australia, Shropshire, Warramunga* and *Arunta*—under Farncomb in *Australia*—were to be part of Vice Admiral J. B. Oldendorf's Bombardment and Fire Support Group of the U.S. Seventh Fleet. Farncomb quickly grasped 'the voluminous operation orders that emanated from the American command' and executed them flawlessly.

Off Luzon and in the Lingayen Gulf, between 5 and 9 January 1945 *Australia* was successively hit by five kamikaze aircraft. Casualties and damage were severe, but the ship completed her scheduled firings before withdrawing for repairs. Oldendorf described her performance as inspirational. Although Farncomb was wounded, he remained on duty. He was appointed C.B. (1945) and awarded the U.S. Navy Cross. On 22 January he hoisted his broad pendant in *Shropshire* and next month witnessed the bombardment and occupation of Corregidor Island. In May, June and July the Australian Squadron supported landings at Wewak, New Guinea, and at Labuan Island and Balikpapan, Borneo. Farncomb was relieved by Collins on 22 July in Manila and flew to Sydney.

Following a stint (August to September 1945) as flag officer-in-charge, New South Wales, Farncomb became commodore superintendent of training at Flinders Naval Depot, Westernport, Victoria. Next year he was appointed commander of the U.S. Legion of Merit for his services with the Seventh Fleet in 1944-45. He went back to sea in November 1946, initially as commodore commanding, then as flag officer commanding H.M.A. Squadron (Fleet). On 8 January 1947 he had been promoted rear admiral. He ensured that the fleet met its commitments in the postwar period which saw reductions in personnel and ships.

By 1949 Farncomb was frustrated, bored with continual official entertainment and drinking more than was wise. Appointed head of the Australian Joint Services Staff in Washington in January 1950, he seemed unable to curb his drinking and was recalled in November. He was transferred to the Retired List of Officers on 7 April 1951. Vice Admiral Sir Richard Peek later criticized the Naval Board for the destruction of Farncomb's career. The burdens and strains of nearly six years of uninterrupted command at sea and of increasingly responsible posts in wartime had been severe. The Naval Board could have rested him after the war but chose not to do so.

Farncomb gave up alcohol completely. He learned Latin to enable him to study for the Barristers' Admission Board examinations.

Admitted to the Bar on 6 June 1958, he developed a reasonably busy practice in Sydney and subsequently joined the solicitors, Alfred Rofe & Sons. As a lawyer, he showed the same penetrating and analytical mind and the industry and ability which had characterized his years in the navy. Heart disease eventually led to his retirement. Survived by his wife, Farncomb died on 12 February 1971 in St Vincent's Hospital, Darlinghurst, and was cremated with Anglican rites; his ashes were scattered at sea from his last flagship, H.M.A.S. *Sydney*. It has been announced that a Collins-class submarine is to be named after him; the Australian War Memorial, Canberra, holds his portrait by Harold Abbott.

Admiral Sir Louis Hamilton, chief of Naval Staff in 1945-48, had regarded Farncomb as 'the best senior officer' in the R.A.N., an opinion shared by others. Aloof and reserved, Farncomb never sought popularity, although the young Trevor Rapke [q.v. Julia Rapke] was one who experienced the charm, humour and 'rich culture' of the private man. Sailors respected 'Fearless' for his fair play, justice and courage, and many who served under him in World War II called themselves 'Farncomb men'.

F. M. McGuire, *The Royal Australian Navy* (Melb, 1948); F. B. Eldridge, *A History of the Royal Australian Naval College* (Melb, 1949); G. H. Gill, *Royal Australian Navy 1939-1942* (Canb, 1957), and *1942-1945* (Canb, 1968); C. Coulthard-Clark, *Action Stations Coral Sea* (Syd, 1991); T. R. Frame et al (eds), *Reflections on the RAN* (Syd, 1991); A5954/1, item 857/6, A3978/8, item Farncomb, H. B. (AA, Canb); interviews and correspondence held by author (Strathfield, Syd).

ALAN ZAMMIT

FARQUHARSON, MARIE LANGLEY (1883-1954), schoolteacher, journalist and community worker, was born on 15 February 1883 at Manly, Sydney, second of eight children of native-born parents Robert John Hinder, schoolteacher, and his wife Sarah Florence, née Mills. Marie grew up at Maitland where her father was headmaster of East Maitland Boys' High School. His residence was also home to fifteen boarders; Sarah ran her large household with 'regularity, care and exactness'. Marie's younger sister Eleanor Hinder [q.v.9] believed that their mother's orderly approach to her responsibilities encouraged her daughters to develop an ability to organize efficiently their time and resources; it was to serve them well.

Educated at West Maitland Girls' High School, Marie became a pupil-teacher at West Maitland Superior Public School in 1900, attended Hurlstone Training College on a full scholarship in 1905, then returned to West Maitland. From January 1907 she taught in

Sydney at the Riley Street Kindergarten, Surry Hills, a poor, working-class suburb. On 17 June 1911 at her father's school she married with Presbyterian forms John Gordon Farquharson (d.1954), an accountant. While living at Lismore, she bore two daughters, Sheila (b.1914) and Rona (b.1916). In 1914 she organized and became the first secretary of the local branch of the British Red Cross Society. On her return to Sydney in 1923, she worked as city correspondent for a group of country newspapers.

Becoming interested in the work of the National Council of Women of New South Wales, she met Mildred Muscio [q.v.10] through Eleanor. During her long association with the council, Mrs Farquharson held the honorary positions of interstate secretary (1925-26), State secretary (1926-32, 1940-41, 1953-54), international secretary (1928-40) and life vice-president (1946); she was also international secretary for Australia (from 1943). She was appointed to the advisory committee of the Unemployment Relief Council in 1930 and, through the N.C.W., ran a sewing-depot for unemployed women. In 1936-38 she was honorary secretary of the Women's Advisory Council and of the Women's Executive Committee for Australia's 150th Anniversary Celebrations. Joint foundation honorary secretary (1939) and president (by 1940) of the Women's Voluntary Services, she was an executive-member of the Australian Comforts Fund; in World War II she worked full time, co-ordinating teams of volunteers; in 1945 she was supervisor of the comforts depot. She was a founder and deputy-president of the Far West Children's Health Scheme and a member of the Sydney University Settlement's supervised playgrounds committee.

'Beautiful and vivacious as a girl', Marie continued to take pride in her appearance and dressed smartly in well-cut clothes. Her sister Eleanor described her as 'valiant', and noted 'she shared her problems and concerns with no one. She lived her own life in a very special way, reserving the time when the family was in bed for her own reading and thinking'. Survived by her daughters, Marie died on 29 December 1954 at her Neutral Bay home and was cremated with Methodist forms.

National Council of Women of NSW, *Biennial Report*, 1926-1950; *SMH*, 16 Aug 1930, 25 Apr 1945, 30 Dec 1954; teachers' records (NSW Dept of Education Archives, Syd); Hinder papers (ML).

LYN BRIGNELL

FARRAN-RIDGE, CLIVE (1886-1962), psychiatrist and pathologist, was born on 16 November 1886 at Woollahra, Sydney, eldest son of Richard Charles Ridge, grazier, and his wife Helen Margaret, née Farran. Educated at Sydney Grammar School, he graduated from the University of Sydney (B.Sc., 1908; M.B., 1915; Ch.M., 1917). Ridge (who later styled his surname Farran-Ridge) served as a captain (from 1915) in the Royal Army Medical Corps in World War I and continued his medical career in England, obtaining a diploma of psychological medicine (1921) from the University of London. In 1925, while an assistant medical officer at Stafford County hospital, he co-authored a paper about the positive effects of insulin-induced coma on the control of psychotic behaviour. The case report failed 'by a hair's breadth' to draw out the full implications of the treatment, and it was not until 1933 that Manfred Sakel of Vienna initiated coma-insulin therapy.

Returning to Australia, Farran-Ridge joined the Victorian Lunacy Department on 8 January 1929 and succeeded R. S. Ellery [q.v.] as pathologist in 1931. Six years later Farran-Ridge introduced Sakel's treatment at the Mont Park Mental Hospital. Stressing the importance of research, he initiated an extraordinary number of projects into aspects of biological psychiatry. He investigated the blood bromide levels of manic depressives, female sex hormones, and the cerebrospinal fluids and serum of patients undergoing malarial treatment for neuro-syphilis; he examined the urine, blood sugars and cholesterol of epileptics; and he devised an experimental treatment with sulphosin for dementia praecox. In addition, he maintained his efforts against the persistent outbreaks of infectious diseases in mental hospitals and continued to conduct post-mortem examinations. To assist him in these undertakings he had a laboratory staff of only two technicians. John Cade [q.v.13] commented that 'it is almost impossible to understand how so much routine and research work could have originated therein'.

Tall and solidly built, Farran-Ridge was 'held in some awe' by his colleagues 'not only because of his dignity and reserve, but also for his felicitous turn of phrase'; he was 'obsessive' in the precise use of words. His magisterial personality was the subject of many tales. (William) Beattie Smith [q.v.11] lecturer (1932) at the University of Melbourne, he was a founding fellow (1938) of the Royal Australasian College of Physicians. Wherever he went, he was a passionate horticulturist, planting vast numbers of trees and organizing vegetable gardens to improve patients' diets. Cade saw him as one 'whose restless imagination defeated his persistence . . . he had too many irons in the fire' and 'missed fame by a whisker'.

Although Farran-Ridge was anxious to resume clinical practice in 1940, he continued to superintend mental hospitals at Beechworth (1940-42), Ararat (1942-46) and Ballarat (1947-51). Tired and disillusioned, he retired in 1951. By then he believed that most of the ideals he valued in medical care were 'in the present state of the country . . . obviously unattainable'. Farran-Ridge died on 7 June 1962 at Mont Park and was cremated. He was survived by his wife Edith, née Braham, whom he had married on 5 October 1928 at St Philip's Anglican Church, Sydney. Clive's brother Thornleigh (1894-1938), known as Tom Farranridge, was a brilliant and popular teaching surgeon in Sydney.

G. L. McDonald (ed), *Roll of the Royal Australasian College of Physicians*, 1, 1938-75 (Syd, 1988); *MJA*, Nov 1938, p 927, May 1973, p 1057.

GEOFF BROWNE

FARRAR, PHOEBE ELIZABETH (1868-1960), bushwoman, was born on 19 December 1868 at Fish River, near Yass, New South Wales, daughter of Henry Wright, a labourer from England, and his native-born wife Martha, née Bauldrey. Nothing is known of Phoebe's early life until 1882 when she sailed to Normanton on the Gulf of Carpentaria with Jack and Mary Ann Farrar, employees of the pastoralist John Costello [q.v.3].

Having leased land between the Macarthur (McArthur) and Roper rivers in the Northern Territory, Costello organized an expedition that year to bring stores, equipment, cattle and horses to his property from the Gulf ports of Normanton and Burketown. Aged 13, Phoebe drove a wagon some 620 miles (1000 km) to the Limmen River where Costello established his station, Valley of Springs. From 1890 the Farrars managed the property with Phoebe's help. Conditions were extremely harsh: the homestead was a collection of huts made from pandanus trunks, thatched with paperbark, with earth floors, doors of greenhide and a bough-shed kitchen.

Assisted by their son Robert, by 1901 Jack and Mary Ann were managing Nutwood Downs station. That year Phoebe gave birth to Robert's son. In 1902 they made a 700-mile (1125 km) round trip to Palmerston (Darwin) to have the child baptized. On the way they called at the Elsey; Jeannie Gunn [q.v.9] described their visit in *We of the Never-Never*. Phoebe married Robert on 30 August 1904 with Anglican rites at Christ Church, Palmerston; they were to have three more children.

Bob and Phoebe next worked on Hodgson Downs station. They were among the few Whites employed on pastoral properties in the Territory where most of the labour was performed by Aborigines. Like numerous Aboriginal women, Phoebe was a competent stockwoman and a skilled rider. Slim but strong, she broke horses, tailed cattle in wild scrub country, worked at musters, and was adept at roping, throwing, branding and shooting. Her cooking was often done at night. She also made furniture and equipment for use in the house and in camps.

In 1925 the Farrars bought land at Brocks Creek. Phoebe drove a mob of cattle there and chose a site for the homestead, which she called Ban Ban Springs. About 1935, while branding cattle, she was charged by a bull and badly gored; it was two days before a doctor reached her; she was taken to Darwin and underwent an operation on her broken hip. Returning home, she continued to ride until late in life. She was again hospitalized from 1956. Survived by her two sons and a daughter, she died on 19 August 1960 in Darwin Hospital and was buried with Catholic rites in Darwin general cemetery. On her death certificate her occupation was recorded as 'housewife': the term did not incapsulate her seventy-eight years of making bush camps, droving, mustering, and mothering. Her family remembered that she had been able to 'fold a buffalo hide like other people could fold a piece of paper', and that nothing kept her down.

S. Baldwin (ed), *Unsung Heroes and Heroines of Australia* (Melb, 1988); H. Radi (ed), *200 Australian Women* (Syd, 1988); *Herald* (Melb), 23 Aug 1960; *SMH*, 24 Aug 1960.

LENORE COLTHEART

FARROW, JOHN VILLIERS (1904-1963), screenwriter and film director, was born on 10 February 1904 at Marrickville, Sydney, and christened Jack, son of native-born parents Joseph Farrow, a tailor's trimmer, and his wife Lucy, née Savage (d.1907), a dressmaker. In 1908 Joseph married Ethel McEnerney who died in 1912, after giving birth to their daughter. Leaving the children with his mother and sister, Joseph served in the Australian Imperial Force in 1915-16. Jack was educated at Newtown Public School and Fort Street Boys' High School (February 1917 to June 1918), then began a career in accountancy. He claimed to have run away to sea in an American barquentine, sailed 'all over the Pacific', and fought in revolts in Nicaragua and Mexico. He gained an enduring love of yachting. Reaching the United States of America, he enrolled at the Jesuits' St Ignatius College (University of San Francisco) in 1923, but left after one month.

A chance voyage in the South Seas with the film-maker Robert Flaherty aroused Farrow's interest in writing for the screen. Re-entering the United States, allegedly by jumping ship at San Francisco, he found his way to

Hollywood where from 1927 his nautical expertise brought him work as a script consultant and technical adviser. He had already earned minor recognition as a poet and writer of short stories. From DeMille Productions he moved to Paramount Pictures Inc. where he crafted easily delivered dialogue for foreign stars of silent films. For two years he wrote screen plays for Charles A. Rogers, an RKO Radio Pictures Inc. producer. During an interlude in Tahiti Farrow compiled an English-French-Tahitian dictionary and wrote a novel, *Laughter Ends* (New York, 1933). Passing through London, he was signed by Associated Talking Pictures to script *Woman in Chains* (1932). He also collaborated on the English version of G. W. Pabst's opera-film, *Don Quixote* (1933).

Back at Hollywood, Farrow was arrested early in 1933 in a Federal government drive against 'aliens' in the industry. He was placed on five years probation for violating immigration laws—his passport described him as a Romanian consular official and his visa had expired. Joining Metro-Goldwyn-Mayer in 1935, he wrote and directed new scenes for a film that was eventually retitled *Tarzan Escapes* (1936), but was replaced as director after problems with the censors. Farrow and his wife Felice, née Lewin, had been divorced. Converted to Catholicism, he married Tarzan's Jane, the 25-year-old Irish actress Maureen Paula O'Sullivan, on 12 September 1936 at Santa Monica, after she had received a Papal dispensation to marry him. Despite Farrow's reputation as a hell-raiser, the marriage lasted until his death, fortified by seven children, and a regime of regular church-going.

A belated fruit of his Tahitian sojourn was a biography of Fr Damien, *Damien the Leper* (New York, 1937), which was frequently reprinted and translated into thirteen languages. An officer (1938) of the Order of St John (knight of justice 1955), Farrow was appointed a knight grand cross of the Order of the Holy Sepulchre of Jerusalem by Pope Pius XI, and maintained an interest in Catholic educational institutions. He produced a 'frank history of the papacy', *Pageant of the Popes* (New York, 1942), and later wrote a biography of St Thomas More (1954).

From 1937 Farrow had made the transition to respected director. His output for several studios in the late 1930s was prolific. Notwithstanding his $75 000 a year contract with RKO, he was determined to serve in World War II. Submitting that he was 'a fairly competent seaman', he was appointed acting lieutenant in the Royal Canadian Naval Volunteer Reserve in March 1940 and was assigned to intelligence, censorship, press liaison and archival duties as controller of naval information. He went to sea on anti-

submarine patrols before he was invalided out of the service early in 1942. Retiring as an honorary commander, Farrow entertained men from R.C.N. ships visiting Los Angeles and (a citizen of the U.S.A. since 1947) was appointed honorary C.B.E. in 1953.

Having been harnessed to the war effort by major studios, Farrow won the New York Film Critics' Circle award and an American academy award nomination for *Wake Island*, a box-office 'smash' in 1942. *The Hitler Gang* (1944) was a more sophisticated documentary drama on the Nazi rise to power. He also directed the highly regarded *Two Years Before the Mast* (1946). Over the next five years most of his best work appeared, notably the *film noir* classic, *The Big Clock* (1947), *Where Danger Lives* (1950) and *His Kind of Woman* (1951).

A conservative Catholic, Farrow had little to fear from McCarthyism; he helped to mobilize resistance to an attempted purge of the Screen Directors' International Guild in 1950. Thereafter, working for several different studios, he made a sequence of mostly undistinguished films from which *Hondo* (1953) stands out for its sympathetic portrayal of the American Indian, Cochise. As co-writer of *Around the World in Eighty Days*, Farrow shared the Oscar for best screenplay in 1956. There were a few more disappointing films, a failed project on the life of Christ, and some television direction; but his attention turned increasingly to his family and charitable work.

Farrow died suddenly of coronary vascular disease on 27 January 1963 at his Beverly Hills home and was buried in Holy Cross cemetery; his wife and six of their children survived him. His daughter Mia had just begun her film career, against his wishes. In twenty-two years Farrow directed some forty films, making an Australian contribution to international cinema unmatched and still little known in his homeland.

A. Walker, *The Shattered Silents* (NY, 1978); E. Katz, *The Film Encyclopedia* (NY, 1979); D. Shipman, *The Story of Cinema*, 2 (Lond, 1984); C. R. Koppes and G. D. Black, *Hollywood Goes to War* (Lond, 1988); *Fortian*, 1962, p 15; *Cinema Papers*, 77, Jan 1990, p 32; *Herald* (Melb), 29 Mar 1932; *SMH*, 30 Jan, 10 Feb, 29 Mar 1933, 27 Feb 1934, 14 July 1947, 9 June 1962, 30 Jan 1963, 5, 9, 10 Sept 1994; *New York Times*, 29 Jan 1963; Roy Canadian Navy personnel records (copies held by ADB, Canb).   CAMERON HAZLEHURST

FARWELL, GEORGE MICHELL (1911-1976), author and traveller, was born on 3 October 1911 at Bath, Somerset, England, elder son of George Douglas Farwell, motor engineer, and his wife Eleanor Grace, née Jones. George attended a number of schools, in later years recalling with affection the Progressive School at Battersea, which encouraged creativity, and with abhorrence the Cardinal Vaughan School, Westminster, which he described as Dickensian, 'its burly, black-robed brothers obsessed with faith, but strangers to charity or hope'. He was rescued from this agony by his uncle, the prominent barrister Tyldesley Jones, who paid for his tuition at Seafield Park, near Southampton.

His mother died in the year that Farwell left Forest School, Walthamstow, prematurely at 17; his father died some months later, leaving him and his brother a small bequest from investments. Disenchanted with clerical work and six months on the dole in Depression-ridden London, in 1933 George joined an expedition to search for buried treasure in French Polynesia. The search came to nothing, but it gave him an eighteen-month idyll in Tahiti—'so enchanting I could hardly believe it real'—and it nourished a wanderlust that propelled him into new adventures for the rest of his life.

Farwell arrived in Sydney in 1935. With his bequest, good looks and sense of style, and an aptitude for making useful contacts, he savoured the city's café society for eight months before being motivated to work, taking jobs as a deckhand, casual wharf labourer and goldminer. He also began writing adventure stories for the *Sydney Mail* and acting in radio serials. Drifting into freelance writing, he used his experiences as raw material, subsequently noting that he made as much from writing about gold as digging for it. But his first few years in Australia were lean times. On 15 February 1938 at the district registrar's office, North Sydney, Farwell married a secretary Grace Patricia Minty; they were to have two children. Patricia found the early days of marriage special and exciting, but George found marriage a folly that was 'not amenable to rational explanation', and left it in 1953, although he was often absent for long periods before then. They were divorced in 1958.

The outback had become an obsession and the setting for most of Farwell's books, articles and radio broadcasts, as he travelled constantly through Australia, later visiting North and South America, Europe, South-East Asia and the Pacific Islands, sometimes for months. His first book, *Down Argent Street* (Sydney, 1948), was about Broken Hill, and his favourite was *Land of Mirage* (Melbourne, 1950), the story of the Birdsville Track and its people. Articles or books inevitably succeeded his travels, for his twin loves—travel and writing—fed on each other. *Last Days in Paradise* (London, 1964) followed a return to Tahiti and *Mask of Asia* (Melbourne, 1966) a stay in the Philippines; the latter won the Rothmans-Moomba Festival book award

in 1967 for the Australian book of the year. He published twenty-two books, including biographies of Charles Sturt and E. D. S. Ogilvie [qq.v.2,5], and the autobiographical *Rejoice in Freedom* (Melbourne, 1976).

Books were only a portion of his considerable literary output. Farwell contributed to magazines and newspapers, broadcast short stories and talks, and wrote some fifty documentary features for the Australian Broadcasting Commission. He spiritedly supported the Fellowship of Australian Writers (president 1944) and fought against the miserly fees proffered to freelancers. While continuing to freelance, he edited *Australian New Writing* (1943-46), the monthly *Australasian Book News and Library Journal* (1946-48) and Australian National Airways Pty Ltd's monthly, *Air Travel* (1949-51); he wrote for the Commonwealth's News and Information Bureau (1952-58) and the Adelaide *Advertiser* (1958-62); and he was public relations officer for the Adelaide Festival of Arts (1959-64) and for the Australian pavilion at Expo 67, Montreal, Canada.

A capable, professional author without academic literary pretensions, Farwell chose to write about real people and places, and did it with great clarity and with insight, yet to describe him as a travel writer does not do his work justice. H. M. Green [q.v.] considered that Farwell's short stories, *Surf Music* (Sydney, 1950), 'remind one of Lawson' [q.v.10] and thought that his radio play, 'Portrait of a Gentleman'—included in Leslie Rees's anthology, *Australian Radio Plays* (1946)—was 'as good as anything Farwell has written'.

Tall and distinguished, with a neat moustache, Farwell was noted for his good manners and even temper, and enjoyed a wide circle of friends, particularly in literature and the arts. He had a great talent for living, and a distaste for the commonplace and ordinary. At home he preferred to spend his time and money on paintings, food and wine, and played host around a large dining-table at convivial dinner parties, often lasting well into the night.

At the bride's home at Cremorne, Sydney, on 6 September 1958 Farwell married a journalist Noni Grace Irene, née Rowland, the divorced wife of S. J. Baker [q.v.13]. They had no children, and George saw the relationship as a partnership of 'staunch mates in the battle to survive'. Noni willingly supported him in his priorities: freedom to travel and freedom to write. Survived by his wife, and the son and daughter of his first marriage, he died of a ruptured dissecting aneurysm on 6 August 1976 in his home at Kingswood, Adelaide, and was cremated. His ashes were scattered on the Birdsville Track. A selection of his work between 1946 and 1976, *Farwell Country* (Melbourne, 1977), was published posthumously. Andrew Fabinyi [q.v.] wrote:

'It is hazardous to predict the future fame of a writer and his books. I believe however that the essence of George Farwell's writing ... will become an integral, and much enjoyed, part of the body of Australian literature'.

G. Farwell, *Farwell Country* (Melb, 1977), introd A. Fabinyi; K. S. Inglis, *This is the ABC* (Melb, 1983); *SMH*, 2 Mar 1944, 23 Nov 1945, 9 Nov 1951, 30 Apr 1966, 8 Jan 1977; *Australian*, 2 Dec 1971; *Advertiser* (Adel), 7 Aug 1976; M. Farwell, unpublished biog of Farwell (held by author, Stirling, Canb); H. de Berg, George Farwell (taped interview, 16 July 1969, NL); information from Mrs N. Farwell, Adel.   STUART INDER

FATNOWNA, HARRY NORMAN (1897?-1967), sugar-farmer, lay preacher and community leader, was born probably in 1897 on Palms estate, near Mackay, Queensland, fourth of five children of Solomon Islanders John Kwailiu Abelfai Fatnowna [q.v.8] (d.1906), plantation labourer, and his wife Maggie Orrani. In 1906 Maggie married her kinsman Luke Logomier (d.1919), a lay preacher at St Mary's Anglican chapel, Farleigh. Harry was educated at the local school and became a labourer at Palms. By 1918 he owned a small cane-farm at Farleigh. On 20 February that year at Holy Trinity Church, Mackay, he married a Solomon Islander Grace Kwasi; they were to have fifteen children. Succeeding his stepfather as lay preacher at St Mary's in 1919, Fatnowna attended the Anglican synod at Townsville in 1921 and was held in high regard in the Church. By 1922 the family had moved to Eulberti, a farm near Eimeo owned by Peter Christensen, where they remained for thirty-four years, working for the local farmers and growing their own crops.

Despite attempts by the Anglicans to retain him, in the early 1920s Fatnowna was converted to Seventh-day Adventism and took half his congregation with him. In 1925 he organized the building of the first Adventist church in the district. With his eldest son Norman, he proselytized among the Islanders: by the 1930s there were three more Adventist congregations. A gifted orator, and a dynamic and respected leader, Fatnowna helped to strengthen members of the Islander community in the rural areas around Mackay who suffered from poverty and racial discrimination. In 1932-34 he opposed the establishment of a segregated primary school for Islanders at Walkerston and helped to clear crown land at Nulla, near Bloomsbury, for an Islander farming settlement. Later in that decade Fatnowna obtained a perpetual lease of 13 acres (5 ha) for his family at Etowrie; in 1956 he moved with them to Andergrove where they bought 5 acres (2 ha).

His accounts-book and diary, kept from 1939 to 1961, revealed a methodical, careful man. The Fatnownas had much in common with others in the Islander community, but in some ways they were exceptional. In typical fashion, their Eulberti home was grass-thatched and constructed in Malaitan style, with a men's house and a main house. Yet the family was comparatively affluent, possessing a horse and sulky, bicycles and later a utility car; they also had a piano, and Fatnowna took and developed his own photographs. His children, who became leaders in the Adventist Church, were well educated by rural standards of the time. In 1932 Norman had been the first Islander to attend Mackay High School.

Mixing with leading Europeans in the district, Harry numbered the barrister W. A. Amiet [q.v.13] and the politician Ernest Evans [q.v.] among his friends. Fatnowna remained an elder of the Farleigh Adventist Church until silenced by a stroke in 1962. Survived by his wife, seven sons and three daughters, he died of broncho-pneumonia on 25 June 1967 at Mackay and was buried in the local cemetery. A street in Andergrove was named after him.

N. Fatnowna, *Fragments of a Lost Heritage*, R. Keesing ed (Syd, 1989); P. M. Mercer, The Survival of a Pacific Islander Population in North Queensland, 1900-1940 (Ph.D. thesis, ANU, 1981); registers of Holy Trinity Anglican Church, Mackay, Qld; H. N. Fatnowna accounts-book (copy held by author, Univ Qld); personal information.   CLIVE R. MOORE

FEINT, ADRIAN GEORGE (1894-1971), artist, was born on 28 June 1894 at Narrandera, New South Wales, eldest of three children of native-born parents Samuel Feint, stationer, and his wife Catherine Charlotte, née Flood, grand-daughter of Edward Flood [q.v.4]. From childhood Adrian was interested in drawing and decorated his Narrandera school exercise-books at night. In 1912 he entered the Sydney Art School where he studied under Julian Ashton and Elioth Gruner [qq.v.7,9]. Feint enlisted in the Australian Imperial Force on 21 January 1916, served with the 15th Field Ambulance on the Western Front from February 1917 and was praised in September 1918 for the gallantry he displayed near Péronne, France. He was granted three months leave in 1919 to study at the Académie Julien, Paris.

Discharged on 12 October 1919, Feint returned to the Sydney Art School which was noted for its teaching in 'black and white'. He worked extensively for Sydney Ure Smith's [q.v.11] advertising agency, Smith & Julius, and provided decorations and cover designs for his magazines, *Art in Australia* (1928-40) and the *Home*. Regarded as having impeccable taste, Feint (with Walter Taylor) directed Grosvenor Galleries between 1924 and 1928. In the late 1920s he depicted himself as a connoisseur surrounded by *objets d'art* in his etched self-portrait, 'The Collector'.

Feint's first etchings—figure studies such as 'Scarf Dance', views of Sydney and his earliest bookplates—had been produced in 1922 and exhibited with the Society of Artists, Sydney, and the Australian Painter-Etchers Society. He showed his first wood-engravings in 1927 while studying design with Thea Proctor [q.v.11]. His bookplates, including those produced for Olive King, Dorothea Mackellar, J. L. Mullins, Frank Clune [qq.v.9,10,13] and the Duke and Duchess of York, attracted local and worldwide attention, culminating in an exhibition at the Library of Congress, Washington, D.C., in 1930. His decorative penwork and designs for private press books, such as those published by the Australian Limited Editions Society, were also highly praised. He painted tropical fish and parrots on the glass panels for the Australian pavilion at the New York World's Fair (1939).

Despite such recognition, Feint still sought acceptance as an oil-painter. He had begun to exhibit paintings in 1929 with the Society of Artists, of which he became a member (1931). With the support of (Sir) James McGregor, a close friend and patron, he virtually gave up commercial art in 1938 to concentrate on oil-painting—receiving technical advice from Margaret Preston [q.v.11]. The best of his still life and landscape paintings have affinities with surrealism, but it is of the decorative English variety (as practised by Edward Wadsworth) rather than the French. Feint's paintings received critical acclaim in the 1940s and 1950s; Ure Smith published *Adrian Feint Flower Paintings* in 1948. Douglas Dundas described his flower-pieces as 'flower arrangements meticulously designed, superbly painted, and set in a related environment of time and space'. Some of Feint's works, such as 'The Jetties, Palm Beach' (1942) and 'Happy Landing' (1944) are potent images, but his reputation continues to be based on his graphic art.

A 'remarkably handsome man, always immaculately but discreetly dressed', Feint lived austerely, though 'early economies had enabled him to acquire beautiful examples of furniture, painting and other objects' for his Elizabeth Bay flat. He died on 25 April 1971 in St Vincent's Hospital and was cremated with Anglican rites. His portrait by Nora Heyson is held by a private collector in Sydney.

Bookplates by Adrian Feint, introd J. L. Mullins, exhibition cat (Syd, 1928); *The Bookplates of Adrian*

Feint (Washington, US, 1930); Aust Ex Libris Soc, *Bookplate Artists*, 1 (Syd, 1934); G. Caban, *A Fine Line* (Syd, 1983); *Art and Aust*, 9, no 2, 1971; *SMH*, 23 Nov 1939, 26 June 1948, 18 Nov 1955, 28 Apr 1971; H. de Berg, Adrian Feint (taped interview, 18 June 1963, NL); A. Feint archive (Aust National Gallery, Canb).   ROGER BUTLER

FELAN, ALBERT JOHN (1919-1968), public relations officer, was born on 3 October 1919 at Annandale, Sydney, elder son of native-born parents Albert Carlyle Felan, clerk, and his wife Irene Alma, née Wheeler. Raised at Queenscliff, Bert became a promising tennis player and competed in the New South Wales Lawn Tennis and Hardcourt Tennis associations' championships. He was then 5 ft 8½ ins (174 cm) tall, with brown eyes and dark hair. Employed as a travelling salesman, he volunteered for the Militia on 1 August 1940. After postings to veterinary and heavy-transport units, he joined the Australian Imperial Force as a lance sergeant in December 1942. Thereafter, he served with the Australian Army Postal Service at home, and in Papua, New Guinea and New Britain. Promoted warrant officer in March 1945, he was commissioned lieutenant on 15 August. He transferred to the Reserve of Officers on 27 August 1946.

While on leave, on 28 October 1944 at St Mary's Catholic Cathedral, Sydney, Felan had married Pearl Josephine Grogan, a receptionist. After the war they lived first at Roseberry and then at Ashfield. He worked for Lynam's Ice Cream, Ampol Petroleum Ltd and was a country sales representative for other firms. Travelling for A. Abrahams & Sons Pty Ltd, sack and (polythene) bag merchants, he was involved in a motorcar accident near Forbes in October 1960 which left him a paraplegic. He stayed with his estranged wife at Narrabri, confronted the reality that he would spend the rest of his life in a wheelchair and in 1962 entered Mount Wilga, the Commonwealth Rehabilitation Centre at Hornsby.

Felan moved into his parents' home at Queenscliff and in September 1964 began working for the Wheelchair and Disabled Association of Australia. A foundation employee at the House With No Steps, Belrose, by June 1966 he was its director of public relations. His dynamic and witty personality, intense interest in people and events, boundless energy and resourcefulness equipped him well for the post which was both difficult and demanding. Felan initiated and planned functions and events to promote the organization, spoke in clubs, conducted tours of the House With No Steps, took charge of bazaars, fêtes and other community activities, and also prepared statements and articles for publication in the press. In 1967 he successfully worked with ATN-7 staff to present a television documentary entitled 'Seven Days' which showed the association's revolutionary approach to the needs of people with disabilities.

A courageous and determined man, Felan was respected for his ability to get on with people. His mind was keen and alert, his sense of humour always evident. Cheerful in spite of constant pain, he faced his disabilities with fortitude. Survived by his wife, son and two daughters, he died of renal failure on 14 April 1968 in Royal Prince Alfred Hospital, Sydney, and was buried in Frenchs Forest cemetery.

Wheelchair and Disabled Assn of Aust (Syd), *Progress*, May 1967, p 8, *and* undated cutting with A. Felan obituary from that magazine, p 6, held in ADB file; *Referee*, 30 June, 14 July 1938; information from Mr J. Felan, Palm Cove, Qld.

SHIRLEY J. WHITE

FELDT, ERIC AUGUSTAS (1899-1968), naval officer and colonial official, was born on 3 January 1899 at Cardwell, Queensland, eighth child of Swedish-born parents Peter Feldt, cane-farmer, and his wife Augusta, née Blixt. Educated locally and (in 1912) at Brisbane Grammar School, Eric won selection for the 1913 entry of cadets into the Royal Australian Naval College, Osborne House, Geelong, Victoria (subsequently at Jervis Bay, Federal Capital Territory). He was chief cadet-captain and gained colours for Rugby Union and athletics before graduating as midshipman in January 1917.

Sent to England, in April 1917 Feldt joined H.M.S. *Canada*. In October 1918 he was posted to H.M.S. *Victory* and in March 1919 to H.M.A.S. *Swordsman*, in which he returned to Australia. He was promoted lieutenant in February 1920 and in January 1921 transferred to the cruiser, *Melbourne*. Seeing little future in the severely reduced R.A.N., he resigned on 30 October 1922 and was placed on the Retired List.

On 15 February 1923 Feldt became a clerk in the public service of the mandated Territory of New Guinea. By 1924 he was a patrol officer. Rising to district officer, he served in different parts of the Territory. At St Andrew's Anglican Church, South Brisbane, on 10 January 1933 he married Nancy Lynette Echlin, a journalist; they were to remain childless. Appointed acting warden (Morobe Goldfields) on 12 November 1935 (confirmed April 1936), Feldt lived at Wau and administered the mining ordinance as the Territory's chief warden. A staff of inspectors, geologists and surveyors assisted him; the giant Bulolo Gold Dredging Ltd was one of the companies under his jurisdiction.

In 1928 he had been promoted lieutenant commander. He transferred to the Emergency List in April 1939. Four months later the director of naval intelligence, Lieutenant Commander R. B. M. Long [q.v.], offered him the post of staff officer (intelligence), Port Moresby. Feldt's assignment would be to activate and extend the coastwatching screen across the north-eastern approaches to Australia which would warn of hostile incursions by sea or air. Having accepted, he was mobilized on 8 September and arrived in Port Moresby that month. Travelling by air, sea and on foot, he visited key sites in Papua, New Guinea, the Solomon Islands and the New Hebrides, meeting coastwatchers and bringing officials and civilian planters into the service. Additional 'teleradio' sets were distributed.

Feldt was appointed supervising intelligence officer, North Eastern Area, in May 1941 and transferred to Townsville, Queensland, with a naval intelligence officer in, respectively, Port Moresby and Rabaul, at Tulagi in the Solomon Islands and at Vila in the New Hebrides. When the Japanese entered the war in December, the coastwatchers showed their worth by transmitting warnings of air-raids to defenders in Rabaul —before its capture in January 1942—and then to those in Port Moresby. After the Americans invaded Guadalcanal in August, coastwatchers alerted them to the approach of Japanese aircraft from Rabaul and Kavieng, New Ireland, enabling American planes to be in position to outfight the faster Zeros.

From early 1942 the majority of the coastwatchers were in enemy territory. Because of naval parsimony, Feldt experienced difficulty in supplying them with stores and equipment. The co-operation of the Royal Australian Air Force in dropping supplies was one source of encouragement. Initially, Feldt had only one staff member at headquarters; often compelled to leave Townsville, he had to delegate the supply operation and routine intelligence work to his assistant. The stress and strain of the job began to affect Feldt's health. While visiting Guadalcanal in March 1943, he suffered a coronary thrombosis.

After recovering, Feldt was stationed in Brisbane and carried out duties with the Allied Intelligence Bureau. He had been promoted acting commander in July 1942, but the R.A.N. reduced him to his substantive rank in August 1943. In February 1945 he was appointed naval officer-in-charge, Torokina, Bougainville, and in May regained the rank of acting commander. Returning to Brisbane in June, he was demobilized on 29 September. He had been appointed O.B.E. in 1944, his only reward.

Feldt retired from the New Guinea administration and lived in Brisbane on a pension. In 1946 he published *The Coast Watchers* (Melbourne), the definitive story of the service. That year he was secretary of the United Service Club. He described himself as 'that oddity of inheritance, a dark Swede, thin, bull-necked and with thinning hair, vehement and forthright . . . [who] never yet called a man a stupid bastard unless he failed to adopt my views within five minutes of my expressing them'. Survived by his wife, he died of myocardial infarction on 12 March 1968 at his New Farm home and was cremated; his ashes were scattered at sea near the Coastwatchers' Light, Madang, Papua New Guinea. Feldt had been remarkable for his ability to get the best out of his coastwatchers, those rugged individualists popularly known as 'the Islanders'. Expecting loyalty, he also gave it and never spared himself.

F. B. Eldridge, *A History of the Royal Australian Naval College* (Melb, 1949); G. H. Gill, *Royal Australian Navy 1939-1942* and *1942-1945* (Canb, 1957, 1968); *Courier-Mail*, 14, 15 Mar 1968; I. F. G. Downs, personal records of life in the Territory of New Guinea (held by Mr Downs, Chevron Island, Qld); personal information.

J. C. H. GILL

FENBURY, DAVID MAXWELL (1916-1976), public servant, was born on 24 March 1916 at Subiaco, Perth, third child of David Percival Fienberg, railway official, and his wife Beatrice Amelia, née Conroy, both Australian born. David was to register his change of name to Fenbury by deed poll in 1960. After attending the Christian Brothers' Aquinas College, he entered the University of Western Australia (B.A., 1937) where he edited (1936-37) the *Pelican.* On 28 September 1937 he was appointed a cadet patrol officer in the Australian administration of the mandated Territory of New Guinea. From his posts in New Britain and the Aitape sub-district, he wrote reports and observations that revealed a wider outlook than was generally expected from a junior officer.

Granted leave to enlist, on 29 October 1941 Fenbury joined the Australian Imperial Force; he was commissioned lieutenant in November 1942 and posted to the Australian New Guinea Administrative Unit. In 1942-45 he led soldiers and Papua New Guinea police on guerrilla operations, and reconnaissance and fighting patrols, in Japanese-held territory. He was promoted captain, awarded the Military Cross and mentioned in despatches. In 1946 he was seconded to the British Colonial Service with which he spent fourteen months, in East Africa and at the Colonial Office, London; he had first-hand experience of the Tanganyikan native authority system. After his A.I.F. appointment terminated on 3 June 1947, he was appointed to lecture at the Australian School of Pacific Administration, Sydney. On 15 May 1948 at St Mark's Anglican Church, East Brighton, Melbourne, he married Joan Marion Brazier (d.1964).

In 1949 Fenbury became senior native authorities officer in the Department of District Services and Native Affairs, responsible for introducing a native local government policy to the Territory of Papua and New Guinea. Basing himself at Rabaul, he created a model for the Australian administration of Papua New Guinea: his initial instructions to his officers encompassed a broad area of local government, including village courts, to prepare the people for self-government. He developed the Tolai Cocoa Project by using the political machinery of local government councils to finance and control economic development. Councils were also established at Hanuabada, Port Moresby, and on Baluan Island in the Manus group where the New Way cargo cult of Paliau Maloat was absorbed.

Fenbury's approach aroused opposition from the minister for territories (Sir) Paul Hasluck who advocated a policy of uniform political gradualism. Like many of the country's expatriates, Hasluck also opposed the proposal for local courts. In 1955 Fenbury was recalled to operate from Port Moresby. There was a rapid expansion of local government, but council activity was restricted to an Australian shire model that excluded local courts and economic development.

That year, having successfully appealed against the appointment of another officer, Fenbury was made a district commissioner with responsibility for policy and planning in the new Department of the Administrator. He found it difficult to accept the attitudes of those who did not share his sense of priorities. In 1956-58 he served as the Australian government's nominee (as area specialist) to the secretariat of the Trusteeship Council of the United Nations, New York. On his return, he was appointed executive-officer for district services in the Department of the Administrator and in 1962 was promoted to head the department. On 30 March 1966 he married Helen Mary Sheils in a civil ceremony in Port Moresby.

Openly critical of government policy and practice, particularly the rejection of local courts, Fenbury expressed his views in official submissions, in seminars and journal articles, and through pseudonymous contributions and letters to newspapers. In July 1969 he was surprised to learn that he had been removed from the politically sensitive headship of the Department of the Administrator and appointed secretary of the new Department of Social Development and Home Affairs, a position which he occupied until his retirement on 26 March 1973.

Fenbury had the rare ability to inspire fresh

ideas and the administrative competence to carry them out. His certainty in the correctness of his judgement made it difficult for him to compromise with those in high places who did not share his vision. His contribution to the Australian trusteeship of Papua New Guinea was immense. In 1974 he accepted a visiting fellowship at the Australian National University, Canberra, where he began work on his book, *Practice without Policy* (1978). He died on 14 May 1976 from injuries received when he was hit by a bus at Leederville, Perth, and was buried in Karrakatta cemetery. His wife, and the son and daughter of his first marriage, survived him.

P. Hasluck, *A Time for Building* (Melb, 1976); I. Downs, *The Australian Trusteeship Papua New Guinea 1945-75* (Canb, 1980); *PIM*, July 1976; *SMH*, 10 Aug 1971, 18 May 1976; *Post-Courier*, 16 Jan, 26-28 Mar 1973, 17 May 1976; *West Australian*, 17 May 1976; Fenbury papers (NL); information from Mr A. Fenbury, Perth.

IAN DOWNS

FENSTON, ESMÉ (1908-1972), journalist, was born on 29 July 1908 at Annandale, Sydney, youngest of three children of native-born parents Henry Lovell Woolacott, furniture salesman, and his second wife Jane Kate, née Wilmot. Esmé was educated at a private college at Drummoyne and in 1921 at Sydney Girls' High School. At the age of 17 she took a job as a reporter on the magazine, the *Triad*, where her half-brother Les Woolacott was employed. (He was the son of her father and his first wife, whose marriage had ended in divorce.) Esmé next worked on the women's pages of the *Daily Guardian* and *Daily Telegraph Pictorial*. In the garden of her parents' home at Cremorne on 15 February 1930 she married with Presbyterian forms 31-year-old Jack Fenston, an education officer. A former officer in the British Army, he later became circulation manager of the *Land* newspaper. After her marriage, Esmé Fenston edited the women's pages of the *Land*. She joined the staff of John Fairfax [qq.v.4,8] & Sons Ltd's *Sydney Mail* in August 1933 and was soon its social editor.

In May 1938 she resigned, having received 'a very attractive offer' from the *Australian Women's Weekly*, founded in 1933 and published by (Sir) Frank Packer's [q.v.] Consolidated Press Ltd. She was one of several talented newspaperwomen, including Dorothy Drain, Adele ('Tilly') Shelton Smith and Joyce Bowden, recruited before World War II by Alice Jackson [q.v.] and George Warnecke. Unlike Drain, Shelton Smith and Bowden who became her friends as well as colleagues, Fenston was not a reporter on the magazine, but concentrated on sub-editing. In 1944, however, she wrote an article, 'Who Will Do the Housework?', in which she suggested that there could be problems ahead when men returned from war and women 'wanted to discard the duster and earn pay envelopes of our own'.

Jack's ambition to be a herb-farmer led the Fenstons in 1940 to move from a flat at Mosman to West Pennant Hills. At a party she was presented with a card—produced by the artists at the *Weekly*—showing her being dragged to Pennant Hills by a caveman. The Fenstons lived comfortably there, in a timber house surrounded by trees. The house, designed by her elder brother Frank Woolacott [q.v.], featured a huge fireplace. On the walls the Fenstons hung paintings by Sali Herman, Pro Hart and Norman Lindsay [q.v.10], collected by Jack who was to become friendly with the art dealer Rudi Komon. Her colleagues often spent the weekend as house guests with 'Jackie' and 'Ezzie'. Although they often found Jack infuriating, they acknowledged his cheerful personality and his knack, especially during the war years, of obtaining scarce goods. He supplied the *Weekly*'s staff with eggs and, an even rarer commodity for the time, sanitary pads.

One of their neighbours was the barrister (Sir) Garfield Barwick who was entertained by the Fenstons' contrasting personalities and became a close friend. He found Jack 'coarse but she was refined. Jack swore like a trooper or truck driver, and liked to shock if he could'. Esmé was 'ladylike, gentle, pure minded, quiet and confident. She did not like anything improper but had a good sense of humour. When Jack went off she would say, "Now Jack, that's a bit high"'. Fenston's workmates did not think her husband was her intellectual equal, but it was, nevertheless, a good and companionable marriage. When the *Weekly* bought a personality quiz from an overseas magazine, the staff first tested the questions on themselves. Drain and Fenston answered identically, except for the last question: 'Do you usually do what you want?' Drain wrote 'Yes' and Fenston 'No', telling Drain that she usually did what Jack wanted. The couple were to remain childless. Fenston made a fuss of her niece Jill and sewed clothes for the child. Packer's son Kerry thought that the *Weekly* was Esmé's baby.

In June 1950 Fenston succeeded Jackson as editor of the *Weekly*; its circulation had reached 750 000, its cover price was sixpence, and in two months the magazine would move to full rotogravure printing. Some of its staff were surprised that she had been offered the editorship. They did not believe that Packer knew how smart she was, how clear in her thinking. Her close friends detected an additional quality—she was innocent without being naive. She had simple tastes—she liked gardening, embroidering linen and making her own underwear—yet she brought to her job a sharp mind, a perceptive nature and common sense.

Fenston's office was spartan. Most days she ate at her desk, the lunch brought to her by one of the copygirls or cadet reporters, among them Ita Buttrose. Fenston was not a star editor and confided that she did not like having her photograph taken. Nor did she want to appear on television, thinking that people would be disappointed by her manner —by the gap between who she really was and what they expected an editor to be. Fenston was not a beauty. She had poor skin, a long chin, a broad forehead and wore heavy-rimmed spectacles; her best feature was her striking chestnut-coloured hair.

Her secret was her empathy with the readers, the suburban families of Australia. Fenston knew what the market wanted without being too far in advance of it. Her motto was that the *Weekly* did not attempt to lead public taste, but merely reflected it. She edited the magazine in its best years—the Menzies [q.v.] years—before colour television was a competing medium and at a time when the *Weekly* was as much a colour newspaper (with a strong male readership) as simply a women's magazine. Fenston gradually moved the magazine with the times, introducing articles on the contraceptive pill in 1964 and on women's knowledge of sex in 1968. Both issues sold well, in excess of 800 000. She told a market researcher that half the magazine was devoted to service features, such as cooking, sewing and knitting, because 'women's lib notwithstanding, the facts of life are that most women in jobs . . . must also do their own chores'.

Packer and Fenston spent a great deal of time with each other at work, even appearing conspiratorial to senior staff. He admired her talent, judgement and dedication, his admiration fuelled by the *Weekly*'s ability to attract substantial advertising and cover-price revenue, and to carry the rest of the company. Packer said that the *Weekly* paid everyone's salary, that it was the milk cow and Fenston the milkmaid. Packer himself oversaw the publication. After him she was the most senior executive in the company and, according to Packer's son Kerry, 'ran the *Women's Weekly* as if it were her own business'. She knew how to manage Packer and stood up to him while most turned to jelly. When he announced that brown envelopes were too expensive and that parcels were to be delivered wrapped in paper and string, she agreed, but pointed out that the *Weekly* would need a new staff member to wrap the parcels. Packer abandoned the plan.

Fenston also knew how to control other executives. When asked in the company tap-room, where executives gathered for drinks after work, if she was aware of a particular news event, she was likely to reply, 'the pictures are coming in tomorrow'. Kerry Packer knew that 'whatever you suggested, she had already thought of it'. Her staff respected her, despite her subtle way of loading them with work, and called her, affectionately, 'Mrs Fen'. She arrived at the office before them and finished after them. To some degree, she was not worldly; she presumed the best of people, never raised her voice, never appeared to lose her temper. The most emotion she displayed was to replace the telephone receiver after an irritating conversation and merely sigh; if very displeased, she rolled her eyes and muttered 'Oh God, Oh Montreal'.

Unhappy with Esmé's distance from the city, Packer bought her a large house near the Lane Cove River where the Fenstons entertained. They employed a housekeeper and chef, Susan Roth, who became a friend of them both. The three subsequently moved to a two-storey house at Darling Point. In the 1950s the Fenstons visited England, at Packer's expense. Jack went ahead by ship, and Esmé flew after, as Packer did not want her away from the office for too long. She loved London and told staff who went there, 'If you don't like London, don't come back'. Although she often talked of retiring, her salary continued to rise and the Fenstons' way of life was governed by her increasing financial security. Packer offered her a car. She accepted, obtained a licence, but seldom drove, as her husband was not happy about her driving.

In 1967 she was appointed O.B.E. for services to journalism. After Jack's death on 16 February 1969, Esmé bought a house at Mosman, overlooking Chinaman's Beach, where Roth cared for her. Fenston's staff believed that she kept excellent health and thought Packer was fussing when he suggested she should go to hospital after a bout of pneumonia. She entered the Mater Misericordiae, North Sydney. She died there of myocardial infarction on 16 April 1972 and was cremated with Anglican rites at a private ceremony. One confused, elderly relation distressed the mourners by asking repeatedly, 'Where's Esmé?' Fenston's estate was valued at $87 428. Joyce Bowden helped to clean the empty house. In the wardrobe she found eight hats and remembered how her former boss often had to rush to David Jones [q.v.2] Ltd to buy a hat when Packer asked her to lunch at the last minute. A memorial service was held at St James's Church, King Street. Barwick, then chief justice, was asked by Packer if he would 'go and speak for Esmé'. Packer said that he himself would become 'too emotional'. Fenston was a modest woman whose twenty-two years as editor of the most successful publication of its day was built on the foundations of a calm personality, sound financial knowledge, an affinity with her readers and a strong working relationship with her employer.

D. McNicoll, *Luck's a Fortune* (Syd, 1979); D. O'Brien, *The Weekly* (Melb, 1982); *Aust Women's Weekly*, 3 May 1972; *SMH*, 10 June 1967; E. Fenston file (John Fairfax Group Pty Ltd Archives, Syd); Syd Girls' High School Archives; information from Sir Garfield Barwick, Nth Turramurra, Mrs J. Bowden, Woollahra, Miss D. Drain, Glebe, Mrs J. Woolacott, Mosman, and Ms I. Buttrose, Syd, Mrs J. Curnow, Dural, NSW, Mr D. McNicoll, Mr K. Packer and Mrs D. Swain, c/- Aust Consolidated Press, Syd.   VALERIE LAWSON

FERGUSON, JEAN ELSIE (1909-1979), hospital matron, was born on 15 July 1909 at Guildford, Perth, sixth child of John Frederick Geary Robinson, pastoralist and racehorse-owner, and his wife Elsie Sarah, née Coppin, both Western Australian born. Jean spent her early years at Tampina, the family's Belmont home, and at Coongan station near Port Hedland. Educated at Guildford and at Perth College, in 1930-33 she trained at (Royal) Perth Hospital ('never worked so hard in my life') and was then employed in hospitals in Perth and at Brookton. She joined the Australian Army Nursing Service Reserve in January 1939 while proceeding to a midwifery certificate from the King Edward Memorial Hospital, Subiaco.

Appointed a staff nurse in the Australian Imperial Force on 22 April 1940, Sister Robinson reached England in July. Next month she was posted to the 2nd/3rd Australian General Hospital at Godalming, Surrey. She arrived in the Middle East in March 1941 and served in hospitals in Palestine and Egypt before returning to Australia in early 1942. From May she was in Queensland, nursing at military hospitals at Warwick and Toowoomba.

On 25 February 1943 at the Presbyterian Church, Tenterfield, New South Wales, she married John Boyd Ferguson, a captain in the A.I.F.; he was to die on 7 September in the Liberator disaster in Port Moresby. Promoted captain in August, Sister Ferguson was allotted for duty with the 2nd/11th A.G.H. and sailed for Port Moresby in October. She worked under canvas at Buna, Papua, and at Madang and Aitape, New Guinea, where malaria was rife, and was proud to wear regulation grey slacks, safari jacket, boots, gaiters and a slouch hat.

Back in Perth in February 1945, Ferguson was posted to the 110th Military (Hollywood) Hospital, Nedlands. On 12 March 1947 she relinquished her A.I.F. appointment and became matron when the hospital was transferred to the Repatriation Department that year. She had a tidy eye and once ordered that drip-bottles be shrouded lest the sight of blood should distress visiting dignitaries. In 1954 Queen Elizabeth II commented that Hollywood was more homely than other repatriation hospitals. As lieutenant colonel and principal matron (later assistant-director, army nursing service), Citizen Military Forces, in 1947-64 Ferguson organized the Royal Australian Army Nursing Corps in Western Command. She was awarded the Associate Royal Red Cross in 1953, appointed M.B.E. in 1963 and received a Florence Nightingale medal in 1969.

Dedicated to progress in the nursing profession and to postgraduate training, Ferguson spelt out her vision in 1958 in delivering the sixth annual oration to the New South Wales College of Nursing. She was a member (1965) of the Commonwealth Repatriation Department's committee of inquiry into nursing services, twice president of the Western Australian branch of the Royal Australian Nursing Federation, a foundation fellow of the State branch of the College of Nursing, Australia, and a member of the War Widows' Guild. Short and plumpish, with blue eyes and brown hair, Ferguson was vivacious and enjoyed company, but never remarried. She was a regular race-goer, played bridge, and swam and gardened at her Dalkeith home. Afflicted with blindness and suffering from multiple sclerosis for some years, she died on 30 January 1979 in Hollywood Hospital and was cremated with Anglican rites.

Milady, Jan 1949; *Listening Post*, Mar 1979; *West Australian*, 7 Nov 1943, 17 July 1953, 12 Sept 1958, 17 July 1961, 15 July 1965, 20 July 1968, 4 May 1969, 5 Feb 1979; *Daily News* (Perth), 5 Aug 1953; *Sunday Times* (Perth), 8 June 1958; Mrs W. Birman, taped interview with Miss V. Hobbs (held by ADB).   WENDY BIRMAN
VICTORIA HOBBS

FERGUSON, JOHN ALEXANDER (1903-1969), trade unionist, politician and public servant, was born on 31 May 1903 at Glen Innes, New South Wales, son of native-born parents Alexander Ferguson, miner, and his wife Mary, née Hannon. When only 6 he heard the Tingha tin-mine whistle announce the death of his father in an accident. Jack was sent to live with his grandparents at Howell, near Inverell. Seven years later he was reunited with his mother at Annandale, Sydney. He completed his schooling, tried various trades and spent a spell on the wallaby before marrying 18-year-old Beatrice Doreen Jago on 25 July 1925 at the Baptist Church, Stanmore.

In 1926 Ferguson joined the New South

Wales railways and the Communist Party of Australia. Within the Australian Railways Union he supported the State secretary Arthur Chapman, an independent-minded radical, and his successor Lloyd Ross. Becoming a close ally, the knockabout Ferguson was a good foil to the serious, taciturn Ross. From 1934 Ferguson organized the union's previously neglected membership in western New South Wales; Ross occasionally accompanied him on 'the red terror', an Indian motorbike with a side-car which Ferguson taught himself to ride on his first journey of 1200 miles (1930 km). In 1941 he became the union's district organizer at Tamworth and in 1943 succeeded Ross as State secretary.

With Ross, Ferguson had quit the C.P.A. in 1940. Both joined the Australian Labor Party. From his union base, Ferguson—'an intelligent, dapper, personable man, with a little of the doctrinaire leftist still in him'—rose quickly through the party machine. He was appointed to the Legislative Council in 1945 and elected president of the State branch of the A.L.P. in 1947. He forged a close working relationship with Prime Minister Chifley [q.v.13] who used his influence to have Ferguson elected federal president of the A.L.P. in 1950.

Ferguson had hoped for unity within the A.R.U., but by 1945 was accusing communists of planning to overthrow him. In 1949 he became a symbolic villain for the communist newspaper, *Tribune*, over his key role in ensuring that New South Wales railworkers defied the A.R.U.'s pro-communist national executive and carried coal declared 'black' by the striking members of the Miners' Federation. Unenthusiastic about the activities of the industrial groups, Ferguson maintained —this time in the face of furious hostility from the pro-'grouper' *News Weekly*—that Labor could not use 'totalitarian' means to defeat communism. Nor, in his view, did the Catholic Church have the right to interfere in Labor affairs. A strong coalition of groupers and a vengeful A.W.U. general secretary Tom Dougherty [q.v.] moved to take control of the State branch of the A.L.P. Ferguson resigned all union, parliamentary and party positions in April 1952 to take up the State Labor government's controversial offer of the chairmanship of the Milk Board.

As chairman, Ferguson was credited with ending seasonal rationing and with stabilizing marketing, despite recurring complaints about milk prices. He emphasized the importance of scientific research and programmes such as artificial insemination in improving the supply and quality of milk. In 1969 he was appointed honorary governor of the Dairy Husbandry Research Foundation within the University of Sydney. He was a fellow (1944-46) of the university senate, a director (1958-

69) of Royal North Shore Hospital and president (1959-69) of Royal National Park Trust.

He never quite lost touch with the bush: on his retirement from the Milk Board in June 1968, Ferguson declared that he would 'ride-about' the State for two weeks—with a camp-oven and billy-can in the back of his car. Survived by his wife, four of his five daughters and two of his three sons, he died of hypertensive heart disease on 2 August 1969 at his Lane Cove home and was cremated with Presbyterian forms. Jack Ferguson had said that he learned early lessons in class hatred on the mining-fields. He overcame obstacles of class and family suffering to fight for a better deal for fellow workers, but his ideal of working-class unity was out of step with the polarized factionalism of Labor in the 1950s.

L. F. Crisp, *Ben Chifley* (Melb, 1961); R. Murray, *The Split* (Syd, 1984); M. Hearn, *Working Lives* (Syd, 1990); *People* (Syd), 22 Nov 1950; *Railroad*, 17 Nov 1942, 9 Mar 1943, 5 Apr, 28 June 1946, 9 May 1952, Sept 1969; *SMH*, 25 Nov 1943, 1 Dec 1944, 25 May 1949, 30 Sept 1950, 13 Oct 1951, 27 Jan, 23 Apr 1952, 4 Nov 1959, 16 Nov 1960, 14 Jan 1961, 17 June 1968, 17 June, 3 Aug 1969; *Tribune* (Syd), 2, 30 July, 3 Aug 1949; *Daily Telegraph* (Syd), 23 July 1949; *News Weekly*, 17 Oct, 28 Nov 1951, 26 Mar 1952; *Worker* (Syd), 2 Apr 1952; *Sun-Herald*, 3 Aug 1969; ARU State Secretary's Report to State Council, 27 May 1946 (held at NSW branch, ARU office, Syd); family information.
MARK HEARN

FERGUSON, SIR JOHN ALEXANDER (1881-1969), bibliographer and judge, was born on 15 December 1881 at Invercargill, New Zealand, eldest of five children of Rev. John Ferguson [q.v.8], Presbyterian minister, and his wife Isabella, née Adie, both Scottish born. Educated at Invercargill until his father was called in 1894 to St Stephen's, Phillip Street, Sydney, John continued at the William Street Public School, then was privately tutored by James Oliver. At the University of Sydney (B.A., 1902; LL.B., 1905; D.Litt., 1955) Ferguson was a contemporary of H. M. Green [q.v.], and graduated in arts with first-class honours and the university medal in logic and mental philosophy.

Admitted to the Bar on 27 May 1905, Ferguson soon developed a sound practice, principally in Equity and industrial law, and contributed to the *Commonwealth Law Review*. He appeared before the High Court of Australia and the Privy Council, most of his briefs being in the areas of industrial and constitutional law. In 1934 he became the first lecturer in industrial law at the university. When the Industrial Commission of New South Wales was reconstituted in 1936,

Ferguson was appointed a judge, an office he held until starting a years leave in December 1951 prior to his retirement.

During his seventeen years on the bench Ferguson dispensed justice with grace and was the author of many improvements in industrial awards. In a tribute, A. C. Beattie, the president of the Industrial Commission, described him as 'a modest innovator', 'something of a radical in his day', and 'a model of tolerance and courtesy'. Ferguson's gentleness of manner and independent spirit gained him the respect of the legal profession and of opposing parties in industrial issues.

His early interest in Australian history and bibliography, which was to be his major preoccupation, had been fostered by his marriage on 2 January 1907 to Bessie (d.1937), daughter of George Robertson [q.v.11], bookseller and publisher. The wedding, with Presbyterian forms, took place at Halstead, the Robertsons' holiday home at Blackheath in the Blue Mountains. Ferguson spent his lunch hours browsing in second-hand bookshops; his interest in books, libraries and Australian history grew apace. In 1914 he joined the (Royal) Australian Historical Society and began book-collecting in a serious way, an activity assisted by his father-in-law: Ferguson had to move in 1922 from his home at Greenwich to a larger house at Hunters Hill to provide more room for his books. Representing his 'personal and scholarly interests', his library included books, newspapers, periodicals and pamphlets, encompassing law, bibliography, publishing, religion, mission material in the vernacular languages of the Pacific islands, New Guinea and New Zealand, works on Captain Cook [q.v.1] and R. L. Stevenson, military history, crime, convicts, transportation and literature. He encouraged scholars, whom he welcomed to his home, to use his collection. 'J.A.' to friends such as C. H. Bertie, George Mackaness and T. D. Mutch [qq.v.7,10], he continued to be referred to by his fellow collector (Sir) William Dixson [q.v.8] as 'young Jacky Ferguson'.

In 1917 Ferguson had published the first part of *A Bibliography of the New Hebrides and a History of the Mission Press* (part II, 1918; part III, 1943) which reflected his interest in the Presbyterian Church, of which he was an elder (from 1912) at St Stephen's and procurator (1921-36). His article on 'Studies in Australian Bibliography' in the *Journal and Proceedings* of the R.A.H.S. in 1918 foreshadowed the *magnum opus* that he was to undertake: the seven-volume *Bibliography of Australia*, 1784-1900, published by Angus [q.v.7] & Robertson Ltd's Halstead Press and known to librarians and bibliographers simply as 'Ferguson'. He aimed to include an accurate description of every book, pamphlet,

broadsheet, periodical and newspaper relating in any way to Australia, wherever they were printed, and to provide historical and bibliographical notes. The first volume was published in 1941 and volumes appeared at irregular intervals, the seventh and last being published in 1969, shortly after his death.

Closely involved with the R.A.H.S., Ferguson contributed to its journal and was president in 1922 and again in 1940-42 when he was able to implement an earlier plan to acquire a building, History House, for its headquarters. With Green and Mrs A. G. Foster, he had a limited edition, *The Howes and their Press*, printed by Ernest Shea [q.v.11]. Ferguson married Dorothy Kathleen Johnston, a 29-year-old secretary, on 16 July 1945 at St Stephen's. A trustee (from 1935) and president (1963-67) of the Public Library of New South Wales, he remained on its governing body until 1969, and was made an honorary member of the Library Association of Australia in 1958. He was also president of the Captain Cook's Landing Place Trust and a member of the La Pérouse [qq.v.1,2] Monuments Reserve Trust. Ferguson was appointed O.B.E. in 1957 and knighted in 1961, but treasured equally his R.A.H.S. fellowship, bestowed in 1927. The National Library of Australia, Canberra, recognized his contributions to bibliography and to libraries with an exhibition in his honour in 1965 that coincided with the biennial conference of the Library Association.

'A reserved man, steeped in the traditional Presbyterian virtues', Ferguson had 'an engaging grin' and could appreciate a joke. In his eighties his 'spare, slightly stooped, sober figure' could be seen at his special desk in the Mitchell [q.v.5] Library. Survived by his wife, and their son and daughter, and by the daughter and two of the three sons of his first marriage, he died on 7 May 1969 at his Roseville home. In conformity with his simple, frugal and considerate life, he had left instructions that his obsequies should take the form of a private cremation from an undertaker's chapel, without prior public announcement; he added the wish that 'those at a distance or hindered by age' should not attend. His eldest son George became publishing director of Angus & Robertson, John followed in his father's footsteps as a lawyer and Colin was killed in 1943 while serving with the Royal Australian Air Force. Sir John's collection of Australiana passed to the National Library and is housed in the Ferguson room.

G. D. Richardson, *The John Alexander Ferguson Memorial Lecture 1975* (Syd, 1977) and for bibliog; *JRAHS*, 62, pt 2, Sept 1976, p 73; *Hist Studies*, 14, no 54, Apr 1970; H. de Berg, Sir John Ferguson (taped interview, 1962, NL).

R. ELSE-MITCHELL

FERGUSSON, MAURICE ALFRED (1895-1975), army officer and grazier, was born on 5 December 1895 at Caulfield, Melbourne, third son of Ernest Fairchild Fergusson, a bank manager from Mauritius, and his Victorian-born wife Alfritha Elizabeth, née Turner. Educated at University High School, Maurice worked as a jackeroo and completed compulsory military training before enlisting in the Australian Imperial Force on 24 August 1914. He sailed for Egypt in October as a gunner in the 1st Field Artillery Brigade, was promoted bombardier in March 1915 and landed at Gallipoli on 25 April. While recovering from a bullet-wound, he developed enteric fever and was hospitalized in England from September.

In July 1916 Fergusson was sent to the Western Front and joined the 10th F.A.B. next month. Six feet (183 cm) tall and weighing 13 st. 4 lb. (84 kg), he was commissioned in December and promoted lieutenant in May 1917. He was wounded at Messines, Belgium, on 7 June and mentioned in dispatches. On 8 August 1918 near Cérisy-Gailly, France, he saved his battery's guns and the lives of many of his men; he was awarded the Military Cross. For his actions throughout the period February to August, he won a Bar to his M.C. In the latter month he was accidentally injured and transferred to hospital in England. He was to be granted a disability pension for the injury, but voluntarily surrendered it in 1922.

On 6 January 1916 at the Church of St Edward the Confessor, Hound, Southampton, Fergusson had married Effie Hazel Skinner who accompanied him to Australia where his A.I.F. appointment terminated on 25 March 1919. After working in the country in New South Wales and Victoria, he bought a dairy-farm at Whittlesea in 1927 and was a member of the local shire council from 1930 to 1934 (president 1931-32). As an Independent United Australia Party candidate, in 1932 he unsuccessfully contested the Legislative Assembly seat of Evelyn. In 1934-39 he managed branches of a pastoral company in New South Wales and Victoria.

Serving in the Militia in 1926-32 and again from 1936, Fergusson was given command of the 8th (Indi) Light Horse Regiment and promoted lieutenant colonel in 1939. He was seconded to the A.I.F. and took command of the 6th Divisional Reconnaissance (later Cavalry) Regiment on 13 October. 'A man who spoke only when necessary, and then forcefully', he was nicknamed 'Ruthless' after telling his troops that he would be ruthless with any soldier who appeared incorrectly dressed. He was firm and austere, trained the unit well, and set high standards of personal conduct and technical efficiency. The regiment reached the Middle East in February 1940. On 9 March 1941 Fergusson was seriously wounded in the siege of the Italian stronghold of Giarabub, Libya, and was repatriated in June. For his services in Cyrenaica, he was awarded the Distinguished Service Order and mentioned in dispatches.

Fergusson returned to the Middle East in November. He commanded the 2nd/17th Battalion in January-February 1942 in Syria and embarked for Australia in March. Promoted temporary brigadier next month, in 1942-44 he successively led the 1st and 2nd Armoured and the 2nd Infantry brigades. In New Guinea, from August 1944, he commanded the 8th Infantry Brigade in operations around Madang and Wewak, and was once more mentioned in dispatches. Back home, on 16 October 1945 he transferred to the Reserve of Officers as honorary brigadier.

In 1946 Fergusson stood as a Liberal Party candidate for the Senate, but was defeated. That year he bought Corio station near Inverell, New South Wales; in 1949 he moved to Moreton Bay, a farming and grazing property near Leadville. He maintained his political interests, holding executive positions in the party, and enjoyed shooting, golf, tennis and billiards. Retiring to Sydney in 1966, he gave generously of his time to Legacy, the Big Brother Movement and the Girl Guides' Association. Fergusson died on 27 September 1975 at Dunedoo and was buried at Moreton Bay. His wife survived him, as did four of their six sons; three had served in the A.I.F., including Terence who was killed in action in 1942 in Papua.

G. Long, *To Benghazi* (Canb, 1952) and *The Final Campaigns* (Canb, 1963); S. O'Leary, *To the Green Fields Beyond* (Syd, 1975); 'What We Have— We Hold!' (Syd, 1990?); *SMH*, 17 Aug, 30 Sept 1946; War diaries of 4th Division Artillery Headquarters, 6th Division Cavalry Regiment, 2nd/17th Aust Infantry Battalion, 2nd Aust Armoured Brigade Headquarters and 2nd *and* 8th Aust Infantry Brigade Headquarters (AWM); Dept of Veterans' Affairs records (Canb); information from Mr D. Fergusson, Epping, and Mr M. Fergusson, Dunedoo, NSW.   J. B. HOPLEY

FERNIE, NORMAN (1898-1977), engineer, was born on 18 June 1898, at Leederville, Perth, fourth child of Alexander Fernie, a carpenter from Victoria, and his wife Mary Elizabeth, née Renkin. Norman attended Scotch College (1910-11), Perth Modern School (1912-14) and the University of Western Australia where he studied engineering (B.Sc., 1920; B.E., 1923; M.E., 1936). On 12 July 1921 he married Iris Evelyn Weston at the Presbyterian Church, Subiaco. Fernie had joined the Department of Public Works that year and was employed on the development of water supplies from rock catchments in the eastern wheatbelt. In 1930 he became district engineer at Northam with the task of restoring the 328-mile (528 km) water-supply pipeline to Kalgoorlie. He devised a method of refurbishing the buried pipeline by re-laying it above ground which enabled complete reconstruction in a decade. For this work he was awarded the R. W. Chapman [q.v.7] medal by the Institution of Engineers, Australia.

On leave of absence from the department in 1935-36 and 1938-39, Fernie designed and supervised the construction of sewerage schemes for the municipalities of Northam and Kalgoorlie, the first such undertakings in the State outside Perth. In 1939 he was seconded to the Department of Industrial Development and Employment; two years later he was appointed director of industrial development. He was largely responsible for establishing several strategically important, government-owned enterprises—notably the Chandler alunite industry (1943), the Wundowie wood distillation and charcoal ironworks (1948) and the Chamberlain tractor factory (1949)—together with a wide range of smaller, privately-owned businesses. During his directorship Fernie served on about thirty boards, committees and panels, most of which he chaired.

On 31 July 1950 he resigned from the public service to accept the managing directorship of Griffin Coal Mining Co. Ltd which operated several underground mines at Collie. When major new seams were discovered in 1953, Fernie pressed for the development of open-cut mining. In the midst of a prolonged miners' strike against open-cut work, the Brand [q.v.13] government signed a new three-year contract with Griffin on 16 December 1960. Earlier that year the company had formed a joint-venture to export low-grade iron ore, after processing it into sponge iron using char derived from Collie coal. By this means Fernie hoped to bypass the Commonwealth's 22-year-old embargo on the export of iron ore. Although the ban was lifted in December 1960 and an export agreement was signed next March, the project did not proceed because of richer deposits in the Pilbara region. In August 1963 Fernie retired from Griffin 'under medical advice'. His struggles to overcome union and government resistance to open-cutting had exacted their toll.

A thin, ascetic-looking man, and a lifelong Labor supporter, Fernie pursued his policies with a commitment and vigour that often made him a controversial figure. He served on the university senate (1943-45), as a State electricity commissioner (1949-53) and as chairman of the Western Australian division of the Institution of Engineers (1943). Survived by his wife, daughter and two sons, he died on 25 May 1977 at Claremont and was cremated with Congregational forms.

P. Firkins (ed), *A History of Commerce and Industry in Western Australia* (Perth, 1979); J. S. H. Le Page, *Building a State* (Perth, 1986); B. Moore, *From the Ground Up* (Perth, 1987); *West Australian*, 17 June 1957, 9 Sept 1963, 22 Dec 1973, 2 Feb 1974, 5, 20 Jan, 27 May 1977; files of WA Depts of Industrial Development *and* Mines *and* Public Works, *also* N. Fernie, Personal note, Feb 1976 (WAA); Auditor's Dept (WA), Report on the Wood Distillation, Charcoal, Iron and Steel Industry, 1967, *and* A. C. Harris, Oral history transcript, 1976, *and* R. G. Hartley, Norman Fernie—Engineer, 1898-1977 (ts, BL).

RICHARD G. HARTLEY

FERRES, HAROLD DUNSTAN GORDON (1885-1978), army officer, grazier and farmer, was born on 4 September 1885 at Ararat, Victoria, fifth child of Robert Ferres, a native-born civil servant, and his wife Caroline Elizabeth, née Tonkin, from England. In 1894 the family moved to the Gippsland district and took up farming. Nicknamed 'Pung', Harold attended Alberton State School and became a good footballer, cyclist and horseman. He cleared and improved grazing blocks around Toora, and raised cattle. An acclaimed shearer, he worked on stations as far away as North Queensland.

On 13 January 1915 Ferres enlisted in the Australian Imperial Force. Commissioned on 29 May, he sailed to Egypt and briefly served in the 5th Battalion before transferring to the 57th Battalion in February 1916. The unit arrived in France in June and next month fought in the battle of Fromelles. In August Ferres was promoted captain and posted to the 58th Battalion. He was mentioned in dispatches for outstanding conduct as a company commander from July to September. Suffering from fever, he was evacuated to a hospital in London in April 1917 and did not return to the 58th until October. On the night of 13-14 March 1918, near Messines, Belgium, he led a successful raid against enemy trenches and was awarded the Military Cross. After the Germans broke through the front line east of Hamel, France, on 4 April he organized defences to prevent them from reaching the Somme Canal; for this work he won a Bar to his M.C.

Promoted temporary major in May 1918 (substantive in September), Ferres was again mentioned in dispatches. On 2 September he commanded his battalion in an attack against Péronne. Although he was severely wounded in the thigh, he continued to direct the assault, despite intense pain and loss of blood. His quick decisions and resolute actions led to the taking of the strongly defended town, with minimal casualties to his own men. He was awarded the Distinguished Service Order. While recovering from his wound in Scotland, on 16 December 1918 he married Joanna Mary Scott Todd with United Free Church forms at her mother's Edinburgh home; they were to have four children.

Back in France, Ferres commanded in turn the 58th and 59th battalions as temporary lieutenant colonel. In May 1919 he embarked for Australia where his A.I.F. appointment terminated on 29 December; as major, he was placed on the Reserve of Officers in 1922 and transferred to the Retired List in 1925. One of the A.I.F.'s most decorated soldiers, he maintained links with his battalion association, but avoided publicity and 'was reticent about his own deeds'. In 1919 he had resumed farming on a new property near Emerald, Victoria; he devoted the rest of his life to his family and his passion for the land. 'To him, the outside world was unimportant'. He was never idle and had stern words for those who were. Predeceased by his wife, he died on 5 July 1978 at Kallista and was cremated with Anglican rites; his daughter and two of his three sons survived him.

C. E. W. Bean, *The A.I.F. in France*, 1916-18 (Syd, 1929, 1933, 1937, 1942); Ferres Family (comp), *Bath and Beyond* (priv pub, np, 1988); AWM records.   NEIL SMITH

FERRIER, SIR HAROLD GRANT (1905-1976), marine engineer and business leader, was born on 26 August 1905 at Drummoyne, Sydney, second son of Robert Robinson Ferrier, a marine engineer from England, and his native-born wife Elizabeth Ferguson, née Grant. Robert, who was of Scottish descent, established the firm of Ferrier & Dickinson in the early 1900s and later Electric Control & Engineering Ltd. Educated at Drummoyne Superior Public and Sydney Grammar schools, Grant was apprenticed with his father's companies. He travelled to Britain where, from 1926 to 1930, he gained experience in marine engineering with Weir, Drysdale Ltd at Glasgow, and in Belfast. On returning to Australia, he worked as a jackeroo before managing pastoral properties in western New South Wales; in his spare time he enjoyed surfing, rowing, riding and polo. In 1934 he was recalled to take control of his father's companies. Thereafter, his hankering for life on the land was restricted to enjoying several acres at St Ives, where he lived after he married Alice Heather Mitchell (d.1948) at St Stephen's Presbyterian Church, Sydney, on 21 May 1936. From the 1950s he owned a small farm at Moss Vale.

Although Ferrier was a trained engineer and a member (from 1945-46) of the Institute of Marine Engineers, his industrial career was essentially in management and in organizations that represented manufacturing interests. The family companies were linked with Weir, Drysdale Ltd from 1945 and amalgamated in 1947 to form Federated British Engineers (N.S.W.) Ltd (Federated Industries Ltd, 1957). Beyond the family companies, Ferrier was chairman of Pioneer Spring Co. Ltd (Pioneer Industries Ltd, 1962) and Commonwealth Portland Cement Co. Ltd (Associated Portland Cement Manufacturers [Australia] Ltd, 1964), and a director of York Air Conditioning and Refrigeration (Australasia) Pty Ltd and Ernest Hiller Holdings Ltd, clothing manufacturers. At St Stephen's on 25 November 1949 he married Margaret Barkell, née James, a 32-year-old divorcee with two daughters. In the late 1950s the family moved to Woollahra.

From 1948 to 1950, as State president of the Metal Trades Employers' Association, Ferrier rose to prominence during a time of industrial unrest. He was subsequently federal president (1950-53) of the Australian Metal Industries Association and represented Australian manufacturers at the coronation of Queen Elizabeth II in 1953. A councillor (from 1949) of the Chamber of Manufactures of New South Wales, he became its vice-president in 1961 and president in 1964; in the following year he was president of the Associated Chambers of Manufactures of Australia. In the mid-1950s, as a member of the Australian delegation, he began to attend the annual conferences of the International Labour Organization, held in Geneva. One outcome of this activity was a personal friendship with Albert Monk [q.v.], president of the Australian Council of Trade Unions. Another was his election as president in 1966 of the International Organization of Employers—he was the first Australian to occupy the position. He had been appointed C.M.G. in 1964 and was knighted in 1969.

A convinced supporter of the tariff and arbitration systems, the twin pillars of Australian manufacturing development, Ferrier advocated legislation requiring importers to deposit a proportion of the value of intended imports as a means of checking what he referred to as 'speculative imports' and of providing information on prospective trends. He criticized the 1948 amendments to the Commonwealth Conciliation and Arbitration Act (1904) for separating basic wage determination and the establishment of skill margins: the seemingly arbitrary decisions made by conciliators in regard to margins often ran counter to his views on encouraging young people to acquire skills through apprenticeships and technical education. None the less, he thought that the Australian wage-regulation system generally reconciled the interests of capital and labour. He was much opposed to what was later called 'enterprise bargaining' which he believed was favoured only by communists as a means of promoting industrial militancy.

Sir Grant belonged to the Royal Sydney Yacht Squadron and Royal Sydney Golf Club, as well as to the Commonwealth Club, Canberra. He spent his last years at Leura in the Blue Mountains. Survived by his wife, and by the daughter of his first marriage, he died of cancer on 28 July 1976 in hospital at Katoomba and was cremated.

Chamber of Manufactures of NSW, *Manufacturers' Bulletin*, 27 Sept 1963; *SMH*, 27 Jan 1948, 17 May 1949, 25 Feb 1950, 1 Jan 1964, 3 June 1966, 14 June 1969, 31 July 1976; information from Mrs G. Litchfield, Coroo, Cooma, NSW.

JOHN PERKINS

FIDLER, JOHN ROY (1891-1973), surveyor, businessman and politician, was born on 8 August 1891 at Gladstone, Tasmania, one of eight children of Joseph Fidler, police constable, and his wife Hannah, née Quinn. After his father was transferred to Burnie in 1901, Jack completed his education at the local state school and began training as a surveyor with the Van Diemen's Land Co. in 1906. Enlisting in the Australian Imperial Force on 11 August 1915, he was posted to the 6th Field Company, Engineers, and sailed for Egypt in November. He was sent to France in March 1916; five months later he was commissioned and transferred to the 7th Field Company. For his deeds on 20 September 1917, east of Ypres, Belgium, when he organized the digging of a communications trench while under heavy fire, he was awarded the Military Cross. Fidler was wounded in action on four occasions and, following the Armistice, fell seriously ill with bronchopneumonia. On 19 July 1919 he married Lydia Maud Brown (d.1958) at St John's Anglican Church, Launceston, Tasmania.

Re-employed by the Van Diemen's Land Co. on a retainer until his retirement as its chief surveyor in October 1956, Fidler undertook additional work for Associated Pulp & Paper Mills Ltd, mining companies, the Public Works Department and private subdividers. Surveying roads and boundaries introduced him to some of the best stands of milling-timber in the State, and, from the 1920s until 1962, he developed a business interest in sawmilling, for some years in partnership with his brother Burnie. With (Sir) Gerald Mussen and A. K. McGaw [qq.v.10], Jack Fidler set up Forest Supplies Pty Ltd to supply A.P.P.M. with timber for pulping and boiler fuel; he was the new company's first general manager (1937-43). In November

1946, standing as a Liberal, he was elected to the House of Assembly for the seat of Darwin (later Braddon). A member of the standing committee on public works, he was defeated in the elections in October 1956.

Fidler served on the Burnie Municipal Council (1957-66) and the local hospital board; he also belonged to the Burnie Club, the Agricultural and Pastoral Society, the Rotary Club and the Boy Scouts' Association. His other interests ranged from bowls to pigeon-racing: he was past president and a life member of the Burnie Athletic Club, a prominent cyclist, keen axeman, and champion of the Seabrook Golf Club. On 11 July 1959 at the Methodist Church, Burnie, he married a widow Ethel Mary Aiton, née Hugo (d.1972). Fidler had a pleasant and engaging personality, but perseverance was his greatest attribute. In parliament he had argued strongly for building a road to link the west and north-west coasts. To prove a point, in his early seventies he contracted to survey the route, and did it himself, largely on foot, assisted by a man and a boy. In 1966 he was appointed M.B.E. Survived by one of the two sons of his first marriage, he died on 17 March 1973 at New Norfolk and was cremated. He is remembered for the Pinnacle Road to the top of Mount Wellington, and for a section of the Murchison Highway where, at the Waratah end, a memorial plaque was unveiled in June 1974.

K. Pink, *The Carnival* (Burnie, Tas, 1986); *Advocate* (Burnie), 13 Dec 1963, 19 Mar 1973, 14 June 1974, 19 Mar 1986; *Mercury* (Hob), 19 Mar 1973; information from Mrs J. Fidler, Hob, and Mr K. Pink, Burnie, Tas.

PETER MERCER

FIELD, FRANK (1885-1961), army officer and engineer, was born on 8 September 1885 at Crayford, Kent, England, son of John Christopher Field, dairyman, and his wife Frances Elizabeth, née Simpson. Frank attended Marshall's School, Erith, and the London County Council School of Science, Woolwich, before completing an apprenticeship in mechanical engineering at the Royal Arsenal, Woolwich. At the local register office on 17 November 1906 he married Harriet Elizabeth Bell, a schoolteacher. He was employed in War Office workshops in the British Isles (1907-12) and Jamaica (1912-18), and was a demonstrator in mechanical engineering at University College, Southampton, in 1921 when he was admitted as an associate-member of the Institution of Mechanical Engineers, London.

Emigrating to Australia, Field was commissioned captain, Permanent Military Forces, on 20 August 1923; two months later he was sent to England for two years training as an inspector of ordnance machinery. In December 1925 he was appointed ordnance mechanical engineer, North-Eastern Area, and was based in Sydney. He was posted to Army Headquarters, Melbourne, in 1937 and promoted lieutenant colonel next year. Following the outbreak of World War II, in 1940 he was appointed temporary colonel and director of mechanization, Australian Army Ordnance Corps (director of mechanical maintenance from May 1942).

The repair and upkeep of equipment had become pivotal to military operations. In 1942 the British formed a new corps, the Royal Electrical and Mechanical Engineers, to take over engineering duties and harness all available technical skill. Planning began for a similar reorganization of the Australian Military Forces. Field brought to the task broad administrative ability, and a knowledge of staff duties and headquarters methods. The Corps of Australian Electrical and Mechanical Engineers, formed on 1 December 1942, was largely his creation. Appointed head of corps and its first director of mechanical engineering, he was promoted temporary brigadier in February 1943. A friend wrote that he set by example a high standard for his officers to follow. He was cautious in delegating responsibility, but then he 'gave total loyalty and support'. Frankie was not at all the typical regimental officer, and he had a rather English reserve that was, for some, not easy to understand. He did not fraternize with his subordinates nor, very readily, with his peers; but he was 'the right officer in the right appointment at the right time'.

Field relinquished his appointment in December 1944 and was transferred to the Retired List on 9 September 1945. Having been seconded to the Department of Labour and National Service in 1944, he was manpower controller of Commonwealth scientific personnel. Next year he joined the United Nations Relief and Rehabilitation Administration with which he served as associate field director for Manchuria and subsequently deputy-director and chief of supply for China as a whole. From 1947 to 1955 he was South-West Pacific representative of the United Nations International Children's Emergency Fund. He had been chairman (1943) of the Victoria division of the Institution of Engineers, Australia, and president (1943-44) of the Institution of Automotive and Aeronautical Engineers. Survived by his daughter, he died on 19 November 1961 at Camperdown, Sydney, and was cremated with Anglican rites.

T. Barker, *Craftsmen of the Australian Army* (Bathurst, NSW, 1992); *Bulletin*, 28 July 1948; AWM records; personal information.

J. P. HALDANE-STEVENSON

FIELD, JOHN (1899-1974), army officer and engineer, was born on 10 April 1899 at Castlemaine, Victoria, only son and eldest of three children of John Woodhouse Barnett Field, brewery employee, and his wife Emily, née Bennett, both native-born. John senior was a Militia officer who rose to colonel and served in the Australian Imperial Force in World War I; years earlier, he had brought his infant son, wrapped in blankets, to be acclaimed by the regiment in which young John later served as a boy-bugler. Educated at Castlemaine High and Technical schools, at the age of 15 Field was apprenticed to Thompson [q.v.12] & Co. Pty Ltd, engineers; he became senior designing draughtsman, specializing in centrifugal pumps and pumping-plants. At Christ Church, Castlemaine, on 11 October 1922 he married with Anglican rites Kate Corlett, a schoolteacher. Next year he was commissioned in the 7th Battalion, Militia.

In 1926 Field was appointed draughtsman in the faculty of engineering at the University of Tasmania. While lecturer in engineering, drawing and design (from 1927), he studied part time for his B.E. (1941). Continuing in the Citizen Military Forces with the 40th Battalion, by 1936 he was a major, intelligent and forward-looking: in 1932 he had won the army's gold-medal essay competition with his paper, 'The New Warfare', dealing with the influence of modern technology on tactics.

As World War II approached, Field worked full time on mobilization plans for Tasmania before transferring to the A.I.F. on 13 October 1939. Promoted lieutenant colonel, he commanded the 2nd/12th Battalion in Britain (June to November 1940), North Africa (December 1940 to August 1941) and Syria (September 1941 to January 1942). His battalion took part in the defence of Tobruk, Libya, from April to August 1941.

Returning to Australia, in May 1942 Field was promoted temporary brigadier and given command of the Militia's 7th Brigade. In July he was made commander of Milne Force, consisting of his own brigade and all naval, land and air units in the region of Milne Bay, Papua; he brought energy and his engineer's experience to the task of constructing airstrips, roads and camps. He reverted to his brigade command next month when Major General C. A. Clowes [q.v.13] arrived to take over the augmented force. The 7th Brigade helped to repulse the Japanese landings in August-September and Field was awarded the Distinguished Service Order.

The brigade was recalled to Australia in late 1943 and sent to New Guinea in July 1944. Field had a lucky escape in September when an aircraft carrying him from Lae to Madang crashed in the mountains; he and his party trekked for nine days before reaching safety. Between November 1944 and the cessation of hostilities in August 1945, the 7th Brigade was part of Lieutenant General (Sir) Stanley Savige's [q.v.] II Corps on Bougainville. Field was appointed C.B.E. (1946) for his part in this campaign. He was twice mentioned in dispatches in World War II.

Back in Australia, Field was courted by both major political parties as a parliamentary candidate, but politely declined their approaches. In October 1945 he took a post in Melbourne assisting Savige who was co-ordinator of demobilization and disposal, and succeeded him in June 1946. Field transferred to the Reserve of Officers on 27 November. Next month the State Electricity Commission of Victoria appointed him assistant general superintendent for Yallourn; he became general superintendent in 1951. A powerful figure in Yallourn (where he was known as 'The Brig'), he was chosen in 1963 to head the La Trobe Valley territory, comprising the combined Yallourn and Morwell projects on which over 7000 workers were employed.

Field had been an able, methodical, reliable and consistent officer. Savige considered him the best of his commanders on Bougainville and wrote of him: 'He never sought the spectacular any more than he was spectacular himself'. Lifted out of relative obscurity by the opportunities of war, Field rose to the occasion and benefited in peacetime, though he was frustrated in his wish for further promotion within the S.E.C. After overseeing a large expansion in production in the La Trobe Valley, he retired to Melbourne in 1964. He had been active in Legacy and the C.M.F. (substantive brigadier 1949), and maintained contact with many of his old comrades.

Well read, and a capable artist in his spare time, Field was a warm, family man, who had illustrated his wartime letters to his children with humorous cartoons. He was—like his hero Sir John Monash [q.v.10]—a most professional citizen-soldier. Field died on 12 May 1974 at St Kilda and was cremated; his wife and three daughters survived him.

D. McCarthy, *South-West Pacific Area—First Year* (Canb, 1959); G. Long, *The Final Campaigns* (Canb, 1963); B. Maughan, *Tobruk and El Alamein* (Canb, 1966); *Stand-To* (Canb), vol 5, no 5, Sept-Oct 1956, pp 2, 43, vol 6, no 1, Jan-Feb 1957, p 9; J. Field, Warriors for the Working Day (memoirs, incomplete ms, AWM); Field papers (held by Mrs B. Hooks, Brighton, Melb, *and* AWM).

PETER LONDEY

FIELD, THOMAS ALFRED (1874-1944) and HERBERT (1878-1955), meat exporters and graziers, were born on 9 May 1874 and 12 August 1878 at Erith, Kent, England, eld-est and second of six children of Thomas Alfred Field, butcher, and his wife Eliza Jemima, née Jaques. In 1885 the family emigrated to Sydney. Young Tom left school to work in his father's growing retail and wholesale butchering business which he and his brothers Herbert and Sydney inherited in 1900. Under the general direction of Tom, they began to acquire grazing properties and to channel resources into the firm's wholesale and export businesses. At St James's Catholic Church, Forest Lodge, on 26 June 1900 Tom married Leontine Mildred Clark. On 9 May 1906 at St Andrew's Anglican Cathedral, Sydney, Herbert married Nellie Pointing, an attractive, 20-year-old concert pianist and quite a different character from her husband.

During World War I the Field brothers controlled about one-third of Sydney's wholesale meat business through their own company and through their interests in James Elliot & Co. Ltd and the Francis Meat Co. Ltd. In 1917 Tom was criticized by the Necessary Commodities Commission for alleged monopoly trading. Later that year, as chairman of the Wholesale Meat Trade Committee, he dealt successfully with widespread strike and industrial action. In 1923 the brothers established T. A. Field Ltd, frozen meat exporters, with listed assets of £1 100 000; Tom was chairman, and Herbert and Sydney directors.

By 1931 T. A. Field Ltd had grown into a meat and pastoral empire, with headquarters in Thomas Street, Sydney, and interests extending throughout eastern Australia. Three years later, however, the brothers divided the assets and formed their own pastoral companies. Tom retained a half-interest in T. A. Field Ltd and received stations valued at £810 000, among them Belalie, Warrana, Bimble, Burrawang and Congi. His private business interests included the 200 000-acre (80 100-ha) Willandra station and its famous merino stud (purchased in 1912 with the Vickery family), and, from 1930, Lanyon (on the Murrumbidgee near Canberra) which he developed as the family's country home and rural showpiece. Field's wool clips were among the world's largest combined offerings under one ownership.

Hard working and confident, he was solidly built and had a forthright gaze. With a cigar in hand, he displayed success, and was respected by his employees. He was also a thinker, with a good memory and firm ideas about the industry. In a company memo he wrote that 'the key to successful business is careful finance'. Field's frequent rounds of his properties kept him away from his family for many weeks. He was one of the first pastoralists to own his own aeroplane.

In spite of his position in the meat trade, Field and his second wife Jessie Tennant rarely went out socially. In 1933 he suffered a severe heart attack. Next year he visited Europe. On his return he took little part in the business. Survived by his wife and their two sons and three daughters, Tom died of heart disease on 29 January 1944 at Warrawee and was cremated with Anglican rites. Although his assets were sworn for probate at £354 641, he had shrewdly reduced his dutiable estate to £8330. Lanyon was resumed by the Federal government in 1974 after protracted litigation in the High Court of Australia.

Herbert also played an important role in the Field business. Following the company split, he received over 250 000 acres, including Giro, Merrowie, Red Hill and Widgiewa stations. He remained a director of T. A. Field Ltd with a quarter-interest until he disposed of all his shares in 1938. His own company moved into the sheep and wool trade, with a head office in George Street, Sydney. Merrowie, near Hillston, became a prominent merino stud and Red Hill, near Tumut, was best known for its Herefords. Herbert ran his properties very much as a business investment. A serious man who discouraged waste, he asserted that 'a set of brains in a sheep is worth a threepence'. He meticulously checked the bookwork and took a pragmatic approach to problems, generally seeing issues in black and white. Stocky in build, with fine, thinning hair, he had a stern, unsmiling demeanour.

Herbert's private life was more extravagant. In 1915 he bought a large house at Ashfield Park and in 1927 moved his family to another grand house, at Bellevue Hill, which he also named The Bunyas. He lavished fine gifts upon his wife and children. Nellie took a great interest in racing; her horse, Blue Legend, won the Australian Jockey Club's Doncaster (1946 and 1947) and Epsom (1946) handicaps. Survived by his wife, daughter and two sons, Herbert died on 4 October 1955 at Bellevue Hill and was buried in Waverley cemetery. His estate was sworn for probate at £43 783.

P. Jarratt, *T. A. Field—a history* (Syd, 1991); *Butcher*, 30 Nov 1917; *Pastoral Review*, 16 Mar 1922, 16 Feb 1944, 16 May 1953, 15 Oct 1955, 18 May 1962, July 1975; *SMH*, 3 Sept, 5 Oct 1955; *Daily Telegraph* (Syd), 5 Oct 1955; deceased estates of T. A. Field, A 73739 no 20/3428 *and* H. Field, B 128752 no 20/6185 (NSWA); information from Mr R. Field, Syd, Mr A. Field, Coolah, Mrs N. G. Lowe, Bowral, and Mr T. Hanrahan, Grafton, NSW.

J. S. SEARS

FIELDER, DOROTHY VIVIENNE (1890-1972), teacher of bridge, was born on 5 June 1890 at Leichhardt, Sydney, daughter of New Zealand-born parents William Phillips Webb, draftsman, and his wife Mary Elizabeth, née Simpson. At Lawson House, Zetland, on 11 July 1914 Dorothy married with Congregational forms James Blaine Fiedler, a motor-car salesman from the United States of America. By 1916 they had changed their surname to Fielder.

In the 1920s Mrs Fielder learned to play contract bridge by correspondence with the American expert Ely Culbertson. From January 1930 she taught both auction and contract bridge in the 'Bridge Studio' at David Jones [q.v.2] Ltd's Elizabeth Street department store, five days a week from 10.00 a.m. to 5.45 p.m.; lessons cost 3s. 6d. (or 30s. for ten) and included morning or afternoon tea. Within a fortnight she added 'post prandial' rubbers of bridge from 7.00 to 9.00 on Friday nights. Her practice sessions on Wednesday and Friday afternoons were invariably crowded. For several years she ran a regular competition—with substantial prize-money—on the last Monday of the month. David Jones's catalogues promoted her as 'a prominent expert providing Bridge Tuition at very moderate rates'.

Through her connexion with Culbertson, in April-May 1932 Fielder officiated as games captain for the first international bridge competition played in Sydney: at David Jones she directed the local section of the competition which was organized by the National Bridge Club of America and conducted in forty countries. By 1934, in Sydney alone, 128 players competed in what was known as Olympic Bridge; Mrs Fielder continued to supervise the Sydney section until 1939. In 1933 she had been referee-in-chief for the first interstate contract bridge competition, between teams from Victoria and New South Wales. Over three days, 120 hands of bridge were played at David Jones, in two daily sessions open to the public. Following this match, bridge associations were formed in all States and in the Australian Capital Territory.

Believing that women had the capacity to play bridge as well as or better than men, Fielder encouraged them to enter competitions. In an article in David Jones's Spring/Summer catalogue of 1932-33 she revealed her passion for contract bridge by describing the last trick of the hand: 'a good discard at this stage of the game could nicely accompany a rich man into the Kingdom of Heaven'. Although her husband seldom played, she prescribed bridge as a recipe for matrimonial happiness: 'I have seen more than one marriage, failing for lack of common interest, being saved when the couple take up bridge together'.

Mrs Fielder taught and directed play at David Jones until the early 1950s, then gave private lessons at her Point Piper home until the day before she died. It was claimed that she had taught more than ten thousand people. She also played and demonstrated canasta, but declared that, while enjoyable, it would never supplant bridge. Survived by one of her two sons, she died on 15 August 1972 at Point Piper; she left her body to the University of Sydney for medical research.

David Jones Ltd (Syd), *The Heart of a Great City* (Syd, 1934); *Bridge Mag of Aust*, 6 July 1933; *Aust Women's Weekly*, 27 May 1950; *SMH*, 27 Nov 1929, 8, 24, 30 Jan 1930, 24 Jan 1934, 19 May 1939, 22 Aug 1972; Mail order catalogues, Spring and Summer, 1929-39 *and* news-cuttings books, 1929-39 *and* D. Fielder staff card (David Jones Ltd, Syd, Archives); information from Mr J. R. Fielder, Wahroonga, Syd.   RACHEL GRAHAME

FIELDING, UNA LUCY (1888-1969), neuroanatomist, was born on 20 May 1888 at Wellington, New South Wales, eldest of five surviving children of native-born parents Rev. Sydney Glanville Fielding, Anglican clergyman and author, and his wife Lucy Frances, née Johnson. The family moved to Windsor in 1893. Una attended a small private school there, and from 1900 St Catherine's Clergy Daughters' School, Waverley. An able student, in 1907 she won a bursary to the University of Sydney (B.A., 1910). For some six years she taught French and English as a governess, and at Kelvin College, Neutral Bay, and Ravensworth, Gordon. Determined to study medicine, she returned to university (B.Sc., 1919; M.B., Ch.M., 1922); she worked (1919-23) as a part-time demonstrator in the department of anatomy, resident medical tutor at Women's College and resident medical officer at the Renwick Hospital for Infants.

In July 1923 Una Fielding sailed for England where she became a demonstrator in the department of anatomy at University College, London, headed by (Sir) Grafton Elliot Smith [q.v.11]. At first she was not a continuously paid member of staff and 'trimmed hats at nights' to finance her own studies: 'I knew that I must prove myself'. She soon gained a reputation for her superb competence as a teacher of practical neurology and for her encyclopaedic knowledge of the subject. In 1927 she spent a term in the United States of America as demonstrator in neurology at the University of Michigan, Ann Arbor; in 1928-29 she was seconded to the American University of Beirut, Syria (Lebanon), as acting-professor of histology and nervous anatomy. From 1928 she lectured in neurology at U.C.L. As well as teaching pre-clinical medical students, she helped to supervise postgraduates; she also taught anatomy and physiology of the nervous system to psychology undergraduates and elementary physical anthropology to students of archaeology and Egyptology.

A member (from 1923) of the Anatomical Society of Great Britain and Ireland, in 1925 Una Fielding had read her first paper to the society, on the brain of the marsupial mole, *Notoryctes*. In 1927 and 1928 she published papers on the ovary, with A. B. Parkes and F. W. R. Brambell, but her most notable collaboration was with Professor Gregor Popa. Her observations on the brain of *Notoryctes* led to the hailed discovery of the vascular link between the hypothalamus and the pituitary gland. She and Popa published their joint findings in medical journals between 1930 and 1935.

On 1 October 1935 Una Fielding was appointed reader in neurological anatomy (neuroanatomy from 1937) at U.C.L. She hoped at last to write a major book on comparative anatomy, but the death in January 1939 of H. H. Woollard [q.v.12], Elliot Smith's successor, and the onset of World War II left her with even heavier teaching responsibilities. As acting-head of the anatomy department she organized the evacuation of all medical students and most staff to a house at Leatherhead, Surrey. In London her detailed drawings and notes for her book were lost in bombing-raids. Colleagues later claimed that her role in holding the medical faculty together was never properly acknowledged. She herself wryly summed up her role as at once 'head of department & anatomical Mrs. Mop, tutorial Mrs. Mop, and often domestic Mrs. Mop'.

Anxious to make a change, she resigned in April 1947 to become assistant-professor of anatomy at the new Farouk 1st University, Alexandria, Egypt. On 31 December 1951 she was dismissed as part of the Egyptian government's action against expatriates; she left Egypt in February 1952, forced to abandon the results of her latest research. In London she returned to teaching as visiting lecturer in neuroanatomy at St Mary's Hospital and St Thomas's Hospital medical schools. In September 1965 she was appointed to the Hunterian Museum of the Royal College of Surgeons to reorganize and summarize Elliot Smith's 1902 catalogue of the nervous system. A member of the British Federation of University Women, she lived at Crosby Hall, Chelsea. She died on 11 August 1969 in hospital at St Pancras.

Brown eyed, and dark haired in youth, Una Fielding was remembered as a tiny woman, always dressed in neat, dark clothing, and wearing a jaunty hat even while lecturing. Friends enjoyed her 'complete unconcern for appearances'. Though never robust, she retained a great zest for life and a lively interest in the modern and topical. She was well versed in literature and the arts, and was a stimulating conversationalist with a great sense of fun. As a teacher she had no problems of discipline: students, whom she treated as fellow scholars, sensed her uncompromising integrity.

Roy College of Surgeons of Eng, *Annual Report*, 1965-66 and *Annals*, 45, July-Dec 1969; *British Medical J* and *Lancet*, 30 Aug 1969; *MJA*, 13 Dec 1969; Aust Federation of Univ Women (Syd), *Newsletter*, no 32, Dec 1969; *J of Anatomy* (Lond), 106, no 2, 1970, p 209; *The Times*, 21 Aug 1969; *SMH*, 8 Dec 1923, 6 June 1925, 23 Sept 1969; U. L. Fielding papers (Roy College of Surgeons of Eng L, Lond); S. G. Fielding papers (ML); Univ College Lond Personnel Dept records; information from Prof R. E. M. Bowden, Lond.   SALLY O'NEILL

FIENBERG, DAVID MAXWELL; *see* FENBURY

FINCH, FREDERICK GEORGE PETER INGLE (1916-1977), actor, was born on 28 September 1916 at South Kensington, London. His putative father was George Ingle Finch, a research chemist from Australia. George was attached to the Imperial College of Science and Technology, London, served with the Royal Field Artillery in World War I and later became a famous mountaineer. Peter's mother was English-born Alicia Gladys Finch, née Fisher. Her husband divorced her in 1920 on the grounds of her adultery with Wentworth Edward Dallas Campbell, an Indian Army officer and Peter's real father. The full circumstances of his birth were not revealed to Finch until he was in his mid-forties.

George and his sister Dorothy had assumed custody of Peter before the divorce. They subsequently dispatched him to their mother Laura who presided over a salon of artists and musicians at Vaucresson, near Paris. Abandoning Continental sophistications for sub-continental simplicities, in 1925 she embarked on a pilgrimage to Adyar, the Theosophical community near Madras, India, with Peter in train. His waif-like aura and wafer-thin body proved irresistible, at least in the spiritual sense, for Adyar's twin panjandrums Dr Annie Besant and 'Bishop' C. W. Leadbeater [q.v.10]. From Dr Besant, Peter had lessons in meditation; 'Bishop' Leadbeater was more noted for his lessons in masturbation. Early in 1926, not unwillingly, the young Finch (without his grandmother) joined a shipload of Theosophists bound for their Australian headquarters in Sydney.

At their Garden School at Balmoral, Peter first learned to read and write English. He soon had to quit this progressive establishment when Laura's estranged husband Charles, a pillar of bourgeois rectitude, dis-covered his 'grandson's' existence in Sydney and removed him to the family home at Greenwich Point. Peter attended the local public school until 1929, and, over the next three years, North Sydney Intermediate Boys' High School. These institutions provided him with his earliest opportunities to show off his versatile dramatic talents. While working as a copy-boy for the *Sun*, he developed a taste for popular writing which might have developed into a career in journalism. He produced romantic verses, and yarns and sketches with a bush or army setting, several of which appeared in the *A.B.C. Weekly* in the early 1940s.

Travelling from the age of 19 with the tent-shows of George Sorlie [q.v.12], Finch had played in both variety and legitimate theatre. His acting interests were nurtured by the small, semi-professional repertory companies in Sydney. From 1937 he was under contract to the Australian Broadcasting Commission and later sought by Macquarie Broadcasting Services Pty Ltd because of his adaptable accent and richly resonant voice which—according to one commentator—'dripped sex appeal'. He won Macquarie awards for the best radio actor in 1946 and 1947, worked as a producer and as a compere, and wrote scripts based on his own fiction.

His luxuriantly wavy hair and his facial features—penetrating eyes, high cheekbones, tulip-shaped mouth, solid curving jawline—made him 'a natural' for the screen. He had taken prominent roles in several Australian feature films from the late 1930s, including *Dad and Dave Come to Town* (1938). Enlisting in the Australian Imperial Force on 2 June 1941, Finch served as a gunner in the 2nd/1st Anti-Aircraft Regiment in the Middle East (1941-42) and in Darwin (1942) where he entertained the troops with impromptu shows known as 'Finch's Follies'. He was then posted to concert parties throughout Australia and was granted leave to appear in some wartime documentaries for the Department of Information and in Charles Chauvel's [q.v.7] feature film, *Rats of Tobruk* (1944). Promoted sergeant, he was director of the Army Theatre Unit at Pagewood, Sydney, when discharged medically unfit on 31 October 1945. At St Stephen's Anglican Church, Woollahra, on 21 April 1943 he had married the Russian ballerina Tamara Rechemcinc ('Tchinarova'), a principal dancer with the Borovansky [q.v.13] company; they were to have one daughter.

After the war Finch kept up the tradition of touring theatre with the Mercury Mobile Players which performed in factories during the workers' lunch-hour. Its repertoire included serious drama and there was a theatre-school attached to it where Finch became a treasured teacher. He also prepared lectures on the history of Australian theatre for the Sydney University Dramatic Society. In a limited way, the Mercury enterprise provided an experimental model for an Australian national theatre. In August 1948 his performance in an English version of Molière's *Le Malade Imaginaire* so impressed the touring Sir Laurence (Lord) Olivier that he offered him a theatre contract, on the strength of which Finch left for London next year.

Another early patron was the English director, Harry Watt, who persuaded Ealing Studios to give Finch his first part in British films (in *Train of Events*, 1949). For a few years Finch successfully combined cinema with theatre, sharing the stage with the likes of Dame Edith Evans, (Sir) John Mills, Orson Welles and Claire Bloom. In addition, he worked for British Broadcasting Corporation radio and television programmes; but, after landing his first movie lead in the Hollywood production of *Elephant Walk* (1954), he concentrated almost exclusively on film.

His talents as a film actor were as versatile as in radio and theatre, and gained him international recognition. In 1947 he had been assistant-director of a documentary on Arnhem Land Aborigines, *Primitive People* (1949), an experience which stood him in good stead when, in 1959, he wrote and directed a fictionalized documentary on a young boy's life on the Spanish island of Ibiza: entitled *The Day* (1960), it won him awards in 1961 at film festivals at Venice, Italy, and Cork, Ireland. Although he only returned briefly to Australia for the shooting of *The Shiralee* and *Robbery under Arms* (both released in 1957), Finch had already made himself into something of a symbol of Australian maleness through his appearance as Nevil Shute's [q.v. Norway] hero, Joe Harman, in *A Town like Alice* (1956). In this role he most embodied the world's idea of the 'typical' Australian man—lean, intrepid and laconic—and won the first of several British Film Academy awards for best actor. Yet both his face and his voice were sufficiently flexible to attract demand for a vast range of character types: he won British academy awards for his portrayal of the title character in *The Trials of Oscar Wilde* (1960) and of the homosexual Jewish doctor in *Sunday Bloody Sunday* (1971).

Finch clearly radiated a catholic sensuality, though his character off the screen was quite assertively heterosexual. It was for his relationships, in his maturity, with a series of 'leading ladies' that he attained worldwide notoriety. An affair with Vivien Leigh, which began during the making of *Elephant Walk*, helped to precipitate the breakup of his marriage to Tamara. Following their divorce, he married a 25-year-old South African actress, Yolande Eileen Turnbull ('Turner'), on 4 July

1959 at the register office, Chelsea; they lived mainly in London and had a son and daughter. Press rumours in 1964 of a relationship with the singer Shirley Bassey proved the last straw for this marriage. Finch was to find greater stability in his relationship with Mavis 'Eletha' Barrett, with whom he lived from 1966 at her home in Jamaica; they had a daughter in 1969, were married in Rome on 9 November 1973 and remained together. Finch died of myocardial infarction on 14 January 1977 at Los Angeles, California, United States of America, and was buried in Hollywood Memorial Park. His wife and children survived him. Posthumously, he won British and American academy awards, as well as a Hollywood 'Golden Globe', for his role as the crazed television anchorman, Howard Beale, in *Network* (1976).

H. Porter, *Stars of Australian Stage and Screen* (Adel, 1965); D. Shipman, *The Great Movie Stars* (Lond, 1972); T. Faulkner, *Peter Finch* (Lond, 1979); E. Dundy, *Finch, Bloody Finch* (Lond, 1980); Y. Finch, *Finchy* (Lond, 1980); M. Pate, *An Entertaining War* (Syd, 1986); Univ Syd Union, *Union Recorder*, 3 Apr 1947; *Woman's Own*, 23 Sept 1961; *Good Housekeeping*, 100, no 5, Nov 1971, p 89; *The Times*, 10 Nov 1973, 15 Jan 1977; *SMH*, 16 Jan 1977; Finch papers (NL).

I. M. BRITAIN

FINCKH, ALFRED EDMUND (1866-1961), pathologist and *maître d'armes*, was born on 31 May 1866 in Sydney, second of four children of Hermann Finckh, a watchmaker and jeweller from Stuttgart, Württemberg, and his Swiss-born wife Sophia, née Moesch. The family moved from Surry Hills to North Sydney. From 1873 Alfred was educated at Reutlingen and remained in Germany to learn watchmaking. In 1885 he returned to New South Wales and worked as a jackeroo at Coonamble before studying arts and medicine on and off at the University of Sydney (M.B., 1905). While employed as a part-time assistant at the Technological Museum, he published several papers.

In 1898 Finckh was asked by Professor (Sir) Edgeworth David [q.v.8] to lead the third Royal Society expedition to Funafuti, Ellice Islands (Tuvalu). Completing the coral-reef boring proved exceptionally demanding, but, after four months, a final depth of 1114½ ft (340 m) was reached. With the government hydrographer Gerald Halligan [q.v.9], Finckh mapped parts of the reef, and dredged lagoon and reef samples. He detailed the distribution of reef organisms, the formation of reef rock and the growth rates of algae and corals. His paper was included in the Royal Society's monograph on the expedition's results. Awarded a research grant by the Royal

Society, in 1901 he investigated the Great Barrier Reef from Cooktown to Lizard Island, using a whaleboat and Aboriginal crew.

Having served as a resident medical officer at Sydney Hospital in 1905, Finckh studied pathology in Berlin, at Hamburg and at St Mary's Hospital, London. Back home in 1908, he was honorary pathologist (1912-18) at Sydney Hospital, and also at the Women's Hospital and the Anti-Tuberculosis Dispensary in 1914. His main energies during this period, however, were directed towards establishing the Sydney Clinical Research Laboratories at 227 Macquarie Street—one of the first private pathology practices in Australia. He was to continue in practice until the age of 90. Imbued with a zealousness that demanded the best diagnosis and treatment of patients, Finckh stressed basic aspects of medicinal and laboratory practice in regular letters to medical journals. He introduced the Wassermann test for syphilis to Sydney amid scepticism and outright mistrust. At St James's Anglican Church, Hyde Park, on 14 July 1913 he had married Melissa Dorcas Slade. In 1917 he designed and built their home at Mosman where he entertained the Naturalists' Society of New South Wales and specialized in growing native Australian plants.

To acquire and maintain physical, mental and emotional fitness, Finckh perfected and rigorously practised fencing as a discipline. He painstakingly taught 'Academic Fencing' in rooms at the rear of the Australia Hotel and described his method in three books. Founder of the Sydney Fencing Club and the Australian Amateur Fencing Federation, he belonged to the International Fencing Federation. He reluctantly gave up competitive foils after participating in the State championships in 1938, but continued as a teacher and critic. At the Olympic selection trials in 1959 and 1960 he deplored in biting tones the '*pauvre escrime*', calling out 'Fisticuffs!', 'It's a circus!' and 'You can't blame *them*, of course. It's the man who *taught* them!'

The embodiment of a healthy, disciplined mind in a healthy, disciplined body, Finckh was a lean, spry man, slightly deaf, with a wry sense of humour that often bubbled into his medical correspondence. Pistol-shooting accompanied his fencing prowess. He never appeared to worry, although in World War I he was subjected to snide anti-German comments, despite his Australian birth. His motto was 'Be Content'. Survived by his wife, son and daughter, he died on 2 September 1961 at Mosman and was cremated.

Hist Records of Aust Science, 7, no 4, June 1989, p 393; *Search*, 20, no 1, 1989, p 27; *Sth Pacific J of Natural Science*, 11, 1991, p 15; *SMH*, 1 July 1933, 22 Mar 1960, 9 Sept 1961; information from Dr D. Holt, Mosman, Prof E. Finckh, Univ Syd; Mr M. Finckh, Blackheath, NSW.

CAROL CANTRELL

FINDLAY, RETA MILDRED (1893-1954), businesswoman, was born on 11 July 1893 at Waterloo, Sydney, youngest of four children of native-born parents William James Carrad, bookbinder, and his wife Mary Elizabeth Jane, née Sinclair. Educated at Fort Street Model School, Reta had a passion for the theatre, spent considerable time painting and sketching, read widely in her father's extensive library and designed clothes which she persuaded others to make. On 19 May 1923 she married George Lanark Findlay at St Mark's Anglican Church, Darling Point. Prompted by the needs of his import business, the couple moved to Melbourne about 1930. Through 'force of circumstances', Reta began work as a commercial artist for a colour-printing and advertising firm, and rapidly rose to publicity manager.

In 1937 she became advertising manager for Georges Ltd, a department store in Collins Street. That year she travelled to Europe to attend fashion showings in London and Paris, and to find new ideas and merchandise. After her return, the store concentrated on retailing the most up-to-date women's fashions, promoting the work of leading European and American designers. The public face of Georges also changed under her direction. The store's logo was redesigned by the sculptor Clifford Last; window displays became elegantly sparse and dramatic; Georges' print advertisements were distinguished by their bold and economic use of artists' sketches and cleverly written copy; and mannequin parades were introduced.

Dissuaded by her employer from leaving Australia permanently, Findlay was sent in 1939 to the United States of America to survey the retail trade. She came back to Melbourne shortly after the outbreak of World War II, organized fund-raising benefits for the Australian Red Cross Society and established a women officers' club at Georges. A committed worker for charity, she was a life governor of the Queen Victoria and (Royal) Children's hospitals.

When, in January 1946, Findlay was appointed associate-director of Georges, she was one of the few female board-members of an Australian public company. During her travels through Europe and the U.S.A. that year, Georges' advertisements featured her 'Air Mail Diary' on a range of topics, including fashion and culture. This novel approach was typical of her talent for creating subtle and effective publicity. In 1949 she acted as general manager of Georges and in September 1950 was made a full director. Next year she left Australia, intending to settle elsewhere; by 1952, however, she had returned to assist with Georges' preparations for the impending royal tour. Her coronation windows drew large crowds of admirers.

Neat and slimly built, Reta was, by her own description, a 'plain' woman. Yet, always impeccably groomed and dressed in the latest fashion, she set the trend for fashion-conscious Melburnians and her outfits often caused a sensation. Her staff knew her as Miss Findlay; her business manner was described as calm and serene. She was, none the less, one who set and achieved her objectives. Blessed with a fertile imagination and a vivacious personality, she could get on with anyone, regardless of background, sex or position. Her flair for fashion promotion, publicity, display and for fostering talent transformed Georges.

Reta Findlay died of atherosclerotic cardiorenal failure on 14 June 1954 in East Melbourne. On 17 June Georges was closed until 1 p.m. while almost all its staff attended her funeral service at St Paul's Cathedral. She was cremated. Her husband survived her; they had no children.

K. Dunstan, *The Store on the Hill* (Melb, 1979); *People* (Syd), 12 Aug 1953; *Sun News-Pictorial*, 26 June 1946, 15, 18 June 1954, 7 Sept 1956; *Herald* (Melb), 29 Apr 1947, 17 Apr, 15, 17 June 1954; *Argus*, 6 Sept 1950, 15 June 1954; *Age* (Melb), 15, 16 June 1954; information from Mr K. Carrad, Port Macquarie, NSW.   ROGER LEONG

FINK, ESME MARY SORRETT (1894-1967), who became the rani of Pudukota (Pudukkottai), was born on 15 September 1894 at Malvern, Melbourne, younger daughter of Wolfe Fink (d.1914), a barrister and Shakespearian scholar from Guernsey, Channel Islands, and his Tasmanian-born wife Elizabeth, née Watt. Molly, as she was always known, was a niece of Benjamin and Theodore Fink [qq.v.4,8]. Although baptized a Catholic, she attended (1904-09) Lauriston Girls' High School. A golden-haired society beauty, with blue eyes, an 'oval, ivory-skinned face' and 'pouting pomegranate lips', she had charm and character. On a visit to Sydney in April 1915 she met Marthanda Bhairava Tondiman (b.1875), rajah of the southern India principality of Pudukota, who followed her from the Australia Hotel to the Hydro Majestic at Medlow Bath in the Blue Mountains where their love affair blossomed. Following their marriage on 10 August that year at the office of the government statist, Melbourne, they encountered sustained hostility from the Australian press. The government of India—with the endorsement of King George V—refused to recognize the marriage or permit the rani to be designated 'Her Highness', and recommended that her entertainment by British officials in India (and Australia) be as private as possible.

After a honeymoon in the United States of America, Molly arrived in her husband's principality late in 1915. She was received enthusiastically by his subjects, but remained in Pudukota barely five months: the attitude of the British government to her marriage rendered her position untenable, and an attempt was made to poison her with oleander leaves when it was discovered that she was pregnant. The rajah's suspicions centred on the palace. He took Molly to Ootacamund. Denied permission to buy a house there, they left India on 16 April 1916; she was never to return.

In Sydney they rented St Mervyns, a waterfront mansion at Double Bay, and on 22 July Molly gave birth to a son, Marthanda Sydney. In self-imposed exile, the rajah became prominent in racing circles in Melbourne and Sydney; his gelding, King Mostyn, netted over £1000 in prize-money and Old Mungindi won the Grand National Steeplechase (July 1917). Molly's closest friends in Sydney were Ada Holman, the wife of the premier, and Ethel Kelly [qq.v.9].

Determined to press their case for recognition, the Tondimans left Australia in August 1919. He gained an interview with Lord Willingdon, governor of Madras, who asked Lord Cromer to help one 'so intensely loyal and *white* in his ways'. The rajah joined Molly in London on 7 November. By the end of 1920 it was clear that the British government would not acknowledge their son as the heir to the principality. The rajah accepted a regency, in return for substantial financial 'compensation' and annual allowances for himself and Molly.

In September 1922 they bought the villa, La Favorite, at Cannes, France. There they cultivated the friendship of the famous, including Edward Molyneux, Elsa Maxwell, the novelist William Locke, and (Sir) Cecil Beaton who sketched and photographed Molly for *Vogue*. Celebrated for her sparkling jewels and 'glittering parties', she was described by Nancy Beaton as 'a very generous woman, madly extravagant'. The rajah died suddenly on 28 May 1928 and was cremated with Hindu rites in London, after Molly and her son were refused permission to fly his remains to India.

From the 1930s Molly lived mainly in London; she visited France frequently and stayed in the United States in 1929, 1937-38 and in 1940-44. During World War II, with her income frozen, she worked, illegally, at the fashionable New York clothing store, Bonwit Teller & Co. She also collected money for the United Service Organizations for National

Defence; although she was accused of embezzlement, she was cleared by the Federal Bureau of Investigation. She was estranged from her son following his imprisonment in 1945 for stealing jewellery. In 1967 she donated her lavish wardrobe, which included classic gowns by Callot Soeurs, Paquin, Patou, Vionnet, Schiaparelli and Chanel, to the Museum of Costume, Bath, England. Survived by her son, Molly died of cancer on 20 November that year at Cannes. Her ashes were placed with the rajah's at Golders Green crematorium, London.

E. Duyker and C. Younger, *Molly and the Rajah* (Syd, 1991), and for bibliog; *Smith's Weekly*, 4 June 1927.
EDWARD DUYKER
CORALIE YOUNGER

FINK, LEO (1901-1972), manufacturer and Jewish welfare worker, was born on 31 October 1901 at Bialystok, Poland, then part of the Russian Empire, eldest son of Mordechai Fink, manufacturer, and his wife Masia, née Jablonska. Educated at Zeligman's Gymnasium, Bialystok, Leo worked in a pioneer corps in Palestine for two years and in 1922-26 studied civil engineering in Berlin and at Altenburg, Germany. He then joined his family's woollen-mill at Galatz, Rumania, but the business was not a success.

In 1928 Fink and two of his brothers emigrated to Victoria and went to a farm at Berwick which had been established to assist Jewish settlement. After a year they moved to Melbourne to start a family business: the venture led to the formation of United Woollen Mills Pty Ltd and United Carpet Mills Pty Ltd. Fink returned to Bialystok where, on 20 September 1932, he married MIRIAM (MINA) Waks (1913-1990). She accompanied him to Melbourne.

Drawn to the Kadimah—a society dedicated to maintaining interest in Jewish history, and Yiddish language and culture—Fink was a committee-member (from 1938) and president (1940). In 1943-47 he presided over the United Jewish Overseas Relief Fund, set up to assist survivors of the Holocaust. Under his leadership it quickly became the largest Jewish organization in the country. From the end of World War II the U.J.O.R.F. also helped those who had lived through the atrocities of Nazism to emigrate and settle in Australia. Melbourne became the focus of the movement and Fink a leader in combating government and public pressure to limit levels of Jewish immigration. He developed a close relationship with Arthur Calwell [q.v.13], minister for immigration in the Chifley [q.v.13] government.

Because much of its work involved resettlement issues, the U.J.O.R.F. merged with the Australian Jewish Welfare Society in 1947 to form the Australian Jewish Welfare and Relief Society. Fink was elected president of the new body, a position he held until 1960. During this period he filled various roles on both the Victorian Jewish Board of Deputies and the Executive Council of Australian Jewry. He travelled frequently to Europe and the United States of America, raising funds for the A.J.W.R.S.'s immigration programme and representing Australia at Jewish conferences. In 1963 Australian Wool Industries Pty Ltd, of which Fink was founding chairman, opened a factory at Ashdod, Israel, to process Australian wool.

Fink's support for multiculturalism brought him into conflict with those who espoused assimilation, as well as with some local Zionists who considered that Jewish migrants should have been encouraged to go to Israel rather than Australia. In 1959 the Hebrew Immigration Assistance Service, U.S.A., granted him an award of honour. Survived by his wife, son and daughter, he died of cancer on 20 September 1972 at Fitzroy and was buried in Melbourne general cemetery. Three buildings bear his name: a block of A.J.W.R.S. units for the elderly, at St Kilda, and the Kadimah Hall, and Jewish Holocaust Museum and Research Centre, both at Elsternwick. His widow Mina, who had been a director (1947-76) of the A.J.W.R.S. and president (1967-73) of the National Council of Jewish Women, was appointed M.B.E. in 1974.

S. D. Rutland, *Edge of the Diaspora* (Syd, 1988); H. L. and W. D. Rubinstein, *The Jews in Australia*, 1-2 (Melb, 1991); *Aust Jewish News*, 29 Sept 1972; Aust Jewish Welfare and Relief Soc reports and minute-books *and* United Jewish Overseas Relief Fund, Annual Reports (Aust Jewish Welfare Soc Archives, Melb); Vic Jewish Bd of Deputies *and* Executive Council of Aust Jewry, Annual Reports (Aust Jewish Hist Soc Vic Inc Archives, Melb); W. M. Lippmann papers (Jewish Welfare Soc, Melb, Archives); L. and M. Fink papers (Univ Melb Archives).
RODNEY L. BENJAMIN

FINNAN, FRANCIS JOSEPH (1897-1966), politician and public servant, was born on 23 September 1897 in Crown Street, Sydney, son of native-born parents Thomas Joseph Finnan, compositor, and his wife Margaret, née Gorman. Frank spent much of his childhood in The Rocks area where his grandfather was licensee of the Hero of Waterloo hotel. Educated at St James School, Glebe, and St Aloysius' College, Milsons Point, until the age of 14, he worked as a messenger for the Sydney Tramways Office before travelling around the shearing sheds as tar-boy, rouseabout and woolclasser. He joined the

Australian Workers' Union in Queensland and became involved in trade-union politics and the Australian Labor Party. On 11 October 1926 he married with Catholic rites Rita Irene Puig at Mary Immaculate Church, Waverley, Sydney.

Moving to the Lithgow district, Finnan conducted a liquor business and cultivated strong links with the coal-mining unions. During the Depression his business declined. He returned to Sydney, joined the Miners' Federation newspaper, *Common Cause*, as a commission agent, then obtained a post on the business staff of the *Labor Daily*. After that newspaper was taken over by Consolidated Press Ltd in the late 1930s, he remained as a liaison officer.

As an A.L.P. candidate, in May 1941 Finnan won the Legislative Assembly seat of Hawkesbury by only 130 votes; in rural areas he asked people to vote for 'Finnan, the Farmers' Friend'. Having fostered the building of a hospital at Gosford, he was its first president (1946). He held Hawkesbury until May 1950 when boundary changes forced him to move to the inner-Sydney electorate of Darlinghurst, a safe Labor seat. When it, too, was abolished before the 1953 elections, he unsuccessfully contested Albury.

Elected to cabinet in February 1947, Finnan served as minister in charge of tourist activities and immigration; from March 1948 until February 1953 he held the portfolios of labour and industry, and social welfare. His responsibilities included pricing policy—an unpopular task in an electorate increasingly impatient with lingering price controls from World War II—and he chaired the interstate conference of prices ministers. He was also a member of Taronga Zoological Park Trust and a councillor (elected by the Legislative Assembly) of the New South Wales University of Technology.

As a reward for his long political loyalty and effectiveness in difficult portfolios, in 1953 Finnan was gazetted president of the Hunter District Water Board. The controversial political appointment was resisted strongly because it infringed established practice of promotion from within the board. In a sermon on the coronation of Queen Elizabeth II the Anglican dean of Newcastle, Rev. W. A. Hardie, strayed from his subject to denounce Finnan's nomination as a blatant example of political corruption and 'spoils for the victor'. A public meeting endorsed by a substantial majority a resolution condemning Finnan as unqualified for the post.

Finnan's diplomacy and relaxed administrative style gradually conquered public and institutional resentment, although criticism sometimes surfaced about his closeness to trade unionism and his laxness with staff. Seemingly 'able to extract money from the Treasury at will', he used his political connexions to negotiate favourable financial arrangements with the State government for the extension of water services in the Hunter Valley, particularly for constructing the Grahamstown reservoir. He also made money available for extensive sewerage works so that retrenched miners could be employed. In 1960 he was appointed C.B.E. When he reached the statutory retiring age in 1962, the government passed special legislation enabling him to continue for another term. He retired in 1964.

Accepted as a Novocastrian, Finnan was a council-member (1959-66) of Newcastle University College (University of Newcastle from 1965), chairman of the Hunter Valley Research Foundation, a member of the Newcastle Regional Development Committee and of the Newcastle International Sports Centre Trust, and a director of the Mater Misericordiae Hospital, Waratah. Lively, with 'a sparkling sense of humour', he was 'a big, beefy man with a red meaty face, bushy eyebrows and silky silver hair'. Throughout his life he was 'infuriated by bureaucracy in any form'. A member of the Journalists' Club, he enjoyed gardening, angling and good food. He died of cancer on 21 March 1966 in the Mater hospital and was buried in Sandgate cemetery. His wife and daughter survived him.

C. Lloyd et al, *For the Public Health* (Melb, 1992); *PD* (NSW), 22 Mar 1956, p 4409; *Newcastle Morning Herald*, 8, 19 Sept 1964, 22, 24 Mar 1966; *Bulletin*, 3 Oct 1964.   C. J. LLOYD

FINNIS, DOROTHY MARY KELL (1903-1970), physiotherapist, was born on 10 March 1903 at Unley Park, Adelaide, daughter of Alfred Edward Simpson, a draughtsman in the civil service, and his South Australian-born wife Frances Isabella, née Kell. Educated at Walford House School, Mollie edited the school magazine and was head prefect in 1920. After two years study, in 1924 she obtained the diploma of the South Australian branch of the Australasian Massage Association. She worked part time at the Adelaide Children's Hospital for twenty years while also practising privately. At the hospital, cases of anterior poliomyelitis had been treated with rest, splinting and passive movements, but she was among those who developed a new treatment by adding the active re-education of individual muscles. She made a major contribution during the 1937-38 and subsequent polio epidemics.

Her well-informed interest in music combined with a deep religious faith to provide a background to her happy marriage. On 6 January 1945 in St Peter's Anglican Cathedral, Adelaide, she married a widower,

Rev. (later Canon) Horace Percy Finnis (d.1960), the organist and the bishop's vicar. In 1944-64 Mrs Finnis was a part-time lecturer in physiotherapy at the University of Adelaide and a part-time supervisor of students' practical work in paediatrics at the Adelaide Children's Hospital. A member (1948-58) of the hospital's house-committee, she was to be granted life membership in 1965. She made a special contribution to the treatment of spastic children and in 1944-58 served on several committees of the Crippled Children's Association of South Australia. The sole president (1945-57) of the Spastic Children's Parents' Group and its successor the Crippled Children's Auxiliary (Spastic Group), she was appointed M.B.E. in 1953.

Professionally, Mary Finnis's most original contribution was in appreciating that some so-called idiopathic orthopaedic deformities could have a neurological cause resulting in abnormal tone. She helped undergraduates and senior graduates to understand her concept of the need to look at the whole person before planning treatment. A sweet-faced, plump, quietly spoken woman, she had a pretty wit, but was not a born teacher. Once she formulated an idea, Finnis was never side-tracked. Although her students did not always receive strong directives, they came to appreciate her innovative mind. In 1952-65 she was the university's representative on the Physiotherapists' Board of South Australia; she was also a foundation member (1958) of the Physiotherapy Society of South Australia.

An avid reader, from 1932 Finnis had belonged to the Tatlers Club, a literary society. She and her husband were foundation members (1932) of the Friends of St Peter's Cathedral and remained active in the group until 1954. In the following year they moved from the cathedral vicarage to Rose Park. Mrs Finnis continued to treat patients until shortly before her death. She died of myocardial infarction on 19 May 1970 in the Royal Adelaide Hospital and was buried in North Road cemetery, Rosebery; she had no children.

SA Branch Physiotherapy Newsletter, July 1970; Friends of St Peter's Cathedral, Minute-books, 1932-55 (Mort L); information from Miss J.-M. Ganne, Netherby, and Mrs M. C. Saddler, Wattle Park, Adel.   JOYCE GIBBERD

FINNIS, HAROLD JACK (1889-1980), administrator, was born on 29 August 1889 at Parkside, Adelaide, son of John Mercer Finnis (d.1909), civil servant, and his wife Florence Matilda, née Lockwood. Captain John Finnis [q.v.1] was Harold's grandfather. Educated by a governess, at Malvern Grammar and Unley Public schools, and at Muirden [q.v.10] College for Business Training, in 1905 Harold entered the State public service as a junior clerk. As a young man he read papers on religious subjects, sang in choirs, and joined literary societies and model parliaments; in 1911-13 he also attended lectures on economics and botany at the University of Adelaide. At Manthorpe Memorial Church, Unley, on 26 December 1914 he married with Congregational forms Gladys Muriel James; they were to have a daughter and a son.

In 1911 Finnis had moved from the Produce Department to the Agriculture Department; four years later he was assistant-secretary to the Advisory Board of Agriculture, librarian, and editor of the *Journal of Agriculture*; by 1921 he was secretary to the board. The work of the board grew and he claimed responsibility for two innovations: the establishment of women's branches (1917) and a press news service—'both in the face of official opposition'. In 1925 he was appointed secretary of the Royal Agricultural and Horticultural Society of South Australia. Next year he directed his first show at Wayville. As secretary (until 1955) and director-secretary (1955-59), the 'unflappable' Finnis presided efficiently and firmly over increasingly larger and more complicated annual shows, rising attendances, the construction of buildings, new uses for the grounds and, to some extent, also over his governing council. He was appointed M.B.E. in 1939.

During World War II the showgrounds were used for defence purposes. From 1940 to 1946 Finnis was secretary of the Business Administration Committee which reported to the Department of Defence Co-ordination. In 1947 he resumed his administration of the R.A.H.S.S.A.'s affairs, oversaw the restoration of buildings and grounds, and, despite continuing austerity, held the first postwar show. His personal qualities 'contributed towards the marked progress' of the organization. Through the society, he assisted the wine industry, stud breeders and country show societies, and fostered relations between primary producers' organizations.

Finnis was a founder of the Adelaide Rotary Club and president (1939-40) of the Rotary Club of Australia. With his work on the Libraries Board of South Australia (1942-74) and the board of commissioners of the National Park (1943-63), his civic service became more varied and demanding. He was a governor (1947-69) of the Adelaide Botanic Garden, a council-member (1950-75) and president (1950-53) of the State branch of the Royal Geographical Society of Australasia, president (1957-68) of the Pioneers' Association of South Australia and chairman (1961-75) of the State working party of the

Australian Dictionary of Biography. As office-bearer, member, or founder, he was associated with numerous other organizations, including the Liberal and Country League, and became known as 'Adelaide's busiest man'.

A commanding figure, over six feet (183 cm) tall, Finnis had a no-nonsense, time-saving, but punctilious manner, especially during meetings. He dressed conservatively, belonged (from 1944) to the Adelaide Club and drove a Jaguar motorcar. Somewhat patrician in outlook, he was friendly and courteous, and liked the company of those who shared his enthusiasms. Gardening and collecting Australiana were lifelong interests; he also found time for historical research, and gave talks and published papers on his findings. His official, civic and private activities complemented each other in his concern for the progress, well-being and history of South Australia. Survived by his wife and daughter, he died on 19 August 1980 in North Adelaide and was cremated.

C. and M. Kerr, *Royal Show* (Adel, 1983); *Public Service Review*, June 1920; *Observer* (Adel), 21 May 1921, 19 Dec 1925; *Advertiser* (Adel), 2 Jan 1939, 21, 22 Aug 1980; Finnis papers (Mort L); N. Adams, interview with H. J. Finnis, 7 Sept 1969 (D5573/5 sound, Mort L).

G. L. FISCHER

FISHER, BETTIE (1939?-1976), singer and Aboriginal theatre administrator, was born possibly in 1939 at Berry, New South Wales, daughter of Leslie Amburlah and his wife Christine, née Connolly. Bettie belonged to the Jirrinja people on the Greenwell Point Mission; her totem was Mirrigan (dog). In the mid-1940s she moved with her family to Newcastle and attended Cardiff Public School until she was expelled at the age of 12. Her marriage to a man named Fisher ended in divorce. Bettie Fisher had seventeen years (c.1954-71) experience as a jazz and blues singer on the New South Wales and Queensland club circuits. On 2 December 1962 she sang *Up a Lazy River* and *Basin Street Blues* on 'Bandstand' on television station TCN-9. In the 1960s she appeared with Jimmy and Freddy Little in the first all-Black show to do the club rounds. She joined (1971) the executive-committee of the Foundation for Aboriginal Affairs, a non-government funded Aboriginal rights organization.

In 1974 Bettie Fisher became administrator of the newly established Black Theatre Arts and Cultural Centre in a Redfern warehouse leased from the Methodist Church for $15 000 a year. The centre was an Aboriginal initiative that received—after sixteen months of lobbying—minimal government funding ($9200) from the Department of Aboriginal Affairs in 1975 and in the following year a grant from the Federal government of $86 000. With the help of friends such as Tom Hogan and Kevin Cook from the Australian Builders' Labourers Federation, she renovated the old warehouse and developed a theatre and studio area. The centre ran drama classes under Bryan Syron, held workshops for inner-city Blacks in modern dancing, tribal dancing, writing for theatre, karate and photography, and provided a venue for new Aboriginal drama. Under Fisher's direction a dance company of five girls and two boys was formed.

The first play staged at the theatre, *The Chocolate Frog*, was written by Jim McNeil; due to Fisher's initiatives, it was the subject of workshops conducted for inmates of Sydney prisons. Another of the earliest plays to be performed at the centre was *The Cake Man*, written by Robert Merritt from Erambie Aborigines' Reserve, Cowra, and directed by Bob Maza, with Black leads taken by Justine Saunders and Zac Martin. The centre also functioned as an informal meeting-place for Redfern Blacks who previously had few places in which to gather, save for the local pubs where they encountered prejudice from the Whites and aggression from the police.

Fisher contacted touring international Black artists to invite them to perform at the Black Theatre. Despite resistance by a number of non-Aboriginal entertainment managers, visitors included Russand Roland Kirk, Roberta Flack, the band, 'Osibisa', and the Ghanaian drummers. Following the death of her lover Alan King, she and Tom Hogan held a marriage ceremony in 1972 at the Black Theatre hall. A physically striking woman, tall and robust, with dark skin and green eyes, she had presence, as well as a passionate commitment to Black rights. Fisher was involved in negotiations with the Department of Education to introduce 'Aboriginality' to schools. She hoped that representatives from each major Black organization, together with Black performers and painters, would visit schools to address students and demonstrate the richness of their culture. In April 1976 she took part in the opening of an 'Aboriginal Embassy' in Mugga Way, Canberra.

Earlier that year Maza had claimed, 'It's easy to attack her because she's a loud-mouthed woman, rough, arrogant, independent of men and has this animosity for whites. But she needs support rather than attack. She's got a raw sort of courage . . . You've got to give her her due: she's a real boots-and-all campaigner'. Bettie Fisher died of coronary arteriosclerosis on 12 May 1976 at Royal South Sydney Hospital and was cremated; her ashes were interred in the Methodist section of Botany cemetery.

Aboriginal Affairs Mthly, 1, Oct 1974; *Mereki*, 1, 15 Nov 1974, p 25; *Identity*, July 1975, p 28, July 1976, p 13, Oct 1976, p 10; *Theatre Quarterly*, Summer 1977, p 98; *SMH*, 11 Jan 1975, 13 May 1976; *Sun-Herald*, 22 June 1975; *National Times*, 12-17 Jan 1976, p 26; information from Mr T. Hogan, Glendale, and P. Fiske, Bondi, Syd.

ANNA COLE
WENDY LEWIS

FISHER, CHARLES DOUGLAS (1921-1978), headmaster, was born on 8 October 1921 at Repton, Derbyshire, England, third of six sons of Rev. Geoffrey Francis (Baron) Fisher, headmaster of Repton School and later archbishop of Canterbury, and his wife Rosamond Chevallier, née Forman. Educated at Marlborough College, Charles was commissioned in the Royal Regiment of Artillery in July 1941 and served in Egypt, Sicily and Italy during World War II. At the University of Oxford (B.A., 1948; M.A., 1953) he represented Keble College at rowing and Rugby Union football, presided over the junior common-room, was a live-wire Christian and 'chiefly organized...."Foot-the-ball" contests of sturdiness and agility between the Gentlemen of Cambridge and the Sportsmen of Oxford'. Tallish and strongly built, round faced and keen, he loved activity. He was a practical joker whose laugh 'gurgled to the surface' then exploded infectiously.

On 15 April 1952, at Canterbury Cathedral, Fisher married Anne Gilmour Hammond. From 1948 to 1955 he taught at Harrow School and in 1955-61 was senior master of Peterhouse, at Marandellas in his wife's homeland, Southern Rhodesia (Zimbabwe). Briefly back in England, at Sherborne School, he moved to Adelaide in 1962 to became headmaster of Scotch College which he transformed, economically and educationally, by adding a new junior school, science laboratories and a chapel, and by instituting a comprehensive outdoor programme and making strong staff appointments.

In the same way, from 1970 to 1973, Fisher put the Church of England Grammar School, East Brisbane, on a better footing: he promoted new educational ideas, raised academic standards, strengthened financial management and established close rapport with staff, parents and boys. He increased the number of houses from six to sixteen to improve pastoral care, stimulated music, created an art department and introduced electives in Asian languages, defensive driving and bachelor cooking. Anne took parties of boys from the school—and some girls—on weekend camps. The boys were 'darling' to her and she was 'Mum'—a restless mum, radical in middle age.

Although strongly opposed to dogma, paraphernalia, symbolism and verbiage in religion, Charles was a conservative. Yet, after moving to Victoria in 1974 on his appointment as headmaster of Geelong Church of England Grammar School, where there were already some girls, he embraced co-education. He found it an asset in music, art, drama and debating, as well as financially. Faced by falling enrolments, he recognized that his previous attitudes were archaic and supported the school council's decision to amalgamate with two girls' schools, Clyde and The Hermitage, despite contingent problems at G.G.S.'s alpine outpost, Timbertop. He skilfully promoted the change as a great educational experiment.

The administrative tasks were forbidding: numbers rose to 1600 on four widely spread sites, and new amenities and new rules were needed. Attitudes had to be changed among a previously male-dominated staff. But in the testing situation Fisher seemed 'as indestructible as a red gum' and remarkably relaxed. His laugh, his cheery, bespectacled face, his participation in plays and his determination to know every pupil at the Corio campus by name, earned him support.

Apart from increased classroom and boarding accommodation, and a theatre, the major building undertaken at this time was a resource-centre, later named the Fisher Library. It was partly funded by the Federal government whose centralism he loved to castigate. Like any meddling with independent schools, the 41-page questionnaire from the Australian Schools Commission in 1974, on which calculations of affluence affecting recurrent grants were based, made him fume. So he worked hard in support of the G.G.S. Endowment Trust, launched in 1976, hoping that it would be a hedge against fee increases and government influence.

Fisher was a manager rather than a thinker. Despite personal optimism, he was pessimistic about encouraging young people to think independently when so many were obviously destined to work in hierarchical institutions. His rather bland desire for his school was that it should balance the development of individuality with the inculcation of attitudes and skills useful to the community, the nation and the world.

Secretary-treasurer (1965-75) and treasurer (from 1976) of the Headmasters' Conference of the Independent Schools of Australia, Fisher was also chairman of the education committee of the Australian Council for Rehabilitation of [the] Disabled. The complexity of G.G.S. and the move to co-education absorbed most of his energy, and the long distance to Timbertop may have claimed his life: while making a routine visit, he died on 5 December 1978 when his car left the road and hit a tree near Kanumbra. Survived by his wife, four sons and two daughters, he was cremated. G.G.S. and C.E.G.S., Brisbane, hold his portraits by Charles Bush.

W. Bate, *Light Blue Down Under* (Melb, 1990); Geelong C of E Grammar School, *Corian*, 104, no 1, May 1979; *Sunday Mail*(Brisb), 22 Oct 1972; *Courier-Mail*, 3 Sept 1977.   WESTON BATE

FISHER, JOHN (1910-1960), journalist, was born on 7 June 1910 in South Melbourne, fifth of six children of Scottish-born Andrew Fisher [q.v.8], prime minister, and his wife Margaret Jane, née Irvine, from Queensland. The family moved to London in 1915. Apart from one year in a state school at St Kilda when the Fishers revisited Melbourne in 1921, John was educated in England, from 1922 to 1929 at Merchant Taylors' School, London. Having travelled in Europe, in 1930 he returned to Melbourne where (Sir) Keith Murdoch [q.v.10] gave him a cadetship on the *Herald*.

In 1934 Fisher's life was transformed by the arrival in Australia of Egon Erwin Kisch [q.v.], a Czechoslovakian communist who had been invited as a star delegate to the All-Australia Congress of the Movement Against War and Fascism, to be held in Melbourne in November. The Federal government prohibited Kisch from landing and the case became a *cause célèbre*. As publicity manager of the Kisch reception committee, Fisher helped to have the ban overturned. Kisch sailed for Europe in March 1935 and Fisher accompanied him. During the voyage he provided material for Kisch's witty and perceptive book, *Australian Landfall* (London, 1937). Fisher was one of its English translators.

From 1935 Fisher was based in Moscow: he worked as sub-editor on the *Moscow News*, published an article in *International Literature* (October) and in Paris attended the first International Congress of Writers for the Defence of Culture. In 1936 he moved between Moscow, Brussels, London and Berlin. Following the insurrection in Spain in July, he was active in the Republican cause. At Barcelona in 1937 he was Australian representative on the World Committee for Aid to Republican Spain, and was liaison officer between that body and the Spanish Relief committees in Melbourne and Sydney. In August he co-organized the British Empire press delegation to Madrid. Back in Australia next year, he spoke on public platforms about his Spanish experiences.

Politics were Fisher's passion and journalism his trade. He was assistant foreign editor of the *Labor Daily* (Sydney), then Canberra correspondent for the communist newspaper,

Tribune, from September 1939 until it was banned in May 1940. Seeking to enter Federal parliament, in 1939 he had tried unsuccessfully to gain Labor Party pre-selection for his father's old seat of Wide Bay, Queensland, before standing in New South Wales in 1940 as State Labor candidate for Hume and receiving only 4.9 per cent of the vote.

In Canberra he had met Elizabeth Skelton, a stenographer on the Hansard staff; they were married on 19 August 1941 at the registrar general's office, Sydney. On 6 June 1942 they sailed for Vladivostok, *en route* to Moscow where Fisher freelanced and was the Australian Broadcasting Commission's war commentator. The A.B.C. terminated his regular broadcasts in January 1943. That month he became press attaché to the Australian legation at Kuibyshev; Beth worked as its clerical officer.

After the cessation of hostilities in Europe the Fishers shifted to Prague. John continued freelancing and Beth was employed by the publishers, McGraw-Hill. Told to leave Czechoslovakia in 1949, he spent the next years in London. The couple separated and were to be divorced in 1959. He settled in Sydney in 1954. Although he had brief stints as a sub-editor, his days in journalism were over. His application in 1955 for a position with the United Nations Educational, Scientific and Cultural Organization was blocked by the Department of External Affairs because of an unsatisfactory security assessment and a negative report by the Department of Labour and National Service.

Tall, extremely thin and ascetic, Fisher was a serious, selfless and impulsive man who tried 'to make the world a better place'. His only interest outside politics was in Shakespearian drama. He took a job as a mailsorter in the General Post Office, Sydney. Survived by his two sons, he died of coronary vascular disease on 25 August 1960 at Plympton, Adelaide, and was buried in Centennial Park cemetery.

Worker's Weekly, Mar, Apr 1939; *Tribune* (Syd), 1 Sept 1939, 8 Sept 1939-Apr 1940; A989, item 1943/845/10/2, A472/1, item W16406, A1066/1, item PI45/226, A1068/1, item IC47/22/18/1 and A1838/261, item 2154/1/14 (AA, Canb); W. Powell, Draft and notes for B.A. Hons thesis on John Fisher, Univ Syd, c1984 (copy held by author, O'Connor, Canb); information from Mrs B. Fisher, Cairns, Qld.   AMIRAH INGLIS

FISKEN, ARCHIBALD CLYDE WANLISS (1897-1970), grazier and politician, was born on 11 March 1897 at Ballarat, Victoria, son of Archibald James Fisken, grazier, and his wife Beatrice May, née Wanliss, both Victorian born. Educated at E. N. Marryatt's Church of

England Grammar School for Boys, Ballarat, at Ballarat College and at Geelong Church of England Grammar School, he was commissioned in the Royal Field Artillery on 27 August 1916. A letter of recommendation from his Geelong Grammar headmaster, F. E. Brown [q.v.7], praised Clyde's leadership qualities, noting that he possessed 'a fine public spirit and . . . is thoroughly manly'. Fisken served with the 281st (London) Brigade on the Western Front in 1916-18 and with the occupation forces in Germany in 1919. For keeping 'his guns firing with great determination' during an enemy attack, he had been awarded the Military Cross in 1918. He was wounded that year and promoted lieutenant.

On his return, Fisken absorbed himself in managing Lal Lal, the family property at Yendon, where merino sheep and Shorthorn cattle grazed on 10 000 well-watered acres; the property had long been famous for its Shorthorns. He had inherited conservative traditions, both a sense of place and property, and of community service. Lal Lal had been in the family since 1846; the family name, through his father and grandfather, had been continuously represented in the Buninyong Shire Council from 1864. Elected to the council in 1922—the year before his father's death and his inheritance of Lal Lal—Clyde remained on it until his death, and was president in 1931-32, 1946-47, 1957-58 and 1966-67. He was prominent in the Ballarat Agricultural and Pastoral Society. In 1927 he had donated the Fisken Cup as a perpetual sports trophy for competition between primary school students, the meetings being held initially at Lal Lal. Fisken himself was an effective batsman with the Golden Point Cricket Club. On 20 February 1924 at Mona Vale Chapel, Ross, Tasmania, he had married with Anglican rites Elspeth Anne Cameron, daughter of a prominent Tasmanian wool producer.

At the 1934 Federal elections Fisken won the House of Representatives seat of Ballarat for the United Australia Party. During the campaign he declared himself to be 'an ordinary business man' and 'no professional politician'. He refuted claims that he was a 'snob' and 'unapproachable' by citing his cricketing activities. Handsome, with strong features, full lips and a moustache, Fisken startled the House when he rose to make his maiden speech in 'full morning dress and white spats in a great splash of sartorial splendour'. But his concerns were serious enough. He was greatly troubled by unemployment, believing that 'humanitarian reasons alone' demanded a solution to the problem and that 'all the ills of the country would be rectified' if it were solved. He also worked for the expansion of repatriation benefits. With a reputation for common sense rather than for oratory, he was

mentioned as a ministerial possibility, but decided not to re-contest Ballarat in 1937. He gave as the reason a commitment to his appointment as founding chairman (1936) of the Australian Meat Board, but Canberra's political intrigue was uncongenial to him.

The Meat Board's primary role was in regulating meat exports, mostly to the British market. Fisken served as chairman until the board was reconstituted in 1946. In his first six years of office he endeavoured to increase Australian meat quotas to Britain and to expand the market for Australian beef in North America; in addition, he negotiated wartime contracts with Britain. From 1943 the board's role was largely superseded by the wider wartime powers given to the Meat Industry Commission, to which Fisken was appointed. In 1943-45 he acted as deputy-controller of meat supplies for Victoria.

Fisken was chairman of Dennys Lascelles [qq.v.4,5] Ltd, a director of the Commercial Union Assurance Co. and chairman of its Victorian board, and a life member, trustee and council-member for thirty-five years of the Royal Agricultural Society of Victoria. Much of his time and effort was directed towards the establishment of a tertiary education institution at Ballarat. In 1958 he was appointed O.B.E. and in 1963 he was elevated to C.M.G. While formal and reserved in his public manner, he was an affectionate parent. He was deeply attached to Lal Lal, which was his consuming hobby as well as his work. Fisken died there on 20 June 1970 and was cremated; his wife, son and three daughters survived him.

Meat Producer and Exporter, June 1970; *Ballarat Courier,* 28 Dec 1935, 22 June 1970; *Sun News-Pictorial,* 22 June 1970; family papers held by and information from Mrs P. Fisken, Yendon, Vic; information from Mrs J. Nevett, Mount Helen, Vic.

GEOFF BROWNE

FITZGERALD, SIR ADOLF ALEXANDER (1890-1969) and GARRETT ERNEST (1894-1970), accountants and educators, were born on 26 October 1890 and 30 June 1894 at Collingwood, Melbourne, third and fourth children of Victorian-born parents Michael Fitzgerald, hatter, and his wife Mary Ann, née Cravino.

Alex (he eschewed his first Christian name early in life) showed intellectual promise, winning a scholarship to Box Hill Grammar School where he was captain and dux in 1905. While employed as a clerk in a hardware merchant's firm, he studied accounting, then joined the public accountants Oxlade & Mackie (from 1923 Fitzgerald & Tompson), becoming a partner in 1915. At St Peter's

Anglican Church, Eastern Hill, Melbourne, on 18 October 1916 he married Ivy Alice Brunstein. In 1927 Fitzgerald became a councillor of the Commonwealth Institute of Accountants (State president, 1928-30, 1935-37; general councillor, 1936; president, 1940-41). As editor (1936-54) of the *Australian Accountant*, the official journal of the institute and its successor, the Australian Society of Accountants, he raised the standard of writing and publication.

Fitzgerald had represented his profession in discussions in 1924 with Professor (Sir) Douglas Copland [q.v.13] on the proposed introduction of a degree in commerce at the University of Melbourne. When the course began in 1925, he enrolled as one of its foundation students, simultaneously beginning his academic career as an assistant-lecturer in accounting. Graduating among the university's first bachelors of commerce in 1927, he continued to lecture in and direct the accounting courses part time until 1954. He was then appointed Gordon L. Wood [q.v.] professor of accounting, a post he filled with distinction until 1958. His books, *Statistical Methods as Applied to Accounting Reports* (1940), *Analysis and Interpretation of Financial and Operating Statements* (1947), *Classification in Accounting* (with L. A. Schumer 1952) and *Form and Contents of Published Financial Statements* (with his brother Garrett, 1948) were pioneering efforts in Australian accountancy, while the textbook which he edited, *Intermediate Accounting* (1948), influenced teachers and students for over twenty years.

In 1936-37 Fitzgerald was a member of the royal commission on water supply in Victoria and in 1939 financial adviser to the State's economic committee of inquiry into the Victorian Railways. In 1941-45 he was a councillor for the City of Box Hill. During World War II he was a member of the Army Accountancy Advisory Panel (1942-43) and of the Capital Issues Advisory Committee (1942-46). After the war he chaired (1945-60) the Commonwealth Grants Commission. His influence— exerted through direct discussions with government officers, through comments in the commission's annual reports, through public addresses which drew attention to advances in accounting generally and existing deficiencies in government accounts, and through the influence of his own teaching— produced considerable improvements in governmental financial reports at both State and Federal levels.

In addition, Fitzgerald was chairman (1953-59) of the Dairy Industry Cost Investigation Committee and a member (1955-69) of the State Electricity Commission; in 1953-55 he was also a member of the Defence Business Board and business adviser to the Department of the Army. In 1959-60 he chaired an inquiry into Post Office accounts and in 1962-65 served on (Sir) Leslie Martin's committee on the future of tertiary education in Australia. Appointed to the Decimal Currency Council in 1957, Fitzgerald was its chairman from 1960. He was a director of numerous companies, and held such varied posts as chairman (1962-65) of the Business Archives Council, Victorian division, member (1960-64) of the Fulbright scholarship advisory committee, and president (1961-65) of the University of Melbourne's Graduate Union.

An able administrator, Fitzgerald delegated tasks to, and inspired loyalty in, those working with him. His personal and professional strengths were punctuality, precision with answers, clarity with staff directions, and careful time-management. Despite his achievements, he was modest and courteous in manner, except when he was involved in barracking for his favourite team— Essendon—in the Victorian Football League. His writing, like his lectures, displayed a clarity and organization of thought and language which had a great appeal and carried conviction to his audience. He was about 5 ft 7 ins (170 cm) tall and slimly built; a portrait painted in 1959 by Jack Carington Smith [q.v.13] and held by the University of Melbourne makes him appear more dour than he really was. Fitzgerald was appointed O.B.E. in 1953 and knighted in 1955.

Sir Alexander was the outstanding figure of his time in Australian accounting. He was welcomed as a lecturer throughout Australasia by practitioners as well as academics, to whose notice he brought the latest overseas developments. While most of his contemporaries still looked to England for professional guidance and example, he was aware of more progressive developments in North America. In 1966 he retired from the accountancy firms Fitzgerald, Gunn & Partners and Fitzgerald, Gunn & Solomon. Next year the Australian Institute of Management awarded him its (Sir) John Storey [q.v.] medal. Predeceased by his wife (d.1964) and survived by their three daughters, he died on 22 August 1969 at Box Hill and was cremated. His estate was sworn for probate at $141 631.

Alexander's younger brother Garrett left school at 14 to work as a clerk in an insurance company. On 8 October 1915 he married Flossy Heather Maddick with Presbyterian forms at Collingwood; they were to have one child before being divorced in 1930. Enlisting in the Australian Imperial Force on 3 March 1916, he served (from November) with the 38th Battalion on the Western Front. He was commissioned in May 1917, wounded in action that month and invalided to England; promoted lieutenant in September, he rejoined the battalion three months later. In March 1918, near the Somme, France, he led a patrol which killed or captured more than thirty enemy soldiers without the loss of any of his men. His A.I.F. commission terminated in Australia on 23 December.

After the war Garrett Fitzgerald worked in the Taxation Department while studying accounting. He became an employee in his brother's firm in the early 1920s and a partner in 1930. Having graduated from the University of Melbourne (B.A., 1926; B.Com., 1927), he tutored and then lectured in accounting at the university from 1927 to 1947. With A. E. Speck, he co-authored *Accounts of Holding Companies* (1946). At St Andrew's Presbyterian Church, Box Hill, on 19 March 1931 he had married Maude de Pelsenaire, a clerk. He was a councillor for the City of Heidelberg in 1938-48 and in 1950-52 (mayor, 1945-46). Mobilized in the Militia in 1939, he served until 1942, rose to temporary lieutenant colonel and was assistant director, ordnance services, 4th Division.

In 1942 Fitzgerald was elected to the Victorian council of the Commonwealth Institute of Accountants (State president, 1946-47). As a member (from 1950) and president (1951-52) of the general council, he was instrumental in the merger with other professional bodies to form the Australian Society of Accountants (now the Australian Society of Certified Practising Accountants); he was president (1955 and 1956) of the A.S.A.'s general council and State president (1964). He spent much time and energy in trying to achieve a co-ordinated accountancy profession and to establish its statutory recognition.

Federal, State and municipal governments also benefited from his services: he was commissioner (1945-48) of the Melbourne and Metropolitan Board of Works, a member of committees of inquiry into salaries and allowances of State (1954, 1964) and Federal (1955, 1959) parliamentarians, chairman (1956) of a committee of inquiry into the Victorian Housing Commission and auditor (1958-60) of the City of Melbourne.

Five ft 4 ins (163 cm) tall and solidly built, Fitzgerald was good-humoured, and fond of telling jokes and stories. He was a devotee of the performing arts, an opera-lover and a patron of the National Theatre Movement. If somewhat more outgoing than his brother, he was no less modest about his own achievements. Tolerant of different views, and patient and understanding with his clients, he was not always punctual and sometimes worked intermittently, but he completed most assignments on time. He was appointed C.M.G. in 1965 and retired in the following year. Survived by his wife, their son and daughter, and by the son of his first marriage,

he died on 5 October 1970 in East Melbourne and was cremated with Anglican rites.

R. J. Chambers, L. Goldberg and R. L. Matthews (eds), *The Accounting Frontier* (Melb, 1965); G. H. Burrows, 'Glimpses of A. A. Fitzgerald', in J. St G. Kerr and R. C. Clift (eds), *Essays in Honour of Louis Goldberg* (Melb, 1989); *Aust Accountant*, 39, Oct 1969, p 453, 40, Nov 1970, p 61; *Univ Melb Gazette*, Nov 1969; *Herald* (Melb), 10 Feb 1955, 26 July 1960, 13 July 1966, 1 Aug 1968, 22 Aug 1969; *Age* (Melb), 27 Aug 1960, 25 May 1967, 22 Mar 1968, 23 Aug 1969; family information.

G. H. BURROWS
L. GOLDBERG

FITZGERALD, JAMES; *see* GERALD

FITZGIBBON, GRAHAM FRANCIS ('SMACKA') (1930-1979), jazz musician, hotelier and restaurateur, was born on 12 February 1930 at Mordialloc, Melbourne, second child of Francis Michael Thomas Fitzgibbon, clerk, and his wife Minnie Margaret, née Mitchell, both Victorian born. His elder sister Maggie was to become an actor in Britain and Australia, and a jazz vocalist. Graham attended St Bede's College, Mentone, until the age of 14 when he was apprenticed to a mechanic. During his childhood he had learned the ukulele, playing and singing with his mother who was his earliest influence, as was the music of Al Bowlly, George Formby, Bing Crosby and Louis Armstrong.

Switching to the banjo, 'Smacka' formed his own band, 'The Steamboat Stompers'. He performed with various Melbourne-based groups, notably that of Frank Johnson, with whom he made his first recordings in 1951. Working at the Darnum Hotel, he gained experience which enabled him to become licensee of the Commercial Hotel, Warragul, in partnership with his parents. While at the Darnum, he had released his first album under his own leadership, *Frisco Joe's Good Time Boys*, which established his name as the 'singing barman'. In 1958, after his father died, he and his mother moved to Wycheproof and took over the Royal Mail Hotel.

At St Patrick's Cathedral, Melbourne, on 31 October 1959 Fitzgibbon married with Catholic rites 19-year-old Faye Mentha Hommelhoff. He took a job as a life-insurance salesman and, with his wife, ran the Druids Hotel in South Melbourne. In 1969 he bought the lease of La Brochette, a small restaurant at Kew, and turned it into Melbourne's first jazz restaurant. Increasingly well known through his work on television, he appeared in such shows as 'Sunnyside Up', 'The Penthouse Club' and 'In Melbourne Tonight'; Graham Kennedy recorded an album with him. Fitzgibbon's success was consolidated with the opening in 1971 of a new restaurant, Smacka's Place, in North Melbourne. In 1972 he sang the title-song for the film, *The Adventures of Barry McKenzie*; as a record, this song began a string of his consistent popular sellers. Plump and smiling, 'Smacka' was a genial public figure and took part in the Keep Australia Beautiful campaign. While engaged in this work in 1977, he was prosecuted for playing music in the streets of Frankston; the case was a *cause célèbre*.

That year Fitzgibbon, a longtime sufferer of melanoma, collapsed during a broadcast on radio station 3LO; the cause was subsequently diagnosed as brain tumour, for which he twice underwent surgery. He died of a cerebral haemorrhage on 15 December 1979 at South Melbourne and was buried in Brighton cemetery. Frank Traynor's 'Jazz Preachers' played at the packed funeral service at St Mary's Star of the Sea Church, West Melbourne. 'Smacka' was posthumously named Melbourne's 'King of Jazz' for 1980. He was survived by his wife, daughter and three sons; three of his children became jazz musicians.

B. Johnson, *The Oxford Companion to Australian Jazz* (Melb, 1987); J. Mitchell, *Australian Jazz on Record 1925-80* (Canb, 1988); *Sun News-Pictorial*, 24 May 1977, 15, 17, 20 Dec 1979; *Herald* (Melb), 1 Sept 1977, 15 Dec 1979; *Age* (Melb), 12 June 1970, 11 Jan 1977, 17, 20 Dec 1979, 14 Jan, 28 Mar 1980; family information.

BRUCE JOHNSON

FITZGIBBONS, LILY KATHLEEN PATTIE (1892-1978), schoolteacher, bus proprietor and hotelier, was born on 28 August 1892 at Wellington, New South Wales, eighth of ten children of William McCarthy, an English-born engine driver, and his wife Ellen Catherine, née Sakey, from New Zealand. While teaching at Bathurst, she met Michael Alphonsus Dominic Fitzgibbons who was employed in the New South Wales Government Railways and Tramways, where Lily's father worked. The two men had served as engine driver and fireman, respectively, with Ben Chifley [q.v.13]. The railway strike of August-September 1917 changed their lives, their aspirations and their place of residence. On 14 July 1920 Michael, then a chauffeur and mechanic in Sydney, married Lily at St Joseph's Catholic Church, Newtown; their three children were born between 1921 and 1926.

It was not long before the business acumen, characteristic of the Fitzgibbons' partnership, came to the fore. Recognizing the need to serve the rail transport system, Lily and Michael established White Buses with money borrowed from their parish priest. Lily kept the books and handled the finances; Michael and his staff drove and maintained a fleet of up to fourteen vehicles. Like their future benefactor (Sir) Frederick Stewart [q.v.12], the Fitzgibbons began to pose a challenge to State rail and tram services. In 1928 they applied to extend their routes from Campsie to Central Railway Station. This endeavour embroiled them in the royal commission held that year which investigated allegations of bribery (the 'case of pipes') by an agent to further the application. Although the Fitzgibbons were exonerated, their business faced bleak prospects with continued government discouragement, high licence fees and the onset of the Depression. Placing their children in boarding schools, they sought new careers as hoteliers. In 1936 they took over the Kirrabelle Coolangatta, the first of many Queensland hotels on which they placed their stamp; they later ran hotels at Southport, Toowoomba, Wandoan, Eight Mile Plains and Mooloolaba. In 1944, at the request of the brewery company, Castlemaine, Perkins Ltd, they moved to the Hotel Daniell, George Street, Brisbane, to cater for American army officers. From that time their reputation for hospitality and good service was consolidated.

Precise, practical and a disciplinarian, Lily made financial and domestic management her forte. It was customary for 'Mrs Fitz' to count the individual pats of butter to be served at breakfast, and to insist that her dining-room staff remain until all the silver was accounted for. Alongside recipes for drinks and the reminder that 'essence cannot cause fermentation but dirt can and usually does', she inscribed in her notebook the maxim which characterized her working life: 'Don't take anything for granted. The price of success is vigilance and thoroughness'. After her husband died in 1967, Lily maintained her links with the hotel industry as licensee of the Hotel Daniell. In retirement, as consultant to two generations of Fitzgibbons engaged in the industry, she encouraged the same entrepreneurial flair, meticulous attention to detail and penchant for hospitality that had characterized her working partnership with Michael. She died on 10 July 1978 at Sunnybank and was buried in Nudgee cemetery; her daughter and two sons survived her.

J. T. Lang, *The Great Bust* (Syd, 1962); J. Iremonger et al (eds), *Strikes* (Syd, 1973); Roy Com of Inquiry into ... Michael Alphonsus Dominic Fitzgibbons ..., *PP* (NSW), 1929-30, 1, p 1035; *Qld Hotels Assn Review*, May 1956, July 1961, Sept 1963, Aug 1967; *Courier-Mail*, 12 July 1978; *Catholic Leader*, Aug 1967, Aug 1978; family papers (held by Mr K. Mann, Rochedale, Brisb); information from Mr B. Fitzgibbons, Raby Bay, Qld, Mr and Mrs V. Fitzgibbons, Attadale, Perth, and Mr K. Mann.

HELEN TAYLOR

FITZPATRICK, AILEEN (1897-1974), community worker, teacher and social work educator, was born on 17 August 1897 at Warialda, New South Wales, daughter of native-born parents Stephen Thomas Fitzpatrick, schoolteacher, and his wife Julia, née Hamilton. Educated at public schools in the country and at Sydney Girls' High School, Aileen passed the Leaving certificate in 1915. She studied classics at the University of Sydney (B.A., 1919) and was employed by the Department of Education.

After teaching classics at Parramatta, Albury, Sydney Girls' and Fort Street Girls' high schools, Fitzpatrick resigned in 1927 to become organizing secretary in Sydney for the Country Women's Association of New South Wales. She developed an interest in community services and was a member of the National Council of Women's standing committee for education which reported that year on the need to establish training for social workers in New South Wales. Following the establishment (1929) of the Board of Social Study and Training, she was initially associated with it in an honorary capacity before being appointed to a salaried position (director) in 1932. Fitzpatrick taught industrial history and casework. Over the next eight years, fifty-three women and one man received the board's certificate in social work.

A large, effusive person with an ability to win over those who mattered, Fitzpatrick gained the approval of professors Tasman Lovell and Harvey Sutton [qq.v.10,12], influential members of the board. Aided by grants from the Carnegie Foundation for the Advancement of Teaching, she went abroad in 1933 to investigate social work in Europe and the United States of America. She again returned to the United States in 1935 with fifteen students to extend her examination of methods of training. Fitzpatrick developed close ties with the American schools and that year became a member of the American Association of Social Workers; she invited Porter R. Lee, director of the New York School of Social Work, to visit Sydney in 1937. Back home, she helped to establish the Council of Social Service in 1935 and the Australian Council of Schools of Social Work in 1938.

Fitzpatrick's achievements as director were overshadowed by the discord that arose with Katharine Ogilvie and Helen Rees, two leading social workers who were responsible for setting up the New South Wales Institute of Hospital Almoners in 1937. They had gained professional qualifications outside Australia, and criticized the board for the standards of its course and the calibre of its teaching staff. Encountering a want of confidence among her colleagues and the withdrawal of some board-members' support,

Fitzpatrick resigned in 1940 when the board's training course was taken over by the university.

She operated out of 5 Hamilton Street (the board's previous address) and turned her attention to the growing refugee problem. Backed by Sir Benjamin Fuller [q.v.8], Julia Corless and Russell Henderson, from 1940 she ran a service for refugees as a subsidiary of the Australian United Nations Assembly. The agency was eventually incorporated in 1949 as the Australian Council for International Social Service. Fitzpatrick was director and presided over services involving family reunion, a foreign language library and an integration programme for the intelligentsia. The work of the organization flourished, but, with increased migration to Australia in the 1950s, A.C.I.S.S. needed the support of overseas affiliates and additional funds to function effectively. When William T. Kirk, president of International Social Service, visited Sydney in 1954, Fitzpatrick sought to have A.C.I.S.S. formerly recognized as a branch of I.S.S. The report of Florence Boester, an I.S.S. representative, favoured affiliation on the whole, while pointing out that casework and management standards had to improve. The lack of formal qualifications of the director and her staff were seen as a disadvantage. A.C.I.S.S. was affiliated in 1955; Fitzpatrick again bowed to pressure from her colleagues and resigned.

A pioneer of social work, she achieved much by her energy and charm, but met her match in other forceful women intent on directing the way in which the profession should develop. Fitzpatrick continued her refugee-work from the Sir Benjamin Fuller Foreign Language Memorial Library. She died on 23 June 1974 at her Eastwood home and was cremated.

R. J. Lawrence, *Professional Social Work in Australia* (Canb, 1965); Bd of Social Study and Training of NSW, *Annual Report*, 1930-40; *SMH*, 26 Mar, 2 Apr 1935, 6 May 1950, 19 Mar 1953, 27 June 1974; F. Boester, Review of the Structure, Administration and Programme of the Australian Council for International Social Service (1954, ms, International Social Service L, Syd); files of Dept of Social Work, Univ Syd (Univ Syd Archives); information from Country Women's Assn Office, Syd; information from Dr N. Parker, Melb, Miss H. Halse Rogers and Mrs E. Cliffe, Cremorne, Mrs A. Bury, Vaucluse, Mrs N. Fleming, Castlecrag, Dr I. Wade Fitzpatrick, Mosman, Syd, and Mr H. Gilchrist, Canb.
KERRY REGAN

FITZPATRICK, BRIAN CHARLES (1905-1965), journalist, historian, socialist and defender of civil liberties, was born on 17 November 1905 at Warrnambool, Victoria, seventh of eight children of native-born parents Peter John Charles Fitzpatrick, schoolteacher, and his wife Marie Louise, née Callister. His father's parents were Irish, his mother's Scots and Manx. Books and music were prominent in the children's upbringing. By 1914 the Fitzpatricks were living in Melbourne at Moonee Ponds, Brian attending the local state school. Peter died in 1919 and his eldest son Frank [q.v.] took over much of the family responsibility; Brian rebelled against him. From 1916 he had attended Essendon High School where he won a scholarship to the University of Melbourne (B.A. Hons, 1925).

In 1922-24 Fitzpatrick concentrated on philosophy and sociology, and gained exhibitions, prizes and scholarships. His chief activities in 1925 were as a founder and chief of staff of *Farrago*, the student newspaper, and also as a founder of the Melbourne University Labor Club. The conversion was recent: he had been a special constable during the police strike. He was carrying out research into revolutionary organizations in Australia, contributing to the *Age*, *Bulletin* and Melbourne *Punch*, and associating with D. J. Cameron [q.v.7] and other Labor leaders.

Fitzpatrick left for England in July 1926, intending to study the British co-operative movement. However, after an adventurous year in London as a journalist, he worked his passage home as a steward. In 1928-30 he was a journalist on the Sydney *Daily Telegraph*, then returned to Melbourne for a year. At this time he had literary ambitions, writing poems and a largely autobiographical novel, 'The Colonials'; though promising, it could not find a publisher. *Songs and Poems* (1931) was later an embarrassment, but part of 'Cenotaph' was anthologized. In 1931-32 he was leader-writer and assistant-editor of the short-lived Sydney Labor daily, the *World*.

At St Patrick's Catholic Cathedral, Melbourne, on 27 August 1932 Fitzpatrick married Kathleen Elizabeth Pitt, a university tutor; they returned from Sydney in 1933 to live at Kew before moving to Toorak. He had been appointed to the *Herald* as a feature writer. For a while he was a reformed character, shunning his drinking-mates at the Swanston Family Hotel, but the marriage broke up in 1935 and divorce followed on 28 October 1939. He married Dorothy Mary Davies on 25 July 1940 at the office of the government statist, Melbourne. In late 1935 Fitzpatrick had left the *Herald* and abandoned his literary aspirations in favour of historical research, commitment to political activism and defence of civil liberties.

As a socialist in a period when capitalism seemed to have broken down, Fitzpatrick held the basic view that politics was primarily 'a struggle between the organized rich and the organized poor', and that only the latter had social justice on their side. In 1940 he gave evidence as an expert witness before the Commonwealth Court of Conciliation and Arbitration on the need to increase the basic wage and later appeared in support of the 40-hour week. He could be seen as a fellow traveller of the Communist Party of Australia, especially when the Soviet Union won so much respect during the years of World War II, but, though influenced by Marxism, he would never obey any dogmatic system and knew that assumption of revolution was absurd. Favouring state enterprise and nationalization of monopolies, he had hopes of the Australian Labor Party which he joined in 1942. If he had a political hero it was Maurice Blackburn [q.v.7]—but he and Blackburn were soon expelled from the party. Fitzpatrick worked for eighteen months in 1942-44 in the Rationing Commission and the Department of War Organization of Industry. He served, as well, on the Prime Minister's Morale Committee and advised H. V. Evatt [q.v.] on his referendum proposals of 1944. But by the end of the war he had lost almost all faith in the A.L.P. and recognized that capitalism would survive.

From 1936 to 1945 Fitzpatrick had concentrated on historical writing. He was initially refused funding by the university, but won the Harbison-Higinbotham [q.v.4] prize (£100) in 1937 and 1939. Backed strongly by Professor R. M. Crawford, in 1938-40 he held a major research scholarship (£200 per annum), and in 1940-42 and 1944-45 a £500 annual grant. His most significant historical works were published in this period: *British Imperialism and Australia, 1788-1833* (London, 1939), *The British Empire in Australia* (1941), *The Australian People, 1788-1945* (1946), and the stopgap, quickly written *Short History of the Australian Labor Movement* (1940). In 1943 external examiners on behalf of the university rejected his application for a D.Litt. degree, a judgement glaringly inconsistent with the standard accepted for other historians.

Knowing that Australians could not recognize their capacity to develop as a nation without better understanding of their history, Fitzpatrick had been idealistically devoting himself to sustained historical writing, and for the first time provided a left-wing interpretation which deeply influenced the postwar generation of young academic historians who were extending the teaching of Australian history in universities. He introduced large areas of knowledge for discussion. His style, while often wordy and pedantic, included many effective passages of finely expressed insight.

Fitzpatrick had been stirred into action by the Book Censorship Abolition League (1934

-35) for which he began his career as a public speaker. In reaction to alarming anti-democratic legislation, in 1935 Max Meldrum, (Sir) John Barry [qq.v.10,13], (Sir) Eugene Gorman [q.v.] and others formed the Australian Council for Civil Liberties, with Herbert Burton as president; Fitzpatrick drafted the constitution. In January 1937 A.C.C.L. published *The Case against the Crimes Act*, written by Barry, Gorman and Fitzpatrick, which was followed by a series of powerful booklets. The council's campaign to allow Mrs Mabel Freer to enter the country was successful. In 1938 A.C.C.L. opposed the Federal government's attempt to apply the Transport Workers Act (1937) to wharf labourers on strike, and increasingly gave attention to the maltreatment of Jewish refugees.

Branches (or parallel organizations) were founded in every State. Fitzpatrick had become the driving force simply because he was contributing much more than anyone else; he established a legal panel and carried his proposal that the executive establish a secretariat with himself as general secretary, effectively taking the council to the left, away from its varied liberal supporters. Conflict followed, especially over legislation for a national register in 1939, which led to the defection of several prominent members. Blackburn replaced Burton, and Fitzpatrick gathered other Labor politicians—Frank Brennan [q.v.7], A. D. Fraser, E. J. Ward [qq.v.], Evatt and Reg Pollard—as active supporters. From 1939, for twenty years, Fitzpatrick wrote the periodical leaflet, *Civil Liberty*.

After the outbreak of World War II, A.C.C.L. was wracked by internal conflict over the National Security Act (1939) and the outlawing of the Communist Party. Although continually criticized for making unauthorized statements, Fitzpatrick consolidated his position. Following Russia's entry into the war, the advent of a Federal Labor government and Japanese attack, he modified his stand on civil liberties, but fought administrative injustices as strongly as ever. He supported his revered friend Evatt over maintaining the internment of some members of the Australia-First Movement, while using his influence to bring about the release of thousands of other internees. His campaign for just treatment of refugees—many of them anti-fascist—was one of his finest achievements. In the later anti-communist years, marked by the attempt to ban the Communist Party and by the royal commission into the Petrov affair, A.C.C.L. survived. It came to be a one-man band. Fitzpatrick's wide range of contacts, knowledge of the law and administrative procedures, and his persuasiveness were formidable. His support in individual cases of injustice, which were often entirely non-political, won the respect of politicians of integrity like Harold Holt [q.v.] who often acted on his advice.

From 1946 Fitzpatrick settled into the role of freelance radical publicist. His scanty income was based on a regular political article in *Smith's Weekly* (1941-49) and a weekly broadcast on radio 3XY. He undertook hack work for the Australian Broadcasting Commission and the *Australian Encyclopaedia*, and wrote regularly for the *Rationalist* (1954-65). *Meanjin* and other cultural journals could pay little for his numerous articles and reviews. His wife's earnings as a secondary and tertiary teacher were critical. Occasionally he was commissioned for minor literary or political writing, or for 'ghosting', and he sometimes worked as a mailsorter or examination supervisor. He eked out a little income from his propagandist monthly publication, the *Australian Democrat* (1947-50), from *Australian News-Review* (1951-53) and from *Brian Fitzpatrick's Labor Newsletter* (1958-65).

No friend of the British Empire, Fitzpatrick had long been an Australian nationalist; Vance and Nettie Palmer [qq.v.11], whom he had met in the mid-1930s, had a profound influence on him. They were the models for natural, self-respecting Australianism, and showed a primary concern for development of the arts. Fitzpatrick's close friends Barry, W. Glanville Cook and C. B. Christesen were of like mind. In his later years he focussed on the growing American influence on Australian foreign policy and on America's economic penetration, and was among the first to campaign against involvement in Vietnam. After Russia's invasion of Hungary and Nikita Krushchev's revelations, Fitzpatrick's sympathy for the Soviet Union had dwindled.

In the mid-1950s Fitzpatrick hankered to resume historical work and applied for academic and journalistic posts. Supported for eighteen months by a grant from the Social Sciences Research Council, he wrote *The Australian Commonwealth* (1956). Idiosyncratic and entertaining, both a long pamphlet and a reference work, it was hardly conventional history, more a statement of the preoccupations of the 'old left'. Thrice invited to apply for university lectureships, he was unsuccessful despite strong support: the chief reasons were political prejudice and alarm at his frequent drunkenness (which rarely prevented his customary early morning start to concentrated work). Requests for grants for research were likewise refused. He responded amiably to the reinterpretation of Australian economic history by Noel Butlin, and in a *Meanjin* article (1963) demolished the alleged 'Counter Revolution in Australian Historiography'.

Fitzpatrick contributed significantly in three areas, as defender of civil liberties, historian and political maverick. He was a man of many contradictions. As his biographer Don Watson remarked, he was 'a cold-hearted Marxist and a soft-hearted liberal. . .a utopian and a pragmatist', fundamentally a rebel against authority. His energy, power of concentration, determination and speed of writing were phenomenal.

He was of average height, portly, with a florid and eventually ravaged face. His charm, wit and mannered courtesy were notable; he objected to indecent conversation. He turned a polite face to critics, believing that 'circumstance is the arbiter of men's opinions'; thus he held 'malice towards none'. A remarkable range of citizens attended his testimonial dinner in 1964. Survived by his wife and their daughter and son, both noted scholars, he died of hypertensive coronary vascular disease on 3 September 1965 at Tamarama, Sydney, and was cremated. Portraits by Graeme Inson and George Luke are held by the family.

D. Watson, *Brian Fitzpatrick* (Syd, 1979) *and* for bibliog and listing of writings; Fitzpatrick papers (NL).   GEOFFREY SERLE

FITZPATRICK, FRANK LIONEL (1895-1972), businessman, was born on 8 August 1895 at Purnim, Victoria, third of eight children of native-born parents Peter John Charles Fitzpatrick, schoolteacher, and his wife Mary Louise, née Callister. Brian [q.v.] was his younger brother. Educated at Cudgee and Winchlesea state schools, and at Ballarat High School, in 1912 Frank joined the finance branch of the Department of Defence as a clerk. On 30 August 1915 he enlisted in the Australian Imperial Force. He was the middleweight boxing champion in his camp and on board the troop-ship, *Ballarat*, in which he sailed to Egypt in December. While serving with the 6th Machine-Gun Company near Passchendaele, Belgium, Fitzpatrick was wounded on 8 November 1917. In the attack at Framerville, France, on 9 August 1918, he braved concentrated fire to recover a gun and bring it into action; he was awarded the Military Medal. He rose to sergeant and was discharged in Australia on 21 June 1919.

Returning to the Department of Defence, Fitzpatrick qualified as an accountant in 1921. He resigned next year to work in the office of a new concrete-product company of which he was appointed manager in 1924. At the Presbyterian Church, Malvern, on 12 January 1926 he married Violet Esme May (d.1961), a stenographer. From 1929 to 1960 he was general manager of Rocla Pipes Ltd. In 1932 he promoted the introduction of rubber ring joints for high-pressure concrete pipes, an innovation adopted throughout the world. During World War II he guided Rocla in the development of post-tensioned concrete pipes; the technology was exported to North America, Europe and India in the late 1940s and 1950s. Appointed a director in 1949, Fitzpatrick was chairman (from 1964) of the company which in 1960 was renamed Rocla Industries Ltd. He had seen the enterprise grow from shareholders' funds of £50 000 in 1930 to $13 million when he retired from the board in 1970.

With wide interests, Fitzpatrick served many societies and institutions. He was a councillor (1942-63) of the Victorian Chamber of Manufactures and a member (1949-60) of the Melbourne Rotary Club. President (1951-52), councillor and honorary fellow (1964) of the Australian Institute of Management, he was awarded its (Sir) John Storey [q.v.] medal in 1966. Fitzpatrick was appointed a councillor (1957) of the Institute of Public Affairs and a fellow (1960) of the Australian Society of Accountants. A councilmember of the Victorian Society for Crippled Children and Adults, he was foundation president (1960) of the Sheltered Workshops Advisory Council of Victoria. In 1961-72 he was a councillor of Women's College at the University of Melbourne.

A director from 1955 of Moulded Products (A'sia) Ltd (from 1967 Nylex Corporation Ltd) and its chairman in 1958-71, Fitzpatrick was also a board-member of Coates & Co. Ltd, Gas Supply Co. Ltd, Kingsley Industries Pty Ltd and John Webster Industries Pty Ltd. Throughout his working life he earned the respect of his colleagues and employees. A humble and compassionate man who treasured integrity and honesty, he enjoyed public speaking and imparting his homespun philosophies. Some of his maxims were: 'Speak of "we", not "I"'; 'Faithfully keep all promises, even little ones'; 'In all situations just quietly do your best'; 'Never allow fears or worry to overwhelm you'; 'Do not postpone or evade action'; and 'In business decisions remember that diversification is getting into something you know nothing about'.

Fitzpatrick was intensely interested in management, particularly in relationships with employees. He regarded careful and close communication with all workers as basic, and urged that authority be delegated and strict attention be given to efficiency. He also introduced annual assessment of senior executives, advocated that they speak more than one language and insisted that they travelled abroad on economy fares. In addition to lecturing on management practices, he wrote articles for technical colleges, training institutions and professional bodies. Regarded as a leader in management technique, he worked as a business consultant after his retirement from Rocla. Apart from his native English, Fitzpatrick spoke French and German, and knew some Italian and Spanish. His hobbies included walking, gardening and cooking. In 1971 he was appointed C.B.E. and named Melbourne Rotary's man of the year. Survived by his son, he died on 3 March 1972 at his Mitcham home and was cremated.

IPA Review, Jan-Mar 1972; *Herald* (Melb), 6 Mar 1950, 10 Apr 1963, 3 Oct 1970, 3 Mar 1972; *Sun News-Pictorial*, 10 June 1971; information from Mr and Mrs M. Fitzpatrick, Bonnie Doon, Sir Peter Derham, Red Hill, and Mr F. Lawson, Sorrento, Vic, Sir Rupert Hamer, Canterbury, Melb, and Sir Eric Neal, Paddington, Syd; family papers (held by Mr M. Fitzpatrick). DAVID H. HUME

FITZPATRICK, RAYMOND EDWARD (1909-1967), businessman, was born on 10 November 1909 at Canterbury, Sydney, third child of native-born parents William Joseph Fitzpatrick, farmer, and his wife Lucy, née Mead. Aged 13 and barely literate, Ray left Milperra Public School to collect bottles and work as a truck driver's offsider. When the Depression bankrupted his employer, Fitzpatrick was given the truck in lieu of back wages and started a business career which embraced transport, excavation, plant hire and metal supply. On 17 February 1932 he married Helen Beattie McLean at St Matthew's Anglican Church, Bondi; he was to divorce her in February 1940. At St Mark's, Brighton-Le-Sands, on 10 August that year he married Clare Isobel Summergreene.

Of robust build and forthright demeanour, Fitzpatrick was sometimes known as 'Mr Big of Bankstown'. From 1943 his business activities were subject to allegations of impropriety and corruption. His opponents, led by Charles Morgan, Labor member for Reid in the House of Representatives, claimed that Fitzpatrick flouted wartime building restrictions and illegally interfered in the tendering process at Bankstown Municipal Council. In April 1944 Fitzpatrick was fined £75 for two breaches of the National Security (Supplementary) Regulations. A Labor supporter, he had provided motorcars for Morgan on polling day in 1940.

Fitzpatrick and Morgan became bitter enemies. The latter believed that Fitzpatrick was a sinister figure who enjoyed covert assistance from individuals within the security services and the office of J. J. Dedman [q.v.13], minister for war organization of industry. Fitzpatrick contended that Morgan's motives were personal and pecuniary. Aiming to unseat Morgan, in 1946 'big Fitzie' was the 'unseen power' behind J. T. Lang's [q.v.9]

successful campaign for Reid, reputedly organizing Liberal Party preferences for Lang.

By the 1950s Fitzpatrick's diversified interests included building, sand and gravel cartage, dredging and the racing industry (it was said that he was able to influence the results of the Harold Park 'trots'). A wealthy man without pretension, he was the archetypal 'rough diamond'. For all his dabbling in shady affairs and willingness to use fisticuffs against rivals, in sections of Bankstown he commanded an 'almost mystical loyalty' not solely based on intimidation. He was a generous employer with a compassionate streak, and once proclaimed enigmatically: 'I've never robbed a worker in my life'. At the Christmas parties he held in the yard of his works at Bankstown, his truck drivers and plant-operators rubbed shoulders with lawyers and judges, politicians and high-ranking policemen, city businessmen and local aldermen.

As proprietor of the *Bankstown Observer*, he engaged the editorial services of Frank Browne, a right-wing journalist, to 'get stuck into' Morgan (who had been re-elected for Reid in 1949 and made virulent attacks on Fitzpatrick in parliament). Several articles alleged that Morgan had been involved in an 'immigration racket' before World War II. With Prime Minister (Sir) Robert Menzies' [q.v.] support, Morgan succeeded in having Fitzpatrick and Browne brought before the parliamentary standing committee of privileges which found that the articles were designed to 'influence and intimidate' a member of parliament, and concluded that a breach of privilege had occurred. Summoned to the bar of the House, Fitzpatrick apologized 'humbly'. In June 1955, by votes of 55 to 11 (Fitzpatrick) and 55 to 12 (Browne), the House of Representatives sentenced both men to three months imprisonment. They applied to the High Court of Australia for writs of habeas corpus, but the court decided that they had been 'validly gaoled' and refused leave to appeal to the Privy Council.

The case was seen by many observers as flouting the normal processes of the law and as an abuse of civil liberties. One newspaper observed that the 'roughneck contractor' was reportedly 'petrified and so lacking in education as to be tongue-tied'. Released from Goulburn gaol in September, Fitzpatrick continued to attract controversy. In October the Department of Taxation fined him £8465 for evasion of income tax. Further allegations were made in the New South Wales parliament in 1958 that he had been involved in corrupt behaviour in the tendering and building of Sutherland Shire Council's road to the Kurnell oil refinery.

Fitzpatrick's business career acquired the

trappings of respectability. He sold his extensive quarrying and contracting business to the Rio Tinto Co. Ltd in 1960; with the proceeds he formed Fitzpatrick Industries Pty Ltd. In 1966 he purchased 27 000 acres in the Wolgan Valley for breeding cattle. For ten years he suffered from diabetes. Survived by his wife and their two daughters, he died of cerebrovascular disease on 5 December 1967 at St Vincent's Hospital, Darlinghurst, and was buried in Pine Grove cemetery, Eastern Creek. His estate was sworn for probate at $732 785.

F. C. Green, *Servant of the House* (Melb, 1969); C. J. Lloyd, *Parliament and the Press* (Melb, 1988); G. Souter, *Acts of Parliament* (Melb, 1988); *J* (Senate), 1954-55, 1, p xxxviii; *PD* (H of R), 3 May 1955, p 352, 16 May 1955, p 1114, 10 June 1955, p 1625; *Cwlth Law Reports*, 92, 1954-55, pp 159, 171; *SMH*, 5 Apr 1944, 23-25 June, 5 Oct 1955, 2 July 1958, 5 May 1966, 25 Apr 1968; The Charlie Morgan Story (ms, nd) and other papers held by Mr K. B. Morgan, Belfield, Syd; Autobiography by Mr C. J. McKenzie, Epping, Syd.

ANDREW MOORE

FLAKELAR, ANDREW ARCHIBALD (1946-1967), surf lifesaver and electrician, was born on 22 October 1946 at Coledale, near Wollongong, New South Wales, only son and youngest of three children of native-born parents Archibald Charles Daniel Flakelar, railway fettler, and his wife Vera Louisa Florence, née Thompson. Andrew belonged to a family which had originally come from Germany, and grew up in a modest home on the poorer side of the railway-line. He enjoyed the simple childhood of a small community on the Pacific Ocean coast, played sport with some skill, and was a cub and a boy scout. After attending Coledale Public and Bulli High schools, he took up an artisan apprenticeship in the signals' branch of the New South Wales Government Railways; his training partly involved travel to major workshops in Sydney. He became a keen fisherman, sometimes line-fishing from his long, wooden surfboard, well out to sea.

An ardent member of Coledale Surf Life Saving Club from the age of 14, Flakelar made many friends there, developed a strong sense of mateship and formed a responsible attitude towards family and society. His parents knew him as a loving and supportive son, while his elder sisters relied on him as a cheerful brother and baby-sitter. He had a casual friendship with a girl in Sydney. Genial and serious minded, he was an outstanding member of his club and an excellent swimmer, fearless in the surf, with a professional attitude towards safety equipment and procedures.

Flakelar was patrol captain at Coledale Beach on Boxing Day, 1967. Although the swell ran high, he decided to open the beach. Flags were erected in the middle section of the beach, away from an obvious rip at the northern end. Seven club members began swimming in the ocean. A big swell drove the majority back to shore, but Charlie Trivett appeared to be in difficulty. Flakelar quickly put on the surf-belt and plunged into the waves, with his comrades feeding out the surf-line. Having reached the area where Trivett was struggling, Flakelar raised his hand, and his good mate Jim Spence pulled on the rope to draw him closer to Trivett. Spence told the police: 'I saw Trivett get out on the rocks and I saw Jim McRombie dive in to assist him. I saw them both get out ... Eddie Patmore came over and said, "Andrew has disappeared, pull him in quickly". We started hauling in pretty fast ... When we [were] about waist high in the water we picked up Andrew. He had no movement'.

Although Flakelar was given mouth-to-mouth resuscitation until an ambulance arrived, he never regained consciousness. A coronial inquiry concluded that he 'was accidentally drowned while attempting a rescue under difficult conditions'. Most probably, the surf-line had snagged on an underwater shelf of rock and Andrew was drowned while being reeled back to the beach.

Amid the tragedies which come to a small community, Flakelar's death was particularly noticed and felt. He appeared to symbolize a generation of young Australians who served in the beach corps. In the happy phrase of the coroner, he was 'a shining example' of 'this group of dedicated men'. Members of the Coledale Surf Club still recall Andrew, and his photographs hang proudly in the clubhouse.

A small monument at Coledale Beach commemorates his sacrifice. The Surf Life Saving Association of Australia posthumously awarded Flakelar its highest honour, a silver medallion 'for rare feats of bravery in the surf'.

Illawarra Mercury, 27-29 Dec 1967, 12 Jan 1968; Coroner's Report and Depositions, Police Report and Post-mortem documents (copies held by author); Coledale Surf Life Saving Club, records; Surf Life Saving Association of Australia, *Annual Report* (1967-68); family information.

D. M. SCHREUDER

FLECKER, HUGO (1884-1957), medical practitioner, radiotherapist, toxicologist and natural historian, was born on 7 December 1884 at Prahran, Melbourne, third son of Austrian-born George Flecker, publican, and his wife Emma, née Ziffer, from Hungary. The family moved to Adelaide where George managed the South Australian Hotel. Educated at Prince Alfred College, Hugo matriculated fourteenth in his class of fifteen, winning a prize for music despite congenital nerve deafness. He enrolled in medicine at the University of Adelaide in 1904 before transferring to the University of Sydney (M.B., Ch.M., 1908). After graduating, he was variously demonstrator in anatomy at the University of Sydney, honorary anaesthetist at the Royal Hospital for Women, Paddington, and honorary physician at the Mater Misericordiae Hospital, North Sydney.

In 1911 Flecker travelled to Britain where he qualified L.R.C.P. (London) and became a fellow (1912) of the Royal College of Surgeons, Edinburgh. Back home, he served in the Militia until 20 August 1914 when he was seconded to the Australian Imperial Force as captain, Australian Army Medical Corps. In Egypt and on the Western Front he worked in hospitals and as medical officer of units in the field. His A.I.F. appointment terminated in Australia on 28 April 1917. Remaining on the Reserve of Officers, he was to rise to major and to perform full-time duty at the 116th Australian General Hospital, Charters Towers, Queensland, in 1942-43. At St Philip's Anglican Church, Sydney, on 21 April 1917 he married Thelma Hensler Emma Malvina Arnold. From 1918 he practised at Temora, New South Wales.

In 1921 Flecker shifted to Collins Street, Melbourne, and set up as a radiotherapist, using apparatus said to develop 2500 volts. About 1923, in an attempt to obtain his own supply of radioisotopes, he journeyed by camel to Radium Hill, South Australia, where he searched for radioactive ore with a gold-leaf electroscope. Honorary radiologist (from 1923) at the Austin Hospital for Incurables and (from 1926) at the Homoeopathic (later Prince Henry's) Hospital, he was honorary demonstrator in radiological anatomy (from 1927) at the University of Melbourne. In 1932 Flecker established himself as a radiologist and radiotherapist at Cairns, Queensland. He was one of the few specialists north of Brisbane. Thorough and painstaking, whenever possible he brought his X-ray findings to the referring doctor for discussion. He took his diploma in radiology (Sydney) in 1937 and became a fellow of the Faculty of Radiology (England) in 1939.

Excelling in botany, zoology and toxicology, in 1936 Flecker described the first fatal case of coneshell poisoning in Australia, and continued to report the effects of scorpion and snake venoms on human victims. His practice at Cairns developed into a centre for radiological opinion, and for diagnosis or advice about snakebite, jellyfish stings, scorpion bites and toxic plant ingestions. He published accounts of two cases of survival from Aus-

tralian taipan bites, but his international fame rested on his research into poisoning by jellyfish. Concerned at the unexplained deaths of swimmers, Flecker identified the cause as the box jellyfish (named *Chironex fleckeri* in 1956), one of the world's most venomous creatures. In the *Medical Journal of Australia* (April 1945) he described another jellyfish envenoming which he termed the 'Irukandji Syndrome', later traced to the box jellyfish, *Carukia barnesi*; his subsequent paper in the same journal (July 1952) became a classic of its type.

Having been active in the Field Naturalists' Club of Victoria from 1921, Flecker developed extracurricular interests in natural history. As foundation president (1932-45) and vice-president (1946-57) of the North Queensland Naturalists' Club, he influenced the documentation and study of the region's flora. The club became a vigorous group, bridging the enthusiasm of amateur collectors and the scrupulousness of taxonomic botanists. More than fifty new species of plants were described during Flecker's presidency; with his encouragement, the club acquired its own herbarium. In 1933-48 he instituted and co-ordinated a census of plants indigenous to the area as a cumulative supplement to the *North Queensland Naturalist*. At least six new species were named in his honour, including the rare and beautiful orchid of Mount Bellenden Ker, *Dendrobium fleckeri*, and a new halophytic wattle, *Acacia fleckeri*. From 1935 until 1937 he wrote a nature column in a Cairns weekly newspaper. His advocacy of conservation and his enlightened approach to ecology—he was concerned with the problems of soil erosion and the spread of noxious, introduced weeds—marked him as a pioneer of the 'Green Movement'.

Known affectionately as 'Fleck' within the medical profession, he was a quiet, meticulous man, courteous to all. He 'enjoyed nothing more than to be surrounded by a group of people while he demonstrated the tentacles of a sea-wasp or the texture of a cedar leaf'. A member of the Queensland branch of the British Medical Association and of the Australian and New Zealand Association of Radiologists, and a fellow of the Royal Geographical Society of Australasia, he also found time for philately and was a prominent Freemason. Flecker died on 25 June 1957 at Cairns and was buried in the local cemetery; his wife, son and daughter survived him. That year he was posthumously awarded the J. P. Thomson [q.v.12] medal of the R.G.S.A. and in 1971 the Flecker Botanic Gardens, Cairns, were named in his honour.

P. S. Short (ed), *History of Systematic Botany in Australasia* (Melb, 1990); J. Devanny, *Bird of Paradise* (Syd, 1945); *People* (Syd), 30 Dec 1953; *MJA*,

30 Nov 1957, p 809; *Memoirs of the Qld Museum*, 27, no 2, 1989, p 567; *Courier-Mail*, 26 June 1957.

JOHN H. PEARN

FLEETWOOD-SMITH, LESLIE O'BRIEN (1908-1971), cricketer, was born on 30 March 1908 at Stawell, Victoria, third child of Fleetwood Smith, a newspaper manager from India, and his native-born wife Frances Alice, née Swan. Frances had edited the *Pleasant Creek News and Stawell Chronicle* after the death of her father, the founding editor; her elder son Walter ('Jim') edited the paper in 1931-61, making ninety-three years of family involvement with it. Leslie was educated at Stawell Primary School and in 1917-24 at Xavier College, Melbourne, where he was a successful first XI cricketer.

When he returned to Stawell to play for the local club, his bowling prowess attracted the attention of the St Kilda club, for whom he played (as Fleetwood-Smith) in 1930-33 before joining the Melbourne club. He first represented Victoria against Tasmania over Christmas 1931 and made his Sheffield Shield debut against South Australia in the following year. His first Test was against South Africa at Durban in 1935, and he went on to play ten Tests, touring South Africa once and England twice (1934 and 1938). He had also participated in a private, non first-class tour of North America in 1932, capturing 249 wickets at 8 apiece.

In Shield cricket for Victoria, Fleetwood-Smith took 246 wickets at 24.6, returning some remarkable analyses, including 15 for 226 against a strong New South Wales side in 1935, and 7 for 17 and 8 for 79 against Queensland in 1936. He took 597 wickets at 22.6 in all first-class cricket. In Test matches he took 42 at 37.4, including 10 for 239 against England at Adelaide in 1937, and, on the other side of the ledger, 1 for 298 in 87 overs at The Oval in 1938, having had (Sir) Leonard Hutton (364) missed at 40.

A left-armer who bowled off-breaks as well as his natural leg-break, he had extraordinary powers of spin, strengthening his arm and hand by squeezing a squash ball. His capacity to bowl the unplayable ball, with one of which he dismissed Walter Hammond—so often his destroyer—at Adelaide in 1937 (effectively to retain the Ashes for Australia), was unmatched in an era of great Australian spin bowlers. Unfortunately, his concentration sometimes strayed, and not only when bowling. Fielding, he would give vent to eldritch whoops and bird-call imitations, and practised golf strokes. Batting, he would often ignore his side's or his partner's needs.

Fleetwood-Smith was handsome, wore a moustache and had thick, oiled black hair; he successfully pursued (and was equally successfully pursued by) many women. At St Mary's Catholic Church, East St Kilda, on 28 February 1935 he had married Mary Gertrude, daughter of H. C. Elliott, a prosperous soft-drink manufacturer and Melbourne alderman. Cited as co-respondent in a divorce case in June 1946, Fleetwood-Smith was divorced by his wife in May 1947. On 9 July 1948 at the office of the government statist, Melbourne, he married a milliner Beatrix Maie Collins (who was not involved in either case).

Having enlisted in the Australian Imperial Force on 28 May 1940, Fleetwood-Smith was promoted warrant officer and served briefly at the Physical and Recreational Training School, Frankston, before being discharged on medical grounds on 4 February 1941. Following a final club season in 1945-46, he retired from cricket. His cricketing occupation gone, and his position as a salesman with his father-in-law's firm lost, he began to drink more heavily, sustaining his habit by short-lived jobs, cadging, and, eventually, theft, for which he was charged—together with vagrancy—in Melbourne in March 1969. He was by then living and sleeping in the derelicts' community on the banks of the Yarra River. The charge of theft was dropped, that of vagrancy adjourned for a year. Old friends, colleagues, and admirers, among them Sir Robert Menzies [q.v.] and Sir Henry Bolte, aghast at his circumstances, subscribed funds for his rehabilitation. He gave up drinking, was reconciled with his wife and obtained more regular employment. But the years of dissipation had wrecked his health. He died of cancer on 16 March 1971 at Fitzroy and was cremated. His wife survived him; there were no children.

J. Pollard, *Australian Cricket* (Syd, 1982); G. Growden, *A Wayward Genius* (Syd, 1991); *Wisden Cricketers' Almanack*, 1972.

W. F. MANDLE

FLETCHER, JACOB (1892-1970), public servant, was born on 15 February 1892 at Jeffcott West, near Donald, Victoria, second of three children of Jacob Fletcher, a farmer from England, and his native-born wife Elizabeth Ann, née Buchanan, a former schoolteacher. Educated at Donald Higher Elementary School, on 6 August 1906 young Jacob joined the Postmaster-General's Department as a telegraph messenger. In 1910 he became a postal-assistant at Leongatha; next year he was promoted telegraphist and transferred to Queensland.

Rejected once on medical grounds,

Fletcher enlisted as a sapper in the Australian Imperial Force on 31 January 1916. He was then 5 ft 6 ins (168 cm) tall, with a sallow complexion, hazel eyes and black hair. In 1916-18 he served on the Western Front with the 3rd Divisional Signal Company and in 1919 as a temporary sergeant with the War Records Section, London. Returning to Melbourne, he was discharged on 5 January 1920 and resumed his Commonwealth Public Service career with the Department of Health. In 1927 he moved to Canberra. Following terms as private secretary to Sir Neville Howse and (Sir) Henry Gullett [qq.v.9], Fletcher was appointed in 1930 to the correspondence and records branch, Department of Trade and Customs.

From 1933 he worked in the trade treaties and agreements branch. Because of Japan's importance as a buyer of Australian wool, the Lyons [q.v.10] government began discussions in 1934 with the Japanese who wanted a treaty of friendship, commerce and navigation. Fletcher assisted in the negotiations until 1936. In that year the Federal government announced its trade diversion policy which limited Australia's rayon and cotton imports from Japan in favour of British manufactures to ensure access to Britain's markets for Australian beef and other primary products. When Japan retaliated, Fletcher took part in efforts to settle the dispute. During the mid-1930s he also helped to conclude trade agreements with Belgium and France.

In 1941-44 he was based in Washington as his department's chief delegate to the economic mission exploring the possibility of a trade agreement between Australia and the United States of America. F. L. McDougall [q.v.10], who met him there, thought him 'a good chap'. Fletcher also gave advice on matters of principle in regard to Lend-Lease arrangements. Back home, he rose to director of his branch in 1946. In the following year he was one of the Australian government's key advisers at trade discussions in Geneva. The U.S.A. proposed to reduce its tariffs by 50 per cent in exchange for the abolition of the system of Imperial preferences, but the delegations from Britain and the dominions only offered modest concessions in scaling down their existing arrangements.

Fletcher was promoted director of research in 1951 and assistant comptroller-general (trade) in 1954. He was appointed I.S.O. in 1957, the year of his retirement. A bachelor, he continued to live in the Hotel Wellington, Barton, as he had done from the 1940s. He died on 27 January 1970 in Canberra Hospital and was cremated with Anglican rites.

R. J. Bell, *Unequal Allies* (Melb, 1977); H. C. Coombs, *Trial Balance* (Melb, 1981); S. McIntyre,

The Succeeding Age (Melb, 1993); *Canb Times*, 13 June 1957, 29 Jan 1970; D. N. Lee, From Fear of Depression to Fear of War, (Ph.D. thesis, ANU, 1991); Fletcher papers (NL). 　　　DAVID LEE

FLETCHER, JANE ADA (1870-1956), teacher, ornithologist and author, was born on 18 September 1870 at Stonefield station, near Penshurst, Victoria, eldest of three daughters of Price Fletcher, a grazier from England who was later agricultural editor of the *Queenslander*, and his Victorian-born wife Sarah, née Cooper. Jane's early life was spent on Russell Island, Queensland, and at Acacia Grove, a sugar plantation at Mackay. When the family moved to Cleveland (Queensland), she was educated in Brisbane. Following their mother's death in 1889, the sisters returned to depression-ravaged Victoria and lived with relations at Bundoora. In 1892 Jane escaped 'Granny's acid tongue' by taking work on an aunt's farm at Wilmot in north-western Tasmania. Four years later she became a teacher of sewing (initially without pay) at West Kentish primary school; by 1899 she had qualified as a head teacher and was appointed to set up a school at Upper Wilmot. She supported her father (who died in 1906) and subsequently taught at Cleveland (Tasmania), Springfield, Woodbridge and Forcett.

From her mother who was a keen botanist and her father who was a dedicated ornithologist, Jane had inherited a love of nature. She and her younger sister Sarah ('Ivy') travelled everywhere by bicycle—notwithstanding their ankle-length dresses—and frequently waded in the swamps about Cleveland where they took a particular interest in rails and crakes. A foundation member (1901) and later a life member of the Royal Australasian Ornithologists' Union, Jane Fletcher wrote and published many papers on the birds of her districts. At Cleveland she was the first to find the nesting of Eurasian coots; in 1912 at Springfield she found a new species for mainland Tasmania, the golden-headed fantail-warbler or barley-bird; at Eaglehawk Neck, where she retired and opened a guest-house, she was the first in the State to record (1925) the gentoo penguin. Her notes were published in *Emu*. She undertook field-work for the Australian-born ornithologist Gregory Mathews [q.v.10], but this activity ceased in 1936 when she was severely injured in an accident. In 1934 she had been the first woman to deliver a lecture to the Royal Society of Tasmania, of which she was a member.

Fletcher also wrote a number of successful books for children. The two earliest—*Stories from Nature* (London, 1915) and *Nature and*

Adventure in Australasia for Boys and Girls (London, 1916)—were followed by a *Brochure of Nature Study: Suggestions and Experiments for use in Schools* (1933). She produced several supplementary readers, among them *Tommy's Ride on the Emu* (Melbourne, 1925, 1948) and *Wanna* (Melbourne, 1939). A member (1953) of the Tasmanian Historical Research Association, she wrote such booklets as the *Military History of Eaglehawk Neck* (1946) and *A Brief History of Port Arthur and the Tasman Peninsula Outstations* (1947). Her lifelong interest in the Aborigines resulted in *Little Brown Piccaninnies of Tasmania* (Sydney, 1950), the most popular of her books for children; her work also appeared as supplements in *Tasmanian Education*—'Aboriginal words as place names in Tasmania' (1953) and 'Notes on the dialects of some of the Aboriginal tribes of Tasmania' (1953). Late in life she published another booklet, *The Stone Age Man of Tasmania* (1954), and a book, *Tasmania's Own Birds* (1956). She died on 15 April 1956 at Eaglehawk Neck and was cremated.

H. Anderson, *The Singing Roads*, 1-2 (Syd, 1969, 1970); J. Marcus (ed), *First in their Field* (Melb, 1993); *Emu* (Melb), 56, 1956, p 149; *Tas Country*, 4 July 1986, p 15; *Mercury* (Hob), 16 Apr 1956; Fletcher papers (OL); Fletcher file (TA); personal information.   LEONARD WALL

FLICK, WILLIAM ALBERT (1890-1980), pest exterminator, was born on 14 February 1890 at Lismore, New South Wales, second of eight children of native-born parents William Flick, a self-styled 'Richmond River Pioneer' and dairy-farmer, and his wife Sarah, née Atkin. His grandfather Jacob Flick had emigrated from Alsace, and the family developed interests in cedar-getting, timber-shipping, cattle-dealing and dairying.

Albie grew up on his father's farm at Ewingsdale, Byron Bay, and was educated locally. At the Pacific Hall, Mullumbimby, on 3 February 1915 he married with Anglican rites Phyllis Pearl Jamison (d.1977). The couple began experiments to rid their Tyagarah dairy-farm of termites. Building on their experience of bee-keeping, they saw the possibility of using working termites to poison the queen. Eventually they developed an arsenical compound, a 'secret' red powder, fine enough to be carried, eaten and spread by grooming throughout a colony. It effectively exterminated termites on their own and surrounding properties. The process was patented in 1937.

Phyllis had quickly recognized the commercial potential. Bill, as he was known to his associates, began acquiring testimonials and charging for his services from about 1918; he

also trained others in Sydney and Brisbane. The Flicks moved to Glen Innes in 1924, for the sake of their daughter's asthma, and then to Perth to treat pest problems in underground telephone cables. Each time they left trained 'Flickmen' to carry on the work. They drove back from Perth and in 1928 settled at Hornsby, Sydney. In the 1930s W. A. Flick & Co. successfully expanded into the cyanide fumigation of cockroaches and bedbugs in ships and hotels. During World War II the business expanded as a protected industry, with government contracts for pest control in hospitals and barracks.

Flick continued to do some of the eradication work himself, and introduced his sons to it. He remained unsophisticated, with a reputation for honesty and good humour, and valued his relations with clients. A strong man of middle height, he enjoyed sport, particularly tennis and fishing, and demonstrated his woodchopping skills at the Royal Easter Show into the 1930s. It was at the show that a sign-writer came up with the slogan, 'Remember —one flick and they're gone'. On billboards and radio the catch-phrase made the company a household name and gave a particularly entomological edge to the word 'flick' in Australia.

After the war the firm's hectic growth and loose control necessitated reorganization. The business was incorporated as W. A. Flick & Co. Pty Ltd, more staff were recruited and Flick passed the management to his sons. Although he remained chairman of directors, he had effectively retired by 1950. The company continued to expand on the basis of eradication rather than prevention, diversifying into allied areas such as crop-spraying, and introducing organochlorines and organophosphates. Fifteen overseas branches were established, mainly around the Pacific.

In semi-retirement at Newport, Flick became a keen lawn bowler and an active Freemason. He was appointed O.B.E. in 1972. Survived by his daughter and three sons, he died on 10 May 1980 at his Newport home and was buried in Mona Vale cemetery. When the family sold out in 1986, W. A. Flick & Co. had long been Australia's largest pest control company, and one that was among the largest in the world.

W. Flick, *A Dying Race* (Ballina, NSW, 1935); Flick Pest Control, *Property Protector* (undated issue, held in ADB file); *SMH*, 3 June 1972, 24 Dec 1964, 13 May 1980; information from, and family papers held by Mr W. G. Flick, Turramurra, Syd.
                                        RICHARD WHITE

FLINN, MARY (ISABEL) (1894-1959), teacher and housewife, was born on 1 February 1894 in East Melbourne, second daughter of Christopher Flinn, clerk, and his wife Marion, née Scott, both Victorian born. Isabel (a name she adopted) was educated at Presbyterian Ladies' College (1908-12) where she was prominent in the debating society and the Christian Union, and won an exhibition in her final examinations. At the University of Melbourne (B.A., 1916; M.A., 1918; Dip.Ed., 1919) she majored in philosophy, attracting Professor W. R. B. Gibson's [q.v.8] attention with a 'neat solution of a complicated problem in Formal Logic'. She graduated with first-class honours and was awarded a Hastie scholarship. In 1917 Flinn was appointed to tutor in philosophy at Ormond [q.v.5] College; she also taught at Trinity and Queen's colleges, as well as taking students in mathematics at P.L.C. and Melbourne High School. In addition, she gratuitously taught classes in psychology for the Workers' Educational Association and for the Free Kindergarten Union of Victoria.

In recommending her for a lectureship in education and psychology at the University of Queensland in December 1920, Gibson wrote that she had 'an eminently first-class mind, enthusiastic in its inner springs, keen and penetrating'; from the unanimous testimony of her students, he concluded 'she must be a quite exceptionally good teacher'. One of her students was William Macmahon Ball. In *More Memories of Melbourne University: undergraduate life in the years since 1919* (1985) he described how Miss Flinn transformed him in two months from unrelieved failure to confidence. Before moving to Queensland, Flinn helped to found the Public Questions Society at the university and was active in the Lyceum Club. After three years teaching, she resigned from the University of Queensland in 1924. On 26 March that year at Queen's College Chapel, Parkville, she married 34-year-old Cyril Stanley Shaw Yarwood, a Methodist minister and her ex-student at Queen's.

Without formal employment while she bore and raised four children, Mrs Yarwood was typical of a generation of women whose careers were cut short by marriage. In 1943 she was appointed to the staff of Woodstock Girls' School, Albury, New South Wales. Students felt privileged to be taught by her, and remembered her comments on the implications of the dropping of the first atomic bomb. Many others were touched by her serenity, wisdom and courage. She resigned in December 1949 to accompany her husband to Wollongong where he had taken a teaching post. Isabel enjoyed bush walking and gardening, played golf with her sons, and took a delight in solo whist and operatic music. When a friend regretted the fate of flowers in the Yarwood garden, Isabel—who was attracted to Stoicism—replied: 'we enjoy its beauty now, but we must accept the cycle of life and death, not only for flowers but for ourselves'. Following a long absence from Christian practice, she became an active member of the Presbyterian Church, Thirroul. Survived by her husband, daughter and three sons, she died of acute pancreatitis on 11 September 1959 in the district hospital, Bulli, and was cremated.

H. Dow (ed), *More Memories of Melbourne University* (Melb, 1985); Presbyterian Ladies' College (Melb), *Patchwork*, 1908-12, *and* Archives; Univ Melb Archives; family papers (held by author, Waverton, Syd).   A. T. YARWOOD

FLOCKHART, DAVID JOHN (1889-1964), Presbyterian clergyman and administrator, was born on 11 December 1889 at Waterloo, Sydney, son of John Flockhart, a blacksmith from Scotland, and his native-born wife Catherine, née McGee. David was educated in public schools and worked in business before deciding to study for the Presbyterian ministry. Having attended night-school, he entered the University of Sydney (B.A., 1917; M.A., 1919) where he won the professor's prize for philosophy in 1916 and graduated with first-class honours in logic and mental philosophy. He tutored in Hebrew and in 1919 was awarded the Mitchell prize at the Presbyterian Theological Hall, St Andrew's College.

At St Stephen's Church, Phillip Street, on 15 November that year Flockhart married a clerk, Jean Isabel Ingram (d.1955). In February 1920 he was ordained and inducted into the charge of Tamworth. He ministered at St Andrew's, Newcastle, from 1923 to 1927, and at St John's, Wahroonga, from 1927 to 1956. In his first year he encouraged his congregation to establish the Wahroonga Preparatory School, and, throughout his ministry at St John's, taught divinity at Knox Grammar School.

A trustee (1927-60) of the Presbyterian Church of New South Wales, Flockhart served on numerous committees, particularly those associated with the administration of Church structures and with the training, placement and support of the ministry. He was a council-member of Knox Grammar School (1929-64), St Andrew's College (1941-56) and Presbyterian Ladies' College, Pymble (1949-64). At the Theological Hall he taught homiletics—as Steel [q.v.6] lecturer —in 1935-37, and theology in 1941-44 and 1953. He served as a chaplain with the Australian Military Forces in 1940-41 and on occasion acted as troubleshooter in cases of congregational crisis. Flockhart was elected moderator of New South Wales for 1949-50. As a representative (1926-59) at the General

Assembly of the Presbyterian Church of Australia, he contributed to a wide variety of committees and was convener (1942-57) of the assembly's Canberra executive. He was moderator-general for 1957-59 and promoted moves towards church union.

Combining social conservatism with theological liberalism and ecumenism, Flockhart abhorred radical political policies and urged a return to God and Christian moral principles to counter economic and social ills. In the controversy over the liberal theology of Professor Samuel Angus [q.v.7], he staunchly defended Angus. Flockhart was highly respected as an energetic, clear-headed and strong-willed administrator, and as a scholar. Younger ministers often regarded him with awe. In his parishes he was held in affection and esteem for his preaching and energetic leadership. One parishioner described him as 'a brilliant preacher and a prince among organisers'.

Flockhart enjoyed playing bowls and belonged to the New South Wales Masonic Club. He suffered a severe stroke in 1958, struggled on to complete his term as moderator-general, but never fully recovered. Survived by his son and daughter, he died on 20 July 1964 in Ballina Private Hospital, Gordon; after a service at St John's, Wahroonga, he was cremated.

C. A. White, *The Challenge of the Years* (Syd, 1951); B. Mansfield and F. Richardson, *Knox* (Syd, 1974); *NSW Presbyterian*, 30 Jan 1930, 7, 21 June, 11 Oct 1933, 20 May 1949, 5 Apr, 20 Sept 1957, 7 Aug 1964; *Procs of the General Assembly of the Presbyterian Church of Aust in the State of NSW*, 1931, p 64, 1955, p 214, 1965, p 18.

JOAN MANSFIELD

FLOREY, HOWARD WALTER, BARON FLOREY OF ADELAIDE AND MARSTON (1898-1968), medical scientist, was born on 24 September 1898 at Malvern, Adelaide, third and youngest child and only son of Joseph Florey, a boot manufacturer from England, and his second wife, native-born Bertha Mary, née Wadham. Educated at the Collegiate School of St Peter and the University of Adelaide (M.B., B.S., 1921; M.D., 1944), Howard sailed for England in 1921 as a Rhodes scholar. At the University of Oxford (B.A., B.Sc., 1924; M.A., 1935), he studied in the honour school of physiology under Sir Charles Sherrington who became an 'influential guide and friend'. Florey transferred in 1924 to the University of Cambridge (Ph.D., 1927; M.A.; 1928), spent ten months (1925-26) in the United States of America, then worked in London.

While a student in Adelaide, Florey had met MARY ETHEL HAYTER Reed (1900-1966).

After a prolonged correspondence she joined him in London. They were married on 19 October 1926 at Holy Trinity parish church, Paddington; the marriage was to be unhappy, due in part to her poor health and in part to his intolerance. From 1927 Florey lectured in the pathology department at Cambridge where he worked on his doctoral thesis on the flow of blood and lymph. In 1931 he was appointed professor of pathology at the University of Sheffield. Four years later he moved to a similar post at the Sir William Dunn school of pathology, Oxford; he was to remain in it until 1962 when he resigned to become provost of The Queen's College.

Florey's appointment to the Oxford chair was a milestone in the history of pathology in the British Empire because, for the first time, a man trained in experimental physiology who looked at pathology as disordered physiology attained a position of influence in the subject. Encouraged by Florey's presence, a succession of young Australians went to the Oxford department for their postgraduate education.

Although Florey made advances in many fields of experimental pathology, by far his greatest contribution to science was the development of penicillin as a systemic antibacterial agent, thus inaugurating the antibiotic era. At Cambridge he had studied natural antibacterial substances, notably lysozyme, an enzyme that had been discovered by (Sir) Alexander Fleming in 1922. Recognizing the need for biochemical expertise to purify the enzyme, Florey recruited (Sir) Ernst Chain to his research team.

In 1938-39 Florey and Chain jointly initiated a systematic investigation of the biological and biochemical properties of antibacterial substances produced by bacteria and fungi. They eventually selected penicillin, discovered by Fleming in 1928, for detailed examination. It proved so promising in experiments on mice infected with streptococci and staphylococci that all the resources of the laboratory were devoted to its production on a scale that would allow testing on humans. The difficulties in wartime Britain were immense, but, due to the enterprise of Florey's team and a variety of 'Heath Robinson' contraptions, enough penicillin was prepared to carry out clinical trials in 1941. The results were so dramatic that assistance was sought from British industry, which proved inadequate to the task. Penicillin for the treatment of war casualties was first produced in the United States of America. Its effects were miraculous.

Despite living in Britain since the age of 23, Florey remained Australian in accent and outlook. In 1944 he visited Australia to discuss the local production of penicillin and to report on the state of medical research in the country of his birth. He produced a paper that played a major role in establishing the Australian National University. From 1947 to 1957 he was closely connected with the development of the university, particularly of the John Curtin [q.v.13] School of Medical Research. Offered the directorship of the school in 1948, he temporized and did not finally decline until 1957. Meanwhile, as 'adviser' to the school (1948-55), he was effectively its non-resident head. He opened the school's permanent building in 1958 and became chancellor of the university in 1965.

Florey was reserved, but sure of himself. A splendid experimentalist, he had no liking for speculation or abstract ideas. He was intensely hard-working and expected the same devotion from his colleagues and students. Although he had no time for administrators—'paper-shufflers', as he called them—when thrust into senior administrative positions he proved to be an excellent chairman. He was a man of vision and above all a man who got things done: 'few people can have made better use than Florey of eminence stemming from a major role in a great discovery'. Outstandingly successful as president (1960-65) of the Royal Society, London, he reorganized the institution, greatly expanded its research-professorship programme and secured magnificent new premises at 6 Carlton House Terrace.

As a boy and a young man, Florey had been good at sport and he continued to play tennis with enthusiasm into his fifties. Outside the laboratory, his main enjoyment was travel, and from his earliest days at Oxford he took every opportunity to go abroad, delving into the history, architecture, art and music of the countries he visited; he relished the extensive travel that he undertook as a result of the fame of penicillin and his connexion with the A.N.U. He was an enthusiastic photographer; he relaxed with classical music; and in later life he found pleasure in painting and in cultivating a rose garden at his Marston home in Oxfordshire.

Florey had been elected a fellow of the Royal Society in 1941, for work done before the practical use of penicillin had been demonstrated. Subsequently, the contributions of the drug to human health and well-being were so immense and so obvious that honours and awards were showered upon him. He was knighted in 1944, won (with Chain and Fleming) the Nobel prize for physiology and medicine in 1945, was appointed to the French Légion d'honneur in 1946, was awarded the U.S.A.'s Medal of Merit in 1948, and received numerous medals and prizes from societies in England and abroad, as well as honorary degrees from many British, Australian and other universities. In 1965 he was created Baron Florey of Adelaide and Mar-

ston. That year he was appointed to the Order of Merit.

Author or co-author of some two hundred scientific papers, Florey edited *Lectures on General Pathology* (London, 1954), which went through four editions, and co-authored the massive two-volume treatise, *Antibiotics: A Survey of Penicillin, Streptomycin, and Other Antimicrobial Substances from Fungi, Actinomycetes, Bacteria and Plants* (Oxford, 1949). On 6 June 1967 at the register office, Oxford, he married a divorcee Margaret Augusta Jennings, née Fremantle (d.1994), a long-time colleague in his Oxford laboratories. Survived by her, and by the son and daughter of his first marriage, he died of myocardial infarction on 21 February 1968 at his Queen's College lodgings and was cremated. He had made no fortune, for in the 1940s patenting of penicillin was against ethical medical principles; his estate was sworn for probate in England at £29 786.

A suburb in Canberra is named after Florey and his likeness adorned an Australian $50 note; a research institute in Melbourne, a lecture theatre and professorship in the John Curtin school, and a joint Royal Society-A.N.U. lecture and travelling fellowship bear his name. In England his name is attached to a fellowship at Lady Margaret Hall, Oxford, and to a building belonging to The Queen's College. A memorial tablet was unveiled at St Nicholas's parish church, Marston, in 1980, and a commemorative stone in Westminster Abbey was unveiled in November 1981. There are portraits of Florey by Frederick Deane in the Sir William Dunn school, by Henry Carr in the Royal Society's apartments, by Allan Gwynne-Jones in the University of Adelaide and by (Sir) William Dargie in Florey's old school. A head in bronze by John Dowie has been placed in North Terrace, Adelaide.

Ethel Florey was born on 1 October 1900 at Stanmore, Sydney, fourth child of John Hayter Reed, bank manager, and his wife Joanna Agnes, née Du Vé, both Victorian born. Educated at Tormore House School, Adelaide, and the University of Adelaide (M.B., B.S., 1924; M.D., 1950), she interrupted her medical career to raise her children. She worked with the Oxford Regional Blood Transfusion Service in 1939-41, then took part in clinical trials of penicillin conducted at the Radcliffe Infirmary, at military hospitals and at the Birmingham Accident Hospital. Although dogged by deafness and ill health for most of her life, she was an extremely determined woman and from 1939 led an active professional life. After collaborating with her husband in the book, *Antibiotics*, she published under her own name a companion work, *The Clinical Application of Antibiotics* (London), in four volumes: the first (1952) dealt with penicillin, the succeeding three (1957-61) with other antibiotics. Lady Florey died of myocardial infarction on 10 October 1966 at Marston and was buried at Fairspear House, Leafield, Oxford.

DNB, 1961-70; L. Bickel, *Rise Up to Life* (Syd, 1972); G. Macfarlane, *Howard Florey* (Oxford, 1979); T. I. Williams, *Howard Florey* (Oxford, 1984); *Biog Memoirs of Fellows of Roy Soc* (Lond), 17, 1971, p 255 *and* for publications; *British Medical J*, 2, 1966, p 1013; *Lancet*, 2, 22 Oct 1966, p 913; Florey archives (Medical Research Council *and* Roy Soc, Lond, *and* ANU).

FRANK FENNER

FLOWER, PATRICIA MARY BRYSON (1914-1977), crime novelist and television playwright, was born on 23 February 1914 at Ramsgate, Kent, England, one of four children of James Bullen, hotel porter, and his wife Jessie Sarah, née Bryson. Pat left Worthing County High School in 1928 when the family emigrated to New South Wales. They lived at Kyogle, and then in Sydney. At the district registrar's office, Paddington, on 22 December 1937 she married Bruce Douglas Jiffkins, a messenger. In the 1940s she worked as secretary for the New Theatre League, writing radio plays and revue sketches in her spare time.

Six weeks after she divorced Jiffkins, Pat married Cedric Arthur Flower, a painter, on 4 March 1949 at the registrar general's office, Sydney. While they were in England from 1950 to 1955, she began to write crime novels, the first of which, *Wax Flowers for Gloria*, appeared in 1958. She published at least one crime novel every two years until 1975, moving from detective stories such as *Goodbye Sweet William* (1959)—featuring Inspector Swinton, her Australian 'Maigret' character—to psychological thrillers, among them *Cobweb* (1972), *Slyboots* (1974) and *Crisscross* (1976). Some of her books were translated into French and German.

Back in Sydney, Pat Flower worked as an advertising copywriter until 1963 when she began to write full time. By 1961 she was also writing film and television scripts, including (with Cedric) *From the Tropics to the Snow*, produced by the Commonwealth Film Unit in 1965. Her play, *The Tape Recorder*, a Pinteresque piece for an actress and tape recorder, was televised by the Australian Broadcasting Commission in 1966 and produced in colour by the British Broadcasting Corporation in 1967. She won the 1967 (Dame) Mary Gilmore [q.v.9] award for 'Tilley Landed on our Shores', a comic version of Governor Phillip's [q.v.2] 1788 expedition. An adaptation of her novel, *Fiends of the Family* (London, 1966), for A.B.C. television won an 'Awgie'

award in 1969 from the Australian Writers' Guild. In the late 1960s some of her television plays were screened in the A.B.C.'s 'Australian Playhouse' series. She also wrote scripts for commercial television. In 1971 the Flowers again visited Europe where Pat gathered further material for her suspense novels. Returning to Sydney in 1972, they took separate flats at Paddington, so that she could concentrate on her writing.

Pat Flower was an amusing companion with a dry wit. Her husky voice retained a slight English accent, and she was attractive in an angular, understated way. From early childhood she wore glasses. She suffered from insomnia and arthritis for many years and was increasingly isolated as her health deteriorated. The two sides of her writing—comedy and horror—reflected aspects of her personality, with her novels becoming progressively darker. On the night of 1/2 September 1977 she died from the effects of poisoning by pentobarbitone, intentionally taken. Her husband survived her.

Scholarly interest in crime writing led to the republication of *Vanishing Point* (1993) and several critics have championed Flower's later novels as among the best of the genre in Australia. At the time of her death, however, she was remembered as one of the first Australian writers able to make the transition from the novel and radio play to the formal requirements of television writing.

D. Latta (ed), *Sand on the Gumshoe* (Syd, 1989); P. Flower, *Vanishing Point*, afterword by M. J. Tolley and P. Moss (Adel, 1993); *Aust Women's Weekly*, 1 July 1958, p 29; *Aust Author*, 10, no 1, Jan 1978, p 43; *SMH*, 28 Aug 1958, 27 Jan 1968, *Bulletin*, 21 Oct 1972; *Age* (Melb), 17 May 1975; Flower papers (ML); information from Mr C. Flower, Werri Beach, NSW.   SUSAN LEVER

FLYNN, JAMES ALOYSIUS FOEDUS (1899-1969), ophthalmic surgeon, was born on 30 May 1899 in Sydney, fourth child of John Flynn, a medical practitioner from Ireland, and his native-born wife Maud May, née Witton. Of their nine surviving children, the six sons formed a remarkable group: they each attended Marist Brothers' High School, Darlinghurst, studied medicine at the University of Sydney and achieved eminence in their profession. All were prominent in university affairs and sport, particularly hockey and rugby, and in professional and community organizations.

The eldest, MICHAEL RICHARD (1893-1957), surgeon, was born on 19 October 1893 at Bairnsdale, Victoria, and graduated B.A., 1914; B.Sc., 1916; M.B., Ch.M., 1920; M.D., 1931. Awarded a Walter and Eliza Hall [qq.v.9] travelling fellowship in 1920, he studied in England; from August 1921 to December 1924 he was a fellow at the Mayo Clinic, United States of America (M.S., 1925, University of Minnesota). He distinguished himself as a practical surgeon, holding appointments at Royal Prince Alfred, Lewisham and the Dental hospitals, and lectured at the university's faculty of dentistry. A fellow of the Royal Australasian College of Surgeons, he was a skilled anatomist and speedy operator. He was prepared to take on difficult surgical procedures—particularly in the head, neck and thorax—well before modern technology made these areas readily accessible. Dick, as he was known, died of cerebral oedema on 11 December 1957 at Lewisham and was buried in Waverley cemetery; his wife Roma Theresa, née O'Dea, survived him.

JOHN JOSEPH WITTON (1895-1955), dermatologist, was born on 26 August 1895 in Sydney, won a Blue for hockey and graduated B.A., 1916; M.B., Ch.M., 1924. He rose through the ranks to lieutenant in the Australian Imperial Force and in 1917-18 served with the 30th Battalion on the Western Front; he was awarded the Military Cross for an action at Foucacourt, France, in November 1918 which left him blind in one eye. Flynn turned to medicine, studied dermatology in London and became a leading figure at Sydney and Lewisham hospitals. A part-time specialist (from 1940) and consultant dermatologist to the Royal Australian Air Force, he reached the rank of honorary group captain. He was an executive-member (from 1942) of the St John Ambulance Association; he played bowls at Royal Sydney Golf Club, belonged to the Australian Jockey and Sydney Turf clubs, and owned several winning racehorses. Serving on the Medical Board from 1944, he was its president when he died of a coronary occlusion on 6 December 1955 at his Bellevue Hill home. His wife Mary Amelia, née Bridge, and daughter survived him.

James graduated M.B., Ch.M. in 1922. Following residency at Sydney Hospital, he undertook training in ophthalmology at its eye department and in Britain, gaining diplomas of ophthalmology (Oxford) and ophthalmic medicine and surgery (R.C.P. & S.) in 1925. Returning to Sydney next year, he was appointed to Royal Prince Alfred and Lewisham hospitals. On 16 January 1929 he married Ranee Mary Gertrude Adams (d.1959) at St Mary's Cathedral. Their only child Ann was to die of diphtheria. Flynn was a fellow (from 1930) of the R.A.C.S., a founder (1938) and president (1939) of the Ophthalmological Society of Australia, and a fellow (1940) of the Royal Society of Medicine, London.

A surgeon lieutenant in the Royal Australian Naval Reserve, Flynn began full-time service on 2 September 1939 and joined H.M.A.S. *Australia* next month (as ophthal-

mologist specialist from December); the ship spent time with the British Home Fleet in 1940 and took part in the Dakar expedition in September. He was posted ashore in April 1941 and worked in Sydney establishments until demobilized on 1 March 1946 as acting surgeon commander. After the war he was consultant ophthalmologist to the R.A.N. and was promoted honorary surgeon captain on his retirement in 1957.

Flynn had given special attention to eye problems associated with naval war service, including night vision and solar retinal damage. His article, 'Photo-retinitis in anti-aircraft lookouts' in the *Medical Journal of Australia* (1942), was a lucid application to clinical practice of what had previously been rather obscure scientific knowledge. He and J. C. Eccles, in 'Experimental photo-retinitis' (*M.J.A.*, 1944), reported well-designed and carefully performed experiments that revealed new information about solar retinal damage.

Despite his busy professional life, which included clinical practice, as well as teaching and examining at the University of Sydney, Flynn sat on the editorial committee of *Oph-thalmologica*, published at Basel, Switzerland. He belonged to the Australian, Royal Sydney Golf, Australian Jockey and Rose Bay Bowling clubs, the Royal Agricultural and Art Gallery societies of New South Wales, the Australian Elizabethan Theatre Trust and the National Trust of Australia. Courteous and kind, he was unruffled in both manner and dress. On 10 January 1962 at St Joseph's Church, Edgecliff, he married Sarah (Sari) Mary, née Purcell, widow of his fellow ophthalmologist, Adrian Odillo Maher. Survived by his wife, James died of a coronary occlusion on 15 July 1969 at his Darling Point home and was buried in South Head cemetery.

His younger brother LEOPOLD RUPERT (1901-1983), consultant physician, was born on 25 March 1901 in Sydney and graduated M.B., Ch.M. in 1924. On the death of his father in 1926, Leo took over his general practice in College Street. After being admitted to membership of the Royal Australasian College of Physicians in 1939, he became a Macquarie Street consultant. A conservative, thorough and sympathetic physician, he was an influential figure at Lewisham and St Margaret's hospitals. During World War II he was a part-time specialist with the R.A.A.F. Medical Branch. He belonged to the A.J.C. and Vaucluse Bowling Club. Leo died on 12 December 1983 at his Darling Point home; his wife Dorothea Mary, née Hickey, and their two sons and three daughters survived him.

GREGORY STEPHEN (1911-1978), ophthalmic surgeon, was born on 8 January 1911 in Sydney and graduated M.B., B.S. in 1935. He was an honorary at Lewisham Hospital, a foundation member of the O.S.A. and one of the first fellows in ophthalmology of the R.A.C.S. Having served in the Citizen Military Forces, in 1942 he was seconded to the Australian Imperial Force. He performed specialist work in the 121st Australian General Hospital, Katherine, Northern Territory, the 2nd/7th A.G.H., Lae, New Guinea, and the 110th A.G.H., Perth, and was a major at the end of the war. Predeceased by his wife Mary Margaret, née Curtis, Greg died of myocardial infarction on 10 July 1978 at his Wollstonecraft home; his son and three of his four daughters survived him.

Another brother Francis Stanislaus (b.1906), an ophthalmic surgeon and missionary priest, was widely known as 'Flynn of the North' and was honoured for his medical work among Aborigines. Two of the Flynn sisters became Brigidine nuns.

G. E. Hall and A. Cousins (eds), *Book of Remembrance of the University of Sydney in the War 1914-1918* (Syd, 1939); *MJA*, 4 Feb, 28 Apr 1956, 25 Jan 1958, 13 Dec 1969, 20 Oct 1979, 15 Sept 1984; *Trans of Ophthalmological Soc of Aust*, 1, 1969 (James Aloysius Flynn memorial number); Roy A'sian College of Physicians Archives (Syd); J. A. F. Flynn naval record, series A6769 (AA, Canb); family information.   G. L. McDONALD

FOCKEN, CHARLES MELBOURNE (1901-1978), physicist and museum director, was born on 23 October 1901 at Kan Lung, Hong Kong, third of four sons of Charles Fredrick Focken, marine engineer, and his wife Elizabeth Edwards, née Gray. After Charles senior died from injuries sustained in a typhoon, the family settled in 1908 at Middle Park, Melbourne, where Charles attended the local state school. His studies at Wesley College (1914-18) and at the University of Melbourne (B.Sc., 1923; B.M.E., 1931), with residence at Queen's College, were studded with first-class honours, exhibitions, scholarships and prizes. Colours in tennis (a lifelong relaxation) and widespread leadership in student affairs saw him named as Rhodes scholar for 1923.

At Lincoln College, Oxford (D.Phil., 1926), Focken studied physics. Two events in England were decisive in his career. One was research under Sir Ernest (Baron) Rutherford at the Cavendish Laboratory, Cambridge, which helped win his appointment in 1926 as the first Beverly-Mackenzie lecturer in physics at the University of Otago, New Zealand. The other was meeting Elizabeth Sills whom he married with Methodist forms in Queen's College chapel, Parkville, Melbourne, on 21 December 1927.

Of less than average height, Focken had an athletic figure; premature baldness enhanced his image as an intellectual, and a ready, engaging smile led to cherubic comparisons. Although he never became a relaxed or stimulating speaker, his carefully prepared lectures imbued students with the importance of a logical approach. He had a zest for administration and was influential in the university and in learned societies. In 1933-35, as the New Zealand Commonwealth Fund fellow, he studied geophysics at the Colorado School of Mines, United States of America (M.S., 1935). He was to publish *Lord Rutherford of Nelson* (Auckland, 1937) and *Dimensional Methods and their Applications* (London, 1953).

Promoted reader in 1950, Focken left New Zealand next year on his appointment as director of the Museum (from 1960 Institute) of Applied Science of Victoria, Melbourne. In 1953 he studied methods of museum display and administration in Britain and Northern Europe, and produced an influential report. The 'dynamic' Focken brought museum display into modern mode, secured extra staff and funds, persuaded government to complete the Swanston Street wing and established a radio-carbon-dating laboratory. His instant action in preserving H. V. McKay's [q.v.10] historic smithy prompted a £20 000 donation from the Sunshine Foundation to erect a planetarium at the museum. During planning for the move of the National Gallery of Victoria, debates on the allocation of areas found Focken at variance with his chairman, the strong-willed F. M. Read; believing he had lost the confidence of the trustees, Focken resigned in December 1961.

In November he had accepted an invitation from the United Nations Educational, Scientific and Cultural Organization to be chief of a mission to establish the Malta College of Arts, Science and Technology at Valetta. With typical energy, Focken began the first courses in temporary premises in 1962. The project was almost completed on his retirement in 1966 and became the New University of Malta (1978). Returning home in 1967, Focken lived quietly at Kew. He died on 15 August 1978 at East Hawthorn and was cremated; his wife and two of their three daughters survived him.

N. H. MacNeil (ed), *The History of Wesley College 1920-1940* (Melb, 1941); W. P. Morrell, *The University of Otago* (Dunedin, NZ, 1969); W. Perry, *The Science Museum of Victoria* (Melb, 1972); St Columb's (Hawthorn, Melb), *Columban*, Sept 1978; *Herald* (Melb), 1 June 1935; Official files (Museum of Vic, Melb); student records (Queen's College Archives, Univ Melb); Focken's diary, note-books and papers (held by author, Burwood, Melb) *and* personal information; information from Mrs L. Athan, Vermont, Melb, and Prof D. N. F. Dunbar, Canb.   F. J. KENDALL

FOLETTA, GEORGE GOTARDO (1892-1973), hosiery and knitwear manufacturer, was born on 30 January 1892 at Northcote, Melbourne, eldest son of Victorian-born parents Henry Gotardo Foletta, a stonemason of Swiss extraction, and his wife Gertrude, née Bright. Henry repaired the depression-ravaged fortunes of his family by starting a successful fancy goods commission-agency.

George was educated at Princes Hill State School and South Melbourne College. He joined the firm in 1909, studied accountancy at night-school, and gradually assumed control of all the Foletta book-keeping, advertising and marketing operations. The flair for design that sparked his interest in advertising the firm's imported hosiery also influenced his own style of life. After he married saleswoman Alice Myra Cooper on 13 March 1915 at the Methodist Church, North Carlton, they built a Californian bungalow, one of the earliest of these unconventional houses in Melbourne.

In 1917 George A. Bond [q.v.7] began manufacturing silk stockings in Sydney, attempting to overcome Australian prejudice in favour of imported hosiery, but it was not until the end of the boom in 1920-21 and the crash that destroyed 50 per cent of the soft-goods import-houses that the hosiery market was opened to increased local manufacture. Backed by his father and a friend Frank Levy, in 1920 Foletta set up the Atlas Knitting and Spinning Mills Pty Ltd in a small hall at Brunswick. Levy was chairman, George Foletta was general manager and his father was a director. With six fine-gauge machines on line by April 1921, Atlas's 'Prestige' brand, high-quality, circular-knit silk hosiery made such a spectacular and profitable entry into the industry that, despite a falling share market, the firm was able to go public as Prestige Ltd in April 1922.

The next few years at Prestige saw friction between board-members: the Folettas wanted the company to persevere with top-of-the-range lines, but the majority faction—led by A. G. Staley and the company's bankers—believed a low-to-medium quality range should be produced. Father and son resigned from the board in 1922 and George went to manage the company's Sydney office. When he returned to Melbourne he found that Prestige, relocated in a new factory at East Brunswick, was making heavy losses in the face of renewed foreign competition. He persuaded the demoralized board to restructure around a quality-first marketing policy. By 1924, when George A. Bond & Co. Ltd was liquidated, Prestige was back in the black. About this time the company became the first Australian knitter to make fully-fashioned silk stockings, outselling the best imported brands and giving Prestige dominance of the local hosiery market.

With the arrival of British-trained Leslie Gough in 1926, Prestige entered its period of greatest expansion. By 1933 it was spinning its own silk yarn, had diversified into lingerie and commenced business in New Zealand; three years later it was spinning imported rayon filament into hosiery yarn. Foletta was managing director (1937-48), chairman (from 1943) and governing director (from 1948) of the Prestige group of companies. In 1944 the company branched out into weaving. Twenty years on, Prestige took over its major competitor, Staley's Holeproof Industries Ltd. In 1968 the Prestige-Holeproof group was the largest knitter in the country, producing a complete range of men's, women's and children's clothing. On 29 July that year Foletta and his board reluctantly recommended acceptance of the offer of Dunlop Australia Ltd to take over the group, and he retired as chairman and governing director.

Foletta was a leading figure in the Australian Industries Protection League, and a co-founder and president (1951-56) of its successor, the Australian Industries Development Association. He was notable as an entrepreneur, a battler of overseas combines and a fighter for Australian manufacturing. In 1962 he was appointed C.M.G. Although he described his younger self as 'a bit of an idealist, a silly kid, a radical', he seemed to the reporter who interviewed him at the time of his retirement to his Tudor-style mansion, with its art collection and bearskin rugs, to be a hard man, slight, wiry and younger than his 76 years. A strong believer in family virtues, he employed two of his brothers at Prestige. None of his sons chose to work in manufacturing, but Foletta's sense of family extended to his factories where Prestige provided elaborate amenities for the employees. Survived by his wife and three of their four sons, he died on 25 April 1973 at Ivanhoe and was cremated; his estate was sworn for probate at $298 316. In 1975 his family history, *Woven Threads*, was privately printed. Five years after Foletta's death, Dunlop discontinued the Prestige brand.

Prestige Ltd, *Ideals* (Melb, 1932); *Herald* (Melb), 29 July 1950, 30 July 1952, 11 July 1968, 30 Apr 1973; *Sun News-Pictorial*, 12 July 1968; Holeproof Ltd, Holeproof. The Corporate Story (ts, nd, Pacific Dunlop Ltd collection, Melb).

AIRLIE WORRALL

FOLEY, JAMES JOSEPH (1886-1975), De La Salle Brother, educationist and administrator, was born on 6 August 1886 at Killenaule, County Tipperary, Ireland, son of Patrick Foley, farmer, and his wife Johanna, née Corcoran. Jimmy entered the De La Salle novitiate at Castletown on 8 September 1903 and took vows on 22 November 1904, adopting the religious name Jerome. After teacher-training at the Order's college at Waterford, he taught in 1903-07 at Ardee where he decided to volunteer to serve in Australia.

In response to appeals to the Order to extend its educational work from New South Wales, Foley and two other brothers arrived in Melbourne on 4 February 1912. Next day they started teaching in a parish hall at Malvern; by Easter they had moved into a new building in Stanhope Street West. Transferred to New South Wales in 1913, Brother Jerome was appointed director at Ashfield, Sydney (1920), and at Armidale (1922). He returned to Victoria in 1923 and—while serving as director at De La Salle, Malvern (1923-24) and St Ignatius' School, Richmond (1924-28)—studied part time at the University of Melbourne (B.A., 1926). From 1929 until 1946 he had charge of the religious community and was headmaster of De La Salle College, Malvern (a secondary school since 1926), housed in new buildings in Stanhope Street East.

Foley was an inspirational teacher, his first loves being the natural sciences and mathematics. In 1930 he visited nearby convents after class, helping nuns in parish schools to teach science with simple experiments, many of which he devised himself. He had a lively character and intellect, and was a voracious reader, especially when walking along his favoured garden paths within the college grounds. Short in stature, he was a bundle of energy and an enthusiastic gardener. He walked miles at weekends, a distinctive figure with his T. S. Eliotish 'wopsical' hat planted squarely on his head. In the baking summer of 1942 he led by example, digging slit trenches in the clay of the main schoolyard.

In 1946-58 Foley was the Order's provincial for Australasia and Papua; he represented the Australian province of the general chapter of Brothers in the mother house in Rome in 1956. During his provincialship ten schools were founded, extending the Order to Papua, New Zealand and three other States in Australia, and a teachers' training college, Oakhill, was opened at Castle Hill, Sydney.

A model Irish-Australian, Foley was loyal to both countries. His support of the Australian Labor Party stemmed from his Irish background and from his membership of an Order devoted primarily to the education of boys from lower-middle and working-class families. He confided his private opinion that Archbishop Mannix [q.v.10] had made a tactical mistake in aligning himself with the Democratic Labor Party after Labor split in 1955. Deeply religious and a 'commonsense'

Catholic, Foley was reticent about himself; with the limpest of handshakes, he was perhaps at his best conversationally, while relaxing in the company of his dogs. His frailties included partisan and sometimes mildly abusive barracking at football matches, and shifting the baseline in a tennis game—if it were to his advantage. After retiring to Oakhill and then to Boystown, Beaudesert, Queensland, he died on 9 September 1975 in Brisbane and was buried in Castle Hill cemetery, Sydney.

Br Aloysius, *The De La Salle Brothers in Australia 1906-1956* (Syd, 1956); G. McNamara, *Brother Paul* (Syd, 1966); De La Salle College, *Blue and Gold* (Melb, 1975); De La Salle Archives, Malvern, Melb; personal recollections.

S. M. INGHAM

FOLEY, THOMAS ANDREW (1886-1973), politician, general labourer and contractor, was born on 26 April 1886 at Charters Towers, Queensland, son of Andrew Foley, labourer, and his wife Margaret, née McKeegan, both from Ireland. Educated at the local state school until the age of 14, Tom later studied at night-school. His various occupations, in North Queensland and New South Wales, included labouring on wharfs, in canefields, timber camps, metalliferous mines, and in railway and building construction. He subsequently worked as a contractor, supplying sleepers to the railways. In these diverse activities Foley honed his union and political experience. By 1919 he was an organizer for the Australian Workers' Union and a member of the Blair Athol (near Clermont) Workers' Political Organisation. At St Joseph's Catholic Church, Capella, on 23 March 1920 he married Christina Madeline Pianta.

In a by-election on 20 December 1919 Foley had won the Legislative Assembly seat of Leichhardt for the Australian Labor Party. As a result of redistributions, the seat was changed three times—to Normanby (1931), Belyando (1949) and Barcoo (1958)—while Foley held it. He was a passionate proponent of his electorate's coal and gemstone mining, and its closer settlement schemes linked with farming and grazing. An advocate of the conservation of fodder to create a reserve against drought, he was equally aware of the need for forestry conservation, but accepted a continuation of the koala and possum fur-trade—regulated by licences. Foley was always a strong supporter of socialism which, for him, embraced state enterprises, co-operative farming ventures, leasing land in preference to granting freehold, nationalized banking, industrial democracy and a union-based council to control industry. His speeches incorporated wide-ranging research and he often used comparative material to illustrate his arguments.

After Labor returned to power under William Forgan Smith [q.v.11], Foley served as government whip (1932-36). On 17 December 1936 he was appointed secretary for mines; he upgraded the education of mine inspectors and managers, and improved ventilation and safety measures. While secretary for labour (1939-44), he established co-ordinating mechanisms for postwar employment. As secretary for health and home affairs (1944-47), he introduced E. M. Hanlon's [q.v.] free hospital scheme. Under Foley's auspices the Queensland Health Education Council and the Queensland Radium Institute were established. Slim in build and of middle height, Foley had a generous nature; he was regarded as deliberate and reliable in his parliamentary duties, but became enmeshed in controversy.

In December 1946 a charge against Foley, concerning illicit tobacco discovered in his garage, was dismissed by a magistrate. Two men, one of them Foley's brother-in-law, were found guilty of possession of the contraband. When Foley was acquitted, the government promptly abandoned its undertaking to establish a royal commission into the affair, but one lasting inheritance was his euphonious nickname 'Fine Cut' Foley. As secretary for public lands (1947-56), he introduced legislation for closer-land and war-service settlement. Allegations of maladministration and corruption within the Lands Department appeared in the *Worker* in 1955 and were aired in the Senate next year. The Gair [q.v.] ministry established a royal commission to investigate the matters and Foley surrendered his portfolio on 6 April 1956. Having received an interim report, the government decided to prosecute Foley before a magistrate in the police court. Once again he was found not guilty. On 14 June, however, he resigned from cabinet when the commission found him guilty of corrupt conduct. The chairman of the Land Administration Board, V. R. Creighton, who had given evidence against Foley, was summoned before the bar of the parliament to explain his behaviour and later dismissed by cabinet. Foley was expelled from the A.L.P. in October. Following the 1957 split, he was accepted as a member of the newly formed Queensland Labor Party, for which he successfully held Belyando. Although he continued to address a plethora of subjects in parliament, he faced the dilemma of having to defend his former policies. At the time of his defeat at the elections in May 1960, Foley had sat in parliament for a continuous term of forty years.

He retired to Coochiemudlo Island in Moreton Bay where he farmed pawpaws. Survived by his daughter and two sons, Foley died on 5 February 1973 in South Brisbane and was buried in Nudgee cemetery.

C. Lack (comp), *Three Decades of Queensland Political History, 1929-1960* (Brisb, 1962); D. J. Murphy et al (eds), *Labor in Power* (Brisb, 1980); R. Patrick, *A History of Health and Medicine in Queensland 1824-1960* (Brisb, 1987); ALP (Qld Branch), *Caucus Minutes, 1919-57*; *PD* (Senate), 15 Feb-17 May 1956; *PP* (Qld), 1956-57, 2, pp 733, 877; *Courier-Mail*, 8 Nov, 6 Dec 1946, 2 May 1956, 6-7 Feb 1973; *Worker* (Brisb), 25 July, 1, 8, 15, 22 Aug, 19 Sept, 3, 31 Oct, 14 Nov 1955, 20 Feb, 12, 19 Mar, 18 June 1956; information from Mr T. A. Foley, Brisb, Mr J. E. Duggan, Toowoomba, Mrs D. Foley, Coochiemudlo Island, Qld, and Mrs G. Swoboda, Brisb.   TIM MORONEY

FOLL, HATTIL SPENCER (1890-1977), politician, was born on 30 May 1890 at West Brixton, London, second child of John Hattil Foll, journeyman butcher, and his wife Kate Elizabeth, née Lamb. Educated at Clapham Collegiate and Holy Trinity schools, Clapham, in 1909 Harry (who disliked the name Hattil) and a friend Guy Middleton emigrated to Queensland where they obtained work on Darr River Downs station, near Longreach. One year later they found jobs as bookkeepers with the coach-builder G. F. Dauth at Beenleigh. Foll wrote for the local newspaper and enjoyed singing, playing the piano and acting in amateur theatricals.

In 1911 he became a clerk in the office of the Queensland commissioner for railways. Enlisting in the Australian Imperial Force on 18 August 1914, Foll sailed to Egypt with the 3rd Field Artillery Brigade and on 25 April 1915 landed at Gallipoli. On 19 May he was wounded in the head and leg, but rejoined his unit in July. Leaving the peninsula in August, he returned to Australia and was discharged medically unfit on 15 February 1916. He had married Evelyn Bush Mousley on 1 December 1915 at All Saints Anglican Church, Brisbane; they were to have a son who died in infancy and four daughters.

Briefly private secretary to the State politician John Adamson [q.v.7], secretary for railways, Foll held office in the Returned Soldiers' and Patriots' National Political League. In May 1917 he was elected to the Senate as a Nationalist candidate. His parliamentary committee-work reflected his interest in military, financial and administrative matters. He served as government whip in 1926-29 and 1932-37, and Opposition whip in 1929-31. From the 1920s he lived in Sydney.

Promoted to cabinet, Foll relinquished his directorships of Mt Isa Mines Ltd and New Guinea Goldfields Ltd. He was minister-in-charge of war service homes (1937-38), held the portfolios of repatriation (1937-39), health (1938-39) and interior (1939-41), and was a member of the War Cabinet (1939-41). As minister for information in 1940-41, he established the Australian News and Information Bureau, New York, and also effected savings in government advertising. In World War II he was a captain in the Volunteer Defence Corps. He was prominent in the parliamentary attacks on General Sir Thomas Blamey [q.v.13] in 1944-45. Having lost the endorsement of the Queensland People's (Liberal) Party for the 1946 general elections, he left the Senate in June 1947.

Next year he bought Eathorpe, a sheep-grazing property near Armidale, where he lived until 1957 when he retired to Port Macquarie. Foll was short and stocky, with blue eyes and wavy, dark brown hair. A sociable man and an astute observer of people and events, he was fond of travel and liked 'grass-roots' politics. He held moderate views, had an analytical mind and a keen sense of humour, and was a confident public speaker. To the end of his life he remained mentally and physically active, enjoying tennis, golf, bowls and especially swimming. Survived by his wife and daughters, he died on 7 July 1977 at Port Macquarie; following a state funeral, he was cremated.

G. Long, *The Final Campaigns* (Canb, 1963); J. Hilvert, *Blue Pencil Warriors* (Brisb, 1984); *PD* (Cwlth, Senate), 16 Aug 1977, p 3; *Port Macquarie News*, 11 July 1977; information from Mrs S. Moore, Tanah Merah, Qld.   ELAINE BROWN

FONG, SYDNEY (KONG SHAN [SOU] KIN) (1878-1955), merchant, was born on 24 November 1878 at Long Foon village, Toishan district, Kwangtung, China, son of Kong Gen Mi, farmer, and his wife Yu See. Details of his early life and first marriage are unknown. His wife remained in China when he emigrated to Western Australia, arriving in September 1896. He lived and worked at Broome for two years before shifting to Perth.

In 1901 he moved to Geraldton and was employed by his uncle Fong Lang who had established the Wing On Woo & Co. store. While working there, he learned to read and write in both Chinese and English, adopted the forename Sydney and eventually took over the business. Fong brought his daughter Irene (1907-1972)—who was born during his first visit to China—to Geraldton about 1909. After his wife died in February 1914, he married Ellen Louisa Ah Moy (1895-1939) at St Peter's Anglican Church, East Melbourne, on 2 December that year. They were to have seven children. Two of his sons were educated at Scotch College, Perth, another

learned woolclassing at Bradford, England, and the fourth studied in Hong Kong.

Located in Marine Terrace, Geraldton, by 1916 Sydney Fong & Co. consisted of a general store (which stocked groceries, fruit and vegetables, wine, spirits and tobacco), a fuel agency, a ship's chandlery, an import and export agency, and a small market garden which provided the store with fresh produce. In the 1920s and 1930s the firm employed a staff of ten. Fong developed a reputation for good service and fair trading; on occasions, when customers were in difficult circumstances, he quietly cancelled their debt. He supplied the district's farmers and acted as an agent for the Geraldton fishing industry, provisioning boats and dealing with seafood buyers. Fong engaged in business with European and Chinese wholesalers in Perth and Fremantle, and kept meticulous accounts in English and Chinese. Progressive and far-sighted, he was reported to have held the first petrol agency in the town and was a foundation member of Geraldton Beach Camps Ltd which built small cottages for holiday-makers.

On 16 May 1944 Fong married Lucy Ann Chung Gon at the Presbyterian Church, Oatlands, Tasmania. A highly respected member of the Geraldton community, he was an elder of St John's Presbyterian Church; he also served on the cemeteries' board and belonged to the bowling club. He continued to give generous financial support to the Church and in the 1930s had been responsible for building a church in the village of his birth. Survived by his wife, by the daughter and adopted son of his first marriage, and by the four sons and three daughters of his second marriage, Fong died on 9 December 1955 at Geraldton. He was buried in Utakarra cemetery after a large funeral at which the moderator of the Presbyterian Church of Western Australia officiated.

A. Atkinson (comp), *Asian Immigrants to Western Australia 1829-1901* (Perth, 1988) *and* Chinese Labour and Capital in Western Australia, 1847-1947 (Ph.D. thesis, Murdoch Univ, 1991); *Geraldton Guardian*, 10, 13 Dec 1955; ts synopsis of interview by R. Jamieson with W. Moy, 1981 (BL); Sydney Fong, Geraldton, 1932-1940 (ts of interview by R. Jamieson with M. Limon, 15 Feb 1983, BL); S. Fong papers (BL); information from Mr L. Fong, Winthrop, and Ms L. Meredith, Noranda, Perth, Mr A. Fong, Geraldton, WA, and Ms D. Quay, Syd.   ANNE ATKINSON

FORBES, ADA LORNA (1890-1976), actress, was born on 1 February 1890 in North Melbourne, second of three children of Victorian-born parents Wilson Duff-Forbes, actor-producer, and his wife Ada Emily

Windson, née Lawrence, actress. A fourth-generation actress, Lorna Forbes (as she was always known) made her stage debut at the age of 5 as Little Willie in *East Lynne*. She was educated at Methodist Ladies' College, Kew. After taking her first professional part (as a 15-year-old) in *Two Little Sailor Boys*, staged at Ballarat, she travelled throughout Australia as an understudy in her father's company. On 20 October 1910 at St James's Anglican Church, Glen Iris, she married an English-born musician, Frederick Charles Chute Chapman, whom she had 'looked [at] across the footlights, and loved'.

Having a strong interest in Shakespeare, in 1916 Forbes was invited to join the Allan Wilkie [q.v.12] Company with which she first appeared as Queen Elizabeth in *Richard III*. Olivia in *Twelfth Night* was her favourite role, but she also played a wide range of other Shakespearian characters, including Portia, Cleopatra, Mistress Page, Goneril and Hermia. She performed in Greek drama and took character roles, playing Madame Arcati in Melbourne's first production of *Blithe Spirit*.

Between 1924 and 1957 she ran the Lorna Forbes School of Drama in Melbourne. When Wilkie disbanded his players in October 1930, she formed a company with Alexander Marsh and toured Tasmania, staging melodrama and farce. During the 1930s Forbes played character roles in musical comedies such as *The Vagabond King*, *Du Barry* and *The Student Prince*. From 1934 she appeared in radio plays and serials produced by the Australian Broadcasting Commission and by Dorothy and Hector Crawford. She was noted for her part in the series, *Coronets of France*.

In 1941 she established the Lorna Forbes Repertory Players which performed drawing-room comedies at different venues. Four years later, with the amateur producer and engineer Sydney Turnbull, she founded the Melbourne Repertory Theatre Group at the Middle Park theatre where one of her pupils, Ray Lawler, produced his first play, *Hal's Belles*. She acted in and directed several productions until the group's demise in 1949 when she became involved in a teaching venture called Theatre Workshop. In 1955 she understudied Dame Sybil Thorndike during her tour of Australia in *The Sleeping Prince* and *Separate Tables*. Aged almost 70, Forbes scored success in the small part of Mrs Burnside in the American comedy, *Auntie Mame*. Further character parts came in *The Music Man* and *The Sound of Music* before arthritis forced her to retire in 1962. Predeceased by her husband, she died on 26 May 1976 at East Camberwell and was buried with Catholic rites in Boroondara cemetery.

Forbes's stage career was limited in its success. Despite her stage presence and deep, richly expressive voice, she had been overshadowed in Wilkie's company by his star (and wife), Frediswyde Hunter-Watts. From 1942 Lorna was affected by intense grief at the death of her only child, the actor Russell Chapman, on active service with the Royal Air Force. Her greatest contribution to the theatre was in repertory, and in teaching voice and stagecraft at a time when there were no formal state-run drama schools.

H. Porter, *Stars of Australian Stage and Screen* (Adel, 1965); *Listener In*, 5 Nov 1938; *Examiner* (Launc), 28 Nov 1930; *Mercury* (Hob), 6 Jan 1931; *Age* (Melb), 5 Sept 1953, 1 Feb 1976; Melb Repertory Theatre papers (La Trobe collection, SLV); information from Ms J. McGrath and Ms A. Fulton, Camberwell, Ms P. Kennedy, Hawthorn, and Mr R. Lawler, St Kilda, Melb.   MIMI COLLIGAN

FORBES, SIR DOUGLAS STUART McGREGOR GORDON (1890-1973), banker, was born on 6 February 1890 at Bulimba, Brisbane, fifth child of William Forbes, master mariner, and his wife Amelia, née Moir, both Scottish born. Educated at Brisbane Central Boys' School and by a private tutor, Douglas won prizes for his copperplate handwriting that was later to become a professional legend. In August 1906 he joined the Royal Bank of Queensland as a junior clerk; appointed manager of its Yarraman branch in August 1913, he was one of the youngest bank-managers of the period. Next year Forbes moved to the Queensland National Bank; he served in fourteen country branches and was manager at Hughenden, Maryborough and Bundaberg. In these pioneering days he slept under bullock-drays at Texas, opened a branch at Goomeri in a tent in the backyard of an hotel, and lived in a number of sugar-towns. On 9 April 1917 he had married 19-year-old Grace Isabel Fallon at St James's Anglican Church, Toowoomba.

In September 1928 Forbes was appointed branch manager in Sydney and five years later chief inspector at head office, Brisbane. He took over from M. G. Haymen as general manager in May 1937. Already respected for his 'exceptionally sound judgment', he also succeeded Haymen as chairman (1937-47) of the Associated Banks of Queensland and as its representative on the board of the faculty of commerce at the University of Queensland. Following the Federal parliament's Banking Act (1945), Forbes recognized that the Queensland National Bank faced an uncertain future. In January 1948 he successfully negotiated a merger with the National Bank of Australasia, an arrangement extremely favourable to his shareholders. Forbes filled one of two new positions on the board of directors of the National Bank of Australasia and was chairman (1948-67) of its Queensland board of advice. The latter body reflected his strong 'Queensland-first' philosophy and, when faced with suggestions of control from the south, he was able to exploit State parochialism to resist Prime Minister Chifley's [q.v.13] proposal for bank nationalization.

As a consequence of his general managership of the Queensland National Bank, Forbes was managing director (1940-73) and chairman (1955) of the Millaquin Sugar Co. Ltd, and chairman (1940-62) of the Queensland National Pastoral Co., both of which were formed to manage interests acquired by the bank from clients during times of recession and drought. Having joined the board (1944) of Castlemaine Perkins Ltd (another client of the bank), he became that company's non-executive chairman (1958); by successfully moving the appointments of (Sir) Edward Stewart and (Sir) Byrne Hart, he so altered the composition of Castlemaine's board as to give external, non-executive directors a 3:2 majority. Forbes sat, as well, on the boards of Queensland Oil Refineries Pty Ltd, BORAL Ltd, Anglo-Australian Corporation Pty Ltd, Queensland Trustees Ltd, Raub Australian Gold Mining Co. Ltd and Brisbane Television Ltd (BTQ-7).

Highly respected for his business acumen, his objectivity in dealing with issues, his command of the English language and his public-speaking ability, Forbes was adept at handling meetings of shareholders and very careful with shareholders' funds. Furthermore, he was so patently meticulous and disciplined that these traits affected the manner in which other directors on his boards carried out their duties. When he had lived in country areas, he cannily raised money for community organizations by means of concert companies whose proceeds attracted government subsidies. In the 1930s he was a member of the Committee of Eastern Trade, established to stimulate commerce with Asia. During World War II he served on the Essential Supplies and on the Patriotic Fund committees, and was treasurer of the Polish Red Cross and the Young Women's Christian Association Services appeals. He was a trustee of the Queensland Cancer Fund, the Brisbane Amateur Turf Club and the Royal Queensland Golf Club. In 1964 he was knighted.

Sir Douglas was a devoted and protective family man, though avowedly averse to inactive retirement, 'dusting the cheese for mum'. Survived by his wife and daughter, he died on 22 June 1973 in Brisbane and was cremated. His estate was sworn for probate at $511 406, a considerable residual sum of which was left equally to the Presbyterian and Methodist churches.

Notable Men of Queensland (Brisb, 1950); G. Blainey, *Gold and Paper* (Melb, 1958); National Bank of Australasia Ltd (Melb), *Nautilus News*, 127, Autumn 1964, 1, July 1973; *Courier-Mail*, 18, 20 Mar, 30 Apr, 1 May 1937, 23 June 1973; *Telegraph* (Brisb), 18 Mar, 30 Apr 1937, 25 June 1973; *Age* (Melb), 29 Mar 1937; *SMH*, 8 May 1937; press-cuttings (held by Mr R. Parkes, Greenslopes, Brisb).

DAVID WATSON

FORD, ATHELSTANE RUSSELL (1901-1979), engineer, was born on 28 August 1901 at Waitara, New South Wales, second son of native-born parents Herbert Macquarie Ford, engineering draftsman, and his wife Priscilla, née Russell. Educated at Sydney Church of England Grammar School (Shore), Athel studied civil engineering at the University of Sydney (B.E., 1923). He joined the Department of Public Works in March 1923 and was employed as an engineering assistant, initially on the Chichester Dam project and then on the River Murray projects at Wentworth, Hay and Maude. On 22 January 1927 he married Ruby Gray Crang with Presbyterian forms at her parents' home at Wentworth. Over forty-three years he worked on many major engineering works across the State, among them the south-west tablelands' water supply, the Cowra, Bega and Maitland sewerage systems, and the development of safe fishing ports along the coast.

After serving as a district engineer at Port Kembla and Coffs Harbour, Ford entered the harbours and rivers branch in 1947. He was enthusiastic about his profession, maintained an interest in current research in his field, and in 1956 undertook a postgraduate course in statistics and hydrology at the New South Wales University of Technology. As principal engineer (harbours and rivers) from 1957 until 1962, he largely concentrated on projects in the Port of Newcastle, including deepening the harbour and reclaiming land to create Kooragang Island for industrial development, described by Ford as one of the largest reclamation projects in the world. He was a member of the Newcastle Port Development Committee and the Hunter Valley Conservation Trust. In 1961 he and J. C. C. Humphrey, assistant-director of the D.P.W., toured England, Holland, France and the United States of America where they visited universities and hydraulic laboratories to inspect engineering developments relating to siltation problems and coastal river-flood mitigation schemes. In a paper presented to the Hunter District Water Board engineers, Ford described his trip as 'quite an eye opener'.

He was appointed deputy chief engineer in 1963 and promoted chief engineer in March 1964. Self-effacing, but full of energy and verve, he was a committed member of the Presbyterian Church and acknowledged by his colleagues as a 'Christian Gentleman'. Ford dressed in a navy blue suit, even in the field, and was stiff with his junior staff. He was preoccupied with mathematics and on journeys enjoyed calculating the speed of a train by timing how long it took to pass a set number of telegraph poles. A member of the Institution of Civil Engineers, London, and the Institution of Engineers, Australia, he presented papers to these and other organizations. On his retirement in August 1966, he returned to Wentworth. In the following year, to honour his contribution to the public works at Newcastle, a new tug was named the *A. R. Ford*. Survived by his wife, daughter and two sons, he died on 30 December 1979 at Curlwaa and was buried in Wentworth cemetery.

J. Armstrong, *Shaping the Hunter* (Newcastle, NSW, 1983); L. Coltheart, *A Guide to the History of the Public Works Department of New South Wales* (Syd, 1991); Dept of Public Works (NSW), *Annual Report*, 1962; Dept of Public Works Staff Assn (NSW), *Stateworks*, 11, no 5, Oct 1966, p 20, 12, no 5, 1967, p 13; *Sunraysia Daily* and *SMH*, 1 Jan 1980; L. Coltheart, New South Wales Ports and Rivers (ms, held by author); information from Mr M. N. Clarke, Enfield, Syd.   LOUISE CHAPPELL

FORD, CHARLES EDGAR (1881-1961), Organist, composer and music examiner, was born on 26 November 1881 at Upper Penn, Staffordshire, England, one of six children of Samuel Ford, a builder and teacher of music, and his wife Alice Phoebe, née Showell, a singer. Edgar received basic musical training from his father, a 'Professor and Teacher of the Art of Voice-Production, Singing, and Elocution', who conducted elementary and choral classes at the Wolverhampton Free Library. Father and son toured England giving recitals in 1894-95 after Edgar had developed into an accomplished soprano with a range of almost three octaves. Educated at Wolverhampton Technical School and through the Burlington Correspondence College, he moved to London, studying the organ under Alfred Madeley Richardson at Southwark Cathedral (where Samuel Ford was assistant-organist in 1903-08) and composition under Dr Charles Herbert Kitson.

At New College, Oxford (B.Mus., 1908; D.Mus., 1913), Ford set to music A. W. E. O'Shaughnessy's ode, 'We Are the Music Makers', and wrote a musical composition on Alfred, Lord Tennyson's poem, 'The Skylark', as part of his doctoral requirements. On 25 August 1909 at the parish church of St Peter the Apostle, Kent, he had married Agnes Ruth Miller (d.1972). Earning a living

as a music teacher, in 1917 he was appointed organist and choirmaster at the parish church, Roehampton. He took a lively interest in the National Union of Organists' Associations which published his *Te Deum Laudamus* in G Minor as a supplement to its quarterly *Record* that year. In 1918 the *Record* published his essay, 'The Sacred and Secular in Music: Their Interdependence', which argued for greater catholicity in the use of music in church. Three years later he became organist at St Saviour's Church, Ealing.

As an examiner (from 1920) for Trinity College of Music, London, Ford was able to indulge his love of travel; his examinations of young Indian princes and princesses boosted his fund of anecdotes. He was a distinguished-looking man of average height, with 'a fairly deep' voice, who was meticulous about appearance and speech. Strong minded and independent, he was well read, and enjoyed company and playing bridge. While he continued to be an active composer, it was in the capacity of an examiner that he had first visited Australia in 1917. Ford is said to have been a divorcee and to have married in South Africa in 1926 Judith Beryl Keane (1894-1979), a poet from Western Australia. In 1941 they took up residence in Perth where he was organist at St Mary's Catholic Cathedral and gave numerous recitals. For the next thirty years his examining tours took him interstate and to Asia, Africa and New Zealand.

Romantic and conservative in style, and displaying fine craftsmanship, Ford's compositions included many pieces for piano and organ, solo and part-songs, as well as some larger choral works, such as his two Masses with organ, and several cantatas with orchestra, notably *Zuleika* and *The River*. Inspired by the Swan River, the latter cantata was a setting—for soprano, mixed chorus and orchestra—of words by his wife. He also set some of her poems as solo songs with piano. His chief orchestral compositions were *Springtime in Puppet Land, Bushland Magic, Strange Nullabor, Tawarri*, the suites *Summertime* and *Rhapsody of God*, and an uncompleted symphony.

Survived by his wife, and by the son and daughter of his first marriage, Ford died on 19 July 1961 at Peppermint Grove and was cremated. The University of Western Australia, the State Library of Western Australia and the Australian Broadcasting Corporation, Sydney, hold most of his compositions. Through their estate, the Fords established a fund to support musical activities at the University of Western Australia.

W. A. Orchard, *Music in Australia* (Melb, 1952); J. Glennon, *Australian Music and Musicians* (Adel,

1968); J. Murdoch, *A Handbook of Australian Music* (Melb, 1983); *Music and Dance*, 52, no 3, Sept 1961; *Who's Who in Music and Musicians' International Directory* (Lond), 1962; *Wolverhampton Chronicle*, 31 May 1916; *Herald* (Melb), 22 Oct 1935, 3 Apr 1940; *West Australian*, 20 July 1961, 17 July 1979; information from Miss C. Ford, Morar, Inverness-shire, Scotland.

FRANK CALLAWAY

FORD, LESLIE HUNTER (1915-1964), rural entrepreneur and politician, was born on 19 January 1915 at Molong, New South Wales, second son of Australian-born parents George Ford (d.1936), farmer, and his wife Lena Olga, née Hunter. Educated at Amaroo Public and Orange High schools, Les ran a Golden Fleece fuel agency at Orange from 1936 and worked as a share-farmer. On 11 January 1941 he married Rhoda May ('Peggy') Hawke at the Methodist Church, Orange. Having been rejected as medically unfit for aircrew in 1940, he enlisted in the Royal Australian Air Force on 19 July 1941. He served as a mechanical transport fitter, completed a tour with No.1 Repair and Salvage Unit at Daly Waters, Northern Territory, then transferred to the stores depot at Dubbo, New South Wales, where his family joined him.

Following his demobilization on 14 November 1944, Ford purchased Skerman's Motors, a General-Motors' dealership at Dubbo, which he developed into a prosperous business. He was also chairman of Ganarrin Meat Service Pty Ltd, a wholesale meat and butchery undertaking. Later he bought land for fattening sheep, including Hazelgrove, a 432-acre (175 ha) property on the Macquarie River.

In 1946 Ford learned to fly a Tiger Moth, journeyed to the United States of America and bought a light aircraft which he used in attending to his diversified business interests. He installed two-way radio equipment in his plane and insisted on landing at Mascot, like the international traffic. In 1960 he bought a Piper Apache and flew it extensively while touring the U.S.A. He became president of the Aircraft Owners & Pilots' Association of Australia in January 1962 and was vice-president for the Pacific region.

An alderman (from 1947) on Dubbo Municipal Council, Ford was elected mayor in 1950 and held the position until 1964. Under his guidance, the city grew as a regional centre with the opening of the abattoir complex in 1954 and the design of the War Memorial Civic Centre. In November 1955 he was appointed O.B.E. for his work and leadership during the floods in March that year. A 'man of vision and infectious enthusiasm', Ford was so completely identified with the progress of the area 'that he was known widely and affectionately throughout the State as "Mr. Dubbo"'. He was elected to the Legislative Assembly for Dubbo in 1959 as a Liberal, but spent his time in Opposition. J. B. Renshaw believed that 'being a backbencher must have been tiresome for such an irrepressible man'.

Generous and hospitable, Ford had played representative cricket and tennis for western New South Wales, and was subsequently a council-member for the western division on the New South Wales Lawn Tennis Association. He was a member of the Dubbo Methodist Church trust and a Rotarian. Survived by his wife and four sons, he died of coronary disease on 17 December 1964 at Kurrajong and was cremated. The L. H. Ford Bridge, spanning the Macquarie River, is a monument to him.

PD (NSW), 26 May 1965, p 3; *SMH*, 3 Mar, 22 Nov 1955, 31 Jan 1960, 2 Feb 1962, 18 Dec 1964; information from Mrs R. M. Ford, Fairlight, Syd, who holds newspaper-cuttings. ROSSLYN FINN

FORNACHON, JOHN CHARLES MACLEOD (1905-1968), wine microbiologist, was born on 28 December 1905 at Wayville, Adelaide, third son of Charles Louis Fernand Fornachon, a Swiss-born electrical engineer, and his second wife Elizabeth Macpherson, née Robertson. John was educated at Golden Grove Public School and the Collegiate School of St Peter. In 1922 he entered Roseworthy Agricultural College where he studied oenology and viticulture (Dip.Ag., 1925), subjects he later pursued at the University of Adelaide (B.Ag.Sc., 1934; M.Sc., 1943). At the request of the Wine Overseas Marketing Board (later Australian Wine Board), in 1934 the university began research into the diseases of wine and wine spoilage. As investigating officer, Fornachon began work in November under Professor (Sir) John Cleland [q.v.8]. Next year the project was moved to the Waite [q.v.6] Agricultural Research Institute at Urrbrae and was administered by the Council for Scientific and Industrial Research. Fornachon's facilities were sparse: 'an incubator, microscope, a few reagents and glassware, some bench space, and not much else'. At St Andrew's Anglican Church, Walkerville, on 9 August 1938 he married Barbara Frances Hamilton.

Awarded a C.S.I.R. studentship, that year Fornachon sailed with his wife for California, United States of America, where he undertook eleven months research before participating in an international wine congress in Germany. He was not to spend another study leave abroad until 1954. The findings of his first major research were published by the Australian Wine Board as *Bacterial Spoilage of Fortified Wines* (1943). A second edition (1969) contained a foreword by Bryce Rankine which described the book as 'a classic in oenological research' and 'of inestimable value to the Australian wine industry'.

In 1941 Fornachon had begun to examine flor yeasts. His work, released in biannual reports to winemakers, was funded by the Australian Wine Board and the Commonwealth Scientific and Industrial Research Organization, and culminated in *Studies on the Sherry Flor* (1953). The book helped to 'place Australian sherry on world standards' and is still the definitive study (a second edition appeared in 1972).

Fornachon next turned his skills to investigating malolactic fermentation, about which very little was known in 1957 when he published a paper on the subject. Like his other projects, this research had practical benefits for winemakers. In 1955 the Australian Wine Research Institute had been opened at Urrbrae, with Fornachon as director of research. He filled the position 'with distinction' until his death. These years were particularly busy ones for him. His commitments included wine judging throughout Australia (he was chairman of judges in Adelaide) and lecturing part time in wine microbiology at the University of Adelaide and at Roseworthy Agricultural College. In addition to publishing eighteen research papers in 1936-68, he wrote an account of the State's wine industry for the book, *Introducing South Australia* (1958); he also compiled the English-language section of a new edition of the *Lexique Vitivinicole International* for the Food and Agricultural Organization of the United Nations in 1963. In that year he was Regent's lecturer at the University of California at Davis, gave a paper on malolactic fermentation to an international symposium in Bordeaux, France, and was a member of the Australian delegation to meetings of the committee of experts on wines and spirits of the Council of Europe.

Tall (6 ft 5 ins, 196 cm) and thin, with a craggy face, curly hair and glasses, Fornachon was a shy, quiet man with a ready sense of humour. He was a member (1951) of the American Society of Oenologists and president of the South Australian branch of the Australian Institute of Agricultural Science. His colleagues were impressed by his scientific objectivity and intellectual honesty, his deeply inquiring mind, and his modesty. A practical scientist, he preferred laboratory research to paperwork at his desk. He died of myocardial infarction on 25 August 1968 in Royal Adelaide Hospital and was cremated; his wife, son and daughter survived him. The library at the Australian Wine Research Institute was named in his honour.

Aust Grapegrower & Winemaker, no 239, Nov 1983; V. Hankel, 'John Charles Macleod Fornachon: a tribute', *Aust Wine Research Inst Technical Review*, no 55, Aug 1988, p 6, *and* for Fornachon's publications; *Advertiser* (Adel), 27 Nov 1939, 26 Aug 1968; information from Mrs E. Mortimer, Largs Bay, Adel.   VALMAI A. HANKEL

FORRO, FERENC ISTVÁN (1914-1974), Jesuit priest and chaplain, was born on 20 March 1914 at Hajós, Hungary, son of Ferenc Nébl Forro and his wife Maria, née Kohl. His twin became a Franciscan priest. Following five years at high school, on 30 July 1930 young Ferenc entered the novitiate of the Hungarian province of the Society of Jesus in Budapest where he completed the normal courses of humanities and philosophy. From 1938 he studied theology at Szeged, and was ordained priest on 22 June 1941. For the remainder of World War II he was successively based at Kolozsvár (Cluj, Romania), as chaplain and catechist (1942-43), and at Hódmezöovásárhely where he taught in the Jesuit high school. In 1945 he returned to Budapest for his tertianship (third year of spiritual training). Back at the theological seminary at Szeged, he served as minister (procurator) in 1946-47 while preparing for the Chinese mission in Hopeh province.

Father Forro was sent to China in 1948, first to Chabanel Hall, Peking (Beijing), and later to Villa Flor, Macao. After being driven out of China by the communists, he was posted to Australia in 1950 to minister to Hungarian immigrants. Making Sydney his base, he worked (1950-54) from St Francis Xavier's, Lavender Bay. In 1954 he moved to St Louis School, Claremont, Perth, which became his centre until 1959 when he returned to Lavender Bay for a pioneering period of pastoral work that lasted ten years.

Called Frank by his friends, Forro was an attractive and witty priest whose pastoral work among the Hungarian community in Australia was to have lasting results. Despite his lack of formal training and his frail health, and despite frequent misunderstandings and disappointments, he became an encouraging and popular rallying-point for a widely dispersed and politically divided community. His leadership showed itself in his capacity to work cheerfully and effectively with a great variety of Hungarians and Australians, clergy and lay. With the Hungarian Ursuline nuns, he founded the St Elizabeth homes for the aged, initially in Perth and then in Sydney. He and his fellow chaplains provided spiritual, emotional and social support for the scattered and demoralized *émigré* community. It was often a heartbreaking and thankless task, particularly in the early period of forced assimilation. Forro's indomitable kindness, impish grin and sincere interest comforted hundreds of Hungarian-Australian families in every State, and he gave an extraordinary example of personal devotion, practical charity and applied modern urban missionary skill to his Catholic confrères.

In 1968 Forro suffered a coronary occlusion. He spent a year in Canberra before being recalled to Europe in October 1970 to live as chaplain to the convent of the 'English Ladies', the Institute of the Blessed Virgin Mary (Mary Ward Sisters) at Schrobenhausen, Bavaria, West Germany. Plans were in train for his return to Australia when Forro died at the convent on 13 January 1974; he was buried in the Jesuit cemetery at Pullach, near Munich.

E. F. Kunz, *Blood and Gold* (Melb, 1969) and *The Hungarians in Australia* (Melb, 1985); J. Jupp (ed), *The Australian People* (Syd, 1988), p 94; *Jesuit Life*, July 1974, p 28; Society of Jesus Archives, Hawthorn, Melb.   J. EDDY

FOSKETT, RUSSELL GEORGE (1917-1944), airman, was born on 7 May 1917 at Roseville, Sydney, third of four children of Edward George Foskett, accountant, and his wife Dora Mabel, née Cotterill, both native-born. Educated at Hornsby Junior Technical School, Russell studied accountancy and worked as a clerk in the credit department of the Shell Co. of Australia Pty Ltd. As a young man, his consuming passions were scouting and hockey. He was a Rover and master of lone scouts. A member of the Gordon district hockey club, he also represented the State. The entire family was involved in the sport: Edward was an umpire, on Saturday nights they used the dining-table to analyse matches, and the backyard was given over to practice games.

Enlisting in the Royal Australian Air Force on 18 September 1940, Foskett embarked in December for Southern Rhodesia where he qualified as a pilot under the Empire Air Training Scheme. In June 1941 he was promoted sergeant and next month joined No.80 Squadron, Royal Air Force. The unit flew Hurricanes and operated in North Africa from October. Foskett was quick to adjust to his new role and was soon regarded as arguably 'the most prominent' of the Australians serving with R.A.F. squadrons in the Middle East. Commissioned in March 1942, he was promoted acting flight lieutenant in July and appointed a flight commander next month. Donald Jack, his commanding officer, was to observe: 'This rapid promotion exemplified the man, who was a born leader. He had everything required; enthusiasm, aggression, humour, a zest for life and boundless energy'.

On 3 November 1942, in the battle of El Alamein, Foskett 'led his squadron in an attack on a formation of Stuka dive-bombers, heavily escorted by fighters . . . seven Stukas were shot down, a further eight were probably destroyed and several others were damaged'. Foskett dispatched two enemy aircraft before his own was hit; he made a forced landing in a minefield, was rescued by the army and resumed flying duties next morning. He was awarded the Distinguished Flying Cross.

Leaving the squadron in March 1943, he was promoted acting squadron leader in May and given a brief rest from operations as a staff officer at No.209 Group headquarters, Haifa, Palestine. In October he was posted to command No.94 Squadron, R.A.F., a mixed Commonwealth unit which included an additional contingent of Yugoslavian pilots. Foskett flew Hurricanes and later Spitfires. Initially based at El Adem, Libya, in October 1944 he took the squadron to Kalamaki, Greece, where it harried retreating German columns.

Foskett's record as a fighter pilot and commander was outstanding. He was credited with 6½ enemy aircraft destroyed. For his work with the Yugoslavian airmen, in 1944 he was awarded the wings of the Royal Yugoslav Air Force by King Peter II and was mentioned in dispatches. On 31 October that year, while returning to base, Foskett's Spitfire developed engine trouble over the Aegean Sea between the islands of Skiathos and Skópelos. He bailed out, but was too low for his parachute to open. His body was recovered and he was buried at sea. Foskett's younger brother Bruce, a navigator in a Royal Canadian Air Force squadron, had been killed over Berlin eight months previously. Russell Foskett's name was inscribed on the Malta Memorial (for airmen with no known graves); he was appointed O.B.E. posthumously in 1945.

J. Herington, *Air War Against Germany and Italy 1939-1943* (Canb, 1954); information from RAF Personnel Management Centre, Innsworth, Gloucester, *and* Air Hist Branch, Lond, *and* RAAF Hist Section, Canb; information from Mr D. Jack, Glasgow, Scotland, Miss N. Foskett, Waverton, and Miss E. Foskett, Longueville, Syd; Foskett family papers (held by author, Sandy Bay, Hob); AWM records.   P. J. SCULLY

FOSTER, FRANCIS HENRY (1888-1979), pastoralist, businessman and politician, was born on 16 January 1888 at Brighton, Sussex, England, eldest of four children of Colonel Henry Foster, farmer of Merton Vale, Campbell Town, Tasmania, and his wife Blanche Laura, née Keach. John Foster [q.v.1] was Francis's grandfather. Educated at the Launceston Church Grammar School, Francis entered Trinity College, University of Melbourne (B.C.E., 1911). He practised only briefly as a civil engineer, at one time under (Sir) John Monash [q.v.10], before travelling to England with his family in 1912 where he inspected industrial establishments. Next year he motored through western Queensland with his friend Douglas Fraser [q.v.], visiting pastoral properties connected with the Collins [q.v.3] family. Both trips stimulated Foster's commercial interests and aspirations. Having been commissioned in the Militia in 1915, he transferred to the Australian Imperial Force on 27 February 1918 and served in France from September with the 4th Field Company, Engineers. He returned to Australia as a lieutenant and his A.I.F. appointment terminated on 22 August 1919. At St David's Anglican Cathedral, Hobart, on 11 December 1929 he married Patricia Ainslie Wood.

The wartime death of his brother, John, committed Foster to managing the family's Tasmanian farming interests, which included Fosterville, Merton Vale, the Mersey Estate, Cape Portland and (from 1932) Mineral Banks. From 1933 to 1947 the family also owned Langi-Kal-Kal, near Ballarat, Victoria. In 1925 Foster had bought Monkira station in Queensland's Channel country from Sir Sidney Kidman [q.v.9]; in 1937 he acquired a significant shareholding in the North Australian Pastoral Co. Pty Ltd, of which he was to remain a director until 1971. Monkira was brought into the company in 1939.

Approachable and unassuming, Foster was a systematic and practical man, with a keen intellect and a quiet authority. He was chairman (1935) of the Tasmanian Meat Board and the State's inaugural representative (1936) on the Australian Meat Board; he was also a committee-member (1932-66), president (1941-44) and treasurer (1948-66) of the Tasmanian Farmers', Stockowners' and Orchardists' Association. Appointed to the Tasmanian Wool Committee in 1939, he was, as well, vice-president of the Graziers' Federal Council in 1944. As a Nationalist candidate, Foster was elected for Wilmot to the Tasmanian House of Assembly in February 1937; he was defeated in December 1941.

Although politically and socially conservative, Foster was always interested in scientific developments, and receptive to new technological ideas and investment opportunities. He was chairman of many Tasmanian companies, among them Perpetual Insurance & Securities Ltd, Perpetual Trustees, Executors & Agency Co. of Tasmania Ltd and

Murex (Australasia) Pty Ltd. In Victoria he was a director of Prestige Ltd and Industrial Engineering Ltd, and founding chairman (1950-71) of Industrial & Pastoral Holdings Ltd. Foster served on the Agricultural Bank of Tasmania's postwar land development committee in 1941-51 and on the board of inquiry into Bass Strait Islands transport facilities in 1948-49. He chaired (1943-49) the Tasmanian committee of the Council for Scientific and Industrial Research, and was a governor (1962-75) of the Ian Clunies Ross [q.v.13] Memorial Foundation, Melbourne, a trustee (1948) of the Tasmanian Museum and Art Gallery, and chairman (1949-51) of the board of The Hutchins School. Survived by his wife, two sons and four daughters, he died on 31 May 1979 at his Hobart home and was cremated; his ashes were placed in the family vault at Cornelian Bay cemetery.

M. Kowald and W. R. Johnston, *You Can't Make it Rain* (Brisb, 1992); family papers (held by author).   WILLIAM F. FOSTER

FOSTER, FREDERICK CHARLES (1907-1976), pianist and entertainer, was born on 20 July 1907 at Reigate, Surrey, England, youngest of five children of Charles Foster, master house-decorator, and his wife Minnie, née Woodley. In 1912 the family emigrated to Brisbane. Fred's cherished piano lessons with Erich John at Albert Kaesar's music store in George Street were paid for by his elder sister. He gained experience playing the organ at church and providing background music for silent movies at the Lyric Theatre. Even then, he was inclined to 'jazz up' proceedings. One of his first professional engagements was in 1925 with radio-station 4BK where he was guided by the musical director Don Bennett. Later, as the anonymous 'Rambling Pianist' on 4BH, Foster played requests and became the toast of Brisbane, though his identity was a closely guarded secret. At Hill End Presbyterian Church on 25 April 1930 he married shop-assistant Florence Edith Howe; they were to have two children before he divorced her in 1949.

During the 1930s Foster was part of Brisbane's top dance band, 'The Jumping Jacks'. Each member played at least four instruments and took turns with vocals, using cardboard megaphones for amplification in large venues such as City Hall. With the 'Kit Kats', he was acclaimed by audiences at Lennon's Hotel and the Trocadero Ballroom for playing American-influenced jitterbug and jazz music of the 'Big Band' era. Freddy next joined the Broadway Dansant New Orchestra. As few musicians earned enough from their talents, he worked as a salesman at Littledyke & Son

Pty Ltd, furniture manufacturers. On 31 December 1941 he enlisted in the Royal Australian Air Force. He served as a stores clerk and with a supply unit in Papua (1943-44), but was primarily employed on welfare activities in Australia. Commissioned on 22 April 1944, he was demobilized as flying officer, Administrative and Special Duties Branch, on 26 November 1945.

Although Foster returned to Littledyke's intermittently, retail shortages encouraged his greater involvement in entertainment. In 1950 he won a national song-writing competition organized by *Tempo* music magazine with his composition, *You've Gone*, developed from his experience in Papua where erratic mail had caused loneliness and depression. Assisted by Charles Porter (later a prominent member of the State Liberal Party), he broadcast children's bedtime stories incorporating imaginative sound effects. Foster was the local accompanist for broadcasts on commercial radio's 'Australia's Amateur Hour'; he taught piano at King House, Queen Street, provided commentary at The Speedway and played an accordion on the riverboat taking Saturday-night revellers to Lone Pine. On 17 January 1950 he had married a telephonist Phyllis Maude Gray with Methodist forms in Brisbane; she divorced him in April 1958. At the Presbyterian Church, Ann Street, Brisbane, he married a widow Patricia Catherine Bidner, née Streek, on 6 June 1958; their marriage was dissolved in 1973.

The small and dapper Freddy was engaged by BTQ-7 television station in 1959. He launched *The Two Sides of Freddy Foster*, a recording of favourite melodies which he promoted by playing excerpts in local stores; his devotion to poodles (he was a life member of the Poodle Club of Queensland) was reflected in the cartoon on the album's cover. Foster was also president of the Queensland Motor Sporting Club and a member of the Corinda Bowling Club. Suffering from diabetes mellitus, he died of a coronary occlusion on 11 October 1976 at Sherwood and was cremated with Anglican rites. The son and daughter of his first marriage survived him.

Truth (Brisb), 18 May 1930; *Courier-Mail*, 13 Oct 1976; undated clippings (1974-75?) from *Village News* held by Mr B. C. Foster, Corinda, Brisb, who also provided information.

JENNIFER HARRISON

FOSTER, JOHN FREDERICK (1903-1975), university administrator, was born on 28 March 1903 in South Melbourne, eldest son of Victorian-born parents Frederick William Foster, salesman, and his wife Annie Louisa, née McCann. Educated at Wesley College, of which he was dux, and the University of Melbourne (LL.B., 1925; LL.M., 1928; M.A., 1932), John was articled to Sir Arthur Robinson [q.v.11] and admitted to the Bar on 2 May 1927. In the following year he was appointed tutor and vice-master of Queen's College at the university. The master, Walwyn Kernick, fell gravely ill in 1932 and Foster gave up his practice at the Bar to serve as acting-master. His devotion and loyalty to the college in crisis attracted sympathy in 1934 when he was passed over in favour of Raynor Johnson as master. On 4 December that year Foster married Winifred Betty Bedggood (d.1967) at the college chapel with Methodist forms.

He spent 1935-36 in England, making a survey of British universities as part of a report by the vice-chancellor, (Sir) Raymond Priestley [q.v.11], on the future development of the University of Melbourne. Secretary (1936-47) of the Australian Vice-Chancellors' Committee, in 1938 Foster was appointed registrar at the University of Melbourne, the youngest person ever to hold that office. He ably assisted Priestley's successor (Sir) John Medley [q.v.] in implementing Priestley's proposals for the expansion of teaching and research, and from 1939 in the more challenging task of placing the institution on a war footing. Between 1938 and 1947 the number of students at the university trebled, and he won widespread popularity through his rare combination of academic training, administrative ability and friendly manner.

In 1947 Foster went to London as secretary of the Universities Bureau of the British Empire (from 1948 the Association of Universities of the British Commonwealth, and from 1964 the Association of Commonwealth Universities). An indefatigable worker, talker and traveller, he committed himself enthusiastically to his tasks. During his term of office (1947-70) member institutions increased from 70 to 180 and the association became an important forum for debate. It developed procedures for staff selection, student enrolment, the servicing of liaison committees and the administration of the Commonwealth Scholarship and Fellowship Plan, of which Foster was secretary (1959-70). He was also secretary (1947-64) of the Committee of Vice-Chancellors and Principals of the United Kingdom, British secretary of the Council of Europe Committee for Higher Education and Research, executive-secretary (1953-70) of the Marshall Aid Commemoration Commission, secretary (1966-70) to the Kennedy Memorial Trust and trustee of the British Institute in Paris. Appointed C.M.G. in 1964 for his services to higher education, he was awarded honorary degrees from seven Commonwealth universities, the one he most cherished being the LL.D. (1975) from Melbourne.

Tall, portly, quietly spoken and affable, Foster was a traditionalist who loved the ritual of English public life, yet he remained proudly Australian. Walking and cycling through the English countryside were his favoured recreations. On 2 January 1968 he had married Margaret Sarah Bate at the parish church, Worlingworth, Suffolk. He died on 24 September 1975 in his thatched cottage, Farthingale, at Worlingworth, and was buried in the local churchyard. His wife, vice-principal of St Gabriel's College of Education, London, survived him, as did the son and two daughters of his first marriage.

O. Parnaby, *Queen's College* (Melb, 1990); G. Serle, *Sir John Medley* (Melb, 1993); *Wyvern Mag*, 1932; *The Times*, 6 Oct 1975; Sir Charles Wilson, address at memorial service for John Foster, 12 Dec 1975, *and* correspondence from Sir Albert Sloman (held by author, Caulfield, Melb); family information.
OWEN PARNABY

FOUCHÉ, FRANÇOIS (1890?-1968), wrestler and entrepreneur, was born reputedly on 13 June 1890 at Goshen, Indiana, United States of America, one of seven children of parents employed in a circus. Information about his early life, based solely on Fouché's testimony, carries an aura of legend. He claimed that his father was a French cavalry officer who formed an aerial circus troupe, and that he himself had graduated from Michigan State University, served as an officer in the United States Army Medical Corps and competed in an Olympic Games. Fouché became a professional wrestler after World War I. With a commanding physical presence, he was about 6 ft 2 ins (188 cm) tall, big boned and athletic, weighing about 18 stone (114 kg) in peak condition. He worked the international circuit and competed against the best, but was consistently modest about his wrestling skill, often observing that he was never in the class of the few at the top.

On 5 September 1938 he arrived in Hobart with several other wrestlers. Three thousand people attended the first match of what was billed as 'one of the most experienced and best performed wrestlers' to visit Tasmania. Intelligent, educated and articulate, with a soft voice and a great sense of fun, Fouché was a showman among showmen. In personal encounters he invariably charmed people, but Hobart already had its wrestling favourites and it was his lot to play the villain. He paraded the city streets and promoted his role with such enthusiasm that he was remembered as having 'arched across the Hobart scene like a rainbow in a leaden . . . sky'. He was not to know then that he would spend the rest of his life in Tasmania and that his super-

ficial theatrical reputation would become fixed in the minds of many citizens, helping to make him at all times a controversial figure.

'Big Frank' set up a gymnasium in Hobart, and conducted radio sessions on diet and health before abandoning wrestling to become the proprietor of a coffee-lounge. He bought a large house in fashionable Sandy Bay where he was later joined by Marjorie ('Mitzie') Myra Arnold (1911-1982), a former 'Tivoli girl' with whom he lived in a devoted domestic relationship. During World War II he opened the Stage Door Canteen, an unlicensed dine-and-dance cabaret in Elizabeth Street which was popular with American troops. There, on 23 August 1942, Leslie Appleton died following an exchange of blows with Fouché. Two days later Fouché was charged with manslaughter. Brought to trial, he was acquitted on 26 September on the ground that he had acted in self-defence. The evidence showed that Appleton had been the attacker and that Fouché hit him only once, but his reputation never recovered from the publicity.

Fouché closed his nightclub in December 1946 and bought farming land at Old Beach, a place then isolated from the city by low-grade rural roads. On that site he planned to build an American-style luxury hotel, with a golf course and casino, to be 'the most outstanding recreational resort in Australia'. Having secured a provisional hotel licence in December 1947, he began work, using day-labour. When the hotel was no more than a crude steel-and-concrete frame, a crisis developed. Fouché had raised his £41 500 mortgage finance through the Tasmanian Public Service Superannuation Fund Board, but in a report to parliament in June 1949 the attorney-general condemned the transaction and the board resigned. The new board refused Fouché any further advances and he brought an action against it in the Supreme Court. The judgement, delivered in September 1950, barred him from receiving any additional payments and ordered him to repay with interest the £21 900 already received. On 26 December 1951 a fire at his partly finished hotel at Old Beach (which was insured by the mortgagees for £25 000) caused losses estimated at £60 000 to £80 000. Fouché then appealed to the High Court, which in March 1952 upheld the previous judgement of the Supreme Court.

In 1953 Fouché opened a licensed beer-bar at Old Beach, but never appeared to recover financially. His house was slowly taken over, from the entrance hall inwards, by building materials and he lived a reduced existence, farming and still planning for the future. He died on 19 July 1968 in a motorcar accident at Glenorchy and was cremated.

W. McNally, *Man from Zero* (Melb, 1973); B. Ross, *H. V. Biggins Headmaster Extraordinary* (Hob, 1986); *More of Don Norman's Old Photographs* (Hob, 1993); *People* (Syd), 16 Dec 1953; *Mercury* (Hob), 6, 9, 15 Sept 1938, 25, 26 Sept 1942, 17 June, 30 Sept 1950, 26 Dec 1951, 1, 7 Mar 1952, 8 Dec 1965, 25 June, 20 July 1968, 2 May 1981; *Herald* (Melb), 20 July 1968; *Australian*, 27 July 1968.   B. M. WICKS

FOWELL, JOSEPH CHARLES (1891-1970), architect, is said to have been born on 2 August 1891 at Albany, Western Australia, son of Charles Wellesley Fowell, sometime clergyman of the Church of England, and his wife Frances Elizabeth, née Pemberton. Joseph was educated in England at the Dominican Preparatory and Fauconberge Grammar schools, Beccles, Suffolk; his boyhood interests included oil-painting and sailing. At Beccles he was articled to an architect F. E. Banham, but completed his training in London with Travers & Mileham. As an assistant with Gibson, Skipworth & Gordon (later with Atkinson & Alexander and others) he helped to design banks and country houses. In 1914 he became an associate (fellow 1930) of the Royal Institute of British Architects.

On the outbreak of World War I, Fowell was refused entry to the navy (having lost the use of one eye); through persistence, he was eventually commissioned in the Royal Naval Volunteer Reserve on 20 December 1915. He served with the Auxiliary Motor Boat Patrol in the English Channel, the North Sea and the Mediterranean. On 14 August 1919 at the Servite Church, Kensington, London, he married with Catholic rites 39-year-old Ettie Spong Horne (d.1939).

They came to Sydney late in 1919. Fowell worked as first-assistant in the private practice of Professor Leslie Wilkinson [q.v.12] with whom he formed an enduring friendship. In 1926 Fowell became an assistant to H. E. Budden. Kenneth McConnel and Fowell (partners 1928-39) won a competition in 1928 to design B.M.A. House (1933 bronze medal, R.I.B.A.). Their joint design for St Anne's Shrine, Bondi, received the 1935 Sulman [q.v.12] award. Fowell was primarily responsible for the design of over forty churches in New South Wales and Victoria, including Catholic churches at North Sydney (1937), Parkes (1939) and Neutral Bay (1941). In enlarging (1934) St Charles's Church, Ryde, he was credited with the first significant architectural expression of Catholic liturgical change. He planned the altar to be free-standing, to join the congregation with the celebrant. His design (1941) for St Philip Neri's, Northbridge, was a further step in liturgical change and influenced later architects. Not content to leave details to others, he designed and supervised the execution of furnishings, sacred vessels and ornaments, and collaborated with sculptors, painters and stained-glass craftsmen.

At St Joseph's Catholic Church, Neutral Bay, on 8 December 1939 Fowell married Eileen Stella Hunt. A fellow (1931) of the Royal Australian Institute of Architects, he was vice-president (1941-42 and 1946-47) of the New South Wales chapter and was to receive its gold medal in 1962. Intermittently, he was also a member of the Board of Architects. In 1950 he was a founder of the Blake prize for religious art and was subsequently life president of the Blake Society. Continuing his leadership in design, Fowell remained senior partner of the firm, which was joined by J. L. S. Mansfield [q.v.] (1939), D. C. B. Maclurcan (1946) and O. R. Jarvis (1962); one unusual commission from 1946 involved refitting passenger ships released by the navy. In the 1960s the firm completed large projects such as the Sydney County Council building (1960), and the Gladesville and Tarban Creek bridges (R.A.I.A. civic design award, 1965).

An accomplished draftsman with a fine feeling for line and colour, Fowell studied life drawing under Desiderius Orban in the 1950s. Four of Fowell's water-colours, painted in the Mediterranean during World War I, were accepted by the Australian War Memorial, Canberra. He was reserved, astute and introspective. His assistants remembered his white hair, his kindness, and his soft-pencil sketches—smudged with cigarette ash—over their drawings. Survived by his wife and the son of his first marriage, he died on 3 July 1970 at his Bayview home and was buried in Northern Suburbs cemetery.

Fowell, Mansfield, Jarvis & Maclurcan, History of the Firm (priv print, Syd, 1960); N. Fowell, *The Sirius Letters*, N. Irvine ed (Syd, 1988); *Architecture in Aust*, 1 Jan 1928, p 6, 1 Sept 1936, p 212, Aug 1970, p 609; *Building* (Syd), 12 Mar 1928, p 43, 24 Aug 1939, p 35, 24 Apr 1941, p 18, 24 Dec 1942; *Building Materials and Equipment*, Aug-Sept 1968, p 45; P. Martin, Fowell, Mansfield, Jarvis & Maclurcan, 1929-1970 (B.Arch. thesis, Univ NSW, 1988); J. C. Fowell documents (held by Fowell, Mansfield, Jarvis & Maclurcan Partnership Pty Ltd, St Leonards, Syd); N. D. Fowell (comp), family history (ms held by Mr J. Fowell, Wynnum West, Brisb).
                                        PETER REYNOLDS
                                        PAMELA MARTIN

FOWLER, JACK BERESFORD (1893-1972), actor, producer and director, was born on 21 July 1893 at Ultimo, Sydney, fourth son of Frank Harry Fowler (d.1893), a musician from England, and his wife Fannie Adèle, née

Ellard, a native-born actress. In 1896 Fannie moved with her sons to Melbourne where they lived in turn at Elsternwick, Brighton, Armadale and Hawksburn; she took in boarders and sometimes acted under the names of Mrs Fanny Fowler or 'Ethel Adele'. Jack was educated at Hawksburn State School and grew to be an omnivorous reader, an ardent theatre-goer, and a follower of cricket and football. As a child, he appeared in amateur productions of Gilbert and Sullivan, though he could not sing. He worked as a messenger boy for a dental supplier, then as a dentist's assistant until he was sacked.

Despite signs of deafness, which became acute, Fowler acted in Gregan McMahon's [q.v.10] Melbourne Repertory Company in 1911-14, making his debut at the Turn Verein Hall, East Melbourne, as Foldal in Ibsen's *John Gabriel Borkman*. In 1914 he toured with the J. C. Williamson [q.v.6] company. He acted with and was assistant stage manager for Nellie Stewart [q.v.12] in David Belasco's *Du Barry* and Paul Kester's *Sweet Nell of Old Drury*. Fowler also toured with the Bert Bailey [q.v.7]-Julius Grant company as Billy Bearup in *On Our Selection*, based loosely on the stories of 'Steele Rudd' [q.v.8 A. H. Davis].

On 10 July 1916 he enlisted in the Australian Imperial Force. He served with the 3rd Pioneer Battalion in Britain and France, performed in concert parties for the troops and was discharged on 28 August 1919 in Melbourne. Fowler rejoined Bailey and Grant before directing an amateur revival of *John Gabriel Borkman* in which he played the title role, probably his best part. He worked with Allan Wilkie's [q.v.12] company for nearly three years as an actor and stage-manager. From Wilkie he inherited something of the expansive acting style and much of the 'stage business' contrived by the actor-managers Sir Frank Benson and Sir Herbert Beerbohm Tree.

In 1925 Fowler founded the Art Theatre Players. He used amateurs and drama students in productions of plays by Ibsen, Strindberg, Shaw, Chekhov, Galsworthy and Coward, and in dramatizations of Dickens. 'J.B.' and his mother were frequent performers. Under his direction *Miss Julie* premiered in 1928 and *Richard II* in 1936. His *Richard II* gave a generation of Victorian schoolchildren an unforgettable, but not always favourable, introduction to Shakespeare. In later years he played John of Gaunt with his chain-mail jerkin adorned by a huge hearing-aid. Dickens's Vincent Crummles was put in the shade by 'J.B.' who was not only actor-manager, director and star of most of the plays he put on, but also advertising-manager and canvasser, trudging city streets with printed cards advertising forthcoming

attractions. Even more, he was ticket-seller, electrician and stage-hand. Stories of his improvised productions became legendary; most were true. Performers sometimes met for the first time on stage.

With his broad shoulders, there was something almost pugilistic about his stance, offset by a romantic, leisurely drift in the way he walked. His manner was Edwardian, courtly, his charm touched with the anxiety of a deaf man trying not to miss out. On stage, he seemed to have everything against him: deafness, a harsh voice which lacked any modulation, a slight speech impediment and a determination to promote plays that commercial managements would not touch. But the Art Theatre Players was an oasis in Melbourne's cultural desert. He was well cast as Bottom the weaver in *A Midsummer Night's Dream* perhaps because he had much in common with Bottom's innocence, egotism and penchant for playing all the parts. His Borkman had a dark, haunting magnetism, and there was a grainy mischievousness about his Burgess in Shaw's *Candida* which made it a comic delight. He last appeared as the grave-digger in *Hamlet* at the Union Theatre, University of Melbourne.

With Sylvia Archer, Fowler wrote the play, *General Sir Hector MacDonald* (1942), a defence of a Scottish soldier who had killed himself in 1903 after accusations of homosexuality. It received a public reading in Melbourne but was never performed on stage. He published a novel, *A Puppet's Mirage* (1957), a theatrical history, *Stars in my Backyard* (1962), an autobiography, *The Green-Eyed Monster* (1968), and *A Must for Dolly*, a sequel to Shaw's *Man and Superman*. His impressive collection of autographed letters, documents and photographs was sold off to help him survive. He succeeded W. A. Osborne [q.v.11] as president of the Melbourne Shakespeare Society. Never married, he harboured a passion for some of his leading ladies and had a long relationship with Sylvia Archer.

Despite his deafness, isolation and poverty, Fowler never seemed to despair, although he was bitter when Melbourne's newspapers no longer reviewed his productions. Gallant, indomitable and quixotic, he was mercifully oblivious of criticism. He died on 17 July 1972 at Albert Park and was cremated. 'J.B.' was no radical protesting against the corruption of commercial theatre; he simply carried the torch for a threatened tradition and saw no need for an apology to justify his position.

J. Murray, *The Paradise Tree* (Syd, 1988); *SMH*, 6, 27 Jan, 6 Feb 1934, 26 May, 18 Aug 1962; *Herald* (Melb), 3 Oct 1953, 7 July 1964; *Sun News-Pictorial*, 9 Jan 1967, 21 July 1972; personal knowledge.   PETER O'SHAUGHNESSY
                                              BARRY O. JONES

FOWLER, JACK RADNALD 'MICK' (1927-1979), seaman, jazz musician and green ban activist, was born on 12 October 1927 at Auckland, New Zealand, son of Felix John Gordon Fowler, waterside worker, and his wife Cecilia Mary Kathleen, née Gollop, both New Zealand born. Brought to Sydney as a child, he was employed in turn as a newsboy, a fruit-picker and a hairdresser. When he enlisted in the Australian Military Forces on 4 March 1946 he was described as being 5 ft 10 ins (178 cm) tall, with hazel eyes and dark hair. Following his training, he embarked in August 1947 for service with the British Commonwealth Occupation Force, Japan, and next month was attached to the 67th Battalion (later the 3rd Battalion, Royal Australian Regiment) at Kure. He returned to Sydney in August 1949 and was discharged on 8 September.

Joining the Seamen's Union of Australia and the Communist Party of Australia, Fowler (generally known as 'Mick') entertained shipmates and comrades with the ukulele, drums and bazooka, playing traditional songs of working-class struggle. As drummer in the Southern Cross Jazz Band, he visited Moscow in 1957 for the sixth World Festival of Youth and Students for Peace and Friendship. Back in Sydney, the band took part in May Day marches. Fowler performed his repertoire at picket lines, and pioneered jazz sessions at factory gates and in hotels. He played the drums and ukulele when he recorded with 'Three Strings and a Dash' (1970) and his own group, 'The Fowlhouse Five & One' (1972-73).

Returning from a voyage in April 1973, he reached his rented flat at 115A Victoria Street, Potts Point, to find the premises boarded up and sold to F. W. Theeman's Victoria Point Pty Ltd. Fowler's plight became a *cause célèbre* for the green ban movement when, with the help of some fifty comrades, he repossessed and barricaded the property. Supported by residents' action groups and trade unionists opposed to the redevelopment of Victoria Street, Fowler announced that the aim of this *ad hoc* coalition was 'to preserve a place in the inner city for low income earners'. He formed 'The Green Ban'd' and recorded *Green Bans Forever* (1975). 'The Battle of Victoria Street' lasted for three years, and involved court challenges, harassment and confrontations between green ban militants and security personnel retained by Theeman. With his moustache, 'boxer's nose, rasping, confidential voice and energetic eyes', Fowler became a prominent figure in Sydney. He was eventually evicted from his home after a legal judgement against him in May 1976. Although ostensibly a victory for Theeman and his associates, the campaign imposed pyrrhic costs on the developers and served as a beacon for green ban mobilization.

Fowler continued to go to sea, but the events had gradually affected his health. He remained depressed over the sinister disappearance in July 1975 of his close friend and fellow activist, Juanita Nielsen [q.v.], and urged that further investigations be conducted into the case. While working as a greaser in the *Australian Pioneer*, he died of a coronary occlusion on 11 August 1979 at Dampier, Western Australia. Over seven hundred mourners in Sydney heard tributes from former comrades as the cortège, accompanied by a jazz band, stopped outside his old address in Victoria Street *en route* to Eastern Suburbs crematorium.

Seamen's Journal, Apr 1957, p 1, May 1959, p 119, Sept-Oct 1979, p 180; *SMH*, 4 May 1973, 19 Feb, 6 May 1976, 16, 18 Aug 1979; *Sun-Herald*, 19 Aug 1979.   RICHARD MORRIS

FOWLER, JOSEPH (1888-1972), businessman and municipal councillor, was born on 28 February 1888 at Bagworth, Leicestershire, England, one of thirteen children of John Fowler, groom, and his wife Mary, née Ash. With his brother Sydney, in the early 1900s Joseph worked in a fruit-preserving business run by an uncle at Maidstone, Kent, and continued with the firm after 1908 when it was relocated at Reading. At St Andrew's parish church, Leicester, on 7 September 1910 he married a nurse, Elizabeth Harris (d.1965); they emigrated in 1913 and settled at Camberwell, Melbourne.

Encouraged by his commercial experience, and by the variety and quality of fruit in Australia, Fowler set up a fruit-bottling business in the rear of his small house in Burke Road. Trading as J. Fowler & Co., by 1915 the company had begun producing home-bottling kits which contained a sterilizer, bottles, lids, rings and a thermometer. To acquire the capital to establish a factory, Fowler travelled the district, selling his kits door-to-door from the back of a cart. In 1920 he bought a shop at the corner of Power Street and Burwood Road, Hawthorn, and registered his business as a private company.

During the Depression his kits became a household name. In 1934 Fowlers Vacola Manufacturing Co. Ltd was registered as a public company. Housewives, nationwide, were urged to bottle their own fruits and jams by 'Mrs B Thrifty', the dainty cartoon character who graced the firm's advertisements. Numerous recipes and instruction books, such as *From Orchard to Bottle the Fowlers Way*, advertised the necessary preserving equipment, extending to jelly bags and juice extractors. Australian-made glass and imported steel and rubber were used in the production of Fowlers Vacola Bottling Outfits.

Determined to put something back into the community which had supported him so well, in 1933-60 Fowler represented Yarra Ward on the Hawthorn City Council (mayor 1938-39 and 1945-46). He served as vice-president of Swinburne Technical College (1942) and of the Hawthorn branch of the Australian Defence League (1943); he was also a Rotarian, and a warden and vestryman of St John's Anglican Church, Camberwell.

Changed demands in World War II encouraged Fowlers Vacola to diversify their product. Canned goods were manufactured for allied troops in the South Pacific. In 1953 new buildings and plant, including a giant pressure-cooker, were installed to increase productivity: from that time Fowlers Vacola sold canned and bottled food throughout Australia and abroad. By 1960 the factory occupied more than $122\,000$ sq. ft ($11\,330$ m^2) and further expansion was to occur when the firm moved to Nunawading. Fowler retired in 1961, but remained chairman of directors; his son Ronald succeeded him as managing director.

Variously described as a generous, jovial man with a sense of humour, and as a strict and astute manager whose company was his life, Fowler was renowned for his straight business dealings and his 'no-nonsense' attitude. Survived by his son and daughter, he died on 24 April 1972 at Camberwell and was cremated. His estate was sworn for probate at $204 424. On Ronald Fowler's death in 1978, the company was bought out by the Sydney firm, Hooper Baillie Industries Ltd; it in turn sold to Sabco Ltd of South Australia; in 1994, when Sabco went into receivership, Australian Resource Recovery Technologies re-established Fowlers Vacola Australia Pty Ltd's headquarters in Melbourne.

Food Preserver, Sept 1960, Feb, May 1965; *Eastern Suburbs Standard*, 27 July 1960, City of Hawthorn Centenary 1860-1960 supp; *Age* (Melb), 1 Aug 1960, 26 Oct 1965, 9 Sept 1978, 26 May 1993; *Sun News-Pictorial*, 27 Apr 1972, 12 Mar 1975; Fowlers Vacola advertising material (SLV); Hawthorn City L vertical files; family information.   VICTORIA PEEL

FOWLER, LAURA MARGARET; *see* HOPE

FOWLER, ROBERT (1888-1965), surgeon and soldier, was born on 5 March 1888 at East Smithfield, London, son of Walter Fowler, surgeon, and his wife Alice, née Wacher. The family emigrated to Victoria in 1891, and lived at Echuca and then at Bendigo. Proceeding from Caulfield Grammar School to the University of Melbourne (M.B., B.S., 1909; M.D., 1912), Robert was Beaney [q.v.3] scholar in pathology in 1911 and assistant-lecturer in pathology in 1912. At the Melbourne Hospital, he was successively resident medical officer, honorary assistant pathologist (1911-12) and honorary clinical assistant (1912).

Having served (from 1910) in the Citizen Military Forces, on 20 August 1914 Fowler was appointed captain, Australian Army Medical Corps, Australian Imperial Force. Two months later he embarked for Egypt. On 12 January 1915 at El Maʿâdi he married Melbourne-born Elsie Walshe. At Gallipoli in September he assumed command of the 1st Light Horse Field Ambulance. From February 1917 to January 1918 he commanded the 4th L.H.F.A. in the advance through Palestine. As temporary colonel and assistant-director of medical services, Australian Mounted Division, in October he faced the 'shambles of Damascus'—when '[m]alaria, dysentery, thirst and starvation were in sole control'—and met T. E. Lawrence. Appointed O.B.E. (1919) and thrice mentioned in dispatches, in 1920 Fowler returned to Australia where his A.I.F. appointment terminated on 8 September.

He became a fellow of the Royal College of Surgeons, England, in 1920 and of the American College of Surgeons in 1924. A foundation fellow (1927) of the Royal Australasian College of Surgeons, in 1931-34 he was honorary surgeon to the governor-general Sir Isaac Isaacs [q.v.9]. Fowler continued to serve in the citizen forces between the wars. His assessments of the potential for patients to be evacuated by air, and of the military importance to Australia of tropical medicine, were to prove prophetic. In 1936-37 he was group captain and deputy-director of medical services, Royal Australian Air Force. He commanded the 117th Australian General Hospital, Toowoomba, Queensland, in 1942-43, and was D.D.M.S., Victorian Lines of Communication Area, in 1943-44.

Fowler's reputation as 'the uncrowned king of gynaecology' was built at several Melbourne hospitals, especially the Alfred where he was honorary gynaecologist (1924-48) and established a famous clinic. In 1926 he had convened an obstetric inquiry for the Victorian branch of the British Medical Association. His 'pioneering work in the treatment of uterine cancer' included Australia's first Wertheim hysterectomies.

Fowler was also a pioneer of medical statistics in Australia. For the Anti-Cancer

Council of Victoria, he had set up in 1939 a central cancer registry which collated data from six major hospitals. In 1955 he drew upon the data to assert 'the positive association of lung cancer and tobacco smoking'. Ten years later his paper was deemed to be 'the most important Australian contribution in this field'. The council established an annual Robert Fowler travelling scholarship.

Colleagues commented on Fowler's late-Victorian elegance, his 'beautiful operative methods' and his 'happy knack of inspiring his assistants'. He was described as 'lithe and rangy in build with a lean, aquiline face, fit frame for his keen and active brain'. A member (from 1932) of the University of Melbourne's standing committee of convocation, he was appointed warden of convocation in 1959 and a council-member in 1962. He died on 8 May 1965 at South Yarra and was buried in Melbourne general cemetery; his wife, son and two daughters survived him.

A. S. Walker, *Medical Services of the R.A.N. and R.A.A.F.* (Canb, 1961); A. M. Mitchell, *The Hospital South of the Yarra* (Melb, 1977); L. Gardiner, *EV Keogh, DCM, MM, MBBS, FRACP* (Melb, 1990); A'sian Medical Congress (British Medical Assn), *Trans of the Third Session* (Syd), 2-7 Sept 1929; *MJA*, 29 July 1939, p 155, 21 Nov 1942, p 455, 21 July 1951, p 69, 2 Apr 1955, p 485, 11 Sept 1965, pp 469, 597; *Age* (Melb), 12 May 1965; Fowler's war diary (copy held in Roy A'sian College of Surgeons archives, Melb).   COLIN SMITH

FOWLER, STANLEY (1895-1961), fisheries researcher, was born on 23 November 1895 at Williamstown, Melbourne, seventh child of Victorian-born parents Robert Fowler, fitter, and his wife Emily Sarah, née Booley. Stanley left his state school to take a job as a clerk with the Victorian Railways. On 17 October 1914 he enlisted in the Australian Imperial Force and that month embarked for Egypt with the 5th Battalion. He was wounded on 25 April 1915 at Gallipoli and again on 25 July 1916 at Pozières, France, where he was severely injured in the head and legs. Invalided home, he was discharged on 30 May 1917 in Melbourne.

After lengthy periods in hospital, Fowler joined the Commonwealth Bureau of Commerce and Industry in March 1920. At Scots Church, Melbourne, on 19 November 1921 he married Agnes Maud Lewis with Presbyterian forms; they were to remain childless and were later divorced. In 1927 he was appointed investigating officer with the Development and Migration Commission. He played a key role in organizing the Australian Fisheries Conference which recommended in 1929 that a federal body be established to conduct a 'scientific, statistical and practical investigation of the fisheries, aimed at their commercial exploitation'. Transferring to the Council for Scientific and Industrial Research as fisheries officer in 1935, he was involved in discussions that led to its fisheries investigations section (later fisheries division) being formed in 1937. Fowler immediately joined the new section.

He was concerned that much of Australia's coastline had 'not been explored in a fisheries sense'. With the co-operation of the Royal Australian Air Force, in 1936-39 and 1942-46 he undertook a series of aerial observations of pelagic stock in coastal waters. Fowler spent hundreds of hours in the air, photographing often vast and previously unknown shoals of fish, including such species as the Australian salmon and bluefin tuna. The results were brilliant. His photographs—some 10 000 in all—are still frequently consulted by fisheries scientists and others interested in the Australian coastline.

Equally conscious of the importance of seagoing exploration, Fowler had been instrumental in the C.S.I.R.'s decision to purchase the research vessel, *Warreen*, in 1933; he was on board for her maiden cruise in 1938 and on numerous occasions thereafter. He welcomed the commercial application of scientific findings and never lost an opportunity to publicize the results of his investigations. Chairman (1940-41) of the Co-operative Fishermen's Association of Victoria Ltd, he enjoyed a close rapport with fishermen and respected their views, though they did not always accord with those of the scientists in the C.S.I.R. His conviction that an abundance of fish awaited exploitation in Australian waters embroiled him in a dispute with his scientific colleagues in 1941.

Fowler's later years with C.S.I.R. were not happy. Promoted principal research officer in 1946, he was overlooked that year for the new position of head of the division's exploration section. He took early retirement in July 1948 on the grounds of ill health, but agreed to compile notes to accompany his photographs; he continued to correspond with newspapers and fishing organizations, and wrote occasional scientific articles for journals. Suffering from atherosclerosis, he died of a coronary occlusion on 22 January 1961 at the Anzac Hostel, Brighton, and was cremated.

T. C. Roughley, *Fish and Fisheries of Australia* (Syd, 1957); V. Mawson et al (eds), *C.S.I.R.O. at Sea* (Hob, 1988); *Pacific Fisherman*, Aug 1942; *Fisheries Newsletter*, Oct 1942, Dec 1948, Mar 1961; Roy Zoological Soc of NSW, *Procs*, Sept 1947; *WA Naturalist*, Mar 1948, Oct 1961; CSIRO Archives, Canb (Series 120, 155, 1007); information from Mr R. Laurent, Cabarlah, Qld.

JOHN LAURENT

FOX, JOHN; *see* JUAN

FOXALL, HENRY GEORGE (1884-1966), engineer and surveyor, was born 7 October 1884 at St Leonards, Sydney, second son of English-born parents Edward William Foxall, accountant, and his wife Margaret Nerissa, née Dobbie. Named after Henry George [q.v.4], Harry was captain (1900-01) at Fort Street Model School; he remained a keen student of English and Roman history, Shakespeare and the classics. At the University of Sydney (B.E., 1906) he was awarded the Deas Thomson [q.v.2] scholarship for geology in 1904, and gained first-class honours in practical metallurgy and assaying next year. Foxall's assistantship with Professor (Sir) Edgeworth David [q.v.8] in the geological survey of Newcastle coalfields led to publications on isolated augite crystals at Gerringong and to notes on the microscopic and crystallographic characteristics of pseudomorphglendonites.

After spending four and a half years working in Queensland mines and at a refinery at Port Kembla, New South Wales, he returned to Sydney in 1910 and joined the staff of his uncle, S. R. Dobbie. In 1912 Foxall passed the land surveyors examination. At Port Kembla on 6 November that year he married with Catholic rites Eugenie Mary Hanley (d.1925); they were to have two sons and two daughters. Dobbie took him into partnership in 1914. Foxall's developing expertise and innovatory methods were shown in his publications (1916) on graphical methods to solve survey problems, in his plane table applications to underground exploration and in his use in the 1930s of aerial photography for mining surveying. His work included reports on the prospects of finding oil in Timor (1911) and Papua (1925), on hydro-electric resources on Vita Levu, Fiji (1935), and on the search for oil around Roma, Queensland. When Dobbie retired in 1936, A. J. Lines (d.1959) joined the firm.

From 1917 Foxall had also lectured on surveying, while employed part time at Sydney Technical College; he insisted that his pupils received a solid grounding in mathematics. His lecture notes, illustrated by his pupil Alan Wood during the Depression, were expanded into Foxall's *Handbook for Practising Land and Engineering Surveyors* (1958). Joint-editor (1919-21) of the *Surveyor*, he was a councillor (1922-49), president (1924-25 and 1944-46) and an honorary fellow (1949) of the Institution of Surveyors, New South Wales. He was appointed to the Board of Surveyors of New South Wales in 1929 and in the 1930s was vice-president of the Town and Country Planning Institute.

At St Andrew's Anglican Church on 11 January 1928 Foxall had married a clerk, Margaret Mabel Reeves. An unassuming gentleman of the old school, with sober habits and high principles, he had a keen sense of humour and the ability to talk and debate on many subjects. Madge and Harry sponsored musical evenings at their Chatswood home. A member of Roseville Golf and Elanora Country clubs, he belonged, as well, to bowling clubs at Gordon and Newport. His elder son Geoffrey entered into the partnership in 1959; his younger son Ian was engineer for surveys with the Snowy Mountains Hydro-electric Authority in 1955-61. Harry Foxall died on 22 April 1966 at Mona Vale District Hospital and was cremated with Anglican rites; his wife and the children of his first marriage survived him.

Surveyor (Syd), Feb, Dec 1916; *Aust Surveyor*, 14, Sept-Dec 1952, p 85, 21, June 1966, p 821; Roy Soc NSW, *J and Procs*, July 1904, p 404; *NSW Geological Survey Records*, 8, 1905, p 161; *SMH*, 1 Feb 1924; information from Messrs G. Foxall, Castle Hill, I. Foxall, East Lindfield, A. Wood, Killara, and Brig D. Macdonald, Syd.   JOHN ATCHISON

FRAME, ANDREE MARCELLE (1910-1967), masseuse and childbirth educator, was born on 17 March 1910 in Paris, second child and only daughter of Robert Crooke, a teacher from Australia, and his French wife Alice Louise, née Legat. Emigrating to Victoria on the eve of World War I, the family—which was to include three more sons—maintained French as the language spoken at home. When Marcelle started school at Cockatoo, she was sent home for want of English. Her secondary education was at the Academy of Mary Immaculate, Fitzroy, where she was dux (1926-27) of the Intermediate and Leaving classes.

After completing school, Marcelle trained as a masseuse, attending classes in anatomy and physiology at the University of Melbourne. In 1931 she gained a diploma from the Masseurs' Registration Board of Victoria. At St Kilda on 23 May 1940 she married, with Methodist forms, William Frame, an engineer. Three years later she had a mastectomy which left her with insufficient strength to practise some aspects of physiotherapy. For a time she worked for the cosmetic firm Cyclax Ltd. Widowed in 1952 and childless, Mrs Frame continued to work, though increasingly as a beautician.

In 1959 she visited the Lamaze clinic in Paris to study its techniques for natural childbirth. She returned to Melbourne full of excitement at the possibilities. At her South Yarra flat she drew together a group of her clients to practise the new method of preparation for childbirth—psychoprophy-laxis. Clients and colleagues were struck by her dynamism and energy which belied her small stature. Her vivacity and charm were accompanied by intense determination, and a strength of character and purpose that was needed to combat the opposition, not merely of the majority of doctors, but of some physio-therapists who challenged the effectiveness and rigour of her approach. In many ways she stood outside the conventional health pro-fessions, but eventually won respect for the care and commitment she gave to her clients.

Frame's clients were so enthusiastic about the birth experiences they achieved under her tuition that they formed the first formal group in Australia to reform birth practices. Established in 1961 as the Association for the Advancement of Painless Childbirth, it be-came the precursor of a wide network of childbirth reform groups, many of which were loosely affiliated as branches of the Childbirth Education Association (the name adopted in 1965), of which she was patron. Her other interests included art and music, and she was an active member of the Alliance Française.

Marcelle Frame lived only to see the initial acceptance of her cause rather than the wide-spread development of childbirth preparation programmes that occurred during the 1970s. She died of cancer on 8 February 1967 at Heidelberg; her will bequeathed her body to the University of Melbourne for medical research.

Herald (Melb), 10 Feb 1967; information from Mr M. Crooke, Chapman, Canb.

KERREEN M. REIGER

FRANCIS, SIR JOSIAH (1890-1964), poli-tician and army officer, was born on 28 March 1890 at Ipswich, Queensland, second child of native-born parents Henry Alfred Francis, draper, and his wife Ada Florence, née Hooper. Educated at Christian Brothers' Col-lege, Ipswich, Jos held a commission in the senior cadets. In February 1908 he joined the Queensland Department of Justice as a clerk.

On 1 April 1916 Francis was appointed second lieutenant in the Australian Imperial Force. He sailed for England in October and served with the 15th Battalion on the West-ern Front from April 1917. Wounded in the shoulder in March 1918, he was hospitalized in England before rejoining his unit in September. In the following month he was promoted temporary captain (substantive in November). His A.I.F. appointment termin-ated in Australia on 16 September 1919.

Involving himself with issues affecting for-mer servicemen, Francis presided over the Ipswich sub-branch (1920-21) and the More-ton district (1920) of the Returned Sailors' and Soldiers' Imperial League of Australia; in the early 1920s he was a member of the or-ganization's State managing council. He was elected to the House of Representatives in 1922 as the Nationalist candidate for More-ton and was to hold the seat until 1955. At the Central Congregational Church, Ipswich, on 26 April 1927 he married Edna Clarke Cribb; they were to remain childless.

Dubbed a 'plodder' for much of his political life, Francis was a member of various parlia-mentary committees and of the royal com-mission on national insurance (1923-27). In J. A. Lyons's [q.v.10] United Australia Party government he was assistant-minister for de-fence and minister in charge of war-service homes in 1932-34, and minister without port-folio—in charge of war-service homes and assisting the minister for repatriation—in 1934. He promoted the concerns of returned service personnel, not only because of his commitment to their welfare, but also because he understood their politics. Unashamedly following R.S.& S.I.L.A. policy, in the late 1920s he had supported the estab-lishment of pension appeals tribunals for ex-servicemen; in 1933 he secured a reduction in the interest rate on loans for war-service homes from 4.5 to 4 per cent.

In March 1943 Francis moved an amend-ment to the Australian soldiers' repatriation bill allowing for a full pension to be paid to veterans suffering from pulmonary tuber-culosis, whether or not their condition could be attributed to war service. The change complied with the policy of the Australian La-bor Party (then in power), but it fell to Francis to bring the matter before the House. Not one voice was raised against the amendment which ended twenty-five years of bitter argu-ment over the plight of ex-servicemen with tuberculosis and ushered in a far-reaching precedent.

With the return to government of the Liberal and Country parties in 1949 under (Sir) Robert Menzies [q.v.], Francis was min-ister for the army (1949-55) and the navy (1949-51 and 1954-55). He ensured that his departments received significant budgetary allocations and was respected by the military chiefs. In 1951 he supported the Naval Board's recommendation that the govern-ment accede to a British request for the air-craft-carrier, H.M.A.S. *Sydney*, to be sent to Korean waters. That year he spent Christmas with Australian troops in Korea.

At a diplomatic reception in Tokyo immedi-ately afterwards, Francis was alleged to have confiscated the film of a press photographer who captured him 'clinking champagne glasses with the Russian Ambassador (Gen-eral Kislenko)'. Francis warned Australian soldiers against marrying Japanese women, arguing that the brides faced immigration restrictions and social rejection if they were allowed into Australia; he added the rather spurious observation that French wives of World War I soldiers had generally been unable to settle down in their new country. While normally not pretentious, he liked to wear a top hat, thereby attracting derisive comments from Labor members in the House.

Appointed Australian consul-general in New York in 1956, Francis built up useful contacts for his country, particularly in American banking and industrial circles. He was knighted in 1957 and retired to Brisbane four years later. Sir Josiah retained an interest in sporting activities and was patron of the Point Danger branch of the Surf Life Saving Association of Australia from 1924 until his death; in 1926 he had saved a boy from drowning at the St Kilda baths, Melbourne. Survived by his wife, Francis died on 22 February 1964 at Toowong and was cremated with Methodist forms. Menzies paid tribute to his 'humanity and understanding'.

G. L. Kristianson, *The Politics of Patriotism* (Canb, 1966); R. O'Neill, *Australia in the Korean War 1950-53*, 1 and 2 (Canb, 1981, 1985); C. Lloyd and J. Rees, *The Last Shilling* (Melb, 1994); *Brisb Courier*, 1 Jan 1932; *Sun News-Pictorial*, 2 Jan 1952; *Herald* (Melb), 21 Oct, 3 Dec 1960; *Sunday Mail* (Brisb), 23 Feb 1964; *Age* (Melb), 24 Feb 1964.
                                    JACQUELINE REES

FRANCIS, MARIA MAY; *see* BRODNEY

FRANK, KENDALL THOMAS (1904-1951), wireless operator and engineer, was born on 21 November 1904 at Mornington Mills, Western Australia, fourth child of native-born parents Henry Joseph Frank, inspector, and his wife Alice, née Templar. Little is known of Ken's childhood and education, other than that in 1920 he studied physics at the Kalgoorlie School of Mines. In December 1927 he joined Amalgamated Wireless (Australasia) Ltd as a ship's radio-operator and served in the M.V. *Kangaroo*. Four months later he transferred to the Coastal Radio Service in which he gained the reputation of being 'a genius', 'a brilliant larrikin' and 'the fastest operator of all time'. He read Morse code at the extraordinary speed of seventy words per minute. It was even said that he was capable of receiving Morse while rolling a cigarette and holding a conversation.

From December 1928 when Frank was posted to the A.W.A. radio station at Port Moresby, that town became his home. He assisted the A.W.A. engineer responsible for constructing a new high-frequency station (opened in March 1931) which was to provide direct communication with Sydney. In 1934 Frank returned to Sydney where he worked with A.W.A.'s engineering department in developing radio for aviation. Back in Papua, in October 1935 he set up radio-station 4PM, making many of the transmitting components himself; from December he was officer-in-charge of Port Moresby Radio. At Ela Protestant Church, Port Moresby, on 3 September 1938 he married a divorcee, Prudence Wildby, née Jeffrey; they were to have a daughter before being divorced.

Following the outbreak of World War II, Port Moresby Radio played a crucial role in military communications in the South-West Pacific Area. Apart from operating special communication channels for the army and navy, the A.W.A. staff—under instructions from the Royal Australian Navy—marshalled hundreds of outpost teleradio stations throughout the territories into an intelligence network. Reporting via Port Moresby Radio on a secret frequency, coastwatchers provided information from behind enemy lines on movements of Japanese troops, ships and aircraft. This system was to help allied forces to turn the tide of the war in the Pacific.

To escape bombing raids, the radio station was moved in February 1942 to Wonga, about five miles (8 km) beyond the town, and an emergency backup station was installed at Eilogo, thirty miles (48 km) away. As officer-in-charge at Wonga, Frank also built a station for the army at Rouna, providing direct communication with Land Headquarters in Melbourne. In June he installed another station at Bisiatabu, through which communication was to be maintained with the 7th Division on the Owen Stanley Range. As allied forces won back the islands, he built a series of radio stations for General Douglas MacArthur's [q.v.] successive forward headquarters. Once hostilities ended, Frank was responsible for rebuilding several war-damaged coastal radio stations in New Guinea. In 1947, soon after the Overseas Telecommunications Commission (Australia) took control of Australia's external radio-communication services, he was appointed officer-in-charge, Papua and New Guinea.

On 26 May 1950, at the general registry office, Port Moresby, Frank married another divorcee, Sybil Molly Bingham, née Denyer. He died from injuries received in a motorcar accident on 21 August 1951 at Woodstock, Queensland, and was buried with Catholic rites in Townsville cemetery; his wife and daughter of his first marriage survived him.

E. Feldt, *The Coast Watchers* (Melb, 1975); I. Mackay, *Broadcasting in Papua New Guinea*

(Melb, 1976); J. Sinclair, *Uniting a Nation* (Melb, 1984); L. Durrant, *The Seawatchers* (Syd, 1986); Overseas Telecommunications Com (Aust), *Transit*, Sept 1951; Overseas Telecommunications Veterans Association (Aust), *OTVA Newsletter*, Nov 1981; Officer's history (staff life assurance), Oct 1946-Aug 1951 (OTC, Aust, Archives, Syd); information from Mr G. Cupitt, Revesby, Syd, Mr P. J. Chapman, Ettalong Beach, NSW, and other former members, Coastal Radio Service.

L. L. DURRANT

FRASER, ALEXANDER JOHN (1892-1965), politician, was born on 22 August 1892 at Fairfield, Melbourne, third child of Simon Fraser, constable, and his wife Jane, née McLennan, both Scottish born. As a youth, Alex was of robust build and excelled at sport; on leaving Kyneton College, he played Australian Rules football for the Melbourne club. On 12 July 1915 he enlisted in the Australian Imperial Force. Commissioned in March 1916 and posted to the 10th Machine-Gun Company, Fraser reached the Western Front in November. In the battle of Messines, Belgium, on 7 June 1917 he rushed forward alone, and, although seriously wounded, continued to fire on the enemy; he was awarded the Military Cross. Invalided home in early 1918, he left the A.I.F. on 30 April, but briefly resumed his appointment from October that year to January 1919.

At St Andrew's Presbyterian Church, Kyneton, on 15 March 1919 Fraser married Ivy Elizabeth Hume (d.1928). On 12 January 1929 at Scots Church, Melbourne, he married Catherine Boyd (d.1953). He became involved in the development of the dairy industry in Gippsland, first as manager of the produce department of the Gippsland and Northern Co-operative Co. Ltd, then as London organizer (1927-28) for the Australian Producers' Wholesale Co-operative Federation, and finally as general manager (1929-37) of the Great Southern Co-operative Co. Ltd. He was also president of the Dairy Factory Managers' Association and a director (1930-37) of the Australian Sunny South Service Co. Pty Ltd. In 1937-46 Fraser was chairman of the Victorian Transport Regulation Board and during World War II concurrently chaired the State Liquid Fuel Control Board.

In May 1946, while secretary (1946-48) of the United Country Party, Fraser was appointed to the Senate by the Victorian parliament to fill the casual vacancy caused by the death of R. V. Keane [q.v.]. Defeated in the Federal elections in September that year, Fraser joined the Liberal and Country Party in 1949 and next year won the Victorian Legislative Assembly seat of Grant. On 19 September 1952 he was one of six Liberals who alleged that bribes had been offered to induce them to refrain from voting on the previous day against T. T. Hollway's [q.v.] no-confidence motion. Appearing before the ensuing royal commission, he refused to give evidence in support of his affidavit. He was defeated in the December elections, but was returned in 1955 as the L.C.P. member for Caulfield East and represented Caulfield from 1958. At Ewing Memorial Church, East Malvern, on 30 July 1955 he had married Ilene Blackley.

Initially chairman of committees (1955-56) and minister without portfolio (1956-59) in (Sir) Henry Bolte's L.C.P. government, Fraser later served as minister of State development (1959-64) and minister of forests (1959-61). He was an efficient administrator and a skilful negotiator. As a local member, he looked after his constituents with zeal, thoughtfulness and generosity. Outside parliament he chaired the National Parks Authority, the Central Planning Authority and the La Trobe Valley Development Advisory Committee. He maintained his interest in sport; and he regularly attended Ewing Memorial Church. Fraser died on 9 July 1965 at Malvern and was cremated; his wife survived him, as did two daughters and one son of his first marriage, and the son of his second. The elder son of his first marriage, who was his namesake, had been killed on 19 May 1944 while serving with the Royal Australian Air Force.

K. West, *Power in the Liberal Party* (Melb, 1965); *PD* (Vic), 14 Sept 1965; *Sun News-Pictorial*, 30 Mar 1929, 31 Jan 1948, 5, 10 Oct 1952, 9, 13 July 1965; *Age* (Melb), 28 Apr 1937, 24 Aug 1942, 27 May 1944, 22 Nov 1946, 2 Apr 1949, 28 Mar 1956, 7 July 1964, 10 July 1965; *Herald* (Melb), 9 Oct 1952, 1 Sept 1962, 12 July 1965; personal information.

L. H. S. THOMPSON

FRASER, ALLAN DUNCAN (1902-1977) and JAMES REAY (1908-1970), journalists and politicians, were born on 18 September 1902 at Carlton, Melbourne, and 8 February 1908 at Derby, Tasmania, sons of Donald Fraser, a Victorian-born surveyor, and his wife Constance Marie, née Hadrill, from Denmark. Allan spent much of his childhood in Tasmania in circumstances which he subsequently described as of 'modest comfort'. His father preached the economic philosophies of Henry George [q.v.4] in the Hobart Domain and supported the Australian Labor Party until 1916 when he became an adherent of W. M. Hughes's [q.v.9] National Labor (later National) Party. Allan was also strongly influenced by the social principles set out in Robert Tressell's novel, *The Ragged Trou-*

sered Philanthropists (London, 1914), which he read at the State High School, Hobart.

Leaving school at 17, Allan Fraser joined the Hobart *Mercury* as a cadet journalist and built close contacts with the A.L.P.'s Tasmanian branch. He moved to Melbourne in 1922 as a political reporter for the *Argus*, then to Canberra in 1929 as head of the Sydney *Sun*'s bureau. At the Presbyterian Church, Glebe, Sydney, on 31 March 1931 he married a sculptress Eda Kathleen Bourke. In 1933 he was based in London, working as a cables sub-editor for *The Times*. Back in Australia, he had another brief stint with the *Sun* before editing *This Century of Ours* (Sydney, 1938), a history of the Dangar [qq.v.1,4] family. Fraser resumed journalism in a junior position with the Sydney *Daily Telegraph*. Active in the Australian Journalists' Association, he had been secretary, treasurer and president of the Victorian district between 1926 and 1929, and was treasurer of the New South Wales district in 1937-38.

In 1938 Fraser was sacked by the *Daily Telegraph*. He accepted the post of secretary to R. J. Heffron [q.v.] who led the breakaway Industrial Labor Party opposed to the State A.L.P. leader J. T. Lang [q.v.9]. Fraser acted as publicity officer for Heffron's party and was credited with helping to formulate the strategy which eventually overturned Lang's political machine. Following a term as news editor and leader-writer for the *Daily News*, he returned to the Federal Parliamentary Press Gallery in 1940 as political correspondent for Ezra Norton's [q.v.] *Truth*, and was engaged in lobbying activities for his employer. When Norton's *Daily Mirror* began publication in 1941, Fraser became its political correspondent. He was president of the Canberra sub-district of the A.J.A. in 1941-44.

Defeating Jessie Street [q.v.], in 1943 Fraser gained pre-selection as A.L.P. candidate for the Federal seat of Eden-Monaro, a large rural electorate in south-east New South Wales that adjoined the Australian Capital Territory. Although Eden-Monaro had a consistent history of returning non-Labor members, he won it through a combination of 'vigorous personal electioneering' and the national swing to John Curtin's [q.v.13] Labor government at the 1943 elections. Fraser quickly established a reputation for political competence, but his prospects were impaired almost from the start by his independence and a disposition to criticize his own party.

His maiden speech emphasized the threat to individual freedoms posed by wartime controls and led to his chairmanship (1944-46) of the national security regulations advisory committee. Yet, he was said to have been the first Labor back-bencher to declare his sup-

port for Prime Minister J. B. Chifley's [q.v.13] controversial bank nationalization proposals in 1947. Fraser was elected to the executive of the parliamentary Labor Party in 1951 and was Opposition spokesman on social security.

In that year he joined the A.L.P.'s Federal leader H. V. Evatt [q.v.] in an energetic and ultimately successful appeal to the electorate to vote 'No' in the referendum—initiated by (Sir) Robert Menzies [q.v.]—to give the Commonwealth powers to outlaw the Communist Party of Australia. This close relationship with Evatt did not last, with the party leader antagonizing Fraser by pledging in 1954 that a Labor government would abolish the means test on pensions within three years of its election. Fraser had reminded the party of the dangers of rash promises on social security matters and Evatt had not consulted him before announcing the policy.

After Evatt issued a statement in October denouncing disloyal elements in the A.L.P., Fraser made a highly critical radio broadcast, warning that Evatt's actions 'could split the party from end to end. It has happened before and thrown the party into the political wilderness for years'. He believed that Evatt should have taken his charges to the A.L.P. federal executive and federal conference instead of 'wildly flinging allegations' about in the press.

Fraser's conduct brought him into an alliance with anti-Evatt elements of the federal caucus, although he had reservations about the implications for civil liberties that might stem from the virulent anti-communism of the industrial groups. In 1955 he clashed with his party as a whole over the gaoling by parliament of Raymond Fitzpatrick [q.v.] and Frank Browne for breaching parliamentary privilege. Defying a caucus directive not to debate the case further, Fraser moved in the House that the two men be released from prison. His brother Jim was the only A.L.P. member to support him. Following Labor's defeat at the 1955 elections, on 13 February 1956 Fraser opposed Evatt for the leadership, but was defeated by 58 votes to 20. As a consequence he lost his high ranking in the caucus executive, obtaining only the ninth of ten posts balloted next day.

As his years as a parliamentarian progressed, Fraser became increasingly interested in foreign affairs, particularly the emerging conflict in Vietnam. From the beginning, he opposed the sending of Australian forces to the Republic of Vietnam (South Vietnam) and, as spokesman for foreign affairs, had some influence in shaping the A.L.P.'s policy for the 1966 election campaign. The party was decisively beaten at the polls and Fraser, who had made the withdrawal of Australian troops the dominant issue in Eden-Monaro, lost the seat which he had held for twenty-three years. He won it back in 1969, but did not seek a place on the caucus executive and retired at the end of his term in 1972. In 1974 he was elected to the A.C.T. Legislative Assembly as an Independent. The A.L.P. had refused him pre-selection because of his age, and the A.C.T. branch expelled him from the party for technically opposing its endorsed candidates. He was appointed C.M.G. in 1977.

A reticent man who found social gatherings an ordeal, Fraser had developed into an attractive politician, making extensive and innovative use of radio broadcasts to cultivate support in his sprawling electorate. He was a resonant speaker with distinctive articulation who brought a luminous intellect and a passionate disposition to the practice of politics. His effectiveness, however, was tempered by the assertion of an unqualified independence which kept him at odds with party discipline and cost him the sustained support of his colleagues, much as they admired his gifts. Late in life he bleakly remarked: 'To a very large extent, my career [in politics] has been futile'. Survived by his wife and son, he died on 12 December 1977 in Canberra and was cremated.

Jim Fraser was educated at Launceston High School. He worked as a chainman and axeman in his father's surveying team, and as a teacher in Victorian state schools in 1927-35. Carrying his swag to New South Wales, he found a job as a journalist at Glen Innes. On 29 January 1942 he enlisted in the Australian Imperial Force and served twice with New Guinea Force, first in the 2nd/1st Field Regiment, Artillery (1943), then in the Public Relations Field Unit (1945). Promoted sergeant on 29 May 1945, he was discharged on 25 March 1946. He was employed as a journalist in the Department of Information, Canberra, in 1946-48, and as press secretary and private secretary to Senator N. E. McKenna [q.v.] in 1948-51.

Because the A.C.T. did not have a seat in Federal parliament until 1949, Jim helped his brother Allan who had agreed to represent the interests of Canberra people. Gradually, Jim took over the bulk of the work, becoming a member (1949-51) of the A.C.T. Advisory Council and winning the A.C.T. seat in the House of Representatives in 1951. As member for a Territory, Fraser had limited voting rights until November 1966. He combined Federal and what was in effect State and local government representation with the duties of unofficial ombudsman in a rapidly growing constituency which mingled both urban and rural interests, and still found time to serve on parliamentary committees and participate in parliamentary debates.

A big, forthright man with a gregarious manner, Jim lacked the rich political talents of his elder brother, but commanded respect for his effective and conscientious performance of one of the heaviest representative responsibilities ever imposed on an Australian politician. On 1 August 1959 at St Andrew's Anglican Church, South Brisbane, he had married Helen Whitten Rowland, a bookseller. He died of cancer on 1 April 1970 in Canberra; accorded a state funeral, he was buried in Canberra cemetery with Presbyterian forms. His wife and son survived him.

D. W. Rawson and S. Holtzinger, *Politics in Eden-Monaro* (Lond, 1958); *Canb Times*, 2 Apr 1970, 13 Dec 1977; Helen K. Fraser, Allan Fraser and the Australian Labor Party: A dissenting member and his party (M.A. thesis, Univ Auckland, 1980); A. Fraser personal papers (NL).   C. J. LLOYD

FRASER, DONALD LOVAT (1875-1962), mining entrepreneur, was born on 8 August 1875 at St Giles, London, second child and eldest son of William Fraser, tanner, and his wife Annie, née Grieve, both Scottish born. Harold [q.v.] was his younger brother. The family emigrated to Queensland in the *Highflier* in 1878. William established a fellmongering business at Rockhampton in 1879 and later speculated in mining ventures. Educated locally, at an early age Donald became interested in gold-mining. In 1898 he joined the rush to the Yukon Territory, Canada, encountering the hardships of that 'perpetual land of snow and ice'. He trekked through a pass on the Alaskan border where some hundred adventurers had been swallowed up in a single snowslide, pegged his claims, and tried to persuade his father to form a company, raise £500 and share in 'the greatest boom . . . that the world has ever seen'. Within three years the odds had turned against the miners. While Fraser failed to make a fortune and lost his quartz-mine to a claim jumper, he gained valuable experience during his years in the Yukon.

He returned to Rockhampton in 1903, his fascination with mining unabated. In subsequent prospecting throughout Central Queensland he added coal to his interests. Although the mighty Bowen Basin coalfields had been lightly tapped in the 1890s, lack of markets had stifled development. In 1911 Fraser applied for leases in the Blackwater area, but his Mammoth Mine syndicate exhausted its small capital within a year in sending 300 tons of coal to be tested by the British Admiralty: despite a favourable assessment, no orders were placed. The Mount Morgan Gold Mining Co. Ltd took an option on the lease in 1912, then relinquished it and turned to Baralaba.

Giving his occupation as assayer and metallurgist, Fraser enlisted in the Australian Imperial Force on 28 November 1914 and was posted to the 5th Light Horse Regiment. He embarked for Egypt next month and served at Gallipoli from May until July 1915 when he was evacuated to England with enteric fever. In November 1916 he was transferred to the 42nd Battalion and sent to the Western Front. Commissioned in January 1917, he was seconded in October as intelligence officer, 11th Brigade headquarters. On 21 April 1918 he witnessed the action in which the German air-ace, Baron von Richthofen, was shot down. Fraser was given leave in England from March to September 1919 to study the manufacture of cement. His A.I.F. appointment terminated in Australia on 13 December.

In 1921 he sold his Mammoth Mine lease and next year established the Rangal Mine at Blackwater which was to produce 110 000 tons of coal by 1934. Still attracted to gold, in 1933 Donald and his brother Harold began to sink shafts at Crocodile Creek, near Rockhampton, and in the following year were instrumental in floating the Crocodile Creek Dredging Co. in Melbourne. Over four years they recovered 2352 ounces of gold. Donald bought the dredge in 1938 and, operating as Resarf Gold Dredging Co., salvaged another 1408 ounces by 1944 when mining ceased. A member of the Rockhampton Stock Exchange, he had sold all his coal interests, including the Excell Colliery at Bluff, by 1941.

Six ft (183 cm) tall, blue eyed, good looking, but modest, Fraser was reputed one of the most adventurous men ever raised in Rockhampton. A member (from 1910) of the Australasian Institute of Mining and Metallurgy, he attended the sixth Commonwealth Mining and Metallurgical Congress, held in Canada in 1957, and was welcomed back at the Klondike as one of its earliest prospectors. Fraser's success as an entrepreneur was confirmed by his generous and often anonymous donations to numerous Queensland and Rockhampton charities, churches and schools. At Scots Church, Melbourne, on 10 February 1931 he had married 38-year-old Cora Armstrong Macleod; she died in childbirth the following year. Fraser died on 19 October 1962 at Rockhampton and was buried with Presbyterian rites in the local cemetery. He had recognized and drawn attention to the resources of the Bowen Basin coalbeds long before foreign investment made them a major national asset.

Notable Men of Queensland, 1950; L. McDonald, *Rockhampton* (Brisb, 1981); *Morning Bulletin*, 20, 22, 25 Oct 1962; J. G. 'Battler' Pattison press-cuttings, series 5, no 37, series 7, no 21 *and* 'Breaking up Gold Dredging', nd, press-cutting (Rockhampton and District Hist Soc collection); Fraser/Macaree papers (Rockhampton Municipal L); R. S. Archer papers (ML); personal information.

LORNA MCDONALD

FRASER, DOUGLAS MARTIN (1888-1968), pastoralist and company director, was born on 9 December 1888 at Malvern, Melbourne, second of three sons of (Sir) Simon Fraser [q.v.4], squatter, and his second wife Anna Bertha, née Collins. Fond of cricket and football, Douglas was educated at Melbourne Church of England Grammar School and Trinity College, University of Melbourne (LL.B., 1911). On 3 March 1913 he was admitted to the Bar. At Tamrookum station, Beaudesert, Queensland, on 10 February 1915 he married with Anglican rites his cousin Marion Dorothea Jane (d.1963), daughter of R. M. Collins [q.v.3]. They built their first home at Mundoolun, on the Collins's 12 000-acre (4860 ha) property near Beaudesert. Enlisting in the Australian Imperial Force on 7 March 1918, Fraser reached Egypt in July and briefly served with the 5th Light Horse Regiment in Palestine. He was discharged on 21 March 1919 in Egypt, then returned to Queensland and his pastoral responsibilities.

In 1919-36 Fraser was managing director of the family company, John Collins & Sons, which, from the 1860s to 1941, owned fourteen stations. He was also successively a director, managing director and chairman of Collins, White & Co. Pty Ltd which owned Eulolo, Beaudesert and Strathfield stations until 1968. His most significant involvement was with the North Australian Pastoral Co.; his uncle, William Collins [q.v.3], had been an original partner in that concern. Fraser was a director (1932-68), managing director (1936-56) and chairman (1936-67) of N.A.P. The company owned Alexandria cattle-station in the Northern Territory and, during Fraser's time, purchased several Queensland properties (Marion Downs, Monkira, Coorabulka and Glenormiston). A director (1924) and chairman (1951) of Moreheads Ltd, in 1956 he administered its amalgamation with Elder, Smith [qq.v.4,6] & Co. Ltd, of whose Queensland board he became chairman. He was, additionally, chairman of the Queensland Meat Export Co., a director of the Australian Stock Breeders Co. and a member of the advisory council of the General Accident, Fire & Life Assurance Corporation Ltd.

Known as 'DM', he had an enormous capacity for work. He distrusted machinery, and was no judge of cattle and horses. His strength lay in the legal training that enabled him to negotiate favourable technical conditions for his companies' properties, as in the case of proving the N.A.P.'s 'residency' in the Northern Territory which brought taxation concessions. Five ft 7 ins (170 cm) tall, Fraser was forceful, arrogant and pigheaded—a dynamic person 'who could tell you a lie with a twinkle in his eye'. Nevertheless, he could also be warm hearted and generous, and was remembered as 'always a good touch for broke ringers and drovers' recovering after a binge in the 'big smoke'. He commuted weekly to Brisbane, but also contributed to his local community as a Beaudesert shire councillor and member of the hospital board. Fraser was president (1947) of the Queensland Club, chairman of the Society of St Andrew and a member for thirty-seven years of the board of Emmanuel College at the University of Queensland.

Survived by his two daughters and one of his two sons, he died on 16 May 1968 at Mundoolun and was buried in the family cemetery. His nephew Malcolm Fraser was prime minister of Australia in 1975-83.

M. Kowald and W. R. Johnston, *You Can't Make It Rain* (Brisb, 1992); *Brisb Courier*, 9 Jan, 15 Feb 1915; *Beaudesert Times*, 12 Feb 1915; *Qld Country Life*, 14 May 1959, 23 May 1968; Fraser family papers (held by Mr W. Fraser, Mundoolun station, near Beaudesert, Qld); Nth Aust Pastoral Co Pty Ltd records (Brisb).   MARGARET KOWALD

FRASER, HAROLD LIVINGSTONE (1890-1950), aviator and grazier, was born on 21 December 1890 at Rockhampton, Queensland, twelfth child of William Fraser, woolscourer, and his wife Annie, née Grieve, both Scottish born. Educated locally, Harold spent eighteen months apprenticed to an architect, but, with the exploits of his brother Donald [q.v.] before him, was not happy in an office. He chose instead to train in the pastoral industry as a jackeroo on Portland Downs, a huge sheep-station in the central west of the State, and at 24 was its overseer.

Enlisting in the Australian Imperial Force on 15 January 1915, Fraser embarked for the Middle East in May. He served with the 5th Light Horse Regiment at Gallipoli from September to December and in the Sinai campaign of 1916. In July he was promoted temporary sergeant; on 5 August at Katia he was wounded in the right shoulder. Selected for the Australian Flying Corps, he was commissioned in April 1917, joined No.1 Squadron as a pilot in June and was promoted lieutenant in September. He supported the advance through Palestine by patrolling, by engaging in photographic, reconnaissance and bombing missions, and by participating in five aerial fights. For his part in the operations to December, he was awarded the Military Cross. In April 1918 he was sent to

hospital and invalided to Australia where his A.I.F. appointment terminated on 30 July.

Fraser obtained a selection block in the Richmond district of north-west Queensland and began wool-growing and dealing in sheep. On 4 July 1922 he married Alethea Marion King at St Stephen's Catholic Cathedral, Brisbane. Following severe drought and low wool-prices, he abandoned his block about 1927. He obtained a civilian pilot's licence, bought a Cirrus Mark I Moth, VH-UFU, and 'barnstormed' around Rockhampton and the central west. Black Bridge Flat near the Fitzroy River was his base, and along the coast he used beaches for landing-grounds.

Inspired by his example, half a dozen aspiring young aviators formed the Rockhampton Aero Club and began grubbing stumps from a disused racecourse for a landing-strip. When their Connor Park Aerodrome opened on 2 March 1930, 'Captain' Fraser gave an exhibition of stunt flying, demonstrating the 'Immelmann turn' which the German air-ace had used on raids over France. With another pilot, Fraser established a training school. Backed by local businessmen, next year he formed Rockhampton Aerial Services Pty Ltd, of which he was managing-director and chief pilot. In a Genairco biplane he flew passenger services between Rockhampton and Brisbane: the inaugural flight took 6½ hours.

Services were soon extended to mine-payroll and weekly newspaper deliveries in Central Queensland. On a return flight from Clermont on 19 July 1936, Fraser's DH50 lost its engine and propeller at 4000 feet (1220 m). The *Morning Bulletin* reported that, after a free-fall of 3000 feet (900 m), he 'manipulated the controls to stop the machine going into a spin' and by 'a series of falling-leaf manoeuvres . . . came down on a flat in a bit of open country'. He walked 15 miles (24 km) to Capella where the local publican was startled by his 'queer looking clothes' and 'bloody great silk scarf'. Having downed a stiff whisky, Fraser nonchalantly caught a train back to Rockhampton. Financial problems, exacerbated by the loss of his plane, forced the sale of Rockhampton Aerial Services to Airlines of Australia that year. Fraser returned to the land, buying a cattle property at Dingo where he privately flew a De Havilland twin-engine aircraft. For a number of years he was associated with his brother Donald in successful gold-mining at Crocodile Creek. In 1946 Harold moved to Greystonlea cattle-station, Kingaroy.

After being trapped by fire in Greystonlea homestead, Fraser died of burns on 1 November 1950 in Kingaroy District Hospital and was cremated with Anglican rites; his wife, son and two daughters survived him. A plaque (1961) at Connor Park airport commemorates him as a pioneer of civil aviation.

L. McDonald, *Rockhampton* (Brisb, 1981); *Evening News* (Rockhampton), 14 Feb, 1 Mar 1930; *Morning Bulletin*, 27 Feb, 3, 6, 17 Mar 1930, 23 July 1936, 8 Nov 1958, 10 Apr 1992; *Peak Downs Telegram*, 25 July 1936; *Age* (Melb) and *Courier-Mail*, 2 Nov 1950; J. F. Hobler, The Birth of Aviation in Rockhampton (ms, 24 Feb 1978, held by author, Rockhampton); family information.

LORNA McDONALD

FRASER, JAMES McINTOSH (1889-1961), motorman, trade unionist and politician, was born on 12 March 1889 at Forres, Morayshire, Scotland, son of James McIntosh Fraser, ploughman, and his wife Elspet, née Anderson. Educated locally, young James was employed as a gardener at Gordon Castle, Fochabers, and as a munitions worker at the Royal Arsenal, Woolwich, London, before he emigrated to Western Australia. On 6 April 1912 at St Andrew's Presbyterian Church, Perth, he married Ellen Simmons, a domestic servant; they were to have five children. During World War I he tried to enlist in the Australian Imperial Force; when he was rejected, he returned to Britain and regained his job at Woolwich arsenal.

Back in Perth after the war, Fraser worked as a motorman with the Western Australian Government Tramways; he held office in the Tramway Employees' Union and from the 1920s served on the State executive of the Australian Labor Party. In 1929-37 he was a member of Perth City Council, representing Victoria Park Ward. Elected to the Senate in 1937, he was minister for external territories (October 1941 to September 1943), and held the portfolios of health and social services from 21 September 1943 to 18 June 1946. He led for the government in the Senate debates on the pharmaceutical benefits and the unemployment and sickness benefits bills (1944), and was the 'immediate ministerial architect' of Labor's broad programme to improve social security.

As acting-minister for the army in 1945, Fraser became involved in controversy over the employment and administration of Australia's military forces in the South-West Pacific Area. In April he visited New Guinea, New Britain and Bougainville to investigate claims of lack of equipment and low morale; on his return, he rejected most of the complaints, but admitted that shipping shortages had delayed the granting of leave and the supply of some matériel. Opposition senators alleged that he had avoided the front line and had spent most of his time with senior officers. Stung by the innuendo, he declared in the House, 'there are no cowards in my family'. His three sons served in the A.I.F. in World War II: Eric was captured by the Japanese in Singapore; Keith died in 1941 while a prisoner of war in Germany.

Fraser was minister for trade and customs from 18 June 1946, but was defeated in the caucus ballot for the second Chifley [q.v.13] ministry and on 1 November rejoined the back-bench. Towards the end of his career he emerged as a trenchant critic of H. V. Evatt [q.v.]. In October 1954 Fraser seconded George Cole's [q.v.13] motion that all leadership positions be declared vacant, claiming that Evatt did not understand the party, could never lead it to victory and was 'the best "how to vote" card Menzies and Fadden [qq.v.] ever had'.

Somewhat austere and angular in appearance, Fraser was quietly spoken and an 'able and level-headed' administrator who was popular with his colleagues. In that he was working class, Catholic (converted 1951) and a trade unionist, he was typical of many Labor politicians of his generation. In 1959 he retired from the Senate. He died on 27 August 1961 at Victoria Park, Perth, and was buried in Karrakatta cemetery; his wife, one of his two daughters and two of his sons survived him.

PD (Cwlth), 26 Sept 1938, p 181, 10 Feb 1944, p 50, 16 Feb 1944, p 223, 26 Apr 1945, p 1082; *PD* (Senate), 30 Aug 1961, p 243; *Argus*, 6 May 1944; *Herald* (Melb), 26 Apr 1945; *West Australian*, 28 Aug 1961; information from Mr P. C. Grundy, Campbell, Canb.

ANDREW LEE

FRASER, JOHN (1945-1968), national serviceman and army officer, was born on 12 January 1945 in Brisbane, son of James Grant Fraser, a motor trimmer from Scotland who became a prominent Gold Coast businessman, and his second wife Leonora Jean, née Shaw, who was born in New South Wales. Educated at St Joseph's College, Nudgee, and at The Southport School, Johnny studied medicine for a term in 1964 at the University of Queensland. One of the best-known junior Rugby Union footballers in Queensland, he played for the Combined Great Public Schools first XV and for the firsts at both his schools. He was employed as a cadet with the Australian Estates Co. Ltd when he was called up for national service on 29 September 1965.

Selected for officer-training, Fraser was sent to Scheyville, New South Wales, where he was described as 'steady', 'intelligent' and 'possessing leadership qualities'. In April 1966 he was commissioned second lieutenant in the Royal Australian Infantry Corps and posted to the 2nd Battalion, Royal Australian Regiment. Next year he successfully applied for an extension of his national service to enable him to be considered for a one-year deployment to the Republic of Vietnam

(South Vietnam). In October 1967 he was transferred to the 3rd Battalion, R.A.R. As commander of 'C' Company's No.9 Platoon, he sailed with the battalion to Vung Tau in December. Known for his 'gap-toothed ever-ready grin', Fraser often led the singing of the 3RAR's ballad, 'There Won't be Many Coming Back'.

In March 1968 the unit began Operation Pinnaroo—probably the most dangerous it conducted in South Vietnam—with the object of capturing and destroying bases of the People's Liberation Armed Forces (Viet Cong) in the Long Hai hills. The Viet Cong designated this area the Minh Dam Secret Zone. Its natural caves and subterranean streams provided a haven from which they launched raids and propaganda missions into the surrounding countryside. By 19 March 'C' Company occupied the Hon Vung foothills where it began to locate and neutralize enemy mines and booby traps.

On 24 March 1968 No.9 platoon was engaged in clearing a safe lane along a gully towards a suspected tunnel entrance. During this slow and deliberate phase, Fraser accidentally triggered a captured M16 anti-personnel mine which had been placed by the Viet Cong to protect the tunnel's mouth. The M16 was of American manufacture and designed to jump about 3 ft (90 cm) into the air before exploding. When he heard the mine arming, Fraser deliberately used his body in an effort to smother the effects of the blast and minimize injuries to those members of his platoon who were close by. The explosion fatally wounded him and seriously injured three of his men. As he lay on the ground, he told his comrades not to approach him because there were more mines around him. Fraser died that day while being evacuated by helicopter; the other wounded soldiers recovered in hospital. He was buried with Catholic rites and military honours in the Allambe Garden of Memories cemetery, Nerang, Queensland. A park in which he had played as a child, near his home at Surfers Paradise, was named in his memory.

R. F. Stuart (ed), *3RAR in South Vietnam 1967-1968* (Syd, 1968); S. Baldwin (ed), *Unsung Heroes and Heroines of Australia* (Melb, 1988); *SMH*, 26 Mar 1968; *Gold Coast Bulletin*, 27 Mar 1968; *Sun* (Syd), 29 Mar 1968; Commander's diary, 1st Aust Task Force, Vietnam, 1-31 Mar 1968 (AWM).

MICHAEL BOYLE

FRASER, KEITH AIRD (1893-1952), railway engineer and commissioner, was born on 9 January 1893 at Neutral Bay, Sydney, eldest of four sons of native-born parents JAMES FRASER (1861-1936), railway engineer, and his wife Maria Elizabeth, née Firth. James was born on 20 August 1861 at Braidwood. Educated at Sydney Grammar School, he joined the New South Wales Government Railways and Tramways in 1881 and rose to be engineer-in-chief for existing lines (1903-14), assistant-commissioner for railways (1914-16), chief railway commissioner (1917-29) and transport commissioner (1931-32). He was largely responsible for beginning the electrification of Sydney's suburban network and for the first stages of the city railway. James Fraser died at Pymble on 28 July 1936.

Keith attended Sydney Grammar School, joined the N.S.W.G.R. as a cadet draftsman in February 1911 and was a junior surveyor on the Waterfall-Otford deviation in 1914. He enlisted in the Australian Imperial Force on 19 December 1915 and was commissioned on 16 March 1916. Briefly based in Egypt and England, he served on the Western Front with the 4th Divisional Engineers from October. Lieutenant Fraser returned to Australia in 1919 as education officer in a troop-ship; his appointment terminated on 29 July.

At St Peter's Anglican Church, Neutral Bay, on 9 March 1920 he married Muriel Hopkins; they were to have one son. As resident engineer on the city railway (1922-32) under the exacting J. J. C. Bradfield [q.v.7], Fraser supervised the construction of Sydney's underground railway lines and the building of Museum, St James, Wynyard and Town Hall stations. He was transferred to South Sydney (1932) and Sydenham (1934); promoted supervising engineer in 1936, he oversaw the building of the new Hawkesbury River railway bridge in 1939.

On 4 April 1940 Fraser was appointed lieutenant colonel in the A.I.F. He commanded the Australian Railway Construction and Maintenance Group, and embarked for England in May. For some six months the unit was stationed in Woolmer Forest, Hampshire, and built a number of large storage sidings, passing loops and other traffic facilities. The A.R.C.M.G. reached the Middle East in March 1941. Assisted by a South African unit, in September the group began surveying a new military railway from Haifa, Palestine, through Beirut to Tripoli, Syria. The Australians had the task of building a 95-mile (153 km) section, beginning five miles (8 km) south of Beirut and ending at Tripoli. Fraser's 'expert knowledge, initiative, resource and drive' overcame the inherent difficulties of making deep cuttings through hard rock, and constructing high embankments and numerous bridges. At first only hand-tools were available, and mechanical equipment arrived slowly. Helped by the 61st South African Tunnelling Company, African labour battalions and civilian workers, they completed the line by December 1942, six months ahead of schedule. 'Fraser was almost solely responsible for the survey, layout and supervision' of a major piece of construction, described as 'among the more remarkable engineering feats of the war'. An 'officer of outstanding merit' whose quiet confidence impressed members of his own and other units, he was mentioned in dispatches and appointed O.B.E. in 1943. He transferred to the Reserve of Officers in Sydney on 10 July.

In 1945 Fraser was nominated as 'director of civil engineering of railway standardisation', but New South Wales failed to ratify the agreement with the Commonwealth government. As deputy chief civil engineer (from 1946), he paid an extended visit (1946-47) to Britain and Europe to study railway practices. In 1950 he was promoted chief civil engineer for the State's railways. On 5 February 1952 he was appointed commissioner. The railways were starved of money and feeling the competition of road transport and the airlines. He had very definite ideas, freely expressed, as to the direction in which he wished to take the State's railway system, and he felt confident that it would be profitable by 1956, provided the government allocated funds to replenish rolling stock, to complete the Eastern Suburbs railway and for the electrification of lines to Wallerawang, Newcastle, Port Kembla and Goulburn. The day would come, he said, when 'a man could sit down to dinner on a long-distance train in New South Wales and enjoy a glass of beer with his meal'. He did not live long enough to implement his reforms. Survived by his wife, he died of cerebrovascular disease on 23 August 1952 at Royal Prince Alfred Hospital and was cremated.

B. Maughan, *Tobruk and El Alamein* (Canb, 1966); J. Gunn, *Along Parallel Lines* (Melb, 1989); *SMH*, 14 Nov 1950, 2, 4 Feb, 10 July, 24, 25 Aug 1952; Railway staff personal history cards 11/16610 (NSWA).   J. D. WALKER
MARTHA RUTLEDGE

FRASER, SIR KENNETH BARRON (1897-1969), surgeon and soldier, was born on 28 March 1897 at Hughenden, Queensland, eldest child of Hugh Barron Fraser, a civil engineer from England, and his native-born wife Clara Emma, née Jones. Kenneth was educated at Brisbane Grammar School where he was dux, medallist (1915) and champion athlete (1914, 1915). He studied medicine for a year at the University of Queensland before transferring to St Andrew's College, University of Sydney (M.B., Ch.M., 1921). During his university years he won Blues for cricket, football and athletics, and represented Queensland and New South

Wales as a hurdler and sprinter. A lifelong sportsman, he was to be a referee at Great Public Schools athletics meetings in Brisbane for decades. After a year as a resident medical officer at Royal Prince Alfred Hospital, Sydney, in 1923 Fraser returned to Brisbane and began general practice. On 17 July 1929 at St John's Anglican Cathedral he married 21-year-old Edith Mary Patricia Lloyd Hart.

Paediatrics was Fraser's greatest interest. He held a part-time appointment at the Brisbane Children's Hospital between 1923 and 1957. A tutor and lecturer (1938-57) in paediatric surgery at the University of Queensland, he became the medical school's first graduate when awarded a master of surgery degree (1940) for a thesis on the treatment of harelip and cleft palate. This subject retained his attention and was the source of most of his publications.

In 1923 Fraser had joined the Citizen Military Forces as captain, (Royal) Australian Army Medical Corps. He commanded the 7th Field Ambulance (1934-35, 1936-39) and rose to lieutenant colonel in 1935. Transferring to the Australian Imperial Force on 12 October 1939, he reached Britain in June 1940 with command of the 2nd/3rd Field Ambulance. That month he was promoted colonel and appointed assistant-director of medical services, A.I.F. in the United Kingdom. He commanded the 2nd/2nd Australian General Hospital in the Middle East between January 1941 and February 1942, and was mentioned in dispatches. Back home, he was deputy-director of medical services, Queensland Lines of Communication Area, from 1942. His A.I.F. appointment terminated on 19 February 1946, but he continued to serve as D.D.M.S., Queensland Command, in the C.M.F. Retiring in 1954, he was promoted honorary brigadier next year and was honorary colonel, R.A.A.M.C., in 1957-62.

After World War II Fraser resumed his practice. He promoted paediatric education through his membership of the university's medical faculty board and its advisory board on paediatric studies, and as a board-member of the (Royal) Brisbane and South Coast hospitals. Having failed to secure funding for a chair in paediatrics in 1949, he invoked the emergency funding provisions of Sir Keith Murray's report on Australian universities (1957) to press for its establishment. Fraser was adamant that the new department be known as Child Health: he believed that 'emphasis on the nutrition and development of normal healthy children should be as great as on the treatment of sick children', and held that 'teaching was needed on cerebral palsy, intellectual impairment and on aspects of child health in obstetrics and gynaecology and social and preventive medicine'. Sitting (1956-66) on the university senate, he successfully promoted degree courses in pharmacy and physiotherapy. He remained involved in paediatric teaching until his death; the Brisbane Children's Hospital named a ward in his honour in 1965.

A founding member of the Red Cross Blood Transfusion Service, Fraser served (1958-66) on the State executive of the Royal Flying Doctor Service of Australia; he helped to consolidate the St John Ambulance Brigade in Queensland and was appointed a knight of the Order of St John (1959). He was a foundation member and president (1958-59) of the Australian Paediatrics Association, a councillor (1936-37, 1947-53) and president (1952) of the British Medical Association (Queensland branch), a fellow (1940) of the Royal Australasian College of Surgeons and a member (1968) of the American College of Surgeons. In addition, he was a council-member (1960-63) of the Australian National University, a member of the Anti-Cancer Council, a trustee of the Gowrie [q.v.9] Scholarship Trust Fund, an executive-member of the State branch of the English Speaking Union and a member of the Subnormal Children's Welfare Association. Appointed C.B.E. in 1953, he was knighted in 1958.

Sir Kenneth was known for his 'forceful, practical, outgoing personality which could move mountains' and for his cheerful, infectious laugh. Although sometimes irascible, he never harboured grudges. His young patients loved him: he made a great show of surreptitiously offering children jelly beans while parents and ward sisters pretended not to notice. Survived by his wife, two sons and two daughters, he died on 24 June 1969 at Clayfield and was cremated. A portrait by Graeme Inson is held by the family.

K. Willey, *The First Hundred Years* (Melb, 1968); R. L. Doherty (ed), *A Medical School for Queensland* (Brisb, 1986); J. H. Pearn, *Focus and Innovation* (Brisb, 1986); R. Patrick, *A History of Health and Medicine in Queensland 1824-1960* (Brisb, 1987); *MJA*, 1 Nov 1969; *Courier-Mail*, 12 June 1958, 26 June 1969; *Telegraph* (Brisb), 25 June 1969; Univ Qld Archives.

HELEN GREGORY

FRASER, 'SNOWY' (1891 ?-1953), Aboriginal tracker, was born probably in 1891 at Llanrheidol station, Winton, Queensland; his father was Willie Fraser, stockman, and his mother's name has variously been given as Minnie or Lizzie. Early in his career Snowy was attached as a tracker to Kynuna station, near the Diamantina River, north-west of Winton. It is possible that he was the 'Tommy' Fraser who, on 1 January 1915, signed (with his mark) an agreement to work with the Diamantina Lakes police station, in the vicinity of Snowy's birthplace. The duty statement required that he serve as a 'Native Tracker', make himself generally useful and obey all reasonable commands for three years. In return he received a wage, accommodation, some clothing and other benefits.

A noted horse-rider, Snowy Fraser competed in provincial races and had at least one major win to his credit. In 1922 a memorandum from the police commissioner advised his staff that the chief protector of Aborigines was opposed to Aboriginal trackers engaging 'in professional sport of any kind'. Participation in sporting gatherings, he argued, brought trackers into contact with the 'wrong class of people' and prize-money unsettled them 'in their regular avocations'. In the 1920s Fraser spent nine years as a tracker, based at Townsville. After an application to the chief protector of Aborigines had been approved, on 1 June 1927 at St Andrew's Anglican Church, Longreach, he married a housemaid, Nellie West, daughter of an Aboriginal stockman. She had a daughter, Rachel, born in Brisbane in 1922; Snowy's son, Archie, was born at St George in 1928.

On 1 November 1940 Fraser travelled from Cherbourg Aboriginal Settlement to take a post with the Police Department as a tracker attached to Oxley station. Described as approximately 50 to 55 years of age, of slight build, about 9½ stone (60 kg) in weight, single, and a fair horseman, he became widely recognized for his exploits. He once amazed Oxley troopers by tracking a safe-blower along a bitumen roadway and leading police to 'his cache of loot under a railway bridge'. At this time trackers were paid between £8 and £10 per month, plus keep. On 1 April 1943 he was promoted to corporal and qualified for an additional five shillings a week. About 1945 he was presented with a radio by the local police inspector as a retirement gift, but was apparently allowed to remain attached to the force and continued to lead periodic searches for missing persons. While visiting Cherbourg, Fraser died of pneumonia on 10 May 1953 and was buried in the local cemetery with Baptist forms. His son survived him. A brief obituary in the *Australian Evangel* referred to Snowy as a well-known identity; among those who attended his 'very big funeral' were six of Oxley's mounted police and their colleagues from Brisbane. The *Courier-Mail* paid tribute to Fraser's exceptional skills, acknowledging that 'dozens of children owe their lives to him and his hawk-like vision in bush searches'.

W. R. Johnston, *The Long Blue Line* (Brisb, 1922); *Aust Evangel*, June 1953, p 5; *Courier-Mail*, 12 May, 28 July 1953; Qld Police Museum, Brisb, Aborigines, Memorandum of Agreement *and* Circular Memorandum, no 1220, 8 May 1922

(A/44883 *and* 205M, QA); Oxley Tracker Station, A/44867-68 (QA); Community and personal history unit, identification cards, Cherbourg (Dept of Family Services and Aboriginal and Torres Strait Islander Affairs, Brisb); information from Ms R. Wie, Aust Inst of Aboriginal and Torres Strait Islander Studies, Canb.   YSOLA BEST

FREDERICK, WILFRED HENRY (1900-1977), headmaster and professor of education, was born on 24 November 1900 at Williamstown, Melbourne, son of Rev. Henry Wendel Frederick, Methodist clergyman, and his wife Harriet Prisca, née Cole, both Australian born. Wilfred was educated at Victorian primary schools and at Castlemaine and Geelong high schools before spending two years as a junior teacher at Williamstown and Geelong West primary and Geelong high schools.

In 1920 Frederick entered Melbourne Teachers' College to pursue studies at the University of Melbourne (B.A., 1923; M.A., Dip.Ed., 1925) where his 'earnestness and zeal', and his ability in sport, music and drama, impressed those who knew him. Appointed to Horsham High School (1924) and then to Northcote (1929), he was seen as an outstanding teacher and 'a man of strong character'. During a year abroad in 1930 he completed diplomas at the University of Paris and at its Institut Britannique, and taught at Watford Boys' Grammar School, England, where he was offered, but refused, a permanent post.

Returning to Melbourne in 1931, Frederick spent two years at the teachers' college, tutoring university-enrolled arts students in French, and science students in English. His closer association with the University of Melbourne began in 1932 when he was appointed lecturer (senior lecturer from 1945) in method of modern languages; he also had charge of modern languages at University High School. For fourteen years he helped to transform the approach to the teaching of the subject through his membership of the French and Italian standing committees, through his publications—*Modern Languages in Secondary Schools* (1937), edited for the Australian Council for Educational Research, and (with F. G. Kirby) *Lectures Choisies* (1942), together with many articles in educational magazines—and through his inauguration in 1931 of the 'French for Schools' programmes for the Australian Broadcasting Commission, which in 1943 were extended nationally. In this project he was assisted by his wife Frances Moyna, née Dimond, previously music mistress at St Margaret's School, Berwick, whom he had married on 25 August 1934 at the Methodist Church,

Armadale. His lecturing responsibilities extended to general methods of teaching, education for leisure, and examinations, while in 1944 he started a course on method of teaching religious education.

From 1947 to 1956 Frederick was headmaster of Wesley College, Prahran, a position in which he had been interested when it was previously vacant in 1938. He brought not only his teaching skills and a lifelong interest in sport (having represented Victoria in interstate tennis), but also a real devotion to the school. To a school assembly he said, 'I can't remember a time when I didn't want to come to Wesley'. There were some who questioned the appointment of a person without a private school background, some who were disturbed by his strict attitude to issues such as alcohol on the premises, and some who found the pace of change and his insistence on democratic discussion difficult to accept. But these critics were largely converted by his enthusiasm and charm. A forestry camp was established at Chum Creek, individual school prizes were replaced, community service was introduced as an alternative to cadets, compulsory sport was abolished, a school counselling-service was begun, remedial teaching commenced, and a Student Representative Council and a Parents' Association were initiated. He helped to disentangle the relationship with Box Hill Grammar School, to investigate the possible sale of the Prahran site and to purchase land at Syndal for the expansion of the school. Important as these changes were, it was more for his personal interest in each boy, his enthusiasm in teaching, his magnetic presence in assemblies, and the doggerel he wrote to commemorate school events that many remembered him.

In 1956 the council of the University of Melbourne invited Frederick to succeed Professor G. S. Browne [q.v.13] in the chair of education, indicating that 'a wider and more fruitful opportunity for serving the educational needs of the State' might be available in this position. With some hesitation he accepted. He had been interested earlier in chairs in Hobart and in Wellington, New Zealand, before his appointment to Wesley, but it was difficult for him now to leave the school he loved so well. From 1957 to his retirement in 1966 he faced two major problems—rapidly increasing numbers of students and a gross shortage of staff, particularly at the professorial level. Aware that many schools were disastrously short-staffed, he resisted the imposition of a student quota until 1964. In a faculty not significantly smaller than engineering, with five chairs, or medicine, with seventeen chairs, the burden on a single professor of education was considerable.

Besides discharging his faculty responsibilities, Frederick was a member of the Council of Public Education and two of its sub-committees, and of eight sub-committees of the professorial board; he chaired the council of University High School, the Commonwealth Scholarships Board (1951-70), the Schools Board (1957-65) and its successor, the Victorian Universities and Schools Examination Board (1965-66); and he was a council-member of Monash University. He was elected a fellow and councillor (1960-72) of the Australian College of Education. At every level he argued for five additional chairs for his faculty, but, despite promises made, he remained the sole professor of education. He took particular interest in the establishment, within the faculty, of the University Teaching Project, with its consulting service to other departments aimed at improving curricula and teaching techniques, a development unique in Australia. Frederick may not have fully understood those who saw research as more important than preparation of teachers for their classroom role, but he maintained a vision of what education could achieve, he aroused in students something of his own enthusiasm for teaching, and he eloquently argued the cause of education in the university and the wider community.

Frederick was always a teacher. His presence was commanding and his grooming immaculate. The lecture for him was 'a process of electrification', and he always argued for 'retention of zest' and 'the gift of undiminished appetite in education'. He was concerned about the 'loss of conviction in society' and the need 'to lift the level of aspiration of many youngsters'. An ardent public advocate for education and for teaching, he was much sought as a speaker for school events and after-dinner addresses. His interest in public speaking continued long after his retirement, and he entertained many with his carefully polished and articulate presentations. Words were a joy to him, and in writing and speaking he used them to full effect.

Many of Frederick's convictions came from his strong faith and consequent church involvement in bodies such as the Joint Board of Graded Lessons of Australia and New Zealand, the Methodist Young People's Department, the Methodist Men's Society of Victoria and Tasmania, and the Council for Christian Education in Schools. Survived by his wife, son and daughter, he died on 24 April 1977 at Heidelberg and was cremated. A memorial window in Wesley College chapel was dedicated on 14 September 1980.

G. Blainey et al, *Wesley College* (Melb, 1967); Frederick papers *and* Univ Melb Council minutes *and* Professorial Bd minutes *and* Education Faculty minute-books (Univ Melb Archives); Education Dept (Vic) records; Wesley College Archives.

N. G. CURRY

FREDRICKSEN, CARL THEODORE (1873-1966), showman and cinema commissionaire, was born on 28 November 1873 at Majorca, Victoria, sixth child of Carl Fredrickson (d.1906), a musician from Russia, and his English-born wife Mary Louisa, née Smythe (d.1923). Educated at Fitzroy State School, he began work as a child, beating a drum outside the Lyceum Theatre, Lonsdale Street. Two days later he was dismissed, following complaints from the Melbourne Hospital across the road. At age 11 he had a song-and-dance act at the Bijou Theatre, then travelled Australia with a circus before returning to sing in a grand opera chorus at the Bijou. Assisted by his younger brother Ernest, he transformed the William Tell legend into a vaudeville act. He set three rifles at the points of a triangle; using a fourth rifle and taking sight with a mirror, he fired over his shoulder, hitting the trigger of the first fixed rifle which discharged the others in sequence, the last of which shattered a ball balanced on his head. This feat he performed in many Melbourne theatres. About 1901 he achieved fame with his Bourke Street ghost-house of illusions and horrors.

In 1908, two years after Carl Hertz introduced moving pictures to the Opera House (later the Tivoli), Hoyts' first picture-house opened, directly opposite in St George's Hall, Bourke Street. Fredricksen, the 'Sultan of Spruikers', was engaged. His distinctive voice projected through the noise of a busy street and his repertoire of alliterative incantations soon captured audiences for the 'flicks': 'a surprising series of skits, screaming sallies and silly situations; satisfactory, startling, swiftly speeding scenes, surprisingly stupendous, side-splitting scenarios, sparkling snappy stunts, sensational, superb, spectacular, sympathetic, soul-stirring screen stories'. Hoyts' Deluxe Theatre replaced the single-storeyed St George's Hall in 1914. 'The Man Outside Hoyts' watched as former patrons marched past on their way to the Great War. Australian born and of part-Danish descent, he anglicized 'Carl' to 'Charles' and also changed the spelling of his surname to Fredricksen as anti-German feeling mounted. He concealed his age, 'always my best publicity stunt', and postponed retirement in 1939 as another generation marched past to World War II. This time he saw faces he had first known as babes in arms at matinees. The theatre was remodelled as Hoyts Esquire in 1948. Charles remained.

The octogenarian singer, showman and sharp-shooter, having treated Melbourne to forty-eight years of *spreken* from one Bourke Street pitch, retired in September 1956. With his pencil moustache, his smart blue uniform adorned by lavish gold trimmings, his gloves, cane and an endless flow of patter, the strutting figure had filled many roles in popular sayings, but the actual man remained an enigma. The proprietors of novelty shops in the city knew him as a maker of papier-mâché theatre masks; a handful knew him as a maker of ventriloquists' dolls. At St Peter's Anglican Church, Eastern Hill, Melbourne, on 30 August 1910 he had married Letitia Ferris Hutchins (d.1954), a dressmaker. In later years he 'lived a butterfly life', travelling home and back between sessions to keep her company. Two months after her death, he married Agnes Jane West on 12 May 1954 at St Luke's Anglican Church, North Fitzroy. He was persuaded to make several comebacks, the last outside the Tivoli in 1965. Predeceased by his wife, he died on 7 August 1966 at his North Fitzroy home and was buried in Melbourne general cemetery. He had no children.

People (Syd), 2 Jan 1952; *Argus* (Melb), 20 Nov 1954, 14 Sept 1966; *Herald* (Melb), 14 Sept 1956, 31 Dec 1965; *Sun News-Pictorial*, 18 Mar 1960, 8 Aug 1966; information from Mrs G. M. Wisken, Blackburn, Melb; personal information.

KEITH R. GROOM

FRENCH, HUBERT CHARLES (1882-1961), businessman, was born on 24 October 1882 at Battle Creek, Michigan, United States of America, second child of Edgar French, civil engineer, and his wife Ruth Emma, née Van Syoc, both from Ohio. Educated at the local public school and at the Detroit College of Law, Michigan, in 1903 Hubert became a partner in a contracting firm. He married Clara Casterton (d.1910) and had a son who died in infancy. On 19 July 1911 he married Mildred Gillespie (d.1959) at Toronto, Canada; he was to be naturalized in 1920. Indulging his interest in things mechanical, he entered a speedboat-manufacturing partnership at Toronto, then managed (1913-19) a building supply company. In 1919 he joined Ford Motor Co. of Canada Ltd and in 1922 was appointed assistant sales manager.

In 1923 French was sent to investigate Ford's Australian operation. He revealed himself as an acute observer with a caustic tongue and a practical man's respect for thoroughness. A heavy smoker, he had curbed a gambling addiction only when it threatened his marriage, and consoled himself for having to spend Christmas in Australia with the thought that it was 'a land of liquor and sunshine'. But the influence of a puritanical upbringing persisted in his disdain for the slothful, 'easy living, luxury loving' independent Ford distributors. This outlook, coupled with his discovery of the expanding presence of General Motors (Australia) Pty Ltd (General Motors-Holden's [q.v.9] Ltd from 1931), convinced him of the necessity for 'opening our own business in Australia'.

Ford Motor Co. of Australia Pty Ltd opened at Geelong in 1925 with French as managing director. At first the firm did not prosper, due in part to intensified competition and a backlog of superseded models, and in some degree to French's egalitarian style of management. While generally conservative, he was keen to foster a 'free and easy spirit . . . between employer and employee'; he was criticized by a Ford-Canada executive for relying on his 'genial personality' to secure cooperation instead of using 'more severe, less likeable methods'.

Staunchly loyal to the parent company, French protected its export business by resisting political pressure in the 1930s to manufacture vehicles in Australia. When threatened with the prospect of a state-owned industry, he submitted a proposal in 1945 which the Federal government preferred to that of G.M.H., principally because it involved trucks as well as cars. Fearing buyer resistance to local products, French demanded substantial financial and tariff support—which was refused on the grounds of cost and because it would have breached Australian trade agreements. To counter competition from G.M.H., in 1949 he announced a four-stage programme for increasing local content in Ford vehicles, but retired as managing director in 1950 before its completion. He remained chairman of the board until 1951, after which he served as a director.

Tall and burly, with a soft-featured, square face, French was a stickler for routine, an ardent proponent of the work ethic, and a keen golfer and swimmer. Although he had few close friends, he was gregarious and well liked by his many acquaintances. He speculated on the stock exchange and was briefly part-owner of an unsuccessful Collins Street business that sold custom-made corsets. Survived by his two daughters, he died on 4 April 1961 at Geelong and was cremated with Presbyterian forms. His estate was sworn for probate at £99 429.

M. Wilkins and F. Hill, *American Business Abroad* (Detroit, Michigan, US, 1964); *Austra-Ford Gazette*, Apr 1961; Federal Government Dept of Business and Consumer Affairs, correspondence files, Aust Industry Motor Car, Local Manufacture, 1938-46, A425, item 1946/245 (AA, Canb); Federal Government Trade Services and Industries Branch, general correspondence files, 1942-58, MP394/1, item 5/8/151, pts 1-5, MP267/1, item 5/5/400, pt 2 (AA, Melb); H. C. French papers (held in Archives of Ford Motor Co of Aust, Campbellfield, Melb); French family papers (held by H. W. McKewan, Mission Beach, Qld); information from Mrs D. Maynard, Point Piper, Syd. JOE RICH

FRENCH, JOHN ALEXANDER (1914-1942), soldier and barber, was born on 15 July 1914 at Crows Nest, near Toowoomba, Queensland, third of five children of Albert French, hairdresser, and his wife Lucy Fanny May, née Donaldson, both native-born. Educated at Crows Nest State School and Toowoomba Technical College, Jack entered his father's barber-and-tobacconist business. On 22 October 1939 he enlisted in the Australian Imperial Force and was posted to the 2nd/9th Battalion, then being formed at Redbank. Quiet, unassuming and of a serious disposition, French was a 'big fair chap', a good sportsman and well liked. He gave his religion as Presbyterian.

Sailing from Sydney in May 1940, he spent five months in Britain before reaching the Middle East in December. In March 1941 the 2nd/9th assaulted the Italian stronghold at Giarabub, Libya. From April to August the battalion took part in the defence of Tobruk before moving to Syria where it performed garrison duties. French became an excellent soldier. He was promoted acting corporal in December and his commanding officer, Lieutenant Colonel C. J. Cummings, saw him as a future officer. The 2nd/9th returned to Australia in early 1942 and left again in August, bound for Papua. By mid-month the unit was established at Milne Bay.

On 26 August 1942 a Japanese invasion force landed on the north shore of Milne Bay, east of K.B. Mission. The 2nd/9th moved into the K.B. area on 2 September and on the following day continued east along the coast towards the Goroni River. French was in 'B' Company which crossed the river on 4 September to attack Japanese positions from the rear. A fierce engagement ensued. Three enemy machine-gun posts retarded the section's advance. Ordering his men to take cover, French made his way forward and destroyed one of the posts with grenades; he returned for more grenades and used them to demolish the second strong-point; armed with a Thompson sub-machine gun, he attacked the third gun-pit, firing from the hip as he went. Although he was badly wounded, he kept going, silenced the post and died in front of it. His action saved casualties among his comrades and assured the success of the attack. He was posthumously awarded the Victoria Cross.

French was buried in Port Moresby (Bomana) war cemetery. His grieving fiancée Dulcie McCahon said that she 'knew he would always carry out his duty regardless of his safety'. Jack's elder brother Eric served in the A.I.F. On 11 August 1943, while flying with the Royal Australian Air Force, their younger brother Gordon was killed in action over Europe. The governor-general, Field Marshal Sir William (Viscount) Slim [q.v.], opened and dedicated the John French, V.C., Memorial Library at Crows Nest on 18 July 1958.

D. McCarthy, *South-West Pacific Area—First Year* (Canb, 1959); L. Wigmore (ed), *They Dared Mightily*, second ed revised and condensed by J. Williams and A. Staunton (Canb, 1986); C. Baker and G. Knight, *Milne Bay 1942* (Syd, 1991); *Courier-Mail*, 15, 16 Jan 1943; *Argus*, 15 Jan, 13 Mar 1943; *Crows Nest Advertiser*, 21 Jan 1943; AWM76, B188 (AWM).

ANTHONY STAUNTON

FREUND-ZINNBAUER, ALFRED; see ZINNBAUER

FREWER, JOHN (1883-1974), Anglican bishop, was born on 1 November 1883 at Fulletby, Lincolnshire, England, third son of Rev. George Ernest Frewer, a clergyman of the Church of England, and his wife Louisa Charlotte, née Charsley. Raised in the parish of Brede, Sussex, where the Frewers undertook promotional work for the colonial churches, John was educated at the King's School, Canterbury, and Selwyn College, Cambridge, but did not complete his degree. He subsequently studied at Lincoln Theological Hostel. Made deacon on 14 June 1908, he was ordained priest on 6 June 1909 by Edward King, bishop of Lincoln. Frewer served his curacy at St Nicholas's, Skirbeck.

In 1911 he arrived in Western Australia to serve as domestic chaplain to Frederick Goldsmith [q.v.9], bishop of Bunbury, his uncle by marriage and his godfather. Goldsmith thought that his nephew's experience of the Lincolnshire port area equipped him for chaplaincy work with labourers in the new rural diocese. Following a stint (1913-16) as rector of South Bunbury, in 1916 Frewer was professed as a member of the Brotherhood of St Boniface, at Williams, and became its warden in 1919. He was appointed a canon of St Paul's Pro-Cathedral, Bunbury, in 1922. The Bush Brotherhood was never a large band, but it attracted several committed celibate priests to itinerant work in a largely agricultural diocese.

In January 1929 Frewer was named as second bishop of North-West Australia, succeeding Bishop Trower [q.v.12]; he was consecrated on 9 April in St George's Cathedral, Perth, and enthroned in the Pro-Cathedral at Broome on 28 April. With the exception of the Diocese of the Arctic in Canada, Frewer's diocese (666 000 sq. miles, 1.7 million km^2) was the largest within the Anglican communion, yet its population in 1929 did not exceed 30 000 and included only 5000 Whites. The bishop was required to discharge the services of a parish priest in many of the remote towns he visited regularly. In Geraldton he helped to establish two hostels for high school students and pioneered the work of the Missions to Seamen; he also took an active interest in the Forrest River Mission, near Wyndham, and dedicated two dozen church buildings throughout the diocese. Despite his physical isolation, he maintained active links with the wider Church and was vice-president (1930) of the Australian Church Union.

From his base in the pearling port of Broome, where he occupied a sparsely furnished three-room house, Frewer made extensive use of air transport in the 1950s. After his one thousandth flight with MacRobertson Miller [qq.v.11 Robertson, 10] Airlines Ltd, he was awarded a gold pass in 1959. He possessed a phenomenal memory, and recalled the names and anniversaries of many parishioners in his scattered flock. Not until 1961, however, when his establishment of clergy reached the statutory minimum of eight, was he able to convene a synod of his own diocese. Next year he presided over the laying of the foundation stone of the Cathedral of the Holy Cross at Geraldton, the new diocesan seat. In 1957 he had been appointed C.B.E.

Frewer did not marry, and was able to supplement his small salary from a private income, although he lived frugally. An amateur actor and keen sportsman in his youth, he continued to play tennis and to swim, between episcopal duties. In 1965 he retired to Perth. He died on 7 December 1974 at Mount Lawley and was cremated; his ashes were placed in Geraldton cathedral.

F. Alexander (ed), *Four Bishops and their See* (Perth, 1957); E. W. Doncaster, *Spinifex Saints* (Perth, 1985); *SMH*, 24 Aug 1963, 10 Dec 1974; *West Australian*, 19 Dec 1974; C. P. Holden, Ritualist on a Tricycle: Frederick Goldsmith, Church, Nationalism and Society in Western Australia, 1880-1920 (Ph.D. thesis, Univ Melb, 1993); Frewer's personal papers (held by Archdeacon E. W. Doncaster, Aldinga Beach, SA); Frewer diaries (BL).   PETER BOYCE

FRISDANE, MARIANNE MATHY-; *see* MATHY, MARIANNE

FRITH, PHILIP RAYMOND (1900-1976), schoolteacher, was born on 8 May 1900 at St Johns Wood, London, foster child of Charles Henry Frith, clerk, and his wife Louisa, née Hill. Little is known of Philip's early life other than that he claimed to have won a scholarship to Dulwich College, London, and to have served as an artilleryman in the British Army late in World War I before working as a physical-education instructor. In 1926 he emigrated to Western Australia where he was employed as a clerk at Busselton. At the local Congregational Church on 9 June 1927 he married 18-year-old Noreen Joyce Connelly; they were to have a daughter before being divorced in 1931. He moved to Queensland and in January 1930 was appointed head teacher of the government school on Mabuiag Island, Torres Strait.

Within months Frith had transformed the previously neglected native-school. Noting his 'genius' for organization and abounding energy, inspectors praised him for his firm but kindly manner, and for the prompt and willing obedience he secured from his pupils. All admired the wealth of material he prepared, 'endeavouring to reproduce in the classroom the larger world beyond the Island': driftwood models of a complete railway system, a main road with congested traffic, Sydney Harbour Bridge, ships, skyscrapers and lighthouses, supplemented by his own crayon drawings and other illustrative matter. In 1934 he was transferred temporarily to the Murray Island school as teacher-superintendent. Next year he established a training school at Mabuiag for advanced pupils from the neighbouring islands, and provided 'refresher' courses for local teachers and branch managers. Besides his school duties, Frith had assumed responsibility for the welfare and well-being of some three hundred Mabuiag Islanders. Acting as far as possible through the 'native' council and police, to whom he offered advice, he gave first aid to the sick, arbitrated in family quarrels or land disputes, and supervised village development, garden culture, sanitation, and the operation of luggers engaged in obtaining trochus and pearl-shell.

From 1940 Frith taught in Aboriginal schools at Cherbourg and Woorabinda settlements, Queensland. In 1944 he was appointed government teacher on remote Saibai Island in Torres Strait. There, as instructed, he opened a small hospital which also served nearby Dauan and Boigu islands. Having taken leave in 1946, he again taught at Mabuiag and was then posted to the primary school at Badu, the most prosperous and developed island in the Strait. In 1947 he reopened the secondary school which drew pupils from all the islands of the group. For the first time in his life, he came to feel a sense of belonging, to the community and to his vocation. In May 1965 he retired to Cairns, Queensland, after he had given 'a lifetime of service for the advancement of Torres Strait Islanders'.

Survived by his wife Frances Annie, née Rooney (who had been the Badu government nurse), and their son and two daughters, Frith died on 13 October 1976 at Cairns and was buried with Anglican rites in Belgian Gardens cemetery, Townsville.

Chief Protector of Aboriginals (Qld), *Annual Report*, 1931, 1935, 1938; *PIM*, 23 Nov 1932, 22 Feb 1933; Director of Native Affairs (Qld), *Annual Report*, 1946-47, 1947-48, 1948-49, 1953-54; *People* (Syd), 3 June 1953; EDU/Mission Schools, Reports of Inspections of Native School at Mabuiag, Departmental records file, B.M., 19 June 1927, *and* items 52234 of 1931, 45325 of 1932, 29211 of 1934, 59527 of 1935 (QA); Chief Protector of Aboriginals (Qld), office file, Abgls Staff, item 29/1803 *and* Isls Torres Strait, 1933, 1934, items 34/6293 and 6361 (QA); information from Mrs A. F. Frith, Cairns, Qld, who holds duplicate of Report of Inspection of Torres Strait School at Badu Island by Inspector Pyle on 8, 9, 12, 13 June 1961.

MARGARET LAWRIE

FROST, CHARLES LESLIE (1897?-1971), Aboriginal leader, was born probably on 22 July 1897 at Peak Hill, New South Wales, son of Charles Frost, labourer, and his wife Jane (Jenny), née Solomon. Of mixed descent, young Charles belonged to the Wiradjuri people. By 1924 he was living at Dubbo and working as a labourer for the Main Roads Board. He was described as 'a tall, thin, erect, laughing' and carefree young man.

On 27 June 1937 Frost opened the public meeting at Dubbo that launched the Aborigines Progressive Association and drew attention to the serious situation of Aboriginal reserves. Having ensured that Aborigines comprised half the membership, the founders set out the objects of the association: to advocate the abolition and reconstruction of the Aborigines Protection Board, to secure improvements in living conditions on the board's reserves, to obtain the repeal of discriminatory legislation, and to achieve the granting of full citizen rights for Aborigines, with direct representation in parliament. In July 1938 the A.P.A. split; the Dubbo section was headed by William Ferguson [q.v.8] and the La Perouse section by John Patten [q.v.11]. Frost was elected president of the Dubbo association, with George Carr the local secretary and Ferguson the organizing secretary.

By 1950 Frost had moved to Condobolin and lived on the mission station. At the town's Methodist Church on 1 July 1950 he married a widow Marcie Bright, née Briar, who was also of mixed descent; they were to remain childless. In 1953 he was employed as a slaughterman by one of the local butchers, and was regarded as a regular, dependable and willing worker. That year he leased a block of land from the Condobolin Municipal Council and was endeavouring to build a house and to take up market gardening. His plans were delayed by a hernia operation. From 1958, although described as an invalid pensioner, he remained active. He was an eloquent writer, possibly due to his attendance in 1961 and 1964 at the summer school run by

the Australian Board of Missions at Tranby Aboriginal Co-operative College. With seemingly endless energy, he applied in 1968 for government assistance to build a boomerang factory. The dream did not eventuate, but he was regarded as a skilled craftsman of Aboriginal ornaments.

Survived by his wife, Frost died on 9 October 1971 at his Condobolin home and was buried with Presbyterian forms in the Methodist section of the local cemetery.

J. Horner, *Vote Ferguson for Aboriginal Freedom* (Syd, 1974); D. Horton (ed), *The Encyclopaedia of Aboriginal Australia* (Canb, 1994); Aborigines Welfare Bd, correspondence files, 1945-69 (NSWA); J. Gordon, taped interview with C. L. Frost, 24-25 Oct 1968 (archive audio tape no 1914, Aust Inst of Aboriginal and Torres Strait Islander Studies, Canb).

V. M. JOHNSON

FROST, CHARLES WILLIAM (1882-1964), politician, was born on 30 November 1882 in Hobart, fourth of six children of William George Frost, gentleman, and his wife Ailsa, née Cregg. In 1853 William had left his family's home, Wentworth Park, Surrey, England, and emigrated to Van Diemen's Land. With an incomplete education at the University of Oxford and his Chartist beliefs, he found difficulty in gaining employment. He turned to farming and eventually settled at Premaydena. Most of the legacy he received from his family's estate was embezzled by a solicitor. Educated at Koonya and Margate state schools, Charles left at 13 to help on his father's farm. A year or two later he walked along the Linda Track to join his elder brother Arthur in the mines on the island's west coast; while working at the Iron Blow mine, he became involved in labour politics.

At All Saints Anglican Church, Hobart, on 3 October 1906 Frost married Ruth Hornsey Young; they were to have four children. He bought an orchard at Margate and undertook contract work to supplement his income. During World War I he cleared a path and erected an electric power-line between New Town and Electrona, south of Margate, making poles from the timber he felled. He performed similar work in other parts of the State. In the mid-1920s he took part in an expedition to the Bulolo goldfields in the mandated Territory of New Guinea, but soon came home.

Frost had joined a producers' marketing arrangement, formed in 1917 and incorporated on 14 May 1918 as the Port Huon Fruit Growers' Co-operative Association Ltd; he became a director in 1923. His experience in this organization and his membership of the Australian Labor Party dominated his subsequent political life. In 1924-27 and 1929-30 he was a member of Kingborough Municipal

Council (warden 1925-27 and 1929-30). Unsuccessful as a Labor candidate for the Franklin district in the House of Assembly in 1928, he won the Federal seat of Franklin at a by-election in December 1929. He was defeated in 1931 but returned in 1934.

In the House of Representatives Frost supported strong protection for Tasmania's rural industries, advocated better shipping and telephone services for the State, and promoted measures to improve housing and employment opportunities. A tough, fearless and fair debater, he loyally adhered to A.L.P. policies. In 1935 he was a member of the Australian delegation to the Empire Parliamentary Association's conference in London and in 1937-40 sat on the joint parliamentary committee on public works. He was elected to the executive of the federal parliamentary Labor Party in 1940.

When Labor came to office in October 1941, Frost was appointed minister for repatriation and minister in charge of war service homes. Although he introduced the Australian soldiers' repatriation bill (1943) which, when enacted, increased benefits to returned service personnel, his administration was criticized by sections of the press: *Smith's Weekly* called him 'Hoar' Frost. In 1946 he lost his seat by 73 votes to the Liberal Party's candidate C. W. J. Falkinder.

Having been a member of cabinet's subcommittee on whaling, Frost hoped to see the industry re-established in Tasmania. His contribution was so well regarded that it was rumoured he would be selected to head a proposed Australian whaling commission. Instead, in 1947 he was appointed Australian commissioner (high commissioner from 1948) to Ceylon (Sri Lanka). Prime Minister (Sir) Robert Menzies [q.v.] terminated his appointment in 1950 and Frost retired to New Town.

Survived by his wife, two sons and a daughter, he died on 22 July 1964 in St John's Hospital, Hobart, and was buried in Cornelian Bay cemetery. His son S. C. H. ('Jack') Frost had been a prisoner of the Japanese in World War II and was a Labor minister in the Tasmanian House of Assembly in 1972-76.

M. Lowe (comp and ed), *Days Gone By in the Channel*, 1 (priv pub, Hob, 1993); C. Lloyd and J. Rees, *The Last Shilling* (Melb, 1994); information from Messrs S. C. H. Frost, Bruny Island, and D. Frost, Margate, Tas.   R. J. K. CHAPMAN

FRY, ALFRED NARROWAY (1892-1979), cornet player, cartage contractor and farmer, was born on 11 March 1892 at Mount Egerton, Victoria, fourth child and elder of twins of Bertram Waterman Fry, an English-born bricklayer, and his wife Annie, née Narroway, from South Australia. Raised in a strict Methodist home, Alf and his brothers were taught to play the cornet, baritone and euphonium; they joined a junior band and participated as individuals in competitions at State level. Bertram took them on long bush expeditions, allowing Alf and his twin Ernest to carry firearms from the age of 9. About 1904 the family moved to Coolgardie, Western Australia. Alf worked locally as a clerk for the stockbrokers Hummerston & Co., at Albany for Dalgety [q.v.4] & Co., and with the Fremantle Harbour Trust.

Five ft 9 ins (175 cm) tall with grey eyes and brown hair, Fry enlisted in the Australian Imperial Force on 23 September 1914 and sailed for the Middle East with the 3rd Field Artillery Brigade. He served at Gallipoli, where he was wounded, and on the Western Front. In 1918 he completed flying training and on 18 December was commissioned in the Australian Flying Corps. Promoted lieutenant in March 1919, he arrived home in January 1920 and his appointment terminated on 20 April.

After captaining the 8th Battery football team during World War I, Fry played Australian Rules for South Fremantle. He also belonged to the Perth City Brass Band and came third in the State's solo cornet championship in 1922. That year he bought land at Quininup in partnership with James Kerath. When group settlement of English immigrants began at Northcliffe in 1924, Fry secured a contract to carry equipment and supplies there from the railway station at Pemberton, 20 miles (32 km) away, and to convey the settlers' dairy-farm produce on his return journeys. For nine years in his Vulcan truck he encountered appalling road conditions in winter and the danger of mechanical failure in any month. Tales abounded of the transport and illicit sale of liquor, of Alf's irrepressible humour and of his stentorian cornet blasts on his early morning departures. At St Paul's Anglican Pro-Cathedral, Bunbury, on 6 April 1926 he married a hospital matron Beryl Eileen Norton (d.1949); they were to have a daughter and two sons.

Having won the Western Australian soprano cornet championship and been second player in the winning sextet in 1926, he partnered E. J. McCormack next year to win the duet championship on euphonium and cornet. Fry played in countless recitals and performed *The Last Post* and *Reveille* at ex-servicemen's funerals far and wide. In 1933 the railway extension to Northcliffe made cartage contractors redundant: Alf joined a short-lived wheat-farming venture at Nungarin before returning to his Quininup farm. A fire on Anzac Day 1954 destroyed the home and most of his possessions. He rebuilt on the same site.

For twenty-two years Fry had belonged to Manjimup's football club and cricket association. He was president (for five years) of the local Returned Services League band, inaugural president of the Quininup Workers' Club and a district bushfire officer. In 1975 he moved to Moonya Lodge, a home for the frail aged. Survived by his sons, he died on 4 June 1979 at Manjimup and was buried in the local cemetery.

J. P. Gabbedy, *Group Settlement*, 2 (Perth, 1988); *People* (Syd), 5 Mar 1958, p 38; *Blackwood Times*, 6 Jan 1922; information from Mr J. P. and the late Mr W. Rooney, Manjimup, Mr A. and Mrs M. Hulcup, Quininup, and Messrs R. and M. Cutting, Upper Warren via Manjimup, WA; personal information.

H. D. EVANS

FRY, HENRY KENNETH (1886-1959), anthropologist and medical practitioner, was born on 25 May 1886 in North Adelaide, fourth child of Henry Thomas Fry (d.1899), warehouseman, and his wife Margaret Hannah, née Phillips. Kenneth was educated at Prince Alfred College and the University of Adelaide (B.Sc., 1905; M.B., B.S., 1908; M.D., 1934); as South Australian Rhodes scholar for 1908, he proceeded to Balliol College, Oxford, where in 1912 he obtained another B.Sc. and diplomas in public health and anthropology. Next year he succeeded Herbert Basedow [q.v.7] as chief medical inspector of Aborigines, based in Darwin. Fry made several trips to remote localities to assess Aboriginal health. He kept a journal of his expedition to Melville and Bathurst islands in which he described a Tiwi *pukumani* burial ceremony; in 1914 he sent thirty-four ethnographic objects, including a canoe and four burial poles, to the Pitt Rivers Museum, Oxford.

Appointed captain in the Australian Army Medical Corps, Australian Imperial Force, on 20 August 1914, Fry sailed for the Middle East with the 3rd Field Ambulance. He was at Gallipoli in 1915 before being sent to France in March 1916 as deputy assistant director of medical services, 2nd Division. For supervising the evacuation of the wounded while under constant shell-fire at Pozières and Sausage Valley in July-August, he was awarded the Distinguished Service Order. In October 1917 he was promoted lieutenant colonel and given command of the 13th Field Ambulance. Returning to Adelaide, on 21 October 1918 he married Dorothy Editha Deeley with Anglican rites at the Church of the Epiphany, Crafers. By January 1919 he was back in France as temporary colonel and A.D.M.S., 5th Division. His A.I.F. appointment terminated on 26 December. He was thrice mentioned in dispatches.

At Eastwood, Adelaide, Fry established a private practice in a house of his own design which incorporated a surgery, laboratory and one of the first X-ray units in the State. From 1920 he lectured in materia medica and therapeutics in the neurology department at the university. He was also an honorary physician at the Royal Adelaide Hospital and an official visitor to Parkside Mental Hospital. A member (from 1923) and president (1938) of the Royal Society of South Australia, he was a founding fellow (1939) of the Royal Australasian College of Physicians. With Archibald Watson, (Sir) John Cleland, Robert Pulleine, Frederic Wood Jones and Draper Campbell [qq.v.12,8,11,9,13], Fry had formed the Board for Anthropological Research in 1925.

In August 1929, at the height of a major drought, he travelled by train to Alice Springs and, at Hermannsburg, joined the board's fifth expedition to Central Australia. Medical members of the team successfully treated the Aborigines for scurvy and received tribal status which facilitated their future research in the region. Fry assisted the ethnologist Norman Tindale in taking unique film records and in gathering sociological data, and conducted psychological and sensory tests. He devised a succinct but flexible framework to record Aboriginal classificatory kinship systems. Termed the 'Fry Framework' by Tindale, it enabled the documentation of varying kinship structures across Aboriginal Australia. Tindale's 'Fry Frameworks' for two hundred Aboriginal groups are held in the South Australian Museum, as are Fry's anthropological notebooks. Fry accompanied the board's expeditions to MacDonald Downs (1930), Cockatoo Creek (1931), Mount Liebig (1932), Ernabella (1933), Diamantina (1934), the Granites (1936) and Nepabunna (1937). In the 1930s he also helped Tindale to record Aboriginal sites on the Coorong with the Tangane elder, Milerum [q.v.10].

The first Oxford-trained anthropologist to work in Australia, in 1930-57 Fry published over twenty scientific papers on Aboriginal kinship, psychology and mythology. In London in 1931 he lectured to the Royal Anthropological Institute of Great Britain and Ireland. His contributions to *Oceania* impressed A. P. Elkin [q.v.] who in 1935 urged the Federal minister for the interior, Thomas Paterson [q.v.11], to appoint Fry as a medical anthropologist to the Aborigines of Central Australia. Fry decided, however, that he could not work under C. E. Cook, the chief protector of Aborigines then in Darwin.

From 1938 Fry was a part-time public health officer for the City of Adelaide; soon after taking up his post, he formulated plans for the mass radiological examination of South Australians. In 1937 he had moved to Crafers in the Adelaide Hills where he devoted much of his time to the care of a reserve of native vegetation which now bears his name. The clear skies enabled him to pursue his hobby of astronomy. He continued to write about Aborigines and in 1951 joined the last of the board's major expeditions, to Yuendumu in Central Australia. Survived by his wife, son and daughter, he died on 22 July 1959 at Stirling and was cremated.

Fry note-books and manuscripts *and* N. B. Tindale manuscripts (SA Museum, Adel); Fry papers (Mort L); file re appointment of NT medical anthropologist, CRS A1, 1935/4434 (AA, Canb); information from Mr J. Fry, Crafers, Adel, and Lady Gillian Cave, Aldeburgh, Suffolk, Eng.

PHILIP JONES

FRY, THOMAS PENBERTHY (1904-1952), lawyer, was born on 19 June 1904 in Brisbane, only son and elder child of James Porter Fry, commercial traveller, and his wife Sarah (Sadie), née Chegwin, both native-born. James was to become an optician, a member (1918-32) of the Legislative Assembly and a lieutenant colonel in the Australian Military Forces. Educated at state and private schools in Brisbane, Thomas entered the University of Queensland (B.A. Hons, 1926; M.A., 1927) where he joined the debating and dramatic societies; he represented (1922-24) the university in Rugby League and in July 1926 refereed a football 'test' between Queensland and New South Wales schoolboys. In 1925 he had been commissioned lieutenant in the Militia.

Travelling to England in 1927, Fry was admitted to Magdalen College, Oxford (B.C.L., 1929) and played Rugby Union for the university against Cambridge. His study at the Academy of International Law in The Hague led to a diploma in 1928. Next year he moved to Harvard University in the United States of America; noted as 'exceedingly industrious and able', he was awarded a doctorate of juridical science (1931).

Admitted to the Queensland Bar on 9 September 1931, Fry combined a varied practice with part-time teaching in social science at the University of Queensland (1932-35) and external examining for the University of Sydney's law school (1932-34). His 'impatiently restless energy' led him to become chairman of the Queensland Historical Society's editorial committee and president (1935) of the Queensland Soccer Council; Fry was also a founder of the Queensland branch of the Australian Institute of International Affairs (president 1932-40, 1947-48) and honorary secretary of the Australian and New Zealand Society of International Law. Some felt that he led 'a rather uncoordinated existence'.

In 1936 he was appointed lecturer in his university's new law school. Small staffing meant a heavy workload: Fry taught constitutional and criminal law, Equity, torts, and property and conveyancing. He employed 'a modified case method of teaching and preferred seminars to the traditional lecturing system'; students found him helpful and kind hearted. Visiting London, he married Orma Howard Smith on 25 January 1937 at St Margaret's parish church, Westminster.

Fry had remained in the Militia, served as honorary aide-de-camp to the governor of Queensland, Sir Leslie Wilson [q.v.12], and was mobilized in 1939. Transferred as major to the Australian Imperial Force on 15 June 1940, he performed the duties of judge-advocate, Middle East (1940-42); he was promoted lieutenant colonel in January 1941 and mentioned in dispatches. Back home, from June 1944 he headed a team in the Directorate of Research (and Civil Affairs), consolidating the laws of Papua and New Guinea. He ceased full-time service on 11 September 1946 and that year returned to the University of Queensland as a senior lecturer. Because he 'trod on many toes', his talents did not receive full recognition by the State's legal profession.

In 1948 Fry resigned to take charge of the Sydney-based legal research section, Department of External Territories, where he continued his earlier work on the laws of Papua and New Guinea, and began their revision. His minister from 1951, (Sir) Paul Hasluck, considered him 'a singular man with exceptional gifts', but recognized the degree to which he lacked 'worldly practicality'. They shared a happy and mutually respectful working relationship. Survived by his wife and two daughters, Fry died of a cerebral haemorrhage on 23 September 1952 in Canberra and was cremated.

P. Hasluck, *A Time for Building* (Melb, 1976); E. Smith, *The Australia Card* (Melb, 1989); *Aust Law J*, 16 Oct 1952, p 316; *Univ Qld Law J*, 2, Nov 1952, p 86; *Queenslander*, 6 June 1929; *Courier-Mail*, 4 Feb 1932, 8 July 1940, 11 Nov 1942, 31 Jan 1948, 25 Sept 1952; s135, staff files, Univ Qld Archives.

IAN CARNELL

FULLAGAR, SIR WILFRED KELSHAM (1892-1961), judge, was born on 16 November 1892 at Malvern, Melbourne, only son and eldest of three children of Thomas Kelsham Fullagar, merchant, and his wife Sarah Elizabeth, née Law, both native-born. Educated at Haileybury College, Brighton, where the headmaster C. H. Rendall [q.v.11] regarded him as his most brilliant student, in 1910 Wilfred entered Ormond [q.v.5] College, University of Melbourne (LL.B., 1915; B.A., 1925; LL.M., 1925). He won a Wyselaskie [q.v.6] scholarship in classical and comparative philology and logic, and graduated with first-class honours and the Supreme Court judges' prize. Fullagar's love of the classics was enhanced by Professor T. G. Tucker [q.v.12] and was abiding: he continued to read Greek and Latin literature, and to compose Latin poetry. His friend Sir Owen Dixon [q.v.] was later to say that Fullagar's classical training gave 'an added distinction to his writings'.

While articled to the Melbourne solicitor J. W. McComas, Fullagar enlisted in the Australian Imperial Force on 28 October 1916. He served in France with the 7th Field Artillery Brigade from May 1918, rose to sergeant and in 1919 was granted six months leave in England to study law. On 11 October that year he married Marion Frederica Dorothea Lovejoy (d.1941) at the register office, Fulham, London; he returned to Melbourne in January 1920 and was discharged from the A.I.F. on 8 February.

Fullagar was admitted to practice on 1 October 1920. He worked initially for the Department of Repatriation and for the Commonwealth Immigration Service because, as a young married man, he felt he could not afford the cost of setting up as a barrister. In 1922, however, with financial assistance pressed upon him by (Sir) John Latham [q.v.10] and Dixon, he took that step, signing the Bar roll on 7 April and reading with (Sir) Charles Lowe [q.v.]. Fullagar was rapidly successful, and able to repay Latham and Dixon within the year. He soon developed a formidable reputation, especially in the fields of Equity and constitutional law. His judicial colleague Sir Arthur Dean [q.v.13] was to write of him, he 'was not an advocate in the accepted sense and no one would think of briefing him in the Criminal Court or before juries', but 'as a sound and learned lawyer, as a brilliant expositor of the law, he was unrivalled'.

In 1928-45 Fullagar served on the Bar committee and in 1940-45 as a vice-president of the Law Council of Australia, giving generously of his time to the development of the profession. An inspiring teacher, he lectured at the University of Melbourne in the law of wrongs and the law of procedure (1923-28), and in constitutional law (1943-45); between 1945 and 1951 he was a member of the university council. He was also a director (1939-45, chairman 1944-45) of the Equity Trustees, Executors & Agency Co. Ltd, a trustee (1940-45) of the Edward Wilson [q.v.6] bequest and a director (1942-45) of Argus & Australasian Ltd.

After a mere eleven years at the Bar, in September 1933 Fullagar had been appointed King's Counsel. Within months, there was speculation in the press that he was about to be appointed to the Supreme Court of Victoria. He probably declined one or more such offers over the next few years, apparently on financial grounds, before finally accepting in July 1945. On 8 February 1950 he was made a justice of the High Court of Australia, a position he was to retain until his death. His judicial work was of the highest quality, but he sat on the bench in a period when there was relative stability in doctrine and principle in both public and private law, and his views on some matters were to be overtaken by later High Court opinion. In 1955 he was appointed K.B.E.

At the Presbyterian Church, South Yarra, on 4 July 1942 Fullagar had married a nurse Mary Florence Taylor. He was of middle height and thickset, with a full face, blue eyes, and dark hair touched with ginger. A quiet, modest, gentle, friendly man, with a delicious sense of humour and (as Dixon put it) 'a most lovable nature', he commanded respect and affection. His principal recreations in later life were reading, gardening, bowls, trout-fishing and walking (he had joined the Wallaby Club in 1933); he wrote light verse, and was fond of the Scottish pipes and the works of Gilbert and Sullivan. Fullagar died of cerebral thrombosis on 9 July 1961 in the Freemasons' Hospital, East Melbourne, and was cremated with Presbyterian forms. His wife survived him, as did four of the five sons of his first marriage; his son Richard followed him to the bench of the Supreme Court of Victoria in 1975. Monash University established a lecture series in 1968 to honour Sir Wilfred's memory.

On Fullagar's death, Prime Minister (Sir) Robert Menzies [q.v.] acknowledged 'his mastery of the law'. To Dixon, Fullagar 'had combined, with a remarkable legal erudition, great resources of scholarship. His judgments commanded the admiration of lawyers, not only for their penetration, their soundness and their correctness, but for the exposition of legal principles in an almost unequalled English style'. Justice Felix Frankfurter, of the Supreme Court of the United States of America, felt 'a personal loss', so close had been his sense of 'professional communion'. In a judgement in the House of Lords relying heavily on Fullagar and delivered a few months after his death, Viscount Simonds spoke of the deprivation which would be experienced by 'all who anywhere are concerned with the administration of the common law'. Such tributes are rare.

A. Dean, *A Multitude of Counsellors* (Melb, 1968); R. Campbell, *A History of the Melbourne Law School 1857 to 1973* (Melb, 1977); *Cwlth Law Reports*, 103, 1959-60; *Aust Law J*, 35, 27 July 1961, p 85; *Herald* (Melb), 5 Jan 1932, 9 Dec 1933, 28 Sept 1935, 6 Mar 1968; *Argus*, 31 July 1945; *Sun News-Pictorial*, 26 Sept 1933, 4 Feb 1950, 13 July 1961;

Age (Melb), 4 Feb 1950, 11 July 1961; information from Mr Justice R. Fullagar, Judges Chambers, Supreme Court of Vic.   R. L. SHARWOOD

FULLARTON, ALEXANDER HAMPTON (1910-1964), jockey and horse-trainer, was born on 10 June 1910 at Ascot Vale, Melbourne, second child of Victorian-born parents Robert Fullarton, horse-trainer, and his wife Rubina Susan, née Hampton. Educated at Moonee Ponds West State School, Alex was apprenticed to the trainer Bill Leyshon at Flemington and was twice leading apprentice in Victoria. He had his best win on the flat in the inaugural King's Cup of 1927 at Flemington, riding Leyshon's Spear Maiden; the Duke and Duchess of York were in attendance.

Increasing weight forced Fullarton to become a jumps jockey. His success was swift and spectacular. At his second ride over fences he won the Victoria Racing Club's 1929 Grand National Steeplechase at Flemington on the Harry Gabell-trained Sandhurst. He rode Polygonum to victory in the V.R.C.'s Grand National Hurdle in 1932, captured a second steeple on Woodlace in 1934 and won the first of two Australian hurdles on Dress Suit in 1937. Fullarton's second victory in that race as a jockey came in 1944 when he rode Benghazi as an amateur, four years after he had retired as a professional jockey to concentrate on training.

In his career as a jockey, Fullarton recorded about 700 wins, some 200 of them over the jumps. Redditch was perhaps the best jumper that he rode; he had the mount when the champion was killed in a fall at Flemington in the Grand National Steeplechase of 1935. Fullarton avoided serious injury during his hazardous career, but his younger brother Don was killed in February 1957 while schooling Mungaroo over the steeplechase fences at Flemington.

From his stables by the Maribyrnong River at West Essendon, Fullarton produced a steady stream of winners. He schooled all his horses personally, an unusual preference partly explained by his continuing love of riding. His recreation was riding to hounds. Fullarton had won the Great Eastern Steeplechase at Oakbank, in the Adelaide Hills, as a jockey on Kenjin in 1934. He trained four further winners of the race: The Feline (1948 and 1951), Teedum (1956) and Moonacoota (1961). Teedum had also won the 1953 Australian Steeplechase. The Feline was the best of Fullarton's jumpers. Among its successes, the small, plain gelding had won the Australian Hurdle (1947), the Grand National Hurdle (1948) and the Warrnambool Grand Annual Steeplechase (1950). Fullarton trained another Australian Hurdle winner,

Elastin (1949), and part-owned Victory March, winner of the Grand National Hurdle (1943). He is the only person to have trained, ridden and owned winners of the Grand National Hurdle.

At the registry office, Collins Street, Melbourne, on 14 March 1933 Fullarton had married Edna Annie Hastings, a Tivoli dancer. On 28 March 1964 at Oakbank, where he had two strong fancies engaged for the local meeting, he collapsed and died of myocardial infarction. Survived by his wife and three sons, he was cremated. Fullarton and The Feline had Melbourne metropolitan jumps races named in their honour.

Herald (Melb), 22 June 1938, 11 Apr 1944, 28 May 1949, 28 Mar 1964; *Argus*, 22 July 1940, 27 Feb 1957; *Sun News-Pictorial*, 23 Oct 1940, 1 July 1942, 30 Mar, 16 Apr 1964; *Age* (Melb), 30 Mar 1964; *Sporting Globe*, 1 Apr 1964.

                 PETER PIERCE

FULLER, BRYAN CECIL (1888-1956), barrister, Presbyterian layman and tennis administrator, was born on 17 August 1888 at Dunmore, New South Wales, thirteenth child of George Laurence Fuller, a farmer from Ireland, and his native-born wife Sarah Cunningham (Conyhame), née Miller. A brother of (Sir) George and C. D. Fuller [qq.v.8], Bryan was educated at Scotch College, Melbourne, and St Andrew's College, University of Sydney (B.A., 1910; LL.B., 1913). He was admitted to the Bar on 8 May 1913 and was associate to Chief Justice Sir William Cullen [q.v.8]. Three years later Fuller began practice as a barrister with Alexander Thomson, K.C.

On 14 December 1916 at Christ Church Cathedral, Grafton, Fuller married 20-year-old Isabel Mary Deane. Developing an extensive practice in commercial law, he was regularly briefed over many years as senior counsel for the State commissioner of railways. He was appointed K.C. on 30 March 1938 and was an acting-judge of the District Court from October to December. Fuller was also a councillor (from 1936) and treasurer (1939-46) of the New South Wales Bar Association; he represented the association on the university's faculty of law and served as vice-president (1950-51) of the Law Council of Australia.

A leading Presbyterian layman, Fuller was a council-member of Knox Grammar School (1923-45) and St Andrew's College (from 1921; chairman, 1938-55). In 1936 he was appointed procurator of the General Assembly of the Presbyterian Church of Australia and in 1937 of the Presbyterian Church in New South Wales. A committee-man *par excellence*, he was notable for his grasp of the law, both civil and ecclesiastical, for his vast experience of committee procedure (which he brought to bear 'impartially and firmly'), and for his remarkable knowledge of people and places.

Fuller's chief recreation was tennis. He was a councillor (from 1921) and vice-president (1926-36) of the New South Wales Lawn Tennis Association. As president from 1936, he was responsible for transferring the association's courts from Double Bay to White City, Rushcutters Bay. He frequently clashed with Sir Norman Brookes [q.v.7] and challenged Victorian domination of the Lawn Tennis Association of Australia. In 1946 Fuller accused Arthur Calwell [q.v.13] of 'gross abuse of his executive powers' in refusing passports to the Australian squad who wanted to compete at Wimbledon.

A man of wide interests, Fuller was a leading member and a long-term vice-president of the University Club, which he joined in 1909; on the death of Sir Percival Halse Rogers [q.v.11] in 1945, he was elected president. He also belonged to the Australian Club. Struck by a motor vehicle in Bent Street on 23 March 1956, he died in Sydney Hospital that day from the injuries he had received and was cremated. His funeral service at St Stephen's Church, Macquarie Street, was attended by one thousand people. He was survived by his wife, daughter and son (Sir) John Bryan Munro Fuller, government leader (1968-76) in the Legislative Council.

A. Dougan (comp), *The Andrew's Book* (Syd, 1970); S. E. Emilsen, *A Whiff of Heresy* (Syd, 1991); *NSW Presbyterian*, 6 Apr 1956, p 1; *SMH*, 25 Mar, 12 Sept 1936, 31 Mar, 6 Apr, 15 June, 20 Oct 1938, 6 Sept 1939, 25 July 1945, 27, 28 Mar, 4 Apr 1946, 28 May, 13, 25 June 1947, 18 May 1949, 6 Aug 1951, 24 Mar 1956.   SUSAN EMILSEN

FUNNELL, WILLIAM (1891-1962), public servant, was born on 8 June 1891 at Goulburn, New South Wales, son of native-born parents William Funnell, railway employee, and his wife Jessie Anne, née Worchurst. Educated at South Goulburn Public School, young William joined the local office of the New South Wales Government Railways and Tramways in 1906 as an apprentice clerk in the traffic branch. From July to November 1912 he worked, on detachment, as an instructor with the railway and tramway ambulance corps in Sydney; on his return he was promoted clerk. At St Aidan's Anglican Church, Annandale, Sydney, on 3 April 1915 he married Gladys Evelyn Walsh.

Transferred next year to head office, Sydney, in 1921 Funnell was appointed special staff officer, first class, and liaised between the railway commissioners and Walter Edmunds [q.v.8], the royal commissioner who inquired into the administration of the State's railway and tramway services, and into the repercussions of the 1917 transport strike. After giving evidence for thirty-three days in the witness-box, Funnell was praised by Edmunds for his ability, energy, impartiality and knowledge. As chairman of the railway strike adjustments board, in 1925 Funnell began the difficult task of restoring the seniority of workers who had been dismissed in 1917 and subsequently re-employed in lower grades. He was a member (1927) and chairman (1931) of the staff board before becoming chief staff superintendent (in 1932).

In February 1942 he was released to take the Commonwealth post of assistant director-general of manpower and controller of national service offices, under W. C. Wurth [q.v.]. A few months later Funnell reported on the use of manpower in the departments of air and the army. To meet wartime labour shortages, he recommended the extensive employment of women in traditional male occupations. He succeeded Wurth as director-general in October 1944. Funnell assured the premiers' conference in August 1945 that demobilization would be speedy. Prime Minister Chifley [q.v.13] commended his work and asked that he continue in office with the new duty of assisting the Public Service Board to establish the Commonwealth Employment Service.

Resigning from the railways, Funnell was appointed secretary of the Commonwealth Department of Labour and National Service in March 1946. He attended the thirtieth session of the International Labour Conference in Geneva in 1947 and visited the United States of America on his journey home. From 1951 he was chairman of Commonwealth Hostels Ltd, a post he held until his death. Faced with a succession of protests from British immigrants who were discontented with their accommodation and increased tariffs, he resolved the rows and settled the related disturbances. In 1954 he was appointed I.S.O. Funnell was 5 ft 11 ins (180 cm) tall, with brown hair, brown eyes and 'Mephistophelian' eyebrows; he enjoyed chess, gardening and tennis. His genial manner, humanity and mental acuity equipped him to settle all manner of disputes. Survived by his wife, daughter and two sons, he died on 25 October 1962 at Castlecrag, Sydney, and was cremated.

SMH, 2 Sept 1922, 13 Sept 1944, 27 Apr, 21, 24 Aug 1945, 6 Mar, 2 May 1946, 23 Nov 1952, 10 May, 12, 15 June 1953, 10 June 1954, 26 Oct 1962; *Smith's Weekly* (Syd), 23 Sept 1944; Railway Staff Personal History Cards, employees born before 1900, 11/16552-745 (NSWA); Use of Manpower in the Department of Air. The Funnell Report, May 1942, A5954, items 468/5-6 *and* Mr W. Funnell to

I.L.O. Conference Geneva, 1947-48, A1068, item T47/134 (AA, Canb).　　　　　ANTHEA KERR

FURNELL, HERBERT GIBLIN ('HARRY') (1898-1973), gynaecologist and army officer, was born on 24 October 1898 at Maryborough, Victoria, son of George William Furnell, a gaol-governor from England, and his second wife Florence Ellen, née Herbert, who was born in New South Wales. After winning scholarships to Geelong Church of England Grammar School and to Trinity College, University of Melbourne (M.B., B.S., 1921; D.G.O., 1932), 'Harry' played Australian Rules football for the Carlton club. He served his residency at St Vincent's Hospital, then entered private practice at Abbotsford. At St Joseph's Catholic Church, Malvern, on 12 April 1924 he married Marguerite McLean.

In March 1923 he was appointed lieutenant, (Royal) Australian Army Medical Corps, Militia, and came under the influence of Colonel Rupert Downes [q.v.8]. By 1932 Furnell was a major, commanding the 10th Field Ambulance; in 1936 he was promoted lieutenant colonel. His civilian career also blossomed. In 1927-29 he had studied surgery in London and Edinburgh, and obstetrics and gynaecology in Dublin and Vienna, before specializing as a gynaecologist. A fellow (1927) of the Royal College of Surgeons, Edinburgh, he was to be elected to fellowships of the Royal Australasian College of Surgeons (1958) and the Royal College of Obstetricians and Gynaecologists, London (1965).

Furnell was among the first to join the Australian Imperial Force in October 1939. Given command of the 2nd/2nd Field Ambulance, he made it 'a magnificent unit, with a sense of purpose amongst all ranks'. He sailed for the Middle East in April 1940. In the advance through Libya in January 1941 'he was continually forward supervising [the] collection of wounded under enemy fire'. On 27 January, in an air-raid near Derna, he saved the life of a wounded soldier by getting him into a slit trench and maintaining pressure on a severed artery. Furnell was awarded the Distinguished Service Order.

Promoted temporary colonel on 16 February 1941 (substantive in August), he transferred to 9th Division headquarters as assistant-director of medical services. At Tobruk, from April to October 1941, he provided medical support to a garrison, initially over 35 000 strong, and to some 10 000 prisoners. His success in caring for the wounded and in maintaining the health of the force was a remarkable achievement.

Furnell's hard training after Tobruk prepared his medical units for the El Alamein campaign of July-November 1942. In the battle which opened on 23 October he established forward surgical centres for the early treatment of severe injuries and evacuated some casualties by air. His arrangements were 'a triumph of organization and detailed planning, all medical units working as one great team'. For his achievements in the Middle East, he was appointed C.B.E. (1943) and thrice mentioned in dispatches.

Returning to Australia in early 1943, Furnell was promoted temporary brigadier and posted as deputy-director of medical services, I Corps and New Guinea Force. He took up his command on 4 July 1943 in Port Moresby and spent much of the next two years moving between his respective headquarters in a war in which disease and the terrain matched the hostility of the Japanese. Twice mentioned in dispatches, he transferred to the Reserve of Officers on 21 July 1945. While rebuilding his civilian practice, in 1946-51 he performed part-time duty in the Citizen Military Forces as D.D.M.S., Southern Command, Melbourne, and (briefly in 1947-48) acting director-general of medical services at Army Headquarters. In 1962 he was appointed an honorary colonel of the R.A.A.M.C.

Furnell was honorary gynaecologist and consultant gynaecologist (from 1960) to St Vincent's Hospital, and dean (1953-57) of the hospital's clinical school. He was involved in planning the Mercy Maternity Hospital (opened in 1971) and in the establishment of a chair of obstetrics and gynaecology at the University of Melbourne. President (1955) and treasurer (1962-72) of the Victorian branch of the British (Australian) Medical Association, he was largely responsible for financing the building of the Medical Society Hall, Parkville. He was a board-member of the British Medical Insurance Co. and the Australasian Medical Publishing Co. Ltd. In 1956 he chaired the medical committee for the Olympic Games. After visiting Indonesia in 1964, he recommended sending a surgical team to train medical students in that country.

Survived by his wife, son and daughter, Furnell died on 22 November 1973 in East Melbourne and was buried in Springvale cemetery. A wartime comrade W. W. Lempriere remembered his courage, endurance, high principles, sense of humour and egalitarianism. Sir Geoffrey Newman-Morris wrote of his kindness and gentleness, and of the firmness and decisiveness with which he served 'the profession he loved and adorned so well'.

A. S. Walker, *Middle East and Far East* (Canb, 1953) and *The Island Campaigns* (Canb, 1957); *MJA*, 6 Apr 1974, p 546; *Age* (Melb), 17 Feb 1965; information from Mrs C. Partos, East Brighton, Melb.　　　　　　　　　　　　　　A. J. HILL

G

GABB, JOEL MOSES (1882-1951), politician and preacher, was born on 21 November 1882 at New Glenelg, Adelaide, eldest of nine children of Charles Henry Gabb, a plasterer from England, and his native-born wife Hannah, née Whittaker. Educated at St Peter's Anglican School, Glenelg, Moses was an adherent of the United (later Australian) Labor Party, reputedly chalking the names of its candidates on the footpath at the age of 12. He became a grocer before undertaking Methodist home mission work (from 1905) on Kangaroo Island and at inland pastoral stations. In 1908 he spent a few months at Prince Alfred College studying for the ministry.

Sent to conduct a mission on the Murray River, Gabb travelled by motorboat to hold regular services between Swan Reach and Loxton, using loudspeakers to preach to communities along the banks and bluffs. He retired from missionary work because of doctrinal differences and did not enter the ministry, but he had established a reputation as a 'fighting parson' who responded vigorously to any intrusion or insult, either to himself or the cloth. On 9 October 1912 at Bath Street Methodist Church, Glenelg, he married Florence Ethel Hobbs; they opened a grocery business at Yatala (Alberton). Standing as an A.L.P. candidate, in 1919 he defeated P. M. Glynn [q.v.9], the sitting member for Angas in the House of Representatives and a minister in W. M. Hughes's [q.v.9] Nationalist government. Gabb lost the seat in 1925 and regained it in 1929.

Too idiosyncratic in his personal and political style ever to submit comfortably to the yoke of Labor caucus discipline, Gabb was essentially an agrarian socialist, a rare creature in the party's ranks. His political career was dominated by two pronounced personal quirks: a passion for calling regular quorums, and an undeviating commitment to the frugal administration of the Federal government, particularly its parliament. Neither quality endeared him to fellow politicians. He described his colleagues as 'too tired and too indifferent' to watch the interests of taxpayers. According to Gabb, the quorum bell forced members to do the work they were paid for, rather than spending time in the billiards and refreshment rooms. Prime Minister Scullin [q.v.11] privately urged him to desist from an overly punctilious observance of the quorum rule, but he declined. On one notable occasion he was derided by members from both sides when he was caught outside the chamber on a quorum call.

In May 1920 Gabb had earned fame as a political populist for refusing to accept a pay rise, claiming that he had contracted with his electors to serve them for £600 a year. By October 1922 he had forfeited £965 and at the elections in December he campaigned on the slogan 'Gabb did not Grab'. He practised economical management of parliament in outlandish ways, such as constantly stalking the corridors to turn off electric lights. He also urged the closing of the parliamentary dining-room, claiming that members were too lazy to walk to their hotels for meals. In January 1931 he resigned from the A.L.P. and from March was aligned with the breakaway group led by Joseph Lyons [q.v.10], a man he admired.

Unlike other A.L.P. defectors, Gabb did not join Lyons's United Australia Party. Nevertheless, with the backing of the South Australian Emergency Committee, which had been a principal agent in establishing the U.A.P., Gabb was re-elected. He supported the government, but sat as an Independent. His crusade to reduce parliamentary salaries led to Charles Hawker's [q.v.9] resignation from the ministry in September 1932. Showing an inclination towards extreme right-wing politics, Gabb once declared that parliament should be shut down and that he ought to be allowed to act as a Mussolini. He retired in August 1934. In 1938 he unsuccessfully stood as an Independent for the seat of Light in the House of Assembly.

Despite his eccentricities and onomatopoeic surname, Gabb was not a particularly colourful or personable politician. One press report described him as 'having a remarkable faculty for dullness ... a sort of inverted alchemist afflicted with an ambition for turning gold into lead'. He committed suicide by cutting his throat on 6 March 1951 at his Alberton home. Survived by his wife, two sons and one of his two daughters, he was cremated. His estate was sworn for probate at £9435.

Uniting Church in SA Hist Soc, *Newsletter*, 30, Aug 1986, p 2; C. J. Lloyd, The Formation and Development of the United Australia Party, 1929-37 (Ph.D. thesis, ANU, 1984); Gabb papers (NL).

C. J. LLOYD

GADSDON, SIR LAURENCE PERCIVAL (1897-1967), businessman and mayor, was born on 24 March 1897 at High Ongar, Essex, England, twin son and eldest of eight children of Frank Benjamin Gadsdon, master carriage-builder, and his wife Mary Gertrude, née Ashdown. Laurence was educated at Haberdashers' Aske's Hampstead School, London. The family emigrated to Western Australia in 1913 and settled at Victoria Park, Perth. Enlisting in the Australian Imperial Force on 25 May 1915, Gadsdon joined the 12th Battalion at Gallipoli in August. That month he was wounded and evacuated to Egypt. There he became critically ill with tetanus. Invalided to Australia, he was discharged in Perth on 23 June 1916. He was a foundation member (1916) of the State branch of the Returned Sailors' and Soldiers' Imperial League of Australia, and later served two terms as vicepresident. Employed by Wilson Gray & Co., a firm of stonemasons which later did the facework on the war memorial in King's Park, he was to become its senior partner and managing director.

In 1918 the Gadsdons moved to Cottesloe where they helped to form the North Cottesloe Surf Life-Saving Club; Laurie was its first secretary. A member (from 1925) of the State branch of the Surf Life Saving Association of Australia, he was its secretary (1931-34) and president (1937-46). In addition, he was a founder (1924) and committee-member of the Cottesloe Tennis Club, and also promoted hockey in Western Australia, coaching his sister Kathleen who captained the local and State team. At Christ Church, Claremont, on 26 October 1929 Gadsdon married with Anglican rites Hilda Mary Hedges; another marriage ceremony was conducted, at Hilda's request, by Fr John Fahey [q.v.8] at Star of the Sea Catholic Church, Cottesloe, on 26 October 1957. Involved in community affairs with the same energy that characterized his participation in sport, Gadsdon had been elected to the Cottesloe Municipal Council at the age of 25 and served as mayor from 1945.

Of middle height, with blue eyes and dark brown hair, Gadsdon was a practical man, 'open-faced and friendly', and rarely seen without his beloved pipe. He had strong qualities of leadership and a keen sense of business, and established a rapport with a wide range of people. During World War II he was honorary director of communications for the Civil Defence Council. A member (1945-60) of the Metropolitan Local Government Association (president 1952), he was an enthusiastic town planner. Due to his initiative, in 1950 the Cottesloe council purchased Claude de Bernales' [q.v.8] magnificent mansion, Overton Lodge, for use as a war memorial hall and civic centre. Gadsdon continued to enjoy swimming and tennis, and took up golf; he belonged to the Royal Commonwealth Society. In 1960 he was knighted.

Ill health forced Sir Laurence to retire as mayor on 25 October 1961. Survived by his wife and daughter, he died of hypertensive heart failure on 7 August 1967 at Claremont and was buried in Karrakatta cemetery with Methodist forms. His estate was sworn for probate at $337 766.

A. C. Lloyd and A. Ferguson (comps), *Leading Personalities of Western Australia* (Perth, 1950); E. Jaggard, *A Challenge Answered* (Perth, 1979); *Cottesloe Spectator*, 21, 28 Mar, 1 Apr, 2 May, 4 July 1929; *West Australian*, 11 June 1960, 26 Oct 1961, 8 Aug 1967; *Daily News* (Perth), 7 Aug 1967; Cottesloe Municipal Council minutes, 1924-61 (Cottesloe Town Council); RSL Archives (Perth); information from Lady Gadsdon, Shenton Park, Mr G. F. Gadsdon, Crawley, and Mrs J. Hunt, Coral Bay, WA.　　　　　RUTH MARCHANT JAMES

GAFFNEY, FRANCIS XAVIER (1877-1970), Marist Brother and Rugby coach, was born on 2 December 1877 in Cardiff, Wales, sixth of seven children of Patrick William Gaffney, customs officer, and his wife Elizabeth Mary, née Griffin, both Irish born. After his father's death, the family emigrated to Brisbane in 1884. Educated with his five male siblings at the Christian Brothers' College, he and his brother Tom helped to form the Gregory Rugby Football Club. Frank played first grade (1889-1905) as half-back with the Gregory, North Brisbane Electorate, Toowong Electorate and Christian Brothers football clubs before entering the Society of Mary (Marist Brothers) at Hunters Hill, Sydney, on 17 April 1906.

Having completed his novitiate at Mittagong, Gaffney took the religious name Henry, and taught briefly in Sydney at St Mary's Cathedral Boys' School and at St Patrick's Boys' School, Church Hill. In 1910 he joined the staff of St Joseph's College, Hunters Hill, where he soon had his juniors playing sparkling Rugby. He taught in 1915-18 at New Norcia, Western Australia, and returned to the primary school at St Joseph's in 1919. Three years later he somewhat reluctantly agreed to coach the two senior teams.

In 1923 Brother Henry's first premiership team—and one of 'Joey's' greatest ever—scored 250 points to 25 in the seven competition games. Between 1922 and 1953 (except during World War II) his first XV won eighteen Athletic Association of the Great Public Schools of New South Wales premierships (four shared) and were runners up four times, averaging in 181 games 26 points for to 6 against; his second XV won 15 premierships (4 shared) and were runners up 9 times. Many of his schoolboys later played Rugby and Rugby League for New South Wales and Australia.

His reputation resulted from his mastery of all aspects of the game and, not least, his uncanny knack of picking early potential.

Insisting on fitness, safe handling, deadly tackling and fast, strong running in the open game, Gaffney made a cardinal rule of 'possession, position and pace'. The 'Wizard of Hunter's Hill' infused into the game a spirit of selflessness, co-ordination and comradeship: we 'have no outstanding players—we produce teams, not individuals'. He told his boys in the cerise and blue, 'Better an honourable defeat, than a mean victory'.

The historian, former English international and Australian selector G. V. Portus [q.v.11] summed up Gaffney's style of Rugby: 'His teams exploit a great variety of modes of attack. They use quick transfers to the wingers, the short punt through, a timely cross-kick, a burst through by five-eighth or centre, the reverse movement to the waiting forwards ... to you, Brother Henry, in the immortal words of the Sentimental Bloke, "I dips me lid"'. A kindly man of strong faith and simple piety, Gaffney regarded his coaching skill as 'a gift from Heaven', a means by which he could influence boys to lead happy and worthy Christian lives. To him, Rugby was a powerful influence in moulding character and developing manly virtues.

Still 'nippy' on his feet in 1951, Brother Henry could be seen ducking, with his soutane flying, into the scrum to explain a special point. He retired as coach in mid-1954 because of a leg injury, but remained at the college. His many friends and ex-students welcomed him at matches and valued his football judgement and advice. He died on Christmas Day 1970 at the Mater Misericordiae Hospital, North Sydney, and was buried in the Field of Mars cemetery, Ryde. One week later it was announced that he had been appointed O.B.E.

G. V. Portus, *Happy Highways* (Melb, 1953); J. Pollard, *Australian Rugby Union* (Syd, 1984); *Sporting Life* (Syd), May 1949, p 19; *People* (Syd), 9 May 1951; *Marist Mthly*, Mar 1971, p 8; *St Joseph's College Annual*, Dec 1971, p 36; *Referee*, 19 Aug 1937; *Smith's Weekly* (Syd), 14 Oct 1950; *SMH*, 26 Dec 1970; *Catholic Weekly*, 31 Dec 1970; Archives, St Joseph's College, Hunter's Hill, Syd.

G. P. WALSH

GAFFNEY, THOMAS NOEL BURKE-; see BURKE-GAFFNEY

GAGAI, KAPIU MASI (c.1894-1946), pearler, boatman, mission worker, carpenter and soldier, was born about 1894 probably on Mabuiag Island, Torres Strait, Queensland, second son of Newa Gagai and his wife Kubi. Kapiu belonged to the Kodal (crocodile) clan and the Badu tribe, and was later adopted—in the Islander way—by a married couple No-

moa and Kaidai. Taken to Badu Island as a child, he received a basic education at the local school, religious instruction from London Missionary Society and Church of England missionaries, and was trained as a carpenter. From the age of about 15 he worked as a swimmer-diver, sailing in the Islander-owned pearling lugger, *Wakaid*.

On 22 December 1915 at Bethlehem Church, Badu, Gagai married with Anglican rites a local woman Laina Getawan (d.1923), daughter of Getawan and Dabangai; they were to have three daughters. In June 1921 Rev. James Watson recruited him to join the staff of (South) Goulburn Island (Methodist) Mission, Northern Territory, as a boat captain and lay mission worker. Gagai's wife and children accompanied him there. He later worked at Milingimbi Mission. At Goulburn Island Mission on 26 October 1929 he married Mujerambi (Marjorie), daughter of Alfred Joseph Voules Brown, trepanger and trader, and Mumuludj, an Iwaidja-speaking Aborigine; Kapiu and Mujerambi were to have ten children.

In April 1932 Gagai took his family back to Badu where he was employed as a carpenter and went to sea in another Islander-owned pearling lugger. The anthropologist Donald Thomson [q.v.] hired him in May 1935 to take charge of the auxiliary ketch, *St Nicholas*, which he sailed off Arnhem Land. Thomson named Kapiu Point, near the entrance to the Koolatong River, in his honour, but this name has not been officially recognized. When Thomson left the Territory in 1937, Gagai resumed his former occupations at Badu before operating a punt for the Queensland Main Roads Commission.

Despite being over-age and classified as medically unfit, he enlisted in the Australian Military Forces on 27 October 1941 and immediately joined the 7th Military District's Special Reconnaissance Unit, commanded by Thomson. Gagai was boatswain of the unit's armed vessel, *Aroetta*, which patrolled the coast of Arnhem Land in 1942-43. He was twice placed in charge of an outpost at Caledon Bay, became an expert Vickers-gunner and was promoted acting sergeant. In recommending him for a decoration, Thomson praised his sense of responsibility, devotion to duty, leadership, loyalty, unselfishness and the example he set for others. The unit was disbanded in mid-1943 and Gagai was posted to the Torres Strait Light Infantry Battalion on Thursday Island.

In late 1943 he was seconded to the 11th Infantry Brigade and took part in a hazardous expedition led by Thomson in Netherlands New Guinea. Thomson subsequently wrote:

I well remember the quiet, steadfast courage of Sergeant Kapiu ... [who] was a first-class waterman. He was strong and he had no nerves. He could work and when the tension was over he could sleep like a log. He did not fret and worry and waste nervous energy . . . He was powerful—massive is a better word —impassive; even stolid. But he could laugh —a laugh halfway between the angels and Rabelais.

Thomson, Gagai and another soldier were wounded when New Guineans attacked the party close to Japanese outposts on the Eilanden River. After recovering in hospital at Merauke from a deep machete cut to his neck, Gagai returned to Thursday Island. From January 1944 he was with No.14 Australian Small Ship Company, supervising Islander and Aboriginal soldiers, and occasionally piloting small craft in Torres Strait and around Cape York. He served in the Torres Strait Light Infantry Battalion from March 1945 until he was discharged on 28 March 1946.

Gagai was 'a loyal churchman' and a chorister who loved his people's traditional songs and dances. Big and strong, he was kind, patient and wise, and greatly respected by the Islanders, Aborigines and White Australians who knew him. He spoke Kala Lagaw Ya, English and some Aboriginal languages, and had a detailed knowledge of Torres Strait waters and the coasts of Cape York and Arnhem Land. Like other Islanders in the A.M.F., he did not receive the same pay and conditions as his White counterparts. Gagai died of lobar pneumonia on 21 August 1946 at Thursday Island and was buried in Badu Island cemetery. His wife and seven of their children survived him, as did two daughters of his first marriage.

L. Lamilami, *Lamilami Speaks* (Syd, 1974); J. Beckett, *Torres Strait Islanders* (Canb, 1987); *Geog J*, 119, pt 1, Mar 1953; J. Rich, Sergeant Kapiu (ms held by author, Epping, Syd); D. Thomson papers (Museum of Vic *and* Mrs D. Thomson, Eltham, Melb); Methodist Overseas Mission records, Northern Australia papers (ML); AWM 54, item 741/5/9 (AWM); information from Mrs B. Sagigi and Ms D. Alexander, Cairns, Mr W. Nona and Mr Y. Panuel, Badu Island, Qld, and the late Mr N. Mast.   JENNY RICH

GAIR, VINCENT CLARE (CLAIR) (1901-1980), railway clerk and premier, was born on 25 February 1901 at Rockhampton, Queensland, eighth child of John Alexander Gair, a prison warder from Scotland, and his wife Catherine Mary, née Maguire (d.1950), a nurse from Ireland. Catherine became prominent in local politics as a supporter of the fledgling Labor Party and young Vince often accompanied her to political meetings. Edu-cated at Leichhardt State School and St Joseph's Christian Brothers' College, Rockhampton, in January 1916 he followed his brother Joseph into the Queensland Railways and was employed as a clerk on £48 per annum. The family moved to South Brisbane that year. Gair was allowed a transfer and was to remain in the railways for sixteen years. He joined the Australian Labor Party, held branch office, and served as a campaign director in State and local government elections. For recreation he played Rugby League football. On 14 July 1924 at St Mary's Catholic Church, South Brisbane, he married a 31-year-old clerk, Florence Glynn, whose death on 29 October 1929 left him deeply depressed. He returned to his parents' home with his young daughter Gloria; she suffered from epilepsy and was to die in 1941.

Increasingly dissatisfied with his post and resenting lack of promotion, Gair turned his ambitions to a political career. In 1931, after a robust pre-selection, he became Labor's candidate for the Legislative Assembly seat of South Brisbane. Next year he defeated the attorney-general N. F. Macgroarty [q.v.10] and entered parliament at the age of 31. Because he was outside the Australian Workers' Union coterie which dominated Queensland Labor politics in the 1930s, Gair did not benefit from the patronage of Premier William Forgan Smith [q.v.11] and spent a decade on the back-bench. He was regarded as a good parliamentary performer, but made relatively few speeches, preferring to minister to his economically depressed electorate. Although he was elected caucus secretary in 1935 and was appointed chairman of committees in 1941, he was not prominent in the A.L.P. organization and did not become a member of the Queensland Central Executive until 1944. Impatient at being excluded from the ministry, Gair considered joining the Royal Australian Air Force in early 1942, but on 16 September was appointed secretary for mines in F. A. Cooper's [q.v.13] government. When the former premier Forgan Smith congratulated him and declared that it had always been his intention to promote him to cabinet, Gair bluntly replied, 'Well you took long enough, you old bugger'. Gair was secretary for mines until 15 May 1947 and held the additional portfolio of labour and employment (labour and industry from 1947) from 27 April 1944 until 10 May 1950.

On 27 December 1944 at the Church of the Holy Spirit, New Farm, Gair had married Ellen (Nell) Mary Sexton; she had recently been in a religious Order before taking a job as a clerk. While some conservative Catholics were scandalized, Archbishop (Sir) James Duhig [q.v.8] wrote to Gair in March 1945 denying he had ever declared that he would not marry them and wishing them both well. In

1953, when proposing the Gairs for a private audience with Pope Pius XII, Duhig described them as 'excellent Catholics'.

In January 1948 Gair had been proud to introduce a 40-hour week for the majority of workers in Queensland. Yet, during the meat-workers' (1946) and railwaymen's (1948) strikes, he urged a confrontationist strategy against the militant unions and in cabinet supported declarations of a state of emergency. In negotiations with employers and unions, Premier E. M. Hanlon [q.v.] overshadowed his labour minister who, unlike Hanlon, had never held senior office in a trade union. The unexpected defeat of E. J. Walsh [q.v.] at the general election in 1947 enabled Gair to contest the deputy-premiership. He won by one vote—a victory which was to change the course of Queensland politics. On 10 May 1950 Gair became treasurer. He acted as premier during the ailing Hanlon's absences, successfully representing the State at a premiers' conference and loan council meeting. When Hanlon died in office on 15 January 1952, the governor Sir John Lavarack [q.v.] asked Acting-Premier Gair whether he could form a new administration. After consulting his cabinet colleagues, but not caucus, he replied in the affirmative and was sworn in as premier on 17 January 1952.

Electorally popular, Gair won the 1953 and 1956 elections by handsome margins. The first three years of his premiership were placid: his standing in the party was high, industrial conflict had waned, economic conditions had stabilized and the Opposition was weak. In 1953 he and his wife travelled to England for the coronation of Queen Elizabeth II, and Gair attended important sugar-industry negotiations. Despite his attachment to Ireland, he was such a staunch monarchist that he shipped home the chairs which he and Nell had been allocated for the coronation in Westminster Abbey.

Gair's last two years in office were traumatic, and culminated in his dramatic expulsion from the A.L.P. in 1957. As premier, he had been keen to break the longstanding hegemony of the Australian Workers' Union within the A.L.P. At the same time, he also attempted to restrict the influence of the A.W.U.'s traditional opponents—the left-wing Trades and Labor Council and its affiliated unions. To achieve his ends, Gair tried to use the right-wing A.L.P. industrial groups which had been established in Queensland in 1946 to fight communism in the union movement. The battle for control of the A.L.P. was waged both within and outside the party. Gair's relationship with the A.W.U., and especially its secretary R. J. J. Bukowski [q.v.13], degenerated to such an extent that the union eventually formed an unholy alliance with the T.L.C. to bring him down. The

issue around which the anti-Gair forces coalesced was the decision of the 1956 Labor in Politics Convention to direct the government to legislate during the next session of parliament to extend three weeks annual leave to all workers under State awards. Gair resisted the demand, both on the grounds of economy and because it was constitutionally improper for the convention to determine the timetable of government legislation.

Following a year of intense conflict and complex political manoeuvrings, Gair was summoned to appear before the Q.C.E. on 24 April 1957 to show cause why he should not be expelled from the party for failing to give effect to a conference resolution. Despite a skilful and impressive self-defence, he was expelled; the vote was 35 to 30. He secured the unqualified support of all his ministers, save deputy-premier J. E. Duggan, then made an unsuccessful attempt to negotiate a coalition with the Country Party leader (Sir) Francis Nicklin [q.v.]. Gair gathered his supporters into the Queensland Labor Party which, with twenty-five members, was the largest single parliamentary party, but his government was defeated over a supply bill on 12 June 1957. In the elections on 3 August a coalition of Country and Liberal parties ended more than a quarter-century of continuous Labor rule. Gair retained his South Brisbane seat, but lost it to the A.L.P. in May 1960. As a former public servant, he was entitled to seek reinstatement and in October was appointed a liaison officer in the Department of Labour and Industry, with a salary of £2500 per annum, plus expenses. He resigned in 1961 to stand for the Senate. Unsuccessful, he was again reinstated and again resigned to contest the Senate election in December 1964. Having won, he attained the leadership of the Democratic Labor Party (with which the Q.L.P. had merged in 1962) by outmanoeuvring the Victorian senator, F. P. V. McManus.

The Liberal-Country Party coalition's majority afforded him little opportunity in the Senate to press the D.L.P.'s family-oriented domestic policies or its stridently anti-communist foreign policy. Gair's early speeches concentrated on the alleged inequities of Federal funding for the States, particularly Queensland. In 1967 he combined with the rebel Liberal senator R. C. Wright to draft the 'No' case against a referendum proposal to break the nexus provision in the Australian Constitution (section 24) governing the size of the Senate and House of Representatives. Gair regarded the defeat of the referendum in May 1967 as a major achievement. He and McManus were joined by two new D.L.P. senators (J. A. Little from Victoria and C. B. Byrne from Queensland) in the elections that year and the party secured the balance of power in the upper chamber. This development, combined with the perceived importance to the coalition of D.L.P. second preferences in elections for the House of Representatives, greatly enhanced Gair's status. He clearly relished his influence, regularly harrying the government on such issues as increased postal charges and controversial 'V.I.P.' flights, and vilifying the A.L.P. for what he saw as its communist sympathies. In 1968 he thwarted Prime Minister (Sir) John Gorton's attempt to call an early election and in 1969 forced the government to harden its stance on Soviet influence in the Indian Ocean.

Australia's involvement in the Vietnam War assisted Gair in advocating the D.L.P.'s hawkish policy on forward defence, which included the acquisition of nuclear weapons. The D.L.P. reached the zenith of its influence in 1970 when a fifth senator (J. T. Kane from New South Wales) was elected. Thereafter the party went into decline. The visit to China in 1971 of President Richard M. Nixon of the United States of America, and the election of the Whitlam Labor government in December 1972 indicated a changing political climate, to which the D.L.P. failed to adapt. Despite his reputation as a skilful and pugnacious campaigner, Gair performed poorly at the 1972 elections. D.L.P. strategists severely misread the mood of the public and claimed that a Labor victory would open the floodgates of pornography and pollute Australian society. With his earthy humour and coarse language, Gair was not a credible advocate for such a campaign and was ridiculed in the media. Although the D.L.P. retained its position and numbers in the Senate, he became alienated from his colleagues who were embarrassed by his aggressiveness and heavy drinking. He compounded his problems by regularly criticizing the Liberals' leader (Sir) Billy Snedden who, he alleged, was incapable of leading a 'flock of homing pigeons'. In January 1973 Gair told the D.L.P. federal executive that he intended to stand down, but vacillated before succumbing to intense pressure from his colleagues. Citing ill health as the reason, he resigned as leader on 10 October 1973 and declared that he would retire when his Senate term expired in 1976.

To improve Labor's chances of winning an additional Queensland seat in the Senate, Prime Minister Whitlam recommended Gair for appointment as ambassador to the Republic of Éire. Gair delayed his formal resignation and (Sir) Joh Bjelke Petersen, the premier of Queensland, confounded Whitlam's scheme by advising the governor to issue writs for five rather than six Senate places. On 1 April 1974 an embittered Gair was appointed ambassador by his erstwhile political enemies, and was expelled from the D.L.P. The en-

suing storm of protest provided a pretext for the coalition and the D.L.P. to try to block supply in the Senate. Whitlam countered by obtaining a double dissolution. At the polls on 18 May the government was returned and all four remaining D.L.P. senators were defeated.

During the political furore, Gair had left on 2 May to take up his appointment, which proved a disaster. The feisty ex-Senator was not suited to diplomacy. He refused his officials' advice, antagonized the Irish Department of Foreign Affairs and his fellow heads of mission, and addressed the British ambassador as 'You old bugger'; his inappropriate behaviour also led to the resignation of some female members of staff. Moreover, he persisted in making public comments on Australian domestic politics. The coalition was finally provoked when he repeated his criticisms of Snedden; Andrew Peacock, minister for foreign affairs in the new Malcolm Fraser administration, recalled him on 21 January 1976. In an angry response, Gair rhetorically asked if this was the thanks he got for having kept the Liberals in power. He returned to Brisbane on 12 March and withdrew from public life. Survived by his wife and their two sons, he died on 11 November 1980 in South Brisbane; he was accorded a state funeral and was buried in Nudgee cemetery. Vince Gair was above all a controversial figure. Rotund, chubby faced, 5 ft 6 ins (168 cm) tall and 'invincibly amiable', he was nicknamed 'Friar Tuck'. While never a great policy innovator, in his prime he was a consummate political tactician and negotiator who 'could be wilful, impatient and . . . arbitrary'.

F. Mines, *Gair* (Canb, 1975); D. J. Murphy et al (eds), *Labor in Power* (Brisb, 1980); B. J. Costar, 'Vince Gair' in D. J. Murphy et al (eds), *The Premiers of Queensland* (Brisb, 1990); *PD* (Senate), 3 Apr, 8 Apr 1974; *Telegraph* (Brisb), 26 Jan 1952, 13, 14 Jan 1977, 16 Nov 1980; *Nation* (Syd), 16 Apr 1966; *Australian*, 4 Apr 1974; *National Times*, 11 Oct 1981; Gair papers (NL); Trades and Labour Council of Queensland, Minutes, 1950-57 (Fryer Memorial L); Qld Parliamentary Labor Party, Caucus Minutes, 1952-57 (Parliament House, Brisb); family information.   B. J. COSTAR

GALEA, PERCIVAL JOHN (1910-1977), gambler and illegal casino operator, was born on 26 October 1910 at Musta, Malta, one of four children of John Galea, later a railway fettler, and his second wife Mary, née Saliba. John had had six children by his first marriage. The family emigrated to Sydney about 1912, settling at Woolloomooloo. By 1924 Perce was a newsboy outside Central Railway Station and already betting in threepences. He started as a milkman with the New South

Wales Fresh Food & Ice Co. Ltd at Ultimo in 1926 and was eventually employed as a driver. Advised by Rodney Dangar, a customer, to back his horse Peter Pan in the 1934 Melbourne Cup, Galea won £150. At St Mary's Cathedral, Sydney, on 18 February 1933 he had married Beryl Catherine Jones. By 1939 he was working as a wharf labourer.

During and after World War II, when Sydney was teeming with British and American sailors, Galea operated as a registered bookmaker at the Wentworth Park greyhound races and ran baccarat schools with Samuel Lee [q.v.] and Sid Kelly, 'a notorious criminal'. About 1949 Galea invested £2500 in Lee Enterprise Pty Ltd and was made a director; he worked at Sammy Lee's Theatre Restaurant as a host and staff supervisor. In evidence given in 1952 to the royal commission of inquiry into the liquor laws (1951-54), he admitted to buying beer on the black market.

Notwithstanding the royal commission, Galea became co-proprietor and manager of the Roslyn Social Club, Elizabeth Bay. Husky voiced, with a crooked smile, he catered for the well-to-do and averred that only legal card games were played. On 22 March 1953 the police raided the premises and arrested forty-six baccarat gamblers, among them Jack Davey [q.v.13]. Galea was fined £75 for occupying a common gaming-house and thereafter took 'appropriate steps'. Once the police cooperated by giving advance warning before a raid, he could afford to invest in expensive fixtures such as roulette wheels. He remained untroubled by the authorities, save for the Department of Taxation: in 1970 he was named in the taxation commissioner's report to parliament and penalized for understating his income by £49 964 between 1955 and 1963.

From the mid-1950s Galea had also run the Victoria Club, Kings Cross, which moved nearby and was renamed the Forbes Club in 1967. The casino 'offered baccarat, roulette, blackjack and craps, free food and alcohol, and a bevy of glamorous hostesses in skimpy evening dresses who doubled as late night escorts'. It was a fashionable place to be seen for show-business personalities, sportsmen, leading politicians and lawyers; boxers worked as doormen and there were no fights. Taking full advantage of hundreds of American servicemen in Sydney on rest-and-recreation leave from the Vietnam War, Galea and his syndicate (Eric O'Farrell, Ronald Lee and Reginald Andrews) operated other luxurious gaming-houses. The Bridge Club (1974-76) at Double Bay had weekly operating expenses of $16 000 which allegedly included $5000 in bribes paid directly to the police; it was relocated at Bondi Junction as the Telford Club (1976).

Galea had been in financial difficulties when he won £12 000 in a lottery in 1957. His flamboyant career on the turf began as his winnings snowballed. In 1961 he bought and sold his first racehorse, Sugarfoot, and soon registered his colours—black jacket with an orange Maltese cross, orange armbands and black cap. A compulsive punter, he ignored his doctors' warnings not to bet in large sums following his first heart attack in 1962. When his colt, Eskimo Prince, won the Sydney Turf Club's 1964 Golden Slipper Stakes and returned to a great reception, Galea (who had won some £33 000) scattered banknotes to the crowd. Eskimo Prince went on to win the Rosehill Guineas and the Australian Jockey Club's Sires' Produce Stakes, but Galea reputedly lost £40 000 after the horse was unplaced in the A.J.C. Derby. Betting as much as £25 000 on a single race, he was soon known as 'The Prince'. He was a suntanned man of middle height with greying hair who took pride in his appearance, owning dozens of handmade suits and pairs of shoes. His other good horses included Indian Prince, Count Rajan and Sir Serene. In 1976 he was elected a provisional member of the Australian Jockey Club.

In 1950 the Galeas had settled at Coogee. They were devout Catholics. He was generous to the Church in Sydney, a friend of Cardinal (Sir) Norman Gilroy [q.v.] and staged an annual party for crippled children. A member of Clovelly Life Saving Club, he swam daily—winter and summer—and was a handball champion for seventeen years. Galea's luck held. He and his family shared the $200 000 Sydney Opera House lottery prize in 1975. To the end of his life he enjoyed a cup of tea, and watching boxing at the Stadium and games of Rugby League.

Galea died of coronary heart disease on 14 August 1977 at St Vincent's Hospital, Darlinghurst, and was buried in Botany cemetery. His wife and two sons survived him; she inherited his estate, sworn for probate at $422 952. Although Galea was a warm-hearted friend, 'adored by punters, esteemed by the press . . . his reputation also instilled fear into bookmakers, bad debtors and underworld operatives'. In 1985 it was alleged that the illegal casinos had 'provided colossal cash flows to the underworld and enabled organised crime to consolidate its power' in Sydney.

Royal Commission of Inquiry into the Liquor Laws and Allied Subjects: Minutes of Evidence, 2 (Syd, 1954); D. Hickie, *The Prince and the Premier* (Syd, 1985); E. Whitton, *Can of Worms* (Syd, 1986); *SMH*, 23 Oct 1970, 23 Nov 1975; *Herald* (Melb), 4 Aug 1977, 22 Oct 1982; *National Times*, 4 Jan 1981.
                                    MARTHA RUTLEDGE

GALLARD, MARK EDWARD (1899-1971), journalist and newspaper executive, was born on 29 April 1899 at Marsfield, Sydney, fifth of twelve children (nine of them boys) of native-born parents Silas James Gallard, orchardist, and his wife Lucy, née Hicks. The children grew up on the family's virtually self-sufficient 15-acre (6 ha) farm. On leaving Ryde Public School, Mark helped in the orchard and joined the Militia in 1916. Transferring to the Australian Imperial Force on 8 February 1918, he was posted to the 35th Battalion on 20 October, and spent nine months in France and England. He was discharged in Sydney on 8 October 1919 and found work as a clerk. His eldest brother Bertram had died from wounds in 1915; his youngest brother Clive was to be killed in action in Malaya in 1942.

Against his parents' wishes (as his fiancée was not a Baptist), on 16 July 1921 Gallard married Emily Young (d.1981) at the Baptist manse, Lewisham. In the 1920s he began reporting on sporting events and identities for Sydney newspapers, and contributed twenty-one episodes of a serial, 'The Millionaire Schoolboy', to the *Boys Weekly* in 1927. Having been news editor of the *Daily Telegraph Pictorial*, he was hired by Ezra Norton [q.v.] in 1933 as editor of the weekly newspaper, *Truth*. It had built its reputation on a recipe of sport, crime, scandal and prurient court cases.

Gallard widened the paper's appeal with more family features, but Norton (who had a sharp, often foul tongue and was given to bullying his staff) ensured that its raciness continued. In May 1935 the Full Court fined the company £200 and Gallard £50 for contempt of court over *Truth*'s publication of a picture of the alleged murderer in the celebrated 'Shark arm case'. Gallard's counsel (Sir) William Owen [q.v.] argued in mitigation that it 'was not always easy for an editor to carry out his employer's policy'. *Truth*'s sales increased from 196 000 in 1932 to 248 000 in 1938. In the latter year Gallard was appointed a director of Truth and Sportsman Ltd and sent on an eight-month world tour to help plan a new afternoon daily.

His work ensured the successful launching on 12 May 1941 of the *Daily Mirror*, a rival to the *Sun*. As editor-in-chief, Gallard exchanged active journalism for management; as Norton's right-hand man, he proved a loyal, competent and steadying influence. Norton trusted him to ensure that his editorial policies were carried out and that business matters requiring political support were tactfully handled. While he suffered under the unpleasant side of Norton's personality and attempted to shield the staff from its excesses, he genuinely respected Norton's independence, drive and expertise. The long and effective association with Norton was the major accomplishment of Gallard's career.

Like his chief, Gallard was a private man. A stocky 5 ft 6 ins (168 cm), with brown hair and deep brown eyes, and a heavy smoker, he kept his own counsel and was always polite and quietly spoken. Less well known was that he was generous to anybody in need and a dedicated family man, whom his growing son found 'more like a brother than a father'. Errol Coote, a *Truth* colleague, dedicated his book, *Hell's Airport* (1934), to Mark Gallard, 'One of the Whitest Men I Know'. Ion Idriess [q.v.9], another friend, regularly inscribed copies of his new books to him.

Following his retirement in 1955, Gallard remained on the board until 1958, when to his bitter disappointment Norton unexpectedly sold out to a company controlled by John Fairfax & Sons [qq.v.4,8] Pty Ltd. Gallard sometimes spoke of writing his memoirs, but lost interest in the idea. Survived by his wife and son, he died on 27 January 1971 at Ryde and was cremated with Anglican rites.

E. Baume, *I've Lived Another Year* (Lond, 1942); W. Olson, *Baume, Man and Beast* (Syd, 1967); *Newspaper News*, June 1935, Mar and Nov 1938; *SMH*, 25 May 1935; *Sunday Mirror* (Syd), 31 Jan 1971; information from Messrs K. Gallard, West Pennant Hills, G. Reading, Castle Hill, T. J. Gurr, Turramurra, Syd, and C. Buttrose, Lindfield, NSW.   STUART INDER

GALLEGHAN, Sir FREDERICK GALLAGHER (1897-1971), army officer and public servant, was born on 11 January 1897 at Jesmond, New South Wales, son of native-born parents Alexander Dunlop Galleghan, crane driver, and his wife Martha, née James. Educated at Cooks Hill Superior Public School, Newcastle, Frederick was a studious lad. In August 1912 he joined the Postmaster-General's Department as a telegraph messenger; fascinated by all things military, he resolved that he would one day exchange his red cap for that of a senior army officer.

After seven years in the cadets, on 20 January 1916 Galleghan enlisted in the Australian Imperial Force. Posted as a corporal to the 34th Battalion, he sailed for England in May. Six months later he was promoted sergeant and sent to the Western Front. Twice wounded in action (June 1917 and August 1918), he was invalided home and discharged medically unfit on 3 March 1919. That he had been denied a commission in the A.I.F. put a chip on his shoulder which gave rise to a tendency to ride rough-shod over officers junior to himself.

At the Baptist Tabernacle, Cooks Hill, on

18 November 1922 Galleghan married a theatre employee Vera Florence Dawson (d.1967); they were to remain childless. Having been employed on clerical duties in the post office, in 1926 he transferred to the Department of Trade and Customs, and in 1936 to the investigation branch of the Commonwealth Attorney-General's Department, Sydney. In September 1919 he had been gazetted temporary lieutenant in the Militia. A lieutenant colonel by 1932, he successively led the 2nd-41st, 2nd-35th and 17th battalions. He joined the A.I.F. on 18 March 1940 and on 17 October was appointed commanding officer of the 2nd/30th Battalion, 8th Division.

Galleghan wanted his battalion to be, and to be seen to be, the embodiment of all that was finest in the Australian army. To achieve his aim, he ordered strenuous training and spared no one—officers, men, or himself. In July 1941 the unit sailed for Singapore. On 14 January 1942 at Gemas, Malaya, Galleghan conducted a brilliant ambush of a superior Japanese force. For his part in the encounter and the subsequent well-executed withdrawal, he was awarded the Distinguished Service Order. He became a prisoner of war when the British surrendered on 15 February. With the removal of senior officers from Singapore in August, he assumed command of the A.I.F.; from March 1944 he was deputy commander of all allied prisoners in Malaya. It was for his role at Changi that he was to achieve lasting fame.

Known as 'Black Jack' because of his dark complexion, black hair and piercing brown eyes, Galleghan was a formidable figure, six feet (183 cm) tall, erect, and with a rock-like countenance. His stern expression and military bearing radiated an aura of command. One junior officer represented many when he wrote: 'We were far more frightened of "B.J." than of the Japanese'. 'His personality', said another, 'left no room for half measures. He did not necessarily seek your regard or goodwill'. Somewhat surprisingly, his harsh discipline earned him the affectionate respect of his men and the grudging admiration even of those who felt the full weight of the occasionally unreasonable exercise of his authority.

Galleghan realized that survival depended on morale and that discipline was the basis of morale. His strict orders—thought by some to border on the absurd for a prisoner-of-war camp—saved countless lives. It was his fate to be remembered most for what he valued least. 'You are not going home as prisoners', he barked in his husky voice, 'you will march down Australian streets as soldiers'. Back home in October 1945, he refused to associate with prisoner-of-war organizations and urged his old battalion to follow his example.

In taking this stand he probably did the survivors of the 8th Division a disservice.

Mentioned in dispatches, Galleghan was promoted colonel and temporary brigadier (with effect from April 1942) before he transferred to the Retired List on 3 January 1946. In the following year he was appointed O.B.E. He had been raised to inspector (1945) in the investigation service and in 1947 became deputy-director, in charge of the Sydney office. In 1948-49, as honorary major general, he headed the Australian Military Mission to Germany. Displaying an unexpected gift for diplomacy, he chaired the fourth session of the general council of the International Refugee Organization, served on its executive-committee and helped displaced persons to emigrate to Australia. On his retirement from the public service in 1959 he was appointed I.S.O. He was honorary secretary (1959-70) of the Royal Humane Society of New South Wales, State chairman (from 1963) of the Services Canteens Trust Fund and an honorary colonel (1959-64) of the Australian Cadet Corps.

'Black Jack' always remained the battalion commander, even wearing a miniature colour patch of the 2nd/30th on his major general's uniform. He had a softer side which, for the most part, he took pains to conceal: when his men returned to Changi from the Burma-Thailand Railway he had been so moved by the toll of death and the desperate condition of those huddled before him that he was unable to speak and in tears marched silently between their lines. In 1969 he was knighted for his services to war veterans. On 8 December that year at St Clement's Anglican Church, Mosman, he married a widow and State commandant of the Voluntary Aid Service Corps, Persia Elspbeth Porter, née Blaiklock; Sir Frederick's old soldiers showed their pleasure by calling him 'The Shah of Persia'. Survived by his wife, he died on 20 April 1971 at his Mosman home and was cremated with Anglican rites.

A. W. Penfold et al, *Galleghan's Greyhounds* (Syd, 1949); L. Wigmore, *The Japanese Thrust* (Canb, 1957); S. Arneil, *Black Jack* (Melb, 1983); E. E. Dunlop, *The War Diaries of Weary Dunlop* (Melb, 1986); P. Adam-Smith, *Prisoners of War* (Melb, 1992); *As You Were*, 1947, 1948; *People* (Syd), 30 Dec 1953; AWM records.   DAVID GRIFFIN

GALLOP, EDWARD ROBERT COWPER (1893-1969), engineer and public servant, was born on 5 June 1893 at Toowoomba, Queensland, third child of English-born parents Edward Gallop, bank accountant, and his wife Lena, née Rommett. Young Edward was educated at Sydney Church of England Grammar School (Shore) and joined the

Department of Public Works on 24 August 1911. He became a field-assistant in 1912 and was licensed as a surveyor in 1916. On 7 April 1916 he enlisted in the Australian Imperial Force. He reached England in July 1917 and served in France with the 3rd Field Company, Engineers, from March 1918 to January 1919.

Discharged in Sydney on 2 June, Gallop returned to the Department of Works as a surveyor in the Murray River waters branch. In July 1921 he was promoted supervising mechanical engineer (grade 2) and transferred to water supply and sewerage. At St John's Anglican Cathedral, Brisbane, on 10 December 1928 he married Augusta Dorothy Picton Greenish, a nurse. From November 1936 he was employed as supervising local government engineer in the Department of Works and Local Government. In 1941 he was assigned to the administrative staff of the State War Effort Co-ordination Committee (which was created to speed up the production of charcoal, the base fuel for producer gas—the only effective substitute for petrol); he was also co-ordinating engineer for New South Wales (1942-45) with the Allied Works Council.

On 11 July 1945 Gallop was appointed permanent head of the Housing Commission of New South Wales, having stipulated that he bring several of his Allied Works staff with him. Hampered by persistent shortages of labour and building materials, by mid-1947 the Housing Commission had completed only a few hundred dwellings. Soon after his appointment, the first Commonwealth and State housing agreement provided effective finance to ameliorate a shortage estimated at 69 000 dwellings in Sydney alone. Despite the Menzies [q.v.] government's preference for state-assisted home-purchase from 1949, Gallop remained convinced that there would always be a need for public housing and maintained that rental accommodation should remain the first priority.

Given the level of emergency, the aggressive and authoritarian traits ascribed to Gallop by his colleagues were appropriate for the task. Under his chairmanship the commission gained a reputation for ruthlessness, especially for impinging on planning controls of the Cumberland County Council and of various municipalities. For economy and efficiency, Gallop kept his own staff small and employed contract labour for building. He did not welcome interference and took pride in describing the commission as the first home-building organization empowered to plan every detail from land acquisition to construction. Slum clearance was the one area where he seemed unable to cut through the demands of competing vested interests.

When suspended in 1949 by the minister for housing, Clive Evatt, over the principles employed in allocating prime land, he refused to accept the decision on the ground that it had no legislative basis. Backed by Premier James McGirr [q.v.], Gallop prevailed. After attempting to abolish the commission in 1953, Evatt resigned from the Cahill [q.v.13] ministry on 1 April 1954. These events ensured the Housing Commission's bureaucratic independence from excessive political manipulation.

In housing styles Gallop appeared to favour individual brick-and-tile bungalows, but he also presided over the construction of thousands of timber and fibro cottages, as well as crisis-accommodation in converted military camps. Flats were limited to 10 per cent. Through Gallop's determination and administrative skill, 45 000 dwellings were provided by the time he retired in 1958. In that year he was appointed C.B.E. He belonged to the North Sydney Bowling, Royal Automobile and Schools clubs, and enjoyed fishing. Survived by his wife and son, Gallop died on 12 June 1969 at his Cremorne home and was cremated.

NSW Housing Com, *Homes for the People* (Syd, 1947) and *Housing in New South Wales* (Syd, 1957) and *Annual Report*, 1942-62; J. Roe (ed), *Twentieth Century Sydney* (Syd, 1980); M. Kelly (ed), *Sydney, City of Suburbs* (Syd, 1987); Cwlth Housing Com, *Final Report*, 25 Aug 1944; *NSW Contract Reporter*, 74, no 28, 9 July 1969, p 5; *Aust J of Administration*, Sept 1989; *SMH*, 10 Dec 1936, 3 Mar 1942, 7 June 1945, 13 June 1947, 8, 9, 16, 17 June, 8 Sept, 19, 20, 27 Oct, 5 Nov 1949, 8 July 1953, 4 May 1955, 21 Feb 1957, 31 May, 12 June, 16 Oct 1958.

ROSEMARY BROOMHAM

GALVIN, LESLIE WILLIAM (1903-1966), politician, was born on 30 April 1903 at Woollahra, Sydney, son of native-born parents Leslie Arthur Galvin, commercial clerk, and his wife Ethel, née Tisdale. Educated at Petersham Commercial School and, after his family moved to Melbourne, at Scotch College, Hawthorn, Bill was apprenticed in the Victorian Railways as a fitter and turner. In 1929 he transferred to the Bendigo railway workshops where he took an active interest in trade union affairs, becoming president of the local branch of the Australian Railways Union and twice president of the Bendigo Trades Hall Council. On 9 April 1932 at her Preston home he married with Presbyterian forms Annie Edith Ruby, a clerk.

In 1939 Galvin was elected to the Bendigo City Council. Mayor in 1944 and 1945, he continued to live in a small, four-roomed weatherboard house in a working-class suburb. He resigned from the council in 1952. About that time a journalist reported: 'He smokes, likes a beer, has a bet now and then and is a keen sport'. Galvin played interstate cricket for the railways in his youth and claimed that he bowled a fair googly. In later life he was president of the Golden Square Football and the Commonwealth Athletic clubs, and of the Bendigo Athletic Carnival. In addition, he played A-grade pennant bowls and was a keen golfer. For an aspiring local politician, this involvement in sport was a decided benefit in a provincial community. His wife also took a keen interest in local affairs and was a special magistrate of the Children's Court.

Galvin's preference was to enter Federal parliament, but in 1945 his friend John Cain [q.v.13] convinced him to stand for the Legislative Assembly in a by-election for Bendigo. At the declaration of the polls on 29 May, Galvin assured Bendigo's electors that he would work for all residents, not merely Labor voters. In 1945-47 he was given the chance to do so as president of the board of land and works, commissioner of crown lands and minister of water supply. A staunch supporter of country interests, he energetically promoted soldier-settlement schemes and the extension of irrigation projects, and saw work commence on the Cairn Curran and Rocklands dams.

Following the Cain government's defeat in November 1947, Galvin was elected deputy-leader of the Opposition. He continued to advance country interests and in 1951 sat on the select committee which investigated the Egg and Egg Pulp Marketing Board. When Labor was returned in December 1952, Galvin became chief secretary and deputy-premier, defeating W. P. Barry [q.v.13] and S. M. Keon for the latter position. Next year he was acting-premier while Cain attended the coronation of Queen Elizabeth II. During the Labor Party split, Galvin remained loyal to the traditional party. Learning that Cain favoured A. E. Shepherd [q.v.] as his successor, Galvin shifted his support in caucus and cabinet from Cain to Barry. After a bitter campaign, Galvin lost the seat of Bendigo by twelve votes in 1955. The defeat robbed him of one chance to lead the Labor Party.

On Cain's death in 1957, Shepherd became leader of the Opposition. Although Galvin regained Bendigo in 1958, his leadership ambitions suffered a further blow that year when he was injured in a motorcar accident a few days before the vote that made C. P. Stoneham the successor to Shepherd. Galvin continued to support country interests, and in 1959-62 sat on the distribution of population committee. In 1964 he retired from parliament due to ill health. He died of hepatic cirrhosis on 1 July 1966 at Bendigo and was cremated; his wife and two sons survived him.

Jovial, bald and bespectacled, Bill Galvin

was a large man with a raucous laugh. He was a keen interjector in the House, but opponents agreed that his interjections were made in a friendly vein, and that he could take a knock as well as give one. Sir Henry Bolte said of him: 'I often wondered whether Bill Galvin was Bendigo or Bendigo was Bill Galvin'.

R. Murray, *The Split* (Melb, 1970); K. White, *John Cain and Victorian Labor 1917-1957* (Syd, 1982); *PD* (Vic), 7 Sept 1966, p 41; *Labor Call*, 4 Dec 1947; *Age* (Melb), 9 Jan 1953, 2 July 1966; *Argus*, 17 Aug 1953; *Sun News-Pictorial*, 2 July 1966.   CHARLES FAHEY

GALWAY, MARIE CAROLA FRANCISCA ROSELYNE (1876-1963), charity and civic worker, and governor's wife, was known by those Christian names, although at her birth on 5 January 1876 at Mayfair, London, she was registered as Mary Charlotte Frances Roslyne. She was the only daughter of two leaders of the English liberal Catholic movement, Sir Rowland Blennerhassett, Irish baronet and parliamentarian, and his wife Countess Charlotte Julia de Leyden, a biographer and historian from Bavaria. Marie Carola attended private schools and convents in Bavaria, France and Switzerland, and read extensively in six languages. On 28 November 1894 she married Baron Raphael d'Erlanger (d.1897), a French biologist who built his own laboratories at the University of Heidelberg; they were to have a daughter and a son. Returning to England, the baroness worked for the sick and destitute, helping to found (and later chairing) a committee which advised on proposed parliamentary legislation affecting women or children.

On 26 August 1913 in the Royal Bavarian Chapel, London, she married Sir Henry Lionel Galway [q.v.8]. Six weeks later he was appointed governor of South Australia and took office on 18 April 1914. Lady Galway's gifts as a public speaker were soon appreciated throughout the State. She inaugurated the Adelaide branch of the Alliance Française, and gave literary and historical talks to the Poetry Recital Society, the Victoria League in South Australia and kindred bodies. Rapt audiences thronged her lectures on modern languages at the universities of Adelaide and Melbourne. Lady Stanley, wife of the governor of Victoria, thought her 'a *wonder*' because she could discourse on '*any* subject—religious, philosophical, political, artistic or scientific'. Lady Galway supported children's hospitals and orphanages, the District Trained Nursing Society and the Young Women's Christian Association. She apologized for being 'more of a slavedriver than a patroness', but her enthusiasm, new ideas, friendly manner and willingness to shoulder some of the burdens won admiration. She inspired the South Australian Catholic Women's League to seek greater public recognition and did much to make Catholics more socially acceptable in Australia's most Protestant State.

At the request of Lady Helen Munro Ferguson [q.v.10], the wife of the governor-general, in August 1914 Lady Galway founded the South Australian division of the British Red Cross Society; it was to assist the sick and wounded, and establish a missing persons bureau. She directed this organization until 1919, as she did the Belgian Relief Fund for which she produced the *Lady Galway Belgium Book* (1916). Founding president of the League of Loyal Women, a body that supplied comforts for servicemen, she also persuaded the Institute of Accountants in South Australia to train sixty female book-keepers as temporary replacements for male clerks who had enlisted. Despite her husband's zeal in fomenting hysteria against Australians of German descent, no one seemed to mind that she was half German. She travelled widely, addressed hundreds of meetings, wrote thousands of letters and helped to raise over £1 200 000 for patriotic causes. For her efforts she was awarded the Belgian médaille de la Reine Elisabeth and the médaille de la Reconnaissance Française, and was appointed dame of grace of the Order of St John and C.B.E. (1926). Before her departure in January 1919 (fifteen months ahead of her husband) the State's women war-workers gave her a diamond and opal necklace. Adelaide's leader-writers noted that her arresting personality, untiring activity and oratorical power had enabled her to exercise a real influence over the trend of public thought, and that she had 'raised the whole status of women in public life'.

Back in Britain, Lady Galway resumed her former duties. She chaired the Mothercraft Training Society, the Consultative Committee of Women's Organisations and the women's committee (1924-25) of the British Empire Exhibition, Wembley, and served on the governing bodies of hospitals, schools and universities. She contributed an essay, in which she urged women to build on the advances they had made since 1914, to *A Book of South Australia* (Adelaide, 1936) and revisited Australia in 1937-38. Her son, twice wounded in World War I, was killed in action in Libya in 1941; her husband died in 1949. Lady Galway published a memoir, *The Past Revisited* (London, 1953). Survived by her daughter, she died on 29 June 1963 at St Merryn, Cornwall. Charity workers, educationists, nurses and England's Catholic intelligentsia attended her requiem Mass at the Church of the Immaculate Conception, Farm Street, London.

P. A. Howell, 'More Varieties of Vice-Regal Life', *J of Hist Soc of SA*, 9, 1981, *and* for bibliog; *Hist Forum*, 13, no 3, Dec 1991, p 29; League of Loyal Women records, press-cuttings book, V 1294 (Mort L).
                                      P. A. HOWELL

GANDON, SYDNEY JOHN (1889-1959), banker, was born on 4 December 1889 at Glebe, Sydney, son of native-born parents Peter Joseph Gandon, general importer, and his wife Caroline Janet, née Benton. Educated at Fort Street Model School, in 1906 Sydney was employed as a probationary cashbook clerk at the head office of the Bank of New South Wales; he became a junior in the securities department and then a manager's clerk. At St James's Anglican Church, Sydney, on 3 November 1920 he married Eileen Breathour Weekes; they were to remain childless. In the 1920s he undertook a variety of tasks before being promoted to assistant to the chief inspector in 1926 and appointed a sub-inspector in 1929.

From March 1929 to June 1931 Gandon was relieving secretary in the bank's London office; from September 1931 he acted as assistant-manager until returning to Sydney in 1932. His London experience gave him a broader perspective of the Depression in Australia. As manager (1934-36) of the main Melbourne office and as inspector (1936-39) of the Victorian division, he became closely linked to policies of the bank's general manager (Sir) Alfred Davidson [q.v.8]. Like Davidson, Gandon was a strong advocate of an independent Australian central bank. He also saw a vital role for private banks in the shaping of Australia's monetary policy, especially in setting interest rates and developing lending guidelines.

On 9 October 1939 Gandon was appointed chief inspector for New South Wales. During World War II he endeavoured to ensure that the bank carefully executed government policies. By the time he became assistant general manager in 1948, the war had changed Australian banking. The Federal Labor government determined interest rates, fixed the exchange rates and controlled all movements of capital in and out of Australia. The commercial banks were required to obtain a licence, to supply the Commonwealth Bank of Australia (which served as a central bank) with detailed accounts of their activities, to maintain compulsory deposits with the central bank, and to invest in public loans or securities only with central bank consent.

In 1947 the Chifley [q.v.13] Labor government attempted to nationalize the private banks. Faced with this threat, the private banks agreed that the Bank of New South Wales should co-ordinate their campaign and challenge the validity of the Banking Act (1947) in the High Court of Australia, notably under section 92 of the Constitution. Gandon had most of the responsibility in the long legal fight which ended when the Commonwealth government's appeal was dismissed by the Privy Council on 26 July 1949.

Appointed general manager on 21 July 1950, Gandon hoped that the Liberal government headed by (Sir) Robert Menzies [q.v.], who had opposed bank nationalization, would remove the central banking functions from the Commonwealth Bank and create a new entity free from political influence. Menzies, however, believed that private banks should be strictly regulated, and continued such wartime policies as the control of interest rates and lending policies. In November 1952 Gandon criticized the government's proposed banking reforms and specifically called for a 'strong, impartial, separately constituted central bank'. He also complained that the Commonwealth Bank continued to have a competitive advantage. His statements received sharp rebuffs from the government.

Gandon began retirement leave on 1 July 1954. In December he was appointed a director of the Australian Metropolitan Life Assurance Co. Pty Ltd. He had a strong passion for things English, particularly English literature, the English language and English music. An active sportsman, he enjoyed cricket, tennis and golf. He lived at Neutral Bay and belonged to the Union and Australian clubs in Sydney, and to the Melbourne and Australian clubs in Melbourne. Survived by his wife, he died of cancer on 1 November 1959 in Royal Prince Alfred Hospital, Sydney, and was cremated; his estate was sworn for probate at £51 365.

R. F. Holder, *Bank of New South Wales* (Syd, 1970); C. B. Schedvin, *In Reserve* (Syd, 1992); *Etruscan*, 4, no 1, June 1954; *Financial Review*, 18 Oct 1951, p 23; Westpac Banking Corp Archives, Syd.   STEPHEN SALSBURY

GARD, MARGARET; see GRANDI, MARGHERITA

GARDNER, CHARLES AUSTIN (1896-1970), botanist, was born on 6 January 1896 at Gressingham, Lancashire, England, son of George William Gardner, farmer, and his wife Sarah, née Stone. In 1909 the family emigrated to Western Australia where they later selected land at Yorkrakine. Keenly interested in botany, Charles developed a deep love for the Australian bush. About the age of 19 he moved to Perth, worked for the National Bank of Australasia and studied landscape painting under J. W. Linton [q.v.10].

In the Western Australian Museum's library Gardner pored over George Bentham's [q.v.3] seven-volumed *Flora Australiensis* (London, 1863-78). Encouraged by the wildflower painter Emily Pelloe [q.v.11] and the government botanist Desmond Herbert [q.v.], he built up his own herbarium and in 1920 was appointed a collector for the Forests Department. Next year he joined an expedition to the Kimberleys which led to his *Botanical Notes* (1923); subsequent papers described and illustrated the botany of the inland Kimberley region for the first time. In 1924 he became a founding member of the Western Australian Naturalists' Club and on 1 July he transferred to the Department of Agriculture as an assistant to W. M. Carne [q.v.7] whom he succeeded as economic botanist and plant pathologist in July 1926. Gardner accepted the dual post of government botanist and curator of the State's herbarium on 1 January 1929.

An unflagging publicist, he gave radio talks, spoke at public meetings and lectured on plant systematics at the University of Western Australia from 1924 to 1962; his lectures were ideal for the student of taxonomy, but deadly dull for others. In 1930 Gardner published his *Enumeratio Plantarum Australiae Occidentalis: a systematic census of the plants occuring in Western Australia*, the only inventory available for the next fifty years. He served (1937-39) as Australian botanical liaison officer to the herbarium, Kew Gardens, London. President (1941-42) of the Royal Society of Western Australia, he was awarded its Kelvin medal in 1949. The abbot of the Benedictine monastery at New Norcia assisted him to learn Latin.

Gardner's ambition to publish a comprehensive 'Flora of Western Australia' never succeeded beyond the *Gramineae* (1952) which dealt with the grasses of the State. His perfectionism and inability to co-operate with other botanists—especially those who possessed university qualifications—provided obstacles to the huge project. A series of papers on native trees portrayed his interest in the eucalypts and in 1956 he joined the veterinarian H. W. Bennetts [q.v.13] in publishing *The Toxic Plants of Western Australia*. Gardner retired as government botanist on 5 July 1960. He was awarded the (W. B.) Clarke [q.v.3] medal of the Royal Society of New South Wales in 1961 and appointed M.B.E. in 1965. Suffering from Parkinson's disease, he died on 24 February 1970 at Subiaco and was buried in Karrakatta cemetery with Catholic rites.

Charles Gardner was an individualist who had a vast knowledge of Western Australian flora which was unfortunately not recorded. Most of his information on Latin names, geographical distribution, plant geography and the biology of the western flora died with him. His greatest legacy, apart from his publications, was the wealth of plant specimens, estimated at 9000 to 10 000, which he added to the collections to form the Western Australian Herbarium. He had also been instrumental in convincing the State government to set aside large reserves for conserving flora; one of them, near Tammin, bears his name.

J of Agr of WA, 1, no 8, Aug 1960, p 747; *Vic Naturalist*, 87, June 1970, pp 145, 173; *J of Roy Soc of WA*, 53, 1970, p 63; *WA Naturalist*, 11, no 7, Aug 1970, p 168; *Nature Walkabout*, 8, no 1, Mar 1972, p 7; WA Museum, *Your Museum*, 2, no 3, Dec 1974; *West Australian*, 6 July 1960, 18 July 1961, 25 Apr 1964, 12 June 1965, 11 Aug 1967, 26 Feb 1970, 2 Dec 1972; *Countryman* (Perth), 13 Apr 1961; *Daily News* (Perth), 25 Feb 1970; Dept of Agr of WA, List of Gardner's publications, 1923-62 (ts, Roy Botanic Gardens, Melb).

N. G. Marchant

GARGETT, THOMAS BRENAN FEMISTER (1898-1975), architect, was born on 2 May 1898 in Brisbane, eldest of four children of Queensland-born parents Alfred Thomas Gargett, postal officer, and his wife Alexandrina, née Femister. While attending Brisbane Grammar School, Brenan applied for the position of apprentice with local architects H. W. Atkinson & C. McLay that was advertised on the headmaster's door. On 22 July 1914 he joined their Adelaide Street practice, which then included A. H. Conrad [q.v.13]. As the 'pupil', Brenan learned to type letters and specifications, and used the 'horrible "letter press"' as a means of keeping records. In 1916 the partnership acquired the contract to build the Trades Hall—its first major public building—and in 1918 the firm became Atkinson & Conrad. Gargett was a student member (1917) of the Queensland Institute of Architects and won its student prize in 1919. Employed as a draftsman, he was among the first to gain a diploma of architecture (1923) from the Brisbane Central Technical College. At the Congregational Church, South Brisbane, on 17 September 1926 he married Lorna Gertrude Robertson. Three years later he registered as an architect.

Having helped to design the Church of England Grammar School buildings (1917), East Brisbane, the Congregational Church (1925), Annerley, and St Alban's (1928), Wilston, Gargett designed his family home, Nymboida, at Annerley. He considered his finest work the memorial library (1934) and studio (1936) at Somerville House Girls' School, South Brisbane. The partnership of A. H. Conrad &

T. B. F. Gargett was formed in 1939 (following Atkinson's death) and survived the uncertain building climate during World War II. In 1943-45 Gargett supervised a civilian drafting office for the Corps of Engineers, United States Army, and formed some useful connexions with the defence forces. The postwar boom brought commissions for two major hospitals, and projects for governments and various religious denominations: clients included the Brisbane and South Coast hospitals board, the Commonwealth Bank, the Anglican Church, Queensland Newspapers and the Metropolitan Fire Brigade. After Conrad's heart attack in 1952, Gargett briefly managed the office single-handed.

He was a member (1950-70) of the Commonwealth Building Research and Development Advisory Committee. In 1958 Conrad & Gargett joined six other companies as founding members of the Brisbane Development Association, initiated by Sir John Chandler [q.v.13]. Gargett's manner and philosophies determined the essentially conservative nature of the partnership which grew to be one of the largest architectural firms in Brisbane. Earnest and unwaveringly methodical, he ensured that sound and tested principles were maintained: any suggestion to incorporate flat roofs was unthinkable, as 'B.G.' insisted that 'flat roofs leak'! His colleagues and staff saw him as a practical person, thorough and fair. He was charming with clients, but his dress sense was less meticulous than his professional methods. An associate (1930), fellow (1935), president (1960-61) and life fellow (1970) of the Royal Australian Institute of Architects, he was twice president (1946-48 and 1958-60) of its Queensland chapter. Gargett died on 10 September 1975 at Toowong and was cremated; predeceased by his wife, he was survived by their two sons.

D. Watson and J. McKay, *A Directory of Queensland Architects to 1940* (Brisb, 1984); *Sunday Mail* (Brisb), 28 July 1974; *Courier-Mail*, 11 Sept 1975; Bd of Architects of Qld records (Brisb); P. Keating and G. Plunkett, History of Conrad & Gargett (unpublished notes, Conrad & Gargett Pty Ltd archives, Brisb); information from Messrs P. Gargett, D. McPhee and P. Keating, Conrad & Gargett.

R. J. Riddel

GARLAND, THOMAS (1893-1952), trade union official, was born on 1 June 1893 at Glasgow, Scotland, son of James Garland, ironworker, and his wife Agnes, née Weldon. The experience of being sent to primary school barefoot and hungry sparked Tom's determination to improve the social system and began what became a lifelong crusade.

Indentured at an early age, he first tasted trade unionism when he organized and led fellow youths in the engineering shops on Clydeside. From 1910 he was an apprentice fitter with A. & J. Inglis, engineers and shipbuilders; later that year he joined the Royal Naval Volunteer Reserve. When war broke out in August 1914 he began full-time service as an engine-room artificer, and completed his apprenticeship in that capacity. He went to sea in H.M.S. *Drake* (1914-15) and *Caroline* (1915-16), and saw action in the battle of Jutland. From November 1916 he trained boy artificers at Portsmouth, England, until invalided out of the navy on 25 September 1919.

Attracted by Australia's promise of peace and prosperity, Garland emigrated to Victoria in 1921 and worked for the State Electricity Co., first as a leading hand constructing the Yallourn to Melbourne power network, then as a fitter at the Yallourn plant. At St Brigid's Catholic Church, North Fitzroy, on 9 February 1924 he married Edith Mary Downey. A local shop steward for the Amalgamated Engineering Union, he was dismissed from his job for his part in establishing a combined unions' committee to represent the workers. With his wife he moved to Adelaide, where he worked for Holden's [q.v.9] Motor Body Builders Ltd.

In 1928 Garland gave the initial lecture at the Marx-Engels Club. Next year he was elected president of the Adelaide district committee of the A.E.U. and was its delegate to the United Trades and Labor Council of South Australia. Attracted by its promise of a better society, he joined the Communist Party of Australia and was on the council responsible for the waterside workers' strike in 1930. He was also secretary of the Unemployed Prisoners Relief Committee which assisted those arrested in the 'beef riot' of 10 January 1931. After organizing two effective strikes, he was sacked by Holden's in 1932.

Garland put his personal comfort and that of his family second to his fight for workers' rights. His struggle to achieve a better society found expression in factory-gate meetings, in pamphlets such as *Contrasts* (1932) and *The Slums of Adelaide* (1940), in newspaper articles and in radio broadcasts. Standing on a communist, socialist or independent ticket, he was defeated in elections for the House of Assembly (1933 and 1941), the House of Representatives (1934) and the Senate (1940). Although self-educated, he was a trenchant debater. His mordant wit, principled and passionate views, and oratorical skills made him an entertaining speaker. At the University of Adelaide in 1934 he debated the motion 'That in the opinion of this house Communism, so far from being a men-

ace, is a necessity to any civilised country', and lost by only seven votes.

In May 1933 Garland had become secretary of the Anti-War Council (from 1934 Council Against War and Fascism). In 1935 he was a U.T.L.C. delegate to the Australasian Council of Trade Unions congress which declared 'uncompromising hostility to capitalist wars'. Following Hitler's and Stalin's non-aggression pact in August 1939, Garland's house was raided and documents were seized. The incident in no way deterred him. At Prospect, on 26 June 1940, he addressed a meeting of the League Against Conscription, thereby contravening the regulations of the National Security Act (1939); in November he was convicted and fined. By 1942, however, after Germany had invaded Russia, and Australia was directly threatened by Japan, Garland publicly criticized opponents of conscription.

World War II applied a strong brake to industrial disputation, while providing opportunities for employers to challenge workers' wages and conditions. Meanwhile, concern that economic depression might recur with the resumption of peace led some people to plan for reconstruction. Garland directed his energies towards both issues. He fought to maintain industrial working conditions, and helped to resolve several major disputes, including those at Holden's in 1944, and the railways and tramways strikes in 1945. In the latter year he resigned from the C.P.A., citing a difference over tactics in dealing with 'liberal bourgeois organisations' as the reason. The difference arose mainly from his membership of Common Cause, a movement based on 'a common denominator of patriotism and self sacrifice' which aimed to implement a better postwar society. After Garland and the Rev. Guy Pentreath had each published his vision for the future in the Adelaide *Mail* in August 1942, Garland and J. W. Wainwright [q.v.12], with twelve others, founded the movement. Common Cause sought a better deal for workers and a more peaceful society. The movement initially attracted support from a wide spectrum of South Australians, but was disbanded in 1949.

In 1937-46 Garland had been secretary of the Gasworkers' Union, the first C.P.A. member to be a trade-union secretary in the State. He led the 'stay-in' strikes that advanced his members' conditions. President (1936-37 and 1943-45) of the U.T.L.C., he became its secretary in 1946 and immediately resigned from all positions which he thought might compromise his office. The succeeding years witnessed a period of tension and dispute between workers and employers. In 1949, following a newspaper campaign against him and a swing towards a more conservative U.T.L.C., Garland lost the secretaryship.

Again he paid for his activism, finding it difficult to obtain work, but he was finally offered the post of secretary-clerk at the McKechnie Iron Foundry.

Although he was short in stature, Garland's energy and willingness to argue for his convictions made him appear a much larger man. In his efforts to improve social outcomes, he gave little thought to his own employment security or material well-being. These attributes led many to regard him as being 'without peer' in the union movement. He suffered from heart disease and attributed it to the extreme conditions he had endured between decks as an artificer. Survived by his wife, son and daughter, he died of coronary thrombosis on 14 February 1952 at his Kilkenny home and was cremated. On hearing of his death, George Ball wrote:

His spirit still survives
and beckons to the fight,
to help our comrades in distress
and win the cause that's right.

J. Moss, *Sound of Trumpets* (Adel, 1985); *Torch*, 31 July 1946; *JHSSA*, 16, 1988; *Herald* (Melb), 21 Oct 1940; *Worker's Weekly*, 14 Sept 1934; *Mail* (Adel), 15, 29 Aug 1942; *Advertiser* (Adel), 16 Jan, 16 Nov 1940, 5 Apr 1944, 15 Feb 1952; J. Playford, History of the Left Wing of the South Australian Labour Movement, 1908-36 (B.A. Hons thesis, Univ Adel, 1958); information from Mr T. E. Garland, Tea Tree Gully, Mrs P. Haseldine, Brooklyn Park, Mr H. Kranz, Wattle Park, and Mr and Mrs E. Johnston, Adel.   MARTIN SHANAHAN

GARRAN, JOHN CHEYNE (1905-1976), grazier and historian, was born on 21 September 1905 at Prahran, Melbourne, second of four sons of Sydney-born (Sir) Robert Randolph Garran [q.v.8], secretary to the Attorney-General's Department, and his wife Hilda, née Robson, from England. Educated at Melbourne Church of England Grammar School, John studied arts for one year at the University of Melbourne. In 1925 he rowed in the Victorian VIII. That year he began work as a jackeroo on Mossgiel station, near Mossgiel, New South Wales, and rose to overseer before 1929 when he took up his own property, Bonshaw, in the Federal Capital Territory. He later added nearby Erindale to his holding.

On 26 September 1932, at the chapel of his old school, Garran married Elsie Pearl Chrisp; they were to have a daughter before being divorced in 1938. Enlisting in the Australian Imperial Force on 1 June 1940, he was sent to Malaya in February 1941 as a corporal in the 8th Divisional Supply Column. He was captured in February 1942 and compelled to work on the Burma-Thailand Railway. Released in August 1945, he returned to Australia and was discharged from the A.I.F. on 3 December.

Garran had specialized in raising sheep for wool and mutton, but he also grew crops, ran some cattle and kept a number of pigs. Thoughtful and scientific in his approach, in 1937 and 1938 he was awarded master farmer certificates for 'skill and enterprise in diversified farming'. In 1948 he won the New South Wales Agricultural Bureau's progressive farmer competition. Next year he travelled overseas to study the latest methods of agriculture. On 7 December 1955 at St Paul's Anglican Church, Canterbury, Sydney, he married a 38-year-old dietician Winifred Ellen Wilson; they were to have two sons and a daughter.

Chairman of the board of Canberra Community Hospital in the late 1940s, Garran was also an executive-member of the Graziers' Association of New South Wales and of the Australian Capital Territory division of the Arts Council of Australia. He performed with and was president (1953-56) of the Canberra Repertory Society: 'because of his own deafness, he was always very conscious of the need to project clearly and this added weight to his utterances both on and off stage'.

From 1970 Garran contributed articles on the wool industry to the journals of the Canberra and District and the Royal Australian historical societies. With his knowledge of sheep-breeding, he became sceptical of previous interpretations of the development of the Australian merino and believed that John Macarthur's [q.v.2] role in founding the industry had been overrated. He set out to write a thorough account of the historical and genetic development of the merino. His manuscript was to be completed by Leslie White and published as *Merinos, myths and Macarthurs* (Canberra, 1985).

Six ft 4 ins (193 cm) tall and loose limbed, Garran had a subtle sense of humour and was unfailingly courteous. Despite suffering prolonged dysentery as a prisoner of war, 'honest John' had been a model of duty, self-sacrifice and devotion to his mates. He bore no lasting hatred towards the Japanese. As a historian he displayed practicality, common sense and perseverance. Survived by his wife and the children of both his marriages, he died on 5 January 1976 at Red Hill, Canberra, and was cremated.

R. R. Garran, *Prosper the Commonwealth* (Syd, 1958); A. Edgeworth, *The Cost of Jazz Garters* (Canb, 1992); *Canb Hist J*, Mar 1976; *Country Life*, 15 Mar 1946; *Bulletin*, 16 Apr 1947; *Canb Times*, 7 Jan 1976; information from Mr R. Garran, Griffith, and Mrs W. E. Garran, Deakin, Canb.

C. C. CRESWELL

GARRETT, Sir ALWYN RAGNAR (1900-1977), army officer, was born on 12 February 1900 at Northam, Western Australia, second child of Alwyn Garrett, a bank accountant from South Australia, and his Swedish-born wife Maria Carolina, née Wohlfahrt. Ragnar was educated at Guildford Grammar School. He entered the Royal Military College, Duntroon, Federal Capital Territory, in 1918 and was company sergeant major of the Corps of Staff Cadets in his final year (1921). Appointed to the light horse, Garrett held junior regimental and staff positions throughout the 1920s and early 1930s, save for a two-year attachment (1923-25) to the British 2nd Dragoon Guards at Bangalore, India. At St Peter's Anglican Church, Glenelg, Adelaide, on 9 September 1925 he married Shirley Lorraine Hunter, a nurse. He served on the staff of 'G' Branch at Army Headquarters, Melbourne, in 1936-37, then attended the Staff College, Camberley, England.

At the outbreak of World War II he came back to Australia and in November 1939 was appointed captain in the Australian Imperial Force. By June 1940 Major Garrett was again in Britain, on the staff of the 18th Australian Infantry Brigade; he was promoted lieutenant colonel on 16 September and briefly commanded the 2nd/31st Battalion. Sent to the Middle East in February 1941, he took part in the campaigns in Greece and Crete in April-May as a staff officer with the 19th Brigade and Savige [q.v.] Force. After further postings to Australian and British formations, mostly armoured, he returned home early in 1942.

Promoted temporary colonel in April, Garrett was senior operations officer on the staff of the 1st Armoured Division until October when he became director of armoured fighting vehicles, Land Headquarters, Melbourne. In September 1943 he joined the staff of I Corps. From December that year to October 1945 he was brigadier, general staff, successively on the headquarters of I Corps, II Corps, New Guinea Force and, again, II Corps: for most of this period he was in New Guinea or on Bougainville. He was appointed C.B.E. (1945) for his 'abounding energy, devotion to duty, and his ability to create and maintain a co-operative spirit within the Staff'. Having commanded the 8th Infantry Brigade during its repatriation and demobilization, in June 1946 he was posted as commandant of the Staff College, Queenscliff, Victoria.

In March 1947 Garrett was sent to Japan for duty with the British Commonwealth Occupation Force. He made his principal contribution as brigadier-in-charge of administration, a post he filled from July 1947 to October 1949, in which time the force was gradually scaled down and its areas of responsibility contracted. Back at Queenscliff in December, he began a longer term as commandant of the Staff College. Following a stint (August 1951 to January 1953) in charge of Western Command as temporary major general, he was made deputy chief of the General Staff. In October 1954 he was promoted temporary lieutenant general (substantive 16 December) and took over Southern Command, Melbourne. He was appointed C.B. in 1957.

Appointed chief of the General Staff on 23 March 1958, Garrett presided over a period of intense activity and change in the structure of the army, beginning with the disbandment of the national service scheme in 1959. The abolition of many longstanding units of the Citizen Military Forces—an emasculation seen by some critics as the regulars' revenge for Militia dominance in the years between world wars I and II—and the conversion of the army to the five-sided 'Pentropic' organization were intended to increase the service's flexibility and rationalize its resources.

Garrett was elevated to K.B.E. in 1959 and transferred to the Retired List on 1 July 1960. He was a man of great personal charm and polish. His had been a model staff officer's career, entailing little opportunity for troop command. One of the few officers of his generation with extensive experience in armoured warfare, he held a succession of increasingly senior administrative jobs which culminated in his appointment to head the army. His tenure as C.G.S. was marked by considerable turbulence, especially over reform of the C.M.F., but the changes which he implemented were to prove transient.

In retirement Sir Ragnar was principal (1960-64) of the Australian Administrative Staff College, Mount Eliza, and chairman (1965-70) of the Western Australian Coastal Shipping Commission. He retained his contacts with the army through appointments (1960-65) as honorary colonel of the Royal Australian Regiment and the Royal Western Australia Regiment. Predeceased by his wife, he died on 4 November 1977 at Mornington, Victoria; he was accorded a military funeral and was cremated. His son and daughter survived him.

R. N. L. Hopkins, *Australian Armour* (Canb, 1978); *Canb Times*, 11 Nov 1965; *Bulletin*, 29 June 1960.
                                                    JEFFREY GREY

GARRETT, THOMAS HUGH (1890-1943), public servant, was born on 18 October 1890 at Dalton-in-Furness, Lancashire, England, second of five children of James Edward Garrett, mines manager, and his wife Mary Cowling, née Vincent. In 1895 the family emigrated to Zeehan, Tasmania. Tom attended the local school of mines and in 1905 was employed as a telegraph messenger in the Postmaster-General's Department. Promoted in turn to clerical positions in the Hobart offices of the Department of Trade and Customs and of the Department of Defence, in 1916 he rejoined Trade and Customs in Melbourne. While attached to the public trustee's office, Garrett worked for the custodian of enemy property and controller of the clearing office (enemy debts). He married Annie Atherton on 25 February 1918 at St John's Anglican Church, Launceston.

On secondment to the Development and Migration Commission, in 1927-28 Garrett examined voluntary organizations involved with immigration. His detailed, incisive reports criticized the performance of the New Settlers' League of Australia; he also recommended that the Commonwealth cease subsidizing the efforts of the Returned Sailors' and Soldiers' Imperial League of Australia to find jobs for former Imperial servicemen.

Garrett was officer-in-charge of commercial intelligence (1929-30), Department of Markets and Transport, and chief clerk and accountant (1930-32), Department of Transport, before moving to Canberra as senior clerk, miscellaneous administrative section, Department of the Interior. He enjoyed overseeing and leasing out Canberra hotels, and agitated his devout wife by telling her that he would love to run a pub. Promoted chief clerk in 1936, he was closely involved with immigration issues. In 1936-37 the department was embroiled in controversy following the government's decision to refuse Mrs Mabel Freer entry to Australia. Freer was a British woman who had 'conceived an affection' for a married Australian army officer when he was stationed in India. After taking a stand on moral grounds, cabinet relented.

Wishing to be seen to be humanitarian, but determined to restrain numbers, in December 1938 J. A. Lyons's [q.v.10] government announced that 15 000 European refugees would be admitted to Australia over the next three years. Garrett had been promoted assistant-secretary in April. He toiled on mountainous case-work, and visited Britain and Europe in 1939 to assess the situation. His reports included harsh generalizations on the unsuitability of many Jews as immigrants, particularly those living in Poland. Tragically, only a modest number of Jews were allowed into Australia in 1938-39. Politicians and public servants, among them Garrett, were preoccupied with administrative neatness and constrained by the policy that refugees should be readily 'absorbed into the Australian community without affecting living standards and without detrimental effect to Australian workers'.

Garrett was highly regarded and as 'hard as nails': a colleague once said, 'he must be human, I heard him laughing with one of his kids'. It was assumed that he would succeed J. A. Carrodus [q.v.13] as head of the department, but the stresses of 1939 had impaired his health. Survived by his wife, son and three daughters, he died of a coronary occlusion on 23 June 1943 in Canberra Community Hospital and was buried in Canberra cemetery.

M. Blakeney, *Australia and the Jewish Refugees 1933-1948* (Syd, 1985); *PD* (Cwlth), 1934-36, p 1768; *Canb Times*, 16 Dec 1932, 24 June 1943; *Argus*, 17 Feb 1939; P. Bartrop, *Australia and the Holocaust 1933-1945* (Melb, 1994); A220/1 item S32/99, 160, A432/85 item 1936/1360, item 1943/1139, A461 item A349/3/5 pt 2, A659 item 1947/1/2109, A5954/1 item 973/13, CP211/2 item 98 pt 2, *and* CP290/1 bundle 1/16 (AA, Canb); AA P437/1 item 1912/843 (AA, Hob).
                                                    IAN CARNELL

GARSIDE, FREDERICK CHARLES (1887-1970), railways commissioner, was born on 5 February 1887 at Burwood, Sydney, son of Eli Garside, an engine driver from England, and his native-born wife Eleanor, née Coleman. Educated at Goulburn, Frederick joined the New South Wales Government Railways and Tramways in May 1903 and completed his apprenticeship as a fitter at the Eveleigh Workshops, Sydney, in 1908. He was based at Nyngan as fitter-in-charge when he married Treasure Mabel Coombs on 27 September 1911 at St Andrew's Anglican Church, Lismore. In 1914 he transferred to Newcastle as assistant outdoor superintendent, responsible for the availability of locomotives.

Because of his Christian Science faith, Garside was a strong non-unionist and did not take part in the railway strike of 1917. In the consequent restructuring of the service, his promotion to district inspector displeased the returning strikers. Opposition from fellow workers led him to seek a position outside the mechanical branch and in 1920 he was made a member of the Railways Suggestions, Inventions and Economies Board, Sydney. He became acting-comptroller of stores in 1922 (comptroller from 1923), a move that brought him close to T. J. Hartigan [q.v.]. In an attempt to lessen sectarian reactions to the Catholic Hartigan's promotion to commissioner, Garside was appointed assistant-commissioner for railways on 29 December 1932.

Sensitive and retiring, Garside deliberately isolated himself from the rank and file. His frequent public addresses tended to be to select groups, such as the Institute of Transport (of which he was chairman, New South Wales centre, 1937-38) and to the Institute of Public

Administration (State chairman 1938-40). He and Hartigan effectively reorganized the deficit-ridden railways in the 1930s. During World War II much of the routine work of the commissioner's office fell to Garside who was a sound manager of planning and finance, but he had little success in negotiating with the unions and probably never fully understood the harsh reality of the footplate or the permanent way.

On 1 October 1948 he succeeded Hartigan as commissioner; Reg Winsor [q.v.] was appointed assistant-commissioner. Friction between them came to a head in January 1949 when Winsor supported efforts by the Railway Salaried Officers' Association to have Garside removed from office because of the way he had handled promotions, transfers and dismissals. Garside's intransigence was blamed for two strikes by members of the Australian Railways Union in October 1950. He had clashed with successive Labor ministers for transport Maurice O'Sullivan and W. F. Sheahan [q.v.], arguing that the precarious state of railway finances in the postwar period stemmed from inadequate government investment rather than from poor administration. Keen to preserve the independence of the commissioner in decision-making, he resisted attempts to place him more firmly under ministerial control. This battle was lost in 1950 when the government passed the transport and highways bill; Winsor was made director of transport and highways, and became his superior.

Garside retired on 5 February 1952. He neither smoked nor drank. In his personal life he preferred retirement and study to an aggressive search for power, and he was perhaps a little out of his depth as commissioner. Strikes, unreliable services, outdated equipment and political controversy marred his term of office. The problems that occurred during his commissionership, and his earlier tendency to allow Hartigan to overshadow him, have tended to blur his significant achievements as assistant-commissioner. Survived by his four daughters, he died on 24 July 1970 at his Roseville home and was cremated with Christian Science forms.

J. Gunn, *Along Parallel Lines* (Melb, 1989); Report by EBASCO Services Incorporated, 5 Nov 1957, *PP*(NSW), 1957-58, 3; *Railway Advocate*, 20 Aug 1970, p 3; *Sunday Herald*, 20 Jan 1952; *SMH*, 23 Jan 1952.   R. M. AUDLEY

GARTRELL, HERBERT WILLIAM (1882-1945), professor of mining and metallurgy, was born on 14 August 1882 at Maitland, South Australia, son of English-born parents William Pascoe Gartrell, blacksmith,

and his wife Martha, née Finch. Educated at the Collegiate School of St Peter, Adelaide, on a scholarship, and at the University of Adelaide (B.A., B.Sc., 1902), in 1903 Herbert won the Tate [q.v.6] memorial medal for his fieldwork in geology. Two years later he was awarded an Angas [q.v.3] engineering scholarship which enabled him to travel to North America. He worked for mining companies in Idaho, United States of America, and British Columbia, Canada, and studied mining at Columbia University, New York (M.A., 1905). In 1910 he was the first lecturer in mining engineering at the University of Adelaide, where he was to teach for the rest of his life. At St David's Anglican Church, Burnside, on 8 December 1910 he married Evangeline Murphy.

On 11 December 1916 Gartrell enlisted in the Australian Imperial Force. He served in France in 1918 in the 1st Tunnelling Company, Royal Australian Engineers, and the 257th Tunnelling Company, Royal Engineers; he was commissioned in August that year and promoted lieutenant in January 1919; his A.I.F. appointment terminated in Adelaide on 10 August. Gartrell published *An Introduction to Mining Finance* (1923), as well as several papers in the *Proceedings of the Australasian Institute of Mining and Metallurgy* during the 1920s and 1930s. In 1934 he took on the additional posts of director of the Bonython [q.v.7] laboratories, South Australian School of Mines and Industries, and of consultant to the Commonwealth Council for Scientific and Industrial Research. He achieved considerable support from the Australian mining industry as his courses won growing national and international recognition. In 1939 he was appointed professor and in 1943 the Broken Hill Proprietary Co. Ltd made a gift of £15 000 to endow his chair.

Gartrell was an active member of the A.I.M.M. and its president in 1941. Believing that 'It is good for a lecture to provide a student with food (for thought), better if it provide him with an appetite . . . all education is self education', he defined the degree in mining engineering as 'a licence to go out and learn'. He was an outstanding teacher who followed with fatherly care the careers of his students. They knew him affectionately as 'Spog'. He and his wife belonged to the Luhrs Road Congregational Church, South Payneham, and gave generously to deserving causes, among them the Adelaide Legacy Club. Gartrell had a clear vision of the nature of the world and of the role he could best play in it. He also had a wry and sometimes caustic manner of expression, especially when he was debunking hypocrisy or humbug: 'Mining prospectuses are frequently obviously fraudulent, since experience has shown no bait is too crude for large sections of the public'.

Survived by his wife and adopted son, Gartrell died of a dissecting aneurism of the aorta on 8 June 1945 at Parkwynd Private Hospital, Adelaide, and was buried in Centennial Park cemetery. In 1985 a number of his former students established the Gartrell School of Mining, Metallurgy and Applied Geology at the South Australian Institute of Technology.

V. A. Edgeloe, *Engineering Education in the University of Adelaide* (Adel, 1989); D. A. Cumming and G. C. Moxham, *They Built South Australia* (Adel, 1986); A. Aeuckens, *The People's University* (Adel, 1989); Univ Adel, *Calendar*, 1910-15; A'sian Inst of Mining and Metallurgy, *Procs*, no 124, 1941, July 1945; information from a number of Gartrell's former students.   E. D. J. STEWART

GASK, ARTHUR CECIL (1869-1951), dentist and novelist, was born on 10 July 1869 at St Marylebone, London, fourth of five children of Charles Gask, merchant, and his wife Fanny, née Edis. Arthur's sister Lilian was to become a writer of children's stories. Educated at Merchant Taylors' School, he trained as a dentist at the Royal Dental and Middlesex hospitals and gained his licence (1891) from the Royal College of Surgeons. On 10 August 1898 he married a dentist's daughter Florence Mary Tippett in the parish church, Tormoham, Devon; they were to have four children. Gask worked at St Vincent's Home, Torquay, then as a dental inspector in industrial schools and in 1905-08 at the Harrogate Infirmary, Yorkshire. He divorced his wife on 19 July 1909 and on 13 September that year married the children's nursemaid Marion Elizabeth Maltby at the register office, West Ham, London. On the birth of their first son in 1910, Gask described himself as a journalist.

Accompanied by Marion and their two sons, and by a daughter of his first marriage, Gask emigrated to Adelaide in 1920. He set up practice in rooms on North Terrace where he was among the first in the city to carry out extractions with gas. Six ft 3 ins (191 cm) tall, slim and moustached, he was suave and successful, and enjoyed telling his captive patients 'off-colour' jokes. He was amiable, but eccentric, and made kleptomaniac raids on his local pharmacist. Although he was an agnostic, Gask liked to discuss religion. While waiting for his patients, he began writing crime fiction.

He paid for the publication of his first novel, *The Secret of the Sandhills* (1921), which sold the print-run of one thousand copies in three weeks. Herbert Jenkins Ltd, London, republished it next year. By 1926 about 30 000 copies had been sold and the firm handled all English editions of his work, which was to comprise some thirty-four novels. His famous detective hero Gilbert Larose first appeared in *Cloud, the Smiter* (1926). Gask's style was pacy and sometimes titillating. He published, on average, at least one book a year until his death. *The Red Paste Murders* (1923) was considered for a film and *The Dark Highway* (1928) was praised in *All About Books* as 'virile and gripping'. *The Jest of Life* (1936) recorded the migration of an Adelaide dentist's soul to several leading citizens. In 1931 *The Lonely House* (1929) was republished in New York by Macaulay Co. which brought out four more of his books, including one in another genre, *The Master Spy* (1937). Gask's work was translated into several European languages, serialized in newspapers and broadcast on radio. He also wrote short stories.

In 1933 Gask retired to write full time at rural Kooringa where he named his property Gilrose; he later returned to Adelaide and lived at Walkerville. Despite illness, he completed *Crime Upon Crime* (1952). Survived by his wife and their two sons, and by the two sons and one of the daughters of his first marriage, he died on 24 June 1951 in North Adelaide and was cremated. *The Secret of the Garden* (1924), republished in 1993, is notable for its mischievous social criticism of Adelaide; H. G. Wells regarded *The Vengeance of Larose* (1939) as Gask's 'best piece of story-telling . . . It kept me up till half-past one'.

P. Depasquale, *A Critical History of South Australian Literature, 1836-1930* (Adel, 1978); *All About Books*, Jan 1929; *Advertiser* (Adel), 21 May 1926, 27 June 1951; *Mail* (Adel), 20 Sept 1947; *Chronicle* (Adel), 20 July 1950; information from Mr P. D. Moss, St Peters, Adel, and the late Mr G. Gask.   MICHAEL J. TOLLEY

GATES, MINNIE MAY (1878-1966), community worker and women's leader, was born on 13 September 1878 at Willoughby, Sydney, fourth of nine children of English-born parents Robert Forsyth, currier, and his wife Stephana, née Gates. Educated at Miss Emily Baxter's Argyle School, Minnie spent her childhood in the comfort and security of a large family home. After her father's tanning business was forced to close about 1900, memories of the family's sharply reduced circumstances remained with her.

On 27 March 1901 at the Wesleyan Church, Chatswood, she married Edmond Charles Gates (d.1953), a dentist. By 1928 she was the mother of six children and honorary secretary of the Women's League of New South Wales. That year she formed a special committee of fifteen women to provide friendship and practical assistance to country girls coming to Sydney to seek employment. Under Mrs Gates's direction, the committee's clubrooms in Hosking Place were developed as the means of offering 'sisterly help' through counselling, training, clothing, food and money.

Mrs Gates was elected honorary secretary (later president) of the Council for Social and Moral Reform in 1929 and was accepted as an associate of the National Council of Women of New South Wales. Entering her fifties, comparatively well-off, with a husband who supported her activities, she was very much at the height of her powers. She was a good-looking woman of medium build, with a strong personality, an authoritative air, the ability to organize and a skill for public speaking. Her work as treasurer (1929-54) of the N.C.W. reflected her continuing interest in securing for women a more prominent role in public life: she constantly urged equal access to areas of education, training and employment traditionally set aside for men.

As the Depression deepened, Mrs Gates managed to persuade the N.C.W. to direct virtually all its employment-relief funds for 1931-32 towards maintaining a twelve-bed hostel in Bligh Street for homeless young women. Worried by costs, in 1934 the N.C.W. baulked at moving the hostel to new quarters in York Street, withdrew its financial support and placed responsibility for the hostel's administration in the willing hands of Mrs Gates. From that time the Big Sister Movement, as her committee had become known, was formalized; Mrs Gates was its founder-president until her death.

Under her direction, the movement expanded to assist elderly disadvantaged women. Hostels were established at Pennant Hills (1936) and Burwood (1953). Money was always scarce, obliging the B.S.M. to depend on fund-raising, donations and voluntary help. Mrs Gates donated furniture from her home at Longueville to equip the Pennant Hills hostel. In 1958 the Minnie Gates Hostel for elderly women was opened at Cronulla, close to where she and her husband had moved in 1941.

Maintaining the family tradition set by her grandfather and father, Mrs Gates was a member (1940-60) of the board of Royal North Shore Hospital; she pressed for a child-care centre within the hospital's grounds and in 1960 had the pleasure of opening the Minnie Gates Playground. During World War II she had also worked for the Australian Red Cross Society. In 1941 she was appointed M.B.E.

In spite of her busy life, she had not learned to drive a motorcar, and neither she nor her husband ever owned one. Even in her late seventies, she made the three-hour return trip to the North Shore by train. She was a lifelong teetotaller and kept fit by swimming each morning at Cronulla beach. Survived by her two daughters and three of her four sons, Minnie Gates died on 30 August 1966 at Caringbah and was cremated.

National Council of Women of NSW, *Seventy-Five Years, 1896-1971* (Syd, 1971); G. Sherington, *The Royal North Shore Hospital, 1888-1988* (Syd, 1988); E. Braitling, *The History of the Big Sister Movement* (Syd, 1991); National Council of Women of NSW, *Minutes*, 1929-58; *Herself*, 2, no 3, 5 July 1930; *SMH*, 30 Sept 1929, 30 May, 5 Aug 1930, 4 Feb, 3 Mar 1931, 3 July 1934, 20 Apr 1935, 4 Sept 1936, 28 Sept 1938, 26 Sept 1939, 12 June 1941, 28 Sept 1943, 31 Aug 1966; *Sun-Herald*, 16 Oct 1960; information from Mrs G. Gates, Syd, Dr R. B. Gates, Cronulla, and Miss J. F. Arnot, Double Bay, Syd.

ALISON PILGER

GAWLER, JOHN STEVENS (1885-1978), architect, was born on 20 May 1885 at West Ham, Essex, England, son of John Miller Gawler, insurance clerk, and his wife Kate, née Stevens. The family emigrated to Melbourne in 1886. Educated at Brighton State and University High schools, young John began his career as office-boy with an estate agent before working for an architect and becoming a junior draftsman. His employer granted him articles without a fee. In 1903 Gawler was awarded a bronze medal by the Royal Victorian Institute of Architects for a drawing of part of the Melbourne law courts.

In 1907 he left Melbourne with a two-year contract to oversee a building project at Canton (Guangzhou), China; he continued on a working tour of the world, returning home in 1912. In September he was appointed Walter Burley Griffin's [q.v.9] representative. Gawler's first major commission may have been Wenley House, Flinders Lane. Another of his early works, St Agnes's, Black Rock (1913), was the forerunner of a substantial body of work for the Church of England. On 7 March 1914 at St Agnes's he married American-born Ruth Miller Woodworth, whom he had met on his travels. That year he entered into partnership with Walter A. Drummond and accepted a part-time position as an assistant-lecturer at the University of Melbourne.

From 1917 to 1919 Gawler served in the Australian Imperial Force and saw action on the Western Front (1918) as a sapper in the 10th Field Company, Engineers. Appointed lecturer in architecture at the University of Melbourne in 1920, he immediately pressed for and obtained a temporary building (towards the cost of which his own firm donated £16 360). He drafted proposals for the establishment of a four-year degree course, introduced in 1928, and was elected dean of the faculty in 1938.

The practice of Gawler & Drummond was prolific, though undistinguished. The firm designed a range of domestic, industrial, commercial and church buildings, as well as the metallurgy school at the university. The only technically interesting aspect of its work was the early use of brick-veneer construction in the McRorie house (1916) at Camberwell, almost certainly the result of Gawler's time at Chicago, United States of America, where the method was popular. The most distinctive work was the Deaf and Dumb Society's church at Jolimont (1929). From 1918 the largest client was the Fitzroy department store, Ackmans Ltd, with its associated factories: the proprietors' satisfaction was reflected in the endowment of a travelling scholarship for architecture students. In 1941 E. S. Churcher replaced Drummond as Gawler's partner.

Gawler was more important as an educator, activist and reformer rather than as a designer. He served as a council-member of the Shire of Nunawading and later (1927-51) of the City of Box Hill, and was president (1948-50) of the Municipal Association. As controller of building permits with the Department of War Organization of Industry from 1940, he was responsible for the approval of civil-construction work in Victoria. In 1943 Prime Minister Chifley [q.v.13] made him deputy-chairman of the Commonwealth Housing Commission, which reported next year.

Appointed foundation chairman of the Town and Country Planning Board in 1946, Gawler formally retired from his practice. In that year the chair of architecture, for which he had consistently pressed, was established by the university, with an endowment from the *Age*. As a part-time member of faculty, Gawler was ineligible to apply for the chair; he tactfully resigned and remained on excellent terms with Brian Lewis, the new professor. In 1949-53 Gawler was a part-time member of the Victorian Housing Commission.

In 1951 he declined reappointment to the T.C.P.B. and made another trip abroad. He remained, however, a member of the Central Planning Authority, on which he had previously represented the board. A fellow (from 1922) of the R.V.I.A., he was awarded the Sir James Barrett [q.v.7] medal in 1959 for his contribution to town and country planning. Gawler published his memoirs, *A Roof Over My Head*, in 1963. Survived by his wife, three daughters and two sons, he died on 6 September 1978 at Mitcham and was cremated. His estate was sworn for probate at $215 235.

Sun News-Pictorial, 27 Aug 1945, 22 Dec 1949, 23 Feb, 29 Mar 1951; *Age* (Melb), 5 Feb 1959; M. Lewis, The Development of Architectural Teaching in the University of Melbourne (ts, 1970, Architecture L, Univ Melb).   MILES LEWIS

GEDDES, CHARLES MATHERS ('JOCK') (1904-1979), Salvation Army officer and military chaplain, was born on 12 March 1904 at Torry, Kincardineshire, Scotland, son of William Geddes, journeyman iron-moulder, and his wife Amelia, née Paterson. Educated locally, by the age of 14 'Jock' was a boy-bandsman with the Gordon Highlanders. He later helped an uncle who was a fish-buyer, but by the early 1920s was unemployed.

Emigrating to Queensland in 1923, Geddes worked for farmers on the Atherton Tableland until he acquired a team of horses and a tractor with which he began contracting. Through the Salvation Army, he met and was deeply influenced by Ensign Matt Cross who had lost both his legs in World War I. Geddes was further inspired by a mystical experience in which he believed he saw Christ. Deciding to become a Salvation Army officer, he entered the training college in Sydney and was commissioned in January 1929; following appointments in North Queensland, he resigned in 1931 and found jobs as a labourer. At the Salvation Army Hall, Mackay, on 17 February 1932 he married Stella Cork. Next year he was reinstated as a captain in the Salvation Army. He held a succession of posts in Queensland and spent two years (1937-39) in Sydney.

On 9 March 1940 Geddes was appointed chaplain in the Australian Military Forces; in November he embarked for the Middle East as a Red Shield representative. He was attached to the 7th Division (from November 1940) at sea and in Palestine, to the 6th Division (from January 1941) in North Africa and to the 9th Division (April to June) in the defence of Tobruk, Libya. After a month in hospital in Cairo, he was assigned to I Corps Signals in Syria. In March 1942 he returned to Australia. Later that year, from his depot in Port Moresby, he distributed Red Shield supplies—Salvation Army comforts—to troops fighting in Papua: in addition to tea and tobacco, he provided words of reassurance.

Transferring to the Australian Imperial Force in January 1943, Geddes served in New Guinea that year and in the hospital ship, *Wanganella*, in 1945; for much of 1944 he was in hospital. He ceased full-time duty on 6 January 1947 in Australia. In 1947-50 he commanded Salvation Army corps in Queensland country towns and rose to major. From November 1950 to April 1951 he was an immigration chaplain, based in Britain. Having subsequently held posts in New South Wales, in January 1955 he was sent to Japan as commissioner, Red Shield services; he also worked in Korea before his repatriation in March 1956.

In 1957 Geddes was appointed territorial evangelist for eastern Australia. He retired because of poor health in January 1959, but in the following year became a rehabilitation officer in Sydney. Returning to active service in 1964 and promoted brigadier (1965), he carried out counselling work until his final retirement on 15 March 1969. In 1976 he was admitted to the Order of the Founder, the Salvation Army's highest award. For the last twenty years of his life he was corps sergeant-major at Sydney Congress Hall.

Geddes had been a boxer in his youth. A 'complex mix of sanctified clown and adventurer for Christ . . . generous to a fault and too quixotic to be always prudent', he was admired for the dynamism of his personality and the strength of his faith. When a drunk spat on him during a street meeting, he told the crowd, 'I've been given a decoration for service to Jesus. But he had better not do it again'. Geddes died on 6 November 1979 at Arncliffe and was cremated; his wife and four daughters survived him.

W. Cairns, *Padre Jock O.F.* (Canb, 1975); *War Cry* (Melb), 8 Dec 1979; information from Salvation Army Headquarters, Syd.   BARBARA BOLTON

GEIGER, KURT (1915-1972), businessman, was born on 11 March 1915 in Vienna, son of Eugen Geiger, merchant, and his wife Elsa, née Glaser. As a young man, Kurt served behind the counter of his family's drapery business. Educated at Waser Gymnasium, in 1933-38 he studied medicine at the University of Vienna. On 19 May 1938 he married Czech-born Olga Trenschina, née Hochwald, in Vienna. Fleeing from Hitler's anti-Semitism, they reached Melbourne on 31 August; Kurt's parents and sister, who remained in Austria, were killed by the Nazis.

Unable to afford to continue his studies at the University of Melbourne, Kurt leased a small shop in Collins Street; in October he set up K. O. Geiger Pty Ltd and began to sell imported handbags. Business was brisk in the weeks before the Melbourne Cup, but then it slackened and Kurt spent two years as a window-dresser for a jeweller while Olga ran the shop. Realizing the benefit of selling matching handbags and shoes, in 1941 the Geigers established Mascot Shoes Pty Ltd, opening their first store in Degraves Street. Kurt was naturalized on 22 June 1944.

In 1945 he travelled through Britain and North America, learning more about the trade and selling shoes on commission. Returning with a licence from a large English company, he bought a shoe factory in 1951 and improved both its machinery and craftmanship. Three years later he owned seven outlets; by 1957 he had five hundred employees.

A man of good taste, immaculately groomed and fashionably dressed in English suits, Geiger was chairman (1959-60) of the Museum of Modern Art of Australia, head of an appeal (1961) for the Royal Australasian College of Surgeons and a director of the National Theatre of Australia Ltd. He was also a member of the Victoria Racing and the Victoria Amateur Turf clubs.

In 1955 Geiger Holdings Pty Ltd and its subsidiaries had merged with Melbourne's oldest retail draper, Hicks Atkinson Pty Ltd, as an alternative to a public float. Geiger was appointed managing director. In 1958, at his instigation, Reid Murray Holdings Ltd made a successful takeover bid for Hicks Atkinson, valuing it at £1.75 million. Geiger became a director of Reid Murray. From 1960 he sold most of his R.M.H. shares (and those of his wife), provoking a confrontation with the company's chairman, Robert Reid, which led to Geiger's resignation from the board in April 1962.

The Geigers left Australia in September 1963, shortly before the collapse of the Reid Murray organization. In April 1964 they opened a shoe salon in New Bond Street, London. Olga returned to Melbourne in 1967 and set up her own handbag shop in Collins Street. She died from an overdose of barbiturates on 9 March 1969 at Toorak. At the register office, Westminster, London, on 31 August 1971 Geiger married Irmgard Steinberg, a consultant. Survived by his wife and by the three daughters of his first marriage, he died on 8 August 1972 at Westminster. His Australian estate was sworn for probate at $920 861.

People (Syd), 20 Oct 1954; *Herald* (Melb), 7 Jan 1956, 1 Oct 1958, 2 Oct 1959, 7, 9 Apr 1962, 9 Apr 1964, 28 Feb 1966, 12 July 1967, 11 Aug 1972; *Nation*, 11 Oct 1958; *Age* (Melb), 4 Oct 1961, 18 Nov 1966; *Bulletin*, 14 Apr 1962; *SMH*, 7 Dec 1963, 23 Apr 1964; Geiger naturalization file (AA, Canb).   DAVID JEFFERSON

GELLERT, LEON MAXWELL (1892-1977), soldier, poet and journalist, was born on 17 May 1892 at Walkerville, Adelaide, third child and elder son of James Wallis Gellert, an Australian-born clerk of Hungarian descent, and his wife Eliza Anne, née Sutton. A sturdy child who was indulged by his mother and 'flogged' by his Methodist father, Leon eventually acquired enough knowledge of self-defence from the Young Men's Christian Association to throw the astonished parent on his back. He remained grateful to his father for introducing him to books, starting with *Coral Island*, but resented James's refusal to sponsor his education beyond Adelaide High School.

Leon became a pupil-teacher at Unley Public School. Financially assisted by an uncle, he attended University (Teachers') Training College, and passed modern European history and education (1912) and English language and literature (1913) at the University of Adelaide. Gellert taught physical education at Hindmarsh Public School until, eighteen days after the outbreak of World War I, 'dancing and singing', he enlisted in the Australian Imperial Force. In his troop-ship in the Aegean he diverted himself by writing verse. As a lance sergeant with the 10th Battalion, he landed at Gallipoli on 25 April 1915. Wounded by shrapnel, and suffering from septicaemia and dysentery, he was evacuated to Malta in July and thence to London. He was diagnosed as having epilepsy, repatriated and discharged medically unfit on 30 June 1916. In November he re-enlisted in Adelaide, only to be discharged almost immediately, but the suspected tendency to epilepsy was not borne out in later life. He returned to teaching, at Norwood Public School.

Meanwhile, Gellert revised and added to his overseas verse. *Songs of a Campaign* (1917) was hailed by the *Bulletin* as one of the best verse collections to have 'come out of the war to the English language'; it won the university's Bundey [q.v.3] prize for English verse, and, before the year was out, Angus & Robertson [qq.v.7,11] Ltd published a third and enlarged edition, illustrated by Norman Lindsay [q.v.10]. Australia's closest approximation to a Brooke or Sassoon, Gellert looked the part, particularly in Lindsay's 1918 depiction of him as a knightly seraph. He was of strong build and middle height, with a fair complexion, grey eyes and light brown hair; sometimes, to his annoyance, his features were described by the press as 'sensitive'.

In the best of his verse Gellert used everyday language to express what would later be termed 'a perplexed disillusionment with the soldier's lot'. But he did not maintain the impetus. *The Isle of San* (1919), a cycle of 120 poems published as a limited edition, again illustrated by Lindsay, dealt with 'Youth's eternal awakening to the failure of ideals'. There were few reviews and H. M. Green [q.v.] subsequently declared that Gellert's 'best verse is almost all in his first book'.

Poetry gave way to journalism, and in due course to expected disillusion. Soon after his marriage to Kathleen Patricia Saunders on Christmas Day 1918 at St Margaret's Anglican Church, Woodville, he joined him in

Sydney where Gellert taught English at Cleveland Street Intermediate High School until 1922. He took over a column, 'The Man in the Mask', in *Smith's Weekly*, and was introduced by Lindsay to an artistic and literary circle which included Sydney Ure Smith and Bertram Stevens [qq.v.11,12]. When Stevens died in 1922, Gellert replaced him as co-editor of *Art in Australia* and became a director of Art in Australia Ltd, which also published the *Home*.

The company was acquired in 1934 by John Fairfax & Sons [qq.v.4,8] Ltd. Ure Smith and Gellert retained their co-editorships until the former resigned in 1938. Gellert was sole editor of the *Home* from that year until its closure in 1942. He was then put in charge of the *Sydney Morning Herald*'s magazine and book pages. Although deprived of the magazine pages in 1945, he retained the title of literary editor and wrote a graceful column, 'Something Personal', for the Saturday book pages; from 1949 he contributed a widely read humorous column to the *Sunday Herald* (later the *Sun-Herald*) and, following his retirement from Fairfax in 1961, the *Sunday Telegraph*. His Sunday columns, republished in *Week after Week* (1953) and *Year after Year* (1956), were usually set in Burran Avenue, Mosman, where he had built a cliff-top home in 1922. They portrayed him as a bespectacled curmudgeon—a far cry from Lindsay's angelic dry-point or Norman Carter's [q.v.7] courtly oil painting of 1923.

The Gellerts' only child and grandchild had died in childbirth during the 1940s. After his wife's death in 1969, he returned to Adelaide and spent his last years with a beloved pet dachshund in a house at Hazelwood Park that he called Crumble Cottage. He died on 22 August 1977 at Toorak Gardens and was cremated.

A. Limb, *History of the 10th Battalion A.I.F.* (Lond, 1919); *SMH*, 23 Aug 1977; K. C. Harper, Leon Gellert (filmed interview, 1975, Aust Council L, Redfern, Syd); audio tapes (Univ Qld Art Museum); Gellert *and* Lionel Lindsay *and* Ure Smith papers (ML); John Fairfax Group Pty Ltd Archives, Syd. GAVIN SOUTER

GENDERS, DOROTHY EDNA (1892–1978), Anglican deaconess, was born on 27 July 1892 at Launceston, Tasmania, younger daughter of William John Genders (d.1901), merchant, and his first wife Lilly Louisa, née Westbrook (d.1892). Educated locally, Dorothy belonged to a church-going family whose generosity extended to the poor and needy. She was guided by her stepmother Mabel (née Brownrigg), her grandfather J. C. Genders and her paternal aunt Marion Louisa Holmes [q.v.9] whom she visited in Perth in

1912. While there, Genders felt called to enter the Church. After serving in St John's Mission House at Launceston, she went to Sydney in 1917, studied at Deaconess House and attended classes at Moore Theological College, and undertook pastoral work. Made deaconess in 1919, she gained a licentiate (1925) from the Australian College of Theology, but was rejected for missionary service because of her small physique and apparent frailty.

In 1928 Genders again visited the Holmes family in Perth. Next year, on Archbishop Le Fanu's [q.v.10] invitation, she returned to work as the rector's assistant at St Barnabas's Church, Buckland Hill; she also trained aspiring deaconesses. Although her stipend was small, she had adequate private means to build a cottage in McCabe Street, Mosman Park, in which she sheltered the destitute and shared a generous table. At the archbishop's request, she moved in 1931 to St Bartholomew's, East Perth, where she took responsibility for pastoral work in the absence of an incumbent rector. She turned the rectory into a refuge for deserted women and children, battered wives and prostitutes; police brought distressed women to the rectory at all hours, knowing that its doors were always open. In 1948 the refuge received 240 destitute women.

Visitations took 'Sister Dorothy' to St Hilda's, North Perth, the Children's Court, the Child Welfare Department, hospitals, private homes and Fremantle Gaol. While 'We who for our evil deeds do worthily deserve to be punished' was her favourite collect for women prisoners, her compassion prevailed. Genders held regular prayer-meetings, taught Sunday School, counselled neighbours and was a life member of the Girls' Friendly Society. Setting off for the bus at 7.30 most mornings, she was 'a quick stepping . . . figure, no more than 5 feet [152 cm] tall, grey frock and cape, and small black hat and veil, a string bag containing books and magazines in her hand. She greeted everyone with a smile and a cheery wave'. At home she taught her budgerigar to recite 'The Lord's Prayer'.

In the 1950s Genders was attached to St Luke's, Cottesloe. Despite some local resistance, she bought the house next to her cottage for destitute people; the sparsely furnished rooms invariably contained a cupboard full of tinned food. She cooked the evening meal, occasionally entertained friends and had a small chapel built on to the front of her own home. The 'tiny woman with a big heart' was appointed M.B.E. in 1970. Genders retired to Meath House, Trigg. She died on 27 August 1978 at the Home of Peace, Subiaco, and was cremated. The Genders' Library at Meath House, the Genders' room at Wollaston College, Mount Claremont, and the Dorothy Genders' Retirement Village, Mosman Park, commemorate her.

Deaconess (Syd), 15 Feb 1927; *Cathedral Notes* (Perth), Sept 1933; *WA Church News*, 46, no 4, 1948; *Anglican Messenger* (Perth), Oct 1978; *Examiner* (Launc), 11 Jan 1901; *West Australian*, 2 Sept 1978; note-books and cuttings (held by Mrs J. Lang, Mosman Park, Perth).   WENDY BIRMAN

GENEFF, GEORGE (1897-1977), market gardener, boxer, contractor and philanthropist, was born on 27 October 1897 at Popovo, Bulgaria, eldest of ten children of Ilia Genev, market gardener, and his wife Nadezda, née Kamburov. In response to vacillating markets the family moved via the Black Sea between Varna and Odessa, Russia. A voracious reader, George advanced quickly in Bulgarian and Russian schools. His mother taught him the Orthodox scripture and tales of his people's struggle against the Turks. By accompanying his father to the markets, he learned how to buy and sell and save. In 1907 Ilia emigrated to Western Australia; his family followed, arriving in February 1911.

The Geneffs lived at Innaloo, Perth, in an iron-roofed, timber-framed shack, the walls of which were lined with bags, before moving to Day Dawn near Cue. George was soon proficient in English. At 15 he cut wood along the Kalgoorlie pipeline and followed John ('Snowy') Flynn's boxing troupe around the goldfields. A short, sturdy fellow, he weighed ten stone (64 kg), was clean shaven and had a fair complexion. In 1914 'Kid George' was given a chance in the ring against a welterweight champion, Jimmy Sullivan. That year Geneff bought 50 acres (20 ha) at Osborne Park on which he established a market garden. By day he worked; at night he studied the art of boxing, and exercised with a punching-ball and a skipping-rope. He fought at His Majesty's Theatre, Perth, and, at the Royal Agricultural Show, took on Percy Button [q.v.13] in exhibition bouts. In 1915 Geneff appeared in fights at the Hippodrome, Sydney, before he went cane-cutting near Bundaberg, Queensland. Boxing lost its appeal for him when he decided that past champions had nothing to show for their glory except 'bruises, flat noses, cauliflower ears and dull minds'.

Returning penniless to Perth, he again turned to wood-cutting and saved his fare to Bulgaria where he married his cousin Elenka Ivanoff on 19 April 1923. Short of money, he paid for his wife's passage to Australia in the *Moreton Bay*, accompanying her as a stowaway. Based at Osborne Park, Geneff prospered as a wood and garden contractor. He survived the Depression through good management, low fees and wise use of his assets.

Acquiring more property, he expanded his business to include lime-burning, using the waste for road construction. From the Balcatta quarry he supplied limestone for the façades of Winthrop Hall and the Lake Karrinyup Country Club. During World War II he did contract work for the Albany and Busselton aerodromes.

As secretary of the Osborne Park-Scarborough-North Beach Ratepayers Association ('the Vigilants'), he charged the Perth Road Board in 1935 with maladministration and corruption, particularly in regard to the Scarborough Beach promenade, and won an action in the Supreme Court against the board's engineer. In that year Geneff was elected as Osborne Park's representative on the board; he was also a member of the Australian Labor Party's metropolitan council. In the late 1950s his philanthropy extended to building the Nadezda Hospital at Innaloo and clubrooms for the Sorrento Surf Life Saving Club; he bought and dispatched two fully-equipped ambulances to Bulgaria, pressed for scholarships for children from low-income families and donated £125 000 for a centre for the elderly at Osborne Park that now bears his name. Closely associated with the development of Sorrento, in 1962 he built the Nookenburra Hotel. The Geneffs twice revisited Bulgaria, but George's roots were firmly transplanted in Australia. Survived by his wife and two sons, he died on 4 November 1977 in Royal Perth Hospital and was cremated with the forms of the Uniting Church.

L. A. Easton, *Stirling City* (Perth, 1971); Osborne Park, Scarborough Beach, North Beach Vigilant Cte, *Vigilant* (Perth), 11 Apr, 13 Nov 1935, 16 Apr 1936; *West Australian*, 10 Feb, 8-10 Mar 1935, 31 Mar, 22 Apr, 10 May, 5 July 1936, 25 Apr 1937, 5 Aug, 7 Nov 1977; *Daily News* (Perth), 21, 23 Apr 1935; M. Thomas, Along the Plank Road through Njookenbooroo to Scarborough Beach (ts, 1989, Perth, BL); G. Geneff, A Biography of the Shepherd Boy (ts, 1986, WAA); information from and scrap-books and clippings held by Mr J. Geneff, Osborne Park, Perth.   WENDY BIRMAN

GENTILE, DORIS MAY (1894-1972), writer, was born on 30 October 1894 at Woolwich, Sydney, second daughter of Harry Charles Dinham, a silver-engraver from London, and his Tasmanian-born wife Ida Margaret, née Pybus. Doris began writing at an early age and published a story in the children's pages of the *Australasian* when she was 7. Usually written under the name of 'D. Manners-Sutton', her work subsequently appeared in the *Australasian*, the *Sydney Mail*, the *Tasmanian Mail* and the *Sunraysia Daily*. In 1923 she published her first novel, *A Marked Soul*, a melodramatic tale involving the transmigration of souls, with the action

moving from penal Van Diemen's Land to the trenches of France.

Intent on high adventure, Dinham left Australia in June 1925. In South Africa she worked as a publicity officer for the United Tobacco companies and published stories in local newspapers. After exploring the Kalahari Desert, she journeyed from Cape Town to the Congo. Her time in Africa was to produce two novels, *Black God* (London, 1934) and *The Last Secret* (London, 1939): both had Africans as the protagonists. Although virtually unnoticed in Australia, *Black God* received widespread acclaim and was chosen as the New York Book of the Month.

In mid-1926 Dinham sailed from the Congo for London where she worked for the *Morning Post*. During 1928 she studied French in Paris and drama in Vienna. Next year she moved to Italy; she attended various universities and pursued competence in a range of languages. She continued to publish short stories, supplementing her income with money earned from dancing engagements and loans from her friend Ella McFadyen, the children's writer. At Benghazi, Cyrenaica (Libya), on 6 June 1934 Doris married Salvatore Gentile, a Sicilian engineer. Marriage and motherhood did not retard her travels, which included a promotional visit to North America in 1936. She was in Britain when World War II broke out, but returned to Sicily in April 1940.

Doris Gentile's movements over the early years of the war are difficult to trace. She left both Sicily and her marriage, and made an unsuccessful attempt to escape with her children to Switzerland. From 1943 to 1946 she lived at Civiglio, Italy, a small village in the hills above Como. Lacking means of adequate subsistence and with two children to support, she made some money by giving clandestine English lessons, but she and her children were malnourished and often hungry. In April 1946 Gentile regained her British nationality and was repatriated to England. Two years later she emigrated to Canada where a friend had organized an editorial position for her with Longmans Green & Co. at Toronto. When her work did not prove satisfactory she returned to London. Although her papers include manuscripts for a number of novels, plays, film scripts and short stories, she published nothing after the war. In 1970 she followed her children to New South Wales. Survived by her daughter and son, she died on 16 May 1972 in Prince Henry Hospital, Sydney, and was buried with Methodist forms in the Anglican section of Botany cemetery.

In a letter written in 1946 to her family in Australia, Gentile made some amazing statements about her life at Civiglio, specifically that she had played some part in the downfall of Mussolini, that she had fought with the partisans and that she had been arrested and tortured. In the fragmentary drafts of two autobiographical novels, 'No Time for Love' and 'The Sawdust Republic', on which she was working in the early 1960s, she told the same story, but as yet there is no other evidence either to confirm or confound these claims. It is possible that she played some role with the partisans and in assisting Allied prisoners of war to escape to Switzerland. The rest of her assertions seem somewhat extravagant.

A small, pretty woman, with a tiny waist and red hair, she had learned early to play with her age and social status. Her marriage certificate and all subsequent documents gave her birth date as 1908; her visiting card bore a coronet and introduced her as the Contessa Dorina Gentile. The various accounts that she gave of her travels in Africa contained much of the bizarre and much inconsistency. Gentile was headstrong, intent on creating an extraordinary life of independence and adventure. She wrote truly in 1945, in a fragmentary diary: 'If I have done nothing else with my life, I at least have made of it something fantastique like a fairy story'. The question remains as to whether the 'fantastique' is the life or the story.

Australian, 13 Oct 1973; *SMH*, 30 Sept 1926, 3 Feb 1927; D. M. Gentile papers (ML); W. P. Hurst papers (LaTL); A1066/1, item 1C45/20/1/2/33 (AA, Canb); family information.   Ros Pesman

GEORGE, Sir ROBERT ALLINGHAM (1896-1967), air force officer and governor, was born on 25 July 1896 at Cromarty in the County of Ross and Cromarty, Scotland, twin child of William George, inspector of the poor, and his wife Mary, née Allingham. Educated at Invergordon and Inverness, in 1914 he enlisted in the Seaforth Highlanders. He was sent to France and commissioned in 1916 in the Gordon Highlanders. Next year he transferred to the Royal Flying Corps as a pilot and in 1918 was awarded the Military Cross for his night bombing and strafing exploits. Appointed to a permanent commission in the Royal Air Force in 1919, he served in India until 1924, then at the Cadet College, Cranwell, Lincolnshire. At the parish church, Caythorpe, on 3 May 1927 he married 18-year-old Sybil Elizabeth Baldwin.

On graduating from the R.A.F. Staff College in 1931, George took command of No.33 Squadron at Bicester, Oxfordshire, and won acclaim for developing the new technique of dive-bombing. He was senior air staff officer, Singapore, 1934-37, air attaché, Ankara (1939-44) and Athens (1939-41), air officer commanding, Iraq and Persia, 1944-45, and air attaché, Paris, from 1945. Appointed

C.B.E. (1944) and C.B. (1948), he was promoted substantive air vice-marshal in 1950 and elevated to K.B.E. on his retirement from the R.A.F. in 1952.

In August that year Sir Robert was appointed governor of South Australia. He and Lady George arrived in Adelaide on 22 February 1953. In a speech of welcome Premier (Sir) Thomas Playford noted that governors were expected to be 'an inspiration in times of danger'. George rose to the challenge after Adelaide's worst earthquake damaged Government House and many other buildings in March 1954, a fortnight before Queen Elizabeth II made her first visit to the city. He did so again in January 1955 when bushfires destroyed fifty homes, including the vice-regal summer residence, Marble Hill. Trapped by the flames for two hours, the Georges and their staff lost their personal effects and were lucky to escape with their lives.

George was admired for his bravery, but his impatience, polo-playing and habit of carrying a fly-whisk as well as a cane on parade did not endear him to the masses. He was appointed K.St.J. (1953), K.C.V.O. (1954), grand master of the Grand Lodge of Freemasons (1956) and K.C.M.G. (1958). Lady George encouraged charity workers, but upset educationists and feminists. Opening laboratories and classrooms at a girls' college, she claimed: 'the most important thing for a girl is to learn how to run a home well' and suggested that 'many wars might have been prevented' if women had 'kept their menfolk better fed and more contented'. Although annoyed by Sir Robert's demands for a swimming pool and a personal helicopter, the premier upheld the dignity of the governor's office. When a cook's action for the recovery of her wages appeared in the Supreme Court lists as *Badcock* v. *Air Vice-Marshal Sir Robert Allingham George*, Playford funded an out-of-court settlement by inserting a line for £500 in the 1956-57 budget on condition that Badcock's solicitor D. A. Dunstan and his Australian Labor Party colleagues in parliament gave an undertaking not to debate that item during the budget's passage through the legislature. Conservatives were enraged when an A.L.P. maverick S. J. Lawn reneged and tried to raise a public outcry about the governor's treatment of his staff. Playford showed his contempt for the Opposition by extending George's term.

Sir Robert retired to England in 1959 and became a director in London of the Bank of Adelaide and the Australian Estates Co. Ltd. Survived by his wife, daughter and three sons, he died on 13 September 1967 at St Marylebone after being struck by a motorcar.

PD (SA), 3 Oct 1956, p 865; *Advertiser* (Adel), 26, 27 Aug 1952, 19, 21, 24 Feb, 1 Apr, 4 June

1953, 3, 4 Jan 1955, 15 Feb 1956, 11 Mar, 5 Nov 1957, 8 Mar 1960; *News* (Adel), 28 Aug 1952, 23 Feb 1953, 1 Mar 1954, 25 Jan, 4 Oct 1956; *Sunday Mail* (Adel), 28 Apr 1956; *Herald* (Melb), 14 Sept, 17 Nov 1967; information from Hon D. A. Dunstan, Norwood, and Hon R. R. Millhouse, Unley Park, Adel.   P. A. Howell

GERALD, JAMES (1891-1971), comedian, was born on 2 January 1891 at Darlington, Sydney, seventh son of native-born parents Stephen Australia Fitzgerald, a cutter who became an actor, and his wife Mary Ann, née Ingram. A nephew of J. D. Fitzgerald [q.v.8], Jim played truant from school to watch acrobats practising on the sandhills behind Centennial Park, learned to tumble and haunted his uncles' circus. Three of his brothers went on the stage as 'Max Clifton', 'Lance Vane' and 'Cliff Stevens'. About 1898 he joined Oscar Pagel, a strongman in Fitzgerald Bros' Circus, travelled with his troupe to South Africa, and then toured Africa, Asia and North America.

Back in Australia by 1908, Fitzgerald tented with several circuses; as 'Diabolo' he was billed as the first man to loop the loop on a motorcycle. Five ft 7 ins (170 cm) tall, with blue eyes and black hair, he joined the Fullers' [qq.v.8] vaudeville circuit in 1912 as 'Jim Gerald', an acrobat and wire-walker. On 21 July 1913 at St Peter's Anglican Church, Wellington, New Zealand, he married Esther Patience Futcher, a 27-year-old actress known as 'Essie Jennings'. A knockabout act with his wife, 'The Actress and the Paperhanger', made his name as a comedian.

Fitzgerald enlisted in the Australian Imperial Force on 5 May 1916 and served in Mesopotamia as a driver with the 1st Australian and New Zealand Wireless Signal Squadron. Discharged on 12 October 1918, he returned to the Fullers' circuit and was soon asked by (Sir) Benjamin Fuller to write and produce his own revue sketches. He had seen the funny side of soldiering in Mesopotamia and his act, 'The New Recruit', remained popular for years. Unlike his contemporaries Roy Rene and George Wallace [qq.v.11,12], Gerald was 'unashamedly international' in his work. Almost every Christmas he played the dame in pantomimes. He made some thirty silent films in the United States of America in 1928, and was influenced by Charlie Chaplin whom he greatly admired.

When the Fullers folded in 1933, Gerald continued to play six-month seasons in Sydney and Melbourne under various managements. In 1935-36 he appeared in several revues at the Garrick Theatre, London, including *Don't Spare the Horses*. Returning to Sydney, in May 1936 he featured in *Shout for Joy*. One critic wrote that he 'cannot particu-larly sing nor does he know much about dancing, but he is undoubtedly a master of patter, of quick, well-timed delivery and retort'. Gerald signed a contract with the Australian Broadcasting Commission in February 1939; he starred in 'Jim and Jitters' with Jim Davidson's A.B.C. Dance Band and conducted the Saturday 'After-Dinner Show'. Next year he formed his own radio-production firm.

On 10 April 1941 Gerald was appointed honorary lieutenant colonel in the A.I.F. Placed in charge of the Entertainment Unit, he embarked for the Middle East on 1 September in the *Queen Elizabeth*. A shrewd organizer and an experienced producer, he gathered Davidson and his band, comedians, singers, jugglers, acrobats and trick cyclists, as well as backstage technicians, 'among them costume designers, seamstresses and electricians'. At his headquarters at Tel Aviv, Palestine, he recruited a female chorus line. The first performance at Gaza of *All in Fun* was 'received with rapturous applause'.

Home again in October 1942, Gerald transferred to the retired list on 31 December. He joined the Tivoli circuit and appeared in the revue, *Stripped for Action* (1943). In 1951 he played the happy roué in *Ladies' Night in a Turkish Bath*. He shared top billing with Wallace in *Thanks for the Memory*, at the Princess Theatre, Melbourne, in 1953 and toured for three years in that revue. He was 'as uproariously funny as ever though not as spry' in *The Good Old Days* (Sydney, 1957). Next year he retired to St Kilda, Melbourne. Gerald enjoyed watching any kind of sport, but his passion was for motoring: he owned a succession of cars which he drove across America, through Europe, the Middle East and Britain, and all over Australia. After Essie's death in 1969, he moved into a home at Rosebud. He died there on 2 March 1971 and was cremated. 'Jim Gerald was probably best remembered for his versatility—as a big-eared oaf in baggy pants and shapeless hat, as a seemingly rubber-boned and pathetically droll clown and as Australia's greatest pantomime dame.'

K. Burke (ed), *With Horse and Morse in Mesopotamia* (Syd, 1927); N. Bridges and F. Crook, *Curtain Call* (Syd, 1980); M. Pate, *An Entertaining War* (Syd, 1986); P. Parsons (ed), *A Companion to Theatre in Australia* (Syd, 1995); *Wireless Weekly*, 17 Feb 1939; *ABC Weekly*, 16 Dec 1939, p 60; *Aust Women's Weekly*, 26 Nov 1949; *People* (Syd), 1 Aug 1951; *Bulletin*, 5 Aug, 9 Sept 1926, 28 May 1930, 3 May 1933; *SMH*, 9 Nov 1928, 31 Oct 1935, 29-30 May 1936, 27 May 1939, 11 Apr, 10 June, 24 Oct, 25 Dec 1941, 13 Oct 1942, 17, 20 Apr 1943, 3 Mar 1971; *Daily Mirror* (Syd), 28 Nov 1973.

MARTHA RUTLEDGE

GEROE, CLARA; see LAZAR

GIBB, Sir CLAUDE (1898-1959), engineer, was born on 29 June 1898 at Queenstown, Adelaide, third of five children of John Gilbert Gibb, a South Australian-born carter, and his wife Caroline Elizabeth, née Dixon. Educated at Alberton Public and Lefevre's Peninsula High schools, Claude won a cadetship to the South Australian School of Mines and Industries where, in 1915-17, he studied mechanical and electrical engineering. He worked for the Adelaide Cement Co. Ltd as an electrician before enlisting in the Australian Imperial Force on 5 December 1917; initially an air mechanic in the Australian Flying Corps, he was based in England from April 1918 and commissioned as a pilot in February 1919.

Next year Gibb obtained a post as senior research assistant to Professor (Sir) Robert Chapman [q.v.7] at the University of Adelaide and found time for further study (B.E., Dip.Appl.Sc., 1923; M.E., 1932). An Angas [q.v.3] scholarship enabled him to return to England in 1924. There he joined the engineering firm, C. A. Parsons & Co. Ltd, at Newcastle upon Tyne as a student apprentice; within five years he was a director and by 1938 general manager. At the Baptist Chapel, Totnes, Devon, on 26 December 1925 he had married Margaret Bate Harris (d.1969); they were to remain childless.

During World War II Gibb's work on steam turbines led to his employment in 1940 at the Ministry of Supply. He became director-general of weapons and instruments production (1941) and was said to have averaged two hours sleep per night. In 1943 he 'left guns to work on tanks' and helped to produce the Centurion. Returning to Parsons, as chairman and managing director from September 1945, over the succeeding years he also chaired A. Reyrolle & Co. Ltd, Parolle Electrical Plant Co. Ltd and Anglo Great Lakes Corporation Ltd, and was chairman and joint managing director of the Nuclear Power Plant Co. Ltd, Pyrotenax Ltd and Savage & Parsons Ltd. He realized the importance of developments in the peaceful use of atomic energy: Parsons supplied the turbo-alternators and gas-circulating blowers at Calder Hall, Risley.

Although Gibb found it difficult to delegate responsibility, he had prodigious energy, a flair for publicity, astuteness, wide experience and 'amiable pugnacity'. He was knighted in 1945. In 1956 he was appointed K.B.E. and elected a fellow (vice-president 1957) of the Royal Society. The universities of London and Durham awarded him honorary D.Sc. degrees. Sir Claude was vice-president (1945-51) of the Institution of Mechanical Engineers, London, and twice received its Thomas Hawksley medal. An easy and natural speaker, he was much in demand. In 1954 he delivered the first Robin memorial lecture at the University of Adelaide on 'The Engineer in the Community'. His twenty-two publications included 'The Stresses in floors of elevated cylindrical tanks' (1923), 'The influence of operating experience on the design and construction of turbines and alternators' (1936), and the admired 'Report on Investigation into the failure of Two 100-MW Turbo-Generators' (1955).

At 49 Gibb recovered from a severe coronary thrombosis, as he did five years later from a second and a third. He continued to travel and work as hard as ever, and collapsed and died on 15 January 1959 at Newark airport, New Jersey, United States of America.

DNB, 1951-60; D. A. Cumming and G. C. Moxham, *They Built South Australia* (Adel, 1986); *Biog Memoirs of Fellows of Roy Soc* (Lond), 1959, p 47; *Cwlth Engineer*, Feb 1959, p 86; *Advertiser* (Adel), 1 Jan 1947, 27 Sept 1954, 17, 19 Jan 1959; *The Times*, 17, 21, 24 Jan 1959.

GWENYTH C. MOXHAM

GIBSON, ALEXANDER BOYCE (1900-1972), philosopher, was born on 10 March 1900 at Hampstead, London, eldest son of William Ralph Boyce Gibson [q.v.8], lecturer in philosophy, and his wife Lucy Judge, née Peacock. 'Sandy' was educated (1913-16) at Melbourne Church of England Grammar School and graduated with first-class honours in classics from the University of Melbourne (B.A. Hons, 1920). He then went to Balliol College, Oxford (B.A., 1923; M.A., 1926), where he read philosophy; his tutor A. D. (Baron) Lindsay had a lifelong influence on him.

In 1923 Boyce Gibson (as he was commonly known) was appointed an assistant-lecturer in philosophy at the University of Glasgow; two years later he became a tutor for the Workers' Educational Association in Staffordshire, England. At St Columba's Church, Chelsea, London, on 2 April 1925 he married Kathleen Grace Derham with the forms of the Church of Scotland. In 1927-35 he lectured in philosophy at the University of Birmingham; his much praised book, *The Philosophy of Descartes* (London), appeared in 1932.

Succeeding his father as professor of philosophy at the University of Melbourne in 1935, Gibson found that the department was small in numbers and generally an intellectual backwater. During his thirty-one year tenure it attained an international reputation for philosophical originality and liveliness. In the 1940s and 1950s he made a number of appointments of young philosophers from Cambridge and Oxford who were enthusiastically committed to the new kind of philosophical inquiry, sometimes called 'linguistic analysis', which derived from the teaching and work of Ludwig Wittgenstein, then at Cambridge. Gibson himself had little intellectual sympathy with this philosophical movement, but he was nonetheless responsible (partly by design, partly by accident) for creating one of the major centres of the movement outside Cambridge and Oxford. In 1948 he was awarded an honorary D.Litt. from the University of Cambridge.

Gibson was, however, very much a pluralist in philosophy and tried to balance the strong analytical tendencies in the department by appointing young scholars of other philosophical persuasions. In 1949 he wrote: 'At present there are two main approaches to philosophy: the metaphysical and the positivist. My own view is that philosophy has everything to gain from their interfructification and I have built a department out of their differences of opinion'. Throughout the 1950s and 1960s there was a certain amount of tension between Gibson's pluralist department and John Anderson's [q.v.7] monistic department at the University of Sydney, although Gibson, in an ecumenical spirit, also appointed one well-known Andersonian to his staff.

No doubt because of his father's Continental background, Gibson always took a lively interest in contemporary European philosophy, and encouraged some of the younger members of his staff to take phenomenology and other French and German philosophical movements seriously. He did this at a time when most English-speaking philosophers tended to dismiss Continental philosophy as so much 'bad poetry'. His own philosophical interests were broad. Attentive to the philosophy of education, to the philosophy of art and to the work of the classical philosophers, he introduced generations of his first-year students to the mysteries of Plato's *Republic*, lecturing passionately on the Form of the Good and the allegory of the cave.

Gibson's enduring interest was in the philosophy of religion. He was a Christian (his paternal grandfather had been a Wesleyan Methodist minister) but he always thought of himself as a 'doubting Thomas': he held that doubt and belief were elements of any religious position, and had to be maintained in (a favourite phrase) 'fruitful tension'. As he put it in his last—and best—work, *The Religion of Dostoevski* (London, 1973): 'It was the novels of Dostoevski which, by excluding the "natural" and "rational" religion in which I was reared, started me off as a Christian-in-process . . . They have shown me that religious faith and philosophical doubt in a sense belong together'.

In a book completed after his retirement in 1966, *Theism and Empiricism* (London,

1970), Gibson argued against the philosophical prejudice that 'it is impossible to be empirically acquainted with the non-empirical'. If we take a sufficiently broad view of 'experience' there is no *a priori* reason, he argued, why the grounds of theism cannot be disclosed in human experience. He was suspicious of the classical rational 'proofs' (and 'disproofs') of the existence of God, and held that religious belief must derive from lived experience. It was Plato, he claimed, who invented the split between reason and experience, a split that had been widened and formalized as a dogma by the seventeenth-century philosophical rationalists and empiricists.

Although a very shy man, Boyce Gibson showed great personal warmth and loyalty to those who knew him well. He also had a nice sense of humour. Again, despite his reserve, he loved academic life, and, as dean (1939-41) of the faculty of arts and chairman (1949-52) of the professorial board, he enjoyed the devious twists and turns of university politics. Survived by his wife and daughter, he died on 2 October 1972 at Surrey Hills and was cremated.

S. A. Grave, *A History of Philosophy in Australia* (Brisb, 1984); J. T. Srzednicki and F. D. Wood (eds), *Essays on Philosophy in Australia* (Boston, US, 1992); *Univ Melb Gazette*, Mar 1966; *Age* (Melb), 18 Dec 1934; *Sun News-Pictorial*, 20 Nov 1937, 18 June 1948.   MAX CHARLESWORTH

GIBSON, AUBREY HICKES LAWSON (1901-1973), businessman and patron of the arts, was born on 4 May 1901 at Kew, Melbourne, third child of John Gibson, a manager from Scotland, and his English-born wife Ellen Ann Meares, née Lawson. Educated at Melbourne Church of England Grammar School, Aubrey proceeded to the University of Melbourne where he passed in one subject, graphics. He also attended the National Gallery of Victoria school, for one year.

On 3 February 1930 Gibson married Marjorie Isabel Kimpton at the chapel of his old school; they were to have a daughter and a son before being divorced. After working as a salesman for Hoover products, in January 1933 he established A. H. Gibson (Electrical) Co. Pty Ltd, distributors of electrical appliances and parts. Having been appointed lieutenant in the Melbourne University Rifles in 1922, Gibson continued to serve in the Militia and rose to major. On 13 May 1940 he was seconded to the Australian Imperial Force. He performed adjutant and quartermaster-general duties in the Middle East (1940-42) and Australia, and transferred to the Reserve of Officers as lieutenant colonel on 13 May

1945; he was made honorary colonel on the Retired List in 1951. In Colombo, on 19 September 1947, he had married Gertrude Jean Balfour.

In 1949 his business was converted to a public company, A. H. Gibson Industries Ltd, with Gibson as chairman and managing director, but it was delisted in 1959. Additional business commitments included serving as chairman and managing director (1955-64) of Consumer Services Ltd, and as director of Volkswagen (A/sia) Ltd (1961-67) and Hoover (Aust.) Pty Ltd (1964-70). As a sideline, he farmed land at Berwick.

Gibson became prominent as a patron of the arts. A founding director (1954) of the Australian Elizabethan Theatre Trust, he was Victorian chairman (1955-67), president (1968-71) and chairman of the board (1971-72). This commitment entailed membership of the boards of the Australian Opera, the Australian Ballet and the Australian Council for the Arts. As A.E.T.T. representative on the board of the University of Melbourne's Union Theatre Repertory Company, later the Melbourne Theatre Company (deputy-chairman 1960-68), he was forceful in securing and refurbishing its Russell Street Theatre base.

Dedicated to the fine arts in particular, Gibson was a trustee (from 1956), treasurer (1957-59) and deputy-chairman (1959 and 1962-64) of the National Gallery of Victoria. He was a councillor (1951-56) and trustee of the Victorian Artists Society, he received the medal of the Society of Artists, Sydney, in 1965, and he was a member (from 1966) of the Britannica Australia Awards Committee. Although his renowned personal collection was strong in Australian paintings and sculpture, it was international in span, and included silver works—featured in his book *The Rosebowl* (1952)—native carvings, furniture, *figurines historiques* and Oriental works, among them Japanese scrolls. In addition to being a co-founder, with Joseph Burke, of the Society of Collectors of Fine Arts, he was a councillor of the National Trust of Australia (Victoria) from its foundation in 1955. His clubs included the Naval and Military, Athenaeum, Savage, Metropolitan Golf, Victoria Racing and the Commonwealth (Canberra).

Rather than an innovator, Gibson was an imaginative, energetic, forceful, successful and generous promoter of the causes he espoused. His was a dynamic contribution to Australia's cultural development and well-being. He died on 26 March 1973 at Prahran and was cremated; his wife and their son survived him, as did the son of his first marriage. His estate was sworn for probate at $835 442. Portraits by Bryan Kneale and Noel Counihan are in the family's possession; a sketch by Louis Kahan is in the Clem

Christesen collection, University of Melbourne, and another is held by the artist.

J. Sumner, *Recollections at Play* (Melb, 1993); *Art and Aust*, 2, no 3, Dec 1964; *Canb Times*, 16 Dec 1965; *Australian*, 24 July 1969; *Age* (Melb), 29, 30 May 1973; Gibson papers *and* A. H. Gibson Industries Ltd file, Stock Exchange of Melb collection (Univ Melb Archives).   FRANK STRAHAN

GIBSON, DOROTHY (1899-1978), teacher, communist and peace activist, was born on 4 July 1899 at Malvern, Melbourne, younger child of John Moir Alexander, a manufacturer's agent from Scotland, and his Victorian-born wife Ellen Mary, née Forbes. John was a successful vigneron and wine merchant, and a committed socialist. Dorothy was educated at Korowa girls' school—for which, despite her disapproval of private schools later in life, she retained the deepest affection —and at the University of Melbourne (B.A., 1920; Dip.Ed., 1924).

For the next ten years she was involved in new education. In 1924-28 she taught at the Rev. John Lawton's [q.v.10] experimental school, St Andrew's College, Kew. She travelled to England twice to pursue her interest in progressive education. Her teaching experience at the school for the children of Soviet Embassy and Trade Legation staff in London in 1933 led to her being invited to teach at the Anglo-American school in Moscow in the following year. 'A miracle has been achieved there', she wrote of the Soviet Union; her uncritical devotion dated from this experience, and was reinforced by her visits in 1953, 1962, 1967 and 1971.

Europe in the 1930s had an immense effect on Dorothy. The Depression, the rise of fascism and the threat of war affirmed her pacifist stance, which she had acquired from her father during World War I. On her return from Moscow in 1935, she abandoned plans to start a school and directed her energies to the anti-war movement and to friendship with the Soviet Union. It was at this time that she turned to Marxism, which came to her 'like a flash of light, an illuminating truth'. She was an executive-member of the Victorian Council Against War and Fascism, and then joined the International Peace Campaign, of which she was Victorian assistant to the secretary, Constance Duncan [q.v.]. Dorothy served as vice-president of the Friends of the Soviet Union and in 1936 joined the Communist Party of Australia which, she stated, 'gave direction and hope to my life'.

On 4 October 1932 at the registrar's office, Collins Street, Melbourne, she had married Donovan Charles Clarke, a 24-year-old teacher; they were divorced in 1936. At the office of the government statist, Queen

Street, on 16 March 1937 she married Ralph Siward, son of W. R. B. Gibson [q.v.8] and brother of A. B. Gibson [q.v.]. Ralph was a scholarly man who became a leading communist theoretician and orator. Their devotion to one another lasted almost forty-one years, until Dorothy's death. They had no children.

At the outbreak of World War II Mrs Gibson worked for the temporarily illegal C.P.A. before holding the post of secretary to the Australian-Soviet Friendship League. During the Cold War period her skills came to the fore. She was an executive-member and full-time organizer of the two main peace organizations initiated by the communist movement: the Australian Peace Council, established in 1949, and its successor, the Congress for International Co-operation and Disarmament, set up in 1959. She organized congresses, petitions, marches, meetings, leaflets and pamphlets, and wrote letters to the press and to peace groups.

A self-effacing woman, Gibson was successful in broadening the peace movement by involving people of diverse backgrounds, political affiliations and faiths. She worked closely with the three 'peace parsons', Frank Hartley [q.v.], Alfred Dickie and Victor James. Her enthusiasm inspired the young, especially during the campaigns against conscription and the Vietnam War.

Unswerving in her political loyalties, Gibson did not allow the revelations of Stalinist atrocities, the crushing of the Hungarian uprising in 1956, or the Soviet tanks in Prague in 1968 to shake her confidence in communism and the Soviet Union. Although she regretted the large exodus of party members in those years, she continued to woo them into some activity; few could resist her persuasion. Her handsome face beamed at the minutest success, and she infused people with both optimism and admiration.

Gibson's political zeal was tempered by her love for her Australian and Scottish family, and by the pleasure she took in her garden and the Australian bush. She admired books, films and paintings of the heroic, uplifting kind, but could be critical of art that served no ideological purpose. She dreamed of a socialist Australia and a world free from war. To achieve these ends she worked tirelessly, even while debilitated by arthritis and angina. Survived by her husband, she died on 6 January 1978 at Prahran and was cremated.

R. Gibson, *One Woman's Life* (Syd, 1980); J. Sendy, *Ralph Gibson* (Melb, 1988); *Age* (Melb), 22 Aug 1980; R. and D. Gibson papers (NL) and file (Univ Melb Archives); E. Quick, interview with S. Murray-Smith, 1982 (tape and video held by author, Mount Eliza, Vic).

NITA MURRAY-SMITH

GIBSON, FREDA EVELYN (1908-1977), flying doctor, was born on 7 February 1908 at Fullarton, Adelaide, twin daughter and third child of South Australian-born parents Albert Paul Oscar Ehmcke, engineer, and his wife Flora Evelyn, née Stoyel. Freda was educated at Walford House and Poltoonga schools, and at Presbyterian Girls' College where she was a prefect, played in the top hockey, basketball and tennis teams, and was dux (1925). She then studied medicine at the University of Adelaide (M.B., B.S., 1931). At Scots Church, North Terrace, on 3 February 1933 she married a fellow graduate Dr Robert Welch ('Roy') Gibson (1907-1948) and later that year joined him in general practice at Ceduna where they used a cottage hospital, staffed and equipped by the Anglicans' Bush Church Aid Society. The Gibsons were the only doctors in the far west and often travelled long distances on rudimentary roads to cope with all kinds of emergencies. Both of them were courageous, decisive and competent.

A new B.C.A. hospital was built at Ceduna in 1937. In the following year the Flying Medical Service was inaugurated. Its Fox Moth biplane, capable of carrying a pilot, a doctor and a stretcher, enabled the Gibsons to reach patients quickly—if there were a landing-strip available or one could be hastily prepared—and saved them much driving and fatigue. They regularly visited the small hospitals at Penong, Cook and Tarcoola (which were all equipped, and often used, for emergency surgery), as well as the Koonibba Aboriginal Mission and outlying settlements. At Cook, patients frequently helped to clear goats from the airstrip. All dispensing had to be done from Ceduna until 1948. The Gibsons' practice flourished. During Roy's lengthy bouts of sickness, Freda managed alone: she performed intricate surgery under primitive conditions in station homesteads, took blood for transfusions, attended accidents and ran her growing household.

When her husband was absent on part-time duty in Adelaide with the Australian Army Medical Corps in World War II, Freda again shouldered the burden of the 80 000 sq. mile (207 200 km^2) practice. She also acted as quarantine officer and sometimes boarded ships (off Thevenard) by Jacob's ladder, a risky feat for a non-swimmer. With her children, she took her turn at watching for enemy vessels. She had a gun and knew how to use it. In the 1920s a man had threatened her father with an axe. Freda politely told him to put the axe away or she would shoot him in the arm; he ignored her and she coolly winged him. She found flying-work relaxing and refreshing, and was expert at adjusting the throttles as the pilot swung the propellers. In one three-year period she made 214 flights, covered 37 683 miles (60 643 km) and treated 2769 patients; her journeys ranged from 23 to 350 miles from Ceduna. Freda was appointed O.B.E. in 1946.

The Gibsons worked together until Roy's death in 1948; he was widely mourned by a widespread community cheered to learn that Freda would continue. In 1951 she was joined by Dr Merna Mueller. Coober Pedy was added to the list of the towns they visited and the B.C.A. opened a wireless base linked by transceivers to the out-hospitals, stations and homesteads. Gibson left Ceduna in 1954 to practise at Fullarton. On 11 May 1968 at St Ignatius' Catholic Church, Norwood, she married Mervyn George Kennedy, an accountant and a widower. She continued to work part time, but her health slowly deteriorated. A tall, slender woman with prematurely white hair and an indomitable spirit, she had been the first woman flying doctor in Australia. With the help of the B.C.A. Sisters, whom she frequently praised, she saved many lives and healed countless people. She gave unstinting service to her patients, some of whom avowed that the mere presence of 'Dr Freda' made them feel better. Survived by her husband, and by the son and two daughters of her first marriage, she died on 12 June 1977 in Royal Adelaide Hospital and was cremated. Her estate was sworn for probate at $135 453.

Greater than their Knowing (Adel, 1986); Presbyterian Girls' College (Adel), *Black Watch*, 1924, pp 3-7; *Real Aust*, Dec 1933, Jan 1937, June 1938, July 1954, Oct 1940, Dec 1949; *Advertiser*(Adel), 1 Jan 1946; Bush Church Aid Soc Council, Minutes, 14 Mar 1968; information from the late Miss F. Dowling.   MARY MCHUGH

GIBSON, GLADYS RUTH (1901-1972), educationist and women's leader, was born on 29 December 1901 at Goodwood Park, Adelaide, eldest of four children of James Ambrose Gibson, a travelling collector for the South Australian Blind and Deaf and Dumb Institution, and his wife Emma, née Keeley. Educated at Goodwood Public and Unley High schools, Ruth began work in 1919 as a student-teacher at Goodwood. Her mother died in 1923, after three years of illness. Ruth assumed most of her responsibilities and became the centre of strength in a closely knit family, remaining so all her life. She obtained her diploma from the Teachers' Training College and studied part time at the University of Adelaide (B.A., 1937; Dip.Ed., 1940).

In 1921 Miss Gibson had been appointed to Westbourne Park Public School. She later taught at primary and technical high schools in Adelaide and in the country before becoming inspector of girls schools (1941) and of secondary schools (1952). At a conference of the Australian and New Zealand Association of Institutes of Inspectors of Schools, held in Perth in 1954, she delivered a paper, 'Education's Part in International Understanding'. During her early career she had been influenced by Adelaide Miethke [q.v.10], and brought energy, dedication and commitment to women's education. Like Miethke, she promoted the careers of promising young teachers. A member of the Public Examinations Board (1942-63) and of the Technical High Schools Curriculum Board, she convened the English and social studies committees of the latter. She was a foundation member, honorary treasurer and a fellow (1963) of the Australian College of Education, a founder of St Ann's College, University of Adelaide, and president (1960-61) of the South Australian University Women Graduates' Association. She retired from teaching in 1961.

While influential and respected within her profession, Gibson was better known for her work with the National Council of Women—at the State, national and international levels. In 1938 she had been one of ten Australian delegates (and their secretary) to the jubilee conference of the International Council of Women, Edinburgh. As South Australian president (1950-54) of the N.C.W., she arranged and headed a women's welcome to Queen Elizabeth II in 1954. Gibson was president (1952-56) of the National Council of Women of Australia and vice-president (1953-56) of the international body. The Federal government had selected her as an official guest at the coronation in 1953, and as a representative at the 10th and 11th sessions of the United Nations Commission on the Status of Women, held in Geneva (1956) and New York (1957); at the 1957 meeting she was elected rapporteur to the commission. These sessions examined women's access to education, economic opportunity, tax and legal questions, and the nationality of married women. Gibson travelled extensively to attend conferences and executive meetings of the International Council of Women, and of the United Nations Educational, Scientific and Cultural Organization.

Her wide interests also led to her involvement as an office-bearer in the State division of the United Nations Association of Australia, in the Soroptimist and Lyceum clubs, Adelaide, in the Good Neighbour Council of South Australia and in the State section of the Royal Flying Doctor Service of Australia. In addition, she served on selection committees for Churchill fellowships and nursing scholarships. These duties never overshadowed her concern for individuals, shown in her many practical acts of kindness and consideration. She was a devout Anglican. Gibson lived in East Terrace, and enjoyed carpentry, gardening and motoring. Although not radical in her views, she was a feminist of her day and a believer in social justice. No position she held was a sinecure: she worked at all of them, and was impressive both as a chairwoman and a public speaker. Tall and strongly built, she dressed impeccably and had considerable presence. Some found her intimidating, but those who knew her appreciated her intelligence, warmth and humour, her generous and unpretentious nature, her skill as a hostess and her attachment to her family.

Gibson had been appointed O.B.E. in 1953 and was elevated to C.B.E. in 1970. She died of cancer on 23 August 1972 at Belair and was cremated. In 1974 a bronze sundial was erected in her memory at the Adelaide Festival Centre; from 1977 the Ruth Gibson memorial award has assisted women to further their studies and careers.

Greater than their Knowing (Adel, 1986); *Education Gazette of SA*, 2 Oct 1972, p 319; *Advertiser* (Adel), 19 Dec 1961; National Council of Women (SA) Archives, Adel; information from Miss J. M. Young, Myrtle Bank, Adel, and Mr C. L. Gibson, Westbourne Park, Adel, who holds a ms about Ruth Gibson's life. PHILIPPA L. FLETCHER

GIBSON, RICHARD MAXWELL (1921-1980), physician, was born on 21 December 1921 at Strathfield, Sydney, third of four sons of Norman Maxwell Gibson, a medical practitioner from Queensland, and his Sydney-born wife Dorothea Mary Agnes, née Burkitt. Educated at Trinity Grammar School, Summer Hill, and at Wesley College, University of Sydney (M.B., B.S., 1944), Richard was appointed resident medical officer at Royal Prince Alfred Hospital in 1944. At St Philip's Anglican Church, Sydney, on 28 December 1945 he married Alison Ruth Macfarlane, a physiotherapist. In 1945-46, as a captain in the Australian Army Medical Corps, he served in the hospital ship, *Manunda*, and at the 113th Military Hospital, Concord.

After a brief period in general practice at Bathurst, in 1948 Gibson joined the staff of (Royal) Newcastle Hospital as resident medical officer, becoming registrar next year. In 1951 he was admitted to membership (fellow 1968) of the Royal Australasian College of Physicians. As staff physician in the hospital's department of medicine from 1954, he was associated with cardiology, psychiatry, gastroenterology and paediatrics. He was appointed director of the department in 1961 and director of geriatric medicine in 1970.

Gibson's absorbing interest in the discipline of geriatrics arose from a survey which he and Grace Parbery (a social worker) had conducted into the needs of disseminated-sclerosis sufferers in the Hunter Valley in 1950. In partnership with Parbery and a multi-disciplinary team, and with the support of the medical superintendent Christian McCaffrey [q.v.], he pioneered a hospital-based service for treating chronically disabled and elderly people, integrating the facilities of the hospital and the community. Known as the 'Newcastle Experience', it incorporated in-patient care and a wide range of domiciliary services, including home nursing, housekeeping, an equipment loan service, the adaptation of dwellings, a retraining unit and a day centre. Gibson promoted correct diagnosis, careful assessment of social needs, good clinical management, rehabilitation and maintenance. Close liaison was maintained with the patient's family doctor and relations, whom Gibson regarded as members of his team.

He enthusiastically advocated the 'Newcastle Experience' on economic, medical and compassionate grounds, interstate and overseas, in the media and at conferences. A member of the advisory committee of the Hospitals Commission of New South Wales, Gibson was a foundation member and president of the Australian Association of Gerontology, a founder and council-member of the Australian Geriatrics Society, chairman (Asia-Oceania region) of the International Association of Gerontology and a member of the National Advisory Council for the Handicapped. In 1965 he was appointed O.B.E. He co-ordinated (from 1973) programmes for chronic disability in the Hunter region for the Health Commission of New South Wales and became regional geriatrician in 1974.

A tall, imposing man, Dick Gibson inspired loyalty in his staff, and confidence and affection in his patients. After his marriage was dissolved in October 1977, he married a divorcee Judith Clift Adams, née Adams, on 17 December that year at the Newcastle registry office. He died of a ruptured abdominal aortic aneurysm on 23 May 1980 at Royal Newcastle Hospital and was cremated with Anglican rites; his wife survived him, as did the son and three daughters of his first marriage. The service he and his team developed was at the national forefront and abreast of that in Britain. His work influenced the direction of geriatrics in Australia and is commemorated by the annual Dick Gibson lecture at the University of Newcastle, the R. M. Gibson travelling fellowship and the R. M. Gibson Scientific Research Fund, all sponsored by the Australian Association of Gerontology.

S. Sax (ed), *The Aged in Australian Society* (Syd, 1970); H. Attwood and R. W. Home (eds), *Patients, Practitioners and Techniques* (Melb, 1984); L. Butler (ed), *Chris McCaffrey* (Newcastle, NSW, 1985); Roy Newcastle Hosp, *Annual Report*, 1949-81; *MJA*, 5 Oct 1957, p 485; *Lancet*, 2, 1965, p 284; *Newcastle Morning Herald*, 26 May 1980; Gibson papers (Auchmuty L, Univ Newcastle). MARGARET HENRY

GIBSON, ROGER BARRACLOUGH (1909-1977), mechanical engineer, was born on 31 May 1909 at Mosman, Sydney, third child of Alexander James Gibson [q.v.8], an engineer from London, and his native-born wife Marion Ellen Florence, née Hitchman. Educated at Sydney Church of England Grammar School (Shore), Roger graduated in engineering technology at the University of Sydney (B.E., 1934). On 24 August 1934 he married Myrna Rosamond McNaghten Dickey at the Shore chapel; they were to be divorced in 1957. After working for the Australian Gas Light Co., in 1937 he joined his father's engineering consultancy firm, Julius [q.v.9], Poole & Gibson, despite some rumblings from the old guard that his irreverent wit and humour were not compatible with the serious profession of engineering. Using a hydraulic model especially built for the purpose at Sydney Technical College, he helped his father in making intensive calculations to increase the discharge capacity of Burrinjuck Dam, thereby ensuring its safety in time of flood.

Having been commissioned lieutenant in the Militia, Gibson was seconded on 1 January 1941 to the Australian Imperial Force. In 1941-43 he served with the Australian Army Ordnance Corps in the Middle East. Back home, he was promoted major and in 1944-45 was electrical and mechanical engineer, Northern Territory Lines of Communication Area Workshops. He transferred to the Reserve of Officers on 3 November 1945 and rejoined his father's firm.

Gibson's originality in design and his imaginative approach to problems involved him in a diverse range of engineering projects: the design of coke ovens and conveyor systems for the Mount Pleasant and Illawarra collieries, the design and development of aircraft undercarriage support and cargo-handling equipment for Qantas Empire Airways Ltd, and of power-operated hangar doors at Mascot airport (a technology transferred to the United States of America), solving pumping-station problems at Mildura and adapting mechanical designs for amusement equipment at Luna Park, Sydney. For many years he also served as the firm's expert on engineering valuation in New Zealand (in regard to earthquake insurance), notably for New Zealand Forest Products Ltd. He married a widow Marjorie Cecilia Cudmore, née Carroll, on 22 June 1963 at the district registrar's office, Chatswood.

One of Gibson's last major projects was the detailed design of special mechanical devices for the Sydney Opera House which included winch systems for television-light battens, loudspeakers, glass-wall cleaning mechanisms, and the 'lenticular' or doughnut-shaped acoustic cloud reflectors in the concert hall.

He loved machinery and gadgets, and was a lively innovator. For a problem requiring imagination rather than disciplined engineering, 'you sent for Gibson'.

A tall, dark-haired man who frequently displayed his teeth in laughter and vivid speech, Gibson was a witty raconteur with an eye for the human and the absurd. Sharp minded and articulate, he was often sought by the legal profession to act as an expert witness, work he responded to with relish. He died of a ruptured aortic aneurysm on 31 December 1977 at his Waverton home and was cremated; his wife survived him, as did the daughter of his first marriage.

M. Anderson and P. Cochrane, *Julius, Poole & Gibson* (Syd, 1989); personal information.

ANN MOYAL

GILBERT, JEANETTE ANNE (1883-1960), educationist, was born on 3 August 1883 at Red Hill, Brisbane, eleventh child of James Gilbert, a Scottish-born clerk, and his wife Lucia Christina, née Peterson, from Denmark. Educated at Petrie Terrace Girls' and Infants' School, and at Brisbane Girls' Grammar School, in January 1902 Jeanette became a pupil-teacher at her old primary school. She returned there in 1909, after teaching in schools at Bundaberg (1905-08) and Pinkenba (1908-09). Appointed in 1912 to the recently opened Gympie High School, she was transferred in 1916 to the Central Technical College, Brisbane.

In 1912 Miss Gilbert had enrolled as an external student at the University of Queensland (B.A., 1917). Promoted in 1918 to the staff of the Teachers' Training College, Brisbane, she was granted leave in 1922 to complete a diploma of education at the University of Melbourne. For a Queensland woman teacher to hold such qualifications was then uncommon. In July 1923 she rejoined the staff of the T.T.C. where she lectured in teaching method, theory of education, music and needlework. She was promoted to senior lecturess in January 1937. A more than competent pianist, she was a superb needlewoman and published a textbook, *Needlework and Garment-making for Schools* (1934, 1944). Although her 16- to 17-year-old female students were daunted, even cowed, by the worked-buttonhole and the repair of the three-cornered tear, they long remembered the presentation and content of her lectures.

Miss Gilbert's influence went beyond routine instruction into the realm of ethics. Duty —to pupils, employer and, lastly, self—was paramount in her view of the aspiring teacher's armoury. Hard work was obligatory, not demeaning, and the student-teacher worth her salt had to sew her own clothes—beautifully, for preference. Distressingly often, Miss Gilbert observed breaches of general deportment in the way that students answered the telephone, entered a room or wrote a letter, and her scheduled lecture was occasionally abandoned to enable her to deal at length with some mass violation of the code of behaviour. The fact that she was still fine-tuning these nuances of etiquette and decorum as late as World War II, without fear of rebellion or ridicule, indicated the awe in which she was held. Yet, she was known to have joined her infants on the floor at story-time, to have shown kindness to the student far from home, and to have been a safe repository for confidences and a loyal support to colleague or friend. The respect that student-teachers had for her gradually evolved into affection.

Tall, but not slim, Miss Gilbert was stately and regal in the manner of King George V's consort: like Queen Mary she was never seen to smoke, seldom to eat, and never to tire. She retired in July 1944. Due to the low monetary worth of female professionals of her time, she lived out her remaining years very privately in the old-fashioned, genteel endeavour of making ends meet. She died on 16 March 1960 in South Brisbane and was buried with Presbyterian forms in Toowong cemetery.

N. R. Anderson, *Kelvin Grove Forty Years 1942-1981* (Brisb, 1981); S. Pechy and P. Thomas, *Telling Tales* (Brisb, 1992); J. Gilbert staff card, History Unit, Qld Dept of Education, Brisb; Brisb Girls' Grammar School Archives; Univ Melb Archives; Univ Qld Archives; Gilbert family papers (held by Mr A. Graham, Atherton, Qld).

DORIS H. SWAN

GILES, BORONIA LUCY (1909-1978), journalist, was born on 25 August 1909 at Collie, Western Australia, third child of Arthur Sanderson, an engine driver from England, and his Queensland-born wife Jessie Mary, née Cosham. Because of the peripatetic nature of her father's employment, 'Bonnie' was educated at various primary schools. From Subiaco State she won a scholarship in 1922 to Perth Modern School where she spent four and a half years. In 1927 she enrolled in arts at the University of Western Australia, studying part time while working for a motorcar firm. Next year she was employed as a cadet by the *Daily News*. She began a diploma of journalism in 1929, struggled until 1931 to balance work and study, but failed to complete the course. At St George's Anglican Cathedral, Perth, on 30 December 1932 she married Robert Owen Giles, a fellow journalist; they were to have five children.

Under the pseudonyms of 'Peg Peggoty' and later 'Auntie Nell', Bonnie Giles showed her flair for creative writing in the children's section of the *Daily News* and used her own drawings to complement her poems and short stories. In 1935 she adopted the pen-name 'Mary Ferber' from the writer Edna Ferber whom she admired. 'Mary Ferber' was to become a household name. She wrote what was essentially a 'Dorothy Dix' column, and its perceptive and critical comments attracted a wide and mixed readership. In an answer to a woman who complained that a husband in her street was avoiding wartime service, she responded: 'And I bet you send white feathers, too'. Giles managed to combine family life with her career as a journalist. Her other regular columns ranged from recipes for cooking to interviews with noted Western Australian families. In the latter years of World War II she began a weekly commentary on current affairs which was characterized by her 'sometimes hard hitting, sometimes whimsical approach'. For nearly twenty years the column was 'a Monday must for her admirers'.

Working tirelessly for disadvantaged people, Giles used her public standing and her articles to foster charitable causes. She sought a home for a blind, slow-learning Aboriginal boy from the country who had to be taken daily to the School for the Blind; she appealed for layettes for poor and unmarried mothers; and she requested radios for old-age pensioners. Administrative opportunities helped her to achieve her philanthropic goals. In March 1959 she was appointed to the State's Health Education Council. For ten years she edited *Our Children*, the magazine of the Slow Learning Children's Group. The minister for education made her a member of the Investigating Committee on Left-School Youth, a committee formed to consider the problems and further education of young people. She also addressed women's clubs on a host of topics.

Giles retired from journalism in 1969. Survived by her husband, two sons and two of her three daughters, she died of a ruptured dissecting aneurysm on 2 May 1978 at her Maylands home and was cremated.

Daily News (Perth), 5 Sept 1969, 5 May 1978; Perth Modern School Archives; student records, 1927-31 (Univ WA Archives); information from and family papers held by Mrs C. Lyall, Darlington, and Mr A. Giles, Gooseberry Hill, Perth; information from Mr D. Giles, Wembley, Perth.

JAN RYAN

GILL, GEORGE HERMON (1895-1973), mariner, journalist, naval officer and war historian, was born on 8 March 1895 at Fulham, London, son of William Hermon Gill, printer's compositor, and his wife Alice, née Clark. Educated in London and at Scarborough, Yorkshire, in April 1910 George went to sea as an apprentice with George Thompson & Co. Ltd's Aberdeen Line. In 1914 he obtained his second-mate's certificate and in December came to Australia in the *Themistocles*; on her return voyage she carried to Egypt troops of the second contingent of the Australian Imperial Force. Gill served at sea with the Aberdeen Line throughout World War I and rose to second officer; in 1921 he gained his master-mariner's certificate.

Emigrating to Melbourne in 1922, he joined the shore staff of the Commonwealth Government Line of Steamers. On 2 June 1923 he married ESTHER PATERSON (1892-1971) with Presbyterian forms at her Middle Park home; they were to remain childless. Gill resigned his post in 1929 and took Esther on a visit to England. Back at Middle Park—where they were to spend the rest of their lives—he turned his hand to freelance journalism, specializing in sea stories and nautical matters. From October 1933 he was employed as a reporter on the *Star*. With Frederick Howard, in 1934 he won a prize of £250 for the film scenario they based on Howard's novel, *The Emigrant*. Gill's 'Walter and Hermon' series of 'breathlessly unpunctuated sketches' in the *Star*, and later the *Argus*, were popular for their 'well observed, gentle ribbing of middle-class suburbia in the 1930s'.

Gill had been appointed lieutenant in the Royal Australian Naval Volunteer Reserve in 1927. Promoted lieutenant commander in June 1936, he was mobilized on 4 September 1939 and sent to Newcastle, New South Wales, for duty with the Examination and Naval Control services. In February 1940 he was posted to Navy Office, Melbourne. As publicity censorship liaison officer in the Naval Intelligence Division, he established cordial relations with the press. In 1943 he was appointed M.B.E. He jointly edited the series of books, *H.M.A.S.* (Canberra, 1942-45), took charge of the N.I.D.'s naval historical records section and in 1944 was chosen to write the naval volumes of the proposed official history of Australia in World War II. After revisiting England in 1945, he ceased full-time service on 14 November. Promoted commander in June 1947, he was transferred to the Retired List in 1953.

In 1947 Gill had become editor of the journal, *Navy*. From the early 1950s he edited the South Melbourne *Record*, an independent suburban weekly. He also wrote *Three Decades* (1949), a history of the State Electricity Commission of Victoria. Meanwhile, he worked on his volumes of the official history and, as G. Hermon Gill, published *Royal Australian Navy 1939-1942* and *Royal Australian Navy 1942-1945* (Canberra, 1957, 1968). The books were favourably reviewed, and he was praised for the balance and clarity of his narrative which set detailed descriptions of the R.A.N.'s operations against the wider backdrop of the war. Since 1981 Michael Montgomery and members of the *Sydney* Research Group have used circumstantial evidence to challenge Gill's account (in his first volume) of the loss of the cruiser, H.M.A.S. *Sydney*, but their criticisms have not overturned his general conclusions.

Five ft 9½ ins (177 cm) tall and of medium build, Gill had fair, curly hair and a florid complexion. As a historian, he was meticulous and avoided pedantry. Nor did he stand on formality. He was highly regarded in naval circles for his knowledge of the R.A.N., and his friends appreciated his kindly demeanour and the warmth of his personality. He died on 27 February 1973 in East Melbourne and was cremated with Anglican rites.

Esther Paterson was born on 5 February 1892 at Carlton, Melbourne, second child of Scottish-born parents Hugh Paterson, artist, and his wife Elizabeth Leslie, née Deans; the artist John Ford Paterson [q.v.5] was Esther's uncle and the dramatist Louis Esson [q.v.8] her cousin. She was educated at Oberwyl school, St Kilda, and studied painting at the National Gallery of Victoria school in 1907-12. Best known for her street-scenes and landscapes, she found further avenues for her talents in commercial art, book-illustrating and cartooning. Her portraits of uniformed and civilian officers, including Rear Admiral (Sir) Victor Crutchley and Commodore (Sir) John Collins, were reproduced in the *H.M.A.S.* series and in magazines, and have been shown at the Australian War Memorial, Canberra. The National Gallery of Victoria and the Geelong Art Gallery hold some of her work.

Paterson was a council-member (1954-68) of the Victorian Artists Society, a fellow (1949) of the Royal Society of Arts, London, and president (1966) of the Melbourne Society of Women Painters and Sculptors. She died on 8 August 1971 at Middle Park and was cremated with Anglican rites. Her younger sister Elizabeth (Betty) Deans Paterson (1894-1970) was also an artist, cartoonist and book-illustrator.

M. Montgomery, *Who Sank the Sydney?* (Syd, 1981); *The Lu Rees Archives*, 8th issue (Canb, 1987); T. Frame, *HMAS Sydney* (Syd, 1993); *SMH*, 3 May 1969; *Age* (Melb), 1 Mar 1973; Paterson family papers (NL).   TOM FRAME

GILL, GEORGE ROYDON HOWARD (1887-1974), solicitor, churchman and sportsman, was born on 10 April 1887 at Highgate Hill, Brisbane, second child and only son of Queensland-born parents James Howard Gill [q.v.4], crown solicitor, and his wife Annie Louise, daughter of George Appel [q.v.3]. James's premature death in 1899 left the family in straitened circumstances. Roy, as he was familiarly known, was educated at South Brisbane State School and, on a scholarship, at Brisbane Grammar School (1901-03). He was articled to the solicitor Reginald MacDonnell King [q.v.9] in 1904 and admitted to practice on 3 May 1910; eight months later King took him into partnership. At St Andrew's Anglican Church, South Brisbane, on 24 June 1914 Gill married Vera Idoline Heaslop (d.1972).

While King was a member (1920-35) of the Queensland Legislative Assembly and deputy-premier in 1929-32, Gill and King's son Stephen (admitted to partnership in 1927) carried on the practice. A council-member of the Queensland Law Association (1924-29), and of its successor, the Queensland Law Society (1929-59), Gill was president in 1934-36 and in 1943-44, the only person to occupy the position twice. In 1958 he was appointed M.B.E. He retired from King & Gill in 1964. After years of service, in 1966 he retired from the Queensland Solicitors' Board and from the board of the law faculty, University of Queensland. Held in high esteem by his colleagues as an authority on legal ethics, he was frequently sought for advice on problems in that area.

Having been blinded in his left eye in 1908, Gill concentrated on rowing for sporting relaxation and next year was selected in the Queensland eight-oared crew. He later turned to administration, managed the State's King's Cup crews, chaired (1919-29 and 1936-66) the Queensland Rowing Association (later Queensland Amateur Rowing Council) and was president of the Australian Amateur Rowing Council when Queensland hosted the King's Cup. Meanwhile, he belonged to the Commercial Rowing Club, of which he was successively chairman, president and patron.

A dedicated Anglican layman and synodsman from the suburban parish of Coorparoo, in 1932 Gill was elected to the Brisbane diocesan council. From 1937 he was chairman of committees of the diocesan synod until he retired in 1968; during this time he also served on general and provincial synods. In addition to being a member of The Southport School council, he served on numerous Church committees. He held office in charity organizations and welfare-service bodies, and gave his time to help people without reward. Survived by his three sons, Gill died on 13 December 1974 at Mount Gravatt and was cremated. Two further generations of the family continued the tradition of practising as solicitors.

S. Stephenson (comp), *Annals of the Brisbane Grammar School, 1869-1922* (Brisb, 1923); H. Gregory, *The Queensland Law Society Inc, 1928-1988* (Brisb, 1991); C of E, *Diocese of Brisbane Year Book*, 1969; *Qld Law Soc J*, Jan 1975; *Courier-Mail*, 17 Dec 1974; personal information *and* Gill family records (held by author, Indooroopilly, Brisb).

J. C. H. GILL

GILLAN, HELEN ELIZABETH (1873?-1955), voluntary worker and social reformer, was born probably in 1873 at Glendonald, Victoria, third of six children of Alexander Gillan and his wife Elizabeth, née Galloway, both from County Antrim, Ireland. Helen was educated at the local school, where her father was a teacher.

One of an expanding number of women to earn their living in white-collar clerical and administrative jobs in the early twentieth century, Gillan was also involved in social reform and welfare through her association with the National Council of Women of Victoria, on which she represented the Women Clerks and Typistes' Association. From 1927 to 1951 she was honorary treasurer of the State branch of the N.C.W. In 1929 she travelled to England and Scotland where she undertook a study of one of her greatest interests, the care of intellectually disabled children; on her return, she spoke on the subject at N.C.W. meetings. Another of her particular interests was the reform of laws relating to marriage and divorce; in 1933 she represented the council at a meeting of the Alimony Reform Association.

That year she became honorary treasurer of the Women's Centenary Council, set up largely by the N.C.W. in protest at the Victorian government's all-male Centenary Celebrations Council. Among other things, the council was responsible for the construction of the Pioneer Women's Memorial Garden in the Domain, Melbourne, and for the publication of the *Centenary Gift Book* (1934). Her activities extended beyond Victoria: in 1931 she had also been elected honorary secretary of the National Council of Women of Australia.

Gillan's major contribution to public life was her work during World War II with the Women's Voluntary National Register. Recognizing the importance of unpaid labour to the impending war effort, the Federal government established the register on 24 March 1939 in an office in the Melbourne Town Hall. The scheme was administered by the N.C.W., largely through the efforts of Gillan herself as honorary registrar and that of her long-time friend 'Minnie' Williamson as honorary secretary. Thousands of volunteer women workers contributed their labour in the evenings as clerks and typists for government service and production departments. The task undertaken by Gillan and Williamson was a massive one; by November 1944, when it officially closed, the Victorian office had recorded some 30 000 names.

At the end of World War II Gillan compiled *A Brief History of the National Council of Women of Victoria, 1902-1945*, chronicling the activities of the organization to which she had contributed so much. In 1945 she was listed among a handful of N.C.W. members who had been awarded the council's gold badge for long service. A bespectacled woman of kindly appearance, Helen Gillan never married, and little is known of her private life or family. In 1951 she retired to Nyora, Gippsland. She died on 30 October 1955 in a convalescent hospital at Loch and was cremated with Methodist forms.

F. Fraser and N. Palmer (eds), *Centenary Gift Book* (Melb, 1934); A. Norris, *Champions of the Impossible* (Melb, 1977); K. Darian-Smith, *On the Home Front* (Melb, 1990); *Argus*, 27 Mar 1929; K. F. Gray, The Acceptable Face of Feminism: The National Council of Women of Victoria, 1902-18 (M.A. thesis, Univ Melb, 1988); National Council of Women of Vic papers (held by the council, Melb).   KATE GRAY

GILRAY, COLIN MACDONALD (1885-1974), headmaster, was born on 17 March 1885 at Broughty Ferry, Forfarshire, Scotland, fourth of five children of Thomas Gilray (1851-1920) and his wife Annie, née Macdonald. Thomas was a brilliant graduate of Edinburgh High School and University. After teaching English at Glasgow High School and University College, Dundee, in 1889 he was appointed professor of English language and literature at the University of Otago, New Zealand; his family followed him to Dunedin in 1890.

Dunedin made Colin Gilray. He was educated at Otago Boys' High School and attended Moray Place Congregational Church. At the University of Otago (B.A., N.Z., 1906) he gained first-class honours in English and German and a second in classics, his main study under Professor G. S. Sale. Gilray was president of the student union, an actor and debater, and uncommonly popular. About 5 ft 10 ins (178 cm) tall and weighing 12 stone (76 kg), by the age of 19 he was established as a great Rugby Union footballer who became a legendary representative of Otago Province; he refused an invitation to join the All Blacks on their first tour of the British Isles, but played against Australia. He was also an outstanding athlete, winning the intervarsity long-jump three times.

Elected New Zealand Rhodes scholar for 1907, Gilray took a second class in 'Greats' at University College, Oxford (M.A., 1910); Professor J. Cook Wilson and E. F. Carritt, philosophers both, were his most respected teachers. As a Liberal, always an Asquithian who regarded Lloyd George as a cad, he campaigned against the House of Lords with his lifelong friend (Sir) Andrew McFadyean. Gilray played Rugby for Oxford and Scotland, and captained London Scottish; a historian of Rugby placed him 'very close to inclusion in my super-class of centres'. In 1910-13, while reading for the Bar (admitted 1913) at the Middle Temple, Gilray taught at Mill Hill School, London, whose headmaster was Rev. (Sir) John McClure, the famous Congregationalist. Mill Hill and McClure stamped him for life.

Gilray returned to Dunedin in 1913 and practised law at Milton. Early in 1916 he enlisted in the British Army; in July he was commissioned in the Rifle Brigade and took part in the disastrous Somme offensive; he was wounded on 13 November. Promoted captain, he was awarded the Military Cross and invalided to England in September 1917. He had favoured a compromise peace. He then trained officer-cadets at Aldershot. On 24 November he had married Ethel Muriel Standish at the parish church, Haslemere, Surrey.

In 1919 Gilray resumed practice at Milton, savouring the peace of rural life. He hankered for England, but in 1922 accepted the headmastership of John McGlashan College, Dunedin. He energetically built up the new Presbyterian school to high academic standards, was innovative in developing science and music, and was himself a gifted teacher, especially of Shakespeare. He was a leading member of the university council. A serious accident in 1931 left him with one leg shorter than the other.

At 49 Gilray accepted the post of principal of Scotch College, Melbourne, in succession to W. S. Littlejohn [q.v.10]. When welcomed in July 1934 he assured the boys assembled in the quadrangle that he too had cold feet. Moving from a school of about 200 pupils to one of about 1500 meant that he could do little more than rule and administer, and could not hope to attach a name to most boys; but he revelled in taking occasional classes in religious education or English. Under the chairmanship of Sir Arthur Robinson [q.v.11] the school council had a strong finance-committee which, with Gilray, made important building extensions before World War II: the Littlejohn Chapel, a boarding-house, the Mackie hall and library. To his dissatisfaction, the school continued to grow in size. He very deliberately developed art, music and theatre; the appointment of the dynamic musician John Bishop [q.v.13] had lasting effects. With his fellow headmasters Father Hackett, (Sir) Francis Rolland [qq.v.9,11] and (Sir) James Darling, with whom he had much in common, Gilray stressed to the boys that privilege implied responsibility and public service, and endeavoured to clamp down on exaggerated press publicity of sporting fixtures. Darling found him the only headmaster with whom he could cheerfully watch an inter-school match—he was such a good winner and loser. The virtual offer of the Mill Hill headmastership came too late.

Gilray imposed military command on his staff: on principle, he kept aloof, issued orders and held few staff meetings. He rejected proposals to increase his salary and was reluctant to increase those of his staff, for it would mean higher fees. To many boys he seemed frightening, like the Metro-Goldwyn-Mayer lion; fundamentally a shy man, he was sometimes irascible. Senior boys who got to know him considered him to be the very model of a gentleman and of good manners.

The war was a testing time. Senior boys leaving found Gilray and other old-soldier staff to be unusually tender. When the military authorities ordered Wesley College to vacate its premises, Gilray promptly invited Wesley's headmaster N. H. MacNeil [q.v.10] to join them at Scotch. They did for two harmonious years—a remarkable feat of organization.

A devout man who often preached in chapel, Gilray observed: 'We want teachers who are students, always becoming better fitted for their tasks . . . The teacher at his best knows that it is God's work that he is trying to do'. He often referred to the Book of Amos and the Acts of the Apostles for their guidance on social justice. In chapel the un-Presbyterian *Book of Responsive Prayer* was used, as at Mill Hill. He waxed hot at any hint of anti-Semitism. He supported the school chaplain Rev. Stephen Yarnold [q.v.] against those who wanted him dismissed for his left-wing views, and nurtured the rare students who sensed a call to the ministry.

Gilray was a liberal humanist, kind despite the gruffness, modest and self-effacing. Privately he mimicked staff and boys, and dreamed of some day playing Othello. Literature remained his passion—Jane Austen, and the works of the great poets, including Robert Bridges' 'Testament of Beauty'.

In 1939-52 Gilray had been a member (chairman, 1949-52) of the standing committee of the Headmasters' Conference of the Independent Schools of Australia; on his retirement in 1953, he became executive-officer for ten years, encouraged to 'do any work within his power'. In 1951 he had been appointed O.B.E. As deputy-chancellor (1954-58, 1959-61) of the University of Melbourne (LL.D., 1956) he presided over its centenary celebrations. As a committee-man he did not intrude his views, but they usually prevailed. He was a member (1961-65) of (Sir) Leslie Martin's committee on the future of tertiary education in Australia. Gilray remained convinced that the best foundation for 'leaders-to-be' was classics, mathematics, and some science.

Predeceased by his wife (d.1968) and survived by their daughter, he died on 15 July 1974 in East Melbourne and was buried in Box Hill cemetery.

G. H. Nicholson (ed), *First Hundred Years* (Melb, 1952); J. W. Hogg, *Our Proper Concerns* (Syd, 1986); G. Serle, *Colin Gilray* (forthcoming); McFadyean papers (Lond School of Economics L).

GEOFFREY SERLE

GILROY, SIR NORMAN THOMAS (1896-1977), Catholic cardinal, was born on 22 January 1896 at Glebe, Sydney, second of six children of William James Gilroy and his wife Catherine, née Slattery, both native-born and of Irish descent. William was a tailor's cutter who for some time ran unsuccessfully a business of his own. Norman attended the convent schools of the Sisters of the Good Samaritan and the Sisters of Charity, and Marist Brothers' Boys' School, Kogarah. He interrupted his brief schooling to work for an estate agent at the age of 12 and left finally at 13½.

The family was solidly Roman Catholic, but not active in Church affairs. Norman was always exact in observance, but was never an altar server and had no early thoughts of priesthood. An interest in the Marist Brothers was frustrated by his family circumstances. On 16 December 1909 he joined the Postmaster-General's Department as a telegraph messenger. With coaching, he passed the telegraphist's examination next year and in 1912 was appointed to Bourke in the State's far west. He was relieving at Narrabri in 1914 at the outbreak of World War I. Refused his parents' permission to enlist in the Australian Imperial Force, he was allowed to volunteer for transport service as a telegraphist. On 2 February 1915 Gilroy sailed for Egypt as junior wireless officer in the transport, *Hessen (Bulla)*, which carried zinc concentrates, 100 troops and 400 horses. His diary of the voyage showed a shrewd understanding of men, remarkable in a youth of 19. While maintaining his own strict standards of total abstinence, he mixed well with all types and developed an affectionate respect for Australian servicemen.

275

On 25 April 1915 *Hessen* was off Gallipoli, and at 4.30 a.m. Gilroy heard the first shots of the campaign. Having landed the 26th Indian Mountain Battery, *Hessen* was ordered to Imbros and was used as a hospital ship for horses and mules. More than once she came under fire. Ordered back to Alexandria and thence to England, *Hessen* reached Greenhithe, Kent, on 4 July after several submarine scares. Gilroy's six weeks in England were a time of critical decision. He met Father Davidson, with whom he formed a close friendship, and took part in parish affairs, especially at a youth club. Gilroy divided his remaining time between visits to theatres and to Church services. Sailing for Australia on 15 August, he reached Melbourne on 8 October. He returned a new man, and to old circumstances.

The postmaster-general decided that too many telegraphists had joined up, and Gilroy was ordered to resume his duties—as a clerk at Lismore, New South Wales. There he came under the influence of the cathedral administrator Monsignor Terence McGuire, founding president of the Manly Union, an association of priests from St Patrick's College who wanted the 'Australianisation' of the Australian Church. McGuire asked Gilroy if he had thought of the priesthood. He replied that he had, but had rejected it on the grounds of his own unsuitability and his family's financial straits. McGuire reassured him on the first point and promised to find a way around the second.

In 1917 Gilroy went to St Columba's Seminary and Foreign Missionary College, Springwood, to begin studies, but in 1919 was transferred to the Pontifical Urban College of Propaganda Fide, Rome, where Australian bishops could claim some free places. He lived in close association with students from Asia, Africa and the Middle East. A strong element of Propaganda training was *romanità*, a Roman sense and loyalty, centred on the person, as well as the position, of the Pope. Gilroy embraced the tradition with total simplicity, an uncomplicated acceptance which did not penetrate the complexities of the mechanisms. His theology was not profound, merely an academic fleshing out of his existing faith and devotion. Ordained priest 24 December 1923, he was granted his doctorate in theology the following year.

On his return in 1924, Gilroy was appointed to the staff of the Apostolic delegation in Sydney led by Bartolomeo Cattaneo, who had come in 1917 to implement a Roman policy recently laid down in *Maximum Illud*, an encyclical on missions by Pope Benedict XV, which called for indigenous hierarchy and clergy in missionary countries. Cattaneo applied the policy rigidly, despite the arguments of local Irish bishops that the cultural problems of missionary countries did not exist in Australia. Before he had left Rome, Cattaneo had known at Propaganda what an Irish prelate called a 'group of bouncing Australian students', who told him of Irish-Australian tensions. With Gilroy, some of these young men became the advance guard of the Australian hierarchy.

Six years experience in the delegation gave Gilroy a thorough understanding of the workings of the Australian Church. In 1930 he returned to Lismore as secretary to Bishop John Carroll. Although he did some pastoral work, he had never been a curate or a parish priest when, on 10 December 1934, he was nominated bishop of Port Augusta in South Australia. The pastoral problems of such a diocese widened his experience of his country. He toured the remote areas, West Coast, Riverland and the desert north (travelling by camel); he introduced the Holy Name Society for Catholic men, and, despite the Depression, started a diocesan monthly newspaper; he learned techniques of pastoral integration that were to serve him well.

On 1 July 1937 Gilroy was nominated coadjutor to Michael Kelly [q.v.9], archbishop of Sydney, with the right of succession. His appointment was a culmination of the Roman-Australian-Irish conflict and a source of tension with the more senior Irish bishops, especially Archbishop Daniel Mannix [q.v.10] of Melbourne. Gilroy succeeded to the see on 18 March 1940 and found a vast diocese which had slipped from the faltering hands of his elderly predecessor. He believed simply that the Code of Canon Law, promulgated as he began his priestly studies, contained the simple answer to all pastoral problems. He visited each parish regularly, scrutinized its spiritual, administrative and financial condition, demanded reform, and retired or moved pastors who neglected the required changes. In those early years he acquired a reputation as an 'iron man' and trained his voice to project his piety and firmness with orotund diction. In later years his standards remained as exacting, but his compassion for those who failed was widely recognized.

His term as archbishop of Sydney began in wartime. Gilroy did not often make the public statements expected of public figures. When he did, they were not always well judged. In 1943 he joined with other church leaders in Sydney in putting forward 'A Christian Outlook in National Life', a statement on postwar reconstruction in a just and charitable society which the signatories saw only in the Fatherhood of God and Brotherhood in Jesus Christ. Less felicitous was his intervention in the controversy surrounding the bombing of Rome in July 1943. Gilroy, the simple patriot, was outraged by the threat to the Vatican and the shrines of Roman Catholicism. He spoke of his ideal of the Allied leaders being shattered, and organized a protest to Churchill and Roosevelt as well as to the Australian government. Not all his fellow bishops concurred, and his outspoken criticism jarred the harmony of the Australian war effort.

On 18 February 1946 Pope Pius XII named him cardinal with the title of the ancient church of the Four Crowned Martyrs. Gilroy was the first Australian-born so elevated. His invariable sense of dignity adorned the ceremony of the cardinalate, while his simplicity of manner removed any suggestion of pomp. He represented the Vatican as papal legate at important Church functions in India, Japan and the Philippines. The first postwar decade was the high point of his career. In between the splendid occasions of his new role, Gilroy presided over the rapid expansion of his diocese to meet the demands of population growth. In addition to providing churches, schools and institutions, he developed the devotional life with sodalities, guilds and clubs to an extent that may have fostered a ghetto mentality. While he disapproved of the independence of the Catholic Women's Association (later St Joan's Social and Political Alliance), he encouraged a devotional and social approach in the Catholic youth organizations, and maintained an uneasy relationship with the Melbourne-based Jocist style of Catholic Action.

Much of his energy was devoted to Catholic education. By 1971 he had 366 schools with 115 704 pupils. Beyond a conviction of the necessity for schools, he had no theories of education. His contribution to the expansion crisis of the 1950s and 1960s was a rigid regionalization and direction of resources. Despite the increase in personnel to 751 Brothers and 2992 nuns, and the new influx of lay teachers made possible by restored sharing in public funds, he had to preside over the failure of his Church to offer Catholic schools to all urban Catholic children. Always suspicious of secular universities, he dreamed of establishing a Catholic university. Two hundred acres were set aside at Beacon Hill for an Australian Notre Dame, but he had not faced the practical difficulties of the project. In 1971 he entrusted Warrane College at the University of New South Wales to the conservative Opus Dei association. More successful had been his effort to establish a pontifical faculty of theology at Manly. Roman approval was given in 1954, but again failure to face practical difficulties limited its growth in his time.

The confrontation with communism in Australia focussed increasingly on the industrial groups within the Australian Labor Party and the episcopally sponsored Catholic Social Studies Movement ('the Movement') presided over by B. A. Santamaria in Melbourne.

The uneasy alliance between the A.L.P. and the Church was much easier in New South Wales than in Victoria. Cardinal Gilroy was from a Labor background and sympathized with Labor objectives, though he viewed all politics and politicians from the point of view of Church interests and was to maintain good relations with the Liberal premier (Sir) Robert Askin from 1965. Personally friendly with J. J. Cahill [q.v.13], he looked upon him and other Roman Catholic cabinet members as Catholics who could do good for the Church. When H. V. Evatt [q.v.] precipitated the Labor split of 1955, a division followed within the Catholic Church over the proper way of maintaining the opposition to communism. Gilroy was prepared to go as far as possible to keep lines of communication with Labor intact. The poet James McAuley [q.v.], a recent convert to Catholicism, but disdainful of Labor, was 'in open and rancorous dispute' with him over politics, and depicted him in *Captain Quiros* (1964) as one whose 'right hand blessed the victims of his left'.

From July 1954 to October 1956 a series of meetings of the Australian hierarchy and its committees failed to resolve issues of dispute on national or diocesan control of 'the Movement' and the extent of lay autonomy in political decision-making by Catholic Action groups. Gilroy opted firmly for full episcopal control and local independence. In New South Wales he believed the Church was in a solid position with the State Labor government. Both he and Mannix appealed twice to Rome for a resolution of the crisis. The final decision was made on 3 November 1957. Although ambiguously disclosed, the ruling resulted in the displacement of the episcopal Catholic Social Studies Movement with the lay National Civic Council.

At the second Vatican Council (1962-65) Gilroy was appointed to the council of presidency, a position of great historical significance. He exercised his functions as director of debates with efficiency and firmness. The council changed direction, however, and a group of more theologically open moderators superseded the presidents in the critical role of directing the council. Gilroy was thorough and dutiful in studying and discussing issues, but he was theologically by-passed by the council. He welcomed the initiative, yet felt it should be left to the Pope and the Roman Curia. He implemented the decisions loyally, if generally without conviction or enthusiasm. He sanctioned the vernacular liturgy while confessing his own regret. He accepted the new impulse to Church unity, but remained eirenic rather than ecumenical. He saw many priests and religious leaving their roles, and wept. He became suspicious of theologians who debated what he took for granted. He could not cope with the reaction to Pope Paul

VI's encyclical, *Humanae Vitae* (1968), on marriage and means of birth control.

Cardinal Gilroy was appointed K.B.E. in 1969. In December 1970 he welcomed his friend Pope Paul VI on the first papal visit to Australia. It cast a glow of an older splendour over the last months of his episcopate. With relief, he tendered his resignation on his 75th birthday, 22 January 1971. Sir Norman moved to the priests' section of St John Vianney Villa, Randwick, run by the Little Sisters of the Poor. There he devoted himself to prayer and charity, regularly visiting the frail with the Coogee Brown Sisters. Having battled the onset of age and ill health with dignity, he died on 21 October 1977 in Lewisham Hospital and was buried in the crypt of St Mary's Cathedral. Churchmen and politicians testified to his contribution to Australian life. Archbishop (Cardinal) Freeman described Gilroy's episcopate: 'He combined prayer and action . . . moving from one to the other with no pause between'.

A. W. Jose, *The Royal Australian Navy 1914-1918* (Syd, 1928); *Acta et Documenta, Concilio Oecumenico Vaticano II Apparando*, series 1 (Antepraeparatoria), 2: *Consilia et Vota Episcoporum ac Praelatorum*, pt 7 *America Meridionalis—Oceania* (Vatican City, 1961); G. Williams, *Cardinal Sir Norman Gilroy* (Syd, 1971); B. A. Santamaria, *Against the Tide* (Melb, 1981); G. Henderson, *Mr Santamaria and the Bishops* (Syd, 1983); E. Campion, *Australian Catholics* (Melb, 1987) and *A Place in the City* (Melb, 1994); *Social Survey*, May 1955, p 5; *Catholic Documentation*, Dec 1955, p 58, Sept 1957, p 45, Mar 1962, p 51, June 1964, p 31; *Labour Hist*, 36, 1979, p 39; Gilroy papers: official (St Mary's Cathedral Archives, Syd, *and* Brisb Archdiocesan Archives), personal (held by Rev L. Bayliss, Moonah, Hob) *and* diaries at Gallipoli (ML) *and* in Rome (St Mary's Cathedral Archives, Syd); information from the late Mrs C. Bayliss, Rev L. Bayliss, Rev H. Slattery, Maroubra, and Rt Rev I. Burns, Avalon, Syd.　　　　　T. P. BOLAND

GLASHEEN, JOHN PATRICK (1901-1954), schoolteacher, public servant and football administrator, was born on 19 January 1901 at Condobolin, New South Wales, son of native-born parents John Patrick Glasheen, baker, and his wife Marcella, née Hennessy. Educated at the Christian Brothers' High School, Lewisham, Jack trained (1918-19) at Hereford House and was sent in July 1919 to Mount Fairy Public School. On 2 January 1926 at the Cathedral of St Peter and St Paul, Goulburn, he married with Catholic rites Mary Alena Carney, a saleswoman. He gained a diploma in economics and commerce from the University of Sydney (1927) and became an associate-member (1938) of the Chartered Institute of Secretaries.

In the 1920s Glasheen emerged as one of the leading pro-Labor figures in the Assistant Teachers' Association, 'all afire with a great zeal to set the affairs of the world in order'. He was treasurer (1929-32) of the New South Wales Public School Teachers' Federation and secretary (1937-41) of the Teachers' Building Ltd. His passion for reform found a vocational outlet with his appointment in 1931 as teacher-in-charge of the day commercial school, established as part of Sydney Technical College to assist unemployed school-leavers. The change was a shrewd one in terms of his career: five years later he was made lecturer-in-charge of the technical education branch's new commercial studies department, which grew to an enrolment of over 5700 students by 1949 when he was promoted assistant-director of technical education (buildings and plant).

Assisted by L. T. Latter, Glasheen had written a textbook, *Whitcombe's Practical Book-Keeping with Exercises* (1933), and he was E. B. Smyth's junior co-author of *Intermediate Accountancy* (1936); both works ran to numerous editions. Glasheen was a member (from 1947) of the development council which planned the New South Wales University of Technology and was appointed to the university's council on its inauguration in 1949. From the early 1940s he had served on the State's Aborigines Welfare Board and also advised C. R. Evatt, minister for education, (1941-44). From 1947 until his death 'Glash' was president and a selector of South Sydney District Rugby League Football Club, 'the pride of the League'. In these years Souths won four premierships (1950, 1951, 1953 and 1954) and were twice runners-up (1949 and 1952). His wife owned and ran a hotel in the South Sydney area.

Five months before the elections which he was expected to lose, Premier James McGirr [q.v.] secured Glasheen's appointment in January 1950 as a member of the Public Service Board. Glasheen's Labor leanings gave rise to mutterings about political patronage, despite his undoubted administrative abilities. The government was returned in June and further controversy surrounded the selection of Glasheen in December as a trustee of the National Art Gallery of New South Wales. There were suggestions that a knowledge of book-keeping and the Rugby back-line sat ill with an appreciation of Bruegel or Buvelot [q.v.3].

Glasheen was seen as one of the State's more principled and forthright public servants. Regarded as an 'ambitious, tough boss', and a 'strong leader' who spoke his mind, he was considered to be fair and was respected for his determined pursuit of policies. Contradicting his physical appearance, his administrative style owed more to the drive of the front row than the nimble sidestep of the half-back, and his knack of selecting sound subordinates was evident in both the public service and sporting arenas. His major contribution lay in the development of commercial education in New South Wales, but many older members of the accountancy profession remembered him with ambivalent feelings. Illness cut short his role in educational policy and administration on the Public Service Board, although he did pave the way for an amendment (1955) to the Public Service Act (1902) which allowed for the appointment of an 'educationist' as the fourth member of the board.

Survived by his wife and daughter, Glasheen died of cancer on Christmas Eve 1954 at his Bronte home and was buried in Waverley cemetery. Senior members of the government, public service and labour movement attended his funeral.

H. Missingham, *They kill you in the end* (Syd, 1973); B. A. Mitchell, *Teachers, Education, and Politics* (Brisb, 1975); I. Heads and T. Brock, *South Sydney* (Syd, 1995); NSW Public Service Bd, *Annual Report*, 1950-54; *SMH*, 1, 2, 4, 6 Feb 1951, 28 Dec 1954.   Ross Curnow

GLASSOP, JACK LAWSON (1913-1966), journalist and author, was born on 30 January 1913 at Lawson, New South Wales, fifth child of Sydney-born parents John Glassop, shire clerk, and his wife Lillian Mary, née Witney. In 1918 John was appointed town clerk of Newcastle. Educated at Hamilton Boys' Intermediate and Newcastle (Boys') High schools, in 1930 young Jack was employed as a reporter on the *Newcastle Morning Herald and Miner's Advocate*. On 3 June 1940 he enlisted in the Australian Imperial Force and served (1940-43) in the Middle East, spending some eighteen months in Cairo on the army newspaper, the *A.I.F. News*. Back in Australia in February 1943, he worked for two years with the army's press unit on another service newspaper, *Table Tops*, published at Atherton, Queensland. While in Cairo he had been inspired by the role of the A.I.F. in the 1941 defence of the Libyan port of Tobruk, and had begun to write a novel, *We Were the Rats* (Sydney, 1944).

Following his discharge from the army on 9 August 1945, Glassop rejoined the *Newcastle Morning Herald*. On 24 April 1946 he found himself famous when a Sydney magistrate held that certain passages in *We Were the Rats* were obscene and imposed a £10 fine on the publishers, Angus & Robertson [qq.v.7,11] Ltd. During the proceedings the chief police witness, Sergeant Roy Munro, had testified that the word 'bloody' in the text was offensive to him. On 13 June Judge Studdert dismissed an appeal, ruling that thirty-one pages of the book were 'legally obscene' and de-

scribing passages in chapter 31 as 'just plain filth'.

On 3 May 1946 at Christ Church Cathedral, Newcastle, Glassop married with Anglican rites Beryl Agnes Regan who nursed in a mental hospital; they moved to the seaside resort of Norahville, near Wyong. After his next novel (about life in a fishing village) failed to find a publisher, he joined the *Sydney Morning Herald*, living in Sydney and later in Canberra. From October 1950 to March 1951 he was a war correspondent in Korea. Over the next nine years he worked successively on the Sydney *Daily Mirror* and *Truth*, the Melbourne *Truth*, and in Adelaide as chief-of-staff of Truth & Sportsman Ltd and (from 1960) as a feature writer on the *Advertiser*. Divorced in 1956, he married Alison Esau on 5 January 1962 at the office of the principal registrar, Adelaide.

Meanwhile, he continued to write fiction: a children's tale, *Susan and the Bogeywomp* (1947), a racing novel, *Lucky Palmer* (1949), an abridged version of *We Were the Rats* (1961) and *The Rats in New Guinea* (1963). His accurate and candid reportage were more impressive than his creativity and skill in handling plot, thematic development, or characterization. The two war novels were heavily indebted to the recollections of veterans of Tobruk and the New Guinea campaigns, which Glassop meticulously recorded in interviews (he was never in Tobruk or New Guinea). For *Lucky Palmer*, about the seedy side of the world of racing and gambling, he drew on his own knowledge and experience. In 1965 he was awarded a Commonwealth Literary Fund grant to work on a novel on Captain Cook [q.v.1].

Five ft 9 ins (175 cm) tall, with a 'muscular body', Glassop had a 'mobile face', 'almost Orientally sloping hazel eyes' and a 'prominent jaw'. His journalism and his war novels both reflected his devotion to 'the Anzac legend'. A compulsive gambler for many years, he displayed 'an enormous zest for living'. While playing golf, he died of a coronary occlusion on 4 November 1966 at Mount Osmond and was cremated. His wife survived him; he had no children.

D. Stewart, *The Flesh and the Spirit* (Syd, 1948); R. Gerster, *Big-Noting* (Melb, 1987); *Southerly*, 6, no 4, 1945, p 49, 7, no 1, 1946, p 57; L. Glassop, 'The "We Were the Rats" Case', *Overland*, no 19, 1960-61, p 38; *SMH*, 16 Dec 1944, 25 Apr, 14 June, 14 Sept, 7 Dec 1946; *Advertiser* (Adel), 5 Nov 1966; H. de Berg, Lawson Glassop (taped interview, 30 Oct 1966, NL).   J. T. Laird

GLEESON, JOHN PHILIP BERCHMANS (1910-1969), Jesuit priest and educationist, was born on 4 April 1910 at Glebe, Sydney, son of native-born parents Edward Lawrence Gleeson, grazier, and his wife Mary Ann Elizabeth, née Fitzpatrick. Philip was educated at Xavier College, Kew, where he was captain (1929) and distinguished himself at sport. In 1930 he entered the Society of Jesus, at Greenwich, Sydney, and in 1932-35 studied philosophy at Loyola College, Watsonia, Melbourne. He completed a bachelor of arts degree at the University of Melbourne in 1934 (although he did not graduate until 1950), and then taught at St Ignatius' College, Riverview, Sydney, and at the new St Louis school in Perth. Four years study of theology followed at Canisius College, Pymble, Sydney. Ordained priest on 8 January 1944, he pronounced his final vows as a Jesuit on 15 August 1947.

In 1946 Gleeson went to Newman College, University of Melbourne, as dean and college tutor in philosophy. He remained there until 1949, when he travelled to Oxford to study philosophy at Campion Hall. Renal illness hampered his work, but he obtained a B.Litt. (1951). After visiting Europe, he returned to Melbourne and in 1952 became the first Australian-born headmaster of Xavier College.

In December 1953 Fr Gleeson was appointed rector of Newman College. He was happiest and most effective during his eight years there. A careful and financially stringent administrator, he made provision for maintenance, renovation, and further building at the college, including the Kenny [q.v.9] wing. He succeeded in greatly increasing student numbers. Gleeson had a close acquaintance with individual students, and was intent on their personal flourishing, although he was almost other-worldly, often uneasy in company and upheld traditional discipline. Not all students appreciated the fact that 'his idealism was conveyed with . . . earnestness and singlemindedness', but he could not be denied respect.

Twice called to be acting provincial superior of the Jesuits in Australia, from 1962 to 1966 Gleeson was rector of Campion College, the Jesuit house of studies at Kew; he was concurrently tutor at Newman and treasurer of the Australian Jesuit province. In 1967 he went to the Provincial headquarters at Hawthorn, while continuing his tutorial work and the giving of spiritual direction. He had become ill with cancer, and he was hospitalized intermittently. Next year he seemed to be recovering so well that he accepted an offer to study once again at Oxford. He died of cancer on 24 February 1969 at Beckenham, London.

Gleeson was one who made the most of his gifts. Except when ill, he was uncommonly vigorous. He was a good driver, but a reckless speedster. Short, close-knit, prim and brisk,

he had a precise mind and was quick-witted, and he worked very hard all through his adult life. His inclinations were in part polemical, but his deepest commitment was religious, and he was much in demand for religious retreats. A 'sharp, alert man of action with too much energy for long-term planning or change', he relished minimizing chaos and magnifying order.

G. Dening and D. Kennedy, *Xavier Portraits* (Melb, 1993); Newman College, Univ Melb, *Newman Mag*, 1985.   PETER STEELE

GLEW, CYRIL ALLERTON (1891-1973), headmaster, was born on 30 April 1891 at Brunswick, Melbourne, son of Victorian-born parents Edward Manning Glew, carpenter, and his wife Sarah Alicia, née Latimer. About 1900 the family moved to Subiaco, Perth. Cyril was educated at Perth Boys' School and encouraged by his headmaster Joseph Parsons [q.v.11] to become a teacher. Appointed a monitor at the school in 1906, Glew entered Teachers' College, Claremont, in 1909 and was sent as an assistant to Bunbury State School in 1911. Within a year he was transferred to Worsley.

For some twenty years Glew's conduct and ability were intermittently criticized by headmasters, superintendents and inspectors who commented on his failure to prepare lessons, his 'feeble' control of his class, his inability to relate to students and the distractions of his extracurricular activities. Recommended for a transfer, on 12 April 1912 he was dispatched as head teacher to the school at Manjimup, a place where conditions were rough, and where his mother and incapacitated father joined him. In 1916 an inspector investigated complaints of Glew's irregular attendance at school, his poor discipline, and his all-night drinking and gambling sessions at the local hotel. The nickname 'Sticky', by which he was fondly known in later years, was recognized as indicative of a lack of respect. Although most parents supported him, he was disciplined, his salary was reduced one grade and he was transferred, first to Peringillup and then to Golden Ridge, near Kalgoorlie.

A small, spare, energetic and enthusiastic man who wore thick-rimmed spectacles, Glew married Clarice Alma Campbell, née McNamara (d.1948), a widow, on 20 December 1919 at St Matthew's Anglican Church, Boulder. After teaching at two other goldfields schools, he was appointed to Pemberton State School in 1927. There his career reached a turning-point. Although the Department of Education continued to question his involvement in community work, he planted pines on land granted to the school, examined the feasibility of introducing trout hatcheries in the district, helped to advance the establishment of a butter factory, and contributed to sporting clubs and welfare organizations. While head teacher of Cannington (1933-35) and of West Northam (1936-38), he studied part time at the University of Western Australia (B.A., 1937; Dip.Ed., 1939). He achieved some success in standardizing James McRae's [q.v.10] intelligence tests for children.

Following a year at Albany in 1939, Glew became head teacher of Collie District High School in 1940. His love of learning and the humanities won praise and led to his appointment in 1944 as head of Perth Boys' School. He gave intellectual leadership, improved the library, encouraged the study and performance of music, supported the cadets and competitive sport, and filled the school with works of art. He initiated regular meetings of headmasters, furthered his involvement in youth organizations and won the respect of the business community. He knew the names of all his boys and followed their later careers with interest.

On 14 February 1951 Glew married Myrtle Amy Manson at St Margaret's Church, Nedlands. After retiring in 1956, he undertook voluntary rehabilitation work with prisoners. In 1964 he was appointed O.B.E. Survived by his wife, he died on 13 August 1973 at Nedlands and was cremated. J. K. Ewers [q.v.] regarded him as 'the finest headmaster I've worked under'.

J. K. Ewers, *Perth Boys' School, 1847-1947* (Perth, 1947); J. Williams, *As it was in the Beginning*(Manjimup, WA, 1992); Univ WA, *Convocation News*, Oct 1973; *West Australian*, 30 Oct 1933, 30 Sept 1948, 11 Apr 1956, 13 June 1964, 16 Aug 1973; Education Dept (WA), AN 45/5 Acc 1059/389/44 [restricted] (WAA).

OWEN F. WATTS

GLOUCESTER, HENRY WILLIAM FREDERICK ALBERT, DUKE of (1900-1974), governor-general, was born on 31 March 1900 at York Cottage, Sandringham, Norfolk, England, third son and fourth of six children of Prince George, Duke of York, and his wife Princess (Victoria) Mary of Teck. After preparatory schooling at St Peter's Court, Broadstairs, Prince Henry was educated at Eton and the Royal Military College, Sandhurst. He attended the University of Cambridge for nine months in 1919-20 and joined the 10th Royal Hussars, British Army, in 1921. A good athlete, he enjoyed cricket, long-distance running, tennis, Rugby Union football and riding to hounds, and represented his university and regiment at polo. In 1934 he visited Australia for Victoria's centenary celebrations and acquired a reputation in

some quarters for insobriety. On 6 November 1935 at Buckingham Palace, London, he married Lady Alice Christabel Montagu-Douglas-Scott (b.1901), daughter of the 7th Duke of Buccleuch; they were to have two children, Prince William (1941-1972) and Prince Richard (b.1944).

Following the abdication of his eldest brother King Edward VIII in 1936, Gloucester suspended his military career to share the royal family's public duties. In 1938 he contemplated making himself available for a term as governor-general of Australia, but his younger brother George, Duke of Kent, was nominated to replace the Earl of Gowrie [q.v.9]. During World War II the Duke and Duchess of Gloucester worked hard—he usually visiting troops, she hospitals. He toured British defences at Gibraltar in 1941 and 1942, and Ceylon (Sri Lanka), India and North Africa in 1942.

That year the Duke of Kent was killed in an air crash. On 15 November 1943 Prime Minister John Curtin [q.v.13] announced that Gloucester had been chosen to succeed Gowrie, whose term had been extended because of the war. Since party policy was that the post should be filled by Australians, the appointment caused concern in Labor circles, and surprised approval in the press and among conservatives. Arthur Calwell [q.v.13] informed Gowrie of the duke's alleged poor reputation. But Curtin, who met Gloucester in England in 1944, and had experienced his own problems with alcohol, 'thought that the presence in Australia of a member of the Royal Family would influence the despatch of British Divisions and equipment to the Pacific'. To many, the appointment of a member of the royal family reaffirmed 'the supreme importance of the Crown as the centre and symbol of Empire unity'.

After a voyage in a blacked-out passenger liner, during which they were in danger of attack by enemy submarines, the Gloucesters arrived in Sydney on 28 January 1945 and the duke was sworn in at Canberra two days later. They found the heat, the snakes, the rats, the flies and the isolation of Yarralumla (their official residence) a strain, but put up a brave public show. The two very young children were popular with the Australian public and helped to break down formality. The duke and duchess joined happily in Australia's celebrations of the victory in Europe in May and in the Pacific in August. Gloucester had brought his own Avro York aircraft. Although the duchess did not enjoy good health, theirs was a vigorous tour of duty, involving constant travel, flights to all States and a visit to Papua and New Guinea (interrupted by Curtin's sudden death) and to Norfolk Island.

Taller than his brothers, the moustached Gloucester looked comfortable in the uniform of his office; he was less at ease as a dinner-party host. Having served two years in the post, he left Sydney on 17 January 1947, returning by air to England to fulfil official duties there during the visit to South Africa of his brother King George VI. While not the most popular occupant of the office, Gloucester had exercised his public duties conscientiously and without controversy. The Australian (Sir) William McKell succeeded him, at which Gloucester is said to have exclaimed: ' "Then it seems I have wasted my bloody time" (in cementing Australia's links with the monarchy)'.

In Britain the duke continued to devote his public life to supporting hospitals, youth work and farming. He represented the Crown abroad on several occasions, and visited Australia again with the duchess in 1965. Survived by his wife and younger son, he died on 10 June 1974 at his home, Barnwell Manor, Northamptonshire, and was buried in the royal mausoleum, Frogmore, Berkshire.

DNB, 1971-80; N. Frankland, *Prince Henry Duke of Gloucester* (Lond, 1980); Alice, Duchess of Gloucester, *The Memoirs of Princess Alice* (Lond, 1983); *Labour Hist*, no 34, May 1978, p 68; *SMH*, 16 Nov 1943, 1 Aug 1946; *Sun-Herald*, 26 Feb 1978.

CHRIS CUNNEEN

GLYNN, NEVA CARR; *see* CARR-GLYN

GODDARD, THOMAS HERBERT (1885-1967), medical practitioner, was born on 26 March 1885 at Newcastle, New South Wales, third of seven sons of Alfred Russell Goddard, a coach-painter from England, and his Irish-born wife Eliza Jane, née Cowan. Tommy was educated at East Maitland Boys' High School and the University of Sydney (B.A., 1904; M.B., 1914). Appointed medical officer to the Mount Bischoff Mine, Waratah, Tasmania, in 1914, in the following year he became resident medical officer at the General Hospital, Hobart. On 19 January 1916 at St George's Anglican Church, Burnie, he married Dagmar Charlotte Jones. Goddard had been promoted superintendent of the hospital in 1915. Following a staffing dispute in 1917 between the Tasmanian government and the local branch of the British Medical Association, he resigned in solidarity with the B.M.A.; with characteristic 'sweet reasonableness' he remained until his replacement was acquainted with the patients.

In 1915-18 Goddard served as an honorary captain in the Australian Army Medical Corps, Militia. He then worked as officer-in-charge of the quarantine station at Barnes Bay, Bruny Island. After a suspected influenza contact had been disembarked from H.M.S. *New Zealand* with Admiral Lord Jellicoe on board, Goddard recorded the 'great privilege' of 'standing in our small motor boat to salute the victor of Jutland'. Goddard commenced general practice in Hobart in 1919. Next year he became honorary physician to the Tasmanian Sanatorium for Consumptives and gradually developed his interest in tuberculosis. Early in 1935 he represented the Tasmanian government at a meeting in Canberra to discuss control of the disease; in that year he also visited centres in Britain, Switzerland and the United States of America to study tuberculosis. He established a chest clinic at the Royal Hobart Hospital in 1937 which provided the foundation for the State's tuberculosis campaign. In 1945 Goddard was appointed State director of tuberculosis. Over the next five years Tasmania introduced a voluntary, then a compulsory, community X-ray survey, and set up a central case register.

As president of the local branch of the B.M.A., in 1947 Goddard delivered the annual address, providing a comprehensive description of the administration, organization, logistics and results of tuberculosis control in Tasmania. He was a member (1915-56) of the St John Ambulance Brigade, director (1917) of Red Cross in Tasmania and was appointed a knight of the Order of St John (1945). President (1925) of the Alliance Française and, in the 1930s, honorary consular agent for France, he had a burning passion for the cause of the Free French in World War II. With a tremendous enthusiasm for life, irrepressible cheerfulness and selflessness, he played the cello and royal tennis, and was honorary medical officer to the Tasmanian Football League and medical officer to the 111th Australian General Hospital. In 1955 he was appointed C.B.E. He retired two years later.

Following his wife's death, Goddard lived with his daughter and son-in-law at St Raphael, France. He died there on 17 February 1967 and was cremated; his daughter survived him.

C. Craig, *Launceston General Hospital* (Hob, 1963); W. G. Rimmer, *Portrait of a Hospital* (Hob, 1981); R. M. Porter and T. C. Boag, *The Australian Tuberculosis Campaign* (Melb, 1991?); A. J. Proust (ed), *History of Tuberculosis* (Canb, 1991); *MJA*, 22 July 1967, 20 Sept 1993; *Mercury*, 1 Jan 1941, 20 Feb, 3, 13, 15 May 1967; T. H. Goddard, The Struggle Against TB in Tasmania 1905-1950 (TA); information from Mrs J. Papin-Jalouste, St Raphael, France, Drs L. A. F. Young and I. MacGowan, Sandy Bay, Mr G. D. Brown, Battery Point, Hob, Mr K. Drake and Dr C. B. McDonald, Hob.

K. S. MILLINGEN*

GODFREY, ARTHUR HARRY LANGHAM (1896-1942), army officer and auctioneer, was born on 26 January 1896 at Camberwell, Melbourne, second child of Charles Edward Rowlandson Godfrey, a bank clerk from India, and his Victorian-born wife Isabel Frances, née Langham. Educated at Central College, Geelong, Arthur was employed as a clerk and served in the Militia with the 70th Infantry (Ballarat Regiment). On 11 January 1915 he enlisted in the Australian Imperial Force; he was posted as a reinforcement for the 5th Battalion and promoted sergeant in March.

Next month Godfrey sailed for Egypt where he was attached to A.I.F. Headquarters. Commissioned in March 1916, he was sent to the 58th Battalion; the unit was transferred to the Western Front in June and he was promoted lieutenant in August. Near Petillon, France, on the night of 17/18 September, he led a raiding party against a section of the German trenches. Although he encountered 'strong opposition', he 'secured identifications and laid two charges of gun cotton. He was the last to leave, and then carried back a wounded Sergeant'. Godfrey was awarded the Military Cross. From December 1916 to May 1917 he served as adjutant of the battalion.

In 1917-18 Captain Godfrey performed staff duties, first at the headquarters of the British 48th Division, and then at those of the 15th and 14th Australian Infantry brigades. He was gassed in May 1918 and evacuated to England. On 15 June that year at St John's Episcopal Church, Edinburgh, he married Mabel Sophia Barrett-Lennard. Returning to the 14th Brigade in France in July, he was detached that month to the 30th American Division with which he remained until the Armistice. His A.I.F. appointment terminated in Australia on 27 July 1919.

Between the wars Godfrey lived at Newtown, Geelong, worked as an auctioneer for Strachan & Co. Ltd, stock and station agents, and was an active Freemason. He resumed his involvement with the Citizen Military Forces as captain (1920) and major (1925) in the 23rd Battalion. In 1927 he was promoted lieutenant colonel and commanded the unit (1927-29) and the composite 23rd-21st Battalion (1929-32 and 1935-39). Seconded to the A.I.F. on 13 October 1939, he was given command of the 2nd/6th Battalion which embarked for the Middle East in April 1940 and trained in Palestine from May.

The 2nd/6th relieved a British battalion outside Bardia, Libya, on 28 December. For his part in the next eight days of operations, culminating in the successful attack (3-5 January 1941) on the fortified town, Godfrey was awarded the Distinguished Service Order and mentioned in dispatches. His brigade com- mander (Sir) Stanley Savige [q.v.] praised his example 'as a soldier and a man'. The battalion took part in the assault on Tobruk on 21-22 January. Promoted colonel and temporary brigadier (20 January), Godfrey relinquished his command of the 2nd/6th on the 28th and became commander, in turn, of the Tobruk Lines of Communication Sub-Area and the A.I.F. Reinforcements Depot.

On 13 March 1941 he was appointed to command the 24th Brigade. Between April and September he led the formation with 'ability and purposefulness' in the defence of Tobruk; he was awarded a Bar to his D.S.O. and again mentioned in dispatches. The brigade held defensive positions in Syria in January-June 1942 before being moved to Egypt to help block Axis forces advancing towards Cairo. From July the 24th Brigade fought at Tel el Makh Khad, and attacked Ruin Ridge where the 2nd/28th Battalion was captured. The battle of El Alamein, a turning point in the war, began on 23/24 October. Godfrey directed the brigade's operations until the evening of 1 November when his tactical headquarters received a direct hit during an enemy artillery barrage. Seriously wounded in the abdomen, he died on 4 November 1942 and was buried in El Alamein war cemetery. He was mentioned in dispatches a third time. His wife, daughter and three sons survived him.

Godfrey was remembered as 'happy go lucky, always smiling', a 'good mixer and a very sincere man'. Resourceful, courageous and compassionate, he administered discipline firmly and fairly. A former adjutant said of him, 'he had the priceless gift of being able to move about, and be equally [at] home with all ranks . . . He was a fine commander too, clear and incisive'. Godfrey was the most senior A.I.F. officer killed in action at El Alamein.

A. D. Ellis, *The Story of the Fifth Australian Division* (Lond, 1920); C. E. W. Bean, *The A.I.F. in France*, 4 (Syd, 1933); J. D. Yeates and W. G. Loh (eds), *Red Platypus* (Perth, 1946); G. Long, *To Benghazi* (Canb, 1952); H. Gullett, *Not as a Duty Only* (Melb, 1976); B. Maughan, *Tobruk and El Alamein* (Canb, 1966); D. Hay, *Nothing over us* (Canb, 1984); information from Messrs F. Carew, Birregurra, Vic, and R. J. Homer, Melb.

JAMES WOOD

GODSON, JOHN ROBERT (1949-1979), petrol-tanker driver, was born on 2 August 1949 at Warren, New South Wales, son of native-born parents George Robert Godson, a market gardener from a long-standing local family, and his wife Laura Rae, née Hammond. With his younger sister Susan, John helped his parents on the family's 50-acre (20 ha) farm, Orange Grove, and was educated at Warren Central School.

Tall and bespectacled, with dark brown hair, Godson was apprenticed to a builder and did contract work on nearby farms. On 13 February 1971 at St Andrew's Presbyterian Church, Warren, he married a 17-year-old local girl Jennifer Anne Poidevin. They set up house at 12 Wilson Street; their sons Damien and Craig were born respectively on 15 August 1973 and 15 December 1974. Jenny described John as being 'a dedicated member of the community . . . good, kind, strong and reliable. He had great integrity. He lived for his family'. To support them, John took additional work delivering petrol around the countryside for Mobil Oil Australia Ltd.

Extended hours away from home put pressure on the marriage and a long-planned family holiday was at last taken in June 1979. New South Wales was in the grip of a railway strike and travelling was difficult. The Godsons stopped at Yass to visit the boys' maternal grandmother and then moved on to Sydney to see the sights. On 9 June, with their Sydney hosts the Harris family, they went to Taronga Zoological Park, returned to the city for dinner and embarked by ferry for a night at Luna Park, 'Just For Fun'.

Jenny recalled that, after several hours enjoying the various attractions, 'It was nearly time for us to leave, the boys asked John if they could have another ride on the Ghost Train and the River Caves. He agreed and the Harrises and I went to get ice creams'. Godson and his boys boarded a carriage and passed through Hell's Doorway into the twisting corridors of the Ghost Train, followed by four 13-year-old students from Christian Brothers' College, Waverley. The building erupted in flames. The charred bodies of John Godson and his sons were found huddled together in a cul-de-sac, the bodies of the four schoolboys close by. He and his sons were buried in Warren cemetery. Luna Park remained closed until 1982.

Persistent allegations circulated in the 1980s that the Ghost Train fire had been deliberately lit at the instigation of entrepreneurs who wanted to redevelop the prime harbour site. Backed by journalists, Jennifer Godson urged the police to reopen the inquiry in 1985, but the Corporate Affairs Commission was unable to unravel the ownership of Harbourside Amusements Pty Ltd (lessees of the park from 1980). Although the National Crime Authority in 1987 described the original police investigation as 'inadequate' and as rendering the coronial inquest 'ineffective', it failed to discover the cause of the fire. John Godson was thrust into prominence by the extraordinary circumstances of his death.

Public Hist Review, 1, 1992, p 50; *Daily Telegraph* (Syd), 11 June 1979; *Daily Liberal and Macquarie Advocate* (Dubbo, NSW), 11, 14-15, 19 June 1979; *SMH*, 11 June, 23-25, 29-30 Aug, 4 Sept 1979, 17-18, 30 Oct, 18 Nov 1985, 12 June, 9, 12, 28 Oct 1987.   MARTIN SHARP

GOFFAGE, JOHN WILLIAM PILBEAN ('CHIPS RAFFERTY') (1909-1971), actor, was born on 26 March 1909 at Broken Hill, New South Wales, son of John Goffage, an agent from England, and his native-born wife Violet Maud Edyth, née Joyce. Nicknamed 'Chips' by his schoolmates, he was educated in country towns and at Parramatta Intermediate Boys' High School. He learned to ride and to box, and developed a lifelong love of painting. Apprenticed as an ironmoulder at the Clyde Engineering Co. Ltd, Sydney, he left to roam through the eastern Australian bush as a drover, shearer and boundary rider; he later worked as a deckhand in coastal boats and as an assistant in a Sydney wine cellar. He sold poems and stories to newspapers and magazines, and the occasional water-colour painting. At St Stephen's Presbyterian Church, Macquarie Street, on 16 November 1935 he married Colina Jean Stewart Ferguson, a 19-year-old dental nurse; they ran an ice-cream parlour before they were divorced in March 1941.

With his thin build and height of 6 ft 6 ins (198 cm), and an irreverent sense of humour, Goffage first entered show business as a magician's assistant, then was hired as an extra in a film, *Come up Smiling* (1939), produced in Sydney. He attracted attention in a small role as a gangling member of a slapstick bushfire-fighting team in *Dad Rudd, M.P.* (1940), and was promptly cast as the comic lead in *Forty Thousand Horsemen* (1940), Charles Chauvel's [q.v.7] much-publicized tribute to the Australian Light Horse in the Sinai desert campaign of World War I. An outstanding commercial success at home, the film screened favourably in Britain and the United States of America, bringing 'Chips Rafferty' (the screen-name Goffage adopted) instant fame in Australia.

On 28 May 1941 at the registrar general's office, Sydney, Goffage married Ellen Kathleen Jameson, a 37-year-old dressmaker. Known as 'Quentin', she was to be his close and constant companion until her death on 27 May 1964. They had no children. On 29 May 1941 Goffage had enlisted in the Royal Australian Air Force. He was amiable, unaffected and popular with the airmen. Commissioned in the Administrative and Special Duties Branch in April 1943, he performed welfare and entertainment duties in Australia and New Guinea. On secondment, he acted in several Australian propaganda films for the

Department of Information, including *South West Pacific* (1943), and in a second feature film for Chauvel, *The Rats of Tobruk* (1944), in which he again played one of the leading roles, this time as a member of the A.I.F. in North Africa. He was demobilized with the rank of flying officer on 13 February 1945.

Rafferty's first postwar film, *The Overlanders* (1946), marked a turning-point in his career. He was cast by British director Harry Watt in the role of a bushman who headed a team which drove a vast herd of cattle across northern Australia beyond the reach of possible Japanese invaders. With a brilliant background in documentary, Watt was determined to create authentic Australian characters in his factually based drama. Under his perceptive and disciplined direction, Rafferty moulded the character of the tough, laconic Australian bushman which he continued to play, with minor variations, for the rest of his life, both in public and on screen. Following a postwar decline in local production, Rafferty took numerous roles in British and American films made on location in Australia, most notably *Bitter Springs* (1950), *Kangaroo* (1952), *Smiley* (1956) and *The Sundowners* (1960). Like many Australian actors, he went overseas to find work; he was given parts in *The Loves of Joanna Godden* (1947), *The Desert Rats* (1953) and *Mutiny on the Bounty* (1962).

In 1952 Rafferty had joined an Australian documentary film-maker, Lee Robinson, to produce a totally local film, *The Phantom Stockman* (1953), a 'Western' with Rafferty in his standard bushman role. Although crudely produced, the film was profitable, and Rafferty and Robinson formalized their partnership in a company, Southern International; they developed an ambitious production programme for film and television designed to revitalize the ailing local industry. After *King of the Coral Sea* (1954), directed by Robinson and starring Rafferty as a Torres Strait pearl fisherman, Southern International secured French finance for three films, among them *Walk into Paradise* (1956) with Rafferty as a New Guinea patrol officer.

He was also active in the administration of the company's projects and in selling the completed films. An outspoken advocate of government support for the film and television industries in Australia from the 1950s, he was a man of strong opinions, strongly expressed, and a Freemason. Not only did he risk personal resources in Southern International, but he used his considerable public image to take a patriarchal role in the local film community. Despite his efforts, his film company foundered and ceased production in 1959. He continued to work as an actor at home and abroad in films such as *They're a Weird Mob* (1966) and *Double Trouble* (1967)

with Elvis Presley. He also made numerous guest appearances on Australian television, in variety shows, in Australian series like 'Skippy' (1970), and in American series which included 'The Wackiest Ship in the Army' (1967) and 'Tarzan' (1969). In 1971 he gave one of his finest performances—and his last in a feature film—as an outback policeman in *Wake in Fright*. Chips died suddenly of lung disease and heart failure on 27 May that year at Elizabeth Bay, Sydney, and was cremated with Anglican rites.

As an actor, Rafferty owed much to a tradition of comedy going back to Pat Hanna [q.v.9] and his series of 'Diggers' stage shows in the 1920s. After his screen character was remodelled by Watt in *The Overlanders*, Rafferty abandoned broad comedy and emerged as a stereotype of the Australian outback male, becoming identified with the character more thoroughly than any other actor of his generation. To the film critic of the *Sydney Morning Herald* (30 September 1946), he was 'the Australian Everyman', in speech, action and character'. For the postwar generation he symbolized essential Australian qualities, and was both honoured (M.B.E., 1971) and reviled for his association with heavy drinking and cultural crudity.

A. Pike and R. Cooper, *Australian Film, 1900-1977* (Melb, 1980); B. Larkins, *Chips, the Life and Films of Chips Rafferty* (Melb, 1986); *Film Weekly*, 13 Sept 1945, 3, 10 Oct 1946; *People* (Syd), 8 Oct 1952; *Walkabout*, 19 Oct 1970; *Continuum*, 1, no 1, 1987; *Australian*, 12 Nov 1969; *SMH*, 1 Jan, 29 May 1971; *Canb Times*, 29 May 1971; *Sunday Telegraph* (Syd), 8 June 1986; *Daily Mirror* (Syd), 26 Oct 1988; personal information.   A. F. PIKE

GOLDBERG, FRANK (1889-1958), businessman and advertising pioneer, was born on 7 July 1889 in London, seventh son of thirteen children of Woolf Goldberg, tailor, and his wife Fanny, née Klein. Frank was educated at the Bayswater Jewish Schools. In his autobiography, *My Life in Advertising* (privately printed, Sydney, 1957), he wrote: 'by tradition, the seventh son is a lucky child. But fortune was a little tardy in showing its favour to me. In my youth, I had to labour unrelentingly'. He quarrelled with his father over the sterner tenets of Jewish law and in 1903 left home to became an apprentice compositor at the *Jewish Chronicle* in the East End. Advised to live abroad for the sake of his health, he reached Wellington, New Zealand, on 27 November 1910.

Next day Goldberg went to work in Veitch & Allan's department store. He sold a large assortment of mechanical toys to Mrs Abraham Levy, and received both a 10 per cent commission and an invitation to dine with the Levys. In 1912 he worked for the *Hutt & Petone Chronicle* before peddling a device called the Oxypathor which promised to relieve gout, arthritis, rheumatism and colic. That year the Levys helped him to establish an advertising agency in Wellington with a £5000 contract to place the advertising for their clothing business. At the time most people 'regarded an advertising agent as a mixture of charlatan and medicine man'. The Levys had no such qualms. Delighted by Goldberg's *chutzpah*, Mrs Levy responded, 'What a salesman!', when he asked if he could marry her daughter Agolda. Their wedding took place on 16 June 1915 at the Synagogue, The Terrace.

Goldberg handled the launch of G. R. R. Nicholas's [q.v.11] aspirin in New Zealand in 1916. After visiting his own siblings in the United States of America in 1921, he picked up the New Zealand account for Goodrich tyres. About 1925 he established a small office in Sydney. Having crossed the Tasman more than fifty times by 1927, in that year he moved the headquarters of the Goldberg Advertising Agency Ltd to Sydney and opened a branch in Melbourne. His major accounts over the next thirty years included the Gramophone Co. (His Master's Voice), Tooth [qq.v.6] & Co. Ltd (beer), Godfrey Phillips' (Australia) Pty Ltd (cigarettes), John Walker & Sons Ltd (whisky) and General Motors Corporation (Chevrolet and Pontiac).

Following a visit to Max Factor in California, U.S.A., Goldberg introduced his cosmetics to Australia in the 1930s. Factor had offered to fit Goldberg (who was balding in middle age) with a toupee. The agency launched the *Australian Women's Weekly* for Consolidated Press Ltd in 1933, won the advertising account for the United Australia Party and, from the 1940s, handled Liberal Party business. Goldberg played down value and price in his advertisements, preferring to emphasize the promise: 'Bring Romance into Spending' was one of his catchphrases. In the 1930s he opened a radio department which produced plays, Bible stories and the popular series, 'Shocking Shakespeare'. By 1940 the agency had offices in Sydney and Melbourne, and in Wellington and Auckland, New Zealand.

A member of the Federal government's War Effort Publicity Board, Goldberg was deputy-chairman (1946-53) of the Australian Advertising Council. He had no sons, but liked male company, playing golf, tennis and bowls. At his cottage at Blackheath in the Blue Mountains he spent many hours talking to his son-in-law Harry Woolf who eventually became managing director of the agency. Goldberg belonged to the Royal Automobile Club of Australia, Tattersall's, the New South Wales Masonic, Millions and the American National clubs.

On a trip to New Zealand in 1953 Goldberg suffered a minor stroke (he drank Scotch and smoked heavily) which led to his partial retirement. Survived by his wife and two daughters, he died of cardiac and cerebrovascular disease on 10 January 1958 at Rose Bay and was buried in Rookwood cemetery. Ten years later the firm was sold to the British company, Masius, Wynne-Williams Ltd.

Newspaper News (Syd), 24 Jan, 7 Feb 1958; *SMH*, 31 Jan 1936, 11 Jan 1958; Goldberg personal file (John Fairfax Group Pty Ltd Archives, Syd); information from Mr H. Woolf, Vaucluse, and Mrs C. Walker, Bellevue Hill, Syd.

VALERIE LAWSON

GOLDMAN, MAURICE DAVID (1898-1957), linguist and professor of Semitic studies, was born on 13 January 1898 at Kolo, Poland (then part of the Russian Empire), son of Arie Lejb Goldman, retail merchant and scholar, and his wife Golda, née Kozminska. Maurice was educated at gymnasiums at Gostynin and Lodz, graduating in 1917. For three semesters he studied medicine at the University of Warsaw and attended several language seminars in his spare time. In 1920 he transferred to the University of Berlin (D.Phil., 1925) to read Islamic culture and Oriental languages under Professor Eugen Mittwoch. About 1922 Goldman married Fela Hermeon (d.1932) in Berlin. He subsequently lectured in Hebrew, Aramaic, Islamic culture, Arabic and Ethiopic at various tertiary institutions in Germany. In the summer of 1935 he travelled to Palestine, Arabia, Egypt, Algiers, Morocco and Tunis.

Coming from a rich cultural mix, Goldman was a remarkable linguist. He spoke modern Hebrew, Polish and German in his daily intercourse; he had been taught ancient Hebrew by his father and Russian by his Russian-born mother; he had studied French, classical Greek and Latin at school; and he mastered all the Semitic languages. In sum, he had a working knowledge of forty languages. While in Germany he published several articles and books, including a Hebrew grammar.

In 1938, after making a subtle comparison between the prophet Mohammed and the Führer, Goldman narrowly eluded the Gestapo—but not before he had ensured that his students had completed their examinations. Travelling on his Polish passport, he visited London, then left for Australia where he had a sister living at Horsham, Victoria. He disembarked in Melbourne on 2 January 1939.

Throughout World War II Goldman served as an interpreter and consultant in the censor's office, Department of the Army,

Melbourne. He was naturalized in 1944. He taught at Temple Beth Israel, St Kilda, was active in establishing Bialik College, North Carlton, and was a guest lecturer at the University of Melbourne where his erudition convinced Professor A. R. Chisholm, dean of the faculty of arts, that he was 'a man of genius'. Dr Greta Hort [q.v.] and other senior colleagues concurred and—although all the outward forms of a university appointment were scrupulously observed—what amounted to a personal chair was created for Goldman in 1945, initially subsidized by a benefaction from the Jewish businessman, Abraham Sicree.

Professor Goldman fitted well into the intellectual climate of (Sir) John Medley's [q.v.] humanizing era at the university. In 1950 Goldman initiated discussion which led to the formation of the Fellowship for Biblical Studies and the *Australian Biblical Review*, and was credited with promoting 'the first Jewish-Christian interfaith dialogue'. A foundation member (1956) of the Humanities Research Council, he remained an active participant in international conferences, even during his final illness. He claimed to have developed a new method of teaching languages: since his method required an intimate knowledge of several cognate languages in their historic and modern variations as well as cultural associations and nuances, few could put it into practice as effectively as did its inventor.

In Berlin, Goldman had been in touch with Zionist leaders; in Melbourne, he supported the Labour Zionist movement, was a member of B'nai B'rith and belonged to the Liberal Synagogue, St Kilda. He served on the school council of Mount Scopus College, wrote a primer for children, and contributed articles to *Australian Jewish News* and *Australian Biblical Review*, and a short chapter to *Light out of France* (Sydney, 1951). His lifelong work on a dictionary of Ethiopic languages remained unfinished.

Goldman was 5 ft 6 ins (168 cm) tall, weighed over 14 stone (89 kg) and had a 'poker face'. He disregarded the warnings of his medical adviser, smoked heavily scented cigars and took no exercise. A widower with no children, he employed a non-Jewish housekeeper. He entertained friends with philosophical discussions, vintage wine, inexhaustible anecdotes and crossword puzzles which he compiled in a range of languages, and he spoke Aramaic to his cat. Goldman died of cancer on 14 September 1957 at his Moorabbin home and was cremated. He left his fine library and the bulk of his estate to the university for the benefit of the department of Semitic studies.

A. R. Chisholm, *Men Were My Milestones* (Melb, 1958); H. L. and W. D. Rubinstein, *The Jews in Aus-*

tralia (Melb, 1991); *People*, 13 Feb 1952; *Who's Who in World Jewry* (NY), 1955; *Leo Baeck Inst Yearbook* (NY), 1956, 1967; *Univ Melb Gazette*, Nov 1957; *Great Synagogue Congregational J*, May 1980; *Age* (Melb), 16 Sept 1957; information from Mrs S. Freadman, East Melb, Sr A. Goldman, Rome, Rabbi J. S. Levi, St Kilda, Melb, Mr B. Rechter, Monash Univ and Mrs L. Carrington, Lyneham, Canb.

NINA CHRISTESEN

GOLDSMITH, ADRIAN PHILIP ('TIM') (1921-1961), public servant, airman and business-manager, was born on 25 April 1921 at Waverley, Sydney, second son of Sidney Goldsmith, a native-born clerk who became a timber merchant, and his wife Philippa Mary, née Scott-Coward, from England. Called 'Tim' by his mother, he was educated at Newington College and—after the family shifted to Avoca Beach during the Depression—at Gosford High School. In July 1937 he took a job as a clerk in the New South Wales Department of Works and Local Government.

On 16 September 1940 Goldsmith enlisted in the Royal Australian Air Force and trained as a pilot. In June 1941 he was sent to England where he served briefly as a sergeant pilot in No.234 and No.242 squadrons, Royal Air Force. He married Dorothea Rosemary Britton on 10 December that year in the parish church, Tuckingmill, Cornwall; they were to remain childless.

Moving to Malta in February 1942, Goldsmith joined No.126 Squadron, in which he flew Hurricanes and later Spitfires. On 21 April he shot down a Messerschmitt Bf 109 and damaged a second; during the first fortnight in May he destroyed six more enemy aircraft; his tally of German and Italian aircraft rose quickly. He was awarded the Distinguished Flying Medal on 15 May and commissioned that day. On 15 June he attacked a large enemy formation, destroying two planes and probably a third in only ten minutes. For this action he was awarded the Distinguished Flying Cross. When his tour ended in July, his 'kills' numbered 12¼. He subsequently received permission to wear a Maltese cross for his contribution to the island's defence.

Having spent a short term instructing in England, Goldsmith returned home and by January 1943 was a flight commander in No.452 Squadron, R.A.A.F. Between March and September, while operating from Strauss, near Darwin, he added four Japanese aircraft to his score. On 2 May he had been shot down: he parachuted into the sea and spent twenty-four hours in an inflatable dinghy before being rescued. Promoted acting flight lieutenant in September, he was posted to instructional duties at Mildura, Victoria, in April 1944. He was an acting squadron leader when his appointment was terminated on medical grounds on 31 May 1945. With 16¼ officially credited 'kills', he was one of Australia's top aces in World War II; his unofficial total was 19¼.

In 1943 Goldsmith's wife had been reported missing, believed killed, while voyaging to Australia. At St Mary's Catholic Church, Concord, Sydney, on 23 October 1944 he married an army nursing sister, Doris May McGrath. They lived at Burwood. A large man—6 ft 1 in. (185 cm) tall—with vivid blue eyes and an outgoing personality, he worked as a salesman. He joined Commonwealth Oil Refineries Ltd (later B.P. Australia Ltd) in 1946 and moved around New South Wales before returning to Sydney as State marketing-manager. Following an operation for ileo-caecal volvulus, he died of peritonitis on 25 March 1961 at the Sydney Sanitarium and Hospital, Wahroonga, and was cremated with Anglican rites; two years later his ashes were scattered over the Timor Sea. His wife, son and daughter survived him; a second son was born in October 1961. Ray Honisett's portrait (1987) of Goldsmith is held by the Australian War Memorial, Canberra.

J. Herington, *Air War Against Germany and Italy 1939-1943* (Canb, 1954); *Age* (Melb), 14 Dec 1942, 11, 18 May 1943; *Sun-Herald*, 26 Mar 1961; RAAF Hist Section, Canb; information from Mrs D. M. Goldsmith and Mrs J. Reeves, Hackett, ACT.   MARK LAX

GOLDSMITH, HERBERT STEPHEN (1884-1956), engineer, was born on 15 August 1884 at Maryborough, Queensland, sixth child of English-born parents ALFRED JOSEPH GOLDSMITH (1848-1928), engineer, and his wife SARAH (1846-1940), née Forster. In 1884 Alfred joined W. F. Harrington [q.v.9], T. Braddock and J. F. Wood to float the engineering company, John Walker & Co. Ltd (Walkers Ltd from 1888), at Maryborough. The Goldsmith family moved to Brisbane in 1891. Alfred developed the firm's manufacture of sugar- and mining-industry equipment, then expanded into shipbuilding and the construction of dredges for the State government. A contract to build ocean-going cargo vessels was negotiated with the Federal government in 1918. Walkers Ltd supplied locomotives for most of Australia's railway systems during Alfred's term on the board, from 1904 until his death on 4 June 1928.

Sarah had been born on 11 February 1846 at Gateshead, Durham, England, daughter of Stephen Forster, chain manufacturer and later foundry proprietor, and his wife Isabella, née Bainbridge. In 1853 the family emigrated to Sydney where Stephen established Forster

& Sons, a manufacturing business. In her parents' home at Harrington Street on 7 June 1873 Sarah married Alfred Goldsmith with Congregational forms. Soon after the family moved to Brisbane she became active on the committee of the Lady Musgrave Lodge, an organization which provided low-cost, non-sectarian Christian accommodation for single women, especially immigrants. Mrs Goldsmith met most of the immigrant ships and personally interviewed many of the girls. In 1892 the lodge erected its own building in central Brisbane. As president (1903-31) of the committee, Mrs Goldsmith organized bands of volunteers to help eliminate a £4000 mortgage on the building. From 1931 she continued to serve as honorary president. Survived by three of her six sons and one of her two daughters, she died on 21 January 1940 at Sherwood and was buried in Toowong cemetery.

Educated at Brisbane Grammar School, Herbert completed an apprenticeship with Walkers Ltd and carried out hydrographic survey-work for the Rockhampton Harbour Board. On 21 September 1908 he joined the dockyards and workshops branch of the New South Wales Department of Public Works as a draftsman and was based at Cockatoo Island, Sydney. At St Paul's Anglican Church, Maryborough, on 6 February 1911 he married Mary Hope Jean Henty. On 4 December 1915 Goldsmith was appointed designing engineer for the State government's new dockyard at Walsh Island, Newcastle; in 1919 he was promoted principal designing engineer. He returned to Walkers at Maryborough as general manager in May 1921. At the onset of the Depression (during which the firm's labour force fell from the hundreds to sixty-four, and half-time work was introduced) he travelled to England where he negotiated a contract to produce diesel engines, under licence to a British company, but with the right to incorporate local design improvements. This plan to become a substantial manufacturer of large engines was frustrated when tariff protection was modified by the Ottowa Agreement (1932).

Throughout World War II Goldsmith guided a massive recovery. His company's employees soared to over one thousand, most of whom were engaged in shipbuilding, especially in the construction of frigates and corvettes for the Royal Australian Navy. In the buoyant postwar expansion Camerons Ltd, an iron-foundry at Mackay, was acquired, and new premises were built for Walkers at Maryborough where one of Goldsmith's sons became manager.

Herbert Goldsmith was an associate (1919) and member (1926) of the Institution of Mechanical Engineers, London. Respected by his staff, he was popularly known as 'The

Chief'. He inspected each of the firm's workshops regularly, but did not interfere in management, although he often made suggestions to drafting staff and his works manager. After thirty-one years as general manager, he retired to Brisbane in 1952 and continued to serve as a director of the firm. He enjoyed boating. Survived by his wife, daughter and three sons, he died on 12 June 1956 at Yeronga and was cremated with Methodist forms.

Walkers Ltd, *Annual Report*, 1885-1908; Aust Railway Hist Soc, *Bulletin*, no 19, 1968, p 229; *Maryborough Chronicle*, 15 Apr 1884, 22 Nov 1887, 13 Feb, 8 Nov 1888, 1 May 1946, 14 June 1956; *Wide Bay News*, 31 July 1886; *Queenslander*, 14 May 1921; *Daily Mail* (Brisb), 7 July 1921; *Brisb Courier*, 23 Jan 1940; Lady Musgrave Lodge, Annual Report, 1906-40 (OL).   JOHN D. KERR

GOLLAN, HERBERT ROY POLLOCK (1892-1968), journalist, soldier, trade commissioner and diplomat, was born on 29 August 1892 at Gawler, South Australia, son of Robert Harper Gollan, evangelist, and his wife Harriett, née Wilson. Educated at Bendigo Central School, Victoria, Roy served an apprenticeship in the printing trade before working as a journalist, first with the Hamilton *Spectator* and then the Geelong *Advertiser*.

On 26 October 1914 Gollan enlisted in the Australian Imperial Force; he was posted as a corporal to headquarters staff, 3rd Light Horse Brigade, and embarked for Egypt on 1 February 1915. At Gallipoli (May to September) he was promoted staff sergeant and employed as brigade clerk. Struck down by fever, he was evacuated to a hospital in Wales, but by February 1916 was back in Egypt. In June he was commissioned, transferred to the 58th Battalion and sent to France. Moved to the 54th Battalion, he was wounded in January 1917 and hospitalized in Britain. He rejoined his unit in April.

Promoted captain in May 1917, Gollan spent most of the remainder of the war on the 15th Brigade's headquarters. He won the Military Cross for his efforts as staff captain, particularly in the Polygon Wood offensive, near Ypres, Belgium, in September-October. While acting as brigade major in 1918, he prepared orders for the September attack on the Hindenburg line, near Bellicourt, France, and was awarded the Distinguished Service Order. He was twice mentioned in dispatches and his A.I.F. appointment terminated in Australia on 5 October 1919. In the 1920s and 1930s he was active in the Militia, rising to major (1928).

Gollan had returned to the *Advertiser* in 1919 as chief of staff, but left Geelong for Melbourne to be a reporter on the *Argus*. At the Baptist Church, Bendigo, on 17 April 1920 he married Muriel May Hyett, a music teacher. Having been employed as a subeditor on the *Evening Sun*, he joined the publicity office of the Victorian Railways in 1925. Next year he transferred to the Victorian Government Tourist Bureau; by 1927 he was its manager. Two years later he became assistant general manager of the *Argus* and the *Australasian*. In 1931 he was president of the Victorian Travel League. He was managing editor (1933-36) of the Melbourne *Star* and manager (1936-37) of the *Argus* and the *Australasian*.

In 1937 Gollan went to India as representative of the Australian National Travel Association; he and his wife lived at Bombay. After nominating himself, in 1940 he was appointed Australian government trade commissioner in India. He was stationed at Calcutta until early 1941 when he moved to New Delhi to take on the additional function of advising Sir Bertram Stevens [q.v.12], Australia's representative on the Eastern Group Supply Council. In 1942 he succeeded Stevens and—based at Simla—held the post until 1945. Promoted senior commissioner, Gollan returned to Calcutta in October that year and moved to Bombay in July 1946. 'He believed in the positive, direct approach and in his highly egotistical way' did much to foster his country's interests.

Appointed Australian high commissioner to India in October 1948, Gollan proved to be a competent diplomat. From his office in New Delhi he worked hard to develop Australian-Indian relations, but was sometimes disappointed at a lack of response from both countries: on one visit to Australia he remarked that his service in India was 'a long sentence'. Following his retirement in April 1952, he settled at Emerald, Victoria. He died there on 28 March 1968 and was cremated. His wife survived him; they had no children.

Herald (Melb), 5 Nov 1927, 22 Jan 1931; *Newspaper News*, 2 Sept 1929; *Argus*, 4 May 1937, 20 Nov 1948; A. R. Taysom, History of the Australian Trade Commissioner Service, 3 (ts, Canb, 1983, NL); AWM 43, item A306 (AWM).

PHILIP DORLING

GOLLAN, ROSS FRANCIS (1902-1961), journalist, was born on 2 October 1902 at Bowral, New South Wales, eldest child of native-born parents Colin Gollan, schoolteacher, and his wife Nellie (Ellen), née Sullivan. Ross attended Sydney Boys' High School, edited the school magazine, was a prefect and played Rugby in the first XV. At the University of Sydney (B.A., 1923; M.A., 1925) he edited *Hermes* and won the 1923

Wentworth [q.v.2] medal for the best undergraduate essay.

Joining the *Sydney Morning Herald* as a cadet on probation in 1923, Gollan made a strong impression as a persistent news gatherer and as an accurate, clear and concise writer with 'the faculty of drawing a man'. On 11 November 1926 at the district registrar's office, North Sydney, he married a fellow journalist Sylvia Stewart Russell, daughter of A. G. Stephens [q.v.12]. She died in childbirth on 4 January 1930. Left with an infant daughter, Gollan married Valmai Fitzroy Clack at Christ Church Cathedral, Newcastle, on 29 April 1931; they were to have three children. Midway through 1928 he had transferred to Newcastle where he made a name as a balanced reporter with a good political mind. After twelve years of covering the tumultuous coal troubles, he moved back to Sydney and was then sent to Canberra as Federal parliamentary roundsman.

During the early part of 1941 Gollan used his column to attack a prime ministerial aspirant (Sir) Percy Spender who was to blame him for undermining his political reputation. Gollan also criticized Prime Minister (Sir) Robert Menzies [q.v.] for being out of touch with the electorate and was credited with having influenced (Sir) Arthur Fadden's [q.v.] rise to power by promoting him as the obvious successor to Menzies. When Fadden became prime minister, Gollan enjoyed a period of influence and prestige that lasted but forty days until John Curtin [q.v.13] took office on 7 October 1941.

Having rejoined the rank and file of the press gallery, Gollan remained a significant force in political reporting. A colleague described him as 'a square built, untidy man who gave the Sydney Morning Herald the reverent loyalty that others reserve for their church'; he was widely read and a good talker, a likeable fellow who thought big and had strong views. Although he approved of Curtin, Gollan increasingly criticized the government and by 1944 denounced its 'resurgent partyism' and the crippling war restrictions. His obituary of Curtin, resented by the Australian Labor Party, presented a sharp assessment of the prime minister's strengths and weaknesses.

In 1946 Gollan was recalled to administrative staff head office, Sydney, but, after disagreements with his superiors, was moved in 1949 to the circulation department as manager. From 1960 he wrote a daily column, 'Sydney Spectator', which provided witty comment on people and events. Survived by his wife, their son and two daughters, and by the daughter of his first marriage, he died of a coronary occlusion on 11 November 1961 in Prince Henry Hospital and was cremated with Anglican rites. Gollan, who had worked for the *Herald* for thirty-eight years, was a man of widely divergent qualities, admired for his scholarship, extraordinary literary knowledge and his great interest in sport.

H. H. Wiedersehn (ed), *An Outline History of the Sydney High School* (Syd, 1933); A. Fadden, *They Called Me Artie* (Brisb, 1969); P. Spender, *Politics and a Man* (Syd, 1972); G. Souter, *Company of Heralds* (Melb, 1981); V. Lawson, *Connie Sweetheart* (Melb, 1990); *New Journalist*, 11 Nov 1973, p 11; *Newcastle Morning Herald*, 6 Jan 1930; *SMH*, 27 Jan, 14, 21, 28 July 1941, 15 May 1944, 6 July 1945, 25 May 1960; *Sun-Herald*, 12 Nov 1961; M. Gollan, Notes on Ross Gollan (ts, held by ADB); A. D. Reid, Oral history tape, TRC 121/40 (NL); personal file for R. Gollan (John Fairfax & Sons Ltd Archives, Syd).   KATHLEEN DERMODY

GOLOUBEV, NIKOLAI PAVLOVICH (1888-1965), medical practitioner and community leader, was born on 5 January 1888 at Okhansk, Perm province, Russia, son of Pavel Goloubev, schoolteacher, and his wife Natalie, née Sobolev. Nikolai attended senior school at Tobol'sk, Siberia, and in 1909 entered Tomsk University (M.D., 1918). Called up in 1915, he served as a junior intern in military hospitals at Tiumen and Tomsk. Having been discharged on 4 April 1918, he passed his final university examinations before being mobilized in June by the White Russian army and allotted to the Vanguard Field Hospital. Goloubev retreated on the 'Icy March' from Omsk across Siberia (September 1919-March 1920) with the remnants of the White forces, eventually reaching Chita, Transbaikal. He was chief doctor at various field-hospitals and assistant-commissioner (1920-22) for the All Russian Union of Towns Committee.

With his wife Anna Alexandria and their son, he settled at Suifenhe (Pogranichnaya station), Manchuria, on the Chinese Eastern Railway where he opened his own hospital in October 1923; he also became official medical officer to the Chinese Maritime Customs Service. In 1930 he moved to Harbin and practised at the German-Russian hospital. The Japanese and Soviet Union's invasions of Manchuria, and the Chinese Civil War, created a volatile political climate for the large and impoverished Russian community. Goloubev headed a number of charitable organizations and often jeopardized his own safety by interceding with the authorities on behalf of his compatriots. He joined the Harbin branch of the Chinese Trade Union of Railway Employees, and was chief of the surgical ward (1945-49) and consulting physician (1949-53) at the Central Hospital, Chinese Changchun Railway; he also lectured on surgery at the medical school, was director of the trained nurses' courses and belonged to the Scientific Association of Russian Doctors.

Divorced from Anna, in 1953 Goloubev married Elisavetta Blavdzevich, née Shefranovskaya, at Harbin; she was a widow with three children. He retired on an old-age pension in April 1956 and arrived in Sydney with his family on 24 December in the *Changte*. Appointed vice-chairman of the Eparchy [Diocesan] Refugee Committee by Bishop Savva of Australia and New Zealand, he helped Russian newcomers in Sydney. In August 1957 he was nominated to a committee that considered appeals to enter Australia, and gave useful and humane advice based on his knowledge of some of the applicants from Harbin. Many of his former patients, who had managed to reach New South Wales, organized a petition to the Department of Health requesting recognition of Dr Goloubev as their qualified medical practitioner. This petition was 'met with kind consideration and approval', and he established a surgery in 1959 at Strathfield where he continued to practise until his death. A humanist and a devout Christian who worshipped at the Russian Orthodox Cathedral of St Peter and St Paul, Strathfield, he was wise and tolerant, and generous with his time and money.

Goloubev changed the spelling of his surname to Goloubeff and was naturalized in 1962. He wrote poetry, painted in oils, played chess and belonged to the Sir Benjamin Fuller [q.v.8] Foreign Language Memorial Library. Stocky in build, with grey-blue eyes, he was an outstanding figure among his countrymen in Australia. He died on 9 December 1965 at his Strathfield home and was buried in Rookwood cemetery. His wife survived him, as did the son of his first marriage who had emigrated with Anna to Tasmania.

Edinenie (*Unification*, Syd), 24, 31 Dec 1965; naturalization file, SP1122/1 item N61/37113 (AA, Syd); family information from Mr M. Kokot, Bondi, Syd.
J. A. ZANADVOROFF*

GONINAN, ALFRED (1865-1953) and RALPH WILLIAMS (1874-1948), engineers, were born on 29 May 1865 and 12 June 1874 at St Just in Penwith, Cornwall, England, sons of Alfred Goninan, grocer and later tindresser, and his wife Rebecca, née Thomas. The brothers were apprenticed locally to N. Holman & Sons. Alfred spent several years as a marine engineer. He married Annie Charleston on 12 November 1889 at the parish church, St Erth; in 1891 they followed her siblings to Australia. Having worked at Port Pirie, South Australia, and Hill End, New South Wales, in 1899 he established an engineering business at Wickham, near Newcastle, with his brother Ralph who had reached Australia in 1894 and worked at Port Pirie, Broken Hill, New South Wales, Western Australia and New Guinea. On 15 March 1900 at her mother's Hill End home Ralph married Ellen Jane Thomas with Wesleyan forms. After her death, he married a widow Bertha Maude Cregan, née MacDonald, on 20 March 1937 at St James's Anglican Church, Sydney.

A. Goninan & Co. Ltd had been incorporated as a public company in 1905, with Alfred and H. Charleston as joint governing directors. The firm experienced difficulties during World War I in supplying their customers. In 1917 Alfred helped to establish Commonwealth Steel Products Co. Ltd at Waratah, mainly to produce railway wheels and axles which could no longer be imported from Belgium. In that year he visited the United States of America to buy machinery, one of seven overseas trips he made to obtain equipment and new ideas. Goninan & Co. moved to more convenient freehold land at Broadmeadow in 1919 and built a flourishing business in general engineering. By 1926 the brothers were joint managing directors and Alfred was chairman. They made pitheads, boilers, wagons and a huge, cast 41-ton block for the district's coal trade.

Alfred helped to established Henry Lane (Australia) Ltd at Hamilton and was a director of Non-Metallics Ltd. In 1930 he stood unsuccessfully as the National Party's candidate for the seat of Newcastle in the Legislative Assembly. Unable to meet a large personal overdraft during the Depression, he was eased out of his firm in 1933 with a small *ex gratia* pension and some recriminations. Under Ralph as managing director, the company reached its peak in the 1940s and was one of the largest in general engineering in Australia, employing over seven hundred people and with three years of orders in hand. He retired in 1946 and was succeeded by his eldest son, also named Ralph (d.1972). Goninan died on 16 May 1948 at the Mater Misericordiae Hospital, Waratah, and was cremated with Methodist forms; his wife survived him, as did the two sons and three daughters of his first marriage.

The family, particularly Alfred, were proud of their Cornish heritage and of being 'Cousin Jacks', as Cornishmen were called overseas. His daughter Alfreda, a noted artist, married Radoje Marcovitch, a Yugoslav diplomat and journalist who became a casualty of World War II. In 1941 she returned to Australia with her children to join her father and in the early 1950s encouraged him to write his memoirs. Another daughter Edmée married Thomas Hamilton, a prominent Newcastle surgeon. Alfred died on 25 August 1953 in his home at Chatswood, Sydney, and was cremated with Anglican rites; his three sons and three of his four daughters survived him. Alfred Goninan was a creative engineer who saw Newcastle as a 'Ruhr of the Antipodes', but he lacked the financial capacity to realize his vision. The closing of the foundry in 1985 marked the end of an era in general engineering, but the firm still bears his name—though owned by Howard Smith [q.v.6] Ltd—and is Australia's largest maker of rail-cars.

L. E. Fredman (ed), *A Cousin Jack in Australia* (Newcastle, NSW, 1992); *Newcastle Morning Herald*, 18 May, 26 June 1948; *SMH*, 26 Aug 1953; personal information.   L. E. FREDMAN

GOOCH, GEORGE GORDON (1893-1967), pastoralist, company director and philanthropist, was born on 1 June 1893 at Yankee Town station, near Carnarvon, Western Australia, son of George Joseph Gooch, pastoralist, and his wife Fanny Grace, née Snook. Partially crippled by poliomyelitis at the age of 2, Gordon attended Scotch College, Claremont, in 1906-12 and stayed on to teach commercial subjects. From 1914 he gained experience in sheep-breeding as a jackeroo at Koonoona and at Winnininnie, South Australia. Back in the West, he worked briefly on his father's stud, Bacton, near Mingenew, before returning to manage Wandagee, the family's sheep-station in the Gascoyne. He inherited Wandagee in 1923, owned Cobra in 1926-28 and acquired Wahroonga in 1948. At Wandagee, Gooch had introduced Koonoona rams to produce big, robust merinos carrying long, strong wool which topped the district's prices in 1917 and 1918. At St Mary's Anglican Church, West Perth, on 7 February 1923 he married Doris Hilda Irene ('Girlie') Campbell.

An able and enterprising pastoralist, Gooch was also an astute businessman. He was a member of the Australian Woolgrowers' Council and the Graziers' Federal Council of Australia, and vice-president of the Pastoralists' Association of Western Australia. In addition, he was a director of Elder, Smith [qq.v.4,6] & Co. Ltd, West Australian Newspapers Ltd, Caris Holdings Ltd, Caris Bros Pty Ltd, Leroya Industries Pty Ltd, the West Australia Trustee, Executor & Agency Co. Ltd and the Pastoral Labour Bureau. While president (1957) of the Royal Agricultural Society of Western Australia, he oversaw a large building programme which included a new members' stand.

Beyond his commercial commitments, Gooch gave practical and financial support to the disabled and disadvantaged, particularly children. Shy of publicity, he quietly donated large sums to the Crippled Children's Society, Lady Lawley Cottage and other charities. He was a long-term patron of the Paraplegic Association and served on the executive-committee for the first Commonwealth paraplegic games, held in Perth in 1962. Scotch College benefited substantially from Gooch's generosity. President (1928-30, 1945-48) of the Old Scotch Collegians and a member (from 1944) of the college council, he chaired the committee for the memorial hall appeal. In 1954 he and his wife contributed £14 000 for a new sports pavilion; that year he was made a life member of the college council. He was appointed C.M.G. in 1958.

In his later years Gooch walked with crutches. Although unable to play, he retained a passionate interest in watching sport. He was patron of the Gascoyne Racing Club, and closely associated with the Perth Polo Club and the Nor' West and Murchison Cricket Association. A genial man of medium build, with an open face and twinkling eyes, he was friendly and hospitable, and never indulged in alcohol. He belonged to the Weld, West Australian and Carnarvon clubs. Survived by his wife, son and three daughters, he died on 1 May 1967 at Shenton Park and was cremated; his estate was sworn for probate at $252 254.

F. W. Gunning, *Lure of the North* (Perth, 1952); *Elders/GM Weekly* (Perth), 4 May 1967; Paraplegic Assn (Perth), *Fortitude*, May 1967; Scotch College (Claremont, Perth), *Scotch College Reporter*, 1967; *West Australian*, 12 June 1958, 17 Oct 1963, 2 May 1967, 4 Jan 1968; *Countryman* (Perth), 17 Sept 1959, 4 May 1967.   WENDY BIRMAN

GOODCHILD, JOHN CHARLES (1898-1980), artist, was born on 30 March 1898 at Southwark, London, fourth of nine children of John Goodchild, journeyman lead-glazier, and his wife Jessie Mary, née White. Young John was educated at the Strand School and found it humiliating to be a scholarship-boy. In 1913 the family emigrated to South Australia where he took several jobs, including sign-writing. Enlisting in the Australian Imperial Force in 1917, he served on the Western Front with the 9th Field Ambulance. While in hospital near Le Havre, France, in 1918, he sent his sketches to the *Digger* and was later commissioned to contribute pen-drawings for *Where Australians Rest* (Melbourne, 1920).

After World War I, Goodchild attended the South Australian School of Arts and Crafts, and produced *Adelaide in Pen and Ink Drawings* (1920). He studied at the Central School of Arts and Crafts, London, in 1921 before returning to Adelaide. To 'keep the pot boiling' he became a commercial artist and taught etching at the School of Arts and Crafts. In 1923 he held a one-man exhibition of his etchings in Adelaide and showed his work in

Sydney with the Australian Painter-Etchers' (and Graphic Art) Society, of which he was vice-president. At St Augustine's Anglican Church, Unley, Adelaide, on 22 April 1926 he married Doreen Rowley. They sailed for London where they attended the Central School —Doreen studying clay-modelling, John engraving and lithography. Early in 1929 they established a studio in Adelaide and John began exhibiting his water-colours with the (Royal) South Australian Society of Arts; he was to be its president (1937-40).

A small, compact figure, with a brisk and bustling gait, Goodchild had 'an eye like a hawk and a fist as steady as a rock'. He readily made the transition from drawing and etching to water-colours. His traditional landscapes, street scenes and architectural views revealed his understanding of tone and form, mastery of line and highly developed sense of colour. Among the best is 'Gateway, Quirinal Palace' (1928), held by the Art Gallery of South Australia. He also produced furniture, panels in bas-relief, the lamps and pylons for the Adelaide City Bridge (opened 1931), and he painted, in oils, a series depicting the Australian offices of Elder, Smith [qq.v.4,6] & Co. Ltd. Shrewd and irascible, he believed that accurate draughtsmanship was the basis of all great art. His work shows extraordinary competence. It is held by major Australian galleries, the Library of Congress, Washington, and the British Museum, London.

Goodchild was a board-member (1938-53 and 1960-69) of the Public Library, Museum and Art Gallery (from 1940 National Gallery of South Australia) and principal (1941-45) of the School of Arts and Crafts. In March 1945 the Australian War Memorial, Canberra, commissioned him as an official war artist. Attached to the Royal Australian Air Force, he painted several water-colours which are compositionally dramatic, particularly 'Oxfords at 3000 feet over Strathbogie Ranges, Victoria'. On 2 September he was present at, and took a cinefilm of, the signing of the Japanese surrender aboard the American battleship, *Missouri*, in Tokyo Bay. In 1946 he was cartoonist for the Adelaide *News*. He travelled restlessly and frequently. Survived by his wife, daughter and two sons, he died on 9 February 1980 at his Highbury home and was cremated.

A. Carroll, *John C. Goodchild 1898-1980*, exhibition cat (Adel, 1981); J. Brooks and D. Goodchild, *John C. Goodchild 1898-1980, His Life and Art* (Adel, 1983); *Sunday Mail* (Adel), 17 Feb 1980; *Advertiser* (Adel), 22 Feb 1980; J. C. Goodchild file 206/002/032 *and* Goodchild family scrapbook (AWM); John Charles Goodchild, oral hist tape 150, 24 Nov 1965 (NL); information from Ms J. Hylton, Norwood, and Mr J. Dowie, Dulwich, Adel.

JOYCE GIBBERD

GOODWIN, JOHN THOMAS HILL (1865-1950), surveyor and community leader, was born on 28 October 1865 at Yelta, near Mildura, Victoria, son of Rev. Thomas Hill Goodwin, an Anglican clergyman from England, and his Irish-born wife Letitia Going, née Pennefather. Educated at Melbourne Church of England Grammar School, John served as a pupil-surveyor and draughtsman with the Victorian Department of Lands and Surveys. From 1891 he practised privately in Victoria, save for stints with the Western Australian and Victorian governments in 1896-99 and 1907-10 respectively. He also qualified as a civil engineer.

On 5 April 1893 at Christ Church, Ballarat, Goodwin had married Harriet Mary Turton (d.1933). Commissioned (1891) in the Victorian Military Forces, in 1910 he was appointed lieutenant, Corps of Australian Engineers, Militia. Although he volunteered for active service in World War I, he was retained in Australia and retired from the Militia in 1920 as honorary lieutenant colonel.

Having entered the Federal Department of Home Affairs in 1910, Goodwin handled property transactions on behalf of the Commonwealth in regard to defence, quarantine, and posts and telegraphs. Five years later he was promoted chief surveyor and estates officer (subsequently surveyor-general and director of lands). In addition, he was officer-in-charge of the administration of the Federal Capital Territory (1916-24) and a member (1921-25) of the Federal Capital Advisory Committee which made recommendations for the building of Canberra. After the Federal Capital Commission was formed to control the city's development, in January 1925 he was seconded to it as lands officer, but returned to the public service that year. Rather than leave Canberra, he retired on 31 December. He held a grazing lease for a few years and presided over the Federal Territory Lessees' Association before resuming private surveying.

Appointed M.B.E. in 1927, in his semi-retirement Goodwin retained a deep attachment to his adopted city, becoming involved in community service and local politics. He helped to form (1929) the Horticultural Society of Canberra and was acting-president (1938-39) of the local division of the Australian Red Cross Society. Keenly interested in swimming, tennis, cricket and rifle-shooting, he assisted in the organization of these activities and was also a Boy Scouts' commissioner. As a foundation member of the Canberra Relief Society, he did much to alleviate suffering during the Depression.

Goodwin was an elected member of the F.C.T. (Australian Capital Territory) Advisory Council in 1931-43 (chairman 1936-41) and of the Canberra Community Hospital board in 1938-48. He served on the National Capital Planning and Development Committee in 1939-41. From 1930 he had been a special magistrate, Court of Petty Sessions, and for many years carried out the duties of coroner. Selfless and genial, 'Goodie' was a 'father figure to the city'. He died on 18 September 1950 in Canberra and was buried in the graveyard of the Anglican Church of St John the Baptist, Reid. His name is commemorated by Goodwin Retirement Villages Inc. which provides accommodation for Canberra's aged. Two of his three sons survived him; the eldest, Brigadier S. T. W. Goodwin, had been killed in action in New Guinea in 1943.

F. M. Johnston, *Knights and Theodolites* (Syd, 1962); L. Wigmore, *The Long View* (Melb, 1963); J. Gibbney, *Canberra 1913-1953* (Canb, 1988); Lands and Surveys Branch, Dept of Home Affairs, *Annual Report*, 1912-13, p 20; *Canb and District Hist Soc J*, Dec 1970, p 9; *Queanbeyan Age*, 8 Dec 1925; *Canb Times*, 13 May 1927, 18, 31 Jan 1929, 26 Nov 1930, 12 Oct 1933, 19, 20 Sept 1950, 12 Mar 1963.   JACK TAYLOR

GOOSSENS, SIR EUGENE AYNSLEY (1893-1962), conductor and composer, was born on 26 May 1893 at Kentish Town, London, eldest of five children of Eugene Goossens (d.1906), a violinist and opera conductor of Belgian birth, and his wife Annie Elizabeth Mary Agnes, a singer and daughter of the operatic basso Thomas Aynsley Cook. His paternal grandfather, another Eugene, had also been a violinist and conductor. Young Eugene was given music lessons at home before being sent in 1901 as a boarder to St Francis Xavier School at Bruges, Belgium; from 1903 he attended the Muziek-Conservatorium twice a week and was trained in violin and *solfège*. Having rejoined his family in 1906 at Liscard, Cheshire, he continued his studies at the Christian Brothers' Institute and at the Liverpool College of Music. He developed a particular passion for steam locomotives and ocean liners which he was to retain throughout his life.

In 1907 Goossens' violin playing gained him the Liverpool scholarship to the Royal College of Music in London. His professors were S. A. Rivarde (violin), J. St O. Dykes (piano), (Sir) Henry Wood (theory) and Sir Charles Stanford (composition). Although he was a nervous performer, Goossens quickly established a reputation for his stylish student compositions. He was awarded the Musicians' Company's silver medal in 1911 and in the following year was made an associate of the R.C.M. After graduation he worked as a vi-

olinist in theatre bands, in the Queen's Hall Orchestra and in various string quartets. He was rejected for military service in World War I on medical grounds; his brother Adolphè (a gifted horn player) perished on the Somme.

At the short-notice request of (Sir) Thomas Beecham, in 1916 Goossens conducted *The Critic*, an opera by Stanford. Goossens' success at his formal début encouraged Beecham to use him as his unofficial deputy, an arrangement which continued for almost a decade and which led to more prominent engagements directing Diaghilev's Les Ballets Russes and the Carl Rosa Opera Company at Covent Garden. At the register office, London, on 18 November 1919 he married Dorothy Millar, née Dodsworth, a divorcee. They had three daughters before the marriage ended in divorce in 1928. In June 1921 Goossens had assembled a virtuoso orchestra under his own name to give concerts of contemporary music in London. These included a critically acclaimed first concert performance in England of Stravinsky's *Le Sacre du Printemps*, with the approving composer in attendance. The *Evening News* referred to the young conductor as 'London's Music Wizard'.

Invited by George Eastman, the 'Kodak King', in 1923 Goossens became conductor of the Rochester Philharmonic Orchestra in New York State, a post which also involved teaching at the Eastman School of Music. The position was seasonal, allowing him to conduct the great orchestras of Philadelphia, Boston, New York and San Francisco, and he returned to Europe each summer for additional appearances, including the premières of his major compositions. On 5 January 1930 at North Congregational Church, Detroit, Michigan, he married Janet Lewis, fourteen years his junior. They were to have two daughters before being divorced in 1944.

In 1931 Goossens succeeded Fritz Reiner as permanent conductor of the Cincinnati Symphony Orchestra, a post he retained for the next fifteen years. Appointed to the Légion d'honneur in 1934, he was by then a recognized figure in international music. As a composer he was placed alongside his British contemporaries (Sir) William Walton, (Sir) Arthur Bliss and Ralph Vaughan Williams. Goossens was happy to exploit his authority as a conductor to champion new music in his programmes. A tall, handsome and immaculately dressed figure with thinning, swept-back hair, he conducted in the grand charismatic manner with a long baton and large beat. His management of orchestras was firm, but always based on an immense practical knowledge of instrumental technique and on his prodigiously detailed memory of a vast, wide-ranging repertoire.

On 18 April 1946 at Paris, Kentucky,

Goossens secretly married an American divorcee Marjorie Foulkrod, née Fetter (b.1912). After a well-received tour of Australia later that year, during which he conducted the State orchestras, Goossens was invited by (Sir) Charles Moses, the general manager of the Australian Broadcasting Commission, to become the first permanent conductor of the Sydney Symphony Orchestra. In addition, he was offered the directorship of the New South Wales State Conservatorium of Music. When he accepted the concurrent posts, the two salaries gave him a combined income greater than that of the prime minister.

Goossens returned to Australia in July 1947 and set about his new tasks with characteristic energy and decisiveness. Having vowed, on arrival, to make the S.S.O. 'one of the six best orchestras in the world', he soon jettisoned its weaker members and engaged or promoted younger players. The orchestra responded to his deep musicianship and skill as a trainer; the public (and critical) response was enthusiastic to the point where subscriptions soon doubled, and the A.B.C. was able to attract soloists and conductors of the first rank to perform with its orchestras. Goossens introduced Australian audiences to more than fifty major works which had previously been ignored or considered too challenging. He also championed local composition, giving many first performances, among them the world première (1946) of John Antill's *Corroboree.*

At the conservatorium, Goossens insisted on an immediate lift in standards, failed whole classes, dismissed staff, and traded on his reputation in Europe to recruit new teachers. He disbanded the mediocre conservatorium choir, conducted the senior orchestra himself and staged a series of ambitious opera performances, including his own *Judith* for which he selected a little-known Sydney stenographer, (Dame) Joan Sutherland, to make her operatic début in the title role. Whenever possible, he taught the diploma classes in harmony, counterpoint and composition; his students included Richard Bonynge, Maureen Jones, Brenton Langbein, Geoffrey Parsons and Malcolm Williamson. Despite his rigorous, uncompromising style of teaching, Goossens was an encourager, unfailingly generous with letters of introduction for talented young musicians who wished to further their studies abroad.

By the early 1950s Goossens had established himself as a major local celebrity: he was featured conducting Tchaikovsky in the newsreels; his free outdoor concerts attracted crowds of 25 000; and his tireless agitation for a performing arts centre in Sydney helped to push the State government into planning the Sydney Opera House on Bennel-

ong Point, the spectacular site that Goossens had first suggested. He directed a series of historic sessions for EMI (Australia) Pty Ltd which produced the first commercial recordings of the S.S.O. Notwithstanding a punishing schedule, he took on the presidency of the State council of the Federated Music Clubs of Australia, published the first volume of his projected autobiography, *Overture and Beginners* (London, 1951), and continued to compose and to pursue his hobbies of photography and painting. In 1955 he was knighted.

At a more private level, a lifelong interest in pantheism and the occult led Goossens into friendship (from 1952) with the notorious Sydney 'witch' and artist Rosaleen Norton [q.v.] and her lover, the poet Gavin Greenlees. He frequently visited their flat at Kings Cross. This rather indiscreet association came to the notice of the police in October 1955 and an undercover vice-squad investigation secured a bundle of letters from Goossens to Norton which the police considered sufficiently incriminating to support a charge of 'Scandalous Conduct'. When Goossens returned to Sydney on 9 March 1956 from an extended European tour, his baggage was searched at the airport by customs officers and found to contain more than one thousand indecent photographs, as well as books, masks, incense and a quantity of strip film. He was taken to police headquarters where he made a signed statement.

At the prosecution in Sydney on 22 March he was too ill to appear. His counsel J. W. Shand [q.v.] pleaded guilty, on his behalf, to having imported prohibited goods. Moses gave evidence as to his good character, but Goossens received the maximum fine, £100. He immediately resigned both his posts and returned to England two months later. The *Sydney Morning Herald* in its editorial commented: 'The end of his career has been pitiful beyond measure'.

Goossens was briefly reunited with his wife on his return to Europe in May, but they were soon living apart. In failing health, he took a variety of rented accommodation in London, including a room at the Colonnade Hotel. At his invitation, he was joined by a young pianist from Adelaide, Linda Main, who was his support and companion for the remainder of his life. News of the scandal surrounding his departure from Australia had reached Europe and he struggled to find regular work as a concert conductor. When Bonynge visited Goossens he found him 'absolutely destroyed. It was tragic'. Nevertheless, the British Broadcasting Corporation and several gramophone companies remembered his particular skill with complex, unfamiliar scores and engaged him to direct a series of significant studio recordings.

Taken ill in Switzerland while visiting two

of his daughters, Goossens died of rheumatic heart disease and a haemorrhaging gastric ulcer on 13 June 1962 in Hillingdon Hospital, Middlesex, on the night of his return to London; he was buried with Catholic rites in St Pancras and Islington cemetery, North London. A substantial, but somewhat cool, obituary in *The Times* described his conducting as 'urbane, civilised and immensely professional'. His five daughters survived him. Goossens left his residual estate 'including all & every copyrights and royalties lawfully arising from my works to my faithful companion and assistant Miss Linda Main'.

Although he was a highly skilled and prolific composer, Goossens' music has been criticized as 'lacking in sap' and exhibiting 'singular unmemorability'. His works were much performed between the wars but his output has fallen into neglect and its often severe technical demands tend to resist revival. Perhaps because he spent so much time conducting the music of more talented contemporaries, his own compositions display impressive eclecticism without finding a distinctive personal voice. The restless quality in his larger works tends to undermine the impact of their striking thematic and formal design. Goossens' early mastery of orchestral colour—the scherzo *Tam o'Shanter* (1916) and *Sinfonietta* (1922)—derived from Richard Strauss and Claude Debussy, while his chamber pieces echo the French musical impressionists of the late nineteenth century. His most important and distinctive works are the *Symphony No. 1* (1940) and *Symphony No. 2* (1942-44), two operas, *Judith* (1929) and *Don Juan de Manara* (1935), both to librettos by Arnold Bennett, and the *Concerto for Oboe* (1927), composed for his brother Léon. In 1991 the A.B.C. named a new studio in Sydney after Goossens in belated recognition of his contribution to music in Australia.

R. Norton and G. Greenlees, *The Art of Rosaleen Norton* (Syd, 1952); D. Ewan (ed), *Musicians since 1900* (NY, 1978); S. Sadie (ed), *The New Grove Dictionary of Music and Musicians* (Lond, 1980); P. Sametz, *Play On!* (Syd, 1992); C. Rosen, *The Goossens* (Lond, 1993); *Current Biog* (NY), 1945; *People* (Syd), 20 June 1951, p 11; *SMH*, 27 May, 14, 19 Aug, 19 Nov 1946, 6 May 1947, 17 Apr 1949, 20 Nov 1954, 15, 23 Mar, 12 Apr 1956, 14 June 1962, 26 Oct 1973; *The Times*, 14 June 1962; Archives of NSW State Conservatorium of Music, Syd, Muziek-Conservatorium of Bruges, Belgium, Roy College of Music, Lond, Eastman School of Music, Rochester, NY, ABC Document Archive, Syd, Attorney-General's Dept of NSW *and* John Fairfax Group Pty Ltd, Syd; transcripts of interviews (1992) with Dame Sidonie Goossens, Det Sgt H. Trevennar, Mr Richard Bonynge and Dame Joan Sutherland (held by author, Hunters Hill, Syd); information from Miss Renée Goossens, France.

DAVID SALTER

GOPINKO, JASCHA (1891-1980), violin teacher and orchestra conductor, was born on 15 December 1891 near Mogilev, Ukraine, Russia, son of Jewish parents Hirsch Gopinko, cloth manufacturer, and his wife Esther, née Maltke. Probably tutored at home, at 16 Jascha won a violin competition in Moscow. He was a student of Pawel Kochanski's virtuoso classes at the Conservatory, Warsaw. To avoid being drafted into the Russian army, he went to sea and reached Melbourne in the *Orvieto* in August 1914. Although he was fluent in Russian, German and French, Gopinko spoke no English. In Sydney a Russian stranger befriended him and housed him with his family. Gopinko washed bottles in a factory before moving to Kurri Kurri. He was 'a terrible miner' and often poor, but his violin playing prompted fellow workers to ask him to teach their children.

Gopinko's enthusiasm for chamber music led him to found and conduct the Kurri Kurri mandolin orchestra, composed of miners. He began to instruct students in other instruments. Having founded the Cessnock Symphony Orchestra, he toured the region as its conductor. A varied classical repertoire gave players the opportunity to perform with visiting professional soloists like Joseph Post [q.v.] or to play solo themselves. At the Eastern Suburbs Central Synagogue, Sydney, on 16 June 1929 Gopinko married 23-year-old Rebecca Snidermann; he taught her to play the cello and she became his devoted helper. He was naturalized in 1930. In time his students began to win prizes locally and at the City of Sydney Eisteddfod; many were to occupy leading positions in orchestras and ensembles at home and abroad. Ernest Llewellyn (later director of the Canberra School of Music) was his most notable early success; other students included Leslie Chester, Ronald Ryder, Donald Blair and Nelson Cooke.

In 1936 the Gopinkos moved to Sydney where Jascha rented a studio at W. H. Paling [q.v.5] & Co.'s buildings in Ash Street and taught unusually long hours. Twice a week he taught at Maitland. For many years Rebecca nursed him for an undiagnosed chronic ailment with the diet she daily brought by public transport. Consciously Jewish and liberal in outlook, the Gopinkos seldom attended the synagogue and lived in relative isolation, but the weekly ensemble rehearsals in their Double Bay home attracted uninvited footpath audiences. Gopinko gave advice freely to teachers who sought it, but had no time for the networks, the gossip and the envy which, he believed, characterized the musical profession. A dark-haired, attractive man of middle height, with a high forehead, fine hands and the eyes of a dreamer, he had a sense of humour and enjoyed being a tease. He built his tuition around a student's temperament and physique. Regardless of timetables, a lesson only finished when a specific goal was reached. His wife cooked meals for pupils (who frequently boarded free of charge) because 'You don't play well unless you feel good'.

Possessing perfect pitch, Gopinko avoided excessive vibrato and sentimentality, played with controlled passion and warmth, and sought to match style to a composer's 'intentions'. His student orchestra's 'clean attack and dignity of style' won praise. Its players learned to sight-read one another's scores, and took turns in performing solos at concerts which he arranged, sometimes for causes such as the Food for Britain Appeal (1948). Despite increasing deafness, Gopinko retained a few students in his eighties. Llewellyn placed him beside Leopold Auer, one of the greatest string teachers in the world. Survived by his wife, Gopinko died on 4 July 1980 at Rose Bay and was buried in Rookwood cemetery.

Aust Musical News, Sept 1935, Feb 1937, Oct 1939, Oct 1945, Feb, Nov, Dec 1947, Jan 1948; J. Gopinko naturalization file, A1/1, item 1930/2121 (AA, Canb); information from Mrs R. Gopinko, Double Bay, Syd, who also holds a tape of an ABC radio interview with J. Gopinko, 1972, and a collection of photographs, papers and news-cuttings.
                                    HELGA M. GRIFFIN

GORDON, COLIN ERNEST SUTHERLAND (1907-1960), headmaster, was born on 24 December 1907 at Berbice, British Guiana, son of John Richard Colin Gordon, sugar-planter, and his wife Hilda, née Sloman. Colin was educated at Charterhouse, England, where he was made head of his house, captain of athletics and cricket, and a prefect; he was particularly influenced by the headmaster (Sir) Frank Fletcher and by a young teacher (Sir) James Darling. In 1926 Gordon entered Christ Church, Oxford (B.A., M.A., 1938). He was elected president (1930) of the university's athletics club, and represented Britain in the high jump at the 1928 Olympic Games in Amsterdam, and British Guiana at the 1930 British Empire Games at Hamilton, Canada. From 1930 to 1931 he taught at Trinity College School, Port Hope, Ontario.

In 1931 Darling brought Gordon to Victoria to teach Latin and English at Geelong Church of England Grammar School. Appointed a housemaster (1935), Gordon became one of his key allies in transforming the school, and a close friend. He was a popular and versatile master, and wrote a Latin textbook. At St John's Church, Toorak, on 4 January 1940 he married Patricia Hayward Newbigin. In that year he taught classics at The King's School, Parramatta, Sydney. Ap-

pointed lieutenant in the Citizen Military Forces in December, he was found to have chronic malaria and was transferred to the Unattached List in May 1941. On 20 January 1942 he was commissioned in the Administrative and Special Duties Branch of the Royal Australian Air Force. He rose to acting wing commander. As chief rehabilitation officer at Air Force Headquarters, Melbourne, he showed 'outstanding foresight' in formulating demobilization policy. His appointment terminated on 19 November 1945.

In that year he was selected to be headmaster of the Collegiate School of St Peter, Adelaide, the first layman to hold the position. When he took office in 1946 the school, of about seven hundred pupils, was somewhat run down and in need of vigorous leadership. Six ft 3 ins (191 cm) tall, austerely handsome and with an air of lithe energy, Gordon brought organizational talent, zest, penetrating insight and a forceful personality to the task. Improvements were made to the fabric of the school, but he gave first priority to the quality of the teachers. He progressively recruited a strong staff, whose professional development he fostered, and he made an innovative appointment of a full-time psychologist responsible for educational guidance. Assessment and reporting throughout the school were systematized. In addition to demanding excellence in both academic work and sport, Gordon tried to ensure that each boy, especially those not in the A forms or first teams, achieved his best.

Although demand for places grew intense, he withstood pressure to enlarge the school. Particularly at the outset, he had a tense relationship with the governors, who resisted change and expected deference to be shown towards members of Adelaide's establishment. A member (from 1948) of the Adelaide Club, Gordon had no time for the snobbery of a small provincial elite. He was sometimes brusque with parents and lectured them on speech days about upholding the moral standards which the school was endeavouring to instil. Bishop Robin [q.v.] supported him and became a spiritual mentor. Assisted by an outstanding chaplain T. B. Macdonald, Gordon strengthened the religious life of the school. His integrity, and occasional brutal honesty, won loyalty from staff and senior boys. His style was autocratic, but informal and consultative. Ideas from the staff were welcomed—at first invariably challenged, and, if persuasive, adopted with enthusiasm.

By 1951 Gordon had established a confident, competitive, Spartan tone that stressed effort and service—sensitivity or imagination were little valued. Next year in Britain he visited leading public schools, and broadened and mellowed his outlook. He returned determined to give the arts and social issues a greater place in the school's life, and convinced that the narrowing pressures of public examinations—especially the dominance of mathematics and science—must be overcome. He introduced a two-year Leaving Honours course which widened the range of subjects and devoted time to non-examination studies, including current affairs.

A member (from 1950) of the council of the University of Adelaide, Gordon helped to promote a chair of education. As chairman (1957-59) of the Headmasters' Conference of Australia, he countered political criticism of independent schools, and was a national advocate of their essential attributes and their right to exist in a democracy. In 1959 he was a founder of the Australian College of Education. By this time he was dying of cancer, but continued working. His speech day report in December was a veiled farewell. He welcomed pupils and parents to 'the last formal rites of the school year', expressing 're-lief that a long and arduous course has been run'. He asked those leaving to 'treasure memories of close companionship, of understanding, trust and loyalty'.

Survived by his wife and two daughters, Gordon died at St Peter's College on 22 August 1960 and was cremated. In many ways he had exemplified the classic headmaster of an English public school, but, unlike his predecessors, he was a colonial with a tinge of egalitarianism who wholeheartedly adopted Australia as his home. While he could be relaxed and humorous with close colleagues, most boys admired him from a distance as a stern and awesome figure. A Stoic who concealed his emotions and did kindnesses by stealth, he was dedicated to his vocation and upright in character. He bequeathed to St Peter's a sense of standards and purpose which sustained it under less distinguished leadership. A portrait by Ivor Hele is held by the college.

J. W. Hogg, *Our Proper Concerns* (Syd, 1986); W. Bate, *Light Blue Down Under* (Melb, 1990); *St Peter's College Mag*, 1945-60, especially Dec 1960; *Current Affairs Bulletin*, 2 Dec 1957, p 14; *Advertiser* (Adel), 26 June 1945, 23 Aug 1960; K. Peake-Jones, A Memoir of C. E. S. Gordon (ts, 1980, held in St Peter's College Archives); information from former colleagues and pupils, among them Sir James Darling, Armadale, Mr G. L. Cramer, Surrey Hills, Melb, and Mr F. H. Schubert, Erindale, Adel.   IAN D. BRICE

GORDON, LEE LAZER (1923-1963), entrepreneur and rock'n'roll promoter, was born on 8 March 1923 in Detroit, Michigan, United States of America, son of Louis Gordon, retailer, and his wife Jennie, née La Pate. Educated locally at Highland Park High School, and at the University of Miami (Bach-elor of Business Administration, 1944), Lee developed a chain of sixty electrical stores across the country. He twice married—and was twice divorced from—the same woman.

Moving to Sydney about 1953, Gordon began merchandising for Royal Art Furnishing Pty Ltd, attracting customers with American sales techniques such as mystery tunes and telephone quizzes. He soon realized that there was an Australian market for live performances by international entertainers and set out to arrange tours by American pop idols: Frank Sinatra played to full houses at the Sydney Stadium in January 1955, Frankie Laine arrived next month and Johnnie Ray received a tumultuous welcome in March. Ray's animated behaviour on stage and the adulation he received were to be characteristic of subsequent visits by rock'n'roll stars.

In January 1957 Gordon organized a tour by 'Bill Haley and the Comets', whose recording of *Rock Around the Clock* was already a best-seller. On the same bill Gordon included 'The Platters', 'Big Joe Turner', LaVern Baker and 'Freddie Bell and the Bellboys'. The show opened at Newcastle, then played to capacity houses in Sydney, Brisbane, Adelaide and Melbourne. Over three weeks 300 000 patrons saw the performances, and Gordon offered Haley $US 100 000 to stay for an additional week.

Gordon's productions came to be known as 'Big Shows'. In October 1957 'Johnny O'Keefe [q.v.] and the Dee Jays' were the first Australians to be included, opening a show which featured the Americans 'Little Richard', Gene Vincent and Eddie Cochran. Gordon gradually increased the number of local acts. In 1958 Lee Gordon Records Pty Ltd began recording pop songs (later under the Leedon label). A close friend of Gordon, O'Keefe was one of the company's artists and was also responsible for signing other Australians, among them 'Lonnie Lee', Barry Stanton, Laurel Lea and 'The Crescents'. Artists used the studio facilities of Festival Records Pty Ltd, to which Gordon subsequently sold Leedon.

At Kings Cross, Sydney, Gordon converted a cinema into a discotheque called The Birdcage. He was credited with introducing the striptease club and drive-in restaurant to the city, as well as 'the first Australian Jazz Festival'. Due to his initiative, a club was established for teenage fans of the rock'n'rollers 'Col Joye and the Joy Boys'. Gordon brimmed with ideas that never materialized, including bringing Elvis Presley to Australia, making a film starring Sammy Davis junior, building an Aboriginal village as a tourist attraction, staging a bullfight and opening a casino.

In the course of his career he made and lost

several fortunes. It seemed that he enjoyed taking risks and one associate claimed that he did his best work when 'broke'. Gordon estimated that he made £3 million by bringing American entertainers to Australia, and lost it all in unsuccessful investments. Some reporters saw him as overly generous and gullible; others alluded to his shadowy connexions. A small, dark man, he radiated self-confidence. In later years, however, his friends believed that he deteriorated physically, allegedly due to alcohol, drugs and financial pressures. He is also said to have suffered from mental breakdowns.

On 23 January 1962 at Acapulco, Mexico, Gordon married Arlene Topfer, a Queensland-born dancer and model; Frank Sinatra was best man. In May 1963 in Sydney a petition against Gordon was dismissed in the Bankruptcy Court. Next month he was charged with attempting to obtain the drug pethidine without a prescription. He left the country on 20 July. A warrant for his arrest was issued on the 22nd for failing to appear before the Central Court of Petty Sessions, but the offence was considered too minor for the authorities to seek his extradition.

After a brief time in the United States, Gordon travelled with his family to London. There he approached the theatrical promoter Harold Davidson looking for work and saying that he wished to make a fresh start. Gordon died of a coronary occlusion on 7 November 1963 at Kensington and was cremated. His wife and daughter survived him; Arlene gave birth to his son in 1964. By the time of Gordon's death, his only apparent assets in Australia were a small interest in the Sound Lounge in William Street, Sydney, and part-ownership of a Kings Cross all-male revue.

J. Oram, *The Business of Pop* (Syd, 1966); B. Rogers (with D. O'Brien), *Rock'n Roll* (Syd, 1975); J. Bryden-Brown, *JO'K* (Syd, 1982); M. Sturma, *Australian Rock'N'Roll* (Syd, 1991); *Music Maker*, Dec 1963, p 4; *Observer* (Syd), 30 May 1959; *Nation*, 5 Nov 1960; *Daily Mirror*, 11, 12 Nov 1963; *SMH*, 12, 14 Nov 1963; information from Ms J. L. Gordon, Double Bay, Syd.   MICHAEL STURMA

GORMAN, SIR EUGENE (1891-1973), barrister, was born on 10 April 1891 at Goornong, Victoria, eldest of three children of Patrick Gorman, a native-born storeman, and his wife Mary, née Mulcair, from Ireland. Educated at St Joseph's College, Hunters Hill, Sydney, he was articled to two Bendigo solicitors. In Melbourne on 5 May 1914 he was admitted to practise as a barrister and solicitor.

Enlisting in the Australian Imperial Force on 4 September 1915, Gorman was commissioned in June 1916 and served on the Western Front (from December) with the 22nd Battalion. At Bullecourt, France, on 3 May 1917, he led his company in an attack and, although seriously wounded, remained at his post. For these actions he was awarded the Military Cross. He was promoted temporary captain in January 1919 and his A.I.F. appointment terminated in Australia on 20 October. His book, *With the Twenty-Second* (1919), contained an introduction written by General Sir William (Baron) Birdwood [q.v.7].

On 6 September 1920 at St Patrick's Catholic Cathedral, Melbourne, Gorman married Parisian-born Marthe Vallée (d.1966), whom he had met during the war. When their son Pierre was born deaf in 1924, they devoted themselves to having him taught lip-reading in Melbourne and Paris. Pierre was to complete a doctorate at the University of Cambridge and to become an international authority on the problems of disability.

Having returned to the Bar after World War I, Gorman built up a large commercial and criminal practice, winning recognition as one of the best criminal barristers of his time. A contemporary observed: 'Gorman's quips and loudly whispered asides were sometimes as effective as his rapid and . . . musical voice, which could be threatening, terrifying, demanding, soothing, persuasive, cajoling or pleading, as the occasion required. His vocabulary was good and he enhanced it whenever he could by apt classical quotations'. He took silk in 1929.

Two years later Gorman unsuccessfully stood for the Legislative Council as an Independent for Melbourne Province. A defender of civil liberties and an opponent of censorship, he was an early supporter of the Book Censorship Abolition League, founded in 1934. He was a foundation member (1935) and vice-president of the committee of the Australian Council for Civil Liberties, initiated by Brian Fitzpatrick [q.v.] and others. An influential adviser (from 1935) to the Country Party premier (Sir) Albert Dunstan [q.v.8], in 1936 Gorman acted as emissary for Dunstan and persuaded Sir Thomas Blamey [q.v.13] to resign from his post as chief commissioner of police rather than face dismissal. Largely due to Gorman's prompting, in 1944 Dunstan appointed Sir Edmund Herring chief justice of the Supreme Court of Victoria.

In 1940 Gorman offered his services as an honorary commissioner, Australian Comforts Fund, and in April sailed for the Middle East. He retired from active practice at the Bar, his reputation as Victoria's greatest trial lawyer still unchallenged, but retained rooms at Equity Chambers, Bourke Street. In December he arranged for Christmas fare to be sent forward to troops massing for the assault on Bardia, Libya, and in July 1941 he took over the Hotel Metropole in Beirut and converted it into a soldiers' club. Back in Australia in 1942, Gorman was appointed Australian consul-general for the Netherlands East Indies. Before he could take up the post, the Japanese had occupied the islands. He was then mobilized as temporary brigadier and appointed chief inspector of army administration. In 1944-45 he commanded the A.I.F. Reception Group, United Kingdom, which repatriated Australian soldiers who had been prisoners of war in Europe. Home again, he transferred to the Reserve of Officers in November 1945. Like A. A. Conlon [q.v.13], he built up a personal network of powerful friends in business, politics, the law, charities and the armed services, and was close to Blamey.

Reflecting on Gorman's wide interests, a parish priest said: 'The law could not contain him. He was too dynamic, too restless, too versatile to be tied down to any one category. He had consuming drive and energy, charm of manner, a keen sense of humour and was brim full of "joie de vivre"'. Honorary consul (1949-55) for Greece in Victoria, he was awarded the gold cross of the Greek Red Cross and was appointed a knight commander of the Royal Order of the Phoenix (1953). Gorman was also a successful punter and owner who raced his horses under the name 'G. Ornong'; he was a committee-member (1937-49, 1951-64) of the Victoria Racing Club and sat on its disciplinary tribunals. He was, as well, president (1948-72) of the Opportunity Youth Clubs and in 1968 of the Australian branch of International Social Service. As chairman (1956-68) of the Commonwealth Dried Fruits Export Board, he played an important role in negotiating co-operative marketing arrangements with the United States of America, Iran, Greece and Turkey. He became a director of 'Truth' and 'Sportsman' Ltd, and for many years wrote an anonymous column, 'Topical Taps', in *Truth*. In addition, he was Australian chairman of London Assurance, deputy-chairman of Unity Life Assurance Ltd and a director of Yellow Cabs of Australia Ltd. He invested in Preston Motors (Holdings) Ltd and in real estate, and owned a 2000-acre (809 ha) sheep farm at Rochester. His interest in primary industry had led him in 1929 to form the Primary Producers' Restoration League.

'Pat' Gorman enjoyed his status as an elder statesman in the legal profession. On several occasions he came out of retirement: at the royal commission on bribery charges in State parliament (1952), at the Petrov inquiry (1954) and to defend the racehorse trainer Harry Bird in 1969. Generous with advice to young lawyers, politicians and business people, according to his secretary he ran 'the biggest free advisory legal service in Melbourne'. In 1961-62 he took the part of a judge in a television series, 'Consider Your Verdict'. He played bridge, travelled frequently, and kept up a voluminous correspondence with friends in Australia and abroad. His dictated memoirs remain unpublished. Gorman was a 'cultural Catholic', though not a devout one.

Appointed C.B.E. in 1960, he was elevated to K.B.E. in 1966. He was deeply opposed to capital punishment, and wrote eloquently in the *Herald* that year against the execution of Ronald Ryan [q.v.]. Sir Eugene died on 19 July 1973 in East Melbourne and was cremated; his son survived him.

J. Hetherington, *Blamey* (Melb, 1954) and *Blamey, Controversial Soldier* (Canb, 1973); D. Watson, *Brian Fitzpatrick* (Syd, 1979); J. Epstein, *No Music by Request* (Syd, 1980); S. Sayers, *Ned Herring* (Melb, 1980); J. Sendy, *Melbourne's Radical Bookshops* (Melb, 1983); K. Anderson, *Fossil in the Sandstone* (Melb, 1986); *Herald* (Melb), 25 Apr 1931, 26 Aug 1942, 15 Dec 1949, 8 Sept 1953, 23 July 1954, 7 July 1966, 8 Apr 1972, 19 July 1973; *Sun News-Pictorial*, 20 Mar 1940, 13 Apr 1942, 11 June 1966, 13 Oct 1967, 10 Apr 1972, 20 July 1973; *Age* (Melb), 6 May 1941, 15 Mar 1962, 20 July 1973; information from Mrs P. Coldham, Kooyong, Melb; personal information.   BARRY O. JONES

GOSSE, GEORGE (1912-1964), naval officer and designer, was born on 16 February 1912 at Harvey, Western Australia, elder child of native-born parents William Hay Gosse, farmer, and his wife Muriel, née Davidson. W. C. Gosse [q.v.4] was George's grandfather and (Sir) James Gosse [q.v.] his uncle. An artillery officer in the British Army during World War I, William was awarded the Military Cross; he was killed in action in 1918. His widow died two years later, leaving George and his sister in the care of their paternal grandmother.

Educated at the Collegiate School of St Peter, Adelaide, in 1926 Gosse entered the Royal Australian Naval College, Jervis Bay, Federal Capital Territory. A member of his family described him as 'so like his father, gay, feckless, fearless and gregarious'. He gained colours for hockey and on graduating was awarded the prize for engineering (theory). From January 1930 he successively served in the cruisers, H.M.A.S. *Australia* and H.M.A.S. *Canberra*, and in May was promoted midshipman. In July 1931 he took passage to England for further sea-training and courses with the Royal Navy.

Initially, Gosse was appointed to the battleship, H.M.S. *Ramillies*, in the Mediterranean Fleet. His training included an air-course in H.M.S. *Glorious* and destroyer-training in H.M.S. *Worcester*. In September 1932 he joined the R.N. College, Greenwich. Proximity to the attractions of London, the company of young Adelaidians on 'grand tours', and a passion for sports cars brought about his undoing. Having failed the examination for lieutenant, he was sent home and his appointment terminated on 30 October 1933.

Gosse 'knocked about', resisting the temptation of serious employment. In the chapel of his old school on 1 October 1938 he married Diana Skottowe. On 21 October 1940 he enlisted as an ordinary seaman in the Royal Australian Naval Volunteer Reserve. He was commissioned sub lieutenant in April 1941 while posted to H.M.S. *King Alfred*; in December he joined H.M.I.S. *Hooghly* at Calcutta, India, as mine disposal officer. Official reports noted his reliability, keenness and ingenuity. Always cheerful under difficulties, he got on well with officers and men, and exhibited 'a daring character and a good knowledge of mines in which he is very interested'. He was made provisional lieutenant in February 1942.

From late 1944 Gosse served in H.M.S. *Vernon (D)* at Brixham, Devon, England, the base for the R.N.'s port-clearance diving operations in Europe. Described at this time as sporting a bold, black beard, he had soft green eyes and a softer voice, and was somewhat of a law unto himself. Yet, he was inventive and had a fascination with things mechanical. Although he had qualified as a shallow-water diver in January 1945, he lacked practice when he went to Germany to begin underwater mine-disposal operations at Bremen, following its capture in April.

In command of Naval Party 1571, Gosse directed a search for mines laid by the retreating Germans in the waters of Bremen's Übersee Hafen. On 8 May his men found 'a D-type mine with additional fittings'. Known as the 'Oyster', it was pressure operated, with acoustic and magnetic units incorporated in its detonation train. At about 6 p.m. next day Gosse dived on the mine. Even with the aid of a waterproof torch, he could not see the device in the mud and proceeded to work by touch. He also had difficulty in stabilizing his buoyancy and had to secure himself to the mine's marker-buoy rope to keep his depth steady.

Gosse used tools which he had improvised, removed the primer release and then extracted the primer 'about eighteen inches [46 cm] down a two-inch tube'. He had interrupted the detonation train and the mine was safe. While he was releasing himself from his makeshift tether, there was a small explosion. Later examination of the landed mine showed that water had entered through the primer tube and operated a mechanism designed to respond to changing water pressure and trigger the detonator if the mine were raised. Gosse rendered safe two more 'Oyster' mines at Bremen. In 1946 he was awarded the George Cross. Having been promoted acting lieutenant commander on 30 September 1945, he was demobilized on 20 March 1946.

Back in Adelaide, Gosse invented many practical household gadgets and fittings, but lost interest once he had met the challenge of concept and design: for the most part, his work was unspectacular. He was president (1946-48) of the Sporting Car Club of South Australia. In 1953 he was chosen as a member of the coronation contingent which went to England in H.M.A.S. *Sydney*. Survived by his wife and two daughters, he died of a coronary occlusion on 31 December 1964 at Maslin Beach and was cremated.

F. B. Eldridge, *A History of the Royal Australian Naval College* (Melb, 1949); J. Grosvenor and L. M. Bates, *Open the Ports* (Lond, 1956); F. Gosse, *The Gosses* (Canb, 1981); V. Smith, *A Few Memories of Sir Victor Smith* (Canb, 1992).

I. McL. CRAWFORD

GOSSE, SIR JAMES HAY (1876-1952), businessman, was born on 21 December 1876 at Kent Town, Adelaide, second son of William Christie Gosse [q.v.4], an English-born surveyor, and his second wife Agnes, daughter of Alexander Hay [q.v.1]. William died in 1881, leaving his widow with three small children. Educated (1886-96) at the Collegiate School of St Peter, James excelled at football and rowing. In 1894-1905 he played as a ruckman for Norwood Football Club (president 1920) and represented the State five times. 'A giant in the boat', in 1902-05 he rowed in the South Australian VIII and was president (1924-31) of Adelaide Rowing Club.

On leaving school, Gosse was employed as a clerk at George Wills & Co. Ltd; he was to remain with the firm for fifty years and rise to managing director. He also became a director and chairman of the boards of the Adelaide Steamship Co. Ltd and the Bank of Adelaide, and was a board-member of News Ltd, the Executor Trustee & Agency Co. of South Australia Ltd, G. & R. Wills & Co. Ltd and James & Alexander Brown [qq.v.3] & Abermain Seaham Collieries Ltd. Chairman of the Australian Association of British Manufacturers, he was president of the South Australian Chamber of Commerce, the Boy Scouts' Association and St Peter's Collegians' Association (1937-38), as well as being a governor (1917-38) of his old school.

In 1907 Gosse had joined the Adelaide Club. At St Andrew's Anglican Church, Walkerville, on 29 April 1908 he married 21-year-old Joanna Lang, daughter of Tom Elder Barr Smith [q.v.11]; they lived at St Margarets, Parkside. Gosse was intensely interested in his forebears, and kept up a friendship with his English cousins, among them the critic (Sir) Edmund Gosse. Travelling throughout Australia, and frequently abroad, James Gosse belonged to the Melbourne, Union (Sydney), Weld (Perth) and Queensland clubs. He was gregarious, hospitable—'On we go!' was his favourite toast—and a great promoter of his State. In 1911-18 he was manager of George Wills & Co. in Perth. Returning to Adelaide, he served as honorary consul (1923-52) for Denmark and was appointed to the Order of the Dannebrog (1936).

A bustling, forthright and active man, irascible and genial by turn, Gosse was much sought after for his zest and entrepreneurial skills. He was never idle or detached from the causes he adopted. President (1923-31 and 1935-47) of the Royal South Australian Zoological and Acclimatization Society, on Sundays he carried a basket of stale bread to distribute as he walked around the cages discussing affairs with the director. From 1933 until his death he was a councillor of the local branch of the Royal Geographical Society of Australasia. In 1947 he was knighted. As chairman (1940-52) of the State's Fauna and Flora Board, he fostered its Flinders [q.v.1] Chase wildlife sanctuary on Kangaroo Island and holidayed there annually. He was a member (from 1939) of the board of the South Australian Museum and in 1948 gave the State government 3000 acres (1200 ha) to the Coorong to restore the sandhills to the condition depicted by George French Angas [q.v.1]. Survived by his wife, daughter and four sons, Sir James died on 14 August 1952 at Stirling and was cremated. His nephew George Gosse [q.v.] won the George Cross and a grandson Alexander Downer entered Federal parliament.

F. Gosse, *The Gosses* (Canb, 1981); Adel Rowing Club, *The First 100 Seasons* (Adel, 1982); *St Peter's College Mag*, 7 May 1937, Dec 1952; *PRGSSA*, 53, 1951-52; *Advertiser* (Adel), 19 Oct 1948, 14 Aug 1952.   FAYETTE GOSSE

GOTTSCHALK, ALFRED (1894-1973), medical scientist, was born on 22 April 1894 at Aachen, Germany, third of four sons of Benjamin Gottschalk, merchant, and his wife Rosa, née Kahen. Alfred's medical course, begun in 1912 and undertaken at the universities of Munich, Freiburg im Breisgau and Bonn (M.D., 1920), was interrupted by World War I, in which he served in the medical corps of the German Army.

In 1923 he was employed as an assistant to Professor Carl Neuberg at the Kaiser Wilhelm Institute for Experimental Therapy and Biochemistry, Berlin. Gottschalk married Elisabeth Bertha Maria Orgler on 1 August that year in Berlin. Three years later he was appointed director of the biochemistry department at the general hospital, Szczecin, but was forced to relinquish the post in 1934 because of political upheavals in Nazi Germany. (Originally Jewish, he and his family had converted to Catholicism.) After practising medicine privately, in 1939 Gottschalk left Germany with his wife and son; they travelled to Liverpool, England, and thence to Melbourne. His wife left him in 1950.

From 1939 to 1959 Gottschalk worked as a biochemist at the Walter and Eliza Hall [qq.v.9] Institute, initially on the biochemistry of yeast and from 1947 with (Sir) Macfarlane Burnet in investigating the enzymic activities of influenza virus. Having shown that the viral 'receptor-destroying enzyme' was a neuraminidase, Gottschalk began a study of glycoproteins, on which he became a world authority. He edited *Glycoproteins. Their Composition, Structure and Function* (Amsterdam, 1966). In 1942-48 he had also taught at the Melbourne Technical College. Naturalized in 1945, he was registered as a medical practitioner in Victoria next year. At the University of Melbourne (D.Sc., 1949), he was awarded the David Syme [q.v.6] research prize in 1951. That year he was elected a fellow of the Royal Institute of Chemistry, London, and of the Royal Australian Chemical Institute whose H. G. Smith [q.v.11] medal he won in 1954. A fellow (1954) of the Australian Academy of Science, he served as secretary (1954-58) of its Victorian group.

On his retirement in 1959, Gottschalk moved to the John Curtin School of Medical Research, Australian National University, Canberra, and continued active benchwork until 1963 when he returned to Germany. He became a guest professor and foreign scientific member (from 1968) at the Max Planck Institute for Virus Research, Tübingen, where he continued to work on glycoprotein biochemistry. The University of Münster awarded him an honorary M.D. in 1969. Gottschalk's scientific work was characterized by his dedication, and by his meticulous attention to detail in the design and execution of experiments and in their description for publication. He insisted on the same standards for his assistants and students; some found his close supervision difficult to tolerate. Outside the laboratory, he was a man of broad interests and interesting conversation, with a subtle sense of humour and a great fund of anecdotes.

Survived by his son, Gottschalk died on 4 October 1973 at Tübingen and was buried there. His scientific publications comprise 216 papers and four books. He is commemorated by the Gottschalk medal, awarded annually by the Australian Academy of Science.

M. Burnet, *Walter and Eliza Hall Institute 1915-1965* (Melb, 1971); *Records of the Aust Academy of Science*, 3, no 1, Nov 1974, p 52; *Age*, 7, 19 Apr 1962; *Sun News-Pictorial*, 21 Apr 1962; Gottschalk papers (Basser L); AA 58/14108, Dept of Immigration (Central Office) (AA, Canb).

FRANK FENNER

GOTTSHALL, BENJAMIN BÉLA VOJTECH (1907-1978), rabbi, was born on 30 August 1907 at Szeged, Transylvania, Hungary, eldest of five children of Rabbi Samuel Gottschall and his wife Jenni Eva, née Schayer (Scheuer). In 1908 Samuel became rabbi to the 'status quo' community at Eperjes (from 1919 Presov, Czechoslovakia). Benjamin began his education at the local Catholic Gymnasium, proceeded to the theological seminary of 'status quo' Judaism, Budapest, and studied Egyptology at Loránd Eötuös University. While reading medicine for eight terms at the Comenius University of Bratislava, Czechoslovakia, he also attended an orthodox *yeshivah*. He supported himself by training and conducting the Bratislava synagogue choir. Deciding on a rabbinical career, he entered the seminary at Breslau, Germany (Wroclaw, Poland), thus studying in turn in Hungarian, Czech and German, as well as Hebrew and Yiddish. In 1936 he received his rabbinical diploma at Breslau.

Posted next year as rabbi to Louny, Bohemia, Czechoslovakia, Gottschall married Margareta Glässner on 1 September 1938 and ministered there until 1942 when the Jews of Louny were sent to the ghetto camp of Theresienstadt. He worked in the morgue and secretly conducted religious services. For this 'offence', in October 1943 he and his wife were transported to the concentration camp at Auschwitz-Birkenau, Poland, and sent to 'Family camp BIIb'. Gottschall distinguished himself by teaching survival techniques (such as always marching in the middle of a column) to his group of inmates and ministering to their psychological and spiritual needs. Discovery would have meant instant execution. On 1 June 1944 he was sent with 999 others as slave labourers to a synthetic petrol plant at Schwarzheide, near Dresden, where he continued his forbidden ministry. His wife was moved to Bergen-Belsen where she died. He was liberated in May 1945, suffering from tuberculosis. The monks at Louny had safeguarded his books, papers and furniture.

Late in 1945 Gottschall became communal rabbi to the surviving Jews in Prague, and assistant successively to Dr Deutsch and Rabbi Sicher, chief rabbis of Czechoslovakia.

On 24 November 1946 in Prague he married Johana (Jana) Práger—daughter of a rabbi from Topol'čany—whose entire family had also perished in the Holocaust. In July 1949 the Gottschalls fled the communist regime, and reached Sydney in the *Surriento* on 6 September with one child and another soon to be born.

While learning English, Gottschall worked in a factory. In May 1950 he succeeded Isack Morris [q.v.] as rabbi to the Newcastle Hebrew Congregation. The family was naturalized as Gottshall in 1955. From 1958 to 1962 he ministered to the Wellington Hebrew Congregation in New Zealand. As chief rabbi of Queensland (1963-67), he enjoyed representing the Jewish community at official functions; the diminutive rabbi was seen on television blessing the towering President L. B. Johnson. Returning to Sydney in 1967, Gottshall served at Kingsford-Maroubra synagogue from that year until he retired due to illness in 1973.

Both he and his wife were active in communal and civic endeavours during all his ministries. His decision to serve small congregations strengthened those communities. In March 1950 he had organized a memorial service for Czechoslovakian Jewry, which he repeated whenever he resided in Australia (and which was to continue in tribute to him). Survived by his wife, and by their son and daughter, Gottshall died of cancer on 28 April 1978 at Woollahra and was buried in Rookwood cemetery. Four decades after their release, his fellow inmates from the camps recalled with warmth his influence on them.

S. S. Caplan, 'Psychological and Spiritual Resistance in Nazi Concentration Camps: The Example of Rabbi Benjamin Gottschall', *Aust J of Politics and Hist*, 31, no 1, Mar 1985; *SMH*, 14 Mar 1979, 26 June 1985; taped interviews, 1980-82, with Dr E. Morgan, Messrs P. Lom and K. Neubauer, and Rebbetzen J. Gottshall, all of Syd (held by author, Northbridge, Syd); naturalization file, A446/123 items 55/10718-19; information from Terezin Archive, Israel.

SOPHIE CAPLAN

GOUGH, ELEANOR LILIAN GLADYS (1887-1967), teacher of dressmaking, was born on 21 February 1887 at Bathurst, New South Wales, second of six children of native-born parents Henry Alexander Gough, sheriff's officer, and his wife Amy Margaretta, née Riley. While living at Maitland, in 1905 Eleanor passed the junior public examination by private study. She trained in dressmaking, probably at the local technical college, before being recruited in 1913 by the Department of Public Instruction to teach at Paterson and Gresford. Transferred to Sydney Technical College as assistant-teacher of dressmaking and millinery, she took up her appointment in 1917. Four years later she began studying part-time at the University of Sydney (B.Ec., 1925). Succeeding Mary Roberts [q.v.11] in 1925 as lecturer-in-charge of the department of women's handicrafts, she was based in new premises in the old Darlinghurst gaol, later renamed East Sydney Technical College.

Miss Gough presided over far-reaching changes to the syllabus. Although the primary aims of the women's handicrafts department were to train teachers and to improve domestic skills, specific vocational courses, beginning with professional cutting and power machining, had been introduced for women in industry. Courses were extended in rural areas by the better organization of circuit teaching. In country towns a successful series of women's handicraft courses usually attracted other subjects and often led to the establishment of branch technical colleges. Gough's responsibilities soon became heavier than those of many of her better-paid male colleagues. In addition to overseeing a major city school, she supervised a network of metropolitan and country classes, circuit classes and correspondence lessons. Under her direction, the courses increased in popularity and waiting-lists grew longer. The enrolment of 635 in 1918 had risen to 2461 by 1930; by the time of her retirement in 1951, she had charge of 10 778 students.

As president of the Technical College Vocations Club for staff, students and former students, Gough helped to set up a cafeteria (1927), a reading circle, a small library and a store; social activities included excursions and dances; and wider contacts were formed. For many years she served on the editorial sub-committee of the *Technical Gazette of New South Wales*. Assisted by some of her colleagues, she also published two textbooks, *Processes in Dressmaking* (1928) and *Principles of Garment Cutting* (1941).

During her twenty-six years as head of her department, Gough coped with the combined effects on her department of the Depression, World War II and educational expansion, particularly under the Commonwealth Reconstruction Training Scheme. A slight, refined and delicate woman, she was respected for her efficiency, general calmness and the dignity with which she handled her job. She moved with serenity, usually dressed in one of her superbly cut suits, with her cloche hat pulled fashionably down. She died on 10 August 1967 at Mosman and was cremated with Anglican rites. In 1956 the Vocations Club had established the Miss E. L. Gough scholarships in recognition of her activities.

Technical Gazette of NSW, 16, pt 1, 1928, 17, pt 1, 1929; *SMH*, 13 Dec 1934; D. Feltham, History of the School of Fashion in the Department of Tech-

nical and Further Education, 1886-1986 (M.Ed. thesis, NSW Univ Technology, 1986); TAFE records, History Unit (Dept of Technical and Further Education, Syd).

JOAN E. COBB

GOURGAUD, PERCIVAL ALBERT (1881-1958), public servant, was born on 3 October 1881 at Norton Diggings, near Gladstone, Queensland, second son of Claudius Gourgaud, a schoolteacher from France, and his English-born wife Mary Jane, née Barnes. Educated at state schools, he worked as a drover and taught himself shorthand with the aim of becoming a court reporter. In 1901 he joined the Postmaster-General's Department in Brisbane as a junior clerk; four years later he transferred to the Department of Home Affairs, Melbourne. At St Joseph's Catholic Church, South Yarra, on 2 March 1908 he married Elizabeth Anne Malcolm, a dressmaker; they were to have six children.

From 1912 to 1916 Gourgaud lived in Canberra and was involved in its early development. Back in Melbourne, he transferred to the Department of Works and Railways, and in January 1917 was chosen as the first secretary of the River Murray Commission. It oversaw irrigation, flood control and navigation, and supervised construction projects largely carried out by the States; in 1919 work began on the Hume Reservoir. In 1927 he accompanied the department's chief engineer on a trip to investigate developments in the United States of America. When Gourgaud relinquished the secretaryship in October 1928, the commissioners praised his ability and service.

With the knack of making himself useful to politicians, in 1911-12 and 1916-23 he had been detached for short periods as secretary to the Federal ministers King O'Malley (twice), P. J. Lynch, W. A. Watt, (Sir) Littleton Groom and R. W. Foster [qq.v.11,10,12, 9,8]. Gourgaud was in a party that accompanied the Prince of Wales during his Australian visit in 1920 and that year travelled to Geneva where he was secretary to the Australian delegation to the first assembly of the League of Nations. In the 1930s he cultivated the friendship of Prime Minister Joseph Lyons [q.v.10].

On 11 June 1929 Gourgaud had been promoted secretary of the Department of Works and Railways and moved to Canberra. The Depression restricted operations and in 1932 the department was amalgamated with Home Affairs and Transport to form the Department of the Interior. In the new organization Gourgaud was appointed assistant-secretary, responsible for works and services. He was deeply hurt by being unable to provide more than sustenance employment in the Canberra region to family men whom he knew to be good workers. A nominated member (from 1930) of the Australian Capital Territory Advisory Council, he was appointed O.B.E. in 1937 and retired in 1946.

Gourgaud was a short, handsome man who dressed well and tended to be fussy. His interests were his family, gardening and golf. He preferred to be known as Percival and only his grandchildren were allowed to call him Percy. Concern for his son Claudius, a prisoner of war in World War II, and the early death of his eldest daughter Gwen placed great strains upon him. Survived by his wife, two sons and three daughters, he died on 30 August 1958 at Canberra Community Hospital and was buried in Canberra cemetery with the forms of the Churches of Christ.

J. M. Powell, *Watering the Garden State* (Syd, 1989); *SMH*, 1 Feb 1937; *Canb Times*, 1 Feb 1937, 1 Sept 1958; A151/1 box F-G, A151/3 box 1, A2925/1 1937 (AA, Canb); information from Mrs B. Chew, Cook, Canb.   JAN McDONALD

GRAHAM, MARGARET (1889-1966), kindergarten teacher and broadcaster, was born on 5 June 1889 at Ballarat, Victoria, fourth of six children of Scottish-born parents John Graham, tailor, and his wife Maggie, née MacKeddie. In 1893 the family settled at Leederville, Perth. A gentle woman with a love of children and a talent for handicrafts, Margaret completed a course at the Kindergarten Training College, West Perth, in 1916. Placed in charge of the Free Kindergarten, Pier Street, in 1921, she moved to the Mount Hawthorn Kindergarten School as director in 1926.

Following the Japanese occupation of the Netherlands East Indies, fear of air-raids on Fremantle and Perth led the State government to close its kindergartens early in 1942. Olga Dickson's suggestion for a radio programme for kindergarten-aged children was first taken up by a commercial station in Fremantle which proposed two fifteen-minute sessions a week. Members of the executive of the Kindergarten Union of Western Australia appointed Mrs Catherine King, daughter of Professor Walter Murdoch [q.v.10], to call on the State manager of the Australian Broadcasting Commission, Conrad Charlton. Accompanied by Molly McGibbon, she persuaded him to let her and her colleagues try a daily programme and 'Kindergarten of the Air' was inaugurated on 19 February. After two kindergarten teachers had been tested as comperes, Miss Graham's performance on the third day of the trials won her the position. On 23 February she began her first programme, with a pianist and two children. According to King, Graham was 'a complete natural. She wasn't glamorous, she was hope-lessly sincere, we couldn't have . . . made her into anything but what she was . . . a modest and inspired amateur'.

To the 'Kindergarten of the Air', Graham brought qualities which assured its success. Her sessions, which started at 9.30 a.m. and ran for twenty minutes, were unrehearsed and all involved children participating in the studio. She spoke to 'thousands of unseen children . . . just as intimately and caringly as to the little group in her studio', and never talked down to them. Children throughout Western Australia loved her voice. Country children often wrote letters to her, and, when holidaying in Perth, were welcome visitors to the studio. Charlton realized that the programme's popularity was largely due to her and asked that the Kindergarten Union resist the temptation to bring other teachers into the session. With her piano accompanist Mrs Jean McKinlay, Graham produced *Dance and Sing* (n.d.), a book of the songs and music used in the programme. She remained director at Mount Hawthorn and her radio fee was paid not to her but to the Kindergarten Union. 'Kindergarten of the Air' became the model for the A.B.C.'s national programme which commenced on 3 May 1943. Perth's own session, protected by the two-hour difference in time, retained its independence.

Graham also gave short talks on the A.B.C.'s women's session, providing advice about young children's behaviour and learning problems, and on the clothing, games and books that were appropriate for them. In 1956 she was appointed M.B.E. By 1960 she was frail and weary, but continued to broadcast until her final session of 'Kindergarten of the Air' for Christmas 1960. Within a year of suffering a disabling stroke, she died on 25 January 1966 at Mount Lawley and was cremated with Presbyterian forms. In 1967 the arts and crafts wing of the new Kindergarten Teachers' College, West Perth, was named in her memory.

D. Popham (ed), *Reflections* (Perth, 1978); J. Lewis, *On Air* (Perth, 1979); K. S. Inglis, *This is the ABC* (Melb, 1983); *West Australian*, 2 Jan 1956, 26 Jan 1966, 3 June 1967; C. King, Margaret Graham —MBE (ts, June 1967, WAA); Broadcasting, Kindergarten of the Air, 2308A/147 (WAA); interview with C. H. King, oral hist programme, 1976 (BL); information from Dr J. Graham, City Beach, Perth, and Mrs J. McKinlay, South Perth.

                              SUE GRAHAM-TAYLOR

GRAHAMSLAW, THOMAS (1901-1973), public servant and soldier, was born on 3 March 1901 at Townsville, Queensland, only son and eldest of six children of James Gray Grahamslaw, a tinsmith from Scotland, and his native-born wife Annie, née Meldon.

Educated at state schools in North Queensland, in 1911 he followed his parents to Papua where his father had found work as a plumber. Thomas was sent to the new, one-teacher school for White children in Port Moresby, but left at 14 to become a grocer's-boy in the British New Guinea Development Co. Ltd's store. In 1916, after many government officers had enlisted for service in World War I, he joined the Territory's public service as a cadet clerk on £1 a week.

In a civil service of fewer than 140 people, Grahamslaw was given numerous responsibilities. As acting-collector of customs at Daru from 1924, he was the only member of his department in the Western Division; subsequently based on Woodlark Island, he was also mining registrar, inspector of native labour and gaoler. On 15 April 1939 at the Church of Our Lady of the Rosary, Port Moresby, he married May McLean, a schoolteacher; they were later divorced.

When the Japanese threatened Papua in early 1942, Grahamslaw was collector of customs and postmaster at Samarai. Ordered to Port Moresby on the suspension of civil administration in February, he saw Australian soldiers and airmen looting the town. In that month he enlisted in the Militia. He was posted to the Papuan (later Australian New Guinea) Administrative Unit, commissioned and appointed district officer of the Northern District. At Buna when the Japanese landed in July, he was soon behind enemy lines as their forces advanced through Kokoda. To bring help to stranded troops, airmen and missionaries, he made an extraordinary lone walk across Papua to Abau on the south coast.

Grahamslaw instructed Australian troops before they fought on the Kokoda Track, reconnoitred difficult country and helped to organize Papuan carriers, whom he praised for their dedication and fortitude. The Japanese were progressively cleared from the Northern District. Promoted temporary major, he reopened administration headquarters at Higaturu in October, and began re-establishing government control and services. He continued to recruit labourers for the army and worked with American divisions moving into combat. In his reminiscences of his A.N.G.A.U. service (Pacific Islands Monthly, March-May 1971) he left a poignant description of the hangings of twenty-two Papuans convicted of crimes during the Japanese occupation. He was appointed O.B.E. (1943) for his part in the Papuan campaign.

Transferring to the Australian Imperial Force in January 1943, Grahamslaw took over the Lakekamu District early next year and patrolled the Goilala country. From mid-1944 he commanded the Southern Region, and was responsible for the administration of virtually all Papua and of New Guinea south of the Markham River. He was promoted temporary lieutenant colonel in January 1945 (substantive in September). In October he handed control to the first postwar administrator (Sir) Keith Murray [q.v.] and ceased full-time duty on 4 February 1946.

After the war Grahamslaw was superintendent of stores (1945) in Port Moresby, assistant-collector of customs (1949) and chief collector (from 1955). He served as a member of the Legislative Council in 1955-60 and was appointed to the Executive Council in 1960. One of the few 'deskmen' to have the respect of field-staff, he was the 'popular old-time public servant' to the press and, affectionately, 'Uncle Tom' to his subordinates. Grahamslaw was fluent in several local languages and had a deep concern for the people of Papua. Of middle height and strongly built, he had played tennis and cricket as a young man, and belonged to the Port Moresby Golf Club for thirty years. In 1961 he retired to New South Wales. On 25 October that year he married a widow Mary Emilie Chase, née Williams, at the Congregational Church, Vaucluse, Sydney. Survived by her, he died on 16 December 1973 at Gosford and was cremated with Catholic rites.

J. Tudor (ed), *Pacific Islands Year Book and Who's Who in the Pacific Islands* (Syd, 1968); *PIM*, Feb 1974; *SMH*, 17 Dec 1973; Grahamslaw papers (NL); information from Mrs M. Baldwin, Caloundra, Qld.
                                                        H. N. NELSON

GRANDI, MARGHERITA (1892-1972), opera singer, was born on 10 October 1892 at Harwood Island, New South Wales, and registered as Margaret, second daughter of Bernard Gard, engine driver, and his wife Catherine, née Ryan, both native-born. Maggie attended Harwood and Yamba public schools; after the family moved to Tasmania in 1903, she was educated by the Presentation Sisters at St Mary's School, Hobart. It was when she sang in the St Mary's Cathedral choir that her voice first attracted attention. By the age of 17 she possessed 'a contralto voice of unusual depth and quality'. Recognizing her great potential, a number of influential Hobart citizens—among them a former premier (Sir) John Evans [q.v.8] and Monsignor Gilleran of St Mary's Cathedral—formed the Maggie Gard Committee to finance her musical studies in Europe.

Aided by a successful farewell concert organized by the committee, Gard left for Paris in January 1911 to study with Mathilde Marchesi, a former teacher of (Dame) Nellie Melba [q.v.10]. Gard's initial studies were curtailed by a bout of typhoid fever, contracted on her arrival, but Marchesi pronounced favourably on her voice and Maggie began lessons with Jean de Reszke. In Hobart, the Maggie Gard Committee continued fundraising and a syndicate of eighty shares at £5 each was subscribed to meet her expenses. Sponsored by Sir John McCall [q.v.10], the Tasmanian agent-general in London, she entered the Royal College of Music in September 1912. In February 1914 she was awarded an open scholarship (worth £100 a year); she became a pupil of Plunket Greene and remained at the college until June 1917. In the following year she enjoyed a successful London début. Having returned to Paris to study for a year with Emma Calvé, she made her Continental début in 1921 as a mezzo-soprano at the Opera-Comique in Massenet's *Werther*. Her stage name, Djemma Vécla, was an anagram of her teacher's surname. She was subsequently engaged to sing Carmen, and in 1922 created the title role in the première of Massenet's *Amadis* at Monte Carlo, Monaco. After this season of opera she went to Milan, Italy, where her principal vocal teacher was Giannina Russ. About this time, Margaret married Giovanni Grandi, scenery designer at La Scala opera house.

After an absence of ten years, during which her daughter Patricia was born, she resumed her career as Margherita Grandi. In 1932 she sang Aida at the Teatro Carcano, Milan. The role firmly established her as a dramatic soprano (the repertoire into which she had moved) and led to performances in opera houses throughout Italy. She appeared in seasons of opera in Cairo, The Netherlands and Budapest. In 1934 she sang the role of Elena in Boito's *Mefistofele* at La Scala, Milan. Following one of her most famous performances as Verdi's Lady Macbeth at the Glyndebourne Festival, Sussex, England, in 1939, critics agreed that she was 'magnificently voiced' and hailed her as 'not only an exceptionally fine singer, but also a notable tragic actress'. At the outbreak of World War II Grandi returned to Italy where she reputedly helped the partisans. The war curtailed her burgeoning career. Her major performances during this time were at Venice in 1940 as Maria in the Italian première of Strauss's *Friedenstag*, and in Rome three years later as Octavia in Monteverdi's *L'Incoronazione di Poppea*.

She returned to Britain in 1947 to recreate the role of Lady Macbeth at the Edinburgh Festival, and to sing Puccini's Tosca and Donna Anna (in Mozart's *Don Giovanni*) at the Cambridge Theatre, London, when her voice was described as 'rich, flexible and perfectly modulated'. Over the next two years Grandi appeared regularly with the New London Opera Company where she worked with her husband who was director and designer. In 1949 she shone as Diana in (Sir) Arthur Bliss's *The Olympians* at Covent Garden, then returned to Edinburgh as Amelia in Verdi's *Un Ballo in Maschera*. Her stage farewell was made in 1951 as Tosca—a fitting finale for her grand dramatic flair and rich voice.

Survived by her daughter, Grandi died on 29 January 1972 at Milan, never having returned to her native Australia. She left few recordings as she was in her fifties by the time she entered the studio: they include excerpts from Verdi's *Macbeth, La Forza del Destino* and *Don Carlos*, and from Offenbach's *Les Contes d'Hoffmann*.

B. and F. Mackenzie, *Singers of Australia* (Melb, 1967); S. Sadie (ed), *The New Grove Dictionary of Music and Musicians*, 7 (Lond, 1980) and *The New Grove Dictionary of Opera*, 2 (Lond, 1992); *Record Collector*, 1978; *A'sian Sound Archive*, no 8, Sept 1989; *Mercury* (Hob), 23 Jan 1911, 10 June 1939, 8 Sept 1947, 16 May 1972; *Weekly Courier* (Launc), 26 Jan, 6 Apr 1911, 11 July 1912, 5 Mar 1914, 7 Nov 1918, 14 Jan, 14 Apr 1921; *Tas Mail*, 25 Jan 1912; information from Roy College of Music, Lond.

JILL WATERS

GRANT, GWENDOLYN MURIEL (1877-1968), artist, was born on 24 May 1877 at Ipswich, Queensland, elder daughter of Montague Henry Stanley, a station-manager from Scotland, and his Irish-born wife Maud Annie Kirkpatrick, née Craig. Following her mother's death in 1879, Gwendolyn was raised by maternal relations in Brisbane. Her father made visits from his rural base and her childhood was a happy one. Educated at the Misses Clark's School, Toowong, she studied art at Brisbane Technical College under Godfrey Rivers [q.v.] and entered the (Royal) Queensland Art Society's annual exhibition in 1899. While employed as a governess on several stations in North Queensland from 1902, she continued painting and exhibiting, and in 1906 held a successful solo exhibition at the Kent Buildings, Brisbane.

In 1907 Miss Stanley made the challenging journey to Melbourne where she studied for five years at the National Gallery schools under Bernard Hall, Frederick McCubbin and Leslie Wilkie [qq.v.9,10,12]. She returned to Brisbane in 1912, shared a studio with Vida Lahey [q.v.9], served on the council of the Q.A.S. and taught art classes. Liberal, fashionably bohemian and with an active intellect, she was not awed by contention. On 22 November 1915 at Taringa she married with Presbyterian forms William Gregory Grant (d.1951), an artist later estimated by Lloyd Rees to be 'the most dynamic painter' in Brisbane. While raising her two children (b.1917 and 1920), 'Stan', as she was called by her husband, maintained her professional life. She was affable, ambitious and tenacious, and her soft voice belied her self-confidence. Granddaughter of Montague Stanley (a member of the Royal Scottish Academy), she was well-connected in local society and, with her husband, played competition golf. She was president (1923) of the local Lyceum Club and wrote on art for the *Daily Mail*. Mrs Grant exhibited regularly with the Victorian Artists Society and the Society of Women Painters, New South Wales; she staged fifteen solo exhibitions and held four joint-exhibitions with her husband.

She regularly entered for the Archibald [q.v.3] prize and from 1920 her reputation as a portrait painter was gradually established. An academic Impressionist, concerned with light and its effects, she once contended that a painting should convey 'the artist's thoughts to the onlooker so clearly that no title is needed'. Her many depictions of domestic subjects were inspired more by models of female 'independence'—based on 'the notion of a femininity of which the moral inspiration was the home and family'—than by any popular themes in contemporary painting. Grant continued to teach art at the Brisbane Technical College until she was 75. Survived by her son and daughter, she died on 17 April 1968 at Herston and was cremated. Her studies of Sir James Blair and Professor B. D. Steele [qq.v.7,12] are held by the University of Queensland; another portrait, 'Winter Sunshine', was purchased by the Queensland Art Gallery in 1938.

V. Lahey, *Art in Queensland, 1859-1959* (Brisb, 1959); L. Rees, *The Small Treasures of a Lifetime* (Syd, 1969); K. Bradbury and G. R. Cooke, *Thorns & Petals* (Brisb, 1988); B. Larner, *A Complementary Caste* (Surfers Paradise, Qld, 1988); K. Bradbury and A. Grant, *Gwendolyn and W. G. Grant, their Art and Life* (Brisb, 1990); B. Macaulay, *Partners in Art* (Brisb, 1990); *Courier-Mail*, 18 Apr 1958; A. Philp, The Society of Women Painters 1910-1934 (M.A. thesis, Univ Syd, 1990).

KEITH BRADBURY

GRATTAN, CLINTON HARTLEY (1902-1980), journalist, author, historian and commentator on foreign affairs, was born on 19 October 1902 at Wakefield, near Boston, Massachusetts, United States of America, son of Leonard Grattan, journeyman baker, and his wife Laura, née Campbell, both from Nova Scotia, Canada. His forebears were Scots, English, Irish and French-Swiss, the patronymic supposedly being changed from Gratteau to Grattan. Hartley deeply admired his maternal grandfather, a subsistence farmer and mineworker. His family background contributed to his pro-labour views and to his sense of being something of an 'outsider' in American society, though he always identified strongly, if critically, with the better aspects of American democracy.

Failing to gain a place at Harvard University, Grattan nevertheless valued his Alma Mater, Clark College, Clark University (A.B., 1923), Worcester. His most influential teacher was Harry Elmer Barnes, a polymath and a crusader for radical causes. Grattan saw himself as inheriting the left-liberalism of Barnes and others who sought to harness the social sciences in a struggle for social justice. By temperament, background and education, Grattan became a dissenter with a liking for combative polemics and a belief in ranging across the disciplines. He was a proponent of American cultural independence in the debates of the 1920s and subsequently a supporter of parallel impulses in Australian culture.

In 1925 he took up journalism in New York, having already begun writing iconoclastic articles on American literary figures for H. L. Mencken's *American Mercury*. On 22 October 1926, in New York, Grattan married with Unitarian forms Beatrice Kuper, an actress who used 'Kay' as her stage surname; they were to be divorced in 1937. He published three books in 1929 and more followed. While pursuing a career as an Americanist, he had visited Australia in 1927 when he accompanied Beatrice who was touring with the musical, *Sunny*. He devoted himself to learning about the 'new' country—which he felt could not be as dull as it seemed—by collecting books and reading widely in its literature. Although he made no contact with the intellectual community, he regarded Australia as a fascinating 'experiment' in democracy. The outcome was a slim booklet, *Australian Literature* (Seattle, 1929), one of the earliest attempts to synthesize nineteenth- and twentieth-century literary history so as to establish what was characteristically 'Australian'.

His essay earned the immediate interest of such writers as Miles Franklin, Nettie Palmer and Katharine Susannah Prichard [qq.v.8,11] because it detected a promise of distinctiveness in Australian literature and did not see it as a branch of Anglo-European culture. In his voluminous later writing, much of it in leading New York journals and newspapers, he expanded his interests into socio-cultural questions, politics, economics and international relations. The span and tone of his work appealed to Australian artists and intellectuals who promoted their country's independence in the 1930s and 1940s.

Among them were people whom Grattan met on his next and most substantial visit to Australia—made possible by a grant from the Carnegie Corporation—in December 1936-September 1938: besides Franklin, Palmer and Prichard, he met H. V. Evatt, Brian Fitzpatrick, Brian Penton [qq.v.], Sir Herbert Gepp, P. R. Stephensen [qq.v.8,12], W. G. K. Duncan, W. Macmahon Ball, and the economists Colin Clark and (Sir) John Crawford, his friend thereafter. Through Geoffrey Remington [q.v.], Grattan forged links with the Australian Institute of Political Science. He published influential articles in the institute's journal, the *Australian Quarterly*, on Joseph Furphy [q.v.8] (as an inspirational radical nationalist) and on Australian society's lack of self-definition and direction. Grattan lamented the country's conservatism in the late 1930s.

Following a speculative and influential article, 'An Australian-American Axis?' in *Harper's Magazine* (May 1940), he again visited Australia for nearly two months in 1940. His brief was to report on wartime conditions and opinion in Australasia. He produced a 49-page typescript, 'Australia and New Zealand Today', which was confidentially circulated in both countries, and which summed up their situations and future possibilities. *Introducing Australia* (New York, 1942) resulted from both his 1936-38 and 1940 tours. An accessible, professionally informed, generalist study, the book was widely read and served not only to introduce Australia to Americans, but, as Franklin pointed out, to interest Australians in their own country. It also appealed to younger nationalists, such as Geoffrey Serle and Stephen Murray-Smith.

In the mid- and late 1930s Grattan had moved farther to the left, without becoming a communist supporter. He married a former sweetheart Marjorie Sinclair Campbell on 3 June 1939 at Philadelphia, Pennsylvania. In January 1942 he was appointed an analyst with the Board of Economic Warfare, Washington, a sign at last of his official recognition as an American expert on Australian affairs. Chaired by Martin Dies, a committee of the U.S. House of Representatives (which was investigating un-American activities) accused Grattan of being both a communist and a Nazi sympathizer, forcing him to resign in April. This bitter disappointment threw him back on freelance journalism in New York. He consequently experienced financial difficulties and moved with his family to nearby Katonah.

After being employed by the Ford Foundation in the 1950s, Grattan produced *The Southwest Pacific to 1900* and *The Southwest Pacific Since 1900* (Ann Arbor, Michigan, 1963) which he and Sir Keith Hancock regarded as his *magnum opus*. The work was an ambitious synthesis and drew on a lifetime's study. It was well received, but some reviewers pointed out its limitations as a generalist history in which the component parts —Australia, New Zealand, 'the Islands' and Antarctica—tended to coexist separately. The approach, especially in 'the Islands', lacked a post-colonial perspective that characterized the work of later historians.

In 1964 the University of Texas at Austin bought Grattan's vast collection of Australiana and South Pacificana, which had become legendary among his steady stream of visitors from Australia. He accepted a post at the university as curator of his collection, with some lecturing duties in history; later made professor, he retired in 1974. On his seventh and final visit to Australia in 1977, he received an honorary LL.D. from the Australian National University in belated recognition of his contribution to the study of Australian culture. Survived by his wife, and their son and three daughters, he died on 25 June 1980 at Austin.

Grattan's wish that his ashes be scattered over Sydney Harbour testified to his extraordinarily enduring attachment to Australia. The country's most important foreign observer, he was, as Serle has said, its most persistent, productive and embracing.

D. Oliphant (ed), *Perspectives on Australia* (Austin, Texas, US, 1989); L. Hergenhan, *No Casual Traveller* (Brisb, 1995), and for publications; *Meanjin Q*, 33, no 3, Sept 1974, p 229; *Overland*, 121, Summer 1990, p 70; J. J. Healy, Bibliography of Grattan's Writings (ms) *and* Grattan papers (Grattan Collection, Harry Ransom Humanities Research Centre, Univ Texas at Austin).

LAURIE HERGENHAN

GRATWICK, PERCIVAL ERIC (1902-1942), soldier and prospector, was born on 19 October 1902 at Katanning, Western Australia, fifth son of native-born parents Ernest Albert Gratwick, postmaster, and his wife Eva Mary, née Pether. After Ernest died in 1911, the family battled to make ends meet. Percy attended state schools at Katanning, Boulder and Perth, and left school at 16. He worked in Perth, at one stage as a messenger at Parliament House, until about 1922 when he went north to the Pilbara and learned droving and blacksmithing on Indee station, 30 miles (50 km) south of Port Hedland. Then he moved to Yandeyarra station, 30 miles farther south, as a stationhand. He gradually built up a droving plant, got a team of mostly Aboriginal stockmen together, and took contracts. Stopped by drought in 1931, he turned to prospecting while employed part time on White Springs station, next to Yandeyarra. In the mid-1930s he settled at nearby Wodgina, a tantalite mine, blacksmithing, prospecting and occasionally working cattle for White Springs. He was his own man, well used to looking after himself in that tough country.

Early in World War II Gratwick tried to enlist in the Australian Imperial Force, but was rejected because his nose had been broken years before. He paid a lot of money to have it fixed, tried again, and was accepted on 20 December 1940. After training he sailed from Perth on 5 July 1941, leaving instructions that his horses not be sold or destroyed. In September he joined the 2nd/48th Battalion under siege at Tobruk, Libya. 'I'm home and pleased and proud to be able to piss in the same pot with such a fine crowd', he told his brother. A month later the 2nd/48th was sent to Palestine. In June 1942 it arrived in Egypt, and in July fought at Tel el Eisa. Gratwick was held in reserve, rejoining his battalion on 10 August. Its next battle, his first, was El Alamein.

Just after midnight on 26 October the 2nd/48th attacked Trig 29, a slight elevation overlooking flat, rocky country even barer than the Pilbara, and powerfully defended by the Germans. Gratwick's platoon was pinned down by heavy fire: its leaders were killed, and it was reduced to seven men. The ground ahead sloped down then up, and both slopes were dotted with mortar and machine-gun posts. As he had done all his adult life, Gratwick asked no one what to do. His mates saw him rise suddenly into the German fire and charge forward, a grenade in one hand, rifle and bayonet in the other. A German sub-machine-gunner stood up and opened fire on him, but Gratwick reached the nearest post and hurled in two grenades, killing its occupants, including a mortar crew. Then he charged the sub-machine-gunner's post. He was mortally hit as he reached it, but silenced the occupants before he died. Inspired, his mates advanced, the Germans fell back, and the ground was captured. Gratwick was posthumously awarded the Victoria Cross.

Percy Gratwick was 5 ft 10 ins (178 cm) tall and of medium build, quiet and resourceful, a practical joker, a bachelor who loved children, a bushman who thought city people had profit-and-loss minds. He measured people by their actions. He lived and died by that belief. In Perth, and in the desert country he came from, people honoured his memory. About 1948 a hill on White Springs was named Mount Gratwick, in 1956 the Gratwick Soldiers' Club was opened at Campbell Barracks, Perth, and in the 1960s Port Hedland named its hall, its swimming pool and a street after him. Gratwick, too, lies in the desert, in El Alamein war cemetery, plot 22, row A, grave 6.

J. G. Glenn, *Tobruk to Tarakan* (Adel, 1960); J. H. Gratwick, *The Gratwick Saga* (priv print, Perth, nd); B. Maughan, *Tobruk and El Alamein* (Canb, 1966); L. Wigmore (ed), *They Dared Mightily* (Canb, 1963); Army Museum of WA, *News-Sheet*, 25 Oct 1991; *West Australian*, 29 Jan 1943; *Argus*, 30 Jan 1943; *Age* (Melb), 4 Mar 1943; P. Gratwick letters 1940-42 (held by Ms V. Gratwick, Nollamara, Perth); information from Mrs G. Chadd, West Perth, Mr B. Gratwick, South Perth, Ms F. K. Chadd, Shenton Park, Perth, and Mrs J. Murray, Esperance, WA.   BILL GAMMAGE

GRAY, DOROTHY MARY; *see* MANSOM

GRAY, GEORGE HENRY (1903?-1967), politician, accountant, farmer and soldier, claimed to have been born on 2 October 1903 at Hay, New South Wales, son of George Henry Gray, bank manager, and his wife Priscilla Maud Kerr, a native-born schoolteacher. Raised by his maternal grandmother on her family's farm at Lewis Ponds, near Orange, young George was educated at Burwood Public School, Sydney, before taking a job in a grocery store at Thornleigh. In the early to mid-1920s he held a post as a customs officer at Shanghai, China, and was a corporal in the Shanghai Volunteer Corps.

Returning to Australia about 1926, Gray moved to Queensland, worked on a farm at Cooyar and became an organizer for the Douglas Social Credit Party. On 4 August 1939 he led thirty-seven members of the League for Social Justice in a raid on Parliament House, Brisbane, demanding that the government reduce unemployment and improve conditions for primary producers. Arrested for unlawful assembly, he was acquitted at the subsequent trial, as were his accomplices. He later maintained that he had been spying on the league for Federal intelligence authorities.

Mobilized in the Citizen Military Forces on 29 May 1940, Gray served in units of the Australian Army Ordnance Corps in Queensland, Papua and New Guinea. He was commissioned in the Australian Imperial Force in May 1942 and transferred to the Reserve of Officers on 12 December 1944 as a captain. At All Saints Anglican Church, Woollahra, Sydney, on 20 April that year he had married a 19-year-old clerk Elsa Noeline Braham ('Bray') Stratton. Back in Brisbane, he was employed as an accountant with the Queensland Cement & Lime Co. and owned a mixed business at Bowen Hills which was run by his wife.

In 1946 the family moved to Toowoomba. There, Gray managed Co-operative Sales and Service Co., joined the Australian Labor Party in 1945 and stood unsuccessfully in 1949 for the city council. Forming the Roseneath Pastoral Co. with two friends in 1950, he began dairying at Mulgowie, near Laidley. Misfortune attended the venture: no crops could be planted during six months of frequent rain and in May 1951 Gray's house burnt down. Secretary of the Tully River District Canegrowers' Executive, in 1955 he became secretary of the Rockhampton Agricultural Society.

Such was Gray's involvement in community activities that, when elected to the House of Representatives for the seat of Capricornia in 1961, he belonged to twenty-two associations and societies. Returned in 1963 and 1966, he worked tirelessly for his electorate, emphasizing the needs of Central Queensland and promoting the Capricornia New State Movement. In parliament he spoke on 'an extraordinarily wide range of subjects', but his chief interests were northern development and defence. His design for a combined tank and tank-carrier received serious consideration by army officers.

Gray was a slim, active man, with brown hair, grey eyes and a fair complexion. A teetotaller and an elder of the John Knox Presbyterian Church, Rockhampton, he was devoted to his family and compassionate towards those in need. Although quiet by nature, he enjoyed a yarn and had a gentle sense of humour. He died of pulmonary oedema on 2 August 1967 at Rockhampton and was buried in North Rockhampton cemetery; his wife, three sons and three daughters survived him. Bray Gray was a Rockhampton City Council alderman (1973-91) and served eight years as State secretary of the Australian Local Government Women's Association.

C. Lack (comp), *Three Decades of Queensland Political History, 1929-1960* (Brisb, 1962); L. McDonald, *Rockhamptom* (Brisb, 1981); *PD* (Cwlth), 15 Aug 1967, p 4; *Courier-Mail*, 5, 8, 15, 23, 24 Aug, 1 Sept 1939; *Canb Times*, 26 Aug 1966; *Age* (Melb), 11 Oct 1966; *Morning Bulletin* (Rockhampton), 3 Aug 1967; *Sunday Truth* (Brisb), 6 Aug 1967; information from Mrs B. Gray and Mrs P. West, Rockhampton, and Mr S. Tutt, Landsborough, Qld.

ELAINE BROWN

GRAY, KENNETH WASHINGTON (1899-1962), oil geologist, was born on 24 October 1899 at Hornsey, Middlesex, England, son of George Washington Gray, woollen commission merchant, and his wife Emily, née Pearson. Educated at the Leys School, Cambridge, in 1918 he served as an artillery cadet and was commissioned in the Royal Field Artillery.

Next year Gray entered Jesus College, Cambridge (B.A., 1921; M.A., 1925), where he graduated with third-class honours in the natural science tripos. He joined the geological staff of the Anglo-Persian Oil Co. Pty Ltd in 1922. During his first seven years with the firm he took part in a number of surveys in the Middle East, mostly in Persia (Iran). His mapping of the Haft Kel and Haft-i-Safid structures contributed to the discovery of these oilfields. With G. M. Lees, in 1925-26 he made the first major reconnaissance survey of Oman and South-East Arabia. After visiting Albania, Gray studied at the University of Vienna (Ph.D., 1930) and wrote his thesis on geological aspects of Central and Eastern Persia. Between 1930 and 1935 he carried out field-surveys in Persia, Albania and Yugoslavia. At the parish church of St Mary Magdalene, Addiscombe, England, on 28 June 1933 he married Doris May Fairweather.

Gray came to Australia in 1935 to make a general appraisal of the country's oil prospects for Commonwealth Oil Refineries Ltd. Three years later he was appointed chief geologist of the Australasian Petroleum Co. Pty Ltd and Island Exploration Co. Pty Ltd to work in Papua and the mandated Territory of New Guinea. When the Japanese invaded Papua in 1942, he was transferred to Ahwaz, Persia, as area superintendent. In 1946 he returned to Papua and walked over the Kokoda Track to undertake a geological reconnaissance.

In 1949 Gray returned to the Melbourne head office of the Australian operations of Anglo-Iranian Oil Co. Ltd where he was appointed managing director of C.O.R. and a representative of Anglo-Iranian Oil. He retired in 1953, but continued doing consulting work for the British Petroleum Co. of Australia Ltd and serving as Anglo-Iranian representative on the boards of the Papuan exploration companies. He edited 'Geological Results of Petroleum Exploration in Western Papua', published in the *Journal of the Geological Society of Australia* (1961).

Widely read and cultured, Gray was a member of the Geological Society of Australia (vice-president 1954-55), the Royal Society of Victoria (honorary secretary 1954-55), the Royal Central Asian Society and the American Association of Petroleum Geologists. He died of a hypertensive cerebrovascular accident on 29 November 1962 at St Georges, Adelaide, and was cremated; his wife, son and daughter survived him. His geological reports are mostly unpublished, but his work in Persia had made a significant contribution to recording the geology of that country.

R. Ferrier, *History of the British Petroleum Company, I, 1901-32* (Cambridge, 1982); Cwlth Oil Refineries Ltd, *Accelerator*, no 139, Oct 1949, no 161, June 1953; Roy Soc Vic, *Annual Report*, 1962, and *Procs*, 76, 1963; *BP Shield*, Feb 1963; *Herald* (Melb), 4 May 1935, 12 Oct 1949; *Argus*, 15 Oct 1949.

FRANK K. RICKWOOD

GRAY, ROBERT (1902-1942), naval officer, was born on 26 June 1902 in South Melbourne, elder son of Victorian-born parents Robert Gray Ovens, traveller, and his wife Alice Jane Jago. She and her sons subsequently took the surname Gray. Young Robert was educated at South Melbourne College and Scotch College where he topped his class in 1911. He joined the Royal Australian Naval College, Jervis Bay, Federal

Capital Territory, as a cadet midshipman on 31 December 1915.

After spending 1920-21 in H.M.A. ships *Australia* and *Melbourne*, Gray was sent to Britain for courses and further sea-training. He attended the Royal Naval Engineering College, Keyham, Devonport, in 1923-24 and returned to Australia in 1926 as engineer lieutenant. In that year, and again in 1929-33, he performed instructional duties at Flinders Naval Depot, Westernport, Victoria. Having served in *Platypus* and *Canberra* in 1926-29, he was promoted engineer lieutenant commander in 1932 and commissioned H.M.A.S. *Waterhen* in 1934. On 12 February that year he married Betty Alyne ('Alice') Crooke at St John's Anglican Church, Darlinghurst, Sydney.

Strongly built, Gray was an accomplished athlete and played Rugby Union football. He was a sociable person and a good messmate, but a stern disciplinarian who earned, and kept, the respect of his men. As senior engineer (1934-37) in H.M.A.S. *Canberra* he was repeatedly recommended for accelerated promotion; on 30 June 1937 he became engineer commander. Following a posting to H.M.A.S. *Penguin*, where he was responsible for the maintenance of ships in reserve, he sailed to England in H.M.A.S. *Albatross* in 1938. He joined H.M.S. *Amphion* as engineer officer in January 1939 and remained with her when she was recommissioned as H.M.A.S. *Perth*.

From the outbreak of World War II *Perth* was successively on the American and West Indian, Australian, and East Indian stations. In December 1940 she joined the 7th Cruiser Squadron in the British Mediterranean Fleet. On 28 March 1941, in the early stages of the battle of Matapan, the squadron encountered a superior Italian force. Evading enemy shells, the cruisers attempted to draw the Italians towards the British battle fleet. *Perth*'s engine-room and boiler-room staffs were required to make maximum speed while maintaining a thick smoke-screen. Their success was attributed almost entirely to Gray's 'grim and cheerful resolution and to his exceptional powers of leadership coupled with outstanding technical ability'. He was awarded the Distinguished Service Order and mentioned in dispatches (1942).

Gray's commanding officer, Captain Sir Philip Bowyer-Smyth, R.N., wrote of him in September 1941: 'He has shown himself to be undeterred by misfortune, ready and quick to improvise and of outstanding coolness, determination and courage under stress. Never defeated and never loses heart'. *Perth* was in Australian waters when Japan entered the war in December. Sent to help in the defence of Singapore and the Netherlands East Indies in February 1942, she was sunk off Java, at the northern entrance to Sunda Strait, on 1 March. Gray was officially declared missing, presumed drowned. His wife and 2-year-old son survived him.

A3978 T7, item: Gray, R. (AA, Canb); information from Messrs R. Gray, Malvern, Melb, W. Gray, Geelong, Vic, K. Baker, Red Hill, and J. Willis, Watson, Canb.   DARYL FOX

GRAY, THOMAS (1905-1941), stockman, soldier and poet, was born on 14 April 1905 at Onslow, Western Australia, third of seven children of Richard Vickers (also known as Gray), a White, Australian-born labourer, teamster and horse-breaker, and his Aboriginal wife Ida, née Harris. After Richard died in 1913, Ida married Ted Payne. In the 1920s members of her family lobbied State politicians for citizenship rights for part-Aborigines. Ida instilled in her children the view that education was the path to social emancipation for Black Australians. Educated at Onslow State School, Tom developed a love of poetry and proved to be a fine athlete.

Finding work as a drover, stock-handler and bushman, Gray learned to recite more than one hundred poems and composed his own verse in the saddle. He often inscribed his lines on the blades of disused windmills and jotted them on the sides of water tanks for passers-by to read. The only piece ever published, 'Crosses', was to appear in the *A.I.F. News* (Cairo, 13 September 1941) after his death. By the mid-1930s Gray was employed as senior stockman at Anna Plains station. A respected racehorse-trainer, he won the Port Hedland and Marble Bar cups on several occasions. In addition, he owned thirty stockhorses and was in demand throughout the region for his droving skills. His gentle and patient techniques as a horse-breaker were unorthodox but effective; one of his friends noted that the quicker, harsher methods of other breakers produced animals with mouths like mules and temperaments to match.

For an Aboriginal Australian of the time, Gray was relatively affluent. Most Aborigines only entered the homes of Whites as domestic servants, yet he was a welcome dinner-guest from Port Hedland to Derby, appreciated for his generosity of spirit, sense of humour and philosophical bent. He lived with Yarni at Anna Plains, and had a son Donald and a daughter Winnie; with Josie Roe from Broome, he had a son Tom.

In 1935 Gray was hired to accompany a party of police which trekked some 3000 miles (4800 km) through inhospitable country pursuing those who had murdered a dogger Daniel O'Brien in the Great Sandy Desert. Gray acted as quartermaster, tracker, stockhandler, pathfinder and—in concert with the police blacktrackers—intermediary between the policemen and nomadic Aborigines. He was also instrumental in the arrest of one of the killers.

On 10 August 1940 Gray enlisted in the Australian Imperial Force. Having trained at Northam, he sailed for the Middle East in April 1941 as a reinforcement for the 2nd/16th Battalion. Comrades in camp and the troop-ship recalled that he recited poetry, including A. B. Paterson's [q.v.11] 'The Man From Snowy River' and Rudyard Kipling's 'If—', and remembered his exploits at two-up. He joined the battalion on 16 June in Syria. In his short time with the unit he became 'quite the most loved man among us'.

Following fierce fighting against Vichy French forces around Damour, Lebanon, Gray was leading prisoners back to his lines on 6 July 1941 when he was killed by fire from a machine-gun post. He was buried in the Beirut 1939-1945 war cemetery.

M. Uren, *A Thousand Men at War* (Melb, 1959); J. Hardie, *Nor'Westers of the Pilbara Breed* (Port Hedland, WA, 1981); R. Hall, *The Black Diggers* (Syd, 1989); *Boomerang* (Perth), 31 Aug 1942; *Daily News* (Perth), 28 Dec 1935; AN 5/3, Police Dept Acc 430, file 6862/1935 (waa); information from Mr S. Gray, Mrs L. Stearne, Mrs J. Ballinger, Mr K. Norrish, Mr P. Carew-Reid and Mr F. Cousens, care of author, Yanchep, WA.

ROD MORAN

GREAVES, FLORENCE TURNER; *see* BLAKE, FLORENCE

GREAVES, WILLIAM CLEMENT (1897-1973), grazier, was born on 10 September 1897 at Monomeith, Victoria, third child of William Clement Greaves [q.v.9 E. Greaves], grazier, and his wife Mary Flora, née McLellan, both Victorian born. The family was prominent in pastoral, agricultural and church affairs. Young Will attended Scotch College, East Melbourne, then helped to manage his father's Gippsland properties during World War I. On 7 March 1929 at St Andrew's Presbyterian Church, Geelong, he married Margaret Marion Morrison Sanderson; they settled at Caldermeade, a homestead originally built by the pioneer Alexander Macmillan which developed into a showplace with its avenue of lambertiana pines and its extensive hawthorn hedgerows.

In 1925-59 Greaves was a member of the Cranbourne Shire Council (president 1928-29, 1936-37, 1946-47 and 1954-55). His wide knowledge of the people and history of the district, coupled with his financial insight, helped to create a prosperous rural community of which he became elder statesman.

His civic interests extended beyond the shire. An executive-member of the Gippsland Municipalities Association, he took a prominent role in its affairs, including sponsoring Charles Daley's *The Story of Gippsland* (1960). Greaves was also president of the West Gippsland Regional Committee and served on many local deputations and committees. Like his father, he was a director and leading shareholder in the Gippsland & Northern Co-operative Co. Ltd and a staunch believer in producer co-operatives.

Reared from boyhood in the traditions of the Royal Agricultural Society of Victoria, Greaves followed his father on its council in 1937 (vice-president 1951-54), and was a prominent figure in the ring during showtime as well as a successful exhibitor. In 1959 he led a journalists' tour of Gippsland, run by the R.A.S. He was twice president of the British Sheep Breeders' Association of Victoria, and a councillor on its federal body. A regular judge of cattle, sheep and horses at shows throughout the Commonwealth, he was president (1924-26, 1933-34) of the Lang Lang show committee, and promoted and supplied cattle to the Lang Lang rodeos in 1943-65. He was appointed O.B.E. in 1960.

A kindly, earnest man, Greaves also had the decisive authoritarian bearing of the well-regulated landholder. He was superintendent (1919-59) of the Lang Lang (Presbyterian) Sunday School and a president of the Kooweerup (later Westernport) Memorial Hospital. In 1955, when he was shire president, a photograph was taken of him with his three sisters, presidents respectively of the local Presbyterian Guild, the Country Women's Association's arts and drama committee, and the Woman's Christian Temperance Union of Victoria. His son Mac (William McLellan) succeeded him on the shire council and was its president in 1962-63. Will Greaves continued to fatten cattle and breed Border Leicester sheep at Caldermeade until retiring to the Melbourne suburb of Oakleigh in 1967. Survived by his wife, daughter and two of his three sons, he died on 9 August 1973 at Malvern and was buried in Lang Lang cemetery.

N. Gunson, *The Good Country* (Melb, 1968); J. Ridgway and J. Lowden, *Rodeo at Lang Lang* (Kilmore, Vic, 1976); *Herald* (Melb), 12 May 1959; *Kooweerup Sun*, 22 July, 5, 19 Aug 1959, 12 Sept 1962; *Korumburra Times*, 19 Aug 1959; *Country Leader*, 4 Sept 1959; *G & N Co-Operator*, 22 July 1965.

NIEL GUNSON

GREEN, CHARLES HERCULES (1919-1950), army officer, was born on 26 December 1919 at Grafton, New South Wales, second of three children of Hercules John

Green, dairy-farmer, and his wife Bertha, née Deville, both native-born. Educated at Swan Creek Public and Grafton High schools, he began working for his father in 1933. Young Charlie showed initiative and enterprise by acquiring two draught-horses to undertake ploughing and road-building contracts. On 28 October 1936 he enlisted in the 41st Battalion, Militia; he rose to sergeant in 1938 and lieutenant in March 1939. A keen horseman and cricketer, he was 6 ft (183 cm) tall, with brown hair, a dark complexion and brown eyes.

Seconded to the Australian Imperial Force on 13 October 1939, Green was posted to the 2nd/2nd Battalion. He was based in the Middle East from February 1940, but missed the operations in North Africa (December 1940-January 1941) due to an accidental injury. His initiation into battle occurred on 18 April at the Piniós Gorge, Greece. In the subsequent retreat he evaded capture, made a hazardous journey through the Aegean Islands and Turkey, and reached Palestine by 23 May. These experiences proved formative, and he was to contribute a sensitive account of the campaign in Greece to *Nulli Secundus Log* (Sydney, 1946). A fellow officer recalled that the 'Troops would follow Charlie anywhere because he understood them and they understood he was fair dinkum'; another soldier remembered how Green had carefully explained tactics to his men, his cool demeanour and husky voice conveying reassurance.

The 2nd/2nd spent periods of garrison duty in Syria and Ceylon (Sri Lanka), then returned to Australia in August 1942. Because Green had injured his foot and contracted typhoid in Ceylon he did not take part in the Papuan campaign. He was promoted substantive major in September and posted in December as an instructor to the First Army's Junior Tactical School, Southport, Queensland. At St Paul's Anglican Church, Ulmarra, New South Wales, on 30 January 1943 he married Edna Olwyn Warner; Colonel (Sir) Frederick Chilton, his commander in Greece, was best man.

Resuming regimental duties in July 1943, Green was seen as the 'natural successor' to Lieutenant Colonel C. R. V. Edgar [q.v.] in command of the 2nd/2nd, but the appointment went to an outsider, Lieutenant Colonel A. G. Cameron [q.v.13]. Green's selection as second-in-command helped to ease tensions. In December 1944 the unit embarked for New Guinea. Promoted temporary lieutenant colonel on 9 March 1945 (substantive in September), Green was given command of the 2nd/11th Battalion; at the age of 25 he was probably the youngest officer to command an Australian battalion in World War II. Between May and July the 2nd/11th participated in the attack on Wewak and in operations around Boram. Green was awarded the Distinguished Service Order (1947).

He was demobilized on 23 November 1945, but found that the transition to civilian life was not easy. Returning to Grafton, he worked as a clerk with the Producers' Co-operative Distributing Society Ltd, studied accountancy part time and from April 1948 commanded his old Militia battalion. On 6 January 1949 he joined the Permanent Military Forces. When the government committed the 3rd Battalion, Royal Australian Regiment, to the conflict in Korea, Army Headquarters decided that it should be led by an officer with a distinguished record in World War II. Green was plucked from the course at the Staff College, Queenscliff, Victoria, and sent to Japan on 8 September 1950 to take command.

Moving to the Republic of (South) Korea that month, the Australian unit formed part of the 27th British Commonwealth Brigade. 3RAR advanced northwards, defeating enemy forces at Yongju on 22 October, at Pakch'on, Democratic People's Republic of (North) Korea, on the 25th-26th, and at Chongju on the 28th. Next day the battalion repulsed a North Korean counter-attack and occupied positions on a ridge overlooking the Talch'on River. During the evening of the 30th an enemy shell exploded near Green's tent, severely wounding him in the abdomen. His death on 1 November 1950 'cast a pall of gloom over his battalion'. He was buried in the United Nations memorial cemetery, Pusan, South Korea. His wife and daughter survived him. The United States of America awarded him the Silver Star (1951).

Green's career as a commander had been exemplary, and serving soldiers are still inspired by it. A cairn at the 41st Battalion's barracks, Lismore, commemorates him, as does a United Nations emblem on the gates to the Swan Creek farm where he spent his youth.

G. Long, *Greece, Crete and Syria* (Canb, 1953) and *The Final Campaigns* (Canb, 1963); S. Wick, *Purple Over Green* (Syd, 1977); R. O'Neill, *Australia in the Korean War 1950-53*, 2 (Canb, 1985); O. Green, *The name's still Charlie* (Brisb, 1993); M. Barter, *Far Above Battle* (Syd, 1994); J. Galloway, *The Last Call of the Bugle* (Brisb, 1994); information from Mr R. Argent, Syd.   MARGARET BARTER

GREEN, FRANK CLIFTON (1890-1974), parliamentary clerk, was born on 26 June 1890 at Mole Creek, Tasmania, son of Joseph Richard Green, schoolteacher, and his wife Kate Elizabeth, née Reardon. As a boy, Frank knew life in the bush, both in the Western Tiers and the Huon Valley, an upbringing which shaped his character. Educated at Cygnet State School and at Queen's College, Hobart, he entered the Crown Law Department in 1909. Two years later he was appointed clerk-assistant in the House of Assembly. Meanwhile, he made a name for himself as a footballer and cricketer. A socialist, he was moved more by sentiment than doctrine. His literary interests were formed by Rudyard Kipling, Hilaire Belloc and G. K. Chesterton, and later supplemented by the poets of World War I. At St Joseph's Catholic Church, Hobart, on 29 April 1914 he married Florence Agnes Kearney.

On 2 September 1915 Green enlisted in the Australian Imperial Force and was posted to the 40th Battalion. He was commissioned in January 1916, sailed for England in July, reached the Western Front in November and was promoted captain in May 1917. For his work, especially in the offensive at Messines, Belgium, in June, he was awarded the Military Cross. After his A.I.F. appointment terminated on 7 October 1919, his commander Sir John Gellibrand [q.v.8] arranged for him to write *The Fortieth: A Record of the 40th Battalion, A.I.F.* (1922). Green's war experience profoundly affected his outlook and strengthened his faith in egalitarianism.

Having resumed work at parliament in October 1919, he fell out with a minister and transferred to the Federal parliament on 1 April 1921 as clerk of papers. Green became a close friend of Frank Anstey [q.v.7], but was shocked by the sectarian violence in Melbourne and by the repercussions of the expulsion from parliament in November 1920 of Irish-born Hugh Mahon [q.v.10]. In 1925 Green was appointed clerk of records. Following the Federal parliament's move to Canberra in 1927, two clerks of the House, W. A. Gale [q.v.8] and J. R. McGregor, died in quick succession, and Green was promoted clerk-assistant under E. W. Parkes. Unlike most people, he took the change from city to bush easily and found recreation in fly-fishing and rabbit-shooting, through which he made many friends, including politicians, bureaucrats, pressmen and trade union officials.

Green welcomed his old friend Joe Lyons [q.v.10] to Canberra, following Labor's election in 1929, but, as the Depression deepened, he watched with dismay as the Scullin [q.v.11] government stumbled to defeat in December 1931. Privy to Lyons's growing disillusionment, he said he understood why Lyons crossed the floor. During the 1930s Green's conviction grew that parliament was in decline. More than ever he sought solace in the bush. In 1937 he became clerk of the House. He saw Lyons's government crumble and his health deteriorate under the weight of events and faction-fighting. Green never got on well with (Sir)

Robert Menzies [q.v.]. Some thought him indiscreet in making friends among members of the press gallery and with communist trade union officials such as Ernest Thornton and James Healy [qq.v.]. Gregarious and a great raconteur, by this time Green was a popular figure of Rabelaisian strength. When World War II broke out and members of his staff (among them Jack Pettifer and Gordon Reid) enlisted, he protected their interests. He gave moral support to his friend John Curtin [q.v.13], especially in 1942 while the prime minister endured sleepless nights dwelling on the safety of Australian troops returning from the Middle East.

From 1945 Green watched Ben Chifley's [q.v.13] struggle for stability amid industrial strife, ideological differences and growing dissension in the Labor Party. The return of Menzies in 1949 further dispirited him. From then on it was all downhill—the controversy over the proposed dissolution of the Communist Party of Australia, the Petrov affair, and the gaoling of Frank Browne and Raymond Fitzpatrick [q.v.] for breach of parliamentary privilege. The death of Green's son (an only child) in a drowning accident was the worst blow. In 1953 he had dutifully attended the coronation of Queen Elizabeth II in London. He retired in June 1955 and returned to Hobart. In 1959 he was appointed C.B.E.

President (1961-64) of the local branch of the Royal Society for the Prevention of Cruelty to Animals, and an active conservationist, Green was also founding chairman of the Australian Dictionary of Biography's Tasmanian working party. He edited *A Century of Responsible Government: 1856-1956 (Tasmania)* (1956), and wrote *The Tasmanian Club, 1861-1961* (1961) and his memoirs, *Servant of the House* (Melbourne, 1969). Survived by his wife, he died on 12 September 1974 at New Town and was cremated.

E. Lyons, *So We Take Comfort* (Lond, 1965); R. Gibson, *My Years in the Communist Party* (Melb, 1966); L. Haylen, *Twenty Years' Hard Labor* (Melb, 1969); *People*, 7 June 1950; *Hemisphere*, 3, Dec 1969; *VHM*, 46, no 1, Feb 1975; *Canb Times*, 4 June 1955, 13 Sept 1974; *SMH*, 13 Sept 1955; *Mercury* (Hob), 13 Sept 1974; Green papers (TA); personal information.   W. A. TOWNSLEY

GREEN, HAROLD GODFREY (1909-1978), research journalist and indexer, was born on 29 November 1909 at Kalgoorlie, Western Australia, son of Solomon Aaron Green, an electrical engineer from London, and his Adelaide-born wife Alice Maude, née Jacobs. As a child, Harry lived in Melbourne with his impoverished, widowed mother and was educated (1919-24) at Melbourne

Church of England Grammar School, possibly through the generosity of Sol Solomon, her wealthy and close relation.

Sixteen years employment with David Syme [q.v.6] & Co. Ltd was interrupted on 2 June 1941 when Green enlisted in the Australian Military Forces. He performed clerical duties in Australia and was promoted corporal before being discharged on 21 May 1946. At Wesley Church, Melbourne, on 7 November 1953 he married Stephanie Taylor (1891-1974), an artist who had studied at the National Gallery school, and who lectured on art on the radio and at the National Gallery of Victoria. In 1955-60 Green organized and administered the *Age*'s reference library.

As his career developed, Green worked mainly in the establishment of efficient information-retrieval systems for a variety of employers, including the Commonwealth Department of Shipping and Transport, the Municipal Officers' Association of Australia and several large commercial companies. In 1971 he joined the Commonwealth Department of Trade and Industry as a research journalist; he retired in 1974, after establishing a comprehensive cataloguing system. He was a member of the Australian Journalists' Association and the Library Association of Australia.

Throughout his working life Green indexed books as a part-time interest. He was employed by many publishers, among them Butterworth & Co. Ltd, Thomas Nelson Australia Pty Ltd, Oxford University Press and Sun Books Pty Ltd. His enthusiasm led him to establish an Australian branch of the Society of Indexers in 1971; next year he became the society's Australian corresponding member and organized correspondence courses in indexing. He was chairman (1971-75) of the Society of Indexers in Australia (Australian Society of Indexers from 1976). Following his retirement, Green continued indexing, and writing historical novels, none of which was published. At the Methodist Church, Glen Iris, on 18 October 1975 he married Maud Ethel Myers, née Waite, a 65-year-old widow. They moved from Melbourne to live at Maryborough.

A quiet, self-effacing man with a gentle personality, H. Godfrey Green earned the respect of those who knew him. His colleagues valued his efficient and meticulous record-keeping and indexing. Of the latter he once wrote: 'Book indexing is a stimulating and satisfactory vocation with adequate rewards and a sense of personal satisfaction. The indexer's task is the important one of producing what might be described as a guide to a book without which the book is almost useless. His job is a lonely one, like that of a poet or an author'.

Green died of a ruptured aortic aneurysm on 24 April 1978 at Maryborough and was cremated; his wife survived him.

Aust Soc of Indexers Newsletter, Sept 1978; *Age*, 26 Apr 1974; information from Mrs S. Hatcliffe, California Gully, Vic.   MARJORIE MORGAN

GREEN, HENRY MACKENZIE (1881-1962), journalist, librarian and literary historian, was born on 2 May 1881 at his grandfather's home, Ecclesbourne, Double Bay, Sydney, eldest of seven children of native-born parents George Henry Green, bank manager, and his wife Agnes Isabella, daughter of James Norton [q.v.5]. He was also descended from a number of early pioneers, among them John Blaxland, Alexander Kenneth McKenzie and Thomas Walker [qq.v.1,2]. Harry attended (1890-98) All Saints College, Bathurst; he was dux of the school, distinguished himself in sport and contributed to the school magazine, the *Bathurstian*. At the University of Sydney (B.A., 1902; LL.B., 1905) he graduated with first-class honours in logic and mental philosophy. President of the university union and editor (1905) of *Hermes*, he was awarded a Blue for athletics and was prominent in football, boxing and rowing. He won the university prize for English verse (1903, 1904), the Beauchamp [q.v.7] prize for an English essay (1904, 1906, 1907) and the Wentworth [q.v.2] medal (1904). In 1907-08 he travelled in Europe, reading, writing and studying art, music and drama. He was admitted to the Bar in Sydney on 24 February 1908, but never practised.

Beginning work (for thirty shillings a week) in 1909 with the *Sydney Morning Herald*, where C. E. W. Bean [q.v.7] was a colleague, Green was employed by the *Daily Telegraph* in 1910-20. Although 'Saturday's work was fairly easy and Sunday's quite easy', he discovered that his hours had no limit. Nevertheless, he appreciated the rigorous training in accuracy, speed and versatility that he received, particularly from Charles Theakstone of the *Herald* and F. W. Ward [q.v.12] of the *Telegraph*, and progressed to writing leading articles and book reviews. At St Mark's Anglican Church, Darling Point, on 9 August 1911 he had married Maria Eleanor Watson, a university graduate who shared his literary interests; they were to have two daughters. 'Sundays' at their Killara home became a meeting-place for poets, novelists, academic colleagues and students.

In 1911 the Australian Journalists' Association was formed. Green helped to draft the constitution of the New South Wales branch and retained a long-term relationship with the association. Responsible for 'War Notes' (1914-17) in the *Telegraph*, he published short stories, articles, literary criticism and verse in the *Bulletin, Hermes, New Triad* and the *Lone Hand*; his work later appeared in the *Australian Quarterly* and *Australian Highway*. On 25 March 1918 he enlisted in the Australian Imperial Force; he embarked for Europe on 14 October but only reached Cape Town when the Armistice was signed; characteristically, while at sea he drew on the ship's company to produce a literary magazine, the *Wyreemian.*

Green succeeded John Le Gay Brereton [q.v.7] as librarian at the University of Sydney in 1921. Extraordinarily energetic, he built up the Australian holdings of the Fisher [q.v.4] Library virtually from scratch, often searching in second-hand bookshops, establishing valuable archives and maintaining communication with numerous Australian writers. The professional standing of the library increased markedly during his administration; academic qualifications were made a condition of permanent appointment; and the Fisher was probably the first Australian library to make use of microphotography.

Prominent in Sydney's literary circles, Green belonged to the Casuals Club. He knew C. J. Brennan, Arthur Adams, Miles Franklin, (Dame) Mary Gilmore, A. G. Stephens and Bertram Stevens [qq.v.7,8,9,11], and enjoyed close relationships with Hugh McCrae [q.v.10], Brereton and R. D. FitzGerald. Living at Killara allowed him to indulge his love of the bush and outdoor activities, and he frequently undertook long bush walks in various parts of New South Wales. The effects of these activities were remarked upon by A. D. Hope who recalled Green's large head and 'nordic eye', his 'neat hard frame' and the 'colouring of a man who works a lot with his hands and spends time out of doors'; Louis Kahan's sketch, first published in *Meanjin* (1961), emphasized the same youthful traits.

Librarianship represented merely the core of Green's activities. He delivered university, extension and Workers' Educational Association lectures, gave talks to literary societies such as the Shakespeare Society of New South Wales and the Australian English Association, marked essays and corrected papers for university and public examinations, judged competitions on literary subjects, and belonged to the British Drama League, the Fellowship of Australian Writers and the Sydney P.E.N. Club. In addition, he regularly spoke on radio for the Australian Broadcasting Commission, and was president (1941-43) of the Australian Institute of Librarians and patron of the Australian English Association. When the Commonwealth Literary Fund lectures were established in 1940, Green was one of the handful of lecturers with any thorough knowledge of Australian litera-

ture whose talents were employed. Meanwhile, much of his lecturing was unpaid or underpaid, a condition that he deplored but tolerated.

By 1930 Green's lectures on Australian literature were recognized as a required part of a university course. In 1933 he applied for the chair of English literature at the university; despite support from some influential individuals, he was unsuccessful. Besides his uncollected short stories, essays and articles, Green's publications were extensive. Poetry was his first interest, but he wrote at least one unpublished novel, 'The Aluminium God', and was represented in *Australian Short Stories* (1928), edited by George Mackaness [q.v.10]. Green's verse was collected in two volumes, *The Happy Valley* (1925) and *The Book of Beauty* (London, 1929), which were well received by his contemporaries: P. R. Stephensen [q.v.12] described *The Book of Beauty* as 'a significant episode in the evolution of Australian consciousness'; other friends made flattering comparisons with Yeats and Keats. In later life Green retained a keen interest in the genre, recognizing and encouraging younger poets such as Hope. Green also edited the 1943 volume in Angus & Robertson [qq.v.7,11] Ltd's annual *Australian Poetry* collections, as well as *Modern Australian Poetry* (1946). His critical and historical writing included *The Story of Printing* (1929); with (Sir) John Ferguson [q.v.] and Mrs A. G. Foster, *The Howes and their Press* (1936); five lectures, *Australian Literature: A Summary* (1928), *The Poetry of W. B. Yeats* (1931), *A Midsummer Night's Dream* (1933), *Kendall* (1933) and *Wentworth as Orator* (1935); a study of Brennan (1939); and *Fourteen Minutes* (1944), a collection of his own radio talks.

Green divorced Eleanor in 1944. On 16 May that year, at the district registrar's office, Ashfield, he married 28-year-old Dorothy Auchterlounie, a poet and future literary critic; they lived at Glenbrook in the Blue Mountains and were to have a son and a daughter. After Green retired in 1946, he received a pension of £312, augmented in 1951 by a small C.L.F. pension. The family moved to Melbourne when Dorothy began lecturing at Monash University in 1961.

To this point, Green's most significant contribution as a literary historian was *An Outline of Australian Literature* (Sydney, 1930) which provided a more comprehensive and chronologically more extensive view of the field than Nettie Palmer's [q.v.11] *Modern Australian Literature* (1924). Concentrating on creative writing from the beginning of European settlement to 1928, Green drew on years of research and personal experience, discussing such little known writers as Henry Handel Richardson [q.v.11], establishing numerous pioneer judgements which have largely stood the test of time, and demonstrating a variety which amazed contemporary *cognoscenti*. From 1939 to 1951 he contributed an annual survey of Australian literature to *Southerly* and in 1951 published *Australian Literature 1900-1950*.

His two-volume *A History of Australian Literature Pure and Applied* eventually emerged in 1961. By 1954 the manuscript had been completed to 1950, but was so delayed in publication that Green added short accounts of later works up to 1960. In the dedication he acknowledged his wife's contribution in their remarkable literary partnership, conceding that her 'critical suggestions, not always received with due gratitude, have made all the difference'.

In her 1984-85 revision, Dorothy described the *History* as 'a primary source'; by then it had become part of the literature it studied. A cornerstone of all later histories, it concentrated on creative writing and emphasized the links between Australian and European culture, but it also included critical surveys of the literature of science, psychology, economics, philosophy, journalism, history, biography, travel and reminiscence; if these aspects appeared quaint and old-fashioned in the critical climate of the 1960s, they have regained their appeal.

A man of his time, particularly in his dual allegiance to Britain and Australia, Green became more radical in his social views in old age. His students and colleagues remembered him as 'impulsive and generous, irascible at times, but scrupulously fair'. He was noted for his drive, energy and gusto, and his forceful but kindly personality. Survived by his wife and the children of both his marriages, Green died on 9 September 1962 at Box Hill and was cremated with Anglican rites; his estate was sworn for probate at £1037.

W. A. Steel and C. W. Sloman, *The History of All Saints' College, Bathurst, 1873-1934* (Syd, 1936); *Meanjin Q*, 20, no 4, Dec 1961, pp 431, 441; Univ Syd Union, *Union Recorder*, 42, 11 Oct 1962, p 227; *Aust Book Review*, 1, no 6, June 1962, p 48; *Aust Lib J*, 12, Mar 1963, p 53; *Overland*, 83, Apr 1981, p 60; *Island Mag*, 33, 1987, p 51; *SMH*, 7 Mar 1947, 5 Apr 1921, 11 Sept 1962, 30 Mar 1985; *Age* (Melb), 20 Jan, 10 Sept 1962, 2 May 1981; D. Green ms collection (Aust Defence Force Academy L, Canb); D. Green papers *and* H. M. Green correspondence (NL); D. and H. M. Green papers (restricted and unsorted, NL); family information.

JOY HOOTON

GREEN, ISOBEL ALICE; *see* MENZIES, FRANK GLADSTONE

GREEN, WILLIAM ALLAN McINNES (1896-1972), civil engineer and town clerk, was born on 24 January 1896 at Port Adelaide, son of Thompson Green, riveter, and his wife Margaret, née Kelly. Educated at Adelaide High School, Allan joined the South Australian Railways on 11 March 1914 as a draftsman. He enlisted in the Australian Imperial Force on 20 March 1916, served on the Western Front in 1917-18 with the 2nd Tunnelling Company and was promoted temporary sergeant in January 1919. Following his discharge in Adelaide on 27 February 1920, he resumed his former employment, while studying part time at the South Australian School of Mines and Industries and at the University of Adelaide (B.Eng., 1928).

Resigning from the railways on 9 June 1928, Green became designer and computer to the Adelaide City Council. He was associated with the design of many large works, assisted in the reconstruction of the city's markets and baths, and provided advice on amending the State's building codes. On 5 April 1932 he married Edyth Irene Thomas with Congregational forms at the Stow [q.v.2] Memorial Church, Adelaide. An associate-member (1932) of the Institution of Engineers, Australia, and an associate (1934) of the Royal Australian Institute of Architects (fellow, 1945), he moved to Tasmania in 1934 as assistant-engineer, architect and building surveyor to the City of Launceston where he designed a number of public buildings and remodelled the town hall.

On 17 May 1937 Green was appointed building surveyor to the Perth City Council. In October 1945 he formally succeeded W. E. Bold [q.v.7] as town clerk. Public criticism of Bold's administration, chiefly stemming from D. L. Davidson [q.v.13], the commissioner for town planning, had culminated in 1938 in a royal commission which found that Bold had grown careless in his responsibilities. Green's appointment was intended to restore credibility to the office of town clerk and to revive the spirit of planning in the State. Gifted with a breadth of knowledge, sincerity and a great capacity for industry, Green grew to understand how the City of Perth operated. In 1952 he toured Europe and North America, and saw for himself what could be done by decisive civic action.

With Green's encouragement, Professor Gordon Stephenson (from England) and J. A. Hepburn prepared an ambitious exercise in regional planning: published as an advisory plan in 1955, their report formed the basis of the Perth Metropolitan Region Scheme (1963). Meanwhile, it was Green's confidence that the city could build the basic sporting venues—a stadium, a swimming pool and a residential village—that made Perth's bid for the 1962 British Empire and

Commonwealth Games a successful one. He then took a leading role in marshalling the city's resources, in co-ordinating and supervising the works programme, and in designing the Perry Lakes Stadium and the Beatty Park Aquatic Centre.

As town clerk and Perth's chief executive-officer, Green was renowned for his ability to master long and complex agendas. It was said that his will lay behind every important decision. Green was generally inaccessible to the press. He argued that, since he could always make his views known to the Perth City Council, there was no need for him to be in the public eye. The absence of overt party politics in local government in the council favoured his no-nonsense, straightforward approach. As an engineer he was quick to grasp essentials, as an architect he had a flair for seeing things as a whole, and as an administrator he believed in thorough preparation and research. He was either the designer or the adviser for practically every building constructed by the city council between 1944 and 1966. In 1963 he was appointed C.M.G. His appointment was extended to 1966, by when he was three years beyond the stipulated age for retirement. He was Western Australia's most experienced, qualified and versatile local government officer.

Green was a kindly, perceptive, articulate and resolute man who, in serving the city council to which he was devoted, found a congenial place in which to develop and practise his talents. He died on 5 September 1972 at Shenton Park and was cremated with Anglican rites; his wife and two daughters survived him.

Local Government J of WA, 1972, p 14; M. Webb 'The Inaugural Allan McInnes Green Oration', *Local Government Administration* (Perth), 20, no 13, 1983, p 17; *Daily News* (Perth), 24 Feb 1960, 14 Jan, 28 July 1962; *West Australian*, 24 Feb 1966, 8 Sept 1972; Perth City Council, staff files, W. A. McI. Green (WAA).   MARTYN WEBB

GREENAWAY, SIR THOMAS MOORE (1902-1980), physician, was born on 1 June 1902 at Kogarah, Sydney, eldest of four sons of native-born parents Thomas Clarence Greenaway, mason's labourer, and his wife Dorothy Mary, née Lawrence. Educated at North Sydney Boys' High School, young Thomas claimed to be 19-year-old Reginald Thomas Gordon Greenaway when he enlisted in the Australian Imperial Force on 18 May 1918. Reaching Britain after the Armistice, he was briefly stationed in France with the 3rd Battalion in 1919.

Back home, Greenaway entered the University of Sydney (M.B., Ch.M., 1925); he was president (1923) of the undergraduates'

association, won the A. E. Mills [q.v.10] prize for medicine in his final examinations and tutored at St Andrew's College in 1927-28. At Royal Prince Alfred Hospital he was resident medical officer (1925-26) and medical registrar (1926-27). On 26 November 1927 he married Lavinia Figtree at St James's Anglican Church, Sydney. In 1928 he joined (Sir) Charles McDonald's [q.v.] general practice at Hurstville. Greenaway was appointed honorary clinical assistant at R.P.A.H. that year and honorary assistant-physician in 1929.

In 1934 he sailed to London where he attended courses, did the rounds—particularly at Guy's Hospital—and gained membership of the Royal College of Physicians (fellow 1951). On his return to Sydney, he practised as a consultant in Macquarie Street. He had been appointed captain, Australian Army Medical Corps, Militia, in 1925. Promoted major in 1932, he was honorary consulting physician to two army hospitals during World War II. Meanwhile, he conducted his busy practice and maintained his unit at the R.P.A.H. In 1948 he became a senior honorary physician at the hospital and was to hold that position until he reached the retiring age of 60 when he was made honorary consulting physician. Although he supported the postwar development of special units in R.P.A.H.'s department of medicine, he did not participate to a large extent, remaining a general physician with a specific interest in endocrinology.

A foundation fellow (1938) of the Royal Australasian College of Physicians, Greenaway was a member of its board of censors (examiners) in 1944-58 and censor-in-chief from 1954 to 1958. He upheld the college's standards for admission, while showing candidates the humane side of the examiners. Following terms as honorary treasurer (1949-50), member of the executive-committee (1949-50 and 1954-63) and councillor (1949-54), he was president of the college in 1960-62. He served on its New South Wales committee from 1949 to 1964.

In addition, Greenaway was a member of the board of directors of R.P.A.H. (1953-73), of the Medical Board (1963-73) and of the council of the State branch of the British Medical Association (1941-44). He tutored (1932-48), then lectured (until 1962), in clinical medicine at the University of Sydney, besides attending to his hospital duties. Although his primary association was with R.P.A.H., he was also a consulting physician at the St George, Ryde and Marrickville hospitals. In 1968 he was made an honorary fellow of the Royal Australian College of General Practitioners. He was knighted that year.

Greenaway's few publications were clinical rather than scientific, but he appreciated the importance of clinical science, and a number of laboratory tests were routinely performed in his rooms. As medicine grew more technologically based, his example and teaching ensured that the patient was never forgotten. He was a superb practitioner of clinical medicine and set high standards. Those close to him, including students, residents and registrars, greatly enjoyed the association, and his rounds were popular and inspiring.

A tall man who retained his youthful good looks, Greenaway was erudite, engaging and witty. His charm was matched by his dedication and by a deep appreciation of the needs of his patients. That he was cultured and able to relax enhanced his professional worth. In his early years he had attended church regularly. He was able to quote from the Bible, and had a wide knowledge of literature, especially of Shakespeare. From 1940 to 1952 he lived at Cronulla and played tennis on Sunday afternoons at his home; he belonged to the Australian, Royal Sydney Golf and Elanora Country clubs.

About 1960 Greenaway began to suffer from Parkinson's disease. Aided by medical and surgical treatment, and exhibiting great courage, he continued to see patients until 1977. He died on 30 October 1980 at Terrey Hills and was cremated. His youngest brother Lawrence, who had entered the Anglican ministry after retiring from the Royal Australian Air Force, conducted the memorial service in R.P.A.H. chapel. Sir Thomas was survived by his wife, two daughters and son John who became a senior physician at the R.P.A.H. Graeme Inson's portrait of Greenaway is held by the R.A.C.P.

Munk's Roll, Royal College of Physicians (Lond, 1984); G. L. McDonald (ed), *Roll of the Royal Australasian College of Physicians*, 2 (Syd, 1994); *MJA*, 16 May 1981; funeral address by Dr G. L. McDonald *and* other records (archives of Roy A'sian College of Physicians, Syd); information from Dr J. M. Greenaway, Syd.   ROBERT A. B. HOLLAND

GREEN[E], ALICE JANE (1863-1966), headmistress, and ANNE ELIZA (1869-1954), artist, were born on 26 July 1863 and 27 September 1869 at Bridport, Dorset, England, second and fifth of eleven children of John Ily Green, master carpenter, and his wife Ellen Webber, née Greenham. Devoutly Methodist, the family later moved to Cardiff, Wales, where most of the children were educated. Alice qualified at the London Day Training College and taught at a large secondary school in Wales. Anne studied at the Battersea Training School, London, before they both emigrated to Queensland in 1892 with other members of the family to join their father who had preceded them three years

earlier. Alice was appointed to the staff of Rockhampton Girls' Grammar School; in 1895 she and Anne established a private school at Tenterfield, New South Wales. In January 1901 they founded the Moreton Bay High School for Girls, at Wynnum, Brisbane; their father had designed and built the three-storey wooden premises overlooking the bay.

While she was teaching at the school, Anne pursued her career as an artist. She studied at Brisbane Technical College under Godfrey Rivers [q.v.11] and in 1911 travelled to England. In London she attended the South Kensington Art School, and was awarded a prize for still life, a diploma and a medal by the Royal Society of Arts. In 1912 she visited Paris where she met Emile Jacques-Dalcroze, founder of a pedagogic system of eurhythmics. After her return, Moreton Bay schoolgirls gave a public display of eurhythmics in the presence of the governor Sir Matthew Nathan [q.v.10].

Back in Paris in 1924, Anne established her own studio, and became an associate-member (1924) and member (1928) of the Société Nationale des Beaux-Arts. She exhibited regularly at the Petit Salon, and at the New Salon from 1921 until 1939. Her work was given some prominence and bought by collectors. Like her close friend Bessie Gibson [q.v.8], she often painted in the Impressionist manner. Anne spent World War II in England, setting up a studio at Southampton and exhibiting at the Royal Academy. Ill health forced her to return to Queensland in 1946. Better known in France and, to a lesser extent, in Britain, she held her first Australian exhibition at Finney's Art Gallery, Brisbane, in 1950. She died on 2 July 1954 at Wynnum and was buried in Bulimba cemetery. Her work is held by the Queensland Art Gallery, and is represented in major institutional and private collections.

From 1901 Alice had been headmistress of Moreton Bay High, a select secondary school, fully-owned and ultimately operated by the Greene sisters who had added a final e to their surname. Initially accepting no more than thirty pupils, they provided education for the daughters of country families and missionaries, and took a few day-girls. A kindergarten and primary section were added later. Boarders might be as young as 5 or 6, and many returned home only for Christmas. In 1910 a new wing, including a library, was built. Following Anne's departure in 1911, three other sisters joined the staff. Moreton Bay High claimed to have one of the first music schools in Queensland—housed in a separate building; it was directed by Hilda, a piano teacher, who held a licentiate (1909) from the Royal Academy of Music, London, and was an associate-member of the Royal

College of Music. Elsie Greene taught French and mathematics; when Alice retired in December 1943, Elsie was appointed acting principal. Helah managed the domestic arrangements, and taught violin and cello. Instruction was pursued with initiative and openness to advanced methods, but, as far as Alice was concerned, 'it was the business of every girl to aim for correct vowel sound'.

The Greene family was prominent in Wynnum and Brisbane society. Two brothers, Samuel and John, were mayors of Wynnum, the former in 1913 and 1917, the latter in 1922. Samuel was an alderman (1938-41) and John was lord mayor (1931-34) of Greater Brisbane City Council. Alice belonged to numerous committees and worthy organizations, and was instrumental in founding a local ladies' swimming club. In 1945 the school was presented to the Methodist Church and subsequently incorporated (as Moreton Bay College) in the Presbyterian and Methodist Schools Association. 'Strong, loving and gracious', Alice died on 8 January 1966 at Wynnum and was cremated.

Wynnum Jubilee Celebrations Souvenir (np, nd); Wynnum District Chamber of Commerce, *Back to Wynnum* (Wynnum, Qld, 1933); J. A. Watts, *Exhibition of Pictures in Oils by Anne Alison Greene*, cat (Brisb, 1950); V. Lahey, *Art in Queensland, 1859-1959* (Brisb, 1959); Qld Art Gallery, *Five Queensland Women Artists*, exhibition cat (Brisb, 1975); C. Ambrus, *The Ladies' Picture Show* (Syd, 1984); B. Larner and F. Considine, *A Complimentary Caste*, exhibition cat, Centre Gallery, Surfers Paradise, Qld (Surfers Paradise, 1988); Moreton Bay College (Wynnum, Brisb), *Old Moretonian*, 1967; *Queenslander*, 18 June 1921; *Brisb Courier*, 2 July 1927; A. J. A. Greene, The Founders Speak, no 6 (ts of radio broadcast on 4QR, 11 Dec 1945, held by OL).

KEN WALLER

GREENE, ANNE (1884?-1965), known as Mother Mary Gertrude, missionary and nurse, was baptized on 18 May 1884 at Killard (Doonbeg), County Clare, Ireland, ninth of twelve children of Thomas Greene, a farmer of Ballaha, and his wife Bridget, née Clancy. Nothing is known of Anne's early education. Emigrating to Western Australia at about the age of 21, she completed her novitiate at the Convent of St John of God, Subiaco, and took the religious names Mary Gertrude. She trained as a nurse at the Order's hospital and studied midwifery at King Edward Memorial Hospital, Subiaco.

Small and wiry, with soft brown eyes that conveyed compassion, Sister Mary Gertrude ministered as both ward and theatre sister at Subiaco and Kalgoorlie, before nursing for two years at Ballarat, Victoria. In 1929 she volunteered to serve at the Order's foundation in the north of Western Australia where no fewer than four of her siblings had preceded her. Sister Mary Bernadine (baptized Emilia on 11 November 1882, d. 25 February 1923) had gone to the mission at Beagle Bay in June 1907 when the Order first sent volunteers to take charge of the Aboriginal women and girls who had been attracted there by the work of the Cistercian monks and their successors the Pallottine Fathers. Sister Mary Bernadine was joined by her sisters, Sister Mary Matthew (baptized Catherine on 13 September 1881, d. 1 April 1978), Sister Mary Brigid (baptized Susan on 30 April 1879, d. 16 May 1968) and Sister Mary Gabriel (baptized Margaret on 31 July 1886, d. 10 February 1984).

On her arrival in 1929, Sister Mary Gertrude initially taught in the school at Broome, then went to the Beagle Bay mission. The Sisters worked in Spartan conditions, offering health care, education and counselling. Their patients included Aboriginal people suffering from Hansen's bacillus (leprosy). At intervals from 1930 the Sisters offered to staff a leprosarium, if the State government were prepared to establish one in the North-West. Much indecision and lobbying occurred before Sister Mary Gertrude and several Sisters received permission in 1937 to work with 340 patients housed near Derby. Almost one-half of these people proved to be suffering from other diseases and were moved to the Derby Native Hospital for treatment. The Sisters cared for the remainder, alleviating as much distress as possible and brightening the leprosarium with cheerful proficiency. After Broome was attacked by Japanese aircraft on 3 March 1942, they moved with their patients into the bush for two weeks.

In 1947 Sister Gertrude was made provincial superior of the North-West, an appointment that brought with it the title of Mother. Her new responsibilities obliged her to stop working in the leprosarium. Next year she was appointed M.B.E., one of the first secular awards given to a St John of God Sister in Australia. Gentle and quietly spoken, Mother Gertrude served as provincial until 1953, and again in 1956-62, following which she became superior of the St John of God Convent, Derby. Early in 1965 her commitments took her to Broome. She died there on 20 February that year as a result of injuries received in a motorcar accident and was buried in the local cemetery.

M. Durack, *The Rock and the Sand* (Lond, 1969); W. S. Davidson, *Havens of Refuge* (Perth, 1978); *WA Record*, 25 May, 15 June 1907, 2 May 1908, 25 Feb 1965, 24 Feb-1 Mar 1984; *Herald* (Melb), 10 June 1948; *West Australian*, 10 June 1948, 24, 27 Feb 1965; M. A. Daly, Healing Hands (ts, Derby, WA, c1980); information from Srs A. Neary and A. Maria, Perth, and Ms L. O'Connell, Brisb.

CATHIE CLEMENT

GREENER, HERBERT LESLIE (1900-1974), journalist, author and Egyptologist, was born on 13 February 1900 at Wynberg, Cape Town, South Africa, only son of Herbert Greener, a captain in the British Army, and his wife Helen Olive, née Bennett. Leslie was educated in England, at Matfield Grange, Kent, and Felsted School, Essex. He attended the Royal Military College, Sandhurst, graduated in 1918 and served for five years as an officer in the Indian Army. On 21 December 1925 at the registrar's office, Waihi, New Zealand, he married Alice Gwendoline Rhona McKenzie, née Haszard (d.1931), a divorcee and an artist. Greener worked as a journalist in New Zealand and Australia, then studied art at the Académie Julian, Paris, in 1927-28. While teaching art and French at Victoria College, Alexandria, Egypt, he completed a year of external study with University College, London. From 1931 he was employed as an epigraphist at Luxor, Egypt, by the Oriental Institute of the University of Chicago. At the British consulate general, Cairo, on 5 May 1934 he married 24-year-old Margaret Lillian Edmunds (d.1958). They came to Sydney in 1936 where for several years he was again employed as a journalist.

On 15 April 1940 Greener enlisted in the Australian Imperial Force; commissioned in November, he was sent to Malaya with the 8th Division in February 1941. He was a captain and divisional intelligence officer when captured by the Japanese on 15 February 1942. Returning to Australia late in 1945, he transferred to the Reserve of Officers on 24 November. During his time as a prisoner of war in Changi camp, Singapore, he had illustrated a children's book written by a fellow prisoner David Griffin, *The Happiness Box* (Sydney, 1947; Singapore 1991); intended as a Christmas present for the children in the camp, it was buried until Greener's release. He went back to journalism in Sydney and wrote two books based on his war experiences, *He Lived in My Shoes* (1948) and *No Time to Look Back* (New York, 1950). Two children's books followed: *Moon Ahead* (New York, 1951; London, 1957) and *Wizard Boatman of the Nile* (London, 1957). Foundation director (1949-54) of Adult Education in Tasmania, Greener resigned to work as a freelance writer and broadcaster. He was awarded a Commonwealth Literary Fellowship in 1957 and taught creative-writing classes on behalf of adult education. Greener asserted that he was 'pagan' in religion and an independent thinker in politics, willing to encourage international understanding.

Following the death of his second wife, he returned to Egypt in 1958. Until his retirement in 1967 he worked with the epigraphic survey department, Oriental Institute of the University of Chicago, during its annual expeditions to Luxor. His experiences were the catalyst for *High Dam over Nubia* (London, 1962) and *The Discovery of Egypt* (London, 1966). In 1967 he lost most of his possessions, including precious manuscripts and photographs, when bushfires swept through south-eastern Tasmania, destroying his home at Longley. At that time he was absent in Egypt, a place to which he continued to return each year, working for the University of Pennsylvania on the Ikhnaton Temple project. On 30 July 1968 at the registrar's office, Hobart, he married Dorothy Chung, née Henry, a 33-year-old divorcee with whom he had been living for the previous ten years. Chairman (1968) of the Tasmanian Historical Research Association, Greener collaborated with the photographer Norman Laird in writing *Ross Bridge and the Sculpture of Daniel Herbert* (1971). He then used his research to write a novel, *Tea for a Stranger*, which was published posthumously in 1975.

Survived by his wife, and by the son of his second marriage, Greener died on 8 December 1974 at the Repatriation General Hospital, Hobart, and was cremated. His last project, *Discovering Egypt with Leslie Greener* (1976), was issued as a kit for senior school students. A portrait of Greener by Jack Carington Smith [q.v.13] won the Helena Rubinstein [q.v.11] award in 1966 and is in the Tasmanian Museum and Art Gallery, Hobart.

M. Giordano and D. Norman, *Tasmanian Literary Landmarks* (Hob, 1984); *National Geographic*, 138, no 5, Nov 1970, p 634; *Contemporary Authors* (Detroit, US), 2, 1978; *Mercury* (Hob), 9 Dec 1968, 1 July 1970, 30 Aug, 9 Dec 1974, 28 Feb 1976; information from Mrs D. Greener, Sandy Bay, Hob.   MARGARET GIORDANO

GREENHALGH, ARTHUR RODELLA (1896-1972), showman, was born on 2 December 1896 at Southern Cross, Western Australia, fourth child of William Greenhalgh, produce merchant, and his wife Daisy Sarah, née Planz, both from England. The family moved to Kalgoorlie, then to St Kilda, Melbourne, to Armidale, New South Wales, and to Mackay, Queensland, where William ran a hotel-booth on the showgrounds. Billing himself as 'Captain Greenhalgh' or 'Dead Shot Bill', in 1909 he and his two younger children started travelling as a sharp-shooting act in tented, sideshow alleys on the dusty, country-town circuit. Arthur acquired some education on the way, at Charters Towers and, though he was not a Catholic, at St Joseph's School, Woollahra, Sydney. His first appearance at the Royal Easter Show was in 1910 with 'Volta, the Electric Marvel'.

Describing himself as an auctioneer from

Bondi, Greenhalgh married 19-year-old Es-mée Georgina Burt at the district registrar's office, Waverley, on 18 December 1923; they remained childless and later separated. For many years he lived with Fuchsia Lillian Lup-ton (d.1963). Arthur had branched out on his own in 1924, working with rodeos and boxing troupes. In 1928, with Fred Clare, an Amer-ican, he began importing acts for Australian shows, including the 'Wall of Death' motor-cyclists, 'the Reckless Jacksons'. In August one of these daredevil riders, Texas-born ERNEST JACKSON IBSCH, (c.1896-1965), known as 'Jack Jackson', bought out Clare. Greenhalgh & Jackson became one of Aus-tralia's leading sideshow entrepreneurs, presenting acts like 'Tam Tam the Leopard Man', 'Dennis O'Duffy, the Irish Giant', and 'Chang, the Pin-headed Chinaman'. In 1934 Greenhalgh made the first of his many over-seas tours to recruit novelty acts for his tent shows.

The outbreak of World War II put a tem-porary end to show business and in 1943 Greenhalgh bought the Beach Hotel, New-castle, where he housed 'the Snake-charmer', 'the Skeleton Man' and others who were stranded for the duration. Arthur liked to spin a tale: he claimed that 'the Giant' washed the windows (without a ladder), 'the Midget' tapped the barrels, and 'the Fat Lady' and 'the Tattooed Lady' jointly presided over the kitchen. Appointed a justice of the peace, Greenhalgh was a notable identity at New-castle, where he invested in a block of flats and was a patron of community organizations, such as the Police-Citizens Boys' Club and the local surf lifesaving club. The owner of sev-eral racehorses (including True Leader, win-ner of the Doomben Ten Thousand in 1953), he was a member of the Australian Jockey Club, turf clubs in Sydney, Brisbane and New-castle, Tattersall's clubs in Sydney and New-castle, and of the latter's Masonic club. He visited Melbourne annually for the racing season, seeing fifty-six Melbourne cups in succession up to 1970. He was also a keen lawn bowler.

Greenhalgh was short, with a bustling man-ner. A 'red-faced, chubbily important little figure' with the voice of the sideshow spruiker, he usually sported a large, diamond tie-pin in his cravat and a ring on his index finger. After the enforced idleness of wartime came a boom, and Greenhalgh's tents re-sumed their journeys to shows and raceday carnivals from Brisbane to Perth. His busi-ness involved the employment of 'freaks', but he acquired a reputation for honesty. 'In the old days when acts were scarce and money was scarcer, we could always turn a swaggy into a wild man of Borneo and get away with it. Now we think nothing of spending a few thousands on air passages in order to sign up a

new act.' In 1947 they engaged 'Zandau, the Quarter-man', an American Negro born with-out hips or legs. Greenhalgh and Jackson owned mechanical rides, the 'Wall of Death' and the 'Wild West Show'. They also em-ployed waxworks exhibitors, Chinese acro-bats, magicians, jugglers, 'the Wonder Boy Canadian Glass Blower' and other attractions which flanked Jimmy Sharman's [q.v.11] box-ing tents in the alleys at Sydney's Royal Easter Show and various carnivals. There, youths gawped at the exotic, saw-dusted wonders. Sample-bags or fairy floss in hand, children implored parents to let them do the same.

Greenhalgh was a founder (1935) and president (1950) of the Showmen's Guild of Australasia. His partner Jackson died in Syd-ney on 2 May 1965. By then Greenhalgh had become patron of the guild. Less peripatetic, he ruled his motley empire mainly from the hotel. He died on 20 February 1972 in Royal Newcastle Hospital and was cremated with Anglican rites; most of his estate was bequeathed to his long-time friend Bert Anderson, manager of the Beach Hotel.

People (Syd), 11 Apr 1951, p 43; *Outdoor Show-man*, Nov 1960, p 1, Nov 1962, p 24, July 1965, p 1, Apr 1966, p 20, Mar 1972, p 15, June-July 1978, p 15, Oct-Nov 1980, p 15; *SMH*, 25 Oct 1947, 2 Apr 1950 (Roy Easter Show supp), 3 May 1965, 21 Feb 1972; *Newcastle Sun*, 25 Oct 1968; *Newcastle Morn-ing Herald*, 21, 23 Feb 1972.

CHRIS CUNNEEN

GREENWOOD, ETTIE GWENDOLINE (1906-1977), benefactress, was born on 8 September 1906 at Mount Victoria, New South Wales, fourth daughter and fifth child of native-born parents Henry Herbert Green-wood, police constable, and his wife Clara Jane, née Porter (d.1923). Clara was a sister of George Benjamin Porter, a grazier at Forbes. In 1911 George bought Marchmont, a property near Ilfracombe in Queensland, previously held by R. G. Casey [q.v.3], which then ran over 34 000 sheep, 85 cattle and 90 horses. Clara and her sister Sarah were part-owners. Ettie was educated at the Bowral branch of Sydney Church of England Girls' Grammar School; she left about 1924, with prizes in music and needlework. In 1928 she visited San Francisco, United States of America.

George Porter died, a bachelor, in 1930. Ettie became one of his beneficiaries, as did her sisters Ida, Mary and Edith, and her brother Gordon. Ettie lived with her siblings at Marchmont for much of the 1930s and 1940s. The Greenwoods held additional interests in Garches, The Rand, Fortuna and

Grant, respectively in the Longreach, Ilfracombe, Mitchell and Barcaldine districts. They were a close family and the sisters adored their brother. Ettie was a small, slim, gentle woman, well groomed and dressed; she held definite views and ideas, and was gifted with common sense.

By the 1940s two of Ettie's sisters had married and shifted elsewhere. About 1947 Ettie and Edith moved into a large, white house, which they named Marchmont, at 38 Marine Parade, Southport. Gordon remained at Ilfracombe until about 1958 when he joined his sisters. Edith died in 1967 and Gordon two years later. Both were unmarried. Ettie inherited the pastoral properties which she sold in 1970. She made a minor investment in two racehorses, Torbunda and Flamont. From this time she lived alone, cultivated a large garden with hired help, but increasingly spent most of her days indoors.

Miss Greenwood died on 7 June 1977 at her Southport home and was cremated with Anglican rites. It was only after her death that the extent of what she had left the living became known. Her estate, sworn for probate at $1 084 119, was bequeathed to the Queensland Institute of Medical Research in a legacy to be known as the Edith and Gordon Greenwood Medical Research Fund. The money has mainly been used for cancer research.

Qld Country Life, 29 Oct 1970; *Telegraph* (Brisb) and *Courier-Mail*, 22 Nov 1977; documents relating to Marchmont pastoral property (ANUABL); information from Dr P. R. Patrick, Jindalee, Qld.

ALISON PILGER
CHRIS CUNNEEN

GREENWOOD, IVOR JOHN (1926-1976), politician and barrister, was born on 15 November 1926 in North Melbourne, eldest of three children of Victorian-born parents Bartlett John Greenwood, boiler-maker, and his wife Joy Olive, née Vickers. Ivor was educated at Hartwell and Mont Albert Central state schools, Scotch College and the University of Melbourne (LL.B., 1949). After graduating, he was an associate, successively, to two justices of the High Court of Australia, (Sir) Frank Kitto in 1950 and Sir Owen Dixon [q.v.] in 1950-52.

Admitted to the Victorian Bar on 1 March 1951, Greenwood soon established a reputation as a scholarly but practical barrister, working principally in the fields of commercial and local government law. For some time he shared chambers with a future governor-general (Sir) Ninian Stephen. On 3 December 1960 at St Mark's Anglican Church, Camberwell, Greenwood married Lola Poppy Roney, a research officer.

Because he did not view the law as a means of making money, he devoted much of his time to voluntary activities designed to enhance the standing of the profession and its social usefulness. Honorary secretary (1963-68) of the Law Council of Australia, Greenwood was also involved in the Law Association for Asia and the Western Pacific, in the hope that the rule of law would become firmly entrenched in the countries of that region. He did not, therefore, achieve the material success that would have been his had he confined himself to the usual activities of a barrister. His practice, however, was extensive enough for him to be regarded as an extremely sound lawyer. He became a leader of the junior Bar before being appointed Q.C. in 1969.

It was not the law, but politics, that was Greenwood's abiding interest. Initially, he had been prominent in the Young Liberal (and Country) Movement before participating in student politics at university where his eloquent opposition to communism endeared him to the hierarchy of the Liberal Party. President (1947) of the Melbourne University Liberal Club, he helped to wrest the Students' Representative Council and the student newspaper, *Farrago*, from left-wing control. The presidency (1949) of the S.R.C. was a further laurel and he was identified as a rising star in the party.

His life in politics was to be beset with controversy. From his undergraduate days he pursued issues of principle, even at the cost of personal friendship, and he was equally dogged in maintaining his political convictions. He had no qualms about opposing Prime Minister (Sir) Robert Menzies' [q.v.] attempt to outlaw the Communist Party of Australia by referendum in 1951, though it put him at odds with prevailing sentiment in the Liberal Party. Greenwood took this action on the grounds of civil liberties. In supporting his friend Alan Missen who was under threat of expulsion from the party for the same reason, he said: 'this referendum ... is completely contrary to all that liberalism stands for'.

In 1952-68 Greenwood was a member of the party's State executive (vice-president 1966-68). He found himself opposed to the majority of his colleagues in 1961 when he again sided with Missen who was acting as solicitor for a political candidate expelled from the Liberal Party. In defending Missen's right to give legal representation to anyone who requested it, Greenwood was motivated by a concern for the freedom of the individual.

Nominated under section 15 of the Constitution to fill the casual vacancy occasioned by (Sir) John Gorton's transfer to the House of Representatives, Greenwood entered the Senate in 1968 and was to be returned at four elections. He was minister for health from March to August 1971 in (Sir) John Gorton's administration, then attorney-general until the defeat of (Sir) William McMahon's government in December 1972. Deputy-leader of the Opposition in the Senate in 1972-75, Greenwood was spokesman on attorney-general matters and the Australian Capital Territory. In December 1975 the Liberal and Country parties regained power under Malcolm Fraser: Greenwood was appointed deputy-leader of the government in the Senate, and minister for environment, housing and community development.

Although Greenwood maintained his interest in civil liberties throughout his career, there were some who thought that he had begun to move to the right once he entered parliament. As attorney-general, he asserted that there was no evidence to support Labor Party allegations that a right-wing Croatian terrorist organization was operating in Australia; his uncompromising approach to law-and-order issues earned him the nickname 'Ivor the Terrible'; and, in the mid-1970s, he showed a distinct lack of enthusiasm for such initiatives as the liberalization of the divorce laws.

Greenwood's apparent assumption of the mantle of a social conservative distanced him from his old friend Missen who had remained on the left wing of the Liberal Party. For his own part, Greenwood could have claimed that he had not changed, and that popular issues should not be slavishly followed lest they undermine institutions which were of greater long-term value to individuals. He was a conservative in that he opposed change unless an overwhelming and logical case were made out for it. Nevertheless, in 1976 he was looking forward to the opportunities his new portfolio presented for 'fashioning [and] moulding' an improved quality of life for Australians.

In May Greenwood fell gravely ill; two months later he was relieved of his ministerial duties. It was a severe blow for the Liberal Party. There were those who thought that he could have transferred to the House of Representatives and that the office of prime minister was not beyond his reach. While somewhat dour in appearance and sombre in manner, he was highly principled, intelligent and articulate. In whatever cause he took up, he was known for his meticulous research and preparation for debate, his forceful and dogmatic presentation, and his absolute conviction. He did not engage in personal abuse. The strongest remark he made of an opponent was, 'But he means well'. Greenwood was devoted to his family and loyal to his staff. He was a lay preacher at the Church of Christ, Hartwell, Melbourne. Survived by his wife, son and daughter, he died of an acute heart attack with anoxic cerebral complications on 13 October 1976 at Parkville and was cremated.

A. Hermann, *Alan Missen* (Canb, 1993); *SMH*, 26 Oct 1971; *Age* (Melb), 26 June 1972, 1 Jan 1976; *Canb Times*, 14 Oct 1976; personal information.

N. A. BROWN

GREGG, SIR NORMAN McALISTER (1892-1966), ophthalmologist, was born on 7 March 1892 at Burwood, Sydney, youngest of six children of native-born parents James Gregg, auctioneer, and his wife Mary, née Miller. Brilliant scholastically and on the sporting-field, Norman was educated at Homebush and Sydney grammar schools, and at the University of Sydney (M.B., Ch.M., 1915). At university he gained many academic distinctions; he was president of the undergraduates' association and a director of the university union; he was awarded Blues for cricket and tennis in his first year; and he also belonged to the baseball and swimming teams, and to a local ice-hockey team. In 1913-14 he thrice represented New South Wales in cricket (his team-mates included Victor Trumper, Herbert Collins, Arthur Mailey [qq.v.12,8,10] and Charles Macartney) and once represented the State in tennis; but for World War I, membership of the Davis Cup team was within his reach.

Having completed medicine with first-class honours, Gregg went to England and on 23 March 1915 was commissioned temporary lieutenant in the Royal Army Medical Corps. He served on the Western Front (1915-18) with the 7th Battalion, East Yorkshire Regiment, and with the 52nd Field Ambulance (June 1918 to March 1919). Promoted temporary captain (1916) and acting major (1919), he won the Military Cross (gazetted 1919). Back home, he was appointed resident medical officer at Royal Prince Alfred Hospital. A 'tall, lithe and vigorous young man', he returned to England to train as an ophthalmologist. In 1922 he gained the diploma of ophthalmic medicine and surgery (R.C.P.& S.) after working as house surgeon at Moorfields Eye and the Royal Westminster Ophthalmic hospitals, and at the Birmingham and Midland Counties Eye Hospital where he impressed the paediatrician (Sir) Leonard Parsons.

In 1923 Gregg set up practice in Macquarie Street, Sydney. That year he was appointed ophthalmic surgeon at Royal Prince Alfred Hospital and held the same post from 1925 at the Royal Alexandra Hospital for Children; he was consultant at the latter from 1950 and at the former from 1952. At St Stephen's Presbyterian Church, Phillip Street, on 10 October 1923 he had married Haidée Margaret, daughter of Duncan Carson [q.v.7]. Their two daughters became physiotherapists.

Gregg talked easily to his patients, and kept a tin of sweet biscuits for the children.

His alert clinical observations and inquiring mind enabled him to make his outstanding discovery about rubella. On 15 October 1941 in Melbourne he delivered a paper on 'Congenital Cataract following German Measles in the Mother' to the Ophthalmological Society of Australia which was published in its *Transactions*. His ethical approach to the care of his patients was poignantly shown when he subsequently revealed that he had not made a slit-lamp examination in his cases because he considered that he was not justified in subjecting babies to an anaesthetic for the necessary length of time.

His friend (Sir) Lorimer Dods stressed how his colleague's willingness to listen to 'that excellent clinical observer—the mother' yielded important information. Gregg's original paper—which emphasized such defects as cataracts and congenital heart disease, but did not include any statement about deafness —was reported in Sydney's popular press on a Monday morning. Before lunch that day two mothers had telephoned to say that they had suffered from rubella during the early stages of their pregnancies and that, while their children were deaf, they were not suffering from any of the defects he had enumerated. He went on to publish 'Further Observations on Congenital Defects in Infants following Maternal Rubella' in the *Transactions* of the O.S.A. (1944).

Gregg's findings had major implications for clinical medicine, basic research and public health. His work, and that of other studies confirming his initial observations, showed that rubella, previously regarded as a mild infectious disease, could cause cataracts and other significant birth defects if susceptible women became infected in the first few months of pregnancy. His discovery stimulated rapid development in the field of teratology and offered hope for primary prevention of some birth defects. It also stimulated research workers in the laboratory to isolate the rubella virus, although this was not achieved until 1962. A vaccine was later developed to protect young women against rubella before they reached their reproductive years.

Despite his large private practice, Gregg did more than his share of the work at his two hospitals. He was a fellow of the Royal Australasian College of Surgeons (1934), president of the Ophthalmological Society of New South Wales (early 1930s) and of the Ophthalmological Society of Australia (1944-45), and lectured (1940-51) at the university on diseases of the eye. As vice-president (from 1946) and president (1959-66) of the board of management of the Royal Alexandra Hospital, he oversaw significant changes to improve children's comfort, such as the removal of restrictions on visiting hours and 'the

brightening of the whole atmosphere of the hospital, doing away with the institutional look and giving it a comfortable, friendly, homelike atmosphere'. Dods wrote that the hospital owed 'an unmeasurable debt to him for his inspiring and clear-thinking leadership, his skilful chairmanship of a rapidly increasing number of committees, and his tireless and enthusiastic attendance at innumerable intramural and extramural hospital functions'. Gregg helped to found the Ophthalmic Research Institute of Australia and was vice-president of the Children's Medical Research Foundation.

His many awards included the University of Adelaide's Shorney prize (1946), and the Charles Mickle fellowship of the University of Toronto (1951), Canada, awarded annually to 'the member of the medical profession who has done most during the preceding ten years to advance sound knowledge of a practical kind in medical art or science'. Knighted in 1953, Gregg was elected a fellow of the Royal College of Obstetricians and Gynaecologists, London (1952), and of the Royal Australasian College of Physicians (1953). He was awarded honorary doctorates—of medicine by the University of Melbourne (1952), science by the University of Sydney (1952) and science by the Australian National University (1958). The American Academy of Ophthalmology and Otolaryngology conferred an honorary fellowship on him in 1955.

In December 1957 Gregg received an invitation from an Italian pathologist Professor Alfonso Giordano to be nominated for the Nobel prize in physiology and medicine for 1958. His reply showed his modesty and a revealing self-assessment of his own work: 'I must confess that it comes as a great surprise and rather a shock that my name should even be considered . . . I feel it only fair to you to inform you that I have really no serious publications except those on Rubella as I have found very little time or inclination for writing during a very busy life'. In 1964 Gregg shared a Britannica-Australia award for medicine with Dame Kate Campbell, the Melbourne paediatrician.

A committee-member (from 1941), captain (1944-47) and president (1952-56) of Royal Sydney Golf Club, Gregg was 'a recognised authority on the Rules of Golf', 'an energetic and forceful administrator', and 'a great stickler for club protocol and customs'. He was an alert, friendly and extroverted man, seemingly enthusiastic about everything, who also belonged to the Australian Club. Sir Norman died on 27 July 1966 at his Woollahra home and was cremated. His wife and daughters survived him.

Gregg's discovery that rubella in early pregnancy caused cataracts and other birth defects was a most important advance in medicine, but there are few symbolic reminders of him and his achievements. The Royal Australian College of Ophthalmologists named a triennial lecture and a prize in his honour. Dods said of Gregg: 'Like so many truly great men, he retained throughout his life a natural humility, and remained a simple, uncomplicated person with a special love for his home and his many friends—a most sympathetic and understanding man of impeccable integrity and unceasing devotion to duty'. (Sir) William Dargie's portrait of Gregg is held by the family.

G. E. Hall and A. Cousins (eds), *Book of Remembrance of the University of Sydney in the War 1914-1918* (Syd, 1939); D. G. Hamilton, *Hand in Hand* (Syd, 1979); G. L. McDonald (ed), *Roll of the Royal Australasian College of Physicians*, 1, 1938-45 (Syd, 1988); P. A. L. Lancaster, 'The eyes have it: Norman McAlister Gregg and Congenital Rubella', in B. Heagney (comp), *Rubella* (Syd, 1992); *MJA*, 10 Dec 1966, p 1166; *Aust J of Science*, 29, no 4, Oct 1966, p 104; *Trans of the Ophthalmological Soc of Aust*, 26, 1967 (Norman McAlister Gregg memorial number); *SMH*, 30, 31 July 1951, 30 Aug 1952, 28 July 1956, 8 Mar 1958, 4 Oct 1961, 20 Oct 1964; *The Times*, 28 July 1966.

PAUL A. L. LANCASTER

GREGORY, CECIL ALBERT (1894-1974), journalist and map publisher, was born on 30 April 1894 at Forbes, New South Wales, son of Albert Edward Gregory, a draper from London, and his native-born wife Isabella, née Lowe. Educated at Bathurst Superior Public School, Cec taught himself shorthand from a Pitman's book. As a cub reporter (from 1909) on the *Bathurst Times*, he excelled at making notes from the long speeches that the newspaper subsequently reproduced in full; he also gave instruction in shorthand at the local technical college. He won the Bathurst Motor Cycle Club's Byrne Challenge Cup in 1916 and displayed an early fondness for adventuring on the roads.

Joining the staff of the Sydney *Daily Telegraph* in 1921, Gregory wrote regional and rural supplements; he later became a sub-editor and then picture editor. In 1923 he produced the *Daily Telegraph Guide to Sydney* which included coloured maps. At Christ Church, Enmore, on 16 September 1922 he married with Anglican rites Sylvia Evangeline Dowling. His wife and two daughters were eventually involved in the mapping business, especially the tedious task of checking the names of streets.

In April 1925 Gregory was elected to the council of the National Roads and Motorists' Association. Next year he was appointed director of the touring and publicity departments. From 1927 to 1932 he edited the *Open Road* magazine. His low salary was off-set by his retention of the right to publish and profit from his guide books, which would be distributed by the N.R.M.A. An active participant in transport debates, he convinced the N.R.M.A. in 1928 to initiate a road-safety campaign and in 1931 was secretary of the Modern Transport Federation of Australia, a lobby group that favoured private buses over state-run trams and trains.

Gregory established the 'Road Before You', a series of strip maps, using the cartography of H. E. C. Robinson [q.v.11] Ltd, but gave the maps added authenticity by driving over the routes himself. He quickly appreciated the potential advertising revenue in publishing maps, directories and guidebooks. Resigning from the N.R.M.A. in June 1933, he set up the Australian Guide Book Co. with the cartographer Clive Barrass. In November 1934 the first *Gregory's Street Directory of Sydney and Suburbs* was produced. Designed to fit into the glove-box of a motorcar, it was vastly superior to the annual *Wilson's Authentic Director*, a small, thick and clumsy volume.

By 1940 Gregory—who prided himself on writing his own text—had produced an Australian school atlas, street directories of Newcastle and Adelaide, a road guide to New South Wales, a fishing and camping directory, and a handbook of stock owners and agents, and *Gregory's 100 Miles Round Sydney*. Publishing was constrained during World War II, but he did bring out a series of sheet maps on particular battles, sold in newsagencies. With a shrewd eye for likely demand, he published *Gregory's Modern Building Practice in Australia* (1944) and in the late 1940s produced guides to the Hume, Pacific and New England highways, the Jenolan caves, the Blue Mountains, and the States of Victoria and Queensland. Stemming from his frustration at the lack of tourist guides on holidays abroad, he published maps of Papua and New Guinea (1949) and Hong Kong (1953). His fortunes rose with the extraordinary growth in car ownership in the 1950s. The Gregory Publishing Co. Pty Ltd remained small and efficient, and used nearby printers.

Six feet (183 cm) tall and 13½ stone (85.7 kg) in weight, the bespectacled Gregory, with his straight, jutting nose and outgoing sense of humour, was a prominent figure in transport and motoring circles. His close friendship with (Sir) William Walkley [q.v.] of Ampol Petroleum Ltd led to a contract to provide maps to that company. Gregory served as general secretary (1935-52) of the Service Station Association of New South Wales and produced its magazine, *Sales and Service*. A keen swimmer and sportsman, and a member of the New South Wales Masonic Club, he had wide-ranging hobbies, from pig-shooting to home movies. In the late 1940s he attended a performance by the hypnotist 'Franquin' and became fascinated by the subject: developing his own abilities in the art, he induced individual and group trances in his Fairlight home, and maintained that hypnotherapy could be valuable in treating anxiety, fear, depression and insomnia.

Survived by his daughters, Gregory died on 17 August 1974 at Fairlight and was buried in Northern Suburbs cemetery. By the time he had sold the firm to Publishers Holdings Ltd in 1962, he was the best-known street-directory and tourist-guide publisher in Australia, dominating the market in New South Wales and having a considerable share in other States. 'Gregory's' was by then a household name.

Pix, 14 May 1949; *People*, 19 Nov 1952; *Daily Telegraph* (Syd), 11 Aug 1985; L. Hovenden, The Motor Car in New South Wales 1900-1937 (M.A. thesis, Univ Syd, 1981); information, news-cuttings and family records provided by Dr and Mrs J. Bosler, Tamworth, NSW, and Mrs M. D'Arcey, Sunrise Beach, Qld.   PETER SPEARRITT

GREIG, GWENDOLINE; *see* VARLEY

GREIG, MAYSIE COUCHER (1901-1971), romantic novelist, was born on 2 August 1901 at Double Bay, Sydney, daughter of Dr Robert Greig Smith, a bacteriologist from Edinburgh, and his English-born wife Mary, née Thomson. Educated at Presbyterian Ladies' College, Pymble, Maysie joined the staff of the *Sun* in 1919 before sailing for England in the following year. She was employed by Manchester evening newspapers and by October 1922 had a column, 'The Woman's View' (later 'Through the Eyes of a Woman'), in the salacious *Empire News*. Her first serial was accepted by the *Daily Sketch*.

At the parish church, Painswick, Gloucestershire, on 14 July 1923 Maysie Greig-Smith married Ernest Roscoe Baltzell, an American Rhodes scholar whom she accompanied to New York. She worked at Boston where, as Maysie Greig, she published her first novels, *Peggy of Beacon Hill* (1924) and *The Luxury Husband* (1927); both were filmed at Hollywood. Her marriage ended in divorce in 1929. While living at Greenwich Village, New York, she married a writer Delano Ames; they, too, were to be divorced (1937). After spending four years travelling, especially to such 'strange and little known countries' as Yugoslavia and Albania, they settled in England, with a home in London and another, Yew Tree House, in the village of St Mary Bourne, Hampshire. Wherever they stayed, Maysie managed to 'inveigle the best recipes from the cook' and often made Hungarian and Al-

banian dishes. Golden haired, blue eyed and ravishingly attractive, she rode and played tennis. By 1934 she was the most prolific woman novelist of the day. She published up to six books a year (mostly with Collins in England and Doubleday in New York), often set in the exotic places that she had visited; she also wrote thrillers as 'Jennifer Ames', and occasionally used 'Ann Barclay' and 'Mary Douglas Warren' as pseudonyms.

On 3 May 1937 at the Municipal Building, Manhattan, New York, Maysie married Maxwell Alexander Murray (1900-1956), an Australian-born journalist; they returned to England where the birth of their child in 1940 did not interrupt Maysie's flow of novels. In 1948 the family settled in Sydney and Maysie added a house at Vaucluse to her other residences. Working some six hours a day with a dictaphone, she continued to produce four books a year and looked on serial rights as a pleasant extra. Some of her later novels had Australian settings, including *One Room for His Highness* (1947), *French Girl in Love* (1963) and *Doctor on Wings* (1966). Max wrote detective stories which were serialized in the American *Saturday Evening Post*; *The Right Honourable Corpse* (New York, 1951) was set in Canberra.

Listing her recreations as tennis, bridge and literary associations, Greig was president (until 1966) of the Sydney centre of International P.E.N.; she revived the group, and attended conferences in Tokyo (1957) and at Bled, Yugoslavia (1965). She also belonged to the Society of Women Writers of New South Wales, the Fellowship of Australian Writers and the Romantic Novelists' Association (England). On 22 June 1959 at the registrar general's office, Sydney, Maysie married Jan Sopoushek, a printer from Budapest and a widower. She sold her Vaucluse home in 1966 and thereafter lived in London. Survived by her husband and by the son of her third marriage, she died of an embolism on 10 June 1971 in a nursing home at St Marylebone.

Maysie Greig flung 'her own vivid personality', humour and enthusiasm into telling a good story. Heeding Delamore McCay's [q.v.10] advice to 'write every sentence as though I were to cable it to England at my own expense', she wrote over 220 novels with an unusual economy of words. She invariably gave her stories happy endings 'because I believe that happiness is the greatest virtue in the world and misery the greatest sin'. For forty years her books were best sellers on both sides of the Atlantic. Her novels were translated into French, Dutch, Portuguese, Swedish and Icelandic.

J. Vinson (ed), *Twentieth-Century Romance and Gothic Writers* (Lond, 1982); L. Henderson (ed), *Twentieth-Century Romance and Historical Writers*

(Lond, 1990); *Home*, 20 Nov 1948, p 15; *Newspaper News* (Syd), 2 Jan 1950, p 11; *Observer* (Syd), 18 Feb 1961, p 9; *Star* (Melb), 28 May 1934; *SMH*, 24 Mar 1955, 3 Oct 1957, 27 July 1958, 12 June 1971; *Sun-Herald*, 21 June 1959, 19 Dec 1965; *Herald* (Melb), 10 Jan 1966.   MARTHA RUTLEDGE

GRENDA, ALBERT FRANCIS (1889-1977), cyclist, was born on 15 September 1889 at Portland, Tasmania, one of eight children of German-born parents Carl Grenda, farmer, and his wife Adeline, née Totenhofer. In 1895 the family moved to Mathinna. 'Alf' left the local school at an early age to help on his father's farm. His four brothers excelled at conventional sports such as football, running, woodchopping and cricket, but Alf took to cycling; when he won his first race, at Scottsdale in 1907, he commented that it was much easier than chopping wood. He raced successfully in Melbourne in 1909 and in Sydney in 1910. Next season he won the Australian one-mile (1.6 km) championship and then showed enough brilliance in the Sydney six-day race to impress American promoters. In 1911 he visited the United States of America and returned there under contract for the following season.

In 1912 he defeated the cycling wizard Frank Kramer in a match race. Although Grenda came second in the world professional sprint championship that year, he teamed with Walter De Mara of Cleveland, Ohio, to take the world tandem crown, thus becoming, arguably, 'the first Australian to win a world's championship' in cycling. Big, strong and well proportioned, Grenda was over six feet (183 cm) in height and was dubbed 'The Tall Tasmanian'. A legend in an era when most cyclists earned only a few pounds a week, he drew large crowds and his versatility brought him a handsome living. In search of even better money, he resumed six-day racing; he and his compatriot Alfred Goullet were considered to be the greatest team on the American six-day circuit. At Newark Velodrome, with three different partners, in 1914 Grenda set world records for the one and two mile (3.2 km) tandem (1 minute 40 seconds and 3 minutes 35 seconds respectively) in 1914, and for the three-mile (4.8 km) event (5 minutes 19 seconds) in 1915. In her parents' home at Harrison, New Jersey, on 21 December that year he married Isabel Crawford. They settled in Tasmania in 1919, but returned to America in 1921.

Grenda subsequently made several brief visits to Australia, including one in 1925 when 55 000 spectators flocked to see him ride in the six-day contest in Sydney. In 'Curly' Grivell's opinion, he was a remarkable all-rounder who 'could win any event on the programme' —or, more appropriately—'all events on the programme'. Grenda ceased competitive cycling in 1926, bought an orange grove at Hollywood, California, in 1930 and took American citizenship. He retired from his business in 1955 and moved to Costa Mesa, Long Beach. Survived by his son and two daughters, he died on 30 May 1977 at Paradise, California, and was cremated.

His nephew Ron Grenda, who was also a versatile competitor with a style uncannily similar to his uncle's, won the Latrobe wheels race (1961), gruelling six-day events (including one at Launceston) and national sprint titles. Ron's son, Michael, combined sprint power and endurance to win numerous Tasmanian and national titles, as well as gold medals in the 4000-metre team pursuit at the Commonwealth (1982) and Olympic (1984) games.

H. ('Curly') Grivell, *Australian Cycling in the Golden Days* (Adel, 1954); R. and M. Howell, *Aussie Gold* (Brisb, 1988); *Sunday Examiner Express*, 24 Dec 1966, 4 Feb 1984; *Advocate Weekender*, 19 Aug 1972; *Northern Scene*, 20 Feb 1979; *Examiner* (Launc), 8, 10 Oct 1982, 2 May 1983, 19 May, 6 Aug 1984, 22 Mar 1986; *Advocate* (Hob), 27 Dec 1984; *Sunday Examiner*, 26 Mar, 31 Dec 1989; news-cuttings from US papers and information from Mrs A. Stumbaugh, Magnolia, California, US, and Mrs J. Parry, Beaumaris, Melb.

ALEXANDER TRAPEZNIK

GREY-SMITH, SIR ROSS (1901-1973), solicitor and racing administrator, was born on 22 July 1901 at St Kilda, Melbourne, fourth child of Victorian-born parents Francis Grey Smith, solicitor, and his wife Sybella Ann, née Ross. Francis was the third son of Francis Grey Smith [q.v.6]. From 1911 Ross spent ten years at Melbourne Church of England Grammar School, not leaving until the age of 20 because of his value as an oarsman —he was captain of boats in 1920-21. He completed the articled clerks' course at the University of Melbourne, was admitted to the Bar on 1 June 1926 and joined his father as a solicitor in Frank Grey Smith & Son.

As a student, Ross had found time to excel in sport. He was a member of the Commonwealth Golf Club's pennant team in 1922, and was accomplished at tennis and shooting. Later he took to more expensive hobbies, including aviation, and was a committee-member (1931-32) of the Royal Victorian Aero Club. This interest was soon displaced by hunting: he joined the Melbourne Hunt Club and by 1932 belonged to the committee of the Oaklands Hunt Club. At Christ Church, South Yarra, on 14 January that year he married with Anglican rites Bettine Alberta, daughter of Charles Fairbairn [q.v.8]. She, too, was an enthusiastic and competent rider. In 1935 they won a steeplechase at Flemington with their hunter, Blue Boy.

The hunt clubs were enmeshed in the network which dominated the administration of horse-racing in Melbourne, and in 1935 Grey Smith was invited to join the committee of the Moonee Valley Racing Club. Three years later he resigned to contest a vacancy on the committee of the ruling Victoria Racing Club. Against two older candidates, he won by one vote, his prestige boosted by the timely win of his colt, Tactical, in the 1938 Ascot Vale Stakes. He raced his horses in partnership with his wife Betty, her brother James Valentine Fairbairn [q.v.8] and Fairbairn's wife Peggy.

Commissioned on 2 July 1940 in the Administrative and Special Services Branch of the Royal Australian Air Force, Grey-Smith —as he had styled himself from about 1936—was chief instructor at the School of Administration, Laverton. He served at bases in New Guinea, the Netherlands East Indies and Borneo, rose to temporary squadron leader and was demobilized on 30 October 1945. During World War II he remained a nominal member of the V.R.C. committee and in 1942 High Road, which he owned with his wife, had won the V.R.C. St Leger Stakes.

After the war Grey-Smith took an interest in several charitable organizations, among them the Old Colonists' Association (president 1948-49), the (Royal) Children's Hospital and the Royal Victorian Institute for the Blind; his wife was treasurer of the Queen Victoria Hospital, vice-president of the Isabel Henderson [q.v.9] Free Kindergarten and a committee-member of the Royal Academy of Dancing. Although he resumed his legal practice, became vice-chairman of the jewellers, William Drummond & Co. Ltd, and presided over the Society of Notaries in 1960-62, his main interest remained the V.R.C. He was vice-chairman in 1959 and succeeded Sir Chester Manifold [q.v.] as chairman in 1962. Throughout his seven years in the chair, Grey-Smith devoted time and energy to staunching the decline in racecourse attendances that stemmed from the introduction of legal off-course betting. In 1960 he had chaired a promotions sub-committee which successfully organized the centenary celebration of the Melbourne Cup and which saw the beginnings of commercially sponsored races in Australia. He also lobbied effectively for the establishment of the Racecourses Development Fund; it channelled money from the Totalisator Agency Board into the provision of improved facilities at racecourses. In 1966 he was knighted.

Sir Ross remained a committee-member of the V.R.C. until his death. A tall and stately man, carefully groomed, he looked well in morning dress on opening days of the annual spring carnival. In some quarters he had a reputation for abruptness, but Keith Dunstan fairly said: 'He had the marvellous ability of being able to maintain firm control, yet get on with people—indeed, everybody he met'. Grey-Smith and his wife had no children and lived quietly at South Yarra in the company of their beloved dogs. Survived by his wife, he died on 14 July 1973 in Melbourne and was cremated. A portrait by Harold Freedman is included in the History of Racing mural at Flemington Racecourse.

C. A. Grant, *500 Victorians* (Melb, 1934); Melb C of E Grammar School, *Liber Melburniensis* (Melb, 1965); D. L. Bernstein, *First Tuesday in November* (Melb, 1969); J. Pacini, *A Century Galloped By* (Melb, 1988); *Age* (Melb), 14, 17 May 1938, 28 Aug 1962, 23 July 1969, 16 July 1973; *Sun News-Pictorial*, 16 July 1973.   ANDREW LEMON

GRIBBLE, ERNEST RICHARD BULMER (1868-1957), Anglican missionary, was born on 23 November 1868 at Chilwell, Victoria, eldest of nine children of English-born parents John Brown Gribble [q.v.4], a miner who became a missionary, and his wife Mary Anne Elizabeth, née Bulmer. Educated at The King's School, Parramatta, where he excelled at sport but was academically 'backward', he left in 1885 hoping to join the New South Wales Artillery. His parents dissuaded him. In January 1886 he went to Western Australia to help his father establish a mission on the Gascoyne River in the State's North-West. When the enterprise was abandoned, Ernie worked as a stockman and drover until parental pressure and a salary of £60 per annum enticed him to accept the curacy of Tumbarumba, New South Wales. In 1892 he was summoned to help his ailing father at Yarrabah Aboriginal Mission, near Cairns, Queensland, and found himself in charge after his father died on 3 June 1893. Driven by filial obligation and guilt, Gribble reluctantly embraced a missionary career. He was made deacon on 21 December 1894 and ordained priest on 1 January 1899. At St John's Anglican Church, Cairns, on 18 April 1895 he had married Emilie Julie Wriede; they were to have three sons.

His theology was a mix of High Church Anglicanism and muscular Christianity. A Social Darwinist in attitude, Gribble was paternalistic and authoritarian: compulsory church attendance, the Protestant work ethic and the Europeanization of Aboriginal culture prevailed on his missions. He segregated the sexes, confined children in dormitories, and satisfied his thwarted military ambition through regimentation, uniforms, paradeduty and mission police. Recalcitrants were imprisoned or given corporal punishment.

Aided by legislation to enforce the removal of Aboriginal children to the mission, the population of Yarrabah rapidly increased. Yet, an embryonic indigenous Church also emerged to provide Aboriginal missionaries, synod representatives and the deacon James Noble [q.v.11]. Such achievements won Gribble acclaim. Missionaries were sent to study his methods; he led expeditions in 1902, 1904 and 1905 to pioneer the Mitchell River mission, and was invited to establish others. In 1900 he had been appointed absentee warden of the mission on Fraser Island; he imposed his system there until the mission closed in 1904 and most of its people were transferred to Yarrabah. In June 1907 he and his wife separated. Gribble became involved with an Aboriginal woman; their daughter was born in September 1908. As a vocal opponent of miscegenation, he was tormented by the affair and suffered a mental and physical breakdown. The Church demanded his resignation from Yarrabah and he 'retired' on 17 June 1910.

In 1911-13 he served as rector at Gosford, New South Wales, where he wrote 'Life and Experiences of an Aboriginal mission to the Aborigines' for the *Gosford Times* (1915). He then took charge of the Forrest River mission, in the far north of Western Australia, which relied on forced removals to build a permanent population. There he became a vocal protector of Aborigines who were abused by local pastoralists and police. In 1926 he helped to expose a massacre of Aborigines by a punitive police expedition; his demands for justice attracted international publicity and led to a royal commission (1927). Although its verdict entrenched Gribble's reputation as a champion of Aborigines, he was plagued by episodic depression and accusations of maladministration. In 1925 his licence had been temporarily withdrawn after mission staff and the local doctor reported that he was mentally unstable. Lean and virtually bald, with intense blue eyes, Gribble had 'altogether the appearance of a bushranger'. In 1928 A. P. Elkin [q.v.] described him as a 'conceited, uncouth tyrant' who ran a 'stud farm' for breeding natives. In June the Australian Board of Missions found Gribble guilty of financial mismanagement, authoritarianism, violation of Aboriginal traditions and an 'obsession with sexual morality'. Gribble's dismissal was sealed when he concealed from the police the complicity of a mission resident in a tribal murder. He left the mission on 20 November and defended his record in three autobiographical works: *Forty Years with the Aborigines* (Sydney, 1930), *The Problem of the Australian Aboriginal* (1932) and *A Despised Race: the Vanishing Aboriginals of Australia* (1933).

From 1930 Gribble was Anglican chaplain to the government Aboriginal settlement at Palm Island, Queensland. His rivalry with the Catholics fostered sectarianism, but he quickly acquired a large congregation by initiating an active social life centred on his church; he even used his dog to herd parishioners into services. While his authoritarianism persisted, his campaigns for Aboriginal rights won him respect. In 1939 he established the James Noble Fund to give Palm Islanders access to secondary education. He corresponded with William Ferguson and worked with William Cooper [qq.v.8] for Federal control of Aboriginal affairs, and was made a life member of the Australian Aborigines' League. Elevated to canon in June 1941, Gribble was appointed O.B.E. in 1956. He was a prolific contributor to Church journals; his memoirs, 'Over the Years' and 'The Setting Sun', were published in the *Northern Churchman* (1932-34, 1945-47). Although elderly, frail and almost deaf, he refused to retire from Palm Island. In 1957 the Church forcibly removed him to Yarrabah where he died on 18 October that year and was buried in the mission cemetery.

Roy Com into the Alleged Killing and Burning of Bodies of Aborigines in East Kimberley and into Police Methods when Effecting Arrests, *PP* (WA), 1927, 1 (3), p xvii; *Missionary Notes*, May 1895, Sept 1900, June 1901; *WA Church News*, Jan 1914, Aug 1925; Aust Bd of Missions, *ABM Review*, July 1916, Dec 1918; *Northern Churchman*, Dec 1931, Nov 1938, Jan 1942, Feb 1944; C. M. Halse, The Reverend Ernest Gribble and Race Relations in Northern Australia (Ph.D. thesis, Univ Qld, 1992); Palm Island Journals of E. R. Gribble (Nth Qld Diocesan Archives, Townsville); Forrest River Mission Journals (BL); Bd of Missions in Syd *and* in WA, Correspondence and Minutes, *and* Gribble papers (ML).

CHRISTINE HALSE

GRIEVE, RACHEL (1885-1977), weaver, **DAVID** (1886-1951), jeweller and metalworker, and **EDITH** (1892-1972), illustrator, were born on 18 February 1885 and 4 July 1886 at South Yarra, Melbourne, and on 12 November 1892 at Surrey Hills, three of seven children of Henry David Grieve, a commercial traveller from Scotland, and his Canadian-born wife Rachel, née Tweed. David studied mathematics at the Working Men's College, Melbourne. Declared medically unfit to enlist in the Australian Imperial Force, he travelled to England to work in the armaments industry on the staff of Vickers Ltd at Barrow-in-Furness. After World War I had ended, he visited his maternal relations in Ontario, Canada, where he was joined by Rachel and Edith. In May 1920 the three Grieves moved to Detroit, United States of America; David designed machines and tools associated with the fast-growing automotive industry.

Edith had studied under Bernard Hall [q.v.9] at the National Gallery of Victoria's art school, Melbourne. At Detroit she worked as an illustrator for American companies and for an advertising agency. Rachel had been employed as an infant-teacher in Melbourne and later as a photographic retoucher before abandoning her career to take over the running of the family home. In the U.S.A. she studied psychology, but lost interest when she saw an exhibition of Scandinavian weaving at the international exposition, held at Chicago in 1933-34. Her interest in weaving awakened, she studied broomstick weaving with Nellie Sargent Johnson at Wayne University, Detroit.

Designing and building most of his own equipment, David Grieve developed skills as a cabinet-maker, metalworker and lapidary. From the 1920s he made some of the furniture and metalwork (such as flatware and silver objects) used in the family's house. He also produced jewellery and metalwork for sale in a Detroit shop. His enthusiasm was heightened by his weekly visits in the 1930s to the Cranbrook Academy of Art, Bloomfield Hills, Michigan. Founded in 1932 with the Finnish architect Eliel Saarinen as its president, the academy had craft studios and master craftsmen for cabinet-making, silver and iron work, bookbinding and weaving. Pupils came to Cranbrook to work with members of the largely European-born faculty which included Charles Eames, Florence Knoll and Eero Saarinen.

When David's health was affected by the cold climate, the Grieves returned to Melbourne in November 1937 and settled at Camberwell. During World War II David worked as a tool designer for Charles Ruwolt [q.v.11] Pty Ltd at Richmond. Following the war, he established his studio in the garden of the family home, and designed and made small machines for industry. He continued his hobby, occasionally exhibiting with the Arts and Crafts Society of Victoria. At this time most of his work was made for personal use, for his sisters, or as gifts for family friends. The jewellery frequently incorporated semiprecious stones and, like the metalwork, adhered to the principles and style of the Arts and Crafts movement. Edith worked as a freelance illustrator; Rachel pursued a career as a weaver and instructor in weaving.

With Jessie Vasey [q.v.], Rachel helped to establish the War Widows' Craft Guild in 1945. She taught weaving at the guild and—under the Commonwealth Reconstruction Training Scheme—to men of the Royal Australian Air Force in hospital at Ascot Vale. For much of her life she exhibited, demonstrated, judged, broadcast and wrote numer-

ous articles about weaving. She was active in the spinners' and weavers' and the embroiderers' guilds, and in the Arts and Crafts Society of Victoria. Highly regarded for its precision and finesse, her weaving was frequently used for official and state gifts to visiting dignitaries. As a promoter of her art, she advised: 'Are you ripe for a nervous breakdown? Don't call a Doctor, buy a spinning wheel!' The family was close-knit. David designed and constructed looms for his sister, and worked with her for the war widows; Edith designed her sister's weavings and her brother's metalwork.

David Grieve died of pulmonary oedema on 5 June 1951 at Camberwell; Edith died there on 30 March 1972; Rachel died on 2 July 1977 at Surrey Hills. They were buried in Box Hill cemetery, the sisters with Presbyterian forms. The work of all three is represented in the collections of the National Gallery of Australia, Canberra. David and Rachel are also represented in the collection of the National Gallery of Victoria.

Aust Home Beautiful, Jan 1948; Cwlth Oil Refineries Ltd, *Accelerator*, Oct 1950; *Herald* (Melb), 11 Aug 1970, 4 July 1977; Grieve papers (National Gallery of Aust Archives).   JOHN MCPHEE

GRIFFITH, STURT DE BURGH (1905-1979), engineer, patent attorney, air force officer and journalist, was born on 15 August 1905 at Manly, Sydney, son of Arthur Hill Griffith [q.v.9], a patent attorney and member of the Legislative Assembly who had emigrated from Ireland, and his native-born wife Mildred Carrington, née Smith. Educated at Sydney Church of England Grammar School (Shore), Sturt studied electrical and mechanical engineering at the University of Sydney (B.E., 1928) and gained six months practical experience at the Pyrmont works of the Colonial Sugar Refining Co. Ltd. He entered his father's firm of patent attorneys, Griffith & Hassel, was admitted to practise in 1930 and became a partner.

After serving in the senior cadets and the Militia, Griffith had joined the Citizen Air Force in December 1925 and obtained a 'distinguished pass' in his pilot training at Point Cook, Victoria. He was commissioned in April 1926 and attached to No.3 Squadron at Richmond, New South Wales. Sent to Canberra to take part in the ceremonies to mark the opening of Parliament House in May 1927, he survived two perilous landings with minor injuries. During a flight over Sydney in August 1928, he was forced to ditch his aircraft in the harbour when the engine failed. He transferred to the C.A.F. Reserve in 1934 as a flight lieutenant. On 23 April 1937 he married Winnifred Morris Marshall at St Philip's

Anglican Church, Sydney; they were to remain childless.

In September 1939 Griffith was mobilized for full-time service in the Royal Australian Air Force. He led No.22 Squadron at Richmond in 1940-41 before being sent to Canberra where he commanded the Royal Australian Air Force Station and the School of Army Co-operation. 'Slightly under average height and of sturdy build', at this time he was described as 'a man of firmly-held convictions, swift and decisive in the expression of them'. He was promoted temporary wing commander in October 1941 and awarded the Air Force Cross in January 1942.

Later that month Griffith was posted as commander of the R.A.A.F. Station, Darwin. He took office less than three weeks before the first Japanese air-raid on the town. At 9.37 a.m. on 19 February the R.A.A.F. operations room received a message that a large formation of aircraft had crossed Bathurst Island and was heading towards Darwin. Believing that the planes could have been American, Griffith did not order the alarm until 9.58 a.m. Within seconds, enemy bombers arrived from the south-east. With their fighter escort, they destroyed naval, military, air force and civilian targets, and departed at 10.40 a.m. A second raid from 11.55 a.m. to 12.20 p.m. concentrated on the R.A.A.F. Station and aerodrome, inflicting serious damage.

Observed to have been 'rattled' by the onslaught, Griffith gave an imprecise, oral order that his staff was to assemble 'half a mile [0.8 km] down the road and half a mile into the bush'. The instruction was distorted as it passed from person to person and men disappeared in various directions: 278 of them were still missing on 23 February. On the afternoon of the 19th, Hudson bombers had been prevented from taking off because Griffith was unable to arrange a ground-to-air wireless link.

In the reports (March and April) of his commission of inquiry into the events of that day, (Sir) Charles Lowe [q.v.] was unable to determine who was to blame for the delay in raising the alarm, but he found that Griffith 'must take some responsibility'. In addition, he held Griffith to be partly at fault for the R.A.A.F.'s general unpreparedness for attacks from the air. Reserving his strongest criticism for Griffith's conduct after the second raid, he described his performance as incompetent and lacking in leadership. Air Vice Marshal W. D. Bostock [q.v.13] reviewed Lowe's findings for the Department of Air. He stated that air-raid warnings were the function of Area Combined headquarters and concluded that it should share the blame for the delay. Moreover, he noted that most of the responsibility for shortcomings in equipment, facilities and personnel in Darwin had to be borne by the department, by the air officer commanding, North-Western Area, and by his chief of staff.

Griffith's difficulties had been accentuated by a cumbersome command structure which superimposed both Area Combined and R.A.A.F. North-Western Area headquarters on his station headquarters, thereby constraining his authority. His decision to assemble his men away from the base, though badly executed, had been reasonable, given the circumstances. None the less, he never held another operational command.

From April 1942 Griffith commanded No.7 Squadron at Bairnsdale, Victoria. In June he was posted to No.5 Maintenance Group, Sydney, where he filled senior administrative and technical staff positions, and was promoted temporary group captain in December 1943. That month he took command of No.1 Aircraft Depot, Laverton, Victoria. Transferring back to the reserve in October 1945, he resumed his work as a patent and trademark attorney and as a consultant engineer. He was a councillor (1932-51) and president (1947-48) of the Institute of Patent Attorneys of Australia.

In 1950 reports of Griffith's road tests on motor-vehicles began appearing in the press and he was soon appointed motoring correspondent for the *Sydney Morning Herald*. Junior staff brought vehicles to his home at Leura in the Blue Mountains and sat 'in terror beside him as he hurled the cars around his set course', gathering data which was entered into stylized reports. At the *Herald* his copy was treated as 'sacred'. A colleague described his work as 'very technical, very accurate, totally objective', and of such standing that his report could mean the difference between the success or failure of a new model. Compilations of his articles, *Sturt Griffith's Road Tests*, appeared annually for some years from 1959. He continued to be employed by the *Herald* until December 1976. Survived by his wife, he died on 14 December 1979 at the Repatriation General Hospital, Concord, and was cremated.

D. Lockwood, *Australia's Pearl Harbour* (Melb, 1966); D. Gillison, *Royal Australian Air Force 1939-1942* (Canb, 1962); A. Powell, *The Shadow's Edge* (Melb, 1988); *Smith's Weekly* (Syd), 10 Jan 1942; *SMH*, 18 Dec 1979; AWM records; private correspondence.   E. D. DAW

GRIFFITHS, GLYNDE NESTA (1889-1968), author and philanthropist, was born on 4 July 1889 at Double Bay, Sydney, youngest of three daughters of Frederick Close Griffiths, a merchant from London, and his native-born wife Annette Agnes, daughter of J. S.

Willis [q.v.6]. Grand-daughters of George Richard Griffiths [q.v.1], Nesta and her sisters Gwyneth (1885-1940) and GWENDOLEN WINIFRED (1886-1968) grew up at Point Piper and were educated privately (by special teachers for different subjects) with their cousins, the daughters of E. W. Knox [q.v.9]. Frederick died in 1907, leaving his affairs in confusion: Gwyneth and Nesta taught dancing at Westwood school and Gwendolen taught mathematics. In 1910 Gwyneth married Henry Dunster Baker, the American vice-consul in Sydney.

Small, 'with blue eyes and long golden-red hair', Nesta 'enjoyed theatre, music, books, travelling, paintings and early morning swims at Nielsen Park'. She played tennis and—like Gwendolen—belonged to Royal Sydney Golf Club. After their mother's death in 1929, the sisters acquired a spacious flat in Silchester, Bellevue Hill, where they lived companionably for the rest of their lives. Starting with little money, Gwendolen invested shrewdly on the stock market and their flat was gradually filled with antique furniture, paintings and *objets d'art*. They remained careful in their daily life, but were very generous to their friends. For many years a committee-member of the Bush Book Club of New South Wales, Gwendolen enjoyed reading the *New Yorker*. She joined the Queen's Club. Nesta, who drove the car, was a foundation member of the Macquarie Club. They regularly attended the High Church services at St James's, King Street. Accustomed to roaming the world from an early age, they sailed in cargo boats, 'motored from the western shores of France to old Vienna' and 'climbed the towers of Rhenish castles'. Britain, Japan, Java, South Africa and North America (including Alaska) were among the places they visited.

Their absorbing interest was other people's lives. A member (from 1923) of the Royal Australian Historical Society, Nesta combed through old books and documents in the Mitchell [q.v.5] Library and History House, and engaged in field-work: she and Gwendolen stayed, sometimes for weeks, at the country homes of their friends and relations. Nesta's first book, *Point Piper Past and Present* (1947), was a limited edition published by S. Ure Smith [q.v.11]. It was followed by *Some Houses and People of New South Wales* (1949), *Some Southern Homes of New South Wales* (1952) and *Some Northern Homes of N.S.W.* (1954). Although her books suffered from lack of editing, the absence of indexes, the omission of references, and occasional inaccuracies, she preserved 'the recollections of an earlier generation'. Her habit of 'strewing bright irrelevances' gave the books much of their charm. She revived interest in the architect John Verge [q.v.2]

and created awareness of an endangered heritage.

Generations of children climbed the stairs to have afternoon tea with 'the Griffi'—as they were affectionately, if disrespectfully, known—and were allowed to touch the treasures. Milk was served in a 'creamer' (a jug in the shape of a cow). The sisters invariably changed for dinner and swept into the kitchen to cook in long dresses. Both were enthusiastic bridge players and entertained friends at home or at one of their clubs.

Taller, and more astringent, exacting and down-to-earth than her sister, Gwendolen was the kinder; Nesta, who asked impertinent questions and indulged in malicious gossip about those of whom she disapproved, could look almost vixenish. They died at Silchester in 1968, Gwendolen on 13 January and Nesta on 4 June; both were cremated. Admiring the work of Sir Lorimer Dods, they had contributed handsomely to the Children's Medical Research Foundation. Nesta bequeathed the residue of her estate, sworn for probate at about $300 000, to the foundation; Gwendolen preferred to provide for Dods's grandchildren.

G. N. Griffiths, *Point Piper, Past and Present*, introd by C. Simpson (Syd, 1970); H. Rutledge, *My Grandfather's House* (Syd, 1986); *SMH*, 19 Oct 1935, 11 Oct 1939, 11 Sept 1947, 12 Feb, 5 July 1949, 20 Dec 1952, 20 Nov 1954, 16 Aug 1968, 5 June, 7 Nov 1968, 10, 11 Apr 1976; *Australian*, 21 May 1976; Griffiths papers (held by Mrs C. Simpson, Bellevue Hill, Syd); information from Mrs V. Brannon, Newport, Nth Carolina, US; family and personal information.   MARTHA RUTLEDGE

GRIFFITHS, JENNIE SCOTT; *see* SCOTT GRIFFITHS

GRILLS, CAROLINE (1888?-1960), poisoner, was born probably in 1888 at Balmain, Sydney, daughter of George Mickelson, labourer, and his wife Mary, née Preiers. On 22 April 1908 at the district registrar's office, Balmain South, she married, with her father's consent, Richard William Grills, a labourer; they were to have five sons and a daughter. Two of the boys died tragically, one as a result of typhoid contracted while working as a lifesaver at Maroubra beach. The Grills moved into a succession of rented houses in the city and the Randwick area, during which years Richard was employed as a real-estate agent. After the death of her father in 1948, Caroline inherited and moved into his home at Gladesville. Known as Aunty Carrie by her extensive family, she was a short, 'dumpy' woman who wore thick-rimmed glasses. She frequently visited her in-laws and friends, making tea, cakes and biscuits for them.

On 11 May 1953 Grills was arrested and charged with the attempted murder of her sister-in-law Mrs Eveline Lundberg and Lundberg's daughter Mrs Christine Downey, both of Redfern; the attempt had been made with thallium, a poison commonly found in rat bait. The symptoms of thallium poisoning included loss of hair, nervous disorders, progressive blindness, loss of speech and eventual death. Both Downey and Lundberg suffered these symptoms for some time, re-covering only when Mrs Grills did not visit. They were not alone. In 1953 Sydney was in the grip of thallium panic. From March 1952 until the arrest of Grills there had been forty-six cases of reported thallium poisoning, in-volving ten deaths. In the few months after her arrest there were further reported cases of thallium poisoning, among them one of a prominent footballer.

Further investigation led police to charge Grills with four murders and one attempted murder. All of the victims, with the exception of a friend of her mother, were in-laws. Police speculated that her poisoning spree had be-gun in 1947 with the murder of her step-mother. Exhumation of the bodies of two victims revealed traces of thallium. While the police believed that a strong circumstantial case existed to substantiate murder, they only proceeded with the original charge of attempting to murder Mrs Lundberg.

At her trial in the Central Criminal Court, Grills professed her innocence, claiming that police had pressured her relations to convict her and that she 'helped to live, not kill'. Her behaviour in court, marked by outbursts of laughter, reinforced ideas that she was a mal-evolent killer. On 15 October 1953 she was found guilty of attempted murder and sen-tenced to death. Although her appeal was dismissed by the Court of Criminal Appeal in April 1954, her sentence was commuted to life imprisonment. She was admitted to the State Reformatory for Women where she spent the next six and a half years.

Rushed to Prince Henry Hospital, Grills died of peritonitis on 6 October 1960 and was cremated with Anglican rights; her husband, daughter and three of her sons survived her. 'Aunt Thally', as she was popularly known, remains an enigma. The undercurrents of envy, anger or revenge that pushed her to kill so many of her family can only be guessed at. She was a disquieting case, a matronly figure who did what all favourite aunts were meant to do—serve tea and cakes.

J. Holledge, *Australia's Wicked Women* (Syd, 1963); R. Hall, *Clues Under the Microscope* (Syd, 1982); A. Dettne et al, *Infamous Australians* (Syd,

1985); *SMH*, 12 May, 8-10, 13, 14, 16, 24 Oct, 12 Dec 1953, 13, 27 Feb, 10 Apr 1954; *Daily Tele-graph* (Syd), 12 May, 16 Oct 1953; *Daily Mirror* (Syd), 2 Nov 1973; Supreme Court (NSW), Depo-sitions, 1953, *and* Court Reporting Office (NSW), Criminal Cases, 1953 (NSWA); Prisons Dept (NSW), Register of Deaths.   STEPHEN GARTON

GRIMWADE, GEOFFREY HOLT (1902-1961), business leader, was born on 19 Sep-tember 1902 at Caulfield, Melbourne, fourth of five sons of Melbourne-born parents Ed-ward Norton Grimwade [q.v.9], merchant, and his wife Phelia Maud, née Whittingham. Born into the business dynasty founded by his grandfather Frederick Sheppard Grimwade and Alfred Felton [qq.v.4], Geoffrey followed his father, uncles and brothers to Melbourne Church of England Grammar School in 1912. War soon disrupted family life. His uncle Ha-rold Grimwade [q.v.9] embarked a colonel and returned a general, and his three elder brothers all enlisted: one, Risdon, was killed at Gallipoli, and when the eldest, Fred, was shot down, wounded and captured in France in 1916, his parents took Geoff and his younger brother to London for some months while they sought, with eventual success, re-patriation of the prisoner from Germany. Geoff returned to school until 1920 without further incident, apart from his alleged re-sponsibility for an explosion which wrecked the chemistry laboratory.

By the time F. S. Grimwade died in 1910, the family business had become a network of enterprises manufacturing chemicals, glass bottles and industrial gases as well as phar-maceuticals. (Sir) Russell Grimwade [q.v.9], the uncle with whom Geoff was to be most closely associated in business, insisted that he follow his example by taking a science degree. Entering Trinity College, University of Mel-bourne (B.Sc., 1923), Geoff completed his degree without particular distinction, ex-celled at tennis, football, athletics and golf, and made himself conspicuous riding a motor-cycle. In 1924 he went to Emmanuel College, Cambridge (B.A., 1927), became president of the Hawkes Club, and gained Blues for tennis and, most notably, golf. Recognized as one of the best amateur golfers in Europe, he led Cambridge to a famous victory in 1927, de-feating Oxford's Harry Oppenheimer in a dra-matic play-off. Grimwade financed holidays on the Riviera by judiciously backing himself against rich but less skilled golfers on Medi-terranean courses. His appetite for sport and for gambling was never to diminish, though the extent of the latter activity was to be known only to his closest friends.

He shared with his father a reserved, at times forbidding, demeanour, but where Nor-ton was bookish, with some interest in the arts, Geoff was extrovert, philistine, energetic, and caustic in wit, although companionable in private enjoyments. Dark, and of middle height, he did not look athletic, despite his sporting skills, but had a powerful physical presence.

On 17 February 1931, four years after his return from Cambridge, Grimwade married Mary Lavender ('Pie') Stuart at St John's Anglican Church, Toorak; they settled in a flat at South Yarra before acquiring their main residence, at Toorak. Four daughters—but to Geoff's regret no sons—were born between 1937 and 1946, the year the Grimwades acquired a property at Rye which became a centre of family life at weekends and holidays. Geoff was never a keen farmer, though he took a scientific interest in improving soils with trace elements.

Competition in a difficult market and a threat of overseas takeover had led in 1929 to the formation of Drug Houses of Australia Ltd, a holding company for seven firms in five States. Geoff's father Norton was the first chairman, but the family's interests were diluted, even in the Victorian operations of Felton, Grimwade & Duerdins Pty Ltd, which Geoff joined. In December 1928 he replaced his father on the board of Australian Oxygen and Industrial Gases Pty Ltd, of which his uncle Russell was chairman. Russell soon enlisted him as managing director of a new venture, Carba Dry Ice Pty Ltd; Geoff negotiated the right to manufacture the 'gas which could be wrapped in newspaper' in Britain in 1929, on an eventful trip which included return through the New York stock-market crash and a Pacific cyclone. He admitted very large personal losses in the crash, but soon demonstrated his outstanding business skills and strategic sense in successfully establishing Carba. When Australian Oxygen was merged into Commonwealth Industrial Gases Ltd in 1935, he transferred to the new board, and Carba (which by 1938 was healthy enough to expand into South Australia) and C.I.G. were his main business responsibilities for some time. In 1936 he also joined the board of J. Bosisto [q.v.3] & Co. Pty Ltd, pioneer producers of eucalyptus oil.

After the outbreak of World War II Grimwade enlisted in the Australian Imperial Force, but before completing training he was sent to the United States of America in 1941 to negotiate agreements for the manufacture of optical glass in Australia, and was discharged from the army when he returned in 1942. In that year he became involved, with (Sir) Leslie McConnan [q.v.], in the establishment of the Institute of Public Affairs. Convinced that Australian interests, and especially business, had been ill-served by all the political parties, Grimwade threw himself into the I.P.A.'s role as an initiator of debate

and formulator of policy, chairing (from 1943) its industrial committee which drafted a detailed postwar programme as 'an alternative to socialism' and which became a de facto executive. He had strongly independent views, distinctively Australian despite family links with Britain, and insisted that the programme include several proposals, especially in the fields of labour relations and profit-sharing, unwelcome to traditional conservatives. Hard working, blunt to the point of tactlessness, and 'terribly persistent', he eventually prevailed. His further insistence that the I.P.A. have no formal party association—despite pressures for involvement in the collapse of the United Australia Party, the 1943 election and the 1944 referendum—was another crucial contribution to its independent development. Grimwade welcomed the establishment of the Liberal Party of Australia, and became a close friend of his Mornington Peninsula neighbour Harold Holt [q.v.], but had no taste for political life, nor perhaps the necessary skills, though he did improve his limited ability in public speaking. He believed the work of the I.P.A. itself to be so important that for a time it might have tempted him from the world of business.

Grimwade felt a special responsibility to continue family business activities, since none of his brothers and only two of his cousins (one of whom died young) entered the firms. As his father and uncles retired, he took many of their roles, though not the whole range Norton had played as the senior of the brothers. Geoff had little to do with Australian Glass Manufacturers Co. Ltd or its successor Australian Consolidated Industries Ltd, in part because he disliked W. J. 'Gunboat' Smith [q.v.11], its managing genius. Geoff replaced his father on the board of Cuming [q.v.8] Smith & Co. Ltd, though not as chairman.

In 1942 Grimwade had joined the board of D.H.A. and in 1950 was appointed chairman and managing director. Modernizing the company's unwieldy structure and strategies became his principal task, symbolized in moving from the old headquarters in Flinders Lane to Bourke Street. He shared Russell's curiosity about new products, producing a sunscreen cream in the 1950s, but his major projects for Drug Houses were international joint-ventures in chemicals and manufacturing, including a large petrochemical plant in Sydney. He gradually reduced his involvement in Carba and even in C.I.G.

Grimwade's stature as one of the ablest businessmen of his generation was earned, not inherited, and extended beyond the family businesses. After an early involvement in Victorian Insurance Co. Ltd, he joined the Victorian board of the Australian Mutual Provident Society in 1939, became its chairman in 1945 and was appointed to the principal board in Sydney in 1957. A member (from 1951) of the new board of the Commonwealth Bank, he quickly developed a warm respect for its governor, H. C. 'Nugget' Coombs. Grimwade also became one of the few men equally at home in the business worlds of Sydney and Melbourne, with (Sir) James Vernon, (Sir) Vincent Fairfax, (Sir) Colin Syme and (Sir) James Forrest among his close associates. His other business interests included Courtaulds (Aust.) Ltd, Wrightcel Pty Ltd and Kempthorne Lighting Ltd.

Work never absorbed all Geoff Grimwade's prodigious energy. Like other Grimwades, he gave much time to the Walter and Eliza Hall [qq.v.9] Institute of Medical Research, joining its board in 1948 and becoming chairman in 1958. (He did not, however, feel sufficiently at ease with either art or charity to succeed Russell on the Felton [q.v.4] Bequests' Committee, on which there had been a Grimwade since its inception.) Geoff continued to play competitive sport throughout the 1930s, and golf all his life; he was a member of the Royal Melbourne and president (1956-61) of the Sorrento golf clubs. Keen on duck-shooting, he nevertheless took a camera on safari in Africa rather than a gun. He attributed his excellence at billiards to nights spent playing compulsorily with his father 'when I wanted to be out chasing girls'. A member of the Union (Sydney), Australian and Melbourne clubs, he was president of the Australian Club at 49, an unusually young age. Geoff became increasingly interested in racing, joining the committee of the Victoria Amateur Turf Club in 1959 and owning several horses, including Khyber (he was addicted to rhyming slang) which won at 20/1 carrying £1000 of its owner's money and a jockey who had a heart attack before weighing in. Grimwade remained a prodigious gambler, in the market and at play. His holidays at Rye always included a poker school, and he also played frequently in Sydney where he once took from (Sir) Frank Packer [q.v.]—whom he incongruously nicknamed 'Dainty'—£5000 on the turn of a single card. With Pie he played bridge. He claimed that his records, which were meticulous, showed he won slightly more than he lost at gambling, and he certainly enjoyed it, as he did smoking, and drinking his favourite 'mallet'—one part of French to five of gin—habits which no doubt contributed to the increasingly ruddy complexion which earned him the nickname 'Purp'.

Grimwade was appointed C.M.G. in 1960. On 22 February 1961, in Sydney on a business trip, he was found dead of a coronary occlusion in his room in the Australia Hotel. His death, at the height of his influence, was a significant loss to business, and in particular to D.H.A. which became the first major Australian victim of overseas asset-strippers a few years later. Survived by his wife and daughters, Grimwade was cremated. His estate was sworn for probate at £388 239.

C. D. Kemp, *Big Businessmen* (Melb, 1964); J. R. Poynter, *Russell Grimwade* (Melb, 1967); *IPA Review*, Jan-Mar 1961, p 13; Company papers of Drug Houses of Aust Ltd *and* Cwlth Industrial Gases Ltd (Univ Melb Archives); Carba Dry Ice Pty Ltd papers; family information.   J. R. POYNTER

GRISHIN, DMITRY VLADIMIROVICH (1908-1975), university teacher and author, was born on 12 September 1908 at Kamyshin, on the Volga River, Russia, eldest son of Vladimir Grishin, schoolteacher and farmer, and his wife Lubov, née Alabuseva. In 1927 Vladimir was arrested as a *kulak*; his wife and four younger children were sent to Siberia. Dmitry, a student at the Pedagogical Institute, Saratov, escaped their fate, but his academic career suffered a setback. Graduating in 1935, he became a schoolteacher and part-time lecturer in Russian literature at the institute.

In Moscow on 9 December 1940 Grishin married Natalia Luzgin, a science teacher. This was his second marriage; the details of his first are unknown. He taught Russian literature at the University of Moscow and was awarded the title *Kandidat filologicheskikh nauk* for his thesis on 'Early Dostoevsky'. When the university staffs were evacuated from Moscow, Grishin was appointed acting-head of the Russian literature department in Elista, capital of the Kalmyk Autonomous Soviet Socialist Republic. During the *blitzkrieg* of 1942 he and his wife were taken prisoner and assigned to work for a dentist in Berlin. They survived allied bombing and on one occasion were buried in the debris of a demolished house. In March 1945 they fled to Bad Nevenahr and thence to Emden where they obtained an entry visa to Australia.

On 23 September 1949 they arrived in Melbourne. At Bonegilla immigrant camp, Grishin organized protests about substandard living conditions. While employed as a laboratory-assistant at Monsanto Chemicals (Australia) Ltd, Footscray, he began working as a part-time tutor in the department of Russian language and literature at the University of Melbourne. In 1954 he was naturalized. He moved through the ranks of full-time tutor (1953), senior tutor (1954), lecturer (1956), senior lecturer (1962) and reader (1970). Meanwhile, he resumed his research. In 1957 he was awarded a Ph.D. for his thesis on Dostoevsky's *Diary of a Writer*. He published a series of books in Russian: *Dostoevsky's Diary of a Writer* (1966), *Dostoevsky: the man, writer and myths* (1971) and *The Young Dostoevsky* (posthumously, 1977); his collection of Dostoevsky's aphorisms was published in Paris in 1975. An indefatigable participant in international congresses, he was founder and vice-president of the International Dostoevsky Society.

Remembered for the very Russian atmosphere he created around him, Grishin insisted on speaking his native tongue to those who could understand the language and teaching it to those who could not. Students and colleagues invited to his home were treated to a lavish display of flowers; fruit trees and beehives crowded his small garden, and the house was crammed with books, Russian artefacts and his wife's paintings. Musical performances (guitar, balalaika and mandolin) were provided by his sons; Dmitry and Natalia gave poetry recitations and the guests were plied with Russian food. Grishin was an energetic entertainer with his whimsicalities, puzzles and quizzes. Even those who disagreed with his views could not but respect his sincerity, his passionate devotion to his native-land and his infinite capacity for work.

Five ft 11 ins (180 cm) tall, prematurely grey, and blue-eyed, Grishin was usually seen with a large briefcase overfull with papers. His constant companion was a diminutive diary in which he recorded most hours of the day in minuscule writing. In 1973 he retired from the university. He died of coronary vascular disease on 19 September 1975 at his North Coburg home and was cremated; his wife and their two sons survived him, as did the daughter of his first marriage.

A. B. Gibson, *The Religion of Dostoevsky* (Lond, 1973); IDS (Pittsburgh, US), *Bulletin*, 1971, 1973; Dept of Russian, Univ Melb, *Russian Contributions*, 1976; *Univ Melb Gazette*, Mar 1974, Dec 1975; family papers (held by Dr S. Grishin, Art Hist, ANU); information from Dr S. Grishin, Mr V. Grishin, Seaford, Melb, Ms M. Travers, Modern European Languages, ANU, and Prof T. H. R. Rigby, Griffith, Canb.   NINA CHRISTESEN

GROUT, ARTHUR THEODORE WALLACE (1927-1968), cricketer, was born on 30 March 1927 at Mackay, Queensland, son of native-born parents Arthur Edward Grout, police constable, and his wife Theresa Eileen, née Kelly. Wally was educated at Fortitude Valley Primary and Brisbane High schools, then worked as a salesman at A. N. Robinson's sports store in Queen Street. In 1940 he joined South Brisbane District Cricket Club, becoming its wicket-keeper in the following year. Enlisting in the Australian Imperial Force on 27 June 1945, he served at Rabaul, New Britain, from March to August 1946 and was discharged on 11 December. In

1948-50 he played A grade Rugby Union football, handling brilliantly as a full-back. At the Methodist Church, West End, Brisbane, on 27 January 1951 he married Joyce Nelma Cunis, a dressmaking machinist.

From 1952 Grout played for the Toombul District Cricket Club. He had made his début for Queensland in the 1946-47 season, standing in for his idol Don Tallon whom he succeeded in 1955. Grout kept wickets for Queensland in 94 matches, and in first-class games was involved in 587 dismissals (473 catches, 114 stumpings). In 1959-60 he disposed of a world record eight batsmen in one innings (against Western Australia). Early in his career he was skilful enough with the bat to open for Queensland and to make four first-class centuries in his 5168 runs, averaging 22.56; as a bowler he took 3 wickets at 38.33.

In the first of six overseas tours he was selected in 1957 to tour South Africa under Ian Craig's captaincy. Nicknamed 'The Griz' (an abbreviation of 'Grizzling Grunter'), reputedly by Neil Harvey, Grout squatted low behind the stumps where his diving legside catches, strikingly reminiscent of Tallon, were thrillers in four home series of Tests between 1958 and 1964, in England (1961, 1964), and in the West Indies, South Africa, India and Pakistan. He kept wicket for Australia in 51 Test matches, helping to dismiss 187 batsmen (163 caught and 24 stumped). Twice he claimed eight victims in a Test match and his six catches in one innings (against South Africa at Johannesburg) in the 1957-58 season set a record. In five other Tests he disposed of five batsmen in one innings. R. B. Simpson described him as 'the greatest wicket-keeper I ever saw'. Grout made 890 runs at 15.08.

Blunt, but warm hearted and generous, with a rugged sense of humour, Grout made friends easily. He 'oozed confidence in every aspect of cricket' and savoured the big moments in a fine career. To his friend Ernest Toovey, he was a 'typical Australian', disliking 'snobs' or 'big timers', yet 'very fair'—on one notable occasion during a Test against England he refused to take the bails off when Fred Titmus was stranded after colliding with Neil Hawke. In the foreword to Grout's autobiography, *My Country's Keeper* (London, 1965), Sir Donald Bradman confirmed the celebrated resemblance to Tallon, recalling 'the same basic type of footwork, the same "swoop" on the snick, the same inevitability about holding a chance, and even the same air of aggressive intent'. Grout retired from cricket in 1966, worked for Rothman's of Pall Mall (Australia) Ltd and became a Queensland State selector in 1967.

Survived by his wife, daughter and adopted son, he died of coronary vascular disease on

9 November 1968 in Brisbane and was cremated with Baptist forms; his ashes were scattered over the Brisbane Cricket Ground.

J. Pollard, *Australian Cricket* (Syd, 1982); W. Torrens (ed), *Queensland Cricket and Cricketers 1862-1981* (Brisb, 1982); *Aust Cricket*, Dec 1968; Qld Cricket Assn, *Annual Report*, 1968-69; Sth Brisb District Cricket Club, *Annual Report*, 1941/42-1951/52; Toombul District Cricket Club, *Annual Report*, 1952/53-1965/66; *Wisden Cricketers' Almanack*, 1986; *Sunday Mail* (Brisb), 9 Nov 1968; *Telegraph* (Brisb), 9, 11 Nov 1968.

P. J. MULLINS

GROVES, HERBERT STANLEY (1907-1970), Aboriginal activist, was born on 4 February 1907 at Walhallow (Caroona) Aboriginal station, near Quirindi, New South Wales, son of Robert William Groves, a respected Aboriginal shearer, and his wife Alice Jane, née Fox. Alice was a Kamilaroi from Toomelah on the Castlereagh River who had been raised at Walhallow. As a child, Bert lived at Gulargambone and often travelled with his family in the north-west of the State where his father found work. Bert intermittently attended Coonamble Public School, attaining fifth-grade standard; through avid reading and self-education he became highly literate and articulate.

In 1923 Groves was apprenticed to a plumber, but found it difficult to obtain jobs. For a while he worked a horse scoop on the construction of the Dubbo to Werris Creek railway. In 1927 he was engaged by the Aborigines Protection Board as handyman on Bulgandramine Aboriginal reserve. About this time he met William Ferguson [q.v.8] who was seeking support for his campaign against the oppressive policies of the A.P.B. Soon afterwards Groves returned with his young wife Susan Mary Cain, née Marney (d.1967), to the Walhallow reserve as handyman. One of his major tasks was to maintain the pump, windmill and water-supply.

Groves enjoyed his time there, and had good relationships with the manager and staff. He took an interest in the health and education of the children at Walhallow Aboriginal School and became president of the parents' and citizens' association. Agreeing to Ferguson's request to gather information about discrimination and racism, he sought and gained employment as the handyman at Aboriginal reserves (Angledool, Brewarrina and Toomelah) in the north-west; he then moved to Pilliga where the A.P.B. had a timber-mill and was using cheap Aboriginal labour.

Dismissed from the board's service for chairing a meeting of the Pilliga branch of the Aborigines Progressive Association (formed by Ferguson in 1937), Groves found work as a truck driver at Coonabarabran. He enlisted in the Australian Imperial Force on 14 April 1943 and served in Australia. After his discharge on 26 January 1945, he settled in Sydney. He worked as a plumber at Rhodes before being employed by the Public Service Board, at Parliament House. For the rest of his life, however, his real 'work' was Aboriginal advancement. He was prominent in a demonstration against a South Australian pastoralist who had been fined £135 for keeping Aborigines in chains in 1946, and he opposed the establishment of a rocket-range in Central Australia. As a part-time member (1950-54) of the Aborigines Welfare Board, he fought hard to improve the conditions in which Aborigines lived on government stations and reserves throughout the State. In 1952 he was appointed a justice of the peace. An accomplished speaker, he was frequently invited to address church and service organizations on Aboriginal issues, and helped in leadership training courses run by the Department of Tutorial Classes at the University of Sydney.

In 1956 Groves became first president of the Aboriginal-Australian Fellowship (formed in Sydney to bring together Aborigines and Whites); in 1958 he was a founding member of the Federal Council for Aboriginal Advancement. He was president (from 1963) of the revitalized Aborigines Progressive Association and also worked for the Foundation for Aboriginal Affairs. As a trustee of the Aboriginal Children's Advancement Society, he was tireless in fund-raising efforts to build for children the Kirinari hostel at Sylvania Heights and hostels at Newcastle and Manly. The success of the campaign for the 1967 referendum which gave the Commonwealth government power to legislate on Aboriginal matters was a major victory for Groves. He chaired the breakaway section of the Federal Council for the Advancement of Aborigines and Torres Strait Islanders in 1970 when some Aborigines decided to form their own organization, the National Tribal Council. The N.T.C. gave him the Aboriginal name 'Boodjree Be Angar Goolee' (responsible person).

At Tranby Chapel, Glebe, on 7 June 1969 Groves married 21-year-old, German-born Renate Sofia Schieron. Survived by his wife and their two infants, and by three sons and two daughters by his first wife, he died of myocardial infarction on 28 December 1970 in Bankstown hospital and was buried with Methodist forms in Woronora cemetery.

G. Rowe, *Sketches of Outstanding Aborigines* (Adel, 1955); J. Horner, *Vote Ferguson for Aboriginal Freedom* (Syd, 1974); L. Fox, *The Aboriginals*

(Melb, 1978); F. Bandler and L. Fox (eds), *The Time was Ripe* (Syd, 1983); F. Bandler, *Turning the Tide* (Canb, 1989); *Churinga*, July 1965, p 4, Mar 1966, p 1; *New Dawn*, Aug 1970, p 13, Mar 1971, p 2; *Mosa Mag*, 2, 1988, p 45; Aust Security Intelligence Organization, Central Office, Canb, Activities Among Aust Aborigines in Aust, 1939-54, A6122XR1, item 156 (AA, Canb); family information.   ALAN T. DUNCAN

GROVES, WILLIAM CHARLES (1898-1967), educationist and anthropologist, was born on 18 August 1898 at Ballarat, Victoria, second child of William Charles Groves, engine driver, and his wife Sarah, née Gribble, both Victorian born. William completed his matriculation year at Ballarat High School in 1914 and began teaching with the Victorian Education Department. Under age, but fit and well built, he enlisted in the Australian Imperial Force on 15 July 1915. He served with the 14th Battalion in Egypt and France, and was promoted sergeant in August 1916. During the fighting at Riencourt on 11 April 1917, he was captured and remained a prisoner until the Armistice. Repatriated in 1919, he was discharged on 29 June. He was to publish a serialized account of his experiences in *Reveille* in 1932-33.

In 1920 Groves resumed his teaching career and commenced studies at the University of Melbourne (B.A., Dip.Ed., 1928). Idealism and religious enthusiasm (he had long been a keen Anglican churchman) inspired his move to the mandated Territory of New Guinea where, in 1922-26, he taught in the government's new schools for indigenous children near Rabaul. There, on 7 November 1925, he married a fellow teacher Doris Kathleen Frances Smith. He subsequently held a temporary lectureship (1927-31) at Melbourne Teachers' College.

As a fellow of the Australian National Research Council, in 1932-34 Groves undertook field-work in New Guinea and studied cultural adaptation. The product of his research, *Native Education and Culture-Contact in New Guinea* (Melbourne, 1936), was well received professionally. Between 1932 and 1959 he also published more than twenty articles of anthropological significance in *Oceania*, *Walkabout* and other journals. He was elected a fellow (1934) of the Royal Anthropological Institute of Great Britain and Ireland. Groves was an Australian representative at the Carnegie International Conference on education in the Pacific, held in Honolulu in 1936. From 1937 to 1938 he was director of education in Nauru; in 1939-40 he reported on the educational needs of the British Solomon Islands protectorate. Commissioned in the Militia in June 1941, he transferred to the A.I.F. in December 1942 as a major and was attached

to the Australian Army Education service until demobilized after the end of World War II.

Groves was appointed director of education, Territory of Papua-New Guinea, in 1946. He advocated 'an education built upon the traditional culture of the people ... and related to the world of today'. His greatest task, and triumph, was to forge a link between the fiercely independent vernacular schools of the religious missions and the secular schooling which the government was obliged to provide. All the necessary infrastructure of an educational system had to be created from the raw materials of a pre-literate society, or imported. These factors limited his achievement in spite of a comprehensive five-year plan introduced in 1948. An inquiry into the Department of Education in 1953 criticized Groves severely—and often unjustly—for lack of policy and success. He was stung to a voluminous rebuttal, goaded in part by the suspicion that elements in the new Liberal government and the administration in Australia falsely believed him to have communist sympathies. Contention was restrained by (Sir) Paul Hasluck, minister for Territories, who issued a set of objectives to guide development for the remainder of Groves's directorship. Until his retirement in 1958, Groves successfully implemented the new policy. He also served (1949-58) on the Executive Council of Papua and New Guinea, and in 1951 was Australian representative on a United Nations special committee that examined non-self-governing territories.

Back in Melbourne, Groves lectured in education at Burwood Teachers' College and worked on his unpublished anthropological material. In 1959 he gave the Tate [q.v.12] memorial lecture at the University of Melbourne. While holidaying in London, he died of hypertensive cerebrovascular disease on 11 July 1967 at St Marylebone and was cremated. His wife, son and two of his three daughters survived him.

D. J. Dickson, 'W. C. Groves: Educationist' in J. Griffin (ed), *Papua New Guinea Portraits* (Canb, 1978); *PNG J of Education*, 25, no 1, Apr 1989; *Herald* (Melb), 9 May 1934, 17 June 1936, 18 Apr 1940; *SMH*, 1 Aug 1934; *Age* (Melb), 25 Mar 1939; *Sun News-Pictorial*, 5 Aug 1960.

D. J. DICKSON

GUM YUEN; *see* YUEN

GUNN, DONALD (1856-1943), woolgrower and politician, was born on 19 February 1856 at Burnima, near Bombala, New South Wales, eldest son of Donald Gunn, a squatter from Scotland, and his wife Anna Sophia, née Hughes, an English-born governess. Seeking to avoid the free-selection mania in the colony of New South Wales, Gunn acquired Wyaga, near Goondiwindi on the Darling Downs, and took his family to Queensland in July 1861. Wyaga was sold in 1863 in order to acquire runs at North Toolburra near Warwick, and Pikedale near Stanthorpe, but floods and heavy debts forced the sale of North Toolburra in 1868. Young Donald was initially educated by his mother, who 'started us children in the right direction', before attending the National School, Warwick, and Brisbane Grammar School.

In 1873 the youth drove ten thousand sheep to the family's newly acquired Kensington Downs, near Bowen, of which he was to be manager, but his father's forced retirement terminated the project. From 1874 Donald was responsible for the management of Pikedale. The run was fenced and developed for the production of fine wool, and a modern wash-pool was constructed. Native fauna continued to be subjected to recreational *battues* until the mid-1880s. At Stanmore, New South Wales, on 29 December 1880 Gunn married with Presbyterian forms Mary Ann Rattray Deuchar; they were to have three sons and two daughters. Wool 'considered second to none in Queensland' was produced at Pikedale and won several medals in that decade. After his father died in 1885, Donald sold Pikedale to the Queensland Co-operative Pastoral Co. When the company failed three years later, he bought back the debt-ridden station and in 1889 again sold the restocked run, for £35 000. He managed a neighbouring property until 1891, then bought a grazing farm at Boonarga (Boolarwell), near Talwood, only to be successively confronted by floods, the bank crash and the long drought.

Describing himself 'as not so much a Kidsonite as a Morganite', in 1907 Gunn stood as an Independent—opposed to (Sir) Robert Philp [q.v.11], the Australian Pastoral Co. 'and that class'—and won the Legislative Assembly seat of Carnarvon. He championed the small grazier and selector, and advocated railway extension, prickly-pear eradication and 'every progressive movement on the Darling Downs' until his retirement in October 1920. An influential founding member and councillor of the United Graziers' Association of Queensland, he was a veteran member and chairman (1906) of Waggamba Shire Council and president of the Goondiwindi Show Society. He travelled extensively, visited Japan, the Americas and South Africa to study wool production, and published *A Grazier's Travels: Japan and America Visited* (1925). A member of the Royal Geographical and the Historical societies of Queensland, and of the Royal National Association, he wrote an authoritat-ive local history, *Links with the Past* (1937). He died on 24 July 1943 at Kangaroo Point, Brisbane, and was cremated; two sons and a daughter survived him. A charitable, genial and honest man, it was said that 'money could not buy him nor threats coerce him'.

His third son WALTER (1888-1968), born on 19 September 1888 at Pikedale, was educated locally and at Brisbane Grammar School. 'A splendid worker', he managed the family property following his father's election to parliament. On 30 October 1912 he married with Anglican rites Doris Isabel Brown at her parents' home at Gulnarbar, near St George. After a brief partnership with his father at the end of World War I, Walter acquired runs in the Goondiwindi district—Mundine and Kildonan in 1924, and Tarewinnebah in the 1930s. Chairman (1939-52) of Waggamba Shire Council, he presided over various local clubs and donated premises for a museum at Goondiwindi. A thickset man, he was a humorous raconteur, with a passion for showing horses, though he was also president (1951-55) of the Downs and South-West Queensland Racing Association. Walter retired from Kildonan in 1966. Survived by his wife, two sons and one of his two daughters, he died on 13 October 1968 at Ascot, Brisbane, and was cremated; his estate was sworn for probate at $402 799. His son Sir William Gunn was chairman of the Australian Wool Board.

G. O. Armstrong, *Waggamba Shire Story* (Brisb, 1973); *Pastoral Review*, 16 July 1941, p 522, 16 Aug 1943, p 547; *Brisb Courier*, 18 July 1861; *Australasian*, 11 Dec 1926; *Courier-Mail*, 26 July 1943, 20 Mar 1971; *Toowoomba Chronicle*, 26 July 1943; Gunn papers (OL, *and* held by Sir William Gunn, New Farm, Brisb).   M. FRENCH

GUNN, MARY (1884-1967), eisteddfod secretary, was born on 19 December 1884 at Lochdougan cot-house, Kelton, Kirkcudbrightshire, Scotland, daughter of John Maben, a farm servant who became an estate manager, and his wife Agnes, née Davidson. Raised at Moniaive, Dumfriesshire, Mary entered the University of Glasgow (M.A., 1906) and shared the class prize for political economy in her third year. She studied singing at Siena, Italy, and, on 19 September 1906 at the British Consulate General, Florence, married John Gunn (d.1946), a solicitor from Glasgow.

Soon after their arrival in Sydney from Scotland in May 1913, their 6-year-old daughter died of diphtheria. Their second daughter was born that year. Moving to Melbourne, John Gunn was admitted to the Bar on 1 December 1915. Back in Sydney in 1918, he again practised as a solicitor (from 1923).

Mary found Australia a comfortable place in which to live—'and I do like comfort'. In 1932 she was office secretary for the committee—including Roland Foster and Frank Hutchens [qq.v.8,9]—that founded the City of Sydney Eisteddfod. She joined its organizing committee next year and was assistant-secretary until 1942. During the eisteddfods' four-year break in World War II, she helped to raise money for the Australian Comforts Fund, and packed and dispatched Christmas hampers for troops serving overseas. When the eisteddfods restarted in 1946, she was organizing secretary.

Known professionally as Miss Gunn, she was 'a very small but forceful lady'. She handled all the preliminary organizing, booked the halls (twenty-four by 1952), performed the formidable task of co-ordinating the arrangements into a timetable, rostered stage-managers, cashiers and ushers, and engaged accompanists for most sections. Then followed proof-reading a 200-page programme. Frequently at her desk for twelve hours a day in the busy season from July to October, she began work on the next eisteddfod before the current one was over. By 1963 the number of contestants had increased from two thousand to over twenty-six thousand. Sadly, in her eyes, a lack of entries forced the cancellation of the two Welsh sections that year.

Neither a professional musician nor a trained organizer, Mary Gunn depended on 'Reason, logic, method, and imagination'. She 'was a very modest person' who 'tried to avoid personal publicity at all times'. In 1963 she was appointed M.B.E. With little time for hobbies, she once confessed that it would be an 'awful thing to be bored'. As a girl 'one of her favourite delights had been a "three-mile row in a 10ft boat affair up the Clyde"'. Still in office at the age of 82, she died at her Maroubra home on 11 May 1967 and was cremated with Anglican rites; a daughter survived her. In 1987 the City of Sydney Cultural Council and the Friends of the Eisteddfod established the Mary Gunn memorial award, given each year for a different section of the eisteddfod (now renamed McDonald's City of Sydney Performing Arts Challenge).

ABC Weekly, 12 Apr 1952; *SMH*, 1 Jan, 28 Oct 1950, 15 Sept 1963, 13, 16 May 1967; *Herald* (Melb), 12 May 1967.   MARTHA RUTLEDGE

GUNN, REGINALD MONTAGU CAIRNS (1893-1974), professor of veterinary science, was born on 19 October 1893 at Petersham, Sydney, second child of Joseph Robertson Gunn, an accountant from Scotland, and his Victorian-born wife Eva Louisa, née Fosdyke.

'Rex' was educated at Hayfield Preparatory and Sydney Grammar schools, and at the University of Sydney (B.Sc.Agr., 1915; B.V.Sc. *ad eund.*, 1929; D.V.Sc., 1935) where he graduated with first-class honours. He enlisted in the Australian Imperial Force on 8 September 1915 and sailed for England in 1916 as farrier sergeant, Army Service Corps. In November he was sent to the Western Front. Granted leave in February 1919, he was admitted to the Royal (Dick) Veterinary College, University of Edinburgh (B.Sc., 1921). Gunn also gained the diploma and membership of the Royal College of Veterinary Surgeons (honorary fellow 1954), and was awarded a silver medal by the (Royal) Highland and Agricultural Society of Scotland. On 23 November 1921 he married Georgina Ethel Willis (d.1960) at Hillsborough, County Down, Ireland.

After postgraduate courses in Copenhagen and Stockholm, Gunn returned to Sydney late in 1921 to take up an appointment as lecturer in veterinary anatomy and surgery at the university. He managed to combine active teaching with a considerable volume and a wide field of research, including skin, horn and organ grafting, and fertility studies in sheep, particularly the ram. His meticulous studies on artificial seminal ejaculation, artificial insemination of ewes and the characters of spermatogenesis led to practical developments in sheep husbandry. He wrote his doctoral thesis on fertility in sheep. Encouraged and assisted in his work by J. A. Gilruth [q.v.9], he made many contacts throughout Australia with leading sheep studs and studmasters, and published mainly in the *Australian Veterinary Journal* (of which he was business manager).

Gunn's scrupulous scientific approach and his manual skills (which made him an outstanding surgeon) profoundly affected his students; they found him dour and unapproachable, but respected his great ability and, in later life, acclaimed his teaching. Practical surgery classes were known as 'Black Wednesday' when all present 'felt the lash of his acid tongue'. He demanded strict discipline in academic and professional work. Appointed reader in 1945, he succeeded (Sir) Ian Clunies Ross [q.v.13] as professor of veterinary science in 1948. He ruled his department autocratically and his altercations with his professional colleagues were legendary. In 1939 and 1954-58 he was dean of the faculty.

As captain (1922) and major (1931), Australian Army Veterinary Corps, Militia, Gunn had commanded the 2nd Cavalry Mobile Veterinary Section at the university from 1923. In 1933 he became deputy assistant director, veterinary services, 1st Division, and in 1943 was transferred to the Reserve of Officers.

He was president of the Veterinary Association of New South Wales in 1926, the Medical Science Club in 1938-39 and 1957-58, the Australian Veterinary Association in 1941-44 and the Veterinary Surgeons Board in 1942-50. As a consultant, he was closely associated with the Royal Agricultural Society of New South Wales and the Australian Jockey Club. In 1955 Gunn reported to the New Zealand government on the need to establish a veterinary school. That year he was also a member of the United Nations Food and Agriculture Organization's mission to India and Pakistan on veterinary education; in 1961-62 he served on an F.A.O. panel of experts.

Having retired in 1958 to his four-acre (1.6 ha) property, Crathes, on the Nepean River near Penrith, Gunn married 31-year-old Dorothy Ada Milne, a secretary, on 11 January 1965 at St Oswald's Anglican Church, Haberfield. He was a man of slight build, with a serious but bright expression and a well-clipped moustache. Students who came in close contact with him after graduating could not believe that he was their stern and demanding teacher. Survived by his wife and their son and daughter, and by one of the two sons of his first marriage, he died on 1 July 1974 at Crathes and was buried in South Head cemetery, Sydney. The university named a building after Gunn and holds a pen-drawing of him by Norman Carter [q.v.7].

G. E. Hall and A. Cousins (eds), *Book of Remembrance of the University of Sydney in the War 1914-1918* (Syd, 1939); *Centaur*, 1939, p 7, 1947, p 11, 1958, p 18, 1974, p 19; *Aust Veterinary J*, 35, Aug 1959, p 381, 50, Sept 1974, p 415; Univ Syd, *Gazette*, Feb 1975; Gunn papers (held by Mrs D. A. Gunn, Turramurra, Syd, *and* Univ Syd Archives).   ROBERT I. TAYLOR

GURNEY, ALEXANDER GEORGE (1902-1955), cartoonist and illustrator, was born on 15 March 1902 at Morice Town, Devon, England, son of William George Gurney (d.1903), a captain's steward in the Royal Navy, and his wife Alice Birdie, née Worbey. Alice emigrated to Hobart and in 1908 married a police constable James William Albert Hursey, a widower with two children. Alex was educated at Macquarie Street State School, where he showed keen interest in cartooning. At the age of 13 he worked briefly as an ironmonger before being apprenticed for seven years to the Hydro-Electric Department. He attended evening art classes at Hobart Technical College under F. V. E. L. Dechaineux [q.v.8], sent cartoons to the *Illustrated Tasmanian Mail*, the *Bulletin*, Melbourne *Punch* and *Smith's Weekly*, and in 1926 published a book of caricatures of notable citizens, *Tasmanians Today*.

By that year Gurney was working in Melbourne on the *Morning Post*; in 1927, when the *Post* was incorporated into the *Sun News-Pictorial*, he moved to Sydney. He revisited Melbourne and, on 16 June 1928 at Christ Church, South Yarra, married Junee, the 19-year-old daughter of Montague Grover [q.v.9]. Having created 'Stiffy & Mo' [q.v.11 Rene] (based on the two vaudevillians) for *Beckett's Budget* in 1927, two years later he produced a full-page weekly cartoon, 'The Daggs' (later 'Daggsy'), for the *Sunday Times*. Gurney was employed by the *Daily Guardian* and the short-lived Labor newspaper, the *World*, in 1931, and by the Adelaide *News* in 1932. He transferred to the Melbourne *Herald* in 1933 and from October drew 'Ben Bowyang', based on C. J. Dennis's [q.v.8] column, until taking Sam Wells's place as the leader page cartoonist when Wells returned to England in 1934.

By late 1937 Gurney was working from his new home at Elwood. Upon Wells's return in 1939, Gurney created the comic strip 'Bluey and Curley', centred on two larrikin soldiers: the first six instalments appeared on a full page in the *Picture-News* in November and the comic strip was moved to the *Sun News-Pictorial* on 1 February 1940. As an accredited war correspondent, Gurney visited army camps throughout Australia to obtain authentic detail and gain a feel for military life; he contracted malaria in August 1944 while visiting New Guinea.

The strip made 'superb use of Australian idiom and slang', and had an 'instinctive understanding and interpretation of the Australian male'. At the end of hostilities in 1945, Bluey and Curley went to Britain for the Victory march and served in the army of occupation in Japan before resuming civilian life and taking jobs as lighthouse-keepers, lion-tamers, private detectives and so on. The strip was widely syndicated in newspapers in Australia, New Zealand and Canada, but Gurney refused to mellow the Australian nature of Bluey and Curley, which hindered its potential sale to the United States of America. In 1948-49 the strip was adapted as a serial on Sydney radio-station 2SM. Gurney illustrated two books of humorous experiences by a medical friend 'G.P.', *Sickness Without Sorrow* (1947) and *Life With Laughter* (1950). The proceeds of both went to the Food for Britain Appeal. In the late 1930s he had also designed emblems for the South Melbourne and Essendon Australian Rules football teams.

Gurney was a balding, stocky, bespectacled man who generally wore a felt hat. He belonged to the Returned Sailors', Soldiers' and Airmen's Imperial League of Australia, and to the Bread and Cheese, and the Melbourne Savage clubs. His favourite pastimes were fishing and shooting. Survived by his wife, son and three daughters, he died suddenly of heart disease on 4 December 1955 at Elwood and was cremated with Anglican rites. The strip was subsequently drawn by Norman Rice and then by Leslie Dixon until 1975.

V. Lindesay, *The Inked-in Image* (Melb, 1970); M. Mahood, *The Loaded Line* (Melb, 1973); J. Ryan, *Panel by Panel* (Syd, 1979); J. Gurney and K. Dunstan, *Gurney & Bluey & Curley* (Melb, 1986); *Inkspot*, no 21, Spring/Summer 1992, p 26; *Herald* (Melb), 9 Aug 1947, 5 Dec 1955; *Sun News-Pictorial*, 5 Oct 1955, 2 Aug 1975; *News* (Adel), 25 Nov 1975.   STEVE PANOZZO

GURNEY, ARTHUR STANLEY (1908-1942), clerk and soldier, was born on 15 December 1908 at Daydawn, on the Murchison goldfields, Western Australia, fourth of five children of George Gurney, miner, and his wife Jane, née Roberts, both from South Australia. Educated at the local state school and at Stott's Business College, Perth, Stan began work with a real-estate agent. From June 1927 he was employed as a clerk and meter-fixer with the City of Perth Electricity and Gas Department. An enthusiastic cyclist, he won a number of road-races and officiated at fixtures conducted by the League of Western Australian Wheelmen.

Quiet, unassuming, 5 ft 8 ins (173 cm) tall and of solid build, Gurney stated that he was an Anglican when he enlisted on 6 December 1940 in the Australian Imperial Force. In July 1941 he embarked for the Middle East and on 12 September joined the 2nd/48th Battalion at Tobruk, Libya; the 2nd/48th was sent to Palestine in October and to Syria in January 1942.

As part of the 26th Brigade, 9th Division, the battalion was deployed to Egypt in June to meet the threat posed by Axis forces pushing east towards El Alamein. Tel el Eisa lay approximately 10 miles (16 km) to the west, near the coast. The division was ordered to mount an attack on 22 July; the 2nd/48th's role was to capture Tel el Eisa Ridge. Major General Sir Leslie Morshead [q.v.] protested to the British commander-in-chief, General Sir Claude Auchinleck, that the plan was ill-conceived, pointing out that inadequate support would be provided. Because the 26th Brigade had to hold its existing ground, the 2nd/24th and 2nd/48th battalions could each spare only two companies for the assault and these would lack reinforcements. Yet the operation went ahead.

The 2nd/48th's 'D' Company, with Private Gurney in No.17 Platoon, crossed its start-line about 6.00 a.m. on 22 July, came under intense fire and began to take heavy casualties. Using a captured post as a fire-support position, 17 Platoon pushed on. Gurney car-ried a cumbersome Boyes anti-tank rifle. His platoon commander, Lieutenant Jim Wearing-Smith, recalled: 'Stan came up to me and I said, "For Christ sake drop that bloody Boyes, you'll do better with a rifle!"' Within the next few moments Wearing-Smith was critically wounded and the platoon sergeant was killed. Carrying a rifle and bayonet, Gurney rushed over open ground through a hail of fire, bayoneted three Germans and captured their machine-gun post. He then charged a second emplacement, bayoneted two of the enemy and sent back one prisoner. While preparing to attack a third post, he was blown off his feet by a grenade burst. Undeterred, he stormed the position. His comrades saw him 'using the bayonet with great vigour' before he disappeared from view and was killed.

Gurney's body was found and buried in El Alamein war cemetery; he was posthumously awarded the Victoria Cross. In 1994 his family presented it to the Australian War Memorial, Canberra. The Stan Gurney V.C. Memorial Bike Race, held annually in Western Australia, commemorates him.

J. G. Glenn, *Tobruk to Tarakan* (Adel, 1960); B. Maughan, *Tobruk and El Alamein* (Canb, 1966); L. Wigmore (ed), *They Dared Mightily*, second ed, revised and condensed by J. Williams and A. Staunton (Canb, 1986); *Energy Com News* (Perth), Mar 1980, p 13; *West Australian*, 12 Sept 1942; information from and correspondence held by Mr J. Wearing-Smith, Adel.   PETER BRUNE

GUTHRIE, BESSIE JEAN THOMPSON (1905-1977), designer, publisher, feminist and campaigner for children's rights, was born on 2 July 1905 at Rosalie, Church Street, Camperdown, Sydney, only child of native-born parents James Buchanan Mitchell, Mint employee, and his wife Jane Elizabeth, née Coulson. The house, at 97 Derwent Street, Glebe, in which Bessie grew up and lived until her death, was part of the Church of England's inner-city property holdings and became the focus of her lifelong battle against Christian profiteering from the poor. She was reared and educated by her aunts Janet Forbes Mackenzie Mitchell and Margaret Crichton Mitchell—fiercely Scottish spinster schoolteachers, bibliophiles and admirers of the work and ideas of Mary Wollstonecraft—who held firm beliefs on the education of women. 'Never iron men's shirts', said Aunt Janet.

From 1921 Mitchell attended classes at (East Sydney) Technical College. She passed design 3 in 1925, intermediate art in 1927 and gained a diploma in design in 1931, having specialized in industrial and modern interior design. Excited by modernism, by the older traditions of Japanese form and space, and by the decorative treasures of medieval architecture, she began to form her own ideas. Her exhibition of design art at the college in 1930 encompassed plans for individual furnishings, restaurant and dance-pavilion interiors, tapestries and theatre design, and was praised for its innovation by the head of the art school Hedley Rowe.

In the late 1920s Mitchell began to work professionally. After selling designs for modular furniture to various companies, she was employed as furniture draughtswoman with Grace [q.v.9] Bros Ltd's department stores. She also developed a private practice in interior design, in the controversial modernist style. Moving in bohemian and artistic circles in Sydney's inner city, she became friendly with Hal Missingham, Kenneth Slessor [q.v.] and with Dulcie Deamer [q.v.8] who helped to expand her cultural contacts and invited her to write on design for the *Australian Woman's Mirror* in the late 1930s. Bessie quickly tired of working and writing on domestic interiors for the rich and tried to democratize design by applying her ideas to poorer households. Her articles in the *Australian Women's Weekly*, *Australian Woman's Mirror* and *Good Fellows* stressed the merit of freeing domestic space from the clutter and labour-intensive drudgery of the past, advocating greater light and efficiency, utility and beauty, duality of purpose, and even notions of passive solar energy and ecological balance. At St Stephen's Presbyterian Church, Sydney, on 3 January 1935 she married Ivor Ralph Michael Russell, a tailor and a divorcee; she was to divorce him in January 1937.

Her developing leftist political sympathies and her enduring love of writing and book design led Bessie to found her own publishing company, Viking Press, in 1939. She focussed on poetry and anti-war tracts, publishing the earliest works of Dorothy Auchterlonie (later Green), Elizabeth Riddell, Elizabeth Lambert, Harley Matthews, Muir Holburn and others whose books she designed and illustrated. Slessor wrote to her from Cairo in 1940: 'I hope your publishing department is still flourishing, but I still think you'll make more out of thrillers, or books on parsnip-growing, or anything except poetry'. Ultimately it was the wartime paper shortage which ended the venture in 1943.

Mitchell was appointed head draughtswoman at De Havilland Aircraft Pty Ltd's experimental gliders factory before working in aircraft design for the Commonwealth government. In February 1945 she accepted the post of secretary for publicity with the Young Women's Christian Association. From that year she wrote, co-ordinated and broadcast a series of talks on 'Plans For Women In The Post-War World', and organized press, radio and Cinesound News releases, as well as training films directed at young women, war widows and women dismissed from industry to make way for returning servicemen.

While lecturing in design at East Sydney Technical College, for the Workers' Educational Association and for the university's Department of Tutorial Classes, she tackled the oppressiveness of housework. In radio programmes and in her classes she used humorously subversive time-and-motion flow charts, inspired by the goal of eliminating housework (a goal she herself attained in her later life). She continued to undertake private design commissions through the 1940s and early 1950s.

At the district registrar's office, Glebe, on 30 June 1950 she married another divorcee Clive Guthrie, a painter who belonged to the Realist Artists' Group. He had served in New Guinea during World War II and sent her his drawings of the indigenous people. Unlike Bessie who never joined a political party, Clive belonged to the Communist Party of Australia; he also joined the Waterside Workers' Federation of Australia, taking jobs as a painter and decorator. Bessie's political consciousness was never circumscribed by party dogma, though she was influenced by anarchist ideas (particularly the works of Kropotkin). She ranged across a complex terrain of radical cultural ideas centring on form and aesthetics, education and feminism. Community, friendship and loyalty were her core principles.

Money never flowed freely, particularly as Bessie found that her ideas of design did not suit a private consultancy for the well-to-do. Clive's wartime experiences had wrecked his nervous system; he continued to paint and exhibit, and eventually received a repatriation pension. The need for a regular income resulted in Bessie working as a clerk in the Government Insurance Office of New South Wales from 1952 until her retirement in 1972. Her intimate friendship with Dulcie Deamer lasted over forty years, despite immense differences over politics, the role of women, religion and exhibitionism. The two sustained a rich and enduring relationship with Rosaleen Norton [q.v.]. Bessie nursed her husband and her friend until Clive died in 1971 and Dulcie in 1972.

Seemingly constrained by personal circumstances and a dreary job, in the 1950s she opened her house to young girls who were the victims of domestic violence, abuse, drunkenness, homelessness and the welfare system. From the day when one young girl who claimed that she had been raped 'was taken from my home and I was unable to find where she was', Bessie became a crusader for children's rights against the Byzantine madness of the State child-welfare system. She researched every aspect of the Children's

Court, the welfare-home system, Church homes, the morality of existing policies and a large group of individual case histories. She bombarded bureaucrats, journalists and politicians with letters demanding changes and disclosure. Her focus and information were always street-based, her loyalty always to the girls. Over the years her network of contacts grew. Young runaways became adolescent, moved on from homes to gaols, had babies or abortions, disappeared and returned—bashed, drunk, tattooed. Some survived, some did not. She ran what amounted to a private half-way house at 97 Derwent Street where runaway girls could write on the 'message wall', obtain support and receive unconditional love. 'Aunty Bessie's' was a safe house.

As many of the girls survived by violence and crime, mixed with inner-city gangsters and belonged to the *demi-monde*, there was considerable risk to a small, straight-backed woman by then in her late fifties. She had some limited success following the 1961 riots at Parramatta Girls' Training School, obtaining press attention and a public inquiry. The government, however, established a maximum security children's prison at Hay in an old, condemned gaol as the ultimate punishment for rebellious girls: there, enforced silence, shaved heads, solitary confinement and daily humiliations prevailed. Few spirits survived. In her 1962 diary Bessie wrote 'Parramatta must be closed. Hay must be closed'.

She broadened her research to include the institutionalized abuse of females—from babies charged with being 'abandoned' to homeless elderly women. A pattern of denial, evasiveness and misogyny emerged. 'Women can always get a bed with a man', was one response she heard again and again. Bessie joined the Council for Civil Liberties, the Humanist Society and other organizations to tackle specific issues, but met with well-meaning inaction and frustrating liberalism. While president of the Glebe Tenants' Association, she successfully campaigned to convince the Whitlam government to acquire the Glebe housing estate.

In 1970 Bessie Guthrie walked into 67 Glebe Point Road, the political home of the Women's Liberation Movement, with her files and stories. She joined the collective of the newspaper, *Mejane* (first issued in March 1971), and quietly began to educate the predominantly younger women. She published much of her material in *Mejane*, systematized her theories and demands, and worked cooperatively to plan mass protests outside Bidura Girls' Home, the Metropolitan Girls' Shelter, Glebe, and Parramatta Girls' Training School. These demonstrations achieved wide press coverage in 1973-74. She per-

suaded the television journalist Peter Manning to fly a helicopter over Hay children's prison and to produce a full-length documentary, based on her research, for the Australian Broadcasting Commission's 'This Day Tonight' (screened in August 1973). The institution at Hay was closed in 1975. Her campaigns also led to the end of compulsory virginity-testing of girls charged by the Children's Court and to the abolition of the charge of 'exposure to moral danger'. The anarchistic and irreverent flair of her younger co-workers in Women's Liberation rejuvenated Bessie. She thrived on new friendships, was challenged by the passion for new ideas, and found a new family. A practical, non-sectarian campaigner, she profoundly influenced the movement at a critical early stage.

With Anne Summers and others, in March 1974 Guthrie squatted in the two adjoining houses at 73-75 Westmoreland Street, Glebe, to found Elsie Women's Refuge Night Shelter. She worked on the roster, contributed her years of research on homelessness, marched through the streets of Sydney on every International Women's Day and joined the campaign to free Sandra Willson, the State's longest-serving woman prisoner. In the 1977 Anzac Day campaign to draw attention to women raped in wars, Bessie made the decisive breach at the Cenotaph, pushing aside policemen, declaring herself a war widow and allowing groups of women to break police lines.

As a radical freethinker and feminist, she had never sought public office or personal glory. Storyteller, bibliophile, sleuth, gourmet and lover of shopping and cafés, she embodied the spirit of the inner city at its best. She was an 'avid reader of crime fiction, her greatest heroine was Modesty Blaise'. Bessie died on 17 December 1977 at Glebe. Her funeral began as a street meeting outside her home where women told stories of her life's work, and some of her oldest friends, such as Jessie Boyd, mixed with her new young friends. The procession, led by women on motorbikes, with streamers, banners and horn-honking, was stopped on Gladesville Bridge by police who refused to believe that it was a 'real' funeral! Women carried her coffin into Northern Suburbs crematorium, sang over her, and still talk of her with great love and good memories.

In 1978 she was commemorated on a poster (held by the National Gallery of Australia) by Toni Robertson for the first Women and Labour Conference; the caption quoted Bessie's remark in 1971: 'I've been waiting for you women to get here all my life'.

H. Radi (ed), *200 Australian Women* (Syd, 1988); *SMH*, 7 Feb 1924, 18 Sept 1939, 19 Dec 1977; *Tribune* (Syd), 2 Oct 1973; *Nation Review,*

22-28 Dec 1977; *National Times*, 26-31 Dec 1977; Guthrie papers *and* notes of interviews, 1975-77 (held by author, Mongarlowe, NSW).

SUZANNE BELLAMY

GUTTERIDGE, MARY VALENTINE (1887-1962), kindergarten principal, was born on 14 February 1887 at Launceston, Tasmania, eldest of five children of British-born parents Matthew Wilkins Gutteridge, medical practitioner, and his wife Mary Kate, née Penney. When her father accepted a position at the Homoeopathic Hospital, Melbourne, Mary was educated at Faireleight school, St Kilda. Aged 18, she left for England to train as a kindergarten teacher at the Froebel Institute, Roehampton. In 1911 she was appointed principal of the junior school, Church of England Girls' Grammar, Melbourne. Six years later she returned to London where she worked in a nursery school and as a volunteer nurse; she later established a nursery school in Paris for displaced children, with assistance from the Rothschild foundation.

In 1922 Miss Gutteridge was appointed by the Free Kindergarten Union of Victoria to the dual position of acting-principal of the fledgling Melbourne Kindergarten Training College and supervisor of the twenty-four kindergartens affiliated with the union. As principal (1923-36) of the college, she carried out a demanding range of duties, including lecturing, student supervision, advertising and taking care of the domestic minutiae associated with running the student hostel. She extended the period of kindergarten training from two to three years, and made the individual child the focus of teaching. In an effort to improve the health of kindergarten children, she and Dr Vera Scantlebury Brown [q.v.11] facilitated the establishment (1927) of the Forest Hill holiday-home, and the introduction of medical inspections and dental services.

Assisted by a Rockefeller fellowship in 1928, Gutteridge studied at Columbia University Teachers College, New York (B.Sc., 1929), and at child research centres in the United States of America. She also travelled in Britain, Europe, Russia and Asia. Back in Melbourne, she took on an additional role as director (1930) of the State's first nursery school, opened as part of the Keele Street Kindergarten, Collingwood. She created a one-year course in nursery-school education for qualified kindergarten teachers, promoted the study of early childhood with a grant from the Australian Council for Educational Research, and published *The Story of an Australian Nursery School* (1932).

The F.K.U. praised her as 'an invaluable officer' and granted her further study leave in 1933. Once more she went to London where she resigned on the grounds of ill health, though she subsequently returned to Columbia University (M.A., 1937; Ph.D., 1940). Her resignation apparently soured her relationship with the F.K.U. She achieved an international reputation, however, as a scholar and teacher at Columbia, the University of Minnesota and (from 1941) at the Merrill-Palmer Institute, Detroit, where she became head of the department of early-childhood education.

On her retirement in 1952, Gutteridge settled in Brisbane; she continued to assist in kindergartens and children's homes until she grew frail with Parkinson's disease. She died on 15 June 1962 at Wavell Heights and was cremated with Anglican rites. Described as a professional in her field, she was remembered for her 'patrician appearance, her intelligent love of children and her gift of friendship'.

L. Gardiner, *The Free Kindergarten Union of Victoria 1908-80* (Melb, 1982); *Courier-Mail*, 18 June 1962; P. Walford, An investigation made into the contribution of Mary V. Gutteridge to the kindergarten movement in Victoria 1922-1936 (B.Ed. thesis, Inst of Early Childhood Development, Kew, Melb, 1979); Free Kindergarten Union of Vic, Annual Report, 1925-26, 1933-34 (Univ Melb Archives); Gutteridge family papers (held by Mrs N. Gutteridge, Ascot, Brisb).

ELIZABETH J. MELLOR

GUY, JAMES ALLAN (1890-1979), politician, trade union official and butcher, was born on 30 November 1890 at Launceston, Tasmania, son of James Guy, a native-born blacksmith, member (1909-13) of the House of Assembly and senator (1914-20), and his wife Margaret, née McElwee, whose brother G. J. McElwee was a member (1940-46) of the Legislative Council. Educated at Invermay State School, young James worked as a butcher. On 7 June 1916 he married Amy Louisa Adams (d.1951) with Methodist forms at Invermay.

Active in union affairs, Guy was State secretary (1911-16) of the Australasian Meat Industry Employees' Union, treasurer of the Launceston Trades Hall Council, and secretary of the Launceston branches of the Federated Storemen and Packers' and of the Federated Carters' and Drivers' Industrial unions; he was also secretary of the Baking Trade Employees' and the Waterside Workers' federations of Australia. He was, as well, a member of the Butchers' Wages Board (from 1911) and of the Launceston City Council (1928-31), and was appointed an inspector (1940) under the Commonwealth Conciliation and Arbitration Act (1904-34). In 1916 he had been elected to the House of Assembly as an Australian Labor Party candidate for Bass; five years later he became general secretary of the Tasmanian branch of the party.

In J. A. Lyons's [q.v.10] cabinet, Guy served as chief secretary (1923-28), minister for mines (1923-24) and minister for railways (1924-28). Acting-premier from July to December 1926 and deputy-premier until June 1928, he was deputy-leader of the Opposition in 1928-29. Although he was an unspectacular parliamentary performer, his ministerial career was safe and steady. In recognition of his standing in Bass, James Scullin [q.v.11] recruited him to contest the seat in the 1929 Federal elections. On 12 October Guy and Lyons entered the House of Representatives.

In parliament Guy sided with Lyons in his gradual falling out with the Labor caucus, especially on the question of overseas loan repayments. On 13 March 1931, with three other Labor members, they supported a motion of no confidence in the Scullin government. Lyons and his 'little band' left the party to join the Nationalists in forming the United Australia Party which came to office in December with Lyons as prime minister.

Guy spoke rarely in the House and his most significant work was done away from the floor of parliament, though when he addressed the Chamber he often had something interesting to say. As a Labor member he had expressed strong support for a formal conciliation and arbitration process. He thought that an arbitration system and the protection of Australian industries were inextricably linked, and would improve the lot of the ordinary worker: 'We should endeavour to legislate so that every worker shall receive a fair wage for the work he performs, and that the conditions under which he operates shall, in every sense, be fair and reasonable'.

While representing Labor, he had sternly criticized (Sir) Earle Page [q.v.11] for his inadequate knowledge of industrial matters and attacked Nationalist opponents for seeking to protect proprietors who employed sweated labour. In constitutional matters Guy supported the Scullin government's plan to give parliament power to amend the Constitution, asserting that those who saw it as sacred and unalterable impeded the country's progress. He claimed that section 51 of the Constitution posed a major problem for national advancement and suggested adopting the Canadian model which detailed provincial powers and left Federal powers 'untrammelled'.

With his change of party, Guy ceased to talk of such matters and confined his speeches largely to parochial Tasmanian issues, such as the production of potatoes and paper pulp, and the impact of trade upon the island's economy. In 1932 Lyons rewarded him for his loyalty by appointing him assistant-minister for trade and customs. One of Guy's responsibilities was to defend film-censorship provisions which he described as 'both necessary and admirable', for, without them, 'all sorts of puerile and undesirable films could be displayed, to the detriment, not only of our civilization, but of the Christian religion'. He dismissed the campaign by the Friends of the Soviet Union against the banning of the film, *The Five Year Plan*, on the grounds that the film was 'not considered desirable in the public interests'.

At the 1934 elections Guy lost his seat. Eager to return to Federal parliament, he contested Bass in 1937 and Wilmot in 1939, before winning the latter in 1940. He was party whip from 1941 until his defeat at the 1946 polls. In 1949 he was elected to the Senate for the Liberal Party.

Guy's comparatively few utterances in the Senate generally dealt with foreign relations and his perception of a communist threat to democracies like Australia. He saw Josef Stalin's 'ultimate goal' as 'the control of the entire human race'. Fearing 'the southward march of the Communists', he described the sending of Australian troops to Korea and Malaya as crucial if the threat were to be averted. Guy pushed continually for a larger defence vote and supported the introduction of compulsory military training. He was in favour of secret ballots in trade union elections to weaken the power of 'Communist bosses'. Reviled by former Labor friends for his part in bringing down the Scullin government, he responded by chiding them in 1955 for neglecting true Australian ways and being prepared 'to play the game on the Communist side'.

Defeated in the elections that year, Guy left the Senate in June 1956. At the Presbyterian Church, Punchbowl, Sydney, on 12 July 1952 he had married Madge Kernohan, a 61-year-old show-card writer. He was appointed C.B.E. in 1968. In later life he lived at Sylvania Waters and was associated with Twentieth Century Fox Film Corporation (Australia) Pty Ltd and the Motion Pictures Distributors Association of Australia. Survived by the son of his first marriage, he died on 16 December 1979 at Bexley and was cremated.

E. Lyons, *So We Take Comfort* (Lond, 1965); *PD* (Cwlth), 10 Apr 1930, p 1073, 26 June 1930, p 3336, 27 Oct 1932, p 1673, 6 Dec 1950, p 3751, 26 June 1951, p 368, 12 May 1955, p 352; *Aust Worker*, 18 Apr 1928, 18 Dec 1929; *Mercury* (Hob), 28 Dec 1979.   SCOTT BENNETT

H

HACKETT, PATRICIA (1908-1963), theatrical producer, actress and lawyer, was born on 25 January 1908 in Perth, second of five children of (Sir) John Winthrop Hackett (d.1916) [q.v.9], newspaper proprietor, and his wife Deborah Vernon, née Drake-Brockman [q.v.9 Hackett]. In 1918 Deborah remarried and the family moved to Adelaide. Educated in 1919-22 at Church of England Girls' Grammar School (The Hermitage), Geelong, Victoria, and for two months in 1923 at Woodlands Church of England Girls' Grammar School, Adelaide, Patricia matriculated by private study in 1924. Next year she passed two subjects towards a law degree at the University of Adelaide, but was dismissed for sitting her sister's Latin examination. In 1927 Patricia went to London where she passed her final examination in law in 1929. Called to the Bar at the Inner Temple in 1930 and admitted to the South Australian Bar that year, she practised in Adelaide; Don Dunstan was to share her chambers from 1952.

In 1932 Hackett made her theatrical début in the Repertory Theatre's production of Ashley Dukes's *The Man with a Load of Mischief*. Two years later she opened her own 150-seat theatre, the Torch, in the basement of Claridge Arcade, Gawler Place, where she chose the cast, directed and starred in an eccentric repertoire. In September 1934, when the critic Sidney Downer panned her staging of Geza Silberer's *Caprice*, she threw a bottle of ink over him; he sued and she was fined. Hackett revisited England in 1936. She published a book of verse, *These Little Things* (Adelaide, 1938). For up to four months each year until the Japanese invasion in 1942, she stayed in the Solomon Islands; during World War II she raised her sister Verna's son and two daughters in a home at Hackney that Patricia owned with her companion Dr Mildred Mocatta.

Between 1942 and 1948 Hackett was involved in plays for the university's Theatre Guild at The Hut. In 1944 Max Harris reviewed her performance in *Gild the Mask Again*: 'We have now seen Miss Hackett as a Biblical dame, Virgin Mary, a Moon Woman, Salome, a Grey Sword, Queen Elizabeth, and a Renaissance wife. It only remains for her to play a Life of Stalin, Diaghilev and Little Nell. Let the Theatre Guild forget the panther passions of the Hackett demi-monde . . . more stress on Theatre and less on Art'. Hackett threatened a libel action. Harris apologized publicly. Thereafter, with one exception, critics were banned from her second Torch Theatre, in the cellar of her Hackney house.

Adelaide's first salon theatre, the new Torch, opened in 1953 with Christopher Fry's *A Phoenix Too Frequent*. Hackett presented 'short seasons of her exotic and dramatically intense, if antiquated, repertoire', essaying each leading role, producing, and usually making costumes and props. Dunstan and Charles Jury [q.v.] were among the actors. Tall and slim, with long dark hair, Hackett had expressive eyes, a patrician nose and a richly modulated voice. She was an actress of 'remarkable purity', although her performances were occasionally marred by pretentiousness. By nature she was generous, witty, flamboyant, temperamental, outspoken and fiery. Her drive and energy were astonishing.

Hackett's last play, *Legend*, comprised much of her verse and was performed as a fringe production during Adelaide's inaugural Festival of Arts (1960). She died of coronary thrombosis on 18 August 1963 at Hackney and was cremated. In 1965 the University of Western Australia established the Patricia Hackett prize, awarded annually for the best creative writing published in *Westerly* magazine.

On Dit, 30 June, 19 July 1944; *Westerly*, May 1965; *Herald* (Melb), 6 Sept 1934; *Advertiser* (Adel), 28 Mar 1963; C. Ballantyne, A Profile of Miss Patricia Hackett *and* P. Goers, Patricia Hackett (mss, 1984, Performing Arts Collection of SA, Theatre Museum, Adel Festival Centre, Adel); information from Mr J. Cousins, Christies Beach, Mr L. Williams, Hawthorn, Hon D. A. Dunstan, Norwood, Miss J. Cook, Adel, Miss J. Brown, Nth Adel, and the late Mr H. Cullen.

JO PEOPLES

HADDON, ALFRED CORT (1855-1940), anthropologist and academic, was born on 24 May 1855 at Finsbury, Middlesex, England, second child of John Haddon, printer, merchant and Baptist deacon, and his wife Caroline, née Waterman, the author of several books of salutary children's tales. As changing economic circumstances caused his parents to shift about London, Alfred's early schooling was patchy, with time spent at the City of London Middle Class School and at the Nonconformist Mill Hill School. He became a keen amateur naturalist and, on entering the family business, pursued this interest by attending evening-classes in anatomy and zoology at King's College, and in geology at Birkbeck College, London. Alfred had little interest in printing, beyond what it offered the natural scientist—the materials and drafting skills to record his specimens and dissections. Eventually a tutor was employed to prepare him for his university entrance examinations. In 1875 Haddon entered Christ's College, Cambridge (B.A., 1879; M.A., 1882), to read the new natural science tripos, at which he excelled, especially in zoology and comparative anatomy. After graduating, he spent six months at the university's zoological station at Naples, Italy.

On his return to Cambridge, Haddon was made curator of the Zoological Museum. A few months later he was appointed a demonstrator in comparative anatomy at the university. In 1880 he accepted the chair of zoology at the Royal College of Science, Dublin. On 21 September 1881 at the Bunyan Meeting-house, Bedford, England, he married Fanny Elizabeth Rose. In Dublin he focussed on marine zoology. Despite being involved in scientifically important, deep-sea dredging expeditions off the south-west Irish coast, and the success of his publications—especially his major taxonomic revision of British sea anemones—he was dissatisfied. He applied for positions elsewhere, among them the foundation chair of biology at the University of Melbourne (which ultimately went to (Sir) Walter Baldwin Spencer [q.v.12]), and began to plan an expedition to further Charles Darwin's [q.v.1] *The Structure and Distribution of Coral Reefs* (1842). T. H. Huxley [q.v.1], the patron who had helped to secure Haddon's Dublin post, suggested that he go to Torres Strait. The choice triggered an abiding intellectual interest in the area and led ultimately to his conversion to anthropology.

In August 1888 Haddon arrived in Torres Strait. He had always intended doing some ethnographic work there, but collected with such zeal that, on his return to Dublin, he was able to publish a number of papers, the most impressive of which ran to almost 150 pages. These brought him to the notice of Britain's anthropological luminaries. After consultation with Huxley, and without relinquishing his Dublin chair, he returned to Cambridge in 1893 to study anthropology. In 1895 he was appointed lecturer in physical anthropology and in 1897 he obtained his D.Sc. During these years Haddon also planned another expedition to the Strait. This time he took with him a team that included C. S. Myers, W. H. R. Rivers, S. H. Ray, William McDougall, and C. G. Seligman. The expedition, which lasted for seven months in 1898, broke new ground in almost every aspect of its work. Rivers pioneered the use of genealogy to elucidate social systems, ceremonies were reconstructed, informants were cross-checked, speech and songs were recorded on wax-cylinders, and Haddon made some of the earliest ethnographic films. The result was a rigorous and sophisticated regional ethno-graphy, the bulk of which Haddon edited and published in six volumes between 1901 and 1935: *Reports of the Cambridge Anthropological Expedition to Torres Straits*. It remains the seminal work in Torres Strait studies.

In 1900 Haddon was appointed lecturer in ethnology at Cambridge and in the following year was made a fellow of Christ's College. He became reader in ethnology in 1909. Although he never made a clear break with the evolutionary paradigm that dominated nineteenth-century anthropology, his Torres Strait work was largely empirical, with a methodology grounded in zoology. His dedication to intensive field-work distinguished him from the earlier generation of anthropologists, and he had a profound, though often unacknowledged, influence on the development of British anthropology. Haddon's scholarly output was prodigious, and included *The Study of Man* (London, 1895), *Head-Hunters, Black, White and Brown* (1901) and *History of Anthropology* (1910), yet he is best remembered for his Torres Strait publications, and perhaps for *Canoes of Oceania* (Honolulu, 1936-38) with James Hornell. Haddon returned to Torres Strait only once, in 1914. He resigned his readership in 1926, but continued to write until his death. Survived by his son and two daughters, he died on 20 April 1940 at his home in Cranmer Road, Cambridge.

A. H. Quiggin, *Haddon, the Head Hunter* (Cambridge, Eng, 1942); E. S. Fegan, *Bibliography of A. C. Haddon 1855-1940* (Cambridge, 1978); D. Moore, *The Torres Strait Collections of A. C. Haddon* (Cambridge, 1984); *Oceania*, June 1940; Roy Anthropological Inst, *Man*, July 1940; *Obituary Notices of Fellows of the Roy Soc*, 3, 1941; *J of Aust Studies*, 2, 1977; *Canberra Anthropology*, 5, no 2, 1982; *Hist of the Human Sciences*, 5, 1992; A. C. Haddon, Australian and Pacific papers (AJCP microfilms).   STEVE MULLINS

HAENKE, HELEN JOYCE (1916-1978), poet and playwright, was born on 9 May 1916 at Wickham, New South Wales, daughter of native-born parents Walter Charles Petherbridge, medical practitioner, and his wife Lily Myrtle, née Wood. Helen was educated at Methodist Ladies' College, Burwood, where she was a prefect (1933) and competed in the senior swimming team. After training as a commercial artist at East Sydney Technical College, she studied painting under Max Meldrum [q.v.10] in Melbourne. On 9 October 1937 at All Saints Church, Petersham, Sydney, she married with Anglican rites Willis Lynn Haenke, an industrial chemist from Queensland; they were to have three daughters. During World War II Willis was engaged in munitions production in Adelaide and

Melbourne, but returned to Queensland in 1943 to run the family coal-mining concerns. At Ipswich, Helen Haenke became an influential figure in the local community; she used her historic home, Rockton, as a focal point for the creative arts, and held recitals, play readings and concerts there.

She began her writing career by contributing prose and poetry to literary magazines. Throughout the 1950s her short stories appeared in the *Australian Women's Weekly*. Her unpublished play, 'Truth to Tell', won an Ipswich drama competition award in 1960, and in the following decade *Southerly* published her poems and short stories. In 1968-78 Haenke studied a range of arts subjects at the University of Queensland. Several of her unpublished one-act plays—including 'Black Out' (1967), 'First Performance', 'In Memoriam', 'Late Warning', 'Return to the Fray' and 'Time and the Bell'—are held by the university's Fryer Library. She occasionally used the pseudonyms 'Winkle' and 'Inglewick'. Her one-act play, *Firebug*, was performed at Brisbane's Warana Festival in 1978 and published in *3 Queensland One-act Plays for Festivals* that year. Haenke also wrote several full-length plays. The three-act *Summer Solstice* (originally titled *Under the Bridge*) was first performed in 1964 by the Brisbane Arts Theatre, and her 'Anti-thriller in Two Acts', *The Bottom of a Birdcage* (originally *Emoh Ruo*), had its first performance in 1976 and was published in 1978. The Ipswich Little Theatre performed Haenke's last play, *The Passage*, in 1978.

Haenke's first published poem won a *Courier-Mail* competition in 1965. She subsequently published two volumes of poetry: *The Good Company* appeared in 1977; *Prophets and Honour* was published posthumously in 1979. Her writing was characterized by 'wit, compassion, perceptive awareness of people and fine control of language'. She also maintained her musical interests: her libretto for the opera, *The Pied Piper*, was performed in Brisbane in 1971. Impeccably groomed and strikingly attractive, she was a foundation member of the Ipswich Forum Club, an office-holder in the Ipswich Business and Professional Women's Association, an executive-member of the Australian Society of Authors and a board-member (1968-77) of Ipswich Girls' Grammar School. She died of cancer on 7 December 1978 in St Andrew's Hospital, Ipswich, and was cremated; her husband and daughters survived her.

M. Freer (ed), *Square Poets* (Brisb, 1971); *Luna*, 4, no 1, 1979, p 20; Alumni Assn of Univ Qld, *Alumni*, 11, no 1, Mar 1979, p 25; Fellowship of Aust Writers, *Scope*, 24, no 3, Apr 1979, p 4; *Courier-Mail*, 27, 29 Sept 1965, 5 Mar 1976, 30 June, 28 Sept 1978.   DELYSE ANTHONY

HAGAI, FRANCIS (c.1940-1974), cult leader, was born about 1940 at Hahalis, Buka Island, Bougainville district, in the mandated Territory of New Guinea. He completed primary level schooling at St Joseph's, Rigu, and one year of teacher-training for Catholic schools. There was no government school in Buka and Hagai became contemptuous of the Church's failure to provide utilitarian education. He apostatized after allegedly being shamed publicly by a confessor for a sexual sin. Tall, athletic, practical and commanding, Hagai was a militant lieutenant (from 1960) to the visionary president of the Hahalis Welfare Society, 'King' John Teosin, whose sister Magdalena Hapius he married. Hagai was a manager-secretary of the H.W.S. in 1962 and later vice-president.

Although continuous with Buka protest movements from 'German time' (1886-1914), H.W.S.—with some 4500 members in 1965—was not crassly millenarian. Rather, said Hagai, it was an 'idea of working', in which land, labour and profits were pooled to capitalize machinery, trade stores and marketing. Residually Christian, H.W.S. syncretised a *sori lotu* ('sorry church'); it revived putative traditional practices like free love, but was also influenced by contemporary European trends, thus breaking bride price and the control by elders over marriage. Prurient media sensationalized the H.W.S. 'baby garden' in which adolescent girls promiscuously conceived and reared infants. 'We know . . . that we are on the road to hell', said Hagai, 'so we pray to God in our own way so that He will be sorry for us when we die'.

In 1961 a local council was imposed on Buka; the alternative to joining was payment of a head tax. H.W.S. defied the government and in February 1962, with Hagai leading, two 'battles' with the riot squad occurred. Forty Bukas and 25 police were injured; 461 people were arrested. Branded the most dangerous rebels seen in the Territory and compared to the secessionists of Katanga, Congo (Zaïre), Teosin and Hagai were imprisoned in Port Moresby. Leftist organizations in Australia protested against colonial brutality; one provided legal aid. In general the Supreme Court remitted sentences; H.W.S. exulted, but the tax was paid. Not wanting the spotlight on its trusteeship, Canberra cooled the conflict. To impress Teosin and Hagai, they were officially shown the facilities of Port Moresby and its Hanuabada council in action. The administration began building a trans-island road, ensuring prosperity for tree-crops as well as police access. The Church sponsored commercial projects to forestall further alienation; in 1966 Hagai was invited to Sydney by the Anglican priest Alf Clint [q.v.13] to undertake a business course. H.W.S. claimed a double victory and continued to affront the clergy who fulminated against these agents of anti-Christ.

Hagai stood for parliament in 1964 and 1968, but hardly campaigned outside H.W.S. villages and polled only local votes. Council patronage and mission anathemas were too strong, although inter-group relations gradually improved. By the 1970s H.W.S. attempted larger enterprises which failed. As one of its few associates with either mechanical or business skills, Hagai handled its public relations. Yet, while viable, H.W.S. was patently inefficient.

With the approach in 1972-75 of Papua New Guinea's independence, H.W.S. joined mainstream provincial politics. Hagai participated in the dissident 'Bougainville Awareness' seminar in 1972, paving the way for Teosin to join in the dissolution of Australia's 'puppet' local councils in favour of more germane community governments. No longer embattled, Hahalis was so riven by feuds over assets, status and controls that there were credible allegations of foul play when Hagai died on 7 July 1974 at Arawa hospital, ostensibly following a drink-driving motor accident at Basbi, Buka.

Hagai was a virile leader who sought to reconcile liberation from custom with traditional communality. Expatriate allegations that he had been a communist in any Marxist sense were fatuous. His was an autochthonous movement aspiring to modernization through self-rule.

K. Willey, *Assignment New Guinea* (Brisb, 1965); A. M. Kiki, *Ten Thousand Years in a Lifetime* (Melb, 1968); J. Ryan, *The Hot Land* (Melb, 1971); H. Laracy, *Marists and Melanesians* (Canb, 1976); M. and E. Rimoldi, *Hahalis and the Labour of Love* (Oxford, Eng, 1992); *PD* (Cwlth), 21 Feb, 3 Apr 1972; Aust Inst of Political Science, *NG and Aust*, 1, no 6, 1966; *Post-Courier*, 10 July 1974; personal information.

JAMES GRIFFIN

HAIGH, CLAUDE ALFRED (1904-1980), confectioner and bloodhorse-breeder, was born on 19 January 1904 at Mile End, Adelaide, one of three children of South Australian-born Alfred Ernest Haigh, confectioner, and his wife Eliza Ann, née Harvey. The family moved to Mount Gambier. In 1915 Alfred purchased from Carl Stratmann the business in Adelaide which he named Haigh's Chocolates. Claude was educated at Unley High School (1915-19) and trained in bookkeeping. Accounting skills formed the basis of his contribution to Haigh's operations after he was admitted as a partner in 1921. On 8 October 1927 at Pirie Street Methodist Church, Adelaide, he married Gerta Vera Klingner, a schoolteacher; they lived at St Georges and were to have four children.

At his Wootoona Terrace home, Haigh cultivated an impressive bulb-garden. He won prizes at the Royal Adelaide Show, culminating in the Mahomet Allum [q.v.7] cup for daffodils in 1935. Following Alfred's death in 1933, Claude had assumed the managing directorships of Haigh's Pty Ltd and A. E. Haigh Ltd, and transferred the registered offices from the Haigh Building in Rundle Street to the Parkside factory where the chocolates were made. Something of a reluctant confectioner, he steered the family business through the Depression and the difficult years of World War II when the supply of sugar was rationed. In 1950 he purchased a freehold interest in the Beehive building; the site, on the corner of Rundle and King William streets, was an Adelaide landmark, and housed the firm's most prominent shop. On the return in 1951 of Claude's son John from a placement with the Swiss house of Lindt & Sprüngli, Haigh's expanded rapidly due to the importation of German processing plant, the negotiation of cinema concessions and the expansion of retail outlets. With a measure of relief, Claude Haigh surrendered the managing directorship to John in 1959, thereafter giving his unfettered attention to his greatest love, the breeding and racing of thoroughbreds.

Claude had also inherited from his father a modest stable of racing mares on a mixed farm at Mallala. Against prevailing opinion, which favoured the northern flats, in 1934 he selected Balhannah in the Adelaide Hills as the place to establish Balcrest. The stud became home to renowned imported stallions and brood-mares, the most successful of which were the 'taproot' mare, Charivari, the stallion, Shakuni, and Coronation Boy, thrice the leading Australian sire. Haigh frequently visited Britain to select sires. He was president (1960-71) of the South Australian division of the Bloodhorse Breeders' Association of Australia and vice-president (1961-71) of the national body. His involvement in the racing industry led him to be chairman (1969-73) of the Adelaide Racing Club and its genial representative on the Totalisator Agency Board.

Stocky in build, with plump features, Haigh had a quick stride, a bustling energy, and a quiet and modest disposition. In 1975 he suffered a stroke at Morden, an imposing residence set among rose gardens at Stirling which he had acquired in 1946. He moved to North Adelaide in 1978. Survived by his wife, son and two of his three daughters, he died on 28 November 1980 in Royal Adelaide Hospital and was buried in Mitcham general cemetery.

Haigh's Ltd, *Haigh's 50 Years 1915-1965* (Adel, 1965); M. Robert, *History of Morden* (Adel, 1993);

Unley High School Mag (Adel), 1 July, 2 Sept 1919; *Aust Bloodhorse Review* (Richmond, NSW), Oct 1992; *News* (Adel), 8 May 1962, 2 Dec 1980; Roy Agr and Horticultural Soc of SA Archives (Wayville, Adel); information from Mr J. D. Haigh, Springfield, Adel, and Aust Thoroughbred Breeders' Assn, Kingsford, Syd.

ROGER ANDRÉ

HAIRE, NORMAN (1892-1952), medical practitioner and sexologist, was born on 21 January 1892 at Paddington, Sydney, eleventh and last child of Henry Zions, gentleman, and his London-born wife Clara, née Cohen. Henry was a Jewish emigrant from Poland who had changed his surname from Zajac. Educated (on a scholarship) at Fort Street Model School, Norman won prizes for acting, elocution and debating. These loves and their pursuit remained throughout his life; acting was his chosen career, but parental pressure decided otherwise.

Having studied medicine at the University of Sydney (M.B., Ch.M., 1915), Zions held six-month resident appointments at Sydney Hospital and the Royal Hospital for Women, Paddington, where his interest in obstetrics and gynaecology was aroused. He worked briefly in Brisbane and then as superintendent at (Royal) Newcastle Hospital. From 1915 he served part time in the Militia as captain, Australian Army Medical Corps. In early 1919, as ship's surgeon, he visited China and other Eastern countries, and developed a love of Oriental art. Later that year he left for Europe, via Africa, again working his passage. He took what he regarded as a more acceptable surname, Haire, derived from the Polish word 'zając', meaning a hare. One would like to think that the insertion of an 'i' was a display of Norman's ego, for he always had plenty of that.

Arriving in London, Haire was house surgeon at the Hampstead General and North West London Hospital until December 1920. That year he attended a meeting of the Malthusian League. In 1921, when the league established one of the earliest birth-control clinics in Britain, the Walworth Women's Welfare Centre, he was appointed medical officer-in-charge and began working part time in the women's department of the London Lock Hospital. In 1920 Haire had visited Berlin. There he was involved with the Institut für Sexualwissenschaft and its director Dr Magnus Hirschfeld. Haire was later to say that Germany was his spiritual home. He quickly became fluent in the language and introduced a number of German publications on sexual science to the English-speaking world in the 1920s and 1930s. In 1920 Haire had also contacted Havelock Ellis [q.v.4] who was

something of a father-figure to him; they corresponded and met frequently, though Ellis endeavoured at times to distance himself from his protégé.

Haire rapidly became the most prominent sexologist in Britain. In the decades between the wars he was a dynamic figure with incredible involvement and output: he was a member of the British Society for the Study of Sex Psychology, the International Medical Group for the Investigation of Birth Control, and the Eugenics Education Society. As secretary of the World League for Sexual Reform, he organized its third congress (London, 1929), which was remarkable for the number attending, their diversity of country of origin and background, and the range of knowledge of those presenting papers. Haire edited the proceedings (published 1930), a massive 670-page volume. He was president of the league from 1930; following its demise in 1936 due to personal, political and national frictions, he accepted the presidency of the British offshoot, the Sex Education Society. During these years he wrote several books—the most important of which was *Hymen* (1927) —and co-authored and edited others, including the *Encyclopaedia of Sexual Knowledge* (1934) written by 'Costler A' (Arthur Koestler) *et al.* Throughout this period Haire wrote for journals and newspapers, and was involved in sometimes fiery public debate.

In 1925 Haire had established a private practice in Harley Street; his combined residence and consulting rooms were strikingly decorated after the Chinese fashion. He was notoriously an expensive consultant. In the area of birth control he pioneered the Haire vaginal pessary and introduced into Britain an intra-uterine device (the Grafenberg 'silver' ring); in another clinical development, he promoted male sexual rejuvenation by the Steinach operation (bilateral vasectomy). In the mid-1930s he acquired a country estate at Berkhamsted, Hertfordshire. Physically a very large man, Haire did not drink, indeed he disapproved of alcohol, but he had an enormous appetite and joy in food. By the late 1930s he was diagnosed as being diabetic and nephritic. The outbreak of World War II and the real threat to Britain in 1940 led him to return to Australia. He pleaded health reasons, but there were those who thought he was 'ratting out'.

In Sydney in late 1940 Haire began practice in Macquarie Street. He rode in a chauffeur-driven limousine, lectured for the Workers' Educational Association and the New Education Fellowship, and spoke on the wireless. He reappeared as an actor—in 1944 his performance in Bernard Shaw's *The Doctor's Dilemma* (Sydney University Dramatic Society) was acclaimed. His series of educational articles (from 1942) in the weekly magazine, *Woman*, written under the pseudonym 'Wykeham Terriss' (a Brisbane reminder), were a social breakthrough in Australia, openly presenting sex-education, pregnancy and childbirth issues, as well as matters relating to gynaecological disorders and venereal disease. Although much criticized, the articles were good publicity and a steady source of income; he continued them with few interruptions until 1951. Some were to be published in a book, *Sex Talks* (1946). His most renowned appearance, however, was in the Australian Broadcasting Commission's 'Nation's Forum of the Air' (23 August 1944): in a debate on 'Population Unlimited' he and Jessie Street [q.v.] supported the negative and were opposed by Dame Enid Lyons and Colin Clark, an economist. Haire was strongly attacked in the House of Representatives after the debate. By 1946 he was ready to return to England.

In London again, it was a battle. Many of his old associates had died and others did not wish to meet him. He tried to revive the Sex Education Society, and founded and partly financed the *Journal of Sex Education* (1948-52). In 1950 he visited America where he suffered a heart attack from which he never completely recovered. He died of ischaemic cardiac failure on 11 September 1952 in King's College Hospital, London. Haire had never married: some considered him homosexual, but he was never clearly active; others thought him a 'neuter'. Early on he had distanced himself from his religion and family, and in his will he bequeathed the bulk of his estate—sworn for probate in England at £29 988 and in New South Wales at £22 210—including his library and papers to the University of Sydney which founded the Norman Haire research fellowship.

E. Mannin, *Confessions and Impressions* (Lond, 1930) and *Young in the Twenties* (Lond, 1971); J. Weeks, *Coming Out* (Lond, 1977); A. Thomas, *Broadcast and be Damned* (Melb, 1980); K. S. Inglis, *This is the ABC* (Melb, 1983); *PD* (Cwlth), 14 Sept 1944, p 805, 20 Sept 1944, p 1031, 27 Sept 1944, p 1473; *Triad* (Syd), May 1927; *Lancet*, 20 Sept 1952; *J of Sex Education* (Lond), Nov 1952; *SMH*, 24 Aug, 21 Sept 1944, 4, 20, 25 Apr 1945, 24 Sept 1952, 24 Sept 1983; *Herald* (Melb), 13 Sept 1952; *Nation* (Syd), 23 Apr 1960; Roy Aust College of Obstetricians and Gynaecologists L (Melb); Fisher L Archives.

FRANK M. C. FORSTER*

HAKE, HERBERT DENYS (1894-1975), headmaster, was born on 8 November 1894 at Bournemouth, Hampshire, England, elder son of Edwin Denys Hake, preparatory-school headmaster, and his wife Marianne Jane Mease, née Toyne. Denys was educated at Haileybury College, Hertfordshire, where he excelled at cricket, rackets, fives and athletics, and in 1913-14 was head of school. He served (1914-19) in India and Mesopotamia with the 2nd Battalion, Hampshire Regiment, rose to captain (1916) and was mentioned in dispatches. A pensioner at Queens' College, Cambridge (B.A., 1921; M.A., 1927), he took a third in history and represented the university at hockey (Blue), rackets (half-Blue) and cricket. In 1920-25 he averaged 15.91 runs in 38 innings for Hampshire and played against the visiting Australians in 1921. He was runner-up in 1929 in the amateur rackets championship of England.

From 1921 to 1938 Hake was a master at Haileybury College (except in 1927-28 when he taught at St John's College, Johannesburg, South Africa, and in 1936-37 when he directed tours of English schoolboys to Australia and Canada). He was a firm but kindly housemaster (from 1931), knowing his boys individually and, wherever possible, their families. Tall, lean and athletic despite an arthritic limp, he was a striking figure with reddish-gold hair, penetrating blue eyes and a quiet but authoritative voice. He was sane, cheerful and full of lighthearted fun.

In 1938 Hake was appointed headmaster of The King's School, Parramatta, New South Wales. On 27 December, the eve of his departure for Australia, he married Elizabeth Cecilia Barton (1909-1991) at the parish church, Clapham, Yorkshire. A talented singer, she had been Haileybury's first dietitian, and was to strengthen his confidence at critical moments. King's was at a low ebb when Hake took office in January 1939 as its first lay head. Numbers, down from 438 to 266 since 1930, were to rise by 601 in his time. He set about a gradual liberalization, such as his friend (Sir) James Darling was implementing at Geelong Church of England Grammar School, Victoria, and which Hake's predecessor C. T. Parkinson [q.v.11] had failed to achieve.

World War II delayed reform, as did the conservative staff appointed by Parkinson's predecessor E. M. Baker. After 1946 Hake chose younger men, some from England, who brought a more moderate style without rejecting the 'healthy hardiness' seen as the school's chief characteristic. Helped and encouraged by Elizabeth, he fostered music, drama and art, influencing King's through senior boys whom he selected as monitors less for their sporting prowess than their personal quality. He liked games to be played for pleasure, not ultra-competitively. The austerities of boarding-school life were softened, and the sources of discipline shifted towards individual conscience and common sense.

Intelligent rather than intellectual, Hake was a quietly committed Christian who combined personal humility with a strong, if unconscious, moral authority. He was gentle in his handling of people and tenacious in pursuing his larger ends. The largest, for the school, was to move it from restricted sites spread around Parramatta. Having failed in his attempts to relocate it at Mount Keira and Penrith, he surmounted old-boy opposition sufficient to break a lesser man, and was relieved at the support accorded to the school's gradual transfer, from 1954, to nearby Gowan Brae, formerly owned by Sir James Burns [q.v.7]. Hake stayed on as headmaster until December 1964 to ensure continuity.

Hake was a commanding figure in the Headmasters' Conference of the Independent Schools of Australia and its chairman in 1952-54. Appointed O.B.E. in 1961, he was a fellow (1962) of the Australian College of Education and belonged to the Australian Club. In holidays he and his family escaped happily to a cottage on Mount Wilson. His retirement—spent there and at Glenhaven—saw his serenity tested by increasing lameness and blindness. Survived by his wife and three daughters, he died on 12 April 1975 in Royal Prince Alfred Hospital, Sydney, and was cremated. Portraits of Hake by Nea Wimbush and (Sir) William Dargie are held respectively by his family and T.K.S. where Hake House commemorates him.

L. Waddy, *The King's School, 1831-1981* (Syd, 1981); W. Blunt, *Married to a Single Life* (Salisbury, Eng, 1983); J. W. Hogg, *Our Proper Concerns* (Syd, 1986); M. L. Loane, *This Goodly Heritage* (Syd, 1990); *Haileyburian*, 1910-14, June 1975; *The King's School Mag*, May 1975, May 1977, June, Dec 1991; *The Times*, 19 Apr 1975; Canterbury Cathedral (Eng) Archives; The King's School archives, Parramatta, Syd; Hake genealogy (comp by Dr A. G. Serle, Hawthorn, Melb); family information and personal knowledge.

MICHAEL D. DE B. COLLINS PERSSE

HALEY, MARTIN NELSON (1905-1980), poet, essayist, translator and schoolteacher, was born on 7 July 1905 at New Farm, Brisbane, eldest of three children of Nelson Nathan Haley, a hawker from England, and his Irish-born wife Mary Josephine, née Kiely. In 1907 the family moved to Nambour. Martin attended the local primary school and in 1918 entered St Joseph's College, Nudgee, on a state scholarship; a school bursary of £20 allowed him to complete the senior examination in 1921. His experience at St Joseph's was pivotal. At the point of leaving home, he discovered a new home. In his unpublished autobiography Haley recalled an 'astonishing sense of uplift' which sprang from the college's 'fine prospect over the fields, frequent mass, a certain bright cleanliness everywhere, freedom from the parental roof,

friends at hand all the time'. Intellectually it was a period of crucial debate generated by the Anglo-Irish crisis and the aftermath of the Russian revolution.

Employed in a bank, he left in 1925 to become a primary school teacher. His first posting was to Yaronga, and he taught at a succession of small schools in the country before being appointed to Kangaroo Point Boys' School, Brisbane, in 1937. At St Benedict's Catholic Church, East Brisbane, on 19 December 1939 he married Lydia May Egan. Haley subsequently taught in schools at Ithaca Creek, Mount Gravatt, Brisbane South and New Farm. He retired in December 1970. A practical and pragmatic educationist, he was resistant to any change which made learning more difficult for his students.

His literary career had begun in 1933 with articles contributed to the *Catholic Leader*; he also wrote for the *Risen Sun*, a monthly paper for Christian Brothers old boys. He was involved in numerous Catholic societies and maintained a prolific output of non-fictional prose, almost all of it published in Catholic papers and journals. Following his transfer to Brisbane in 1937, he joined the Catholic Poetry Society of Queensland: founded by the poet Paul Grano [q.v.9] in 1934, its members included James Picot [q.v.] and Brian Vrepont. Haley's output comprised original poetry and translations. *Poems and a Preface* (1936) was self-published and received little attention. His later work, including *More Poems and Another Preface* (1938), never established a major reputation. He translated and published several collections of poems from Latin, Greek, French, Spanish and Chinese sources. With languages in which he was not proficient, he depended on prose paraphrases and the advice of friends.

A potent and habitual controversialist, Haley supported causes with a passionate concern. He belonged to a generation which saw a resurgent Catholicism as the only bulwark against communism. He was a staunch supporter of General Franco, and he rejected Darwinian evolution and the philosophy of Pierre Teilhard de Chardin. Poetically, he remained devoted to the idea that metre and rhyme were the cornerstones of form in English-language verse. Haley was active in the Catholic Readers' and Writers' Society from its foundation in 1944, and president (1975) and editor of its journal, *Vista*. Survived by his wife and three daughters, he died on 18 October 1980 at Paddington and was buried in Pinaroo lawn cemetery, Aspley.

Catholic Readers' and Writers' Soc (Brisb), *Vista*, 6, no 1, 1980; *Courier-Mail*, 3 Dec 1970, 20 Oct 1980; Haley staff card, History Unit, Qld Dept of Education, Brisb; Haley collection, Fryer L, Univ Qld.

MARTIN DUWELL

HALFORD, GEORGE DOWGLASS (1865-1948), Anglican bishop, was born on 9 June 1865 at Kensington, London, son of Edward Halford, surgeon, and his wife Frances Jones Trist, née Dowglass. George was educated at Felsted School, Essex, Keble College, Oxford (B.A., 1888; M.A., 1893)— where he rowed and was prominent in the drama society—and Leeds Clergy School. Made deacon in 1890 and ordained priest on 24 May 1891, he was assistant-curate (1890-95) and vicar (1895-97) at St Peter's, Jarrow, Durham. His mentor Bishop Westcott groomed him for the Oxford Mission to Calcutta, India, before persuading him to pioneer a ministry to outback Queensland. Halford's establishment of St Andrew's Mission House in 1897 at Longreach began the Bush Brotherhood movement. He was archdeacon (1899-1907) of the diocese of Rockhampton, but quit the 'weariness and dulness' of the outback in 1902 to become rector of St Paul's Cathedral where he also gained repute as the city's champion exhibitor of gloxinia and caladium. His monastic inclination encouraged him to reorganize St Paul's rectory into a clergy community-house, and in 1907 he set up a short-lived female religious community to care for unmarried mothers from the bush.

In 1907 Halford resigned to return to England. He declined bishoprics in Polynesia, New Guinea and north-west Australia, choosing instead a lectureship at St Saviour's College, Southwark. On 2 February 1909 in Brisbane he was consecrated bishop and on the 9th was enthroned as the second bishop of Rockhampton. Halford spent almost his entire espiscopate maintaining a modest ministry to the White population of Central Queensland. A mission to South Sea Islanders, which he launched at Moores Creek, foundered for lack of resources, but he campaigned strongly for the 'Bible in State Schools' movement. Moved by the willingness of the young for sacrifice in battle, he abandoned his episcopate during World War I to establish an 'emergency corps' to minister to pioneering communities of workmen in railway and mining camps. In 1920 he resigned his bishopric.

By 1923 he had established the Order of Witness at Tingalpa, near Brisbane, which pledged absolute obedience to Archbishop Sharp [q.v.11]. Halford freelanced until 1936, mostly in the Dawson, Burnett and Callide valleys, then being opened to closer settlement. In 1930 he declined work as an assistant-bishop at St Albans, England. He also refused an episcopal ministry in the 170 000 square miles (440 000 km²) surrounding Charleville, leading Sharp to comment that Halford would not go an 'inch' except where he wanted. By 1932 colleagues considered him a drifter, 'neither exercising authority nor under authority'. He studied economics in a slab hut at Monto, and later attempted to introduce the Christian Social Order movement to Brisbane. In 1935 Archbishop Wand [q.v.12] ordered his return from Monto and appointed him canon missioner of the diocese of Brisbane. His supporter J. H. F. Fairfax [q.v.8 R. Fairfax] bought him a house at Wilston, where Halford conducted a legendary ministry to men and boys. He died on 27 August 1948 at Grange, Brisbane, and was cremated.

Happiest roughing it 'as a wandering friar living in a tent', Halford had a larrikin trait which provided his point of contact with men. His reputation as the founder of the Bush Brotherhood sits uneasily, given his dislike of the outback and preference for the coastal bushlands. The refinement in manners which he retained suggested to his obituarist that Queensland was a mistaken destination, Halford's gifts and sensibilities being more suited to the ancient civilizations of India or Japan.

Bush Brother, 44, no 3, Dec 1948, pp 159, 166, 171; *Courier-Mail*, 3 Feb 1909, 26 June 1922, 10, 18 Jan 1923, 28 Aug 1948; R. H. H. Philp, George Dowglass Halford (M.A. thesis, UNE, 1982); A. E. Cocksidge, A History of the Parish of St Alban the Martyr, Wilston (ms, nd, Anglican Diocesan Archives, Brisb); Halford papers (Anglican Diocesan Archives, Brisb).   GEORGE P. SHAW

HALL, ADA; *see* BAKER, ADA

HALL, HESSEL DUNCAN (1891-1976), historian and public servant, was born on 8 March 1891 at Glen Innes, New South Wales, second of four children of native-born parents William Hessel Hall, Wesleyan minister, and his wife Jeannie, née Duncan. Educated at Emu Plains and Penrith public schools, Sydney Boys' High School and the University of Sydney (B.A., 1913; M.A., 1915), Duncan gained first-class honours in both of his degrees. On 1 August 1914 at St Paul's Anglican Church, Chatswood, he married Bertha Sneath, a nurse; they were to have a son and three daughters before being divorced. Hall taught at Teachers' College and North Sydney Boys' High School, then proceeded in 1915 to Balliol College, Oxford (B.Litt., 1920). The report he wrote for his B.Litt. was published as *The British Commonwealth of Nations* (London, 1920).

Encouraged by A. L. Smith, the master of Balliol, in 1917 Hall became secretary to a unionist committee, chaired by Lord

Selborne, that was preparing a federal solution to the Irish problem. Between 1917 and 1920 he tutored in the Midlands and the North under the University of Oxford's extension programme. He described himself as a socialist and was involved with the Fabian Society. After failing to obtain a readership at Dacca, India, he returned to Australia. Rejected for the chair of history and economics at the University of Queensland, he found employment in Sydney, chiefly with the university's department of tutorial classes. He was active in public affairs, worked as a correspondent (1921-25) for the *Manchester Guardian* and led the Australian delegation to the Institute of Pacific Relations conference in Honolulu in 1925.

Hall was professor of international relations at Syracuse University, New York State, in 1926-27. While visiting Geneva in 1927, he joined the staff of the League of Nations and was prominent in efforts to control the opium trade; in 1935 he transferred to the information section and was given special responsibilities for the British dominions. He went back to the United States of America in 1939, took a visiting professorship at Harvard University in 1940 and served on the British Raw Materials Mission, Washington, in 1942-45. For the next decade he was based at the British embassy where he had charge of the North American volumes of the official war history and published *North American Supply* (London, 1955).

After retiring in 1956, Hall continued the work he had earlier begun on a history of the British Commonwealth. He used his acquaintance with the dominions' leaders and his access to unreleased government records to produce the monumental *Commonwealth* (London, 1971). In his first book he had developed the concept of the Commonwealth as 'a free co-operating society of nations' and put forward ideas that influenced the Balfour Declaration (1926). His last book, although over-long, confirmed his reputation as 'the doyen of a school of constitutional historians'. In between, he wrote articles on Commonwealth, Pacific and international affairs, produced *Mandates, Dependencies and Trusteeship* (New York, 1948), and applied psychoanalytic principles to international affairs and politics. In the last-mentioned aspect he was encouraged by his wife Jenny Waelder, a psychoanalyst and divorcee, whom he had married on 10 September 1943.

A talented, creative man whose early political views moderated with age, Hall was noted for his wide interests and 'remarkable powers of analysis and exposition'. He died on 8 July 1976 at Bethesda, Maryland, and was cremated; his wife survived him, as did the children of his first marriage.

SMH, 20 Jan 1921, 30 Apr 1926; *The Times*, 13 July, 3 Aug 1976; Hall papers (NL); J. Le Gay Brereton papers (ML).   B. H. FLETCHER

HALL, IRENE SLATER (1888-1961), hospital matron, was born on 19 July 1888 at Ryde, Sydney, fourth child of native-born parents Moses Slater Hall, farm servant, and his wife Harriett, née Noakes. Irene spent her early life in Sydney and was educated there. In 1907 she began nursing at Ellen Gould's [q.v.9] Ermelo Private Hospital, Dulwich Hill, before starting her training at Sydney Hospital in January 1908. Registered on 9 July 1913, she remained on the staff as a head nurse until she became head nurse and deputy-matron at (Royal) Newcastle Hospital on 1 December 1914. Five months later she was appointed matron. During her forty-three years in office her name became synonymous with the institution which grew from a small district hospital to a large modern one.

A keen horsewoman, Miss Hall rode to and from New Lambton on her weekly inspection of the convalescent home. Possessing a 'certain presence', she was almost six feet (183 cm) tall, endowed with good looks and with eyes that could give a glacial glance or show compassion. Her beautiful handwriting, letters and reports demonstrated her intelligence. A dignified and dedicated woman of great integrity, she continued the Nightingale tradition. In her induction address she told new trainee-nurses that 'you will find that my school can be likened to the British army, there is only one difference—they have slackened discipline, I have not'.

Matron Hall was cutting and severe when she detected infringements of the rules of her training-school or anything less than excellent patient care. She considered it an essential part of training to demand of and enforce upon her nurses a high standard of personal morality, ethics and etiquette. Following the conference of the Matrons' Association of New South Wales, held at Newcastle in 1933, she edited the *Matrons' Handbook of Lectures to Trainees* (1935). In 1950 she published a paper on the 'Importance of Ethics in Nursing' in the *Journal of the First Australian Nursing Conference*.

A skilled administrator, Hall worked tirelessly to improve the status of her profession. She was a council-member (1927-58) of the Australasian Trained Nurses' Association, a foundation member and fellow of the College of Nursing, Australia, president of the State branch of the Florence Nightingale Committee of Australia, and a delegate to congresses of the International Council of Nurses in London in 1937, at Atlantic City, United

States of America, in 1947, and in Rome in 1957. She was also interested in a range of civic and charitable organizations.

Hall was awarded King George V's silver jubilee (1935) and Queen Elizabeth II's coronation (1953) medals, and appointed M.B.E. in 1957. Due to ill health, she retired in 1958, but maintained a keen interest in the hospital and her nursing staff. She died on 11 August 1961 in Royal Newcastle Hospital and was cremated with Anglican rites. The nurses home (built in 1960) was named after her.

A. Armitage, *A Golden Age of Nursing* (Syd, 1991); *A'sian Nurses' J*, 11, no 8, 15 Aug 1913, p 284, 59, no 9, Sept 1961, p 228; *SMH*, 14 Aug 1947, 1 Jan 1957; *Newcastle Morning Herald*, 3 Jan, 22 Feb, 4 Dec 1957, 12 Aug 1961; *Newcastle Sun*, 11 Aug 1961; B. Capper, The History of Nurse Education at Royal Newcastle Hospital: 1891-1991 (M.Ed. Studies thesis, Univ Newcastle, 1991); Newcastle Hospital records, 1914-15, *and* Hall papers (Roy Newcastle Hospital Archives); information from Mrs E. Firth, Fairy Meadow, NSW, Mrs M. I. O'Brien, Lindfield, and Miss J. I. Pollock, Burwood, Melb.   BETTY CAPPER

HALL, WILLIAM JAMES (1877-1951), photographer, was born on 11 May 1877 at Woolloomooloo, Sydney, son of William Frederick Hall, a butcher from England, and native-born Caroline Asimus whom he married in 1883. William senior, who was also a fingerprint expert at Long Bay gaol, set up a photographic studio in Phillip Street, Sydney, in 1890; he moved the business to Hunter Street in 1893 and to Castlereagh Street in 1898. After being schooled locally, young William joined his father to learn the lucrative art and took over the business about 1902. He set up Hall & Co. at 44 Hunter Street in 1904. On 14 August 1901 he had married Alice Rosina Hopson at the Anglican Church of St Simon and St Jude, Bowral.

Hall developed a keen interest in sailing and in sailing craft, and between the late 1890s and early 1930s compiled one of the most valuable marine photographic collections in Australia. The 3000 glass plates, now in the archives of the Royal Sydney Yacht Squadron, give a fascinating picture of competitive and recreational sailing on Sydney Harbour, as well as of the associated social activities. The backgrounds, too, showing old 'ironside' warships and windjammers are of as much interest as the rigs and dress of the boats' crews. These photographs reveal that Hall was both an artistic cameraman and an excellent technician—especially given the limitations of his equipment. Each Monday morning in his shop window he displayed the photographs he had taken of weekend races, much to the delight of yachting enthusiasts.

Quiet and retiring, Hall was perhaps better known as a photographer of livestock. In commercial photographic circles he was generally considered to have pioneered the art in Australia, and to have set a particularly high standard. Some of his best work appeared in a four-volume record of pastoral life, *The Pastoral Homes of Australia* (1910-14). He was a familiar figure at the leading agricultural shows, and in demand with livestock breeders and exhibitors at the Sydney, Brisbane and Melbourne shows. His work was widely published in stud stock advertisements in major pastoral journals, including the *Pastoral Review (and Graziers' Record)*. From July 1928 to December 1929 he made an extended tour of South Africa to photograph merino studs.

Hall's and his firm's interests were not confined to marine and animal subjects; they extended to landscape photography, portraiture, city and rural life, as well as aerial and military work. A widower, he married Edith Hannah Gilkes on 7 December 1940 at St Aidan's Church, Longueville. They lived in nearby Mary Street, overlooking the Lane Cove River. Survived by his wife, he died on 26 August 1951 at St Luke's Hospital, Darlinghurst, and was cremated. The son of his first marriage predeceased him.

J. Toghill, *Sydney Harbour of Yesteryear* (Syd, 1982); A. Davies and P. Stanbury, *The Mechanical Eye in Australia* (Melb, 1985); *Pastoral Review*, 15 Sept 1951; *SMH*, 17 July 1928, 21 Dec 1929, 3 Sept 1947, 29 Aug 1951.   G. P. WALSH

HALL BEST, SIR JOHN VICTOR; *see* BEST, SIR JOHN VICTOR HALL

HALLIGAN, JAMES REGINALD (1894-1968), public servant, was born on 8 November 1894 in East Melbourne, third child of John Joseph Halligan, a printer from Ireland, and his Victorian-born wife Elizabeth Jane, née Rourke. Educated at Christian Brothers' College, East Melbourne, Reg entered the Commonwealth Public Service on 25 October 1911 as a clerk in the Department of External Affairs. In 1916 he transferred to the Department of Home and Territories. For six months in 1922-23 he was relieving accountant at Rabaul, in the mandated Territory of New Guinea, and in 1925 revisited that country to investigate the public service there. In 1927 he gained a diploma of commerce from the University of Melbourne.

In that year Halligan moved to Canberra where, in 1931, he was attached to the new territories branch in the Prime Minister's Department. Promoted senior clerk, in 1933 he became head of his branch and accompanied ministers on numerous visits to the territories. At St Patrick's Catholic Church, Braddon, on 21 November 1936 he married Marjorie Millicent Grosvenor; she had been confidential typist to the prime minister and cabinet, and had been appointed M.B.E. (1934). In 1937 Halligan was acting-administrator of Norfolk Island. He was elevated to assistant-secretary in the Department of External Territories in 1942 and was its secretary from 1944 to 1951.

Known as 'happy Halligan' for his ready smile, he was a short, dapper man, with brown hair, 'sparkling' brown eyes and a quiet nature. He was a keen golfer, a 'social' tennis player and loyal to his friends; he was, as well, a staunch Catholic. Inclined to stubbornness, he had definite opinions, an excellent memory and agility at mental arithmetic. Partly because he was a 'workaholic', he enjoyed good relations with his ministers: Sir George Pearce [q.v.11] had praised him in 1937 for 'his fine work and enthusiasm'.

For all that, Halligan was an unimaginative bureaucrat who showed no evidence that he read the growing literature on colonial administration. In 1940 his branch was condemned by (Sir) Frederic Eggleston [q.v.8] as having 'nobody . . . who is fitted by training and education to run a department with the complicated problems with which this one has to deal' or with 'knowledge of the problems of native administration'. To (Sir) Paul Hasluck, Halligan was 'a devoted, likable and thoroughly good man, helpful, warm-hearted and kindly', but he also saw him as 'a dutiful man for pushing files around . . . so long as the top paper on a file had some suitable minute on it, initialled and dated, he felt that the immediate needs of administration had been achieved'. When Hasluck became minister for territories in 1951, Halligan was passed over as departmental secretary because 'he would not help me to break new ground'.

From 1951 until his retirement on 7 November 1959 he was Hasluck's special adviser. Senior Australian member (1948-59) of the South Pacific Commission, and British and Christmas Island phosphate commissioner for Australia (1952-62), Halligan was appointed O.B.E. in 1960. He died on 21 November 1968 at Canberra Hospital and was buried in Canberra cemetery; his wife and son survived him.

P. Hasluck, *A Time for Building* (Melb, 1976); Eggleston papers (NL); A518, G800/1/1 *and* CP136/1, bundle 1/12 (AA, Canb); information from Mrs M. Halligan, Canb.

ROGER C. THOMPSON

HALLSTROM, SIR EDWARD JOHN LEES (1886-1970), manufacturer, zoological park administrator and philanthropist, was born on 25 September 1886 at High Park station, near Coonamble, New South Wales, eighth of nine children of William Hallstrom, a saddler from England who was of Swedish extraction, and his native-born wife Mary Ann, née Colless, a descendant of John Lees of the New South Wales Corps. Edward was about 4 when his father's farming endeavour failed and the family moved to Sydney. They lived at Waterloo near young (Sir) William McKell, with whom Edward (although never a Labor supporter) formed a lifelong friendship. The Hallstrom parents separated and conditions were hard for the children. At the age of 10 Edward was doing odd jobs to supplement the family income. He left school at 13, to be apprenticed to a cabinet-maker, but continued to study the *Harmsworth Self-Educator*, encyclopaedias and scientific magazines. Intelligent and hard working, he soon had charge of a furniture factory. Several years later he established his own business, manufacturing bedsteads. Fascinated with flying, he was friendly with the pioneer aviators Bert Hinkler and George Taylor [qq.v.9,12]; he built box kites for Taylor and was with him on his inaugural flight at Narrabeen Beach in December 1909.

On a trip to Maryborough, Queensland, Hallstrom met Margaret Elliott Jaffrey, a talented artist who shared his love of animals. They were married with Presbyterian forms on 6 April 1912 at her parents' home at New Farm, Brisbane. Edward was a strict disciplinarian, but his wife and four children idolized him. After reading an early article on refrigeration, he studied every patent in that field taken out since Federation and experimented in a makeshift laboratory in his backyard at Dee Why. He quickly saw the possibilities of kerosene-powered refrigeration for outback stations which relied on the primitive 'Coolgardie safe'. In 1923 he produced his first unit, the Icy Ball absorption refrigerator, a chest model run by kerosene, which he sold in the outback himself. He then diversified into the Silent Knight upright models, run on gas or electricity. To his family's relief, he moved production from the backyard to a rambling site at Willoughby. During World War II the factory produced munitions, as well as refrigerators for the American Army for medical purposes. By the mid-1940s Hallstroms Pty Ltd was turning out 1200 refrigerators per week and employed over seven hundred people, among them members of his family. He subsequently invented a machine for refrigerating anaesthetics which he presented to Sydney Hospital.

His entrepreneurial and inventive abilities

enabled Hallstrom to manufacture an efficient, reasonably priced product at a time when imported refrigerators were costly. For all his softly spoken, affable manner, he was known as 'the Chief', someone whose word was law. Yet, he was a kind man, renowned for close relationships with his employees to whom his personal generosity was legendary. Silent Knight became a household name in Australia, supplying both domestic and export markets, and Hallstrom became a millionaire. The family moved into a harbourside home at Northbridge, although he spent much of the week in a Spartan flat at his factory.

By this time Hallstrom could afford to indulge two passions—a love of birds and animals (a childhood obsession) and philanthropy. With the proceeds of the sale of five hundred kerosene refrigerators in Africa in 1937, he bought two rhinoceroses which he presented to the Taronga Zoological Park Trust. These were the first of many gifts which gave him extraordinary influence. In 1941 he was appointed a trustee of the zoo which he was to dominate for the next twenty-six years. He was vice-chairman (1945-51) and president from 1951 until 1959, when his son succeeded him. As honorary director (1959-67) Hallstrom was still effectively in control.

Hallstrom was the zoo's greatest benefactor and most active trustee—by the time of his death he had made cash donations of over $500 000, in addition to birds and animals. He financed expeditions to New Guinea, Africa and South America, established links with overseas zoos and museums, and set up a private farm at Mona Vale to produce fresh food for the animals. He revelled in and actively sought publicity, and took distinguished visitors to the zoo in his Rolls-Royce (number-plate ZO-000). He also made the zoo more popular by exhibiting animals such as 'King Kong', the gorilla, and 'Nellie', the harmonica-playing elephant, and by introducing a successful breeding programme that included the rare black rhinoceroses which he fed with 'scones spread with butter laced with vitamins'.

By the 1960s Hallstrom's lack of professional qualifications was seen as archaic. As a self-made man accustomed to wielding authority, he clashed with scientists over management practices at the zoo and in 1966 two public inquiries were set up by the minister for lands. While paying tribute to Hallstrom as a 'great philanthropist and nature lover', he was criticized on many grounds: there was no trained zoologist or veterinary surgeon on the staff, and excessive cement had been used in the animal enclosures (which, being easy to clean, reduced parasitic disease). He was deeply offended when Dr Heini Hediger, director of the Zurich Zoologi-

cal Gardens, Switzerland, referred to him in his report as 'a great amateur'. A professional zoologist was appointed director and Hallstrom was made director emeritus. Nevertheless, many of Hallstrom's ideas came from years of practical experience and the zoo's successful breeding programme 'was in itself evidence that the animals were living under suitable conditions'.

The inquiries shook Hallstrom badly. He rejected the notion that an ardent love of animals could be superseded by professional training and that 'scientists found it impossible to communicate with him'. From 1966 he was also under covert surveillance for illegal trafficking in fauna. Four years later, thirty-five people were convicted of that offence and it was thought that Hallstrom may have used his influence to have his involvement concealed. Whatever the truth, in 1968, dispirited and unwell, he donated his personal collection of birds and animals worth more than $20 000 to the zoo. That year his wife died, and he gave $22 000 to the Central Methodist Mission to establish at Leichhardt the Margaret Hallstrom Home for unmarried mothers.

Meantime, in the Territory of Papua and New Guinea, Hallstrom had been involved in several projects, such as coffee-growing and an experimental sheep-breeding station at Nondugl. In 1949 he gave £20 000 and 750 acres (300 ha) to the Commonwealth government to create a trust, setting aside land for the Hallstrom Bird of Paradise Sanctuary from which he developed a worldwide exchange programme. He also donated £10 000 to establish a library attached to the Australian School of Pacific Administration at Mosman, now the Hallstrom Pacific Library. He genuinely delighted in philanthropy, and personally assessed the begging letters with which he was daily besieged. He made countless donations to diverse projects, charities and individuals, but especially for medical research. Large sums went to Sydney Hospital for a cancer clinic and to Royal Prince Alfred Hospital for cardiac research. The Hallstrom Institute of Cardiology at R.P.A.H. was set up in recognition of his generosity. There were also donations to smaller hospitals, and he was a board-member of Sydney and R.P.A. hospitals.

Hallstrom was a fellow of the Royal Zoological societies of New South Wales and London, a member of the New York Zoological Society and a life member of the Royal Australian Historical Society. He belonged to the exclusive Explorers Club, New York. Knighted in 1952, he was named Father of the Year in 1957. He was awarded the gold medals of the Société Royale Zoologique de Belgique (1964) and the Zoological Society of San Diego (1966), and in 1966 was appointed knight commander of the Royal Order of the Northern Star for sponsoring Swedish Expeditions to New Guinea and for assistance to the Royal Museum of Stockholm. A genus of petrels was named *Hallstroma* in his honour by G. M. Mathews [q.v.10].

A teetotaller and non-smoker, Hallstrom was astonishingly active and 'never let his mind lie idle for a minute'. He enjoyed a joke, especially when in mid-life, with his stocky build and heavy glasses, he was often mistaken for H. V. Evatt [q.v.]. He also collected the hats of famous men, including Chaplin, Churchill, Truman, Eisenhower and (Sir) Robert Menzies [q.v.]. An art lover, he presented a collection of bird paintings by John-James Audubon to President Truman for the National Gallery of Art, Washington, and gave paintings to the local R.Z.S. and to Parliament House, Canberra. At St Philip's Church, Sydney, on 14 June 1969 Sir Edward married Dr Mary Mabel Maguire, née McElhone, a widow and an old friend. Survived by his wife, and by the son and three daughters of his first marriage, he died on 27 February 1970 at his Northbridge home and was cremated with Anglican rites. To the public, Hallstrom was a genial philanthropist and animal lover; privately, he could be self-willed and difficult. He was both a significant figure in the history of Taronga Zoo and a practical humanitarian who reputedly donated over $4 million. His estate was sworn for probate at $974 914.

H. Hediger, *Report on Taronga Park Zoo from the Viewpoint of Biology of Zoological Gardens* (Syd, 1966); N. Thompson and J. T. Quinn, *Report on Administrative and Business Aspects of Taronga Zoological Park* (Syd, 1966); E. Hahn, *Zoos* (Lond, 1968); E. Wilksch (comp), *The Naremburn Story* (Syd, 1988); R. Strahan, *Beauty and the Beasts* (Syd, 1991); *Refrigeration J,* Apr 1950; *People* (Syd), 12 Apr 1950; *South West Pacific,* no 17, 1951; *Walkabout,* 31, Oct 1965; *Aust Zoologist,* 15, 1970, p 403; *Nation* (Syd), 5 Oct 1963; *Australian,* 7 May 1986; J. Lawrence, A History of Taronga Zoological Park (B.A. Hons thesis, Univ NSW, 1981); J. Hill, The Silent Knight—The Life and Character of Sir Edward John Hallstrom (ms, held by its author, Milton, NSW); Hallstrom papers (Taronga Zoological Park, Hallstrom Pacific L, Powerhouse Museum and ML).   AUDREY TATE

HALPERN, BERTHOLD (1923-1980), professor of chemistry, was born on 18 June 1923 in Vienna, son of Szymon Halpern, bank official, and his wife Eugenie (Goldy), née Blasenstein. Evacuated to England with a group of Jewish children in 1938-39, he attended Bournemouth Municipal (Technical) College until he was interned; his brother Ossy made his way to Palestine. Berthold was transported to Australia in the *Dunera,* reached Melbourne on 3 September 1940 and was again interned, at Tatura. After serving in the 8th Employment Company, Australian Military Forces (1942-46), mainly in Victoria, Halpern worked as an engineer at Telephone & Electrical Industries Pty Ltd in Sydney and was naturalized on 27 March 1947. Granted war matriculation status, he graduated from the University of Sydney with first-class honours in organic chemistry (B.Sc., 1951) and joined Monsanto Chemicals (Australia) Ltd. At the district registrar's office, Chatswood, on 8 June 1951 he married Margaret Dorothea Bruton, née Libbesson, a secretary and divorcee whose son by her previous marriage he adopted. In 1957 Halpern accepted a Salters Institute scholarship at the Imperial College of Science and Technology, University of London (Ph.D., 1959); he returned to Monsanto as research manager to work on antibacterial agents.

In 1962 he was invited to join Professor Frank Dwyer [q.v.] as senior research fellow at the John Curtin School of Medical Research, Australian National University, Canberra. Following Dwyer's death, in 1963 Halpern took a Syntex fellowship in Mexico City. From 1964 he worked in the instrumentation research laboratory in the department of genetics at Stanford University, California, United States of America, on new methods for detecting extraterrestrial life by using mass spectrometry and gas chromatography to seek amino acids. As a senior investigator for National Aeronautics and Space Administration, he evaluated material collected by the Apollo Lunar and data from the Viking Mars missions; he did not discount the possibility of life on Mars.

Returning to New South Wales in 1970 as foundation professor of chemistry at Wollongong University College (University of Wollongong from 1975), Halpern soon attracted massive research funding and installed a GC-MS computer system. He developed new techniques for sequencing proteins, and for diagnosing metabolic disorders and genetic defects in children, and collaborated on biomedical research with Stanford University and with biochemists in Oslo, Norway. Awarded Queen Elizabeth II's silver jubilee medal (1977), he was elected a fellow of the Australian Academy of Science in 1978. Alone or with colleagues, he published more than 130 scientific papers.

Reluctant to speak about his early years (possibly because his parents may have been murdered by the Nazis), Halpern was an agnostic and essentially a private person, devoted to his family, stamp collecting, bridge, chess and gardening. He remained a loyal supporter of the Collingwood Football Club from the time of his army service in Victoria. His friends called him 'Tiny'—he was over six feet (183 cm) tall. Suffering from chronic asthma and bronchitis, he died of a sudden heart attack on 15 November 1980 at his Mount Ousley home and was cremated. His wife and son survived him. In 1981 the University of Sydney awarded him a D.Sc. A Halpern memorial lecture was established at the University of Wollongong.

Hist Records of Aust Science, 5, no 4, 1983; *Dunera News*, 27, June 1993, p 11; *SMH*, 26 Sept 1970, 2 Nov 1978; *Australian*, 26 Nov 1980; naturalization file, A435/1, item 46/4/2401 (AA, Canb); information from Mrs M. Halpern, Lugarno, Syd.
                                    KLAUS LOEWALD

HALPERN, STANISLAW ('STACHA') (1919-1969), painter, potter, printmaker and sculptor, was born on 20 October 1919 at Zolochev, Poland (now Ukraine), son of Eisig Halpern, engineer, and his wife Berta, née Gutt. In 1938 Stacha enrolled at the School of Commercial and Fine Art, L'vov. When his studies were cut short by the German invasion of Poland, he emigrated via England to Perth in 1939 and later that year travelled to Melbourne where he was employed as a fitter and turner. At the office of the government statist, Melbourne, on 28 August 1943 he married Sylvia Pauline Black, a stenographer; they were to have a daughter before being divorced.

While working at a Melbourne commercial pottery as a mould-maker in 1944-45, Halpern developed an interest in the craft. At this time, too, he befriended Arthur Boyd who, with John Perceval, had established the Arthur Merric Boyd Pottery at Murrumbeena. In 1946-47 Halpern set up a home studio, with the aim of becoming a full-time potter. Despite financial difficulties, he was reasonably successful at selling his work through the Primrose Pottery Shop, Melbourne. On 17 June 1947 he was naturalized. He studied part time at the George Bell [q.v.7] school in 1948-49 and for one term at Melbourne Technical College.

Halpern's first solo exhibition of paintings and pottery, at the Stanley Coe Gallery in 1950, was well received. In 1951 he journeyed to England and Europe where, for the next fifteen years, he led a semi-nomadic existence. Although he produced some pottery, particularly during a stay in the south of France in 1952, this period was occupied primarily with painting. Unlike most Australian artists who travelled to Europe at this time, Halpern was to make a significant contribution to the Paris art scene, and he exhibited frequently in solo and group exhibitions in Paris, Amsterdam and Rome, and at Basle and Milan. His paintings of the mid- to late 1950s were vigorously expressionistic landscapes and streetscapes, painted quickly and

confidently, with thick paint and calligraphic linework. In the late 1950s and early 1960s he completed a series of paintings of beef carcasses, powerful meditations on violence and death, and possibly his most abstract works. At the Brondesbury Synagogue, Middlesex, England, on 24 July 1961 he married 25-year-old Betty Ann Hamilton.

In 1966 Halpern returned to Melbourne. Increasingly, he turned his attention to images of human faces, generally dark, brooding and fragmented. His ceramics, derived largely from European peasant pottery, were wheel-thrown or hand-built from rough terracotta clay with bold, semi-abstract painted decorations. A 'gay-hearted, witty, sensitive man' who was unfailingly generous to friends and young artists, Halpern found Australia 'just as isolated, smug, chauvinistic' as before. The local art world's preoccupation with American colourfield abstraction made his bold European expressionism seem old-fashioned. Nor did his exuberant pottery match a prevailing interest in the refinement and control of Japanese folkcraft and Chinese porcelains. After three productive but unhappy years, he died suddenly of heart disease on 28 January 1969 at Hampton and was buried in the new Cheltenham cemetery. His wife and their two daughters survived him; the daughter of his first marriage predeceased him.

A retrospective exhibition at the National Gallery of Victoria in 1970 failed to generate much public or critical interest. Although two touring exhibitions of his work have been held since his death (Nolan Gallery, Canberra, 1989-90, and Charles Nodrum Gallery, Melbourne, 1993), Halpern remains one of Australia's most unjustly neglected artists.

P. Restany, *Espaces Imaginaires* (Paris, 1957) and *Stanislav Halpern* (Paris, 1961); R. Queneau, *Halpern Peintures* (Paris, 1958); R. Gindertael, *Halpern—oeuvres recentes* (Paris, 1962); National Gallery of Vic, *Stanislav Halpern Retrospective Exhibition*, cat (Melb, 1970); P. Timms, *Australian Studio Pottery and Chinapainting* (Melb, 1986); J. MacFarlane, *Stacha Halpern*, exhibition cat (Canb, 1989); C. Nodrum, *Stacha Halpern survey, 1952-1969*, exhibition cat (Melb, 1993).
                                       PETER TIMMS

HALSE, REGINALD CHARLES (1881-1962), Anglican archbishop, was born on 16 June 1881 at Luton, Bedfordshire, England, only son and youngest of three children of James John Halse, a manufacturer of straw hats, and his wife Gulielma, née Hack. Educated at St Paul's School, London, where he made his mark at cricket and Rugby Union football, and at Brasenose College, Oxford (B.A., 1905; M.A., 1907), Reginald had decided by the age of 17 to seek holy orders. At

Kelham Theological College he was influenced by Fr Herbert Kelly, founder of the Society of the Sacred Mission. Halse was made deacon in 1906, and ordained priest on 21 December 1907 by A. F. Winnington-Ingram, bishop of London, who became the model for his own subsequent episcopate. Halse served in the East End of London as curate (from 1906) of St Saviour's, Poplar, and priest-in-charge (from 1911) of St Nicholas's, Blackwell.

He was leader of an informal fraternity of young, Kelham-trained priests who wanted to serve abroad when G. H. Frodsham [q.v.8], bishop of North Queensland, came to England seeking recruits for his Bush Brotherhood. The fraternity agreed that Halse would go first and that other members would follow. Arriving at Townsville, Queensland, in January 1913, he served as warden of the Brotherhood of St Barnabas and examining chaplain (until 1925) to the new bishop J. O. Feetham [q.v.8]. Under him, Halse and the brotherhood were influential in shaping the Anglo-Catholic ethos of the diocese. His reputation as a preacher grew, and, in the general mission held throughout Queensland in 1917, he conducted five ten-day missions within two months. In 1914 he had established a short-lived boys' school at Herberton which marked his enduring enthusiasm for church schools. After acquiring funds in England in 1919, he was founding headmaster (1920-25) of All Souls School, Charters Towers. Although he was no disciplinarian, his tolerant humanity, enthusiasm for sport, lively preaching and personal interest in each boy won the affection of his students.

Consecrated bishop of Riverina by the archbishop of Canterbury on 29 September 1925 in Westminster Abbey, London, Halse was enthroned in the pro-cathedral at Hay, New South Wales, on 6 January 1926. The vast diocese, covering the far west and south of the State, called for a peripatetic ministry among scattered parishes and often tiny congregations. His easy informality and natural dignity made him a much-loved pastoral bishop. Preaching engagements and missions in parishes and schools often took him beyond his own diocese and earned him the nickname 'bishop of Never-in-'er'. In 1943 he succeeded J. W. C. Wand [q.v.12] as archbishop of Brisbane and was enthroned in St John's Cathedral on 3 November. Wand's leadership had not been widely popular, and Halse interpreted his election as an invitation to pursue his low-key, pastoral style of episcopate. He inherited a large diocese disrupted by World War II, short of clergy, with a part-time assistant-bishop ten years his senior, and encumbered by debt stemming from the Depression.

Showing amazing stamina, Halse coped on only a few hours sleep each night, supplemented by catnaps (sometimes during meetings). His lifelong habit of improvising with inadequate resources stood him in good stead. He wrote his letters by hand, conscripted clergy or students to drive his car and piled several jobs on one person. Yet he never appeared hurried or flustered, and his unpretentious style of life was complemented by the natural dignity and sonorous voice which enhanced his liturgical presence. These qualities, while endearing, led to increasing frustration in the diocese in the archbishop's advancing years. Perhaps because he recognized that he was unable to supply the vision, the strategies and the dynamic leadership needed by the Church in the postwar period, he encouraged active, younger men from whom he drew strength and ideas. In 1946 he appointed an economics graduate Roland St John as registrar of the diocese; his prodigious efforts, aided by inflation, eliminated diocesan indebtedness. Halse also relied on others, among them W. A. Hardie, E. E. Hawkey and I. W. A. Shevill, all of whom became bishops, and he gained energy from his students at the neighbouring St Francis's Theological College.

His episcopate was marked by tolerance and reconciliation. A pioneer in the ecumenical movement, Halse suffered criticism from some Anglo-Catholic friends who were alarmed that his tolerance might lead the Church into pan-Protestantism. In the 1930s he had discussed intercommunion with Protestant leaders and proposed a formula which he hoped might enable the reconciliation of ministries. He welcomed the formation of the World Council of Churches in 1948 and led in the setting up of a regional committee in Queensland. In 1961 he stood alone against the entire provincial synod of Queensland in voting for full communion with what was to be the united Church of North India. His personal friendship with the Catholic archbishop (Sir) James Duhig [q.v.8] laid a foundation for closer relations between their Churches. Halse was a reconciler, too, within the Anglican Church. He supported constitutional autonomy for the Australian Church and his rapport with bishops of different churchmanship helped to overcome suspicion of the proposed constitution. When smouldering discontent at growing Anglo-Catholic practices exploded in the Brisbane synod in 1953, Halse's inflexible calm and wily delaying tactics deflected the fury. His reputation for employing inactivity as an instrument of policy was enhanced.

The same spirit of toleration characterized his approach to public affairs. Disregarding postwar anti-Japanese sentiment, he visited the Japanese Church in 1947 and faced criticism for inviting the Japanese primate to return the visit. Halse opposed communism, but declined to engage in the bitter tirades of a number of Church leaders. He consistently advocated the path of arbitration for the settlement of industrial disputes. Despite his identification with Australian life, Halse never lost his Englishness. In 1947, on the recommendation of the Archbishop of Canterbury, he was awarded an honorary D.D. (Lambeth); in 1962, by which time he was the senior bishop of the Anglican Communion, he was appointed K.B.E. and delighted in being what he thought was the first Anglican bishop outside Britain to be knighted. He died on 9 August 1962 in Brisbane. Large crowds, silently lining the city streets as the cortège moved to St Matthew's cemetery, Sherwood, testified to the community's widespread affection for him. A portrait by Gwendoline Grant [q.v.] and one by Win Robbins are respectively held at Old Bishopsbourne and St Martin's House, Brisbane.

C of E Diocese of Brisb, *Church Chronicle*, Dec 1943, Sept 1962; *Anglican*, 16 Aug 1962; K. Rayner, The History of the Church of England in Queensland (Ph.D. thesis, Univ Qld, 1962); J. Pryce-Davies, Pilgrim and Pastor (ts, 1990, Diocesan Archives, Brisb); personal information.

K. RAYNER

HAMBLY, WILLIAM FRANK (1908-1972), Methodist minister, biblical scholar and college principal, was born on 11 April 1908 at New Norfolk, Tasmania, eldest of four surviving children of Abraham Hambly, a Methodist minister from Victoria, and his Tasmanian-born wife Harriet Bertha, née Webber. Abraham was a harsh disciplinarian and Frank rebelled by running away from home several times. His early education was in Victorian state schools in the various Methodist circuits to which his father was appointed. He then attended Geelong High School and from 1922 was a Corrigan [q.v.3] scholar at Wesley College, Melbourne; following three incidents of truancy, he expelled himself in 1924. Having spent several years in sundry occupations, including working in a chemist's shop, he taught at St Kilda Park State School. He underwent a religious conversion, became a Methodist lay preacher and was received as a candidate for the ministry in 1929.

Hambly entered Queen's College, University of Melbourne (B.A., 1931; M.A., 1933), and graduated with second-class honours in philosophy and sociology. Continuing his theological studies at the Melbourne College of Divinity (B.D., 1942), he was ordained on 8 March 1934 at Wesley Church, Melbourne. In Queen's College chapel on 10 April that year he married Dulcie May Sutherland

(d.1993), a schoolteacher. For the next ten years he served in churches at Yarram, East Malvern and Warrnambool, and in the Methodist Home Mission department. At the age of 36 he was appointed minister of Pirie Street, Methodism's 'cathedral' church in Adelaide.

As a lecturer, Hambly made an enormous impact on the Methodist Church in South Australia. Tall of build, with a protruding chin, he was a fluent and powerful debater at Church conferences. At Pirie Street he showed himself to be one of the most scholarly and eloquent preachers in Australian Methodism. He exerted a great influence on younger men of the ministry in the ordering of church worship, in ecumenical matters and in the exposition of the New Testament, especially St John's Gospel. In 1955 he became president of the Methodist Conference in South Australia. He was elected secretary-general (1960) and president-general (1963) of the Methodist Church of Australasia.

Despite his commitment to Methodism, Hambly fostered closer relations with other denominations. As a student at Queen's College, he had been confirmed in the Anglican Church so that with good conscience he could take communion. In 1958-71 he was chairman of the Joint Commission on Church Union which embraced representatives from the national councils of the Congregational, Methodist and Presbyterian churches. He prepared several documents which provided a basis for the discussions between the three bodies that led to the formation of the Uniting Church in Australia in 1977.

Widely recognized in theological circles as a biblical scholar, Hambly was particularly interested in the doctrine of the church in the Gospel according to St John which had been the subject of his Bevin lectures (1954) in Adelaide. His Johanine study eventually produced a dissertation, 'The Church in the Fourth Gospel', for which he was awarded a D.D. in 1963 by the Melbourne College of Divinity. He was much in demand as a preacher and lecturer, but he spoke with few notes and it was a source of regret to many that he published so little. Apparently because he found it difficult to finalize his thoughts for publication, he placed few articles in learned journals, thus limiting his contribution to international scholarly debate. All that was ever printed was three collections of popular radio talks.

In 1951 Hambly had left Pirie Street Church. Next year he was appointed the first master of Lincoln College, a male residential college at the University of Adelaide. He had to cope with difficulties relating to buildings and to the raising of finance within the Church. Under his leadership the college was securely established and able to expand in the

1960s when government money was made available.

Hambly took part in other activities. In 1964 he led a Church delegation to Fiji for the inauguration of the Fijian Methodist Conference. He was deputy chancellor (1968-71) of the University of Adelaide, president of Adelaide Rotary Club and a member of the Libraries Board of South Australia. A keen Freemason, he attained the rank of senior grand warden. Golf and philately were his major recreations. Survived by his wife and twin sons, he died suddenly of heart disease on 15 April 1972 at Lincoln College and was cremated. One of his sons, Peter, taught French at the University of Adelaide; the other, Frank, became executive-director of the Australian Vice-Chancellors' Committee. Lincoln College holds a portrait of Hambly by Alf Hannaford.

A. D. Hunt, *This Side of Heaven* (Adel, 1985); Methodist Church of A'sia (SA), *Minutes of Conference*, 1972, and *Central Times*, 26 Apr 1972; student records, Wesley College Archives, Melb; information from Dr P. Hambly, Burnside, Adel, Dr F. Hambly, Yarralumla, Canb, and the late Rev. G. T. Inglis.   ARNOLD D. HUNT

HAMILTON, JOHN BRUCE (1901-1968), ophthalmologist, was born on 2 April 1901 in Hobart, son of Clyde Hamilton, merchant, and his wife, Beatrice Lilian, née Paxton. John Hamilton [q.v.4] was his grandfather. Bruce was educated at Leslie House School, Hobart, and the University of Sydney (M.B., Ch.M., 1924). He then went to England where he gained diplomas of ophthalmic medicine and surgery (R.C.P.& S., 1928) and ophthalmology (Oxford, 1929). On his return, he set up practice in Hobart. From 1930 he was, at different periods, honorary or consulting ophthalmic surgeon to the Royal Hobart Hospital, the Queen Alexandra Hospital for Women, and the Royal Tasmanian Society for the Blind and Deaf (later the Tasmanian Institute for the Blind, Deaf and Dumb).

In 1935 Hamilton and Dr W. D. Counsell investigated the prevalence and causes of blindness in Tasmania. After examining 170 cases, they delivered a paper on hereditary eye disease and proposals for alleviating blindness to the National Health and Medical Research Council's meeting in Hobart in 1937, at which Hamilton also recommended that doctors and the public should be educated in genetics and eugenics. Their research was awarded the Royal London Ophthalmic Hospital's Gifford Edmunds prize. Hamilton's *A Guide to Ophthalmic Operations* (London, 1940) was *de rigueur* for surgeons for many years. Characteristically, he paid tribute in the preface to the tutelage of 'George', who had charge of surgical instruments at Moorfields Eye Hospital, London, where Hamilton had been a house surgeon.

Having served in the Australian Army Medical Corps Reserve from 1935, Hamilton was appointed major in the Australian Imperial Force on 4 January 1941. That year he went to the Middle East as ophthalmic surgeon with the 2nd/7th Australian General Hospital. His eye surgery was 'renowned throughout the Army'. Returning to Australia in 1943, he was attached to headquarters, Tasmania Force, before his A.I.F. appointment terminated on 1 November. On 21 April that year at St John's Presbyterian Church, Hobart, he had married Dora Jessie Grant.

Finding that his clinical observations concurred with those of the Swedish ophthalmologist Henrik Sjögren, Hamilton re-issued, with his own foreword and appendix, a paper published by Sjögren in 1933. Entitled *A New Conception of Kerato-conjunctivitis Sicca* (Sydney, 1943), it proved helpful to rheumatologists and immunologists. Hamilton's study of the eye condition of family members used one hundred and eleven pedigrees and earned him an M.D. from the University of Sydney in 1948. Published under the title, *The Significance of Heredity in Ophthalmology—a Tasmanian Survey* (Melbourne, 1951), it attracted the attention of scientists investigating gene location.

Hamilton was a fellow (1931) and State chairman of the Royal Australasian College of Surgeons, a fellow of the Royal Society of Medicine, London, a member and president (1948) of the Tasmanian branch of the British Medical Association and a member of the Australian Medical Association. In addition, he was a life member of the Ophthalmological Society of the United Kingdom and president of the Ophthalmological Society of Australia. He was an active Anglican, a member of the Liberal Party and president (1948-49) of the Hobart Legacy Club. His enthusiasm for history led him to establish the Bligh [q.v.1] Museum of Pacific Exploration at Adventure Bay.

Tall and well dressed, with 'a very real belief in himself and his abilities', Hamilton was a perfectionist for whom no detail was too small to consider, or—as his colleagues and staff often found—to complain about. However arrogant or curmudgeonly his peers might find him, he was usually generous and encouraging to his patients. Survived by his wife, son and daughter, he died of hypertensive heart disease on 11 April 1968 at Sandy Bay and was cremated.

F. Elias, *The Well-being and Education of Visually Impaired Children in Tasmania* (np, 1978); T. Bowden, *The Way My Father Tells It* (Syd, 1989);

Roy Aust College of Ophthalmologists, Tas Branch, *Papers on the Life and Work of Dr J. Bruce Hamilton* (Hob, 1990) *and* for Hamilton's publications; E. J. Smith, *Time is the Builder* (Hob, 1991); *MJA*, 20 July 1968; *Saturday Evening Mercury*, 13 Apr 1968; *Mercury* (Hob), 2 July 1968.

JEAN PANTON
JENNIFER BOND

HAMILTON, MARIE MONTGOMERIE (1891-1955), pathologist and hockey administrator, was born on 7 April 1891 in Sydney, only daughter of Hugh Montgomerie Hamilton [q.v.9], a native-born judge, and his second wife Minnie Redfearn, from England. Marie was educated at Presbyterian Ladies' College, Croydon, where she excelled as an all-rounder and was dux. Nominated to coach her old school's hockey team in 1913, she was treasurer (1914-16) of the New South Wales Women's Hockey Association. Her fiancé was killed at Lone Pine, Gallipoli. In 1918 she entered the faculty of medicine at the University of Sydney (M.B., Ch.M., 1923) and took up residence in Women's College. She captained the university hockey team in 1920, was president of the N.S.W.W.H.A. for twenty-one consecutive terms (1928-48) and chaired (1932-34 and 1945-54) the All Australia Women's Hockey Association. During her terms of office, women's hockey became an international sport.

On graduation, Dr Hamilton worked as a resident medical officer at Royal Prince Alfred Hospital. On 3 June 1926 she was appointed assistant medical officer in the Department of Public Health. There she met the pathologist Dr Elsie Dalyell [q.v.8]. They began work on the treatment of venereal disease in women, a lengthy process in the pre-penicillin era. Late in 1927 they established a venereal disease clinic at the Rachel Forster Hospital for Women and Children, Redfern, and offered treatment and counselling. Hamilton's sympathetic, if forthright, nature endeared her to her clients.

In 1934 she began private practice as a pathologist from the family home at Strathfield where she lived for the rest of her life, attended by her housekeeper. At the R.F.H., Hamilton was an honorary pathologist, and a member of the board and advisory committee; she was also pathologist at the Western Suburbs and the Masonic hospitals. After his father had been killed in an air crash in 1932, she cared for her young nephew Hugh Montgomerie Hamilton. Her needs were simple, verging on the austere, but her home was 'full of family treasures, beautiful china, furniture and old books'. She dressed sensibly rather than fashionably, and was a great believer in soap and water instead of make-up. Her friends were mainly hockey and medical people with whom she enjoyed good dinner conversation, accompanied by a sherry or glass of wine, and occasionally one cigarette —which her nephew later noted was taken with some glee.

Using her position with the N.S.W.W.H.A., Hamilton established an annual fund from which to supply equipment to the R.F.H.'s pathology department. She worked, as well, at the McGarvie Smith [q.v.11] Institute from 1936 on anthrax research. During World War II she was aware of the need for blood-group testing to enable citizens to become donors: she arrived at a hockey oval, armed with hundreds of small bottles and needles, and proceeded to classify the blood of all the women present. Responding to the government's request for people to grow more food, she bought a small dairy-farm near Camden and ran it when she had completed a correspondence course in agriculture.

Hamilton represented medical women on the university's standing committee of convocation from 1939; in 1943 she was the first woman elected to the council of the New South Wales branch of the British Medical Association. She was a foundation member (1928) and president (1948-49) of the Medical Women's Society of New South Wales.

An enthusiastic traveller within Australia, especially on camping safaris to the outback, she also accompanied women's hockey teams overseas. Ill health forced her to return to Australia from one such tour in 1952. She was made a life member of the State and the All-Australia women's hockey associations. Attended by Dr Julia Amphlett, her friend and colleague since university, Hamilton died of cancer on 2 November 1955 at Killara and was cremated with Anglican rites.

L. Cohen, *Rachel Forster Hospital* (Syd, 1972); M. H. Neve, *This Mad Folly* (Syd, 1980); L. Hodges, *A History of the New South Wales Women's Hockey Association* (Syd, 1984); *Aurora Australis*, 1906, 1907, 1908; *MJA*, 14 Feb 1925, 31 Dec 1955; *SMH*, 16 Nov 1942, 26 Mar 1943, 4 Nov 1955; information from Mr H. M. Hamilton, Byron Bay, NSW.

MARION K. STELL

HAMMER, HEATHCOTE HOWARD (1905-1961), army officer, commercial traveller and storekeeper, was born on 15 February 1905 at Southern Cross, Western Australia, second son of Victorian-born parents William Hammer, miner, and his wife Ada May, née Williams. Educated at the Ballarat School of Mines, Victoria, he took a local job before becoming a commercial traveller. At St Patrick's Catholic Cathedral, Melbourne, on 26 October 1935 he married Mary Frances Morrissey, a clerk; they were to have two children before being divorced in 1955. Having joined the Militia in 1923, he was commissioned in the 8th Battalion in February 1926, transferred to the 17th Light Horse (Machine-Gun) Regiment in 1937 and promoted major in 1939.

'Tack' Hammer was seconded to the Australian Imperial Force in May 1940. He sailed for the Middle East in September and carried out instructional duties in Palestine. His posting as brigade major of the 16th Brigade in March 1941 soon brought him the operational experience he craved. After participating in the disastrous campaign in Greece, his brigade built defences in Syria. In January 1942 he was appointed to command the 2nd/48th Battalion, 9th Division; he led the unit with distinction in the fighting at El Alamein, Egypt, from July. His capture of Trig 29 on 26 October was brilliantly planned and executed. In the last attack launched by the division, on 30-31 October, although Hammer was wounded, he took two German prisoners and, when only forty of his men remained, withdrew this remnant and had them dug-in by dawn. One of his soldiers said of him at El Alamein: 'Tack will do us. He's a soldier and a half'. Hammer was awarded the Distinguished Service Order.

Returning to Australia in February 1943, he took command of the 15th Brigade in New Guinea in July. Following strenuous operations which led to the capture of Salamaua in September, Brigadier Hammer was given a brief time to rest and train his men at Donadabu before they joined the 7th Division in the Ramu Valley in January 1944. There they took part in the clearing of the Huon Peninsula and entered Madang on 24 April. Hammer was awarded a Bar to the D.S.O. (for Salamaua) and appointed C.B.E. (for the Ramu).

In December 1944 the 15th Brigade began its move to Bougainville. Even before his troops embarked, Hammer had appreciated the potential problem of morale and discussed it frankly in an address to the whole brigade. On Bougainville he developed amenities such as a sportsground, swimming pool, concert area and rest camp. The 15th went into action in April 1945. When the Japanese surrendered in August, he set up schools and courses to prepare his men for their return to civilian life. Mentioned in dispatches, he transferred to the Reserve of Officers on 29 November 1945.

One of the most thoughtful and successful Australian commanders of World War II, Hammer was a 'tireless, fiery and colourful leader', immaculate in the desert and even in the jungle. 'Hard as nails' was the motto he proclaimed at his first inspection of the 2nd/48th and it inspired his training methods throughout the war. Like Field Marshal Earl Wavell, he understood and expounded the logistical basis of battle: 'Weapons, ammuni-tion and food are treasures in this country', he told his troops on the way to Salamaua, urging them to fight their battles 'wisely'. Evidence of his own wisdom was to be seen in the strict anti-malarial routines in his brigade, which he regarded less as a medical than as a disciplinary problem. He was also an imaginative tactician, as his night operations against the Japanese near Salamaua demonstrated. On Bougainville he employed artillery, tanks and air power with the aim of limiting casualties among his infantry.

As controller of demobilization in Victoria (1945-46), and as an assistant-commissioner for repatriation (1946-47) and a member of the Repatriation Commission from July 1947, Hammer remained close to the ex-service community. Seeking refuge from the 'hurly-burly', he resigned in September and bought a general store at Bright. He returned to the Militia as commander, 2nd Armoured Brigade (1953-56), and was an aide-de-camp to Queen Elizabeth II in 1954. Promoted major general, he commanded the 3rd Division in 1956-59 and was appointed honorary colonel of the 8th-13th Victorian Mounted Rifles in 1959. In the postwar army he threw himself into training with the same creativity and drive that had distinguished his career in the A.I.F.

On 14 January 1956 at the College Church, Parkville, Melbourne, Hammer had married with Presbyterian forms Helena Irena Olova, née Vymazal, an Austrian-born interpreter. Survived by his wife, and by the daughter and son of his first marriage, he died of a coronary occlusion on 10 March 1961 at Brighton and was buried in Springvale cemetery with Anglican rites and full military honours.

G. Long, *Greece, Crete and Syria* (Canb, 1953) and *The Final Campaigns* (Canb, 1963); A. S. Walker, *The Island Campaigns* (Canb, 1957); J. G. Glenn, *Tobruk to Tarakan* (Adel, 1960); D. Dexter, *The New Guinea Offensives* (Canb, 1961); R. Mathews, *Militia Battalion at War* (Syd, 1961); B. Maughan, *Tobruk and El Alamein* (Canb, 1966); *Bulletin*, 27 Aug 1947; *Herald* (Melb), 13 Aug 1947; AWM records; letters held by Brig G. D. Solomon, Farrer, Canb.   A. J. HILL

HAMMOND, THOMAS CHATTERTON (1877-1961), Anglican clergyman and college principal, was born on 20 February 1877 at Cork, County Cork, Ireland, youngest son of Colman Mark Hammond (d.1883), farmer, and his second wife Elizabeth, née Sergeant. Educated at Cork Model School, at the age of 13 Thomas became a railway clerk. His involvement with the Young Men's Christian Association, and a religious conversion, led him to full-time work as a street and mission preacher. Admitted in 1896 to train in Dublin with the Society for Irish Church Missions to the Roman Catholics, three years later Hammond enrolled at Trinity College, Dublin (B.A., 1903). His chief interest, apart from a conservative approach to scriptural studies, was in idealist philosophy. He was made deacon on 20 December 1903 and priested in the Church of Ireland by the archbishop of Dublin on 26 March 1905.

At St Anne's parish church, Cork, on 23 January 1906 Hammond married Margaret McNay, whose family had been closer to him than his own. As curate and, from 1910, rector of St Kevin's, an inner-suburban Dublin parish, he was an effective pastor, but his energies were directed to the wider field of evangelism and to the defence of the Irish Protestant position. He became a prolific pamphleteer, writing with learning and sardonicism. In the art of public speaking he had few equals for pungent and well-ordered eloquence. Hammond was appointed (1919) clerical superintendent of the Irish Church Missions and controlled a large staff engaged in educational, welfare and evangelistic work. He wrote *Authority in the Church* (1921), a study of Anglican episcopacy. In 1926 he toured Canada and Australia, defending the Book of Common Prayer which was then being threatened with revision.

As a result of his growing reputation, Hammond was appointed principal of Moore Theological College, Sydney. While Archbishop Mowll [q.v.] thought the appointment provocative, he looked on him as a key figure in strengthening the diocese. Hammond arrived in April 1936 to find the college understaffed, poorly funded and lacking a distinctive direction. He began a vigorous campaign to improve it. His own teaching, though sometimes mechanical from overwork, was rigorous and systematic. With more staff and buildings (including a new chapel in 1950), he made the college a centre of evangelical Anglican teaching. His *In Understanding be Men* (1936, sixth edition 1968) soon became a standard text and was popular with the laity. Hammond found it disappointing that his mature works —*Perfect Freedom* (London, 1938), a study in Christian ethics, *Reasoning Faith* (London, 1943), on Christian apologetics, and *The New Creation* (London, 1953), on the theology of regeneration—did not command similar support. Many, however, heard his fortnightly broadcasts, 'The Case for Protestantism'.

Hammond easily assumed the role of critic of Roman Catholicism; to so old a campaigner, the local scene seemed rather tame. In a short time he was a well-known public figure, feared and admired for his trenchant wit, his logic and his learning. Professor John Anderson [q.v.7] and he readily engaged in controversy. Hammond was grand chaplain (1943-47, 1950-61) and grand master (1961)

of the Loyal Orange Institution of New South Wales, and grand chaplain (1954-61) of the Federated Loyal Orange Grand Council of Australasia. Rector (1936-61) of St Philip's, he was a canon (from 1939) of St Andrew's Cathedral and an archdeacon without territorial jurisdiction (from 1949).

Administration was not his forte. Advice and advocacy were. He had helped Mowll to deal with the complaints of the liberal Sydney clergy, the 'Memorialists' (1938). A decisive opponent of Anglo-Catholicism, Hammond was a prime mover against Bishop A. L. Wylde (for using part of the Roman Catholic order of service) in the 'Red Book' case (1943-48) which sought, with some success, to place legal restraints on 'ritualist' worship, and he initiated a restrictive ordinance in the Sydney synod in 1949. Hammond championed what he believed to be the Protestant integrity of his Church. It was because he came to think that English canon and case law could no longer guarantee this position in Australia that, in 1955 and afterwards, he supported a constitution for an autonomous Church.

'T.C.' (as he was generally called) was not just an elderly Irishman spending his last years in a new land. He made a solid impact on Sydney Anglicanism. He was loved and feared, revered and reviled—which is what he wanted to be. He brought well-based scholarship to his new post and produced a large number of well-prepared ordinands. His fervour and invective were as effective as his personal kindliness and humour. Hammond retired from Moore College in 1953, but remained at St Philip's. Survived by his wife, three sons and only daughter, he died on 16 November 1961 in Sydney Hospital and was buried in Northern Suburbs cemetery.

M. L. Loane, *Centenary History of Moore Theological College* (Syd, 1955) and *Mark these Men* (Canb, 1985); S. Judd and K. Cable, *Sydney Anglicans* (Syd, 1987); W. Nelson, *T. C. Hammond* (Edinburgh, 1994) *and* for publications; C of E (Syd), *Syd Diocesan Synod Reports*, 1936-61; *SMH*, 8 Apr 1926, 26, 27 June 1947, 17 Nov 1961, 1 Nov 1978; *Aust Church Record*, 23 Nov 1961; *Anglican*, 24 Nov 1961.
K. J. CABLE

HANGER, EUNICE (1911-1972), playwright and schoolteacher, was born on 8 March 1911 at Mount Chalmers, Queensland, third child of Thomas Hanger [q.v.], schoolteacher, and his wife Myfanwy, née Granville-Jones. (Sir) Mostyn Hanger [q.v.] was her brother. Eunice was educated at Gympie High School, where her father was headmaster, and at the University of Queensland (B.A., 1932; M.A., 1940). From 1933 she became an outstanding teacher at her father's school. Transferred to Rockhampton High School in 1940, she joined the local little theatre which was to stage her first plays. In 1948 Miss Hanger was appointed to Brisbane High School and joined the Twelfth Night Theatre Company. Next year she dramatized the novel by 'M. Barnard Eldershaw' [q.v. F.S. Eldershaw], *A House is Built* (1929)— the first play on an Australian subject staged by Twelfth Night. By 1963 she had directed works by Shakespeare, Shaw, Tennessee Williams and Pirandello, as well as several of her own and other Australian plays, for the company. A director of the 'walk and talk' school, she concentrated on the 'correct' use of language, although she welcomed new European plays, particularly those of Beckett and Ionesco.

Hanger's own plays had some popularity in the little theatre movement, particularly her one-act comedy, *Upstage* (London, 1952). Aimed at redressing the gender imbalance in amateur theatre, *Upstage* had an all-woman cast and brought Shakespeare's heroines together on stage, ostensibly to elect 'Miss Shakespeare'. Her major work—the verse drama, *Flood*, set in a tropical bungalow during 'the wet'—won an award in the Playwrights' Advisory Board competition in 1955 and was staged by Twelfth Night on 19 October. Hanger adjudicated drama festivals, organized play-reading groups and was secretary of Twelfth Night, with whom she also acted, notably as Emma in Ray Lawler's *Summer of the Seventeenth Doll*. She was also active in the English Teachers' Association.

From February 1955 until December 1956 Hanger was seconded to the University of Queensland as a temporary lecturer in English; in June 1958 she was appointed lecturer in drama. She also directed and acted with the University Staff Players. Disturbed by a trend she perceived in Australian playwriting towards the three-act realism popularized by *The Doll*, and dissatisfied with the results of subsequent competitions run by the Australian Elizabethan Theatre Trust, she began to accumulate the scripts of unpublished plays and saw herself as a 'wet nurse to the orphans abandoned by the Trust'. Her interest lay in contemporary writing and she relied solely on her own judgement as to what merited collecting.

In 1962-63 she was embroiled in an argument in the *Bulletin* with critics, writers and directors of little theatre companies who challenged her claim that good Australian plays were being neglected. Her activities led to further conflict with Campbell Howard, a rival collector of plays written in 1920-55. Howard's accusation that she had occasionally violated authors' copyright was rejected by the National Library of Australia, which monitored and copied from both collections

and described her procedures as 'punctilious'. The Hanger Collection in the Fryer Memorial Library at the university contains some 2000 scripts.

Accurately identifying the early efforts of major stage-writers of the 1960s, she drew national and international attention to three playwrights—Ray Mathew, David Ireland and Patrick White—whose work she thought went beyond 'flat-footed realism'. She directed Mathew's *A Spring Song* in 1958, and it was the first play published (1961) in the University of Queensland Press's drama series, of which Hanger was general editor. She also directed and published (1964) Ireland's *Image in the Clay*. Despite White's disparaging remark that 'this poring over ephemeral work seems to be a disease to which Australians and Americans are prone', she championed his plays in articles and speeches, including one delivered to an international comparative literature conference in Germany in 1964. She contributed a chapter on drama to Geoffrey Dutton's [q.v.] *The Literature of Australia* (Melbourne, 1964). In 1965 she was promoted senior lecturer.

Eunice lived with her parents for much of her life and assisted her father in writing his memoirs. Her later years were lonely and of another time, out of step with the prosaic male vulgarism, untrained speech and experimental production methods of the post-1968 dramatic renaissance, which she nevertheless continued to support. Hanger's last enthusiasm was for the Italian language and for the playwright Dario Fo, whose work she translated and arranged to have performed in Brisbane over a decade before Fo was acclaimed in the English-speaking world. She died of cancer on 16 October 1972 at Toowong and was cremated with Presbyterian forms. A commemorative volume of her work, *2D and Other Plays*, was published in Brisbane in 1978.

Southerly, 23, no 2, 1963, p 132; *Telegraph* (Brisb), 17 Oct 1972; *Courier-Mail*, 18 Oct 1972; Hanger collection and papers, Fryer L, Univ Qld.   RICHARD FOTHERINGHAM

HANGER, SIR MOSTYN (1908-1980), judge, was born on 3 January 1908 at Rockhampton, Queensland, second of five children of native-born parents Thomas Hanger [q.v.], schoolteacher, and his wife Myfanwy Granville-Jones. Eunice Hanger [q.v.] was his younger sister. Educated at Gympie High School, where his father was headmaster, Mostyn was captain and dux in 1925 and won an open scholarship to the University of Queensland (B.A., 1929; LL.M., 1941). He spent two years as a clerk in the registry of the Supreme Court and another in the office of the registrar of joint stock companies.

Admitted to the Bar on 21 November 1930, Hanger did not begin practice until early 1932. During the Depression, activity in the legal profession declined and he had to wait some fourteen weeks for his initial brief. In his first year he earned only thirty guineas, whereas the rent on his chambers (which he shared with Walter Harrison) was £50. At St Andrew's Presbyterian Church, Brisbane, on 8 April 1936 Hanger married Greta Lumley Robertson. Having completed his masterate, in 1941 he lectured at the university in company law.

On 25 May 1942 Hanger enlisted in the Royal Australian Air Force; he was then 5 ft 7 ins (170 cm) tall and weighed 10 st. 9 lb. (68 kg). In the following month he was commissioned in the Administrative and Special Duties Branch. Promoted acting flight lieutenant in April 1943, he was subsequently adjutant of No.12 Squadron, based at Merauke, Netherlands New Guinea. His appointment terminated on 2 May 1945. Practice moved briskly after the war. Assisted by the preference given by the Commonwealth Crown Solicitor to returned servicemen, Hanger's work grew rapidly and widely within the civil jurisdiction. He took silk in 1950 and successfully appeared as counsel for the plaintiff in a celebrated case in which the architect J. F. Hennessy sued Archbishop (Sir) James Duhig [q.v.8] for non-payment of fees for designing the Cathedral of the Holy Name. On 23 July 1953 Hanger was appointed judge of the Supreme Court of Queensland.

On 5 October 1965, while president (1962-71) of the Industrial Court of Queensland, he ruled against the re-employment of forty-five men by Mount Isa Mines Ltd. The decision prompted an unsuccessful call for his removal by (Sir) John Egerton on the grounds that Hanger's wife held shares in the company. In a controversial judgement in August 1966 Hanger declared invalid the power of the State Industrial Commission to set awards that included a 'compulsory unionism' clause. Appointed senior puisne judge in April 1970, he became chief justice of the Supreme Court on 12 May 1971. Hanger was appointed K.B.E. in 1973. As deputy-governor, he served as administrator of Queensland for short periods in 1972 and 1977. He retired in July 1977.

Survived by his wife, daughter and three sons, Sir Mostyn died on 11 August 1980 at St Lucia; he was accorded a state funeral and was cremated with the forms of the Uniting Church.

B. H. McPherson, *Supreme Court of Queensland* (Syd, 1989); *Aust Law J*, 27, 1952-53, p 248, 45,

1970-71, p 384, 54, Dec 1980, p 758; *Courier-Mail*, 15 July 1977, 12 Aug 1980; M. Hanger, Memoirs (held by Judge J. M. Hanger, Southport, Qld); transcript of procs of the Full Court of the Supreme Court of Qld, 18 July 1977, 12 Aug 1980, *and* of the District Court, Cairns, 12 Aug 1980; information from Judge J. M. Hanger, and Mr R. I. Hanger, Brisb.   M. W. D. WHITE

HANGER, THOMAS (1874-1964), headmaster, was born on 27 January 1874 at Rockhampton, Queensland, son of Richard Hanger, a wheelwright from England, and his Scottish-born wife Elizabeth, née Cherry. Thomas was educated at Bogantungan Provisional and Rockhampton Central Boys schools. Of these years he later wrote: 'A fair measure of the culture of any community is the treatment its parents hand out to their own children and, judged by this test, the community was degraded'. Denied the opportunity of a scholarship to Rockhampton Grammar School owing to his family's poverty, he embarked unenthusiastically upon the grind of a teaching career. In 1887 he joined the Department of Public Instruction as a pupil-teacher at Rockhampton Central Boys' School with an annual salary of £30. He was appointed to Maryborough in 1896 as an assistant-teacher (£114 a year) and returned to Rockhampton Central in 1899. On 2 July 1902 at Murray Street, Rockhampton, he married with Congregational forms Myfanwy Granville-Jones, a fellow teacher.

As head teacher (£200 per annum), from February 1903 he taught at Jericho, near Barcaldine, where he and his wife spent their early married life. Standing on the school verandah, he turned away in pity at the first sight of his pupils' bloodshot and scorched eyes, but it was at this place that he learned to appreciate the scent of bush flowers, 'the beauty of dawn and sunset' and the 'fragrance of the smoke from gum-sticks as the billy boils'. Postings followed at Mount Chalmers (1909-11), Rockhampton North Boys' School (1912-13) and Maryborough West (1914-16). By means of an external course at the University of Queensland (B.A., 1914) he earned a 'garret-room degree' which enabled him to pursue his life's-work as the much respected headmaster of Gympie High School between 1916 and 1940.

The highly centralized educational system influenced and fashioned Hanger, but did not crush his spirit of individualism. He rejected official creeds, yet held firmly to a disciplined code, regarding the school and the teacher as moral forces in an amoral world. Many of his senior pupils—including his son Mostyn and daughter Eunice [qq.v.]—won scholarships to the university. Hanger cultivated a deep love of literature and music, and physical culture became a daily habit. Although he retired in June 1940, he taught, part time, his favourite subject, mathematics, at the Church of England Grammar School, Brisbane, until November 1949. His vivid memoir, *Sixty Years in Queensland Schools*, was published in Sydney in 1963. At the age of 90 he wrote an article for the *Queensland Teachers' Journal* (May 1964) in which he reflected on his career and concluded, 'few men can have richer blessings to count'.

Survived by his wife, son and four daughters, Hanger died on 18 July 1964 at Rainworth, Brisbane; in accordance with his request, he was buried in Jericho cemetery, with Presbyterian forms.

J. Colebrook, *A House of Trees* (Lond, 1988); *Courier-Mail*, 21 July 1964; Hanger staff card, History Unit, Qld Dept of Education, Brisb; Hanger family papers (held by Judge J. M. Hanger, Southport, Qld).   TOM WATSON

HANIGAN, ROSE (1864-1952), known as Mother Francis, Sister of Mercy, was born on 19 October 1864 at Barkers Creek, near Castlemaine, Victoria, sixth child of Irishborn parents John Hanigan, labourer, and his wife Anne, née Cahill, a teacher. Rose left school to become a trainee milliner with McCreery & Hopkins, the leading emporium in Castlemaine. She rose quickly to senior saleslady, but decided to follow a religious vocation. In 1892, at the age of 28, she joined the Sisters of Mercy at Bendigo where she made her vows in 1895, taking the name of Francis. Five years later she led a group of four sisters who were appointed to establish a Mercy foundation at Tatura. Returning to Bendigo, she was superior of the convent in 1911-16. During this period, acting on medical advice, she implemented precautions to protect the Sisters against tuberculosis which was then prevalent in the district.

In 1920, in the wake of the pneumonic flu epidemic, the Order decided to open a private hospital in Melbourne. Coonil, a mansion at Malvern, was purchased and Mother Francis was appointed superior of the founding community. Her resourcefulness was called into play as she attended to renovations, recruiting staff, registering the institution as St Benedict's Hospital and establishing rapport with leading doctors. The early involvement of (Sir) Hugh Devine [q.v.8] ensured that St Benedict's was well known to his surgeon colleagues. In 1948 the Cabrini Sisters took over its management.

After changes in government regulations had enabled the Mercy Sisters to fulfil their long-held objective of opening a hospital with intermediate and maternity wings, in 1930 Mother Francis purchased for the Order a one-acre (0.4 ha) site in East Melbourne. That year, accompanied by her assistant Sister Philippa Brazil, she undertook an inspection tour of hospitals in the United States of America. The architect (Sir) Arthur Stephenson [q.v.12] was commissioned to design the 120-bed Mercy Private Hospital, but work was delayed because of the difficulty in raising finance during the Depression; excavations began in February 1934 and the Mercy opened on 2 December.

Mother Francis won the respect of doctors and contractors. Stephenson regarded his involvement with the hospital as a 'kind of mission'. A young neurosurgeon who met the elderly nun described her as 'a lovely woman . . . only the size of a threepenny bit but with a personality that could fill a room'. Her standards were high and she maintained them rigorously. One of her practices was to visit each patient daily, and they remembered her capacity to discuss any subject with ease. In 1940 the Mercy was declared a first-class hospital: thenceforth trainees did not have to go to other hospitals to gain nursing skills. Having handed over to Mother Philippa Brazil in 1948, Mother Francis died on 28 March 1952 at the Mercy and was buried in Melbourne general cemetery.

M. Ignatius O'Sullivan, *The Wheel of Time* (Melb, 1954); M. G. Allen, *The Labourers' Friends* (Melb, 1989); S. Priestley, *Melbourne's Mercy* (Melb, 1990); *Advocate* (Melb), 29 Nov, 6 Dec 1934; *Age* and *Herald* (Melb), 29 Mar 1952; Convent of Mercy, Bendigo, Vic, register, 1876-1907.
                    MAREE G. ALLEN

HANLON, EDWARD MICHAEL (1887-1952), railway worker, grocer and premier, was born on 1 October 1887 at Paddington, Brisbane, fifth of seven children of London-born Michael Hanlon, drayman, and his wife Mary Anne, née Byrne, from Ireland. Educated at Petrie Terrace State School and Brisbane Technical College, Ned worked as a schoolboy in his father's milk-delivery business. In 1901 he was a message-boy for several barristers before being employed in a grocery shop. During his teens he belonged to the Toowong Workers' Political Organisation and became part of a Labor Party team which addressed political meetings throughout Brisbane. He joined the Queensland Railways Department as a porter in 1903 and was later a shunter. Involved in the development of unionism in the railways with men such as Frank Cooper, Mick Kirwan [qq.v.13,9], Joe Sherry and Tom Brown, he helped to establish the Queensland Railway Union, and was a member and vice-president of its management-committee. The 1912 general strike in

Brisbane was a traumatic experience for Hanlon, who held a seat on the strike committee. Although he was passionately committed to this struggle to preserve unionism, his experiences convinced him of the futility of direct industrial action. When the terms of the settlement of the strike required that he, Cooper, Kirwan and Sherry leave the railway service, Hanlon returned to the grocery business.

He enlisted in the Australian Imperial Force on 11 August 1915, joined the 9th Battalion in Egypt in February 1916, served on the Western Front, rose to sergeant and was discharged on 26 August 1919 in Brisbane. In partnership with his brother Patrick, he set up a grocery business. On 17 April 1922 at St Brigid's Catholic Church, Red Hill, he married Elizabeth Carver (d.1946). Hanlon represented the Paddington district at the 1925 Labor conference which drafted the Australian Labor Party's municipal policy for the first Greater Brisbane Council elections. The intensity and labyrinthine nature of Labor politics in Brisbane's inner working-class suburbs helped to develop in Hanlon an ability to 'mix it'. Contemporaries regarded his 'Irish temper' as one of his chief political assets. In 1926 he won pre-selection from the sitting Labor member for the seat of Ithaca in the Legislative Assembly; he entered parliament on 8 May and held the seat for the rest of his life.

After Labor's landslide defeat in 1929, Hanlon came under notice as an effective, robust parliamentary debater, with a capacity to wound the conservative government of A. E. Moore [q.v.10]. In Forgan Smith's [q.v.11] government Hanlon was home secretary from 17 June 1932 until 5 December 1935 when he became secretary for health and home affairs. As the minister largely responsible for the development and implementation of the A.L.P.'s welfare policies, Hanlon held assumptions and attitudes that had important consequences for the character of Queensland society. Under his administration Aborigines continued to be subjected to 'enforced population transfers, confinement to particular areas under relatively arbitrary and quite authoritarian regimes, excessive moral scrutiny, interference in intimate human relationships, supervised breeding, imposed placement and calculatedly inferior educational training for their children, control over their labour conditions, wages and personal property, and even suppression of their "injurious" or menacing "customs" or practices'. In these ways, Aborigines who, in their 'natural' state—according to Hanlon—were 'about 1,000,000 years behind the white race', were 'protected' by the state.

In Labor folklore Hanlon was credited with having implemented a creative and effective public health policy. He was responsible for the reorganization of health administration and played a significant role in the development of a free public hospital service. The realization of this long-desired Labor party goal was frustrated by subsequent lack of government finance. A premium was placed on preventative health care. Hanlon had a special interest in the health of women and children (expressed largely through government provision of pre- and post-natal facilities) and was a staunch supporter of the work of Sister Elizabeth Kenny [q.v.9]. Recent scholarship, however, has argued that he, in concert with Sir Raphael Cilento, director-general of health and medical services, vigorously pursued a policy of suppressing abortion clinics. In the area of prisoner rehabilitation, Hanlon initiated a system of prison-farms in Queensland.

On 27 April 1944 he became treasurer and deputy to Premier F. A. Cooper. On social issues Hanlon was a strong supporter of the monarchy and the White Australia policy. In economic matters, he fervently embraced large-scale development projects, and subscribed to the values of small business capitalism, with an emphasis on the importance of primary production and decentralization of industry. His understanding of the concept of socialism amounted to little more than the argument that all people ought to share equitably in the results of their labours. It was in the area of industrial relations that he exhibited the nature of many of his fundamental beliefs.

From 7 March 1946 until his death in office in 1952, Hanlon was premier of Queensland. In two major industrial confrontations—the meat industry strike (1946) and the railway strike (1948)—he brought the force of the state to bear in resisting, and attempting to break, these strikes which he believed were fomented and conducted by the Communist Party of Australia. From his viewpoint, members of the C.P.A. were agents of a foreign power hell-bent on destroying democracy, the conciliation and arbitration system, the A.L.P. and the trade unions. Hanlon was a member of the executive-committee of the Queensland Central Executive of the A.L.P. which established the industrial groups in July 1946 and which consolidated and extended their operation in July 1948. He encouraged the 'groupers' in their anti-communist crusade in the trade unions and publicly supported their efforts. A committed believer in States rights, Hanlon identified a number of centralizing tendencies in Australian industrial relations as threatening his government's ability to maintain industrial peace: the extension of the influence of the Commonwealth Court of Conciliation and Arbitration, the growth of federal unions, and the efforts to expand the Federal government's industrial relations powers.

Hanlon feared that the growth of powerful federal unions would mean an ever increasing possibility that Queensland unionists could become involved in industrial disputes which were not local in origin. The coal industry provided a classic example of his attitudes. He was determined to shield the industry from disputes which might arise as a result of what he regarded as an undesirable concentration of power in the central council of the Miners' Federation of Australia. Steps taken by Prime Minister J. B. Chifley [q.v.13] between 1947 and 1949 to establish a national authority to regulate industrial relations throughout the coal industry were quickly rejected by the Hanlon government. Proposals during the late 1940s that the national parliament assume more responsibility for the regulation of industrial matters (through devices which included constitutional changes, reference of State powers and concurrent legislation) were received with scorn. Even milder approaches failed to elicit a positive response. Hanlon refused point-blank to have anything to do with Chifley's efforts to develop closer co-operation and consultation between governments in the area of industrial relations.

In common with other governments in Queensland, the Hanlon administration was the target of allegations of corruption, relating—among other things—to political appointments to the public service and to electoral malpractices. The election result in the seat of Bulimba in 1950 was declared void by Justice (Sir) Alan Mansfield [q.v.] on the ground that fraudulent practices had occurred. Hanlon was a consummate politician in terms of 'getting the numbers'. He had successfully contested the A.L.P. pre-selection ballot for Ithaca in 1926, only to see the Q.C.E. order a fresh ballot after widespread protests alleging irregularities. The second ballot, won by Hanlon, was equally controversial. Newspaper reports suggested that he and his supporters had managed to prevent the inclusion of certain unfavourable postal votes in the count. In 1938 the Protestant Labour Party mounted a campaign against Hanlon. When he again won the seat of Ithaca, the result was challenged by one of his opponents who alleged malpractice. Sitting as Elections Tribunal judge, E. A. Douglas [q.v.] found irregularities sufficient to set aside Hanlon's return, but the decision was reversed on appeal.

In the late 1940s the A.L.P. in Queensland was gravely concerned at falling trends in its voter support. Despite his constant rhetoric about the importance of defending democracy, Hanlon placed a far higher premium on his party's electoral survival. His Electoral Districts Act (1949) created an electoral malapportionment of major dimensions. The State was divided into four zones, with a different number of voters per electorate in each zone. The zones with relatively low voter numbers contained traditional rural Labor strongholds. Expressed in terms of a geographical decentralization of political power, Hanlon's justification was used repeatedly against the A.L.P. in subsequent decades of non-Labor government in Queensland.

Survived by his three daughters and one of his two sons, Hanlon died of hypertensive cardiorenal disease on 15 January 1952 at the Mater Misericordiae Hospital, South Brisbane; he was accorded a state funeral and was buried in Toowong cemetery. Hanlon's legacies are difficult to measure. His savage counter-attack against the unions in 1946, and particularly in 1948, both created and exacerbated personal hatreds, and led to a loss of respect in the trade union movement for Labor politicians. These pressures and tensions played a significant role in producing the 1957 A.L.P. 'split'. The praise bestowed on many of Hanlon's initiatives in health policy and administration has not been extended to his anti-strike activities which involved an assault on civil liberties. One of Queensland's more innovative premiers as far as working conditions were concerned, Hanlon introduced major reforms in important areas, including annual-, sick- and long-service leave. Considering his attitudes towards Aborigines, the monarchy, White Australia, communists, strikes, electoral democracy, 'developmentalism' and States rights, the governments led by Hanlon in 1946-52 had more in common with their non-Labor successors than is popularly imagined.

C. Lack (comp), *Three Decades of Queensland Political History, 1929-1960* (Brisb, 1962); D. J. Murphy and R. B. Joyce (eds), *Queensland Political Portraits 1859-1952* (Brisb, 1978); M. B. Cribb and P. J. Boyce (eds), *Politics in Queensland* (Brisb, 1980); R. Fitzgerald, *A History of Queensland from 1915 to the Early 1980s* (Brisb, 1984); D. Blackmur, *Strikes* (Syd, 1993); *Courier-Mail*, 16 Jan 1952; D. Blackmur, Industrial Relations under an Australian State Labor Government. The Hanlon Government in Queensland 1946-1952 (Ph.D. thesis, Univ Qld, 1986); W. Selby, Motherhood in Labor's Queensland 1915-1957 (Ph.D. thesis, Griffith Univ, 1992).   DOUGLAS BLACKMUR

HANNAFORD, ALFRED (1890-1969), inventor of farming machinery, was born on 23 June 1890 at Wattle Vale farm, near Riverton, South Australia, ninth of ten children of native-born parents John Hannaford, farmer, and his wife Elizabeth, née Shearer. After attending Riverton Public School until sixth grade, Alf worked on the family farm. In its blacksmith's shop he invented and developed a wet-wheat pickling machine fashioned from a railway sleeper: by enabling seed to be dipped in a copper sulphate solution, it helped to combat rust in wheat. His invention was inspired by a machine exhibited at a farmers' conference. 'If I can't make a better one', Hannaford declared, 'I'll eat my hat'. A big, strong, vigorous man, ingenious but essentially practical, he sometimes rose at 2 a.m. to give an idea physical form. The design drawing came later.

At the Methodist Church, Tarlee, on 2 April 1913 Hannaford married Ivy Julia Hill. After a drought in the following year, they moved to Adelaide where he continued to refine the pickler and patented it in 1914; with the help of J. E. Swann, several machines were manufactured. Although the picklers were in great demand, Hannaford worked for H. V. McKay's [q.v.10] Harvester Co. for two years to gain business experience. In 1923 he invented a dry-wheat pickler and in 1924 a combined seed grader and dry-pickler. The latter machine marked a breakthrough in the control of smut and in the cleaning and grading of wheat, and proved popular with farmers in every State; in 1927 the wooden-framed machine was converted to a steel-bodied one, the first of its kind in Australia. Alf. Hannaford & Co. Ltd, established in 1925, built between 500 and 600 machines a year until farmers could no longer afford them during the Depression. The company then introduced a contract scheme, loading the machines on trucks and taking them to farms where they graded and pickled the wheat at a bag-rate charge. By 1933 the firm had two hundred trucks and graders operating; by 1937 it had opened offices in Victoria and Western Australia. In 1944 11 000 farmers had their grain treated by the Hannaford On-Farm Grading Service, producing sufficient seed to cover some five million acres (about two million hectares). Hannaford's five children all worked for the company at different stages.

Committed to improving the quality and yields of Australian crops, in 1937 he had built a clover harvester and begun extensive harvesting of Barrel Clover, which was later named after him. He retired as managing director in 1960 and was appointed M.B.E. in 1961. Hannaford enjoyed travelling, particularly in South Africa and Europe. He was a Rotarian and a Methodist lay preacher. Survived by his wife, two sons and three daughters, he died on 25 August 1969 in the Queen Elizabeth Hospital, Woodville, and was cremated; his estate was sworn for probate at $457 460, from which he bequeathed $320 000 to the Waite [q.v.6] Agricultural Research Institute. He is commemorated by a plaque (1986) in the footpath on North Terrace, Adelaide.

Waite Agr Research Inst, Univ Adel, *Biennial Report*, 1980-81; *Advertiser* (Adel), 31 Dec 1960, 1 July 1970; PRG 155 (Mort L); information from Mrs G. Dunstone, West Lakes, Adel.

KAY HANNAFORD

HANNAH, SIR COLIN THOMAS (1914-1978), air force officer and governor, was born on 22 December 1914 at Menzies, Western Australia, son of Thomas Howard Hannah, public servant, and his wife Johanna, née Frame, both native-born. The family shifted from Bunbury to Perth where Thomas officiated as clerk of the Local Court and later as a magistrate. Educated (1929-30) at the Hale [q.v.4] School, Colin obtained his Junior certificate and excelled at sport. In February 1933 he joined the Militia, serving as a gunner with the 8th Field Battery; six months later he took a post as a junior clerk in the State Public Service and was employed in the Crown Law Department.

On 15 January 1935 Hannah enlisted in the Royal Australian Air Force. Sent as an air cadet to No.1 Flying Training School, Point Cook, Victoria, he gained his flying badge in June 1936 and was commissioned next month. His first posting was to No.22 Squadron at Richmond, New South Wales. Moving to Laverton, Victoria, in May 1937, he joined No.23 Squadron as adjutant. In March 1938 his unit was transferred to the new air base at Pearce, Western Australia. At Christ Church, Claremont, on 5 January 1939 he married Patricia Treacey Gwenyth Gordon with Anglican rites.

Flight Lieutenant Hannah travelled to England in July 1939 for armament training with the Royal Air Force; he began the course less than a week before the outbreak of World War II. Returning to Australia in March 1940, he was employed at No.1 Armament School, Point Cook, and at base headquarters, Laverton. In May he was posted to Air Force Headquarters, Melbourne, for duties on the technical staff. He was promoted acting squadron leader in September. Appointed deputy director of armament in 1941, he rose to temporary wing commander in April 1942.

Arriving at Milne Bay, Papua, in October 1943, Hannah joined No.6 Squadron, a Beaufort bomber unit operating against the Japanese. During a familiarization flight his aircraft strayed over Kiriwina Island and was fired on by allied anti-aircraft batteries: he was fortunate to receive nothing more than a nick in the forehead. He assumed command of the squadron in November, was made temporary group captain in the following month

374

and led No.71 Wing in January-February 1944. Evacuated ill, he spent almost six weeks in hospital at Laverton before rejoining No.6 Squadron at Goodenough Island. In September he became senior air staff officer on the headquarters of Western Area, Perth, and held the command from June 1945 to May 1946.

In 1947 Hannah attended the R.A.F. Staff College, Andover, England, and was subsequently S.A.S.O. at R.A.A.F. Overseas Headquarters, London. Back home, in May 1949 he took over the base at Amberley, Queensland. There, in August 1950, he was given temporary command of No.82 Wing (Lincoln bombers). In 1951 he was appointed O.B.E. He was posted to R.A.A.F. Headquarters in September as director of personal services; from July 1952 he was director-general of personnel. Appointed an aide-de-camp to Queen Elizabeth II, he was largely responsible for planning R.A.A.F. involvement in the royal tour of 1954; that year he was elevated to C.B.E. While studying at the Imperial Defence College, London, he was promoted air commodore in January 1955. He was S.A.S.O., headquarters, Far East Air Force, Singapore, from January 1956 and was appointed C.B. (1959) for his service during the Malayan Emergency.

Returning to Melbourne, in March 1959 Hannah became director-general of plans and policy, and in August led an advance party which began the Department of Air's transfer to Canberra. As D.G.P.P., he represented the R.A.A.F. on the joint planning committee. In December 1961 he was appointed deputy chief of the Air Staff and on 17 May 1962 was promoted acting air vice marshal (substantive, January 1963). After heading Operational Command at Penrith, New South Wales, from February 1965 to December 1967, he took charge of Support Command in Melbourne. On 1 January 1970 he was promoted air marshal and made chief of the Air Staff for what was expected to be a three-year term. He was appointed K.B.E. in 1971.

In January 1972 it was announced that Hannah would be the next governor of Queensland—the first R.A.A.F. member to attain such a position. He was sworn in on 21 March and hailed as 'a young thinking man of action . . . an experienced administrator with a no-nonsense reputation . . . a man with the flexibility of mind and ability to mix with people, so necessary for a Governor'. Nevertheless, by late 1975 he was involved in controversy. Following several petty incidents which had attracted adverse publicity, at a Brisbane Chamber of Commerce luncheon on 15 October Hannah criticized the 'fumbling ineptitude' of E. G. Whitlam's Federal Labor government for placing Australia in 'its present economic state'.

Convinced that Hannah lacked political impartiality, the Commonwealth government advised the Queen to revoke his dormant commission to serve as administrator in the event of the absence or incapacity of the governor-general. The Queensland premier (Sir) Joh Bjelke-Petersen stated publicly that he wanted Hannah's term extended, but it was allowed to expire on 20 March 1977. Hannah had been appointed K.C.M.G. and a knight and deputy-prior of the Order of St John in 1972; in August 1977 he was appointed K.C.V.O.

Sir Colin was stocky in build, with light blue eyes, a fair complexion and straw-coloured hair. He was regarded as a bluff, informal man, who was easy to work with, though he had a 'short fuse'. Survived by his wife and daughter, he died of myocardial infarction on 22 May 1978 at his Surfers Paradise home; he was accorded a state funeral and was cremated. A portrait (1979) by Paul Fitzgerald hangs in the R.A.A.F. officers' mess, Point Cook.

J. E. Hewitt, *Adversity in Success* (Melb, 1980); H. Rayner, *Scherger* (Canb, 1984); C. D. Coulthard-Clark, *The Third Brother* (Syd, 1991); R. E. Frost, *RAAF College & Academy 1947-86* (Canb, 1991); *PD* (Cwlth), 16 Oct 1975, p 2202; *RAAF News*, June 1969, Apr 1972, June 1978; *Courier-Mail*, 16 Oct 1975; *Australian*, 27 Oct 1975, 14 Aug 1976, 22 Mar 1977; information from Air Marshal Sir Charles Read, Bayview, Syd, and Mr J. F. Russell, Essendon, Melb.   C. D. COULTHARD-CLARK

HANNAM, JAMES GEORGE CHARLES (1895-1979), waterside worker, trade unionist and cyclist, was born on 26 October 1895 at Balmain, Sydney, third child of native-born parents James Hannam, butcher, and his wife Elizabeth Maria, née Hartland. A blacksmith by trade, young Jim enlisted in the Australian Imperial Force on 29 August 1914; he was then 5 ft 7 ins (170 cm) tall, with grey eyes, fair hair and an athletic build.

Posted as a driver to the 1st Divisional Ammunition Column, he embarked for the Middle East in October 1914. In Egypt, in September next year, he was sentenced to fifty-six days field punishment for leaving his picquet without orders. He was sent to France in April 1916 and was briefly attached to the 101st Battery, Australian Field Artillery, before returning to the 1st D.A.C. in October. In 1916-19 he was court-martialled on three occasions for absence without leave and related offences; he was sentenced twice to field punishment and once to a years hard labour, most of which was suspended. He was discharged from the A.I.F. on 23 December 1919 in Sydney.

Hannam returned to France as a professional cyclist and came back to Australia in 1924 on contract as 'Jacques Nagel, the Flying Frenchman'. In the parsonage of the Congregational Church, Richmond, Melbourne, on 2 September 1925 he married 19-year-old Doris Ada Louisa Riley. She was the daughter of Tom Riley, secretary and a founder of the Port Phillip Stevedores' Club, one of two branches of the Waterside Workers' Federation on the Melbourne waterfront. Jim joined his father-in-law on the docks and picked up casual work as a wharf labourer: 'We had our own foremen that we used to follow and we knew how many men they were going to take. It was open pick-up. We'd all stand around in the yard and the boss would come on the platform and he'd call your names out, or just point to you'.

Continuing his sporting career under the assumed named of 'Jim Nagel', Hannam regularly competed in cycling events in Victoria. On 1 February 1926, described as the 'champion of France', he was beaten at Geelong by H. K. Smith, holder of the Australian road championship. At the Exhibition oval, Carlton, on the 27th 'the French-Australian J. Nagel' won the ¾-mile (1.2 km) handicap and the five-mile (8 km) scratch for professionals.

In 1928 Hannam was caught up in waterfront industrial troubles which flared with particular violence after the Bruce-Page [qq.v.7,11] government's legislation encouraged non-union labour to work on the wharves. On 2 November at Princes Pier, Port Melbourne, police fired into a crowd of W.W.F. strikers who were bent on driving off 'volunteer' strike-breakers. One waterside worker subsequently died from gunshot wounds, and three, including Hannam, were wounded. Having recovered from the bullet-wound to his arm, Hannam attended the wharf-labourers' pickups for casual work throughout the Depression. When, as often as not, work was not available, he filled in otherwise idle hours training for cycle races. Remaining on the waterfront, he finally transferred at the age of 69 to the reserve 'B' Register in 1964. He died on 9 April 1979 in South Melbourne and was cremated; his daughter survived him.

W. Lowenstein and T. Hills, *Under the Hook* (Melb, 1982); *Maritime Worker*, 29 May 1979; *Age* (Melb), 2 Feb, 1 Mar 1926, 3 Nov 1928; *Argus*, 3 Nov 1928.   RICHARD MORRIS

HANNAN, ALBERT JAMES (1887-1965), crown solicitor and Catholic layman, was born on 27 July 1887 at Lower Broughton, South Australia, and registered as James Garrett Hannan, son of Francis Augustus Hannan, a native-born farmer, and his wife Mary Ellen, née Flynn. Educated at Port Pirie West and Solomontown public schools, at Sacred Heart College, Largs Bay, and at the University of Adelaide (B.A., 1909; LL.B., 1912; M.A., 1914), he graduated with first-class honours in classics. He taught briefly at Unley High School, then enrolled in law at the university, and won two Stow [q.v.6] prizes and the David Murray [q.v.5] scholarship. Known to his friends as 'Tacky' because of the admonition, 'Tace, Hannan' (Be silent, Hannan), that followed his frequent interruptions in Professor H. D. Naylor's [q.v.10] classics lectures, he was articled to George McEwin and admitted to the Bar on 23 April 1913. He immediately joined the Attorney-General and Crown Solicitor's Department as assistant parliamentary draftsman, becoming parliamentary draftsman in 1916 and assistant crown solicitor in 1917.

Enlisting in the Australian Imperial Force on 2 July 1918, Hannan was not called up for duty and was discharged one week after the Armistice. At St Francis Xavier's Cathedral, Adelaide, on 22 February 1919 he married Elizabeth Mary Catherine Rzeszkowski (d.1922). In the archbishop's house, West Terrace, on 7 March 1927 he married Una Victoria Measday, a 33-year-old clerk. Between 1917 and 1925 Hannan taught law part time at the university. He was promoted crown solicitor in 1927 and held the post until his retirement in 1952. Appointed K.C. in 1935, he was president (1937-39) of the Law Society of South Australia. He fervently believed in States rights and was suspicious of any move towards centralism; these views gave a particular zest to his pleadings in constitutional cases. In 1946 he was appointed C.M.G. He successfully represented the South Australian and Western Australian governments in appeals to the High Court of Australia (1948) and the Privy Council (1949) against the Chifley [q.v.13] government's Banking Act (1947). Premier (Sir) Thomas Playford was determined to see Hannan elevated to the Supreme Court bench, but met resistance from the chief justice Sir Mellis Napier [q.v.]. Eventually Napier relented and agreed to Hannan's appointment as an acting-judge on three occasions in 1954-57.

Hannan was a deeply religious man and persistently sought the establishment of a residential college for Catholics at the university; Aquinas College was affiliated in 1947 and a wing of the college was named after him. He was awarded the Cross of Honour *Pro Ecclesia et Pontifice* (1946) and appointed knight of the Order of St Sylvester (1955). In 1953 he registered his change of Christian names to Albert James by deed poll. During World War II he had opposed the Common Cause movement in which prominent communists were involved; he was a key figure in 'A Call to the People of Australia' (1951).

Summary Procedure of Justices in South Australia (Melbourne, 1922), *The Practice of the Local Court in South Australia* (Melbourne, 1934) and the adulatory *Life of Chief Justice Way* [q.v.12] (Sydney, 1960) were Hannan's major publications. He was a council-member (1939-61) of the university, warden (1960) of the senate and a council-member (1949-65) of St Ann's College. A well-known character around Adelaide, he was a likeable and garrulous man, with a fine sense of humour and touches of eccentricity. He belonged to the Adelaide (from 1936) and Modern Pickwick clubs, and was president (1957) of the Commonwealth Club of Adelaide. Survived by his wife and their two daughters, he died on 1 January 1965 in North Adelaide; he was accorded a state funeral and was buried in Centennial Park cemetery.

C. C. Martindale, *The Risen Sun* (Lond, 1929); K. Bullock, *Port Pirie, the Friendly City* (Adel, 1988); S. Cockburn, *Playford* (Adel, 1991); M. M. Press, *Colour and Shadow* (Adel, 1991); *Aust Law J*, 30 Apr 1965; *Aquinian*, 9, 1965; *Aust J of Politics and Hist*, 12, no 3, Dec 1966; *JHSSA*, 16, 1988; *SMH*, 18 Aug 1944, 26 Feb 1948, 10 May 1949; *Sunday Mail* (Adel), 10 June 1959; *Southern Cross* (Adel), 1 Aug 1952, 8 Jan 1965; *Advertiser* (Adel), 2 Jan 1965.   JOHN PLAYFORD

HANNAN, JAMES HENRY (1906-1975), Catholic priest and mission publicist, was born on 22 March 1906 at Gembrook, Victoria, third child of Thomas Evans Hannan, a miner from South Australia, and his Victorian-born wife Edith, née Dyson. Schooled by the Sisters of St Joseph, Yarraville, and by the Marist Brothers at Assumption College, Kilmore, James began seminary training at Corpus Christi College, Werribee. He completed his studies with doctorates in philosophy (1926) and theology (1930) at the Pontifical Urban College of Propaganda Fide, Rome, where he was ordained priest on 8 December 1929. Returning to Australia in 1930, Hannan was assistant-priest at South Melbourne until 1935 when he was appointed director of missions for the Melbourne diocese. Besides raising funds for missions, he operated a correspondence course of religious instruction for Catholics in the outback.

The apostolic delegate Giovanni Panico had noted Hannan as an energetic organizer during the Melbourne Eucharistic Conference in 1934. Through Panico's initiative, in 1937 Hannan was appointed national director of the Pontifical Mission Aid Societies for Australia and Oceania. In this position he acted as executive-officer for a committee of bishops representing the Australian hierarchy. Although based in Melbourne, he travelled widely throughout Australia, overseeing the introduction of a comprehensive and co-ordinated system of mission promotion. In each diocese he worked through a director whose task it was to mobilize support in schools and parishes. From 1938 to 1946 he also edited *Catholic Missions*. He was granted the title of monsignor in 1940.

Under Hannan's direction, membership of the Society for the Propagation of the Faith rose steadily. So did the amount of money collected (£45 000 in 1944). Most of the funds were given to the Aboriginal missions centred on Darwin and the Kimberleys, but a growing amount was allocated to the Pacific Islands, and especially to the Territory of Papua-New Guinea which was to become increasingly important as a mission field after World War II. Foreseeing this development, and aware of the missions' pressing needs for personnel in the era of postwar reconstruction, in 1946 Hannan appealed to the diocesan priests of Australia to volunteer for a term of missionary duty. To set an example, he then resigned as director and went to Bougainville.

Although he had intended to stay for five years, ill health forced Hannan to leave the island in 1948. Following his recuperation, he made a three-month preaching tour of the United States of America that year and was appointed priest of the Melbourne parish of South Yarra. In 1969-74 he served on the editorial board of the *Advocate*. He died of emphysema and chronic bronchitis on 22 August 1975 and was buried in Melbourne general cemetery. His younger brother George had been ordained priest on 18 March 1939 in Rome.

Through his sermons, radio broadcasts and films promoting the cause of Catholic missions, James Hannan became one of the best-known priests in Australia. In helping to generate among Catholics and the wider community a sense of responsibility for advancing the well-being of Papuans and New Guineans, he was also one of the most influential. He contributed significantly to the body of opinion which supported the aid and development commitment to Papua New Guinea that became a distinctive feature of Australian government and church policies in the 1950s, 1960s and 1970s.

C. Halley, *Australia's Missionary Effort* (Melb, 1973); H. Laracy, *Marists and Melanesians* (Canb, 1976); J. Waldersee, *The Four Founders* (Syd, 1983) and *A Grain of Mustard Seed* (Syd, 1983); *Herald* (Melb), 2 Jan 1935, 8 Oct 1937, 1, 2 Apr 1947, 19 Mar 1948; *Sun News-Pictorial*, 10 Mar 1939, 9 Apr 1946, 2 Apr 1947, 11 Apr 1948; *Argus*, 30 Mar 1939; *Age* (Melb), 24 Dec 1940; *Advocate* (Melb), 28 Aug 1975; *Catholic Weekly*, 4 Sept 1975.

HUGH LARACY

HANSEN, GWENDOLINE DOROTHEA JULIE (1896-1971), film censor, was born on 19 February 1896 at Waverley, Sydney, sixth child of Alfred Julius Nielson, an assayer from Norway, and his native-born wife Martha, née Maxwell. Obtaining her Leaving certificate at Parramatta High School in 1915, Gwendoline won a scholarship to Teachers' College (Blackfriars). She joined the New South Wales Department of Public Instruction and in 1918-22 taught book-keeping, business principles, English and history at Meadowbank, Ashfield and Gloucester public schools. At the Methodist Church, Strathfield, on 15 April 1922 she married Herbert William Hansen (d.1928), a fellow teacher. Next year she was employed as a temporary teacher at Hurstville Public School. Gwendoline and Herbert moved to Springwood in the hope that the country air would help him to recover from the effects of gas poisoning in World War I. After her husband's death she returned to Sydney and took classes at Hurstville Central Domestic/Home Science School.

In January 1930 the Scullin [q.v.11] Labor government appointed Mrs Hansen a censor for a one-year term; she replaced Eleanor Glencross [q.v.9] whose earlier appointment had resulted from lobbying by women's organizations for a female representative on the Commonwealth's Film Censorship Board. Glencross publicly protested that Hansen's selection was a political one. The assistant-minister for trade and customs Frank Forde dismissed the charge as baseless and as being unfair 'to a soldier's widow with family responsibilities, who, on her merits, was successful in securing the position' from hundreds of applicants. Hansen rejoined her colleagues Cresswell O'Reilly [q.v.11] and Lionel Hurley on the board in 1932 as part of a new censorship régime under which the major change was the replacement of the liberal Appeal Board by a single adjudicator. In 1933 she was reappointed for a three-year term on a salary of £2 a day, 'subject to appropriate reduction under the Financial Emergency Act 1931-1932'. Thereafter, her contract was to be renewed regularly until her retirement in February 1961.

Guided by the general principles in the Customs (Cinematograph Films) Regulations, she censored an average of 450 films a year and worked with three chief censors, O'Reilly (to 1942), John Alexander (in 1942-56) and Colin Campbell (from 1956). Hansen witnessed many changes in film content, technology and community attitudes during her thirty years in office. In an interview after her retirement she recalled classifying Charlie Chaplin's first 'talkie', remembered the ban imposed on horror films in 1949 and referred to the classification of television programmes from 1956. She also observed that Austral-

ians were becoming more broad-minded, and that films were increasingly more suitable for adults than for children. Hansen was appointed M.B.E. in 1961. Her recreations included surfing, golf and motoring, and later bowling, tapestry and needlework. Survived by her son, she died on 7 January 1971 at the Repatriation General Hospital, Concord, and was cremated with Anglican rites.

I. Bertrand, *Censorship in Australia* (Brisb, 1978); Cwlth Film Censorship Bd, *Report by the Chief Censor*, 1928-60; Hansen papers (held by Mr D. S. Hansen, Chatswood, Syd).

ANDRÉE WRIGHT

HANSLOW, HAROLD (1882-1958), farmer and soil conservationist, was born on 4 October 1882 at Carlton, Melbourne, second child of Harry Hanslow, a goldsmith from England, and his Victorian-born wife Emelyn, née Beer. Educated at Princes Hill State School, young Harold became a rabbiter before travelling in 1904 to Canada where he worked on farms, in mines and as a lumberjack. On his return in 1911, he selected an irrigation block at Koyuga and developed a 'model farm', at first running dairy cattle and later raising fat lambs. A successful and progressive farmer, Hanslow served as a local councillor (1936-38) and as president of the Tongala Agricultural Society. He joined the Victorian Farmers' Union and the Victorian Country Party, of whose central council he became a member. His opposition to the party's entry into coalition governments accorded with (Sir) Albert Dunstan's [q.v.8] views.

In 1938 Hanslow was appointed to the State Rivers and Water Supply Commission to represent the views of irrigators. At that time the commission's senior staff were concerned about the problem of soil erosion, but had no power to redress it. (Sir) Ronald East, the commission's chairman, persuaded Hanslow to accept particular responsibility for soil conservation. Having undertaken an extensive inspection tour of the State, he was quickly convinced of the gravity of the issue. He set himself two major tasks: to convince Victoria's farmers to change their methods so as to promote soil conservation, and to persuade the government to pass legislation which would provide a framework for tackling the broader aspects of the matter. In the former he was highly successful. He had a natural flair for publicity and an understanding of the ways in which farmers could be influenced. In 1940 he donated the Hanslow Cup for the Mallee farm showing the best application of soil conservation principles. During the next decade similar competitions were established in most districts of Victoria. In

1941 he published a handbook, *Better Irrigation*, and a pamphlet on raising fat lambs.

Hanslow was initially less successful in his approaches to government. Indifferent from the outset to any proposals for action, by 1939 Dunstan had become obstinately hostile. In a dramatic sequence of events Hanslow threatened to expose the government's inactivity on soil conservation. Dunstan in turn threatened Hanslow with immediate dismissal from the commission, but Hanslow remained adamant and in 1940 the Soil Conservation Board was established. It had few powers beyond demonstration and persuasion, yet it laid the foundation for systematic soil conservation work in Victoria and was succeeded by the Soil Conservation Authority in 1949. Although Hanslow retired from the S.R.W.S.C. that year, he maintained his active interest in soil-conservation work.

A short, energetic man, he was known as 'the Tongala spark plug' and 'the mighty atom'. He was a notable raconteur whose wide interests included sport and charity work. In 1956 he was appointed O.B.E. Hanslow never married. He died on 1 October 1958 at Mont Albert and was cremated with Anglican rites; his estate was sworn for probate at £19 315.

B. D. Graham, *The Formation of the Australian Country Parties* (Canb, 1966); M. and E. Smith, *Like River Red Gums* (Norlane, Vic, 1981); J. M. Powell, *Watering the Garden State* (Syd, 1989); *Age* (Melb), 4 Oct 1958; *Countryman* (Melb) and *Kyabram Free Press* and *Weekly Times* (Melb), 9 Oct 1958; State Rivers and Water Supply Com correspondence VPRS 6008 (PRO, Vic).   JAN MCDONALD

HANSMAN, FRANK SOLOMON (1896-1972), biochemist and pathologist, was born on 19 November 1896 in Sydney, third surviving son of Abraham Hansman, a boot manufacturer from London, and his native-born wife Alice, née Isaacs. Frank's elder brothers died on active service in World War I. Educated at Fort Street Boys' High School and the University of Sydney (M.B., Ch.M., 1920), he developed an interest in biochemistry while serving as a resident medical officer at Royal Prince Alfred Hospital. He travelled to London where he studied at St Thomas's Hospital and at the Lister Institute of Preventive Medicine. In 1924 he qualified as a member of the Royal College of Physicians.

On his return to Sydney, Hansman joined Arthur Tebbutt in a Macquarie Street practice that specialized in pathology and biochemistry. Although Tebbutt was a reserved man, he and the volatile Hansman remained in harmonious practice for thirty years. At the district registrar's office, Mosman, on 19

November 1926 Frank married Tebbutt's sister, Euphemia (Effie) Joyce (d.1970). Hansman was senior honorary biochemist (1928-51) at R.P.A.H. and honorary director of pathology (1928-58) at the Women's Hospital, Crown Street. He was a foundation fellow of the Royal Australasian College of Physicians in 1938 and of the Royal College of Pathologists of Australasia in 1958. His research ranged widely: renal function and disease, calcium and phosphorus metabolism, and, in particular, the effects of alcohol on human performance.

During World War II Hansman was an honorary major, Australian Army Medical Corps, and visiting medical officer, 113th Australian General Hospital, Concord. With Lieutenant Colonel A. L. Dawson (president) and Sir Norman Paul [q.v.11], he was a member (1942) of the board which identified chromium salts in the dye of khaki uniforms as the cause of a form of dermatitis among Australian soldiers serving in the Middle East and New Guinea. He also belonged to the Australian Red Cross Society's National and New South Wales Blood Transfusion committees.

Convinced that alcohol was a major cause of road traffic crashes, in the 1950s Hansman began a campaign for the introduction of police-conducted tests to determine drivers' blood-alcohol levels. At times almost single-handed in his crusade, he addressed public bodies and wrote scientific articles; he was an active committee-member of the Road Safety Council of New South Wales; and he represented the Federal Council of the British Medical Association in Australia on the Australian Road Safety Council and before a Senate select committee. He overcame much opposition, even from members of his own profession. In spirited correspondence in the *Medical Journal of Australia* he once chided a senior psychiatrist: 'in this important social problem, let us have not "in vino veritas", but "in scripto veritas"'. It took a great deal of persuasion and evidence to induce politicians to support breath-testing at a time when many law-abiding citizens did not deem it anti-social to drive after drinking a considerable amount of alcohol.

Following Victoria's lead six years earlier, in 1968 the New South Wales government introduced the legislation that Hansman had long advocated. Police were empowered to require a driver to submit to a breath test after an accident (if a traffic offence had been committed), or if, from the manner of driving, it could be assumed that the driver had consumed alcohol. Driving a vehicle with a blood-alcohol concentration above 0.08 g (later reduced to 0.05 g) per 100 ml was made an offence. Random breath-testing was introduced in December 1982. The incidence of road accidents dropped significantly. There were 1303 deaths from traffic accidents in the State in 1980 and 581 in 1993. The social behaviour of most citizens altered markedly in regard to drinking and driving.

A smallish, active man, Hansman set high standards and delighted in argument; while he was impulsive and could be abrupt, he was also quietly generous. He had a fluent pen. Happily married, he was a fine host in his waterfront home at Vaucluse. He was chairman of Hansman Pty Ltd and sometimes presented his colleagues with the firm's quality shoes. Ceasing private practice in 1963, he took locum appointments at the Commonwealth Health laboratories at Albury, Rockhampton, Queensland, and Tamworth, New South Wales. On 11 February 1971 at the district registrar's office, Tamworth, he married Betty Joyce Nicholson, a 42-year-old secretary. Survived by his wife, and by the two sons and two daughters of his first marriage, he died on 23 December 1972 at Tamworth and was cremated.

A. S. Walker, *Clinical Problems of War* (Canb, 1952); G. L. McDonald (ed), *Roll of the Royal Australasian College of Physicians*, 1, 1938-75 (Syd, 1988); *MJA*, 4 July 1959, p 27, 23 Mar 1963, p 444, 3 Mar 1973, p 460; *SMH*, 6 June 1950; information from Dr D. Hansman, Adel, and Mr S. Hansman, Cronulla, Syd.   G. T. FRANKI

HANSON, FREDERICK JOHN (1914-1980), police commissioner, was born on 26 May 1914 at Orange, New South Wales, eldest of four children of native-born parents Ernest Frederick Hanson, telegraphist, and his wife Vera Marie, née Teddiman. Educated at the Christian Brothers' St Mary's Boys' School, Burwood, Fred worked as a manufacturing jeweller's assistant (1929-31) before being employed as a porter in the New South Wales Government Railways and Tramways. He joined the New South Wales Police on 7 September 1936 and in the following year was posted to Broken Hill where, in the Sacred Heart Cathedral, he married Carole Louise Whitehall with Catholic rites on 9 November 1938. In 1940 Hanson was transferred to plain clothes duties.

He had served (1932-36) in the Citizen Air Force and obtained his 'A' class private pilot's licence in 1939. On 31 January 1942 he was released to the Royal Australian Air Force. Commissioned on 14 January 1943, Hanson served as a pilot in Britain, the Middle East and Ceylon (Sri Lanka), and was mentioned in dispatches. On 30 January 1946 he was demobilized as acting squadron leader and rejoined the police.

Promoted constable (first class) while on active service, Hanson was briefly posted to the vice squad before being assigned to the police air wing as sergeant (third class). Such rapid advancement, in an organization committed to promotion on seniority, resulted in numerous appeals. The first appeal heard was rejected and the remainder were withdrawn, thereby allowing him to overtake more than a thousand colleagues on the seniority list. Thereafter, he was known as 'Slippery'. When the air wing was disbanded in 1950, Hanson moved to the new No.21 Mobile Division. He returned to Broken Hill in 1953 and was advanced to sergeant (first class) in 1955. He served as inspector (third class) and officer-in-charge at Bega (1959-62) and Wollongong (1962-64), then moved to the Metropolitan Police District as superintendent (third class). After attending the Australian Police College in 1963, he rose to superintendent (first class) and assistant metropolitan superintendent in 1967.

Hanson was appointed assistant-commissioner in 1968, deputy-commissioner on 14 January 1972 and commissioner on 15 November. That year he attended the general assembly of the International Criminal Police Organization at Frankfurt, Germany; in 1974 he visited the Australian police contingent on Cyprus. While commissioner, he introduced merit rating, abolished seniority in executive promotions and established the crime intelligence unit. By objecting to the Police Association's attempt to gain greater access to the Industrial Commission of New South Wales, he sparked contention. He gained widespread approval in 1975 when he instituted aggressive street patrols to counter hooligan activity, but he failed to control illegal gaming which became a major public issue. Next year Hanson sued the Australian Broadcasting Commission for defamation in suggesting that he had a financial interest in an illegal casino at Gosford; the case was settled out of court. Pressured to resign as a result of adverse publicity, he delayed until he was replaced in 1976 by his favoured successor and air wing colleague Mervyn Wood. Allegations of corruption were made against Hanson in the 1980s.

A modest but humorous man, he kept his family life extremely private. He was a renowned practical joker and esteemed by his subordinates for his interest in their welfare, his readiness to delegate responsibility and his unwillingness to be impeded by red tape. Survived by his wife, he died from carbon monoxide poisoning by inhalation on the night of 25/26 October 1980 at his Terrigal home; the coroner dispensed with an inquest and Hanson was cremated.

B. Swanton and G. Hannigan (eds), *Police Source Book 2* (Canb, 1985); *SMH*, 1 Mar, 16 Nov 1972; *Daily Sun*, 25 July 1974, 9 Feb 1975; *Daily Mirror*

(Syd), 9 Feb 1975; *Sun-Herald*, 23 July 1980; NSW Police Dept, Annual Report, 1972-80; Hanson's record of service and stations (copy held by author, Kambah, Canb); information from Mr R. Blissett, Five Dock, Syd, Mrs M. Hanson, Parkes, Mrs L. Jones, Figtree, Mr E. Madden, North Parramatta, and Mr J. Mitchell, Castle Hill, NSW.

BRUCE SWANTON

HANSON, RAYMOND CHARLES (1913-1976), composer and teacher, was born on 23 November 1913 at Burwood, Sydney, youngest of five children of William Hanson, an Australian-born railway engineer, and his wife Lilian, née Bennett, from England. The marriage broke up when Raymond was quite young. At his mother's insistence, he was raised as a Baptist; he was to remain a spiritual person, but his faith later wavered. A sickly child, he suffered from a bronchial complaint and a recurring infection left him almost deaf in his right ear. He listened to his eldest sister practising the piano and began composing at the age of 8. Educated at Burwood Public and Fort Street Boys' High schools, Hanson had to leave high school in third year. Because he was too poor to pay for piano lessons, he was taught gratis by Ann Spillane, and in 1930 gained the licentiate (piano) of the Associated Board of the Royal Academy of Music and the Royal College of Music. Until 1939 he scraped together a living from teaching the piano or working in menial occupations. He was gifted with a fine improvisatory ability and usually composed at the keyboard.

Having presented several recitals of his own works in the late 1930s, Hanson was awarded the Gordon Vickers scholarship in composition at the New South Wales State Conservatorium of Music, but World War II interrupted his studies after only two months. He served in the Australian Military Forces in 1941-46 and rose to sergeant while with the Army Education Service in Tasmania. Through his army service he developed a lasting interest in jazz: he met a number of jazz musicians in the American forces when he formed and arranged a concert party. After the war he resumed his scholarship, studying under Alexander Burnard and receiving encouragement from (Sir) Eugene Goossens [q.v.].

In 1948 Hanson was awarded a fellowship of the conservatorium and began teaching aural training, a subject that would hold a particular fascination for him. In the early 1950s, with Leonard Teale, Roland Robinson and others, he formed the short-lived Australian Cultural Defence Movement which aimed at protecting Australian art from the perceived inroads being made by other cultures, particularly American. The movement eventually faltered under the weight of anti-communist criticism. Hanson recalled that 'culture' was then considered a dirty word, 'associated principally with strong left ideas and more principally with communism'. He believed that his association with the A.C.D.M. and his later involvement with the Australian-Soviet Friendship Society were detrimental to his professional career and the attainment of a salaried position at the conservatorium.

Nevertheless, Hanson had much success as a teacher of aural training, and later harmony, orchestration, and composition. His teaching was influenced by the treatises of Paul Hindemith. Jazz and classical musicians alike respected his ability and dedication, and many sought private lessons from him, among them Don Burrows and Larry Sitsky. Lessons often ended in long discussions of philosophy or politics.

At St Matthew's Anglican Church, Manly, on 15 September 1956 Hanson married Moira Winifred Young (d.1975), a 23-year-old student at the conservatorium. The marriage proved difficult. They moved in turn to five different northern suburbs; he was troubled by failing health as his domestic situation deteriorated. In May 1967, while examining in Canberra, he suffered a heart attack. In September he was appointed senior lecturer in composition at the conservatorium.

An unpretentious man, Hanson was respected by his colleagues. In his prime he was also active in politics and sport, especially cricket. Towards the end of his life, however, he was increasingly depressive in outlook and uncomfortable with people in authority. Whereas in the 1940s his compositions were considered too radical to be popular, by the 1960s he was considered too conservative, a perception he did not resist, though it sorely troubled him. Disenchanted with the *avant-garde*, he remained committed to an empirical and craftsman-like approach to music, revealing traces of English pastoralism as well as the influence of Hindemith. Hanson preferred to explore the freedom, not the stricture, of the twelve-note scale and was fascinated by the consequent possibilities for harmony and linear development.

In 1973 he received a $9000 fellowship from the Federal government to support him while he composed *Jane Greer*, an opera about the Rum Rebellion; James Thomson wrote the libretto; the work was never staged. Hanson was appointed A.M. in 1976. Survived by his three daughters, he died of myocardial infarction on 6 December that year at his Thornleigh home and was cremated.

Hanson's surviving works include several operas, a symphony, and four concerti, of which the trumpet concerto (1948) is best known and was released worldwide by RCA of

Australia Pty Ltd in 1969. His impressive *Piano Sonata* (op. 12), composed between 1938 and 1941, reflects the composer's feelings about the fall of Paris in World War II. Massive and technically difficult, in 1968 it was reworked with the encouragement of the Sydney pianist Igor Hmelnitsky who later recorded it. An oratorio in two parts, *The Immortal Touch* (1976), based on the words of the Indian poet-philosopher Sir Rabindranath Tagore, is the most striking example of Hanson's preoccupation with the metaphysical. He also wrote scores for film, television and radio, and jazz music and arrangements. His failure to attract lasting recognition as a composer resulted from inadequate self-promotion, and from the official and public attitude towards Australian composers which he and others of his generation had to endure.

F. Callaway and D. Tunley (eds), *Australian Composition in the Twentieth Century* (Melb, 1978); *Aust J of Music Education*, 20, 1977, p 29; *SMH*, 1, 5 Oct 1970, 11 Dec 1973, 8 Dec 1976; H. de Berg, Raymond Hanson (taped interview, 31 Aug 1973, NL); information from M. Keogh, Killara, and Mr J. Lloyd, Music Dept, Univ Technology, Syd.

PETER JOHN TREGEAR

HANTON, HILDA MARY (1884-1954), hospital matron, was born on 23 June 1884 at Yankalilla, South Australia, fourth of five children of Walter Hardy Hanton, Wesleyan minister, and his wife Fanny, née Roach. As a young woman Hilda Mary cared for her semi-invalided younger sister, Clarice, and enjoyed painting as a recreation. She trained as a nurse at the (Royal) Adelaide Hospital in 1913-17, receiving a gold medal for first-class passes in her final examinations. A charge nurse from June 1919, Hanton unsuccessfully applied in November for the position of matron of the Memorial Hospital (which was to be opened by the Methodist Church at North Adelaide next year). In January 1920 she was appointed matron of the twenty-bed hospital at Renmark on the River Murray. Its facilities were frequently under pressure, but she coped by careful administration, dedication and resourcefulness. In July 1922 she became matron of the Memorial Hospital: she was to guide its development for the ensuing twenty-five years during which the number of beds increased from 30 to 140.

The hospital provided for private patients receiving medical and surgical treatment, and for maternity cases. Its four-year training programme for nurses was recognized by the Nurses Board of South Australia on which Hanton served as a member (1923-43) of the panel of examiners. Believing that the bedside nurse was the very foundation of the pro-

fession and that a matron should take an active role in the care of patients, she was a familiar figure in the wards. Many women appreciated her support at the birth of their babies and in their first days of motherhood. She visited each patient daily and developed a special bond with occasional, long-term invalids. To the nursing staff Hilda Mary, as she was unofficially known, became a legend. A small woman, immaculately dressed in a white, starched, high-collared uniform and a veil, she set high standards for her nurses. Although in awe of her, they respected her discipline, fairness and kindness.

Involved in the wider affairs of her profession, for twenty years Matron Hanton was a councillor of the South Australian branch of the Australasian Trained Nurses' Association (president 1941-45). She was also a president of the National Florence Nightingale Committee, Australia, and vice-chairman of the Australian Nurses' Christian Movement. The 'continuous and monotonous drive' of the years of World War II made demands on matrons in civilian hospitals through staff shortages and limited finances. After leaving the operating theatre one night, Hanton was accused by air-raid wardens of aiding and abetting the Japanese because lights were visible in the nurses' home.

In 1946 her health declined and she retired one year later. Her successor was K. I. A. ('Kay') Parker [q.v.]. The Memorial Hospital's board of management praised Hanton's 'unfailing courtesy, unwearied devotion, her even, cheerful temperament ... and unexcelled ability'; the Methodist Church extolled her 'magnificent ministry'. In 1948 she was appointed M.B.E. She continued to nurse part time in a small private hospital. Miss Hanton died of cancer on 14 April 1954 in her home at Toorak Gardens and was buried in Mitcham cemetery. Her estate was sworn for probate at £2546.

W. Haseloff, *Inasmuch . . .* (Adel, 1976); J. Durdin, *They Became Nurses* (Syd, 1991); *Advertiser* (Adel), 19, 21, 25 June 1947, 1 Jan 1948, 22 Apr 1954; (Roy) Adel Hospital, Register of appointments, 1884-1920; Memorial Hospital, Minutes of meetings of Bd of Management, 1919-54; Renmark Hospital, Minutes of meetings of Bd of Management, 1920-22; Nurses' Bd of SA, Midwives register, 1922-30, *and* Minutes of Nurses' Registration Bd of Examiners, 1924-63 (SRSA); Florence Nightingale Memorial Cte, SA Branch records *and* Aust Trained Nurses' Assn (SA), Minutes of meetings (Roy Aust Nursing Federation Archives, Kent Town, Adel); information from the late Mr F. Alvey, and Miss M. Hanton, Glenelg, Adel.

JOAN DURDIN

HARDESS (HARDRESS), CATHERINE (1889-1970), artist and designer, was born on

18 November 1889 at Flemington, Melbourne, second daughter of George Henry Hardess, schoolteacher, and his wife Ann Emma, née Taylor, both Melbourne born. Educated at Ballarat and Prahran, in 1919 Catherine was appointed to teach fine art in the girls' school at Swinburne Technical College. Taking leave in May 1923, she travelled to London and studied (1923-25) painting, drawing and ornamental design at the Slade School of Fine Art. In 1926 she returned to Swinburne and continued to teach there until 1934 when she took leave without pay and again sailed for England. She eventually resigned from Swinburne in 1937.

While in England, Hardess worked with Osborne Robinson, costume and decor designer at the Northampton Repertory Theatre, and was subsequently appointed designer at the Tunbridge Repertory Theatre, Kent. She was joined in London in 1935 by Edith 'Mollie' Grove (b.1909) whom she had met at Swinburne. Grove, who was to be her business partner and companion, completed a diploma with the Kensington Weavers. The two women shared a 'studio' life and travelled together. On their way back to Australia in 1939, they visited Scandinavia, Russia, Poland, Hungary and Greece, looking at craft and educational institutions.

They arrived in Melbourne in August and prepared for an exhibition of the fabrics they had woven in London and in their basement studio in Queen Street. Held at the Hotel Australia and opened by (Sir) Robert Menzies [q.v.] in March 1940, the exhibition featured tweeds, dress fabrics, furnishing materials, floor rugs and accessories. Their business was registered as eclarté Pty Ltd, the name being derived from the French *clarté*, prefixed by an additional 'e'(always with a lower case). At about this time Hardess chose to be known as Hardress, perhaps to make her surname sound less Germanic, although she never officially altered it.

The business prospered, soon employing ten and later thirty-five weavers. Melbourne department stores, including Georges Australia Ltd and Henry Buck Pty Ltd, sold clothing made from eclarté fabric, and four new ranges were made available each season. Although more expensive than many imported fabrics, eclarté materials were preferred by the fashion conscious, by those wishing to support Australian industry and especially by Australian couturiers. In 1960 one of eclarté's fabrics won a gold medal at the first Australian Wool Bureau fashion awards. Official gifts were commissioned from eclarté, including lengths of fabric for Queen Elizabeth II as a gift from the Wool Bureau.

In December 1951 eclarté had moved to a larger building at Dandenong which was opened by Menzies, whose government—through the Wool Bureau and the Institute of Management—encouraged and supported the enterprise shown by the two women. Hardress said of their approach to business: 'There is still room in this modern age for the joy and satisfaction of craftsmanship and creative work in happy surroundings. And it can be made to pay. We have proved it'.

Despite large commissions throughout the 1950s, the recession in the textile industry and the difficulty of maintaining the production of high quality, hand-made textiles caused eclarté to scale down its operations and move in 1957 to smaller premises, an old mill at Heathcote. Before resuming work there, Hardress and Grove investigated modern weaving techniques and factory production in Britain.

On their return in 1958, they decided to concentrate on the production of furnishing fabric, co-operating with architects such as Robin Boyd [q.v.13] and (Sir) Roy Grounds, and the designer Fred Ward. Experimenting with a wide variety of weaves and yarn, Hardress sought inspiration for her colour combinations in the Australian landscape, especially its flora. She worked closely with clients, designing individual fabrics to complement each interior as well as the view from the windows.

Local commissions were received from Ormond [q.v.5] and St Hilda's colleges and the faculty of commerce at the University of Melbourne, the John Batman Motel and the Shell Building, and from the Academy of Science, University House and Parliament House, Canberra. Large projects required work to be carried out by more mechanized textile mills. Ensuring the quality of the finished product raised further problems and in 1962 a series of economic setbacks forced the liquidation of eclarté. Hardress died on 4 October 1970 at Lower Plenty, Melbourne, and was cremated.

Craft Aust, Spring 1985, no 3, p 57; *Herald* (Melb), 25 May 1937, 14 Aug 1939, 11 Dec 1951; *SMH*, 12 Nov 1940, 20 Sept 1953; *Sun News-Pictorial*, 19 Dec 1951, 5 Sept 1953; *Age* (Melb), 19 Dec 1951, 27 Sept 1952; information from Miss E. M. Grove, Balwyn, Melb, and Swinburne Univ of Technology, Melb.   JOHN MCPHEE

HARDWICK, HAROLD HAMPTON (1888-1959), sportsman, was born on 14 December 1888 at Balmain, Sydney, younger son of native-born parents George Henry Hardwick, draftsman, and his wife Priscilla, née Herrin. His father taught him to swim with cork water-wings as soon as he could walk and young Harold became a regular at Frederick Cavill's baths where he copied Dick

Cavill's [qq.v.7] new crawl stroke and learned the trudgen for long distances. At 10 he began boxing lessons. From then on, he swam in summer and boxed in winter.

In 1904, while at Fort Street Model School, Hardwick won several swimming championships, played in the first XV and captained the winning lifesaving team. His father's death interrupted Harold's plans to study dentistry; on leaving school, he was apprenticed to a process engraver and was later employed as an accountant. Trained daily after work by W. W. Hill, he joined the Enterprise Swimming Club and in 1907-08 defeated Alick Wickham for the State 100 yards freestyle title. Next season he won the State freestyle titles for the 100, 220 and 300 yards, and for the ¾-mile and 1-mile events.

In 1911 Hardwick represented Australasia at the Festival of Empire in London to celebrate the coronation of King George V. As funds were low, he competed in swimming and boxing. After winning the 100 yards Empire swimming title, two days later, with hardly any training, he stopped the highly favoured English champion William Hazell in the first round, and an hour later won the Empire heavyweight title, halting his Canadian opponent in 2 minutes 35 seconds. Hardwick—who also won the 100, 220 and 440 yards Amateur Swimming Association championships of England—returned home in triumph and was named 'Sportsman of Australia' for that year. At the 1912 Olympic Games in Stockholm he was a member of the Australasian team that won the 4 x 200-metre freestyle event in the unofficial record time of 10 minutes 11.6 seconds; he also won bronze medals in the 400 and 1500-metre freestyle events.

Swimming, boxing, gymnastics, water-polo and lifesaving were Hardwick's main interests (he was a foundation member of the Manly Surf Club), but he also played Rugby Union for New South Wales against a visiting American universities team (1910) and was a member of the Eastern Suburbs premiership team (1913). In 1914 he won the State amateur heavyweight boxing championship and in 1915 signed up with R. L. Baker [q.v.7] for eight professional fights, of which he won four; in the last bout (19 February 1916) he was knocked out by Les Darcy [q.v.8] in the seventh round, though not before he had broken two of Darcy's teeth.

Giving his religion as Catholic, Hardwick enlisted in the Australian Imperial Force on 25 August 1917. After attending wireless-training school, he embarked as a sapper on 24 June 1918 and served with No.2 Signal Squadron in the Middle East. In April 1919 at the Inter-Theatre of War Boxing Tournament at Aldershot, England, he won the heavyweight boxing title; chosen by his fellow competitors, he was awarded a cup for the 'Ideal Sportsman' of the British forces, an honour he highly prized. At the Inter-Allied Games held outside Paris he was a member of the victorious Australian team in the 800-metre relay. He returned home in August and was discharged from the A.I.F. on 14 October.

When Hardwick's application for reinstatement as an amateur was rejected by the New South Wales Amateur Swimming Association he gave up competitive sport. In 1920 he joined the Department of Education as supervisor of swimming and was responsible for organizing holiday swimming schools throughout the State. In 1938 he directed the schoolchildren's display at Australia's 150th Anniversary Celebrations. He retired as deputy-director of physical education in February 1953.

In 1921 Hardwick had been commissioned in the Militia. As temporary lieutenant colonel he commanded the 1st Cavalry Divisional Signals from 1940 until his transfer to the Reserve of Officers in April 1942. At the Scots Church, Sydney, on 6 October 1945 he married with Presbyterian forms Maud Beatrice Hopper, née Harrison, a 65-year-old divorcee. He was foundation president (1949) and a life member (from 1952) of the Union of Old Swimmers. Survived by his wife, he died of a coronary occlusion on 22 February 1959 at Rushcutters Bay and was buried with Anglican rites in Waverley cemetery.

Hardwick was a handsome man, with blue eyes, brown hair and a fresh, olive complexion; he stood six feet (183 cm) tall and weighed twelve stone (76 kg) in his prime. Likeable, generous and unassuming, he was the quintessential sportsman. For his 1911 feats, his name was retrospectively inscribed on the Helms trophy, Los Angeles, United States of America. He is commemorated in the Sport Australia Hall of Fame and by the Harold Hardwick memorial trophy awarded annually to the winner of the New South Wales 100-metres schoolboys' title. It bears the inscription: 'In memory of a great sportsman, soldier and gentleman'.

G. H. Goddard, *Soldiers and Sportsmen* (Lond, 1919); P. Besford, *Encyclopaedia of Swimming* (Lond, 1976); R. and M. Howell, *Aussie Gold* (Brisb, 1988); A. Clarkson, *Lanes of Gold* (Syd, 1990); P. Fenton, *Les Darcy* (Syd, 1994); *People* (Syd), 18 Nov 1953, p 40; *Sporting Traditions*, 7, no 1, Nov 1990, p 61; *Referee*, 12, 26 July, 16 Aug 1911; *The Times*, 1 May, 26 June, 2 July 1919; *SMH*, 10 Dec 1920, 16, 31 Mar 1922, 10 Feb 1953, 24 Feb 1959; Hardwick papers (NL).   G. P. WALSH

HARDY, BENJAMIN GOWER (1898-1944), motor driver and soldier, was born on 28 August 1898 at Marrickville, Sydney, third child of Benjamin Gower Hardy, a perfume manufacturer from England, and his Australian-born wife Emily, née Cole. Ben was described as a 'diligent and consistent' pupil at Randwick Public School. Employed as a driver with Dalgety [q.v.4] & Co. Ltd, he lived at Willoughby with his sister and widowed mother. He never married. A tall, shy man, he repaired appliances and motorcars for his neighbours, brought home stray pets and was a keen fisherman. He was also a marksman with the Chatswood Rifle Club and won its championship in 1926.

On 25 September 1941 Hardy was mobilized as a private in the Citizen Military Forces. Considered too old for active service, he was attached full time to the 7th Garrison Battalion where he soon became recognized as an authority on the Vickers machine-gun. He later served with lines-of-communication and garrison units before being posted in February 1944 to the 22nd Garrison Battalion, based at No.12 Prisoner of War Group, 2 miles (3.2 km) from Cowra.

The 22nd guarded a camp, roughly circular in shape and divided into four segments, containing prisoners of war from Japan, Italy, Formosa and Korea. They were a strange mix: the Italians had with few exceptions settled easily into life at the camp; the Japanese, who found the shame of their capture almost unbearable, were generally sullen and uncooperative. The Italians occupied two sections, Japanese privates and non-commissioned officers were crowded into the third—known as 'B' Compound—and the fourth was inhabited by Japanese officers and a small number of Koreans and Formosans.

About 2 a.m. on 5 August 1944 some 1100 prisoners in 'B' Compound set fire to their huts and attempted to break out, across the barbed-wire entanglements which enclosed them. For a long time they had been hoarding baseball bats, kitchen knives, garden tools and other potential weapons, but the trigger for the eruption had come on the 4th when they learned of an imminent arrangement to separate the N.C.O.s from the privates, who were to be taken to a camp at Hay.

As the Japanese rushed the fences, using blankets to blunt the barbed-wire spikes, their huts exploded in flames. Hardy and Ralph Jones [q.v.] pulled greatcoats over their pyjamas and sprinted to their Vickers-gun which was mounted on a trailer. They reached the gun as hordes of prisoners raced towards it with the intention of turning the weapon against the garrison. With Hardy firing and Jones feeding the ammunition, they manned the Vickers until they were engulfed by their assailants and bashed to death. The Japanese took over the gun and swung it around, but it jammed—probably because they neglected to swing the ammunition belt

with it. Hardy was buried in the war graves section of Cowra general cemetery. In September 1950 he was posthumously awarded the George Cross 'for outstanding gallantry and devotion to duty' in the face of 'an overwhelming onslaught of fanatical Japanese'. His aged mother died a few days after the award was publicly announced and his sister Beatrice was presented with the decoration by the governor-general Sir William McKell.

L. Wigmore (ed), *They Dared Mightily* (Canb, 1963); H. Gordon, *Die Like the Carp!* (Syd, 1978) and *Voyage from Shame* (Brisb, 1994); *Argus* and *Daily Telegraph* (Syd), 1 Sept 1950.

HARRY GORDON

HARDY, KENNETH THOMAS (1900-1970), wine merchant, was born on 23 May 1900 at Mile End, Adelaide, third of five children of South Australian-born parents Robert Burrough Hardy, vigneron, and his wife Esther Lavinia, née Simpson. Thomas Hardy [q.v.4] was his grandfather. Educated (1913-17) at the Collegiate School of St Peter, by the age of 21 Kenneth was managing a branch of Thomas Hardy & Sons Ltd, wine merchants, at Circular Quay, Sydney. On 16 September 1926 he married Kathleen Eleanor Gordon at St James's Anglican Church, King Street. He was later made a director of R. H. Gordon & Co. Ltd, house furnishers. While flying to Canberra with Hugo Gramp [q.v.4] and other vignerons, Kenneth's cousin Thomas Mayfield Hardy was killed in October 1938 when the airliner, *Kyeema*, crashed into Mount Dandenong, Victoria. As the adult Hardy male in direct descent, Kenneth returned home to run the firm.

Although he was untrained in winemaking, he found himself chairman and managing director of a struggling company. World War II brought manpower restrictions, lack of imported replacement machinery and an embargo on wine exports to Britain. Sales in Asia and India vanished in 1941 with the Japanese advance. The wine industry slumped to a fifty-year low, but Kenneth held Hardy's together by calm and dogged faith. Fascinated by the family company's history, he loved the McLaren Vale vineyards and was well liked by his employees.

Hardy was president (1941-48) of the Winemakers' Association of South Australia and succeeded Desmond Du Rieu [q.v.] as chairman (1944) of the Federal Viticultural Council. A member (from 1946) and chairman (1949-58) of the Australian Wine Board, he was also chairman of directors of the Adelaide Bottle Co. Pty Ltd. In 1949 he travelled to Britain where he sought tariff reductions, and to France and Germany where he investigated the production of moselles and burgundies, and examined distribution systems. Next year he was appointed president of the South Australian Chamber of Manufactures Inc. Having helped to establish (1955) the Australian Wine Research Institute at Urrbrae, of which J. C. M. Fornachon [q.v.] was founding director, Hardy sat on the institute's inaugural council and its oenological research committee. In 1959 he again travelled abroad. He was appointed O.B.E. in 1960.

A thickset man, modest and reticent, Hardy overcame the disabilities of a harelip and cleft palate. He enjoyed entertaining visitors, both local and from overseas, among whom were Field-Marshal (Viscount) Slim and the pianist Winifred Atwell. His prescription for guests who suffered hangovers on Sunday mornings was a brandy heart-starter. He liked fishing and golf, and belonged to the Royal South Australian Yacht Squadron and the Adelaide Club (from 1949).

After retiring as managing director in 1965, Hardy remained chairman of the board, which in 1968 funded a collection of books on wine and viticulture at the State Library of South Australia. He died of myocardial infarction on 13 November 1970 at Gilberton and was cremated. He was survived by his wife, daughter and son Robert, production manager and a director of the company. Kenneth's nephew Thomas Walter Hardy was managing director (from 1967) and chairman (from 1970).

R. Burden, *A Family Tradition in Fine Winemaking* (Adel, 1978); Aust Wine Bd, *Annual Report*, 1954-55; Aust Wine Research Inst, *Annual Report*, 1957-58; *Hotel Gazette of SA*, Feb 1960, May 1965; *Winestate*, Mar 1981; *Advertiser* (Adel), 10 Nov, 12 Dec 1949, 5 Dec 1959, 14 Nov 1970; *Bulletin*, 24 Feb 1981; information from Mr R. G. Hardy, Leabrook, Adel.   ROSEMARY BURDEN

HARITOS, EUSTRATIOS GEORGIOU (1888-1974), salt producer and storekeeper, was born on 5 January 1888 at Mitilíni, on the Turkish-controlled island of Lesbos (Lésvos), son of George Haritos and his wife Despina, née Samios. As a young man Stratos worked the salt-pans on the Turkish coast. Fighting on the side of the Greeks in the first Balkan War, he was wounded in 1912 and hospitalized at Piraeus (Piraiévs). A plate was inserted in his head. When he recovered he made his way to Port Said, Egypt, where he was employed for a time as a powder-monkey.

In 1914 construction began on the Pine Creek to Katherine railway extension in the Northern Territory. Haritos somehow learned of the project and sailed to Darwin in the following year. Being a 'useful sort of carpenter', he obtained a job on the Fergusson River bridge. He later lumped coal on the Darwin wharfs and worked in a local restaurant. At the office of the registrar-general, Darwin, on 5 September 1917 he married 17-year-old Eleni (Ellen) Hermanis (d.1966); a Greek Orthodox service was subsequently performed.

About 1919 Haritos formed a partnership with John Sphakanakis, Dick Colivas and others to develop the salt-pans near Ludmilla (Racecourse) Creek. They sold salt to Vestey Bros' Meatworks, buffalo shooters, cattle-stations and butchers' shops. In 1931/32 their four acres (1.6 ha) of pans yielded 150 tons of salt, valued at £1200; by that time Darwin had virtually ceased to import salt. At Racecourse Creek the Haritos family also ran goats and fowls, and grew peanuts and watermelons.

Haritos prospered and by 1941 owned four blocks of land in the town. On one of them (corner of Daly and Cavenagh Streets) he had built a two-storey, fibro shop and residence. He then opened a grocery store which was to become something of an institution. After the Japanese bombed the town in February 1942, he joined his family who had been evacuated earlier. At Mullumbimby, New South Wales, he ran a banana plantation before returning to Darwin and reopening his store in January 1946. By then the Federal government had resumed all land in the town with the intention of establishing a new central business district. Haritos received £6100 as compensation for the acquisition of his properties (an amount was included for war damage and depreciation). When the government abandoned the plan in 1951, he was able to obtain leases on the site of the Daly Street store and another of his former holdings. A family home was completed at Fannie Bay in March that year.

Naturalized on 7 March 1924, Haritos never revisited Greece. He appreciated the security of life in his adopted country, picked up spoken English very quickly, and eventually learned to read and write the language. Despite an uncertain temper, he was highly respected and an important representative of Darwin's Greek community which grew in size and influence. He died on 25 September 1974 in Darwin and was buried in the general cemetery; his four sons and four daughters survived him.

NT, *Annual Report*, 1932, 1933; *NT News*, 27 Sept 1974; interview with J. Haritos (oral hist collection, NTA); F46, F1 1946/159 pt 2, F1 1954/419, F649 S180 pt 2 (AA, Darwin); A1/1 1929/10053, A3 19/1248, A3/1 NT21/4037 (AA, Canb); family information.

HELEN J. WILSON

HARNEY, WILLIAM EDWARD (1895-1962), author and bushman, was born on 18 April 1895 at Charters Towers, Queensland, second of three children of English-born parents William Harney, miner, and his wife Annie Beatrice, née Griffin. In 1897 his father went to Kalgoorlie, Western Australia, to search for gold; when he returned in 1902, work was still scarce. Young Bill attended Charters Towers Central (Boys') School before the family moved to Cairns in 1905. He found a job as a printer's devil with the *Morning Post*, his mother worked as a cook in a boarding-house, and her husband continued on to Mount Molloy where Annie and the children later joined him. Harney and his father then went back to Charters Towers, seeking gold in the mullock-heaps, while other members of the family were employed on cattle-stations.

At the age of 12 Harney set off alone, droving in western Queensland, working on cattle-stations and boundary-riding a section of rabbit-proof fence near the Simpson Desert. Faced with unemployment, on 6 September 1915 he enlisted in the Australian Imperial Force. He trained in Egypt and served on the Western Front in 1916-18 as a signaller in the 9th Battalion. Discharged on 20 June 1919 in Queensland, he travelled west by train, then rode to the Northern Territory; he drove cattle, delivered mail by pack-horse and again worked as a boundary-rider. In 1921 he won £650 in a Melbourne Cup sweep. With the money, he took up land with Johno Keighran at Seven Emus Lagoon, near Borroloola. They made a meagre living by buying and selling cattle and mustering wild herds.

In 1923 Harney was convicted of cattle-stealing and spent three months in Borroloola gaol. He passed the time reading classics of English literature from the local library. Freed on appeal, he gave up his share of Seven Emus station and bought a sailing vessel, the *Iolanthe*, with money from his war gratuity. He and a mate Horace Foster gathered trepang in the Gulf of Carpentaria, and collected and sold salt from land they leased nearby.

On 5 April 1927 at the chapel of the Anglican mission, Groote Eylandt, Harney married 17-year-old Kathleen Linda Beattie, a part Aborigine; their daughter Beatrice (Beattie) was born in 1928, their son Billy two years later. When Linda fell ill with tuberculosis in 1930, Harney sold the *Iolanthe* and took his family inland where conditions were less humid. They roamed extensively in search of work and suffered hardships during the Depression. Linda died in 1932. Next year Beattie developed tuberculosis. Harney had to leave her in hospital in Darwin while he went road-mending and fencing, west of Katherine.

He also maintained an aerodrome on Bathurst Island for a time. Beattie died in 1934. Billy was to drown in 1945, trying to save a child.

From 1940 Harney worked for the government's Native Affairs Branch as acting patrol officer and protector of Aborigines. He resigned in 1947 and built himself a hut on the beach at Two Fellow Creek, near Darwin. In 1941 he had begun to contribute pieces to magazines such as the *Bulletin*, *Walkabout* and *Overland*; he then concentrated on writing books, on his own life, the Northern Territory and the Aborigines. His publications included *Taboo* (Sydney, 1943), *Songs of the Songmen*, with A. P. Elkin [q.v.] (Melbourne, 1949), *Life Among the Aborigines* (London, 1957), *Content to Lie in the Sun* (London, 1958), *Bill Harney's Cook Book*, with Patricia Thompson (Melbourne, 1960), *Grief, Gaiety and Aborigines* (London, 1961), *The Shady Tree*, completed by Douglas Lockwood [q.v.] (Adelaide, 1963), and *A Bushman's Life*, edited by Douglas and Ruth Lockwood (Melbourne, 1990). Coloured with a wealth of bush lore and bush humour, his books attracted a large readership. His acclaimed radio interview (1958) with J. J. M. Thompson [q.v.] on his war experiences was to be published as *Bill Harney's War* (Melbourne, 1983).

Often leaving his home for months at a time, Harney worked as a grader-driver's assistant in Central Australia, as an adviser to the American National Geographic Society's expeditions (1948-54) to Melville Island and Arnhem Land, and on the set of the film, *Jedda* (1955). In 1956 he visited Britain where he gave talks on radio and television. Appointed ranger at Ayers Rock-Mount Olga National Park in 1957, he enjoyed the company of tourists and was able to explain the mythology of Ayers Rock (Uluru) which he had learned from two Aboriginal friends. He retired in 1962.

Although Harney had received little formal education, he taught himself and built up an exceptional knowledge. He communicated easily with the Aborigines and became an authority on their lore, customs, rites and languages. A gregarious and generous person who regarded everyone as equal, he was short and stocky, with hypnotic blue eyes and an expressive face. Above all, he was a superb raconteur. He died of a coronary occlusion on 31 December 1962 in his home, Shady Tree, at Mooloolaba, Queensland, and was buried in Buderim cemetery.

D. Carment and B. James (eds), *Northern Territory Dictionary of Biography*, 2 (Darwin, 1992); Harney papers (held by author *and* NL); personal information.   JENNIFER J. KENNEDY

HARRHY, EDITH MARY (1893-1969), composer and entertainer, was born on 19 December 1893 in London, daughter of Jonathan Harrhy, a council inspector from Monmouthshire, Wales, and his wife Annie, née Rose. Edith always attributed her musical gift to her Welsh heritage. Educated at Shenley House School, London, she began her musical studies early and took her first Trinity College examination at the age of 7. Later, as Ernest Palmer scholar, she entered the Guildhall School of Music, under (Sir) Landon Ronald, where she studied piano, singing, harmony, counterpoint and opera, winning annual scholarships and numerous prizes.

In 1914 Edith left the Guildhall school to tour with the English violinist Mary Law. The duo visited Australia in 1915 and South Africa in 1916, and made some gramophone recordings. In Australia Edith had met William Constant Beckx Daly; they were married on 8 April 1919 at St Andrew's parish church, Whitehall Park, London. From September, they lived with the Daly family in Melbourne, a situation which facilitated Edith's professional life, but caused some strain in the marriage.

During the 1920s Edith accommodated her career to her husband's work as a commercial traveller in pharmaceuticals; she travelled with him, broadcasting and giving recitals for charities, clubs and societies. Her concerts centred on performances of her own compositions, with Edith singing, playing piano and accompanying the other musicians—usually two singers and a violinist. The nursery songs she composed for her two daughters proved particularly appealing and successful.

In 1930-33 the family lived in England where Edith gave recitals in London and the provinces. On her return to Melbourne, she began her work with amateur and semi-professional musical-theatre groups. She was associated with Gertrude Johnson's [q.v.] Australian National Theatre Movement from its inception in 1935, and was its musical director in 1940-48. She also worked as musical director with the Gilbert and Sullivan Society of Victoria, the Q Guild, the Lyric Light Opera Society and—as staff coach and accompanist from 1950—the Melbourne Conservatorium of Music Opera Society. In these years her light operas, *Alaya* and *The Jolly Friar*, had a number of productions, as did her two operettas for children. In addition to her musical activities, Harrhy was a life governor of Prince Henry's Hospital and a member of the Lyceum Club. She died on 24 February 1969 at Oxley, Brisbane, and was cremated; her daughters survived her. The Music Theatre Guild's Edith Harrhy award commemorates her service to musical theatre.

Fair haired and tiny, Harrhy had been acutely conscious of her age and repeatedly gave her year of birth as 1903. She was a gifted coach, a pianist 'of refined and delicate style', a versatile entertainer, beguiling, charming and funny, with a delightful mezzo-soprano voice. She is remembered chiefly for her sweetly simple songs—she claimed to have published (from 1920) two hundred of the thousand she composed. The best known of them, *What The Red Haired Bosun Said*, was recorded by John Brownlee [q.v.7].

A. L. Cohen, *International Encyclopedia of Women Composers* (NY, 1987); K. R. Snell, *Australian Popular Music: Composer Index* (Melb, 1987); L. Marsi (comp), *Index to the Australian Musical News 1911-1963* (Melb, 1990); *Who's Who in Music and Musicians' International Directory* (Lond), 1962; Harrhy papers (NL); information from Mrs H. Coutts, Bermagui, NSW.

KAY DREYFUS

HARRIES, DAVID HUGH (1903-1980), naval officer, was born on 27 June 1903 at Kew, Melbourne, son of David Henry Harries, a stockbroker from Wales, and his Victorian-born wife Vera Lyon, née Cross. Educated at Melbourne Church of England Grammar School, on 1 January 1917 young Harries entered the Royal Australian Naval College, Jervis Bay, Federal Capital Territory. He graduated in 1920 with numerous academic and sporting distinctions, and was immediately sent to England for sea-training and courses with the Royal Navy. In 1924 he was promoted lieutenant.

Serving alternately with the R.A.N. (1925-27 and 1930-33) and the R.N. (1927-30 and 1933-35), Harries spent most of the next ten years at sea. He topped the long navigation course at H.M.S. *Dryad* in 1927, was promoted lieutenant commander in 1932 and attended the R.N. Staff College in 1934. At St Peter's parish church, Cranley Gardens, London, on 23 December 1933 he had married Margaret Emily Street. In 1935 he was posted to Navy Office, Melbourne, and in 1937 joined H.M.A.S. *Australia* as navigating officer. Next year he commissioned H.M.A.S. *Hobart* and in December was promoted commander. Back in England, he commanded H.M.S. *Seagull* from July 1939 to September 1940 when he moved to H.M.S. *Niger* as senior officer, 4th Minesweeping Flotilla.

Between April 1941 and October 1942 Harries served as Australian naval attaché in Washington, D.C.; Sir Owen Dixon [q.v.] appreciated his assistance and praised his work. By December Harries was in England, supervising the transfer to the R.A.N. of the heavy cruiser, *Shropshire*. He was posted as executive officer on her commissioning in June 1943. Leaving that ship in mid-1944, he was

appointed deputy chief of Naval Staff and acting captain in August (substantive 30 June
1945). He commanded *Australia* (1945-46)
and *Hobart* (1946-47) before completing the
1948 course at the Imperial Defence College,
London. In 1949-50 he was captain of the
Sydney shore establishment, *Penguin.*

On 22 April 1950 Harries took command of
the aircraft-carrier, *Sydney*. The ship was deployed to Japan in August 1951 for service
with the United Nations forces against the
Chinese and North Koreans. In October,
while on her first operational patrol, she
equalled the record for a light fleet carrier
with eighty-nine flying-sorties in a day. That
month Harries had the 'unpleasant and unforgettable experience' of riding out Typhoon
Ruth. *Sydney* conducted six more patrols. Her
aircraft supported allied ground forces, spotted for naval bombardments, and bombed and
strafed enemy troops and facilities; British
and American senior officers were impressed
by her performance. She sailed for Australia
in January 1952. For his part in the campaign,
Harries was appointed C.B.E. (1952) and an
officer of the American Legion of Merit
(1954).

In April 1952 he was posted as commodore
superintendent of training at Flinders Naval
Depot, Westernport, Victoria, and in November became second naval member of the
Naval Board. Promoted acting rear admiral
(substantive 7 July 1954), Harries was head
of the Australian Joint Services Staff,
Washington, in 1953-55, flag officer commanding, H.M. Australian Fleet, in 1956-57,
and flag officer in charge, East Australia
Area, in 1958-60. He was passed over for the
post of chief of Naval Staff in 1959, transferred to the Emergency List on 27 June
1960 and appointed C.B. (1961). Settling in
Sydney, he qualified as a chartered accountant.

Intelligent, alert, handsome and physically
fit, 'Darbo' Harries overcame his youthful
shyness, but retained a natural reserve. In his
official dealings, however, he tended to offer
opinions 'out of season', and, in higher administrative posts ashore, occasionally clashed
with senior public servants. He 'stuck by what
he thought was right and was admired for it by
the sailors'. A strict disciplinarian, he
demanded total dedication from his subordinates, but was sympathetic to those who
were 'having a bad trot'.

For recreation, Harries played tennis and
golf, and studied German and Russian in his
spare time; he belonged to the Australian and
Union clubs, Sydney, and the Naval and Military Club, Melbourne. Following a stroke, he
spent the last eight years of his life in a nursing home. He died on 6 July 1980 at Bellevue
Hill and was buried in Waverley cemetery; his
wife and two sons survived him.

F. B. Eldridge, *A History of the Royal Australian
Naval College* (Melb, 1949); R. O'Neill, *Australia in
the Korean War 1950-53*, 2 (Canb, 1985); *Navy
News*, 12 Dec 1958, 17 June, 12 Aug 1960, 11 July
1980; A3978/9, item Harries, D. H. (AA, Canb);
information from Cmdr J. Stacey, Bowral, Vice
Adm Sir Richard Peek, Cooma, and Adm Sir
Anthony Synnot, Yass, NSW.

MIKE FOGARTY

HARRINGTON, EDWARD PHILIP
(1895-1966), balladist, was born on 28 September 1895 at Shepparton, Victoria, fourth
child of Philip Harrington, a farmer from Ireland, and his Victorian-born wife Margaret,
née O'Brien. Ted spent his boyhood and youth
on his father's farm at Boundary Bend, and
completed 'a rather chequered school career'
at Wanalta Creek and Shepparton Central
schools. On 22 February 1917 he enlisted in
the Australian Imperial Force; he was then 5
ft 3 ins (160 cm) tall, his chest measured 32
ins (81 cm), he had blue eyes and brown hair,
and he gave his religious denomination as
Catholic. Harrington sailed to the Middle East
and in August joined the 4th Light Horse
Regiment in Palestine. He took part in the
charge at Beersheba (31 October) and in the
1918 advance to Damascus, Syria, before
being discharged in Australia on 24 August
1919. For much of his remaining life he
required medical attention and received a
repatriation pension.

After the war Harrington 'went broke on a
Mallee farm'. In the 1920s he began contributing to the *Bulletin* and *Labour Call*. Widely
described as the last of the bush balladists—a
term which undervalues the range of his
writing—he once said that he was 'a literary
throwback'. One critic described his ballads
as 'humourous, racy and realistic', but
another, while agreeing that all Harrington's
verse possessed 'a virile, singing, swinging
quality', also pointed to the many poems with
lyrical qualities. At least fifteen were set to
music: eight of them (including 'My Old Black
Billy') by Edith Harrhy [q.v.], and others by
Peter Dawson [q.v.8] who recorded 'The
Bushrangers' and 'Lasseter's Last Ride'.
Harrington, nevertheless, made very little
from any of his verses. In 1940-41 he realized
a total of 24 shillings in royalties, which were
deducted from his advance payment of £12.
He learned a plasterer's trade, worked in munitions during World War II and was later
employed in a canteen at Fishermens Bend.

A foundation member of both the Australian Poetry Lovers' Society (1934) and the
Bread and Cheese Club (1938), Harrington
regularly visited J. K. Moir's [q.v.] weekend
gatherings, always wearing a grey felt hat and
often a dark blue overcoat, and never without
a child's cardboard school-case which was referred to as his 'two-bottle case'. He was

friendly but reserved, and only offered an opinion when asked directly. His closest friends among writers were possibly E. J. Brady and John Shaw Neilson [qq.v.7,10], and, after Harrington had returned to live in Melbourne in 1936, he and Neilson met regularly.

In all, Harrington was the author of five collections of verse—*Songs of War and Peace* (1920), *Boundary Bend and Other Ballads* (1936), *My Old Black Billy and Other Songs of the Australian Outback* (c.1940), *The Kerrigan Boys and other Australian Verses* (1944) and *The Swagless Swaggie and Other Ballads* (1957)—all noteworthy for their restrained social comment and humanism. Besides his poems, he wrote a number of short stories between 1962 and 1965, most of which appeared in *Bohemia*.

Seeing him at Jack Titus's pub in 1962, L. J. Blake observed: 'He looked spry enough but the dreadful cough was with him then. A tiny man with a coat too long and legs so short, but one could see him with emu feather jauntily in his hat and those legs in breeches, a light horseman of the first A.I.F. who fought once at Beersheba'. Harrington died of emphysema and chronic bronchitis on 28 May 1966 in North Melbourne and was buried in Fawkner cemetery. His estate was sworn for probate at $4539.

H. W. Malloch, *Fellows All* (Melb, 1943); Education Dept (Vic), *Vision and Realisation*, L. J. Blake ed, 3 (Melb, 1973); *Overland*, no 3, Autumn 1955, p 8, no 35, Nov 1966, p 50; *Aust Tradition*, 3, no 2, June 1966, p 11; *Lawsonian*, no 369, Apr 1993, p 5; *Sun News-Pictorial*, 8 Oct 1945; *Age* (Melb), 30 May 1966; *Advocate* (Melb), 16 June 1966; S. Murray-Smith *and* C. Goode papers (LaTL); personal information.

HUGH ANDERSON

HARRINGTON, SIR WILFRED HASTINGS ('ARCH') (1906-1965), naval officer, was born on 17 May 1906 at Maryborough, Queensland, second child of native-born parents Hubert Ernest Harrington, solicitor, and his wife Laura Irene, née Barton. W. F. Harrington [q.v.9] was his grandfather. After attending Wychbury Preparatory School, Maryborough, in 1920 'Arch' entered the Royal Australian Naval College, Jervis Bay, Federal Capital Territory, where he excelled scholastically, and gained colours for Rugby Union football and hockey. In 1924 he went to sea as a midshipman in H.M.A. cruisers, *Brisbane* and *Adelaide*.

Later that year Harrington was sent to Britain for training with the Royal Navy and joined the battleship, H.M.S. *Malaya*, in the Mediterranean Fleet. While an acting sub-lieutenant at the R.N. College, Greenwich, he was commended by the Admiralty in September 1927 for an outstanding war-course essay. Back in Australia, he was promoted lieutenant in 1928 and served in R.A.N. ships until 1933 when he returned to Britain on appointment to the cruiser, H.M.S. *Cornwall*, which was deployed to the China Station for three years. Home again, he was a lieutenant-commander (from December 1936) and executive officer (from January 1937) of H.M.A.S. *Swan*.

Following seven months on the staff of the R.A.N. College at Flinders Naval Depot, Westernport, Victoria, on 30 August 1939 Harrington assumed command of the sloop, H.M.A.S. *Yarra*. In August 1940 the ship sailed for Aden. There she was attached to the Red Sea Force. In the war against Iraq (May 1941) she supported troops occupying positions on the west bank of the Shatt al Arab. On 24 May Harrington commanded naval elements of a combined operation at Habib Shawi. He was mentioned in dispatches and promoted commander in June.

When the British moved against Persia on 25 August, *Yarra* sailed down the Shatt al Arab from Basra to Khorramshahr. That morning she sank the sloop, *Babr*, captured two gunboats in the Karun River, and landed troops. On the 29th at Bandar Abbas she saved the burning Italian ship, *Hilda*, and took her in tow. Commodore Cosmo Graham, the senior naval officer, Persian Gulf, observed that, having given Harrington an order, he was able to dismiss the matter from his mind until Harrington reported, 'as is his custom, that the task has been successfully achieved'. Harrington was awarded the Distinguished Service Order.

In November-December *Yarra* was in the Mediterranean, escorting convoys which supplied Tobruk, Libya. By January 1942 she was in the Far East, running between Singapore and the Sunda Strait. On 5 February, near Singapore, the ship suffered superficial damage when the Japanese made an air-raid on the convoy she was protecting. Manoeuvring *Yarra* to the aid of a transport, *Empress of Asia*, which had been stricken in the attack, Harrington 'did a fine rescue job', laying his vessel's bow alongside the liner's stern and taking off 1804 people. He relinquished his command on 10 February and was transferred to H.M.A.S. *Australia* in March as executive officer. For his organization and administration of that ship in the South-West Pacific Area, particularly at Tulagi and Guadalcanal in July-August, he was again mentioned in dispatches. From July 1944 he commanded the destroyer, H.M.A.S. *Quiberon*, in operations chiefly around the Netherlands East Indies.

On New Year's Day 1945 at St Anne's Anglican Church, Strathfield, Sydney,

Harrington married a nursing sister Agnes Janet, daughter of Cyril Legh Winser who had been private secretary to governors of South Australia in 1915-40 and Australian amateur golf champion in 1921. Harrington served in the shore establishment, H.M.A.S. *Penguin*, in 1945-46 and was promoted captain in 1947 while attached to the Department of Defence, Melbourne. His command of the destroyer, H.M.A.S. *Warramunga*, from April 1948 to January 1950 included a three-month deployment to Japanese waters. In 1950-51 he was director of manning at Navy Office, Melbourne. He attended the Imperial Defence College, London, in 1952 and spent the next two years in the Admiralty's Naval Equipment Department at Bath. Home again, he commanded the aircraft-carrier, H.M.A.S. *Sydney*, from 1955 and was appointed C.B.E. in 1957.

As rear admiral (March 1957), Harrington was flag officer in charge, East Australia Area, in 1957-58, second naval member of the Naval Board (responsible for personnel) in 1958-59, and flag officer commanding H.M. Australian Fleet from 1959. He was appointed C.B. in 1962. On 24 February that year he was promoted vice admiral and succeeded Sir Henry Burrell as chief of Naval Staff in Canberra. Harrington was elevated to K.B.E. in 1963.

Over several years before Harrington's appointment as C.N.S., the navy had experienced a series of unrelated accidents with increasingly serious consequences. Then, in October 1963, five junior officers from *Sydney* drowned when the whaler they were sailing capsized near Hook Island, North Queensland. In February 1964 eighty-two lives were lost in a collision between the aircraft-carrier, H.M.A.S. *Melbourne*, and the destroyer, H.M.A.S. *Voyager*, off the New South Wales coast near Jervis Bay. Controversy surrounding these events dominated the second half of Harrington's term.

The tragedies provoked a crisis of public confidence in the navy and heightened concerns outside the service that professional standards had declined since the departure, a decade earlier, of the last British flag officer to be seconded to Australia. Harrington enlisted the support of two ministers for the navy—(Sir) John Gorton (to December 1963) and (Sir) Frederick Chaney (from March 1964)—who were prepared to defend the R.A.N.'s reputation in the face of widespread criticism.

Harrington's personal belief was simply that the service was having a run of bad luck that had to end. In the Naval Board's confidential submission to Federal cabinet on the findings of Sir John Spicer's [q.v.] royal commission into the loss of *Voyager*, Harrington argued that the failures and shortcomings which led to the disaster were unconnected, and could not have been foreseen and prevented. Moreover, he considered that the incident revealed no fundamental flaw in the administration and operation of the R.A.N. He was, however, privately critical of the captains of both *Melbourne* and *Voyager*.

In the wake of *Voyager*'s loss, Harrington obtained permission from the Admiralty for the long-term loan of the destroyer, H.M.S. *Duchess*. He skilfully managed the navy's programme for acquiring equipment, persuading the Chiefs of Staff committee to accept it without major amendment and gaining government approval for the construction of two new frigates, *Swan* and *Torrens*, as permanent replacements for *Voyager*. These achievements revealed his resolution and determination, and reflected the close relationship he enjoyed with senior British naval officers, notably Earl Mountbatten, with whom he maintained a personal correspondence.

Harrington retired on 24 February 1965. Although the R.A.N.'s public standing had declined, levels of government funding remained high and there was no shortage of recruits. It was also to his credit that the navy was in a high state of preparedness to meet the challenges of its involvement (from 1964) in supporting Malaysia against Indonesian Confrontation and of its subsequent operations in the Vietnam War. Meanwhile, he continued the policy of reducing the R.A.N.'s reliance on Britain and increasing its ability to operate with the United States Navy.

A stern disciplinarian, Harrington was regarded by many as an unfriendly man, yet, to those he came to know and trust, he was sympathetic. Most who sailed under him admired his ability. He was driven by ambition and by a determination to do his best, whatever the circumstances. Although old-fashioned in some ways, he was receptive to new ideas and innovative in applying them. All who encountered him took him seriously, but the tufts of hair which he grew on his cheeks provided a source of humour. On noticing a sailor who affected similar whiskers, Harrington said: 'On me they look dignified; on you they look bloody ridiculous'. The sailor was ordered to be clean-shaven.

In September 1965 Prime Minister Sir Robert Menzies [q.v.] appointed Sir Hastings commissioner-general to represent Australia at the Canadian international exhibition, to be held in 1967 and known as Expo 67. Harrington died of hypertensive cerebrovascular disease on 17 December 1965 in Canberra Community Hospital; at his own wish, he was buried at sea off Port Jackson. His wife, two sons and two daughters survived him.

Harrington's brother CHARLES FREDERICK

(1914-1941) was born on 22 June 1914 at Eagle Junction, Brisbane. He was educated at The King's School, Parramatta, New South Wales, and the University of Sydney (M.B., B.S., 1938). Appointed surgeon lieutenant, R.A.N. Reserve, on 1 September 1939, he was mobilized for full-time service in October 1940 and briefly posted to the auxiliary, H.M.A.S. *Wyrallah*, before joining *Yarra's* sister ship, H.M.A.S. *Parramatta*, on the East Indies Station in January 1941. She was transferred to the Mediterranean in June.

An inspirational figure, Harrington trained a crew from his staff in the use of a Vickers machine-gun, mounted it aft and took charge of it in action. East of Tobruk, on 24 June, a force of some fifty enemy bombers attacked *Parramatta* and the sloop, H.M.S. *Auckland*, which was sunk. *Parramatta* recovered survivors as the air-raids continued. Harrington turned the officers' and petty officers' messes into emergency sickbays, and he and his men worked tirelessly in caring for the wounded and those suffering from shock. He was awarded the Distinguished Service Cross (gazetted 1942).

Charles Harrington was presumed lost in action on 27 November 1941 when his ship sank after being torpedoed north-east of Tobruk by the German submarine, U 559. Of *Parramatta's* complement of 9 officers and 151 sailors, all save 23 sailors died.

P. and F. M. McGuire, *The Price of Admiralty* (Melb, 1944); A. F. Parry, *H.M.A.S. Yarra* (Syd, 1944); F. B. Eldridge, *A History of the Royal Australian Naval College* (Melb, 1949); G. H. Gill, *Royal Australian Navy 1939-1942* (Canb, 1957), and *1942-1945* (Canb, 1968); T. Frame, *Where Fate Calls* (Syd, 1992); Harrington papers, H.M.A.S. *Creswell* (Hist Collection, Jervis Bay, ACT); Harrington's personal correspondence and other papers (branch files, Office of the Chief of Naval Staff, Navy Office, Canb).   TOM FRAME

HARRIS, BERTRAND JOHN (1925-1974), astronomer, was born on 2 March 1925 at Patcham, Sussex, England, son of Joseph Bertrand George Harris, a clerk in the civil service, and his wife Dora Winifred Brunsdon, née Barnett. Educated at the Royal Grammar School of King Edward VI, Guildford, John played Rugby, cricket and chess, and competed in the debating team; he matriculated in 1941 and won the Magnus prize for mathematics.

During World War II Harris served (from April 1943) with the Royal Navy, rose to leading seaman and visited Brisbane when his ship put in for repairs. On 20 November 1946 he joined the Royal Greenwich Observatory, London, as a temporary clerk and was promoted temporary scientific assistant next year. At the parish church, Orpington, Kent, on 7 January 1950 he married Ethel Mary Wood, a civil servant. An external student at the University of London (B.Sc., 1952), he was appointed an experimental officer at the observatory on 10 May 1956.

Within a year Harris resigned to take the post of assistant-astronomer to H. S. Spigl at the Perth Observatory. He began work there on 20 May 1957. His initial task was to take responsibility for the observatory's role in the Markowitch International 'moonwatch' programme which aimed to map the precise position of the moon at any given moment for the benefit of space craft. He later took charge of the observatory's main research work—to prepare part of the meridian catalogues, another internationally organized project which set out to produce a comprehensive chart of the position of the stars. In 1961 he visited Canberra and Sydney to discuss with government astronomers his plans for a programme of astronomy at the Perth Observatory; his major interest involved a new plate-measuring machine which the observatories had acquired for their meridian work. Having acted in the post from 5 November 1961, Harris became government astronomer on 24 October 1963. At the meeting of the Australian and New Zealand Association for the Advancement of Science, held in Canberra that year, he was elected a member of the International Astronomy Union.

Following the threatened closure of the Perth Observatory in the early 1960s, government responded to Harris's pleas to move the building to a site at Bickley in the Darling Range, 15 miles (24 km) east of its original location at Mount Eliza. He promoted the new institution by co-operating with observatories at Hamburg-Bergedorf, West Germany, and at Flagstaff, Arizona, United States of America. His encouragement of close relationships between his observatory and the Physics Department at the University of Western Australia and other astronomical institutions resulted in the installation at Bickley in 1967 of a partially automated meridian instrument and an electronic computer.

Harris retained a passion for cricket and reading, and helped to produce plays for amateur dramatic groups. Survived by his wife, son and daughter, he died of a coronary occlusion on 23 December 1974 at his Kalamunda home and was cremated. At a time when other State observatories were being closed, his work had given the Perth Observatory a new direction and purpose that stemmed from a challenging programme of research.

J of the Astronomical Soc of WA, Dec 1974; *Q J of the Roy Astronomical Soc*, 17, 1976, p 520; *West*

Australian, 25 Dec 1974; correspondence files, Perth Observatory, Bickley, WA.

MURIEL UTTING
P. J. JENNINGS

HARRIS, EDGAR CHARLES (1897-1964), publisher, was born on 28 July 1897 at Eaglehawk, Victoria, son of native-born parents Thomas Harris, grocer, and his wife Louisa, née Nichols. He was educated at Eaglehawk State School until the age of 13. After being employed for a year with a solicitor and for a few weeks in a bank, he ran away to Melbourne where he was fascinated by Cole's [q.v.3] Book Arcade. Returning home, he became a telegraph messenger at the Bendigo post office before working as a postman at St Kilda from 1914. A friend introduced him to fine literature. 'It was like finding a new world', Harris said years later.

Enlisting in the Australian Imperial Force on 11 October 1916, he trained in England in 1917, but was sent home and discharged, medically unfit, on 20 February 1918. Harris then resumed his job as a postman, at Gilgandra, New South Wales. He subsequently worked as a billposter in various towns and cities from Mount Morgan, Queensland, to Melbourne. There he became a typist. Gifted with a pleasant, light-tenor voice, he was taken into the chorus in Barry Lupino's pantomime, *Mother Hubbard.* A mild stammer did not affect his singing. He next toured the outback with Randolph Bedford's [q.v.7] troupe. In Sydney he joined the office-staff of David Jones [q.v.2] Ltd and also combed the bookshops. His book, *A Spring Walk: Windsor to Bulli,* was privately printed in 1922.

Having played minor roles with Oscar Asche [q.v.7] in *Cairo* and *Julius Caesar,* Harris found his niche in 1923, working in Melbourne for A. H. Spencer [q.v.12] at the Hill of Content bookshop. He stayed with him for sixteen years during which he helped to sell the significant libraries of Robert Sticht, F. H. Cole and H. L. White [qq.v.12,8,12]. On 3 August 1925 he married a divorcee Frieda Ethel Forwood, née Starr, in a civil ceremony at Carlton.

In 1938 Harris joined George Jaboor who had taken over the Australian agencies for Cambridge University Press. When war in 1939 caused a paper shortage in Britain, Harris suggested printing local editions for their principals. On his recommendation a publishing adjunct, Georgian House Pty Ltd, was founded in 1943; following Jaboor's death in 1946, Harris became its managing director. His books were nicely produced: the Australiana facsimile editions and Australian art monographs were outstanding; the natural history works and the *Australian Junior Ency-*

clopaedia (1951) were all excellent. Leading writers appeared on the Georgian list. Harris stated that the profits on cheap picture books, which he produced for chain-stores, offset losses on quality works. When Robert Close's *Love Me Sailor* (1945) was banned in 1948, Close was gaoled and Georgian House fined.

Harris suffered a severe heart attack in 1955 and publishing was curtailed. Tall, dignified and known as Ted, he was president (1957-58) of the Australian Book Publishers' Association. He was also managing director (1947-64) of E. C. Harris Pty Ltd and the Australiana Society Pty Ltd. Andrew Fabinyi [q.v.] thought him 'one of the most creative publishers in the English-speaking world'. Harris died of ischaemic congestive cardiac failure on 27 September 1964 in East Melbourne and was cremated; his wife and two sons (both in publishing) survived him.

A. H. Spencer, *The Hill of Content* (Syd, 1959); *Age* (Melb), 16 Mar 1963, 29 Sept 1964; E. C. Harris papers (held by Mr B. W. Harris, Middle Park, Melb); personal information.

J. P. HOLROYD

HARRIS, HAROLD LARK (1889-1975), educationist, historian and public servant, was born on 3 March 1889 at Burwood, Sydney, third son of Joseph Harris, grocer, and his wife Adela Jane, née Wellington, both from Cornwall. Harold was educated at Burwood Superior Public School where he became a pupil-teacher in 1905. He spent 1908 at Teachers' College before attending the University of Sydney (B.A., 1912; M.A., 1916; LL.B., 1925) on a scholarship from the Department of Public Instruction which was preparing teachers for the expanding high-school system. Graduating with first-class honours in history, he was posted to Newcastle High School in February 1912. At St Andrew's Anglican Church, Summer Hill, Sydney, on 16 December 1913 he married Elsie Mildred Cavell.

While on the staff of North Sydney Boys' High School (1915-17), Harris resumed his university studies. His first publication, *A Source Book of Australasian History* (with R. G. Henderson, 1917), was a pioneering compilation of documents designed to suit a new high-school syllabus. In February 1918 Harris was appointed a lecturer in history at Teachers' College, joining C. H. Currey [q.v.13] and other highly qualified staff recruited by Alexander Mackie [q.v.10]. Harris contributed a chapter on political and social history to volume 5 of James Colwell's *The Story of Australia* (1925). A member (from 1919) of the Royal Australian Historical Society, he published two articles in its journal in

1926 and 1927. The first was an analysis of the influence of Chartism in Australia; the second was a broad economic history focussed on the 1893 financial crisis in New South Wales.

Harris then began to write for teachers and schools, a field in which, unlike Currey, he had experience. *The Teaching of History in Secondary Schools* (1930), long used as a text for trainee teachers, was followed in rapid succession by books for students in their senior primary and secondary years: *The Story of Australian Industries* (1931), *British and Imperial History from 1688* (1932), *The Economic Resources of Australia* (1933), *Highlights of History* (1933) and *Australia in the Making* (1936). Most of them ran to several editions.

For many years Harris lectured to tutorial classes run jointly by the university and the Workers' Educational Association. He was a member of the Sydney group of Round Table. His interest in economics led to his secondment to the Bureau of Statistics and Economics in 1935-38. He produced *Australia's National Interests and National Policy* (Melbourne, 1938) for the Australian Institute of International Affairs; the work was used by delegates to the 1938 British Commonwealth Relations Conference, held at Lapstone.

Having been promoted to senior lecturer, Harris became an inspector of schools in April 1940. Eleven months later he began a career as director of youth welfare in the Department of Labour and Industry and Social Welfare. Responsible for 'youth employment, including vocational guidance, placement and after care', he established advisory committees throughout the State. His new interests were reflected in *Doing Our Best for Our Children* (1946), a book aimed at parents. He made important contributions on immigration and on decentralization to summer schools of the Australian Institute of Political Science in 1946 and 1948 respectively. In 1948-49 he visited Britain and North America.

In the early 1950s Harris moved from his home at Vaucluse to one at Hornsby. He consistently listed tennis as his sole recreation. Following his retirement in 1953, he served as president of the Marriage Guidance Council of New South Wales and contributed an article on that organization's work to *Australian Quarterly* (1956). Survived by his two sons, he died on 20 March 1975 at Wahroonga and was cremated.

R. White and B. Wilson (eds), *For Your own Good*, special issue of *J of Aust Studies* (Melb, 1991); B. H. Fletcher, *Australian History in New South Wales 1888 to 1938* (Syd, 1993); information from Hist Information Officer, NSW Dept of Education, Syd.   BRUCE MITCHELL

HARRIS, JOHN CASTLE (1893-1967), potter, was born on 13 May 1893 at North Waratah, New South Wales, fourth child of Harry William Harris, a native-born printer, and his wife Lucy Lillian, née Smith, from England. Jack had six years in the volunteer cadets and farmed at Mayfield before enlisting in the Australian Imperial Force on 19 February 1916. He embarked for England in the *Beltana* in May, was promoted sergeant in August and served (from November) with the 36th Battalion on the Western Front. Wounded in action (a gunshot wound to the right thigh) on 13 March 1917, he was invalided to England. He returned to Australia in November and was discharged, medically unfit, on 21 December in Sydney. Almost six feet (183 cm) tall, he was fair haired and blue eyed.

Nothing is known about his education or formal training in the arts. In the 1920s he was known professionally as Castle Harris and made a living from the sale of his punched and embossed leather tablecloths, which often incorporated Australian floral motifs. He described himself as an artist living at Coogee when he married a fellow artist Alice Rochfort, sister of Neville William Cayley [q.v.7], at St James's Anglican Church, Sydney, on 31 December 1923.

In the early 1930s Harris had lessons in clay modelling from Una Deerbon (1882-1972); on a visit to Melbourne in 1935, he worked briefly and informally at the Deerbon Pottery School and was employed at the Premier Pottery at Preston. A number of ceramics, elaborately decorated with dragons, lizards and fish, exist with the signatures of both Castle Harris and Alan James, the principal thrower of the pottery's Remued ware; one with a blue-glazed, frill-necked lizard by Harris is held by the Shepparton Art Gallery.

Harris had a studio in Hunter Street, Sydney, in 1939 and 1940, and another at Toongabbie in the mid-1940s. He seems to have had no time for contemporary, earthy, handicraft ideals or for the 'accepted notion that handcrafted objects should be useful', and therefore kept well clear of the Society of Arts and Crafts of New South Wales. His wares were designed for the gift-shop market. Large, heavily decorated and frequently sculptural, his ceramics featured Australian and grotesque animals, and showed a strong Oriental influence. Some large examples were executed in lattice-work.

About 1946 Harris shifted to the Blue Mountains and established a studio at Wentworth Falls. He later moved to Lawson where he continued his work. Predeceased by his wife, he died on 7 April 1967 in hospital at Wahroonga and was cremated. He had no children.

M. Y. Graham, *Australian Pottery of the 19th and Early 20th Century* (Syd, 1979); J. McPhee, *Australian Decorative Arts in the Australian National Gallery* (Canb, 1982); P. Timms, *Australian Studio Pottery and China Painting* (Melb, 1986).

JOHN MCPHEE

HARRIS, LEONARD BURNIE (1890-1964), newspaper publisher and printer, was born on 12 October 1890 at Burnie, Tasmania, second of three sons of Charles James Harris (1864-1913), journalist, and his wife Isabella, née Wilkinson. Leonard's grandfather Robert Harris (d.1903)—the family patriarch—began his journalistic career in 1845 with the Launceston *Cornwall Chronicle* (later the *Examiner*); in 1875 he moved to Victoria where he established the *Colac Reformer*. After spending three years in Wellington, New Zealand, he joined the staff of the Melbourne *Argus* about 1881. He returned to Tasmania in 1890 to join his sons Charles and Robert (d.1896) in setting up, at Burnie, the *Wellington* (later *Emu Bay*) *Times*. Eight years later they also published the *North-Western Advocate* at Devonport. In 1904 the two newspapers were amalgamated.

Educated at the local school, Leonard joined the Van Diemen's Land Co. in 1905, but worked for the newspaper in his spare time. In 1913 he was appointed a director of Harris & Co. Ltd. When Charles Harris died, Leonard's elder brother Russell succeeded their father as managing editor of the *Wellington Times*. At Burnie on 23 March 1915 Leonard married with Methodist forms Sylvia Geehan O'Brien (d.1938), a milliner; they remained at Burnie and were to have five sons and a daughter. In that year Leonard's younger brother Selby took charge of the company's commercial printing establishment, located at Devonport.

In 1924 Len became manager of the Devonport branch. Under Russell and Len, the *Advocate* won national recognition as a leading provincial daily, and was one of the first in Australia to install an electric-powered lithographic printing plant. In 1935 Russell died, aged 43, and Len in turn became managing director. Although resourceful, he was fully tested during World War II, for newspapers were one of the hungriest consumers of raw materials. On 25 March 1941 at Wesley Church, Hobart, he married Nancy May King, née Ford, a 30-year-old divorcee. In the postwar era the newspaper flourished under his leadership.

A Freemason, Leonard Harris was foundation president of the Burnie Chamber of Commerce (1937) and of the local Rotary Club (1942); he gave freely of his time to organizations allied with newspapers and print-ing. In his youth he had been a sprinter and middle-distance runner; he won the Burnie Gift in 1912, and played A-grade tennis, cricket and football. He was president of the Burnie Athletic Club and a committee-member for forty years. An outstanding golfer and a member of the Tasmanian Golf Council, he regularly won the Seabrook and the Devonport club championships, and represented the State in competitions. Len retired from the executive-managership of Harris & Co. Ltd in 1963 and was succeeded by his second son Lloyd. At the same time Selby retired in favour of his son Geoffrey. Survived by his wife and by three sons of his first marriage, Len Harris died on 4 July 1964 at Wynyard and was buried with Anglican rites in Wivenhoe cemetery. In August 1992 his grandson Nigel Harris joined the company's board of directors.

Cyclopedia of Tasmania (Hob, 1931); *Mercury* (Hob), 8 Apr 1935, 8 July 1964; *Advocate* (Hob), 6 Apr 1935, 29 June 1963, 6 July 1964, 29 Mar 1973; family *and* personal information.

R. A. FERRALL

HARRIS, MARY PACKER (1891-1978), teacher of art, was born on 30 July 1891 at Middlesbrough, Yorkshire, England, daughter of Clement Antrobus Harris, professor of music, and his wife Mary Elizabeth, née Packer, both Quakers. Mary was educated at Morison's and Perth academies, Perthshire, Scotland, and (from 1909) at the Edinburgh College of Art (Dip.Art, Scottish Art Teachers' Certificate, 1913). In 1915 she went to a large school at Buckie, Banffshire, as art mistress and from 1918 held a similar post at the Ayr Academy. Her elder brother Antrobus, a musician, was killed in the trenches in Flanders, Belgium, in 1916. After emigrating to Australia, her younger brother John had joined the Australian Army Medical Corps; he was badly wounded at Gallipoli. John persuaded Mary and her parents to join him in South Australia in 1921.

Next year Miss Harris was appointed to teach at the South Australian School of Arts and Crafts; the job was poorly paid and she felt forlorn during her early years in Adelaide. Gradually gaining in assurance, in 1930 she was asked by the Education Department to teach English literature and the history and appreciation of art at the Girls' Central Art School, a new institution within the School of Arts and Crafts. From these classes came a series of plays—often based on the lives of artists—which were written, acted and presented by her students, with costumes and settings devised from the materials and gardens at hand. She also taught at The Wilderness School and lectured (1937-46) at the

National Gallery of South Australia. Meanwhile, she continued to produce refreshing watercolours, prints, batiks, tapestries and illuminations. Although criticized for her 'muzzy mysticism', she was a constant exhibitor and encourager.

In 1939 Harris organized an art exhibition in Adelaide, 'The Testament of Beauty'. Contributors included Ivor Francis, David Dallwitz and herself. Three years later, in an effort to revitalize the Royal South Australian Society of Arts, some of her students were among those who presented the 'Adelaide Angries' exhibition which was one of the factors that led to the formation of the Contemporary Art Society of South Australia. Harris retired in 1953. A leading member of Adelaide's Lyceum Club and of the Society of Friends, she dressed soberly and was an ardent pacifist, a visionary and a vegetarian.

Harris published *Art, the Torch of Life* (1946), *The Cosmic Rhythm of Art and Literature* (1948) and an autobiography, *In One Splendour Spun* (1971). In the garden of Bundilla, her home and studio at Walkerville, and on the banks of the adjacent River Torrens, she arranged sculptures, mostly of Aborigines, by William Ricketts. The place became a haven for her students, one of whom, Ivor Francis, recorded 'the sense of purpose and happiness her inspired teaching and guidance brought me. What more can one ask of life than to have had a good teacher?' Harris died on 26 August 1978 at Walkerville and was cremated. The Art Gallery of South Australia holds five of her works.

R. Biven, *Some Forgotten, Some Remembered* (Adel, 1976), and *Mary Packer Harris 1891-1978*, exhibition cat (Adel, 1986); *SA Homes and Gardens*, 1 Dec 1948; *Ivor's Art Review*, 1, no 3, 1957; *Kalori* (Adel), Dec 1968, Mar 1972; *Advertiser* (Adel), 3, 9 Apr 1946, 4 May 1954, 4 Dec 1963, 11 Oct 1977, 28 Aug 1978, 31 July 1979; *Australian*, 31 May-1 June 1980; Harris papers *and* L. Arnold, Now in Retirement (ABC radio interview with M. P. Harris, 1969, Mort L); personal information.

RUTH TUCK

HARRIS, NORMAN CHARLES (1887-1963), railways administrator, was born on 10 April 1887 at Moonee Ponds, Melbourne, second child of Victorian-born parents Charles Joseph Harris, civil servant, and his wife Isabella, née McKay. Charles rose to be chief clerk of the rolling-stock branch and superintendent (1920-25) of the refreshment services branch of the Victorian Railways. At Scotch College, East Melbourne, Norman was head prefect, dux in science, mathematics and modern languages, a member of the firsts in rowing, cricket, football and athletics, and a witty contributor to the *Scotch Col-*

legian. In 1906-10 he studied engineering at McGill University, Montreal, Canada, where he graduated M.Sc. During his holidays he earned ten cents an hour with the Canadian Pacific Railway Co.

On leaving McGill, Harris joined C.P.R.'s technical staff and learned about rolling-stock construction, on which he was to become a world authority. In 1911 he returned to Australia to take up a post as an assistant-engineer with the Hydro-Electric Power Co. in Tasmania. On 10 April 1912 at the Presbyterian Church, Armadale, Melbourne, he married Rita May Wilson Moss [q.v. Harris]. His career in the Victorian Railways commenced in 1913 when he entered its way and works branch as a draftsman; one year later he joined his father in the rolling-stock branch.

In 1912 Harris had been commissioned in the Militia. Appointed captain in the Australian Imperial Force on 18 October 1915, he served on the Western Front with the 2nd Divisional Engineers and was promoted major in July 1917. At Pozières, France, in July-August that year, while often under heavy shell-fire, he organized trench improvements and the consolidation of captured works, and was awarded the Military Cross. He won the Distinguished Service Order for his actions on 19 May 1918, near Albert, when again under enemy shelling he supervised the construction of four bridges over the River Ancre, enabling a successful attack to be launched. Twice mentioned in dispatches, he was granted leave after the Armistice to study railway and engineering practices in Britain. He returned to Melbourne in 1919, was promoted lieutenant colonel (1921) in the Militia and held engineering and staff posts until 1928.

Harris had rejoined the rolling-stock branch in 1919; he was promoted assistant chief mechanical engineer (1922) and chief mechanical engineer (1928). Appointed a commissioner of the Victorian Railways in 1933, seven years later he succeeded (Sir) Harold Clapp [q.v.8] as chairman of commissioners. In his first report (1940) Harris suggested that Melbourne should have an underground railway and urged the need for further electrification. During World War II he chaired the transport sub-committee of the Emergency Council for Civil Defence. His greatest peacetime triumph was 'Operation Phoenix', begun in 1950, which saw the refurbishment and replacement of rolling-stock. Thirty new seven-carriage suburban trains came into use from 1956 and were named 'Harris trains'. Maintaining that 'railroading is a team job', Harris was well known for shovelling with the fireman, for his meticulous care of royal trains and for his denunciation of competition from road haulage.

Appointed C.M.G. in 1949, Harris retired in 1950, but remained chairman (1949-51) of the Victorian branch of the Institute of Transport of Australia. A subsequent chairman of commissioners, E. H. Brownhill, said that 'Harris was one of the great railway men of all times'. Having joined the Melbourne Legacy Club in 1935, Harris served on the employment, education and Junior Legacy club committees, as well as the board of management. He was president in 1950. At his home he coached Legacy wards in mathematics and science. Survived by his wife, he died on 3 May 1963 at Brighton and was cremated. His estate, sworn for probate at £28 489, included bequests of £600 to McGill and to Scotch College.

Vic Railways, *Harris Trains* (Melb, 1957); L. J. Harrigan, *Victorian Railways to '62* (Melb, 1962); *Aust Transport*, Feb 1963; *Sun News-Pictorial*, 19 Oct 1949; *Age* (Melb), 9 Apr 1949, 4 May, 20 Sept 1963; *Herald* (Melb), 20 Dec 1944; *Age* file on N. C. Harris (LaTL).   SEBASTIAN CLARK

HARRIS, RITA MAY WILSON (1888-1975), community worker, was born on 24 January 1888 at Brighton Beach, Melbourne, elder daughter of Victorian-born parents Isidore Henry Moss, grazier, and his wife Alice Frances Mabel, née Wilson [q.v.10 Moss]. Having encountered a seven-year drought, the family moved from their property near Dubbo, New South Wales, to Melbourne, and in 1902 Rita entered Presbyterian Ladies' College. Following in the footsteps of her philanthropic mother, in 1907-11 she worked as a voluntary helper at the Carlton Free Kindergarten.

On 10 April 1912 at the Presbyterian Church, Armadale, Rita married Norman Charles Harris [q.v.]. Although they were childless, she had a deep love of children and continually worked for their welfare. At their Brighton home, the Harrises kept open house at weekends, with large tennis parties on Sundays. During World War II numerous servicemen were entertained there. Rita had a gracious personality and the gift of leadership; her energy and enthusiasm drew together many helpers to raise funds for women and children, and she maintained their interest in and dedication to the projects.

In 1920 Mrs Harris had joined the committee of the Collingwood Crèche-Kindergarten. Particularly interested in its educational aspects, she established a sub-committee which was responsible for opening the Collingwood Kindergarten in 1924 in a separate building on adjoining land in Keele Street. As its honorary secretary, she obtained the support of local firms for the kindergarten. A pilot project, the first nursery school and training centre in Victoria, was opened in 1931 in a purpose-built upper storey. Harris was made a life governor of Keele Street Kindergarten in 1939 and was its president in 1946-53. After the kindergarten was moved to the Hoddle Street Housing Commission Flats, it was renamed the Rita May Harris Free Kindergarten in 1955.

An executive-member (from 1933) of the Free Kindergarten Union, Harris chaired the finance committee in 1945-47 and was vice-president in 1947-50. For many years she was the convener of the special efforts committee which virtually kept the F.K.U. afloat. In 1939 she had inaugurated the Silver Door auxiliary to save and recycle waste materials; under her leadership, the scheme expanded to become the F.K.U.'s war effort. When she resigned as convener in 1945, £11 000 had been raised. She was appointed honorary vice-president (1950) of the F.K.U. in recognition of her services to kindergarten work in Victoria.

In 1933 Harris had joined the board of management of the (Royal) Women's Hospital (vice-president 1943-44, president 1945-48). From 1935 she was also president of the hospital's senior auxiliaries. While a board-member, she served on the house, entertainment, and building and finance committees. She came to the presidency at a difficult time in the hospital's history: there was still no relief from the wartime difficulties of staffing hospitals and the nurses had to cope with a postwar baby boom.

Plans were drawn up for a new out-patients' department, for additions to the Gertrude Kumm [q.v.] wing and for an extension of the midwifery department. An X-ray diagnostic plant was installed, a blood transfusion unit was created and the post of medical superintendent was introduced. Despite the energy, thoroughness and courage that Harris brought to her task, the realization of the plans was frustratingly slow, due to lingering wartime shortages. None the less, she furthered the prestige of the hospital to a marked degree until her resignation in 1950. Next year she was appointed O.B.E. In 1958 the new out-patients' department was named the Rita Harris wing.

After her retirement, she worked for an auxiliary which she had formed when her husband was president (1950) of the Melbourne Legacy Club. During her twenty-two years involvement, the auxiliary raised thousands of pounds, of which one-quarter went to Legacy and the remainder to Red Cross. Predeceased by her husband in 1963, Rita Harris died on 21 July 1975 at Middle Brighton and was cremated. Her estate was sworn for probate at $318 490.

C. E. Sayers, *The Women's* (Melb, 1956); M. O. Reid, *The Ladies Came to Stay* (Melb, 1960); L. Gardiner, *The Free Kindergarten Union of Victoria 1908-80* (Melb, 1982); Free Kindergarten Union of Vic, *Annual Report*, 1920-50, *and* Minutes, 1928-50 (held at FKU, Richmond, Melb, *and* in Univ Melb Archives); Royal Women's Hospital (Melb), *Annual Report*, 1930-50; family information.

DIANE B. ALLEY

HARRISON, SIR ERIC JOHN (1892-1974), politician, was born on 7 September 1892 at Surry Hills, Sydney, third child of Arthur Hoffman Harrison, a painter and decorator from England, and his Irish-born wife Elizabeth Jane, née Anderson. Eric left Crown Street Superior Public School at the age of 13 to work in the textile industry and was soon managing one of (Sir) James Murdoch's [q.v.10] factories. Large framed and athletic, Harrison boxed, played football and achieved success as a rower. On 8 October 1916 he enlisted in the Australian Imperial Force. He served on the Western Front with the 5th Field Artillery Brigade from December 1917 and in May 1918 was promoted sergeant. A member of one of the A.I.F. crews that rowed at the Henley Peace Regatta in London in 1919, he was discharged from the army on 10 November in Australia.

At St Stephen's Presbyterian Church, Sydney, on 1 May 1920 Harrison married Mary Cook McCall (d.1941), a typiste. He resumed his employment with Murdoch's Ltd. With no prior political interests, he became active in the All for Australia League and achieved celebrity by forming a branch, with police protection, in J. T. Lang's [q.v.9] bailiwick of Auburn. By 1931 Harrison was a State councillor and chairman of the league's division based on the Federal electorate of Wentworth. In the December general elections he contested the House of Representatives seat of Wentworth for the United Australia Party and decisively defeated W. M. Marks [q.v.10] who had also been endorsed by the party.

Following his re-election in 1934, Harrison was appointed minister for the interior on 12 October, but surrendered the post on 9 November when the U.A.P. ministry was reconstructed to accommodate its Country Party coalitionists. During his four weeks in office he issued the order to prohibit the entry into Australia of the Czech anti-war publicist Egon Kisch [q.v.]. An assistant-minister from November 1938, Harrison received the portfolios of postmaster-general and repatriation in April 1939 after (Sir) Robert Menzies [q.v.] became prime minister and the Country Party quit the coalition. With the negotiation of another coalition in March 1940, Harrison again stood down.

As postmaster-general, he had angered the

Sydney newspaper owners, particularly (Sir) Warwick Fairfax, by approving plans for the Australian Broadcasting Commission to publish a weekly journal. At the elections in September 1940 Harrison had to withstand a strong challenge from the prominent solicitor (Sir) Norman Cowper, whom the proprietors backed. Brian Penton [q.v.] portrayed Harrison in the *Daily Telegraph* as an energetic local member with the 'handgrip of a grizzly bear' and an imagination to match. The *Sydney Morning Herald* observed that he had only two speeches, one on defence and the other on the communist threat. Harrison responded by impugning Cowper's war record. Having defeated Cowper, he was appointed minister for trade and customs, and imposed additional newsprint rationing while endorsing the launch of Ezra Norton's [q.v.] *Daily Mirror*.

Harrison was a constant, admiring and vigorous ally of Menzies. As his leader's support ebbed, he stood by him. Arriving late at the cabinet meeting on 28 August 1941 at which Menzies indicated that he would resign, he burst in and demanded, 'Boss, what are they doing to you?' At the 1943 elections Harrison narrowly defeated Jessie Street [q.v.]. He gained the deputy-leadership of the U.A.P. in April 1944 and retained the post when the Liberal Party of Australia was formed later that year.

In 1940 Harrison had been commissioned in the Militia. Promoted captain, he performed full-time service in 1942-43 as liaison officer with the United States military forces in Australia. When he wore his uniform in Canberra, Labor's E. J. Ward [q.v.] denounced him as a fake soldier and alleged he had been a member of the New Guard. Harrison subsequently raised accusations of ministerial malpractice against Ward. He proved a bruising critic of the Curtin and Chifley [qq.v.13] governments—well informed, persistent, somewhat stilted in delivery, but uninhibited in personal accusation. 'The rapier, laddie, the rapier, not the bludgeon', Menzies, tongue in cheek, once suggested. On 18 October 1944 at St Stephen's, Sydney, Harrison had married Linda Ruth Yardley, née Fullerton, a widow and a businesswoman. She became his political confidant and softened his abrasiveness.

Following the coalition's victory in December 1949, Harrison was given the portfolios of postwar reconstruction (which he relinquished on 17 March 1950) and defence. From April 1950 until March 1951 he was resident Australian minister in London; while there, he handed over defence on 24 October 1950 in exchange for interior, but retained the deputy-leadership of the party to thwart any threat to Menzies' control. Back in Australia, on 11 May 1951 Harrison was appointed minister for defence production, vice-president of the Executive Council and leader of the House. He was an undistinguished administrator of the munitions and aircraft factories. A controversial manager of the legislature, he used the guillotine so brutally that he caused unrest among government back-benchers, though his relations with his Labor counterpart Arthur Calwell [q.v.13] were surprisingly amicable. Harrison had been appointed to the privy council (1952). For a few months in 1955-56 he was minister for the army and for the navy.

In 1954 he had served as minister-in-charge of the royal visit and Queen Elizabeth II invested him K.C.V.O. at its close. Resigning from parliament in 1956, he succeeded Sir Thomas White [q.v.] as Australian high commissioner in London. Harrison was an active promoter of Commonwealth ties and even more outspoken in advocacy of the 'White' Commonwealth than Menzies; he provided the prime minister with palatable accounts of British affairs and was an attentive host during Menzies' regular visits to London. In 1961 Harrison was appointed K.C.M.G.

He and his wife returned to Australia in September 1964 and settled at Castle Cove, Sydney. Sir Eric's last years were overshadowed by Parkinson's disease. Survived by his wife and the three daughters of his first marriage, he died on 26 September 1974 at Chatswood and was cremated with Anglican rites. His estate was sworn for probate at $207 461. A self-made man, Harrison had achieved high office. Beyond his own electorate, which he worked assiduously, he had limited influence in the party organization. With his rugged good looks and powerful personality, he was essentially a politician of parliament, the party room and the public platform, an infighter rather than a strategist, whose qualities complemented those of his leader. He was a man of strong views warmly expressed, shrewd—except on any matter that might be construed as communist subversion—a formidable opponent and a loyal friend, his tendency to pompousness offset by masculine humour.

L. Harrison, *Me Too* (Melb, 1954?); K. Perkins, *Menzies* (Adel, 1968); P. Spender, *Politics and a Man* (Syd, 1972); E. Lyons, *Among the Carrion Crows* (Adel, 1972); G. Souter, *Company of Heralds* (Melb, 1981) and *Acts of Parliament* (Melb, 1988); A. W. Martin, *Robert Menzies*, 1 (Melb, 1993); *Daily Telegraph* (Syd), 6, 13 Sept 1940; *SMH*, 10 Sept 1940, 27 Sept 1974; *Sun* (Syd), 21 Feb 1950; *Canb Times*, 27 Sept 1974; Harrison *and* Menzies papers (NL).

STUART MACINTYRE

HARRISON, HAZEL JOYCE (1905-1970), kindergarten principal, was born on 22 June 1905 at Beaudesert, Queensland, sixth child of Robert Harrison, a Brisbane-born dairyman, and his wife Sarah, née Kerlin, from Ireland. Hazel was educated at a district state school and as a boarder (1916-22) at Brisbane High School for Girls (later Somerville House) where she captained the tennis team, winners of the interschool pennant in 1922. She then enrolled at the Kindergarten Teachers' Training College, Brisbane. After graduating in 1925, she was attached to several metropolitan kindergartens before being appointed director in 1926 of the Rosalie Crèche and Kindergarten.

In 1932 Miss Harrison gained a nursery school teacher's diploma from the Kindergarten Teachers' Training College, Melbourne. Next year she became director of the Keele Street Kindergarten, Collingwood. While there, she embarked on a pioneering investigation of the role of the mother in relation to the needs of infants and young children. In 1939 she moved to South Australia as resident lecturer at the Kindergarten Teachers' Training College, North Adelaide. Her duties involved the supervision of all Kindergarten Union training centres for students in the State. In February 1940 she was promoted director, with responsibility for the management of training activities. Despite a period of ill health and a heavy workload, Harrison presided over the 'most rapid change of philosophical direction in College's career'. Sets of Montessori equipment were consigned to the storerooms and she introduced predominantly American ideas, reshaping the curriculum to conform with similar courses overseas. Having returned to Brisbane for the whole of 1947 to nurse her terminally ill sister, she resigned her directorship in December 1949 and read English and psychology at the University of Adelaide.

Harrison travelled to England in 1953 and completed a course in child development at the Institute of Education, University of London. Next year she joined the Institute of Child Development. Her study of the influence of nursery schoolteaching, especially on parent-child relationships, won high regard and led to her engagement by the Tavistock Clinic, where, as teacher-in-charge (1954-66), she worked with the educationist John Bowlby and examined aspects of the English system of pre-school education. During this period she represented the Australian Pre-school Association at the World Organization for Early Childhood Education.

On her return to Australia in 1967, Harrison was appointed principal of the Kindergarten Teachers' College, Brisbane. Under her leadership the college's curriculum was enhanced and an academic course was introduced of sufficient width and depth to enable students to relate their studies to the practical field. Better organization, innovative teaching methods and the publication for the first time of a college handbook all stemmed from her professional experience. An attractive, pale, well-dressed woman with prematurely greying hair, Harrison was approachable and popular with students. Her dignity, warmth, sensitivity and tenacity of purpose left an indelible imprint. Following a brief illness, she died of heart disease on 29 May 1970 in the Beaudesert Hospital and was cremated with Anglican rites.

P. G. Freeman (comp), *History of Somerville House* (Brisb, 1949); C. Dowd, *The Adelaide Kindergarten Teachers College* (Adel, 1983); C. M. T. Byrne, *Meeting the Needs of Our Children* (Brisb, 1986); *Somerville House Mag*, June 1932, June 1933, Dec 1933, Dec 1944, 1967, 1970; Kindergarten Union of SA, *Annual Report*, 1940-50; *Courier-Mail*, 30 May 1970.   K. E. GILL

HARRISON, HECTOR (1902-1978), Presbyterian clergyman, was born on 5 April 1902 at Northam, Western Australia, third son of Thomas Allan Harrison, a hospital orderly from England, and his South Australian-born wife Hester Ann, née Bray. Educated at Northam State School (dux 1915), at the age of 14 Hector became a Salvation Army bandsman before serving (1918-20) with the Australian Military Forces' Reserve Band in Perth.

In 1922 Harrison entered the Salvation Army Training College, Melbourne. After being commissioned, he worked for two and a half years in the inner suburbs of Richmond, Fitzroy and North Melbourne. Because of his beliefs in regard to the sacraments of holy communion and baptism, he decided to prepare for the ministry of the Presbyterian Church. He studied part time for the Intermediate and Leaving certificates while acting as a home missionary for the Church. Entering Ormond [q.v.5] College, University of Melbourne (B.A., 1930; M.A., 1932), he preached at North Essendon on weekends and obtained his B.D. (1933) from the Melbourne College of Divinity. At St John's Presbyterian Church, Essendon, on 30 May 1931 he married Doris May Sarah Ann Tear.

Appointed to the parish of New Town in Hobart, Harrison was ordained in 1933. Next year he was commissioned as a chaplain in the Militia. In 1936 he transferred to Claremont, Western Australia, whence he accepted a call to be minister of the Church of St Andrew, Canberra; arriving in May 1940, he was to serve this parish until his death. He encouraged corporate worship, visited his parishioners regularly and comforted the sick in hospital; his drive and enthusiasm led to the establishment of new Presbyterian parishes

in the Australian Capital Territory. A counsellor and friend to the highly placed and the humble, he spoke nobly when he conducted Prime Minister John Curtin's [q.v.13] funeral in 1945. Harrison was a part-time chaplain at the Royal Military College, Duntroon, and at the naval depot, H.M.A.S. *Harman*. In 1953 he was appointed O.B.E.

Harrison was moderator of the Presbyterian Church of New South Wales in 1950-51 and moderator-general of the Presbyterian Church of Australia in 1962-64. He was appointed a vice-president of the World Presbyterian Alliance in 1964. While he was on friendly terms with his fellow clergymen in Canberra and believed in spiritual unity among the Christian denominations, he thought that only 'the religious romantic' could envisage 'one great world church'. He criticized the Federal government's efforts in the 1960s to increase state aid to private schools, and he continued to be totally opposed to alcohol and gambling.

Tall, sparely built, soldierly in bearing and with piercing brown eyes, Harrison had a dynamic personality, abundant energy and a keen sense of humour. From an early age he suffered from a hearing disability. He died on 19 November 1978 in Canberra Hospital and was cremated; his wife, son and three daughters survived him. Alan McIntosh's portrait of Harrison hangs in St Andrew's Church.

Presbyterian Church of St Andrew (Canb), *On the Life of the Very Reverend Hector Harrison, O.B.E., M.A., B.D.*, memorial supp of the *Echo* (Canb, Dec 1978); Harrison papers (NL).

GODFREY LAURIE

HARRISON, SIR JAMES WILLIAM (1912-1971), army officer and governor, was born on 25 May 1912 at Camperdown, Victoria, second child of Victorian-born parents James Samuel Harrison, farmer, and his wife Mary Eleanor, née Harlock. Young James was educated at Geelong College and the Royal Military College, Duntroon, Federal Capital Territory, where he graduated in 1932 as an artillery specialist. After spending four years in Melbourne with the 2nd Heavy Brigade, he trained in India and Malaya in 1937-38. Returning to Australia, in May 1940 he was promoted captain and seconded to the Australian Imperial Force. At Christ Church, South Yarra, Melbourne, on 30 September 1940 he married with Anglican rites Patricia Helen MacLean Lennox.

In 1940-42 Harrison served in the Middle East; he mainly performed staff duties and was mentioned in dispatches. Promoted lieutenant colonel, he 'displayed marked ability' while at headquarters, New Guinea Force, from November 1942 to February

1943. He was attached to the Australian Army Staff, London (1943-45), before being posted to the Directorate of Military Operations, Melbourne, where he handled 'many difficult problems' associated with the conclusion of the war and the occupation of Japan. From July 1947 he acted as liaison officer, Long Range Weapons Board of Administration, Melbourne. Having attended the Joint Services Staff College in England in 1948, he became an instructor at the Australian Staff College, Queenscliff, Victoria. In 1951 he was promoted temporary colonel and appointed first commandant of the Officer Cadet School at Portsea.

Promoted temporary brigadier and posted to London in 1954 as Australian army representative, Harrison completed the 1956 course at the Imperial Defence College. In August 1957 he took over Western Command, Perth, as temporary major-general (substantive from September 1959). Appointed O.B.E. (1953) and C.B.E. (1958), he was chairman, joint planning committee, Department of Defence, Canberra (1960-62). He was a member of the Military Board—as quartermaster-general (1962-63) and adjutant-general (1963-66)—and head of Eastern Command, Sydney (from 1966). His competence and friendly manner had made him one of the army's most popular officers.

In 1968 Harrison was invited to become the first Australian-born governor of South Australia. Appointed C.B. in January and K.C.M.G. in October, he was seconded from military duties and installed as governor on 4 December. The salary was unattractive. Steele Hall's Liberal government relieved Harrison of the responsibility for paying his domestic staff's wages when he reached the prescribed age for retiring from the army on 25 May 1969. Sir James was about 5 ft 5 ins (165 cm) tall; his auburn hair had turned grey by the time he took office.

Don Dunstan later concluded: 'Sir James fulfilled his role as Governor quietly and in the traditional way, and left little mark on the State'. Government House social functions were limited in 1969-70 by extensive renovations to the building's fabric and by the hospitalization, first of Lady Harrison, then of her husband. In April 1970 the governor developed angina. He was obviously in pain during the opening of parliament that month and may not have suspected that the speech Hall had prepared for him was to provoke a storm on the ground that it 'politicized' the governor's office: it omitted the usual phrase, 'My Ministers advise me', from a passage threatening the imposition of water restrictions, making it appear that this was his own statement. On 9 May Harrison suffered a coronary occlusion and was ill for two months. In the following year he and his wife set off on an overseas holiday. Sir James died suddenly on 16 September 1971 while flying to Honolulu; survived by his wife and two sons, he was cremated.

D. Dunstan, *Felicia* (Melb, 1981); *Australian*, 23 Oct 1968; *Sun News-Pictorial*, 11 May 1970; *Sunday Mail* (Adel), 5 Sept 1970; *News* (Adel), 18, 22 Sept 1971; Governor's dispatches, 1968-71 *and* press-cuttings books, 1968-71 (Government House, Adel); information from Lady Harrison, Robertson, NSW.
P. A. HOWELL

HARRISON, TRAVIS HENRY JOHN (1901-1977), agricultural scientist and public servant, was born on 4 January 1901 at Pennant Hills, New South Wales, third of nine children of native-born parents Henry Russell Harrison, fruit-grower, and his wife Lillian Mary, née Fox. Henry's property, Cherrybrook Farm, had been established by his Wesleyan parents who were descended from convict pioneers of the district. Educated at Sydney Boys' High School (1913-17) and University of Sydney (B.Sc., 1923; D.Sc.Agr., 1934), Trav was appointed lecturer in botany and entomology at Hawkesbury Agricultural College in 1923. At the Methodist Church, Epping, on 15 April 1925 he married Marjorie Powell Holliday.

His research on the fruit-fly and brown-rot diseases of stone fruits won him a (Sir Benjamin) Fuller [q.v.8] Trust scholarship; he studied at Imperial College, London, in 1930-32 (diploma in plant pathology, 1934). Back in Sydney, Harrison obtained his doctorate for a thesis on brown rot and in 1935 was awarded a King George V silver jubilee medal. He left Hawkesbury college in 1936 and in the following year joined the Federal Department of Commerce and Agriculture. As fruit inspector and research officer, based in London, he suggested measures to improve the condition of Australian fruit arriving in Britain. When World War II interrupted his work, he was employed as government procurement officer (from 1940).

Returning to Australia in 1945, next year Harrison became executive-member and secretary of the Australian Agricultural Council's irrigation production advisory committee. From February 1947 he was director of plant quarantine, Commonwealth Department of Health, Canberra; he was to be promoted assistant director-general in 1964. He endeavoured to protect Australia's agricultural industries from foreign pests and diseases by strengthening existing procedures and by developing the quarantine service as a co-operative undertaking with the States. In 1963-66 he chaired the National Sirex Campaign which succeeded in saving Australia's pine-wood industries.

Having helped in 1951-54 to achieve the plant protection agreement for the South-East Asia and Pacific region under the auspices of the United Nations Food and Agriculture Organization, Harrison fostered it as chairman (1956-60, 1964-67) of the regional international plant protection committee. He conducted special assignments for the F.A.O. in 1966, 1967 and 1970. Elected as an Independent, he was a member (1959-67) and deputy-chairman (1961) of the Australian Capital Territory Advisory Council; he was also a member (1957-67) and chairman (1963-67) of the Canberra Community Hospital board. In 1965 he was appointed O.B.E.

Of medium build, Harrison was a keen sportsman who had won Blues in Rugby Union football and cricket at university. His distinctive sandy-brown hair earned him the nickname 'Rusty'. As a leader, he was firm and determined, hard working and self-controlled, but these qualities were tempered by his cheerfulness, warmth and humility. For fifty-eight years he was a lay preacher in the Methodist Church. A keen gardener and a lover of natural beauty, he retired in 1966 and two years later moved to Rosedale Farm, near Batehaven, New South Wales. He died on 2 April 1977 in Canberra Hospital and was cremated; his wife, daughter and two sons survived him.

H. Barker and R. Hawkins, *Early Wesleyans of Pennant Hills* (Syd, 1983); N. Yeates, *Robert Dickie Watt Kt.* (Coffs Harbour, NSW, priv pub, Syd, 1987); *J of Aust Inst of Agr Science*, 43, nos 3 and 4, Sept/Dec 1977; information from Mrs V. Gait, Cronulla, Syd, Mr G. J. Harrison, Brighton, Adel, Mrs J. M. Thomson, Yarralumla, and Mr J. R. Morschel, Narrabundah, Canb.   D. G. PARBERY

HART, PERCY LLOYD (1874-1944) and GRAHAM LLOYD (1906-1974), judges, were father and son. Percy was born on 20 November 1874 at New Farm, Brisbane, sixth child of Graham Lloyd Hart, a solicitor from India, and his native-born wife Sarah Ellen Cooper, née Roberts. Educated locally at J. S. H. Schmidt's school and at Brisbane Grammar School (1887-93), Percy was a keen Rugby Union footballer and a gymnast. He passed the Barristers' Board examinations and was admitted to the Bar on 22 March 1898. At Wickham Terrace, Brisbane, on 12 July 1904 he married with Presbyterian forms Margaret Beatrice Crombie. Hart built up an extensive practice, especially in Equity, constitutional and ecclesiastical law. On 1 May 1916 he enlisted in the Australian Imperial Force. Commissioned in March 1917, he sailed for England twelve months later and served in France from August 1918 to January 1919, first with the 25th and then with the 26th battalions.

Back in Brisbane, Hart became a legendary figure. His vast fund of knowledge and memory for details—particularly case names and citations—stood him in good stead in court where he excelled in bluffing and was noted for protracting argument in case something might be turned up. He was always willing to help junior members of the profession. In 1933-38 he was an acting-judge of the Supreme Court. Following his dissenting judgement in the Ithaca election case (1938), the government did not offer him a full-time commission. A man of integrity and strong principles, Hart was a councillor of the Bar Association of Queensland and a member of the barristers' examination board. He was an Anglican synodsman and chancellor of the diocese of Brisbane, and president and trustee (1924-42) of Brisbane Grammar School's Old Boys' Association. Survived by his wife, four sons and two daughters, he died of cancer on 10 July 1944 at Clayfield and was cremated.

His eldest child Graham was born on 6 January 1906 at Ascot, Brisbane. Educated at Eagle Junction State and Brisbane Grammar schools, he was described at the latter as being 'industrious and public spirited', qualities he was to display throughout his life. In 1925 he enrolled at the University of Queensland intending to study medicine, but, within a year, went to work on the family property at Longreach; he started as a jackeroo and became an overseer. Returning to Brisbane in 1929, he studied law as an associate to Justice H. H. Henchman and was admitted to the Bar on 6 June 1933. Having been commissioned lieutenant in the Militia, Hart was seconded to the A.I.F. on 15 June 1940. He served with the 2nd/2nd Anti-Tank (Tank-Attack) Regiment in the Middle East (1940-42) and Papua (1942-43), and rose to captain in 1942. His A.I.F. appointment terminated in Queensland on 5 February 1944. At St John's Anglican Cathedral, Brisbane, on 21 July 1942 he had married 23-year-old Helen Constance Bryant.

Hart resumed his varied and successful practice, and took silk in 1953. A member of the Liberal Party, he held the seat of Mount Gravatt in the Legislative Assembly from August 1957 to January 1963. During his years in parliament he made many contributions, particularly in debates on aspects of the law. On 11 February 1963 he was appointed to the Supreme Court bench. Intolerant of delays in the administration of justice, he delivered his judgements promptly. His decisions often reflected his interest in legal history and were illustrated with numerous historical examples to support his analyses. Innate kindness characterized his judgements, as well as his personal relations, and he was held in high regard by the profession.

President (1961-63) of the Bar Association of Queensland, Hart was instrumental in forming the Australian Bar Association, of which he was vice-president (1962-63). As chairman (1959-63) of Barristers' Chambers Ltd, he was largely responsible for the decision to build the Inns of Court in Brisbane because he believed that members of the Bar should lead a collegiate life. He contributed to professional journals, maintained an interest in French literature and was chairman (1967) of the Supreme Court's library committee. A gentle man with an infectious sense of humour, he loved people and had interests that ranged from the Brisbane Agricultural Society to Legacy. He was also prominent in the Anglican synod. Survived by his wife, daughter and two sons, he died of myocardial infarction on 18 April 1974 in Brisbane and was cremated. His three children entered the legal profession.

R. Johnston, *History of the Queensland Bar* (Brisb, 1979); B. H. McPherson, *The Supreme Court of Queensland 1859-1960* (Brisb, 1989); *Courier-Mail*, 11 July 1944, 19 Apr 1974; *Telegraph* (Brisb), 19 Apr 1974; E. J. D. Stanley, A Mingled Yarn (unpublished ms) *and* Supreme Court, Judges' biog files, SCL/JB *and* news-cuttings (Supreme Court L, Brisb).　　　　　　ALADIN RAHEMTULA

HARTIGAN, THOMAS JOSEPH (1877-1963), railways commissioner, was born on 8 December 1877 at Woolloomooloo, Sydney, eighth child of Irish-born parents Michael Hartigan, letter carrier, and his wife Ellen, née Cusack. Educated at the Christian Brothers' High School, Lewisham, in January 1893 Tom joined the New South Wales Government Railways and Tramways as an apprentice clerk. On 26 March 1908 at St Thomas's Catholic Church, Lewisham, he married Imelda Josephine Boylson, a school-teacher. He was promoted chief accountant in 1921 and comptroller of accounts and audit in 1928.

In 1924 Hartigan had appeared before the royal commission into railway and tramway services and pointed out that the major source of the railways' deficit was interest paid on loans. The commission recommended sweeping reforms of the railways' managerial structure. Although it was widely expected that Hartigan would become assistant-commissioner for finance in 1925, the post went to an engineer A. D. J. Forster, provoking suggestions that sectarianism had played a part in the appointment.

In 1929 Hartigan toured Britain, Europe and the United States of America to investi-

gate railway operations. On his return, he clashed with the chief commissioner W. J. Cleary [q.v.8] over accounting procedures. Having avoided involvement in Cleary's conflict (1930-32) with Premier J. T. Lang [q.v.9] and his protégé C. J. Goode, Hartigan was promoted assistant-commissioner in March 1932. Lang's government was dismissed in May and the new minister for transport (Sir) Michael Bruxner [q.v.7] appointed Hartigan commissioner for railways on 29 December. The selection of F. C. Garside [q.v.] as assistant-commissioner appeased the largely Protestant senior ranks of the service, but Hartigan's religion was to remain an issue during his commissionership.

The financial position of the railways improved marginally in the mid-1930s and Hartigan was able to keep critics at bay by pointing to improvements in revenue. In 1936 he was appointed C.M.G. The drought and the 1938 coalminers' strike had adverse effects on the service. Despite the introduction of major economies, and higher charges for fares and freights in March 1939, earnings fell, staff were retrenched and Hartigan was publicly criticized. None the less, he was appointed for a second term on 29 December. He moved quickly to place the railways on a war footing and was largely responsible for preparing for the immense increase in traffic that occurred in 1942-44. From December 1941 he chaired the (Commonwealth) War Railway Committee which co-ordinated services nationally.

After 1945 the substantial surpluses from wartime revenue dwindled. Strikes created chronic shortages of coal; a backlog of maintenance—deferred during the war—began to affect the reliability of equipment; and competition from road and air transport heightened. Workers demanded improvements in pay and conditions. Hartigan's 'gift of the gab' and personal charm, which had helped him achieve generally good relations with the unions, could not prevent a dramatic rise in the number of industrial disputes. His retirement on 1 October 1948 may have saved him from being made a scapegoat for the railways' problems. Yet his management had been competent and the decline of the service had resulted from circumstances over which he had little or no control.

A man of robust health, Hartigan enjoyed an active retirement and continued a long involvement with the Gordon Cricket Club. He died on 2 May 1963 at Mosman and was buried in Northern Suburbs cemetery; his wife, two daughters and two sons survived him.

D. Aitkin, *The Colonel* (Canb, 1969); D. Burke, *Man of Steam* (Syd, 1986); J. Gunn, *Along Parallel Lines* (Melb, 1989).　　　　　　R. M. AUDLEY

HARTLEY, FRANCIS JOHN (1909-1971), Methodist clergyman and peace activist, was born on 11 March 1909 at Rutherglen, Victoria, second of four children of Australian-born parents Francis Robert Hartley, engine driver, and his wife Minnie Annie Theresa, née Green, both active members of the Methodist Church. Soon after his birth the family moved to the Gippsland coalmining town of Wonthaggi where his father worked as a winch driver before opening a tailoring and pressing business.

Frank was educated at the local state and technical schools, and became a proficient artist. With his father's help, at the age of 16 he opened a mercer's shop. He was influenced by both the Methodist Church and the coalmining culture of the town, personified in his mentor Idris Williams [q.v.]. From 1930 Hartley studied at Otira training college and Queen's College, University of Melbourne (B.A. Hons, 1938). He entered the ministry in 1938. At Queen's College chapel on 8 April 1939 he married Marion Forrest Hamilton Thomson Lyon, a Scottish-born missionary and stenographer. His first posting was to the Methodist church at Orbost.

Church and family life were disrupted by the outbreak of World War II. Appointed chaplain in the Australian Imperial Force on 22 August 1941, Hartley served with the 7th Divisional Cavalry Regiment in the Middle East (1941-42) and in the fighting along the Sanananda Track, Papua, in December 1942-January 1943. His book, *Sanananda Interlude* (Melbourne, 1949), documented the tragedy, danger and comradeship of the campaign. In 1943-44 he was a senior chaplain at 7th Division headquarters in New Guinea. He was mentioned in dispatches (1943) and transferred to the Reserve of Officers in December 1945.

Posted to suburban Murrumbeena, Hartley resumed his course (which had been interrupted by the war) at the Melbourne College of Divinity (B.D., 1949). As for many servicemen, readjustment to family and work was not easy. His determination to prevent another war led to an alliance with Rev. Alf Dickie (Presbyterian) and Rev. Victor James (Unitarian). The three became known as 'the peace trinity'. They founded the Australian Peace Council in 1949 and in 1950 organized an Australian Peace Congress in Melbourne.

Hartley's public involvement in peace issues in the Cold War period eroded his popularity as a war hero, especially in the Church. In 1951 he was transferred to the Newport Methodist Church, in the western suburbs, where he found more freedom for his wider activities. That year he attended a meeting in Vienna of the World Peace Council—to which he had been elected a member in 1950—and also visited Rome, Prague and Moscow. His pamphlet, *In Quest of Peace* (c.1952), emphasized the importance of his meetings with the Czech theologian Joseph Hromadka. On his return, Hartley was president of the Democratic Rights Council (founded 1948) which opposed the banning of the Communist Party of Australia. Prime Minister (Sir) Robert Menzies [q.v.] labelled him the 'pink parson'.

Short and stocky, with spectacles and thinning hair, Hartley was a regular speaker on the Yarra Bank. He worked tirelessly for the peace movement in the 1950s, helping to organize the Australian Convention on Peace and War (1953), a church commission report on peace and an Australian Charter of Freedom (1954), as well as travelling to international meetings of the World Peace Council. In 1955 he accepted the additional responsibilities of superintendent of the Prahran Methodist Mission. While there, he promoted community-based services—some in partnership with the voluntary sector and local government—including Meals on Wheels, homes for the aged, crèches, opportunity shops, the Somers [q.v.12] Youth Camp and the Tyabb Training Farm.

Criticism of the Australian Peace Council as a communist front gathered momentum after the organization was proscribed by the Australian Labor Party in 1954. Hartley was described as a 'fellow traveller' for his stands on foreign policy. During the Australia and New Zealand Congress for International Co-operation and Disarmament, held in Melbourne in 1959, the organizers, especially Hartley, Dickie and Samuel Goldbloom, were portrayed by the conservative press as pawns of the Soviet Union. The conference was well attended, however, and resulted in a spirited discussion of issues, especially nuclear disarmament. It marked the high point of the postwar peace movement in Australia. In 1965 Hartley and Dickie were awarded the Joliot-Curie gold medal by the World Peace Council.

The stress of these years affected Hartley's health and he suffered a stroke in 1965 while *en route* to the Helsinki Peace Conference. Undeterred, he won election to the Prahran City Council on a community platform in 1969. He died of cardiac failure on 5 July 1971 at Prahran and was cremated; his wife, daughter and three sons survived him. Hartley was an internationally recognized polemicist for peace in the postwar period; although his advocacy lacked an intellectual dimension, his deep commitment survived formidable opposition.

M. Hartley, *The Truth Shall Prevail* (Melb, 1982); *Aust Left Review*, Apr-May 1967, p 55; Hartley papers (Univ Melb Archives).

RENATE HOWE

HARTUNG, ERNST JOHANNES (1893-1979), professor of chemistry and astronomer, was born on 23 April 1893 at Caulfield, Melbourne, second son of five children of Carl August Ernst Hartung, musician, and his wife Ida Emilie, née Hagenauer. Carl had come to Melbourne from Leipzig, Germany, after fighting in the Franco-Prussian war. His wife was the Victorian-born daughter of F. A. Hagenauer [q.v.4], a Moravian missionary.

Ernst was educated at Wesley College, a school which had produced Walter Rosenhain, (Sir) David Rivett [qq.v.11] and William Sutherland [q.v.12], all of whom became distinguished scientists. At the University of Melbourne, Hartung graduated (B.Sc., 1913; D.Sc., 1919) with first-class honours, and won the Dixson, Kernot and Wyselaskie [qq.v.8,5,6] scholarships. In 1919 he was appointed to a lectureship at the university. World War I had denied him an opportunity to undertake postgraduate studies in Britain or Europe, but in 1922 (Sir) David Masson [q.v.10] and Rivett enabled him to spend twelve months on salary at University College, London. On 25 November that year he married Gladys Gray at the register office, St Giles.

Throughout his long career Hartung was enthralled by light and colour in all their manifestations. Like the Greeks, 'he had the genius to be astonished'. His love of the Australian bushland, first developed on boyhood holidays at Ramahyuck, an Aboriginal reserve in Gippsland founded by his father-in-law, and also at Strathfieldsaye, the home of his cousin Clive Disher [q.v.], was intensified by family friendships with J. W. Lindt [q.v.5], whose mastery of the photography of forest scenes at Narbethong he strove to emulate. In 1926 Hartung's research on the photo-decomposition of silver halides was awarded the David Syme [q.v.6] prize. Demonstrating chemical phenomena to large undergraduate classes, Hartung developed to a high degree the use of screen projections and published *The Screen Projection of Chemical Experiments* (1953). In 1935 he achieved an ambition to record the various forms of Brownian movement in colloidal solution on 35 mm cinefilm, which was copied, with permission, by the Eastman Kodak Co. onto 16 mm film for its World Science Library.

In 1928 Hartung had succeeded Rivett in the chair of chemistry; he held it until 1953. Over this period he devoted much time to the university extension lecture scheme, and, in the 1930s, to the design and construction of a large, new chemistry building. Of tall, spare build, he presented a somewhat stern image to the student body; inspiring respect rather than affection, he was a strict, though fair, disciplinarian. His lecturing style surged with enthusiasm. Hearing his account of a test million-volt flash-over which he had witnessed at Teddington, England, Rivett assured the audience that Hartung's description was even more impressive than the original.

During World War I, Hartung had been ineligible for military service due to defective eyesight, but he made a useful contribution to the local provision of gas masks. Masson, W. A. Osborne [q.v.11] and T. H. Laby [q.v.9] comprised the committee charged with the design task. According to Hartung, Masson was incensed by the action of the 'never-equable' Laby in complaining directly to the attorney-general W. M. Hughes [q.v.9] about the work of his colleagues. The rift which ensued between chemistry and physics lasted until World War II when Laby was chairman of the Optical Munitions Panel. In this capacity he approached Hartung to chair the advisory committee on optical materials, asking if optical glass of the requisite quality and properties could be made in Australia. Hartung proceeded to produce trial batches, using local raw materials for the crucibles and melts, which met the exacting specification. Subsequent large-scale production by Australia Consolidated Industries Ltd under the dynamic leadership of the redoubtable W. J. 'Gunboat' Smith [q.v.11] confounded British experts, production being achieved within ten months instead of the predicted four years, and at a cost of £60 000 instead of the forecast £1 million. 'After that', said Hartung, 'we chemists were Laby's white-haired boys'.

Hartung contributed to other branches of organized science as general president (1927-28, 1929-30 and 1931-33) of the (Royal) Australian Chemical Institute, ex-officio councillor (1943-48) of the Council for Scientific and Industrial Research, and trustee (1950-55) of the Museum of Applied Science, Melbourne. He represented Australia in 1931 at the centenary meeting of the British Association for the Advancement of Science, and in 1941 at the Royal Society and Commonwealth Scientific conferences. Apart from bushwalking associated with photographic excursions, he had no outdoor recreation, except that associated with his presidency, for many years, of the university football club. His stiff, formal academic reserve tended to be put aside during the excitement of the game.

Early retirement in 1953 was part of Hartung's determination to live to his eighties with faculties unimpaired. At his farm at Woodend he established an observatory (30 cm Newtonian reflector). His study of some 4000 stellar objects gave rise to *Astronomical Objects for Southern Telescopes . . . a handbook for amateur observers* (London, 1968); the work had involved countless hours of observation in freezing conditions, a severe test of his great physical stamina.

In his twenty-five years of retirement Hartung was the complete naturalist and warmly accepted as sage of the district. His explicit ambition to remain alive to view the total eclipse of 1976 was fulfilled, as was his cheerful prognostication that the return of Halley's Comet in 1986 would lie beyond his span. Survived by his wife and two daughters, he died on 30 January 1979 at Parkville and was cremated. He was spared the sadness of the total destruction of his beloved Lavender Farm by the Ash Wednesday fires of 1983 when his meticulous diary of some 7000 pages was consumed; only a short copy-excerpt remains.

D. P. Mellor, *The Role of Science and Industry* (Canb, 1958); R. Rivett, *David Rivett* (Melb, 1972); J. Radford, *The Chemistry Department of the University of Melbourne* (Melb, 1978); L. W. Weickhardt, *Masson of Melbourne* (Melb, 1989); *Chemistry in Aust*, 46, no 5, May 1979, p 219; Hartung papers (Univ Melb Archives); family information.   L. W. WEICKHARDT

HARVEY, HENRY JAMES (1901-1966), trade unionist and industrial commissioner, was born on 19 November 1901 in South Brisbane, son of Peter James Harvey, fireman, and his wife Elizabeth Teresa, née O'Toole, both Queensland born. Educated at West End State School, he joined the Department of Lands as a cadet clerk on 13 December 1915 and attended night-classes. From an early age, he had been aware of the labour movement through his father's union activities. After leaving the public service in February 1920, Harry was periodically unemployed; following a brief stint as a hairdresser, he worked as a stoker at the Murrarie meatworks. He joined the Federated Engine Drivers and Firemen's Association of Australasia, rapidly rising to president (1922) of its Brisbane sub-branch. In 1923-33 he was caretaker of the Brisbane Trades Hall where he also served as librarian (until 1935). At St Francis's Catholic Church, West End, on 18 January 1930 he had married Wilhelmina Rowe, a tailoress.

In 1935 Harvey was elected secretary of the Queensland Trades and Labor Council. His activities at Trades Hall involved him with the Federated Miscellaneous Workers' Union and in August 1938 he resigned his T.L.C. post to become secretary of the F.M.W.U. In this capacity he represented a wide variety of occupations, including caretakers, cleaners, messengers, lift-attendants, watchmen, gatekeepers, greenkeepers and even billposters. He was by then identified as a moderate union leader, which assisted his election as T.L.C. president in July 1939, when he won by a record majority against the communist candidate E. J. Hanson. By the time he resigned in 1948 to concentrate on F.M.W.U. duties, communist officials dominated the Brisbane T.L.C. Aligned with the Australian Labor Party, Harvey felt that he lacked support from certain moderate trade unions in the fight against communist control. During World War II ill health precluded him from serving with the armed forces, but he was energetically involved in wartime civil service. In May 1942 he was appointed to the trade union advisory panel of the Federal Manpower Committee. That year he became an air-raid warden. He was a member (1943-45) of the royal commission which recommended the establishment of a central authority to control the production and marketing of fruit and vegetables in the State.

Harvey had been the F.M.W.U. delegate to the Queensland central executive of the A.L.P. in 1928-35. He was a member (1947-49) and vice-president (1948-49) of the party's executive-committee. From 1935 he moved towards the politics of moderation. At the 1932 Labor Convention he had insisted that a Labor government should legislate directly on behalf of workers. In 1947 it was his amendment of a similarly contentious motion which defused a potential clash between industrial and political wings of the party. Although he planned to enter Federal parliament, he withdrew his nomination for the seat of Bowman in 1949 due to 'health reasons'. He was a long-time friend of Premier Ned Hanlon [q.v.] who, in November, appointed him a commissioner of the Industrial Court of Queensland. On the bench Harvey's negotiating skills came to the fore. Whether the dispute involved rail, sugar, transport or electricity workers, he won considerable praise from all sections of the industrial community and the media for his patience and consultative abilities. He was adept at operating behind the industrial and political scenes. Assigned to the northern circuit, he handled three major disputes at Mount Isa mines in 1959, 1961 and 1964-65. The last-mentioned strike—a bitter, divisive battle that lasted eight months—tested his conciliatory skills and took its toll on his health.

A short, thickset man, Harvey was not rancorous by nature; his life revolved around his work and his family. He was a member of the (Royal) Brisbane and South Coast hospitals board, and of the senate (1944-52) of the University of Queensland. He also contributed articles to newspapers, and took part in debates on radio and television. Survived by his wife, son and daughter, he died of myocardial infarction on 7 June 1966 in Royal Brisbane Hospital and was buried in Toowoong cemetery.

C. Lack (comp), *Three Decades of Queensland Political History, 1929-1960* (Brisb, 1962); G. Sheldon, *Industrial Siege* (Melb, 1965); D. J. Murphy (ed), *Labor in Power* (Brisb, 1980) and *The Big Strikes* (Brisb, 1983); P. Mackie and E. Vassileff, *Mount Isa* (Melb, 1989); *Courier-Mail*, 23 Mar, 6, 13 Apr, 9 May 1949; *Telegraph* (Brisb), 9 June 1955; Trades and Labor Council of Qld, Executive Minutes, 1932-38 (Fryer L, Univ Qld); information from, and papers held by Mrs V. Cusack, Aspley, Brisb; documents and news-clippings held by Mr K. Edwards, Geebung, Brisb; information from Mr C. Jones, Windsor, Brisb.　　　　TIM MORONEY

HARVEY, HUBERT HAROLD (1913-1968), sharebroker, was born on 30 November 1913 at Pennington, Port Adelaide, second child of Harold Hernett Harvey, foreman, and his wife Una Frances, née Harrington, both South Australian-born. Educated at Woodville High School and Prince Alfred College (on a scholarship), Hubert worked briefly as a law clerk before the prospects of sharebroking attracted his adventurous spirit. He began as a clerk with Cutten & Co., a small Adelaide firm with Broken Hill connexions. Although lacking formal qualifications, he began to exhibit the extraordinary analytical skills which were to make him legendary in later life, and his energy and enthusiasm impressed his employers. In January 1941, at the age of 27, he was admitted to partnership. On 27 May 1939 at the Methodist Church, Malvern, he had married Constance Norma Oakley, a typist.

Commissioned lieutenant in the Australian Army Service Corps on 24 December 1942, Harvey transferred to the Australian Imperial Force and served at Milne Bay, Papua, with the 2nd Bulk Petrol Storage Company in 1943-44. His appointment was terminated on medical grounds on 4 January 1945.

In August 1943 Harvey had bought a seat on the Stock Exchange of Adelaide. A big man, 6 ft 3 ins (191 cm) tall, with a commanding and engaging personality, great energy and confidence, he returned to professional life and rapidly built a powerful base of commercial contacts in Adelaide and interstate, strengthening and developing relationships with sharebrokers and companies. In July 1946 the firm was named Cutten & Harvey. He was also active in the Junior Chamber of Commerce as national president (1947) and international vice-president (1950). The expanding postwar economy and heavier taxation encouraged family-owned and private companies to seek additional capital through a stock-exchange listing. A persuasive salesman with a flair for balanced risk-taking, Harvey seized the opportunities and soon became the predominant underwriter of capital issues in Adelaide, both for new public floats and for capital raisings by existing companies and

semi-government authorities. By July 1953 he was sole proprietor of his sharebroking business, the largest in Adelaide. He took on three partners in 1955-58, but remained senior partner until his death.

Having floated the fledgling oil-exploration firm, Santos Ltd, in 1954, he was appointed a director and its main financial adviser in 1957; almost single-handed, he raised the capital necessary to keep the company afloat until the discovery in 1963 of natural gas at Gidgealpa. While visiting New York in October 1957 to negotiate with American oil companies for joint-ventures in Santos's leases, he had fallen ill with a perforated ulcer which caused permanent heart damage. After five months he recovered sufficiently to return home, but suffered from severe angina for the remainder of his life. Although slightly tempering his workload, he pursued his interests with characteristic zeal and was a director of United Motors (Holdings) Ltd, Coca-Cola Bottlers and the Natural Gas Pipelines Authority of South Australia. He also owned a grazing property near Keith and invested in a tropical pasture-seed plantation by the Adelaide River, Northern Territory. Power-boating, water-skiing and horse-racing were among his recreations; his best racehorse, Arctic Coast, won the Australian Cup and the Duke of Norfolk Stakes in 1968.

In 1962 he had established the Hubert Harvey Public Charitable Fund; during the next twelve years it distributed over $200 000 to charities, of which $100 000 went to the Crippled Children's Association of South Australia. Survived by his wife, son and two daughters, Harvey died of a coronary occlusion on 17 August 1968 in Darwin and was cremated. His estate was sworn for probate in Victoria and South Australia at $974 399.

R. M. Gibbs, *Bulls, Bears and Wildcats* (Adel, 1988); N. Young, *Figuratively Speaking* (Adel, 1991); *News* (Adel), 17 Aug 1968, 18 June 1974.
　　　　　　　　　　　　　　IAN G. COLYER

HASZLER, CHARLES (1907-1973), medical practitioner, was born on 9 March 1907 at Levoča (Slovakia), then known as Lőcse and part of the Austro-Hungarian Empire, son of Károly Haszler, schoolteacher, and his wife Margit, née Toth. Charles (baptized Károly) was educated at the Humanistic Gymnasium, Budapest, and the University of Budapest (M.D., 1931). He was a member of staff at the university from 1928, first in the Institute of Pathological Anatomy and then in the No.2 Surgical Teaching Hospital. During this period he undertook research in Vienna (1932) and at Heidelberg, Germany (1936-37). Awarded a master's degree in surgery from Budapest in 1935, three years later he won a state commission for research. From 1942 he was chief surgeon at a large country hospital. On 22 October 1935 in Budapest he had married Maria Ilona von Wahlmann-Lüders in a civil ceremony, which was followed by a Catholic service on 2 November 1936.

In mid-1944 Haszler joined the Hungarian Army and served as a divisional surgeon on the Eastern Front. His unit surrendered on 2 May 1945 to American forces in Austria. He was a prisoner of war for two months. After his release he was employed as a surgeon in Bavaria by the American military government; he later worked for the United Nations Relief and Rehabilitation Administration, and for the International Refugee Organization. In 1949 he was accepted as an immigrant to Australia. *En route* he practised as a surgeon for three months in a displaced persons' hospital at Trani, Italy.

Arriving in Melbourne, Haszler took a job as a factory hand with General Motors-Holden's [q.v.9] Ltd at Fishermens Bend. On 15 January 1950 he was appointed to the Department of Public Health, Territory of Papua and New Guinea. At the end of World War II only eight doctors remained in the Territory which was suffering the effects of the war and the consequent neglect of medical work. Haszler was one of thirty-five doctors selected at the request of (Sir) John Gunther, director of public health, to re-estabish health services in Papua and New Guinea.

Haszler served as district medical officer in charge of Mount Hagen hospital until November when he was transferred to Port Moresby as assistant surgeon specialist. In 1953-55 he was assistant district medical officer at Madang. Naturalized in 1955, in the following year he was posted to Port Moresby as surgeon specialist. In 1958 he was transferred to Rabaul as regional medical officer for the New Guinea islands region, a position which entailed work in the areas of policy and administration. He obtained a diploma in tropical medicine and hygiene from the University of Sydney in 1959.

Appointed assistant-director (medical services) in Port Moresby in 1964, Haszler pioneered many initiatives: a local government health service, radio health education programmes, and, most importantly, the first rural health centres staffed and operated by Papuans and New Guineans. He was also responsible for establishing a tuberculosis hospital and for commencing an intensive malaria eradication programme with support schools to train technicians. His direct visits to aidposts and subsequent conferences with local government officials led to improved facilities at the outstations. The fulfilment of his medical ambitions came in the late 1960s with the opening of the Rabaul Community Health Centre.

A big man both physically and mentally, Haszler enjoyed the trust and respect of all who knew him. He and his wife had a deep appreciation of music and the arts, and encouraged Papua New Guinean efforts in these fields. Intolerant of political opportunists, he argued that the introduction of liberal licensing laws had not resulted in alcoholism among the indigenous people. He became the first president of the Papua and New Guinea Medical Society. His research into the disease *pig bel* proved helpful to public health officials.

In 1967 Haszler retired to Wahroonga, Sydney. Survived by his wife, son and daughter, he died of chronic renal failure on 8 September 1973 at Camperdown and was cremated.

E. F. Kunz, *The Intruders* (Canb, 1975) and *The Hungarians in Australia* (Melb, 1985) and *Displaced Persons* (Syd, 1988); *PNG Medical J*, 10, no 2, June 1967; *Sth Pacific Post*, 10 Nov 1950, 1 June 1966, 24 Sept 1973; Haszler photographic collection (NL); family papers (held by Mrs C. Lewis, Roseville, Syd, and Mr H. Haszler, Eltham, Melb); information from the late Mrs M. I. Haszler.

ALBERT SPEER

HATELEY, MARTHA MADGE (1906-1950), air force matron, was born on 13 May 1906 at Murtoa, Victoria, eldest of six children of native-born parents Harry Charles Hector Hateley, farmer, and his wife Ethel, née Woodland. Educated at Murtoa State School, Madge helped on her parents' farm and was prominent in local community life. During the Depression she trained as a nurse at Horsham Base Hospital, then studied midwifery at Ballarat Base Hospital.

Following the outbreak of World War II, in June 1940 the minister for air J. V. Fairbairn [q.v.8] approved the formation of the Royal Australian Air Force Nursing Service. It was to comprise 616 nurses by December 1945. Hateley applied for entry in September 1940 and was appointed staff nurse on 21 October 1941. She served at No.2 R.A.A.F. Hospital, Ascot Vale, Melbourne, before transferring to No.1 R.A.A.F. Hospital, Laverton (later relocated at Wagga Wagga, New South Wales). Promoted sister, group II, on 1 April 1942, she joined No.1 Medical Receiving Station, Daly Waters, Northern Territory, on 6 May. She assisted in major operations performed by the mobile surgical unit; by the end of that month she had helped to care for 131 patients, among them Australian and American armed forces personnel, and Aboriginal and White civilians. In September the station was moved to a new site at Coomalie Creek where canvas marquees were used until new wards were built of bush timber and iron.

Japanese bombers attacked nearby Batchelor in October and the Coomalie airstrip (adjacent to the medical receiving station) in November. The nurses had been ordered to dye their white uniforms in tea to produce a drab colour for camouflage. Heat, insects and electrical storms added to the miserable conditions of the North-Western Area, but the nurses found some relief by occasionally visiting an open-air picture theatre or by attending dances in Darwin, 50 miles (80 km) to the north: due to the scarcity of women as partners, they were on their feet for most of the night. In August 1943 Hateley returned to No.2 R.A.A.F. Hospital where, as senior sister (from 1 December 1944), she had charge of the isolation block. She was posted to No.4 R.A.A.F. Hospital, East Sale, Victoria, in April 1946 and to No.3 R.A.A.F. Hospital, Concord, Sydney, in August. Promoted temporary matron in January 1947, she became provisional matron in September 1948.

Matron Hateley was of slender build and middle height, with fair hair and slightly angular features. Her appearance was immaculate. In 1945 she had been appointed an associate of the Royal Red Cross for her 'outstanding service' in working 'tirelessly and with the utmost cheerfulness' under trying circumstances. Next year she attended Government House, Melbourne, for the investiture. On 12 August 1949 in Sydney her air force appointment was terminated because of ill health. She died of cancer on 11 June 1950 at the Repatriation General Hospital, Concord, and was cremated with Presbyterian forms. Her sister Doris served as an army nurse before working in infant welfare.

They Wrote it Themselves (Melb, 1946); AWM 64 item 53/3, AWM 137 item 2.1 and 2.6, AWM 88; information from Miss D. M. Hateley, Altona, Melb.   HELEN BOXALL

HAUSLAIB, WILLIAM RUSSELL (1897-1970), businessman, was born on 18 May 1897 at Bucyrus, Ohio, United States of America, son of William Housleib, merchant, and his wife Sophia, née Meyers. Rus was educated at Bucyrus High School and in 1915 entered Western Reserve University, Cleveland. In World War I he served with the American Expeditionary Force on the Western Front. After his demobilization he attended the Wharton School of Finance and Commerce, University of Pennsylvania (B.S.E.). About 1921 he married Helen Springer in New York; they were later divorced. Hauslaib (as he spelt his surname) came to Sydney in 1935 when appointed managing director of the automotive importing firm, Ira L. & A. C. Berk Ltd, Australian agents for the Packard Motor Car Co. At St Stephen's Presbyterian Church, Macquarie Street, on 2 February 1937 he married A. C. Berk's daughter Vivienne Berk Audette, a widow with four children. In 1950 he became chairman of the firm.

From his early days in Sydney, Hauslaib took an active part in civic and business organizations, especially those involving American interests and the local American community. He was president (1939-40) of the Chamber of Automotive Industries of New South Wales, a member (1939-41) of the Federal Chamber of Automotive Industries and an executive-member of the Motor Traders' Association of New South Wales. During World War II he served (from 1941) on the State Liquid Fuel Control Board. In 1958 he was appointed chevalier of the Ordre du Mérite Commercial by the French government for fostering trade between France and Australia. While president (1959-60) of the Rotary Club of Sydney, he organized a campaign for more street signs and for visible numbers on every house to assist the police, ambulance and fire brigade. He was president (1946-47) of the Australian-American Association and a director (from 1949) of the United States Educational Foundation in Australia.

His most lasting contribution to the community was made as foundation treasurer (1947) and president (1950-67) of the American National Club. The fledgling club, located in an historic terrace house at 129 Macquarie Street, was established to provide a place to enhance relationships and to promote goodwill in Australian-American commercial dealings. As the club grew, it was able to acquire adjoining buildings on either side. In 1962 a deal was negotiated with a French company, Citra Australia, which purchased the real estate and built a sixteen-storey building—the first high-rise in Macquarie Street—with the club owning and using the top three levels.

Hauslaib also belonged to Tattersall's Club. He enjoyed gardening at his Point Piper home and surfing. Survived by his wife, he died on 29 November 1970 in Royal Prince Alfred Hospital and was cremated; his estate was sworn for probate at $282 443. The American National Club became the American Club of Sydney in 1989 and occupies the same premises.

The First Thirty Years of the American National Club 1947-1977 (Syd, 1977); *MTA Official J*, 15 Jan 1939, p 17, 15 Feb 1941, p 17; *SMH*, 27 May 1936, 19 Jan 1940, 26 July 1941, 14 June 1947, 7 Feb 1950, 8 July, 27 Oct 1959, 4 Mar 1960, 9 Sept 1971; family and personal information.   JAMES H. COLEMAN

HAVILAND, STANLEY (1899-1972), public servant, was born on 13 April 1899 at Kogarah, Sydney, fourth son of native-born parents Cecil Henry Haviland, clerk, and his wife Emily, née Shaw. Educated at Cleveland Street Superior School, Stanley joined the public service in 1915; he became a junior clerk in the Department of Lands and, from 1920, a clerk in the Department of Local Government. On 16 November that year at the Methodist Church, Glen Innes, he married Florence Mary Nunn.

Following the amalgamation of the departments of Public Works and Local Government, Haviland was appointed assistant under-secretary on 1 November 1936. When the departments were separated in 1941, he retained his post in Local Government until promoted under-secretary and permanent head in October 1946. At a time of expansion and extraordinary growth in local government enterprise, he proved an efficient administrator. He served (1945-46) on the royal commission into the boundaries of local government areas in the County of Cumberland, championed stronger local government and advocated the amalgamation of councils. On his retirement in 1960, he was presented with a bound volume containing individual messages of goodwill from over two hundred shire, municipal and county councils.

In a busy and distinguished career Haviland belonged to many boards associated with various aspects of public life. He chaired several committees that were connected with the 1951 Commonwealth of Australia Jubilee and with the 1954 royal visit; he also chaired the Sydney Opera House Executive Committee (1954-61)—which advised the premier on the selection of the site, the design and the construction of the opera house —and the Sydney Opera House Trust (1961-69). In 1957 he was appointed C.B.E. His other interests included the Library Board of New South Wales (on which he served in 1946-60), the State councils of the Royal Institute of Public Administration and the National Trust of Australia, the board of the Australian Elizabethan Theatre Trust, and the Australian Museum and Royal National Park trusts.

Haviland was part-time vice-president (1955-57) and full-time president (1960-65) of the Metropolitan Water, Sewerage and Drainage Board. He promoted staff relations, eased formality, and was involved in improving and beautifying picnic areas at the board's dams. At times, however, he remained a controversial figure because of his silence over criticism of the opera house and the fluoridation of Sydney's water supply. An active Rotarian (1948-72) and president (1958-71) of the St George area of the Boy Scouts' Association, he was a devoted family man, affable,

short and stocky. Haviland was keen on outdoor pursuits, particularly swimming, fishing and bowls. He was meticulous in the layout of his workshop, and the care of his car, his aviaries and his fernery.

Remaining active, he served (1965-67) on the royal commission that inquired into rating, valuation and local government finance; the government accepted its recommendation to establish the Local Government Grants Commission. Ten months after the death of his wife, Haviland died suddenly on 2 June 1972 at his Kingsgrove home and was cremated. His son survived him.

H. E. Maiden, *The History of Local Government in New South Wales* (Syd, 1966); F. A. Larcombe, *The Advancement of Local Government in New South Wales 1906 to the Present* (Syd, 1978); *Syd Water Bd J*, Apr 1955, Oct 1960, Oct 1972; *SMH*, 22 June 1966, 5 June 1972; information from Mr O. Haviland, Willoughby, Mr J. M. Collocott, Castle Cove, Miss R. Williams, Manly, Syd, and Mr A. Morse, Bathurst, NSW.   JACK WATSON

HAWKER, BERTRAM ROBERT (1868-1952), Anglican clergyman, educationist and benefactor, was born on 29 March 1868 at Llandudno, Carnavonshire, Wales, youngest of sixteen children of George Charles Hawker [q.v.4], who had been born in London and become a politician and grazier in South Australia, and his wife Bessie, née Seymour, from Ireland. Bertram was educated at Glenalmond School, Perthshire, Scotland (1882-86), and at Trinity Hall, Cambridge (B.A., 1891; M.A., 1896). He worked with the poor in the East End of London and was made deacon in 1894. After serving as a curate at Stone, Kent, he was appointed honorary chaplain to the bishop of Adelaide in 1895. At St Peter's Cathedral, Adelaide, on 23 July 1896 Hawker married Constance Victoria, daughter of Sir Thomas Buxton [q.v.7], the governor of South Australia. Returning to England, Hawker held curacies in Surrey and Cumberland before being ordained priest on 10 June 1900. For the next four years he was vicar at Isel, Cumberland, his last Church appointment. From 1908 he lived on the Buxton estate, Runton Old Hall, near Cromer, Norfolk.

In 1905, while holidaying in Sydney, Hawker had visited a special school for young children of families living at Woolloomooloo. Convinced that similar institutions were needed in the depressed residential districts of Adelaide, he arranged a series of demonstrations of kindergarten methods at The Briars, his parents' home in the Adelaide suburb of Medindie, and in the Exhibition Building. He claimed that 'childhood play was a powerful vehicle for the formation of social responsibility, ethical awareness, selfdiscipline and other personal and citizenship qualities'. In September he chaired a meeting at the University of Adelaide which founded the Kindergarten Union of South Australia to educate the children of the poor. Its first kindergarten, for children aged 3 to 6, was opened in Franklin Street in February 1906 and was followed by others, all free and privately funded. Independent from the state education system, the kindergartens could be flexible and innovative.

Hawker travelled to Rome in 1911 and called at Maria Montessori's *casa dei bambine*. Impressed with what he saw, he returned to England and set up a Montessori school near his home. Montessori's principles were also adopted by the K.U.S.A., to which Hawker donated £500—£100 for its building fund and £400 to enable the principal Lillian de Lissa [q.v.8] to study in Europe and the United States of America. In 1914 she stayed with Hawker and was opening speaker at the Montessori conference he organized at East Runton.

After World War I he performed voluntary work in Vienna for the Save the Children Fund, London. From 1924 he was a patron of the International Student Movement and he also helped Kurt Hahn to establish (1934) Gordonstoun School, Moray, Scotland. Hawker continued visiting South Australia until 1938, usually staying at Bungaree station where his family affectionately called him 'Uncle Bolshie'. A gentle, sensitive man with a sense of fun, he disliked publicity and never accepted a salary, financial reward or recognition for his work. He liked cooking, gardening and riding; much of his income came from a conserving factory at Lubeck, West Germany, in which he held shares. Survived by his wife and one of his two sons, he died on 14 October 1952 at Thaxted, Essex. His estate was sworn for probate in England and South Australia at £86 197.

C. Dowd, *Adelaide Kindergarten Teachers College*, 1907-1974 (Adel, 1983); T. T. Reed, *Anglican Clergymen in South Australia in the Nineteenth Century* (Gumeracha, SA, 1986); *World's Children*, Nov-Dec 1952, p 227; Dept of Education (SA), *Pivot*, 6, no 3, 1979; *Advertiser*(Adel), 20 Oct 1952; *The Times*, 17 Oct 1952; information from Prof K. J. Cable, Randwick, Syd, Mrs J. Hawker, Clare, SA, and Mr H. Hawker, Wandsworth, Lond, and the late Mr M. S. Hawker.   Dirk van Dissel
     Mary E. B. van Dissel

HAWKINS, HAROLD FREDERICK WEAVER (1893-1977), painter, was born on 28 August 1893 at Sydenham, London, eldest of five sons of Edgar Augustine Hawkins,

architect, and his wife Annie Elizabeth, née Weaver. The cultivated, progressive, but unhappily married parents separated when Harold was 8, after which the boy shared a parental role with his father, a vegetarian and a Fabian, who spoke Esperanto fluently and was severe. In 1906-10 Harold attended Dulwich College where he won the art prize every year. He then proceeded to Camberwell School of Arts and Crafts intending to qualify as an art teacher, but enlisted on 20 April 1914 in the Queen's Westminster Rifles, in premonition of war.

Sent to the Western Front, Hawkins was seriously wounded at Gommecourt, France, on 1 July 1916: 'The whole place roaring with flames, a wonderful sight . . . gas . . . we were to be a sacrificial attack . . . all the men with me were killed . . . I crawled back for two days'. A series of twenty operations saved his arms from amputation, though his right hand remained lifeless and the left became a less-than-full-strength painting hand. After his discharge on 3 February 1919, a disability pension supported his modest needs. In London in 1919-22 he studied at the Westminster Technical Institute and School of Art, and took additional etching classes with Sir Frank Short; he bought a house at Barons Court and there his tenants included his friends Frank Medworth [q.v.] and the painter and poet David Jones. Hawkins's own, mostly unpublished, writing included poetry and a manuscript account of his life, 'My Philosophy' (1968).

In 1923 he held his first solo exhibition and saw his work displayed in the Royal Academy of Arts. On 15 September that year at All Saints parish church, Kensington, he married Irene (Rene) Eleanor Villiers, a 21-year-old artist. For most of the next ten years they lived by the Mediterranean, initially at St Tropez, France (1923-25). Back in England in 1926, he disliked press notices which emphasized his disability; in Malta (1927-30) he adopted the art-name 'Raokin', with which he signed his paintings after 1927, but his working name soon reverted to Weaver Hawkins.

At la Seyne, France (1930-33), Hawkins observed war preparations at nearby Toulon. With his family, he visited Tahiti and Wellington before arriving in Sydney in March 1935 and settling at Mona Vale. Australia became the place for quiet years focussed on his three children. In England he had been called 'a modern Hogarth' for his depictions of everyday working life and leisure; in outer suburban Sydney these subjects became tender and domestic. Morris West met him and recalled: 'My immediate impression was of a quite extraordinary male beauty—fine-boned, bearded visage, with clear untroubled eyes and a ready smile . . . a man at peace with himself and his world'. Usually wearing his home-made leather sandals, Hawkins never donned a tie. He said, 'we are rationalists, socialists and nonconformists'.

Between 1941 and 1972 (when he ceased to paint) he exhibited widely, especially with the Contemporary Art Society of Australia (State president 1952, 1954-63) and the Sydney Printmakers. Hawkins entered works for the Archibald, Sulman [qq.v.3,12] and Wynne prizes, and for the Blake prize for religious art, though he was an agnostic. Solo exhibitions were held at the Macquarie Galleries and elsewhere in 1946-68. In 1953 he was awarded Queen Elizabeth II's coronation medal. His work entered a few public collections and won minor prizes from 1950, but not until a 1976 retrospective exhibition at the Art Gallery of New South Wales did he begin to be assessed as a major artist. After 1958 he lived on the North Shore. Survived by his wife, daughter and two sons, he died on 13 August 1977 at Willoughby and was cremated. Several self-portraits are held by the Raokin Collection, Sydney.

Hawkins's ambitious, sometimes mural-sized, modernist allegories of morality for an age of atomic warfare and global over-population had been so uncommon in Australia when painted that most of his fellow artists were embarrassed by his art. His hardness of form was sometimes assumed to be a result of his injuries, but informal drawings (seldom exhibited) proved that his touch was delicate and sensitive. While his disability might have stimulated his unusual interest in subjects of strenuous work and play, it was his tough mind which chiefly created order out of chaos in works which he hoped might help to make the world a better place: 'I hold that it is possible to create beauty with the intellect'.

D. Thomas, *Project 11: Weaver Hawkins*, exhibition cat (Syd, 1976); E. Chanin and S. Miller, *The Art and Life of Weaver Hawkins* (Syd, 1995); H. de Berg, Weaver Hawkins (taped interview, Dec 1965, NL); Hawkins papers (Art Gallery of NSW L, Syd).   DANIEL THOMAS

HAWKINS, THOMAS JOSEPH (1898-1976), public servant, was born on 15 November 1898 at Carlton, Melbourne, second of ten children of Thomas Hawkins, a detective in the police force, and his wife Mary Frances, née Nash, both Victorian born. Educated at St George's School, Carlton, and St Patrick's College, East Melbourne, young Tom was appointed a staff clerk at Navy Office on 16 August 1915, two years after the formation of the Australian fleet. He studied part time at the University of Melbourne (B.A., 1921;

LL.B., 1926). Slim and 5 ft 11 ins (180 cm) tall, in 1921-29 he played first-grade district cricket in turn for Fitzroy and Carlton as a medium-fast bowler.

During his career, which was to be wholly in naval administration, Hawkins was associated with seventeen ministers for the navy and fourteen chiefs of Naval Staff, beginning with Rear Admiral Sir William Creswell [q.v.8]. By 1939 Hawkins had risen to head 'N' Branch and in that capacity contributed to the part played by the Royal Australian Navy in World War II. He provided the secretariat to the Naval Staff, and was responsible for the main signal office and its cyphering work. In 1948 he succeeded G. L. Macandie [q.v.10] as assistant-secretary and in 1950 took over from A. R. Nankervis [q.v.] as secretary of the Department of the Navy. Hawkins was appointed C.B.E. in 1955.

Endowed with intellect, he could be impatient with lesser minds, and his fiery denunciations of shoddy work were legendary. Hawkins had a high regard for the naval profession and remained watchful for any denigration of its civilian element by those who were poorly informed. As secretary, he ensured that the navy's requirements were properly formulated, then strenuously protected the service's interests against the claims of other government departments. Some naval officers mistook his fighting qualities for hostility, but most—outstandingly Vice Admiral Sir John Collins—valued his support.

Hawkins's experience with ministers for the navy underwent a startling change when Senator (Sir) John Gorton assumed the portfolio in 1958; whereas his predecessors had conducted business from a distance, Gorton immersed himself in the whole range of naval affairs, working full time in Navy Office which was moved to Canberra in 1959. Hawkins earned Gorton's approbation for accommodating this massive change.

At the Church of St John the Baptist, Clifton Hill, Melbourne, on 16 August 1924 Hawkins had married Kathleen Monica Burke, a graduate of the University of Melbourne who taught French in secondary schools. Gently and with humour, she softened her husband's tempestuousness. She lived until 1994, gracious and much loved by their four sons and three daughters, and many 'grands' and 'great-grands'. After his retirement in 1963, Hawkins had returned to Melbourne where he continued his lifelong attachment to the Catholic Church, becoming the parish accountant at East Brighton and a director (1964-76) of the Villa Maria Society for the Blind. He died on 18 September 1976 at Malvern; following a service conducted by his brother Fr James Hawkins, S.J., he was buried in Melbourne general cemetery.

R. Hyslop, *Aye Aye, Minister* (Canb, 1990); M. Pratt, interview with T. J. Hawkins, 1956 (ts, oral history section, NL); R. Hyslop, interviews with Sir John Gorton *and* Sir John Collins, 1988 (tss, AWM); information from Mr T. Hawkins, Chadstone, Melb.   ROBERT HYSLOP

HAY, MARGARET FORDYCE DALRYMPLE (1889-1975), clerk and librarian, was born on Christmas Eve 1889 at Rushcutters Bay, Sydney, eldest of six children of native-born parents Richard Dalrymple Hay, surveyor, and his wife Bessie, née Cheesbrough. Appointed to the Law School at the University of Sydney as a typist in June 1919, Margaret became clerk to the faculty in 1923 and took on the additional duties of law librarian in the following year. Because the Law School had part-time teaching staff, apart from the dean (Sir) John Peden and (from 1921) Professor A. H. Charteris [qq.v.11,7], she assumed a central role in its administration, especially when Peden had responsibilities in the Legislative Council.

A small, fair woman, with soft, sparkling eyes, Miss Hay was trim and efficient-looking in tailored skirts and jackets, soft blouses and colourful scarves. She was quick in mind and body, and impatient only at stupidity or bad manners. Although capable of striking dread in a nervous new employee, she inspired loyalty, respect and affection. A link between students and academics, she assisted the students' law society, was influential in the placement of articled clerks and graduates, and had a close relationship with members of the legal profession and the judiciary. She proposed the publication of *The Jubilee Book of the Law School* (1940), co-ordinated its preparation and initiated a collection of portraits of the staff.

In World War II Hay ran the Law School Comforts Fund which sent selected monthly parcels of books to legal men and law students serving in the forces; she also compiled the *Legal Digest*, a quarterly newsletter combining information on legislative changes and judgements with gossip about members of the profession at home and abroad. In addition, she worked tirelessly to assist those servicemen who were permitted to study law by correspondence, forwarding them teaching notes and textbooks, and arranging tutoring and examinations.

Hay became an associate-member of the National Council of Women of New South Wales and joined the National (later United Australia) Party. She was interested in genealogy and was widely read; Trollope was one of her favourite authors. The *Sydney Morning Herald* published several of her articles and she left some unpublished works, including a biography of Sir Thomas Bavin [q.v.7], a history of T. J. Thompson's family and stockbroking firm, and biographical notes on numerous members of the New South Wales Bar. Her writing revealed a lively—at times acerbic—wit, the skills of an observant raconteur, a generally uncritical appreciation of the legal profession, her patriotism and her political conservatism.

Bridging the gap from the small pre-war school to the large postwar faculty, Hay carried the corporate memory of Law School policy and philosophy, at times perhaps too rigidly, through periods of stress and strain from Peden's deanship to that of K. O. Shatwell. After she retired in December 1953, a farewell presentation enabled her to take a second holiday in her beloved England. In the 1960s she did some part-time work in the law library before entering a convalescent home. She died on 10 December 1975 in the Scottish Hospital, Paddington, and was cremated.

J. and J. Mackinolty (eds), *A Century Down Town* (Syd, 1991); *Univ Syd News*, 1 Mar 1976, p 2; *SMH*, 12 Dec 1975; Dalrymple Hay papers (NL); Faculty of Law minutes (Univ Syd Archives); family and personal information.   JUDY MACKINOLTY

HAY, OLGA JANET (1891-1974), headmistress, was born on 27 September 1891 at Elsternwick, Melbourne, second daughter of Rev. Joseph Hay, Presbyterian clergyman, and his wife Marjory, née Pender, both Scottish born. Her parents were friends of the Henderson family and in 1903-09 she boarded at Oberwyl school, St Kilda, then owned by Isabel Henderson [q.v.9]. Olga began training at Loreto Convent, Albert Park, in 1905 and in 1912 obtained her primary teacher's certificate. In 1911 she had become junior resident mistress under Miss Henderson at Clyde Girls' Grammar School, St Kilda. Miss Hay taught at Ruyton, Kew, in 1912, and at Kambala, Sydney. She returned to Melbourne on the outbreak of World War I and spent two years at Alexandra College, Hamilton. On the advice of her mentor Henderson, in 1917 she bought Horton school, Box Hill, which she sold at the end of the war for twice the price she had paid. In 1919 she became acting-head of Fareleight school, St Kilda, when the headmistress contracted pneumonic influenza.

Having visited the United States of America, Britain and France in 1920, Hay came home to teach at Clyde, by then located at Braemar House, Woodend. She also commenced reading for a degree at the University of Melbourne (B.A., 1924). To fulfil the compulsory practical work in science, she needed to be close to the city and in 1922 was appointed to Methodist Ladies' College, Kew, where she met 'the most democratic group of people I have ever been with in my life'. During the 1920s she was an active member of the Assistant Mistresses' Association.

In 1929-31 Hay spent two years abroad. While in England she gained the Cambridge Teacher Training Certificate and taught at Luton Secondary Girls' School, Bedfordshire. She returned to M.L.C. where colleagues appreciated her personality, her 'outgoing freedom and generosity of spirit', and her eccentricity; the girls liked her dry humour, but feared her sometimes brutal frankness. Besides her teaching, she participated in such extracurricular activities as Bible study, debating and the Walking Club. She also established and organized a library at M.L.C.

From 1937 Hay was headmistress of Clyde. Under her leadership the school continued on the lines set down by Henderson, although Hay gave greater prominence to science, art, music and practical subjects in the curriculum, and introduced interstate excursions. She knew every girl in the school and her influence on each one was more than intellectual: she possessed 'a moral integrity bordering on the puritanical . . . mellowed by charity and sweet reasonableness'. If her forthrightness became irascibility in old age, it was usually tempered by kindness. A member (from 1937) of the Headmistresses' Association and twice its president, she retired from Clyde in 1959. She wrote *The Chronicles of Clyde* (1966), continued her membership of the Lyceum Club and maintained a keen interest in educational matters. Olga Hay died on 29 August 1974 in East Melbourne and was cremated.

A. G. Thomson Zainu'ddin, *They Dreamt of a School* (Melb, 1982); *Cluthan*, Dec 1974; *Age* (Melb), 18 Sept 1974; notes of interviews with O. J. Hay, 22 June 1970, 17 Sept 1971, *and* other papers (held by author, Glen Waverley, Melb).

A. G. THOMSON ZAINU'DDIN

HAYDEN, JOHN GERALD (1901-1960), physician, was born on 3 April 1901 at Ballarat, Victoria, eldest of six children of Edward John Hayden, insurance company manager, and his wife Laura, née Higgins, both Victorian born. John was educated at St Patrick's College, Ballarat, where he was dux, and (on a scholarship) at Newman College, University of Melbourne (M.B., B.S., 1923; M.D., 1925). Graduating with first-class honours, he became resident medical officer, then registrar, at St Vincent's Hospital, Fitzroy. He studied in the United States of America and in 1927 qualified as a member (fellow 1941) of the Royal College of Physicians, London.

In 1928 Hayden began practice as a consultant physician in Melbourne. His first room was in the rear portion of (Sir) Hugh Devine's [q.v.8] establishment at 55 Collins Street. That situation, coupled with Hayden's skill and energy, and aided by Devine's referrals of patients, helped him to acquire a large practice. He was appointed physician to outpatients (1928) and to in-patients (1934) at St Vincent's.

Commissioned in the Australian Army Medical Corps in 1925, Hayden was active in the Militia and commanded the 15th Field Ambulance from 1938. He transferred to the Australian Imperial Force on 1 July 1940 as lieutenant-colonel and was sent to the Middle East in February 1941 as officer-in-charge of the 2nd/7th Australian General Hospital's medical division. In September 1942 he was promoted colonel and placed in command of the hospital. He led the unit in New Guinea in 1943-44 and was subsequently consulting physician, Directorate of Medical Services. In 1944 he was appointed C.B.E. and mentioned in dispatches. Transferring to the Reserve of Officers on 1 December 1945, he served as an army consulting physician from 1948 to 1960.

The years from 1945 were those of Hayden's greatest influence—at the University of Melbourne where he was Stewart lecturer in medicine in 1949-55, at St Vincent's Hospital, in the Royal Australian College of Physicians and in the wider community. His medical knowledge seemed encyclopaedic, his experience was enormous, and his confident, eloquent and expert teaching of both undergraduates and postgraduates made him for a period the star attraction of the St Vincent's Hospital Clinical School. A wise adviser and committee-man at the hospital, he played an important role in setting up St Vincent's School of Medical Research. Hayden was one of the earliest clinicians in Australia to understand the importance of molecular biology in medical science. After interviewing Pehr Edman [q.v.] in Europe, Hayden had no hesitation in recommending him for appointment as the first John Holt [q.v.9 Michael Holt] director of the new research school. In 1956 Hayden was appointed to the second chair of medicine at the University of Melbourne, to be held at St Vincent's.

A foundation fellow (1938), executive-member, vice-president (1952-54) and president (1958-60) of the R.A.C.P., Hayden was also a member of the National Heart Foundation, of the scientific committee of the National Health and Medical Research Council, and of the medical advisory committee of the Hospitals and Charities Commission.

While his public and professional career was marked by success and eminence, Hayden bore heavy trials in his private life. At Newman College chapel on 19 December 1929 he had married with Catholic rites Ida

Margaret Kelly, a nurse; after suffering poor health, she went missing in 1947 and was subsequently presumed dead. With the support of their adopted daughter, he continued with his work in a way that brought him admiration. On 4 March 1953, again at Newman chapel, he married a divorcee Patricia Constance Bell, née Leihy. The later 1950s were a happier period for him, marked by professional and academic honours, but still dimmed by physical troubles. He underwent a gastrectomy for a penetrating stomach ulcer in 1955; his final illness struck him before he had the time to realize his potential as professor of medicine.

'Jack' Hayden, as he was affectionately known at St Vincent's, was a Catholic of deep religious faith. Survived by his wife and their 1-year-old son, and by his adopted daughter, he died of cancer on 26 December 1960 at St Vincent's and was buried in Melbourne general cemetery. His estate was sworn for probate at £29 697. Justus Jorgensen's [q.v.] portrait of Hayden is held by the R.A.C.P.

G. L. McDonald (ed), *Roll of the Royal Australasian College of Physicians*, 1, 1938-75 (Syd, 1988); *MJA*, 15 Apr 1961, p 572; Council of School of Medical Research, St Vincent's Hospital (Melb), minutes; information from Mr F. Hayden, Ocean Grove, Vic; personal information.

BRYAN EGAN

HAYDON, PATRICK MAURICE (1890-1949), Catholic priest, was born on 19 March 1890 at Hornsby, Sydney, youngest of nine children of Irish-born parents Martin Haydon, hotelkeeper, and his wife Bridget, née Purcell. Patrick was educated at St Joseph's Convent School, Granville, St Mary's Cathedral School, Sydney, and St Joseph's College, Hunters Hill. Despite excellent academic prospects, he chose to study for the priesthood at St Patrick's College, Manly, and required dispensation from the canonical age of 24 in order to be ordained on 30 November 1912 at St Mary's Cathedral. In December he was appointed to Queanbeyan in the rural deanery as assistant to Fr Matthew Hogan.

His arrival coincided with the development of the Federal Capital Territory, marked by the official naming of Canberra on 12 March 1913. Haydon acquired a motorbike, visited work depots, and celebrated Mass under canvas at the Cotter River and in temporary huts at Westridge (Yarralumla) and Molonglo (Fyshwick). He later assembled congregations at Acton Hall, the Royal Military College, Duntroon, and Ainslie School. Weekly Sunday Masses began at Acton Hall in January 1925. The traditional 'station' Masses continued for some years at Springbank, home to the Sullivan and Bates families.

When a reorganization in 1917 transferred Queanbeyan to the Goulburn diocese, Hogan returned to Sydney. Only 27 years old and exulting in the title of 'bush priest', on 26 January 1918 Haydon was confirmed as pastor of Queanbeyan. His Catholic pilgrimages to Canberra in 1927, 1928 and 1930 were attended by bishops and other dignitaries. On 30 January 1927 some five thousand people came to the site (at Parkes) which he had negotiated for a national cathedral and episcopal residence. At the gathering on 27 February 1928 he was appointed first pastor of St Christopher's parish, Canberra; he chose this patronal title with regard to the countless visitors he foresaw would travel to Canberra.

Co-operating with other churchmen, Haydon cared for workers and their families during the Depression. His strong leadership promoted social work and fund-raising efforts in the parish, and created deep bonds of loyalty to him. He initiated eight building projects in Queanbeyan and Canberra; St Christopher's Church, Manuka, was opened in 1939. From 1923 he had edited a monthly newsletter, the *Angelus*, in which he revealed his polished style of prose and his extensive scholarship, and he contributed poems and articles to Church publications. Haydon became a confidant to four prime ministers—J. H. Scullin, J. A. Lyons [qq.v.11,10], F. M. Forde and J. B. Chifley [q.v.13]—who were members of his congregation while in the capital. He was appointed vicar-general of the diocese in 1940 and prothonotary apostolic (monsignor) in 1941.

Dame Enid Lyons described Haydon as 'six feet four inches [193 cm] tall and proportionately broad, and every inch pure Australian'. Because of a serious stammer, he kept his sermons short, but his speech impediment was largely 'overcome by the swift beauty of his thought' and his 'natural eloquence'. He died of haematemesis on 19 April 1949 in Canberra Community Hospital and was buried in Canberra cemetery. The Haydon Catholic Centre, Manuka, commemorates him.

W. W. Farmer, *Monsignor P. M. Haydon* (Syd, 1952); E. Lyons, *So We Take Comfort* (Lond, 1965); *Canb Times*, 20, 21 Apr 1949; Archives of (Catholic) Archdiocese of Canb and Goulburn (Archbishop's House, Canb).

BRIAN MAHER

HAYES, EDWARD LEO (1889-1967), Catholic priest and book collector, was born on 23 November 1889 at Frederickton, New South Wales, second of eight children of native-born parents Edward Martin Hayes, schoolteacher, and his wife Bridget Mary, née Flannery. Leo was educated at public schools where his father was headmaster, at Frederickton and at Palmer Island on the Clarence River. He left at the age of 15, worked in an auctioneer's office at Gunnedah until 1908 and was then appointed a clerk with the Darling Downs Co-operative Association, Toowoomba, Queensland. Having studied (from 1911) at St Columba's Seminary, Springwood, New South Wales, he proceeded to St Patrick's College, Manly, where he won a prize for dogmatic theology. On 30 November 1918 he was ordained priest for the Brisbane archdiocese by the Apostolic delegate Bartolomeo Cattaneo in St Mary's Cathedral, Sydney.

While he was assistant-priest (1918-22) at Ipswich, Hayes developed an interest in geology. He was parish priest at Kilcoy (1922-24) before ministering at Taroom (1924-27). Assigned to Chinchilla in 1928, he chose to join Toowoomba after it became a separate diocese in 1929. During his appointment to Crows Nest (1931-50) he was responsible for establishing churches at Haden, Coalbank and Perseverance Creek. He was next based at Oakey (1951-67) where he built St Monica's Church and a new convent school, as well as renovating the convent and presbytery.

Yet is was due to 'his hoard'—the Leo Hayes Collection—that he attained prominence. A 'small gnome of a man' with 'bower bird instincts', Hayes had bought his first book as a 7 year old and begun to gather birds eggs. Ultimately his collection comprised 25 000 books, pamphlets and periodicals (about two-thirds of them Australiana), and 30 000 manuscripts, letters and documents. It also included legal papers, press-cuttings, book-plates, stamps, notes and coins, postcards and photographs, maps, ferns, pistols, cattle-bells and Aboriginal artefacts. Hayes was a self-taught expert in many fields. In 1937, 1938 and 1940 he went on expeditions, organized by the Queensland branch of the Royal Geographical Society of Australasia, to the Carnarvon Ranges, Western Australia; in 1942 he was elected a fellow of the society and awarded its Thomson [q.v.12] medal for his work as geologist and ethnologist. His expertise led to recognition in academic and literary circles, and among the powerful and famous. Hayes's friends and acquaintances included John French [q.v.], Dorothy Cottrell, Dame Mary Gilmore, John Howlett Ross [qq.v.8,9,11], and General Douglas MacArthur [q.v.] who consulted his maps of the Pacific during World War II. Hayes was kindly, gentle and devout; he had the gift of a raconteur and was 'an eloquent public speaker'.

The University of Queensland conferred an honorary M.A. on Hayes in April 1967 and in October acquired the ailing archdeacon's wide-ranging collection (he wanted it to re-main in Queensland) for a nominal price of $20 000. In appreciation, the university established two scholarships in his name, for research in Australian literary or historical sources. He died on 17 November 1967 in St Vincent's Hospital, Toowoomba, and was buried in the local cemetery.

M. Brennan et al, *Catalogue of Manuscripts from the Hayes Collection* (Brisb, 1976); St Patrick's College (Manly, Syd), *Manly*, 6, no 2, Oct 1940, p 37; *Univ Qld Gazette*, 1967-68, p 11; *Footprints*, 3, no 11, May 1980, 3, no 12, Aug 1980; *Bulletin*, 26 Nov 1947; *Catholic Leader*, 2, 23, 30 Nov 1967, 31 May-30 Aug 1970; Catholic Diocesan Archives, Toowoomba, Qld.
CHRIS HANLON

HAYES, HERBERT EDWARD ELTON (1882-1960), Anglican clergyman and heretic, was born on 31 October 1882 at Greenhithe, Kent, England, son of George Herbert Hayes, carpenter, and his wife Eliza Ann, née Jenkins. Herbert was educated at a local Church of England school and at a Nonconformist academy. After five years in the militia, he transferred to the regular army in 1904. When he baulked at military discipline he was sent to Dublin; there he came under the influence of a Protestant mission to Catholics. Quitting the army, Hayes began Baptist theological training at Harley College in 1907, but resigned without completing the course. In 1910 he joined the Egypt General Mission in Cairo; while a genuine missionary, he also acted as an observer for British military intelligence. On furlough in England at the outbreak of World War I, he was called up and served on the Western Front with the Army Ordnance Corps, rising to acting lance sergeant.

During the last years of the war a close association with Rev. P. B. 'Tubby' Clayton—founder of the Toc H movement—led Hayes to change his allegiance to the Church of England. At the war's end he entered Knutsford Ordination Test School. Made deacon in 1919 and ordained priest on 19 December 1920, he returned to Egypt with the Church Missionary Society and took charge of the church and school at Menouf, near Cairo, where he also resumed his undercover work as a political agent. On 15 June 1923 at the British consulate, Cairo, he married Kathleen Blanche Gawler, an Australian-born nurse from the C.M.S. hospital at Menouf. He followed her to her homeland, working his passage as a welfare superintendent in an emigrant vessel.

Commissioned by Clayton to begin the Toc H movement in Australia, Hayes was an enthusiastic, good-humoured and indefatigable promoter of the cause. As first national padre, he travelled throughout the Commonwealth to promote the movement. The Returned

Sailors' and Soldiers' Imperial League of Australia offered him office accommodation in Anzac House, Melbourne. In 1926 his support of British ex-servicemen who were alleging discrimination against them by the R.S.& S.I.L.A. so angered that body that he was forced to move his office to Swanston Street. That year the Toc H leadership was appalled to learn that he had taken part in an inter-communion service with Baptist members.

While Hayes spent leave in England, Egypt and Palestine, Clayton's close associate Rev. Pat Leonard was sent to Australia to take over as national padre. On Hayes's return in 1927, Archbishop Lees [q.v.10] offered him the new parish of Mernda where Hayes proceeded with an unconventional ministry, hectoring the authorities and his congregation. Always a compulsive 'scribbler', he wrote under various aliases for *Smith's Weekly*, the *Bulletin*, *Argus* and *Herald*, as well as publishing at his own expense a dozen or so pamphlets and several small books of verse that included material lightheartedly attacking episcopacy, proposing nudity and advancing pro-feminist views.

Those who sought a pretext for his dismissal found it in the Christmas number of *Labor Call* in 1934, in which Hayes described Jesus as an illegitimate child whose mother's honour had been saved by Joseph. Finding the article immoral, heretical and blasphemous, Archbishop Head [q.v.9] wrote to Hayes asking for an immediate recantation. Hayes refused and was suspended from his duties on 27 April 1935. He faced an ecclesiastical tribunal on 4 June on charges of false doctrine and conduct disgraceful to a clergyman. Emotionally disturbed but unprepared to recant, he was granted an adjournment during which he visited England. Throughout 1935 the case attracted widespread national interest. In December he was found guilty, but, because ecclesiastical courts had no civil jurisdiction in Australia, he could not be compelled to resign. The diocesan authorities dissolved the parish and the vicarage was offered for sale. Mrs Hayes anonymously purchased it.

A short, stocky, sandy-haired man, balding as he aged and 'full of fight and poetry', Hayes continued to conduct services in the empty and decaying wooden church of St Stephen, supported by his wife who bred Irish terriers and did embroidery. He long hoped for reinstatement. Believing himself a 'scapegoat', he attacked his trial in a lengthy pamphlet, *God's Priceless Mountebank* (1935), which confirmed the view of his detractors that he was naive and intemperate, and an embarrassment. Increasingly eccentric and surrounded by a large collection of Egyptian antiquities, he continued his association with Freemasonry and developed an interest in numismatics and the occult. He died on 13 October 1960 at Fairfield and was cremated; his wife survived him.

People (Syd), 2 July 1952; *Smith's Weekly* (Syd), 10 Oct 1931; *Labor Call*, 20 Dec 1934; *Argus*, 25 Feb, 29 Apr, 5 June, 12, 24 Dec 1935; *Herald* (Melb), 28 Feb, 23, 24, 27 Dec 1935, 3 Apr 1936; Hayes papers (NL); information from Miss J. Bassett, Mernda, Vic.   D. C. LEWIS

HAYES, ROMUALD DENIS (1892-1945), Catholic bishop, was born on 30 January 1892 at Malvern, Melbourne, third son of Victorian-born parents Thomas Hayes, grocer, and his wife Mary, née Kilmartin. Romuald was educated at convent primary schools at Malvern and Kyneton, and at Xavier College, Kew, where he was school captain and rowed in the college VIII. From St Columba's Seminary, Springwood, New South Wales, and St Patrick's College, Manly, he proceeded to the Pontifical Urban College of Propaganda Fide, Rome, where he was ordained priest on 10 August 1917. On his return, Hayes was attached to the diocese of Melbourne as a curate at Northcote. In 1920 he became the first Australian to join the St Columban's Mission Society. His initial assignment was with the society's journal, *The Far East*, at Omaha, Nebraska, United States of America. He sailed home in 1921, via China where he visited Columban mission stations. Following his appointment as director of the Australasian province of the Columban priests in 1924, he was based at Essendon where the society established a seminary and consolidated support for its Chinese missions from the Catholic community in Australia.

In January 1932 Hayes was elected to the see of Rockhampton, Queensland. His appointment was a sign of change in the character of the hierarchy of the Church in Australia. From 1930, to the chagrin of the bishops born and educated in Ireland, a process of indigenization had begun from Rome. At Hayes's enthronement on 24 April 1932 Archbishop (Sir) James Duhig [q.v.8] remarked that Hayes was 'amongst what we may call the first generation of Australian born bishops'. Hayes took a keen interest in rural affairs which was reflected in his correspondence with the priests of the diocese. At his invitation, J. J. C. Bradfield [q.v.7] visited the district in August 1939 to examine sites for an irrigation scheme. On 9 April 1940, at a public meeting in Rockhampton, Hayes introduced Bradfield who proposed to establish a 25 000-acre (10 000 ha) irrigation scheme at Wura on the Dee River, south-west of Mount Morgan. A booklet describing the scheme was prepared under Hayes's guidance. As a member of the Central Queensland Advancement League, he wanted to secure development of secondary industry in the region, particularly through provision of reliable water supplies.

The establishment of the National Secretariat for Catholic Action in 1937 and its later subsidiary, the National Catholic Rural Movement, were welcomed by Hayes who was quick to assign full-time chaplains to these organizations. Beginning in January 1941 at the newly completed St Brendan's College, Yeppoon (the first Catholic boys' boarding-school in the diocese), the N.C.R.M. held annual retreats for farmers. Hayes gained support for his ideas of rural reform from the Catholic bishops' social justice statements, especially *Pattern for Peace* (1943), *The Family*(1944) and *The Land is Your Business* (1945). Recognized for his energy, organizing ability and charm, Hayes was a bespectacled and sensitive man of medium build. He valued his privacy, was loath to travel without private facilities and would sooner walk than accept a lift with a woman.

Bishop Hayes died of a coronary occlusion on 25 October 1945 at Rockhampton and was buried in the local cemetery.

The Dawson Valley (Rockhampton, Qld, 1940); *Wura Irrigation Scheme* (Rockhampton, 1940); Catholic Diocese of Rockhampton, *Review*, 6, no 9, Dec 1940, p 3; *Morning Bulletin*, 25 Apr 1932, 26 Oct, 1 Nov 1945; *Central Queensland Herald*, 1 Nov 1945; Hayes papers *and* Circulars to Priests, 30 May 1932-22 Dec 1937, 25 Jan 1939 *and* Bradfield Scheme (Diocesan Archives, Catholic Education Office, Rockhampton).   PATRICK O'CONNOR

HAYLEN, LESLIE CLEMENT (1898-1977), politician, playwright, novelist and journalist, was born on 23 September 1898 at Woodfield, near Queanbeyan, New South Wales, youngest of twelve children of Thomas Haylen, a maintenance man from Ireland, and his Victorian-born wife Catherine, née Day. His parents were small farmers before they moved to Sydney about 1908. Raised as a Catholic, Les was later to lose his faith. He was influenced by his grandfather William Henry Day, who loved literature, and by (Dame) Mary Gilmore [q.v.9], a family friend. In Sydney, he attended high school and began work as a bank clerk.

Enlisting in the Australian Imperial Force on 6 July 1918, Haylen embarked for Europe in October, but the troop-ship was recalled and he was discharged in January 1919. He re-enlisted in June and sailed for London next month as an escort for German prisoners being repatriated in the *Trás-os-Montes*. Back in Sydney in November, he was successively employed as a journalist on the *Sunday Times*, as theatre critic on the *Sun* and as news editor on the *Sunday Times*. At the registrar general's office, Chancery Square, on 30 April 1927 he married Sylvia Myrtle Rogers, a shop-assistant.

They moved to Wagga Wagga where Les was the *Daily Advertiser*'s chief sub-editor and leader-writer. His anti-war play, *Two Minutes' Silence*, was staged in Sydney in 1930. It ran for twenty-six weeks and was enthusiastically reviewed by Kenneth Slessor [q.v.]. In 1933 the McDonagh sisters [qq.v.10] produced a film version of the play. After a brief stint on the Orange *Leader*, Haylen returned to Sydney. In 1933 he joined the *Australian Women's Weekly* as news editor. He wrote the plays, *Change of Policy* (1934) and *Freedom has a Beard* (1937), and three novels about early Australian life, *The Game Darrells* (1933), *The Brierley Rose* (1935) and *Brown Boy Singing* (1940). The novels were serialized in the *Women's Weekly* before their publication as books and their subsequent production as radio serials.

In 1942, when Haylen sought Australian Labor Party pre-selection for the Federal seat of Parkes in south-west Sydney, (Sir) Frank Packer [q.v.] terminated his contract with Consolidated Press Ltd. Haylen was appointed editor of the A.L.P.'s new official newspaper, the *Standard*. He gained the pre-selection in 1943. Shunning official party publicity-material, he wrote his own and unexpectedly defeated Sir Charles Marr [q.v.10] in the elections that year. Haylen's margin was 1020, one of the largest in his twenty-year hold on Parkes.

His maiden speech proclaimed his interest in cultivating 'the spirit of Australianism' through literature, theatre and art, and he sought financial aid for Australian artists and writers. Around parliament, he quickly established a reputation as a *bon vivant*, 'with plenty of charm, wit and a sharp tongue'. No Labor Party machine-man, he was regarded with suspicion by those who were. He was committed to socialism and read widely on the subject. Parish-pump politics bored him and he described formal occasions in his electorate as 'fetes worse than death'; he preferred foreign affairs and economics.

In 1944 Haylen acted as publicity director for the 'fourteen powers' referendum. Next year Arthur Calwell [q.v.13] chose him as chairman of the Commonwealth immigration advisory committee which visited Europe to find new sources of settlers. The committee's report (1946) became the basis for Australia's ambitious postwar immigration programme. He wrote another play, *Blood on the Wattle* (1948), about the Eureka uprising.

Haylen narrowly missed a cabinet post after the 1946 elections. In Opposition from

1949, he was a vigorous and satirical debater in the House. His literary production included pamphlets and occasional verse. He led a parliamentary delegation to Japan in 1948 and caused a stir in Australia by shaking hands with Emperor Hirohito. That year he visited China to arrange for the migration of Europeans from Shanghai. In 1957 he headed a Labor delegation to China and in 1959 published *Chinese Journey*, a glowing account of changes which had taken place under the communists.

As 'Sutton Woodfield', in 1960 Haylen published *A for Artemis*, a satire on politics and the press; he drew in part on his experience with Packer and his feud with the Sydney cartoonist George Molnar. In 1945 Haylen had been appointed to the advisory board of the Commonwealth Literary Fund. He was president (from 1946) of the Fellowship of Australian Writers, and served on the interim council (1960-61) and the council (1961-64) of the National Library of Australia. In 1963 he was a member of a parliamentary delegation to South-East Asia.

A strong admirer of the political leaders for whom he worked, he had supported J. B. Chifley's [q.v.13] attempts to nationalize the banks and settle the 1949 coalminers' strike, advised H. V. Evatt [q.v.] in his crusade against the 'groupers', and showed great loyalty to Calwell. Although Haylen claimed that he was consistent in his socialism, he was dubbed a 'political gadfly' and Labor's 'Artful Dodger' for his volatility. He stood unsuccessfully for the deputy-leadership in 1960.

Haylen's defeat at the 1963 elections was a surprise. He continued writing, and in 1965 and 1976 edited *The Tracks We Travel*, volumes of Australian short stories. In 1965 he also published *Big Red*, a novel about politics in rural Australia in the 1890s. Another play, *The Stormy Blast* (1966), reflected his opposition to Australia's involvement in the Vietnam War. After failing to be elected to the Senate in 1964 and to be pre-selected for his old seat of Parkes in 1965, he wrote his political memoirs, *Twenty Years' Hard Labor* (Melbourne, 1969), which revealed his disillusionment with parliament and the A.L.P., especially its right wing. One reviewer perceptively wrote that Haylen was 'not of the old school of Labor [and] neither was he of the new'. Haylen openly admitted that he would never have entered parliament if he had been able to support his family as a writer.

Survived by his wife and two sons, he died on 12 September 1977 at Lewisham, Sydney, and was buried with Anglican rites in Rookwood cemetery. In their tributes in the House, Haylen's former colleagues recalled his wit, repartee and irreverence. Gough Whitlam remarked: 'Only Australia could have produced him'.

PD (Cwlth), 28 Sept 1943, p 94; *People* (Syd), 18 July 1951, p 40; *Age* (Melb), 3 Dec 1960; *Bulletin*, 2 June 1962; *Herald* (Melb), 29 Dec 1964; *Sun News-Pictorial*, 2 Dec 1963, 1 Nov 1965; *SMH*, 13, 14 Sept 1977; Haylen papers *and* M. Pratt, L. C. Haylen, taped interview, 12 Oct 1976 (NL).

R. E. NORTHEY

HEADING, SIR JAMES ALFRED (1884-1969), farmer and politician, was born on 28 January 1884 at Payneham, South Australia, second child of William Heading, a farmer from England, and his wife Rhoda Sarah, née Cook. Jim was educated at Netherby. About 1909 he moved to Queensland where he farmed at Cobbs Hill, near Murgon. Elected to the Weinholt Shire Council, he played a major role in acquiring a butter factory for the region in 1913; two years later he became chairman of the newly created Murgon Shire Council.

On 18 September 1915 Heading enlisted in the Australian Imperial Force. He joined the 47th Battalion in Egypt and in June 1916 moved with it to the Western Front. His service was interrupted by long periods of convalescence in England as a result of wounds to the leg and the shoulder. In June 1917 he was promoted sergeant. On 12 October at Passchendaele Ridge, Belgium, after all the officers of three companies had become casualties, he took charge. Disregarding personal danger, he placed outposts and connected the flanks; for these actions he was awarded the Distinguished Conduct Medal. At Dernancourt, France, on 5 April 1918 his platoon commander was killed. Heading again took charge and established control of no man's land in the immediate vicinity; he won the Military Medal and was promoted warrant officer. Transferring to the 45th Battalion in May, he arrived home in August 1919 and was discharged on 14 October. On 2 October that year he had married Ruby Jeanie Thomas at the Methodist Church, Clarence Park, Adelaide.

On his farm, Highfields, Heading became a noted stud breeder of Illawarra Shorthorn cattle and Large White pigs. He was chairman of the Queensland Co-operative Bacon Association (1926-57) and of the South Burnett Co-operative Dairy Association (1930-57). President (1951-55) of the Royal National Agricultural and Industrial Association of Queensland, he was a keen supporter of agricultural shows, and a foundation member (1920), president and patron of the Murgon Pastoral, Agricultural and Horticultural Society. He was also a foundation member and president of the local branch of the Returned Sailors' and Soldiers' Imperial League of Australia. Appointed major in the Volunteer

Defence Corps in September 1942, he commanded the 20th Battalion in Queensland in 1942-46.

In May 1947 Heading won the Legislative Assembly seat of Wide Bay for the Country Party; from 1950 to 1960 he represented the newly created electorate of Marodian. He was minister for public works and local government (1957-60) in (Sir) Francis Nicklin's [q.v.] cabinet and his administration was characterized by an expansion of government building, notably new schools. Appointed C.M.G. in 1954, he retired from parliament in May 1960 and was knighted in 1961.

A kindly man, devoted to his family, Heading never lost the 'common touch'. He was fond of cricket and said that the game 'taught players to take defeat or victory in the right spirit'. Survived by his son and three daughters, Sir James died on 9 April 1969 at Murgon; he was accorded a state funeral and was cremated. A park in Murgon is named after him.

C. Lack (comp), *Three Decades of Queensland Political History, 1929-1960* (Brisb, 1962); *PD* (Qld), 1969-70, p 23; *Countryman* (Brisb), May 1969; *Courier-Mail*, 5 May 1950, 10 Apr 1969; *South Burnett Times*, 26 Nov 1980; information from South Burnett Co-operative Assn, *and* Murgon Shire Council, RSL and Horticultural Soc, *and* Royal National Assn; personal information.

G. W. ROBERTS

HEADLAM, FRANK (1914-1976), air force officer, was born on 15 July 1914 at Launceston, Tasmania, son of Malcolm Headlam, farmer, and his wife Hilda Mary, née Burrill, both Tasmanian born. Educated at Clemes College, Hobart, Frank gained his Leaving certificate in 1932. He overcame family objections to a career in the Royal Australian Air Force, enlisted as an air cadet at Point Cook, Victoria, on 16 January 1934, completed flying training and was commissioned in January 1935.

After further courses, in 1936 Headlam was posted as an instructor to No.1 Flying Training School, Point Cook, where in March 1937 he was promoted flight lieutenant. In 1938 he began the first 'long specialist course' in navigation conducted by the R.A.A.F. and passed with distinction. Transferring to Laverton in 1939, he was a flight commander with No.1 and No.2 squadrons and subsequently station navigation officer. Next year he was sent to R.A.A.F. Headquarters, Melbourne, and made squadron leader. On 15 June 1940 he married Katherine Beatrice Bridge at St Paul's Anglican Church, Frankston; they were to have a daughter and son before being divorced.

Headlam returned to Laverton in April 1941 to take command of No.2 Squadron; three months later he was promoted wing commander. In December the squadron's Lockheed Hudson aircraft were deployed to Penfui, near Koepang, Timor, to help in countering Japan's Pacific offensive. Air Commodore J. E. Hewitt, assistant chief of the Air Staff, visited Penfui in January 1942 and noted that the unit was operating under considerable difficulties: 'My own feeling . . . was that we were expecting too much of Headlam and his squadron'. In February Headlam was ordered to withdraw to Darwin.

Following a brief stint at headquarters, North-Western Area, he commanded (1942-44) navigation and air observer schools in Victoria and South Australia, was promoted group captain in December 1943 and completed a course at the R.A.A.F. Staff School, Mount Martha, Victoria. Headlam went back to Darwin in January 1945 as senior administrative staff officer and from January 1946 was officer commanding, North-Western Area. In 1946-47 he was based in England where he attended the Royal Air Force Staff College, Andover. Returning to Australia, he took the post of director of training at R.A.A.F. Headquarters in November 1947.

In December 1950 Headlam was given command of No.90 Wing in Malaya. For several months in 1951 he was commander of the R.A.F. station at Tengah, Singapore, the principal base for operations against communist insurgents. By February 1952 he was senior air staff officer at headquarters, Home Command, Penrith, New South Wales. He was appointed O.B.E. in 1953 and in January 1955 was promoted substantive air commodore. In November he left for London to attend the 1956 course at the Imperial Defence College. Back in Australia, he filled a succession of senior positions, including acting air member for personnel on the Air Board (March to October 1957 and August 1959 to May 1960), air commodore plans (October 1957 to January 1959) and acting deputy chief of the Air Staff (May to June 1960). He had been elevated to C.B.E. in 1958.

Appointed air officer commanding, Operational Command, in January 1961, Headlam was promoted air vice marshal on 29 May. He was sent to Malaya in July 1962 to take command of No.224 Group, R.A.F. 'In December that year the Brunei revolt flared up'; it was quickly subdued—'in large measure due to the effective use of the air forces' under Headlam's command. 'Shortly after, the Indonesians started the operations in Borneo that [formed] part of their confrontation policy.' Headlam was 'responsible for the tactical and air defence operations' which—with other measures on land and at sea—contained 'the Indonesian incursions, and protected the independence of Sabah, Sarawak and Brunei'.

An effective commander and an inspiring leader, he was appointed C.B. in 1965.

After his return, Headlam was deputy chief of the Air Staff in 1965-66 and R.A.A.F. support commander in 1966-67. In January 1968 he went to London as head of the Australian Joint Services Staff. Back home, he retired in August 1971 and lived in Melbourne. On 20 January 1964 at the registrar general's office, Sydney, he had married a widow Vernon Rima Howorth Spence, née Swain, a social worker. Following a long illness, he died of complications arising from cancer on 23 December 1976 in Melbourne and was cremated. His wife and the children of his first marriage survived him.

D. Gillison, *Royal Australian Air Force 1939-1942* (Canb, 1962); J. E. Hewitt, *Adversity in Success* (Melb, 1980); C. D. Coulthard-Clark, *The Third Brother* (Syd, 1991); *Age* (Melb), 4 Dec 1947, 27 Dec 1976; *Sun News-Pictorial*, 3 Dec 1964, 23 June 1965, 17 Aug 1966; *Herald* (Melb), 24 Dec 1976.
                                    BRIAN EATON*

HEALY, EILEEN MARY (1888-1966), best known as Mother Bonaventure, Sister of Mercy, was born on 22 September 1888 at Ballarat East, Victoria, second of five children of Victorian-born parents Michael John Healy, railwayman, and his wife Mary Helena, née Costello, a teacher. Eileen was educated at St Alipius's Primary School and Sacred Heart College, Ballarat East, and at the University of Melbourne (Dip.Mus., 1909; Dip.Ed., 1916). Her three sisters became music teachers. One of them, Gertrude (1894-1984), achieved prominence as a violinist. After studying in Berlin (1914) and London (1914-20), in 1923 Gertrude was appointed principal study teacher in violin at the Albert Street Conservatorium, Melbourne. She later ran a music school at the Sacred Heart Convent, Ballarat East.

At the age of 20 Eileen entered the novitiate of the Sisters of Mercy, Ballarat East, where she was professed three years later as Sister Bonaventure. Working under the noted educationist Mother Mary Xavier Flood, founder of the Aquin (later Aquinas) Training College for Teachers, she helped with the pioneering work in this field. In 1928 she was appointed assistant-superior. As mistress of method (1951-66) Mother Bonaventure prepared hundreds of nuns and other trainees for the apostolate of teaching. From 1952 to 1966 she was also principal of Sacred Heart College, Ballarat East, which offered a full curriculum of humanities, science and commerce. She became mother general in 1956 and a member of the Australian College of Education in 1963.

The establishment of Patrician House (a hostel for undergraduates of the training college), as well as the construction of an increasing number of buildings at Sacred Heart College, four large primary schools in Ballarat, and convents and schools in thirteen Victorian country towns, brought Mother Bonaventure the sobriquet of 'The Builder'. No aspect of school life was overlooked in her endeavours. To expand sporting facilities at Sacred Heart College, she planned a nine-hole golf course on an unused piece of convent property at Mount Xavier—said to be the first public golf course built and owned by a convent—which was opened in 1949. The culmination of her efforts was a senior secondary college at St Martin's in the Pines, Mount Clear; almost on her deathbed, she completed the plans and launched the project for a large day- and boarding-school on the 52 acre (21 ha) site.

As a Sister of Mercy, Mother Bonaventure vowed her life to the service of the poor, the sick and the ignorant. In responding to the social needs of Ballarat, she rearranged and systematized the traditional visitation of the poor by the Sisters and inaugurated the Mercy Home Care and Nursing Service. She was a foundation member of the Australian Federation of the Sisters of Mercy. Mother Bonaventure died on 26 May 1966 at the Sacred Heart Convent, Ballarat East, and was buried in the new cemetery at Ballarat.

Light, July 1966; *Courier* (Ballarat), 27 May 1966; M. P. Welsh, Mantle of Mercy (ms, Convent of Mercy Archives, Ballarat East, Vic); Catholic Education Office records (MDHC).
                                    ANNE FORBES

HEALY, JAMES (1898-1961), trade unionist, was born on 22 March 1898 at West Gorton, Manchester, England, son of Dominic Healy, corporation labourer, and his wife Mary Ellen, née Schaill, a cotton-mill worker. Educated at the parish school of St Francis of Assisi, Gorton, Jim was influenced by his father's Irish republicanism and at age 8 began assisting electoral canvassers for the Labour Party. In 1915 he enlisted in the 8th Battalion, Argyll and Sutherland Highlanders. He was wounded in action on the Western Front and discharged medically unfit in 1918.

Finding regular employment scarce in England, Healy moved to Scotland where he initially worked as a plate-layer with the tramways. At St Cuthbert's Catholic Church, Edinburgh, on 19 July 1919 he married Elizabeth McGowan, a woollen weaver. They emigrated to Queensland with their three young sons in 1925. He found jobs as a fireman and boiler-attendant at the Mackay powerhouse, and from 1927 as a labourer on the town's wharves. In 1928 he was elected to the local committee of management of the Waterside Workers' Federation of Australia and was the union's delegate to the Mackay branch of the Australian Labor Party. Next year he was appointed to the trades and labor council at Mackay and began his first term as branch president of the W.W.F.

Healy became disillusioned with the A.L.P. after witnessing the Queensland Labor government's inability to aid the plight of the unemployed in the Depression. A union-sponsored study trip to the Soviet Union in 1934 reinforced his growing belief that the communists best represented the interests of workers. He and Ben Scott wrote a pamphlet about their experiences, *Red Cargo* (Sydney, 1934), and Healy joined the Communist Party of Australia, remaining a staunch member for the rest of his life.

Working conditions and pay for wharf labourers were poor in the 1930s and the men were divided between two unions, the W.W.F. and the Permanent and Casual Wharf Labourers' Union of Australia. Strikes in 1917 and 1928 had weakened the W.W.F. and there was an influx of non-union labour during the Depression. Healy realized that change was necessary at a national level. He moved to Sydney about 1936 and at the union's all-ports conference in October 1937 was elected general secretary of the W.W.F. In 1939 he transferred its head office from Melbourne to Sydney. Starting with no money, little assets and few prospects, he began to turn the federation into a modern, effective union. He had obtained approval at the 1937 conference for a national policy to be adhered to by all branches and for the establishment of a national journal, the *Maritime Worker*, of which he became editor.

In 1937-38 Healy led public campaigns in support of the Sydney waterside workers' bans against loading scrap metal for Japan and by the Port Kembla men against loading pig-iron destined for the same country. The federation was able to strengthen its position during World War II due to the increased demand for wharf labour and the need to expedite the shipment of war materials. A member (1942-49) of the Stevedoring Industry Commission, Healy secured substantial pay rises for his unionists and the replacement of the 'bull' system (in which overseers selected workers like cattle) by rotating gangs. In return, the W.W.F. executive encouraged the men to put maximum effort into loading and unloading military supplies. Healy again demonstrated his commitment to broader political issues by leading the boycott (1945-49) on Dutch ships carrying goods which could be used to crush the Indonesian independence movement.

Healy's greatest challenge and ultimate triumph was the absorption into the W.W.F. of the rival P.C.W.L.U., a union detested by many of his comrades for having been formed by 'scabs'. This amalgamation—commenced in 1946 and completed in 1955—underlined Healy's determination and his capacity for strategic thinking. In the 1949 coalminers' strike he had been gaoled for contempt of court, after refusing to reveal the location of money withdrawn from the bank to assist the strikers. Sentenced to twelve months imprisonment, he apologized and was released after five weeks. The industrial groups within the unions attacked communist officials in the 1940s and 1950s, but Healy was able to shrug off all challenges to his position. He took an active part in the successful campaign (1950-51) against the Menzies [q.v.] government's attempt to ban the Communist Party.

Menzies' administration introduced the Stevedoring Industry Act (1954) which established a committee of inquiry into the industry and aimed to put an end to the W.W.F.'s monopoly on the supply of wharf labour. Supported by the Australian Council of Trade Unions, the federation struck in protest. Healy appeared before the committee of inquiry and produced evidence to show that high stevedoring charges in Australia stemmed less from excessive labour costs than from collusion between the shipping companies to keep rates as high as possible. None the less, the government pressed ahead in 1956 with new legislation aimed at weakening the federation and the improvements it had gained in working conditions and safety provisions. In 1957 he was appointed to the A.C.T.U. executive as the representative of the transport unions.

Healy died of a cerebrovascular accident on 13 July 1961 in St Vincent's Hospital, Darlinghurst, and was cremated; his wife, daughter and sons survived him. An atheist, he was given a 'comrade's farewell' in the W.W.F. Hall, Sussex Street. Hundreds of mourners filed past the open coffin and *The Internationale* was played. His funeral cortège stretched for nearly a mile and blocked city traffic for more than an hour.

The universal respect for 'Big Jim's' integrity and dedication was demonstrated by the tributes paid to him after his death by his political opponents and spokesmen for the employers. The *Bulletin* referred to him as the 'best single P.R. device the Australian Communists ever had'. As his nickname suggests, he was a large man, and he was often pictured smoking a pipe. Portraits by Newton Hedstrom and Ralph Sawyer are held at the Maritime Union of Australia's offices in Sussex Street. Healy's capacity for analytical thinking, his unflappable personality and his patient persistence were instrumental in unifying the wharf labourers' unions, and in gaining improvements in wages and conditions. He was a communist, and also a democrat. Asked when Australia would become socialist, he had replied, 'When fifty-one per cent of the people think as we do'.

R. Lockwood, *The Story of Jim Healy* (Syd, 1951); T. Nelson, *The Hungry Mile* (Syd, 1957); *In Memory of Jim Healy* (Syd, 1961); V. Williams, *The Years of Big Jim* (Perth, 1975); T. Bull, *Politics in a Union* (Syd, 1977); S. Moran, *Reminiscences of a Rebel* (Syd, 1979); A. Moore (ed), *The Writings of Norman Jeffery* (Campbelltown, NSW, 1989); *SMH*, 14, 18 July 1961; *Bulletin*, 22 July, 12 Aug 1961; C. Ryan, Ships and Sickles: The Communists and three Australian maritime unions 1928-45 (M.A. thesis, Univ NSW, 1986); Waterside Workers' Federation Archives (restricted access) (ANUABL).

RAY MARKEY
STUART SVENSEN

HEALY, MARY (1865-1952), best known as Mother Gertrude, Sister of Charity and hospital administrator, was born on 24 July 1865 in Dublin, daughter of Francis Healy, ironmonger, and his wife Anne, née Carton. Mary accompanied her family to Victoria where she attended Loreto Abbey, Marys Mount, Ballarat, under Mother Gonzaga Barry [q.v.3] and gained some teacher training. She entered the Novitiate of the Sisters of Charity, Sydney, on 5 June 1889 and was professed on 2 October 1891 as Sister Gertrude. That year she began training at St Vincent's Hospital, Darlinghurst; she registered with the Australasian Trained Nurses' Association on 24 July 1903.

In 1910 Sister Gertrude was appointed mother rectress of St Vincent's. Keen to see the institution become a clinical school for the University of Sydney, she set out to expand the hospital and increase the number of specialties. In 1913 work began on new accommodation for nurses. The out-patients' division was extended, with improved X-ray facilities, and an enlarged electro-therapeutical and massage department provided rehabilitation for returned servicemen. Construction of a third storey was completed in 1918. By 1917 nursing staff under Mother Gertrude's direction had risen to thirty Sisters of Charity and eighty trainees. During the 1919 influenza epidemic St Vincent's admitted over 27 000 urgent cases and treated another 70 000 as out-patients. Her term of office ended in 1920.

Following three years managing the Order's adjoining private hospital at Darlinghurst, Mother Gertrude was appointed rectress (1924-33) of St Vincent's Hospital, Melbourne. She expanded fund-raising activities and, in 1927, helped to establish an auxiliary movement. In 1932 she engaged Norma Parker, St Vincent's first qualified hospital almoner. That year Mother Gertrude toured Europe to study advances in the design and administration of modern hospitals. The results of her investigations were incorporated by (Sir) Arthur Stephenson [q.v.12] in a new wing which contained the administrative offices, the X-ray and therapeutic equipment, four operating theatres and six wards. Opened in 1934, it was to be named the Gertrude Healy Wing.

Mother Gertrude came back to Sydney in 1934 to administer St Vincent's Private Hospital. She started a second term as rectress at the much enlarged public hospital in 1943. Her first task was to inaugurate a central surgical service complex. By the mid-1940s the hospital was a leading training school for professionals in related areas of health—physiotherapists (from 1914), almoners (1936), dietitians (1941) and occupational therapists (1946). With the end of World War II, Mother Gertrude planned a massive expansion of St Vincent's to encompass a maternity and a children's hospital, a new intermediate wing and a modern nurses' home. In 1924 she had raised the possibility of the Order running a maternity hospital, but it was not until 1936 that the Sisters were authorized to practise obstetric nursing. Delays and shortages held up construction of the maternity and children's hospitals. Meanwhile, in 1947 Mother Gertrude had again returned to manage the private hospital.

From the early 1940s Mother Gertrude had acted as councillor to the superior general in hospital matters. Her calm, dignified countenance, kindly eyes and gentle Dublin accent made her very approachable. Throughout her nursing life her efforts to achieve excellence in medical care were aimed at benefiting the 'sick poor'. She died on 28 April 1952 at St Vincent's and was buried in Rookwood cemetery. (Sir) Herbert Schlink [q.v.11], chairman of Royal Prince Alfred Hospital, described her as one of the greatest hospital administrators in Australia.

D. Miller, *Earlier Days* (Syd, 1969); B. Egan, *Ways of a Hospital* (Syd, 1993); St Vincent's Hospital (Syd), *Annual Report*, 1910-20, 1943-46; St Vincent's Hospital (Melb), *Annual Report*, 1924-33, Annals of the Sisters of Charity of Aust, 2, 1882-1938, *and* register of nurses, St Vincent's Hospital, Syd, 1882-1910 *and* other material in Sisters of Charity Archives, Potts Point, Syd.

CATHERINE O'CARRIGAN

HEALY, MARY GABRIELLE (1908-1980), Catholic nun, musician and liturgist, was born on 4 January 1908 at Toowoomba, Queensland, eldest of three daughters of Toowoomba-born parents Charles Healy, railway employee, and his wife Cecilia Clare, née McNamara. After primary schooling, Gabrielle won a scholarship which enabled her to enter Lourdes Hill College, Brisbane, in 1922. Having gained an associateship (piano) of Trinity College of Music, London, in 1927, she taught speech and drama in the Holy Name parish, Toowoomba. On 6 January 1929 she joined the Sisters of the Good Samaritan of the Order of St Benedict, at Pennant Hills, Sydney. As Sister Mary Gabrielle, she made her first profession of religious vows on 2 July 1931. She taught music at St Scholastica's College, Glebe, for six years, and then at Hamilton, Victoria (1937), Marrickville, Sydney (1938-41 and 1952-66), Gayndah, Queensland (1942), Canberra (1943-45), Wollongong (1946-51), Manly (1966-77) and Glebe (1978-79), New South Wales.

Meantime, Sister Gabrielle was awarded a licentiate (1932) of the Associated Board of the Royal Schools of Music, London, and a licentiate (singing 1943) and fellowship (1944) of Trinity College. She believed that liturgical music should move people to pray and specialized in the polyphony of the sixteenth century. While carrying out her daily teaching schedule, she embarked upon various musical projects. Gifted with initiative, energy and enthusiasm, she enlisted widespread support for her enterprises which included the spectacle for the Good Samaritan centenary celebrations, held in Sydney in 1957, a number of Passion plays and Gilbert and Sullivan operas, staged at Marrickville, and pageants 'to put Christ back into Christmas', performed at Hyde Park and Long Bay gaol in the 1960s.

In 1958 Sister Gabrielle took part in the United Nations Educational, Scientific and Cultural Organization's seminar on drama in education. She also helped to plan music education for the Australian Broadcasting Commission and was a member of the board responsible for introducing a diploma of sacred music at the New South Wales State Conservatorium of Music. As president of the Singers of David—formed in 1963 by Sisters, Brothers, priests and the laity to promote liturgical music—she arranged Psalm festivals and musical performances (1964-70) at the Sydney Town Hall in which students from Catholic schools and colleges took part. From 1968 the choir regularly performed in the Mass that was televised each month on channel TCN-9 in Sydney and sang at two official Masses during the 1970 visit of Pope Paul VI.

Sister Gabrielle lectured part time at the Good Samaritan Teachers' College and at St Patrick's College, Manly, which conferred on her a diploma of theology (1968). A member of the Institute of Pastoral Liturgy (1970), of the Australian College of Education (1971)

and of the National Liturgical Commission (1975), she was a consultant on the music sub-committee of the International Committee on English in the Liturgy (1976). At Manly in 1977 she helped to organize a liturgical convention on worship.

Her expertise gained Sister Gabrielle the position of adjudicator (1978-79) in instrumental, vocal and choral sections at eisteddfods in Sydney, Darwin and Brisbane. In 1979 she attended the National Association of Pastoral Musicians' convention at Chicago, United States of America, and visited liturgical centres around the world. She died on 17 January 1980 at Lewisham Hospital, Sydney, and was buried in Northern Suburbs cemetery.

Sisters of the Good Samaritan, Manly, 1881-1981 (Syd, 1981); *SMH*, 20 Dec 1963, 18 Jan 1979; *Catholic Leader*, 12 Aug 1979; *Catholic Weekly* (Syd), 27 Jan 1980; M. P. D. McKinlay, Vale, Sister Mary Gabrielle (ts, Good Samaritan Generalate Archives, Glebe Point, Syd).
URSULA TROWER

HEALY, PATRICK BURSELUM (1897-1970), bookmaker, and MARY (MOLLY) ESTELLE (1915-1971), charity worker and socialite, were husband and wife. Pat was born on 8 December 1897 in Perth, fourth child of Patrick John Healy, a bookmaker who rose to be president of his trade union, and his wife Emily Harriett, née Harris, who came from a property-holding Bassendean family. Young Pat worked as a barman. On 17 May 1916 at the Jandakot hall he married with Anglican rites Annie Linda Spencer, a clerk; they had three children before being divorced in 1930.

Shortly after World War I Healy had begun his career as an illegal starting-price 'bookie' in a back lane near a hotel. Granted a licence to field at the Perth trots, he was expelled in the mid-1920s, possibly because he was mixing on- and off-course betting, and probably during one of the Western Australian Trotting Association's purges. His business prospered during the 1920s and 1930s when he operated an illegal betting-shop in central Perth. It is likely that he used bribes to avoid prosecutions, even though his premises were raided regularly. He once said of the police in the 1920s, they 'used to come and have a cup of tea and tell me I had to go off, and I went'. At St Mary's Catholic Cathedral on 5 February 1931 he married 21-year-old Frances Clare Keating; they had two children before she divorced him on 6 October 1938. He married 23-year-old Mary Estelle Coughlan on 29 November that year at the district registrar's office, Fremantle.

Molly had been born on 17 June 1915 in West Perth, fourth child of Patrick Martin

Coughlan, an engine driver from Victoria, and his Western Australian-born wife Sarah Josephine, née Dudley. Apprenticed to a dressmaker at Boan's Department Store, she did some modelling and may have met Pat at a tennis club. He built a mansion for her at Dalkeith; it had a river frontage and they moved in immediately after their marriage. By 1938 his business had made him wealthy.

Following World War II, Healy used a loophole in the law and conducted his betting business by telephone. He became one of the top men, a St George's Terrace commission agent and the financial backer of many of his bookmaking colleagues. In 1954 the State Labor government legalized off-course punting and set up a string of betting shops. Healy was one of the first to be granted a licence. At one stage he employed thirty staff, ran up a yearly phone bill of over £2000 and turned over £1 million annually. He officially retired in 1960 when the Liberal government abolished the shops and established the Totalisator Agency Board. But old habits die hard. In 1970 his last conviction for illegal betting occurred, twenty-four years after his previous one. His lawyer told the court that his client 'did it really for something to do'.

Healy had risen to prominence by taking bets from other bookies who were laying-off to cover their own commitments; about one-half of his turnover was in this form. It was common knowledge that his sources of information could not be surpassed. His enemies, of whom he had many, described him as a very cunning operator—as one fellow 'bookie' put it, 'ruthless, utterly ruthless'. On several occasions from the 1930s he secretly lobbied governments for legalisation and supported whichever party best served his interests. At the royal commission on betting in 1959, he told of big donations to both the Liberal and Labor parties.

What annoyed Healy most was that Perth's Establishment excluded him. Despite his opulence and extravagance, the Weld Club routinely blackballed him. When he heard of one rejection, he exploded: 'If that club was a business, I'd buy it and sack the fuckin' lot of them'. Although he belonged to many sporting clubs, he was forced to remain on the margins of polite society. Molly, however, was at the centre of the social and charity world of Perth's smart set, albeit at the second level of the local social hierarchy. She got there by a combination of Pat's money, and her beauty, generosity and charm. She was known for her extravagance and flamboyance, as was her husband. Their parties were legendary. She dressed beautifully and expensively, frequently in her own creations, and was a regular at opening nights. She strode the catwalk at Perth's major charity functions for nearly thirty years, and regu-

larly graced the fashion and social pages of the local press. Proud of her house and garden which she made available for functions, even to strangers, her one regret was that she never had children. Pat and Molly were generous to their kin, to their friends and to charity. Pat remained on the fringe of Molly's social world, probably by choice. That was a world she seemed to have carved out for herself. Both of them attracted love, envy and contempt in equal measure.

Survived by a daughter of his first marriage, Healy died on 13 December 1970 at Shenton Park. He left the bulk of his estate, sworn for probate at $110 789, to establish a medical research centre at the University of Western Australia. Molly died of cancer on 28 December 1971 at Subiaco; like Pat, she was buried with Catholic rites in Karrakatta cemetery. She had sold the Healy mansion to Alan Bond.

Sporting Globe, 30 Dec 1959; *West Australian*, 4 Feb 1961, 14 Dec 1970, 26 May 1973, 9 Sept 1980; *Sunday Times* (Perth), 2 Jan 1972; C. Fox, Off-Course Betting in Western Australia 1934-1954 (M.A. thesis, Univ WA, 1979); information from Mr W. Latter, Fremantle, Mrs M. Hungerford, Cottesloe, Dr and Mrs C. Georgeff, Crawley, Perth.

CHARLIE FOX

HEAP, AMY ELIZABETH (1874-1956), artist and illustrator, was born on 6 February 1874 at Tonge-with-Haulgh, Lancashire, England, daughter of James Heap, wine merchant, and his wife Amy Elizabeth, née Bamber. Young Amy was initially educated at Bolton, and later attended art schools at Manchester and in London. She received a teacher's certificate in 1895 and a certificate for art instruction in 1897. Sketching tours in England took up some of her time and she may have taught, although her family's circumstances did not make it essential. With her brother Frederick and younger sister Ethel, she emigrated to Western Australia in 1909.

After living on a group-settlement farm at Busselton, they moved to Claremont and thence to Darlington. The sisters joined in the artistic life of Perth and became members of the Western Australian Society of Arts. From 1912 to 1925 Amy irregularly exhibited drawings, paintings, stained pokerwork pictures, metalwork, embroidery and gessowork; the embroidery was designed by Amy and worked by Ethel. In 1912 a local art critic wrote that 'Miss Heap . . . has a greater number and variety of exhibits . . . than any other artist, her work showing an artistic versatility that is remarkable'.

During World War I Heap joined the staff of Western Australian Newspapers Ltd as an artist/photographer. From 1918, as a 'specialist in embellishment', she contributed drawings and photographs to the *Western Mail*, a weekly journal aimed at rural readers which also enjoyed a wide circulation in Perth. Her delicate and graceful drawings provided borders for photographs, poems, articles and short stories. Daisy Rossi commented on 'her arresting and decorative covers . . . her sensitive pen and ink drawings' and the 'delicate refined style' of her water-colours. In 1929, Western Australia's centenary year, Heap's brilliant water-colour, 'Nuytsia Floribunda', or 'Christmas Tree in Bloom', was the front cover of the *Western Mail* annual; equally striking was her water-colour of black swans for the 1932 issue. For a time she and the photographer Fred Flood dominated the visual imagery in the *Mail*'s Christmas editions. Both 'heard happy shepherds chanting by streams in a Western Arcady'; their work emphasized 'the values of stability and social contentment', and had 'no room for sorrow, pain and deprivation'. Amy was 'aristocratic in bearing, manner, and speech; and very, very English . . . "a Dresden china" sort of person, small but very impressive'. Her handwriting was 'precise, neat and self-confident'. Her private life remained that. Independent and a spinster, she drove her own motorcar.

Heap retired from the newspaper about 1934 and went to live with her sister and brother at Albany. In 1933-44 she continued to exhibit on and off with the Perth Society of Artists, of which she was a member. An inveterate traveller, she visited New Zealand, Tasmania and England, where she exhibited in 1938. At the age of 70 she was described as 'indefatigable'. She died on 17 April 1956 at Albany and was buried with Anglican rites in Karrakatta cemetery, Perth. Her works hang in the Albany Town Council chambers, Woodbridge House, Guildford, and the Art Gallery of Western Australia, Perth.

W. Murdoch (ed), *The Westralia Gift Book* (Perth, 1916); J. L. Glascock (ed), *Jarrah Leaves* (Perth, 1933); J. Gooding, *Western Australian Art and Artists 1900-1950* (Perth, 1987); C. T. Stannage, *Embellishing the Landscape* (Perth 1990); *West Australian*, 20 Nov 1912, 8 Oct 1935, 23 Oct 1937, 18 July, 19 Dec 1939, 12 Nov 1940, 18 July 1959; *West Australian Mag* (weekly insert of *West Australian*), 2-8 June 1990, p 16; Heap file *and* WA Soc of Artists' file (Art Gallery of WA, Perth).

DOROTHY ERICKSON

HEARMAN, JOAN; see TULLY

HEDDITCH, MABEL EMILY (1897-1966), mayor, was born on 11 December 1897 at Hambrook, Gloucestershire, England, daughter of Alfred William Flux, farmer, and his wife Emily, née Hill. Educated at Colston's Girls School, Bristol, she studied cheesemaking at a country dairy school in 1914.

During World War I, when her three brothers enlisted (two were killed), Mabel ran the family farm and met Norman Samuel Forward Hedditch (d.1954) who, after serving in France with the Australian Imperial Force, had been assigned to farm-work in England. She emigrated to Victoria in 1921 and they were married on 15 April at St Stephen's Anglican Church, Richmond, Melbourne. They settled on the Hedditch family farm at Cape Bridgewater, near Portland, where they raised seven children and became the fifth generation of the family to run the local post office. Norman was also an estate agent and representative for Goldsborough Mort [qq.v.4,5] & Co. Ltd. His brother Harold Read Hedditch (1893-1974), a member of the Country Party, was to represent Port Fairy and Glenelg (1943-45) and Portland (1947-50) in the Legislative Assembly.

Mrs Hedditch entered into community life with zeal. A foundation member of the Portland branch of the Country Women's Association of Victoria (group president 1947-49, central vice-president 1951, State president 1953-55), she soon gained an insight into the problems of the country women of Victoria. The Melbourne *Herald* described her as one 'who knows and loves the land, the people who live on it, the things that grow in it'. A 'biggish' woman, 'with a bright, happy face, and wavy, light brown hair', she was 'blessed with abundant energy and very good health'. She served on the Portland Town Council in 1949-64 and was mayor in 1956-60, a period of rapid progress.

As treasurer of the town's infant welfare centre, Hedditch saw its new building erected. She directed the Home Help Service, worked for Meals on Wheels, buttered hundreds of scones and sandwiches, and was president of the Old Folks Welfare Committee and an energetic secretary of the Lewis Court Homes for the Aged. In 1954 she was made a justice of the peace and in 1960 she was appointed O.B.E. Survived by her two daughters and four of her five sons, she died of myocardial infarction on 6 January 1966 at her Portland home and was buried in Bridgewater cemetery. Later that month it was announced that she had been granted a citizenship award as Portland's most outstanding woman for 1965.

Aust Municipal J, 45, no 768, Feb 1966; *Sun News-Pictorial*, 7 Sept 1949; *Herald* (Melb), 29 May 1954, 18, 22 Sept 1956; *Age* (Melb), 26 Oct 1954; *Portland Observer*, 7, 28 Jan 1966; *Rainbow News*,

27 July 1971; family papers (held by Mr G. N. Hedditch, Ballarat, Vic).   GWEN BENNETT

HEFFRON, ROBERT JAMES (1890-1978), premier, was born on 10 September 1890 at Thames, New Zealand, and registered as James, fifth of eight children of Irish-born parents Michael Heffron, blacksmith, and his wife Ellen, née Heath. Leaving school at 15, James worked by day at a gold-treating plant and studied metallurgy by night at the local school of mines. By the age of 19 he had saved enough money to follow an elder brother to California, United States of America, where he was variously employed as a builder's labourer, carpenter and mule driver. Having failed to find a fortune on the Yukon, Alaska, he returned to New Zealand in 1912. Heffron joined the New Zealand Socialist Party and in the following year was prominent in the eight-month miners' strike at Waihi. He was appointed an organizer for the Auckland General Labourers' Union and studied law part time at Auckland University College. Giving his occupation as shearer, on 29 December 1917 at the registrar's office, Raetihi, he married Jessie Bjornstad (d.1978), daughter of a Norwegian engineer. To evade military service, he left with his wife for Melbourne.

There, in 1919, Heffron was appointed organizer for the Federated Clothing Trades of the Commonwealth of Australia and joined the Marxist-oriented Victorian Socialist Party. About this time he added Robert to his name. He moved to Sydney in 1921 as secretary of the New South Wales branch of the militant Federated Marine Stewards' and Pantrymen's Association of Australasia, a post he was to hold for ten years. In 1925, at the instigation of Sir George Fuller's [q.v.8] Nationalist government, he was charged with conspiracy in connexion with the Port Lyttelton (New Zealand) seamen's strike, but the charges were dropped for lack of evidence. In these years he abandoned the Catholic faith in which he was raised, became a leading member of the Rationalist Association of New South Wales and later described himself as a 'proselytising rationalist'.

Supporting the official Australian Labor Party headed by Premier John Thomas Lang [q.v.9], in October 1927 Heffron unsuccessfully contested the Legislative Assembly seat of Botany against Thomas Mutch [q.v.10], minister for education, who led a breakaway group in protest against Lang's dictatorial methods in cabinet and caucus. Heffron won Botany in the Lang landslide of 25 October 1930 and retained the seat until 1950 when he was elected for Maroubra. After Labor's defeats in the 1932 and 1935 State elections,

Heffron became the key member of a small group in caucus, and of a large and growing group associated with the Labor Council of New South Wales and its secretary Robert King [q.v.], both of which determined that 'Lang must go'. Heffron's anti-Lang strategy was based on his personal stronghold in his Botany-Maroubra branches and on left-wing trade union rebellion against Lang's autocracy. In turn, Lang based his counter-strategy on his control of the party machine through a small inner group, his domination of a cowed caucus, his majority holding of the newspaper, *Labor Daily*, and the passionate loyalty of most metropolitan branches. Lang's bases of power were seriously eroded by 1938.

As a former member of the Victorian Socialist Party, Heffron was an obvious target of Lang's anti-communist campaign. In a show of left-wing union strength against Lang, King organized a conference of dissident unions on 1 August 1936, attended by Heffron and three other caucus members. In response, Lang summoned a special State A.L.P. conference on 22 August which anathematized and expelled Heffron, King and fourteen trade-union leaders who had attended the industrial conference. They formed the nucleus of the breakaway Industrial Labor Party, commonly called the Heffron Labor Party.

Following the re-election of the Stevens-Bruxner [qq.v.12,7] United Australia Party-Country Party coalition in March 1938, the I.L.P. organized a 'unity' conference for 25 June which called upon the A.L.P. federal executive to recognize it as the official Labor Party. When Heffron's party won two by-elections (Hurstville and Waverley) in March and April 1939, the federal executive (under pressure from the Federal parliamentary leader John Curtin [q.v.13]) sponsored a unity conference at the Majestic Theatre, Newtown, on 26 August. Lang lost the crucial vote (166-205) which restored to caucus the right to elect the parliamentary leader. On 5 September, two days after Britain and Australia declared war against Germany, Heffron, (Sir) William McKell and Lang contested the leadership; McKell won in the second ballot.

McKell's chief strategist R. R. Downing later claimed that Heffron refused to contest the deputy-leadership, partly at the urging of his wife who said: 'Bob, if you can't be Number One, why settle for Number Two?' J. M. Baddeley [q.v.7] retained the deputy-leadership until 1949. McKell led Labor to victory on 10 May 1941. Heffron ranked third in the ministry and was appointed minister for national emergency services, an increasingly important portfolio with Japan's entry into the war in December 1941. He played a key role in marshalling the State's manpower and material resources in support of the national war effort. From June 1944 he was minister for education.

In February 1946 McKell told an increasingly fractious caucus that he intended to resign before the 1947 election. To help Heffron secure the succession, McKell remained a member of caucus—after Prime Minister Chifley [q.v.13] had announced his appointment as governor-general—expressly in order to vote for Heffron. On 5 February 1947, however, Heffron lost by two votes to James McGirr [q.v.] who led Labor to its third successive win on 3 May, with a reduced but comfortable majority. The next three years were marked by widespread industrial turbulence, a damaging coal-strike in 1949, the rising power within the Labor Party of the industrial groups (originally formed to combat communism in the trade unions), and tensions between the State executive and the parliamentary party.

At the elections on 17 June 1950 McGirr's temporizing leadership produced a Legislative Assembly evenly divided between the Labor and Liberal-Country parties (46 members each), and the government relied on the support of two Independent Labor members. On 2 April 1952 McGirr's deputy John Joseph Cahill [q.v.13] was elected leader, with Heffron achieving, at the age of 62, the deputy-leadership which he had refused to contest in 1939. Their seven-year partnership gave the Labor government a renewed period of ascendancy in New South Wales, securing its re-election in 1953, 1956 and 1959. The memory of Heffron's former left-wing associations contributed to the ability of the parliamentary Labor Party to remain publicly united in the face of the turmoil which split the Labor movement in 1955. In New South Wales the split was relatively limited.

As deputy-premier, Heffron remained minister for education; the fact that he was no longer a Catholic was deemed a desirable, if not an essential, qualification for that portfolio. He had set out a comprehensive plan in a book entitled *Tomorrow is Theirs: The Present and Future of Education in New South Wales* (1946). In the crucial postwar years he promoted scientific and technical training, and presided over an era of educational expansion and experiment, in close collaboration for much of the period with his forceful director-general (Sir) Harold Wyndham. Primary school enrolments increased from 330 000 to 570 000, secondary school enrolments from 119 000 to 210 000, and technical college enrolments from 42 000 to 108 000. Heffron carried legislation to establish the New South Wales University of Technology, the University of New England and university colleges at Newcastle and Wollongong; university en-

rolments rose from 5000 to 22 000. He was also secretary for mines from February to September 1953.

On 28 October 1959, six days after Cahill's sudden death, Heffron was elected leader unopposed. The radical of the 1920s and the rebel of the 1930s had become a grandfatherly figure, even a figurehead, presiding sedately over an ageing cabinet and an often turbulent caucus. The octogenarian Lang, through his weekly newspaper, *Century*, revenged himself by lampooning Heffron as 'Mr Magoo', after the short-sighted, accident-prone, American cartoon character. A contemporary journalist noted in the *Bulletin* that 'in the House he tends to ramble on ... although occasionally the old radical has shown his teeth, flashed into anger, and for a few minutes reminded us that this was the great mob-orator who led many bitter strikes'. From being a firebrand in his youth, Heffron had become a 'Homburg-hatted, benign, slow and plummy spoken gentleman'.

In January 1960 he persuaded Downing, his attorney-general, to appoint H. V. Evatt [q.v.] chief justice of New South Wales. Heffron's pedestrian campaign led to the loss of a referendum (29 April 1961) to implement a resolution by the 1958 State Labor conference to abolish the Legislative Council; the vote was 882 512 to 1 089 193. Nevertheless, he was able to exploit the electoral misfortunes of the Menzies [q.v.] Federal government flowing from a credit squeeze which produced 3 per cent unemployment, unacceptable to a community conditioned since the war to full employment. Despite a revived Opposition under (Sir) Robert Askin, Labor increased its majority at the State elections on 3 March 1962.

During the 1962 campaign Heffron had undertaken to hold a royal commission into off-course betting. A bitter dispute arose between Downing, who favoured the concept of totalizator-agency betting, and the chief secretary Christopher Augustus Kelly, who wanted to legalize existing starting-price operators. Downing procured a State-executive demand on Heffron to introduce legislation to set up the Totalisator Agency Board. Outside intervention produced an even greater and far-reaching humiliation in 1963. On 30 September the federal executive declared two measures in the New South Wales budget that provided state aid for non-government schools—funding for science laboratories and a means-tested allowance of £21 a year to the parents of children enrolled from third year at Catholic and other independent secondary schools—to be contrary to Labor policy and instructed the State government to withdraw the proposals. At a time when Menzies had made the Labor Party's alleged control by outside 'faceless men' a dominant political issue, Heffron's failure to resist the federal diktat contributed to increasing discontent with his leadership. He resigned in J. B. Renshaw's favour on 28 April 1964, insisting that 'nobody is throwing me out'. Heffron retained his seat of Maroubra in the 1965 elections, which ended Labor's twenty-four-year rule, and retired in January 1968.

Heffron was granted honorary doctorates of letters by the universities of Sydney (1952) and New England (1956), and of science by the New South Wales University of Technology (1955). He listed golf as his only recreation. In 1947 he had been elected an honorary member of the Royal Australian Historical Society. Survived by his two daughters, he died on 27 July 1978 at Kirribilli and was cremated. At his funeral service in St Stephen's Presbyterian Church, Macquarie Street, James Carroll, the Catholic auxiliary archbishop, paid tribute to Heffron's contribution to the New South Wales education system and to his indirect contribution to the eventual settlement of the historically divisive issue of state aid to Catholic schools.

G. Freudenberg, *Cause for Power* (Syd, 1991); D. Clune, *The Legislative Assembly of New South Wales* (Syd, 1993) and *Parliamentary and Extra-Parliamentary Labor* (Syd, 1995); NZ *PP*, H-19K, 1917; *ALP J*, Feb 1962; *Labour Hist*, no 62, May 1992; *Nation* (Syd), 6 May 1961; *Bulletin*, 3 Mar 1962, 15 Feb, 9 May 1964; Bert Roth collection, Alexander Turnbull L (Wellington, NZ).

ROBERT CARR

HEIGHWAY, FREIDA RUTH; see ABBIE

HEINIG, MARY CHRISTINE (1892–1979), educationist, was born in 1892, probably in New York, daughter of German-born parents Frank Heinig, manager, and his wife Alma. Christine was later reticent about her background and German descent, but is said to have grown up among pioneer settlers at Winnetka, Illinois, where she was educated in a one-room school. After graduating from the National College of Education at Evanston—which was renowned for its Froebelian approach to teaching—and studying at the University of Chicago (Ph.B., 1932), in 1928 she became director of the nursery school at Columbia University, New York (M.A., 1936). Her early publications included *Play; The Child's Response to Life* (with Rose Alschuler, Boston, 1936) and *The Child in the Nursery School* (Melbourne, 1938).

In 1937 Miss Heinig accepted the invitation of the Free Kindergarten Union of Victoria to succeed Mary Gutteridge [q.v.] as principal of the Melbourne Kindergarten Training College for one year. She brought to the position knowledge of recent developments in nursery education and a revitalized approach to Froebelian theory. Her appointment was extended for a further year, during which she attracted more students and improved the quality of instruction. Former students recalled the vivacity, creativity and enthusiasm of her teaching. She initiated in-service programmes, upgraded library facilities, designed experimental equipment, and instilled in students and kindergarten staff the need for a scientific approach to nursery education based on observations of children's development and closer collaboration with parents.

Heinig's influence quickly spread beyond Victoria. Her organizational ability and charm facilitated the foundation of the Australian Association for Pre-School Child Development (later the Australian Pre-School Association) which, in 1938, appointed her its first federal education officer. Her main duty was to co-ordinate the establishment of child-research and demonstration centres in each State and Territory. After a brief visit to the United States of America, she took up her post; she was assisted by Dr J. H. L. Cumpston [q.v.8], director-general of the Commonwealth Department of Health, by State committees and by Lady Gowrie [q.v.9], after whom the centres were subsequently named. Heinig's contribution was both practical and administrative: she influenced the design of buildings, furnishings and equipment, as well as the appointment of staff. As pre-school adviser (from 1943) to the Department of Health, she promoted wartime children's centres (based on existing kindergartens), instigated play-groups and advised on Margaret Graham's [q.v.] successful innovation, 'Kindergarten of the Air'. With Cumpston, Heinig co-authored *Pre-School Centres in Australia* (Canberra, 1945).

Resigning from the A.A.P.S.C.D. in September 1944, Heinig returned to the U.S.A. in the following year. There she continued her involvement in education as an associate (1947-61) in elementary and secondary education of the American Association of University Women. She was described as 'an auburn-haired person with quizzical eyes and quirked lips that reveal an ever-fresh approach to living'. In 1951 she was sent to Germany by the State Department to help establish kindergartens in Berlin; in 1955 she revisited Australia to attend the seventh biennial conference of the Australian Pre-School Association. She died on 23 October 1979 in Alabama, U.S.A. An Australian colleague paid tribute to her 'dynamic . . . attitude', 'breadth of outlook' and 'true sense of the place of child study and pre-school child development in the general march of education'.

L. Gardiner, *The Free Kindergarten Union of Victoria 1908-1980* (Melb, 1982); E. King, *Dreams Become Deeds* (Melb, 1986); *Aust J of Early Childhood*, 5, no 1, Mar 1980; *Age* (Melb), 13 Feb, 20 Mar 1937, 3 Oct 1942, 7 Sept 1944; *Argus*, 15, 17 Mar 1937; *Herald* (Melb), 15 Mar 1937, 9 Nov 1938, 10 Aug 1955; *SMH*, 7 Apr, 10 Nov 1938, 7 Sept, 30 Nov 1944, 21 July, 14, 15 Sept 1955, 8 Nov 1979; *Sun News-Pictorial*, 11 Aug 1955; A. Jackson-Nakano, From the Cradle. A history from the records of the Australian Early Childhood Association 1938-1958 (ms, 1993, Aust Early Childhood Assn, Canb).

ELIZABETH J. MELLOR

HELBIG, EDUARD PAUL (1884-1958), Lutheran missionary, was born on 9 July 1884 at Sedan, South Australia, second child of Friedrich Gotthelf Helbig, farmer, and his wife Emma Elisabeth, née Lange, both South Australian born and of Prussian descent. In 1902 the family moved to a mixed farm near Greenock. Paul attended the nearby Point Pass College. Instead of completing his theological studies, he responded to the call from the Neuendettelsau Lutheran Mission for carpenters to go to German New Guinea. Before leaving South Australia he became engaged to his cousin Ernestine Maria Niemz (d.1953), whom he married in New Guinea on 21 April 1909.

Having reached New Guinea in 1906, Helbig was one of the first Australians to work with German missionary colleagues. In 1908 he took charge of the Lutheran mission's coconut plantation at Salankaua, near Finschhafen, and was responsible for clearing and planting the neighbouring Timbulim plantation. He supervised the building of a wharf at Finschhafen in 1912, and the construction of a road from the coast to the mountain mission centre at Sattelberg. For a brief time he was relief captain of the mission schooner, *Bavaria*. Suffering from malaria and a near fatal attack of blackwater fever, he moved to Sattelberg in 1922. There he supervised buildings for the expanding health-and-school station, while he and his wife were also 'house-parents' for its boarding-students. In 1937 Helbig joined his son-in-law Rev. Georg Hofmann at Asaroka, in the Goroka Valley, when restrictions on mission activities in the Central Highlands were eased. On the outbreak of World War II many of his German colleagues were interned, but Helbig—an Australian citizen—was allowed to stay. Although most expatriates were evacuated following Japan's entry into the war, he remained until civil administration ceased in 1942.

After the war the Lutheran Mission in New Guinea faced a severe shortage of personnel. In recognition of his early theological studies and experience in New Guinea, Helbig was ordained in the United Evangelical Lutheran Church of Australia on 5 August 1945. As soon as conditions permitted, he returned to Asaroka where he remained until 1951 when he retired to Tanunda, South Australia.

A strict vegetarian, Helbig was of slim build and middle height, and with a striking black beard. For much of his life he suffered from asthma, as well as the long-term effects of malaria. 'Papa Helbig' was known as an open, friendly and earnest man, whose benign exterior disguised a more dour and serious inner self. He was fluent in the Kâte language and related well to people, regardless of race; he was also a willing teacher to his New Guinean assistants and versatile in addressing the practical needs of the mission. The old mission houses which stand at Asaroka commemorate his skill.

Helbig died on 2 August 1958 at Eastwood, Adelaide, and was buried in Langmeil cemetery, Tanunda; two of his three sons and one of his two daughters survived him. His eldest son Martin Samuel (1911-1968) was the first ordained Australian Lutheran to serve in New Guinea; a daughter Clara had died in missionary service there.

A. G. Helbig, *Family History of Johann Wilhelm Helbig (1830-1896), His Wife Hannah Catharina Ruciak (1832-1904) and their Descendants in Australia to 1979* (Adel, nd); J. Flierl, *Christ in New Guinea* (Tanunda, SA, 1932); E. A. Jericho, *Seedtime and Harvest in New Guinea* (Brisb, c1961); H. Wagner and H. Reiner, *The Lutheran Church in Papua New Guinea* (Adel, 1986); *Lutheran Herald*, 1 Sept 1945, 8 Aug 1953, 13 Sept 1958; *Queensland Lutheran*, Sept 1958; Lutheran Archives, Nth Adel; Neuendettelsau Mission Archives, Neuendettelsau, Germany; information from Mrs K. Deckelmann, Port Augusta, SA, Mr T. Helbig, Walla Walla, NSW, and Mr D. Rohrlach, Glynde, Adel.

ROBIN RADFORD

HELMORE, BASIL ARTHUR (1897-1973), solicitor and businessman, was born on 28 February 1897 at Newcastle, New South Wales, eldest surviving child of Ernest Arthur James Helmore, a company secretary from London, and his Queensland-born wife Gertrude, née Allbon. Basil attended Cooks Hill Superior Public and Newcastle High schools. In 1913 he topped the State in French and Latin at the Leaving certificate, and that year won a prize for an essay on the first entry into Sydney Harbour of the Australian Fleet on 4 October.

Helmore was articled to William Sparke of the legal firm, Sparke & Millard, in 1914, and passed the Solicitors' Admission Board examinations. His articles having been suspended, he enlisted in the Australian Imperial Force on 5 September 1916. He trained as a gunner and sailed for England in the *Benalla* in November. After further training at Larkhill,

Wiltshire, he served with the 4th Field Artillery Brigade on the Western Front from August 1917. His diaries and letters to his father revealed affection, a passionate nature that was well controlled, and a love of the French language. On 18 October 1918 he was posted for duty with the A.I.F. Education Scheme. He was to maintain an enduring correspondence with the friends he had made, including 'Jacqueline', an attractive member of the French family with whom he had been billeted. He returned to Sydney in June 1919 and was discharged on 14 July.

Back at Newcastle, Helmore completed his articles and was admitted to practice on 19 November 1920. Following the retirement of Millard, he became a partner (1922) in Sparke & Helmore (from 1950 Sparke, Helmore & Withycombe). On 4 November 1922 he married Jessie Wilhelmina Cannington at St Saviour's Anglican Church, Carey Bay, Lake Macquarie. In addition to running a busy practice, Helmore edited four legal textbooks on both real and personal property. Full of drive and energy, he took correspondence courses with the University of London (LL.B., 1933; Ph.D., 1955) and wrote a doctoral thesis on legal proceedings between governments. He was a director (from 1942) of J. & A. Brown [qq.v.3] & Abermain Seaham Collieries Ltd, chairman (from 1948) of City Newcastle Gas & Coke Co. Ltd, president (1957-58) of the Newcastle Law Society and a council-member (1953-60) of the Incorporated Law Institute of New South Wales.

In 1937 Helmore stood unsuccessfully for the Senate as a United Australia Party candidate; in 1948 he was defeated by J. D. Kenny [q.v.] in a by-election for the Legislative Council. Helmore's community activities ranged from diocesan affairs to the Boy Scouts' Association, Freemasonry, Rotary and Legacy. In the late 1940s he joined the Lord Mayor's Committee for the Establishment of an Autonomous University of Newcastle. He was elected to the council of Newcastle University College in 1960 and, on its independence in 1965, to that of the University of Newcastle; he was deputy-chairman (1965-66) and warden of convocation (1967); he chaired the university's by-laws committee and donated prizes to the department of French. In 1971 he was appointed O.B.E.

Throughout his life Helmore was regarded as a brilliant and humorous public speaker, especially after dinner. In contrast to the manner he exhibited in his professional, educational and diocesan involvements, he loved the risqué, and his Rabelaisian stories and *doubles entendres* were accompanied by his unusually high giggle. A member of the Newcastle, United Service (Newcastle) and University (Sydney) clubs, he enjoyed playing bowls. He was 5 ft 7½ ins (171 cm) tall and slim in build, with pleasant features and a demeanour dominated by his smile and infectious laughter. Always ambitious, he was capable of clashing with others and suffered reversals acutely, yet at the end of his life, as at the beginning of his adulthood, he valued friendship highly. Helmore died on 4 November 1973 at his Newcastle home and was cremated; his wife, daughter and two sons survived him.

Newcastle Morning Herald, 4 May 1910, 10 Mar 1950, 5, 6 Nov 1973; *Daily Telegraph* (Syd), 20 July 1912; *SMH*, 23 Jan 1914, 12 June 1971; *Dungog Chronicle*, 13 Apr 1943; *Maitland Mercury*, 15 Apr 1943; Helmore papers (AWM); Univ Newcastle Archives; information from Mr P. Withycombe, Newcastle, Mrs D. M. Bevan, Newcastle, and Mr D. A. Helmore, The Junction, NSW, who holds family papers; personal information.

WARREN DERKENNE

HELY, WILLIAM LLOYD (1909-1970), air force officer, was born on 24 August 1909 at Wellington, New South Wales, third child of Prosper Frederick Hely, storekeeper, and his wife Alice, née Lloyd, both native-born. Bill was educated in public schools at Mudgee, Wollongong and Rozelle before entering Fort Street Boys' High School where he gained his Intermediate certificate in 1926. While employed as a clerk, he studied accountancy part time.

On 16 February 1927 Hely entered the Royal Military College, Duntroon, Federal Capital Territory, as a staff cadet nominated by the Royal Australian Air Force. Graduating on 9 December 1930, he was appointed pilot officer in the R.A.A.F. next day. In 1931 he completed flying training at Point Cook, Victoria, qualifying with a distinguished pass. He filled junior postings at Richmond, New South Wales (1932 and 1936-37), and in Victoria at Laverton (1932-33 and 1937-38) and Point Cook (1933-36). By 1933 he had acquired specialist qualifications in aerial photography.

Promoted flight lieutenant in April 1936, Hely left that month for Western Australia to take part in the North Australian Aerial Geological and Geophysical Survey. On 13 April he lost his way in the Northern Territory and had to make an emergency landing about 90 miles (145 km) north-west of Newcastle Waters; the badly damaged plane and its uninjured crew were found nine days later. During the 1937 survey season Hely was called upon to mount three search and rescue operations in Central Australia. In May and again in September he located downed aircraft, but in November was unable to find a missing prospector. The searches were conducted under trying climatic conditions and over rough and virtually uninhabited country. For his work he was awarded the Air Force Cross.

On 29 November 1938 at St Aidan's Anglican Church, Launceston, Tasmania, Hely married Jean Adie McDonald, a secretary. Next month he embarked for England to enter the Royal Air Force Staff College, Andover. He was promoted temporary squadron leader in September 1939 and was briefly employed in the operations room at headquarters, Coastal Command. Returning to Australia in January 1940, he was posted to R.A.A.F. Headquarters, Melbourne, as staff officer, plans. In January 1941 he was made temporary wing commander and from August was director of operations.

Acting Group Captain Hely went to Darwin in May 1942 to be senior air staff officer at headquarters, North-Western Area, and was involved in planning for the evacuation of Timor. He was director of air staff policy at R.A.A.F. Headquarters from March 1943; in May 1944 he was sent to Merauke, Netherlands New Guinea, to command No.72 Wing. In September he moved to Cairns, Queensland, and formed No.84 Wing which he took to Bougainville in November to provide support for army operations.

In October 1945 he returned to Melbourne and was director of organization and staff duties (1946), director of postings (1946-47) and director of personal services (1947-48). Although the demobilization of the wartime force and the change to peacetime conditions made these posts difficult, Hely displayed 'outstanding qualities'. He sailed to England in December 1948 to attend the course at the Imperial Defence College, London. Back in Melbourne, in January 1950 he took up duty as deputy to the air member for personnel. In September 1951 he was posted to Pearce, Western Australia, as air officer commanding, Western Area, and in April 1952 was made acting air commodore. During the atomic-weapons trials at the Monte Bello Islands in 1952, he was responsible for the many operational tasks allotted to the R.A.A.F. He was appointed C.B.E. in 1953.

Promoted acting air vice marshal in October 1953 (substantive 5 September 1956), Hely became deputy chief of the Air Staff. In January-April 1955 he was acting air member for personnel; from January 1956 he was air officer commanding, Training Command; and in May 1957 he went to Washington as head of the Australian Joint Services Staff. From March 1960 he was based in Canberra as air member for personnel until his retirement on 25 August 1966. He had been appointed C.B. in 1964. Hely continued to live in the capital and was patron of the local branch of the Air Force Association. Survived by his wife and two daughters, he died of cancer on 20 May 1970 in Canberra Hospital and was cremated with R.A.A.F. honours.

J. E. Lee, *Duntroon* (Canb, 1952); G. Odgers, *Air War Against Japan 1943-1945* (Canb, 1957); J. E. Hewitt, *Adversity in Success* (Melb, 1980); C. D. Coulthard-Clark, *The Third Brother* (Syd, 1991); *R.A.A.F. News*, July 1970; *Age* and *Argus* (Melb), 9 June 1938; *Canb Times*, 21-23 May 1970.

BRIAN EATON*

HENDERSON, JOCELYN (1905-1972), conservationist, was born on 11 February 1905 at Albury, New South Wales, third daughter of native-born parents Walter George Henderson, solicitor, and his wife Charlotte Gertrude, née Fleming. Walter wrote short stories with a country setting; his affection for the bush influenced Jocelyn. Nicknamed 'Daph', she was educated at Albury Grammar School and in 1920-21 at the Church of England Girls' Grammar School (The Hermitage), Geelong, Victoria. Unlike her sisters, she was shy and retiring, and returned to work at home. When the family moved in 1931 to Upper Wantagong, a grazing property near Holbrook, she was able to indulge her passions for orchid collecting, bird-watching and studying trees.

In early 1943 Miss Henderson began a crusade to promote reafforestation and soil conservation. She organized thoroughly, read widely, gained the support of numerous bureaucrats and community leaders, and spoke to a range of organizations. She wrote extensively for newspapers, journals and radio, and published *Fire—or water?* (Sydney, 1947), a book on reafforestation and fire control. Her campaign received a mixed reception. Senior Federal and State public servants were largely supportive, for her views coincided with those which they were trying to persuade their governments to adopt. The contrast between administrative enthusiasm and political indifference was most marked in Victoria. In New South Wales there was bipartisan political support for conservation issues, but she encountered scepticism from E. H. F. Swain [q.v.12], chairman of the Forestry Commission.

None the less, she secured several major successes. Many farmers were persuaded to take action on soil conservation and reafforestation, and the State government passed legislation allowing local councils to plant community forests for beautification, soil conservation and as a valuable future crop. She received the most hostile reception close to home. Albury Municipal and Holbrook Shire councils condemned her recommendations as impractical and wasteful. She was subjected to harassment by some aggrieved pastoralists who depended on the summer grazing in the Snowy Mountains that she wished to see abolished to protect the catchments of the Murray and Murrumbidgee rivers.

Henderson maintained her passionate concern for reafforestation, but after 1950 her active involvement declined. She was a founder of the Men of the Land Society (later the Conservation Society of New South Wales). In 1960 she made a world tour to study community and private forestry, and advised the Federal government on legislation to promote forestry schemes. H. A. Lindsay [q.v.] based the character Alison Reeford in *The Red Bull* (London, 1959) on Henderson and her work.

In 1950 Wantagong had been sold, apparently with some family acrimony, and she moved with her parents to Glencraig, a dairy-farm near Robertson. She married Clifford Woodman Squire, a local share-farmer, on 7 January 1961 at St Andrew's Presbyterian Church, Camperdown, Victoria. They bought a property, Green Meadows, near Bundanoon, New South Wales. Short and slightly built, Jocelyn feared cameras, and appeared severe and intense in photographs. In 1967 the Squires retired to Bowral where she died of cancer on 9 November 1972 and was cremated with Anglican rites; her husband survived her. She is remembered by her nieces and nephews, not least for introducing them to the Australian bush.

H. A. Lindsay, Notes on Jocelyn Henderson (Oct 1968, held at ADB, Canb); Conservation Soc of NSW, Death of Noted Conservationist (press release, 20 Nov 1972); Henderson papers (ML); information from Mr J. Henderson and Mrs V. Heriot, Holbrook, NSW, and Mrs D. F. Exon, Chapman, Canb.   JAN McDONALD

HENDERSON, THOMAS (1872-1968), headmaster, was born on 7 December 1872 at Mooloolah, Queensland, second of four children of Thomas Henderson, police constable, and his wife Eliza, née McAteer, both from Ireland. The family moved to the Brisbane suburb of Hemmant where Thomas attended the local state school. In April 1888 he was admitted to the Department of Public Instruction and sent to Kangaroo Point Boys' School as a pupil-teacher; three years later he became an assistant-teacher. He then taught at Ipswich East (1896-97) and Woolloongabba (from 1898) boys' schools. At Holy Trinity Church, Woolloongabba, on 10 April 1901 he married with Anglican rites Maria Ada Mumford, a telephone-operator. From July 1902 Henderson ran the one-teacher school at Glencoe until appointed head teacher of a new

school at Rangeville, Toowoomba, in July 1909. He was transferred to Ascot State School, Brisbane, in May 1920, and remained there for nineteen years.

A competent and progressive administrator, Henderson was unusually innovative and creative. His concept of 'the school beautiful' inspired the establishment of attractive grounds, with gardens, flowering trees, bush-houses, rockeries, fish ponds and vine-covered archways. Adventure playgrounds, planned athletic ovals and games courts were added features. Gymnasiums and swimming pools built at Rangeville and Ascot were among the first in Queensland state schools. Appreciating the value of school libraries, Henderson acquired a separate building at Ascot for use as a library and reading-room. He arranged for one teacher to become an art specialist in order to implement an ambitious programme of art, craft and art appreciation. By drawing on the talents of his staff, he decorated schoolrooms with murals of educational and aesthetic value.

Henderson introduced choral work, and founded a bugle band at Rangeville and a brass band at Ascot. Pupils were consistently successful in external scholarship examinations, winning three Lilley [q.v.5] medals during this period. Sport was encouraged and a competitive house-system introduced. Well in advance of their general acceptance by the Department of Public Instruction, Henderson established project clubs which promoted pupils' interests in poultry, beekeeping, fish, vegetables and flowers. Ascot held its own annual agricultural and horticultural show. He was also instrumental in establishing a model, one-teacher school within Ascot where teachers-in-training spent some time in anticipation of their service in small schools.

A successful amateur sportsman, Henderson turned out for athletics, cricket, football and bowls. He rose to the rank of lieutenant in the Queensland Teachers' Volunteer Corps and was an officer of school cadets. With the help of his colleagues, he produced several textbooks on mathematics, history and geography; for many years he was an executive-member of the Queensland Teachers' Union. 'Hendy's' reputation was built on his ability to develop his staff, to inspire the co-operation of individuals and to involve communities in his work. Many of his achievements were the more impressive for being accomplished during the Depression. Affectionately regarded as the 'Mr Chips' of Ascot School, he retired on 30 June 1939. He died on 12 December 1968 at Clayfield and was cremated; his wife, three daughters and three of his four sons survived him. The other son Trevor Macateer Henderson [q.v.] predeceased him.

N. Guy and H. Sutcliffe, *Ascot* (Brisb, 1995); *Telegraph* (Brisb), 12 Dec 1968; *Courier-Mail*, 13 Dec 1968; teachers' staff cards and other Education Dept records (Hist Unit, Qld Dept of Education, Brisb); Rangeville *and* Ascot state schools records (QA); Henderson family records (held by Mrs R. M. James, Hamilton, Brisb).

HAROLD J. SUTCLIFFE

HENDERSON, TREVOR MACATEER (1905-1967), optometrist and racehorse-owner, was born on 27 August 1905 at Glencoe, on the Darling Downs, Queensland, third son of seven children of Thomas Henderson [q.v.], schoolteacher, and his wife Maria Ada, née Mumford. Trevor was educated at Rangeville State (where his father was head teacher) and at Toowoomba Grammar schools. On leaving school, he was apprenticed to the optical firm, Charles Gamin & Co., Brisbane; by the age of 23 he had established his own flourishing business in the T. & G. Building, Queen Street. On 27 December 1933 at the Ann Street Presbyterian Church, Brisbane, he married Irene Erla Cummins; they were to have two sons before being divorced in 1948.

Managing his business adeptly, Henderson combined financial acumen with a remarkable ability to take advantage of publicity, particularly advertising on commercial radio. It was a controversial approach in what was deemed a conservative profession, but his theme song, *Take a Pair of Sparkling Eyes*, was known in households throughout Queensland. He was a member of the Queensland division of the Australian Optometrical Association and served as a counsellor in 1935. The growth of his business was often at the expense of many other members of the A.O.A., as was his contractual agreement (1941) with the State government—via the Department of Health and Home Affairs—to provide an optical service at country hospitals 'for persons . . . not in a position to pay'. By 1949 Henderson's firm had branches at Ipswich and Toowoomba, and also conducted a large mail-order business, both directly and through agencies.

Already a city identity, Henderson became one of Queensland's most prominent turf sportsmen of the postwar period. He was a leading owner, racing his horses under his gold, pink and black colours in Brisbane and at Toowoomba: among the more noteworthy were Duke Paul, Masefield, Sir Helion and Red Mirth. Henderson was also a part-owner of several other well-known racehorses, including Cobbler's Wax and Glenrowan. At the Church of the Holy Spirit, New Farm, on 7 August 1951 he married with Catholic rites Veronica Emily Carton, a 33-year-old receptionist.

Henderson was a member (from 1940) of Tattersall's Club, Brisbane; a committee-member (from 1958), he was president in 1961-66 and conjointly president of Tattersall's Racing Club. His presidency spanned a period of important change and growth, during which the government's Totalisator Agency Board developed and Tattersalls became a convivial rendezvous, boasting a six-year waiting-list for membership. He was elected to the committee of the Queensland Turf Club in 1966 and served on its licensing and finance sub-committees, as well as on the Metropolitan Galloping Races allocation committee.

Survived by his wife and the sons of his first marriage, Henderson died of hypertension and coronary atherosclerosis on 26 September 1967 at his Hamilton home and was buried in Pinaroo Lawn cemetery with Anglican rites. His estate was sworn for probate at $187 186.

Aust Optometrical Assn, Qld Division, *Notes on the First Fifty Years of Organized Optometry in Queensland, 1908-1958* (Brisb, 1974?); R. Longhurst, *Friendship is Life* (Brisb, 1993); *Courier-Mail*, 27 Sept 1967, 12 Sept 1968; *Telegraph* (Brisb), 27 Sept 1967, 12 Dec 1968.

ROBERT I. LONGHURST

HENNESSY, ERIC CLAUDE (1910-1964), soldier, hospital attendant and stock-and-station agent, was born on 8 September 1910 at Lithgow, New South Wales, son of native-born parents Percy Reginald Hennessy, furnaceman, and his wife Ethel Florence, née Hammerton. Eric attended primary school, possibly at Pine Rocks, and subsequently found work at nearby Orange as an attendant at the (Bloomfield) Mental Hospital. On 21 November 1933 at St Barnabas's Anglican Church, Sydney, he married Betty Agnes de Lautour; they were divorced in 1939. A member of the 6th Light Horse Regiment, Militia, he had been included in the Australian contingent for the coronation of King George VI in 1937.

Soldiering was Hennessy's passion. On 3 November 1939 he enlisted in the Australian Imperial Force and was posted as a sergeant to the 6th Divisional Reconnaissance (later Cavalry) Regiment, a carrier-mounted scouting force. He was commissioned lieutenant in January 1940 during his voyage to the Middle East where his unit trained in Palestine and Egypt.

In the assault against Bardia, Libya, on 3 January 1941, Hennessy acted as a forward observation officer. He waved on Australian troops from a position close to a breach in the Italian wire and was under a heavy barrage for some hours before rejoining his squadron; he was awarded the Military Cross. After Tobruk fell on 22 January, he was one of the first to enter the town. The Italian naval commander, Admiral Massimiliano Vietina, attempted to surrender his forces to him. When Vietina proffered his sword, Hennessy waved it aside, allegedly saying, 'You keep it, mate. I've got enough souvenirs'.

The regiment was sent to Palestine in May and operated against Vichy French forces in Syria in June-July. Back in Australia, in June 1942 the 6th became part of Northern Territory Force, with Hennessy an acting squadron leader. He was promoted temporary major in July. At St Stephen's Anglican Church, Chatswood, Sydney, on 8 December 1943 he married Valmai Amy Searle, an army nursing sister. From October that year his unit had trained in Queensland where it was re-designated the 2nd/6th Cavalry (Commando) Regiment. Promoted temporary lieutenant colonel, Hennessy assumed command on 4 February 1944, achieving a goal he had set himself four years earlier.

In October the regiment embarked for New Guinea. Hennessy led it in action at Aitape and Wewak, and won renown as one of the most capable commanders in the A.I.F. A calm and inspiring leader, colourful, sensitive and a shrewd judge of men, he was much loved by his troops who regarded him as a 'soldier's soldier'. He was 6 ft 2 ins (188 cm) tall, strongly built and had a fair complexion. In May 1945 he fell ill and was evacuated to Australia. He returned to New Guinea in July, relinquished command in December and was transferred to the Reserve of Officers on 12 February 1946. For his part in the campaign he was awarded the Distinguished Service Order.

Finding it difficult to adjust to a peacetime career, Hennessy worked as a representative for Atlantic Union Oil Co. Pty Ltd before becoming a stock-and-station agent at Wellington, New South Wales. In 1954-56 he served on the Wellington Shire Council (deputy-president 1955); in 1956 he stood unsuccessfully as a Liberal Party candidate for the Legislative Assembly seat of Mudgee; he was next employed as a secretary-manager of clubs operated by the Returned Sailors', Soldiers' and Airmen's League of Australia at Woollongong (1957-62) and Bathurst (from 1963). Preferring life in the country, he rejected offers of senior managerial positions with Sydney-based companies. He was active in Legacy and regularly addressed school children on Anzac Day. Survived by his wife, their daughter and two sons, and by the son of his first marriage, he died of myocardial infarction on 14 November 1964 at Bathurst and was buried in the local cemetery.

G. Long, *To Benghazi* (Canb, 1952) and *The Final Campaigns* (Canb, 1963); S. O'Leary, *To the Green Fields Beyond* (Syd, 1975); *Western Advocate*, 16 Nov 1964; War diaries, 6th Divisional Cavalry Regiment *and* 2nd/6th Cavalry (Commando) Regiment (AWM); information from Mr J. Offner, Wellington, Mrs S. McKinnon, Wee Jasper, Mr E. Nunn and Mr R. Rauchle, Orange, NSW.

DARRYL MCINTYRE

HENRY, MAX (1883-1959), veterinary surgeon and army officer, was born on 14 June 1883 at Glebe, Sydney, son of Arthur Henry, who had emigrated from England and become registrar in insolvency, and his native-born wife Martha, née Skillman. Max attended The King's School, Parramatta, as a day-boy (1896-1901) and in 1901 enrolled at the Royal Veterinary College, London, where he won three medals. Qualifying in July 1906, he was admitted to membership of the Royal College of Veterinary Surgeons and undertook postgraduate courses in pathology, bacteriology and tropical diseases.

Henry returned to Sydney and joined the Department of Health in 1907 as dairy supervisor for the Bega area. Next year he transferred to the stock and brands branch of the Department of Agriculture as a veterinary surgeon; he lectured at Hawkesbury Agricultural and Sydney Technical colleges. On 4 August 1910 he married Denise Ramsden Wood at St Paul's Anglican Church, Carlingford. He submitted a thesis to the faculty of veterinary science at the University of Sydney (B.V.Sc., 1912).

A captain in the Militia, Henry was commissioned in the Australian Imperial Force on 11 November 1914 and was posted to No.1 Veterinary Section which established a veterinary hospital at Heliopolis, Egypt. In March 1916 he was promoted temporary major and made assistant (later deputy-assistant) director of veterinary services, 5th Division. Three months later he was sent to France where he was observed on one occasion looking 'miserably cold despite his sheep skin jacket, riding his horse through the mud and slush of the "Somme" area, trying to help his V.O.'s do something to ameliorate conditions arising from their wretched environment'. Promoted lieutenant colonel on 1 May 1918, Henry won the Distinguished Service Order (1919) and was mentioned in dispatches four times for his work on the Western Front. His appointment terminated in Sydney on 8 July 1919.

He rejoined the Department of Agriculture and on 1 January 1924 was appointed chief veterinary surgeon. Henry inherited a very small staff which had provided poor service to stock-owners. Despite opposition and

discouragement from those he was endeavouring to help, his energy, imagination, integrity and perseverance enabled him to establish an effective veterinary service and to
reduce losses due to disease and poor animal
husbandry. He encouraged research, expanded laboratories and field-stations, and
earned an international reputation in epidemiology and as an administrator. In 1940 the
department was reorganized and he was appointed chief of the division of animal industry. His major regret was that he had failed to
eradicate the cattle tick.

Despite his heavy workload as chief veterinary surgeon, Henry had resumed his Militia
service in 1921 and was assistant-director of
veterinary services in New South Wales in
1922-40. He lectured at the university from
1922, mainly on veterinary jurisprudence and
epidemiology, and acted as an external examiner. In 1924 he was foundation president of
the Veterinary Surgeons Board. A member of
the Royal Society of New South Wales, he
also belonged to the Rotary Club of
Sydney.

Largely through Henry's efforts the Australian Veterinary Association had been
established in 1921. He was foundation
honorary secretary (1921-24), federal
council-member (1924-34 and 1941-46), editor of its journal (1925-28) and president
(1926-28 and 1944). In 1938 he visited Europe, Britain and North America, and attended the Thirteenth International Veterinary Conference, in Switzerland. He was
elected a fellow of the A.V.A. in 1945 and
awarded the Gilruth [q.v.9] prize in 1953. Following his retirement from the department in
1947, he acted as general secretary to the
association until 1949. The R.C.V.S. bestowed its diploma of honorary associateship
on him in 1954.

Max Henry was a tall, well-built man, with a
strong moustache and in later years a small,
neatly trimmed beard. His innate shyness
made him appear brusque, but he was gentle
and modest. He loved light opera and the
theatre, as well as bush life and camping, and
had a real interest in native plants extending
back to his youth. Survived by his wife, son
and three daughters, he died at his Chatswood
home on 9 June 1959 and was cremated. His
son John followed him into the veterinary
profession. The A.V.A. library was named the
Max Henry Memorial Library and is housed
at the Elizabeth Macarthur [q.v.2] Agricultural Institute, Menangle.

G. E. Hall and A. Cousins (eds), *Book of Remembrance of the University of Sydney in the War 1914-
1918* (Syd, 1939); *Aust Veterinary J*, 20, Feb 1944,
p 180, 23, Aug 1947, p 226, 29, Aug 1953, p 231,
35, June 1959, p 304; World Veterinary Hist Assn
(Denmark), *Historica Medicinae Veterinae* (issue
published by World Veterinary Congress, Perth),
Aug 1983, p 17; *SMH*, 3 Nov 1920, 12 May 1938,
14 May 1954; W. L. Hindmarsh, Reminiscences
(Aust Veterinary Assn Hist Collection, Harden,
NSW); J. Henry, Recollections of Max Henry as a
father (ts, held in ADB file); The King's School,
Parramatta, Syd, Archives.

ROBERT I. TAYLOR

HENSCHKE, CYRIL ALFRED (1924-
1979), winemaker, was born on 11 September 1924 at Angaston, South Australia,
youngest of twelve children of native-born
parents Paul Alfred Henschke, winemaker
and farmer, and his wife Johanne Ida Selma,
née Stanitzki. His great-grandfather Johann
Christian Henschke had emigrated from Sile-
sia in 1841 and settled at Bethany in the
Barossa Valley. Nine years later he took up
land at Keyneton where he and his son Paul
Gotthard began selling their wine in 1868.
After the turn of the century Paul Alfred produced fortified wines, sold mainly in bulk.

Cyril was educated at Keyneton Public and
Nuriootpa High schools; he often rode his
bicycle from Keyneton to Nuriootpa and back,
a total distance of 25 miles (40 km). On leaving school, he worked in the district's
vineyards and wine cellars, including the
Thomas Hardy [q.v.4] & Sons Ltd winery at
Dorrien, where his interest in bottled table
wines originated. At the Lutheran Church,
Grünberg, on 10 September 1947 he married
Doris Elvera Klemm, a nurse.

One of Cyril Henschke's early tasks when
he started working on the family's Keyneton
property about 1949 was to build more cellar
accommodation. Unlike his father, who combined winemaking with farming, he concentrated on the former and left the latter to his
brother Louis. Cyril took charge of winemaking in 1955 and set out to produce fine table
wines—dry whites and dry reds—but initially
had difficulty selling them. Sales improved
after he entered a national wine show in
Sydney in 1956, where his 1952 Mount
Edelstone shiraz won the first of several
awards. Further success greeted his 1954
Rhine Riesling, ensuring his position as a
leading producer of varietal table wines. His
most highly acclaimed wine, Hill of Grace,
produced from shiraz grapes planted in the
1860s near the Keyneton cellars, was never
shown. During the 1960s he planted grape
varieties—until then rarely grown in South
Australia—such as semillon, traminer and
sylvaner, and made distinctive wines from
them. His winemaking techniques were
characterized by a willingness to experiment.

In 1970 Henschke became the first Australian vigneron to be awarded a Churchill
fellowship, which enabled him to study at

small wineries in Germany, California, South Africa and Britain. Back in South Australia, he became one of the founding 'Barons of the Barossa', a wine fraternity that promoted the region, and was active in the Barossa Winemakers Association. He sought neither fame nor public office, preferring to work quietly in his old stone cellars.

Of lean build and middle height, Henschke was lively, witty and enthusiastic, a generous host and a man of many interests, among them the arts (particularly classical and baroque music), astronomy and geology. Forthright, but courteous and controlled, he read avidly and loved talking to people. He was a member of the local council, an elder of his church, a Jaycee and a Rotarian. Henschke was shot by his wife at their home in the early hours of 13 December 1979; survived by her, their daughter and two sons, he was buried in the graveyard of the Gnadenberg Zion Lutheran Church, Moculta. Doris was charged with his murder, but acquitted in February 1980. Their son Stephen continued the family's winemaking tradition.

G. Farwell, *100 Years of Winemaking* (Adel, 1968); *Wine & Spirit Buying Guide*, Feb 1980, p 23; *Age* (Melb), 11 Feb 1967; *Advertiser* (Adel), 15, 20 Dec 1979; information from Mrs I. Dallwitz, Nuriootpa, and Mr S. Henschke, Keyneton, SA.

VALMAI A. HANKEL

HENTY, SIR NORMAN HENRY DENHAM (1903-1978), politician and wholesaler, was born on 13 October 1903 at Longford, Tasmania, second of four children and eldest son of Victorian-born parents Thomas Norman Henty, storekeeper, and his wife Sarah Nina Lily Mary, née Wilson. A member of the pioneering Henty [qq.v.1,4] family, Thomas had come to Tasmania in 1896. He managed Brown's Store, a grocery at Longford, then moved to Launceston about 1904 where he began a wholesaling business.

Educated at Launceston Church Grammar School, Denham left at the age of 14 to work for his father; he was employed in the office until he became sales representative to the general stores which the firm supplied. In such a small concern there was no opportunity to specialize: he was also shipping and accounts clerk, and delivered invoices and statements by hand as he strolled home after work. Despite the Depression and strong competition, the business flourished, largely due to his efforts and business acumen.

The family made a significant contribution to sporting activities in their provincial community, cricket being a favoured pastime. Denham was a self-taught pianist, much in demand at social functions. He was also an avid bird-watcher who, as minister for customs and excise, was to prohibit (1960) the export of Australian native fauna for commercial purposes. At St Aidan's Anglican Church, Launceston, on 15 March 1930 he married Faith Gordon Spotswood, a schoolmistress; they were to have three sons and a daughter. Faith's strong character and support were to prove invaluable to her husband in his political career.

In the decade after his marriage, Henty reinforced his reputation in the business world for hard work, competence and prudence, and rose to be managing director (1937-50) of T. Norman Henty & Sons Pty Ltd. Because of rheumatic fever, he was unfit for military service in World War II, but served as an enthusiastic member of the Volunteer Air Observers' Corps. He was an alderman (1943-51) and mayor (1948-49) of Launceston City Council and represented the L.C.C. on the council of Launceston Technical College.

A member of the committee that established the Liberal Party of Australia in Tasmania in 1945, Henty joined the party's federal council in 1947. Two years later he was elected to the Senate. Taking his seat in July 1950, he retained it comfortably at the elections in 1951, 1955 and 1961. He fostered the welfare of his constituents, frequently recalling his concern for those who suffered in the Depression and vowing to prevent a recurrence of a similar situation. His commitment extended to personal benevolence; after his retirement he gave his parliamentary pension to charity.

In the Senate, Henty could be a forceful speaker, especially when enthusiastic for a cause, such as improvements to Bass Strait shipping services. His common-sense approach to issues, and his ready friendship and assistance to new or young members of parliament, made him friends on all sides of politics. He was instrumental in expanding the Senate committee system, and initiated select committees on air- and water-pollution in April and May 1968.

Reliable and loyal, Henty was a staunch supporter of (Sir) Robert Menzies [q.v.] who rewarded him with ministerial rank. Henty's portfolios—customs and excise (1956-64), civil aviation (1964-66) and supply (1966-68) —largely reflected his commercial background. Having entered cabinet in 1963, he was deputy-leader of the government in the Senate in 1964-66 and leader in 1966-67. While minister for customs, he liberalized censorship of books and films; through his efforts as minister for civil aviation, the airport terminal at Launceston was modernized.

Retiring from the Senate in June 1968, Henty was appointed K.B.E. that year. Sir Denham was a director of the Equitable Building Society, A. G. Webster & Woolgrowers

Ltd and the Launceston Bank for Savings, whose boards valued his network of contacts. He was a member (1970-71) and chairman (1971-72) of the Launceston General Hospital's board of management and a member (from 1968) of the Overseas Telecommunications Commission (Australia). In 1970 he was made an honorary freeman of the City of Launceston. Survived by his wife, daughter and two sons, he died on 9 May 1978 at Launceston and was cremated; his estate was sworn for probate at $143 813. Henty House and an adjoining waterscape in the Launceston Civic Plaza commemorate him.

M. Bassett, *The Hentys* (Lond, 1954); R. A. Ferrall, *Notable Tasmanians* (Launc, 1980); *Examiner* (Launc), 30 Mar, 8 June 1968, 10 May 1978; *Mercury* (Hob), 8 June 1968, 10, 11 May, 10 June 1978; information from Mr A. S. Henty, Launc, and Mr T. N. Henty, Relbia, Tas.   R. J. K. CHAPMAN

HERBERT, ANDREW DESMOND (1898-1976), professor of botany, was born on 17 June 1898 at Diamond Creek, Melbourne, eldest of three children of Victorian-born parents Andrew Burgess Herbert, fruit-grower, and his wife Winifred Alice, née Connell. Desmond was educated at Malvern State School, Melbourne Church of England Grammar School and the University of Melbourne (B.Sc., 1918; M.Sc., 1920; D.Sc., 1929). At the age of 20 he was appointed government botanist in Western Australia and subsequently lectured part time in agricultural botany and plant pathology at the University of Western Australia. In 1921 he accepted the post of professor of plant physiology and pathology at the University of the Philippines. On 11 December 1922, in Manila, he married his assistant Vera McNeilance, daughter of J. H. Prowse [q.v.11]. Herbert moved to the department of biology at the University of Queensland in 1924 as a lecturer in botany; he was promoted associate-professor (1946), acting-professor (1948) and foundation professor of botany (1948-65). He examined for the State pharmacy board and represented Queensland on the board of higher forestry education.

Two themes, the pathology and biogeography of plants, dominated Herbert's scientific writings. He was attracted to the former because 'bitter pit' was a serious disease in apples on the family orchard. From the time of his appointment in Brisbane he developed plant pathology into a scientific discipline. Through his students, many of whom entered government service, he contributed significantly to the development of Queensland's agriculture. His interest in climate as a major factor controlling the geographical distribution of vegetation was first expressed in his doctoral dissertation and the theme recurred in several of his publications.

Soon after arriving in Brisbane, Herbert became an acknowledged leader of its small scientific community. President of the Queensland Naturalists' Club (1926), of the Royal (1928), the Horticultural (1936-42) and the Orchid (1940) societies of Queensland, of Section M (Botany) of the Australian and New Zealand Association for the Advancement of Science (1932) and of the Queensland branch of the Australian Institute of Agricultural Science (1942), he was granted an honorary D.Sc. by the University of Queensland in 1935. He was an excellent communicator who lectured on horticulture for the Australian Broadcasting Commission and for the Board of Adult Education, and wrote for the *Sunday Mail*; his book, *Gardening in Warm Climates* (Sydney, 1952), was compiled from his articles. Being red-green colour-blind neither diminished his enjoyment of gardening nor inhibited his enthusiasm for judging garden competitions.

During World War II Herbert advised on the selection of sites suitable for research on chemical warfare. With C. T. White [q.v.12] and R. E. P. Dwyer, he wrote *Friendly Fruits and Vegetables* (Melbourne, 1943), a survival manual for members of the Royal Australian Air Force. In 1966 he was appointed C.M.G. A large man with a swarthy complexion, he had a commanding presence which belied a gentle and kindly nature. He was an active Freemason and an accomplished raconteur whose utterances were punctuated by the waving of a pipe from which he was rarely separated. Predeceased by his wife and survived by his two sons and two daughters, he died on 8 September 1976 in Royal Brisbane Hospital and was cremated with Methodist forms; his estate was sworn for probate at $138 805. Herbert's son John Desmond (1925-1978) was a minister (1965-78) in the Legislative Assembly and his daughter Joan Winifred (Cribb) (b.1930) became a noted naturalist and author.

D. P. Mellor, *The Role of Science and Industry* (Canb, 1958); *Univ Qld Gazette*, Dec 1948; Roy Soc WA, *J*, 60, 1977; Roy Soc Qld, *Procs*, 89, June 1978, pp xix, 134; *Qld Naturalist*, 22, nos 1-4, May 1978, p 72, 22, nos 5-6, 1979, p 96; *Courier-Mail*, 15 Dec 1965, 10 Sept 1976; *Telegraph* (Brisb), 9 Sept 1976; Univ Qld *and* Univ WA archives; information from Sir Theodore Bray, St Lucia, Brisb.

H. TREVOR CLIFFORD

HERBERT, WILLIAM SCOTT (1920-1975), tenor, was born on 6 December 1920 at Albert Park, Melbourne, seventh of eight children of Victorian-born parents Frank Harry Herbert, traveller, and his wife Jean

Whatley, née Ingram. As children, he and his siblings gathered at the piano to sing together under the spirited leadership of their father who was of Welsh descent. William was educated at Trinity Grammar School. While a chorister at St Paul's Cathedral, Melbourne, he was influenced by the choirmaster Dr A. E. Floyd [q.v.8] who became his mentor; Floyd was primarily responsible for his development, particularly in oratorio, and for the excellent diction which remained a notable feature of his singing.

In 1939 Herbert made his first public appearance as a soloist in the *Messiah* with the Melbourne Symphony Orchestra. His success was quickly followed by solo performances with choral societies around Australia and with the Australian Broadcasting Commission's orchestras under eminent visiting conductors, one of whom, (Sir) Malcolm Sargent, was so impressed by the musical and technical qualities of his singing that he assisted him to find his first engagements in England. Shortly after his arrival in London in 1947, Herbert appeared at a promenade concert at the Albert Hall and was engaged by the British Broadcasting Corporation. He participated in the inaugural concert at the Royal Festival Hall in 1951 and was soloist in the first performance at a 'prom' of Elgar's *The Dream of Gerontius*, the work with which he was most closely associated. In Europe he was probably best known for the role of the Evangelist in Bach's *St Matthew Passion*.

Although he sang in opera and in concert, it was as a singer in oratorio that Herbert established a wide reputation, frequently appearing at the Three Choirs and the Edinburgh festivals. In 1953 he was a soloist at the coronation of Queen Elizabeth II and in 1958 he was one of four singers from Britain chosen to take part in a concert to celebrate the United Nations which was held in Geneva and transmitted to ninety-eight countries. He had married Jeanne Bethan Harries on 3 May 1952 at St Margaret's parish church, Westminster, London; they were to be divorced in 1964. Herbert toured Australia for the A.B.C. in 1950, 1956 and 1959 before returning permanently in 1963 to take up the post of lecturer in voice at the University of Western Australia. At St Andrew's Presbyterian Church, Perth, on 17 September 1964 he married Rosemary Frances Hunt, a museum artist.

In 1965 Herbert moved to the new Canberra School of Music as lecturer in voice. He took an active role in the musical life of the city, not only as a teacher, but as conductor of the Australian National University Choral Society, soloist with the Canberra Symphony Orchestra and as a recitalist. His wealth of experience, urbanity and wit endeared him to students and colleagues. As an artist he had two important attributes: a love and deep understanding of the music he sang, and a completely professional approach to its performance. Survived by his wife and their 6-year-old daughter, he died of bronchitis and emphysema on 23 December 1975 at Woden Valley Hospital and was cremated with Anglican rites.

B. and F. Mackenzie, *Singers of Australia* (Melb, 1967); J. Glennon, *Australian Music and Musicians* (Adel, 1968); *Canb Times*, 26 Dec 1975.

W. L. HOFFMANN

HERCUS, ERIC OSWALD (1891-1962), physicist, was born on 23 June 1891 at Dunedin, New Zealand, third son of Scottish-born parents George Robertson Hercus, accountant, and his wife Elizabeth, née Elder. Eric attended Otago Boys' High School, Dunedin, and in his final year (1908) won a senior national scholarship.

In 1909 he entered the University of Otago (B.Sc., N.Z., 1912; M.Sc., 1913) where he obtained first-class honours in almost every subject, and senior scholarships in both mathematics and physics. His master's degree was awarded the Cook prize and first class-honours. Supported by a government research scholarship, in 1913 Hercus transferred to Victoria (University) College, Wellington, New Zealand's only university with an active research programme in physics, to work under Professor T. H. Laby [q.v.9]. Laby's passion was precision measurement, and he set Hercus the difficult task of determining the absolute thermal conductivity of air. The work was successfully completed in 1914, though not published until four years later.

Awarded the 1851 Exhibition science research scholarship for New Zealand, Hercus sailed to England and entered Trinity College, Cambridge, in October 1914. He began work in the Cavendish Laboratory under J. J. (Sir Joseph) Thomson on a project on positive rays. Six months later he was appointed a radiography instructor in the Royal Army Medical Corps and sent to Malta. On 21 September 1916 he was commissioned lieutenant, Royal Naval Volunteer Reserve. Posted as scientific adviser on the staff of the flag officer, Dover Patrol, he designed direction-finders for shore-batteries and kept watch in the 'war room' at Dover. He was demobilized on 13 January 1919.

Hercus returned to Cambridge and his work on positive rays. He stayed for only six months before leaving to take up a lectureship at the University of Melbourne, where Laby had held the chair of natural philosophy since 1915. The work in Cambridge came to nothing, but in Melbourne he resumed his collaboration with Laby in a classic redetermination of the mechanical equivalent of heat. The university awarded him a D.Sc. (1928) for his precision measurements in relation to heat. Once this work was completed, his research atrophied and he published only a couple of short and fairly inconsequential papers thereafter.

In her father's home at Christchurch, New Zealand, on 29 January 1924 Hercus had married with Presbyterian forms his second cousin Florence Hercus, a pianist. Promoted senior lecturer (1923) and associate professor (1931), Eric Hercus served as acting-professor when Laby and his successor (Sir) Leslie Martin were on leave. He taught a wide range of topics, chiefly to upper-level students; his lectures, delivered in the softest of voices, were models of clarity. Those on thermodynamics and statistical mechanics eventually gave rise to a useful textbook, *Elements of Thermodynamics* (1947), which was expanded and republished as *Elements of Thermodynamics and Statistical Mechanics* (1951). A tall, spare and retiring man, he willingly shared his knowledge of his subject with those who penetrated his shy exterior.

During World War II Hercus, like his colleagues, took on additional duties. While maintaining his normal teaching responsibilities, he was a member (1940-45) of the Optical Munitions Panel and he participated in work done in his department on the design and manufacture of optical equipment for the armed forces. Later in the war he also lectured on radar to military personnel.

Hercus joined the Institute of Physics (London) in 1923, becoming a fellow in 1929, and took part in the pioneering series of conferences sponsored by the institute's Australian members before World War II. Vice-president (1945) of the institute's Australian branch, he was honorary secretary (1952-55) at a time when the branch was evolving towards becoming the Australian Institute of Physics. He was elected a fellow of the Australian and New Zealand Association for the Advancement of Science and thus a member of the Australian National Research Council in 1946 (joint honorary secretary 1949-50). At the 1951 meeting of the International Union of Physics, held in Copenhagen, he represented Australia.

In 1947-56 Hercus served as his university's representative on the council of the (Royal) Melbourne Technical College (president 1952). He continued to lecture for several years after his retirement in 1956, and acted as a consulting programmer for the early-generation electronic computer, CSIRAC, located at the university. Survived by his wife and son, who was also a physicist, he died suddenly of coronary vascular disease on 30 June 1962 at his Sandringham home and was cremated.

R. Bacon, *The Dover Patrol, 1915-1917* (Lond, 1919); *Univ Melb Mag*, 13, 1919, p 106; *Univ Melb Gazette*, Apr 1957, p 12, Sept 1962, p 9; Hercus papers (Univ Melb Archives); Hercus file (Archives of the Roy Com for the Exhibition of 1851, Imperial College of Science and Technology, Lond); Aust National Research Council papers (NL).

R. W. HOME

HERINGTON, JOHN (1916-1967), war historian, air force officer, public servant and social worker, was born on 3 June 1916 at Coventry, England, fourth of five children of Basil Henry Herington, commercial clerk, and his wife Margaret Ellen, née Dunne. Basil died in 1922 and the strain of caring for her children affected Margaret's health; following her death, John was raised by guardians. After attending Bablake School, Coventry, he entered Downing College, Cambridge (B.A., 1937; M.A., 1941), where he rowed and played Rugby Union football. The master was Admiral Sir Herbert Richmond who encouraged Herington's interest in military and strategic history.

Attracted by the work of Kingsley Fairbridge [q.v.8], Herington joined the Child Emigration Society as a trainee social worker and studied welfare problems in the East End of London. In 1938 he escorted a group of children to Australia and continued his research at the three Fairbridge schools. Powerfully built and 5 ft 10 ins (178 cm) tall, he had brown hair, a broad forehead, lively blue eyes and a firm jaw, features that were in keeping with his witty mind and resolute character.

Herington enlisted in the Royal Australian Air Force on 2 February 1941 and trained as a pilot in Australia and Canada; he topped his class of fifty-one students. Commissioned in September, he was sent to Britain and promoted flying officer. In April 1942 he reached Gibraltar with No.202 Squadron, Royal Air Force Coastal Command. He captained Catalinas on long-range patrols over the Atlantic and the western Mediterranean, and made three attacks on submarines. In March 1943 he was posted as an instructor to No.131 Operational Training Unit in Northern Ireland. On 24 May his Catalina plunged into Lough Erne. He found himself under water, with his right leg protruding through a metal bulkhead; remaining calm, and summoning his strength, he extricated himself and swam to the surface. He suffered massive injuries and subsequently caught pneumonia which prevented his return to duty until March 1944 when he became intelligence officer,

No.10 Squadron, R.A.A.F., at Mount Batten, Devon.

On 20 April 1944 at the parish church of St Mildred and St George, Castleton, Yorkshire, Flight Lieutenant Herington married Freda Elizabeth Robson, a nursing sister who had cared for him in hospital. He was converted from Catholicism to Anglicanism after his marriage. Employed as an education officer from October, he was promoted temporary squadron leader in January 1945 and placed in charge of the historical records section at R.A.A.F. Overseas Headquarters, London. His team researched the war diaries of hundreds of R.A.F. squadrons and produced a preliminary history ('first narratives') of the Australian contribution to each of the R.A.F.'s commands. Herington wrote on Coastal Command.

In 1946 the Commonwealth government appointed him official historian to write a one-volume book on Australia's role in the air war against Germany and Italy. He returned home in 1947 and was demobilized on 24 March 1948 to work full time on the project. Herington's formidable intellect was reinforced by total recall. Able to assemble, collate and edit text in his mind, he wrote steadily, with little alteration. On completing a number of chapters, he obtained approval to publish the history in two volumes: *Air War Against Germany and Italy 1939-1943* (Canberra, 1954) covered operations when the adversaries were evenly matched; *Air Power Over Europe 1944-1945* (Canberra, 1963) dealt with the period when the Allies had gained air superiority over Germany.

The histories were highly technical, given the nature of an air war in which scientific, engineering and design developments had rapidly occurred. Herington's handling of the 'big picture' was masterly, as in the opening chapter of his second volume. The experience of Australians in air operations was used to describe the cutting edge of battle. To preserve balance, he provided statistical tables showing the relationship of the Australian effort to the total number of sorties. Overall, reviews in newspapers and service journals were favourable. Veterans considered that the main object of an official history—to provide an adequate literary memorial—had been well met.

Having rejoined the R.A.A.F. in 1951 as squadron leader, Special Duties Branch, Herington performed intelligence duties in Melbourne while making progress with his histories. He was seconded to the Department of Supply in 1953-54 and placed in charge of security for the atomic-bomb tests in South Australia. Resigning his commission, in March 1954 he was appointed the department's regional security officer for South Australia. In 1957 he was promoted chief

security officer, Melbourne; in 1964 he was posted to London as the department's senior representative. Survived by his wife, four sons and three daughters, he died of cancer on 22 January 1967 at St Marylebone and was cremated; his ashes were interred in the churchyard of St John the Evangelist, Glen Iris, Melbourne.

W. R. Clark, 'John Herington', *Stand-To* (Canb), 11, no 3, July-Sept 1967, p 14; *SMH*, 25 Jan 1946, 27 July 1963, 24 Jan 1967.   W. R. CLARK

HERRON, SIR LESLIE JAMES (1902-1973), chief justice, was born on 22 May 1902 at Mosman, Sydney, second of six children of native-born parents Henry Herron, insurance clerk, and his wife Emily Ethel, née Downie. Leslie was educated at the Church of England Preparatory School, Mosman, Sydney Grammar School and the University of Sydney (LL.B., 1924). He obtained second-class honours, despite being an enthusiastic athlete, oarsman and footballer who played (1922-25) first-grade Rugby Union as breakaway for Western Suburbs Football Club.

Admitted to the Bar on 28 August 1925, Herron read with R. C. Bonney and built up a successful practice (mainly in common law) on the Northern Circuit. He spoke to juries 'in a down-to-earth manner which they could understand' and in consequence 'snatched innumerable verdicts'. At St James's Anglican Church, Sydney, on 6 January 1930 he married Andrée Lorna, daughter of Frank Leverrier [q.v.10], K.C.; they lived at Wollstonecraft until building a home at Castle Cove in 1960. Taking up golf, he played off a handicap of nine at his best and was president (1944-73) of the Australian Golf Club.

Herron was an acting District Court judge in February 1939 and took silk on 20 December. Elevated to the Supreme Court bench on 10 February 1941, he sat mainly in criminal and civil causes, attempting 'to keep the balance between wartime needs of the Executive and the rights of the individual'. He received a death threat in December 1948 for having sentenced Charles Ivan le Gallien to life imprisonment for patricide; given police protection, Herron played golf with his bodyguard. In 1958 he served as royal commissioner, inquiring into the auditor-general's statements concerning Abram Landa, the minister for housing.

Devoting time to the administration of sport, Herron was chairman (1933-39) and president (1943-56) of the New South Wales Rugby Union, foundation chairman (1948) of the Australian Rugby Football Union and chaired the International Rugby Football Board in London in 1957. He was also president of Sydney Grammar School Old Boys'

Union (1948-50) and of the New South Wales Amateur Swimming Association (1949-64), and a member of the New South Wales Olympic Council and the Sydney Cricket Ground Trust (chairman 1970-72).

As senior puisne judge, Herron was acting chief justice (from March 1962) during the illness of H. V. Evatt [q.v.] and was confirmed in office on 25 October. Although he was no great jurist, he brought to his office 'a robust common sense in the enunciation of principles and a broad humanity of approach'. He claimed that 'long and intimate experience with the daily work of this Court . . . and my varied activities in life . . . may have endowed me with that even greater quality of a Judge, namely, sound judgment'. At the Bar he had eschewed appellate work and as chief justice did not relish it, but he presided over the Full Court with great authority.

In administering the business of a rapidly expanding judicature, Herron sought to prevent delays and was grieved that 'litigation resulting from death or bodily injury by motor vehicles has tended to overwhelm the Court'. He was an energetic chairman (from November 1961) of the Law Reform Committee; many of its recommendations were adopted by the Law Reform Commission and embodied in the far-reaching Supreme Court Act of 1970 which 'directed the fusion of law and equity' in an attempt to make litigation 'just, quick and cheap'. Upheld by his Christian faith, Herron conducted his court with consideration, dignity and mercy, especially towards unrepresented appellants. He found the chief justice's private garden at the Supreme Court a retreat where he could 'ponder over cases' or practise his golf swing and putting.

Herron headed appeals for St Vincent's and the Mater Misericordiae hospitals, the National Heart Foundation, the Freedom from Hunger Campaign, the Central Methodist Mission, the Salvation Army and the Bush Children's Hostels Foundation of New South Wales. As president of the State branch of the St John Ambulance Association, he was appointed a knight of the Order of St John in 1964. A Freemason, he was worshipful master (1966-67) of Lodge Royal Empire and a past junior grand warden (1969) of United Grand Lodge of New South Wales. He was named 'Father of the Year' and made an honorary citizen of Grafton in 1963, appointed C.M.G. in 1964 and K.B.E. in 1966, and received an honorary LL.D. (1972) from the University of New South Wales.

'A splendid companion—interested, interesting and with a lively sense of humour', Herron was a member of the Australian, Australian Jockey and the Royal Automobile clubs. He loved veteran cars and travelling in trains, and surfed regularly in summer.

Known to his bowling mates as 'Chook', he belonged to the City and Northbridge bowling clubs, and to the Dead End Kids Bowling Club which raised money for charity. He was a 'big man with a commanding presence and a strong personality'—six feet (183 cm) tall, weighing over fourteen stone (90 kg), with thick white hair. In an occasional address (later broadcast), he condemned as a lawyer the trial of Jesus: a 'legal travesty, leading to judicial murder, swift and pitiless'.

On reaching what he described as 'the age of statutory senility', Sir Leslie retired in May 1972 and began working on a scheme for free legal aid. He had been appointed lieutenant-governor in April 1972 and was administering the government when he died of acute leukaemia on 3 May 1973 in St Vincent's Hospital, Darlinghurst. Accorded a state funeral, he was cremated with Presbyterian forms. His wife and daughter survived him. A portrait of Herron by Graeme Inson is held by the Supreme Court, one by H. A. Hanke by the University of Sydney, and two by Esmé Bell by the Australian Golf Club and Herron's family.

J. M. Bennett, *Portraits of the Chief Justices of New South Wales 1824-1977* (Syd, 1977); *PD* (NSW), 8 Aug 1973, p 9; *NSW Weekly Notes*, 79, 1962, p iii; *Aust Law J*, May 1973, p 282; *State Reports* (NSW), 1974, 1, p viii; *Rugby News*, 12 Mar 1973, p 3; Sydney Grammar School, *Sydneian*, Nov 1973, p 10; *Daily Telegraph* (Syd), 28 Oct 1962; *SMH*, 21 Dec 1939, 3 Dec 1948, 19 Dec 1951, 11 Nov 1961, 4 Nov 1962, 23 Aug 1963, 1 Sept 1965, 1 Jan 1966, 2 Mar 1967, 12 Apr, 2 Aug 1970, 30 Aug 1972, 7 May 1973; *Sun* (Syd), 22 Aug 1963, 29 Jan 1987; Herron papers (ML); information from Mr J. and Mrs S. Crawford, Turramurra, Syd.

MARTHA RUTLEDGE

HESTER, JOY ST CLAIR (1920-1960), artist, was born on 21 August 1920 at Elsternwick, Melbourne, second child of Robert Ferdinand Hester, a bank officer from England, and his wife Louise May, née Bracher, a Victorian-born teacher. Educated at St Michael's Church of England Girls' Grammar School, St Kilda, in 1936 Joy completed one year of an art-and-crafts course at Brighton Technical School. At the National Gallery schools she won first prize (1938) for drawing a head from life. The course was conservative and she abandoned it, preferring to attend life-drawing classes at the Victorian Artists Society, East Melbourne. A founding member of the Contemporary Art Society in 1938, she first exhibited in its inaugural exhibition in the following year. The C.A.S. was to remain her only venue for showing work until she held her first solo exhibition at the Melbourne Book Club Gallery in 1950. On 1 January 1941 at All Saints Church, Greensborough, she married with Anglican rites a fellow artist Albert Lee Tucker.

Between 1938 and 1947 Hester was part of a stimulating and innovative circle of painters —among them (Sir) Sidney Nolan, Arthur Boyd and John Perceval—which was colloquially known as the 'Angry Penguins', after the art and literary magazine of the same name published by John Reed and Max Harris. She was the only woman artist in the group. It met regularly at Heide, the home of the art patrons John and Sunday Reed. Sunday was Hester's closest friend, encouraging her work, supporting her financially and later adopting her first son Sweeney.

Hester drew and rarely painted, favouring the media of brush and ink. It was an unusual choice, one that set her apart from her contemporaries and one that she developed with great skill through her brief career. If it determined her style and method, it also meant that during her lifetime her art received little attention. Drawing was not valued as highly as oil painting and was seen as preparatory to the finished work of art. Further, Hester's method of working—sitting on the floor in company and rapidly producing her drawings —meant that she was viewed as a casual rather than a serious artist.

She chose the human face as her motif, focussing on the eyes. Intense emotions and psychological states were registered with quick, sure, expressionist strokes. Her portraits of friends and family were incisive, while the 'Gethsemane' series (1946-47) concentrated on upward-gazing, hallucinatory heads. Her immediate influences included German Expressionism, the Russian emigrant painter Danila Vassilieff [q.v.], and Picasso. She was also directly influenced by the newsreels shown in 1945 of Nazi concentration camps. Ezra Pound, T. S. Eliot and Judith Wright were her favourite poets. An important early series, 'From An Incredible Night Dream' (1946-47), was inspired by Jean Cocteau's *Opium* (Paris, 1930).

In 1947 Hester was diagnosed as having Hodgkin's disease and given a short time to live. She left her husband and young son, and moved to Sydney with Gray Smith (1919-1991). In the next two years she produced some of her finest drawings: the 'Face', 'Sleep' and 'Love' series. She exhibited these in 1950, together with a selection of her poems, placed on the walls next to the drawings.

From 1948 to 1956 Hester lived with Gray Smith in rural Victoria, first at Hurstbridge, then at Avonsleigh and Upwey in the Dandenong Ranges. Against medical advice she had two more children. She was in remission from Hodgkin's disease until 1956, when the symptoms re-appeared. During her last years she lived at Box Hill, where she had her first studio. There she produced her largest drawings and, for the first time, began regularly signing and dating her work. The image of a large-eyed child, holding an animal, dominated this period, as did the subject of 'The Lovers' (1956-58) where fear and sexual passion were mingled in the embrace between man and woman. In the same years her poetry was concerned with romantic love and with metaphors of the natural world.

Divorced on 14 April 1959, Hester married Gray Smith on 11 November that year at the office of the government statist, Melbourne. She spent increasingly long periods in hospital. Survived by her husband and their son and daughter, and by the son of her first marriage, she died on 4 December 1960 at Prahran and was buried in Box Hill cemetery. There are four portraits of Hester by Albert Tucker, one in his own collection, another in that of Bob Weis in Melbourne, and two in the National Gallery of Australia, Canberra; a self-portrait is in the Georges Mora collection, Melbourne. Her work is represented in major Australian art galleries.

J. Burke, *Australian Women Artists* (Melb, 1980) and *Joy Hester* (Melb, 1983) *and* for bibliog; R. Haese, *Rebels and Precursors* (Melb, 1981); *Art and Aust*, 1, no 4, June 1966, p 40, 1, no 18, Sept 1980, p 68; *Age* (Melb), 7 Dec 1960, 30 Sept 1976, 7 Oct 1981; *Australian*, 12 Oct 1976, 14 Jan 1984.

JANINE BURKE

HETHERINGTON, JACK (JOHN) AIKMAN (1907-1974), author and journalist, was born on 3 October 1907 at Sandringham, Melbourne, younger son of Victorian-born parents Hector Hetherington, grocer, and his wife Agnes, née Bowman. Educated at Sandringham State School and (on a chorister's scholarship) at All Saints Grammar School, St Kilda, Jack left at 16 to join the *Evening Sun* as a copy-taker. His first short story was published in the *Australasian* in 1925, the year in which he moved to the Herald & Weekly Times Ltd as a journalist; by 1934 he was writing a daily column and editing the *Sun News-Pictorial*'s Saturday magazine. Next year he worked his passage to England. Based in London, he survived by writing stories about the Australian outback for popular magazines, and by working as a sub-editor and wire-service reporter. *En route* to Australia, he spent six months in the United States of America with Australian Associated Press.

Late in 1938 Hetherington returned to Melbourne and the *Herald*. In January 1940 he was assigned as a war correspondent and sailed with the Australian Imperial Force's first convoy for the Middle East. He covered the battles of Bardia and Tobruk (January 1941), and witnessed the enemy's surrender at Benghazi (February). His reports were published in newspapers in Australia, by *The Times* and the *Manchester Guardian*, and by the *New York Times* and the North American Newspaper Alliance.

In March 1941 Hetherington accompanied the Australian 6th Division on the abortive expedition to Greece. His was the first allied account of the Anzac Corps' withdrawal; its publication in *The Times* provoked trenchant criticism of the operation. The Greek campaign also generated his first book, *Air-borne Invasion* (London, 1943), about the battle of Crete. Back in Melbourne, on 15 March 1943 at the office of the government statist he married Olive Meagher, née McLeish (d.1966), a 45-year-old divorcee. In that year he published *The Australian Soldier* (Sydney, 1943).

Early in 1944 the *Herald* sent Hetherington to cover the allied invasion of Western Europe. He landed in Normandy on the evening of D-Day, 6 June. After a short time with the British Second Army, he was invalided home where he wrote an unpublished account of the invasion. His only novel, *The Winds Are Still*, won the *Sydney Morning Herald*'s competition for the best war story published in 1947. He had built a reputation as 'one of the outstanding correspondents of the war'. Profoundly respectful of ordinary people caught up in conflict, he wrote in 1956 that 'the courage of the unheroic is the most sublime courage of all'.

In 1945-49 Hetherington was editor-in-chief of the *Adelaide News*. Unhappy as an administrator, he returned to the Melbourne *Herald* as a feature-writer. In 1952 he joined the *Argus* as deputy-editor. Two years later he went to the *Age* to write the 'Collins Street Calling' column; he had recently published his first full biography, *Blamey* (1954). Finding the confines of a daily column too restrictive, he transferred to features and special articles, which encouraged his interest in biography and provided material for a steady stream of books: *Australians: Nine Profiles* (1960), *Forty-two Faces* (1962), *Australian Painters* (1963) and *Uncommon Men* (1965).

He was gradually changing direction from Jack Hetherington, journalist, to John Hetherington, author, a shift manifested in 1956 when he registered his change of name by deed poll. In 1966 he published *Pillars of the Faith*, an anthology of biographies of Victoria's churchmen. At St George's Anglican Church, Malvern, on 25 July 1967 he married Mollie Roger Maginnis, a fellow journalist, and took leave from the *Age* to finish *Melba* with the aid of a Commonwealth Literary Fellowship; in 1968 it won the Sir Thomas White [q.v.] prize for biography. The autobiographical *The Morning was Shining* (London) followed in 1971. Hetherington was appointed O.B.E. in 1972. By that time he had left daily

journalism, partly because he had suffered a heart attack, but mostly because he was challenged and content in writing more substantial work. In 1973 he completed an official biography of Norman Lindsay [q.v.10] which he subtitled *The Embattled Olympian*.

Modest and cheery, Hetherington loved picnics and barbeques, wine and conversation. He was meticulous and hard working. Although racked with lung cancer, he spent his last weekend correcting page-proofs. Writing was his life and his careful craft. Predeceased by the son of his first marriage, he died on 17 September 1974 at Parkville and was cremated; his wife survived him.

Age (Melb), 13 May 1961, 18 Sept 1974; *Herald* (Melb), 17 Sept 1974; Hetherington papers (LaTL, AWM, NLA); Hetherington letters and biog notes (held by Mrs M. Hetherington, Melb).

SALLY A. WHITE

HEY, HARRY (1892-1960), metallurgist and businessman, was born on 20 June 1892 at Horbury, Yorkshire, England, son of Haydn Hey, foreman dyer, and his wife Emma, née Webster. Educated at Dewsbury, Harry later travelled to New Zealand where he undertook research on dairy products. He arrived in Victoria in 1915 and was engaged as an industrial chemist at Geelong. Having joined the staff of the Electrolytic Zinc Co. of Australasia Pty Ltd in 1917, he worked as a research chemist at Risdon, Tasmania, and was then given charge of a research station in South Melbourne. At Christ Church, South Yarra, on 4 January 1919 he married Mardi Soares with Anglican rites.

During (Sir) Herbert Gepp's and H. St J. Somerset's [qq.v.8,12] terms as general manager, Hey supervised the company's pilot plant which was set up in Tasmania to recover zinc and lead concentrates from the ores of the Read-Rosebery mines. In 1927 he visited North America to study milling practices before designing the concentrator at Rosebery. As chief metallurgist (1927-43), Hey stimulated and aided research—carried out at the University of Melbourne under Sir David Masson [q.v.10]—on the electro-chemical characteristics of aqueous solutions of zinc sulphate. Representing several mining companies, Hey directed (1930-39) the work of the flotation research laboratories at the university. Meanwhile, he built up a research organization at Risdon which gained an international reputation in zinc technology. Promoted technical superintendent in 1943, he helped to introduce an extensive programme for modernizing the roasting plants, with the aim of using all the sulphur content of zinc concentrate.

Hey was appointed to the board of Electro-lytic Zinc in 1944; he became general man-ager in 1945, managing director in 1947 and chairman in 1952. He introduced a profit-sharing scheme for employees, encouraged the role played by Risdon and Rosebery in training technicians and tradesmen, won the company's support for educational insti-tutions and presided over the expansion of Risdon to a capacity of 160 000 tons per year. A member (from 1928) of the Australasian Institute of Mining and Metallurgy, Hey was the first chairman (1936-39) of its Victorian branch. From 1940 to 1960 he was a member of the A.I.M.M. council (vice-president 1942, president 1943-44 and 1949). He was deputy-president of the Fifth Empire Mining and Metallurgical Congress in 1951; Essing-ton Lewis [q.v.10] was president. Hey was awarded the institute's medal for 1951 and elected a life member in 1955. He had been awarded the Kernot [q.v.5] medal by the University of Melbourne in 1954.

A member of seven boards of directors, Hey chaired the Commonwealth govern-ment's Explosives and Chemicals Industry Advisory Committee and belonged to the Atomic Energy Commission's business advis-ory group. He published several scientific papers, one of which was the Liversidge [q.v.5] lecture (1931) of the Royal Society of New South Wales. An enthusiastic golfer, he was captain (1952-54) and president (1959-60) of the Metropolitan Golf Club. Two days after an operation for a longstanding hernia condition, he died suddenly on 11 April 1960 in the Freemasons' Hospital, East Mel-bourne. Survived by his wife, daughter and son, he was cremated; his estate was sworn for probate at £90 169.

A'sian Inst of Mining and Metallurgy, *Procs*, Dec 1960; *SMH*, 10 Mar 1947, 26 Jan 1953, 23 Feb 1955; *Herald* (Melb), 28 Mar 1952; *Age* (Melb), 3 Sept 1954, 12 Apr 1960; *Sun News-Pictorial*, 12, 14 Apr 1960; information from A'sian Inst of Mining and Metallurgy, Parkville, Melb.   NOEL KIRBY

HEYDON, SIR PETER RICHARD (1913-1971), public servant, was born on 9 Sep-tember 1913 at Croydon, Sydney, son of native-born parents Vigar Crawford Heydon, schoolteacher, and his wife Emily, née Sinclair. Educated at Fort Street Boys' High School, Peter won an exhibition to the Uni-versity of Sydney (B.A., 1933; LL.B., 1936). After completing articles with the solicitors Vickery & Wilson, he was admitted to the Bar in 1936 but did not practise. In March that year Heydon joined the political section of the Department of External Affairs in Canberra. He served as private secretary to Sir George Pearce [q.v.11] from July to November 1936,

to (Sir) Robert Menzies [q.v.] on his 1938 visit to Britain and Europe, and to S. M. (Viscount) Bruce [q.v.7], the Australian high com-missioner in London, when he came to Aus-tralia in 1939. In September-December Hey-don was liaison officer with the Department of Defence in Melbourne.

His diplomatic career was fully launched in January 1940 with his appointment to the staff of R. G. (Baron) Casey [q.v.13], the Aus-tralian minister in Washington. On 7 March 1942, in Ottawa, Heydon married Muriel Naomi Slater, a Canadian who was Casey's personal assistant. Heydon was one of the external affairs officers whom H. V. Evatt [q.v.] distrusted, apparently because of his prior connexions with Menzies and Pearce. In November Evatt sent Heydon and his Wa-shington colleague (Sir) Keith Officer [q.v.] to the Australian legation in the Soviet Union which opened at Kuibyshev in January 1943. The 'difficult and delicate task' of represent-ing Polish interests in the Soviet Union gave Heydon valuable experience in 1943-44.

Early in 1945 he returned to Canberra where he was briefly in charge of the depart-ment when (Sir) William Dunk and J. W. Bur-ton took leave. Heydon was posted to London in 1947 as head of the external affairs staff at Australia House. From May to October 1950 he was chargé d'affaires in The Hague. That posting was followed by two years as minister in Rio de Janeiro and by high commissioner-ships in Wellington (1953-55) and New Delhi (from 1955). The appointment to New Delhi brought him 'most satisfaction and happi-ness'. Under Prime Minister Jawaharlal Nehru, India was a major force among non-aligned powers. Despite numerous difficulties —India's perception that Australia favoured Pakistan in the dispute over Kashmir, India's sensitivity to Australia's membership (with Pakistan) of the South-East Asia Treaty Or-ganization, the conflicting attitudes of Aus-tralia and India towards the People's Republic of China, Australia's support for Anglo-French policy in the Suez crisis of 1956, and clashes between India and Australia at the United Nations over Australia's trusteeship of the Territory of Papua and New Guinea— Heydon was able to win Nehru's trust.

Back in Australia in 1959 as assistant-(later first assistant-) secretary, he fre-quently acted as departmental head in absences of Sir Arthur Tange. Heydon saw the department grow to a staff of four hundred in Canberra and seven hundred over-seas, and gave particular attention to building its relations with parliament, the press and the universities.

On 6 November 1961 Heydon succeeded Sir Tasman Heyes [q.v.] as secretary of the Department of Immigration. To his new de-partment he brought a broad appreciation of the workings of government, a network of contacts in Australia and abroad, and a concern about the public standing of the immigration programme. He won respect and admiration for his businesslike approach to administration, his tactical sense, his appreciation of what was viable, his capacity in drafting ministerial submissions and his ability to inspire confidence. Conscientious in attending to his duties, he identified priorities, formulated staffing levels, set high standards and developed *esprit de corps*. Both he and his minister (Sir) Hubert Opperman persuaded the government in 1966 to liberalize the White Australia policy. With the aim of ensuring better settlement of immigrants, in 1969 Heydon successfully pressed for the establishment of a committee to facilitate the recognition of foreign professional qualifications. In 1959 he had been appointed C.B.E.; he was knighted in 1970.

A keen reader, especially of history and biography, Heydon wrote a memoir of Pearce, *Quiet Decision* (Melbourne, 1965); he also published biographical essays and articles on immigration and diplomacy. A 'big and exuberant man', and an able public speaker, he was in private conversation a 'splendid (and tireless) raconteur'. His stories were often about the ministers he had served, but he could make himself the butt of his jokes; he related how he once arranged a flag for Evatt's official car in London only to be informed by the minister that it was in fact the flag of New Zealand.

Heydon shared his family's enthusiasm for golf, and retained an interest in cricket and Rugby Union football. He had been troubled by high blood pressure from his mid-thirties though he did not allow it to restrict his enjoyment of life. Survived by his wife, son and two daughters, he died of a myocardial infarction on 15 May 1971 in Canberra; after a service at the Presbyterian Church of St Andrew (where he had been an elder) he was cremated.

L. F. Crisp (ed), *Peter Richard Heydon 1913-1971* (Canb, 1972) *and* for publications; *Canb Times* and *SMH*, 17 May 1971.   J. R. NETHERCOTE

HEYES, SIR TASMAN HUDSON EASTWOOD (1896-1980), public servant, was born on 6 November 1896 at Kent Town, Adelaide, son of Hudson Eastwood Heyes, compositor, and his wife Mary, née Jones. Educated in Melbourne, in 1912 Tasman entered the Commonwealth Public Service as a messenger in the Department of Defence. Next year he joined the Permanent Military Forces and was employed as a staff clerk with the rank of corporal.

Enlisting in the Australian Imperial Force

on 18 March 1916, Heyes served on the Western Front from April 1917, spending twelve months with the 3rd Divisional Signal Company before being posted to the Australian War Records Section and promoted sergeant. He was discharged on 19 August 1919 in Melbourne, resumed his public service employment and was transferred that year to the Australian War Museum at the request of C. E. W. Bean [q.v.7]. On 29 November 1921 Heyes married Ethel Brettell Causer with Anglican rites at Christ Church, St Kilda; they were to have a son and daughter. In 1924-27 he was in England as Australian representative on the historical section (military branch), Committee of Imperial Defence, and carried out research for the Australian official war histories. He returned home via the United States of America, Canada and New Zealand, briefly undertaking research in those countries.

From 1928 he was deputy to the director of the Australian War Memorial, J. L. Treloar [q.v.12]. Having moved to Canberra, in October 1939 he was appointed acting-director in Treloar's absence and oversaw the opening of the A.W.M. in 1941. The minister for the interior J. S. Collings [q.v.8] wrote in 1942 that Heyes possessed 'a first-rate capacity for clear and constructive thinking', as well as 'energy and driving force'; others commented on his organizational skills, decisiveness and capacity for hard work. For a few months in early 1942 Heyes was secretary of the Administrative Planning Committee and for the remainder of World War II was assistant to A. J. L. Wilson, assistant-secretary (policy and supplies), Department of Defence.

In May 1946 Heyes was appointed secretary of the new Department of Immigration. He faced the tasks of building a department from a nucleus of staff inherited from the Department of the Interior, managing an unprecedented level of government involvement in the selection, movement, reception, job placement and supervision of immigrants, and ensuring public acceptance of the radical shift in immigration policy which saw a dramatic increase in numbers from continental Europe. Under Heyes's administration the personnel of the department (excluding employees in migrant camps) rose from 74 in 1946 to 1218 in 1961; staff stationed overseas increased from 14 in 1947 to 390 in 1961; and net migration climbed from 11 200 in 1947 to 89 090 in 1960. In the 1950s permanent and long-term arrivals averaged 122 100 per annum.

Sharing the nation-building vision of Arthur Calwell [q.v.13] and subsequent ministers, Heyes was dedicated to his work. To his staff he spoke of the 'immigration spirit', and publicly stressed the importance of immigration 'to assure this nation of substantial economic growth, security and happiness for years to come'. A man of great personal charm and friendliness, he had a flair for public relations and was aware that the support of community leaders had to be enlisted. He made it his business to sell the programme, not only through the establishment of the Commonwealth Immigration Advisory Council (which represented major interest groups), but also at a personal level: from the outset he ensured that two influential critics of the programme experienced the benefits of immigration by being allocated servants from the new arrivals.

Heyes was committed to the concept of assimilation; he preferred British and Northern European immigrants, and people of 'Aryan' stock; and he defended the White Australia policy. Wishing to avoid public controversy, he exercised a conservative influence on ministers with reformist inclinations. In 1957 he recommended that non-Europeans who wanted to be naturalized should be made to comply with strict terms of eligibility, including fluency in English and evidence of participation in 'normal Australian life'.

Appointed C.B.E. in 1953, Heyes was knighted in 1960. After he retired in 1961, he served on the Commonwealth Immigration Planning Council and the Australian Broadcasting Control Board, and was chairman of directors (1962-69) of Commonwealth Hostels Ltd. In 1962 Sir Tasman was awarded the Nansen medal by the United Nations in recognition of his, and his country's, contribution to the resettlement of refugees. Calwell wrote that 'the name of Tas Heyes . . . ranks with the best and most highly successful departmental heads in the history of our Federation'. Heyes's career was testimony to the fluidity of class barriers in the society of his day and to the opportunity for men of ability with little formal education to rise from relatively humble beginnings. Survived by his daughter, he died on 25 June 1980 at Windsor, Melbourne, and was cremated.

A. A. Calwell, *Be Just and Fear Not* (Melb, 1972); *Reveille* (Syd), 1 Dec 1939; AWM 93, item 22/2/150 (AWM); A664/1, item 609/402/821, A5954/1, item 690/29 (AA, Canb); information from Messrs R. Metcalfe, W. A. Higgie, J. Grant, J. E. Blackie, G. C. Watson, and W. Brown, Canb.

ANDREW MARKUS

HEYMANN, ERICH (1901-1949), chemist and academic, was born on 20 February 1901 at Frankfurt am Main, Germany, son of Hugo Heymann and his wife Emmy, née Elsas. Educated (1907-19) at the Wohler-Real Gymnasium, Frankfurt, Erich worked before and after school to help produce food during World War I; several bouts of pneumonia left him unfit for military service. He studied in the faculty of science, University of Munich, for three months in 1920, then enrolled at the University of Frankfurt (Ph.D., 1924).

From 1924 Heymann was employed as a research-assistant at the Institute of Colloid Science, Frankfurt, before joining the staff of the department of physical chemistry, University of Frankfurt, as senior demonstrator in 1928; next year he was appointed lecturer. In September 1933 Adolf Hitler dismissed Jewish scientists from German universities. Heymann, who was well known in his field, gained asylum in London. He worked for almost three years under Professor F. G. Donnan at the Sir William Ramsay Laboratory for Inorganic and Physical Chemistry, University College. Through the office of the Academic Assistance Council, a Carnegie Corporation grant of £550 per annum, given to the University of Melbourne, brought Heymann to Australia.

Joining the university's chemistry department in June 1936, he was promoted to senior lecturer in 1938 and was naturalized that year. He obtained a D.Sc. (University of Melbourne) in 1939 and became associate-professor in 1945. Although Heymann was at the university for only thirteen years, he made a lasting impact on Australian science in the fields of electrochemistry, colloid and surface chemistry, and the study of molten salts. Sir David Masson [q.v.10] and E. J. Hartung [q.v.] had been involved in colloid and surface chemistry, and (Sir) Ian Wark had carried out research on flotation processes in the department's laboratories. Heymann widened and added depth to the effort. His first project was suggested by Sir David Rivett [q.v.11] who was interested in reducing water evaporation from dams by spreading films of organic materials on the surface. Heymann and his students failed to solve the practical problem, but they did contribute to theoretical understanding of the free energies of surface films on liquids. Their contribution to molten salt chemistry was to provide high quality experimental data on viscosities, electrical conductivity, surface tensions and molar volumes of molten salts.

Big, fresh faced and friendly, Heymann had a style of lecturing and an ease of manner that did much to break down the rigidity between staff and students. It was not until Heymann commenced lecturing to them in 1937 that first-year chemistry students met a teacher who treated them as individuals and showed obvious sympathy for their academic problems. A keen walker, he often spent part of the summer in the Victorian Alps, hiking and writing. His other main recreation was music, the love of which he shared with his students by taking them to concerts and operas.

An associate (1937) and fellow (1944) of the (Royal) Australian Chemical Institute, Heymann was vice-president (1948) of its Victorian branch. In 1942 he was awarded the institute's H. G. Smith [q.v.11] medal and also the Grimwade [q.v.9] prize for industrial chemistry. He gave the Liversidge [q.v.5] lecture to the meeting of the Australian and New Zealand Association for the Advancement of Science, held in Perth in 1947. Entitled 'Potentials at Interfaces', it concluded: 'It is often considered that electrochemistry has achieved a state of completion . . . I . . . hope to have shown that particularly with respect to the origin of potentials and the structure of double layers produced, a large field of fundamental importance is unexplored which merits closer attention'.

While travelling in the United States of America on a Carnegie grant, Heymann died of coronary vascular disease on 22 November 1949 at Chicago, Illinois, and was cremated. His legacy is the strong network of surface and colloid scientists in Australian research establishments and the contributions that they have made to international science and local industry. The R.A.C.I. named its applied research medal for 1986 in his memory.

J. Radford, *The Chemistry Department of the University of Melbourne* (Melb, 1978); R. W. Home, *Physics in Australia to 1945* (Melb, 1990); Roy Aust Chemical Inst, *J and Procs*, 17, 1950, p 45; *Chemistry in Aust*, 48, 1981, p 224.

T. H. SPURLING

HICKS, SIR CEDRIC STANTON (1892-1976), university professor and army catering officer, was born on 2 June 1892 at Mosgiel, New Zealand, son of George Henry Hicks, a New Zealand-born factory worker, and his wife Sarah, née Evans, from England. Young Hicks attended Ravensbourne Public and (on a scholarship) Otago Boys' High schools. While at the University of Otago (B.Sc., N.Z., 1914; M.Sc. Hons, 1915; M.B., Ch.B., 1923), he earned an income by demonstrating chemistry to medical students, lecturing to evening-classes and teaching photography at the Dunedin School of Art; he also won a national research scholarship. In his spare time he played tennis, water polo and Rugby Union football, represented the province in rowing, swam competitively, managed the Otago University *Review* and was an executive-member of the Students' Association.

By his own account, in 1916-18 Hicks served as a non-commissioned officer in the New Zealand Expeditionary Force. He assisted Professor J. K. H. Inglis in the synthesis and production of Chloramine-T for use against meningitis among the troops. Under the Sale of Food and Drugs Act (1908), Hicks was appointed government analyst in 1918 and also worked as police toxicologist for the provinces of Otago and Southland. His earnings helped him to complete his medical degree. Meanwhile, he undertook research into several branches of chemistry and was elected a fellow (1922) of the Institute of Chemistry of Great Britain and Ireland. Awarded a Beit medical research fellowship in 1923, he travelled to England and studied at Trinity College, Cambridge (Ph.D., 1926), where he pursued his interest in the pathology of the thyroid gland.

The fellowship gave Hicks an opportunity to carry out research in Switzerland, Germany and the United States of America. On 8 June 1925 at St Jude's parish church, Kensington, London, he married 21-year-old Florence Haggitt; they were to have two sons before she divorced him on 1 October 1948. In 1925 Hicks successfully applied for the Sheridan research fellowship and Marks lectureship in mammalian physiology, then being advertised by the University of Adelaide. He stated that, although more attractive opportunities might be offered 'to those of us who have come to this part of the globe, it is the duty of those who can to return and work for the Dominions'. He took up the post in April 1926. In January 1927 he was appointed to the new chair of physiology and pharmacology which he was to hold until 1957.

On his arrival in Adelaide, Hicks had bought and begun to restore Woodley, his home at Glen Osmond. During the Depression he studied the dietary patterns of five hundred families receiving relief. The university awarded him an M.D. in 1936 for his thesis on the application of spectrophotometry 'to biochemical, physiological and medico-legal problems'. He was knighted that year. In the 1930s he made several trips to Central Australia to examine the physiology of Aborigines. A member (from 1936) of the Commonwealth Advisory Council on Nutrition (subsequently the nutrition committee of the National Health and Medical Research Council), he took a leading part in surveying the diets of Australian families.

In February 1940 Hicks was appointed temporary captain, Australian Military Forces, and performed part-time duty as catering supervisor, 4th Military District, Adelaide. He was transferred to Army Headquarters, Melbourne, in June. As chief inspector of catering, he began a campaign for applying scientific principles to the feeding of troops. His achievement in overcoming resistance to his proposals was considerable: on 12 March 1943 the Australian Army Catering Corps was formed, largely due to his persistence. Having been promoted temporary lieutenant colonel (1941), he was posted as first director of the corps; by the end of World War II it numbered some 17 000 officers and soldiers. Hicks altered the basis of the allowance for military rations from a monetary to a nutrient entitlement, improved the pay and promotion opportunities of cooks, established schools of cooking and catering, devised new methods for preparing food, supported the service's adoption of the Wiles steam-cooker, and designed jungle-patrol, emergency and air-drop rations.

Hicks's initiatives led to a dramatic reduction in wastage. In 1944 he visited Britain and the U.S.A. to promote his ideas; in November he was seconded to the Australian Imperial Force as temporary colonel. Relinquishing his appointment on 31 January 1946, he was recalled for part-time duty in 1947 and transferred to the Retired List as honorary brigadier on 10 March 1952. The army retained him as a scientific food consultant, in which capacity he supervised the Defence Food Research Establishment at Scottsdale, Tasmania. His 'Who Called the Cook a Bastard?' (Sydney, 1972) gave an account of his experiences in military catering.

On 9 October 1948 Hicks had married with Congregational forms Valerie Irene Hubbard, a 28-year-old trained nurse and a divorcee who had reverted to her maiden name; the wedding took place in her father's home at Peppermint Grove, Perth. Committed to community work, Sir Stanton was president (1958-65) of the South Australian Tuberculosis Association Inc. In addition, he analysed the merits of fluoridation, studied soil conservation, investigated biological approaches to food production and took a close interest in land reform in Italy. Survived by his wife, and by the sons of his first marriage, he died on 7 February 1976 at Glen Osmond; he was accorded a military funeral and was cremated.

D. P. Mellor, The Role of Science and Industry (Canb, 1958); H. Nash, The History of Dietetics in Australia (Canb, 1989); Advertiser (Adel), 9 Feb 1976; Hicks papers (NL); Univ Adel Archives.

HEATHER NASH

HIGGINS, ESMONDE MACDONALD (1897-1960), communist publicist and adult educationist, was born 26 March 1897 at Malvern, Melbourne, second surviving of six children of John Higgins, an accountant from Ireland, and his Victorian-born wife Catherine, née McDonald; his elder sister was Janet Gertrude [q.v.11 Palmer]. Dux and prefect at Scotch College, Esmonde ventured into radical idealism through Frederick Sinclaire's [q.v.11] Free Religious Fellowship. At the University of Melbourne (B.A., 1918; M.A.,

1954) he won many prizes and engaged in the tumultuous debates of 1916-17.

Staunchly opposed to conscription, Higgins enlisted in the Australian Imperial Force on 19 November 1917, forsaking an honours degree. He served in France with the 6th Field Artillery Brigade from October 1918 and was granted leave in February 1919 to read modern history at Balliol College, Oxford, his studies there being endowed by his uncle Henry Bournes Higgins [q.v.9]. At first Higgins enjoyed Oxford but soon abhorred its elitist artificiality. After travelling through the Soviet Union in the summer of 1920, he joined the Communist Party of Great Britain. He obtained second-class honours in qualifying for his degree in 1921, but never graduated; he found his subsequent work with the Labour Research Department in London more satisfying.

Higgins returned to Australia in August 1924. His intent was to work for the Communist Party of Australia's fledgling 'Research Bureau'. The British communist Harry Pollitt hailed him as a putative Australian Lenin. The bizarre circumstances of Australian communism mocked such notions, yet for years Higgins served the C.P.A. as an office-holder and publicist on the Labour Weekly. Sydney was his usual home, but in 1925-26 he lived in Victoria and Western Australia, and in 1928 he was a delegate to the sixth congress of the Communist International in Moscow. His major interest in the early 1930s was the League Against Imperialism.

Increasingly alienated from Stalinism, Higgins changed his life's course. On 3 January 1935 at the district registrar's office, Randwick, Sydney, he married his longstanding lover Marjorie Josephine Gardner; witty and resilient, 'Joy' had a background far removed from her in-laws' Protestant-bourgeois respectability. In 1936 he secured appointment as a Workers' Educational Association lecturer in northern Tasmania. Thence he wrote comradely letters to Trotskyites, but retained party ties for a time. James Normington Rawling [q.v.] saw such behaviour as confirming Higgins's weakness and even his deceit, yet to friends 'Hig' was a source of intellect and delight.

He continued with W.E.A. work—in the Auckland district, New Zealand (1938-41), and through the University of Sydney's Department of Tutorial Classes, at Newcastle in 1941-45 and in Sydney in 1945-63 (from 1950 as assistant-director). Early in his career his lectures fostered social and political awareness; they later became increasingly academic and apolitical. As a teacher and expositor Higgins was always supreme. He wrote well on 'The Queensland Labour governments, 1915-1929' (his M.A. thesis) and on David Stewart and the W.E.A. (1957).

Survived by his wife, son and daughter, he died of cancer on Christmas Day 1960 at his Croydon home and was cremated; his estate was sworn for probate at £1100. In all he did, and failed to do, Higgins told much about his generation.

Aust Highway, Jan 1961, p 9, May 1961, p 32; *Aust Q*, Mar 1961, p 8; M. Roe, 'E. M. Higgins: A Marxist in Tasmania 1936-38', *Labour Hist*, no 32, May 1977; Palmer *and* Baracchi papers (NL); Normington Rawling papers (ANUABL).

MICHAEL ROE

HILL, ARTHUR MACHEN ('BUNG') (1903-1979), gynaecologist and obstetrician, was born on 22 October 1903 at Castlemaine, Victoria, third child of Arthur Machen Hill, medical practitioner, and his wife Emily Maude, née Johnson, both Victorian born. Arthur was educated at Castlemaine South State and Castlemaine High schools, Wesley College and the University of Melbourne (B.M., B.S., 1927; M.D., 1931). After graduating he worked as a resident medical officer (1927-32) at the Alfred, (Royal) Children's and (Royal) Women's hospitals, completed a diploma of gynaecology and obstetrics (1933), and became a lecturer and examiner in those subjects at the university.

Hill was superintendent (1933-35) of the Women's Hospital. There he began his research on post-abortion gas gangrene septicaemia cases, often the result of unsterile termination of pregnancies by unqualified abortionists. Working with the microbiologist Hildred Butler [q.v.13], he established the nature and types of *Colstridium welchii* abortional infections, and developed expertise in diagnosing the severity of the infection and the best application of treatment—hysterectomy surgery or drug therapy. He continued to collaborate with Butler on haemolytic streptococcal infections that followed childbirth.

In 1935 Hill travelled to England and became a member (fellow 1945) of the (Royal) College of Obstetricians and Gynaecologists. Next year he was made a fellow of the Royal College of Surgeons, Edinburgh, and the British Medical Association awarded him the Katherine Bishop Harman prize in obstetrics for his clinical study, 'Post Abortal and Puerperal Gas Gangrene, a report of 30 cases', published in the *Journal of Obstetrics and Gynaecology of the British Empire* (1936). He returned to Melbourne and to the Women's as honorary gynaecological and obstetrical surgeon in 1938.

Appointed flight lieutenant, Medical Branch Reserve, in February 1942, Hill was a part-time consultant with the Royal Australian Air Force during World War II. On 23 October 1951 at the office of the government statist, Melbourne, he married Helen (Ilona) Semark, née Krames, a Hungarian-born divorcee. In 1951-63 he was senior gynaecological surgeon to in-patients at the R.W.H. With Kevin McCaul and Graham Godfrey, he demonstrated the acceptability of the Wertheim operation as treatment of uterine cervical cancer. As a lecturer he was notoriously unpunctual: once, having missed an 11 a.m. lecture, he arrived at 1 o'clock next morning and summoned the students to the labour ward in their pyjamas. Such aberrations were forgiven because he was 'a superb lecturer when he did come'.

Regarded as 'a legend in his own lifetime' and as something of an eccentric, 'Bung' Hill was 'impeccably dressed, with an alert and twinkling eye, a soft voice and a pervasive personality'. It has been suggested that his nickname derived from his childhood when he called out 'bung, bung' while playing with a popgun. One of his many qualities was his great understanding of human nature. His recreations were his family, tennis, listening to classical music, and reading medical, historical, biographical and viticultural literature. He was a dab hand at composing poetry for speeches and birthdays. In April 1953 he displayed his talents as raconteur by delivering a notable speech on the aims and principles of the Royal College of Obstetricians and Gynaecologists' Australian regional council at the Arthur Wilson [q.v.12] Memorial Foundation fund-raising dinner. A *bon vivant* and a connoisseur of wine, he was granted membership (1964) of the Confrèrie des Chevaliers du Tastevin, France. He also belonged to the Viticultural Society of Victoria.

When he retired from the R.W.H. in 1963, Hill was appointed honorary consulting surgeon. Colleagues maintained that his exacting standards had influenced the quality of medicine and the tone and manner of medical life in Melbourne. On his election as fellow of the Royal Australian College of Surgeons in 1974, he was described as 'an outstanding figure' who had published at least thirty papers of merit. The subjects of his articles were diverse, ranging from pelvic lymphadenectomy, through intra-uterine contraceptive device to post-menopausal bleeding. In 1976 Hill was appointed O.B.E. Survived by his wife, daughter and son, he died on 20 January 1979 at Mount Eliza and was buried in St Kilda cemetery. A sculpture of his hands, cast by Alan Martin, is held by the Royal Australian College of Obstetricians and Gynaecologists, Melbourne.

T. Hewat, *The Florey* (Syd, 1990); Roy Women's Hospital (Melb), *Bulletin*, 12, no 1, Feb 1979; *MJA*, 14 July 1979; *Age* (Melb), 23, 25 Jan 1979.

HILERY BELTON

HILL, CEDRIC WATERS (1891-1975), air force officer, was born on 3 April 1891 at Maryvale station, near Warwick, Queensland, fourth child of Edward Ormond Waters Hill, grazier, and his wife Phillis, née Clark, both native-born. At Brisbane Grammar School, Cedric was 'Sluggish at his work, but good natured and honourable'. He learned sheep-farming in New Zealand, took an apprentice-ship with a Brisbane engineering firm, completed a course in shearing-machinery maintenance and began working in sheds around Queensland. After seeing the magic-ian Nate Leipzig perform, Hill studied and practised conjuring; his other interest was flying and he built two gliders before World War I broke out.

Sailing to England, Hill was commissioned in the Royal Flying Corps on 3 July 1915 and by the end of the year was in Egypt with No.14 Squadron. His precision bombing of the reservoir at Bir el Hassana on 27 February 1916 won acclaim, and he was mentioned in dispatches that year. On 3 May anti-aircraft fire forced his B.E.2c down, east of Romani. Using his dismounted Lewis-gun, he traded fire with some Arabs for six hours before sur-rendering and being handed over to the Turks. They took him to the prisoner-of-war camp at Yozgat, Turkey, where he befriended a Welshman, Lieutenant Elias Henry Jones. To entertain their comrades, Hill and Jones communicated with the spirit world by ouija-board, conjured ghostly 'manifestations' and perfected a telepathy act.

Although forbidden to escape by their own superiors, Hill and Jones decided to exploit the greed and superstition of the camp's com-mandant in order to get away. In early 1918 they convinced him that their supernatural informant, 'the Spook', could reveal the whereabouts of buried treasure if he were consulted on the Mediterranean coast—whence they planned to abscond to Cyprus. To justify their removal from the camp, they feigned madness, Hill exhibiting symptoms of 'religious melancholia' and Jones general par-alysis of the insane. A mishap foiled the plan, but the conspirators decided to persist with the ruse of insanity to gain repatriation on medical grounds.

Having hoodwinked the local doctors, Hill and Jones were sent to Constantinople in May. On the way, a fake, double-suicide at-tempt almost cost them their lives, but it helped to lend authenticity to their deception. In hospitals and camps, in and around the capi-tal, they underwent psychiatric examinations and overcame ploys to expose them. With his 'forehead puckered, jaw dropped and mouth open', Hill read from the Bible, and fasted until he became ill from malnutrition and dys-entery. By August he and Jones had been certified insane and approved for an exchange of prisoners with the British. Hill sailed for England on 1 November 1918 and resumed his career in the Royal Air Force.

While again serving in the Middle East, he married a fellow Australian Jane Lisle Mort on 16 March 1921 at Port Said, Egypt, with Church of England rites. Back in England, on 5 October 1930 he flew from Lympne aero-drome, Kent, in an attempt to beat Bert Hinkler's [q.v.9] time for a solo flight to Aus-tralia. A crash on the 18th, when he was taking off from Atambua, Netherlands Timor, for the final leg to Darwin, prevented him from breaking the record. Hill commanded squadrons in Britain and the Sudan, rose to wing commander in 1937 and was given charge of the R.A.F. Station, Tangmere, Sus-sex. Promoted temporary group captain in June 1940, he performed staff and training duties in Britain and had operational com-mands in the Middle East before being placed on the Retired List on 5 January 1944. For the next two years he was a ferry pilot with the Air Transport Auxiliary.

'A friendly, jolly person, tall and very sun-burnt', Hill was an outstanding rifle and pistol shot, a keen skier and photographer, and a member (1933) of the Inner Magic Circle. In retirement in England he took up gliding. Sur-vived by his wife and daughter, he died on 5 March 1975 in his home at Windsor, Berk-shire. His account of his feat of 'malingering', *The Spook and the Commandant* (London), was published later that year.

E. H. Jones, *The Road to En-Dor* (Lond, 1921); T. W. White, *Guests of the Unspeakable* (Syd, 1935); E. P. Wixted, *The North-West Aerial Frontier 1919-1934* (Brisb, 1985); *Magic Circular*, 35, Jan 1941; *Over the Front*, 4, no 2, Summer 1989, p 148; C. W. Hill records (Qld Museum, Brisb); information from Miss P. P. J. Hill, Beaminster, Dorset, Eng.

NEVILLE PARKER*
DARRYL BENNET

HILL, MARY ERNESTINE (1899-1972), journalist and author, was born on 21 January 1899 at Rockhampton, Queensland, only child of Robert Hemmings (d.1910), a factory man-ager from London, and his second wife Margaret Foster, née Lynam, a Queensland-born schoolteacher. Ernestine's childhood was spent in Brisbane where she won a bur-sary to All Hallows convent school. She ap-pears to have been an outstanding student, although she later said that the nuns who taught her had not encouraged her to write. In 1916, however, Hibernian Newspaper Co. Ltd published her *Peter Pan Land and Other Poems*, with a preface by Archbishop (Sir) James Duhig [q.v.8]. Next year she attended Stott & Hoare's Business College, Brisbane, having been coached by her mother for a scholarship there. First in her year, she gained entrance to the public service, and in January 1918 was appointed a typiste in the library of the Department of Justice. She later claimed to have begun preliminary studies towards a law degree at the University of Queensland.

In Sydney in early 1919 Hemmings entered the world of journalism as secretary to J. F. Archibald [q.v.3], literary editor of *Smith's Weekly*, of which she subsequently became a sub-editor. There began her association with R. C. Packer [q.v.11], the newspaper's manager. On 30 October 1924—'the happiest day of my life'—her son Robert was born. He was rumoured to be Packer's son, although he was never publicly acknowledged by him. Ernestine assumed the surname Hill. Robert grew to be a partner in the restless travels on which she based her life's work. About 1931 Hill began a decade of travel writing, primarily for Associated Newspapers, where Packer was managing editor. The colourful and enthusiastic style of her articles led to syndication and to acceptance by other publications such as *Walkabout*.

Her sensationalist reporting in 1931 of the discovery of gold in the Granites, north-west of Alice Springs in the Northern Territory, contributed to a gold rush and a stock-market boom. The failure of this venture left many prospectors stranded and destitute, and Hill was attacked for irresponsible journalism. Many years afterwards she condemned another of her news articles in the *Sunday Sun*, headlined 'Black Baby Saved From Being Eaten' (1932), as the work of 'a wicked and ruthless journalist'. *The Great Australian Loneliness* (London, 1937), her vivid account of travels in the outback and a promotion of the Territory, led to Australian and American editions. *Water into Gold* (Melbourne, 1937), her romanticized history of the Murray River irrigation area and the dried-fruit industry, was praised by reviewers.

In 1932 Hill had met Daisy Bates [q.v.7]. In a syndicated series of articles entitled 'My Natives and I', first published in the Adelaide *Advertiser* in 1936, she recorded Bates's experiences of living in remote desert areas with indigenous Australians. Although Bates did not acknowledge Hill's claim of ghost-writing Bates's book, *The Passing of the Aborigines* (London, 1938), she later confirmed Hill's contribution. Hill's *Kabbarli*, published posthumously (Sydney, 1973), was her personal tribute to Bates.

Hill's only novel, *My Love Must Wait* (Sydney, 1941), was based on the life of Matthew Flinders [q.v.1]. Its completion was subsidized by a Commonwealth Literary Fund fellowship. The book's success was followed by English and American editions, and it later became prescribed reading for school students. Miles Franklin [q.v.8] was awed when its sales reached 60 000, but added the qualification 'pity it is so inaccurate'. Hill's writings were generally popular and respected, and *The Great Australian Loneliness* was used for the orientation of American troops during World War II. In 1940-42 she edited the women's pages in the *A.B.C. Weekly*. She was also a feature-writer on travel for the Australian Broadcasting Commission, and gave radio-talks about her journeys. In June 1942 she was the first creative writer to be appointed a commissioner of the A.B.C.

At this time her son was approaching eligibility for war service. She began a long struggle to have him exempted from conscription on various grounds—his pacificism, her need of him as a research assistant, and his health. It was an unhappy period. Her popularity began to wane and in September 1944 she resigned as commissioner, giving ill health as the reason. In October she wrote to George Mackaness who, with Dame Mary Gilmore [qq.v.10,9], had been among her supporters: 'They have let Bob go'. She resumed her travels. In 1946 she bought a caravan, and she and Bob continued their wanderings. In the following year the novelist K. S. Prichard [q.v.11], who was with her at Coolgardie, Western Australia, wrote that Ernestine 'seems to take...flies and red-backed spiders galore...in her stride. She's a strange otherwhereish creature with big beautiful eyes, a hoarse voice and curious incapacity to argue logically about anything'. Hill's successful story of John Flynn [q.v.8] and the Australian Inland Mission, *Flying Doctor Calling* (Sydney, 1947), preceded *The Territory* (Sydney, 1951)—a colourful and romantic account of Northern Australia and its people—illustrated by Elizabeth Durack.

Despite Hill's great ambitions and voluminous notes for future novels, plays, descriptive works and even film scripts, she published no further books. The last twenty years of her life were dominated by financial worries, and by troubles with her physical and emotional health. She was affected by her poor diet and cigarette smoking; her letters abounded with references to being 'old and done', and mentioned 'breakdown feelings'. Her 'wanderings'—as she called them—continued, but without the same financial or spiritual rewards. Her hopes were centred on what she considered to be her *magnum opus*, a huge novel entitled 'Johnny Wisecap', about the life of an albino Aborigine, which she repeatedly reported as almost ready for publication. She wrote that 'the ideas come thick and fast. I can't sort them out. A forest is here, nearly in bloom'. Her publisher, Angus & Robertson [qq.v.7,11] Ltd, although sympathetic, gradually began to doubt her ability to produce and after 1959 made no further financial commitments.

In 1959 Hill received a Commonwealth Literary Fund fellowship which provided her with a small pension for life, but her personal distress remained. She continued to travel, mainly on the east coast, trying to settle in North Queensland, writing an occasional article and dragging her trunks of notes with her, always restless and unhappy. In 1970 she returned finally to Brisbane and to the care of her family. The effects of malnutrition, emphysema and shortage of money continued to govern her life, as did her inability to cope with the massive collection of notes, manuscripts and photographs from which she still hoped to publish. Survived by her son, she died on 21 August 1972 in Brisbane; in accordance with her wishes, she was buried 'just under a tree' in Mount Gravatt lawn cemetery. The Fryer Library, University of Queensland, and the Queensland Art Gallery hold portraits of her.

K. S. Inglis, *This is the ABC* (Melb, 1983); C. Ferrier, *As Good as a Yarn with You* (Cambridge, UK, 1992); *Advertiser* (Adel), 4 Jan-19 Feb 1936; *SMH*, 23 Aug 1972; M. R. Bonnin, A Study of Australian Descriptive and Travel Writing, 1929-1945 (Ph.D. thesis, Univ Qld, 1980); Hill papers (Fryer L, Univ Qld); information from Mr R. Hill, Trentham, Vic, and Ms M. Morris, Bundeena, NSW.

MARGRIET R. BONNIN
NANCY BONNIN

HILLGROVE, ARTHUR DUNCAN (1909-1979), contractor, was born on 4 September 1909 at Birchip, Victoria, fourth son of Victorian-born parents Donald Hillgrove (d.1920), farmer, and his wife Clara Jane, née Bolden. Educated at Birchip Higher Elementary School, Arthur obtained his Intermediate certificate, but left in 1923 to work as a farm labourer. Five years later he bought a wheat pickler and a truck to handle seed wheat for local farmers; at the same time he acquired a team of horses and successfully tendered for road works with the Shire of Birchip. By the 1940s Hillgrove was a major figure in the district. In 1943 he was elected to the shire council. He was president of the local football club and, for seven years, of the Tyrell Football League. On 6 August 1948 he married Verna Louisa Hill at Dandenong with Methodist forms.

After World War II Hillgrove's business interests grew considerably. 'A.D.', as he was commonly known, embraced technological innovation with enthusiasm. In 1944 he moved into contract shearing with his own team and equipment. Having purchased the latest heavy earth-moving plant in 1948, he serviced local needs by clearing and levelling land and sinking dams; he then successfully tendered for work throughout the State. Among his major projects were drainage contracts for the Geelong Water Trust and the Melbourne and Metropolitan Board of Works, land development at Horsham and Kerang, sewerage works at Shepparton and Robinvale, reservoirs at Hopetoun, Allansford and Churchill, and road by-passes on the Hume and Princes highways. In 1958 he formed A. D. Hillgrove (Constructions) Pty Ltd (from 1965 Transvic Contractors Pty Ltd), with an office in Melbourne. Other enterprises included tin-mining in western New South Wales in 1958 and drilling for water in the late 1960s.

Hillgrove became the largest individual employer in the Birchip area. He gathered a loyal workforce and, from his base, conducted an ever-widening commercial empire. In 1950 his wheat pickling business became Hillgrove Grading Service; by the 1970s it operated fifteen machines in northern Victoria and the Riverina. He bought and developed land in many parts of the State and in the 1950s built up a large holding in the Shire of Birchip, including his father's original selection. In 1950 'A.D.' had entered into a partnership in a hardware store in Birchip, in 1960 he built a large workshop to maintain his machinery and in 1967 he opened a tyre service. He established a branch of J. I. Case (Aust.) Pty Ltd in 1964 and began assembling tractors and auto-headers from imported parts. Branches were opened in other Victorian country towns.

Four times shire president, a government nominee on the Mallee Regional Committee and a foundation member of the Port of Portland advisory committee, Hillgrove was named Birchip's citizen of the year in 1969 and appointed A.M. in 1977. He died of a coronary occlusion on 30 June 1979 at his Birchip home and was buried in the local cemetery; his wife, son and daughter survived him. His estate was sworn for probate at $1 074 161.

J. E. Senyard, *Birchip* (Birchip, Vic, 1970); *Warracknabeal Herald*, 6 July 1979; family papers (held by Mrs J. Living, Birchip, Vic).

J. E. SENYARD

HILLIARD, WILLIAM GEORGE (1887-1960), Anglican bishop and headmaster, was born on 29 May 1887 at Redfern, Sydney, son of native-born parents Alpha Ernest Hilliard (d.1904), a coach-painter of convict descent, and his wife Eleanor Priscilla, née West. Educated at Darlington and Stanmore public schools, and at Sydney Boys' High School (on a scholarship), George developed lifelong enthusiasms for cricket, literature and debating.

He became a pupil-teacher in 1904 and two years later won a scholarship to Teachers' College (Blackfriars) which enabled him to attend the University of Sydney (B.A., 1910; M.A., 1914). In 1910 he joined the staff of Fort Street Model School under A. J. Kilgour [q.v.9].

Influenced by those he met while lecturing part time (1911-16) at Moore Theological College, Hilliard was made deacon in 1911 and ordained priest on 19 December 1912. He served as curate at Holy Trinity, Dulwich Hill, and was appointed headmaster of its new parish school, Trinity Grammar; under his enthusiastic direction, enrolments more than trebled within four years. At St Philip's, Church Hill, on 19 December 1914 Hilliard married Lilian Constance Pearl Wooster. In June 1916 he was appointed rector of St John the Baptist's, Ashfield. A conservative parish council made his first years difficult, adding to the strain of his pastoral work during World War I and the distress he suffered when his wife died in 1918, leaving an infant son. With some relief, in 1926 Hilliard accepted the ministry of the large and evangelical parish of St Clement's, Marrickville. He married Dorothy Kezia Duval on 16 May 1927 at St John's, Ashfield.

In the following year Hilliard returned as headmaster to Trinity Grammar, by then a diocesan school; although he had to contend with a huge capital debt and the Depression, he inspired a sense of unity and purpose in students and staff. A Freemason, he served as grand chaplain (1931-33) of United Grand Lodge of New South Wales. He was a gifted writer and much in demand as a speaker. Appointed a canon of St Andrew's Cathedral, Sydney, in 1932, he accepted the see of Nelson, New Zealand, in October 1934.

Bishop Hilliard needed little urging from Archbishop Mowll [q.v.] to return to Sydney in 1940. As rector of St John's, Parramatta, and co-adjutor bishop, he became a familiar figure in public life. Tall, with a mane of flowing silver hair and a rich resonant voice, he had his own radio programme on 2UW and appeared on such television shows as 'Meet the Press'. He frequently waited on the State government to deplore gambling and Sunday sport. His membership (1953-57) of (Sir) Harold Wyndham's committee on secondary education gave him satisfaction.

As Hilliard aged, his inability to refuse office led to declining health. He tried, often in vain, to combine his parish duties with the heavy demands of public engagements, committee-work and the complex role of diocesan registrar. Survived by his wife and one of their three daughters, he died on 1 March 1960 at Parramatta and was cremated. His portrait by William Pidgeon is held by Trinity Grammar School.

J. West, *Innings of Grace* (Syd, 1987), *and* for bibliog; *SMH*, 10 Sept 1928, 21 July 1932, 15 Dec 1933, 8 Jan 1934, 31 May 1940, 8 July 1947, 7 Mar 1949, 3 Jan 1958, 22 Sept 1959, 2, 4 Mar 1960.

JANET WEST

HINCKS, SIR CECIL STEPHEN (1894-1963), politician, farmer and soldier, was born on 18 February 1894 at Maitland, South Australia, eldest of seven children of native-born parents Henry Stephen Hincks, miller, and his wife Emily Frances Picton, née Parkins. Educated at Port Victoria Public School and the Collegiate School of St Peter (1907-08), Cecil began work in the flour-milling business and was about to try out for Port Adelaide Football Club when World War I commenced. On 19 August 1914 he enlisted in the Australian Imperial Force and was posted to the 10th Battalion. He served at Gallipoli and on the Western Front where he was commissioned in January 1917. Gunshot wounds to his chest and thigh in April led to the amputation of his right leg, a year's convalescence in England and more than one hundred surgical operations over the remainder of his life. At St Mark's parish church, Surbiton, Surrey, on 5 December 1918 he married Gladys Lottie Merritt, the 18-year-old daughter of a caterer; the marriage ended in divorce shortly after he returned to South Australia where his appointment terminated on 13 December 1920.

After being employed at Port Victoria by the Wheat Harvest Board, Hincks set up on his own, managing grain and insurance agencies. In 1928 he bought a farm at Urania. A popular figure, he was a justice of the peace, prominent in sporting, educational and charitable organizations, and a State councillor (1922-46) of the Returned Sailors' and Soldiers' Imperial League of Australia. On 12 March 1935 at the Baptist Church, Alberton, Adelaide, he married Edith May Staples, a 30-year-old clerk. He was elected to the House of Assembly in March 1941 as the Liberal and Country League member for Yorke Peninsula and was to be returned unopposed at every election until his death. He sold the farm and in 1946 moved with his family to Largs Bay. Chairman (1944) of the parliamentary Liberal Party, he was appointed in 1945 to a committee which was charged with inspecting and assessing land for purchase by the Federal government for the resettlement of ex-servicemen.

On 17 April 1946 Hincks was given the portfolios of lands, irrigation and repatriation; he held them until 1 January 1963. Despite his crutches and poor health, he gave himself unstintingly, and received widespread respect and affection. For all that, soldier settlement required a stronger and abler minister, and one more prepared to co-operate with the Department of Agriculture. The demand by soldier settlers for viable blocks soon exceeded the supply and resettlement was painfully slow, even after changes to the scheme in 1948-49. One critic described Hincks as kindly, but weak, 'a gramaphone . . . playing records provided by the Lands Department'. None the less, the minister was always accessible, and keen to assist ex-servicemen and their families. His record term saw the consolidation of the repatriation programme and many related achievements, particularly the Loxton irrigation project.

Hincks was knighted in 1960. Next year he visited the United States of America, Europe and Japan, investigating the bulk-handling of barley and seeking markets for South Australia's salt and iron ore. Survived by his wife and their son and daughter, he died of cancer on New Year's Day 1963 in the Repatriation General Hospital, Springbank, Adelaide. Sir Cecil was accorded a state funeral, which was attended by thousands of ex-servicemen, and was cremated with Anglican rites. The Hincks Conservation Park, Eyre Peninsula, commemorates him.

R. Heinrich, *Wide Sails and Wheat Stacks* (Port Victoria, SA, 1976); *PD* (SA), 12 June 1963, pp 4, 13, 20 Aug 1947, p 344; *Advertiser* (Adel), 18 Apr 1946, 19 Mar 1955, 2-3 Jan 1963; *Maitland Watch*, 31 Jan, 7 Feb 1963; C. Lucas, The RSL in South Australia 1945-1954 (B.A. Hons thesis, Univ Adel, 1963); H. Le Lacheur, War Service Land Settlement in South Australia (M.A. Hons thesis, Univ Adel, 1968); R. Jennings, Independent Members of the South Australian Parliament 1927-1970 (M.A. thesis, Univ Adel, 1982); Liberal Party of SA records (Mort L).   JENNY TILBY STOCK

HINDWOOD, KEITH ALFRED (1904-1971), ornithologist and businessman, was born on 3 July 1904 at Willoughby, Sydney, younger of twin sons and third of four children of native-born parents Alfred Joseph Hindwood, stationer, and his wife Ida Ellen, née Phillips. Keith was educated at North Sydney Public School until the age of 14. In 1928 he set up a wholesale stationery, office supplies and printing business; he was to convert it into a company in the late 1950s and run it until he retired in 1970. At St John's Anglican Church, Darlinghurst, on 29 October 1936 he married Marjorie Goddard, a stenographer.

In 1924 Hindwood had joined the Royal Australasian Ornithologists' Union. The first of 185 articles that he published in its journal, the *Emu*, appeared in 1926: it was a detailed life-study of a distinctive bird, the rock warbler (*Origma rubricata*). Throughout his life he recorded occurrences and aspects of bird behaviour in his comprehensive files. Be-

tween 1928 and 1937 he submitted fifty-two photographs of natural history subjects to the *Sydney Mail* and in 1931-32—as 'Oriole'—wrote a column, 'Nature Notes and Studies', in the *Land* newspaper. He made regular excursions to different bird habitats around Sydney and several camping trips beyond, two to determine the restricted range of the rock warbler in New South Wales.

Interested in historical ornithology, Hindwood belonged to the Royal Australian Historical Society. His honeymoon on Lord Howe Island sparked his enthusiasm to research its ornithological history, including extinct birds. He published the results in the *Emu* and in *The Birds of Lord Howe Island* (1940). He later wrote articles on pioneer naturalists and early colonial artists, among them George Raper [q.v.2]. His other books included *The Waders of Sydney* (with E. S. Hoskin, 1955), *The Birds of Sydney* (with A. R. McGill, 1958), *Australian Birds in Colour* (1966), and *A Portfolio of Australian Birds* (illustrated by William T. Cooper, 1968). In 1960 and 1961 Hindwood joined two colleagues, K. Keith and D. L. Serventy, in the survey vessel, H.M.A.S. *Gascoyne*, on voyages to the Coral Sea. Their conclusions on the birds of the area were published by the Commonwealth Scientific and Industrial Research Organization as *Birds of the South-West Coral Sea* (1963).

Although he was strictly an amateur, Hindwood was recognized as a world authority on Australian birds. Honorary ornithologist (later research associate) at the Australian Museum, Sydney, for over forty years, he was a life member (from 1931) of the Gould [q.v.1] League of Bird Lovers of New South Wales, a corresponding fellow (1938) of the American Ornithologists' Union, president (1939) and fellow (1950) of the Royal Zoological Society of New South Wales, and president (1944-46) and fellow (1951) of the R.A.O.U. In 1959 he was awarded the Australian Natural History medallion.

Kindly, philanthropic and humane, with a jovial sense of humour, Hindwood consistently helped the underprivileged. He also encouraged young people to study birds. Experienced observers sought his guidance and constructive criticism of their manuscripts before publication and obtained information from his files. 'Lofty' Hindwood was 6 ft 3 ins (191 cm) tall, slim and agile. While birdwatching in Royal National Park, he died suddenly of coronary artery disease on 18 March 1971 and was cremated. His wife, daughter and son survived him.

Aust Museum, *Aust Natural Hist*, 15 June 1971, p 54; RAHS, *Newsletter*, June 1971, p 7; *Emu* (Melb), Oct 1971, p 183; Hindwood papers (ML);

information from Mrs M. Hindwood, East Lindfield, Syd; personal information. ERNEST S. HOSKIN

HINTON, HENRY FREDERICK (1909-1978), motorcycle racer and motor mechanic, was born on 31 July 1909 at Aston, Birmingham, England, eldest son of Henry John Thomas Hinton, general labourer, and his wife Nellie, née Hanson. The family emigrated to Sydney soon after World War I and settled at Canley Vale where Harry attended the public school. In the 1920s his father and two uncles owned a motorcycle business, Hinton Bros, at Newtown. Hinton made his competitive début in 1929 in a motorcycle beach-race at Gerringong. His Western Suburbs clubmates dubbed him 'Chisel', a reference to his sharp mind rather than his thin build: he was 5 ft 10 ins (178 cm) tall and weighed just over 10 stone (64 kg). While working as a motorcycle courier in Sydney in 1931, he was involved in a serious road accident and lost his left eye. Restricted vision did not affect his racing career. At St Andrew's Anglican Church, Lakemba, on 5 March 1932 he married Vienie Kathleen Reid, a typiste.

In 1933 Hinton won the 350-c.c. class at the Australian Tourist Trophy races on a gravel-surfaced course at Phillip Island, Victoria, riding a borrowed Norton machine. An official representative (1933-39) for Bennett & Wood Ltd, the Birmingham Small Arms Co. Ltd agent in Sydney, he prepared the modified B.S.A. roadsters (which lacked the design sophistication of some of their rivals) and competed as team leader in road-racing, and in dirt-track and road trials. He won the Australian lightweight event at Bathurst in 1937 and 1940, and the sidecar event at the new Mount Panorama circuit in 1938.

During World War II Hinton repaired Army motorcycles for Bennett & Wood. In his spare time he and Eric McPherson founded the Motor Cycle Racing Club of New South Wales. In 1946 Hinton opened his own motorcycle dealership at Bankstown and switched to Norton machines. He won the 350-c.c. class at Bathurst in 1947 and 1948, and the senior (500-c.c.) Grand Prix five times between 1950 and 1955. Endorsed by the Auto Cycle Council of Australia as an official representative, he competed in the Isle of Man T.T. races in 1949-51, as well as in events in Ireland and Europe; he soon graduated from racing privately entered machines to being factory rider (1949-51) for Norton Motors. In 1949 he had become the first Australian to record a podium finish in a world 500-c.c. championship event by finishing third in the Dutch T.T. A crash in 1951 ended his international career.

Hinton returned to racing by winning two classes at Bathurst over Easter 1952, riding ex-factory Nortons. Next year he won four out of the five solo classes. He was five times Australian motorcycle champion and seventeen times a winner at the annual Bathurst motorcycle-racing carnival. After his retirement in July 1955, he gave his racing machines and wily technical help to his sons, who between them won eight Australian championships. Survived by his wife and two of his three sons, Hinton died of cerebrovascular disease on 9 May 1978 at Belmore and was cremated; his eldest son Harry had died in 1959 in Italy following a motorcycle-racing accident.

A Fistful of Revs (Syd, 1978); D. Cox and W. Hagon, Australian Motorcycle Heroes, 1949-1989 (Syd, 1989); J. Scaysbrook, Motorcycle Grand Prix World (Melb, 1989); Two Wheels, 19, no 2, Oct 1978, p 38, no 3, Nov 1978, p 46; SMH, 10 July 1949, 10 Apr 1955; Report on 1933 Australian Tourist Trophy (published in Australian Cycling and Motor Cycling, undated part of mag held by author, Haberfield, Syd); information from Messrs E. Hinton, Baulkham Hills, R. Hinton, Belfield, R. Challenger, Georges Hall, Syd, and N. Burling, Forster, NSW.   DON COX

HIRSCHFELD, OTTO SADDLER (1898-1957), medical practitioner and university chancellor, was born on 24 March 1898 in Brisbane, eldest of six children of Eugen Hirschfeld [q.v.9], a physician from Prussia, and his Victorian-born wife Annie Sarah Eliza, née Saddler. Otto was educated at the Normal School, Brisbane Grammar School (which he represented at Rugby Union football) and the University of Queensland (B.Sc., 1919; M.Sc., 1921). With Professor T. H. Johnston [q.v.9], he was co-author of 'The Lingulidae of the Queensland Coast', a paper read to the Royal Society of Queensland in June 1919. Hirschfeld then studied medicine at the University of Melbourne (M.B., B.S., 1923). After serving as a resident medical officer at the (Royal) Melbourne Hospital for eighteen months, he returned to Brisbane in June 1924 and entered private practice. On 29 October 1925 at St Andrew's Anglican Church, South Brisbane, he married Joan Mary Eliott, a nurse. His father, who had been German consul in Brisbane, was interned in 1916 and deported in 1920. Although he was permitted to return to Australia in 1927, the family suffered many indignities during these years. As the eldest son, Otto carried the responsibility of being head of the family in Eugen's absence. He never revealed any resentment of the episode.

Having been a physician to out-patients at Brisbane Hospital from 1925, Otto Hirschfeld was appointed a physician to in-patients in

1936 and a senior part-time physician in 1938. In that year he began lecturing in clinical medicine at the University of Queensland. He was subsequently a lecturer in pharmacology and materia medica, in diseases of metabolism, in forensic medicine, and in medicine and pathology. While an examiner in medical nursing, he wrote a manual that was published by the Nurses and Masseurs' Registration Board of Queensland. Hirschfeld was an excellent general physician, with a particular interest in diabetes mellitus and therapeutics; he had charge of the diabetic clinic at Brisbane Hospital in 1937-57. A member (1951) and fellow (1956) of the Royal Australasian College of Physicians, he served on its therapeutic advisory committee. He also sat on the State advisory committee on hospital drugs and surgical appliances, and the poisons schedule committee of the National Health and Medical Research Council, and chaired the committee which prepared the *Brisbane Hospital Pharmacopoeia*.

A huge man, slow of movement and speech, 'needing only a cloak to make him a Chestertonian figure', Hirschfeld was nevertheless highly intelligent, quick witted and keenly observant. He was gifted with the 'common touch' and knew a host of people from all walks of life. Hundreds of medical students who listened to his lectures and attended his rounds of the wards quickly acquired respect and affection for him. They looked on him as a great clinician whose knowledge was tempered with honesty and sense. Showing kindness and understanding, he helped to solve many of their personal problems. His colleagues held his clinical judgement in such regard that he was known as a 'consultant's consultant'. He was a member (from 1950) of the senate of the University of Queensland, deputy-chancellor (1952) and chancellor (from 1953). While he grasped details quickly and had a flair for eliminating non-essentials, his decisions were based on justice and principle. Respected and well liked, he carried out his duties with dignity, diplomacy and courage. In 1956 the University of Melbourne conferred on him an honorary LL.D.

Contract bridge, philately, reading, gardening and horse-racing were his recreations. A foundation member of the Queensland Bridge Association, Hirschfeld was president (1949) of the Australian Bridge Council. In the World Bridge Olympics in 1951 he and his partner won third prize in competition with four thousand pairs. He was a member (from 1927) and president (1940-41 and 1949-50) of the Johnsonian Club, and particularly enjoyed its camaraderie; he also belonged to the Queensland Turf Club. Hirschfeld died of a ruptured aneurysm of the abdominal aorta on 29 May 1957 at Clayfield and was cremated;

his wife, two sons and two daughters survived him. (Sir) William Dargie's portrait of Hirschfeld is held by the University of Queensland.

G. L. McDonald (ed), *Roll of the Royal Australasian College of Physicians*, 1, 1938-75 (Syd, 1988); *Univ Qld Gazette*, Sept 1953, p 2, Dec 1956, p 8, Sept 1957, p 2; *MJA*, 2, Aug 1957, p 223; Univ Qld Medical School, *Trephine*, 5, no 2, 1957, p 102; *Courier-Mail*, 30, 31 May 1957; Univ Qld Archives; information from Dr K. E. Hirschfeld, Brisb.

ROSS PATRICK

HIRSCHFELD-MACK, LUDWIG (1893-1965), artist and teacher, was born on 11 July 1893 at Frankfurt am Main, Germany, son of Ernst Hirschfeld, a manufacturer of leather goods, and his wife Clara, née Mack, both members of the Evangelical Reformed Church. Young Ludwig was encouraged to express his inquisitive nature through art. After attending the Muster gymnasium at Frankfurt am Main, he studied painting and crafts at the Debschitz Schule, Munich, and attended lectures in art history at the University of Munich. Conscripted into the German Army at the outbreak of World War I, he was promoted lieutenant and won the Iron Cross. In 1917 he married Elinor Wirth who brought him into contact with the Society of Friends.

On being discharged at the end of the war, Hirschfeld attended the Stuttgart Academy where he was introduced to colour theory and printmaking. In 1919 he enrolled at the Weimar Bauhaus, studied under Johannes Itten, Paul Klee and Wassily Kandinsky, and was apprenticed to Lyonel Feininger in the print workshop. He qualified as a journeyman in 1922. Early in his career he had adopted his mother's maiden name when signing his works. Hirschfeld-Mack's major preoccupation was with the application of colour theories. It resulted in his colour-light plays, his best-known achievements at the Weimar Bauhaus. Hoping to capture the 'actual' movement implied in the illusionary tensions of abstract art, he built and operated an apparatus that combined moving projections of coloured light, mechanical templates and music of his own composition. He published an explanatory booklet, *Farben licht-spiele, Wiesen-Ziele-Kritiken* (Weimar, 1923), and gave performances in Berlin and Vienna, and at Weimar and Leipzig.

When the Bauhaus was relocated at Dessau in 1925, Hirschfeld-Mack remained at Weimar and taught in schools and teachers' colleges before moving to Berlin in 1934. The rise of the Nazis forced him to leave Germany because of his part-Jewish heritage. In Britain from March 1936, he worked for subsistence societies in Wales, taught in a preparatory school and developed large-scale, projected-light advertising projects. He lent a number of his works to the Museum of Modern Art, New York, for its Bauhaus retrospective of 1938.

In 1940 Hirschfeld-Mack was deported to Australia as an enemy alien in the *Dunera*. He was interned at Hay and Orange, New South Wales, and at Tatura, Victoria. There he made a number of woodcuts that illustrated life under detention. Released in 1942 through the sponsorship of (Sir) James Darling, headmaster of Geelong Church of England Grammar School, Hirschfeld-Mack was appointed its art master. He promoted his pupils' self-knowledge, introduced them to *avant-garde* painting techniques, and encouraged wood-carving, weaving, musical instrument-making, leatherwork and other crafts. Through a colour-coding of strings and keys of guitars and xylophones, he extended the experience of music for many boys. Under his leadership the art school provided scenery, lighting and displays for plays and exhibitions, pottery for charity stalls, sheepskin coats for victims of the war in Europe, and gates and gardens for the school. In 1954 he organized an exhibition of the work of his pupils. His own work had been exhibited at the University of Melbourne in 1946 and at the Peter Bray Gallery, Melbourne, in 1953.

Held in high esteem by both students and staff, 'Dr Hirschfeld', as he was known at Geelong, was an inspirational teacher who consistently propounded the Bauhaus principles of self-knowledge, economy of material and form, and reform of society through art. One pupil Daniel Thomas saw him as a 'serene, quiet man—so fair that he glowed with the pale radiance of saints in stained-glass windows'. Darling said of Hirschfeld-Mack: 'He inspired dozens of boys with his integrity, and enthusiasm. He was an almost perfect man . . . a beautiful character and an original teacher'.

Hirschfeld-Mack's wife had returned to Germany where she died on 11 November 1953. At Glenhuntly, Melbourne, on 4 January 1955 he married with Methodist forms Olive Harrison Russell, a fellow teacher; they retired to Ferny Creek in the Dandenong Ranges in 1957. He continued with his art and taught at various institutions, among them the university and the Kew Kindergarten College. In 1963 he published *The Bauhaus: An Introductory Survey*. Next year he visited Europe and was invited by the Bauhaus-Archiv, Darmstadt, Germany, to reconstruct his colour-light apparatus and demonstrate his colour-light plays, one of which was filmed for the archive. Survived by his wife, and by two of the three daughters of his first marriage, he died on 7 January 1965 at Allambie Heights, Sydney, and was cremated with the forms of the Society of Friends.

N. Draffin, *Two Masters of the Weimar Bauhaus*, exhibition cat (Syd, 1974); N. Underhill, *Ludwig Hirschfeld Mack*, exhibition cat (Brisb, 1977); C. Pearl, *The Dunera Scandal* (Syd, 1983); W. Bate, *Light Blue Down Under* (Melb, 1990); G. Eisen, *The Dunera Experience*, exhibition cat, Jewish Museum of Aust (Melb, 1990); *Form* (Cambridge, Eng), 2, Sept 1966, p 10; *Art and Aust*, 30, no 4, 1993, p 518; P. Stasny, Ludwig Hirschfeld-Mack, Künstler, Kunsttheoretiker und Kunstpädagoge im Gefolge des Weimarer Bauhaus (Ph.D. thesis, Univ Vienna, 1991).
TIM FISHER

HISLOP, JAMES GORDON (1895-1972), physician and politician, was born on 14 August 1895 at Prahran, Melbourne, son of James Hislop, a chemist from Scotland, and his Victorian-born wife Catherine Ann, née Collins. Educated at Scotch College and the University of Melbourne (M.B., B.Sc., 1918), 'Gordy' served in emergency influenza hospitals in Victoria and Tasmania, and in the Children's Hospital, Perth. He travelled to England in 1920 and undertook postgraduate study at the Royal Infirmary, Manchester, Brompton Hospital, London, and the Frimley Sanatorium, Surrey; his interest in chest disease and tuberculosis dated from this time. In 1922 he became a member of the Royal College of Physicians (fellow 1949). Hislop returned to Victoria and was employed at the (Royal) Melbourne Hospital in 1923.

At All Saints Church, St Kilda, on 8 December 1925 he married with Anglican rites Netta Millicent Searll; she accompanied him to Perth where he was medical superintendent (1924-27) of the Children's Hospital. In 1927 he entered private practice as a consultant physician. An honorary physician to in-patients at (Royal) Perth Hospital in 1929-49, Hislop represented the medical staff on the board of management in 1941-48. He was also a fellow (1938) of the Royal Australasian College of Physicians and a member of its State committee in 1946-66. During World War II he was attached to the Civil Defence Council of Western Australia; he was honorary director (1942-46) of emergency medical services, and executive-officer and deputy-chairman of the medical co-ordination committee. In 1950-55 he was an honorary physician at Fremantle Hospital.

Hislop's main medical interests were chest disease (on which he contributed articles to the *Medical Journal of Australia*) and medical education. Active on the editorial committee which published *Clinical Reports*, he was a member (from 1931) and chairman (1959) of the British Medical Association's standing postgraduate committee in Perth. In addition, he was a section vice-president at the

Australasian medical congresses in Adelaide (1937) and Perth (1947). A keen advocate of the establishment of a medical school at the university, he became first chairman of its postgraduate medical education committee in 1959. He was, as well, a governor (1963) and life governor (1966) of the Australian Postgraduate Federation in Medicine.

Elected to the Legislative Council as a Nationalist member for Metropolitan Province in 1941, Hislop was returned as a Liberal in 1946 and remained in parliament until he retired on 21 May 1971. His major concerns were in matters of health—the pasteurization of milk, the qualification and registration of nurses and ambulance officers, workers' compensation, miners' silicosis, and problems of the aged—and in the mechanisms of local government, town planning, electoral reform and Commonwealth-State relations. His greatest disappointment was the repeated failure of his bills to liberalize the abortion laws.

Hislop was flamboyant and dramatic in both his political and medical activities. 'Measured meandering sentences' characterized his rounds of the wards and he was described as 'a Roman emperor in meticulous pin-stripe'. His patients loved him and he was tireless in their interests. He enjoyed reading from his extensive library, gardening and playing bowls, and was a dedicated Rotarian. Survived by his wife, daughter and son, he died on 4 May 1972 at Claremont and was cremated.

Munk's Roll, Royal College of Physicians, 6, (Lond, 1982); G. L. McDonald (ed), *Roll of the Royal Australasian College of Physicians*, 1 (Syd, 1988); P. Firkins, *A History of the Rotary Club of Perth, 1927-1987* (Perth, 1987); *MJA*, 1923, 2, p 514, 1924, 1, pp 282, 527, 1924, 2, p 185, 1925, 1, p 51; Aust Postgraduate Federation in Medicine, *Annual Report*, 1960-69; *WA Graduate Medical Bulletin*, 1972, p 72; Roy Perth Hospital *and* Univ Melb archives. R. A. JOSKE

HOCKING, ALBERT EDWARD (1885-1969), political organizer and businessman, was born on 24 March 1885 at Carlton, Melbourne, second surviving child of Cornish parents Henry Hocking, miner and grocer, and his wife Lavinia, née Mitchell. Educated at Carlton North State School (dux 1898), he was obliged to leave at the age of 14 because his father had lost all his savings in the bank crash of the 1890s. Bert became a mail-boy in a farm-machinery company and studied accountancy at night. Ambitious and precocious, he criticized the financial management of the Carlton Cricket Club and, at 18, was appointed its treasurer; he later played in the first-grade team.

In 1907 Hocking qualified as an accountant and began his career as an independent businessman. Secretary (from 1912) of the Warburton Timber & Tramway Co. Pty Ltd, in 1915 he established the Cambridge Manufacturing Co. Ltd in partnership with his half-sister. His subsequent business interests were diverse, with sand-mining, farming and brass-manufacturing prominent. At St Paul's Anglican Church, Fairfield, on 24 November 1915 he married Eulalie Alethea Essery (d.1957); they eventually settled at Balwyn and were to have four children.

Elected to the Camberwell City Council in 1919, Hocking was defeated in 1922. He was re-elected next year and took office as Camberwell's youngest mayor (1923-25). A justice of the peace in 1923, he organized special constables during the police strike. In 1927 he was beaten by (Sir) Wilfrid Kent Hughes [q.v.] for Progressive Nationalist Party preselection for the seat of Kew in the Legislative Assembly. That year the Hockings moved to Toorak. Hocking owned two city properties by 1929, the year in which he stood unsuccessfully for the Melbourne City Council. He also owned orchards at Healesville, Monbulk and Tresco, and was president (1930-32) of the Fruit Growers and Cool Stores Association of Victoria.

Disillusioned with the deflationary economic and banking policies of the Nationalist Party, Hocking had joined the Victorian Country Party in 1929. He failed to win preselection for a Legislative Council province in 1931, but was elected next year to the United Country Party's central council where he dazzled his colleagues with his dynamism and organizing ability. Rising rapidly in the party (chief president 1933-35), he wielded considerable influence until 1943 and was chairman (1937-42) of the *Countryman*'s board of management. During his presidency he stabilized party funds, and assisted farmers financially by reforming the party's bank-order membership scheme and securing an agreement with Federation Insurance Ltd.

Hocking had opposed the Country Party's participation in the Argyle [q.v.7] ministry. Following the 1935 election, he engineered (Sir) Murray Bourchier's [q.v.7] replacement as parliamentary leader by (Sir) Albert Dunstan [q.v.8] and won acceptance for Tom Tunnecliffe's [q.v.12] proposal that the Country Party form a minority administration, supported by the Australian Labor Party. Dunstan took office on 2 April 1935.

Despite a prickly personal manner, Hocking was popular among farmers and the party's rank and file due to his outspoken criticism of orthodox banking practice; one Federal member of the United Australia Party dubbed him 'the would-be bank wrecker'. Approving of Hocking's views on debt adjustment for farmers, Dunstan appointed him a commissioner of the State Savings Bank of Victoria in July 1935.

Throughout the 1930s Hocking was an indefatigable, if bombastic, publicist for the Country Party. He vigorously opposed those who formed the splinter Liberal Country Party in 1937 in protest at (Sir) John McEwen's [q.v.] expulsion from the party for joining the Lyons-Page [qq.v.10,11] Federal coalition. Hocking and McEwen were bitter enemies, but were later reconciled by their mutual friend (Sir) Arthur Fadden [q.v.].

The political alliance between Hocking and Dunstan disintegrated in 1939 over a controversial pre-selection ballot involving the premier's son. Hocking blocked what he believed to be the unconstitutional method of Arthur Dunstan's selection, and an enraged premier passed special legislation removing Hocking from the board of the State Bank on a questionable legal pretext. The central issue at stake was the party organization's determination to direct the parliamentarians. Hocking and Dunstan were such dominant and combative figures that another major party schism seemed imminent.

'Artful' Albert Dunstan outmanoeuvred his opponent by calling an early State election for 16 March 1940, which the government won. Hocking unsuccessfully contested the difficult seat of Allandale, hoping to confront the premier from within the parliamentary party. At the party's State conference in April, Dunstan challenged the delegates either to expel him or 'stand behind the government'. Faced with this ultimatum, Hocking backed down. He was seared by the mauling.

As his companies won wartime contracts, Hocking became politically less active. He supported the reconciliation with the Liberal Country Party in 1943, but did not stand for central council in 1944. Resigning from the party in December 1948, he urged its members to join him in the new Liberal and Country Party to fight the threat of communism. Although he remained relatively quiescent in party politics in the 1950s and 1960s, he was embroiled, as a board-member, in a controversy surrounding the building and administration of a new hospital at Healesville.

Premier Tom Hollway [q.v.] had reappointed Hocking to the board of the State Bank on 31 August 1949; he served as chairman in 1957 and 1962. He was an attentive board-member, clashing with management over liquidity ratios and with the union over extended hours. Seeking to modernize what he regarded as an old-fashioned bank, he promoted the introduction of new technology. His term expired in 1963.

Hocking was an important figure in the Victorian Country Party throughout the 1930s, but his stubborn and dominating personality (McEwen once called him 'a dictator') was better suited to the world of business than to politics. He made enemies as readily as allies, and preferred issuing orders to negotiating political compromises. Hocking remained an active manager of his many business interests, especially Wm Bedford Ltd, and even began a new venture as a pastoralist at Deniliquin, New South Wales, in 1958. Survived by his two sons and two daughters, he died on 2 August 1969 at Armadale, Melbourne, and was cremated; his estate was sworn for probate at $593 571.

R. V. Jackson and J. G. Crawford (eds), *John McEwen* (priv pub, Canb, 1983); P. Hocking, *Stormy Petrel* (Melb, 1990); R. Murray and K. White, *A Bank for the People* (Melb, 1992); *Liberal Country Times*, 12 Aug 1938, 8 Mar 1940; *Countryman* (Melb), 15, 22, 29 Mar 1935, 22 Oct 1937, 14 Apr 1938, 8 Mar, 12 Apr 1940, 5, 19 Feb, 16 Apr 1943; J. B. Paul, The Premiership of Sir Albert Dunstan (M.A. thesis, Univ Melb, 1961); family information.   B. J. COSTAR

HODGE, GRACE McKENZIE (1888-1980), schoolteacher, was born on 13 May 1888 at Bundaberg, Queensland, sixth of ten children of Scottish-born parents Robert Hodge, bricklayer, and his wife Euphemia, née McKenzie. With their eldest child, the parents had emigrated to Australia in April 1880 and settled at Bundaberg where the developing sugar industry provided employment for builders. Robert selected land in the North Isis district, near Childers, and named their home Auld Reekie. Grace was educated at Bundaberg Central, Cordalba Provisional and Isis Central Mill Provisional School (which had only one teacher), before attending the larger Cordalba State School for her scholarship year. In 1902 she won a state bursary which entitled her to free education at a grammar school and provided an annual allowance of £30 for three years. She chose Maryborough Girls' Grammar School. In 1903 her results were the highest in the class and she was awarded the Melville bursary. At the New South Wales senior public examination in 1906, she gained silver medals in ancient history, English, French and physiology, and a place at the University of Sydney.

Miss Hodge had also qualified for a Carnegie grant (available to children of Scottish emigrants—who excelled academically—to study at a university) and chose to enrol at the University of Edinburgh. During the voyage to Britain the young student was chaperoned by the sister of Andrew Fisher [q.v.8], the Federal member for Wide Bay, who was a friend of Grace's father. Grace graduated

(M.A., 1911) with second-class honours in classics. Her course included Greek and Roman history, Latin, Greek, logic and mathematics. She subsequently studied in Paris and was awarded the Alliance Française certificate for conversation in French.

Having taught at schools in France and Germany to perfect her pronunciation, Hodge returned to Queensland. In January 1912 she was the first female teacher to be appointed to Bundaberg High School. Next year she transferred to the Central Technical College. She taught English, French, German, Latin and Greek in secondary schools at Dalby (1914-16), Gympie (1916-20) and Childers (1921-23). Following settled periods at Rockhampton High (1923-35) and at Maryborough High and Intermediate (Girls) School in 1936-47, she was appointed to the correspondence tuition section of Teachers' Training College, Brisbane, in 1948. From May 1951 she taught at Wynnum High School until her retirement on 13 May 1953. A number of her students established academic careers of their own and remained grateful for her encouragement, friendship and capacities as a teacher.

Grace Hodge benefited from her parents' liberal ideas. Her scholastic achievements were unusual at a time when many girls were not encouraged to seek academic qualifications and when most teachers were trained under the pupil-teacher system. A 'quiet, endearing modesty characterized her classroom and private life'. Aged 92, she died on 17 September 1980 in Childers Hospital and was buried in Cordalba cemetery with the forms of the Uniting Church.

B. W. O'Neill, *Taming the Isis* (Childers, Qld, 1987); Hodge staff card, History Unit, Qld Dept of Education, Brisb; Hodge family papers (held by Mr R. and Mrs A. Pedley, Childers, Qld, and Mrs L. Tuff, Riverside, NSW). BRIAN O'NEILL

HODGETTS, HENRY WARBURTON (1882-1949), sharebroker, was born on 11 June 1882 at Petersburg, South Australia, son of Henry Warburton Hodgetts, telegraph operator, and his wife Emily Mary Armit, née Lees, a postmistress. The family moved to Adelaide where young Harry was educated at the Old College School, Norwood; its principal A. R. D. Leonard paid his fees to attend the Collegiate School of St Peter in 1898. In October that year Hodgetts gained a post-office cadetship. He worked in both the State and Federal departments until 1910 when he became secretary of the Stock Exchange of Adelaide. At St Aidan's Anglican Church, Marden, on 16 October 1912 he married Mary Edith Gordon Gwynne, grand-daughter of E. C. Gwynne [q.v.4]. Hodgetts arranged

collections for patriotic causes and trained with the Stock Exchange's rifle club during World War I. Having bought a seat on the exchange in 1917, four years later he established H. W. Hodgetts & Co and flourished. In 1923 he joined the Adelaide Club.

Following a slump in the early years of the Depression, his business improved in Adelaide's share-trading revival after Britain abandoned the gold standard in 1931; transactions of over £2 million passed through his books in 1934. That year, while a member of the Australian cricket board of control, Hodgetts contracted to employ the New South Wales batsman (Sir) Donald Bradman, who agreed to make himself available for the Kensington, South Australian and Australian teams. Chairman of the South Australian Lacrosse Association and active on many sporting, educational, religious and charitable bodies, Hodgetts was socially prominent and considered to be solidly respectable.

Losses from a Broken Hill agent's business failure and from speculation in wheat futures hit Hodgetts heavily. By 1941 additional losses, including those from underwriting the float of Hotel Darwin Ltd, compounded his problems. He borrowed clients' scrip to secure advances and pawned his Adelaide Club debentures, but interest payments and bankers' demands were pressing. From 1942 Federal wartime controls over stock exchange transactions (against which he had lobbied as a committee-member of the exchange) denied him opportunities to trade out of his difficulties.

On 2 June 1945 Hodgetts advised the exchange that he could not meet his commitments; an examination showed his estate deficiency to be £82 854. The collapse shocked Adelaide: the two hundred and thirty-eight unsecured creditors included the solicitor Guy Fisher (£34 567), the test cricketer Arthur Richardson [q.v.] who lost his life savings, the retired governor-general Lord Gowrie [q.v.9], Bradman and other well-known people. Hodgetts, once a dapper dresser but now shabbier, with 'iron-grey hair and tired features', pleaded guilty in September to false pretences and fraudulent conversion. Even the funds of the Royal Institution for the Blind, of which he was honorary treasurer, had been misappropriated. The judge found that a 'disastrous combination of embarrassing difficulties' had led him to succumb to temptation. On being sentenced to five years imprisonment, Hodgetts wept.

The State government expedited legislation requiring sharebrokers to establish trust funds, keep proper books and produce audited accounts. Hodgetts's downfall prompted questions about the way in which Bradman immediately set up business on his own account, although he had a seat on the

Stock Exchange and was not Hodgetts's partner. After serving most of his sentence, Hodgetts died of cancer on 4 October 1949 in the Magill wards of the Royal Adelaide Hospital; his funeral service was conducted by Rev. A. G. Hay and A. N. Thomas [q.v.12], a former bishop of Adelaide. He was buried in St George's cemetery, Magill. His wife, two daughters and three sons survived him.

R. M. Gibbs, *Bulls, Bears and Wildcats* (Adel, 1988); J. R. Davis, *Principles and Pragmatism* (Adel, 1991); *News* (Adel), 4, 9 June, 7, 11, 12, 14 July, 8, 17 Aug, 7, 10 Sept 1945; *Advertiser* (Adel), 5 June, 9 July, 8, 11 Sept 1945; *Truth* (Adel), 9 June, 21 July, 11 Aug 1945; *Register* (Adel), 1 Sept 1916; Stock Exchange of Adel Cte minute-books and news-cuttings book (Mort L).

R. M. GIBBS

HODGKINSON, LORNA MYRTLE (1887-1951), psychologist and educationist, was born on 13 May 1887 at South Yarra, Melbourne, daughter of Victorian-born parents Albert James Hodgkinson, sugar-planter, and his wife Ada Josephine, née Edmiston. The family settled in the Northern Rivers region of New South Wales. After Albert's death, his wife and daughter moved to Western Australia where Lorna attended Perth Girls' School. In 1903-06 she was employed by the Education Department as a pupil-teacher and took courses to qualify for the 'C' certificate. While working as an assistant (1907-12) at Perth Infants' School, she pioneered a class for mental defectives.

Between 1913 and 1915 Miss Hodgkinson taught at public schools in New South Wales. In 1917 the Department of Public Instruction appointed her to May Villa, near Parramatta, to teach mentally defective girls who were wards of the State. She obtained paid leave in 1920 and travelled to the United States of America where she studied the treatment of retardates. At Harvard University (M.Ed., 1921; D.Ed., 1922), she wrote her dissertation on 'A State Program for the Diagnosis and Treatment of Atypical Children in Public School Systems'. Back in New South Wales, in October 1922 she took up a post created for her by the department as superintendent (later supervisor) of the education of mental defectives.

In evidence before the royal commission on lunacy law and administration in 1923, Hodgkinson asserted that the system for dealing with mentally defective children was mismanaged. Her allegations provoked a public outcry. Albert Bruntnell [q.v.7], who held the portfolio of public instruction, ordered a ministerial inquiry which found against her on all counts. She was suspended from duty for 'disgraceful and improper conduct in making false statements and pretences', specifically in regard to the claims she had made about her formal education to gain admission to Harvard.

An investigation by the Public Service Board confirmed the charges, and in March 1924 Hodgkinson was censured and demoted to regular teaching duties. When she failed to take up her new position, she was dismissed. Impatient and indiscreet, she had fallen victim to the government's sensitivity over its handling of an issue on which there was growing public concern. The evidence that she had falsified her educational background was circumstantial, and the dean of Harvard's graduate school of education wrote a testimonial affirming her standing and achievement.

In April 1924 Hodgkinson advertised for residents to enter a new private school for mentally defective children; with six pupils, it opened later that year as the Sunshine Institute, Gore Hill. Initially a tenant, in 1930 she purchased a portion of the site (previously owned by the Theosophical Society in Australia) and spent the rest of her life building up the establishment to sixty pupils. She and her companion Ruth Nelson holidayed at Mona Vale with the children.

The main influence on Hodgkinson came from her Harvard mentors, especially Walter Fernald, founder of a residential state school in Massachusetts for the feeble-minded. Hodgkinson urged that such children be appropriately classified, segregated from the rest of the community and trained for later economic self-sufficiency. For the 'higher grade' of child, she favoured an additional system of vocational guidance and supervision; she envisaged that the 'less able' should remain—if need be, permanently—in a self-supporting, cottage-colony system. Her first priority, however, was the residential training school.

Despite her definite opinions on the appropriate treatment of retardates, Hodgkinson was a 'very retiring and private person' after her public humiliation. She was not a prominent speaker or writer, nor was she active in the emerging groups of professional psychologists. Nevertheless, she lectured on 'mental hygiene' on radio 2GB (the Theosophists' station) in 1927 and addressed the Australian Racial Hygiene Congress in Sydney in 1929. She had published a two-part article, 'Workers or Wasters: the Feeble-minded in America' in the *Sydney Morning Herald* in 1922 and a summary of an address she gave to the Women's Reform League appeared in the *Woman's Voice* in 1923.

Hodgkinson died of cancer on 24 March 1951 at Gore Hill and was cremated with Anglican rites; her ashes were interred in the grounds of the Sunshine Institute. She had brought to reality on a small private scale the vision she entertained for a large public venture. Immediately before her death she had converted the institute to a non-profit organization under a board of trustees, to whom she bequeathed the bulk of her estate, sworn for probate at £55 812. Renamed the Lorna Hodgkinson Sunshine Home, the institution expanded, while retaining her philosophy of individual care and development.

Roy Com on Lunacy Law and Administration, Report, *PP* (LC NSW), 1923, 1, p 651; Dept of Education, Report on Mental Defectives, *PP* (LA NSW), 1923, 1, p 983; A. M. Turtle, 'The short-lived appointment of the first New South Wales government psychologist, Dr Lorna Hodgkinson', *Aust Hist Studies*, 25, no 101, Oct 1993; A. Distin Morgan and C. Wang, Notes on the history of the Home and the life of Hodgkinson (held at the Lorna Hodgkinson Sunshine Home, Gore Hill, Syd); file on Lorna Hodgkinson (special bundles, box 8/669, NSWA).   ALISON M. TURTLE

HOGAN, HECTOR DENIS (1931-1960), sprinter and refrigeration mechanic, was born on 15 July 1931 at Rockhampton, Queensland, youngest of three children of George Michael Hogan, a labourer who became a storekeeper, and his wife Mary McGeraghty, née Shields, both Queensland born. Hector grew up at Nudgee Beach, Brisbane, and was educated at Marist Brothers' College, Rosalie. He served a five-year apprenticeship as a refrigeration mechanic, riding his bicycle fifteen miles (24 km) to and from his workplace. His athletic ability was noticed at a Young Christian Workers' carnival at New Farm Park and, soon after joining the Brothers' Amateur Athletic Club in 1948, he had several successes in junior ranks. In 1951 he became Queensland Open sprint champion. Next year at the Australian Amateur Athletic Championships in Brisbane he won the 100-yards event in 9.6 seconds, equalling the Australian residential record. The race was controversial because Hogan burst from the blocks to gain an early lead and this characteristic lightning start led to his nickname, 'Hustling Hec'. He came second to John Treloar at the Olympic selection trials and was disappointed not to be selected for the 1952 Olympic Games, held in Helsinki.

Five ft 7 ins (170 cm) tall, stocky and weighing 11 stone (70 kg), Hogan was a versatile performer who competed in the long and triple jumps, and in the 220 yards (200 metres), but it was in the 100-yards and 100-metres events that he excelled. After equalling the world record for the 100 yards (9.3 seconds) and 100 metres (10.2 seconds) on a grass track in Sydney in March 1954, he was confident 'There will be no holding me'. He won the bronze medal in the 100 yards (9.7 seconds) at the Empire Games at Vancouver, Canada, and was fifth in both the 220 yards

and the long jump. On 11 June 1955 at St Paul's Presbyterian Church, Brisbane, he married Maureen Salmon, a hairdresser and daughter of his manager. They moved to Melbourne where Hec prepared for the 1956 Olympic Games. He won both his heats in the 100 metres (10.5 seconds) at the Olympics; in the final he had one of his best starts, but 'went so fast I lost my balance at about 30 metres'. Hogan finished third (10.6 seconds), becoming the first Australian male sprinter to win an Olympic medal since Stan Rowley [q.v.11] at the 1900 Games.

Before the Melbourne Olympics, Hogan had suffered from undiagnosed tiredness and loss of strength. Although he won the national 100-yards championship in 1957 and 1958, to capture seven national titles in succession, he unexpectedly failed to qualify for the 100-yards final at the Commonwealth Games in Cardiff in 1958. He gained a bronze medal, however, as a member of the 4 x 110-yards relay team. On returning to Australia, he moved to Bowen, Queensland, to manage a hotel owned by Maureen's father. When Hogan's health rapidly deteriorated, leukaemia was diagnosed. Survived by his wife and 4-year-old son, he died on 2 September 1960 in Brisbane Hospital and was buried with Anglican rites in Nudgee cemetery.

J. Shepherd, *Encyclopaedia of Australian Sport* (Adel, 1980); *People* (Syd), 28 July 1954; *World Sports* (Lond), Apr, May 1953; *Sporting Life* (Syd), Aug 1953, Apr, May, Aug 1954, Dec 1956; K. Appleton, Hector Hogan (unpublished assignment, Human Movement Studies, Univ Qld); information from Mr M. Hogan, Mermaid Waters, Qld, Mrs M. Berkeley, Sunnybank, Brisb, and Mr T. Booth, Tarragindi, Brisb; Hogan letters and press-cuttings (held by author, Univ Qld).

IAN F. JOBLING

HOGBEN, HORACE COX (1888-1975), public accountant and politician, was born on 20 September 1888 at Magill, Adelaide, son of English-born parents Rev. George Hogben, a carpenter who had become a Baptist minister, and his wife Agnes, née Carmichael. Educated in public schools at Magill and Port Pirie, Horace began work as a junior with Broken Hill Pty Co. Ltd at Port Pirie in 1905. Two years later he moved to Adelaide. While employed as a clerk and company secretary, he represented (1913) the State in hockey, and studied at the South Australian School of Mines and Industries and at the University of Adelaide (associate in commerce, 1915). At the Baptist Church, Parkside, on 4 May 1915 he married Clara Margaret Marion McPharlin. From 1922 he was an accountant and office manager with Cowell Bros & Co. Ltd before setting up his own business as a public accountant in 1930. He was president (1940) of the State division of the Australasian Institute of Secretaries.

Secretary (1930-40) of the Young Liberal League, Hogben was also treasurer (from 1931) of the Emergency Committee of South Australia which opposed the 'financial extremists' in J. H. Scullin's [q.v.11] Federal Labor government. The success of the committee's candidates in the 1931 Federal elections encouraged the State's Liberal Federation and Country Party to amalgamate in the following year to form the Liberal and Country League, of which Hogben was vice-president. From April 1933 to February 1938 he was a member for Sturt in the House of Assembly. Concerned about housing problems during the Depression, in 1934 he and (Sir) Keith Wilson (president of the Y.L.L.) formed a committee to examine the 'shortage of low-price houses and the concomitant of rising rents'. Hogben undertook the research, at the expense of much of his accountancy practice and income.

He subsequently proposed the formation of a housing authority, easier terms for financing prospective home-owners and remedial action to deal with substandard houses, recommendations which were embodied in the South Australian Housing Trust Act (1936), the Building Societies Amendment Act (1938), the Housing Improvement Act (1940) and the Homes Act (1941). The auditor-general J. W. Wainwright [q.v.12] encouraged Hogben to advocate the establishment of a new housing authority which would construct low-cost rental homes. If rents were kept down and workers' wages were lower than those paid in the other States, manufacturing would be attracted to South Australia. The government adopted these policies, gradually increasing the role of secondary industry in the State's economic structure.

Acknowledged as the founder of the South Australian Housing Trust—set up in 1936 as Australia's first public housing authority—Hogben served as its deputy-chairman (1941-67) and saw it become a key agency in promoting the State's industrialization and urbanization under Premier (Sir) Thomas Playford. Hogben was also a director (from 1938) of the Co-operative Building Society of South Australia and a trustee of the Savings Bank of South Australia. Survived by his wife, son and daughter, he died on 18 December 1975 at his Unley home and was cremated. The trust reported that he had combined 'the two broad aims of any Statutory Authority . . . a real and deep concern for people, together with an accountant's appreciation of the need for good financial control'. A portrait by Jacqueline Hick is held by the trust.

D. Jaensch (ed), *The Flinders History of South Australia* (Adel, 1986); S. Marsden, *Business, Charity and Sentiment* (Adel, 1986); R. Linn, *For the Benefit of the People* (Adel, 1989); *Advertiser* (Adel), 2 Apr 1940, 22 Dec 1975.   SUSAN MARSDEN

HOINVILLE, FREDERICK DOUGLAS (1907-1959), skywriter and glider pilot, was born on 26 October 1907 at Kent Town, Adelaide, son of Australian-born parents Frederick Hoinville, a cinematographist of Huguenot descent, and his wife Hilda, née Hales. Educated at Essendon High School, Melbourne, young Fred trained as a fitter and turner; by the age of 35 he had worked in numerous jobs and run several small businesses without settling down to anything. At St Philip's Anglican Church, Auburn, Sydney, on 2 April 1937 he married Gladys Thelma Saunders; they were to have three daughters before being divorced in 1955.

During World War II Hoinville was rejected by the Royal Australian Air Force because of a perforated eardrum, a condition which later healed. While lying on a surfboard off Bondi in 1943, he watched a Gypsy Moth manoeuvring above him and decided to learn to fly. He immediately enrolled for lessons, qualified months later, obtained a commercial pilot's licence in 1948 and bought a Tiger Moth aircraft which he named *Brolga*. Next year he was appointed Sydney secretary of the newly formed Aircraft Owners and Pilots Association of Australia. Teaching himself stunt-flying, he became a barnstormer and gave spectacular displays across the country.

Hoinville was also interested in gliding. A founding member (1946) of the Hinkler [q.v.9] Soaring Club, he was foundation secretary (1949) of the Gliding Federation of Australia. On 11 January 1949 he broke the Australian gliding distance record, covering 221 miles (356 km) from Peak Hill to Collarenebri in 7 hours 15 minutes. On 5 January 1950 he piloted a glider from Parkes to Greenwell Point, near Nowra, achieving a distance of 190 miles (306 km) in 7 hours 45 minutes, and reaching a maximum altitude of 10 100 ft (3978 m). The flight qualified him for the Gold 'C' award of the Fédération Aéronautique Internationale. In 1952 he competed in the World Gliding Championships in Spain. A council-member of the Society of Australian Inventors, he was involved in the 1950s in the production of a 'mini-midget' glider, a craft with a wing-span of 25 ft (7.6 m); he successfully tested a prototype in August 1957, but failed to gain financial support.

In the early 1950s Hoinville had revived the art of skywriting and made it a lucrative venture, initially in Sydney. Flying *Brolga* between 13 000 and 17 000 ft (4000 to 5000 m), he formed words from smoke specially generated from his aircraft. Messages (usually advertisements) composed of letters half-a-mile (0.8 km) long could be read from the ground. Each letter had to be produced in reverse. Hoinville so exploited the winds that, as he shaped a letter, it was blown away from him, enabling him to start the next without moving on. He described his work as 'a mixture of mental arithmetic and split second timing'.

About the mid-1950s Hoinville moved to Melbourne. On 10 November 1956 at Bentleigh he married with Presbyterian forms Grace Mary, née Iggulden, a divorcee and writer; they had a son and three daughters. He was killed on 18 April 1959 when his powered glider crashed at Goulburn, New South Wales; survived by his wife and their daughters, and by two daughters of his first marriage, he was cremated with Anglican rites. His autobiographical *Halfway to Heaven* (Sydney, 1960) was published posthumously.

N. Parnell and T. Broughton, *Flypast* (Canb, 1988); A. Ash, *Gliding in Australia* (Melb, 1990); *SMH*, 24 Nov 1945; *Sun-Herald*, 17 Nov 1957; *Advertiser* (Adel), 20 Apr 1959; *Herald* (Melb), 22 May 1963; *Daily Mirror* (Syd), 21 June 1978.

SYLVIA MARCHANT

HOLDSWORTH, HUBERT AUGUSTUS GORDON (1884-1965), silversmith, painter and printmaker, was born on 4 November 1884 at Odiham, Hampshire, England, second of three sons of Charles Edward Hall Holdsworth, gentleman, and his wife Ellen Louise, née Bostock, both from Yorkshire families connected for generations with the Church of England. Gordon was taught music and art in England before the Holdsworths emigrated to Western Australia in 1900; they established Coplow, a homestead at Hester Siding, near Bridgetown, and became timber-millers. He joined the Western Australian Society of Arts in 1904 and began a career as painter, etcher, sculptor and metalsmith. Said to have studied metalsmithing under J. W. R. Linton [q.v.10], he opened an art school at Bridgetown in 1911. Much of his technique was derived from treasured books and magazines which he read in his rural retreat.

About 1911 Holdsworth received his earliest-known commission, for a brass lectern in St Paul's Anglican Church, Bridgetown. He fashioned an intricate processional cross for C. O. L. Riley [q.v.11], archbishop of Perth from 1914, and, in the years that followed, made 'furniture' for many churches. His work was 'firmly rooted within the Arts and Crafts tradition' and his ecclesiastical metalware exhibited a highly individual approach. Despite the remoteness of Bridgetown, Holdsworth was able to support himself over a sixty-year career. He exhibited his paintings

at the Albert Hall, London, in 1912, and showed his silver regularly in Western Australia and New South Wales. In October 1920 the *Bulletin*'s reviewer wrote that 'Gordon Holdsworth of Westralia sends a casket that might have been Pandora's'. He had held his first solo exhibition in Perth in 1916 and in 1924 was awarded a medal for a brass and enamel lectern, displayed in the British Empire Exhibition, Wembley, London.

A dashing young man with an aquiline nose, a moustache and a goatee, Holdsworth never married. He cared for his widowed mother until her death, carefully applying her make-up for church on Sundays. In later life he was described as 'fey'. John Feeney, an artist who met him in 1961, remarked that he was 'quite extraordinary . . . a complete artistic personality of a vanishing era', and added that 'his work whilst not being particularly modern was of a rare excellence'.

Although Holdsworth suffered severe burns in a fire which destroyed his home in 1953, he continued to be productive. He died on 3 August 1965 at Bridgetown District Hospital and was buried with Anglican rites in the local cemetery. When speaking of Holdsworth, an obituarist recalled the words about Sir Christopher Wren: 'If you would see his monument look around you'. Western Australian churches contain numerous examples of his art. The most notable, usually in brass, silver and copper, are in St Paul's, Bridgetown, St George's Cathedral, Perth, St George's College, Crawley, Perth College, Mt Lawley, St Boniface's Cathedral, Bunbury, and St Mary's, Busselton. His work is also held in the Western Australian Museum, the Art Gallery of New South Wales and the parliament of Western Australia.

J. O'Callaghan, *Treasures from Australian Churches* (Melb, 1985); A. Schofield and K. Fahy, *Australian Jewellery* (Syd, 1990); D. Erickson, Aspects of Stylistic and Social Influence on the Practice of Gold and Silversmithing in Western Australia 1829-1965 (Ph.D. thesis, Univ WA, 1992); Holdsworth file *and* WA Society of Arts papers (Art Gallery of Western Australia); Holdsworth papers (Bridgetown Tourist Bureau Museum); Holdsworth collection (BL photographic records).

DOROTHY ERICKSON

HOLLAND, SIR GEORGE WILLIAM FREDERICK (1897-1962), returned servicemen's leader, was born on 5 January 1897 at Marong, near Bendigo, Victoria, second son of William Henry Vernon Holland, a native-born miner, and his wife Amy Louisa, née Vernon, from England. Educated at the local state school, George joined the Victorian Public Service on 22 August 1913 as a clerk in the office of the curator of estates of deceased persons (later the public trustee's office).

On 19 August 1914 Holland enlisted in the Australian Imperial Force; in October he embarked with the 7th Battalion for the Middle East. Landing at Gallipoli on 25 April 1915, he was wounded in August and evacuated to Egypt. In March 1916 he was sent to France where he was promoted sergeant and wounded at Pozières in July. East of Ypres, Belgium, he took charge on 20-22 September 1917 after his company sergeant major became a casualty. Holland assisted in constructing strong-points and maintaining supplies before he, too, was hit. For his deeds, he was awarded the Military Medal. Returning to Australia in November 1918, he was discharged on 24 January 1919 and resumed his job as a public servant.

On 27 September 1919 at Holy Trinity Church, Marong, Holland married May Hollingworth with Anglican rites. Active in the affairs of the Returned Sailors' and Soldiers' Imperial League of Australia, he was elected president of the Victorian branch in 1929, a position he was to hold for twenty-one years. His main concerns were to help ex-servicemen find employment, to promote their welfare and that of their families, and to develop the league into a strong organization. The principal legacy of his term was the establishment of a network of homes for war veterans and servicemen's widows in Victoria, a scheme which he largely planned and set on a sound financial base. He was appointed C.B.E. in 1938.

While Holland rarely faced serious challenges to his authority at the State level, in the 1930s he was involved in some bitter differences with the national president Sir Gilbert Dyett [q.v.8] over tactics the R.S.& S.I.L.A. should adopt in its dealings with governments. In the late 1940s Holland had several clashes with J. B. Chifley's [q.v.13] administration and accused it of showing preference in employing unionists rather than returned men, particularly in the building trades. None the less, Holland joined with the unions in arguing that married women should give up their jobs to demobilized servicemen. In 1948 the Victorian government appointed him chairman of the Discharged Servicemen's Employment Board. He campaigned against 'the communist menace' and staunchly defended the Returned Sailors', Soldiers' and Airmen's Imperial League of Australia's policy of excluding communists from its membership.

Succeeding Sir Eric Millhouse, Holland was elected national president of the R.S.S.& A.I.L.A. on 24 February 1950. After visiting West Germany in 1951 to investigate aspects of Australia's immigration programme, he publicly supported the entry of Germans into Australia, a sensitive issue in league ranks after World War II. Similarly, in the early 1950s he endorsed calls for the limited rearmament of Japan and stated that, although Australians should remember Japanese brutality in the war, his country needed Japan as an ally against the new communist threat. Holland was knighted in 1953 and appointed K.B.E. in 1961.

The health and welfare of veterans remained his paramount interests. He was close to the Liberal prime minister (Sir) Robert Menzies [q.v.]. On the eve of Holland's retirement in October 1960, Menzies asked him what he most wanted for the R.S.S.& A.I.L.A. He replied, 'free medical and hospital treatment for service pensioners' (by which he meant ex-service personnel who had been awarded pensions in advance of retirement age, but without sickness or injury benefits). Menzies granted the request. In November 1961 Holland was entertained at a cabinet dinner in Canberra at which Menzies presented him with a silver salver etched with the signatures of members of his ministry.

Holland was the last of the World War I soldiers to preside over the R.S.S.& A.I.L.A. He left it in a secure position financially and politically, but an injection of leadership from younger World War II veterans was overdue. From 1956 he was a commissioner of the State Savings Bank of Victoria. Survived by his wife, son and four daughters, Sir George died of coronary artery disease on 14 June 1962 in his East Malvern home and was buried in Springvale cemetery. Sir Arthur Dean [q.v.13], chancellor of the University of Melbourne, who had served with Holland in the 7th Battalion, delivered the eulogy on behalf of the R.S.S.& A.I.L.A.

G. L. Kristianson, *The Politics of Patriotism* (Canb, 1966); P. Sekuless and J. Rees, *Lest We Forget* (Syd, 1986); *Mufti*, 5, no 7, 7 July 1962; *Age* (Melb), 15, 16 June 1962; *Sun News-Pictorial*, 15, 19 June 1962; Returned Services League papers (NL).

JACQUELINE REES
PETER SEKULESS

HOLLICK, RUTH MIRIAM (1883-1977), photographer, was born on 17 March 1883 at Williamstown, Melbourne, youngest of thirteen children of English-born parents Harry Ebenezer Hollick, civil servant, and his wife Frances Jane, née Cole. While studying at the National Gallery school of design in 1902-06, Ruth struck up a friendship with her teacher Frederick McCubbin [q.v.10]. About 1908 she bought a small motorcar and promoted herself in rural Victoria as a freelance photographer specializing in portraits of families and children. She toured the Riverina and the Western District of Victoria, mostly working outdoors with a field camera.

World War I brought the most productive stage of Hollick's career. She operated from her parents' home in suburban Moonee Ponds, assisted by Dorothy Izard, her personal and professional partner. Hollick's work assumed a confident stylishness, characterized by her dramatic composition and free use of light; it became the trademark of her social and fashion photography, much of which was used in advertising and by the *Bulletin* and *Lone Hand*.

When Mina Moore [q.v.10] retired in 1918, Hollick moved into her studios in the Auditorium Building, Collins Street. As her reputation and business grew, she took an entire floor in Chartres House for reception and studios, and Dorothy devised an ingenious shuttle for plates and prints from the darkroom next door. Between 1920 and 1928 Hollick and Pegg Clarke, who specialized in gardens and landscapes, were Melbourne's leading photographers and shared most of the commissions for the *Home* and *Australian* magazines. They were also firm friends (from art-school days) in a quartet which included Izard and Clarke's partner, the painter Dora Wilson [q.v.12].

In 1928 Hollick held a solo exhibition of her portraits of children. Next year she was the only woman whose work was accepted for the Melbourne Exhibition of Pictorial Photography. In 1929 and 1930 she was represented in the pictorial sections of both the Melbourne and Adelaide camera clubs, and her work was shown at least once with the Photographic Society of New South Wales. She exhibited at the London Salon of Photography (1920) and the colonial exhibitions of the Royal Photographic Society of Great Britain (1925 and 1927); in 1932 she was one of six Melbourne Camera Club members who showed in London at the *Amateur Photographer* Overseas Exhibition. By then she was said to have won six silver and numerous bronze plaques in Australia and abroad.

Hollick had no formal training and her style was the result of experimentation. Her particular skill in using available light probably derived from her years on the road, making the best of each situation and being confident of every plate taken. She was 'a hard worker though not a businesswoman: she enjoyed spending, good dressing and parties'.

In the Depression Hollick gave up the city studio and worked again from Moonee Ponds, while also making country trips. With Dorothy, she toured Europe for the first time in 1950. Eight years later she retired. She died on 7 April 1977 at Sandringham and was cremated with Christian Science forms. Collections of her glass plates and original prints are held by the Art Gallery of New South Wales and the National Gallery of Australia.

J. Cato, *The Story of the Camera in Australia* (Melb, 1955); G. Newton, *Silver and Grey* (Syd, 1980); B. Hall et al, *Aust Women Photographers, 1890-1950*, exhibition cat (Melb, 1981); B. Hall and J. Mather, *Australian Women Photographers 1840-1960* (Melb, 1986); *Herald* (Melb), 3 Nov 1928; *Argus*, 31 Oct 1928.   BARBARA HALL

HOLLINWORTH, MAY (1895-1968), theatrical producer and director, was born on 1 May 1895 at Homebush, Sydney, only child of native-born parents William Haley Harper Hollinworth, a wool clerk who became a theatrical producer, and his wife Alice Ida Louisa, née Dansie. May trained as a dancer, but suffered a broken leg; increasing weight put an end to that career. In 1926, while working as a demonstrator in chemistry at the University of Sydney, she began directing plays for the Sydney University Dramatic Society. In 1927 she achieved prominence with a controversial production of *As You Like It* in modern dress and by winning first prize (for her production of Oliphant Down's *The Maker of Dreams*) in a one-act play competition, awarded by Gregan McMahon [q.v.10] of the Sydney Repertory Society.

Appointed resident director of S.U.D.S. in 1929, Hollinworth established her reputation as a top-ranking director in amateur circles with a series of splendidly mounted productions, including Rostand's *L'Aiglon* (1933), Shakespeare's *Twelfth Night* (1937) and Sheridan's *The School for Scandal* (1940). She served (1938-63) on the Playwrights' Advisory Board, established by Leslie Rees to encourage Australian dramatists. In the small S.U.D.S. clubrooms in George Street she directed Australian plays, as well as contemporary ones from overseas such as T. S. Eliot's *The Family Reunion*; she continued her large-scale, classical productions in the university's Great Hall. Although she had worked as a freelance director on Alexander McDonald's *Day Must Break* (1937) at the Theatre Royal and presented Eliot's *Murder in the Cathedral* in the Town Hall in December 1943, Hollinworth believed in ensemble theatre and was happiest with her own company of actors, from whom she demanded and received complete loyalty. She cast them accurately, told them where to move on stage and then left them alone to develop characterization.

After resigning from S.U.D.S. early in 1943, Hollinworth soon drew a nucleus of actors around her to form the Metropolitan Players; Leo McKern, Jane Holland and Enid Lorimer were among them, as were, later, Betty Lucas, Dinah Shearing and Robin Lovejoy. In the remaining years of World War II they mainly presented light comedies and mystery thrillers at army camps and hospitals to entertain soldiers, and in suburban halls to stimulate civilian interest in the theatre.

In 1946 Hollinworth opened the Metropolitan Theatre (seating seventy) in Reiby Place, Circular Quay, using an ex-army amenities boxing-ring for a stage; *Othello*, her first production there, was deemed the 'finest performance of a Shakespeare play in Sydney for many years'. Another critic wrote of the fourth play, Molnár's *Liliom*, 'It is really staggering to see a play of this quality in a tiny hall while the big professional theatres show only trivial and meaningless potboilers'. Hollinworth presented one Australian play each year and began the 1947 season with Douglas Stewart's *Ned Kelly*. She had dreamed of running a professional repertory company, but no commercially viable theatre could be found. In 1949 the Metropolitan Theatre moved to the two hundred-seat Christ Church St Laurence hall. While directing Edward Reeve's [q.v.6] historical drama, *Raymond, Lord of Milan*, in 1950, Hollinworth became seriously ill and was forced to retire.

When her health improved, she was invited to direct at the Independent Theatre by her former rival (Dame) Doris Fitton who regarded her as 'a clever mysterious woman, and I always told her that she worked witchcraft with her actors'. Hollinworth's crowning achievement was her engagement by the Australian Elizabethan Theatre Trust to direct *The Shifting Heart*, Richard Beynon's prize-winning play, which opened at the Elizabethan Theatre on 4 October 1957 and toured Australia next year. Among her great strengths as a director were an excellent use of lighting and the grouping of her actors to form stage pictures which eloquently underlined the playwright's intentions.

During her later years Hollinworth was patron of the Pocket Playhouse Theatre, Sydenham, and an enthusiastic member of the All Nations Club, formed in the 1950s to encourage cultural exchange between immigrants and local citizens. In failing health from 1963, she became interested in the problems of the profoundly deaf and explored the use of theatre as an aid in communication. She died on 19 November 1968 in Royal Prince Alfred Hospital and was cremated with Anglican rites. In her will she bequeathed her house at Stanmore to the Adult Deaf and Dumb Society of New South Wales.

A shortish, square woman, with shrewd, dark eyes and a wide mouth that gave more than a hint of humour, Hollinworth had a cool intelligence and a quiet, commanding personality. She impressed by her achievements, having few words to waste in chat. In an age when talent, aspiration, innovation and tireless hard work received no subsidy, Hollinworth was single-minded in pursuit of excellence. She never married: her colleagues were her family and her life was the theatre.

D. Fitton, *Not Without Dust and Heat* (Syd, 1981); *SMH*, 1 Apr 1946, 12 May 1955, 20 Nov 1968, 22 Feb 1990; *Bulletin*, 9 Oct 1946; *Sun-Herald* (Syd), 17 Mar 1957; information from Messrs W. G. Cassidy, Elizabeth Bay, R. A. Hunter, Stanmore, R. W. Petersen, Longueville, Dr W. H. Steel, Seaforth, Syd, N. McVicker, Mudgee, NSW, and the late I. J. Maxwell; personal information.

LYNNE MURPHY

HOLLOWAY, EDWARD JAMES ('JACK') (1875-1967), trade unionist and politician, was born on 12 April 1875 in Hobart, son of Joseph Holloway, labourer, and his wife Harriet, née Durgess. Joseph was killed in an industrial accident in 1879. Ted was unhappy and rebellious at various Catholic schools until, at the age of 12, he encountered a schoolmaster who encouraged his talents. Holloway worked briefly for a tobacconist in 1888 and then for a stockbroker; in 1890 he moved with his mother to Melbourne and became a bootmaker. In August he attended a public rally in support of the maritime strike. Deeply affected by the hostility of the government and the militia, and by the orderly response of the crowd of 30 000, he was impressed by Chief Justice George Higinbotham's [q.v.4] support for the workers and thought that he stood out like a giant among the 'horde of mental and moral pygmies occupying official positions in the Colony'.

In 1892 Holloway was based at Broken Hill, New South Wales, where he did picket duty in the miners' strike. The violence which he witnessed strengthened his belief in the virtues of negotiation and conciliation. Next year he joined the Western Australian gold rush and frequently went hungry. Returning to Melbourne in 1894, 'Jack' (as he was now called) resumed bootmaking. On 15 February 1900 at Carlton he married Edith Isabel Clarke (d.1963), a 22-year-old waitress; Rev. Archibald Turnbull [q.v.12] officiated. Although raised a Catholic, Holloway held no religious convictions as an adult. In his twenties he read rationalist, radical and socialist texts, and joined Tom Mann's Economic Study Circle which included John Curtin [qq.v.10,13].

Duty led Holloway to abandon theory in favour of practical trade-union work. He represented the Australian Boot Trade Employees' Federation on the Melbourne Trades Hall Council and joined the Abbotsford branch of the Political Labor Council of Victoria. By 1911 he was on the T.H.C.'s executive-committee and was subsequently its chief negotiator. In 1914-16 he held the 'triple crown'—presidencies of the T.H.C., the P.L.C. and the eight-hour day anniversary committee. He was general secretary (1915-29) of the T.H.C., president (1916-22) of the Australian Political Labor executive (Australian Labor Party federal executive) and founding secretary (1916) of Labor's national anti-conscription executive, whose story he was to tell in *The Australian Victory over Conscription in 1916-17* (1966). In 1923 he was an Australian representative at the fifth session of the International Labour Conference, held at Geneva.

After standing unsuccessfully for the Senate in 1925 and for the seat of Flinders in the House of Representatives in 1928, he sensationally defeated Prime Minister S. M. (Viscount) Bruce [q.v.7] for Flinders in 1929. In March 1931 Holloway was appointed an assistant-minister in J. H. Scullin's [q.v.11] cabinet, but resigned in June in protest against the government's adoption of the Premiers' Plan. At the 1931 elections he won the seat of Melbourne Ports; he was to hold it until his retirement in 1951. Minister for health and for social services from October 1941 to September 1943, he was minister for labour and national service from September 1943 to December 1949. In April-May 1949 he was acting prime minister; in 1950 he was appointed to the Privy Council.

A tall, fair man, Holloway became attractively animated when he spoke on subjects about which he cared. His career was filled with reforming achievements. As a trade unionist, he had been responsible for the establishment of the Melbourne T.H.C.'s disputes committee, the successful presentation of the unions' case for a 44-hour week and the resolution of countless industrial conflicts. As minister for labour, he helped to achieve the 40-hour week and 14 days paid annual leave for all workers. In addition, he gave the Commonwealth Court of Conciliation and Arbitration power to fix women's wages, expressing the hope that their rate would never again be less than 75 per cent of that applicable to men. He dissociated himself from Prime Minister J. B. Chifley's [q.v.13] handling of the 1949 coalminers' strike.

Holloway's success was due not only to hard work, but to honesty and sincerity which earned him respect within and without the labour movement. Survived by his son and daughter, he died on 3 December 1967 at St Kilda and was cremated. His estate was sworn for probate at $7087.

A. A. Calwell, *Be Just and Fear Not* (Melb, 1972); P. Hasluck, *Diplomatic Witness* (Melb, 1980); R. McMullin, *The Light on the Hill* (Melb, 1991); *News* (Adel), 17 Oct 1929; *Age* (Melb), 9 Sept 1959; Holloway papers (NL).   D. P. BLAAZER

HOLLWAY, THOMAS TUKE (1906-1971), premier and lawyer, was born on 2 October 1906 at Ballarat, Victoria, third of four sons of Thomas Tuke Hollway, merchant and mayor (1910-11) of Ballarat, and his wife Annie Amelia, née Nicholl, both Victorian born. Young Tom was educated at the Macarthur Street State School and the Church of England Grammar School, Ballarat, where he was a prefect, a promising sportsman and dux in 1924. Fellow students—who included (Sir) Henry Bolte—saw him as witty and debonair, and already interested in a political career. Hollway completed his education at Trinity College, University of Melbourne (B.A., 1927; LL.B., 1929). He was admitted to practice as a solicitor in 1928 and joined R. J. Gribble (later Gribble, Hollway & Heinz) at Ballarat.

Interested in modern poetry, with E. H. Montgomery (a member of the Legislative Assembly in 1948-50) he published a booklet, *The Moderns* (1931), under the joint pseudonym 'C. J. Staughton'. Hollway was also a keen cricketer and a promoter of baseball. At St Andrew's Presbyterian Kirk, Ballarat, on 26 August 1932 he married Sheila Florence Kelsall; they were to remain childless.

In 1927 Hollway had joined the Young Nationalist Organization. As a member of the United Australia Party, in May 1932 he was elected to the Legislative Assembly for the seat of Ballaarat. In 1940 he was rapidly promoted in the ranks of the U.A.P.—first to whip, then deputy-leader, and, on the death of Sir Stanley Argyle [q.v.7] in November, leader. He led the Opposition in 1940-42 when (Sir) Albert Dunstan's [q.v.8] minority Country Party governed with support from the Australian Labor Party.

Retaining his seat in parliament and the party leadership, Hollway enlisted in the Royal Australian Air Force on 21 February 1942. He was commissioned next month and trained as an intelligence officer. In May-August that year he served in Papua with No.100 Squadron before being transferred to the Reserve on 10 July 1943 with the rank of flying officer.

Among Liberal politicians Hollway was exceptional in the extent to which he was prepared to co-operate with the A.L.P. Strongly opposed to the gerrymander which had given the Country Party disproportionate power from the 1920s, he sought Labor's assistance in having it overturned. In 1941 he discussed redistribution with John Cain [q.v.13] and in September 1943 they united in a no confidence motion against Dunstan, assuming that Hollway would then be commissioned to form a government which would effect electoral reform. Hollway was disconcerted when the governor Sir Winston Dugan [q.v.] commissioned Cain to form a government and after four days joined with Dunstan to bring it down.

On 18 September Dunstan formed a 'composite government' in which Hollway served as deputy-premier, minister of public instruction and minister of labour. In October 1945 the Liberal Party (which had replaced the U.A.P.) and the Country Party both split, and a minority government under a dissident Liberal, Ian Macfarlan, took office for seven weeks. Hollway engineered this Liberal Party split, but publicly dissociated himself from it.

Following the defeat of Cain's second ministry, on 20 November 1947 Hollway became premier and treasurer in a Liberal-Country Party coalition. (Sir) John McDonald [q.v.], who had replaced Dunstan as Country Party leader in 1945, was his deputy. A journalist described the young premier as 'a dark, smooth-haired man whose 41 years sit boyishly on him. He is an unpretentious cross between a cheerful country lawyer and a professional politician. He prefers to roll his own cigarettes'. Hollway told reporters that he hated Westerns but liked to 'go to bed with a good murder'; he was a tea-drinker but not a teetotaller; and his design for living included 'a wife, a sense of humour and a garden'.

The coalition broke up on 3 December 1948 after Hollway had forced McDonald to resign for attacking the premier's conciliatory handling of transport strikes. A moderate in the Deakin [q.v.8] tradition, Hollway enjoyed a good personal relationship with the Trades Hall Council's secretary J. V. Stout [q.v.]. Hollway remained as premier and treasurer, changing his party's name to Liberal and Country Party, and persuading some members of parliament to defect from the Country Party.

In the elections on 13 May 1950 Hollway's L.C.P., with 41 per cent of the vote, won 27 seats, the A.L.P. with 45 per cent won 24, and the Country Party with 10.6 per cent won 13. Labor agreed to support a minority Country Party ministry under McDonald in return for adult franchise for the Legislative Council, nationalization of the gas industry and some municipal reforms. Hollway was defeated on a no confidence motion, sought a dissolution of the Assembly which was rejected by the governor Sir Dallas Brooks [q.v.13], and resigned. McDonald became premier on 27 June.

Still opposed to the inequitable electoral distribution, by 1950 Hollway had the support of the executive and State council of the L.C.P., but encountered strong opposition from the Country Party and from influential members of the parliamentary party who, in a closely fought ballot in December 1951, deposed him as L.C.P. leader and elected Leslie Norman.

Despite his charm, Hollway had lost much of the support that he had previously commanded. Colleagues disliked his autocratic style of leadership and regarded him as 'unstable'. His reliance on his wife and a small group of extra-parliamentary advisers was also resented, as was his habit of conducting some parliamentary business in his suite at the Hotel Windsor. A faction, built around (Sir) Arthur Warner [q.v.], plotted against him. With a small group of followers, Hollway was expelled from the L.C.P. in September 1952. Allegations of bribery were made against him and referred to a royal commission of three Supreme Court judges. It adjourned indefinitely when (Sir) Eugene Gorman [q.v.] raised the *sub judice* rule after Hollway had issued writs for libel against the *Age*. (These were later settled on undisclosed terms.)

Labor joined with the L.C.P. to defeat McDonald on the supply bill in the Legislative Council in October 1952. McDonald sought a dissolution, was refused and resigned. Hollway was commissioned to form a minority government, consisting of the eight members of parliament who had left the L.C.P. and joined his Electoral Reform League. Sworn in on 28 October, he was defeated next day in a motion of censure moved by McDonald and supported by the L.C.P. He sought a dissolution which was refused. Brooks recommissioned McDonald as premier and then granted a dissolution.

In the elections of 6 December 1952 Hollway led the Electoral Reform League which contested 15 seats and won 4. He had transferred from Ballarat to Glen Iris, and, with Labor support, defeated Norman in his own seat. He campaigned, as did the A.L.P., on the electoral formula of '2 for 1', that is, for each Federal seat in Victoria to be divided into two State seats. The A.L.P. won office and Cain introduced the '2 for 1' electoral redistribution, adopting Hollway's plan.

The seat of Glen Iris having been eliminated, Hollway stood for the new electorate of Ripponlea in the elections on 28 May 1955. He had lost his zest for campaigning, and relied on support from A.L.P. branch members and strong endorsements from the *Herald* and the *Sun*. (Sir) Edgar Tanner [q.v.] won the seat for the L.C.P., with preferences from the Anti-Communist (later Democratic) Labor Party.

Hollway retired to Point Lonsdale where he became president of its progress association. Travelling to Melbourne, he acted in a drama series on radio. He suffered from cirrhosis of the liver and died of a cerebral haemorrhage on 30 July 1971 at Point Lonsdale; survived by his wife, he was buried in the local cemetery. His estate was sworn for probate at $26 373.

S. Sayers, *Ned Herring* (Melb, 1980); K. White, *John Cain and Victorian Labor 1917-1957* (Syd, 1982); L. Thompson, *I Remember* (Melb, 1989); P. Blazey, *Bolte, a Political Biography* (Melb, 1990); *Politics*, 13, no 2, Nov 1978; *Herald* (Melb), 8 Oct 1941; *Sun News-Pictorial*, 8 Nov 1947; *SMH*, 10 Nov 1947; *Smith's Weekly* (Syd), 11 Mar 1950; *Age* (Melb), 31 July 1971; information from Hon J. Don, Armadale, Melb, and Dr D. Hollway, Gordon, Vic.   BARRY O. JONES

HOLMAN, WILLIAM PROUT (1899-1972), radiologist, was born on 16 September 1899 at Mooroopna, Victoria, youngest of four sons of Charles Holman, schoolteacher, and his wife Eliza Gertrude, née Williams, both Victorian born. Educated at the local state school and (on a scholarship) at Scotch College, Melbourne (1913-18), Bill proceeded to Ormond [q.v.5] College, University of Melbourne (M.B., B.S., 1923), where he was an enthusiastic member of the dramatic society. After a year as a resident medical officer at the (Royal) Melbourne Hospital, he was appointed registrar under L. J. Clendinnen [q.v.8]. Holman moved to Tasmania in 1925 as radiologist to the leading surgeon (Sir) John Ramsay [q.v.11] and practised from rooms in Ramsay's private hospital, St Margaret's, in Frederick Street, Launceston; he was also active in the local dramatic society. On 17 April 1929 he married Mollie Bain at St John's Anglican Church, Launceston.

During the 1930s Holman was responsible for the installation of an advanced deep-therapy machine at the Launceston General Hospital. Keenly interested in the development of new and improved techniques for the delivery of radiotherapy, he played a major role in the formation and administration of the Tasmanian Cancer Committee. A foundation fellow (1938) of the Royal Australasian College of Physicians, he was aware of the plans of (Sir) Peter MacCallum [q.v.], professor of pathology at the University of Melbourne, to establish a cancer hospital in that city. From the 1930s, when he had first used radon needles for treating breast cancer, Holman had pioneered the use of ionising radiation for the disease. For the remainder of his life he continued to search for an alternative to surgical mastectomy. His work attracted international interest and he was elected a fellow of the Faculty (later Royal College) of Radiologists, London, in 1939. That year he became president of the Tasmanian branch of the British Medical Association.

The State government decided in 1943 that Tasmania's radiotherapy services should move towards amalgamation with a centralized institution in Victoria. In 1952 the newly formed Cancer Institute Board of Victoria established Peter MacCallum clinics at Laun-

ceston and in Hobart, over which Holman was given responsibility. He became assistant medical director (1952) of the board and moved with his family to Melbourne; in 1954 he was promoted to medical director. His longstanding interest in cancer of the breast led to a rewarding collaboration with Dr Graham Godfrey and the Royal Women's Hospital. Holman served as an honorary radiotherapist at the R.W.H., the R.M.H. and the Austin Hospital, and as a consulting radiotherapist at the Launceston General and Royal Hobart hospitals. He retired from the board in September 1966, but continued to work with the institute as a specialist radiotherapist. He was a member of the Australian and New Zealand Association of Radiologists, and a foundation fellow (1949) and president (1950) of the College of Radiologists of Australasia (later the Royal Australasian College of Radiologists).

Described as a 'powerful force for the good practice of medicine' and as a 'renaissance man', Holman had a great range of interests, including poetry, drama and history. On his death, he left a small folio of love poems to his wife. He was a practising Anglican and a board-member of the Church of England Girl's Grammar School (Broadland House), Launceston; he enjoyed the mountains and lakes of Tasmania, played golf, showed interest in the developing wine industry and belonged to the Launceston Club. Survived by his wife and four daughters, he died on 12 August 1972 at Canterbury, Melbourne, and was cremated. In 1986 the clinics at Launceston and in Hobart were named in his honour. His eldest daughter became professor of physiology at Monash University, Melbourne.

C. Craig, *Launceston General Hospital* (Launc, 1963); G. L. McDonald (ed), *Roll of the Royal Australasian College of Physicians*, 1, 1938-75 (Syd, 1988); *MJA*, 21 Oct 1972, p 966; *Examiner* (Launc), 19 Aug 1972, 11 Oct 1986; information from Dr L. Hardy Wilson, Bridport, Tas; family information.   MOLLIE E. HOLMAN

HOLMES, EDITH LILLA (1893-1973), artist, was born on 9 March 1893 at Hamilton, Tasmania, third of five children of William Nassau Holmes, a schoolmaster from Ireland, and his wife Lilla Edith, née Thorne, a Tasmanian-born teacher. The family lived at Devonport and Scottsdale before settling on the outskirts of Hobart at Dilkhoosha, 62 Charles Street, Moonah, which remained Edith's home until her death. Her artistic talents were encouraged by her mother who had 'a good sense of colour' and created memorable interiors in their home. Edith studied art at the Hobart Technical College under Lucien

Dechaineux [q.v.8] in 1918-19 and 1922-24, and under Mildred Lovett [q.v.10] in 1925-26, 1928-31 and 1935. She benefited from Dechaineux's emphasis on 'painting in tone' and acknowledged Lovett's encouragement, though her 'modern outlook at first was not well received in Hobart'. In 1930-31 Holmes attended Julian Ashton's [q.v.7] Sydney Art School, under Ashton and Henry Gibbons, where she met George Lambert and Thea Proctor [qq.v.9,11].

During the 1930s Holmes shared a studio in Collins Street, Hobart, with Lovett, Florence Rodway [q.v.11], Dorothy Stoner, Ethel Nicholls and Violet Vimpany. She travelled regularly to Melbourne where she held seven exhibitions (individual and joint) between 1938 and 1951. Her work was favourably received, and thought to be refreshing, particularly by Basil Burdett in 1938 and Rupert Bunny [qq.v.7] in 1941. In Melbourne she met the artists Danila Vassilieff and Eveline Syme [qq.v.], as well as George Bell and Arnold Shore [qq.v.7,11]. Tall and slender, with a striking figure, she had strong features with good bone structure. Her hair was dyed 'a wonderful orange colour and it flowed violently over her forehead almost covering up her bright eyes'. A flamboyant dresser, she sported large, 'old-fashioned hats . . . scarves and wide belts of amazing colour and pattern that allowed her to stand out from the crowd'. She was active in the Victoria League, the English Speaking Union and the Women's Non-Party League of Tasmania, and was a life member of the local division of the United Nations Association.

Holmes exhibited annually in 1927-72 with the Art Society of Tasmania and was a member (1930-52) of its council. A founding member (1940) of the Tasmanian Group of Painters, she also exhibited regularly with them until 1969. She travelled to England and France in 1958, 1960 and 1971, holding an exhibition at Tasmania House, London, in 1958. In an art competition in 1954 to mark Hobart's sesquicentenary she had won a special prize, and in 1972 she secured another, awarded by the Tasmanian branch of the Contemporary Art Society. She loved her natural surroundings, particularly Mount Direction which was visible from her home. Having been inspired in the 1920s by the outdoor work of Lovett and Vida Lahey [q.v.9], she painted in all weather and seasons, especially on a property at Carlton where she had a shack. She also enjoyed painting portraits, particularly of her relations, was 'interested in people and how they dressed', and felt it important to convey their character in her art. An instinctive, joyous painter, she was a vibrant colourist. Two self-portraits from the 1930s—'Summer', an intriguing oil showing three faces, and 'Self Portrait in a Sun Hat'—are in the Tasmanian Museum and Art Gallery.

Miss Holmes died on 26 August 1973 in Hobart and was buried with Anglican rites in Forcett cemetery. Her work is represented in the Australian National Gallery, Canberra, the National Gallery of Victoria, the Devonport Gallery and Art Centre, and in numerous private collections. Dorothy Stoner's portrait of Holmes is held by the Queen Victoria Museum and Art Gallery, Launceston.

J. Burke, *Australian Women Artists 1840-1940* (Melb, 1980); V. Veale, *Women to Remember* (St Helens, Tas, 1981); H. Kolenberg, *Edith Holmes and Dorothy Stoner*, exhibition cat (Hob, 1983); S. Backhouse, *Tasmanian Artists of the Twentieth Century* (Hob, 1988); M. Angus, *Edith Holmes Exhibition*, exhibition cat (Hob, 1986); *Herald* (Melb), 3 Dec 1938; H. de Berg, Edith Holmes (taped interview, 8 Oct 1965, NL); J. Hickey, Notes on Edith Holmes (ms, Hob, 1975, copy held by Tas Museum and Art Gallery); information from Miss E. Brooker, Midway Point, Tas.

SUE BACKHOUSE

HOLMES, JAMES MACDONALD (1896-1966), geographer, was born on 26 February 1896 at Greenock, Renfrewshire, Scotland, son of James Holmes, journeyman slater, and his wife Isabella, née McLeary. In 1919, after three-and-a-half-years service with the Royal Navy, James was exempted from preliminary examinations to enter the University of Glasgow (B.Sc., 1925; Ph.D., 1934) where he was student demonstrator in geology to Professor J. W. Gregory [q.v.9]. Having gained a certificate of distinction in geography, Holmes was admitted as a research student in 1925 and elected a fellow (1927) of the Royal Geographical Society of London. Fond of the outdoors and a good organizer, he was an enthusiastic field-worker and one of the first King's scouts in the west of Scotland. Holmes was lecturer-in-charge of geography (1927-29) at Armstrong College, Newcastle upon Tyne, England. On 26 September 1929 he married Marion ('Muriel') Macdonald (d.1982), with the forms of the United Free Church, at Scourie, Sutherland, Scotland, before taking up an appointment as associate-professor of geography at the University of Sydney, succeeding T. G. Taylor [q.v.12]. From 1930 he also lectured in economic geography.

Despite financial stringency, poor facilities and a degree of official indifference, Macdonald Holmes (as he now styled himself) began —with characteristic energy—important research on soil erosion and regional planning. He was president (1930-33) of the Geographical Society of New South Wales, and edited and extended its journal, the *Australian Geographer*. With John Andrews, he published *Descriptive Geography for Secondary Schools* (1932). In 1933 he gave evidence to the royal commission (chaired by H. S. Nicholas [q.v.11]) into the possible boundaries of new States and became a respected adviser to governments on conservation and planning. Other publications followed: *Regional Atlas of Australia and the World* (1936), *Practical Map Reading* (1941) and *The Geographical Basis of Government* (1944). In January 1945 he was appointed to the McCaughey [q.v.5] chair of geography.

Holmes saw geography as 'the study of land in relation to people'. He built up a strong honours school based on field-projects, often financed by private funds, and worked effectively to create new employment opportunities for trained geographers in the public and private sectors. He gave many talks and contributed to the press on subjects ranging from aviation to international affairs. Such a high profile attracted criticism, the chief of which was the uneven quality of his publications. In addition to numerous articles in local and overseas journals, his later works included *Soil Erosion in Australia and New Zealand* (1946), *The Murray Valley* (1948) and his most successful book, *Australia's Open North* (1963).

From 1935 Holmes had helped to set up the New South Wales section of what became the Royal Flying Doctor Service of Australia, and was vice-president (1947-48) and president (1949-51) of its federal council; his wife founded (1938) and presided (1946-82) over an auxiliary in Sydney to raise funds for the service. Holmes was also president (1940) of the local Linnean Society. Involved with Scottish organizations and the lay administration of the Presbyterian Church, he was an active council-member (1940-66) of Scots College. He and his wife were tireless workers for the Sydney University Settlement. Short and rotund, with a large, oval face and large, expressive eyes, he was a man of great personal charm and persuasiveness. Students found him a friendly teacher, and enjoyed his field-excursions with their evening socials enlivened by Scottish dancing. He retired in December 1961. Survived by his wife and two sons, he died of cancer on 28 August 1966 in St Luke's Hospital, Darlinghurst, and was cremated. The Macdonald Holmes Library in the geography department at the University of Sydney commemorates him.

Aust Geographer, 10, no 3, 1966-68, p 220; Univ Syd, *Gazette*, Oct 1966, p 187; *Scotsman*, 1966, p 24; *Aust J of Science*, 29, no 4, Oct 1966, p 104; *Aust Geographical Studies*, 5, no 1, Apr 1967, p 85; *Geographers Biobibliographical Studies*, 7, 1983, p 51; *SMH*, 8 May, 26, 27 Nov 1929, 15, 19 Aug 1932, 15, 17, 20-22 June 1933, 17, 31 July 1936, 29 Aug 1966.   G. P. WALSH

HOLMES, JOHN DASHWOOD (1907-1973), barrister and judge, was born on 13 May 1907 at Darlinghurst, Sydney, son of Greville Charles Dashwood Holmes, a commercial traveller from England, and his native-born wife Margaret, née Kelly. After being schooled at Christian Brothers' College, Waverley, John went jackerooing. He worked freelance as a radio and press journalist while studying at the University of Sydney (B.A., 1928; LL.B., 1932). Admitted to the Bar on 10 March 1933, he swiftly built up a substantial and wide-ranging practice, especially in constitutional law, commercial law and Equity. In the 1930s Holmes collected Australian books and pamphlets, and compiled an unpublished bibliography on the growth of the Federation movement. At St Paul's Anglican Church, Cobbitty, on 16 March 1938 he married a musician Joan Symons, daughter of George Mackaness [q.v.10]; they were to be divorced in June 1946. On 31 October that year he married a divorcee Margaret Eve Blaxland Robertson, née Levick, at the district registrar's office, Drummoyne. Both marriages were childless. He lived at Drummoyne in the 1940s before moving to Castle Hill and eventually to Blues Point.

As lecturer in constitutional law (1940-50) at the university, Holmes was involved in controversies resulting from Julius Stone's appointment as professor of international law and jurisprudence, and in disagreements with others in the faculty: like R. C. Teece [q.v.12], Holmes represented the interests of the practising profession in the contretemps. He wrote textbooks on war legislation affecting property, the law of money-lending, and the Prices Regulation Act (1948). In numerous contributions to the *Australian Law Journal* he showed the diversity of his legal interests, including a daring argument—advanced in 1934 and vindicated shortly before his death —that the Commonwealth could legislate on companies for the whole of Australia.

During World War II Holmes served on the Aliens' Tribunal. He appeared in many leading constitutional cases before the High Court of Australia and the judicial committee of the Privy Council. Appointed K.C. in July 1948, he later took silk in Victoria and in Queensland. He was a junior counsel for the Commonwealth in the Bank nationalization case (1948) and represented before the Privy Council the successful appellant in *Hughes and Vale Ltd* v. *New South Wales* (1954) in litigation over the freedom of interstate trade. Holmes belonged to the Union Club. To intimate colleagues, he was a staunch and loyal friend, but he was generally reserved.

Actively involved in the corporate interests of his profession, Holmes was a member (1961-62, 1964-65) and president (1965) of the Council of the New South Wales Bar Association, and vice-president of the Australian Bar Association. He was appointed a judge of the Supreme Court on 8 November 1965 and elevated to the Court of Appeal on its opening on 1 January 1966. Known at the Bar for his ability, hard work and compelling sense of duty, as a judge of appeal he added a demeanour that was learned, humane and courteous, witty but never unkind. Yet he could show frustration at the inadequacies of inferior courts. In 1967 he rebuked a magistrate for having rushed headlong into such an irretrievable position that 'the eggs are not only broken; they are scrambled beyond unscrambling'. In another case that year he described the 'terrors' endured by a litigant before a stipendiary magistrate, saying that they illustrated 'how the poor, sick and friendless are still oppressed by the machinery of justice in ways which need a Fielding or a Dickens to describe in words and a Hogarth to portray pictorially'.

Reduced by a debilitating blood disorder that had afflicted him for years and given him a sallow countenance, Holmes died of hepatoma on 21 January 1973 at the Mater Misericordiae Hospital, Crows Nest, and was cremated with Anglican rites. His wife survived him.

J. and J. Mackinolty (eds), *A Century Downtown* (Syd, 1991); *Aust Law J*, 7, 1934, p 372, 39, 1965, p 252, 47, 1973, p 106; *Cwlth Law Reports*, 76, 1948, p 1, 93, 1954, p 1; *State Reports* (NSW), 69, 1967, 247 at 268; *Weekly Notes* (NSW), 86, 1967, 215 at 218; *SMH*, 8 July 1948, 6 Aug, 5 Nov 1965, 14 Nov 1970, 22 Jan 1973; *Sun* (Syd), 8 Nov 1965; Holmes papers (NL); information from Hon J. P. Slattery, Crows Nest, and Hon G. D. Needham, Dural, Syd. JOHN KENNEDY MCLAUGHLIN

HOLMWOOD, RAYMOND ARTHUR (1911-1941), air force officer, was born on 7 December 1911 at Newcastle, New South Wales, second child of native-born parents Arthur Percy Holmwood, public schoolteacher, and his wife Mabel Alice, née Burgmann. After gaining his Intermediate certificate, on 15 February 1928 Raymond entered the Royal Military College, Duntroon, Federal Capital Territory, as a staff cadet nominated by the Royal Australian Air Force. He undertook the 'A' course at No.1 Flying Training School, Point Cook, Victoria, graduated with his 'wings' in December 1931 and was commissioned in the following month.

Having been posted to No.1 Squadron, Laverton, in February 1932 Holmwood joined No.3 Squadron at Richmond, New South Wales, where he quickly demonstrated outstanding leadership qualities. He earned respect for his professional competence, possessed a highly developed sense of duty and was a first-class athlete. These attributes were complemented by his fine appearance: he was 5 ft 10 ins (178 cm) tall, weighed 10 st. 11 lb (68.5 kg), and had straw-coloured hair, blue eyes and a fair complexion. With his 'aquiline features [and] strong chin ... he made a most romantic figure'. On 21 September 1934 at St Mark's Anglican Church, Darling Point, Sydney, he married Margaret Alice, daughter of (Sir) Thomas Gordon [q.v.9].

Holmwood's appointments began to reflect his potential for high command. From December 1935 to February 1936 he was adjutant of No.3 Squadron; in 1936-37 he commanded the Cadet Squadron at No.1 F.T.S.; and he performed staff duties at Air Force Headquarters, Melbourne, in 1937-39. Promoted acting squadron leader, he took over the Intermediate Training Squadron at No.1 F.T.S. in July 1939 and became the squadron's chief flying instructor in April next year when it was expanded and transferred to No.1 Service Flying Training School.

In July 1940 Holmwood was sent to England to serve on exchange with the Royal Air Force. Disembarking in October, he completed an operational conversion course on fighter aircraft, then flew with No.64 Squadron, R.A.F. On 18 December he was appointed commanding officer of No.615 Squadron, based at Kenley, Surrey, and was thus the first R.A.A.F. officer to lead a British squadron in World War II. His appointment was the more meritorious because No.615 had distinguished itself in earlier fighting and its honorary air commodore was Prime Minister (Sir) Winston Churchill. Holmwood was promoted temporary wing commander in January 1941.

On 26 February 1941, during an engagement with enemy aircraft over Waddenhall, a rural district near Petham, Kent, Holmwood's Hurricane was shot down; he baled out of his aircraft but his parachute caught fire. The members of his unit regarded him as 'the very finest type' and his death cast a gloom over Kenley. Survived by his wife and four-year-old son, he was buried in Whyteleafe (St Luke's) churchyard, near Caterham, Surrey.

C. Orde, *Pilots of Fighter Command* (Lond, 1942); *Aircraft* (Melb), 19, no 5, Feb 1941, p 14; *Age* (Melb), 3 Jan, 3 Mar 1941; *Herald* (Melb), 1 Mar 1941. ALAN STEPHENS

HOLT, HAROLD EDWARD (1908-1967), prime minister, was born on 5 August 1908 at Stanmore, Sydney, elder son of Thomas James Holt, schoolteacher, and his wife Olive

May, née Williams, both Australian born. Harold began his education at Randwick Public School and boarded briefly at Abbotsholme, Killara, where he met (Sir) William McMahon, a future colleague and prime minister. Tom Holt left teaching and tried the hotel trade in Adelaide before becoming a travelling theatrical manager. Harold's unsettled years ended when, aged 11, he was sent with his brother Cliff to board at Wesley Preparatory School, Melbourne.

Harold completed his matriculation at Wesley College, excelling more as a sportsman and in theatricals than as a student, although the scholarship he took to Queen's College, University of Melbourne (LL.B., 1930), placed half the weighting on academic attainment and the other half on force of character and athleticism. The undergraduate continued his sporting career, captaining the college in cricket and representing it in football and tennis. He won a college medal for oratory (1930) and was elected president of the sports and social club (1931); he was president of the University Law Students' Society and a member of the university's debating team. Admitted to the Bar on 10 November 1932, he read with (Sir) Thomas Clyne and discovered that there was no future for young barristers during the Depression. In 1933 Holt began a sole practice as a solicitor.

His father's career, meanwhile, was flourishing. Widowed about 1925, Tom joined the entrepreneur F. W. Thring [q.v.12] in 1930 to make feature films, then managed radio 3XY in Melbourne when Thring bought the operating rights in 1935. Cliff took a job as publicity director for Hoyts Theatres Ltd. With an aunt playing comedy in Britain, Harold thus had connexions and interests in film and stage, and in 1935 was appointed secretary of the Cinematograph Exhibitors' Association. A modest income and a widening circle of companions gave the young man the security and sense of belonging his *bon vivant* father could not provide.

Harold found political as well as theatrical friends, including (Dame) Mabel Brookes [q.v.13] and (Sir) Robert Menzies [q.v.]. Holt joined the Young Nationalists and in the 1934 Federal elections stood for the United Australia Party against James Scullin [q.v.11] in the Labor stronghold of Yarra. After contesting another Labor seat in the State elections, he won, at 27 years of age in 1935, a by-election for the secure U.A.P. seat of Fawkner in the House of Representatives. Holt was to retain Fawkner until 1949 when, following a redistribution and the enlargement of the House, he moved to the new seat of Higgins which he was to hold with absolute majorities until his death.

The new member for Fawkner was a dashing figure: of middle height, fit and handsome,

with thick black hair swept back, well-tailored clothes, a ready smile and a natural charm. Shortly after his first election, Holt entered an arrangement with Jack Graham, another young Melbourne solicitor and an Old Geelong Grammarian, to whom he paid a retainer to look after his work. They opened an office at 178 Collins Street, employed a typist and took on industrial work, gaining some business through Holt's cinema and theatre connexions, and from the name he was making in politics. The partnership expanded after World War II into Holt, Graham & Newman, and lasted until 1963 by which time Holt, understandably, was making little contribution.

Following the 1937 elections Holt used parliament as a forum to advocate national physical fitness. On 26 April 1939 he joined the first Menzies government as minister without portfolio, assisting the minister for supply and (from 23 February 1940) the minister for trade and customs. In addition, Holt was briefly acting-minister for air and civil aviation. At 30, he had become the youngest man to hold ministerial office in Federal parliament. His front-bench career was interrupted when Country Party members rejoined the ministry in March 1940. He enlisted in the Australian Imperial Force on 22 May and trained as a gunner, his previous military experience consisting of five years compulsory membership of the Wesley College cadets, three years in the Melbourne University Rifles and fourteen months in the artillery (Militia).

Menzies recalled Holt to Canberra as a result of the deaths of three senior ministers in an air accident on 13 August 1940 and he was discharged from the A.I.F. After the elections in September, he was given a full cabinet post and the new portfolio of labour and national service—in recognition of his tact and easygoing disposition—though his major contribution was to introduce child endowment, earning him the epithet, 'godfather of a million children'.

Holt agonized over but eventually supported the ousting of his mentor Menzies in August 1941. The fallen hero forgave this first and last act of disloyalty. Holt retained his portfolio in the short-lived ministry of (Sir) Arthur Fadden [q.v.], and, when John Curtin [q.v.13] took office in October, sat on the Opposition front-bench as spokesman on industrial relations. He attended an abortive unity meeting of non-Labor leaders in Melbourne in February 1943, but was not a prime mover in the discussions which followed the electoral annihilation of the U.A.P. in August and which led to the formation of the Liberal Party. He did, however, support the decision of the parliamentary party in February 1945 to adopt the name 'Liberal', and he was to be a principal and outspoken champion of the anti-socialist cause in the late 1940s.

Two important events affected Holt at the end of the war. His father died in October 1945 and, on 8 October 1946, ten days after the Liberal Party was heavily defeated at the polls, he married with Congregational forms Zara Kate Fell, née Dickins, in her parents' home at Toorak. The two had courted when he was a law student, but, tired of their quarrelling and his general tardiness, she went abroad, and married a British Army officer stationed in India. Holt later claimed that he had kept away because of his Depression-induced poverty, and was devastated by her decision. After Zara's marriage failed, they restored their relationship, by which time she had three sons, of whom the twins—aged 7 in 1946—were possibly conceived during an earlier reunion with Harold.

Eight frustrating years in Opposition ended with the Liberal victory in December 1949. With the support of Albert Monk [q.v.], president of the Australian Council of Trade Unions, Menzies reappointed Holt minister for labour and national service, and gave him the additional portfolio of immigration which he was to hold until October 1956. Acknowledging Arthur Calwell's [q.v.13] role in developing the immigration programme, Holt added his human touch and flexibility to hardship cases and significantly extended the assisted-passage scheme to non-British migrants. Under pressure from his own party, and conforming to his own beliefs, he maintained a preference for British settlers, but their numbers, as a proportion of the intake, fell in the 1950s. He was also committed to the White Australia policy and, ignoring the evidence he encountered at Commonwealth ministerial meetings, expressed his confidence that it did not cause resentment, in part because of tactful administration.

Holt held the labour portfolio until December 1958. An instinctive conciliator, he established such a good relationship with Monk and moderate trade-union leaders that members of his party accused him of excessive fraternization and damned him as an appeaser. Holt's methods contributed to the trend in which, despite an increase in the number of industrial disputes in the 1950s, there was a substantial decline in the number of working days lost. He also introduced important legislation—most notably, to make secret ballots in union elections mandatory (1951), and to separate the conciliation and arbitration processes from the exercise of judicial functions (1956), thus establishing the modern form of the Federal arbitration system.

His middle years were perhaps his happiest, for the successful minister discovered a liking for overseas travel. He had first ventured abroad in 1948 when he attended a meeting of the Commonwealth Parliamentary Association in London, contrived a visit to Paris and stayed up until dawn. In the 1950s he took part in four meetings of the C.P.A. and was chairman (1952-55) of its general council. He was a guest at the coronation of Queen Elizabeth II in 1953, sat at 'my master's elbow' at a Commonwealth prime ministers' conference in London in 1957 and that year presided over the fortieth session of the International Labour Conference at Geneva. Zara accompanied him on almost all of these trips, with their many stopovers, new political and social contacts, opportunities to swim, dine and party, and even to make the Savoy Hotel in London 'a second home'.

On his travels Holt kept diaries which he circulated among officials and 'chums'. In them, for the most part, he eschewed politics, preferring to recommend restaurants, hotels and countries, and to comment—generously and warmly—on the appearance and attributes of those he met. The diary of his 'Coronation Odyssey' described a C.P.A. luncheon for seven hundred parliamentarians at Westminster Hall where, after gulping 'a couple of quickies', he sat between the Queen and Lady Churchill, listened in admiration to Sir Winston and enjoyed 'an unforgettable experience', not least for finding the Queen 'very easy to talk to, completely natural, charming'. The diarist had an eye for the comic, telling friends back home about the complicated toilet arrangements inside Westminster Abbey to assist elderly peers and their grand wives during a long day.

Holt was an inquisitive and patriotic tourist. On his Geneva visit in 1957 he espied Charlie (Sir Charles) Chaplin at the airport and had a good 'look-see'. Moving on to London, the Holts saw *Summer of the Seventeenth Doll* and both were 'proud of the Australian author, proud of the all-Australian cast, and proud of the country which had produced the types in the play and the types who played them'.

The hard-working and hard-playing Harold astonished everyone with his stamina. Up late on overseas trips, he attended to his papers before dawn, undertook a load of official engagements, and proved to be an effective negotiator and ambassador. His firm chairmanship contributed to the success of the C.P.A.'s Nairobi conference in 1954 at which he found to his delight that he got on well with the Asian members. Equally, at the I.L.C. session in 1957 he deftly handled a post-Suez Egyptian objection to his presidency, and calmly restored order when a Soviet delegate tried to make a propaganda speech after members of the Hungarian delegation were denied recognition.

In 1956 Holt had succeeded Sir Eric Harrison [q.v.] as deputy-leader of the parliamentary Liberal Party, easily defeating R. G. (Baron) Casey [q.v.13], but just beating a New South Wales senator (Sir) William Spooner [q.v.]. Doubts about Holt's mental toughness, and State rivalry, explained the close result which, none the less, gave him the clear inside running to succeed Menzies. The party organization was especially pleased because the new deputy-leader was closer to it than Menzies, even though Holt's chairmanship of the party's revived joint standing committee on federal policy did not make the government more responsive to the organization in policy matters. Parliament also benefited because, as leader of the House, he adopted Harrison's practice of working closely with Calwell, his opposite number.

Holt became treasurer on 10 December 1958 following Fadden's retirement. Treasury generally approved of the appointment: Holt had the requisite seniority and skill in cabinet to win a brief, and he did not have a dangerously independent mind or a personal agenda. While he did not automatically accept everything placed in front of him, and would ask questions, he had little interest in economics and no conceptual grasp. His gift was in talking to people, and persuading them to accept a proposition. His good fortune was to be advised by very able officials.

One of his first legislative acts was to push through the delayed reforms of the Commonwealth Bank of Australia, separating the reserve functions and creating three banks to deal with trading, savings and development activities, all controlled by the new Commonwealth Banking Corporation. As treasurer, he joined the board of governors of the International Monetary Fund, the International Bank for Reconstruction and Development, and the International Finance Corporation, chaired the annual meetings of these organizations in Washington in 1960, and made several visits to the United States of America and Europe to deliver speeches and raise loans, a workload which tested even his endurance without noticeably reducing the social round.

Holt sanctioned Treasury's monumental decision in February 1960 to remove virtually all import restrictions. The failure, however, to maintain strict fiscal and monetary control, and the preference for gradual measures to halt a speculative boom, led in November to another important decision which nearly reversed Holt's steady evolution to the top. He and the Reserve Bank of Australia announced a package of measures amounting to a 'credit squeeze' which drove the economy into a recession and saw unemployment rise to 131 000 by January 1962. On Treasury's advice, Holt argued against early remedial action on the expectation of a quick recovery and on the assumption that inflation was the real enemy. Complaining that the government had acted too late in disciplining the economy and too drastically when it did so, business turned on Holt, the treasury secretary Sir Roland Wilson and finally on Menzies himself.

As a result, the government just scraped back in the December 1961 elections and Holt's vote in Higgins fell by 6.5 per cent. Many Liberals and Liberal-supporting businessmen demanded his removal from the Treasury. Menzies insisted that the credit squeeze was a government decision, and so Holt survived. The prime minister, with the treasurer at his shoulder, sought to retrieve the situation by consulting with business leaders in February 1962 and implementing policies which, very slowly, helped the economy to recover. Holt carried some scars, and he looked nervously at the reaction to his subsequent budgets. In August 1963 he proudly told Sir Howard Beale that he had never received so many favourable private comments from businessmen, while noting that some held unreasonable expectations and accusing them of having studied no more deeply than newspaper editorials.

Holt and the economy kept out of any further serious trouble and the deputy whom Menzies always thought of as 'Young Harold' was the unanimous choice of the party room when 'the great white chief' announced his retirement in January 1966. There was no obvious alternative and the new prime minister, who took office on Australia Day, could boast that he got there without stepping over a dead body. The 'son' had taken over from the 'father', Menzies declared the country to be in good hands, and there was an eagerness in the press and political circles to see if he could make his own mark.

Making only two immediate ministerial changes—both caused by retirements—Holt promoted in Dame Annabelle Rankin the first woman to hold a portfolio in a Federal ministry and in Malcolm Fraser a future prime minister. He did, however, signal a new style by acting more as chairman of a committee, by including the press in his overseas tours and being solicitous to their needs, and by presenting himself in an open and informal manner. The now silver-haired, still fit and good-looking prime minister, photographed in a wetsuit alongside his three bikini-clad daughters-in-law, looked the perfect choice to carry the Liberal Party into and beyond the 'Swinging Sixties'.

One substantial change occurred in March 1966 when Holt's government introduced the most significant modifications (until then) in the White Australia policy, lowering the requirements for non-European entry, residency and citizenship. The reforms reflected his determination to bring Australia closer to

Asia. He made several trips to the region in 1966-67, visiting neutrals as well as friends. His personal style of diplomacy led him into mistakes and risks, such as the decisions to open an Australian embassy in Taiwan and to invite Air Vice Marshal Nguyen Cao Ky, prime minister of the Republic of (South) Vietnam, to visit Australia. Yet, as Gough Whitlam, the leader of the Opposition, pointed out in March 1968: '[h]e made Australia better known in Asia and he made Australians more aware of Asia than ever before'.

This awareness was fostered by the Vietnam War. Inheriting Australia's involvement in the defence of South Vietnam, Holt enthusiastically extended the April 1965 military commitment of 1500 personnel to 8000 in October 1967, and kept urging the Americans to send more forces and to maintain the bombing of the Democratic Republic of (North) Vietnam. He believed that the conflict resulted from China's thrust into South East Asia, that Australians were fighting to repel aggression and to honour treaty obligations, and that the Asian dominoes would fall if South Vietnam collapsed, thereby endangering Australia. Holt also accepted that Britain's impending withdrawal east of Suez meant Australia must secure the effective presence of the U.S.A. in Asia and the Pacific. An increased armed involvement in South Vietnam seemed the appropriate insurance premium.

Holt's personal plunge into the war was also fired by what Zara called 'Harry's most spectacular friendship' with the American president Lyndon Johnson. His off-the-cuff remark at the White House in July 1966—assuring Johnson that a staunch friend would go 'all the way with L.B.J.'—occasioned him embarrassment back home, yet, for Holt, an expression of loyalty did not denote servility. Rather, it reflected the genuine, wholehearted and unsparing relationship between two men who shared many characteristics, and who fortified each other in the face of growing domestic criticism of the war. This hostility distressed Holt without affecting his resolve and its impact was eased when Johnson visited Australia in October 1966, one month before Federal elections which Holt won with a record majority.

Whereas 1966 was a good year, everything seemed to go wrong in 1967. The death of his brother Cliff in March—'a terrible blow'—unsettled him, though he had a natural or developed immunity to sadness. Relieved that he managed to get to Sydney in time for the funeral, he left immediately for a scheduled Asian tour. In Canberra, Whitlam had replaced Calwell as the leader of the Opposition, and his debating skills and quick mind gave him an ascendancy over Holt who, as the year

progressed, lost his customary equanimity while he struggled through his tangled speeches. Labor's by-election victories in July and September hurt him politically. So did his failure to carry the May referendum to break the nexus between the numbers in the House and the Senate, though the simultaneous proposal—to include Aborigines in the national census and to empower the Commonwealth to legislate on Aboriginal affairs—won overwhelming approval.

The more serious wounds were selfinflicted. Holt was not prepared to discipline his own party or the coalition, animosities were rife, and he resisted party pressure for a much needed cabinet reshuffle. He also bungled the 'V.I.P. flights affair' in which the government was accused of misleading parliament over the existence of passenger manifests. Loyalty to a friend, Peter Howson, minister for air, left Holt obviously floundering in the House. Disloyalty, possibly involving Holt's chief whip, and rumours of health problems, were fuelling doubts about his capacity to lead.

'Young Harold' appeared to reach his nadir with the half-Senate elections on 25 November 1967. The government's share of the popular vote of 50 per cent in 1966 fell to 42.8 per cent at a time when hostile anti-Vietnam demonstrations were clearly unsettling him. Yet he ended the political year with a triumph. Immediately before the Senate polls, the government decided not to follow Britain in devaluing the currency. (Sir) John McEwen [q.v.], deputy prime minister and Country Party leader, and a long-standing and good political friend, returned from overseas and publicly attacked the decision, thereby threatening coalition unity. Holt met McEwen in private on 12 December, warned him that, with a few expected Country Party defections, the Liberal Party could and would govern alone if McEwen continued to defy a cabinet resolution, and published a detailed rebuttal of the deputy prime minister's statement.

Despite a year of setbacks, Holt had won a crucial political battle. Worn out, he was not depressed when he left Canberra for the last time on Friday 15 December for a weekend at the family home at Portsea on Victoria's Mornington Peninsula. He intended to come back on Monday, fresh as ever because Portsea always worked a miracle cure, with plans for ministerial changes in the New Year and a major statement announcing a switch in foreign policy giving emphasis to European affairs.

Zara stayed behind in Canberra. Harold played tennis and relaxed with friends throughout Saturday. On the morning of Sunday 17 December 1967 he collected a neighbour Marjorie Gillespie, her daughter and two young men, and together they watched the lone English yachtsman (Sir) Alec Rose sail through the Heads. The party then went to Cheviot Beach where Holt changed into his swimming trunks, said that he knew the beach like the back of his hand, and, soon after midday, entered what everyone later agreed was a fierce and high surf. Harold was seen swimming freely out to sea when turbulent water suddenly built up around him and he disappeared. Help was called, a major rescue operation was mounted, and Zara and the immediate family arrived. By nightfall some 190 people were looking for the prime minister without expecting to find him alive. The search was scaled down on 22 December and officially terminated on 5 January 1968. Holt's body was never found.

A service attended by two thousand official guests was held at noon on 22 December in St Paul's Anglican Cathedral, Melbourne. An estimated ten thousand mourners and Christmas shoppers listened to the service relayed by loudspeakers. The overseas dignitaries included a tearful President Johnson, Harold (Baron) Wilson, the British prime minister, the Prince of Wales and senior representatives of twelve Asian nations. Archbishop (Sir) Philip Strong, the Anglican primate, spoke of 'fidelity' as the mark of the man's life and work, and dwelt on Holt's commitment to Asia, to the maintenance of freedom among free peoples and to the liberation of those living under tyranny. Memorial services were held on the same day or later throughout Australia and in other parts of the world.

Considerable speculation followed Holt's disappearance. Every summer, Australians of all ages do foolish things in the water, and drown. Some commentators, nevertheless, found it impossible to believe that a prime minister, who was not in fact a strong swimmer, who had a sore shoulder and who entered a dangerous sea, could have acted foolishly. His customary fearlessness, a desire to 'show off', the likelihood of his being stunned or dragged down by debris, a simple miscalculation: these explanations were considered insufficiently momentous to match the gravity of the event. Stories circulated that he was distracted by political troubles, or that he had committed suicide, fulfilling his own premonition of not living beyond 60. Those best placed in December 1967 to judge his state of mind remain adamant that Harold, the life affirmer, was in good spirits, and that he was already thinking of a time beyond politics at Bingil Bay, near Innisfail, Queensland, where he and Zara had a shack and a virtually private beach, and which he described as his 'Shangri-La'. The probability is that the prime minister was simply another statistic of an Australian summer.

Harold Holt may not have been a visionary or a profound thinker, but he had worked diligently in serving and celebrating his country. His achievements as a senior minister in the postwar Menzies governments were considerable, he contributed to the nation's standing overseas and he helped his own party achieve a permanence lacking in its earlier manifestations. Overshadowed by Menzies, he had attributes which made him an admirable deputy and, in less turbulent times, a good leader: integrity, a willingness to listen, a sense of what was possible, and a team spirit which made him the least likely of his colleagues to undermine or gossip about the others. He could be stubborn, tough and politically courageous, but never ruthless. Loyal to friends and colleagues, tender towards his opponents and nice to everybody —irrespective of position—this thoroughly decent man was genuinely liked and missed on all sides. That, after thirty-two years in politics, was a remarkable epitaph.

Holt used to tell Calwell of his struggle to find a place and a name for himself. But he also had the capacity to bounce back from adversity. The death of his mother, his father's marriage to Thring's daughter whom Holt himself had escorted, the hardship and disappointments of the Depression years, a near-escape in April 1941 from a hit-and-run driver near Gundagai, New South Wales, an accident which killed his chauffeur and immobilized him less then three weeks before the 1955 elections, and Cliff's death in 1967: these events may have shaken him, but he became so self-absorbed that nothing appeared to touch him too deeply. If he had hoped for a different family life, the one he acquired in 1946 gave him financial security, a devoted wife and three boys who took his name in 1957, looked up to him and found him good fun, even though, given his long absences in Canberra, he was at best a weekend father who never closely followed their progress.

He liked the family to be together, when he was available. Menzies was one of the very few political visitors to the home at Toorak, and his appearances were rare enough. And Holt knew how to relax away from work. He gambled frequently at cards and on the racetrack, and the family needed Zara's fashion business to prosper financially and to buy the Portsea house. He occasionally tried golf and more often played tennis, but the most important outlet was spear-fishing to which the boys had introduced him. He loved the sport and would frequently, and unwisely, seek his quarry some 400 yards from his support-boat and in waters others thought too dangerous.

In many ways he was an ordinary bloke who liked to be liked. Humble, sensitive to criticism, gregarious—without revealing too much of himself—he could mix with anyone.

He thrived on people, and liked women. In 1962 he wrote in his diary of a dinner companion that 'she is still a very lovely woman, but like a very ripe peach which should be eaten without delay'. Provoked by public disclosures that Marjorie Gillespie had been his lover, Zara claimed that Gillespie was just 'one of the queue'. Zara knew of Harry's affairs and tolerated them, but she also deliberately exaggerated the extent of his indulgence. Their marriage survived because the two lived separate lives; and Holt admired, and was lucky to have, such a feisty partner.

Holt was sworn of the Privy Council in 1953 and appointed C.H. in 1967. A memorial plaque has been laid under the waters of Cheviot Beach and a portrait by W. E. Pidgeon hangs in Parliament House, Canberra. Holt's estate was sworn for probate at $92 842.

Z. Holt, *My Life and Harry* (Melb, 1968); D. Whitington, *Twelfth Man?* (Brisb, 1972); G. Whitwell, *The Treasury Line* (Syd, 1986); D. Langmore, *Prime Ministers' Wives* (Melb, 1992); G. Henderson, *Menzies' Child* (Syd, 1994); *Bulletin*, 31 May 1961; L. Brodrick, Transition and Tragedy (B.A. Hons thesis, Macquarie Univ, 1989); Menzies papers *and* Liberal Party of Aust papers (NL); Harold Holt papers (AA, Canb); Andrew Holt papers (held privately); information from Messrs N. Holt and A. H. Holt, Prahran, S. Holt, Toorak, Melb, A. Eggleton, Brussels, P. Bailey, Deakin, Canb, and J. Short, Collingwood, and the Hon P. Howson, Toorak, Melb.   I. R. HANCOCK

HOLYMAN, SIR IVAN NELLO (1896-1957), businessman and airline founder, was born on 9 July 1896 at Devonport, Tasmania, eleventh of thirteen children of William Holyman [q.v.9], mariner, and his wife Honora, née Ballard. Educated at Launceston Church Grammar School, he intended to follow his elder brother VICTOR CLIVE (1894-1934) into a career as a ship's officer in the family shipping company, William Holyman [q.v.4] & Sons Pty Ltd, Launceston, a business founded by their grandfather. Ivan's father, however, saw that he was placed as a clerk in the company's Launceston office in 1911.

Enlisting in the Australian Imperial Force on 18 August 1914, Holyman was posted to the 12th Battalion and was commissioned at Gallipoli in August 1915. He was sent to the Western Front in April 1916 and promoted captain (May 1917). Near Jeancourt, France, on 18 September 1918, 'the splendid fighting company under his command' took more than one hundred prisoners; he was awarded the Military Cross. Thrice wounded during his service, and mentioned in dispatches, he returned to Tasmania where his appointment terminated on 8 July 1919. That year he re-entered the administrative section of William

Holyman & Sons, taking over management of the company on his father's death in 1921. At Launceston on 2 April 1924 he married Enid Colville McKinlay with Presbyterian forms.

It was Victor's vision that led the family into air transport. Born on 27 August 1894 at Devonport, he trained as a pilot in Britain and was appointed flight sub lieutenant, Royal Naval Air Service, in June 1916. He fought on the Western Front, transferred to the Royal Air Force in 1918 and ceased full-time service in February 1920. In 1932 the family bought a three-passenger de Havilland 83 Fox Moth and Victor commenced flights from Launceston to Flinders Island, under the banner Holyman Bros Pty Ltd; the aircraft was named *Miss Currie*, after the principal town on King Island. Following amalgamation with a competitor L. McK. Johnson, Tasman Aerial Services Pty Ltd was formed to fly passengers from Launceston to Melbourne. Johnson was bought out and Holymans Airways Pty Ltd was registered, with Huddart [q.v.4] Parker Ltd and Union Steamship Co. Ltd as partners. Winning a Commonwealth government contract, the company began a mail service to the mainland on 1 October 1934.

On 26 October Victor and ten others were lost over Bass Strait in the recently acquired DH86, *Miss Hobart*. Captain Holyman, as Ivan was commonly known, became the governing force of the fledgling aircraft company. He initiated moves which led in November 1936 to the purchase of Holymans Airways by a consortium of Holyman Bros Pty Ltd, the Orient Steam Navigation Co. Ltd, Huddart Parker Ltd and the Adelaide Steamship Co. Ltd with its associate Adelaide Airways. The new company had been registered in Melbourne in May 1936 as Australian National Airways Pty Ltd. Ivan's brother Dare (1891-1964) became its freight manager.

Absorption of West Australian Airways enabled flights to Perth; the takeover of Airlines of Australia Ltd brought linkage to Cape York, Queensland; Sydney traffic had also been generated, making A.N.A. a nationwide organization. With the purchase of a Douglas DC2 in 1936, Holyman brought the first, modern, all-metal airliner to Australia, and he continued to upgrade his fleet with Douglas aircraft. He also introduced to Australia air hostesses, free flight-meals and the automatic insurance of passengers. An enthusiastic pioneer of the Air Beef Scheme, he built up A.N.A.'s air-freight business to be the largest in the British Commonwealth.

Under Holyman's direction A.N.A. prospered. During World War II the company provided much support to the government and armed services. In 1945 the Chifley [q.v.13] Labor government, applying its policy of acquisition of key industries, moved to nationalize the airline. Holyman fought this proposal through to the Privy Council, and won. The government's reaction was to establish a rival firm, Trans Australia Airlines, which competed for passengers and freight. In 1949 A.N.A. was floated as a public company. By 1956 it was flying 13 million miles (21 million km), carrying more than 600 000 passengers and nearly 50 000 tons of freight.

Regarded as a firm but fair business practitioner, and as a congenial and humane man, Holyman was chairman of Tasmanian Board Mill Ltd, Kilndried Hardwoods Ltd, Herd & Co. Ltd and Australian National Hotels Pty Ltd. He served on the boards of a number of other companies, including Olympic Distributors (Tasmania) Pty Ltd, National Instrument Co. Pty Ltd, Bungana Investments Pty Ltd, McIlwraith, McEacharn [qq.v.10] Ltd, Menzies Hotel Ltd and Goliath Portland Cement Co. Ltd. He was appointed K.B.E. in 1956.

Sir Ivan was a member of the Royal Melbourne and Royal Sydney golf clubs, of the Victoria and Moonee Valley racing clubs, and of the Tasmanian Turf Club; he also belonged to the Launceston Club, and, in Melbourne, to the Australian, Athenaeum, Savage, West Brighton and Naval and Military clubs. While holidaying in Honolulu, he died in his sleep on the night of 18/19 January 1957 and was cremated; his wife, daughter and two sons survived him. On 3 October that year A.N.A. was sold to Ansett Transport Industries Ltd. In 1961 the approach to Hobart airport was named Holyman Drive.

M. Hodges, *Veil of Time* (Melb, 1945); C. Turnbull, *Wings of Tomorrow* (Syd, 1945); *Aircraft* (Melb), Sept 1942; *Age* (Melb), 20 Oct 1934; *SMH*, 14 May 1936, 4 Mar 1946, 31 May 1956, 21, 23 Jan 1957; *Herald* (Melb), 10 Sept 1955, 19 Jan 1957; *Sun* (Syd), 21 Jan 1957; *Mercury* (Hob), 4 Nov 1961; Holyman family papers (Univ Melb Archives).   FRANK STRAHAN

HONE, SIR BRIAN WILLIAM (1907-1978), headmaster, was born on 1 July 1907 at Semaphore, Adelaide, son of South Australian-born parents Frank Sandland Hone [q.v.9], medical practitioner, and his wife Lucy, née Henderson. Brian was educated at Prince Alfred College, Adelaide, where he was senior prefect (1924) and captain of tennis and cricket. At the University of Adelaide (B.A. Hons, 1928) he was prominent in student life and won Blues in cricket, football and tennis. Despite a very large, almost lumbering, frame, Hone was quick on his feet and had remarkable ball sense. During the 1929-30 cricket season he opened the batting for South Australia, scoring a century against Victoria and averaging nearly 50. Solid in defence, he scored heavily off the back foot,

punching the ball with powerful forearms. He was thought to merit Test selection.

In September 1930 Hone went to New College, Oxford (B.A., 1932; M.A., 1938), on a Rhodes scholarship that led to an important friendship with Sir Francis Wylie, warden of Rhodes House. He achieved honours in English—C. S. Lewis was his tutor—through well-organized hard work, and won Blues in cricket and tennis. Twice in three years his mature batting saved the Oxford XI from defeat by Cambridge, the highlight being an innings of 167 in 1932. Next year he was a shrewd and forceful team captain.

From 1933 to 1939 Hone taught at Marlborough College, Wiltshire. Influenced by its master George Turner, he became insatiable in pursuit of good educational ideas and techniques. He hosted discussions about them long into the night, especially when made head of the new department of English. The multifaceted life of a boarding-school intrigued him, and the strength of Marlborough's music and art astonished him. His enduring love of fine printing led him to establish the Marlborough College Press in 1934. He enjoyed being in charge of things and was a meticulous games coach. Along formal English lines, but with a relaxed Australian tone and a schoolteacher's eye, he wrote *Cricket Practice and Tactics* (London, 1937). It was the height of his literary achievement.

The height of Hone's ambition was to run his own school. His father was a diligent agent in looking for openings for Brian's talents. One idea was the wardenship of the new Union House at the University of Melbourne; another, in 1936, was the headmastership of Melbourne Church of England Grammar School. When consulted, George Turner suggested to Dr Hone that Brian needed more teaching experience before tackling a demanding post. He still lacked confidence, Turner thought. Brian's letters in the early 1930s contained much doubt and self-deprecation—the obverse of his energy and drive. It was an innate modesty, with which he had always to struggle, although his marriage on 1 August 1933 to Adelaide-born Althea Enid Boyce at the parish church, Peasmarsh, Sussex, provided an antidote; she was a marvellous blend of support and chiding, respecting his total commitment to a career in education but not afraid to challenge his perceptions and strategies.

Aged only 33, after several attempts at other posts, in 1940 Hone was appointed headmaster of Cranbrook School, Sydney. Small, and in need of his vitality, it was a perfect testing-ground for his desire to apply to an Australian day-school the scholarship, house-system and cultural pursuits of a good English boarding-school. He appointed the young painter Justin O'Brien to the art school and searched for energetic, highly qualified academic staff. To instil new values, against much opposition, he debunked premierships and lowered the prestige of sporting heroes.

That blend of ideals, ideas and organization was Hone's hallmark. Whereas (Sir) James Darling's revolution among boarders at Geelong Church of England Grammar School in the 1930s could be based directly on English experience, Hone had to develop a day-school model. Time had to be stolen for optional enrichment—and staff and boys encouraged to use it well. In pursuit of skills and attitudes that would empower them as adults, he believed that boys must be 'coerced into experience'. Through concern for self-esteem, with a democratic Australian touch, he abolished streaming in all but the cumulative disciplines of languages and mathematics, and insisted that individuals be judged against their potential, not abstract standards. Houses were to be used more for pastoral care than for competitive games, and a housemaster was to be a boy's mentor throughout his time at school.

Eclectic in searching for ways to enliven and inform them, Hone almost imprisoned his staff in meetings, where they were deluged with reading material and his latest views and plans. He was a determined, though genial, taskmaster, who led by example like a team captain on the field. His own awareness of individuals was astonishing. Hone made a name for the school and himself; he was secretary (1945-52) of the Headmasters' Conference of Australia, president of the Sydney Orchestral Society in 1946 and was made a fellow of St Paul's College, University of Sydney, in 1948. His achievements were known to Bishop John McKie who told colleagues on the Melbourne Grammar School council when they were considering applications for a new headmaster in 1950 that the best man in Australia had not applied.

Although not seeking advancement, Hone accepted the challenge when offered the post. Large, celebrated, and solid as its bluestone, Melbourne Grammar was conservative, proud of elite sportsmen and scholars, but neglectful of also-rans. It was a cultural desert. Older teachers challenged Hone's philosophy, as did some senior boys and many —often powerful—former students. His desire, in particular, to reduce the prestige of sportsmen seemed to insult the school's tradition.

From February 1951 the new headmaster prepared the staff for major changes in 1952, along lines well tried at Cranbrook. Houses were revitalized, the curriculum reorganized. Overt discipline was relaxed, but routines were strengthened. Boys were to be kept busy at what interested them, whether through clubs and societies, or on cadet corps

afternoons when they were given the added options of Boy Scouts, St John Ambulance Brigade and, later, qualifying for the Duke of Edinburgh awards. In games the tyranny of cricket, football, rowing and athletics was softened by greater emphasis on tennis, swimming, hockey, Rugby Union and cross-country. The status of first teams was reduced. The uncoordinated were welcomed, just as games players were persuaded to perform in orchestras, choirs and plays. Boys were given significant tasks in the tuckshop, library, bookroom and other areas. They ran the school magazine, rejuvenated thanks to Hone's interest in printing.

Enthused by his vision, the council began an extensive building programme. Its members accepted the link between educational and financial priorities. A new era of delegation and efficiency began. Delegation was a channel for the special talents of staff, who were stretched for the benefit of the school. Hone wanted to make the most of them—as of himself. That was the meaning of life. Several times he was reduced to a state of nervous exhaustion. He recuperated with stimulating overseas visits; on a Carnegie grant in 1955, for instance, he visited sixty schools in Britain and America, made or renewed hundreds of contacts and arranged staff exchanges for years to come.

A major strategy was to attract good staff. He appointed John Brack to the art school and Donald Britton as director of music. To provide a new architectural vision he found Mockridge, Stahle & Mitchell, and involved staff in planning the buildings with special care for the laboratories, the library and a radically different common-room. The superannuation scheme was upgraded, and outside 'contract correctors' increased the efficiency of learning in the humanities. Even so, the school continued to produce many of the State's best young mathematicians and scientists. He was proud of it.

Eager for educational debate, Hone chaired (1954-57) the Headmasters' Conference. He was a founder and fellow of the Australian College of Education, and served on the councils of Monash University (deputy chancellor 1973-74) and the Australian National University, the Schools Board of the University of Melbourne and its successor, the Victorian Universities and Schools Education Board, and the council of Mercer House. With Paul McKeown, he edited a series of essays, *The Independent School* (1967).

Outside education, but important for Melbourne Grammar in terms of his contacts, were memberships of the Melbourne Club, the Melbourne Beefsteak Club, the Boobooks, the Royal South Yarra Tennis, the Wallaby and the Melbourne Cricket clubs. By sharing their political conservatism, he lived in a closed world, though he tolerated some radicals on his staff. 'Tiresome', he would call them, with one of his belly laughs and a despairing shake of his large head. His humanity was palpable, there was so much of him, bent over, perhaps, among the under-15 footballers he coached, finger pointing and arm sweeping to indicate a tactic. His philosophy was 'all care in organization; all trust in execution', but he was so keen on good results that he would often short-circuit the process with concerned interference.

Appointed O.B.E. in 1969, Hone was knighted in 1970, the year of his retirement. He then joined the Commonwealth Secondary Schools Library Committee (chairman 1971-74). Survived by his wife, daughter and three sons, Sir Brian died on 28 May 1978 while on holiday in Paris. A portrait by (Sir) Ivor Hele is held by Melbourne Grammar.

Melb C of E Grammar School, *Liber Melburniensis* (Melb, 1965); J. W. Hogg, *Our Proper Concerns* (Syd, 1986); C. E. Moorhouse, *Challenge and Response* (Melb, 1989); *Independence*, 3 July 1978; *Age* (Melb), 1 Aug 1950, 28 Feb 1969, 27 July 1978; press-cuttings, letters and other papers (held by Lady Hone, Kew, Melb).   WESTON BATE

HONEY, NEREDAH DAISY ST LEON (1879-1960), circus artiste, was born on 5 January 1879 at Carlton, Melbourne, eldest child of native-born parents Frederick Augustus Jones, circus performer, and his wife Margaret, née Leyden. Brought into the family circus, 'Baby Daisy' (aged 2) appeared with her father 'Gus St Leon' in his carrying act. She trained as an equestrienne and became 'everybody's favourite in her great firehoop act'. After settling (1896-98) at Tamworth, the family returned to circus life. Billed as 'Mademoiselle Neredah Leon, the hurricane hurdle rider', Daisy was the star equestrienne in Fitzgerald Bros' Circus in 1899-1901.

The St Leons toured the United States of America with Ringling Bros in 1902-03 and then Mexico with Trevino's Circus. At Pahuca on 10 February 1904 Daisy married Alfred George Honey (d.1970), a London-born gymnast. Following adventures in Central America with its own circus, the family returned to the U.S.A. and worked the Pantages and Orpheum vaudeville circuits. Alfred was partnered by Frank Cherry; Daisy's brothers and 'Mo' Aarons had an acrobatic act.

The two troupes, 'Honey and Cherry' and 'The 5 St. Leons', arrived in Sydney in December 1908 and took vaudeville engagements with Harry Rickards [q.v.11]. On 19 April 1909 'Gus St Leon's Great United Circus' opened under canvas at Liverpool. With 18 wagons and 40 horses, the Great United was one of Australia's leading provincial circuses. The Honeys were performers and equal partners. By 1917 Golda, their first child, had a solo, slack-wire act; her three sisters and three brothers became acrobats, and eventually perfected a spectacular, 'three high' teeterboard act. The Honeys performed in New Zealand in 1920-21 and toured Australia for the last time in 1926 with Wirth [qq.v.12] Bros Circus before sailing for the U.S.A.

They initially appeared in American circus, then settled into regular vaudeville engagements. Enhanced with dancing and comedy routines, the Honeys' acrobatic turn continued until World War II. Daisy and Alfred acquired a family home at Wyckoff, New Jersey. Golda's career ended when she fell from the wire in 1934. Having served in the United States Army, 'The Honey Brothers' had a popular nightclub act and appeared in early American television programmes. By the late 1950s they were operating a party-boat on the south coast of California; their sister Florence ('Coochie') had her own troupe of all-female acrobats in 1963.

Through changing fortunes, Daisy dominated her family. Five ft 3 ins (160 cm) tall and rather stocky in build, with hazel eyes and dark brown hair, she possessed a 'crackly' personality, a sharp sense of humour and a 'deep, hearty laugh'. She liked wearing hats or turbans. While accompanying her children on endless circuits of vaudeville theatres and county fairs, she wrote light verse. Her letters were chatty and mostly 'upbeat', even when things were not going well. In the 1950s Daisy and Alfred retired to southern California. Survived by her husband and children, she died on 8 June 1960 at Oxnard and was buried in the Ivy Lawn cemetery.

M. St Leon (comp), *The Circus in Australia 1842-1921* (Syd, 1981), *Spangles and Sawdust* (Melb, 1983) and *The Silver Road* (Springwood, NSW, 1990); *Variety* (NY), 12 June 1909; *Theatre* (Syd), 1 Aug 1913; *Examiner* (Launc), 26 Feb 1881; *Western Herald*, 16 Nov 1895; *Bulletin*, 21 July 1900; *SMH*, 6 Feb 1909; *Argus*, 13 Feb 1909; *NZ Herald*, 26 Dec 1920; information from Mr M. King, Glebe, Syd, Mrs Z. H. Honey, Davie, Florida, and Mrs P. D. Thomas, Morrison, Colorado, US, and the late Mr A. and Mrs S. St Leon.

MARK VALENTINE ST LEON

HONNER, RICHARD ST JOHN (1897-1962), surgeon and athlete, was born on 30 November 1897 at Maitland, South Australia, eldest of four children of William Honner, a farmer from England, and his wife Ellen Mary Dominic, née Moloney, a schoolteacher. His father later bought a property at Junee, New South Wales, where Dick's love for the land

and horses was bred in him. Inheriting a talent for music from his mother, he developed a lifelong love for the violin, and gained a medal (1913) and a licentiate (1916) from the London College of Music. After primary schooling at Junee, he attended St Joseph's College, Hunters Hill, Sydney, and entered St John's College, University of Sydney (M.B., Ch.M., 1922). He was resident medical officer (1922-23) at St Vincent's Hospital under Sir Alexander MacCormick and (Sir) John McKelvey [qq.v.10].

With characteristic enthusiasm, Honner spent vacations at Junee where he trained as a hurdler and long-jumper on makeshift tracks and pits. He became the Australian and New South Wales long-jump champion. Chosen to compete in the 1924 Olympic Games, he kept a detailed diary of his journey to France and his time there. On reaching Paris, he wrote: 'We are dismayed and heart-broken . . . [with] no ground to train on . . . what a frightful handicap we are up against!' He did his 'worst jump for the last 7 years' and was unplaced.

Embarking with zest upon postgraduate studies at the Middlesex (1924), Poplar and London (1925-27) hospitals, Honner qualified L.R.C.P., London, and M.R.C.S., England, in 1925. He devoted one day a week to athletic training. On 16 June 1926 at the Crystal Palace he broke the 37-year-old British record with a jump of 24 ft 4½ ins (7.43 m). Back in Sydney, on 14 April 1928 at St John's College chapel he married Kathleen Mary Dooley. That year he was appointed honorary gynaecologist at Lewisham Hospital, and in 1931 surgeon and honorary obstetrician at St Margaret's Hospital. While abroad in 1936, he was elected F.R.C.S., Edinburgh, and next year became a fellow of the Royal Australasian College of Surgeons.

On 19 February 1942 Honner was mobilized as a major in the Australian Army Medical Corps. He served in military hospitals, principally at Goulburn and at Alice Springs, Northern Territory. From 1946 he rapidly built up one of the largest obstetric practices in Sydney. His deeply held Catholicism was closely linked with his devotion to medicine: fearless and forthright in the expression of his convictions, he was widely respected for his integrity. Honner's membership of the Medical Guild of St Luke provided him with a forum where he wielded considerable influence. In a series of letters in the guild's *Transactions* he rebutted the views of Dr John Duhig of Brisbane—a free-thinker and fierce critic of Catholic beliefs—with spirit and clarity, disregarding his opponent's disparaging references to himself.

Honner's friends recognized his dynamism and vitality, as well as his mercurial temperament. Although he indulged in humorous sallies and witty repartee, he balanced this side of his nature by a quiet reserve, sensitivity and compassion. His quickness of speech and movement gave rise to his nickname, 'the Tin Hare'. He lived at Woollahra, belonged to the Australian Jockey Club and set up the Marian Pastoral Co. Pty Ltd. While addressing his colleagues at a dinner in the Australia Hotel, he collapsed and died of myocardial infarction on 10 November 1962. Survived by his wife, son and three daughters, he was buried in Waverley cemetery.

St Joseph's College Annual, 1915, p 81, 1916, p 26; *Cerise and Blue*, 1924, p 27; *Transactions of the Medical Guild of St Luke*, no 14, 1963, p 7; *MJA*, 27 Apr 1963, p 634; *Sun* (Syd), 8, 12 May, 2 June 1924; *SMH*, 16 Aug 1924, 28 June 1926; *The Times*, 17, 28 June 1926; *Catholic Weekly*, 20 Dec 1962; R. Honner file, series 71, item 665 (Archives of Roy A'sian College of Surgeons, Syd); R. Honner correspondence (held by Mr D. Honner, Jugiong, NSW).

LEILA BARLOW

HOOK, ALFRED SAMUEL (1886-1963), architect and professor, was born on 24 July 1886 at Heston, Middlesex, England, son of Harry Hook, an 'oil and colourman', and his wife Catherine Elizabeth, née Ashford. After the family moved to Bournemouth, Alfred was educated at Boscombe and at the East Bournemouth Science, Art and Technical School; he later studied architecture in London and qualified as an associate of the Royal College of Art.

An established, if impoverished, architect who found the strain of depending on a small private practice injurious to his health, Hook arrived at Cairns, Queensland, in 1909. He worked for the architect Hervey Draper, but from February 1910 was employed as a draughtsman in the Department of Public Works, Brisbane. On 25 July that year he married 29-year-old Alice Guppy with Methodist forms at the city's Young Men's Christian Association building. Moving to Sydney in 1912, he became a draughtsman with the government architect where he remained for fourteen years and rose to designing architect. Among his projects was the structural design of the steel reinforcement for the country trains concourse at Central Railway Station.

Hook contributed to the foundation of the faculty of architecture at the University of Sydney in 1918 and to the development of its curriculum. From 1922 he lectured there part time. Appointed associate professor of architectural practice and construction in 1926, he was 'the practical man' of the faculty, highly regarded by his students as a lucid exponent of structural mechanics. His book on that subject, written for rural students sitting for the Board of Architects' examinations, was available in manuscript form for some years before its publication in 1943.

His practical approach was also evident in the way he endeavoured to improve architects' salaries and working conditions through the Architects' Association of New South Wales, a group formed as a rival to the conservative Institute of Architects of New South Wales. Elected association president in 1922, Hook helped to reunite the two professional bodies, becoming vice-president of the reconstituted institute in 1924 and president in 1926. Intermittently a member (from 1925) of the Board of Architects, he favoured increasing its powers over matters of practice, professional relations and training so as to free the institute to educate public taste and develop architecture as an 'art vital to people's prosperity'. Because small homes constituted 95 per cent of building enterprise, he reasoned that they should be the focus of architects' attention for they constituted 'a national style' through the sheer weight of their numbers. Rather than the highly ornamented designs beloved by builders in the 1920s, Hook preferred quiet, dignified proportion, balance and restraint. He set up a scheme whereby institute members would provide designs at low cost to those building houses on a modest budget.

A founder of the Royal Australian Institute of Architects which was established to foster national uniformity of architectural practice and status, Hook became its inaugural president in 1929 and its first life fellow (1932). He carried that organization almost single-handed through the Depression and World War II, holding the honorary positions of secretary, treasurer and registrar—sometimes simultaneously—until he retired in 1947.

During the war Hook urged boys and girls leaving school to consider studying architecture in order to prepare for 'an era of building and rebuilding such as had never been seen before'. As professor of architectural practice and construction (1946-51) and dean (1948-49), he oversaw much of the intensified postwar training for ex-servicemen and women. Outside the university, he advised the trustees of the Anzac Memorial, Hyde Park, served many years on the Building Appeals Board (chairman from 1942), arbitrated building disputes and was a long-term member of the executive-committee of the Standards Association of Australia.

Always ready to acknowledge the contribution of a broad range of arts to architecture, Hook was a man of diverse talents. From 1936 to 1945 he gave regular lunch-hour talks on the history of music, using gramophone records given to the university by the Carnegie Corporation of New York. He was a member of the Sydney University Musical Society's choral group and a keen amateur organist who was associated with the installation of the university's War Memorial Carillon (1928) and the foundation of the department of music (1948). A speaker of great wit and charm, Hook was also an accomplished writer; in his retirement he wrote a detective story, *The Coatine Case* (London, 1953), under the pseudonym 'A. J. Colton'. He died at his Randwick home on 19 June 1963 and was cremated with Anglican rites; his wife, son and daughter survived him.

J. M. Freeland, *The Making of a Profession* (Syd, 1971); *J of the Inst of Architects of NSW*, May 1925, p 4, Aug 1925, pp 1-26, June 1926, p 19; *J of the Roy Aust Inst of Architects*, Aug 1925, p 15; *Architecture*, Mar 1926, p 12, Aug 1926, pp 10, 19; *Architecture in Aust*, 52, no 3, Sept 1963, p 156; Univ Syd Union, *Union Recorder*, 1 Aug 1963, p 185; *SMH*, 3-4 Feb, 3 Mar, 2 June, 13 Dec 1926, 30 Sept 1927, 14 Apr, 26 Sept 1928, 3 Jan, 18 Sept 1929, 22 Jan 1930, 8 Sept 1934, 2 Mar 1938, 18 Mar 1939, 10, 23 Dec 1943, 14, 16-17 Mar, 1 Sept 1945, 14 Dec 1954, 9 June 1957, 15 Aug 1959, 5 Aug 1962; Faculty of Architecture Minutes, 1920-1950 *and* an obituary of A. S. Hook (Univ Syd Archives); information from Dr P. Reynolds, Balmain, Syd.

ROSEMARY BROOMHAM

HOOKE, SIR LIONEL GEORGE ALFRED (1895-1974), broadcasting pioneer, radio engineer and businessman, was born on 31 December 1895 at St Kilda, Melbourne, fourth child of Frank William Hooke, a tea merchant from England, and his Victorian-born wife Ethel Margaret, née Kelly. Educated at Brighton Grammar School, where he was a sergeant in the cadets and 'an ardent student of wireless telegraphy', Lionel joined the Marconi company as a marine wireless operator in 1913. In the following year Marconi merged its Australasian interests with those of the Telefunken company to form a new organization, Amalgamated Wireless (Australasia) Ltd.

On Christmas Day 1914 Hooke sailed from Hobart as wireless operator on board the *Aurora* which carried the support party for Sir Ernest Shackleton's proposed crossing of the Antarctic continent. In March 1915 the ship was moored in McMurdo Sound for the winter. An ice-field formed around her. On 6 May it began to move, severing her mooring lines and carrying her northwards. She was trapped in the drifting floes until the ice melted in February 1916. After enduring appalling conditions and attempting to operate inadequate equipment for more than ten months, in March Hooke established contact with the outside world.

Under tow, *Aurora* reached New Zealand

in April. There, he received news that his elder brother Frank had been killed at Gallipoli. Lionel sailed for England and was commissioned in the Royal Naval Volunteer Reserve on 15 December. He served in anti-submarine vessels, commanded armed tugs and later qualified as a pilot. A wartime photograph shows him as an authoritative and confident figure, posed characteristically with one hand in his jacket pocket and sporting the white ribbon of the Polar medal. In 1918 he transferred to the Royal Air Force.

Soon after his return to A.W.A. in 1919, Hooke was promoted Melbourne manager of the Sydney-based company. Recognizing the potential of wireless telephony, in 1920 he helped A.W.A.'s general manager (Sir) Ernest Fisk [q.v.8] to arrange a direct transmission of musical items from Hooke's home at Middle Brighton to Federal Parliament House in the city. The technical achievements of the demonstration were the result of Hooke's drive and initiative, as were the more sophisticated transmissions in 1921-22 which preceded A.W.A.'s announcement that it intended to begin commercial broadcasting.

Under the 1922 Wireless Agreement between the Federal government and A.W.A., the Commonwealth assumed a controlling interest in the firm. In return, the government provided additional capital, promoted A.W.A.'s concept of direct wireless telegraphy between Australia and Britain, and transferred Australia's coastal radio stations to the company. Hooke was in his element with the coastal radio operation, reorganizing and re-equipping the stations. He loved the sea, and travelled abroad by ship whenever possible; on land, he was a motoring enthusiast. His automatic distress transmitter (patented in 1929) improved safety at sea by enabling emergency wireless messages to be sent from ships that did not carry an operator.

In 1925 he was transferred to Sydney as deputy general manager and assisted with the inauguration in 1927 of the profitable beam-wireless telegraph service. He and Fisk formed a close professional relationship, with Hooke gradually assuming a larger executive role. During their partnership A.W.A. acquired an international reputation. At St Andrew's Anglican Church, Brighton, Melbourne, on 15 February 1930 Hooke married Eilleen Clarice Sparks, an actress and a divorcee who had reverted to her maiden name.

He guided A.W.A.'s entry into the manufacture and marketing of the 'Radiola' wireless broadcast receiver. With David Sarnoff, of the Radio Corporation of America, Hooke negotiated a joint venture between A.W.A. and R.C.A. to manufacture radio valves at the Ashfield works of Amalgamated Wireless Valve Co. Pty Ltd, a subsidiary of A.W.A. In World War II the valve company produced defence matériel, including klystrons and magnetrons for radar equipment.

When Fisk retired in 1944, Hooke took over as managing director and faced the difficult task of reorganizing the company whose peacetime staff of 3000 had more than doubled. Unpopular decisions—contrary to A.W.A.'s tradition of continuity of employment—had to be made if it were to remain profitable. He gained the best possible financial outcome for A.W.A. in the negotiations that followed the Commonwealth Telecommunications Conference (1945) which obligated the Australian government to take over the beam wireless service.

Hooke was knighted in 1957 and became chairman of A.W.A. in 1962. He presided over the company's decisions to manufacture television transmitters, television receivers and micro-electronics equipment, and to expand its research into solid-state electronics and optical-fibre communications. Within the company he was held in such regard that it sometimes verged on awe and reverence. Admired for his loyalty to A.W.A. and for the concern he showed for its staff, he appreciated the importance of being visible to all. His visits to the company's factories, his attendance at Christmas parties and his presence at annual balls reinforced the image of a kindly, unfailingly polite and considerate man who was able to inspire his employees.

A senior member (1943) and life senior member (1965) of the Institute of Radio Engineers (later Institute of Electrical and Electronics Engineers Inc.), New York, Hooke wrote several papers and supported the *A.W.A. Technical Review* which published articles by his research staff. He was a director of other public companies, including Kandos Cement Co. Ltd, a fellow (1959-69) of the senate of the University of Sydney, chairman of the electronics and telecommunications industry advisory committee and vice-president (1954-58) of the Chamber of Manufactures of New South Wales. Hooke died on 17 February 1974 at St Leonards and was cremated; he was survived by his wife and son John who succeeded him as chairman of A.W.A. At a memorial service for Sir Lionel at St James's Anglican Church, Sydney, his friend of forty years Monsignor James Delaney delivered the address.

AWA Ltd, *In Memoriam* (Syd, 1974) and *Address by the Chairman of the Bd*, 36th Ordinary General Meeting (Syd, 1944) and *Managing Director's Review*, Annual General Meeting (Syd, 1945); L. Bickel, *Shackleton's Forgotten Argonauts* (Melb, 1982); E. Harcourt, *Taming the Tyrant* (Syd, 1987); *SMH*, 19, 23 Feb 1974; Brighton Grammar School (Melb) Archives.   L. W. DAVIES

HOOKER, SIR LESLIE JOSEPH (1903-1976), real-estate developer, was born on 18 August 1903 at Canterbury, Sydney, son of Nellie Tingyou. From the age of 8 Leslie was raised by Sylvia Pemberton whom he called 'aunt', although she was no relation. Educated in public schools at Canterbury and Beecroft, he began work at 13 in a Japanese import and export company, Mitsui Bussan Kaisha Ltd, before being employed as an assistant-purser in Burns, Philp [qq.v.7,11] & Co. Ltd's ship, *Mataram*, which traded in the Pacific. Back in Sydney, he tried to take advantage of an economic boom, but his first real-estate business, operating out of Martin Place, failed in the mid-1920s.

Leslie changed his surname by deed poll from Tingyou to Hooker in February 1925. He opened a real-estate agency, L. J. Hooker Ltd, at Maroubra in 1928. At St Philip's Anglican Church, Sydney, on 23 June 1934 he married Madeline Adella Price, daughter of a storekeeper. Surviving the Depression, Hooker's agency flourished; by the mid-1930s he had hired his first salesman and opened an office in O'Connell Street in the city. In 1936 he bought the rent roll of Woods & Co., with offices at Kensington and Kingsford. Two years later he moved his headquarters to 98 Pitt Street and in 1939 opened another office at Randwick.

L. J. Hooker Ltd was listed on the Sydney Stock Exchange in July 1947, posting the best real-estate turnover for any company that year. The firm rode the wave of postwar reconstruction, supplying subdivided blocks to land-hungry owner-builders throughout Sydney. In addition, Hooker acquired a taste for taking over suburban real-estate agencies, and for buying hotels in Sydney and country towns through a network of family companies and Rex Investments Ltd (registered 1938, floated as a public company 1948). He gave evidence to the royal commission of inquiry into the liquor laws (1951-54) about his hotel licences and connexion with Tooth [qq.v.6] & Co. Ltd.

Hooker's real-estate activities, including his takeover bids and overseas trips, proved newsworthy. Although he himself seldom contributed to public debate, he did call for the abolition of rent control, arguing that there was little incentive for developers to build new blocks of flats in Sydney when older ones were full of tenants on fixed rents. In 1955 he formed what became Hooker Rex Pty Ltd to embark on developments at Batemans Bay, on the old racecourse in the Sydney suburb of Kogarah and on Queensland's Gold Coast. In 1958 he changed the company's name to L. J. Hooker Investment Corporation Ltd (Hooker Corporation Ltd from 1968) and in 1959 he established Australian Landtrusts Pty Ltd. That year *Nation*

described Hooker as 'the most efficient selling agent of urban real estate in Australian history': the article explained part of his success by the way in which he had recruited young, trained, 'executive-type' salesmen and by his securing two knights, Sir Arthur Fadden and Sir Neil O'Sullivan [qq.v.], as directors of some of his companies.

Continuing to expand, Hooker's perfected the technique of buying undervalued companies that were in financial trouble, keeping their best assets and disposing of the rest. In 1959-60, its greatest takeover year, the firm's main acquisitions included City Investments Ltd (a Brisbane finance company), G. H. Thomas Pty Ltd, Accommodation Australia Ltd (with seven motels), Australian Wool Brokers & Produce Co. Ltd, Mainguard (Australia) Ltd (including Festival Records Pty Ltd), and W. L. Buckland's [q.v.13] pastoral empire with vast holdings in the Northern Territory, Western Australia, Queensland and New South Wales. Hooker took delight in personally announcing these takeovers, and in the fact that—in the larger acquisitions—his company made almost no capital payments, but instead offered shareholders options to buy shares at par in Hooker's at a future date.

Having presided over one of the most breathtaking expansion programmes in Australia's corporate history and been fêted as the nation's 'biggest landholder', Hooker was happy to be publicized as the Sydney financier who rounded off the week by going for a swim. In an expansive mood, he told the *Sydney Morning Herald* that 'Australia is roaring ahead and it is up to us to keep pace with this development ... If we, as an Australian company, don't keep this pace then overseas interests will only too gladly take our place'.

The Menzies [q.v.] government's credit squeeze in November 1961 hit the Hooker corporation which posted its first ever loss in the financial year 1961-62. The company's many subsidiaries had compounded the problem by using short-term borrowing to finance long-term commitments. (Sir) Keith Campbell, a 32-year-old businessman whom Hooker had recruited from his Thomas homes takeover in 1960, became acting general manager in 1962, charged with the financial survival of the company. Unable to raise money locally, Campbell eventually secured backing in the United States of America in 1964, and brought the company to a healthy profit by 1968. The two men got on well. Hooker reputedly 'enjoyed being the front man, the one who attended to the cocktail party circuit but who needed someone back in the office'.

On announcing his retirement from executive positions in the company in 1969, Hooker said: 'I have an instinct, a sixth sense for choosing well in real estate', adding that his recipe for success was to be born with a businessman's brain, to be 'tenacious and determined', and not to believe in bad luck. He observed that parts of Maroubra that he sold in his youth had come to be regarded as treeless and ugly, but he reflected with pride on his company's 'model estates' in the North Shore suburbs of Castle Cove, Killarney and Winston Hills.

Hooker lived at Mosman and belonged to a number of Sydney's leading clubs—Tattersall's, the Australian Jockey and the Sydney Turf clubs. He was a director (1945-64) of Sydney Hospital (vice-president 1965-76), a life governor of the Royal New South Wales Institute for Deaf and Blind Children, and president (1970) of the Council for Integrated Deaf Education. In 1973 he was knighted. Survived by his wife, daughter and two sons, Sir Leslie died on 29 April 1976 at St Vincent's Hospital, Darlinghurst, and was cremated. An agnostic, but 'born a Catholic', he received a requiem Mass in St Mary's Cathedral. By the time of his death he had more than 170 branches throughout Australia, their distinctive red and yellow signs a hallmark of real-estate activity. The Hooker Corporation went into liquidation after the property crash of the late 1980s, but his name survived in a system of over four hundred franchised real-estate outlets.

The name of Hooker had become synonymous with real-estate development. Obituaries portrayed him as a 'champion' of the industry and as a 'great salesman'. In his heyday in the 1950s and 1960s Hooker was criticized for his pro-development push and satirized in Frank Hardy's *Outcasts of Foolgarah* (1971) as 'L. J. Hookem', a self-made, upright philanthropist who exploited black labour on his pastoral properties in the North and was 'the greatest single cause of inflated land prices in the South'.

R. T. Appleyard and C. B. Schedvin (eds), *Australian Financiers* (Melb, 1988); *SMH*, 19 Jan 1956, 8 May 1960, 2 June 1973, 1 May 1976, 13 Mar 1985; *Nation* (Syd), 5 Dec 1959; *Aust Financial Review*, 21 Jan 1960; *Observer* (Syd), 28 May 1960; *Sun-Herald*, 9 Feb 1969; *Bulletin*, 1 Mar 1975; information from Mr D. Hooker, Portland, NSW, and Mr P. Lightfoot, Taringa, Brisb.

PETER SPEARRITT

HOOTON, HARRIET (1875-1960), women's activist and editor, was born on 13 July 1875 at Biraganbil, near Gulgong, New South Wales, second daughter of Thomas Hooton, a miner from England, and his Victorian-born wife Louisa, née Howson (d.1923). Educated at state schools at Geelong, Victoria, Ettie moved to Kalgoorlie, Western Australia, in the 1890s. In 1908 she joined the Perth branch of the Australian Natives' Association. A foundation member of the Women's Service Guild, the National Council of Women of Western Australia and the Perth branch of the Australian Labor Federation (from 1916), she worked hard on their executive-committees.

In 1920 Hooton attended the initial meeting of the Western Australian Parents' and Citizens' Association and became its first secretary. She organized its annual conferences which addressed such issues as the need for better medical and dental attention for school children, the benefits of new technology and 'cinema' in schools, requests for free uniforms and free textbooks, the provision of hostels for children from the country districts, and the pursuit of nature-study and the promotion of arbour days. Hooton travelled to London in 1924 and claimed to have attended the British Labor Women's Conference as a fraternal delegate. She also visited the League of Nations Assembly and the International Labour Office in Geneva. Her trip broadened her vision and heightened her interest in internationalism and world peace.

Back at Mount Hawthorn, a working-class suburb of Perth, she shared with her stepfather the house she had inherited from her mother. As secretary of the Mount Hawthorn Progress Association, she endeavoured to have a local kindergarten established. For some fifteen years from June 1926, she published the monthly *Parents' and Citizens' Broadcaster* from her home. In 1927 she began to edit the women's page of the *Westralian Worker*, using the pseudonym, 'Vision'.

Hooton's honorary secretaryship (1927-47) of the Labor Women's Central Executive involved her in conferences and deputations. The issues which most concerned her and her peers included equal pay for women, better health care for mothers and babies, kindergartens, free milk and free schoolbooks for children, better housing and world peace. Like many other Labor women, she opposed conscription in World War I and was subsequently against compulsory military training. During the Depression she was secretary to Bessie Rischbieth [q.v.11], president of the Citizens' Committee for the Relief of Unemployed Girls. Appointed a justice of the peace (1936), Hooton unsuccessfully sought preselection as a Labor candidate for the Senate in 1937. When May Holman [q.v.9] died in 1939, she took over as president of the Federation of Parents' and Citizens' Associations.

More a Martha than a Mary, Miss Hooton

was a stalwart campaigner for those causes she discovered through women's organizations and the Labor movement. After World War II a new generation of parents and young teachers found her a fine example of the old guard, but with ideas increasingly irrelevant to their world. She died on 21 April 1960 in North Perth and was cremated with Presbyterian forms.

Parents' and Citizens' Broadcaster, vol 1, no 1, June 1926-vol 29, no 111, June-Aug 1939; *Westralian Worker*, 19 Feb 1937; *West Australian*, 5, 7 Aug 1954, 23 Apr 1960; *WA Parent and Citizen*, May 1960, Oct 1971; Records of Education Dept of WA *and* Labor Party *and* Women's Service Guild *and* National Council of Women of WA (WAA); Annual Conference of Parents' and Citizens' Associations, 1922 (BL); Aust Natives Assn records (Perth branch, Mosman Park); information from Mrs M. C. Williams and Mr A. C. Staples, Perth.

MICHAL BOSWORTH

HOOTON, HENRY ARTHUR (HARRY) (1908-1961), poet and philosopher, was born on 9 October 1908 at Doncaster, Yorkshire, England, son of Levi Hooton, railway shunter, and his wife Margaret, née Lester Glaister. Sent to a socialist Sunday School, Harry also attended (1922-23) Christ's College, Finchley. He was brought to Australia by the Dreadnought Trust and reached Sydney in the *Demosthenes* on 28 October 1924 with fifty-nine other boys.

Harry left the Government Agricultural Training Farm, Scheyville, in June 1925 at the age of 17 to carry his swag, 'or rather my port', around Queensland and northern New South Wales. Convicted of unarmed robbery, he spent about eighteen months in Maitland gaol. He eventually settled at Newcastle where, on 3 November 1936 at St John's Anglican Church, he married a clerk Thora Zilma Isabel Hatch who bore him twins. They moved house frequently and were later to separate. Hooton started his serious writing, but finding and keeping work were recurring problems. He took relief work and labouring jobs, sold photographs door-to-door, and wrote of one factory in which he was employed, 'The Egg Board broke my heart'.

Initially a Trotskyist, Hooton participated in the unemployed people's strike at Newcastle in 1939. As a provocative commentator on local and international affairs, he voiced his anarchist opinions in the *Newcastle Morning Herald and Miner's Advocate*. Consequently, he was one of thousands of suspects who were kept under surveillance and was raided by the security police in 1940.

These Poets, Hooton's first book of poetry, was published in 1941. It was widely praised by reviewers, among them P. R. Stephensen [q.v.12] in the *Publicist*. Hooton loved correspondence. His earliest extant letters date from 1936 and were written to Marie Pitt [q.v.11], but his correspondents included Ian Mudie, Rex Ingamells [qq.v.], Max Harris, Oliver Somerville, Harold Stewart, Ted Turner, Clem Christesen and Miles Franklin [q.v.8]. The English writer John Hargraves described Hooton's letters as 'crammed tight with single-spaced margin-crowded eye-swivelling sight-blinding a-to-z key bashing'.

Moving to Sydney in 1943, Hooton accepted a position with Brian Penton [q.v.] on the *Daily Telegraph*. He walked out during the journalists' strike of October 1944 and never returned, taking odd jobs and mainly surviving through the generosity of friends. *Things You See When You Haven't Got a Gun* was published in 1943, but his philosophical writings were ridiculed by local critics. Meanwhile, he produced what he hoped would be a far-sighted, alternative literary magazine. The first issue was roneoed, called simply *No.1* (1943), and contained poems by A. D. Hope and Garry Lyle. A year later *NUMBER TWO* appeared and in 1948 *Number Three*. In 1950 and 1951 Hooton worked on three issues of *MS*.

Never a modernist in the accepted sense, he attacked James Joyce most vehemently. After conflicting with Professor John Anderson [q.v.7], Hooton wrote: 'If someone outside university has an original idea, he's a crank; if someone inside a university has an original idea, it'll be a miracle'. He was influenced by Oscar Wilde's essay, *The Soul of Man Under Socialism*, and produced a four-page pamphlet, *Anarcho-Technocracy* (c.1951).

In 1952 Hooton met Margaret Elliott (later Fink) with whom he lived for seven years at Potts Point. They held regular Sunday soirées. Hooton loved fierce discussion, though often in a humorous and gentle way. There, and in many Sydney coffee shops, he continued to talk, write poetry and work on his unpublished philosophical treatise, 'Militant Materialism'. He contacted like-minded people in Japan, India, South Africa, England, France, New Zealand and the United States of America to aid the creation of what Hooton would call the best magazine in the world—*21st Century, The Magazine of a Creative Civilization*, which appeared in 1955 and 1957. He had another book published in San Francisco, *Power Over Things* (1955).

Moving to Melbourne in 1960, Hooton sorted mail at the General Post Office. Diagnosed as terminally ill with cancer, he was brought back to Sydney by his friends in time to see proof copies of his last book, *It is Great to be Alive* (1961). On his deathbed, he made eleven half-hour tape-recordings. Survived by his son and daughter, he died on 27 June 1961 and was cremated.

S. Soldatow, *Harry Hooton* (Syd, 1990); *Quadrant*, Mar 1993; *National Times*, 24 Aug-1 Sept 1979; Dreadnought Trust, Minute-books, registers of boys and ships (ML); Hooton papers (ML, NL, Meanjin Archives, Univ Melb).

SASHA SOLDATOW

HOPE, JOHN (1891-1971), Anglican clergyman, was born on 5 January 1891 at Strathfield, Sydney, youngest son and tenth child of Charles Hope, a Victorian-born woolbroker, and his wife Mary Hooper, née Kebble, from New Zealand. The family had some distinguished members, including Rev. Samuel Marsden [q.v.2] and the historian Manning Clark. John was educated at Ashfield Collegiate and Sydney Grammar schools. For a year he worked for the New Zealand & Australian Land Co., but the influence of the High-Church rector of Burwood was inclining him towards holy orders.

Full-time duty as missioner and catechist at Burwood was followed by training at St John's Theological College, Melbourne. There Hope was grounded in Gore's incarnational theology and the Anglo-Catholic ideals of social justice. He returned to Sydney, where Evangelical churchmanship generally prevailed, and was made deacon on 12 July 1914 and ordained priest on 17 December 1915 by Archbishop Wright [q.v.12]: 'the most unfortunate thing I ever did', that sorely tried prelate would later admit.

At the time of his deaconing, Hope was engaged to be married. But he was to remain a bachelor, less by inclination than by circumstance. He was a well-set, handsome man, sometimes brusque, yet with charm of manner and a deep understanding of people. Many causes were to claim his support and he took them up rather than analysed them. His preaching was more forthright than eloquent, his mind agile but not intellectual in its leanings. Totally regardless of personal comfort, he was a strident upholder of the poor, and an enemy of smugness and irresponsible wealth.

Hope's first curacy, at middle-class Randwick, did not inspire him. He failed to become a military chaplain, then moved in 1916 to the Anglo-Catholic city parish of Christ Church St Laurence. A breakdown in health led him to accept the sympathetic Archbishop Donaldson's [q.v.8] offer of the Brisbane parish of Clifton. After six years additional experience, Hope returned to Christ Church, first in an acting capacity and, from 1926, as rector.

The old, Gothic-style church in what had slowly become the unfashionable end of the city was to be his final parish. He sought no preferment and was given none. The state appointed him M.B.E. in 1956, the church gave him nothing. In time, however, Hope gained a place of great influence and respect, of affection and notoriety, revered by some, execrated by others—a unique figure in the Church of England in Sydney and a distinguished one beyond. Under his firm leadership, Christ Church adopted the most advanced form of Anglo-Catholic theology and worship. Indeed, Hope went further than most others in England and Australia, using the 'Sarum rite' and the full array of Catholic practice.

While this made Christ Church a vigorous Anglo-Catholic centre, drawing worshippers from afar and influential throughout Australia, it aroused fierce opposition in the increasingly Evangelical Sydney diocese. Hope coped with the barrage of criticism with equanimity. From the mid-1930s he adroitly countered the diocesan synod's efforts to curtail the income from the property of the defunct Christ Church schools. It was a war of attrition that involved court action and interminable synod debates. Hope was a shrewd campaigner, despite his air of simplicity and unworldliness. Eventually, the pressure relaxed in the last years of Archbishop Mowll [q.v.].

At first Hope used open-air missions, complete with liturgical processions, in his parish near Central Railway Station. Throughout his rectorship, his house was open to a motley array of visitors; Bea Miles [q.v.10] often slept on the doorstep. The Christ Church 'Cheeros' for the lonely and destitute became legendary, as did its hospitality for servicemen. Known to his parishioners as Father John, he preached vigorous, blunt sermons on behalf of social justice—pragmatic rather than doctrinaire. He supported Rev. Alf Clint's [q.v.13] work among Aborigines and gave him a house, Tranby, at Glebe. While his church attracted many among the well-to-do, Hope was at heart a slum parson who saw spiritual healing as complementary to his high sacramental worship.

With the advent of Archbishop Gough, Hope retired in 1964 in the knowledge that a sympathetic successor would be secured. Full of years and famous in his generation, he died on 21 June 1971 in Royal North Shore Hospital and was cremated. He left the residue of his estate, sworn for probate at $27 812, to the Order of St Luke the Physician (Australasia).

L. M. Allen, *A History of Christ Church S. Laurence, Sydney* (Syd, 1939); L. C. Rodd, *John Hope of Christ Church* (Syd, 1972); C of E (Syd), *Syd Diocesan Synod Reports*, 1926-64; *SMH*, 31 May 1956, 9 Feb 1964, 14 Dec 1971, 8 Dec 1973; *Australian*, 27 June 1971.   K. J. CABLE

HOPE, LAURA MARGARET (1868-1952), medical practitioner, was born on 3 May 1868 at Mitcham, Adelaide, second of four children of Scottish-born parents George Swan Fowler [q.v.4], grocer, and his wife Janet, née Lamb, both liberal-minded Baptists. Laura was educated privately in Adelaide, England and Germany. Slender, with blue eyes and brown hair, she hid a sense of fun beneath a precise, composed manner. She and her favourite brother James shared strong religious beliefs and a love of reading. On the family estate, Wootton Lea, Glen Osmond, she helped her father to breed leeches for sale to pharmacists. In 1887 she became the first female to enrol in medicine at the University of Adelaide (M.B., Ch.B., 1891); her graduation was applauded by the chancellor (Sir) Samuel Way [q.v.12] and by women suffragists.

In 1892 Dr Fowler was appointed resident medical officer at the Adelaide Children's Hospital for a term of twelve months: the board agreed that 'the spirit of the rules of the Hospital will not be violated by the appointment of a lady'. She performed her duties with 'diligence and ability'. Her application to join the local branch of the British Medical Association was 'the immediate cause' of admission for women.

Influenced by Rev. Silas Mead's [q.v.5] missionary fervour, Laura experienced a 'call' and persuaded her fiancé Dr CHARLES HENRY STANDISH HOPE (1861-1942) to accompany her to India; Mead married them on 4 July 1893 at Wootton Lea and they sailed for Bengal as self-supporting medical missionaries. Laura dedicated her life to this work and to the care of her husband who was 'often poorly'. She and Charles co-operated with other missionaries, mainly at the South Australian Baptist Mission at Pubna where they began. From dawn 'Dr Memsahib' treated queues of patients at the dispensary and visited women in their zenanas, often cycling in her pith helmet. She was welcome wherever she went. Both doctors learned Bengali and Hindi, and took private patients. Charles won repute for eye surgery. Freed from domestic tasks, Laura occasionally participated in mission work and studied plants. James Fowler administered her ample private income and marriage settlement; in their long, affectionate correspondence she sometimes ended her letters, 'Your little sister Smiler'.

In summer the Hopes usually retreated to the hills, or travelled to England or Australia. Following a European holiday, both studied in England at the Liverpool School of Tropical Medicine in 1902. Laura then worked at the New Zealand Baptist Mission Hospital, Chandpur, India. They frequently treated typhoid, cholera and malaria cases. In 1907-09 the Hopes practised at the Bengal Baptist Mission at Kalimpong in the Himalayan foothills; they spent a year at Nairne in the Adelaide Hills before returning to Pubna. In 1914 Laura took medical charge of the Presbyterian St Andrew's Colonial Homes, Kalimpong, which housed over five hundred Anglo-Indian and neglected children.

Again in England, in 1915 the Hopes joined the Scottish Women's Hospitals for Foreign Service and were sent to Serbia where they directed a unit that treated wounded soldiers. Captured in November, they were transported to Hungary by cattle truck and imprisoned for two months. They eventually reached England in 1916, recuperated, and resumed work in Kalimpong. Laura and Charles were each awarded the Serbian Samaritan Cross in 1918. That year Laura left Kalimpong with a woman missionary and travelled by pony for two weeks over steep hills, ministering to fourteen scattered Christian 'parishes'; she came back refreshed 'in body, mind and spirit'. After an Adelaide respite in 1922, she and Charles worked at Faridpur, Naogoan and Kalimpong where Laura rejoiced at gaining a resident Bengali evangelist for the hospital compound. They remained at Pubna from 1929.

Laura was awarded the Kaisar-i-Hind medal shortly before she and her husband retired to Adelaide in 1934. She managed their Erindale household, gardened, and, during World War II, knitted for soldiers. After Charles died she lived with her niece Marion Allnutt [q.v.13]. Laura died on 14 September 1952 in North Adelaide and was buried in Mitcham cemetery. She had no children.

A. Mackinnon, *The New Women* (Adel, 1986); G. B. Ball, The Australian Baptist Mission and its Impact in Bengal 1864-1954 (M.A. thesis, Flinders Univ, 1978); *Baptist Record of SA*, 15 Jan 1935, p 8; *Register* (Adel), 17 Dec 1891; *Express and Telegraph* (Adel), 14 Feb 1916; Fowler papers (Mort L); Children's Hospital, Bd of Management minutes, GRS 1869/1 (SRSA); Univ Adel Archives; information from Mrs N. Susman, Linden Park, Mrs H. Brewster, Norwood, Adel, and the late Mrs M. Rilett. HELEN JONES

HOPE, LOWTHER CHARLES (1892-1969), manufacturer, was born on 4 August 1892 at Fairford, Gloucestershire, England, one of five children of George Marfield Hope, an illiterate gardener and domestic servant, and his wife Mary Ann, née May. Charles was educated at the local Farmers' Endowed and Church of England schools until he was 12 years old. Determined to become an engineer, he helped out at a blacksmith's shop in his spare time. After labouring for two years on his father's farm and attending night-school, he served an apprenticeship in a small coach-

and body-building factory at Fairford. During this period he developed into a resourceful, practical and 'tough' individual, being influenced by his mother who stressed that hard work and independent action would reap their rewards. Aged 17, he was employed as an engineering smith by a vehicle body-building factory at Farnham, Surrey. Six months later he went to Hooper & Co., London, where bodies were made for Daimler and Rolls-Royce. In 1910 he joined his elder brother Stanley at another motor-body works at Coventry.

Concluding that, if he were to make his fortune, he needed to emigrate, Hope read about the British colonies. Australia became his preferred destination, especially after his uncle John May returned from New South Wales with stories of opportunity. Sponsored by May, he reached Sydney in 1912 to find opportunities somewhat limited. He took a succession of jobs in Sydney and at Warialda, and cut sugar-cane along the Richmond River, before finding work, first as a blacksmith, and then in a coach- and body-building factory at Lismore. There, in 1914 he opened his own business, Charles Hope Ltd, making sulkies and motorcar springs. On 11 September 1915 at St Andrew's Anglican Church, Lismore, he married Gladys Hart; they were to have three children. On the outbreak of World War I, he obtained a supply of spring steel and expanded his business (under the trade slogan, 'Hope springs eternal') through agents at Newcastle, Sydney and Brisbane.

In 1921 he visited England to examine engineering and design developments, and to acquire spring-making machinery. He opened the Monarch Engineering Works in Brisbane in April 1924 to manufacture springs for motor vehicles and railway rolling stock; he also diversified into iron and steel fabrication, as well as electroplating. Drawing upon his flair for technology and design, he ordered special presses to meet the demands of various clients. Hope continued to improve his techniques, and learned much from his trips in 1925 and 1929 to Britain and the United States of America. In 1927 he had opened a spring factory in Sydney and soon claimed to be supplying about 80 per cent of springs required by motorcar importers. That year, realizing that profits could be made from producing a light utility vehicle, he sent for his younger brother Harold, a body-designer, and Hope's Body Works Pty Ltd was established. In 1932 the factory and the works were merged. The Depression and a large, unpaid order by General Motors-Holden's [q.v.9] Ltd severely affected Hope's operations. Following a brief entry into the Melbourne market, he concentrated on Queensland. Recovery was helped by Harold who designed a body to fit the new Morris (People's) car.

The design and manufacture of domestic refrigerators became Hope's next challenge. By 1939, with the help of a European designer, he was producing a kerosene-powered, air-cooled, absorption refrigerator. During World War II manufacturing was interrupted to allow his Brisbane factory to service American military vehicles, at considerable profit. Production of the Charles Hope Cold Flame refrigerator resumed in 1946; by 1953 he had supplied over 100 000 households. Charles Hope Ltd, floated as a public company in 1948, kept innovating. A contribution was made to door insulation through development of a laminated plastic, Panelyte, made under licence from 1952. Hope's postwar motor-body business prospered, aided by a Brisbane City Council contract for the bodywork for its buses. In the mid-1950s the company was also assembling Austin 95 motorcars for the British Motor Corporation. By 1960 Hope was prepared to enjoy his success. In that year his company, one of Queensland's largest metal industries, was sold to Australian Consolidated Industries Ltd on the basis of two A.C.I. shares for every three of Charles Hope Ltd's—or, as Hope put it, the equivalent of 'a million and a half b-- quid'. He retired in 1962.

Keenly interested in sport, as a young man Hope had tried cricket, soccer, boxing, bareknuckle fighting and bicycle racing. In 1948 he established the Cotswold Hills Thoroughbred Stud at Toowoomba. President (from 1960) of the Bloodhorse Breeders' Association of Queensland, he remained active in horse- and cattle-breeding after retirement from business and published an engaging autobiography, *Hope Springs Eternal* (Brisbane, 1965). He died on 18 April 1969 at Toowoomba and was cremated; his wife, son and one of his two daughters survived him.

Qld Manufactures Yearbook, 1947-61; *Courier-Mail*, 19 Apr 1969; *Australian*, 22 Apr 1969; files on Charles Hope Ltd *and* Hope's Body Works Ltd *and* Charles Hope Holding Co. Ltd (QA).

W. ROSS JOHNSTON

HOPMAN, ELEANOR MARY (1909-1968), tennis player and administrator, was born on 9 March 1909 at Coogee, Sydney, only daughter and second of three children of native-born parents Charles Ernest Hall, clerk, and his wife Mabel Gertrude, née Tipper. Educated at Claremont College, Randwick, where she excelled at tennis and music, Nell was brought up strictly, in accordance with middle-class, Protestant conventions, and developed strong views about young people's need for discipline. Her own self-discipline was evident in six-hours daily practice at the piano. Studying under J. Hugh

McMenamin, she obtained the licentiate and teaching diploma of the Royal College of Music, London, and won a scholarship to go abroad in 1928, but chose instead a tennis career. Music remained an important part of her life, and she regularly played for enjoyment and relaxation.

Nell was 'spotted' by Davis Cup player, Harry (Henry Christian) Hopman and, when she came to Melbourne in 1930 with the New South Wales junior team, he partnered her in the Australian senior mixed doubles, which they won. She also won the women's doubles title that year and again in 1933. Nell married Harry on 19 March 1934 at St Philip's Anglican Church, Sydney, and moved to Melbourne where he worked (1933-56) as a sports journalist for the *Herald and Weekly Times*. They spent their honeymoon in the *Orford* with the Davis Cup team *en route* to England. On returning to Melbourne, Nell resumed her own tennis career, becoming captain of the Victorian interstate team which remained undefeated for five years.

In 1935 Nell again accompanied Harry to England where he reported on Wimbledon and she wrote occasional pieces for the *Australian Women's Weekly*. They entered the mixed doubles; although unseeded, they reached the finals. The thrill of playing on centre court in her only Wimbledon final remained a highpoint in her life. The Hopmans won the Australian mixed doubles in 1936, and in 1937 when Nell also won Victorian women's doubles titles. Victory in the Victorian singles in 1938 and in the South Australian singles next year raised her national ranking to equal first with Emily Westacott, who defeated her in the Australian championships in 1939. Nell and Harry won the Australian mixed doubles for the fourth time in 1939.

Her confidence had grown with international experience as captain of the Australian women's touring team, which spent nine months in Europe, Britain and the United States of America during 1938. It was only the second time that the Lawn Tennis Association of Australia had sponsored a trip for women, and, since there was no women's equivalent of the Davis Cup, Australia's leading female players had few chances to compete abroad. Hopman took her responsibilities earnestly, demanding discipline and correct dress and behaviour. Yet, Nancye Wynne recalled that she 'was very fair if you did the right thing', and remembered her 'vibrant personality' and the 'great affection' she evoked. Further opportunities for travel were halted by World War II, but the tour had fired Nell's determination to make the L.T.A.A. take seriously international competition for women.

In 1940 Hopman won her only Australian singles title—the hardcourts championship —and also took out the doubles title. Thereafter, wartime work as secretary to the chief of the British liaison staff and as a volunteer at Red Cross House limited her playing to pennant competition. In 1945, however, she won the State doubles title and was again runner-up in the Australian singles in 1947. She and Nancye Wynne (Bolton) then toured Europe and America, Nell paying her way by writing for American, British and Australian magazines. The experience confirmed her determination to open up L.T.A.A.-sponsored coaching and travel opportunities for the next generation of Australian women players. At 37 she was nearing the end of her playing career, though she was to win the South Australian singles again in 1949-50 and the Victorian doubles in 1951. Never having been coached, her style was awkward and unorthodox, and she used the same grip and the same side of the racquet for forehand and backhand. None knew better the need for systematic training of the up-and-coming women players. Election as the first woman councillor of the Lawn Tennis Association of Victoria in 1947 launched her career as a tennis administrator.

Hopman persuaded the L.T.A.A. to invite the reigning Wimbledon champion Louise Brough and another leading player Doris Hart to tour Australia in the summer of 1949-50. She arranged, too, for the new champion Maureen ('Little Mo') Connolly and the American junior title holder Julie Sampson to play in Australia in the summer of 1952-53, as a result of which the L.T.A.A. set up a committee to discuss ways and means of improving the 'poor standards of Australian women's tennis'. Other tennis writers threw their weight behind Nell's campaign, accusing the L.T.A.A. of a 'parochial attitude to women players'. In 1955 the L.T.A.A. did at last send a women's team abroad, under the management of Adrian Quist, but no plans for further tours were forthcoming.

In 1950 Hopman had managed Victoria's Wilson Cup team. Once more, players recollected her stress on discipline—'the girls were fined for leaving a hairbrush out on the dressing table'—but also her sense of fun, her fairness and her enthusiasm. In 1952-54 she was employed by the United States and South Californian Lawn Tennis associations to act as companion-chaperon to Maureen Connolly, then at the peak of her career. It was a successful relationship, Nell approving of Maureen's 'manner and demeanour', and she partnered Connolly to victory in the French doubles in 1954.

In the following years young tennis players began to assert the right to independent travel. A dedicated team-player and amateur herself, Hopman was openly critical of 'private trips overseas'; for her, the game and the team were always more important than the individual. With no children of her own, she failed to understand that younger players' expectations of teachers, coaches and team managers were changing. Moreover, the fact that, at 51, Nell was too far removed in age to be a fun-loving friend as well as a manager lay at the root of the difficulties encountered when she took a team of Australian women players overseas for the L.T.A.A. in 1961. She had guaranteed that the tour would not make a loss; it made a profit of £2500. Margaret Smith, Lesley Turner and Mary Reitano believed that, in consequence, they were overworked, their accommodation and diet were inadequate, and Mrs Hopman behaved like a martinet. When Smith refused to go with the 1962 official L.T.A.A. team under Hopman's management, Nell attributed her attitude to the influence of her trainer Frank Sedgman, her employer Bob Mitchell and the regrettable modern trend towards private tours.

Important though the tours of 1961-62 were in promoting Australian women's tennis, the pinnacle was reached in 1962 when Hopman persuaded the L.T.A.A. and the International Lawn Tennis Federation to support a women's international team-competition similar to the Davis Cup. The first Federation Cup competition was played in London in 1963 and Hopman won for Kooyong the right to stage the cup in Australia in 1965. In addition, she raised £15 000 to sponsor teams from ten nations. Australia won the cup and made a profit of £16 000. In 1962 Hopman was appointed O.B.E. She became the first woman life member of the L.T.A.V. in 1965. About this time she began to suffer severe headaches; in 1966 she underwent surgery for a brain tumour. Although she resumed her administrative work, including the organization of the Country Week championship for which she had been responsible since 1947, she did not recover her previous robust health. Survived by her husband, she died of an intercranial tumour on 10 January 1968 at Hawthorn and was cremated. Her portrait by (Sir) William Dargie is held at the Kooyong clubhouse.

M. Smith, *The Margaret Smith Story*, D. Lawrence comp (Lond, 1965); R. Yallop, *Royal South Yarra Lawn Tennis Club* (Melb, 1984); M. Lake and F. Kelly (eds), *Double Time* (Melb, 1985); *Lawn Tennis in Aust*, 15 Mar, 15 Oct 1937; *Aust Tennis*, 4, no 8, Mar-Apr 1953, p 18, 5, no 5, Sept 1953, p 12, 6, no 4, Apr 1954, p 27; *Herald* (Melb), 20 Mar, 2 June 1962, 28 Nov 1964, 21 July 1965, 10 Jan 1968; *Age* (Melb), 2, 3 Mar, 2 June 1962, 6 Jan 1965, 11 Jan 1968, 20 Apr 1970; *Sun News-Pictorial*, 28 Feb 1934, 17 Dec 1947, 2, 3, 8 Mar 1962, 2 Apr 1962, 11 Jan 1968; *Australian*, 11 Jan 1968.
JUDITH SMART

HORDERN, SAMUEL (1909-1960), stockbroker and grazier, was born on 16 May 1909 at Strathfield, Sydney, only son and third child of native-born parents (Sir) Samuel Hordern [q.v.9], merchant, and his wife Charlotte Isabella Annie, daughter of Sir John See [q.v.11]. From 1912 the family lived at Babworth House, Darling Point. Educated at Cranbrook School (1919-27), in 1929 Sam proceeded to Jesus College, Cambridge (B.A., 1931; M.A., 1939), to study law and economic history. He was active in the college's boat club at the time of its fame, rowing in the winning 1st boat in 1930-31. Back home, Hordern joined the Sydney Stock Exchange in 1934 and the brokers, Buzacott & McKeown (Hordern Utz & Bode after a merger in 1938). On 12 April 1934 at St John's Anglican Church, Toorak, Melbourne, he married June, daughter of Richard Percy Clive Baillieu and grand-daughter of W. L. Baillieu [q.v.7]. They moved into a house designed for them by Leslie Wilkinson [q.v.12] at Bellevue Hill, Sydney.

After serving for a year as a provisional lieutenant in the 2nd Armoured Car Regiment, Militia, Hordern was commissioned in the Australian Imperial Force on 15 June 1940 and posted to the 7th Divisional Cavalry Regiment. He sailed for the Middle East in December and commanded the regiment's No. 13 Troop in Cyprus in 1941. His democratic manner made him popular with his men who affectionately called him 'Sambo'. An unfailing sense of humour and a knowledge of humanity added force to his leadership.

Returning to Australia in March 1942, Hordern embarked for Papua in September. He and his soldiers fought as infantry on the Sanananda Track in December 1942 and January 1943. Posted home again, he was promoted major in August and that month joined the 1st Australian Army Tank Battalion (later the 1st Armoured Regiment) at Milne Bay, Papua, as commander of 'C' Squadron. In operations in precipitous jungle on New Guinea's Huon Peninsula in November-December he reconnoitred enemy positions on foot and kept his tanks up with the leading infantry; his efforts minimized casualties among Australian troops. He was mentioned in dispatches and appointed O.B.E. (1945). Having taken part in the capture of Balikpapan, Borneo, in July 1945, he transferred to the Reserve of Officers on 6 December.

In Sydney, Hordern retired from Hordern Utz & Bode and from the Stock Exchange in 1948 to pursue pastoral interests. At Retford Park, Bowral, he bred stud cattle—as his forebears had done—Shorthorn, Devon, Hereford, Aberdeen Angus, Jersey and Santa Gertrudis. His other livestock included Welsh ponies, Suffolk Punch and Quarter horses,

Ryeland and Southdown sheep, pigs, Labradors, whippets and Pekingese dogs, and pheasants and canaries. Prominent in cattle circles, he was associated with Yulgilbar Pastoral Co. Ltd and in many pastoral companies with interests in developing outback Australia. He was keen to establish Quarter horses in Australia—as well as Santa Gertrudis cattle from King Ranch, Texas, United States of America—through King Ranch (Australia) Pty Ltd and he chaired the Santa Gertrudis (Australia) Breeders Association. Following his death, Retford Park was bought by the King Ranch (Australia) company.

In keeping with family tradition, Hordern was an enthusiastic councillor (1935-50), vice-president (1950-54) and president (1954-60) of the Royal Agricultural Society of New South Wales. When Sydney's Royal Easter Show resumed in 1947, he was acting-chairman for two years of the dog sections. At fiery meetings he persuaded numerous dog clubs to come together under an R.A.S.N.S.W. kennel control club. As the show's ringmaster (1949-54) he was a popular figure, dressed in jodhpurs, hacking jacket and trilby, and mounted on his horse, Christmas. In the early 1950s he instigated moves to form the Equestrian Federation of Australia to represent all independent horse breeds, bodies and disciplines within the scope of the agricultural societies. Foundation president (from 1952) of its federal council, he sought affiliation with the Australian Olympic Federation and the Fédération Equestre Internationale; he set up an equestrian centre at Retford Park and actively sought sponsorship for Australia's first Olympic equestrian team which competed in Stockholm in 1956.

Understanding the mentality of committee-men, Hordern was never dictatorial, but a listener who tried to persuade them to overcome parochial fears and develop a national outlook. He could, however, be notoriously late for meetings, and those who complained brought out the larrikin in him. In 1957, at the Royal Agricultural Society of England's meeting at Norwich, he took the lead in establishing the Royal Agricultural Society of the Commonwealth—under the presidency of the Duke of Edinburgh—for the exchange of knowledge and experience. He was made a life member of the Royal Agricultural Society.

Hordern was a director of the Australian Mutual Provident Society, Perpetual Trustee Co. Ltd, Tooth [q.v.6] & Co. Ltd and Courtaulds (Australia) Ltd, a committee-member of the Australian Jockey Club and a councillor of Cranbrook School. He belonged to the Union, Australian, New South Wales and Royal Sydney Golf clubs, Royal Sydney Yacht Squadron, the Melbourne Club and, in Britain, Leander

Boat Club and The Hawks Club, Cambridge. He was appointed C.M.G. in 1958.

Six ft 5 ins (196 cm) tall and handsome, Hordern was a notable organizer and an eloquent speaker with an outstanding personality. Survived by his wife, daughter and son, he died on 25 July 1960 in Liverpool hospital from injuries received in a motorcar accident and was cremated. His estate was sworn for probate at £690 680. The Samuel Hordern memorial trophy for jumping events was presented to the Bowral Horse Show in 1961 by N. F. Small, driver of the taxi in which Hordern and his wife were passengers at the time of the accident. A posthumous portrait of Hordern by (Sir) William Dargie is held by the R.A.S.N.S.W.

Cranbrookian, 42, no 1, 1960; *Country Life*, 2 July 1955; *Sun-Herald*, 18 Mar 1956; *Sun* (Syd), 25-26 July 1960; *Daily Mirror* (Syd), 25, 29 July, 16 Dec 1960; *SMH*, 29 Aug 1935, 29 Nov 1947, 30 June 1954, 12 June 1958, 26, 27 July, 17 Dec 1960; *Daily Telegraph* (Syd), 29 July 1960; *Bulletin*, 3 Aug 1960; information from Messrs J. Barnes, Binalong, NSW, A. Howie, Killara, and D. A. Pratten, Palm Beach, Syd.   CAROLINE SIMPSON

HORDERN, URSULA MARY (1911-1961), fashion editor, was born on 1 April 1911 at Woollahra, Sydney, fourth daughter of five children of Herbert Henry Bullmore, a native-born medical practitioner, and his wife Elfride Henriette Victoria, née Büttner, from Melbourne. Always known as Mary, she was educated at Ascham School, Edgecliff, and excelled at French and sport. Her family was one of the earliest to build a house at Palm Beach for holidays. On leaving school, she worked as a receptionist for her father, and spent a year at Shanghai, China, with (Sir) Frederick and Laura Maze (her godmother).

At All Saints Church, Woollahra, on 3 March 1932 Mary married Anthony Hordern [q.v.9], a grazier and a widower. They lived at Retford Hall, Darling Point, and at Milton Park, Bowral, where Mary created a famous garden which was opened to the public every spring to aid the Bowral hospital. In the mid-1950s she commissioned the Melbourne architect Guilford Bell to design a round house, Wingadal, at Point Piper (completed 1956); the interiors were created by her friend Marion Hall Best.

Mrs Hordern was fashion editor (1946-57) of the *Australian Women's Weekly*, owned by her brother-in-law (Sir) Frank Packer [q.v.]. In 1946 the magazine decided to bring Paris fashions to Australia in a display of glamour and luxury after the lean, wartime years. She flew to Paris to organize an extensive parade of clothes, with mannequins from the leading

French designers, save for Christian Dior. Over the next three years she produced three more French fashion spectaculars in Sydney, Melbourne and Adelaide which engendered huge publicity and sales for the *Weekly* throughout Australia. Dior's earlier decision to franchise with David Jones [q.v.2] Ltd had caused a social schism between Mary Hordern and Hannah, wife of Sir Charles Lloyd Jones [q.v.9]. In the summer of 1953 they made a public reconciliation as joint hostesses of a grand ball, irreverently referred to as 'The Drapers Ball'.

In 1953 Hordern was a founding member of the Art Gallery Society of New South Wales. She was president of the organizing committee for the French government's exhibition of art and industry, held in a new pavilion at the local Royal Agricultural Society's 1956 Royal Easter Show. Meeting 'frustrations at every turn', such as arguments between the Department of Public Works and the French architect over lighting, she solved the problems directly with H. G. Conde [q.v.13], chairman of the Electricity Commission. She was appointed to the Légion d'honneur in 1957.

Possessing a statuesque figure to wear the clothes she wrote about, Hordern was an attractive woman with presence, brown hair, blue eyes and an acute mind. Her formidable attitude overrode dissenting opinions, and she became a powerful authority on fashion and an arbiter of taste. She dominated her family and associates with an iron hand. Survived by her husband and two daughters, she died of myocardial infarction on 5 June 1961 at her Point Piper home and was cremated; her estate was sworn for probate at £121 964. Mary's only brother Flight Lieutenant James Bullmore had been killed in action on 29 November 1942 over Papua.

B. H. Fletcher, *The Grand Parade* (Syd, 1988); A. Imrie (ed), *1952-1980 Architecture of Guilford Bell* (Melb, 1982); V. Lawson, *Connie Sweetheart* (Melb, 1990); *Aust Women's Weekly*, 26 Apr, 5 July 1947, 21 June 1961; *SMH*, 2 Oct 1933, 16 Nov 1934, 18 July 1954, 6, 7 June, 1 Sept 1961; *Daily Telegraph* (Syd), 6 June 1961; *SMH Good Weekend*, 16 July 1994; Roy Agr Soc of NSW, Minutes, meeting 15 Feb 1956 (Roy Agr Soc, Syd); information from Mrs J. Bancks and Mrs P. Baillieu, Woollahra, and Mrs D. Munro, Bundeena, Syd.

CAROLINE SIMPSON

HORNER, JOHN ADAM (1899-1973), organist, was born on 18 October 1899 at Steps, Lanarkshire, Scotland, son of William Horner, commercial clerk, and his wife Jeanie Pollack, née Adam. Educated mainly in northern England, John began to study accountancy. By the age of 16 he was organist of St Andrew's Episcopal Church, Milngavie, near Glasgow. He joined the Royal Flying Corps in 1917, was commissioned (1918) in the Royal Air Force as an observer and served on the Italian front before being demobilized in January 1919. Intent on a professional career in classical music, he qualified as a licentiate (1919) of the Royal Academy of Music and a fellow (1923) of the Royal College of Organists. In the mid-1920s he was engaged as organist and choirmaster at Woodlands Church, Glasgow, as organist with the Scottish Orchestra Company and as instructor of the University of Glasgow's orchestral society. While teaching organ and pianoforte at the Glasgow Athenaeum School of Music, he was appointed in 1927 to the Elder [q.v.4] Conservatorium of Music, University of Adelaide.

Arriving in South Australia in February 1928, Horner proved to be an organist and teacher of the highest quality. At St Peter's Anglican Cathedral, Adelaide, on 10 December that year he married Marjorie Laura Ball, a musician. In 1929 he began teaching music theory at the conservatorium and commenced a series of part-time appointments as organist and choirmaster in churches: St Peter's, Glenelg (for three years), St Augustine's, Unley (three years), where he composed a set of chimes for the carillon, and Stow [q.v.2] Memorial Church, Adelaide (for twelve years). Throughout the winter months of the 1930s he gave weekly public recitals which ranked him as one of the finest organists in Australia. He was prominent in the establishment and leadership of the Lydian Singers (1935) and the Stow Music Club. With John Bishop [q.v.13], he arranged musical fêtes and boat trips on the River Torrens, leading his students in the singing of madrigals. He belonged to the Savage Club.

During World War II Horner served (1941-45) in Australia with the Administrative and Special Duties Branch of the Royal Australian Air Force and rose to temporary squadron leader. Back at the conservatorium, from 1947 he undertook a heavy load of theoretical teaching for the bachelor of music degree. He was music critic (c.1950-72) for the *Advertiser*, attracting acclaim for articles that embodied subtle and penetrating musicianship, wit and humour, and a readiness to indicate shortcomings in interpretation or performance.

In the closing years of his career Horner was president of the State division of the Arts Council of Australia, music adviser to the Adelaide Festival of Arts, and South Australian delegate (1958) to a United Nations Educational, Scientific and Cultural Organization conference which led to the foundation (1965) of the Australian Society for Music Education. On Bishop's death in 1964, Horner became acting-director of the conservatorium and was elected dean of the faculty of music. He retired in 1966. In 1970 he was appointed O.B.E. Survived by his wife and their adopted son, he died on 10 October 1973 at Toorak Gardens and was cremated.

A. Hewlett, *Cause to Rejoice* (Adel, 1983); A. D. McCredie (ed), *From Colonel Light into the Foothills* (Adel, 1989); Arts Council of Aust, *Q Bulletin*, 4, Dec 1965; *Aust J of Music Education*, Apr 1974; *Register* (Adel), 6 Feb 1928; *Chronicle* (Adel), 7 Nov 1929; *Advertiser* (Adel), 11 Oct 1973; ts of interview with Horner, 24 Aug 1969, D 5573/4 (Mort L); press-cuttings (Univ Adel); information from Mr H. Tidemann, Wattle Park, Adel; personal information.   V. A. EDGELOE

HORNIBROOK, SIR MANUEL RICHARD (1893-1970), master builder, industrialist and company director, was born on 7 August 1893 at Enoggera, Brisbane, and registered as Emanuel, second of seven children of Irish-born parents John Hornibrook, storeman and builder, and his wife Catherine, née Sullivan. In 1896 John took up farming in the Obi Obi Valley, near Nambour; the family returned to Brisbane in 1903 where he set up as a tea merchant and died that year of typhoid fever. Manuel was educated at Nambour, Obi Obi, Bowen Bridge and South Brisbane state schools. A 'big lump of a lad' at the age of 13, he was apprenticed to H. W. Fooks, Adelaide Street, to learn the building and joinery trade. In August 1912 he established his own business as a builder and contractor; his brother Reg joined him in the following year. On 27 November 1915 Manuel Hornibrook married with Methodist forms Daphne Winifred Brunckhorst at her parents' Enoggera home.

From the outset Hornibrook showed the drive and initiative that were to characterize his career, though his business was, from the first, very much a family affair. Four other brothers joined him—Ray in 1918, Eric in 1919, Frank in 1921 and Gus in 1948. The company began carrying out drainage schemes in Brisbane suburbs for local councils in 1918, and then contracted for large sewerage works at Longreach, Roma and other towns in western Queensland. In 1922 the firm excavated the State's first open-cut coalmine at Blair Athol, and constructed water-supply systems for Goondiwindi, Mackay and Rockhampton. By 1926 business had developed to such an extent that M. R. Hornibrook Ltd (a proprietary company from 1932) was formed with a paid-up capital of £25 000. In the late 1920s Hornibrook extended into New South Wales, establishing a subsidiary company (Hornibrook Bros & Clark Co. Ltd) in Sydney in 1938. In 1947 Hornibrook Constructions Ltd was registered

in Papua. Other branches were set up in Victoria and South Australia in the 1950s. Over a period of forty years these companies built wool stores, wheat silos, wharves, sugarsheds, tank farms, water mains, factories and electricity power-stations. They constructed shipping beacons at the entrance to Moreton Bay and at Weipa. A major achievement was the successful completion in the 1960s of the superstructure of the Sydney Opera House, including the sail-like roof.

It was, however, as a bridge-builder that Hornibrook made his reputation. His first sizeable bridge, erected for the Department of Main Roads across the Burrum River in 1925, was the earliest, publicly funded, reinforced-concrete bridge in Queensland. The Hornibrook Highway—a toll road which he launched as a private venture during the Depression—included what was Australia's longest bridge at the time of its construction, and provided full-time employment for hundreds of men. The group built more than one hundred bridges, some of the better-known including the William Jolly [q.v.9], Story [q.v.12] and New Victoria bridges in Brisbane, the Northbridge and Iron Cove Bridge, Sydney, the King's Avenue and Commonwealth Avenue bridges in Canberra, and the Markham River Bridge in the Territory of Papua and New Guinea.

As did (Sir) Leslie Thiess, Hornibrook brought modern, mechanized methods of civil-engineering construction to Queensland and Australia. Reflecting Hornibrook's natural mechanical and engineering instincts, his company established its own workshops for maintaining the heavy machinery which had become an essential part of large-scale contracting. It also developed facilities for designing and manufacturing the specialized tools required for specific contracts. A first-rate craftsman, Hornibrook insisted that his company should employ the best methods in carrying out its work. Nor was he afraid of adopting new techniques, as indicated by his pioneering use of the 'sand island' method of preparing foundations for the piers of the William Jolly Bridge in 1927. His application of air-lock technology to the construction of the piers of the Story bridge provided another model for later contractors.

In February 1955 Hornibrook (Pty) Ltd was floated as a £1 million public company and was heavily oversubscribed. By the following year it was employing over two thousand people. The strength of the Hornibrook group, which stemmed from being the creation of a single, dynamic personality, became a weakness after it was launched as a public company. Lacking a sufficient technical and financial support base, the firm began to lose contracts to its rivals, particularly those from abroad. Hornibrook's individuality could not come to terms with the need for modern financial and management structures in his companies. As a result they were unable to meet the competitive pressure of international contracting. In 1964 Hornibrook Ltd and M. R. Hornibrook (N.S.W.) Pty Ltd were acquired by the British-owned Wood Hall group. Two years later Hornibrook retired as chairman of directors. He did, nevertheless, continue his association with other companies that bore his name, among them the Hornibrook Highway Ltd, and Hornibrook Highway Bus Service Ltd of which he was chairman. He also retained chairmanship of Brisbane Gravels Pty Ltd and remained on the board of the Queensland Cement & Lime Co. Ltd. In search of a challenge of a different kind, in 1955 Hornibrook had bought Omar, a property in South Australia, which he developed for sheep and cattle.

He devoted much time and effort to raising the professional status of civil-engineering contracting in Australia and to improving educational facilities for young men planning to enter it. In 1914 Hornibrook had joined the Queensland Master Builders' Association and was its president in 1922 and 1923; he was president (1926) and a life member (1959) of the Master Builders Federation of Australia; he was also a foundation fellow (1951), councillor and president (1952-56) of the Australian Institute of Builders, and a driving force in the construction of its headquarters at Milson's Point, Sydney. For his contribution to the science and the practice of building, he was awarded the A.I.B.'s first medal of merit (1955). President (1953-59) of the Queensland Civil Engineering Contractors' Association, he was an honorary member (1968) of the Australian Federation of Civil Engineering Contractors and an honorary fellow (1969) of the Chartered Institute of Building (Britain)—the first Australian to be so honoured. He was appointed O.B.E. in 1957 and knighted in 1960.

Known to his associates as 'M.R.', Hornibrook was a big man, not only in physique— he stood 6 ft 2 ins (188 cm) tall and weighed 17 stone (108 kg)—but in personal magnetism, vision and spirit. Courage, ability and determination carried him to the highest levels in his profession. He dominated his immediate environment, had a cool head in crises and did not suffer fools gladly. His lack of formal education was amply compensated by a large measure of common sense, energy and enthusiasm. Hornibrook's warm humanity and interest in people was legendary. He enjoyed golf and bowls, and was president of the Queensland Golf Council. His organizational abilities were always in demand for fund-raising and, in 1931, during his term as president of the Hamilton Bowling Club, a spacious clubhouse was built. Sir Manuel was

a Rotarian and an ardent worker for International House, University of Queensland, of which he was foundation master (1966-70).

Survived by his wife, daughter and two sons, Hornibrook died on 30 May 1970 at the Holy Spirit Private Hospital, Wickham Terrace, Brisbane, and was cremated. His estate was sworn for probate at $230 564.

Men of Queensland (Brisb, 1929); W. Browne, *A Man of Achievement* (Brisb, 1974); *People* (Syd), 19 Oct 1955, p 19; *Building, Lighting and Engineering*, Jan 1960, p 24; *Chartered Builder*, 1, 1970, p 7; *Sunday Mail* (Brisb), 25 Jan, 31 May 1970; *Courier-Mail*, 23 Nov 1957, 1, 20 Jan 1960, 26 Sept 1968, 3 June 1970, 6 Oct 1971.

RAYMOND L. WHITMORE

HORSFALL, ROBERT ALLAN (1909-1974), civil engineer, was born on 20 July 1909 at Somerville, Victoria, son of Francis Arthur Horsfall, civil engineer, and his wife Campbell Isabel, née Donaldson, both Victorian born. Educated at Korumburra Higher Elementary School, Scotch College, Hawthorn, and the University of Melbourne (B.C.E., 1931; B.M.E., 1946; M.C.E., 1949), Bob was employed by the Shire of Korumburra (1931), Mt Isa Mines Ltd (1932-34) and Mt Lyell Mining & Railway Co. Ltd (1934-38). He married Catherine Mary Bowen on 20 December 1934 with Catholic rites at St Patrick's Cathedral, Melbourne. On 11 August 1938 he joined the State Rivers and Water Supply Commission as an engineering assistant.

In 1940 Horsfall was commissioned in the Royal Australian Engineers. He transferred to the Australian Imperial Force on 28 July 1941 and, as a major, commanded the 2nd/4th Field Squadron in New Guinea in 1944. Energetic and resourceful, he was appointed M.B.E. (1945) for his contribution to the rapid construction of the base at Madang. Having served in Borneo in 1945, he relinquished his command in January 1946 and returned to the S.R.W.S.C.

An innovative engineer whose commitment to professional water management meshed perfectly with the developmental ethos of the immediate postwar years, Horsfall exerted considerable influence in the investigations and designs branch. As assistant chief designing engineer (1947), and chief designing engineer and branch head (from 1958), he was associated with almost every major civil engineering project undertaken by the commission until the early 1970s. He contributed to the planning and design of some twenty new large dams, and to the enlargement of eight others, including the Cairn Curran, Glenmaggie, Eildon and Hume storage facilities. Urban water supply proposals, drainage and land reclamation schemes, flood mitigation plans, salinity investigations, irrigation developments, and channel, tunnel, spillway, levee and river diversion schemes throughout Victoria bore his mark. His reputation for engineering versatility and administrative flair was further enhanced by an ability to devise novel, cost-saving design features.

In 1946-47 Horsfall served as deputy-commissioner of the Central Planning Authority and as government nominee (until 1956) on the Central Highlands Regional Committee. At the request of the Federal government, in 1951 he represented Australia at the congress of the International Commission on Irrigation and Drainage, and at a conference of the Economic Commission for Asia and the Far East on flood control, held in India. In 1952 he travelled to England and Germany to finalize contracts for the stage-two construction of the Eildon, Cairn Curran and Glenmaggie dams. He conducted special investigations, appeared frequently before State parliament's public works committee as an expert witness, prepared numerous technical reports, and wrote and spoke widely on water management and associated engineering matters.

On 1 February 1963 Horsfall was appointed commissioner of water supply. Two years later he was promoted to deputy-chairman of the S.R.W.S.C., responsible for design policy and financial oversight of water management. He was ministerial adviser on water trust operations, Victorian representative on the River Murray Commission and a member of the Snowy Mountains Council; he chaired a 1964 interdepartmental committee investigating the economic viability of small-town water supply proposals and prepared draft legislation for the commission. In 1964 he investigated water-supply practices in Europe and attended conferences in Edinburgh and Stockholm. In 1966 and 1968 he again represented Australia at E.C.A.F.E. conferences in Canberra and Bangkok.

Economic rationalists and emerging conservationists alike, however, were increasingly questioning the 'big dams' mentality that so informed government and commission policy. Quietly firm, Horsfall persisted. The Dartmouth Dam, now Victoria's largest water-storage facility, was the last major project on which he worked. Following a period of ill health and some disaffection with the reorientation of resource management, he retired from the S.W.R.S.C. in October 1972. He subsequently accepted consultancies with J. B. Ley & Partners, and with Maunsell & Partners, Melbourne. In 1974 he was appointed I.S.O.

Approachable and generous, the heavy-smoking Horsfall was of middle height and medium build, with dark brown hair and a weather-beaten complexion. He served on many community and professional bodies, including Melbourne Legacy, the 2nd/4th Field Squadron Association (president 1946-55), the Institution of Engineers, Australia, the standing committee of convocation of the University of Melbourne (1955-61) and the Environment Protection Council. He enjoyed tennis and bushwalking as a young man, and remained an enthusiastic crewman and member of the Royal Brighton Yacht Club. Survived by his wife and two of their three sons, he died of hypertensive coronary vascular disease on 16 September 1974 at Fitzroy and was buried with Presbyterian forms in Brighton cemetery.

J. M. Powell, *Watering the Garden State* (Syd, 1989); Dept of Conservation and Environment (Vic), *Water Victoria* (Melb, 1991); *Aqua*, Summer/Autumn 1975, p 14; Horsfall personnel file (State Rivers and Water Supply Com, Rural Water Corp, Armadale, Melb); bib of Horsfall's publications on file at ADB, Canb; family information.

R. WRIGHT

HORT, GRETA (1903-1967), academic and college principal, was born on 25 May 1903 in Copenhagen, daughter of Vilhelm Hjort, astronomer royal, and his wife Anne Margrethe, née Ulrich. Educated at N. Zahle's Skole and at the University of Copenhagen (M.A., 1927) where she won a gold medal, Greta lectured in English at the university for two years. She travelled to England and studied at Newnham College, Cambridge (Ph.D., 1931), before proceeding as Pfeiffer research fellow (1931-34) to Girton College. There she was awarded the Gamble prize for an essay on *The Cloud of Unknowing*, and published *Sense and Thought, A Study in Mysticism* (1936) and *Piers Plowman and Contemporary Religious Thought* (1937).

In June 1938 Dr Hort was appointed principal of University Women's College (later University College) at the University of Melbourne. Diana Dyason saw her as 'almost a caricature of the Girton bluestocking, sparse fine hair drawn into a wispy bun from which it was always escaping, little dress sense and a penchant for thick grey ... stockings'. In accordance with the ideals of the college council, Hort developed in her students the principles of freedom and self-government to a degree greater than in other Melbourne colleges. She tutored in philosophy and fostered high academic standards generally; between two and eight exhibitions and prizes were awarded to U.W.C. students each year during her principalship. Elaine Chong, a student from Singapore, remembered that 'she took the trouble to get to know us individually', but, according to Dyason, there were 'rumblings of student revolt' due to Hort's 'arbitrariness' and 'use of pressure tactics'.

Active in the Danish community, Hort was also president of the Czechoslovak branch of the Red Cross Society, patron of the Australia-Indian Society, vice-president of the Australia-China Society, an executive-member of the Pro-Palestine Association of Victoria, president of the Victorian branch of the Australasian Society of Psychology and Philosophy, and a member (1943-46) of the university council. In addition to teaching, administration and social obligations, she found time for writing; she published *Two Poems* (1945) and *Mamre* (1946), a translation of Martin Buber's essays in religion. She resigned as principal in October 1946 and went with Professor Julie Moscheles to Prague where she undertook research for 'The Plagues of Egypt' (*Zeitschrift fur Alt Testamentliche Wisenschaft*, 1957-58) and 'The Death of Quorah' (*Australian Biblical Review*, December 1959).

In 1957 Hort accepted the chair of English literature at Aarhus University, Denmark. Her familiarity with Australian literature, ballads and bush songs enabled her to pioneer Australian studies in Europe. Brilliant, but eccentric, she edited an anthology of Australian literature for use in Danish high schools and lectured on the subject at German universities. In 1964 she attended a conference on Commonwealth literature, held at Leeds, England. Appointed to the Order of the Dannebrog in 1965, in that year she was awarded the Tagea Brandt prize for outstanding scholarship.

Hort died of a post-operative thrombosis on 19 August 1967 in her home at Risskov, Denmark. A library at University College was named after her in 1992.

H. Dow (ed), *Memories of Melbourne University* (Melb, 1983); *Meanjin Q*, 5, no 2, Winter 1946; *Westerly*, no 4, Dec 1987; *Herald* (Melb), 6 May, 20, 23, 25 June 1938; *Age* (Melb), 21 June 1938, 23 Apr 1966, 5 Sept 1967; H. Brookes papers (NL); Girton College, Univ Cambridge, Archives; information from Lady Derham, Toorak, Melb; personal letters and information.   URSULA HOFF

HOSKING, EDWIN CLEMENT (1896-1966), singer, teacher and folklorist, was born on 4 March 1896 at Hindmarsh, Adelaide, son of Edwin Hosking, a draper from Yorkshire, and his South Australian-born wife Ellen Waller, née Humble. Educated privately and at various public schools, Clem was a boy-chorister in the College Park choir. At the age of 17 he decided on a musical career, and had singing lessons from Miss Mary Wright. He

enlisted in the Australian Imperial Force on 1 April 1916, served on the Western Front from September 1917 as a signaller in the 48th Battalion and was discharged in Adelaide on 6 October 1919.

Studying under Count Ercole Filippini, Hosking moved to Sydney where he was taught by Vincenzo de Giorgio, and by Guido Cacielli at the New South Wales State Conservatorium of Music. In 1921 Hosking opened a studio in George Street and, for more than thirty years, took pupils in singing. He was also in charge of music (1925) at the Pitt Street Congregational Church. In 1920 Filippini had praised his 'very fine baritone voice' and predicted a successful career in opera for his pupil, but, while continuing his studies abroad, Hosking developed a passion for folk-songs and folklore. A member of the Theosophical Society in Australia (1927-38), he was musical director (1926-30) of radio station 2GB.

In 1933 Hosking founded the Sydney Folk Song Choir which he directed until 1952. The choir gave numerous broadcasts and recitals: items were usually interspersed with his informed commentary; on occasions he was a soloist. He was particularly interested in Celtic culture and undertook research into the folk-songs of the Outer Hebrides, which he visited from time to time. Gaining an international reputation as a singer, choir director and lecturer, in 1938 he was created a bard by the Gorsedd of Cornwall and given the title 'Kenyas an Eneson' ('Singer of the Isles') for his services to Celtic music. His influence in creating an awareness of and love for folk-songs was unparalleled in Australia.

During World War II Hosking was honorary director of the Red Cross Concert Unit in Sydney. At Newington College, he was part-time choirmaster (1944-61) and a close friend of the headmaster P. R. Le Couteur [q.v.10] and his wife Emma. Initially, the choristers were conscripts and Hosking found discipline difficult. A mathematics teacher was appointed master-in-charge of the choir to keep order during rehearsals. The standard of singing improved. In 1953 Hosking helped to found an adult listening group, later the Wyvern Music Club, Lindfield.

When the United Nations Educational, Scientific and Cultural Organization's Australian committee for music was formed in 1951, Hosking was invited to become a member. Other spheres of service included the Celtic Society of Australia (president 1941-65), the International Folk Music Council, the Folk Lore Association of New South Wales (Folklore Association of Australia by 1947; president 1946-65) and the New Australians' Cultural Association (vice-president). He published two books on the music of the Outer Hebrides, *Fine Song for Singing* (1951) and

Three Hebridean Songs (1953). In *Old Tales in a New Land* (1957) he outlined the peasant traditions of twelve European countries, many of whose people were postwar immigrants in Australia.

Clement Hosking was of middle height and medium build, and of good bearing. Unmarried, he devoted his life to music and folklore, although he could converse authoritatively on a range of subjects. He was cultured and dignified, 'a charming companion, serenely poised, wise, and warmly human'. His expertise in folklore brought considerable acclaim: Dame Mary Gilmore [q.v.9] lauded his literary gifts, Dulcie Holland wrote a piano piece in his honour and Dr Edgar Bainton [q.v.7] prepared the wording for an illuminated address which he presented to him on his retirement in 1952. As 'Maitri' and 'Kenyas', Hosking contributed paragraphs to the *Bulletin*.

A man of mystic temperament, he studied Catholicism before embracing Buddhism. Hosking lived for many years at Killara, but eventually moved into a Methodist aged-care unit at Leichhardt. He died there of myocardial infarction on 9 October 1966 and was cremated with Buddhist rites. A public thanksgiving service was subsequently held in Newington's chapel. The Celtic Fellowship and the Folklore Association endowed Clement Hosking annual awards for Celtic and Hebridean folk-singing at the City of Sydney Eisteddfod.

J. Glennon, *Australian Music and Musicians* (Adel, 1968); P. L. Swain, *A Quarter Past the Century* (Syd, 1988); *Aust Musical News*, 10, 1921, Aug 1923, Aug 1930, Oct 1951, Apr 1952, June 1952; *Green Room Pictorial*, 1 June 1924; *Theatre* (Syd), July 1925; *Newingtonian*, Aug 1946, Dec 1952, Dec 1961; *Syd Mail*, 20 Apr 1921; *Sun* (Syd), 23 Oct 1935; *Bulletin*, 16 Mar 1955; *North Shore Times*, 7 Aug 1963; Hosking letters, press-cuttings and scrapbooks (NL).   PETER L. SWAIN

HOSKING, RICHARD (1877-1971), physicist and teacher, was born on 1 May 1877 at Ballarat East, Victoria, fifth child of Cornish-born parents Martin Hosking, missionary, and his wife Sarah, née Richards. In 1894 Richard entered Queen's College, University of Melbourne (B.A., 1909; D.Sc., 1913); he was awarded the Kernot [q.v.5] research scholarship in natural philosophy in 1899. Three years later he proceeded to the University of Cambridge (B.A., 1904) as an 1851 Exhibition research scholar in physics. Back in Melbourne, he lectured in science while continuing his studies; his D.Sc. was awarded for a thesis on the viscosity of water.

On 6 December 1905 Hosking had married Lilian Mary Florence Preston at the Palmerston Street Methodist Church, North Carlton. Physics and mechanics master at Sydney Grammar School from 1906, he contributed several articles to scientific journals. In March 1911 he was appointed professor of physics at the newly established Royal Military College, Duntroon, Federal Capital Territory. A neat, trim man who sported a moustache, he was remembered by his students principally for the clarity of his lectures. In early 1914 he agreed to preside over a science club begun by the cadets, but the venture foundered due to disruptions caused by World War I. During the Christmas vacation he assisted Professor (Sir) Thomas Lyle [q.v.10] in the measurement of gauges made in Australia and used for testing locally produced shell-cases.

Retrenched in December 1922 as a result of severe reductions in the staff at Duntroon, in the following year Hosking obtained the post of senior master at Melbourne High School where he taught physics and mathematics. He also lectured in natural philosophy and had charge of laboratory classes at the university in the evenings. In January 1924 he took up a new position with the Royal Australian Air Force as science instructor.

Hosking taught aerodynamics, meteorology, air pilotage and wireless telegraphy to students at No.1 Flying Training School, Point Cook. He later organized classes for airmen about to sit examinations required for promotion and introduced tutorials for all ranks. In 1926 he was elected a fellow of the Institute of Physics, London. The air force expanded during the 1920s and he found his workload increasing. His title was changed to education officer and part of his time was spent at R.A.A.F. Headquarters, Melbourne. Officers were appointed to assist him in 1936 and he was elevated to principal education officer at headquarters.

Taking furlough before his formal retirement in May 1939, Hosking embarked with his wife on an extended overseas tour. In World War II he worked successively as a physicist at the Munitions Supply Laboratories, Maribyrnong, Melbourne, as a consultant to J. W. Handley Pty Ltd, manufacturers of military optical equipment, and, in an honorary capacity, with the R.A.A.F.'s Directorate of Technical Services.

In his final retirement he lived at Elsternwick. Survived by his wife and three sons, he died on 17 May 1971 at Brighton and was cremated. As an army and air force educationist, he had been one of a small number of civilians who made a significant impression on the defence forces before World War II.

J. E. Lee, *Duntroon* (Canb, 1952); C. D. Coulthard-Clark, *Duntroon* (Syd, 1986); R. E. Frost,

RAAF College & Academy 1947-86 (Canb, 1991); *Herald* (Melb), 9 Nov 1938; *Age* (Melb), 20 May 1971; private memoir (held by Mr H. R. Hosking, Gardenvale, Melb).   C. D. COULTHARD-CLARK

HOTCHIN, SIR CLAUDE (1898-1977), businessman and art benefactor, was born on 7 March 1898 at Quorn, South Australia, son of Robert John Hotchin, butcher, and his wife Bertha Mary, née Brown, a tailoress. In 1905 the family moved to Broken Hill, New South Wales. When his father died in 1909, Claude was granted special permission to leave the local school and start work. Moving to Adelaide at the age of 15, he obtained a job in Clarkson Ltd's hardware store. On 4 April 1925 at the Pirie Street Methodist Church he married Doris May Clarkson, the daughter of his employer. Next day the couple moved to Perth to help manage a branch of the firm. After a fire gutted the store in 1932, Hotchin and the co-manager bought the goodwill and name of Clarksons (W.A.) Ltd. In 1940 he became sole manager of the business. The postwar building boom contributed to the success of the company: in 1950 he was able to sell his interests and retire from working life.

Hotchin was important as an art collector and benefactor of public galleries in Western Australia. Believing that 'good pictures are things of beauty and character, naturally they have an influence for good when youth is surrounded by them', he had begun to buy paintings in 1937. Ten years later he opened the Claude Hotchin Art Gallery in Perth and ran it until 1951. In 1948 he inaugurated a competition for Western Australian artists; the prize bore his name and was awarded annually until 1973. Between 1948 and 1977 Hotchin donated an estimated two thousand original paintings to galleries, hospitals and shire councils throughout the State in an effort to 'stimulate art appreciation'. His predilection was for Australian pastoral landscapes. Many of the smaller regional collections have remained unchanged from the time of the first gifts and their essentially conservative holdings continue to exert subtle influence on attitudes to art in the local communities. Royal Perth Hospital and the University of Western Australia were major recipients, and, in 1972, the Art Gallery of Western Australia received an initial bequest of $10 000 with which it established the Sir Claude Hotchin Art Foundation.

An active supporter of the Methodist Church, Hotchin belonged to the Perth Rotary Club (from 1930) and was a founding member (1938) of the Crippled Children's Society of Western Australia. He was a member (1947-64) of the board of trustees of the Public Library, Museum and Art Gallery of Western Australia and chairman (1960-64) of the board of the Art Gallery. In addition, he served on the senate of the university (1951-69) and on the university's McGillivray art bequest committee (1961-73). In 1967 he was knighted. The university awarded him an honorary LL.D. in 1974.

Sir Claude was a tall, impressive and charming man, with a flair for public speaking. He lived at Chartwell, Mundaring, and his recreations included poetry, golf, swimming, motoring and gardening. Survived by his wife and daughter, he died on 3 June 1977 at Albany and was buried with Anglican rites in Allambie Park cemetery. (Sir) Ivor Hele's portrait of Hotchin is held by the Art Gallery of Western Australia.

National Exhibitions Touring Structure (Perth), *Sir Claude Hotchin Art Bequests* (Perth, 1992); *West Australian*, 4 June 1977; J. Gooding, One Man's Vision: A Study of Western Australian Art Collector, Claude Hotchin 1898-1977 (M.Phil. thesis, Univ WA, 1988), *and* for bibliog; Hotchin papers (WAA).   JANDA GOODING

HOUSLEY, TREVOR ALFRED (1910-1968), public servant, was born on 31 October 1910 at Gympie, Queensland, fifth child of native-born parents William Frank Frederick Housley, painter, and his wife Eva Alice, née Carroll. Educated at Gympie High School and the University of Queensland (B.Sc., 1941), Trevor joined the Brisbane office of the Postmaster-General's Department on 15 October 1926 as a junior mechanic (in training). He later worked as a clerk in the personnel and accounts branches.

At St Joseph's Catholic Church, Kangaroo Point, on 16 February 1935 Housley married Susan Maureen Reilly. In the following year he was promoted engineer. During World War II he established telecommunications systems in Papua and New Guinea for the armed services; after returning to Australia he installed radar equipment in warships. In 1946 he transferred to the Department of Civil Aviation as supervising engineer; he rose to chief airways engineer and took a prominent part in the Professional Officers' Association.

Appointed assistant to the general manager of the Overseas Telecommunications Commission (Australia) in February 1951, Housley directed the development of the commission's radio facilities, including the building of major transmitting and receiving stations on the outskirts of Sydney, at Doonside and Bringelly respectively. He was also responsible for preparing O.T.C.'s services to handle the large volume of international communications associated with the 1956 Olympic Games in Melbourne.

As O.T.C.'s general manager (from 1956), Housley led an Australian delegation to London in 1958 for the Commonwealth Telecommunications Conference which recommended the construction of a 'round-the-world' telephone cable system. Following the 1959 Pacific Cable Conference in Sydney—at which he again headed the Australian delegation—he became convener of the Commonwealth Pacific cable management committee, comprising representatives from Australia, Britain, Canada and New Zealand. The committee supervised the building of a high-capacity telephone cable between Australia and North America; the COMPAC service opened on 3 December 1963 and was probably the most important milestone in Australian international telecommunications since the landing of the first telegraph cable at Port Darwin in 1871.

Housley's leadership transformed O.T.C. into a rapidly growing and highly profitable business, gave Australia ample facilities for telephone and data communication with the rest of the world, and made him an international figure in telecommunications. In 1961 he was appointed C.B.E. Next year he was chosen as Australia's representative on the management-committee for the South East Asia cable project which was to link Australia to the Territory of Papua and New Guinea, and to Guam, Hong Kong, Singapore and Malaysia, with connections from Guam to Japan and the United States of America.

In 1958-64 Housley helped to renegotiate financial and operating arrangements between Australia and British Commonwealth countries, and between Australia and other countries with which it conducted substantial telephone business. From 1964 he represented Australia and O.T.C. on the interim communications satellite committee of what was to be called the International Telecommunications Satellite Consortium.

Housley was a gifted telecommunications engineer, an outstanding executive and a brilliant negotiator, particularly at the international level. Six ft 4 ins (193 cm) tall and large framed, with a shock of prematurely white hair, he had a genial personality and a down-to-earth manner. His speech was laconic and drew on a stock of Australian expressions, such as 'up a dry gully' and 'chasing a rabbit while it will run'. He dressed untidily, rarely wore a coat in his Sydney office and had the habit of placing his pipe, often still warm, in the top pocket of his nylon shirts which led to burn-marks and holes through which the stem protruded.

Members of his staff called him Trevor. He knew them all by name, and recalled details of their families and interests without effort. Despite incessant overseas travel, he spent much time visiting O.T.C. stations and branches throughout Australia, talking to, socializing with and enthusing his colleagues. Housley built up corporate morale and encouraged his employees to respond to challenges. He drove people hard, but no harder than he pushed himself, and he remained calm and thoughtful when under pressure.

On 9 December 1965 Housley was appointed director-general, posts and telegraphs, based in Melbourne. A body vastly different in size and culture from O.T.C., the Post Office had considerable industrial and organizational problems with which he had to contend. He died of an intracranial haemorrhage on 10 October 1968 at Kew and was buried in Boroondara cemetery; his wife, son and three of his four daughters survived him.

E. Harcourt, *Taming the Tyrant* (Syd, 1987); OTC, *Transit*, 4, no 1, Feb-Mar 1951, 17, nos 3 and 4, Sept-Dec 1965; *Australian*, 12 Nov 1965, 24 June 1967; OTC *and* Aust Post archives (Telstra Corp L, Paddington, Syd).

GEORGE F. MALTBY

HOWARD, KENNETH PERCIVAL FREDERICK (1913-1976), racecaller, was born on 2 December 1913 at Waverley, Sydney, son of Percival Thomas Howard, a window-dresser from Victoria, and his Sydney-born wife Brenda Florence, née Knight. As a schoolboy, Ken studied racing colours, breeding and records. He became a cadet journalist, probably on *Truth*, before joining radio station 2SM as a messenger-boy; in 1936 he made his first race broadcast from Moorefield as understudy to Reg McKenzie. A few years later Howard moved to radio 2KY. At the district registrar's office, Paddington, on 4 September 1939 he married Iris Adelaide, a hairdresser and daughter of the horse-trainer Joe Cook. In that year he replaced Melbourne radio station 3XY's racecaller Harry Solomons, gaoled for his role in a scheme to defraud starting-price bookmakers.

Back in Sydney in 1941, Howard joined radio 2UE. He also called trotting and greyhound races, and commentated on boxing and wrestling matches. Until 1952 neither the Australian Jockey Club nor the Sydney Turf Club allowed commercial radio stations to describe races from their courses. Howard had to use precarious, off-course vantage points: at Rosehill he broadcast from a tower on an oil-storage tank, at Canterbury from another tower on top of a fowlhouse and at Randwick from the roof of a block of flats. An official threatened him with a shotgun for broadcasting from a tree adjacent to the Pakenham racecourse. For the next meeting the club erected a hessian screen to block his view, but

Howard foiled this move by using a hot-air balloon.

Early Australian broadcasters, led by the Australian Broadcasting Commission's M. A. Ferry [q.v.8], described races in a calm and carefully modulated manner. In contrast, Howard's rising tone of excitement could turn even 'a maiden handicap of hacks into a Homeric struggle'. He was known for such colourful phrases as 'lunging for the wire' and 'London to a brick' (first used during the Blitz). Howard was an extremely accurate caller, naming the position of each horse in the race once every furlong, rather than focussing only on the front-runners.

In the early 1950s he moved to radio 2GB, where he remained. Howard presented Australia's first television turf programmes, including 'Racing Review', on TCN-9 in December 1956. With faith in his own judgement, he earned the nickname ''Magic Eye' for his accuracy in calling the first-placed horse immediately a race had finished. He was not always right, however: in 1968, after he incorrectly called Royal Account as winner of the A.J.C. Derby and Joking as winner of the Epsom, the Victoria Amateur Turf Club replaced him as its broadcaster of the Sydney races relayed to Caulfield.

Howard had been appointed M.B.E. in 1967. He described his last Sydney race at Randwick on 31 December 1973. In retirement, he still called the Bowraville races, but devoted most of his time to fishing, lawn bowls and gardening. Survived by his wife, he died of coronary vascular disease and cirrhosis of the liver on 21 October 1976 at his Nambucca Heads home and was buried in the Catholic section of Botany cemetery, Sydney.

N. Penton, *A Racing Heart* (Syd, 1987); J. Pollard, *Australian Horse Racing* (Syd, 1988); *People* (Syd), 16 Aug 1950; *SMH*, 26 July 1966, 1 Jan 1967, 1 Jan, 26 Dec 1974, 22 Oct 1976, 7, 14 June 1981; *Sun-Herald* (Syd), 13 Oct 1968, 16 Dec 1973; *Herald* (Melb), 14 Oct 1968, 22 Oct 1976; *Daily Mirror* (Syd), 21 Oct 1976; *Sun* (Syd), 2 Jan 1974, 21 Oct 1976; *Wireless Weekly*, 20 Jan 1934; *ABC Weekly*, 18 Jan 1947, p 29.

RICHARD WATERHOUSE

HOWARTH, ROBERT GUY (1906-1974), scholar, literary critic and poet, was born on 10 May 1906 at Tenterfield, New South Wales, second son of native-born parents Arthur Howarth, schoolteacher, and his wife Lucy Elizabeth, née Newling. Guy was educated at Fort Street Boys' High School, Sydney, under A. J. Kilgour and George Mackaness [qq.v.9,10], and was school captain in 1924. He was aged 19 when he married 16-year-old Sylvia Marjorie Beryl Smith, a stenographer, on 27 June 1925 at St Stephen's Anglican Church, Newtown; they were to have three sons before she divorced him in September 1948. He graduated from the University of Sydney (B.A., 1929) with first-class honours, the university medal in English and the Wentworth [q.v.2] travelling fellowship. A non-collegiate student attached to St Catherine's Society at the University of Oxford (B.Litt., 1931), he specialized in seventeenth-century poetry. By the time he was appointed lecturer at the University of Sydney in 1933, he had collected, edited and published in London *Minor Poets of the 17th Century* (for Everyman's Library, 1931), *Letters and the Second Diary of Samuel Pepys* (1932) and *Letters of George Gordon, 6th Lord Byron* (1933).

As a teacher, Howarth was quick to recognize and praise the work of students and colleagues, generous in providing opportunities for their advancement and conscientious in his correspondence. His formal lectures read well in print, but were rather too packed to assimilate easily. In later life he was to persuade colleagues to join him in readings of scenes from plays under discussion. He raised some conservative eyebrows in Sydney by introducing his classes to modernist or contemporary writers, including Hopkins, Eliot, the Sitwells, Joyce, Faulkner and Auden, and to Australian writers, among them Joseph Furphy, Shaw Neilson [qq.v.8,10], Kenneth Slessor [q.v.] and Christina Stead. He invited students to convivial meetings in his rooms at the university, and entertained at his modest home in Young Street, Neutral Bay, where visiting writers from overseas, such as Stephen Spender, rubbed shoulders with Slessor, R. D. FitzGerald, Douglas Stewart, Miles Franklin [q.v.8] and Hal Porter.

Howarth established an international reputation as a specialist in Elizabethan tragedy and Restoration comedy; his contribution to Australian literature was as substantial and enduring as it is underrated. In 1939 he persuaded the Australian English Association to publish under his editorship the journal, *Southerly*. He judged work solely on the basis of literary quality, and announced that the journal would eschew political and ideological considerations. Not only did Howarth influence Australian writing through deciding who would or would not be published in the 1940s and 1950s, but, as a literary critic for both the *Sydney Morning Herald* and *Southerly*, he made decisive assessments of writers as diverse as Christopher Brennan, Hugh McCrae [qq.v.7,10], Furphy, Neilson, Stead and Patrick White.

A 'lyricist, aphorist and satirist', Howarth has been described by Professor A. L. McLeod as a significant Australian poet and a 'master of the "simple and sensuous" love lyric'. The epigrammatic wit and polish of his better verse is illustrated by lines from poem iv in *Spright and Geist* (1944):

'Each parting is a little death',
You said, and died.
But I do more than yield my breath—
I'm crucified.

He also edited or wrote introductions for works by McCrae and Furphy, William Hay's *The Escape of the Notorious Sir William Heans* (Melbourne, 1955) and—with John Thompson [q.v.] and Slessor—*The Penguin Book of Australian Verse* (London, 1958).

In 1948 Howarth was appointed reader in English literature. On 12 November that year at the registrar general's office, Sydney, he married Lilian Irene Shephard, née Flynn, a clerk and a divorcee; they were to be divorced in 1964. He was elected a fellow (1952) of the Royal Society of Literature of the United Kingdom, and was a foundation member (1954-55) of the Australian Humanities Research Council, a member (1950-55) of the advisory board of the Commonwealth Literary Fund and president (1947-55) of the Sydney branch of the English Association. Bitterly disappointed at his failure to be appointed to the Challis [q.v.3] chair of English literature at the University of Sydney, he resigned in 1955 to accept the Arderne chair of English literature at the University of Cape Town.

Awarded grants by the C.L.F. in 1971 and 1972 to prepare an edition of the letters of Norman Lindsay [q.v.10], Howarth returned to Sydney. He suffered a fractured skull when he was struck by a motorcycle in George Street on 30 December 1973 and died on 21 January 1974 in Sydney Hospital; survived by the sons of his first marriage, he was cremated with Anglican rites. He left his will unaltered and his estate to Lilian. She sold his library and manuscripts as a 'collection entire' to the University of Texas, Austin, United States of America. It was a major loss to Australian scholarship. The papers alone fill 75 boxes and the books more than 100 shelves; the collection includes the manuscript of Howarth's *magnum opus* on the dramatist John Webster. The *Letters of Norman Lindsay* (1979) was completed by Anthony Barker.

Southerly, 34, no 2, 1974, pp 107, 112, 34, no 4, 1974, p 385, 49, no 3, 1989, p 363, 49, no 4, 1989, p 649; *Library Chronicle of Univ Texas*, 13, 1980, p 68; *SMH*, 27 Aug 1931, 7 Apr 1933, 12 June 1934, 26 Jan 1952, 21 Dec 1954, 6 Dec 1971, 30 Oct 1972, 23 Jan 1974.   STUART LEE

HOWDEN, HARRY LESLIE (1896-1969), naval officer, was born on 4 July 1896 at Vogeltown, Wellington, New Zealand, son of Patrick Grieve Howden, a merchant from Scotland, and his English-born wife Mary Elizabeth, née Niblett. Educated at Wellington College, as a youth Harry sailed the Pacific in trading vessels. He made his way to England, obtained an appointment in October 1915 as midshipman, Royal Naval Reserve, and went to sea in the battleship, H.M.S. *Benbow*. On 5 October 1916 he transferred to the Royal Australian Navy, joining H.M.A.S. *Sydney* in December 1917.

Postings to H.M.A. ships and to shore establishments in Australia broadened Howden's experience. Promoted lieutenant in May 1919, he completed courses in England in 1923-24. He then commanded the destroyer, H.M.A.S. *Tasmania* (as lieutenant commander from May 1927), and served in H.M.A.S. *Australia* from 1928. On exchange with the R.N. in 1930, he commanded the gunboat, *Mantis*, which operated on the Yangtse River, China. His flair for shiphandling impressed his superiors and in December 1931 he was promoted commander. On 21 May that year at the British consulate-general, Hankow, he had married Vanda Mary Sanders Fiske; they were to have three sons before being divorced.

Returning to Australia, Howden was executive officer of H.M.A.S. *Albatross* (1932-33), H.M.A.S. *Canberra* (1933-35) and Flinders Naval Depot, Westernport, Victoria (from 1935). He was appointed O.B.E. in 1937 and was sent that year to England for duty in the Admiralty's Naval Intelligence Division. On 30 June 1938 he was promoted captain. Home again in October, he had a succession of brief commands until August 1939 when he was given the six-inch-gun cruiser, *Hobart*.

After World War II began, *Hobart* was employed on patrol and escort work east of Suez. In June 1940 she carried troops to British Somaliland. Two months later the Italian invasion forced the British to withdraw to Berbera, where, from 14 to 19 August, Howden supervised the evacuation of 7140 soldiers and civilians in transports and warships. He set up a combined headquarters in *Hobart*, improvised a flotilla of ferrying craft, saw to the comfort of the wounded and organized rescue parties for stragglers—despite air-raids and nightly gales. His 'cheery confidence' proved inspirational and he was elevated to C.B.E. for his role in the operation.

Hobart served with the Australian Squadron between December 1940 and July 1941. Dispatched to the Mediterranean Station, she took part in the relief (August to October 1941) of the Australians at Tobruk, Libya. Following Japan's entry into the war in December, *Hobart* sailed for Australia, but was diverted to Singapore and attached to allied forces attempting to halt the Japanese advance through Malaya and the Netherlands East Indies. Alternately escorting convoys and searching for enemy vessels, 'Lucky Harry' and his ship survived repeated air-attacks. While he enjoyed good fortune, he also showed outstanding skills as a seaman and commander. During each strike he ordered sharp turns and drastic changes of speed which saved the ship. Bombs dropped on 15 February 1942 fell close enough for him to see the 'ugly red flash of their burst and to feel the heat of their explosions across [his] face'. He was mentioned in dispatches. On 1 March *Hobart* sailed for Colombo. In May she was in Australian waters and fought in the battle of the Coral Sea. When Howden's command ended next month, his crew gave him an emotional farewell.

Although flamboyant and a *bon vivant*, Howden was a well-informed and conscientious officer. He took pains to foster the welfare of his subordinates and won their admiration, but he could be tough on those who did not meet his standards. Some saw him as generous and sociable; others accused him of vanity and dogmatism. He was a small, neatly dressed man who kept himself fit by riding, sailing and rowing, but an arterial lesion at the base of the brain precluded further sea service and the opportunity for promotion to flag rank. In 1942 and again in 1943-46 he commanded the new Sydney shore establishment, H.M.A.S. *Penguin*, and oversaw its development. His next posting was as naval officer-in-charge, Fremantle, Western Australia.

Howden retired on 4 July 1951 and spent his time travelling and managing his extensive portfolio of shares. At the district registrar's office, Chatswood, Sydney, on 26 September 1960 he married Freda Sybil Oates, née Harradence, a 46-year-old divorcee. While holidaying in London, he died on 16 February 1969 at Smithfield and was cremated; his wife survived him, as did the sons of his first marriage. He bequeathed almost all his estate, sworn for probate at $2 771 733, to charity.

G. H. Gill, *Royal Australian Navy 1939-1942* (Canb, 1957); *Naval Hist Review*, Dec 1974, p 3; *Herald* (Melb), 20 Sept, 30 Nov 1969; A3978, Howden, H. L. (AA, Canb); information from Prof M. Howden, Cattai, NSW.   DARRYL BENNET

HOWELL, BERTRAM (1893-1961), musician, band-leader and collector, was born on 24 November 1893 at Runcorn, Cheshire, England, son of James Bertram Howell, storekeeper to a general contractor, and his wife Charlotte Helen, née Holness. Educated at

Manchester, Bert claimed to have learned to play the violin from the age of 9 at the Royal Manchester College of Music and to have progressed to playing in the Hallé Orchestra. He emigrated to Melbourne before World War I broke out and formed the Society Jazz Band in 1916. His early professional engagements included appearances at the 'Djin Djin' tearooms, Collins Street, in 1920 and at private parties. In that year he established the Dominant Music Lending Library at 178 Collins Street. Between engagements at the Victory Picture Theatre, St Kilda, he went abroad in 1922 and 1924 to further his musical studies and collect the latest music.

After two phenomenally successful years (from September 1928) at the Ambassadors Theatre, Perth, Howell arrived in Sydney early in 1931 where he took positions in turn at the Capitol and State theatres. An eighteen-month season followed at the Capitol Picture Theatre, Melbourne, before his world tour in 1933. Visiting Cairo, Vienna, Madrid, Paris, Brussels, Berlin, London, New York and Hollywood, he returned to Melbourne with two trunkloads of the latest orchestral music.

Howell adopted Swing, an aggressive new form of music, when it reached Australia in 1936 and quickly spread through the entertainment industry. His band dominated Melbourne radio. Organized as both a big-time theatre and radio unit, it included the city's top musicians who could earn over £15 a week. From September 1935 they combined regular appearances at the Capitol with their 'Shell Show' on radio 3AW. In March 1938 the band moved to the State Theatre until its contract was ended in February 1939. Lured by Sydney's night-life, its members decided to relocate there.

By May 1939, less than two months after starting at the Prince Edward Theatre, the band was appearing at Romano's [q.v.11] Restaurant, Martin Place. The hectic pace continued: a typical day's schedule included two shows at the Prince Edward between feature films, and nightclub work at Romano's between 9 p.m. and 2 a.m. from Monday to Saturday. On Wednesdays the 'Kraft Dilly Revue' (relayed to twenty-three radio stations throughout Australia from radio 2GB) presented the singer Dorothy 'Dilly' Foster with Howell's band, sponsored by the Kraft Walker [q.v.12] Cheese Co. Pty Ltd. At St Peter's Anglican Church, East Sydney, on 1 June 1940 Howell married Jean Bishop Houghton, an 18-year-old law clerk; they were to remain childless and to be divorced in 1956. His song, *Homeward*, written with Varney Monk [q.v.10], was previewed in 1944 in the 'The Anzac Show' at the Prince Edward. At the end of World War II he terminated his engagement and left for England.

While living at Whitstable, Kent, the Howells established an antiques and fine arts business at Canterbury. He had become interested in the fifteenth-century French lyric poet, François Villon, and collected rare editions of his published works in England. Howell returned to Australia in June 1949, corresponded regularly with English and European antiquarian book-dealers, and travelled overseas to supplement his Villon collection. He died of coronary vascular disease on 10 November 1961 at St Luke's Hospital, Darlinghurst, and was buried in Randwick cemetery; his Villon collection, personal papers and ephemera were bequeathed to the Public Library of New South Wales.

A. Bisset, *Black Roots, White Flowers* (Syd, 1987); *Music Maker*, 21 Aug, 20 Sept 1944; *Everyone's*, 12 Apr 1933; *Tempo*, Feb-Mar 1939; *Shell House J*, Sept 1935; *SMH*, 10 Apr 1939, 14 Apr 1962; Howell papers (ML).   JUDY NELSON

HOWEY, GEORGE CAPSTICK (1894-1952), dairy-farmer, was born on 24 March 1894 at Geelong, Victoria, son of English-born parents Albert Edward Capstick, coach-painter, and his wife Agnes, née Langhorn. He was named George Langhorn Capstick, but, after his father's death (1895) and his mother's marriage (1896) to William Howey, he adopted his stepfather's surname. Educated at Northcote State and Warrnambool Agricultural High schools, George worked in Gippsland before managing his mother's property at Swan Marsh. He employed share-farmers for milking and concentrated on increasing production by improved farming methods. On 25 March 1925 at St John's Anglican Church, Colac, he married Una Elizabeth Beatrice Cowley, a schoolteacher.

Active in social and sporting life, Howey identified with people in the district, and resolved to lift the status of the dairy industry and its hard-pressed workers. He aimed to promote the application of science and new ideas, and initiated or supported such organizations as the Victorian Pasture Improvement League, the Victorian United Cow Testing Association (president 1936-40), the Colac Rye-grass Growers' Co. (chairman 1931), and the Colac and District Pastoral and Agricultural Society. As the Depression deepened and very low returns persisted into the 1930s, he realized that farmers should organize to demand a decent living. In 1933, as the United Country Party's candidate, he stood unsuccessfully for the Legislative Assembly seat of Polwarth.

In 1940-52 Howey was president of the Victorian Dairymen's Association. His sincere, friendly, even-tempered manner, his remarkable memory and intimate and practical knowledge of production and marketing, and his ability to express complex issues in simple terms earned the trust and respect of dairy-farmers. By 1943 he had sat on eight different committees and chaired four of them. As a member of the Australian Dairy Produce Board (chairman 1948-52) and a director of the Commonwealth Dairy Produce Equalisation Committee, he was largely responsible for the living standards of dairy-farmers. He represented Victoria on the Joint Dairying Industry Advisory Committee. While his reputation and authority grew, so did the influence of dairymen through the V.D.A. In 1946, 1949 and 1951 he travelled to Europe to investigate and report on the industry for the Commonwealth government.

Even as his influence extended to national and international levels—he was foundation president of the Australian Dairy Federation and vice-president of the International Dairy Federation—Howey retained his strong interest in local affairs. The owner of three farms in the district, he was a director of the Colac Dairying Co. Ltd, deputy-coroner, a justice of the peace, borough councillor (1939-43), a Freemason, a Rotarian and an excellent all-round cricketer. Between trips to Melbourne and Sydney, he valued the occasional day of tranquillity when he went fishing. Survived by his wife, son and three daughters, he died of myocardial infarction on 26 August 1952 at Colac and was buried in the local cemetery. Next year he was posthumously awarded the Australian Society of Dairy Technology's gold medal.

K. Sillcock, *Three Lifetimes of Dairying in Victoria* (Melb, 1972); I. McIntosh, *Forest, Lake and Plain* (Melb, 1988); *Vic and SA Dairy Farmer*, June 1940; *Vic Dairy Farmer*, Sept, Oct 1952; *Camperdown Herald*, 9 May 1925; *Camperdown Chronicle*, 19 May 1925; *Sun News-Pictorial*, 31 Dec 1943; *Leader* (Melb), 20 June 1951; *Age* (Melb), 27 Aug 1952; *Colac Herald*, 29 Aug, 3 Sept 1952; information from Mr I. Howey, Eaglemont, Miss A. Howey, Ivanhoe, and Miss E. Howey, Glen Waverley, Melb, and Mrs H. Smith, Portland, Vic.   L. LOMAS

HOWIE, CLARA WINIFRED (1881-1960), nurse and administrator, was born on 27 June 1881 at Glenelg, Adelaide, fourth of five children of George Cullen Howie, ironmonger, and his wife Clara Jane, née Hotham, both from Scotland. Laurence Hotham Howie [q.v.9] was her eldest brother. Winifred's father died in 1883. Two years later Clara took the children to live with her father Rev. John Hotham, a Congregationalist minister, at Port Elliot where she ran the home as a boarding-house in summer and as a small private school in winter. Winifred trained (1906-09) as a nurse at the Adelaide Children's Hospital and completed a midwifery course at the Queen's Home in 1910. Next year she began work with the District Trained Nursing Society (later District and Bush Nursing Society).

In 1912 Howie was the first nurse sent by the society to Hergott Springs (Marree), 360 miles (580 km) north of Adelaide and 150 miles (240 km) from the nearest doctor. The town was home to a thriving community of Indian and Afghan cameleers, and a photograph shows Sister Howie in her starched nursing uniform, riding a camel. She was obliged to 'live at the public house and ... interview her patients there'. In 1918 she moved to Goolwa where she opened a branch of the D.T.N.S. In the following year she was appointed assistant-superintendent of nurses at the society's Adelaide headquarters; she was its general secretary and superintendent of nurses in 1926-49; Edith Maude Bottrill (d. 12 August 1960) was her deputy (from 1926). Their work involved frequent tours of the country branches. A plump woman, with large, mild eyes and a calm expression, Howie showed unfailing sympathy for the sick poor and handled their problems tactfully.

She was a member (from 1924) of the Australasian Trained Nurses' Association, acting-president (1937) and president (1937-41) of the South Australian branch and its representative on the State Registration Board. In 1936 she joined the centenary committee which published Nursing in South Australia (1938): the book included a tribute to her and to the A.T.N.A. written by Rev. John Flynn [q.v.8]. During World War II the work of the D.T.N.S. was often heavy, monotonous and trying, due to the lack of domestic help in homes and hospitals.

Sister Howie required her outback staff to attend Aborigines living in bush camps and to encourage them to come to the nursing hostels for treatment. She developed a special relationship with Daisy Bates [q.v.7] and corresponded with her for many years. The D.T.N.S. central office acted as a post office for Bates. By 1947 Howie was supervising about thirty sub-branches, and her nurses made 103 000 visits. In 1948 she was appointed M.B.E. Although she resigned in 1949, she continued her care for the sick through the auxiliary of the Royal Adelaide Hospital. Distressed by the news of the death of Miss Bottrill, she died on 13 August 1960 at her Forestville home and was cremated.

J. Durdin, They Became Nurses (Syd, 1991); Port Augusta Despatch, 7 Nov 1913; Advertiser (Adel), 16 June 1937, 19 Oct 1949, 15 Feb 1960; Roy District Nursing Soc of SA, Minutes of Bd Meetings, 1912-49 (held by RDNS, Adel); information from Miss M. Howie, Parkside, Mrs J. Flint, Westbourne Park, and Mrs D. Lines, Blackwood, Adel.
                                        CAROL F. GASTON

HOY, ALICE (1893-1976), educationist, was born on 9 February 1893 at Ararat, Victoria, youngest of eleven children of Rueben Hoy, a Victorian-born blacksmith, and his wife Bridget, née Brennan, from Ireland. Alice was educated at Kensington State and University High schools, and was awarded exhibitions and scholarships to the University of Melbourne (B.A., 1914; Dip.Ed., 1915; M.A., 1916; LL.B., 1927). She graduated with first-class honours, winning the Wyselaskie scholarship in political economy and the Dwight [q.v.4] prize in history.

In 1915 the Education Department sent Hoy to University High, a 'practising school' for trainee-teachers. She gained rapid promotion and in 1924 became mistress of method at Melbourne Teachers' College, with an attachment (1926-49) as senior lecturer at the university's school of education. Having written a textbook, Civics for Australian Schools (1925), she revised it continually and new editions were published almost annually until 1945. In 1938 she studied teacher-training schemes in Britain and North America. Her career culminated in her appointment on 21 December 1949 as principal of the Education Department's new secondary training centre at the university. A strict disciplinarian, she inaugurated a successful training for secondary teachers, whose numbers had been depleted since the abandonment of financial assistance for trainees during the Depression. She retired in February 1958.

Miss Hoy influenced education in Victoria for over fifty years. Although she drew her ideas from numerous schools of thought, she favoured the late nineteenth and early twentieth century English view of education, and had little time for American progressivism. Her loyalty to the work and values of the Education Department, and her steady attention to the implementation of its policies, stemmed from her belief in the efficacy of education for social good and from her faith in the department's ability to advance that goal. Respected by colleagues for her integrity, penetrating intelligence, dry wit, fluent and precise command of language, and 'her stinging sallies', she was also an influential council-member of University Women's College (1936-64), the Australian College of Education (1959-71) and Monash University (interim council 1958-61, council 1961-71). In 1961 she published a history of University High School, A City Built to Music.

Late in life, Hoy received considerable honours: she was made an honorary fellow

(1960) of the Australian College of Education and appointed O.B.E. (1964); the Australian and New Zealand Association for the Advancement of Science awarded her the Mackie [q.v.10] medal in 1967 and Monash University conferred an honorary LL.D. on her in 1972. She died on 4 September 1976 at Pascoe Vale and was buried in Ararat cemetery; her estate was sworn for probate at $302 730. A portrait by Chris White hangs in the foyer of the Alice Hoy Building, Institute of Education, University of Melbourne.

A. H. Ramsay, *Report on Certain Phases of Education* (Melb, 1949); Education Dept (Vic), *Vision and Realisation*, L. J. Blake ed (Melb, 1973); D. Garden, *The Melbourne Teacher Training Colleges* (Melb, 1982); *Univ Melb Gazette*, 1976, no 4, p 15; J. Meabank, A Contract with Education: Alice Hoy 1893-1976 (M.Ed. thesis, Univ Melb, 1988); A. Hoy's record, Education Dept (Vic) Archives.

JULANN MEABANK

HOYSTED, FREDERICK WILLIAM (1883-1967), racehorse-trainer and jockey, was born on 8 May 1883 at Wangaratta, Victoria, fifth of twelve children of English-born Henry Hoysted, trainer, and his Victorian-born wife Winifred Louisa, née Johnstone. Henry's father, also Frederick William, hailed from County Kildare, Ireland. The most famous member of a renowned Australian racing family, young Fred began his career as an amateur jockey at the age of 12, winning his first race (on Wicket) at Bright in 1895 and his first city race at Maribyrnong on Bosnia (trained by his father) in the following year. Soon afterwards he received his only suspension, for failing to ride Wicket out: Hoysted said that he would sooner flog the stewards than a tired horse, and was stood down for a month. Following a fall at Beechworth in 1911, he turned to training—in partnership with his elder brother Henry ('Tib')—from their father's Wangaratta stables. On 21 April 1913 he married Ellen Frances Veronica Dedrick at Wangaratta; they were to have five sons before she died in 1931. Fred was to be affectionately known as 'Father'.

In November 1926 at Albury, New South Wales, his horse, Rakwool, beat the odds-on favourite trained by 'Tib'; the brothers had a disagreement and Fred moved to Melbourne. He took over stables at Mentone and by 1932-33 was the leading metropolitan trainer. Hoysted won or shared the premiership on seventeen occasions, including seven in succession from 1945-46 to 1951-52. Rakwool, which won the Grand National Steeple in 1931 with 11 st. 7 lb. (73 kg), was the first of his many fine fencers. His stables were named Redditch, after his best jumper which won the Grand National Steeple in 1933 with 12 st. 3

lb. (77.5 kg), together with the Australian Steeplechase in 1933 and in 1934 under the huge weight of 12 st. 13 lb. (82 kg). The outcry that ensued when Redditch died (July 1935) in a race fall at Flemington led to the replacement of post-and-rail by brush fences.

Known especially as a champion trainer of two-year-olds (in 1953-54 he won twenty juvenile races), Hoysted had the pick of Melbourne's finest jockeys, among them Harold Badger, Scobie Breasley, Frank Dempsey and Bill Williamson [q.v.]. His horses won numerous feature races, including the Adelaide Cup (Donaster), Doomben Ten Thousand (Ungar), Epsom (Achilles), Newmarket (Gay Queen), Oakleigh Plate (High Title) and the Victoria Racing Club's Oaks (Provoke and True Course), but the Melbourne Cup eluded him. Having taken over the training of Rising Fast, with which he won the Caulfield Cup in 1955, Hoysted saw the outstanding stayer unluckily beaten in that year's Melbourne Cup.

At St Patrick's Catholic Cathedral, Melbourne, on 27 October 1932 he had married Mary Elizabeth Brown, a nurse. The racing dynasty, which began when one Fred Hoysted arrived in Victoria in 1859, continued after his grandson's retirement in 1966: two of 'Father's' sons became successful metropolitan trainers and another, previously a promising jockey, became notorious for his stand against jockeys' use of the whip. Survived by his wife and the sons of his first marriage, Fred Hoysted died on 9 February 1967 at his Mentone home and was cremated with Anglican rites; his estate was sworn for probate at $111 144.

Age (Melb), 3 Mar, 2 May 1948, 10 Feb 1967; *Sun News-Pictorial*, 22 Sept 1948, 1 May 1964, 30 June 1966; *Sporting Globe*, 5, 8, 12, 15 Oct 1966, 18 Jan 1975, 5 Oct 1982; *Herald* (Melb), 1 May 1978.

PETER PIERCE

HUDSON, EDWARD ARTHUR (1921-1980), airman and office supervisor, was born on 17 April 1921 at Rockhampton, Queensland, fifth child of native-born parents Samuel George Hudson, tram conductor, and his wife Susan Catherine, née Holmes. Educated at state schools, Eddie worked as a clerk for the Rockhampton City Council. On 13 September 1940 he joined the Royal Australian Air Force under the Empire Air Training Scheme; he completed courses in Australia and Canada, qualified as a pilot and was promoted sergeant in June 1941. Having finished his advanced training in England, in September Hudson was posted to No.57 Squadron, Royal Air Force, with which he flew Wellington bombers. He was commissioned in April

1942. Two months later he completed a full tour of thirty operations; he was awarded the Distinguished Flying Cross for pressing home attacks at low altitudes.

In April 1943 he began a second tour, with No.460 Squadron, R.A.A.F., flying Lancasters mostly against heavily defended targets in Europe. Next month he took part in a raid over Czechoslovakia which involved 327 heavy bombers. The Pathfinders mistook a large lunatic asylum near Dobrany for the Skoda armament works at Pilsen and only Hudson's aircraft—through careful navigation and determined flying at low level and against the bomber stream—managed to hit the target, returning to base with an excellent photograph. He subsequently completed the required twenty missions and was awarded a Bar to his D.F.C.

Assigned to instructional duties in July, Hudson was promoted acting squadron leader in November and mentioned in dispatches. In 1944 he was selected to fly 'G for George' (a veteran Lancaster from No.460 Squadron) via North America to Australia. The aircraft reached Amberley, Queensland, in November and was to make many flights around Australia promoting the Third Victory Loan. Before that, Hudson took the plane to his home town where he and the crew received a great welcome from his family and friends, and were accorded a civic reception.

Although popular and respected, Hudson was so quiet and unassuming that his successful wartime career came as a surprise to those who had known him earlier, but his comrades in the air force recognized his courage, skill and determination. With dark, curly hair and brown eyes, he was 5 ft 7 ins (170 cm) tall and slightly built, weighing only 8 st. 10 lb. (55.3 kg). While posted to No.38 and No.34 squadrons in 1945-46, he flew transports in Australia, the South-West Pacific Area and Japan. He was demobilized on 22 August 1946 and returned to his civilian job. In the early 1950s he moved to Brisbane where he became office supervisor with U.K. Motors Pty Ltd. At St Patrick's Catholic Church, Rockhampton, on 28 April 1952 he married Mavis Johnston; they were to adopt two children.

Hudson's health deteriorated after the war, obliging him to decline an offer to fly for an international airline. He attributed his disabilities to his R.A.A.F. service, including the effects of exposure to radiation at Hiroshima, Japan, in February 1946. Survived by his wife, son and daughter, he died of histiocytic lymphoma on 7 April 1980 in South Brisbane and was cremated with Anglican rites.

C. Webster and N. Frankland, *The Strategic Air Offensive Against Germany, 1939-1945*, 2 (Lond, 1961); Operations record-book, 460 Squadron, RAAF, 1939-45 (AWM); newspaper-cuttings from *Morning Bulletin* (Rockhampton), nd, including typed extract from 11 Nov 1944 (held by ADB, Canb); information from Mrs M. Hudson, Enoggera, Brisb, Mr J. R. Austin, Pearl Beach, NSW, Mr G. Cousins, Allenstown, Qld, Wg Cdr P. S. Isaacson, Toorak, Melb, and the late Messrs R. F. Friend and C. Hawes.   ALAN FRASER

HUDSON, SIR WILLIAM (1896-1978), civil engineer, was born on 27 April 1896 at East Nelson, New Zealand, seventh of eleven children of James Hudson, a medical practitioner from London, and his New Zealand-born wife Beatrice Jane, née Andrew. Dr Hudson kept a tight rein on his family and expected Bill to study medicine. Bill enraged him when, in his matriculation year at Nelson College, he said that he wanted to be a civil engineer. In a classic case of parental misjudgement, the father told the son destined to become a world leader in his profession, 'Bill, that is about all you are bloody well good for'.

In 1914 Hudson left New Zealand to enter University College, University of London. A brilliant student, he won the Archibald Head medal, gained the college diploma with distinction and in 1920 graduated B.Sc.(Eng.) with first-class honours. His studies had been interrupted by service in World War I. A second lieutenant in the London Regiment, he was wounded in the thigh at Bullecourt, France, in April 1917. He emerged from hospital with a slight limp in his right leg, a limp which only became pronounced when he was tired. To further his interest in hydro-electric engineering, he took a postgraduate course at the University of Grenoble, France.

Hudson's first job was with Sir W. G. Armstrong, Whitworth & Co. Ltd, London, but he returned to New Zealand in 1922 to join the Public Works Department as an assistant-engineer. He was initially employed on railway construction and then on the Mangahao hydro-electric scheme. Between 1924 and 1927 he again worked with Armstrong, Whitworth as engineer-in-charge of construction of the Arapuni Dam. At St Columba's Presbyterian Church, Fairlie, on 28 December 1926 he married 21-year-old Annie Eileen Trotter.

In 1928 Hudson crossed the Tasman to work first for the New South Wales Department of Public Works and then for the Sydney Metropolitan Water, Sewerage and Drainage Board. Appointed an assistant-engineer, he later took charge of construction of the Nepean Dam. In 1931 the Depression abruptly halted the project and he found himself unemployed. 'Not a man to remain idle', he moved his family to New Zealand and set off to try his luck in Britain. He was instantly rewarded. Sir Alexander Gibb & Partners offered him the post of engineer-in-charge of construction on the Galloway hydro-electric scheme in a remote corner of south-west Scotland. The largest project of its kind in Britain, the undertaking was challenging and presented, albeit on a minor scale, some of the problems he was to face in the Snowy Mountains of Australia.

Hudson notified his wife of his success in typical fashion—by a telegrammed directive, 'Come to Scotland'. Arriving at Tilbury, England, with a child in hand, she found another summons, 'Can't get away. Come to Galloway'. Husband and wife finally met at a small railway-station in Scotland. The five years he spent on the Galloway scheme (which he completed a year ahead of schedule) enhanced his growing reputation as an efficient and dedicated leader. With J. K. Hunter, he presented a paper on the scheme to the Institution of Civil Engineers in London and won the Telford premium.

Returning to Sydney in 1937, Hudson was again recruited by the water board as resident engineer for the Woronora Dam project. By 1948 he was the board's engineer-in-chief. In the following year he applied for the post of commissioner of the newly established Snowy Mountains Hydro-electric Authority. Nelson Lemmon, the Federal minister for works and housing, was attracted by Hudson's reputation for building dams on time and at fixed prices, and by the opinion of union officials that, although a 'bit of a slavedriver', Hudson was decisive and fair. When cabinet demanded the usual three nominations, Lemmon handed Prime Minister J. B. Chifley [q.v.13] a slip of paper which read 'Hudson, Hudson, Hudson'.

Appointed on 1 August 1949, at 53 he reached the pinnacle of his career as manager of the Snowy Mountains scheme, responsible for the biggest civil engineering project ever undertaken in Australia and one which the American Society of Civil Engineers would call an engineering wonder of the world. His starting salary was the princely sum of £5000 a year and he was given considerable powers, including direct access to the responsible minister.

Although classed as a statutory body, the S.M.H.E.A. had, to a substantial degree, the freedom of private enterprise, a necessary concomitant of the great task that lay before Hudson. That task, to be performed in a harsh terrain and climate, was to direct operations which would trap the seaward-flowing waters of the Snowy and Eucumbene rivers and drive them westward through long trans-mountain tunnels to irrigate the dry inland plains. In falling through the tunnel systems, the waters would generate electricity for the Australian Capital Territory, New South Wales and Victoria. Ultimately, the work-

force (which peaked at 7300 in 1959) built 16 dams, 7 power stations, 50 miles (80 km) of aqueducts and 90 miles (145 km) of tunnels. Completed in 1974, ahead of schedule, and at a cost close to the 1953-54 estimate of £422 million, the scheme had a generating capacity of 3.74 million kilowatts of hydro-electric power and provided an annual average of 2.36 million megalitres of water for irrigation and other purposes.

To head this vast undertaking, Hudson was the ideal man. While reserved and even shy, he was driven by ambition, and knew how to choose men, how to inspire and how to lead them. Of middle height, lean and sharp featured, he had a full mouth, a prominent nose, bushy eyebrows and alert, steely eyes. He shouldered the responsibility with a crusading zeal which left no doubt that he saw it as the opportunity for which he had waited and prepared all his life.

Engineers and technical staff were in short supply in 1949. Hudson began at once to 'search the world' for skilled workers and found numbers of them in refugee camps in Europe. Two-thirds of all Snowy personnel were to come from overseas. The S.M.H.E.A. employed people of thirty-two nationalities on the job, some of whom had fought against each other in World War II. Hudson imbued them with an *esprit de corps* by extolling the overriding importance of the project—'You aren't any longer Czechs or Germans, you are men of the Snowy'. He won their respect by taking practical measures for their wellbeing, by ensuring that they had good pay, food and quarters, by providing housing for their families and by showing concern for their safety. To stir their pride and sense of camaraderie, he kept them informed, published a staff magazine and even promoted a song, *Snowy River Roll*. Alive to the problems likely to arise with an isolated army of men cut off from normal life, he encouraged sporting activity and camp concerts, and allowed wet canteens.

He ensured that, in the allotment of houses and in all else, the immigrants were given equal opportunity and status with the Australian born. His constant aim was to preempt anything that might impede the work. Wary of politicians, he nevertheless made strenuous efforts to keep them on side and to avoid political interference. He found a powerful ally in (Sir) Robert Menzies [q.v.] who had been critical of the scheme before becoming prime minister in December 1949. In addition, Hudson moved to prevent industrial troubles. One short strike, which he admitted was mainly the fault of management, taught him a valuable lesson. Instead of resorting to the industrial courts, he secured a private arbitrator Stanley Taylor who quickly settled disputes. Each month supervising engineers sat round the table with local union representatives to identify matters liable to cause unrest.

Industrial safety was another vital concern. To reduce the number of accidents causing serious injury and loss of life, Hudson initiated a joint safety campaign which resulted in a dramatic reduction in the accident rate among the authority's and contractors' personnel. He stipulated that no one would be employed unless he signed a statement agreeing to observe prescribed safety precautions and in 1958 he ordered seat belts to be worn in the S.M.H.E.A. vehicles. Failure to do so, after one warning, meant dismissal.

Everything was judged by its 'usefulness to the scheme'. Acting on this key tenet, Hudson was a hard and demanding taskmaster. 'He expected complete loyalty, complete devotion and hard work'. On the other hand, he was fair and always ready to listen to people. Good performances were rewarded with incentive payments. World tunnelling records were broken. But any sign of slackness or idleness roused his quick temper. He once approached a group of workers who appeared to be taking an unauthorised tea-break and sacked them on the spot. The men looked puzzled. One of them said: 'We don't know who you are, but we work for the Main Roads Department'.

Hudson loved work and led from the front, showing stamina, drive and extraordinary industry. He toiled seven days a week, with lights shining in his office at Cooma until the early hours of the morning. He rarely took holidays, and relaxed—when he felt the need —by bushwalking. There was something evangelical about his approach to the Snowy project, which may help to explain the success of his public-relations programme. People in the media found him pleasant, quiet and direct. Thousands of Australians came on tours arranged by the authority and the 'Snowy' became a household word. The project grew to be a source of national pride, a symbol of the burgeoning Australia of the 1960s.

In 1955 Hudson had been appointed K.B.E.; in 1964 he was elected a fellow of the Royal Society, London. Sir William's tenure as commissioner was extended twice and Menzies promised that he would be allowed to finish the task, provided his health held. Menzies' successor Harold Holt [q.v.] did not honour the pledge and Hudson was retired in 1967, on the eve of his 71st birthday. He moved to the suburb of Garran in Canberra. In 1974 he attended a ceremony to mark the twenty-fifth anniversary of the project which had changed the face of Australia.

Among many distinctions, Hudson received the (W. C.) Kernot [q.v.5] memorial medal (1958), the James N. Kirby [q.v.] medal (1962), and the James Cook [q.v.1] medal

(1966) of the Royal Society of New South Wales. He was elected a fellow (1961) of University College, London, and was a foundation fellow (1975) of the Australian Academy of Technological Sciences. Accorded honorary memberships of the Australasian Institute of Mining and Metallurgy (1961) and of the Institution of Engineers, Australia (1962), he was also an honorary fellow (1967) of the Royal Australian Institute of Architects. He was awarded an honorary LL.D. by the Australian National University (1962) and an honorary D.Eng. by Monash University (1968). The Returned Services League of Australia conferred honorary life membership (1968) on him and the Braille Library of Victoria made him a life governor (1976).

Other countries sought Hudson's guidance on water-control undertakings. He gave advice on the Volta River project in Ghana and assisted the United Nations in deciding what money to allot for similar works elsewhere. The first chairman of the Australian committee of the International Commission on Large Dams, he had attended an executive-conference in Moscow in 1962. Such a man never retires. After leaving the Snowy, he held numerous engineering consultancies and presided over organizations whose concerns ranged from inland development and research into welding to combating drug dependence. He headed the National Safety Council of Australia and the New South Wales Road Safety Council (from 1968), and served as a Commonwealth arbitrator on disputes involving engineering.

Through it all, Hudson never forgot the Snowy. He loved attending meetings of the 'Old Hands'—those who had worked on the scheme from the first year—to whom he was known as 'King Billy' or simply 'the Old Man'. Grimly fighting the pain of arthritis as he grew older, Hudson walked the hills behind Garran every day until illness overtook him. Survived by his wife and two daughters, he died on 12 September 1978 at Red Hill, Canberra, and was buried with Anglican rites in Cooma cemetery, close to the project of which he had been 'the heart, soul and inspiration'.

S. McHugh, *The Snowy* (Melb, 1989); M. Unger, *Voices from the Snowy* (Syd, 1989); B. Collis, *Snowy* (Syd, 1990); *Biog Memoirs of Fellows of Roy Soc* (Lond), 25, Nov 1979; *Canb Times* and *SMH*, 14 Sept 1978; Oral Hist Project, Sir William Hudson, TRC 121/5 *and* William Flynn, TRC 308 (NL); information from Lady Hudson and Mrs M. Unger, Garran, Canb, and Mrs G. MacGregor, Avalon Beach, Syd.
ERIC SPARKE

HUGHES, ELLEN MARY KENT; *see* KENT HUGHES, ELLEN MARY

HUGHES, PATERSON CLARENCE (1917-1940), air force officer, was born on 19 September 1917 at Numeralla, New South Wales, eleventh of twelve children of native-born parents Paterson Clarence Hughes, labourer, and his wife Caroline Christina, née Vennel. Young Pat was initially educated at Cooma District (Public) School; after the family moved to Haberfield, Sydney, he attended Petersham Boys' Intermediate and Fort Street Boys' High schools. A good swimmer and footballer, he built model aeroplanes, was keenly interested in electricity and constructed crystal sets. He briefly worked as a junior stock clerk with the jewellers, Saunders Ltd, then in January 1936 joined the Royal Australian Air Force as a cadet at Point Cook, Victoria. Twelve months later he sailed for England to take a short service commission in the Royal Air Force.

Having flown with No.64 (Fighter) Squadron for two and a half years, in November 1939 Hughes was promoted acting flight lieutenant (substantive September 1940) and posted to No.234 Squadron as a flight commander. On 8 July 1940, near Land's End, he led three Spitfires which shot down a lone Junkers 88, the unit's first 'kill'. He and his section destroyed another Junkers south-east of Plymouth on the 28th. Temporarily detached on 1 August to help in organizing No.247 Squadron, he took advantage of the break from flying-duties to marry that day his English fiancée Kathleen Agnes Brodrick at the register office, Bodmin, Cornwall.

Back with his own unit, on 15 August Hughes shot down a Messerschmitt Bf 110 and shared in the dispatch of a second. He was successful on the 16th, 18th and 26th, each time destroying two Messerschmitt Bf 109s. An advocate of closing in for a certain 'kill', he accounted for three Bf 110s on 4 September, two Bf 109s on the 5th and at least one Bf 109 on the 6th. One of his victims on 5 September may have been Oberleutnant Franz von Werra, the flamboyant German ace.

Hughes was the real driving force behind No.234 Squadron. When its members' morale was dangerously low, it was his inspiration that welded the squadron into an efficient fighting unit. His authority in the air was tough and uncompromising, but on the ground Pat remained 'one of the boys'. Between 13 August and 7 September the squadron shot down 63 enemy aircraft and fought to the point of exhaustion. Hughes contributed at least 14 confirmed, 1 probable, 3 shared and 1 unconfirmed shared to this total, and became the highest-scoring Australian fighter pilot in the Battle of Britain. His close-in tactics led to his death on 7 September 1940 during the *Luftwaffe*'s first heavy raids on London. He pounced on a Dornier 17—perhaps he collided with it, perhaps his Spit-

fire was struck by debris from the exploding bomber, perhaps he flew into the firing-line of a Hurricane attacking the same target. The confusion that surrounded the crash remains unresolved. Four days after his death No.234 Squadron was moved to a quieter sector.

Pat Hughes was buried in St James's churchyard, Sutton, Hull. The award of his Distinguished Flying Cross was gazetted in October. At Christ Church, Kiama, New South Wales, his sister Muriel placed a memorial tablet on the graveyard fence.

C. Shores and C. Williams, *Aces High* (Lond, 1966); F. K. Mason, *Battle Over Britain* (Lond, 1969); D. Wood and D. Dempster, *The Narrow Margin* (Lond, 1969); W. Ramsey (ed), *The Battle of Britain* (Lond, 1980); D. Newton, *A Few of 'The Few'* (Canb, 1990); information from and family papers held by Mr W. M. Hughes, Beacon Hill, Syd.

DENNIS NEWTON

HUGHES, RANDOLPH WILLIAM (1889-1955), university lecturer and literary critic, was born on 10 August 1889 at Burwood, Sydney, son of William Henry Hughes, a Sydney-born warehouseman, and his wife Affra Castle, née Bell, from Melbourne. Educated at Sydney Boys' High School, Randolph studied classics at the University of Sydney (B.A., 1913; M.A., 1915) where he was fascinated by Christopher Brennan [q.v.7] and became a friend of A. R. Chisholm. Hughes taught classics (1913-15) at Bathurst High School. On 29 December 1914 he married a schoolteacher Ina Muriel Stanley Hall (d.1941), sister of Elsie Stanley Hall [q.v.9], at the Congregational Church, Waverley; they were to have twin sons. Awarded a travelling scholarship, he sailed alone to London and thence to Cairo. He was commissioned in the Royal Engineers, served (1916) in Egypt and Sinai, and was retained by the Egyptian government on special duties.

In October 1917 Hughes matriculated at New College, Oxford, where he went on to take first-class honours in medieval and modern languages in 1919 (B.A., 1923). From 1920 to 1922 he taught English literature in France, first at the University of Rennes and then at the École Normale Supériere, Paris. In 1922 he was appointed lecturer in French language and literature at King's College, University of London (D.Litt., 1931); he was awarded his doctorate for a thesis on Baudelaire. Following an acrimonious dispute with a colleague, Hughes resigned his post in 1935. For the next twenty years he survived as a freelance writer and by marking examination papers. His health was often poor. He wrote primarily for French and English journals on nineteenth-century literature. His contribution to Australian intellectual life included a major study, *C. J. Brennan* (Sydney, 1934). On the publication of P. R. Stephensen's [q.v.12] *The Foundations of Culture in Australia* in 1936, Hughes savagely reviewed it in the *Nineteenth Century and After*, thereby creating considerable controversy in Australia.

Hughes also wrote articles favourable to Hitler and Nazi Germany. Offered a research post at the Humboldt University of Berlin to study the Nazi régime, he declined because of ill health. He remained a man of the far right, strongly anti-Semitic, and developed ties with Action Française. From 1939 his interests became more purely literary and he spent his remaining years preparing editions of the work of Algernon Swinburne and Dante Gabriel Rossetti; he published Swinburne's unfinished novel, *Lesbia Brandon* (London, 1952).

Highly strung and passionate, Hughes held his beliefs tenaciously, and was a talented scholar and a man of integrity. He called himself both a pagan and a Tory, and was determinedly pro-British and pro-European in outlook. He wore a monocle and gloves, carried a walking-stick and insisted on the proper manners of a gentleman. On 7 August 1942 at the register office, Chelsea, he married a civil servant Dorothy Freda Ayres; he later claimed that she 'basely and dishonourably' deserted him 'at a very critical period' in his life. Survived by one son of his first marriage, he died of coronary thrombosis on 21 March 1955 at Tunbridge Wells and was buried in the local cemetery. His portrait by Edward Wolfe is held by the Dixson [q.v.8] Galleries, Sydney.

A. R. Chisholm, *Men Were My Milestones* (Melb, 1958); *British A'sian*, 20 Aug 1914; *Aust Q*, 27, no 2, June 1955, p 27; *The Times*, 9 May 1955; Teachers' records (NSW Dept of Education Archives, Syd); Hughes papers (ML).

GREGORY MELLEUISH

HUGHES, THOMAS JOHN (1892-1980), politician, was born on 8 September 1892 in South Melbourne, son of Felix Hughes, labourer, and his wife Maria, née Boudan. The family moved to the Western Australian goldfields in 1896 and settled at Boulder. At the age of 14 Tom became a telegraph-boy and remained in the Commonwealth public service until his resignation as an assistant audit inspector in 1922. He played football, and rowed for Western Australia in 1914 and 1920. A strong anti-conscriptionist, he served on the State executive of the Australian Labor Party and was president (1921) of its metropolitan council. In November 1922 he won the by-election for the seat of East Perth in the Legislative Assembly. At

her parents' home in Perth on 20 December that year he married with Catholic rites Lucy Olive Stone (d.1976), a tailoress.

Disappointed at not gaining cabinet office under Philip Collier [q.v.8], 'Diver' Hughes grew increasingly critical of the party's leaders and sided with the workers when the government sent police to the 1925 maritime strike. Although he lacked experience in the industry, he campaigned vigorously for the secretaryship of the Timber Workers' Union; after the job went to May Holman [q.v.9], he sued the *Westralian Worker* for libel. He broke formally with the party in August 1926 and did not contest the 1927 elections. Standing as an Independent Labor candidate for East Perth in 1930, he was defeated.

Hughes went into business as an auditor and accountant, and studied part time at the University of Western Australia (LL.B., 1932). Before he left parliament he had begun promoting lotteries on a 25 per cent commission. This source of income was lost when the State government banned private lotteries in 1930 and two years later set up a Lotteries Commission. Hughes's criticism of the commission led to the resignation of its chairman Alex Clydesdale, a member of the Legislative Council, on the ground of conflict of interest. In May 1934 Hughes unsuccessfully contested West Province for the Legislative Council.

Although threatened with bankruptcy, in February 1936 he stood as an Independent for East Perth against J. J. Kenneally [q.v.9]. With considerable support from the Relief and Sustenance Workers' Union, Hughes won the seat on preferences. Kenneally challenged the result. Hughes resigned, fought a by-election in May and again won. On 27 August he spoke for two and a half hours in the House, levelling accusations of fraud and neglect against members of the Labor government. Parliament unanimously appointed a royal commission which found none of the allegations substantiated. Undaunted, Hughes continued sniffing out corruption. In 1937 he was admitted to the Western Australian Bar. Re-elected for East Perth in 1939, during World War II he urged the abolition of State governments. In 1943 he resigned from parliament to contest the Federal seat of Perth as an Independent, polled over 8000 votes, but was beaten into third place by T. P. Burke [q.v.13]. After suffering a worse defeat at the Federal by-election for the seat of Fremantle in 1945, Hughes abandoned politics to concentrate on his legal practice. He spent his last years in the Home of Peace, Subiaco. Survived by his son and daughter, he died there on 6 November 1980 and was cremated with the forms of the Uniting Church.

Chunky and energetic, Hughes was a rare

example of the larrikin populist in Western Australian politics. 'I've got nothing against socialism and communism', he said, 'but I hate socialists and communists'. While never formally a Lang Labor man, he spoke well of J. T. Lang [q.v.9] and mustered similar support from working-class underdogs. He lost his appeal with the passing of the Depression.

PD (WA), 18 Aug 1926, p 352, 27 Aug 1936, p 221; *V&P* (LA WA), 1934 (A3), 1937 (3); *Westralian Worker*, 21 Feb 1936; *West Australian*, 8, 11 May 1936; C. Fox, The Relief and Sustenance Workers' Union 1933-1934: An Anti-Labor Political and Industrial Organisation (B.A. Hons thesis, Univ WA, 1977).   G. C. BOLTON

HUGHES, TIMOTHY (1919-1976), soldier and farmer, was born on 28 April 1919 at Point Pearce (Bookooyanna) Aboriginal Station, South Australia, son of Aboriginal parents Walter Stanford Hughes and his wife Gladys, née Adams (later Elphick), both agricultural labourers. His father was of Narangga descent and his mother of Kaurna; his grandfather Alfred Hughes had testified before the 1913 royal commission on Aborigines. Tim was educated to fifth grade before working for his father (who was by then a share-farmer on the station) and as a contract shearer. He was an unemployed labourer at Stenhouse Bay when he enlisted in the Australian Imperial Force on 4 December 1939.

Posted to the 2/10th Battalion, Hughes served in Britain in 1940, took part (April-August 1941) in the defence of Tobruk, Libya, and fought in the battle of Milne Bay, Papua, in August-September 1942. In December the unit joined allied forces assaulting Buna. On the 26th, during the advance along the old airstrip, Hughes's platoon was pinned down by machine-gun fire. He volunteered to climb on top of a dispersal bay and, despite coming under concentrated fire from three directions, engaged two Japanese posts with grenades. Armed with a sub-machine gun, he protected his comrades while they took cover; he then made three sorties to silence the enemy's weapons, enabling the platoon to consolidate its position. For these deeds he was awarded the Military Medal.

Usually 'in the forefront of any action', Hughes was wounded at Sanananda on 19 January 1943. He returned to Australia in March, was promoted substantive corporal in June and joined the 31st Employment Company in August. After several spells in hospital with malaria, he was discharged on 5 September 1945. His brother Alfred served (1951-54) in the regular army and fought in Korea with the 1st Battalion, Royal Australian Regiment.

Tim Hughes resumed share-farming for four years at Point Pearce. He was subject to South Australia's Aborigines Act (1934-39) which limited his people's freedom of movement and their access to the benefits of citizenship. As a result of his application, on 18 May 1956 he received exemption from the Act, but deeply resented this 'dog licence' and remained critical of the way in which Aborigines were treated. At the office of the principal registrar, Adelaide, on 2 August 1945 he married Eileen O'Donoghue.

After attending a course at Wingfield Rural Training Centre, near Adelaide, Hughes was involved with the War Service Land Settlement scheme in the south-east of the State. At the urging of his wife and (Sir) Cecil Hincks [q.v.], in 1953 he leased a soldier-settler block of 979 acres (396 ha) at Conmurra. A staunch Methodist, he insisted on Sunday observance and held services in his home before the local church was built. Throughout his life he believed in the value of careful planning and in sticking to his plans. He encouraged his children to gain a good education. Hughes made friends easily, joined in community activities and was highly regarded by his fellow soldier settlers. At first he ran a dairy herd, but soon switched to sheep and trained as a woolclasser. Hard work and determination helped him to make a modest success of his block over a period of twenty-two years, but his stock and plant remained mortgaged to the Lands Department which controlled his finances, allowing him living expenses of only £18 per week. His marriage broke down in 1967. In September that year he suffered a heart attack. A stroke in 1968 prevented him from performing heavy tasks on his property. He and his wife were divorced in 1970.

In 1966 the South Australian government had passed an Act establishing the Aboriginal Lands Trust to ensure that Aborigines held title in their existing reserves and that royalties from mining on these reserves passed to Aboriginal control; the funds were to be used to acquire additional land and to develop land vested in the trust. Hughes was appointed its first chairman. He served until 1973, by which time the trust had grown to include ten members, administering assets worth over $250 000. In 1970 he was appointed M.B.E. Survived by his son and daughter, he died of a coronary occlusion on or about 1 April 1976 at Ardrossan and was buried in Centennial Park cemetery; his estate was sworn for probate at $73 100. His mother Gladys was appointed M.B.E. (1971) and was South Australian Aborigine of the Year in 1984.

C. Mattingley and K. Hampton (eds), *Survival in Our Own Land* (Syd, 1988); P. and B. O'Connor, *In Two Fields* (Millicent, SA, 1991); *Sabretache*, Oct

1977; *Advertiser*(Adel), 30 Oct 1954, 17 Oct 1970, 7 Apr 1976; information from Mr P. Hughes, Adel, Mrs E. Hughes, Quorn, SA, and Mr I. Edwards, Glandore, Adel.   ROBERT HALL

HUGHES, SIR WILFRID KENT; *see* KENT HUGHES, SIR WILFRID

HUGHES-JONES, EDITH (1905-1976), nurse and hospital proprietor, was born on 10 March 1905 at Tungamah, Victoria, and registered as Edith Hughes, second child of Rev. William Thomas Jones, Methodist clergyman, and his wife Agnes Edith, née Hardy, both Victorian born. Educated at Presbyterian Ladies' College, Kew, she undertook her general nursing training at the Alfred Hospital, Prahran, and completed midwifery at the (Royal) Women's Hospital, Melbourne. As a young girl she had developed organizing and delegating skills when her father encouraged her to help at camps run by the Try Boys Homes.

The family lived frugally, and Edith, with her two brothers, was taught the value of hard work and the worth of money. Developing financial flair, she bought Windarra, a private hospital at Toorak where she had served as matron. In 1938 she became matron and owner of Windermere, at Prahran, which she developed into one of Melbourne's best-known private hospitals. She used the freedom and independence which these acquisitions gave her to benefit nursing.

Following the sinking of the hospital ship, *Centaur*, in 1943, Miss Hughes-Jones initiated the Centaur War Nurses' Memorial Trust, of which she was honorary secretary (1943-76), a trustee and a member of its scholarship committee. Her close association with many nurses who were to die in World War II reinforced her dedication and enthusiasm, and lay behind the role she played in establishing (1948) the War Nurses Memorial Centre (later the Nurses Memorial Centre). After the war she also helped to form the trust from which the Annie M. Sage [q.v.] memorial nurses' scholarship was awarded.

As foundation honorary secretary (1946-75) of the Florence Nightingale Committee of Australia, Hughes-Jones devoted many years to promoting postgraduate education for nurses. She was one of the founders (1949) and a fellow (1971) of the College of Nursing, Australia, and its honorary secretary (1950-55) and president (1955-56). In 1957 she was appointed O.B.E. President (1961-66) of the (Royal) Victorian College of Nursing, she was a member of the Victorian Nursing Council. In 1973 she set up Windermere Hospital

Foundation Ltd to provide funds for charitable organizations and nursing education.

Her involvement with the Lyceum Club and the Collins Street Independent Church—as a deacon from 1955 and an elder in 1967—gave her access to influential people who supported her causes. Hughes-Jones loved her home at Olinda; its garden, which gave her great joy, was often thrown open for fund-raising functions. She made enormous demands on those who worked for her and allowed nothing to prevent her from gaining her objectives.

Following a long battle with cancer, Hughes-Jones died on 15 April 1976 at Prahran and was cremated; her estate was sworn for probate at $153 597. At her memorial service Dr Francis MacNab said: 'We knew she was determined, demanding, sometimes insensitive, distorting events and circumstances. But we also knew she was compassionate, grateful, generous, innovative, colourful, approachable, provocative'. Her brother William Eric Archer Hughes-Jones (1902-1976) was a surgeon and chairman (1968-73) of the Royal Melbourne Hospital's board of management.

B. Schultz, *The Seventeenth Patricia Chomley Oration: 'Founders of the College'* (Brisb, 1983); *UNA*, 74, no 2, 1976; *Age* (Melb), 23 Apr 1976; Memorial Service for Miss Edith Hughes-Jones, 24 Apr 1976 (held by Collins St Independent Church, Melb); Nurses Memorial Centre, Melb, Archives.
JENNIFER WILLIAMS

HUISH, SIR RAYMOND DOUGLAS (1898-1970), ex-servicemen's leader and businessman, was born on 7 December 1898 at Clifton, Bristol, England, third of five children of Edward William Huish, liftman, and his wife Amelia Ann, née Goss. The Huishes moved briefly to the United States of America, where 'Bob' (as he was later known) received some education, before returning to England in 1910. In August of that year the family emigrated to Rockhampton, Queensland, the city in which Amelia's relations lived.

Overstating his age by some fifteen months, Huish enlisted in the Australian Imperial Force on 18 August 1915 and was posted to the 5th Light Horse Regiment. In October he embarked for the Middle East. At Katia, Sinai, on 5 August 1916 he was severely wounded in the leg and admitted to hospital. In February 1917 he transferred to the 2nd Light Horse Brigade Signal Troop and took part in the advance through Palestine and Syria. While in the Jordan Valley he contracted malaria and was to suffer recurrent bouts for the rest of his life. Promoted corporal in March 1919, he returned to

Australia and was discharged in Brisbane on 27 September. Huish obtained a job at Rockhampton with Sydney Williams & Co., a windmill-manufacturing firm. At St Paul's Anglican Cathedral, Rockhampton, on 1 November 1921 he married Hilda May Weber, a 23-year-old clerk. In 1927 he was appointed local branch manager of Buzacott (Qld) Ltd, machinery merchants; within a year he became State manager in Brisbane; by 1929 he was managing director. He retired as chairman of directors in 1958.

Following his return to Rockhampton, in 1923 Huish had been active in reviving the local sub-branch of the Returned Sailors' and Soldiers' Imperial League of Australia and was its vice-president (1924). He served on the executive of the central district and was a State councillor and treasurer. From 1930 to 1967 he was State president. In this capacity he was also a trustee of the league's numerous bequests and foundations, including the Patriotic Fund of Queensland, the Naughton Trust and the scholarship fund. Deputy-chairman (1932-50) of the State Repatriation Board, he was an Australian delegate to the British Empire Services League's conference in London in September 1939. During World War II he organized the Volunteer Defence Corps of the Returned Sailors', Soldiers' and Airmen's Imperial League of Australia and was chairman of the State recruiting committee.

In 1949-50 Huish was a member of the royal commission that inquired into the Golden Casket Art Union. At the request of (Sir) Robert Menzies' [q.v.] government, he visited Europe in 1950 to investigate and report on emigration to Australia. From 1960 until 1967 he was deputy national president of the R.S.S. & A.I.L.A. and its successor, the Returned Services League of Australia, and in 1965 led the league's pilgrimage to commemorate the fiftieth anniversary of the landing at Gallipoli. With (Sir) William Keys, he represented the league on a visit to Indonesia and a tour of South East Asia in 1963 and again in 1967, following which he was appointed deputy-chairman of the South East Asia Veterans' Conference which resulted from the visit.

In addition to his work for the R.S.L., Huish was one of Queensland's outstanding businessmen. He was a director of a number of prominent companies, including Cribb & Foote Ltd of Ipswich (from 1937), Queensland Theatres Ltd, Independent Oil Industries Ltd (both from 1938), the Finance Co. of Queensland, W. G. Johnson Pty Ltd, Ipswich Properties Ltd and the Scottish Union & National Insurance Co. A Freemason, he was a fellow (1962) of the Institute of Directors of Australia.

Always a tireless worker, Bob Huish got things done. Once a decision had been made, he pursued it with single-minded purpose. He abhorred compromise, and was impatient with those who suggested it. Despite complete deafness in his right ear, he was a forceful and determined figure at conferences where he was frequently the leader. Huish had joined the league when it was small and disorganized. When he left in 1967 it was a large and influential body. Queensland and national membership numbered 4374 and 24 482 in 1923; by 1963 the figures had increased to 27 124 and 257 209 respectively. Huish was an advocate of National Service training and of an effective system for civil defence. While one of his State's 'best known personalities', he also became known throughout Australia for his outspoken tirades against communism.

Huish was appointed C.B.E. in 1937. Knighted in 1953, he was invested next year by Queen Elizabeth II on her first visit to Brisbane. Sir Raymond died on 26 January 1970 in St Helen's Hospital, South Brisbane, and was cremated; his wife and two daughters survived him.

Queensland and Queenslanders (Brisb, 1936); *Notable Men of Queensland* (Brisb, 1950); G. L. Kristianson, *The Politics of Patriotism* (Canb, 1966); Anzac Day Commemoration Cte (Qld), *Anzac Day* (Brisb, 1970); *Telegraph* (Brisb), 22 July 1950; *Courier-Mail*, 10 May 1967, 27 Jan 1970; R. W. Swartz, Opening Address, RSL State Conference, Mackay, 7 June 1967 (copy held by RSL, Brisb); information from Miss G. Huish, Taringa, and Mrs E. Ashby, Tarragindi, Brisb.

RUPERT GOODMAN

HULME-MOIR, FRANCIS OAG (1910-1979), Anglican bishop, was born on 30 January 1910 at Balmain, Sydney, third of four children of native-born parents Alexander Hugh Moir, shipping accountant, and his wife Violet Beryl, née Hulme. His mother, who had to raise her children in straitened circumstances, prefixed her maiden name to her married surname. Although baptized a Methodist, Frank grew up as a practising Anglican. Living at Randwick, he attended Sydney Technical High School and was employed as a survey draftsman. He lost his job in the Depression and had a difficult time financially. His conversion to a vibrant religious faith by Rev. Herbert Begbie at Willoughby in May 1932 gave him his true vocation.

Rejecting an offer to use his fine bass voice professionally and laying aside an ambition to enter the police force, Hulme-Moir studied part time at Moore Theological College. He was a lay reader at several North Shore parishes and, after a financial struggle, a full-time ministerial candidate. In 1936 he was made deacon and on 28 February 1937 he was ordained priest. At St Stephen's Church, Chatswood, on 10 April that year he married a typiste Ena Dorothy, daughter of Rev. Reginald Smee.

From the outset, Hulme-Moir was marked as a man who would contribute strongly as a churchman. Impressive in appearance and personality, he was a persuasive speaker and an obvious leader of men. Yet there was gentleness and a deep concern for the individual beneath the imposing presence and booming voice. Following a curacy at the strongly Evangelical centre of St Andrew's, Summer Hill, in 1937 he became State secretary of the Church Missionary Society, his vitality and administrative skill helping to reverse the institution's decline. In 1930 he had been commissioned in the Militia. A clear choice for chaplaincy work with the Australian Imperial Force, he served in the Middle East (1940-42) and in New Guinea (1944-45) and Bougainville (1945). He was promoted deputy assistant chaplain-general (1943) and was mentioned in dispatches.

Back in civilian life, Hulme-Moir rose rapidly in the Church. From 1945 he was rector of St Clement's, Mosman, returning to Summer Hill in 1952. He was archdeacon of Ryde (1947-49) and of Cumberland (1949-54), and maintained his military connexion as senior chaplain, Eastern Command. Having turned down two offers of elevation to the episcopate, he succumbed to a plea from the New Zealand diocese of Nelson and was consecrated bishop in Christ Church Cathedral on 11 June 1954.

Hulme-Moir enjoyed New Zealand, of which Nelson was the Evangelical hub; he liked his rural diocese and upheld its churchmanship vigorously but with tolerance. In 1959 he became senior Anglican chaplain to the New Zealand armed forces. It was with reluctance that he returned to Sydney in 1965 as assistant-bishop and dean. Intended to bring a strong Australian-born presence to an apparently English-ruled diocese, his appointment continued after the election of another Australian (Sir) Marcus Loane as archbishop in 1966. Hulme-Moir had declared that he did not seek his own nomination for that post.

To his regret, he found the deanship too much and resigned in 1967. He remained assistant-bishop and accepted appointments as bishop to the armed forces (1965), chaplain to the police force (1966), national chairman of the Church of England Men's Society (1969) and chaplain-general to the army (1974). In a life crowded with visitations, tours, preaching, public engagements and endless committees, Hulme-Moir remained patient, always in control and invariably concerned with the needs of the individual. Retir-

ing in 1975, he joined the Parole Board of New South Wales and remained pastor to countless people. In 1976 he was appointed A.O.

Hulme-Moir died of hypertensive cardiovascular disease on 10 March 1979 at his Collaroy Plateau home and was cremated. His wife, who had supported him in all aspects of his immense ministry, survived him, as did his two sons and only daughter.

M. L. Loane, *Mark these Men* (Canb, 1985); C of E (Syd), *Syd Diocesan Synod Reports*, 1966-79; *Southern Cross* (Syd), Apr 1979; *SMH*, 12 Mar 1979; family information.   K. J. CABLE

HUME, STELLA LEONORA HARRIETTE (1882-1954), radio announcer, director and producer, was born on 4 October 1882 at South Yarra, Melbourne, daughter of Victorian-born parents William Workman Jeremy, draughtsman, and his wife Laura Savina, née Peregalli. Said to be of 'French, Italian, English and Welsh descent', Stella later adopted the name Violet. On 3 October 1905 at the Methodist Church, Mosman, Sydney, she married Ernest James Hume. They moved to Adelaide where Ernest was in partnership with his brother Walter [q.v.9] in manufacturing steel fencing.

While raising her four children, Mrs Hume taught elocution, served as art director of the Adelaide Repertory Theatre, pursued interests in sculpture, music, dancing, singing, and cultivating and arranging flowers, and also appeared in silent films, billed as 'Leonora Starr'. In 1923 her sons Ernest and Jack became fascinated with wireless. Believing in the cultural and educational potential of the new technology, her husband bought a transmitter and ancillary equipment, and set up a studio in their home, Peltonga, on Park Terrace (later Greenhill Road), Parkside. The Humes obtained a permit to make experimental broadcasts. By mid-1924 Stella was 'the voice of 5 Don N', as their station 5DN was known. The station flourished. Live broadcasts were made from the music-room at Peltonga and, by landline, from the Elder [q.v.4] Conservatorium of Music and the University of Adelaide.

One of the world's first female announcers and programme directors, she appeared on 5DN as 'Miss Leonora Starr', elocutionist, and as 'Auntie Stella', a children's storyteller. In 1924 the Humes applied for an A-class licence—which would have enabled them to finance high-quality programmes from listeners' fees—but were disappointed when 5DN received a B-class licence, obliging them to seek revenue by transmitting advertisements. Mrs Hume arranged to broadcast the play, *Lilies of the Field*, in November. In 1925 she engaged and directed approximately one thousand performers and speakers, in addition to orchestras and bands. Her transmissions were received in the United States of America. Because 5DN remained on air later at night than Melbourne and Sydney stations, enthusiasts in eastern Australia tuned in.

A strikingly handsome woman, Stella had a well-modulated voice, a keen sense of humour, a friendly nature and an egalitarian outlook. 5DN performers were unpaid, but were invited to supper at Peltonga before being driven home in one of the family's motor-cars. After her husband died in 1929, she declined to take over 5DN's commercial affairs and moved to Neutral Bay, Sydney, where she occasionally gave radio talks and patented a four-valve 'wireless receiver', the 'Accord Four'. She joined the Theosophical Society and took up spiritualism, allegedly believing that radio would become a medium for communicating with the dead. About 1939 she returned to Adelaide. In the early 1950s she moved to Goulburn, New South Wales.

Survived by her daughter and two of her three sons, Stella Hume died on 3 January 1954 in the Mental Hospital, Kenmore, and was cremated. The National Film and Sound Archive, Canberra, holds recordings of her voice. A cairn at the site of Peltonga commemorates her.

J. F. Ross, *A History of Radio in South Australia, 1897-1977* (Adel, 1978); D. J. Towler, *The First Sixty Years 1924-1984* (Adel, 1984); Hume scrapbook and papers in the 5DN Collection, particularly AUDN, MS 15, 45-72 (National Film and Sound Archives, Canb); Minutes of Evidence of the Commonwealth Royal Commission on Wireless (1926-27, AA, Canb).   NANCY ROBINSON FLANNERY

HUMPHRIES, WALTER RICHARD (1890?-1951), civil servant, was born probably on 16 October 1890, either at Streatham, London, or Purow, Cape Province, South Africa, son of Henry Horan Humphries, stockbroker. On 6 August 1912 Richard was appointed to the Papuan service as a patrol officer. As one of (Sir) Hubert Murray's [q.v.10] 'outside men', he carried out his instructions punctiliously and self-effacingly, setting a pattern for the younger field officers who followed him. In 1916-17 he served as acting assistant resident magistrate on the Lakekamu goldfields. From July to September 1917 he took part in a major overland patrol which travelled from Lakekamu station, Nepa, in the south, to Ioma, in the northern Mambare Division, and explored the country of the warlike Kukukuku people *en route*. At St Mary's Catholic Cathedral, Syd-

ney, on 22 January 1919 he married Ethel Frances Puxley, a civil servant.

Between 1918 and 1941 Dickie Humphries served in turn at Misima and Abau, and as resident magistrate of the Gulf, Delta, Northern and Central divisions. He undertook numerous patrols, some attended with risk, while from 1927 raising his two daughters after his wife had died of blackwater fever. On 6 November 1932 at St Peter's Anglican Church, Wanigela, he married Myra Blanche Hain. In 1935 he conducted an inquiry at Kikori into the deaths of tribesmen who had attacked Jack Hides's [q.v.9] and James O'Malley's Strickland-Purari patrol. He served on the Papuan Executive Council in 1941-42 and 1949-51.

Humphries was articulate and had a literary bent. He wrote humorous and instructive articles for 'southern' newspapers, some serious verse for the *Papuan Courier*, patrol and district reports, and vocabularies of Papuan languages. His *Patrolling in Papua* (London, 1923) was part of an impressive publishing tradition that included the work of such field officers as Wilfred Beaver, C. A. W. Monckton [q.v.10], Hides and Ivan Champion. Cool and brave under threat, Humphries was compact and nimble, his athleticism and vigour matched by an emotional disposition and an uncompromising morality. As a desk officer, he demonstrated the same meticulous competence and energy he had shown in the field. He did not spare his subordinates and could be harsh. Much respected, he was sometimes feared.

In December 1942 Humphries was appointed captain in the Citizen Military Forces and posted to the Australian New Guinea Administrative Unit. Given responsibility for the army's radio station in Port Moresby, he was promoted major (May 1944). In May 1943 he had presided at the trial of 'renegade' Papuans in the Northern Division who had collaborated with Japanese forces; twenty-two of the accused Papuans were executed, to the anger of the people of Higaturu.

Transferring to the Reserve of Officers in July 1945, Humphries served in the administration of the Territory of Papua and New Guinea, from 1950 as director of native labour. During a final tour of inspection before his retirement he was killed at Higaturu with over 3000 villagers and 34 Europeans (including one of his daughters, her husband and their two children) in the eruption of Mount Lamington on 21 January 1951. His wife survived him, as did the other daughter of his first marriage.

J. Sinclair, *Last Frontiers* (Gold Coast, Qld, 1988); *PIM*, Feb 1951; *SMH*, 10, 17 May 1943, 13 May 1978; information from Mr J. B. Bramell, Manly, Mr D. Marsh, Harbord, Mrs A. Marsh,

Dee Why, Syd, Mrs E. Champion, Canb, Mrs E. Champion, Southport, Qld, and Pastor L. Lock, Singleton, NSW.   D. C. LEWIS

HUNT, BRUCE ATLEE (1899-1964), medical practitioner, was born on 23 February 1899 at Glebe, Sydney, eldest of three children of native-born parents Atlee Arthur Hunt [q.v.9], barrister, and his wife Lilian, née Hunt. Educated at Melbourne Church of England Grammar School where he was head of school, Bruce enlisted in the Australian Imperial Force on 24 February 1917. He served on the Western Front in 1918 with the 8th Field Artillery Brigade. In 1919 he studied medicine for a year at King's College, London, before entering the University of Melbourne (M.B., B.S., 1925; M.D., 1928). On 18 August 1926 in the chapel of his old school he married Theodora Maedhail Harper, granddaughter of Robert Harper [q.v.9]. Following a series of appointments in Melbourne hospitals, he qualified in 1928 as a member (fellow 1951) of the Royal College of Physicians. Accompanied by his wife, he furthered his studies in London and Vienna.

In 1930 Hunt set up practice in Perth. That year he helped to found a diabetes clinic at (Royal) Perth Hospital; partly because of his wife's susceptibility to the disease, diabetes was his major specialist interest. Contrary to orthodox opinion, he approved a liberal diet for diabetics, provided their weight was kept under control. He was an active honorary (1931-58) on the staff of the R.P.H. and attained the status of senior physician in 1953. A prime mover in the formation of the Royal Australasian College of Physicians (foundation fellow 1938), he enlivened many advisory committees on public health by vigorous arguments with some of his professional colleagues.

World War II interrupted Hunt's career. Commissioned in October 1939 as honorary squadron leader, Royal Australian Air Force, he transferred to the A.I.F. on 19 August 1941. Next month he sailed to Singapore as a major with the 2nd/13th Australian General Hospital. He was captured when the island fell in February 1942. Sent with 'F' Force to the Burma-Thailand Railway, he proved a devoted physician and worked with impossibly small resources. He was beaten several times by the Japanese for standing up for the rights of sick prisoners of war. Repatriated in 1945, he was appointed M.B.E. (1947) and testified before war crimes tribunals.

After the war Hunt became a powerful if sometimes controversial figure in the Perth medical establishment. He was president (1949-50) of the Western Australian branch of the British Medical Association and vice-president (1956-58) of the R.A.C.P., but was disappointed of the presidency although he sat on the council for sixteen years. He was largely responsible for setting up a clinical research unit at R.P.H. in 1952 and served on the interim faculty when a school of medicine was established at the University of Western Australia in 1957. His teaching was 'intensely practical, utilitarian and egocentric'.

Hunt was a man of proconsular presence, broad shouldered, balding early, with aquiline features; 'portly as he aged', he walked 'in a curious short-stepped impatient shamble'. A classical education when young and a lifetime friendship with the historian (Sir) Keith Hancock left him with a keen appreciation of the humanities. He loved music, especially Bach, and followed the horses, knowledgeably, enthusiastically, but not always profitably. Hunt exercised great charm on men and women, and was an encouraging mentor to the young. His last years were clouded with illness, but his personality remained undiminished. Survived by his wife, daughter and son, he died of hypertensive coronary vascular disease on 29 October 1964 at Applecross and was cremated.

G. L. McDonald (ed), *Roll of the Royal Australasian College of Physicians*, 1, 1938-45 (Syd, 1988); *Roy Perth Hospital J*, Dec 1958, p 456, Dec 1964, p 723; *MJA*, 1 May 1965, p 662, 20 Jan 1973, p 134; *West Australian*, 30 Oct 1964, 20 Sept 1969; E. G. Saint, Bruce Atlee Hunt—A Homage (memorial oration, 1978, ts copy in ADB file); personal information.
                                              G. C. BOLTON
                                              ALEX COHEN

HUNT, HAROLD ARTHUR KINROSS (1903-1977), classical scholar and educationist, was born on 16 March 1903 at Dubbo, New South Wales, third child of Harold Wesley George Hunt, a native-born schoolmaster, and his wife Grace Matilda, née Henderson, who had been born in Germany. His father died within three months of Harold's birth; his mother then trained as a teacher and founded Woodcourt College, Marrickville, Sydney. Educated at Newington College under C. J. Prescott [q.v.11] and at the University of Sydney (B.A., 1924), he graduated with first-class honours in classics and the university medal. A Cooper [q.v.3] travelling scholarship took him to Queen's College, Oxford (M.A., 1926).

In 1927-35 Hunt taught at Melbourne Church of England Grammar School. Senior classics master from 1931, he also directed debating, rowing, rifle-shooting and the cadet corps, and completed a diploma of education (1929) at the University of Melbourne. On

20 December 1928 he married Gwendolen Dinah Fulton Jones (d.1977) at St Stephen's Anglican Church, Penrith, New South Wales.

Hunt joined the staff of the University of Melbourne in 1936 as lecturer in classics. Promoted senior lecturer (1945) and associate-professor (1949), he succeeded C. A. Scutt [q.v.11] in 1955 as professor of classical studies. The department's new name suited Hunt, whose broad interests included numismatics, social history and archaeology; his major concerns were ancient philosophy (especially Stoicism) and Ciceronian studies. He was awarded a Litt.D. by the university in 1950 for his thesis, *The Humanism of Cicero* (published 1954). Sub-dean (1938-41) and dean (1955-57) of the faculty of arts, he was a member of council in 1952-55.

During World War II Hunt had served in the Citizen Military Forces (1942) and as an intelligence officer in the Australian Imperial Force (1942-43). He rose to captain and was involved in devising an intensive course of instruction in Japanese. On this model, in 1946 he pioneered an intensive course in Ancient Greek, flexible enough to serve his department for forty years. A born teacher, he was method lecturer (1945-49) in Latin in the university's school of education. His book, *Training through Latin* (1948), was one result, while other technical publications followed his association (1962-65) with the Australian Council for Educational Research. Hunt was a popular public lecturer with a droll sense of humour, displayed with deadpan face and immaculate timing. He was utterly fearless in singing to crowded lecture theatres his Latin translations of hits from the musicals. His 'special genius for sociability' put many a student at ease.

Councillor (1932), treasurer (1934-42), vice-president (1946-50 and 1955-61), president (1950-54) and patron (1962-77) of the Classical Association of Victoria, Hunt delivered its H. W. Allen [q.v.7 L.H. Allen] lecture in 1963, 1970 and 1973. He was an articulate champion of his discipline and president (1967-69) of the Australian Society for Classical Studies. A foundation member (1954) of the Australian Humanities Research Council, he became sub-editor of *The Humanities in Australia* (edited by (Sir) Grenfell Price, Sydney, 1959). Following retirement in 1969, Hunt published *The Story of Rotary in Australia* (1971), *The Professor and the Possum* (1973), *The Master Printers of Sydney* (Sydney, 1976) and *A Physical Interpretation of the Universe* (1976). He died on 11 April 1977 at Camberwell and was cremated; his son and daughter survived him. An excellent likeness by Rex Bramleigh appears as the frontispiece to *Cicero and Virgil* (Amsterdam, 1972), a festschrift for Hunt edited by John Martyn.

Univ Melb Gazette, Sept 1949, p 72, Mar 1969, p 11, Sept 1977, p 13, Autumn 1993, p 30; Classical Assn of Vic, *Iris*, 1977, p 29; Univ Melb Archives; information from Mr I. K. Hunt, Melb.

K. J. McKay

HUNT, JACOB GEOFFREY (1912-1941), grazier and soldier, was born on 15 April 1912 at Inverell, New South Wales, second child of native-born parents Alexander Hunt, grazier, and his wife Alice Ada Clinton, née Woods. Educated at Bannockburn Public and Inverell Intermediate High schools, Geoff grew up and worked on the family property, Oakwood.

A good horseman and athlete, in January 1939 he joined the local Militia infantry unit, the 33rd Battalion. When World War II began he was determined to enlist in the Australian Imperial Force, but was rejected because he was too short. By March 1940 he was a sergeant in the 35th Battalion, Militia. Hunt finally managed to enlist in the A.I.F. on 14 May; he gave his religion as Anglican; his recorded height of 5 ft 5 ins (165 cm) may have been exaggerated. Posted to the 2nd/13th Battalion and promoted corporal, he sailed with his unit in October for Palestine where further training was undertaken. In February 1941 the 2nd/13th was incorporated in the 9th Division and deployed to North Africa. The battalion was stationed at Beda Fomm, Libya, before withdrawing eastwards and reaching Tobruk by 9 April.

During the siege of the fortress Hunt was a member of the battalion's Pioneer Platoon. He regularly worked alone—or with a small party—out in front of the perimeter posts, laying and repairing the wire, and locating and removing mines and booby traps. Patrolling at night, he made the area his own, becoming familiar with the ground and all the approaches. When the battalion advanced its line on the left of the Salient in May, he went out under machine-gun fire to wire the new position. On other nights he led parties carrying stores to the forward posts. He was known as the battalion's scout and was described as 'outstanding for his energy and courage and resourcefulness'.

The 2nd/13th occupied the right sector of the Salient in June and made preparations to advance the line. Hunt took out squads on two successive nights to clear the vicinity of booby traps. Persistent mortar fire killed or wounded several of his men. Displaying 'exceptional coolness and ability', he extricated the wounded, then returned to continue his task. He was awarded the Distinguished Conduct Medal (gazetted 1942) for this action and for his work over months of the siege. A soldier in his platoon recalled that he had 'a wonderful control over men and we would happily do anything for him. He was energetic like a game fox terrier and quite fearless of any higher ranks, including our tough CO, "Bull" Burrows' [q.v.13]. In July Hunt was promoted lance sergeant.

On 29 November 1941 the battalion moved to Ed Duda in readiness for an attack towards Sidi Rezegh. At dawn the Germans brought down heavy artillery fire on the exposed Australians, causing many casualties. Hunt was one of those hit by shrapnel. He died on the following day and was buried in the Tobruk war cemetery.

G. H. Fearnside (ed), *Bayonets Abroad* (Syd, 1953); B. Maughan, *Tobruk and El Alamein* (Canb, 1966); information from Mr A. C. Hunt, Attunga, and Mr E. C. Woolley, Narara, NSW.

PETER BURNESS

HUNT, RALPH ALEC (1891-1980), engineer and administrator, was born on 13 March 1891 at Brighton, Melbourne, eldest son of Victorian-born parents Henry William Hunt, solicitor, and his wife Wilhelmine Jane, née Rule. Ralph was educated at Brighton and Melbourne Church of England grammar schools, and at the University of Melbourne (B.C.E., 1916). He joined the State Rivers and Water Supply Commission of Victoria as an assistant-engineer in 1915.

On 10 October 1916 Hunt enlisted in the Australian Imperial Force. Commissioned in September 1917, he served in France from April 1918 with the 12th Field Company, Engineers. In May he was promoted lieutenant. At Cérisy-Gailly, on 8 August, he reconnoitred roads and bridges while under heavy fire and was awarded the Distinguished Service Order. Mentioned in dispatches, he returned to Melbourne in August 1919 and his appointment terminated on 12 September. He returned to State Rivers as a design and construction engineer on the Hume Reservoir project.

Hunt married Parisian-born Henriette Kaczka (d.1945) at the registry office, Melbourne, on 24 January 1920. That year he began his career with the State Electricity Commission. Although his early engineering posts were relatively minor, he was one of the pioneers under Sir John Monash [q.v.10] who developed the generation of electricity from brown coal. In 1934 Hunt became an administrator, rising in 1938 to general superintendent, Yallourn. On 31 October 1949 at St Paul's Anglican Church, Warragul, he married Betty May Budge, a 27-year-old trained nurse.

One month earlier he had been unexpectedly catapulted to the top of the S.E.C. as chairman and general manager, the first time

the posts had been combined since Monash's death in 1931. Hunt's war record, early commission links, proven capacity to bring about organizational reform and pleasant manner secured him the dual offices. He was to need all his skills over the next seven years. The commission's supply system had been stretched to its limits in the 1940s. Its unpopular electricity restrictions had provoked political threats to transfer its distribution network to regional supply boards and allocate the brown-coal installations to a separate organization. Severe financial shortages prevented much-needed expansion at Morwell and Kiewa, and in 1956, his last year as chairman, Hunt advised the minister of electrical undertakings (Sir) George Reid that the commission would be unable to accept new load unless its future capital could be assured.

'Sharp-featured, keen-eyed and stockily built', Hunt was committed to the S.E.C. to an extent that left little time for relaxation, other than an occasional game of golf. He was an associate (1922) of the Institution of Civil Engineers, London, and a foundation member (1919) of the Institution of Engineers, Australia. In retirement, he was president (1957-58) of the Old Melburnians, Australian deputy-chairman of Malcolm Moore Industries Ltd, and a member of the committees of management of the Austin Hospital and of the court of directors of the Royal Humane Society. Survived by his wife and their son, and by the son of his first marriage, he died on 26 April 1980 at Mont Albert and was cremated.

H. Gill, *Three Decades* (Melb, 1949); C. Edwards, *Brown Power* (Melb, 1969); *V&P* (LA Vic), 1947 (5); *Age* (Melb), 2 Sept 1949, 17 May 1957; *Smith's Weekly* (Syd), 24 Sept 1949; *A'sian Post*, 27 Oct 1949; M. J. Holmes, The State Electricity Commission of Victoria—a case study in autonomy (M.A. thesis, Univ Melb, 1969); information from Mrs J. Holmes, Mt Eliza, Vic.

DIANE LANGMORE

HUNTER, ALEXANDER (1919-1971), economist and academic, was born on 23 December 1919 at Govan, Glasgow, Scotland, fifth son of Archibald Hunter, foreman shoemaker, and his wife Margaret, née Dykes, a former farm-servant. Alex attended Elder Park Primary and Govan High schools, leaving at 15 to learn his father's trade. During World War II he served abroad with the Argyll and Sutherland Highlanders and the Royal Army Service Corps. Determined not to return to shoemaking, Hunter entered the University of Glasgow (M.A. Hons, 1951; D.Litt., 1966) on a grant. He won the William Tweeddale prize for distinction in political economy and joined the academic staff in

1951. At the office of the district registrar, Hillhead, on 22 December 1947 he had married Thelma Anna Carmela Cibelli, a fellow student and future academic.

In 1952 Hunter moved to the University College of North Staffordshire, Keele, where he taught economics and developed an interest in the implications for welfare of monopolies and restrictive practices. His first publications in 1955 were on this topic. Thereafter, he used his skills in economics to advise public bodies dedicated to promoting workable competition. In 1956 he became a consultant to the registrar of restrictive trading agreements. The experience led to his influential book, *Competition and the Law* (London, 1966), and enabled him to challenge successfully J. K. Galbraith in the *Economic Journal* in 1958-59.

Emigrating with his family to Australia in 1958, Hunter took up a senior lectureship at the University of Melbourne. Despite suffering his first heart attack, he edited *The Economics of Australian Industry* (1963). In 1961 he accepted the chair of economics at the University of New South Wales. He wrote a series of articles on restrictive trade practices, gave evidence to the Tasmanian royal commission which reported (1965) on the issue, and in 1967 was appointed a part-time consultant to the Commonwealth commissioner of trade practices. In 1965 Hunter had moved to Canberra as a senior fellow in the Research School of Pacific Studies at the Australian National University. He transferred to the Research School of Social Sciences next year and was promoted professorial fellow in 1969. He carried out research on the Indonesian economy (particularly oil and population) and the Australian petroleum and shipping industries, published prolifically and attracted international notice.

Hunter was a practical man who modestly hoped to use his training to make the world a marginally better place. He was a well-rounded economist of the type that is unfashionable, but essential, in academia today. Although he made use of theory, he was aware that it was often 'incompatible with practical applications of policy'. He valued the logical basis of his discipline which he skilfully employed—together with evidence (both contemporary and historical), simple statistical measures and a comparative approach—to investigate issues in the field of industrial economics. He wrote in a clear, straightforward and informative manner with the object of persuading public figures and their advisers to his point of view.

Gentle, generous and kind, Hunter was well liked for the 'warmth of his friendship and the melodious lilt and laughter in his voice', and for 'his integrity . . . unpretentious and uncomplaining nature'. His genuine interest in the work of postgraduates from other departments was a rare attribute. While visiting Papua New Guinea as a member of the Territory's commission of inquiry into coastal shipping, he died of a coronary occlusion on 21 May 1971 at Lae and was cremated. His wife, daughter and two sons survived him.

Bulletin of Indonesian Economic Studies, 7, no 2, July 1971, p 95; *Economic Record*, 47, no 119, Sept 1971, p 427, and for publications; *Canb Times*, 22 May 1971; T. S. Swan, Alex Hunter, 1919-71, *and* J. Isaac, Memorial Service to Alex Hunter, Canb, 27 June 1971, *and* T. Hunter, A Very Earnest Lady (tss, held by Dr T. Hunter, Cook, Canb).

G. D. SNOOKS

HUNTER, JOHN GEORGE (1888-1964), medical administrator, was born on 19 September 1888 at Ultimo, Sydney, son of William Fyfe Hunter, a loomturner from Scotland, and his native-born wife Ellen Jane, née Sloane. Educated at Fort Street Model School and the University of Sydney (B.Sc., 1909; M.B., 1915; Ch.M., 1946), John interrupted his studies to act as biologist on (Sir) Douglas Mawson's [q.v.10] Australasian Antarctic Expedition in 1911-14. After graduating, Hunter worked briefly as a resident at the Royal Alexandra Hospital for Children. On 10 February 1916 at St Philip's Anglican Church, Sydney, he married Clarice Mary Walker, a nurse.

As captain, Australian Army Medical Corps, Australian Imperial Force, Hunter served on the Western Front with the 9th Field Ambulance (1916-17) and in England with the 2nd Australian General Hospital (1917-18). He returned to Sydney, went into general practice in turn at Mascot and Botany, and was honorary assistant-physician (1923-29) at Sydney Hospital and honorary physician (1927-29) at Royal South Sydney Hospital. In 1929 he was appointed full-time medical secretary of the New South Wales branch of the British Medical Association. Next year he organized its first postgraduate course for medical practitioners and presided over the official opening of B.M.A. House at 135 Macquarie Street; in 1959 he achieved his aim of clearing the debt on the building.

Hunter was also general secretary (from 1933) of the B.M.A.'s Federal Council in Australia. He taught medical ethics at the university, delivering 'very neat lectures on good manners for medical men'. In 1941 he was mobilized in the Militia as major, and performed staff and medical duties in Sydney until 1943. An outstanding organizer, he helped to establish the Hospitals Contribution and Medical Benefits funds of Australia. For fifteen years he was secretary for Australasia of the World Medical Association and in 1961-64 chaired the Australian Council of Social Service.

In the 1940s Hunter had opposed with 'almost religious fervour' the Federal Labor government's 'free medicine scheme'. Presenting him with the gold medal (1956) of the Australian branch of the B.M.A., the federal president (Sir) Cecil Colville observed that: 'He more than any single person, was responsible for the success of the fight . . . against the Chifley [q.v.13] Government in its attempt to place a galling yoke of subservience on the necks of the members of the medical profession'. In 1957 Hunter was appointed C.B.E. Regarded as the 'chief architect' of the Australian Medical Association which was formed in 1962, he drafted its code of ethics.

Hunter was neither a publicity seeker nor a remote administrator. A man of integrity, he was reserved, modest and loyal, willing to help his colleagues at all times. He retired in 1962 and pursued his hobbies of fishing and gardening. That year the A.M.A. established the J. G. Hunter testimonial fund to finance a prize or scholarship in his honour and to commission his portrait. Painted by (Sir) William Dargie, it hangs in the A.M.A.'s Canberra office. Hunter died on 27 December 1964 in his home at Lilli Pilli, Sydney, and was cremated; his wife, daughter and four sons survived him.

Faculty of Medicine, Univ Syd, *Senior Year Book*, 1946-47; *MJA*, 1 Sept 1962, p 350, 10 July 1965, p 89.   BRENDA HEAGNEY

HURLEY, SIR THOMAS ERNEST VICTOR (1888-1958), surgeon and medical administrator, and LESLIE EVERTON (1893-1967), physician, were born on 3 January 1888 at Ceres, Victoria, and 28 January 1893 at Everton, eldest and fourth sons of Thomas Hurley, state schoolteacher, and his wife Mary Elizabeth, née Scholes, both Victorian born. Educated at various primary schools determined by their father's postings, they both won scholarships to Wesley College, and to Queen's College, University of Melbourne.

At Wesley, Victor gained exhibitions in completing his Leaving certificate and played for the first XI. (Sir) William Upjohn [q.v.], a schoolmate, later wrote that Hurley already possessed the qualities that were to make him an outstanding leader in his field: he was 'alert, merry, fond of fun, good at sport, very good at studies, frank and unafraid to express his opinions, companionable and . . . friendly'. In 1905 he entered the university (M.B., 1909; B.S., 1910; M.D., 1912; M.S., 1913)

where he was awarded exhibitions in pathology, and in medicine and obstetrics.

On graduating, Hurley was appointed resident medical officer (1910) at the (Royal) Melbourne Hospital. It was the beginning of an association with that institution that was to span almost fifty years. In 1911 he became registrar. Next year, as medical superintendent, he supervised the almost total rebuilding of the hospital on its Lonsdale Street site. He was appointed an honorary surgeon to out-patients in 1914. In that year he commenced private practice in Collins Street.

On 20 August 1914 Hurley was appointed captain, Australian Army Medical Corps, Australian Imperial Force, and sailed for Egypt in October. He served at Gallipoli from April to September 1915 with the 2nd Field Ambulance. Promoted temporary lieutenant colonel in March 1916 (substantive 1917), he performed staff duties at A.I.F. Headquarters, London, in 1916-17; he was appointed C.M.G. (1917) and mentioned in dispatches for his 'tact, ability and strenuous work'. In 1917-18 he was on the Western Front, principally with the 2nd Australian General Hospital. His A.I.F. appointment terminated in Melbourne on 11 February 1920.

Before leaving England, Hurley had become a fellow (1918) of the Royal College of Surgeons, England. On 10 June 1919 at St James's parish church, Westminster, he married Elsie May, daughter of G. H. Crowther [q.v.8]; she had come to London as a member of a Voluntary Aid Detachment during the war. Back in Melbourne, they bought a house at South Yarra, from which they moved in 1926 to a larger one at Toorak to accommodate their growing family. Hurley had resumed practice in Collins Street and at the (Royal) Melbourne Hospital out-patients' department.

His ability soon won him additional responsibilities, as lecturer and examiner in surgery at the university, founding secretary (1920-23) of the Surgical Association of Melbourne and assistant to (Sir) George Syme [q.v.12], surgeon to the Victoria Police. On Syme's retirement in 1928, he took over that position and held it until 1956. In 1921 he had been elected to the council of the Victorian branch of the British Medical Association (president 1930), on which he served for the rest of his life, apart from a short interval during World War II. He was a member (1923-48) of the Charities Board of Victoria and a foundation member (1927) of the (Royal) Australasian College of Surgeons. In 1927 he was made honorary surgeon to in-patients at the (Royal) Melbourne Hospital. He was dean of its clinical school in 1929-36.

Hurley followed Basil Kilvington [q.v.] as Stewart lecturer in surgery (1936-46) at the university. As a lecturer, wrote one of his sons who was a medical student, he was 'clear and methodical' rather than inspiring. His lectures were well organized, sound and practical, but they lacked the 'oratorical skill and showmanship' of Sir Alan Newton [q.v.11], the 'mordant wit' of Upjohn and the 'verve' of Victor's brother Leslie. One of his colleagues noted that, as a surgeon, Hurley was 'orthodox and safe', but added that, if the essence of style were to achieve maximum result with minimum effort, he had style. 'One elegant stroke would sever the skin . . . A few confident blows with the blades, and the most brutish of gall-bladders was ripe for the plucking'. Hurley chaired (1936-46) the board of examiners in surgery. Chairman, as well, of the Red Cross Society of Australia in 1939-40, he resigned to take the post of director (director-general from January 1943) of medical services, Royal Australian Air Force.

The infant R.A.A.F. medical service had been controlled by the director-general of army medical services. Hurley developed an autonomous organization capable of meeting wartime needs. One of his earliest actions was to recommend the formation of the R.A.A.F. Nursing Service. He recruited large numbers of medical officers: there were more than five hundred by 1944, reinforced by part-time consultants throughout Australia. The first R.A.A.F. hospitals were established, initially at Laverton and Ascot Vale, and at Richmond, New South Wales.

In late 1940 Hurley instigated and thereafter chaired the Flying Personnel Research Committee to study problems in aviation medicine. Having sent R.A.A.F. officers to Britain to learn Royal Air Force methods, he set up rehabilitation centres which helped aircrew to overcome major surgical, orthopaedic and neuro-psychiatric disabilities, and to return to duty. His medical air-evacuation transport units shifted thousands of battle casualties in the South-West Pacific Area. Appointed C.B. in 1945, he was demobilized on 6 December.

After the war Hurley returned to practice and was a consulting surgeon (from 1947) at the R.M.H. He took on additional professional positions: Victorian representative on the Federal Council of the B.M.A. in Australia, vice-president (president from 1950) of the Walter and Eliza Hall [qq.v.9] Institute of Research, president (1947) of the Medical Legal Society of Victoria, vice-president (1947-51) of the R.A.C.S. and president (1947-57) of the R.M.H. In 1948 he chaired the surgery section of the sixth Australasian Medical Congress, held in Perth.

As federal president of the B.M.A. in 1949-51, Hurley was a conciliatory negotiator between the association and the Chifley [q.v.13]

government over the Pharmaceutical Benefits Act (1947) which was a modest first step towards a national health service. A proponent of a national insurance scheme, Hurley was sympathetic to the proposals of the minister for health, N. E. McKenna [q.v.], but he faithfully represented the views of the B.M.A. He was appointed K.B.E. in 1950. In 1951-53 he was president of the R.A.C.S. On his retirement as president of the R.M.H., the hospital established the Victor Hurley Research Fund.

Much loved within the medical profession, Hurley had 'a broad, open, friendly face which inspired trust and confidence'. His natural charm, equable, quiet cheerfulness, humanity, tolerance and easy sociability made him approachable to colleagues and patients alike. Blessed with the ability to relax and enjoy the company of his fellows, he relished humorous stories and ridiculous situations. He was president of the Naval and Military Club, a member of the Melbourne Club, and he played a 'crisp' game at the Royal Melbourne Golf Club. In later life his home was at Kew, and he treasured holidays with his family at their seaside cottage at Point Lonsdale.

Survived by his wife, two daughters and four sons, Sir Victor died of complications of emphysema on 17 July 1958 at Royal Melbourne Hospital; he was accorded a funeral with R.A.A.F. honours and was cremated. His estate was sworn for probate at £43 550. The R.M.H. holds his portrait by Murray Griffin.

Like his elder brother, Leslie Hurley gained exhibitions in completing his Leaving certificate. In 1911 he entered the University of Melbourne (M.B., B.S., 1917; M.D., 1919; M.S., 1920) where he competed in Queen's College's cricket, football and athletic teams, and won a Blue for lacrosse. On 11 September 1914 he enlisted in the A.I.F. He sailed for the Middle East next month and served at Gallipoli in April-July 1915 with the 2nd Field Ambulance. Sent home to complete his medical course, he gained first-class honours in all subjects and won every exhibition in his final year. He was discharged from the A.I.F. on 16 May 1916. At All Saints Church of England, Clayton, on 15 October 1917 he married Margaret Muriel Atkinson, a nurse.

Following a residency at the (Royal) Melbourne Hospital, he became lecturer (from 1923 senior lecturer) in embryology and histology at the university. (Sir) Albert Coates [q.v.13], one of his students, wrote: 'Diagnosis based on a meticulous interrogation of the patient, the social and family background, painstaking physical examination and then, a resort to special investigation—this was to Leslie Hurley a sacred trust. With no empirical humbug, perhaps less bedside manner than some affected, he was a pioneer in scientific medicine'. From 1924 Hurley was also physician to out-patients at the (Royal) Melbourne Hospital. In 1933, as his practice as a consulting physician burgeoned, he resigned his university appointment. He was made physician to in-patients in 1935.

During and after World War II he was a part-time consultant to the R.A.A.F., practising in the air force hospitals at Laverton and Heidelberg and rising to group captain. While Victor was away, Leslie took over his consulting rooms in Parliament Place; on his return, they practised there together. In 1947-48 Leslie was Stewart lecturer in medicine at the university. He continued his work at the R.M.H. until 1951; Coates predicted that his piercing voice and aphorisms would long be remembered in its corridors.

A devoted family man, Hurley had enjoyed camping holidays with his five daughters and two sons, and trout fishing with his wife. She died in 1945. At Scots Church, Melbourne, on 13 December 1947 he married with Presbyterian forms Olive Marion Johnson, a secretary. He had little interest in social activities outside the family, but did play a weekly game of golf—with more enthusiasm than skill—until prevented by the onset of a long illness which forced him to give up his practice in 1966. Survived by his wife and by the children of his first marriage, he died on 23 May 1967 at Richmond and was cremated; his estate was sworn for probate at $181 057.

G. Blainey et al, *Wesley College* (Melb, 1967); K. F. Russell, *The Melbourne Medical School 1862-1962* (Melb, 1977); G. L. McDonald (ed), *Roll of the Royal Australasian College of Physicians* (Syd, 1988); J. V. Hurley, *Sir Victor Hurley* (Melb, 1989); O. Parnaby, *Queen's College* (Melb, 1990); *MJA*, 4 Oct 1958, 23 Sept 1967; *Smith's Weekly* (Syd), 19 Mar 1949; *Herald* (Melb), 11 Dec 1945, 17 July 1958; *Age* (Melb), 5 Mar, 18 July 1958, 25 Nov 1959; RACS Archives, Melb.

DIANE LANGMORE

HUTCHENS, FRANK LAWRENCE WELLINGTON (1918-1966), steelworks engineer, was born on 28 June 1918 at Cobar, New South Wales, second son of native-born parents John Wellington Hutchens, mining clerk, and his wife Josephine, née Farrelly. In the early 1920s the Cobar mine closed and John moved his family to Waratah, Newcastle. He found a job at the Broken Hill Proprietary Co. Ltd's new steelworks and was later storekeeper and purchasing officer at the nearby works of what became the Commonwealth Steel Co. Ltd (Comsteel). Frank excelled in sport and academic studies, and was dux of the Marist Bros' school, Hamilton. In November 1935 he joined Comsteel as a trainee-

engineer. Having gained an engineering diploma (1940) from Sydney Technical College, in 1942 he was appointed assistant to the superintendent of the mills. At Corpus Christi Catholic Church, Waratah, on 27 February 1943 he married Patricia Mary Rooney, a cook.

Able and industrious, Hutchens was promoted assistant works superintendent in March 1954 and an executive-officer in the following year. Within months he was in charge of planning the introduction to Australia of the cold-rolling process for stainless steel. He made three trips abroad to study the process, assemble data and subsequently check on the progress of plant being manufactured at engineering centres in the United States of America and Europe. The site chosen for the £4 million strip-mill was farmland at Unanderra, close to the section of the Australian Iron and Steel Ltd's steelworks at Port Kembla from where the hot-rolled feed-strip would be obtained.

Hutchens was promoted assistant-manager in 1957 and moved to Unanderra to supervise the construction of the works. A rambling creek was redirected from the property, huge quantities of fill were spread to raise the ground above flood-level, rail and road bridges were erected to give access to the site, and power lines were diverted. His management skills were such that building proceeded according to plan and the plant was commissioned in September 1959, three months ahead of schedule. It was the first large contract undertaken by the new construction company, Transfield Pty Ltd. The Comsteel works was well served by rail and road, and Hutchens ensured that the grounds were beautified with gardens.

In 1961 Hutchens returned to Newcastle. Next year he was appointed general manager of Comsteel. A council-member of the Association of Australian Forging Industries, he joined the Federal government's Export Development Council in 1965 and was invited to chair the Newcastle study-tours committee of the Duke of Edinburgh's third Commonwealth Study Conference. Hutchens was a keen golfer and president of the Steel Works Golf Club. Popular, charming and a gifted speaker, he believed in playing as hard as he worked. He died suddenly of a coronary occlusion on 21 October 1966 while holidaying at Gosford and was buried in Sandgate cemetery, Newcastle. His wife, daughter and two sons survived him.

BHP Review, 35, no 5, Aug 1958, p 10, 40, no 1, Christmas 1962, p 28, 44, no 1, Christmas 1966, p 31; *Daily Telegraph* (Syd), 6 Apr 1960; *Sth Coast Times*, 7 Apr 1960; *SMH*, 12 Apr 1960; *Newcastle Morning Herald*, 22 Oct 1966; B. M. Firth, The Industrialization of Wollongong with special reference to AIS, 1926-1976 (Ph.D. thesis, Macquarie Univ, 1986); information from Mrs P. Hutchens, Jesmond, NSW, and Mr J. C. Hutchens, Caringbah, Syd.   BEVERLEY FIRTH

HUTCHEON, JOHN SILVESTER (1882-1957), cricketer and barrister, was born on 5 April 1882 at Warwick, Queensland, eldest of four children of John McIntosh Hutcheon, a schoolteacher from Scotland, and his Sydney-born wife Elizabeth Sarah, née Silvester. Jack was educated at the local state school and at Toowoomba Grammar School where, in his final year, he made over 1000 runs (average 42) at cricket. On 27 November 1900 he was employed by the Department of Agriculture. He played first-grade matches for the Brisbane, North Brisbane and Toowong clubs, and was selected for the State in 1905. During the 1907-08 season he represented Queensland against an English touring team. At St Mary's Anglican Church, Kangaroo Point, on 17 December 1907 he married Mabel Mary Wilkinson.

A free and vigorous batsman, Hutcheon obtained most of his runs in front of the wicket and, once thoroughly set, scored at a rare pace. He was also a brilliant fieldsman. In 1908-09—his best season—he amassed 1539 runs (average 67) in club and intra-State games, notching six centuries and the highest score made by a Queenslander (259 not out, for Brisbane against Richmond River): he hit 26 off one over, scoring so fast that Brisbane's last 328 runs came up in 126 minutes. In 1910-11 he captained Queensland and played against a South African side that included G. A. Faulkner and C. B. Llewellyn. He turned out for the Rest of Australia against New South Wales in C. T. B. Turner's [q.v.6] testimonial match (1910) and top scored in the first innings with 36 on a bad wicket. Unable to obtain leave of absence, he declined an invitation to join the Australian team chosen to tour New Zealand.

From 1911 Hutcheon was a clerk in the Queensland Agent-General's Office, London; on 26 January 1914 he was called to the Bar at Lincoln's Inn. He returned to Brisbane, entered the Crown Solicitor's Office on 26 November and was admitted to the Queensland Bar on 14 March 1916. Next year he was appointed assistant crown solicitor, but resigned in 1922 to take up private practice. Much of his work was for the Queensland Canegrowers' Council, for which he appeared frequently before the Central Sugar-cane Prices Board. He was appointed K.C. on 27 July 1944 and was president of the Queensland Bar Association in 1952-57.

Best remembered for his hard work as a cricket administrator, Hutcheon represented Queensland on the Australian Board of Con-

trol for International Cricket from 1919 to 1957. A 'snobbish, dictatorial wowser . . . [he] helped give it the reputation for riding roughshod over the wishes of cricketers'. He was also a life member (1923) and president (1926-57) of the Queensland Cricket Association, and chairman (1920-57) of its executive. Queensland was admitted to the Sheffield Shield Competition in 1926, and Hutcheon and Roger Hartigan were credited with securing Brisbane its first Test in 1928. According to Hartigan, 'Hutcheon kept Queensland very much in the limelight'. In 1928-29 Hutcheon was an Australian selector and in 1933 helped the governor Sir Leslie Wilson [q.v.12] to form the local Wanderers' Cricket Club, a social club which regularly toured Queensland country areas and interstate.

Hutcheon had also excelled in tennis, rowing and table tennis, but in later years was always more keen to talk about his exploits in lacrosse. In 1907 at the Melbourne Cricket Ground he played for a victorious national side against a touring Canadian team and he later competed in interstate carnivals; he was president of the Queensland Lacrosse Association (1925-49) and of the Australian Lacrosse Council (1939-46). In 1956 he was appointed C.B.E. Survived by his wife and one of his two sons, Hutcheon died on 19 June 1957 in his home at Albion Heights and was cremated. His brother Ernest also played cricket for the State and wrote *A History of Queensland Cricket* (1946).

J. Pollard, *Australian Cricket* (Syd, 1982); B. Green (comp), *The Wisden Book of Obituaries* (Lond, 1986); *Cricket, A Weekly Record of the Game*, 7 Oct 1911; *Producers' Review*, July 1957; *Wisden Cricketers' Almanack*, 1958; *Brisb Standard*, 21 Sept 1929; *Courier-Mail*, 31 May 1956.

P. J. MULLINS

HUTCHISON, RUBY FLORENCE (1892-1974), politician, was born on 15 February 1892 at Footscray, Melbourne, third of ten children and eldest daughter of John George Herbert, billiard-marker, and his wife Florence Louisa, née Atherton, both Victorian born. When Ruby was 4 years old the family moved to the Murchison goldfields in Western Australia; they lived first at Cue, then at Day Dawn and finally at Meekatharra. Ruby's main schooling was at the Dominican Convent, Cue. On 11 March 1909 in her father's house at Meekatharra she married with Catholic rites Daniel Joseph Buckley, a miner; they were to have three sons and four daughters before their marriage was dissolved on 5 December 1928.

After leaving Meekatharra, Ruby and her children lived together in the timber country of the Hotham Valley, in Perth and at Northam. She earned an income by taking boarders and by dressmaking. Her determination to succeed and her strong-minded approach to the problems of women dated from this period. At the district registrar's office, Perth, on 8 November 1938 she married a 49-year-old labourer Alexander Hutchison (d.1961). After her children had reached adulthood, she attended Stott's Business College (from 1941) and the University of Western Australia's summer schools where she studied public administration, public speaking, psychology and languages.

By her own account, Ruby had first joined the Labor Party at the age of 16. Her interest in politics developed during the years of the Depression and World War II. She stood unsuccessfully as the Australian Labor Party's candidate for Suburban Province in the Legislative Council in 1950 and at a by-election in 1953. When she won the seat on 8 May 1954 and entered parliament a fortnight later, she became the first woman member of the State's Upper House and remained the only woman member until her retirement. Re-elected in 1960, she was returned by North-East Metropolitan Province in 1965. At St Peter's Catholic Church, Bedford, on 14 May 1966 she married Frederick Richard Hugh Lavery (d.1971), a 68-year-old widower and fellow Labor M.L.C.; they were the first husband and wife to serve simultaneously in an Australian parliament. She retired from politics on 21 May 1971 and on 20 September registered a deed to authorize her continued use of the surname Hutchison.

Throughout her parliamentary career Mrs Hutchison pursued a variety of causes, including the right of women to serve on juries, as well as child-welfare, education and housing issues. Committed to the eventual abolition of the Legislative Council, she introduced a number of private member's bills for reforming the electoral system for the Upper House, a chamber which Labor had never controlled. Her most forceful rhetoric was directed at the property franchise for Council elections. In October 1962 she was the second woman member ever to be suspended (Dame Florence Cardell-Oliver [q.v.13] was the first) from either House of the Western Australian parliament, after refusing to withdraw her remark that she was ashamed to be a member of such an undemocratic chamber. Ironically, following the adoption of adult suffrage for the Council in 1965 and the acceptance of redrawn electoral boundaries, Labor's representation diminished during her final term in parliament. Hutchison supported the ideal that governments should be constituted of an equal proportion of men and women.

An active community worker, she was founder (1962) and president of the Western Australian Epilepsy Association, and an inaugural member (1959) of the State branch of the Australian Consumers Association. She was also involved in the Girl Guides, and founder and first chairman of the women's auxiliary of the State's Boy Scouts' Association. Tall and bespectacled, she was a well-groomed woman who usually dressed in neutral colours.

Hutchison died on 17 December 1974 at Shenton Park and was buried in Karrakatta cemetery with Catholic rites; she was survived by two sons and three daughters of her first marriage. Seen by F. J. S. Wise, her leader in the Council, as rebellious and as having an overwhelming enthusiasm for her beliefs, she was a fiery speaker and a tenacious crusader for democratic reform, women's rights and social justice.

PD (WA), 30 Oct 1962, p 2086; *Herald* (Melb), 10 May 1954; *Sun* (Syd), 13 May 1959; *Daily News* (Perth), 25 Oct, 10 Nov 1962; *Weekend News*, 10 Nov 1962; *West Australian*, 29 Oct 1967, 27 Nov 1970, 18 Dec 1974, 4 June 1981; M. Choules, Women in West Australian Parliamentary Politics, 1921-1968 (B.A. Hons thesis, Curtin Univ of Technology, 1988; family information.

DAVID BLACK

HUTTON, MARY (1883-1964), headmistress, was born on 28 October 1883 at Hawthorn, Melbourne, fourth daughter of Colin Fergusson Hutton, a gentleman from Scotland, and his Adelaide-born wife Isabel Jane, née Townsend. Mary was educated at Manningtree Road State School, Hawthorn. At the age of 15, under the instruction of a private tutor, she qualified for matriculation.

A monitor (1899) and pupil-teacher (1900) at Hawksburn State School, she was recognized as 'promising, energetic and useful', and moved quickly through the ranks. At Melbourne Training College she won her trained teachers' certificate in 1904 and the Gladman [q.v.4] prize. Appointed to Cobram in 1906, she gained her infant teachers' certificate that year. Over the next twenty months she taught at five country and city schools. In 1908 Miss Hutton became a secondary teacher at the Continuation School (from 1912 Melbourne High School) and enrolled at the University of Melbourne (Dip.Ed., 1911; B.A., 1914; M.A., 1916). She won the Dwight [q.v.4] prize for education and the Cobden medal for political economy.

By 1918 Hutton was one of a small group of senior mistresses with limited opportunities, for there were then no head-teacher positions available to women within the state secondary system. The reclassification of domestic arts schools as girls' secondary schools in

1925 enabled her to be appointed (1927) headmistress of the Collingwood Domestic Arts School, a task she approached with 'vigour, capacity and ability'. Her job was daunting, for the school had little status and was housed in 'barrack like gloom' in a condemned building.

Hutton succeeded Christina Montgomery [q.v.10] as headmistress of Melbourne Girls' High School in 1934. Following a bequest from Sir Macpherson Robertson [q.v.11], the school moved into new premises at Albert Park in November and its name was changed to MacRobertson Girls' High School. For fourteen years Hutton worked to consolidate her school's reputation for academic excellence and service. She promoted literature and science, a cultured mind, physical health and calm judgement, but had to balance her higher goals with vocational preparation for a world where there were unequal opportunities for girls. She also tried to maintain school spirit when the building was requisitioned during World War II and the pupils were dispersed. After they returned in 1943, she faced higher enrolments, staffing problems and increased traffic noise, but the school's reputation continued to grow.

A tiny (4 ft 11 ins, 150 cm), quiet, reserved woman who served on the Schools Board and the university's committee of convocation, Hutton worked to improve pay and promotion for women secondary teachers. She was an executive-member of the High School Teachers' Association and a council-member of the Victorian Teachers' Union. Her own position illustrated the inequalities she fought: despite consistent assessment as an outstanding head, it was not until 1945 that she was classified as a principal, and even then she was still paid less than her male counterparts. Nevertheless, she considered teaching 'the noblest profession'. Following her retirement as headmistress in 1948, she taught part time at the school for six years.

Hutton's other abiding interest was the Baptist Church, of which she had been a devout member since 1904. In 1951-63 she was a council-member of Kilvington Baptist Girls Grammar School. She died on 20 December 1964 at Fitzroy and was buried in Boroondara cemetery; her estate was sworn for probate at £486. MacRobertson Girls' High School holds her portrait by Alexander Colquhoun [q.v.8].

MacRobertson Girls' High School, *Pallas*, June 1948, Dec 1965; *Vic Baptist Witness*, 5 Mar 1965; *Argus*, 30 Oct, 23 Nov 1948; *Age* (Melb), 21 Dec 1964; Education Dept (Vic) personal record files *and* Teachers' Assn files (Hist Services, Education Dept, Melb); Kilvington Baptist Girls School Council minutes; MacRobertson Girls' High School Archives; Sth Yarra *and* Armadale Baptist Church records; Education Dept (Vic) Archives, series 6007, 10249, boxes 137, 138 and 150, 10274, box 4, 10537, boxes 62 and 64 (PRO, Vic).

JUDITH BIDDINGTON

HYLAND, GLADYS PENFOLD; *see* PENFOLD HYLAND

HYLAND, SIR HERBERT JOHN THORNHILL (1884-1970), storekeeper, investor and politician, was born on 15 March 1884 at Prahran, Melbourne, second son of George Hyland, a Victorian-born painter, and his wife Mary, née Thornhill, from Ireland. Bert attended Caulfield State School until the early deaths of his parents forced him to leave at the age of 12 to take a job in a grocery store at Glenhuntly. After recovering from typhoid fever, he worked in another grocery at Mitcham, then moved to South Gippsland. There he was successively employed in a general store at Welshpool, in a grocery at Beulah and at the Kongwak Butter Factory before establishing his own general store and mixed grocery business at Leongatha. On 8 May 1912 at her parents' home at Galaquil he married with Methodist forms 18-year-old Amelia Mary Barratt (d.1968); their son and daughter were to predecease him, to his deep distress.

As Hyland's business flourished, he diversified into dairy-farming and became a major landowner in the region. He was ruled unfit for war service, but proved a staunch advocate of soldier settlers. Elected in 1923 to the Woorayl Shire Council (president 1928-29), he took an increasingly active role in community affairs, joined the Country Party and served as president of its Central Gippsland district council. His commercial ventures proved so profitable that he was able to retire in the late 1920s and devote himself to community and philanthropic causes.

In 1927 Hyland unsuccessfully contested the newly created seat of Wonthaggi in the Legislative Assembly. Next year he managed Tom Paterson's [q.v.11] successful campaign to retain the House of Representatives seat of Gippsland; he was an ardent supporter of Paterson's controversial dairy-assistance scheme. With the aid of preferences from the Australian Labor Party, in 1929 Hyland defeated the sitting Nationalist for the seat of Gippsland South and entered State parliament. Although he courted electoral disapproval by moving permanently to St Kilda, he became legendary for his services to his constituents: he was an inveterate lobbyist and letter-writer in their interests, and he visited his electorate weekly.

Appointed minister without portfolio in the minority Country Party government of (Sir)

Albert Dunstan [q.v.8] in June 1936, Hyland was promoted to various ministries, both in minority Country Party and in coalition cabinets, until the election of the Cain [q.v.13] government in 1952 brought a temporary halt to the chronic instability of Victorian politics. Hyland's portfolios included transport (1938-43), chief secretary (1943-45), State development (1947-48 and 1950-52), labour (1947-48), decentralization (1948) and transport and prices (1950-52). The internal tensions in the coalition ministries were illustrated when a reluctant Hyland, as chief secretary, was required to introduce a bill in 1944 which brought about a modest reform of Victoria's highly malapportioned electoral system.

When the Hollway-McDonald [qq.v.] coalition collapsed in division in 1948, Hollway blamed Dunstan's scheming for the government's demise. Hyland agreed. To the annoyance of his Country Party colleagues, he helped to keep Hollway in office in 1948-50 by abstaining on crucial parliamentary votes. Allegations of political patronage attended Hollway's appointment of Hyland to chair the La Trobe Valley Development Advisory Committee in 1949. In January that year Hyland had declared himself in favour of an amalgamation of the Liberal Party and the Country Party; he later gave serious consideration to leaving the Country Party and joining the Liberals who had controversially renamed themselves the Liberal and Country Party in an attempt to absorb the Country Party. The central council of the Country Party made moves to expel Hyland, but the crisis abated and he again became a senior minister in McDonald's Country Party government in 1950.

Knighted in 1952, Hyland was elected leader of the parliamentary Country Party in 1955—just in time to contest the elections caused by the A.L.P. split. His leadership was characterized by robust parliamentary and electoral competition with the Liberal Party. In the early years of (Sir) Henry Bolte's Liberal government, Hyland took advantage of the premier's relative inexperience to extract concessions, especially in relation to freight charges. Yet he never managed to adapt his political strategies to the changed environment of majority governments. He railed against Bolte for his alleged Melbourne bias and his lack of effective policies for decentralization. Too often Hyland was given to extravagant and even vituperative language. In a debate in parliament in 1958 he called Bolte 'a mongrel' and referred to another minister as 'a stupid looking goof'; he was suspended from parliament in 1960 for describing the Speaker as being 'as silly as a billy goat'. His regular addresses to Country Party conferences were laced with 'vitriolic' denuncia-

tions of the Liberal Party. Despite these outbursts, Hyland was well liked by most of his parliamentary colleagues.

Following the 1964 elections, he was unexpectedly replaced as parliamentary leader of the Country Party by his deputy George Moss. Hyland's advancing years told against him among the younger Country Party politicians and he failed to be elected deputy-leader. He continued in parliament, served on the Public Works Committee (1964-67) and took a particular interest in the improvement of the facilities at Parliament House.

Bert Hyland retained Gippsland South at fifteen consecutive elections—five of them unopposed. His personal popularity can be gauged by his last election (1967) when he secured the largest majority of any member of the Legislative Assembly. Having decided, at the age of 86, not to contest the 1970 election, he surprised the supervisor of the parliamentary dining-room Elsie Joan Mendoza, née Atkins, a 48-year-old divorcee, by asking her to be his wife. They were married with Methodist forms on 2 January 1970 at his East St Kilda home. Shrewd investments had made Sir Herbert a wealthy man and he continued to support the Helping Hand Association for Mentally Retarded Children. Survived by his wife, he died on 18 March 1970 at Prahran; he was accorded a state funeral and was cremated with Anglican rites. His estate was sworn for probate at $278 653.

R. Wright, *A People's Counsel* (Melb, 1992); *PD* (Vic), 20 Mar 1970; *Countryman* (Melb), 26 July 1929, 30 Jan 1958, 17 June 1964, 29 Jan, 2 Apr 1970; *Age* (Melb), 12 Apr 1961, 21 Mar 1970; *Bulletin*, 4 Aug 1962.   B. J. COSTAR

HYNES, SIR LINCOLN CARRUTHERS (1912-1977), sportsman, radio and television manager, and hospital administrator, was born on 14 April 1912 at Balmain, Sydney, second son and fifth child of native-born parents Rev. Francis William Hynes, Methodist minister, and his wife Mabel Evelyn, daughter of Rev. J. E. Carruthers and niece of Sir Joseph Carruthers [q.v.7]. Lincoln was educated at North Sydney and Sydney boys' high schools where he acquired the name of 'Bob'. Sport was a central part of his life. A fast-medium, left-arm bowler and right-hand, middle-order batsman, he played four seasons for New South Wales from 1935-36. His greatest achievement was to execute a trap, set by his captain Alan McGilvray, to dismiss (Sir) Donald Bradman for a duck, caught at leg slip, at the Sydney Cricket Ground in 1936. Hynes later relished re-telling and re-enacting this dismissal, which loomed larger than his best first-class figures of 6 for

25 against Victoria. He was also a first-grade Rugby Union referee and prominent in the Northbridge Bowling Club, winning the singles, pairs and fours, and becoming patron of the club.

Hynes had enrolled in law at the University of Sydney, but soon left to work for Louis Dreyfus & Co. (1932-35), Neptune Oil Co. Ltd (1935-36), W. Dunlop & Co. Pty Ltd (1936-42) and Independent Oil Industries Ltd (1942-43). At Wesley Chapel, Sydney, on 29 July 1939 he married Enid May Brunskill. Joining the Royal Australian Air Force on 16 March 1943, he was commissioned in the Administrative and Special Duties Branch on 20 May 1944 and promoted flying officer in November. He served at R.A.A.F. Headquarters, Melbourne, and as an area sports officer at Milne Bay, Papua (1943-44), and at the School of Administration, Melbourne.

Following his demobilization on 7 February 1946, Hynes was employed as a part-time sports commentator with radio 2GB and rose to be sales manager of Macquarie Broadcasting Services Pty Ltd. In 1951 he moved to Brisbane to manage radio 4BC for M. F. Albert's [q.v.7] Commonwealth Broadcasting Corporation Pty Ltd, then returned to Sydney in 1956 as general manager of C.B.C., based on radio 2UW with a network of stations in New South Wales and Queensland.

A gregarious individual, Hynes enjoyed the fraternity of cricketers and helped to launch the broadcasting careers of K. A. and R. G. Archer, whom he recruited for radio-stations 4BC and 2UW respectively; Ken Archer later became Hynes's right-hand man in the C.B.C. and succeeded him as its chief executive. Hynes was influential in the Australian Federation of Commercial Broadcasting Stations for many years and its president in 1958-72. He was also closely involved with the introduction of television and was a director (from 1960) and chairman (from 1970) of Darling Downs TV Ltd. His extensive business interests led to his appointments as Australasian chairman (from 1972) of Cook (Thomas) Pty Ltd and as a director (1976) of City Mutual Life Assurance Society Ltd.

Hynes had been associated with the Royal North Shore Hospital from 1960 and was chairman (1968-77) of its board. He helped to raise funds for the hospital chapel (posthumously named after him), and oversaw major hospital extensions. Active in many other associations involved with health care, he was president (1973-74) of the Australian Hospital Association. In 1967 he was appointed O.B.E.; in 1971 he was knighted. Sir Lincoln belonged to the Rotary Club of Sydney, the United Service, the American National and Pymble Golf clubs, the Cricketers' Club of New South Wales and to four bowling clubs. An accomplished musician, he was organist at several Sydney churches; as a baritone, he was highly placed in radio 2GB's 'Australia's Amateur Hour'. He liked gardening at his Killara home. Survived by his wife and three daughters, he died of acidosis on 7 August 1977 at R.N.S.H. and was cremated.

R. Robinson, *From the Boundary* (Syd, 1950); *ABC Weekly*, 5 May 1956, p 14; *Australian Paraplegic*, 6, no 3, Sept 1972, p 39; Aust Cricket Soc, Syd Branch, *Hill Chatter*, 1, no 2, 1974, p 715; Roy Nth Shore Hospital, *Synapse*, no 47, Sept 1977; *SMH*, 31 Oct 1958, 1 Jan 1967, 14 Nov 1968, 12 June 1971, 8 Aug 1977.   R. I. CASHMAN

HYTTEN, TORLEIV (1890-1980), professor of economics and university vice-chancellor, was born on 17 February 1890 at Drammen, Norway, son of Oscar Emil Hytten, a master shoemaker, later bankrupted, and his wife Marie Charlotte, née Knudsen. The eldest of nine surviving children, Torleiv showed ability at school at Tönsberg, but poverty denied him further education in his youth. In 1910 he emigrated to New South Wales. There, among other jobs, he laboured on land reclamation at Newcastle and with a ship chandler in Sydney, before being employed as a truck driver and in other occupations at Broken Hill from 1913 to 1918. An active trade unionist, 'Tom' read the writings of Karl Marx until he was weaned away by a visiting Workers' Education Association lecturer, Herbert Heaton [q.v.9]. With a physique too light for heavy manual work, Hytten turned to journalism and contributed to several newspapers during his time at Broken Hill. In 1918 he 'drifted' to mining towns on the west coast of Tasmania where he wrote for the *Zeehan and Dundas Herald*. Heaton encouraged him to become secretary of the W.E.A. in Hobart. Having matriculated in 1920, Hytten studied at the University of Tasmania (B.A., 1922; M.A., 1929) while working as a journalist on the Labor *World* and the *News*. At Burnie on 11 April 1922 he married Margaret Frances Gill Compton with Presbyterian forms. He was naturalized in the following year.

After a brief experience of journalism in South Australia, in 1926 Hytten was appointed to a temporary lectureship in economics at the University of Tasmania. He associated with a brilliant group of Tasmanian economists which included (Sir) Douglas Copland, James Brigden, L. F. Giblin [qq.v.13,7,8] and Heaton. Giblin, in particular, was an important influence. In 1929 Hytten obtained a master's degree with first-class honours for his thesis on transport economics, and succeeded Brigden as professor of economics. Hytten was an economic adviser (1929-35) to the Tasmanian government and chairman (1932) of the State Employment Council. He accompanied Prime Minister S. M. (Viscount) Bruce [q.v.7] to the League of Nations in 1935. That year he was appointed economic adviser to the Bank of New South Wales; based in Sydney, he regarded his fourteen-year association with the bank as 'the happiest of his life' and belonged (1938-50) to Round Table. Considering himself a pragmatist, Hytten believed that the cost-cutting Premiers' Plan (1931) was the only answer to the Depression, and kept Keynesian views at arm's length. In the late 1940s he worked against J. B. Chifley's [q.v.13] bank nationalization policy.

In 1949-57 Hytten was the first, full-time vice-chancellor of the University of Tasmania. An effective fund-raiser, he was largely responsible for establishing a residence (later named Hytten Hall) for men on the new campus at Sandy Bay. His term coincided with a revolt of Tasmanian academics against low salaries and relatively poor conditions. According to his own account, Hytten's business training in quick decision-making was unpopular with the professoriate. In 1955 a royal commission into the university concluded that the situation required 'a more forceful approach' than Hytten's, and that the vice-chancellor 'preferred to cleave to the Council and to the Chancellor' against the professorial board, instead of taking an independent line. Many blamed Hytten for the summary dismissal in 1956 of Professor Sydney Sparkes Orr [q.v.] who was considered to have been the chief instigator of the commission. Hytten, however, main-

tained that he had been forced by the council, against his better judgement, to remove Orr for sexual impropriety. The case involved principles of natural justice and matters of academic tenure. It dragged on for ten years and led to a national boycott of the university's chair of philosophy.

In addition to producing unsigned government reports, Hytten published in economic and political journals, among them the *Economic Record* and *Australian Quarterly*. He was a board-member (1954-59) of the Commonwealth Bank, an adviser to State and Federal governments, and served on numerous public committees. A foundation member and chairman (1933-39, 1946-47) of the Economic Society of Australia and New Zealand, he was chairman (1956) of the Australian Vice-Chancellors' Committee. Hytten combined 'shrewd observation and the gift of silence'. While sceptical of Christian dogma, he believed in Christian principles. He was appointed C.M.G. (1953), a knight (1951) of the Order of St Olav (Norway) and a chevalier (1957) of the Order of the Crown (Belgium). Following his retirement in 1957, he moved to Aberdeen, Scotland, to be close to his son. Hytten died there on 2 January 1980, survived by his wife and son, the other son having died in infancy.

L. Foster, *High Hopes* (Melb, 1986); R. P. Davis, *Open to Talent* (Hob, 1990); Roy Com on University of Tasmania, Report, *PP* (HA, Tas), 1955 (18), p 56; *People*, 29 July 1953; *Mercury* (Hob), 4 Jan 1980; T. Hytten, To Australia—with thanks (ms, June 1971, Univ Tas Archives).   R. P. DAVIS

I

IBBOTT, NELLIE GRACE (1889-1970), mayor, was born on 20 June 1889 at Leyton, Essex, England, daughter of John Charles Pugh, printing machine manager, and his wife Ellen Beatrice, née Smith. On 26 September 1914, at the local Congregational Church, Nellie married Alfred Thomas Ibbott, a piano-maker. They came to Australia in 1923.

When a by-election was held in April 1928 to fill a vacancy in the Ivanhoe Riding of the Heidelberg Shire Council, Mrs Ibbott narrowly defeated her male opponent and became the first woman on the council. The seat had to be recontested in the August elections; the same two candidates opposed each other, and Nellie won by an increased margin. In 1933 she was nominated as shire president, but was beaten by a male councillor. Heidelberg became a city in 1934 and Ibbott served as mayor in 1943-44. Her election attracted considerable interest: while there had previously been a female shire president (at Gisborne), she was the first woman in Victoria to hold mayoral office.

Ibbott was a familiar figure to the residents as she strode along the streets—well-dressed, wearing flat-heeled tan shoes and carrying a tan leather handbag which contained her notebook. A strong debater in the council chamber, she insisted that she was 'no feminist' and that only co-operation between men and women could achieve anything. Tenacious in her attempts to improve conditions in her area, she initiated approaches to State ministers on such matters as unemployment, increased police protection, improved railway stations and better bus services. She was also responsible for establishing the Heidelberg Benevolent Society. During her time on the council, more emphasis was placed on community services than on the traditional roles of local government—rates, roads and rubbish. Seven baby-health centres were established and Heidelberg claimed to be the first municipality to have implemented widespread immunization against diphtheria. Councillor Ibbott also encouraged the arts in the City of Heidelberg. After twenty-two years service, she was defeated in the elections in 1950.

In 1948 Ibbott had been elected to chair the board of management of the Fairfield Infectious Diseases Hospital. She was at various stages president of the Austin Hospital Auxiliary, treasurer of the Victorian Association of Benevolent Societies and chair of Airlie Maternity Hospital. In addition, she served on the executive of the Victorian Baby Health Centres Association and of the Victorian Council of Social Service. A vice-president of the Liberal Party of Australia, Victorian division, she chaired (1946-48) the central committee of the women's section. In 1949 she was nominated as a candidate for Liberal Party pre-selection for the Senate, but was unsuccessful.

Nellie Ibbott was appointed M.B.E. in 1954. Following their retirement, she and Alfred moved to Mornington where she remained active in party politics. Predeceased by her husband, she died there on 25 June 1970 and was cremated with Anglican rites. She had no children. The City of Heidelberg was slow to honour her. A park in Ivanhoe was named after her in 1984, as was a room in the civic-centre precinct in 1991.

Aust Women's Weekly, 25 Sept 1948; *Heidelberger*, 1 July 1970; *Herald* (Melb), 21 July 1927, 11 Dec 1942, 1 July 1948; *Sun News-Pictorial*, 16 Nov 1932, 1 July 1948, 29 Aug 1950; *Age* (Melb), 2 Sept 1943, 12 Aug 1944, 26 Feb 1949, 10 June 1954; Heidelberg City Council, Minute-books, 1928-50.

JEAN BAKER

INGAMELLS, REGINALD CHARLES ('REX') (1913-1955), poet and editor, was born on 19 January 1913 at Orroroo, South Australia, eldest of four children of native-born parents Eric Marfleet Ingamells, Methodist minister, and his wife Mabel Gwendolen, née Fraser. Due to his father's postings, 'Rex' was educated at schools in country towns, among them Meadows, Burra and Port Lincoln. He then studied at Prince Alfred College (1927-30), Adelaide, and at the University of Adelaide (B.A., 1934). His M.A. thesis was rejected on the grounds that his topic, 'Australian History as a background to Australian Literature', had not been approved. Rather short and slimly built, with fairish hair and a small, military-style moustache, he was friendly and persuasive in manner, but could become intense and dogged in literary argument. On 9 July 1938 at the Methodist Church, Port Broughton, he married Eileen Eva Spensley.

While unsuccessfully applying for a number of academic positions, in 1936-39 Ingamells worked as a public examinations coach, a temporary teacher at Adelaide Technical High School and a part-time lecturer with the Workers' Educational Association; he also taught at Prince Alfred College (1939-42) and Unley High School (1943-45). In 1945 he moved to Melbourne to take a job with George Jaboor, a publishers' representative.

Next year he was employed as a commercial traveller with Georgian House Pty Ltd. By 1955 he was working for Longmans, Green & Co. and about to join United Service Publicity Pty Ltd.

Ingamells had written two volumes of verse, *Gumtops* (Adelaide, 1935) and *Forgotten People* (Adelaide, 1936), before he postulated his 'Jindyworobak' point of view. He claimed to be influenced by L. F. Giblin [q.v.8], T. G. H. Strehlow [q.v.], James Devaney [q.v.13], and finally by P. R. Stephensen [q.v.12] whose *The Foundations of Culture in Australia* (Sydney, 1936) gave him a historical view of the impact of 'overseas' influences on Australian culture. With Ian Tilbrook, Ingamells published *Conditional Culture* (Adelaide, 1938) as a manifesto. The word Jindyworobak—which they took to be an Aboriginal term meaning 'to annex' or 'to join'—was proposed as a symbol 'to free Australian art' from 'alien influences' and 'bring it into proper contact with its material'. Their pamphlet advocated a 'clear recognition of environmental values', a 'fundamental break . . . with the spirit of English culture', and the use of 'only such imagery as is truly Australian', and claimed that 'our writers and painters must become hard-working students of Aboriginal culture'.

This pamphlet, with Ingamells' *Sun-freedom* and the first *Jindyworobak Anthology*, both of which were published in Adelaide in 1938, occasioned substantial debate. The South Australian poet Flexmore Hudson was an early supporter, but drifted away when Ingamells' editorial rigidity (particularly of the anthology) became evident. Ingamells conceded that some people 'will say that . . . I am determined to reject poetically better non-Australian verse in favour of mediocre Australian'. Another Adelaide poet Ian Mudie [q.v.] drifted closer. Like Mudie, Ingamells joined Stephensen's Australia-First Movement (founded 1941), whose political aims were to some extent complementary to the literary ambitions of the Jindyworobaks. Ingamells' politics found expression in his next book, *At a Boundary* (co-authored with his brother John, Adelaide, 1941), and particularly in one of the poems therein, 'The Gangrened People'.

In 1941-42 critics derided Ingamells and the 'Jindys' partly for their political ideology and largely for the pedestrian 'Australian' and 'Aboriginal' verse that the movement was producing. A. D. Hope called the Jindyworobaks the 'Boy Scout School of Poetry'. From this point, the effect of Ingamells and his followers declined and their role in initiating an important discussion tended to be forgotten, despite the fact that the anthology appeared annually until 1953 and Ingamells continued to write prolifically. His verse saga, *The Great South Land* (Melbourne, 1951), a history of Australia from primordial times, which he unwisely advertised as being as long as *Paradise Lost*, won the Grace Leven prize and the Australian Literature Society's gold medal for 1951.

Ingamells died in a motorcar accident on 30 December 1955 near Dimboola, Victoria, and was buried in Payneham cemetery, Adelaide. His wife and three sons survived him. As a lyrical poet, he had a modest talent. As a pamphleteer, although he overstated his case, his arguments on the appropriate language and subject matter for Australian poets deserved attention and got it, as did his views on Aboriginal culture. As an editor and publisher, through his Jindyworobak movement, he was responsible for at least forty-four volumes of poetry and literary comment (apart from periodicals) between 1938 and 1953. His output was achieved through considerable personal and financial sacrifice. Ingamells' self-portrait is held by his son Graeme at Birregurra, Victoria.

B. Elliott, *The Jindyworobaks* (Brisb, 1979); H. McQueen, *The Black Swan of Trespass* (Syd, 1979); C. Munro, *Wild Man of Letters* (Melb, 1984); *Southerly*, 2, no 3, 1941; *ABC Weekly*, 26 May 1956; *Herald* (Melb), 31 Dec 1955; *Argus*, 7 Jan 1956; J. Dally, The Jindyworobak Movement 1935-45 (Ph.D. thesis, Flinders Univ, 1979); Ingamells papers (Mort L *and* LaTL *and* Flinders Univ, Adel); information from Mr J. Ingamells, Leabrook, Adel.   JOHN DALLY

INGLIS, WILLIAM KEITH (1888-1960), professor of pathology, was born on 11 February 1888 at Redfern, Sydney, third son of native-born parents John Thomas Inglis, auctioneer, and his wife Australia, née Renwick. Keith's academic progress through Sydney Grammar School and the University of Sydney (M.B., 1911; Ch.M., 1912; M.D., 1917) was enlivened by his enthusiastic participation in athletics, cricket, hockey and rowing; he was awarded a Blue for being a member of the VIII which won the intervarsity event in 1908. At the Congregational Church, Summer Hill, on 28 August 1914 he married Jessie Fulton McPherson (d.1933); they were to have three daughters and a son.

During his residency at Royal Prince Alfred Hospital, Inglis had impressed his medical and surgical mentors. While demonstrating in the university's pathology department and serving in the Militia as senior medical officer, Bathurst camp, he wrote his M.D. thesis on 'Agglutination After the Administration of Typhoid and Paratyphoid Vaccines' which won the university medal and attracted the interest of the military authorities. On 20 July

1916 he was appointed captain, Australian Army Medical Corps, Australian Imperial Force. By August 1917 he was stationed in France. As a pathologist with the 3rd Australian General Hospital, Abbeville, and the 2nd A.G.H., Boulogne, he performed numerous post-mortem examinations. The problems he encountered with dysentery and trench fever led to his first publications.

In London, from October 1918, Inglis collected and prepared pathological examples (from army surgical and autopsy material) which could be shipped to Australian medical museums. Letters to his wife discussed his increasing fondness for pathological work and his ambition to become a specialist, 'even though the remuneration would be much less ... than I could earn in private practice'. His personal letters also revealed homesickness, as well as scant sympathy for the British Establishment at a time of postwar industrial unrest—'Thank God I am a non-conformist! Thank God I am not an Englishman!' In May 1919 he arrived in Australia with his specimens which were sent to museums in every State. Major Inglis's A.I.F. appointment terminated on 13 July and he returned to the university's pathology department in 1920.

Over the next decade his teaching load, research interests and responsibility for patients all grew, particularly after his appointment in 1922 as honorary pathologist (director of pathology from 1926) at Sydney Hospital. He later argued that his hospital and university posts were complementary, 'for the students who attended my classes at the medical School were thus enabled to make themselves familiar with clinical pathology and the problems of morbid anatomy as revealed by post mortem examinations'.

In the 1920s Inglis published several collaborative studies, but his main preoccupation was with the nature of the pre-cancerous state. His book, *Paget's Disease of the Nipple* (Oxford, 1936), contained a wealth of clinical photographs and micrographs of the same lesions. The cases (which included skin, genital and alimentary lesions, and also breast cancer) were arranged as if in a museum exhibition to show that 'cancers start, not by malignant changes in an individual cell, neighbours of which remain normal, but by neoplastic changes affecting many cells in the same area'. The style was clear and didactic, and his ideas were to retain their currency.

Meanwhile, at Sydney Hospital, Inglis was one of the group responsible for the establishment in 1933 of the Kanematsu Memorial Institute of Pathology, with its charter to promote medical research. The generosity of Toranosuke Kitamura [q.v.9] and fellow Japanese benefactors was matched by the idealism of Sydney Jamieson and Inglis who saw an opportunity to develop a centre of experimental medical research and pathology within a clinical institution. Almost from the start, the concept aroused hostility from administrators in the hospital and the Department of Public Health who believed that research had no place in patient care, and, indeed, was inimical to it. Inglis was part-time director of the institute in 1933-36.

His personal base remained the university's pathology department where in 1936 he succeeded D. A. Welsh [q.v.12] in the chair. Inglis was unwavering in his belief that pathology was the essential basis of clinical training and steadfastly defended the concept that advances in patient care could best be fostered if fundamental research were conducted within hospitals in addition to universities. His influence was pivotal in maintaining the viability of research at the Kanematsu.

With the outbreak of World War II, the responsibility for service pathology at Royal Prince Alfred Hospital fell to Inglis. His opinion in difficult cases was highly valued by his peers. Characteristically, he examined microscope sections and formed a view before reading the clinical history, and his reports always indicated any lingering doubts he had about his diagnosis. This intellectual integrity was the hallmark of his work and it influenced generations of pathologists associated with the Sydney school. Inglis's extra workload consumed his energies and left little time for personal research. He began to write about medical education and entertained hopes that, after the war, academic pathology would assume a greater role in the teaching hospitals. His hopes were dashed when the R.P.A.H. board appointed a non-university pathologist, making clear its rejection of his position on experimental research and its fear of an academic takeover.

At the Congregational Church, Killara, on 15 June 1934 Inglis had married Madge Australia, sister of Ellice Nosworthy [q.v.]. Madge continued the tradition of inviting fourth-year medical students to tea in the garden of the Inglis's North Shore home. Inglis was a founding member (1938) of the Royal Australasian College of Physicians and a director (1946-60) of Sydney Hospital. He retired from the university in 1952. While speaking in defence of the independence of the Kanematsu at a Sydney Hospital board-meeting, he collapsed and died on 26 January 1960; in accordance with his wish, his body was delivered to the university's medical school. His wife survived him, as did the children of his first marriage.

G. L. McDonald (ed), *Roll of the Royal Australasian College of Physicians* (Syd, 1988); *Hist Records of Aust Science*, 6, no 2, Dec 1985; Inglis papers (held by Dr M. Inglis, Mosman, Syd).

YVONNE COSSART

INNES, FREDERICK FORREST (1892-1962), actuary, was born on 23 May 1892 in Hobart, son of Robert Russell Innes, civil servant, and his wife Mary Augusta, née Forrest. Educated at The Hutchins School, Frederick joined the Hobart branch of the Australian Mutual Provident Society in 1909 and began actuarial studies. In 1916 he transferred to head office in Sydney to enable him to sit the examinations of the Institute of Actuaries, London. He was sent to the A.M.P. Society's London branch in 1919 to further his studies and qualified as a fellow of the institute in 1924. At St Paul's parish church, Beckenham, Kent, on 12 July that year he married Flora Ethel May Knight; they were to remain childless.

Returning to Sydney in 1925, Innes was promoted joint assistant actuary in 1931, associate-actuary in 1938 and actuary in 1945. He helped to guide the A.M.P. through the Depression, coped with staff shortages during World War II, and came to terms with the rapid changes to the Society and its unprecedented expansion in the postwar years. There were few independent actuaries in Australia before the 1960s and it was common for those employed by the large life-insurance offices to perform consulting work. Innes advised a number of institutions, including the State Superannuation Board; he and Hubert Vaughan conducted quinquennial valuations of its fund. Innes's most notable task was to prepare, with Samuel Bennett, cost estimates for the Commonwealth's national insurance scheme which was proposed in the mid-1930s but subsequently abandoned.

Innes was competent and conscientious rather than brilliant or innovative. It is possible that he achieved promotion to the most senior actuarial rank because the A.M.P.—which did not believe in recruiting from outside—had no other actuaries in his age group. Precise and somewhat old-fashioned in character, short statured and with bristly hair, he was very respectful towards his elders. He expected the same deference from his subordinates, and was inclined to be resentful when the careers of some of his talented juniors progressed more rapidly than he felt was proper. None the less, he was a kindly man. He was an enthusiastic gardener who invited junior staff to his home at Manly and presented them with his Kurume azaleas.

Between 1925 and 1943 Innes served for more than ten years on the committee of the Actuarial Society of Australasia (president 1937) and was president (1940) of the Insurance Institute of New South Wales. After retiring in July 1953, he continued as consulting actuary to several large superannuation schemes and was a director of Coal Mines Insurance Pty Ltd. He was a Freemason and a member of the New South Wales Club. Suffering from coronary atherosclerosis, he died suddenly on 18 June 1962 in the A.M.P. Building, Circular Quay, and was cremated. His wife predeceased him.

AMP Soc, News and Views, Sept 1953, and Amicus, 1, no 1, 1962; W. C. Balmford, Three Score Years and Twenty (ms, 1976, copy held by author, Macquarie Univ, Nth Ryde, Syd); Actuarial Soc of A'sia, Minute-books, 1915-62 (Inst of Actuaries of Aust Archives, Syd); AMP Soc Bd minute, 2 July 1931 (AMP Archives, Syd).   CLARE BELLIS

IRVING, SYBIL HOWY (1897-1973), founder and controller of the Australian Women's Army Service, was born on 25 February 1897 at Victoria Barracks, Melbourne, eldest of three children of Victorian-born parents Godfrey George Howy Irving [q.v.9], army officer, and his wife Ada Minnie Margueritha, daughter of Frederick Thomas Derham [q.v.4]. As a result of her father's army postings, Sybil lived in every mainland State during her girlhood. 'We got used to all the travelling after a while', she later reflected. 'We had the most travelled canary I have ever known—and each trip we lost another piece of the dinner set'. She was educated at various schools, including Lauriston Girls' High School, Melbourne, which had been founded by her aunts Margaret and Lillian Irving, and the Queen's School, Perth.

In 1924 Sybil Irving accepted the full-time post of secretary of the Girl Guides' Association, Victoria, a position she was to hold until 1940. An effective administrator, she was appointed M.B.E. (1939). Through guiding, she became involved in teaching needlework to girls who had contracted poliomyelitis. In 1935 she helped to set up the Victorian Society for Crippled Children (and Adults); she was a founding member of its council of management and worked voluntarily for the institution until her death.

In World War I Irving had served in a Voluntary Aid Detachment organized by the Australian division of the British Red Cross Society. She was appointed assistant-secretary of the society's Victorian division in 1940, but resigned in the following year when she was invited, largely because of her family background and guiding experience, to establish and administer the Australian Women's Army Service. Having assumed the post of controller (head) of the A.W.A.S. on 6 October 1941, she travelled around Australia by train to recruit officers. Promoted lieutenant colonel in January 1942 and colonel in February 1943, she had more than 20 000 women under her direction when the A.W.A.S. reached its peak strength in 1944.

They were assigned as signallers, mechanics, drivers, storekeepers and stenographers, and to other occupations which the army established for women. Irving relinquished her appointment on 31 December 1946. For ten years from April 1951 she was honorary colonel of the A.W.A.S.'s successor, the Women's Royal Australian Army Corps.

She had drawn heavily upon her own beliefs for her wartime work. Guiding was used as the basis for the new service, a practice which attracted both praise and criticism. Irving distributed to A.W.A.S. officers the prayer attributed to Sir Francis Drake before he went into battle against the Spanish fleet and by which she attempted to conduct her life. One version read:

'O Lord God, when Thou givest to Thy servants to endeavour any great matter, grant us to know that it is not the beginning, but the continuing of the same until it be thoroughly finished, which yieldest the true glory: through Him that for the finishing of Thy work laid down His Life'.

She strongly supported official policy that women in the A.W.A.S. should not bear arms. 'These girls will be the mothers of the children who will rebuild Australia', she argued. 'They must not have the death of another mother's son on their hands.'

A portrait of Irving (held by the Australian War Memorial, Canberra) was painted by Nora Heysen in 1943 and shows a stern-looking woman, with a fair complexion, blue eyes and light brown hair, dressed in the manly uniform of the A.W.A.S. Partly visible by her lap is the uniform's soft, wide-brimmed hat, modelled upon the one which she had worn on the day she first reported for duty at Victoria Barracks in 1941. She chose that shape, rather than a peaked cap, because she considered it to be more feminine. Her dignity of bearing, frequently remarked upon by those who met her, is evident in the painting, but there is no sign of the hopeful eyes or broad smile of earlier photographs.

Her sister Freda Mary Howy Irving (1903-1984), a well-known Melbourne journalist, joined the A.W.A.S. in World War II. Their brother Ronald Godfrey Howy Irving (1898-1965) graduated from the Royal Military College, Duntroon, Federal Capital Territory, in 1919 and served in the Middle East in 1940-42 before returning to Australia where he was director of military training for three years. He retired as a brigadier in 1953.

Sybil Irving was general secretary of the Victorian division of the Red Cross from 1947 to 1959. On her retirement she was granted honorary life membership of the society. In 1960-61 she took a thirteen-month holiday in Britain and Europe, one of her several trips abroad. She met Red Cross workers in Swit-zerland and elsewhere, visited the Women's Royal Army Corps in England and attended the wedding of Princess Margaret, the W.R.A.A.C.'s colonel-in-chief. Back in Australia, Irving worked as a consultant (1961-71) for the Victorian Old People's Welfare Council (later the Victorian Council on the Ageing), organizing elderly citizens' clubs.

After a lifetime of duty, commitment, uniforms and uniformity, Colonel Irving died on 28 March 1973 at her South Yarra home; she was buried with Anglican rites and military honours in Fawkner cemetery. Friends and former colleagues raised funds for a chain of memorials—one in every capital city—which were unveiled between 1977 and 1979. Other memorials include a seat and plaque at Victoria Barracks—her birthplace and that of the A.W.A.S.

P. Adam-Smith, *Australian Women at War* (Melb, 1984); L. Ollif, *Women in Khaki* (Syd, 1981) and *Colonel Best and Her Soldiers* (Syd, 1985); A. Howard, *You'll be Sorry!* (Syd, 1990); *Age* (Melb), 12 Feb 1943, 29 Mar 1973; *Weekly Times* (Melb), 28 Oct 1959; Girl Guides Assn, Vic, miscellaneous biog material on Irving (held by G.G.A.V. Melb).

JAN BASSETT

ISAAC, CYRIL EVERETT (1884-1965), schoolteacher, politician and conservationist, was born on 14 October 1884 at Brunswick, Melbourne, son of Abraham Isaac, a Congregational clergyman, and his wife Mary, née Judd, both English born. Educated at Maldon and Lake Rowan state schools, in 1900 Cyril was sent as a student-teacher to Lee Street State School, North Carlton. From his earliest days there, his ideas on education were entwined with his love of horticulture. A former pupil remembered him as the teacher who 'dug a garden bed in the asphalt grounds of the school and taught the children . . . how to plant seeds and bulbs'. Isaac was subsequently posted to numerous Victorian primary schools, including Ten Mile, near Jamieson, where he met Elizabeth Brown whom he married with Congregational forms on 3 September 1907 in her mother's home at Kevington; they were to have seven children.

Wherever Isaac worked, his schools regularly competed for the annual school garden prize, established in 1903 by the Australian Natives' Association. In 1909 he suggested that teacher enthusiasts in the Bendigo inspectorate should exchange plants; Frank Tate [q.v.12], the director of education, became interested, and in August 1910 the Victorian State Schools' Horticultural Society was launched. Isaac was its first executive-secretary and full-time supervisor (1913-22) of school gardening. He founded the State Schools' Nursery at Hughesdale to provide plants for school gardens and to educate children in horticultural principles. From 1916 he organized a series of flower days that raised £32 309 for the War Relief Fund.

On 14 December 1916 Isaac enlisted in the Australian Imperial Force. He served with the 58th Battalion on the Western Front from December 1917, was commissioned in November 1918 and rose to lieutenant before his appointment terminated on 10 November 1919 in Melbourne. Resigning from the Education Department in 1922, Isaac opened Flowervale Nursery at Noble Park. Elizabeth, a passionate horticulturalist who later propagated a new variegated lilly pilly (*Acmena smithii var. Elizabeth Isaac*), supported him. Isaac was honorary horticultural adviser (from 1934) to Melbourne's Royal Agricultural Show; he was also active in the Victorian Nurserymen and Seedsmen's Association (president 1936-37) and in Associated Nurseries Pty Ltd (chairman 1932-65). In 1928-31 and 1937-40 he was a Dandenong shire councillor.

As the United Australia Party's candidate, in June 1940 Isaac won the Legislative Council seat of South-Eastern Province. He supported the teaching service bill (1946) to ensure sufficient well-trained staff to meet increasing student numbers. His most important work, however, was in forest conservation. Inspired by Judge Leonard Stretton [q.v.], who had investigated the State's disastrous bushfires in 1939, he had initiated in 1944 the Save the Forests Campaign with the support of Sir Herbert Gepp [q.v.8] and the Forests Commission of Victoria. In 1949 the S.F.C. opened a nursery to support community tree-planting days and in 1951 was incorporated as the Natural Resources Conservation League of Victoria. Isaac also pressed parliament to set up a royal commission in 1946 to inquire into forest grazing. His conservation messages were heard on Victorian radio throughout the 1940s and 1950s.

In 1952 Isaac—with Sir Clifden Eager [q.v.] and Sir Frank Beaurepaire [q.v.7]—lost party endorsement for the Legislative Council: all three former U.A.P. members were ousted by younger men who had gained prominence in the Liberal Party's organizational machine. Isaac stood as an Independent, but was defeated. A foundation member of the Victorian National Parks Authority, he was its deputy-chairman (1957-61). In 1956 he was appointed O.B.E. Predeceased by his wife, and survived by three of his four sons and one of his three daughters, he died on 17 September 1965 at Footscray and was cremated.

P. Aimer, *Politics, Power and Persuasion* (Syd, 1974); L. Robin, *Building a Forest Conscience* (Melb, 1991); *Dandenong J,* 5 June 1946; *Conservation News,* Feb 1956; *Victoria's Resources,* 7, no 3, 1965; *Educational Mag,* 17, no 8, Sept 1960; *Herald* (Melb), 11 Sept 1936, 17 June 1940, 6 Apr 1966; *Age* (Melb), 4 Feb 1961, 18 Sept 1965; ts copies of Isaac's radio broadcasts (Natural Resources Conservation League Archives, Springvale, Melb); information from Mrs E. Smith, Bendigo, Vic.

LIBBY ROBIN

ISAACHSEN, SIR OSCAR LIONEL (1885-1951), banker, was born on 8 September 1885 in North Adelaide, eldest of three children of South Australian-born parents Oscar Henry Isaachsen, clerk, and his wife Lydia, née Smith. Young Oscar's paternal grandfather had emigrated from Norway in 1848. His father died in 1890 and his mother remarried. Educated at Sturt Street Public School, Pulteney Street School (dux 1900) and on a scholarship at Prince Alfred College, he competed in football and cricket, and always maintained an interest in sport. He passed first-year English at the University of Adelaide and was a pupil-teacher at Glenelg Grammar School.

In 1905 Isaachsen joined the Bank of Adelaide. His early postings were to McLaren Vale, Unley and Mannum where he met Ella Gertrude Schuetze (d.1976). They were married on 8 December 1910 in the Church of St John the Baptist, Murray Bridge. Manager at Blyth (from 1912) and at Minlaton (from 1915), he joined local sporting bodies and raced dogs with the Minlaton Coursing Club. His betting, and his preference for fishing to churchgoing, incurred the disapproval of the Methodist community of Yorke Peninsula, but the close friendships he made there and his love of fishing lasted for many years.

Port Pirie (1920-23) was Isaachsen's last country posting before he moved to Adelaide in 1924. He rose steadily through the bank's hierarchy to become general manager in 1939. Four years earlier he had visited England, Europe and the United States of America, pursuing his interest in international economics and monetary systems. Throughout 1939-45 he supported the war effort, gave particular attention to staff on active service and their families, and had the Union Jack raised over the bank each day. His four sons joined the Australian Imperial Force; Alan was killed in action in Papua in 1942 and Cedric was awarded the Distinguished Service Order.

During the difficult postwar years of government controls Isaachsen established an important role for the bank in the development of South Australia's economy. He promoted diversification of the primary sector and the growth of manufacturing, and was one of the founders of the Industries Assistance Corporation of South Australia Ltd. His public addresses as president (1945-47) of the Adelaide Chamber of Commerce stressed the importance of private enterprise and the maintenance of individual effort and initiative, and he was alarmed that Australians could 'become serfs of a socialist and possibly communist State'. He defended the basic wage and advocated a stronger Commonwealth Court of Conciliation and Arbitration to ensure industrial peace and goodwill, and to protect the rights of employer and employee. Chairman (1940-50) of the Associated Banks of South Australia, in 1947-49 he led the State's campaign against the nationalization of the banks.

Isaachsen's leadership and financial skills assisted the Lord Mayor's Food for Britain Appeal and the Cancer Appeal Fund, and he was a member (1941-48) of the board of governors of Pulteney Grammar School. Known to his many friends as 'Ike', he had a quick wit and keen sense of humour. He was solidly built, with strong features accentuated by early balding, and he dressed elegantly. Isaachsen especially enjoyed a day at the races, and had an eye for a pretty woman and a good horse. An evening of fine food, with a glass of wine followed by a cigar, was his chosen social occasion, often at the South Australian Hotel or the Adelaide Club, to which he belonged from 1936. He relaxed with a book or his caged parrots.

After retiring in June 1950, Isaachsen was immediately appointed to the board of the bank and elected chairman. His half-brother Alan Augustus West succeeded him as general manager. In the next ten months Isaachsen became a director of City Mutual Life Assurance Society Ltd, United Insurance Co. Ltd, Pascoe Industries Ltd and Adelaide Cement Co. Ltd. In 1951 he was knighted. Survived by his wife, daughter and three sons, he died suddenly of heart disease on 1 May that year in Sydney; after a service at St Columba's Anglican Church, Hawthorn, Adelaide, he was cremated. Sir Oscar's estate was sworn for probate at £26 696.

A'sian Insurance and Banking Record, 22 Sept 1947, 22 Jan, 21 May 1951; *Advertiser* (Adel), 4 Jan, 4 Sept 1946, 6 Sept 1947, 1 Jan, 2 May 1951; *Herald* (Melb), 5 Sept 1947; *Mail* (Adel), 6 Jan 1951; R. A. Potter, 'With Faith and Courage': The Bank of Adelaide 1865-1965 (unpublished ms), *and* Bank of Adel, *Annual Report*, 1934-50, *and* staff records (held by ANZ Museum, Melb); information from Mrs M. E. Crompton, Nth Adel, and Mr O. C. Isaachsen, Kingswood, Adel.

MARGARET L. BLACK

ISAACSON, CAROLINE 'LYNKA' (1900-1962), journalist, was born on 14 September 1900 in Vienna, elder daughter of Emile Jacobson, shipping executive, and his wife Bettina, née Lipmann. Privately educated by a governess who gave her the pet name 'Lynka', Caroline finished her schooling at Highbury Park, London. She had begun writing freelance articles before she met Arnold Isaacson, a 37-year-old lieutenant in the Australian Imperial Force who had participated in the landing at Gallipoli. They were married on 30 March 1919 at the Dalston Synagogue, Islington. In 1926 they sailed with their two children for Melbourne, where Arnold began a long career as a printing manufacturer's agent with Lamson Paragon Ltd.

In 1928 Caroline asked (Sir) Geoffrey Syme [q.v.12], managing editor of the *Age*, for a reporting job. The family needed the money. With her fair complexion, well-modulated English accent and fashion sense, she adapted to writing social notes and was soon appointed editor of the women's pages. She then moved as women's editor to the *Age*'s rural weekly magazine, the *Leader*, where she adopted the nom de plume 'Viola' and began a section called 'The Spare Corner'. Although she employed nannies and housekeepers, and spent little time on domestic chores other than cooking, she held 'womanly pursuits' in high regard. 'The Spare Corner' was conceived as a correspondence and service section for country women who used it to exchange household hints and tales of their lives. Isaacson promoted the exchange with characteristic purpose, travelling throughout Victoria, addressing meetings of the Country Women's Association, speaking with her readers and editing several editions of *For Australian Women: the Leader Spare Corner Book*.

Her energy was not confined to journalism. A foundation member of the Liberal Synagogue, St Kilda, she worked on the Jewish Board of Deputies' programmes, helping refugees from Nazi Germany adapt to Australia. Isaacson was a staunch supporter of the Freeland League for Jewish Territorial Colonisation, which lobbied for the establishment of a Jewish settlement in the North-West of Western Australia, and she taught English to refugees. She was also executive-officer of the British Memorial Fund, and an active supporter of the Country Women's Association, the Young Women's Christian Association and Melbourne's theatrical community.

Early in World War II, Isaacson worked as the *Age*'s foreign news sub-editor. In July 1942 she enlisted in the Australian Women's Army Service and was commissioned lieutenant in October. After a short time as an adjutant, she was transferred to the Directorate of Public Relations; with the rank of captain, she conducted journalists on their visits to army installations. She was placed on the Retired List in September 1943.

In 1945 Isaacson joined the *Argus* as editor of its women's pages. Three years later she became owner and editor of, and reporter for a country newspaper, *Dandenong Ranges News*. Still active in Jewish affairs, she was honorary editor (from 1948) of the *Australian Jewish Outlook* and director of public relations (from 1952) of the Victorian Jewish Board of Deputies. In 1953 she joined her son's firm as editorial director of three suburban newspapers, the *Southern Cross* (Brighton), the *Elsternwick Advertiser* and the *Prahran News*. After her husband died in 1960, she retired and visited Europe and England. She died on 23 January 1962 at Genoa, Italy. Her daughter, the photographer Joan Beck, survived her, as did her son Peter who had served in the Royal Australian Air Force and was thrice decorated during World War II.

Aust Women's Weekly, 31 July 1948; *Herald* (Melb), 26 Jan 1962; *Age* (Melb), 27 Jan 1962; personal papers (held by Mr P. Isaacson, Toorak, Melb); family information.   SALLY A. WHITE

ISLES, KEITH SYDNEY (1902-1977), economist and university vice-chancellor, was born on 4 August 1902 at Bothwell, Tasmania, second son of Sydney Henry Isles, a labourer who became a farmer, and his wife Margaret Ellen, née Knight. Educated at Hobart High School and the University of Tasmania (B.Com., 1925), Keith was employed by the Department of Education from 1922 and taught at Launceston High School. In 1924 he joined the staff of the Collegiate School of St Peter, Adelaide. He studied arts at the University of Adelaide and won the Tinline [q.v.6] scholarship for history (1925).

At St Luke's Anglican Church, Jericho, Tasmania, on 4 September 1926 Isles married Irene Frances Clayton, an English-born schoolmistress. They travelled to England where he entered Gonville and Caius College, Cambridge, in 1927 and graduated (B.A., 1929; M.A., 1933; M.Sc., 1935) with first-class honours. Gaining a Rockefeller fellowship in 1929, he was admitted as a research student, and was awarded the Wrenbury scholarship (1930) and the Adam Smith prize (1932).

From 1931 Isles lectured in political economy at the University of Edinburgh. During this time he published *Wages Policy and the Price Level* (London, 1934) and *Money and Trade* (London, 1935). In 1937 he was appointed to the chair of economics at Swansea University, Wales. He returned to Australia as successor to E. O. G. Shann [q.v.11], professor of economics at the University of Adelaide, in August 1939 and, in collaboration

with B. R. Williams, wrote *Compulsory Saving* (London, 1942). Granted leave from the university in 1942 to become an economic adviser to the wartime Commonwealth Rationing Commission, he was mobilized in the Australian Military Forces in December 1943 and attached to Alf Conlon's [q.v.13] Directorate of Research as a temporary lieutenant colonel.

Isles was appointed to the chair of economics at the Queen's University of Belfast, Ireland, in 1945. Of his several books and numerous academic papers, his most substantial contribution was *An Economic Survey of Northern Ireland* (London, 1957). An extensive investigation undertaken for the British government, it was written in collaboration with Norman Cuthbert, a member of his department at Queen's. In this survey Isles demonstrated his skills and strengths as an applied economist.

In August 1957 he succeeded Professor Torliev Hytten [q.v.] as vice-chancellor of the University of Tasmania. A period of growth saw the introduction of faculties of medicine and agriculture, but was eventually dominated by the turmoil of the Sydney Sparkes Orr [q.v.] case. Having been dismissed as professor of philosophy in March 1956, Orr brought an action against the university. When the Supreme Court of Tasmania gave judgement against him that year, he appealed to the High Court of Australia. The appeal was rejected in May 1957. Unwilling to accept the court decisions as final, Orr and his supporters continued to press the university for a further inquiry.

Even though he had played no part in either the dismissal or the subsequent court hearings, Isles could not avoid becoming involved. In August 1958 he published and distributed a pamphlet—*The Dismissal of S. S. Orr by the University of Tasmania*—in which he gave his unqualified support to the university's handling of the affair and called for an end to academic pressure on the university. Orr brought actions against him for defamation and libel. Contending with strong academic opposition, including a ban on filling Orr's vacant chair, preoccupied Isles for several years. The defamation actions were withdrawn in 1966 when a settlement between Orr and the university was finally reached. In January 1967 Isles was appointed C.M.G. He retired in December.

He received an honorary LL.D. (1963) from the University of St Andrews, Scotland, and an honorary D.Litt. (1968) from the University of Tasmania. At the latter ceremony the university ('a more efficient and happier place than he found it') acknowledged having 'derived enormous benefit from his patience, his wisdom and his selfless dedication'. During 1968 Isles was visiting professor of economics at the New University of Ulster, Belfast, and in the following year received an honorary LL.D. from the Queen's University of Belfast.

Isles belonged to the Tasmanian Club, and listed his recreations as tennis, cricket, golf, motoring and photography. Survived by his wife, son and two daughters, he died on 18 June 1977 at Rose Bay, Hobart, and was cremated.

R. Davis, *Open to Talent* (Hob, 1990); Students' Representative Council of Tas Univ Union, *Togatus*, 26 Nov 1956; *Mercury* (Hob), 20 June 1929, 15 Nov 1938, 20 June 1977; *Herald* (Melb), 11 Jan 1943, 16 June 1967; *Nation* (Syd), 23 Sept 1961; *Sun News-Pictorial*, 19 Aug 1964; *Age* (Melb), 4 May, 4 June 1965; *Examiner* (Launc), 2 Jan 1967.

A. J. HAGGER

IVERSON, JOHN BRIAN (1915-1973), cricketer, was born on 27 July 1915 at St Kilda, Melbourne, second child of Henry William Iverson, an accountant and estate agent from New South Wales, and his Victorian-born wife Edith Joyce, née White. Educated at Geelong College, where he was a fast bowler in the second XI, Iverson turned to golf after leaving school and won the Maldon club championship in 1936. He went jackerooing and then worked in his father's real-estate agency in Melbourne. Enlisting in the Australian Imperial Force on 30 May 1940, Iverson served in the Middle East (1941-43) and in New Guinea (1943-44). He was with the 2nd/4th Light Anti-Aircraft Regiment from January 1942 and rose to lance sergeant before his discharge on 5 September 1945. At St John's Anglican Church, Toorak, on 1 July 1944 he had married Dorothy Jean de Tracy, a typiste.

During his years in New Guinea, Iverson developed his legendary method of bowling, practising with a table-tennis ball that he gripped between his right thumb and bent middle finger, with which the ball was propelled. As a slow bowler, his variety of deliveries proved virtually undetectable. Essentially an off-spinner, he had a quick top-spinner and a well-disguised leg-break. He played sub-district cricket with Brighton. His belated entry into first-class cricket occurred in the 1949-50 season. Always awkward in the field and incompetent with the bat (his highest Test score was 1, his average 0.75), Iverson was 6 ft 2 ins (188 cm) tall and weighed 15 stone (95 kg). While the Australian Test team was in South Africa, he took 46 wickets at 16.6 for Victoria. In the same season he captured 75 wickets at 7 apiece on a tour of New Zealand with an Australian B team.

Iverson's single and remarkable Test series came in the 1950-51 season against England, which Australia won by four matches to one. He did not bowl in the first innings at Brisbane, but took 4 for 43 in the second. In the second Test (played in Melbourne) he took 6 for 73. In the third, in Sydney, Iverson began his second-innings spell with the wickets of (Sir) Leonard Hutton and R. T. Simpson at no cost, and finished with his best Test figures of 6 for 27. After taking 3 for 68, he was injured in the Adelaide Test. He captured 2 for 84 in Melbourne and completed the series with a return of 21 wickets at 15.24. 'Even the great Hutton could not fathom him', Keith Miller wrote, but added 'the miracle man had feet of clay'.

Miller helped to destroy Iverson's 'direction, his confidence, and his late flowering career'. Believing that the Australian and Victorian captain Lindsay Hassett had stopped Iverson from bowling in the nets at New South Wales players in the Australian team to prevent interstate rivals from 'picking' his deliveries, Miller and Arthur Morris disrupted Iverson's line and punished him in an early Sheffield Shield match of the 1951-52 season. Soon afterwards Iverson declared himself unavailable for Victoria, though he toured India with a Commonwealth team in 1953-54 and headed the bowling averages. Miller believed that 'one of the greatest mistakes made by Australia since the war was in not bringing Jack Iverson to England in 1953'. By then, age and lack of confidence, apart from the likelihood of unsuitably slow wickets, were against this one-series wonder —to Miller 'a freak', to the English journalist E. M. Wellings 'the Fabulous Jack Iverson'.

Following a stint as a cricket commentator on radio, Iverson immersed himself in his family's real-estate business until he sold it in 1972. On 23 October 1973 at his Brighton home he shot himself in the head. Survived by his wife and two daughters, he was cremated.

E. M. Wellings, *No Ashes for England* (Lond, 1951); K. Miller, *Cricket Crossfire* (Lond, 1956); A. Wrigley, *The Book of Test Cricket* (Lond, 1965); C. Martin-Jenkins, *The Complete Who's Who of Test Cricketers* (Adel, 1980); J. Pollard, *Australian Cricket* (Syd, 1982); D. Frith, *By His Own Hand* (Syd, 1990); *Canb Times*, 26 Oct 1973.

PETER PIERCE

J

JACKSON, ALICE MABEL (1887-1974), journalist and editor, was born on 15 October 1887 at Ulmarra, New South Wales, fourth daughter and seventh of eight children of William Archibald, a schoolteacher from the New Hebrides, and his native-born wife Clara Amelia, née Baker. After finishing her education at the Sacred Heart Convent, Highgate, Perth, Alice entered the Western Australian teaching service in 1906. Her duties included needlework, on which her inspectors gave mixed reports (she once failed cut-out), but her lessons and discipline were generally commended. In 1914 she was appointed to Kalgoorlie Continuation School and in 1916 to Goldfields High where the inspector found her 'very satisfactory': her teaching of English, history and geography in the junior school was 'thorough, skilful and successful', she was 'a good disciplinarian', and she had rendered 'good service' as editor of the school magazine.

At Mount Lawley, Perth, on 3 May 1916 Alice married with Methodist forms Samuel Henry Jackson (d.1968), then on leave from the 44th Battalion, Australian Imperial Force. He had taught at Perth Boys' Central School. In World War I he won the Military Cross and French Croix de Guerre. Alice's teaching appointment 'lapsed on account of marriage', though she was reappointed to Goldfields High on a weekly salary. She resigned in 1918 and moved with her husband to Sydney where their two children were born. Samuel had retrained as an accountant. It was later claimed that his business failure, occasioned by the Depression, was the reason for Alice's return to paid employment, but she had done so before that.

She was an occasional contributor to the magazine, *Triad*, and in April 1926 was appointed to edit *Cobbers*, a companion publication aimed at a younger readership. It failed to attract advertisers. The proprietor Leslie Woolacott closed *Cobbers* and announced that Mrs Jackson was joining *Triad*. Having 'spread herself frequently on the Plain English and Red Pages of the Bulletin', she 'transferred all her literary activities from the Ancient and Respectable Weekly to the Youthful and Skittish Monthly'. The photograph which accompanied this announcement depicted a youthful-looking 40-year-old, with a smiling expression, a plump face, slightly prominent teeth and thick, dark, softly waved hair. Publicity for the defunct *Cobbers* had emphasized her 'lovable personality' and her 'acute mind well salted with humour'.

Triad promoted itself as Australian in sentiment and cosmopolitan in outlook; at that time it was publicizing birth control. Mrs Jackson wrote book reviews and features. Following a change in the magazine's ownership, she briefly contributed to *Beckett's Budget* before its transformation to a sex and scandal sheet. In 1928 Samuel Jackson was in Wellington, New Zealand; Alice may have taught there.

Back in Sydney, Mrs Jackson was reported to have worked for *Smith's Weekly* and the *Sunday Times*. She moved to the *Daily Guardian* where she introduced (1930) the 'Shopping Bureau', a daily column featuring good buys and bargains. Reader participation was encouraged by cash prizes for 'wise buying'. In February 1931 she took the 'Shopping Bureau' to the *Daily Telegraph*. Four months later *Smith's Weekly* employed her to head a team of women reporters working on an expanded women's section which would include news and editorial comment, as well as the 'shopping bureau' and other service items. The promise was not realized: the novel features were dropped, and the women's section was contracted and confined to household hints, fashion and gossip. Jackson left within six months. George Blaikie named her among several 'bright women', recruited to *Smith's*, who 'promptly declared that they would sick up if they had to write social pap, and set about outwriting the male journalists on every subject anyone cared to name'. In January 1932 the *Daily Telegraph* announced that it was introducing a special weekly section for women, under the direct supervision of Mrs Jackson. As Sydney proprietors bought and closed newspapers and started others, and journalists lost their jobs, Alice remained employed. In the forced toings and froings she gained broader experience than might otherwise have been possible.

The *Australian Women's Weekly* began in 1933. Jackson joined it from the start, while working out her notice at the *Telegraph*. The first issue of the *Weekly* appeared on 10 June. Its founding editor George Warnecke informed readers in November of Mrs Jackson's appointment: 'When The Australian Women's Weekly sees genius it goes after it'. In a celebratory history, Denis O'Brien singled out her 'flair . . . for editorial administration' as her eventual contribution to the *Weekly*'s success. He credited Warnecke with the larger achievement of devising the innovative concept—the *Weekly* was to be as much newspaper as magazine, with special reports on topical matters, and it would give primacy to women journalists.

Jackson had no official designation, but was in effect second-in-charge. She edited and wrote items for 'Points of View', covered selected events and occasionally reviewed theatre (Beatrice Tildesley [q.v.12] was the regular theatre reviewer). Jackson relieved Warnecke of much of the day-to-day administration. With the launch of a Victorian edition in September, and other interstate editions soon after, the production schedule was tight and complex. The *Weekly* was printed on an old press belonging to Labor Papers Ltd. As circulation increased, the need for new machinery became urgent and in December 1934 Warnecke went abroad to choose it. Jackson was left with immediate editorial responsibility. Warnecke did not return until November 1935 and subsequently worked mainly on the *Telegraph*. He remained nominally in charge of the *Weekly*, but Jackson was effectively editor. She formally succeeded him in April 1939. By then the *Weekly*'s editorial hierarchy was entirely female.

The new, high-speed press incorporated rotogravure equipment and gave the *Weekly* a technical edge on its competitors. When the new plant had been installed in December 1936, the magazine's print-run was sixty-four pages, sixteen in full colour. Because the *Weekly* had already outsold its rivals, its remarkable early performance owed more to editorial skill than to printing technology. Circulation rose by 60 000 while Warnecke was abroad and in 1939 exceeded 400 000. The respective contributions of titular and de facto editor cannot be precisely identified. Some of the *Weekly*'s more enduring features were clearly Warnecke's initiatives. He organized a London office through which came European news and a flood of stories about the royal family; he bought 'Mandrake the Magician' cartoon strips and a mass of Hollywood material; and he negotiated rights to best-sellers for serialization. Jackson oversaw the smooth transition from local to national production, establishing editorial offices in other capital cities and arranging an Australia-wide coverage of news attuned to the resonances of nationalism.

Through its reportage of women taking up new work, joining together for reform, protesting on behalf of particular groups (for example, Aboriginal women denied choice in marriage), accepting challenges (such as pioneer air flights) and 'making do', the *Weekly* forged links between Australian women and the hitherto largely masculine image of being Australian. The enterprise of Australian women became a *Weekly* staple, even if an article entitled 'Australian Girl Trains Racing Cheetahs' was an extreme example. The *Weekly* covered balls and fashionable weddings, but its cartoonists often scoffed at high society. There were other elements in the editorial mix: the stuff of dreams—royal pageantry, Hollywood lifestyles, romance, beauty and high fashion—and quantities of practical advice, from recipes and dress-patterns to sexuality. Jackson aimed for a broad readership. O'Brien summed up her term as editor under the heading, 'Gloves go on', and claimed that she gave the *Weekly* a comfortable, middle-class respectability. But that is to miss the point. What the *Weekly* did under Jackson was to enable women to see themselves within a national tradition. Myths of national character and Australian achievement became accessible to them. The emotional force of nationalism underlay the magazine's success.

In an easy transition to wartime conditions the *Weekly* tailored its news content to war needs and the maintenance of morale. The magazine was leaner as a consequence of newsprint rationing and less vulnerable to competitors. By the end of World War II circulation would exceed 600 000. O'Brien alleged that the *Weekly* was 'unashamedly propagandist', but, as Helen Wilson observed, it made a 'conscious effort to put down those prejudices about what was feminine and masculine, to show that femininity was compatible with independence, military activity and heavy manual work'.

The editor's personal contribution to the war effort was to help run the Australian Women's Weekly Club for Servicewomen, opened in January 1943. She was co-president with Gretel Packer, wife of (Sir) Frank [q.v.] who was managing director of Consolidated Press Ltd, the *Weekly*'s publisher. The club provided dormitory accommodation, evening entertainment, meals and a beauty parlour. In 1941 Consolidated Press had conducted a 'Bundles for Britain' campaign, collecting clothes for air-raid victims. Jackson was accredited as a war correspondent and travelled to England in September to inaugurate distribution. She came briefly under official scrutiny when an intercepted cable revealed her report of the 'willingness' of British prisoners of war to work for the Germans. It is unlikely that there was any consequent action. Her husband was on full-time duty with the Australian Military Forces. As temporary lieutenant colonel, he held staff positions in Sydney and was a deputy-director (from 1943) of the security service. Mrs Jackson toured defence establishments in Western Australia and Port Moresby in 1943. She went abroad again, in 1945, to report on the United Nations conference at San Francisco, United States of America, and to inspect war damage in Europe.

Jackson's situation as editor changed subtly after the war. Packer was a 'hands on' owner and, while war work had taken him away from his newspapers, demobilization brought him back to the office. Jackson was under pressure to enlarge the quota of advertising. That was a familiar battle and not in itself sufficient to arouse her disaffection. The recruitment of Mary Hordern [q.v.], Packer's sister-in-law, to write fashion reports may have alienated Jackson, especially when linked to the *Weekly*'s sponsorship of an annual parade of Paris fashions, a scheme about which she was not enthusiastic. Increased proprietorial interference with content was rumoured. When offered the post of editor of the rival *Woman's Day* (*Woman's Day and Home*) in 1950, Jackson accepted and moved to Melbourne. By then the *Weekly*'s circulation was nearing 750 000.

Under Jackson the *Weekly* had become an arbiter of style and fashion, but she always dressed conservatively. Known to familiars as 'Mrs J', she required her reporters to attend social events appropriately attired and she persuaded her employers to pay a dress allowance. No evidence suggests that she valued the homemaking role for herself. The Jacksons shifted house several times. When Samuel was in the army, Alice moved into a city apartment near her office. Her staff respected her and several went with her to *Woman's Day*. She left that magazine after fifteen months. Alice had understated her age and, at 64, may have been tired. Her return to Sydney followed her husband's retirement and his ill health. He had been employed with the Department of External Affairs from 1947 and had served in Japan where he was also Australian representative on the United Nations Temporary Commission on Korea. Mrs Jackson's only other paid employment was as publicity agent for Romano's [q.v.11] Restaurant.

Survived by her daughter and son, Alice Jackson died on 28 October 1974 at Meadowbank, Sydney, and was cremated. Her memory was overshadowed by the reputation of her successor Esmé Fenston [q.v.] as the *Weekly*'s editor. Fenston was ideally placed to benefit from the advent of quality full-colour equipment and the expansion of consumerism in the 1950s. Basic to her attainment, however, was the prior establishment of a national distribution system which made the *Weekly* attractive to advertisers. That had been Jackson's achievement.

G. Blaikie, *Remember Smith's Weekly?* (Adel, 1966); R. S. Whitington, *Sir Frank* (Melb, 1971); D. O'Brien, *The Weekly* (Melb, 1982); H. Radi (ed), *200 Australian Women* (Syd, 1988); *Triad* (Syd), 10 Oct 1926; *Aust Women's Weekly*, 1933-50, esp 14 June 1947; *Woman's Day*, 1950-51, esp 18 Sept 1950; *Newspaper News* (Syd), 1 Jan 1934, 1 Aug, 2 Oct 1950, 1 Oct 1951; *Media Papers*, 15 Feb 1982; *SMH*, 6 Jan 1968, 29 Oct 1974.

HEATHER RADI

JACKSON, JAMES RANALPH (1882-1975), artist, was born on 3 July 1882 at Bunnythorpe, near Palmerston, New Zealand, one of eleven children of George Albert Jackson, a farmer from England who was descended from a family renowned for silversmithing, and his wife Mary Ann Julia, née Leach, who was born in India. Following Mary's death in 1890, the family moved to Darlinghurst, Sydney. The visual spectacle of the harbour made an indelible impression on James. Leaving school at an early age, he was apprenticed to a city decorator and studied drawing in the evenings at the (Royal) Art Society of New South Wales (fellow, 1922; life vice-president, 1965). He also briefly attended J. S. Watkins's art school.

Having failed to enrol with Bernard Hall [q.v.9] at the National Gallery schools in Melbourne in 1906, Jackson went to London and worked under (Sir) Frank Brangwyn who encouraged him to paint thickly and taught him the basic technology. Jackson then spent a year at the Académie Colarossi in Paris, living in the Latin Quarter. He absorbed the principles of Impressionism and travelled through Europe during the summer holidays.

Back in Sydney in 1908, Jackson joined and began to exhibit with the Art Society. His home was on the North Shore where he preferred to paint landscapes and seascapes of Sydney Harbour with the sun on his back. A member (1916-33) of the Australian Art Association, Melbourne, he exhibited regularly and established a strong following there. In Sydney, Jackson taught (1917-26) drawing and painting at the Art Society and arranged many field-camps for his students. In 1920 he held his first solo exhibition at the Gayfield Shaw Art Salon. At St Paul's Anglican Church, Middle Harbour, on 10 December 1924 he married Dorathea Elizabeth Toovey, a 25-year-old typist and one of his students; they were to have a daughter and son before he divorced her in 1947.

In December 1926 he and Dora left for Europe; journeying through France, Italy and Switzerland, they visited Paris and London before travelling through the Pyrenees and Spain. In April 1928 they returned to Sydney. Exhibitions of his new work received wide press coverage and Dora also exhibited successfully. The Depression hit Jackson hard, and in the early 1930s he was forced to let the house he had built at Seaforth and take his family for long periods to the country (around Gloucester) where they could live more economically. There he painted many accomplished landscapes. He was eventually forced to sell the home in Sydney, but by 1936 had settled into a new studio at Mosman.

Jackson was a foundation member (1937) of the Australian Academy of Art with which he exhibited annually until 1946. Meanwhile, he joined the camouflage section of the Department of Defence in 1942 until dismissed when the department discovered his real age—a fact he had always concealed. A 'chirpy little man', 5 ft 3 ins (160 cm) tall, he enjoyed fishing and belonged to the Journalists' Club. Survived by his children, he died on 9 September 1975 at Royal Prince Alfred Hospital and was cremated. He had lived alone for many years, happily independent and satisfied with the long haul of his career. His work is represented in most public and many private collections throughout Australia; the early Impressionist paintings of Sydney Harbour were fluent and superior to his later, prize-winning works.

J. Jackson, *James Jackson* (Syd, 1991); *Art in Aust*, 1917; *SMH*, 24 Aug 1923, 16 Apr 1928, 5 May 1938, 21 Feb 1958, 5 Oct 1961, 14 Sept 1973, 10 Sept 1975.   BARRY PEARCE

JACKSON, JOHN (1913?-1945), soldier, was born possibly on 29 April 1913 at Copmanhurst, near Grafton, New South Wales, son of Kate Jackson, an Aboriginal woman from the Moree district. After leaving school at an early age, Jack worked on dairy-farms around Grafton and served in the Militia with the 41st Battalion. He gave his religion as Catholic and his date of birth as 28 April 1916 when he joined the Australian Imperial Force on 3 March 1941; in the following month he was sent to train at Tamworth. It had been A.I.F. policy that the enlistment of Aborigines was 'neither necessary nor desirable', but the pay and conditions in the army attracted Aboriginal men from country areas. As in World War I, once the demand for manpower increased, the authorities began accepting dark-complexioned recruits of mixed Aboriginal and European parentage.

On their final leave before embarkation, Jackson and fellow soldiers from the Grafton district, E. J. 'Punchy' O'Donohue and John Barnier, were 'given a send-off by their local community in the tiny, unlined weather-board Hall at Alumny Creek'; Jackson had a good voice and sang 'One Day When We Were Young'. He was promoted acting sergeant in August 1941 and sailed for Singapore next month. His posting to the 8th Divisional Provost Company on 30 November entailed a reduction in rank to acting corporal. The provost company's major function was to maintain discipline and their workload increased as the Japanese advanced towards Singapore.

Jackson was in hospital suffering from malaria when Singapore fell on 15 February. Six days later he was discharged and returned to his unit, though his condition necessitated a further period in hospital in May-June. The Japanese were puzzled to find a handful of dark-skinned soldiers among the interned Australians. Aware of the existence of the White Australia policy, they thought that Aboriginal soldiers might be used as informers, but the patriotism and solidarity of these men was no different from that of their comrades of European descent.

In July 1942 Jackson was sent to British North Borneo as a member of a labour force assembled to build an airfield at Sandakan. The prisoners of war were overworked, starved, beaten and denied medical care. Surprisingly, an occasional camp concert was permitted: at one of them, Jacko sang 'Beautiful Dreamer'. By October 1943 some 2500 Australian and British prisoners were held at Sandakan. Due to executions and maltreatment—particularly the forced marches in 1945 through 160 miles (260 km) of mountainous country to Ranau—only six survived. Jackson died on 29 April 1945 at Sandakan. His name is inscribed on the Labuan Memorial, Sabah, Malaysia, commemorating personnel, most of them prisoners of war in Borneo, who have no known grave.

D. Wall, *Sandakan* (Syd, 1992); *Reveille* (Syd), Jan-Feb 1994; *Koori Mail*, 15 June 1994.

DAVID HUGGONSON

JACKSON, JOHN FRANCIS (1908-1942), grazier, businessman and air force officer, and LESLIE DOUGLAS (1917-1980), businessman and air force officer, were born on 23 February 1908 at New Farm, Brisbane, and 24 February 1917 at Newmarket, eldest and fourth sons of Queensland-born parents William James Jackson (d.1935), merchant, and his wife Edith Annie, née Grayson. Both boys attended Brisbane Grammar School. Completing his education at Scots College, Warwick, John toured Europe with the Young Australia League. By 1927 he was working his property, Macwood, 60 miles (97 km) from St George. In 1933 he became the proprietor and manager of Western Queensland Motor Engineering Works, St George, and local representative of the New Zealand Loan & Mercantile Agency Co. Ltd. He learned to fly, bought a Klemm Swallow monoplane and in 1936 competed in the South Australian centenary air-race from Brisbane to Adelaide. That year he joined the Royal Australian Air Force Reserve. At Christ Church, North Adelaide, on 17 February 1938 he married with Anglican rites Elizabeth Helen Thompson.

Appointed pilot officer, R.A.A.F., on 2 October 1939, Jackson embarked for the Middle East in October 1940. He served with No.3 Squadron in Libya, Syria and Cyprus, flew 129 sorties and spent 206 hours in the air in

Gladiators, Hurricanes and Tomahawks. Among his victories, he was credited with destroying three Junkers 87 dive-bombers on 18 February 1941 and another on 5 April; he was awarded the Distinguished Flying Cross and mentioned in dispatches. Flight Lieutenant Jackson returned to Australia in November and joined No.75 Squadron at Townsville, Queensland, in March 1942.

On the 19th he assumed command as acting squadron leader and began moving the unit's Kittyhawks to Port Moresby which had been without fighter protection against Japanese air-attacks. Jackson's leadership and aggression inspired his men. Confronting superior forces, they intercepted enemy raiders and counter-attacked Japanese bases. During a solo reconnaissance on 10 April he was shot down into the sea off Lae and swam ashore. Two New Guineans helped him to avoid the Japanese and guided him on a gruelling, eight-day trek through the jungle to Bulolo. He was then carried to Wau whence he was flown to Port Moresby on 23 April.

'Old John' earned the affection and trust of all who served with him. His 'philosophy, like himself, was rugged, simple, not subject to debate, determined but as true as steel'. On 28 April 1942 he led five aircraft to intercept a Japanese strike. He was killed in the ensuing combat. Survived by his wife, daughter and son, he was buried in Bomana war cemetery. Jackson International Airport, Port Moresby, commemorates him.

On leaving school, Leslie worked briefly in the family business, J. Jackson & Co. Pty Ltd, before purchasing a garage and service station at Surat. He, too, became a pilot. Enlisting in the R.A.A.F. on 6 November 1939, he was commissioned in February 1940 and served with units in Darwin, Singapore and Brisbane. On 28 March 1942 he joined No.75 Squadron. In the defence of Port Moresby he was credited with destroying four enemy fighters and damaging two bombers. Leslie succeeded his brother in command on 29 April. In the battle of Milne Bay (August-September) the Kittyhawks of No.75 and No.76 squadrons played a decisive part in defeating a Japanese invasion force that had been sent with inadequate air support. Jackson accounted for one enemy fighter and was awarded the Distinguished Flying Cross.

After leaving the squadron in January 1943, he held staff appointments in Australia. Between December 1943 and November 1944 he led No.78 Wing (as acting wing commander from September 1944) in operations in New Guinea, New Britain and the Netherlands New Guinea. He was awarded a Bar to his D.F.C. for 'determined and successful attacks on enemy installations and shipping'. Having performed instructional duties in New South Wales, he commanded Air Defence Headquarters, Madang, New Guinea, from June 1945. He was demobilized on 8 February 1946 in Brisbane.

Jackson established Active Service Motors at Roma and bought Western Queensland Motors, St George, from John's widow. On 25 January 1947 at St Andrew's Presbyterian Church, Southport, he married Cynthia Mary Cobb, née Molle (d.1974), a 27-year-old widow. Survived by his three sons, he died of a cerebral haemorrhage on 17 February 1980 at Southport and was cremated with Anglican rites.

D. Wilson, *Jackson's Few* (Canb, 1988) and *The Decisive Factor* (Melb, 1991); Nos 3, 21, 23 and 75 Squadrons, No 78 Wing, No 8 Operational Training Unit, unit hist records (Hist Section, RAAF, Canb); E. Logan, family hist (untitled ms, extracts held by Mr D. Wilson, Chisholm, Canb).

DAVID WILSON

JACKSON, LAWRENCE STANLEY (1884-1974), taxation commissioner, was born on 2 April 1884 at Stepney, Adelaide, son of William Samuel Jackson, an engine driver from England, and his South Australian-born wife Mary, née Norton. Lawrence was educated at Pulteney Street School. In 1903 he joined the Commonwealth Public Service as a clerk in the Postmaster-General's Department. Transferring to Federal taxation office, Adelaide, in 1911, he was to spend the remainder of his working life in taxation administration. On 21 March 1912 he married Hazel Winifred Powell (d.1939) at the Methodist Church, Norwood. He was promoted senior assessor (1916), assistant deputy commissioner, Sydney (1920), secretary in the central office, Melbourne (1925), and deputy-commissioner, Sydney (1929).

In 1932, as the senior Federal taxation officer in New South Wales, Jackson was closely involved in the confrontation between the Commonwealth and State governments which reached its climax in the final days of the premiership of J. T. Lang [q.v.9]. Jackson subsequently revealed (*Sydney Morning Herald*, 12 August 1970) that, on 30 April 1932, the Commonwealth assistant-treasurer (Sir) Walter Massy-Greene [q.v.10] had instructed him and other officials to break into locked floors of the New South Wales government taxation office and remove documents which were being held under guard by the State authorities. Massy-Greene was persuaded to withdraw the order.

Jackson played a major role in the negotiations which achieved substantially uniform taxation Acts for the States and the Commonwealth in 1936. Moving to Canberra, he became second commissioner that year. On 6 May 1939 he was appointed commissioner of taxation. Significant administrative changes occurred during his commissionership, including the establishment of the Commonwealth as the sole authority for assessing and collecting income tax (1942), and the introduction of 'pay-as-you-earn' and provisional taxation (1944). The associated work imposed a heavy burden on him. Although offered reappointment, he retired on 5 May 1946 at the expiration of his term.

Throughout his career Jackson was recognized by his colleagues as a dedicated and conscientious officer. His approach to his work was captured in an application for promotion, made at age 33, in which he wrote that he had 'endeavoured to keep pace with the expert work of the [taxation] department by sacrificing my private time and study to the various taxation acts, and by a complete devotion of the whole of my energies'. In 1949 he was commissioned to edit the official 'Wartime Taxation History 1939-1945'; the two unpublished volumes are held by the Australian Taxation Office Library, Canberra. S. J. Butlin [q.v.13] wrote in a foreword in 1954 that 'the work as a whole bears the stamp of Mr Jackson's passion for accuracy and meticulous attention to detail'.

At St Leonard's Presbyterian Church, Brighton Beach, Melbourne, on 29 April 1944 Jackson had married Phyllis Lee Vale, a stenographer; after his retirement they lived in Melbourne and then in Adelaide. Survived by his wife, and by the two sons and one of the two daughters of his first marriage, he died on 7 August 1974 in North Adelaide and was cremated. His elder son Sir Lawrence Jackson was chief justice (1969-77) of the Supreme Court of Western Australia.

SMH, 29 Apr, 3, 7 May 1932, 22 Oct 1949, 12 Aug 1970; Jackson papers (NL); Jackson file, A6899/1 (AA, Canb).   IAN CASTLES

JACKSON, WILLIAM (1907-1975), orchardist and politician, was born on 28 October 1907 at Dover, Tasmania, eldest of five children of English-born parents Dr William Jackson, gentleman orchardist, and his wife Maud, née Bush. Dr Jackson had studied medicine at Caius College, Cambridge, and represented England at Rugby Union football; a colourful personality and a philanthropist, he was an authority on all branches of gardening. Young William, who was known as 'Tim', was educated at The Hutchins School, Hobart, and began farming at Dover, growing high-quality fruit and vegetables. At St Peter's Anglican Church, Geeveston, on 19 February 1932 he married Nancy Golding Eady, a schoolteacher. A member (1933-34) of Esperance Municipal Council, he was managing director of Port Huon Fruit Growers.

On 1 September 1940 Jackson was appointed sub lieutenant, Royal Australian Naval Volunteer Reserve, and was sent to Britain that month for service under the Admiralty Yachtsmen Scheme. He was navigating officer of H.M.S. *Wanderer* in 1940-43. Back in Australia, from January to August 1944 he was first lieutenant of H.M.A.S. *Kapunda*. In October he took command of H.M.A.S. *Bendigo* which performed minesweeping duties with the British Pacific Fleet. He was demobilized on 6 March 1946 as acting lieutenant commander and became foundation president (1950-59) of the Dover branch of the Returned Sailors', Soldiers' and Airmen's Imperial League of Australia.

Standing as a Liberal candidate, on 23 November 1946 Jackson was returned to the Legislative Assembly for the seat of Franklin. An 'amiable giant of a man', 6 ft 3 ins (191 cm) tall and well liked by all, he was elected deputy-leader of the Opposition in 1951 and leader in 1956. He had barely taken up the leadership when C. A. Bramich, the honorary minister for housing in (Sir) Robert Cosgrove's [q.v.13] Labor government, crossed the floor on 11 September, giving the Opposition a majority. Jackson moved a no confidence motion which was carried 15 to 14, but, lacking political guile, he was outwitted by Cosgrove who adjourned the Assembly and regained office at the elections on 13 October. Hampered by disunity and an 'insidious whispering campaign' against their leader, the Liberals again failed narrowly at the elections on 2 May 1959. Pressure mounted against Jackson and, when the party organization intervened on 19 March 1960, he resigned in protest and was succeeded by (Sir) Angus Bethune. Jackson left the party and sat as an Independent Liberal until May 1964.

After his father's death in 1948, Jackson took up the hybridizing of daffodils, which William had begun in the 1920s. Each year he flowered thousands of daffodil seedlings, selecting just a few hundred for further testing. Only those that passed a three-year trial were named. He exported bulbs to many countries, including Britain, the United States of America, Canada and Japan. Between 1955 and 1963 Jackson won nine Australian Seedling cups in succession and eight Tasmanian cups; his daffodils were awarded the national championship in 1964, 1968, 1969, 1972 and 1973. Following a world tour in 1972, he was satisfied that Tasmania led the world in his speciality—superior pink daffodils.

Survived by his wife, son and daughter, Jackson died on 19 February 1975 in Hobart and was cremated. His wife won a trophy at the World Daffodil Conference, Wellington, New Zealand, in 1976.

K. West, *Power in the Liberal Party* (Melb, 1965); W. A. Townsley, *Tasmania . . . 1945-1983* (Hob, 1994); *Catalogue of Jackson's Daffodils, 1963-75; Saturday Evening Mercury*, 25 Jan 1969, 19 Aug 1972; *Mercury* (Hob), 11 Sept, 6 Oct 1976; *Huon News*, 20 Oct 1990; information from Mr D. Jackson, Surges Bay, Tas.   GEORGE C. WADE

JACOBS, ALFRED NAILER (1897-1976), medical practitioner, was born on 11 July 1897 at Surrey Hills, Melbourne, second child of Henry Atwood Jacobs, a warehouseman from England, and his second wife Amy Lilian, née Scales, from Geelong. Educated at Scotch College and the University of Melbourne (M.B., B.S., 1925), Alfred suspended his studies and enlisted in the Australian Imperial Force on 5 January 1916. He served on the Western Front from September 1917 with the 15th Field Ambulance. At Bellicourt, France, on 29-30 September 1918 he evacuated the wounded for thirty-six hours continuously while under heavy fire and won the Military Medal. After being discharged on 4 September 1919, he completed his degree and worked successively at the Melbourne, the Homoeopathic and the Bendigo hospitals.

In 1926 Jacobs joined the staff of the Fremantle Hospital, Western Australia. Next year he was employed at the State Tuberculosis Sanatorium, Wooroloo, before practising at Yarloop. In the Perth College chapel on 6 January 1929 he married with Anglican rites Eva Ivy May Hurst, a trained nurse. During the early years of the Depression he set up practice at Harvey where he was responsible for the care of some 3500 sustenance workers and their dependants. His observation of human suffering and his experience of having 'virtually . . . to hold a gun to the government's head' to obtain medicines and hospital supplies increased his political awareness and led him to join the Douglas Social Credit Party of Western Australia (vice-president 1933). He was described as 'a clear and incisive speaker' who embodied 'that happy combination of idealism with realism'. In his public lectures and study groups he promulgated the view that the cause of unemployment was the replacement of people by machines. At the Federal elections in 1934 he stood unsuccessfully for the Senate as a Social Credit candidate. He was also to be defeated when he stood for the Legislative Council in 1944 (as a Labor candidate) and 1968 (as an Independent). With (Sir) Walter Murdoch [q.v.10], he was a foundation vice-president (1939) of the Western Australian branch of the Australian Council for Civil Lib-

erties. In reaction to the rise of fascism in Europe, he gravitated to the political left and came under the surveillance of the Commonwealth Investigation Branch and its successor the Australian Security Intelligence Organization.

In 1940 Jacobs moved with his family to Narrogin. There, his practice involved him in the affairs of the local Aboriginal community. He helped to found the Narrogin Native Welfare Committee (later Association) in 1946 and served as its honorary secretary throughout the 1950s. The N.N.W.C. lobbied for better living conditions, higher educational opportunities and full citizenship rights for Aborigines. At the administrative level, Jacobs was often at odds with the Native Affairs Department and campaigned for the Federal government to take charge of Aboriginal affairs. The N.N.W.C.'s attempts to intervene in cases of police brutality against Aborigines also caused friction with local officials. Suffering from tuberculosis, Jacobs spent periods in Hollywood Repatriation Hospital, Perth, in 1947, 1950, 1952 and 1955. At the first federal conference of the Aboriginal Advancement League, held in 1958, he presented the N.N.W.A.'s demands for radical reforms, including land, fishing and mining rights.

Jacobs was frequently reviled, in part because of his identification with the A.C.C.L.'s campaign against (Sir) Robert Menzies' [q.v.] attempts to ban the Communist Party of Australia. He claimed that he had never belonged to the C.P.A., and that he always tried to understand social and political problems from both sides of the political spectrum. His real concerns were with 'civil liberty'—for which he was 'willing to fight tooth and nail'—and with Aboriginal causes. He died on 26 January 1976 at Narrogin and was buried in the local cemetery; his wife, son and three daughters survived him.

G. C. Bolton, *A Fine Country to Starve in* (Perth, 1972); *A Walk through the History of Western Australia 1829-1979* (Perth, 1979); J. A. McKenzie, *Challenging Faith* (Perth, 1993); *MJA*, 1976, 1, p 1018; *Harvey-Waroona Mail*, 31 Aug, 7, 14 Sept 1934; *Reliance Weekly*, 12, 24 Aug 1952; *Narrogin Observer*, 5 Sept 1952, 29 Jan 1976; *West Australian*, 28 Jan 1976; Dept of Veterans' Affairs (Perth), A. N. Jacobs personal file *and* Narrogin Native Welfare Cte, Minutes *and* Correspondence (WAA).   JAN WILSON

JACOBS, MAXWELL RALPH (1905-1979), forester, was born on 25 February 1905 in North Adelaide, son of Isaac Jacobs, schoolteacher, and his wife Bertha Marion, née Shorney, both South Australian born. Educated at Unley High School and the University of Adelaide (B.Sc., 1925; M.Sc., 1936), Max was awarded a Lowrie [q.v.10] postgraduate scholarship to the Waite [q.v.6] Agricultural Research Institute. He was appointed forest assessor in the Federal Capital Territory in 1926 and promoted chief forester in 1928. A Commonwealth scholarship took him to the University of Oxford (diploma in forestry, 1931) and to the Forstliche Hochschule Tharandt, Germany (doctorate in forest science, Technische Hochschule Dresden, 1932).

Returning to Australia, Jacobs was appointed a research officer with the Commonwealth Forestry Bureau, Canberra, in January 1933 and that year made a reconnaissance of the then little-known forest resources of the Northern Territory. On 23 December 1933 he married Phyllis Vesper Quinton (d.1976) at St David's Presbyterian Church, Haberfield, Sydney. He carried out original research on the growth stresses of trees and the effects of wind sway, and experimented with the use of cuttings for propagating radiata pine. His extensive studies of the anatomy of the bud systems and the silvicultural behaviour of various eucalypts in Australia were to be consolidated in his *Growth Habits of the Eucalypts* (Canberra, 1955) which became a standard international text. In 1939 he was awarded a fellowship from the Commonwealth Fund and attended Yale University (Ph.D., 1941), United States of America, where he continued his investigations into growth stresses.

Back home, on 19 March 1942 Jacobs was mobilized in the Militia as a temporary captain and appointed deputy assistant director, engineering services, Army Headquarters, Melbourne. In 1943-44 he performed staff duties in the directorates of engineering stores and of engineering survey, and served briefly in Papua and New Guinea. He transferred to the Reserve of Officers as honorary major on 8 November 1944. Next month he was appointed principal and lecturer in silviculture at the Australian Forestry School, Canberra. Over fifteen years 'the Doc' lectured to and professionally guided more than three hundred undergraduates from Australia, New Zealand, Asia and Africa; they returned his warmth and interest with respect and affection.

Jacobs was acting director-general (from December 1959) of the Commonwealth Forestry and Timber Bureau and its director-general (from May 1961). He played a leading role in establishing the Australian Forestry Council in 1964 and chaired its first standing committee; he also chaired other bodies connected with forestry or the forest industries, among them the timber industries committee of the Standards Association of Australia, and wrote numerous papers and reports on Australian forest policy. In 1966 he was appointed I.S.O.

In 1927 Jacobs had joined the Empire (later Commonwealth) Forestry Association; he was a member (1963-69) of its governing council. A foundation member (1935) of the Institute of Foresters of Australia, he was awarded its N. W. Jolly [q.v.9] medal in 1962 and elected a fellow in 1969. He was made an honorary member of the New Zealand Institute of Forestry (1958) and of the Society of American Foresters (1966).

After retiring from the Commonwealth Public Service in February 1970, Jacobs worked as a consultant to several national and international bodies, including the Food and Agriculture Organization of the United Nations, at whose request he undertook a massive rewrite of its *Eucalypts for Planting* (Rome, 1979). He went on a number of missions abroad, particularly in connection with eucalypts. In addition, he was president of the agricultural and forestry section of the Australian and New Zealand Association for the Advancement of Science, of the Royal Society of Canberra (1948-49) and of the Rotary Club of Canberra (1956-57). His main recreation was golf.

Survived by his two daughters, Jacobs died on 9 October 1979 in Woden Valley Hospital and was cremated. To commemorate his contribution to the discipline, the Institute of Foresters of Australia initiated the M. R. Jacobs fund in 1983. Administered by the Australian Academy of Science, the fund assists individuals to conduct forestry and forest-industry research projects, and to participate in conferences.

Cwlth Forestry Review, 59 (1), no 179, Mar 1980, p 4; *Canb Times,* 12 Oct 1979; personal information.

L. T. CARRON

JACOBY, IAN MATHIESON (1901-1973), financier and hire-purchase pioneer, was born on 27 January 1901 at Mundaring, Western Australia, second of four children of Mathieson Harry Jacoby, an orchardist from Adelaide and a member (1901-05, 1908-11) of the Western Australian Legislative Assembly, and his Victorian-born wife Mary Augusta Maude, née Cresswell. Ian was educated at Thomas Street State School, Subiaco, and Christ Church Grammar School, Claremont, but left when his father died in 1915. Two years later he became a founder of the Christ Church Old Boys' Association.

In busy wartime conditions Jacoby was soon employed in the shipping department of Dalgety [q.v.4] & Co. for a half sovereign each week until he received a better offer (13s. 4d. a week) from McIlwraith, McEacharn [qq.v.10] & Co. at Fremantle. By the age of 20 he had saved more than £500 and was dissatisfied with the low rate of bank interest. In the early 1920s Perth had no finance companies, other than banks which were loath to lend for consumer goods such as motor vehicles. Jacoby reasoned that he could exceed bank interest on his money if he were prepared to provide hire-purchase arrangements or instalment credit. Circumstances proved him correct—by 1927 he was augmenting his salary by some 40 per cent from these dealings.

His activities were noticed by a visiting representative of the American finance company, Industrial Acceptance Corporation, who offered him a job in its Australian headquarters in Sydney. Arriving there in mid-1927, Jacoby met and courted the violinist Hilda Irene Sutton (d.1968), whom he married on 7 September 1928 at St Mark's Anglican Church, Darling Point; they were to have one son before being divorced in February 1943. Jacoby's American directors, in an economy drive, had recalled senior executives and terminated the Studebaker franchise, leaving him in charge on a salary of £1250, plus 3 per cent commission. After the Wall Street crash they cabled Jacoby to put the Australasian subsidiary into liquidation. Instead, he sent a counter proposal that he be given a chance to sell I.A.C. (Australasia) Pty Ltd to Australian investors. The American principals consented, subject to a 31 December 1929 deadline.

Aged 28, with few wealthy contacts, Jacoby studied lists of company directors for prospective investors. He eventually approached the Nathan family who, with interests in Maples piano and furniture stores, and in Lane's and Neal's motors, were well aware of hire-purchase potential. Benjamin Nathan bought the goodwill and outstanding debts owed to I.A.C., making himself chairman and Jacoby general manager. As the Depression bit and bank credit was curtailed, I.A.C.'s lending contracted, but Jacoby managed to pull the firm through, even paying a dividend of 7 per cent in 1931. The company then went from strength to strength as he 'probed with fascination the limits of prudent and therefore profitable lending'.

In 1939 Jacoby was sent overseas to study methods used in the hire-purchase industry in the United States of America and England. He returned with new ideas for funding, though the outbreak of World War II postponed their implementation. On 17 December 1943 at the office of the government statist, Melbourne, he married a divorcee Elsa Antoinette Ruth Dadswell, née Stenning (d.1994), a 33-year-old Australian singer he had met in London; they were to have two children.

Due to Jacoby's careful management, I.A.C. came out of the war about equal in size to its rival, Australian Guarantee Corporation

Ltd. Competition increased, however, with the entry of the industrial finance division of the Commonwealth Bank of Australia—headed by a friend of Jacoby's (Sir) Alfred Armstrong [q.v.13]—which offered credit at 4 per cent, severely undercutting the 6.5 per cent charged by I.A.C. Although in favour of trading banks becoming associated with finance companies, Jacoby was determined to free the latter from the expense of bank credit. He persuaded his directors to list I.A.C. on the Sydney stock exchange in 1948, thus making it the first publicly listed finance company in Australia.

In 1949 Jacoby again went abroad, carrying letters of introduction from the governor of the Commonwealth Bank and Treasury officials. In America and England he encountered new ideas regarding consumer credit; on his return he gained approval to float short-term debentures as a means of raising capital. This move took I.A.C. and other finance companies farther away from the regulatory control of the banking system. In succeeding years Jacoby became an advocate of short-term stock through the financial press; he 'may have been the first to make commonplace the need for maximum returns on funds, and hence for a money market's services'.

By the early 1950s the Nathan connexion with I.A.C. had virtually been severed and Jacoby found it increasingly difficult to work with his conservative directors. In June 1953 he resigned and began a new company, Custom Credit Corporation Ltd, which was listed on 9 July. In a 'dazzling' coup he persuaded the National Bank of Australasia to take 40 per cent of Custom Credit's shares, thereby ensuring nationwide coverage and transforming its borrowing potential. His move soon had other banks scrambling for hire-purchase associations. The new company did extremely well, surpassing by 1959 all but one of its competitors. None the less, by 1962 relations between Jacoby and other directors had soured. He suffered a mild stroke and resigned from the board in early 1963.

On 18 February that year Jacoby registered a new public company, Ready Credit Ltd, in Perth. A caricature, with a brief résumé of his career, appeared in the *Weekend News* (14 September 1963). Within two years friction again occurred between him and his directors; in 1965 he sold out his holdings and 'finished up a healthy benefactor from a company in which others did not do so well'.

Throughout this time Jacoby was still principally domiciled in Sydney, but the death of his 19-year-old son James in 1967 appears to have marked a turning-point. Jacoby returned to Perth. In January 1970 his wife divorced him. He abandoned business pursuits in favour of more leisurely interests, including writing his memoirs and supporting the Claremont Football Club. At the district registrar's office, Perth, on 13 February that year, the man who had declined to have personal details listed in *Who's Who in Australia* married a 45-year-old widow Florentine Sophia Blogg, née De Beers. Survived by his wife, and by the son of his first marriage and the daughter of his second, he died on 25 April 1973 at Shenton Park and was cremated. An obituarist described him as 'the finest financial brain in the country'.

I. Elliott, *Mundaring* (Mundaring, WA, 1983); R. T. Appleyard and C. B. Schedvin (eds), *Australian Financiers* (Melb, 1988); Custom Credit Corporation Ltd, *Annual Report*, 1978 (25th anniversary edition); *Western Mail* (Perth), 19 Sept 1908; *SMH*, 27 Oct 1953, 29-30 May 1967, 20 Jan 1969, 1 May 1973; *Bulletin*, 3 Aug 1963; *Weekend News* (Perth), 14 Sept 1963; *West Australian*, 16 Oct 1967, 28 Apr, 1 May 1973.

PAMELA STATHAM

JAEGER, JOHN CONRAD (1907-1979), mathematical physicist, was born on 30 July 1907 at Stanmore, Sydney, only child of Carl Jaeger, a German-born cigar-manufacturer from South Africa, and his English-born wife Christina Louisa, née Sladden. John was closely attached to his mother and her family, especially her brothers who were engineers in England and South Africa. He won a scholarship to Sydney Church of England Grammar School (Shore) where he gained many prizes and was dux (1923). At the University of Sydney (B.Sc., 1928; D.Sc., 1941) he spent two years in the engineering faculty, then changed to science, and was awarded first-class honours and university medals in mathematics and physics. His first published research (1928), on the motion of electrons in pentane, was carried out under V. A. Bailey, but he was more influenced by H. S. Carslaw [qq.v.13,7].

In 1928 Jaeger proceeded on a Barker [q.v.1] graduate scholarship to Trinity College, Cambridge (B.A., 1930; M.A., 1934); listed as wrangler, he was awarded the Mayhew prize (1930) for proficiency in applied mathematics. He remained in Cambridge until 1935, studying quantum theoretical topics—in part under (Sir) Ralph Fowler—and continuing his interests in pure and applied mathematics. On 23 December 1935 at St John's parish church, Notting Hill, London, Jaeger married Sylvia Percival Rees; they were to be divorced in 1950. In February 1936 he took up the post of lecturer in mathematics at the University of Tasmania; he and Professor E. J. G. Pitman shared the whole of

the teaching until World War II. Although Jaeger gave lectures in pure mathematics, he especially enjoyed expounding applied mathematics to engineers and was an excellent teacher.

Jaeger's return to Australia was marked by a remarkable surge in the number of his publications. He renewed his ties with Carslaw and they co-authored two major books, *Operational Methods in Applied Mathematics* (Oxford, 1941) and *Conduction of Heat in Solids* (Oxford, 1947). The latter became the definitive work in the subject and is still in print. Their research papers on heat conduction included the results of many computations which Jaeger carried out on a hand calculator. The Council for Scientific and Industrial Research drew upon his skills and conceptual grasp in its initial development of an electronic computer.

During World War II Jaeger had been engaged on projects of a more immediately applied nature, such as charcoal production and the problem of why sandstone rollers cracked in newsprint production. He was eventually seconded to C.S.I.R.'s division of radiophysics in Sydney and carried out theoretical work on antenna patterns and wave propagation. Back in Tasmania, he published *An Introduction to the Laplace Transformation* (London, 1949), *An Introduction to Applied Mathematics* (Oxford, 1951) and further research papers on heat conduction. He was promoted associate-professor in 1949 and professor one year later. On 24 October 1950 at the registrar-general's office, Hobart, he married Martha Elizabeth ('Patty') Clarke (d.1978), the university's chief clerk and a member of an old Tasmanian family.

In 1952 Jaeger was appointed to the foundation chair of geophysics in the Research School of Physical Sciences at the Australian National University, Canberra. He immersed himself whole-heartedly in this new field and set about building up research of international standing in the solid-earth sciences. From the beginning, he had the idea of developing a centre for broad geophysical research, which grew to encompass geochemistry. His achievements reflected a breadth of vision, based on deep roots in classical physics, and an extraordinary perspicacity in making appointments.

Overcoming numerous constraints, Jaeger pursued his goal and the Research School of Earth Sciences was established in 1973, shortly after his retirement. The core of this school represented the body of activities he had fostered in geophysics and geochemistry. While research in these areas became internationally orientated, he had also forged links with organizations in Australia: he collaborated with public authorities and mining companies in seismology, rock mechanics, heat flow and geochronology, and was a member of several national committees concerned with earth sciences.

Although Jaeger made excursions into other fields, his personal research at the A.N.U. was mainly in terrestrial heat flow and rock mechanics. The work on heat flow laid the basis for the first comprehensive picture of the regional variations in the geothermal flux in the Australian continent. Rock mechanics dominated the last fifteen years of his scholarship, with particular emphasis on fracture of rocks and friction at sliding rock surfaces. These investigations were complemented by a considerable amount of consulting for mining and civil-engineering bodies, and by the publication, with N. G. W. Cook, of *Fundamentals of Rock Mechanics* (London, 1969). Earlier, Jaeger had written a successful monograph, *Elasticity, Fracture and Flow* (London, 1956). Almost all his books went through several editions.

Jaeger was elected to fellowships of the Australian Academy of Science (1954) and the Royal Society, London (1970); he was awarded an honorary doctorate of science (1975) by the University of Tasmania; he and Cook shared the Rock Mechanics award of the American Institute of Mining, Metallurgical and Petroleum Engineers in 1969; and Jaeger gave the Rankine lecture to the British Geotechnical Society in 1971. In 1963-65 he had acted as head of the school of physical sciences. He retired in December 1972.

In physique Jaeger was tall and, in middle years, of substantial bulk; he had receding hair and wore spectacles. Inclined to be shy and retiring in disposition, he could present a gruff exterior, though it mellowed on closer acquaintance. He enjoyed living in semi-rural surroundings at Oaks Estate, was a connoisseur of old houses and antique furniture, had a fondness for cats and nineteenth-century literature, and collected steam-engines and early farm machinery. Raised as an Anglican, he later showed little interest in conventional religious observance. In his final years he retreated to a remote part of the Tasman Peninsula, about 60 miles (96 km) from Hobart. He died on 15 May 1979 in Canberra and was cremated; he had no children. The Research School of Earth Sciences holds his portrait by Frances Philip.

Biog Memoirs of Fellows of Roy Soc (Lond), 28, 1982, p 163; *Hist Records of Aust Science*, 5, no 3, 1982; Jaeger papers (Basser L); personal information.   M. S. PATERSON

JAMES, ALEXANDER ALEXANDRO-VICH (1882-1976), medical practitioner, was born on 25 January 1882 at Yaroslavl, Russia, son of Jewish parents Alexander Zhemchuzny

and his wife whose name is unknown. Educated at the local Classical Gymnasium and at the Imperial Moscow University (M.D., 1910), Alexander accepted several provincial posts before he was appointed house surgeon at the Imperial Nicholas Military Academy, St Petersburg in 1912. He served with the Imperial Russian Army during World War I. While with the White Russians (1918-20), he superintended the Kuban Cossack army's hospitals. In 1919 he was sent to Paris to study rehabilitation of the war disabled.

On the defeat the southern army, Zhemchuzny was drafted into the Soviet medical service to work as house surgeon (1920) in the military hospital and artificial limbs centre at Rostov-na-Donu. At Ekaterinodar (Krasnodar) he married Zinaida Volkova (d.1961) at the Church of the Trinity on 11 September 1920 (a civil ceremony was conducted on 10 February 1921). Other sources suggest that they were married as early as 1912. He held several government positions in Moscow from 1921 and completed a postgraduate course. As senior medical officer (1926-31) at the Central Hospital of the Chinese Eastern Railway at Harbin, Manchuria, Jemchoojny (as he now styled himself) handled surgical and orthopaedic cases. He declined to return to the Soviet Union and practised privately from 1931. Following the Japanese occupation of Manchuria, he established (1934) a polyclinic at Tientsin (Tianjin), China.

With his wife and younger daughter, Jemchoojny reached Sydney in the *Nankin* in April 1940. He changed his surname to James that year and was naturalized in 1946. Unable to obtain medical registration, he enrolled (1944) as a full-time student in fourth-year medicine at the University of Sydney. A younger colleague wrote of him: 'at sixty-four, his mind is as fresh and agile as his splendidly preserved physique'. Although granted deferred final examinations because of illness, James never graduated. He practised as a physiotherapist and by 1947 had acquired a convalescent home at Thirroul, Wollongong.

In the late 1940s he came under the scrutiny of Australian Security Intelligence Organization operatives who reported that 'members of the Soviet Legation and other pro-Soviets visit James at Thirroul . . . it is reported from the White Russian Community in this state that he is looked upon as a Communist, and in a sense has been ostracised from that Community'. He belonged to the New Russian Club which was regarded as a communist organization.

Eventually, in 1958 James was registered to practise medicine on the basis of his Russian degree; that year he joined the State branch of the British Medical Association. He achieved a measure of fame, or notoriety, for his system of asthma management, on which he wrote a booklet condemning its treatment with drugs 'as futile, hopeless, helpless and harmful'. His own method was based on a somewhat bizarre concept of the causes of asthma being related to mouth breathing, and his treatment consisted of breathing exercises and vibrotherapy.

James's management of patients was aided by his impressive personality and his 'richly accented torrent of words'. He used an old-world consulting-room at Wollongong (at Rose Bay, Sydney, from 1972) which contained a full-length portrait of himself in Eastern dress. Acquiring a large group of asthma patients who improved dramatically with his treatment, he received considerable media support. In 1969 the National Health and Medical Research Council investigated his claims, but stated that there was nothing 'to warrant a full scale objective clinical trial'. He was indignant at the scepticism of the medical profession and battled for years for formal recognition of his methods. Survived by his two daughters, he died on 1 August 1976 at Auburn District Hospital and was buried in Bulli cemetery.

Univ Syd, Faculty of Medicine, *Senior Year Book*, 1945-46, p 104; *MJA*, 1970, 2, p 941; *SMH*, 23 Oct 1970, 23 July, 4-5 Aug 1971, 8 Aug 1972, 3 Aug 1976; naturalization file, A435/1, item 49/4/450 *and* ASIO file, A6119, items 371-2 (AA, Canb); membership records, AMA Archives (NSW Branch), St Leonards, Syd; newspaper-clippings and correspondence (Roy A'sian College of Physicians Archives, Syd).   BRENDA HEAGNEY
                                        BRYAN GANDEVIA

JAMES, BRIAN; *see* TIERNEY, JOHN LAWRENCE

JAMES, JIMMY (MITAMIRRI) (c.1902-1945), tracker, was born about 1902 near Alice Springs, Northern Territory, son of Jimmy Widgedy (also known as Thomas James), tracker. Mitamirri (meaning bandicoot) was of Arrernte descent and received both tribal and elementary education. He became a stockman and was later employed as a steward in coastal steamers. During the 1920s he worked for the police, tracking stolen cattle at Marree, South Australia, and in the Northern Territory, and breaking horses in Adelaide. Jimmy was 'a bit of a doer'. In the mid-1920s he moved to the United Aborigines' Mission reserve near Swan Reach where he supported himself by fishing. On 3 February 1930 in the local Congregational manse he married Alice Disher (d.1934). He raised his three daughters, but his son was placed in Colebrook Home for Aboriginal Children at Quorn. A photograph showed James as a lean, laughing young man in an open-necked shirt and trousers, sitting on a sugar-bag outside his pine-and-hessian shack, nursing two of his children.

He took up lay preaching and football, and demonstrated boomerang throwing at country shows and to tourists on paddle-steamers. From 1937 he and Jerry Mason built cottages for the mission's families; they were paid £1 each for every hut—only after four were completed. In March 1938 both men wrote letters requesting overdue wages. James resumed tracking for the police with no fixed rate of pay. On 7 June, near Berri, he traced a rapist and murderer after searchers had trampled the area for days and dust obliterated most of the evidence. Police claimed that not one in a thousand Aboriginal trackers had 'Jimmy's flair, intelligence and lightning deductive power'.

Now famous, he was invited to perform at the Northern Territory Exhibition in Melbourne Town Hall in July 1938. His travel and accommodation, however, were supervised by the police. He proved a star attraction and in interviews emphasized his reliance on God's help. James also preached in Lygon Street Methodist Church and spoke on radio 3DB: 'I never bend down low', he said, 'just walk slow round and round until I see more'. In the mission church at Swan Reach on 27 August that year he married with Lutheran forms Christina Hunter; they had an elaborate, European-style wedding. She soon deserted him and he was to divorce her in 1942. In 1939 he displayed his skills at a spring carnival in the Fitzroy Gardens, Melbourne; he also performed on stage for a syndicate in Adelaide. He again captured the headlines in January 1940 by recovering a lost 3-year-old girl.

During World War II James moved to Kingston-on-Murray. He successfully pursued eight escapees from the Loveday internment camp by tracking over metal roads from the bumper bar of a car. He died of tuberculosis on 24 December 1945 in the Lady Weigall Hospital, Barmera, and was buried in the local cemetery. His Aboriginal friends and his children were neither allowed to see his body nor attend his funeral. Police Sergeant Ward said, 'Jimmy was a Black man with a white heart'. The people of Barmera collected money to erect a gravestone in 1949. James's son-in-law had learned tracking from him and took his name; he was South Australian Aborigine of the Year (1983) and was awarded the O.A.M. (1984).

C. Mattingley and K. Hampton (eds), *Survival in Our Own Land* (Syd, 1988); M. Jones, *Tracks* (Renmark, SA, 1989); *AFA Annual Review*, 1938;

United Aborigines' Messenger, 1 Feb 1945; *Herald* (Melb), 20, 23 July, 10 Sept 1938, 12 Feb 1982; *Age*(Melb), 1 Aug 1938; Guide to Records Relating to Aboriginal People, Police Dept of SA (restricted), GRG 5/2/1938/1293, 1451, 1910 (SRSA); photograph of J. James (M B44029, Mort L); information from Mrs W. Caddy and Mr B. Whitmore, Barmera, Ms S. A. Flynn, Renmark, Mrs A. Rigby, Glossop, SA, and Mrs M. Wilson, Cheltenham, Adel.   SUZANNE EDGAR

JAMES, JOHN ALEXANDER (1887-1965), medical practitioner, was born on 21 May 1887 at Broughton Creek (Berry), near Nowra, New South Wales, son of Charles Edward James, a Wesleyan clergyman from England who became a Presbyterian minister, and his Sydney-born wife Catherine Hemming, née Hardy. In the late 1890s the family moved to Queensland. John was educated at Brisbane Grammar School where he was a leading Rugby Union footballer, cricketer and rifle-shooter. At the University of Sydney (M.B., 1911; Ch.M., 1915) he was awarded Blues for Rugby and cricket.

After graduating, James worked as a resident medical officer, first at the Royal Prince Alfred Hospital, Sydney (1912-13), and then at the Coast Hospital, Little Bay. On 26 March 1915 he was appointed captain, Australian Army Medical Corps, Australian Imperial Force. He served at Gallipoli with the 5th Field Ambulance, and on the Western Front with the 22nd Battalion, the 1st Australian General Hospital and the 15th Field Ambulance. By 1918 he was deputy assistant director of medical services, 5th Division. Promoted temporary lieutenant colonel in December, he briefly commanded the 4th Field Ambulance. He was mentioned in dispatches and returned to Australia where his appointment terminated on 11 November 1919. In later life in Canberra he retained something of his military bearing and was closely associated with the Royal Military College, Duntroon.

Having resumed employment at the Coast Hospital in 1919, James travelled to England in 1922 to study surgery. He was elected a fellow (1925) of the Royal College of Surgeons. His appointment in January 1926 as medical superintendent of Canberra Hospital was a coup for the Federal Capital Commission; C. S. Daley [q.v.8] had considered it essential 'to have a first-class surgeon in the National Capital'. James supervised the development of the hospital from what was derisively called a 'first-aid-post' to a modern institution with more than 100 beds, a well-equipped operating theatre and an X-ray unit.

On 19 November 1929 at St Stephen's Presbyterian Church, Sydney, he married Sheila Cary, the hospital's theatre sister. After visiting England and Europe in the following year, they established a surgical and general practice at Braddon. James was a fellow (1930) of the (Royal) Australasian College of Surgeons, a visiting and honorary medical officer at Canberra Government (Canberra Community) Hospital, and a member (from 1936) of the Federal Capital Territory's Medical Board. He was described as a 'neat and pretty surgeon' who put 'the welfare of his patients before any consideration of personal prestige'. With a firm but friendly manner, he possessed dignity and charm; although he was reserved, he won the confidence of his patients and their families.

James was a member of the Canberra Chamber of Commerce and a patron of sport. He was appointed O.B.E. (1951) and C.B.E. (1959). In 1963 he ceased practice. Survived by his wife, daughter and two sons, he died on 20 February 1965 in Canberra Community Hospital and was buried in Canberra cemetery. The John James Memorial Hospital, Deakin, was named in his honour.

MJA, 15 May 1965, p 736; *Canb Times,* 23 Feb 1965; information from Dr C. James, Garran, Canb.   ANTHONY PROUST

JAMES, ROWLAND (1885-1962), coalminer and politician, was born on 14 June 1885 at Lambton, New South Wales, youngest of eleven children of Welsh-born parents Moses James, miner, and his wife Mary Ann, née James. Rowley was educated at a public school. He worked in mines in the Newcastle district for twenty-five years, with an interval (1912-16) when he was similarly employed at Collie, Western Australia. At the local Methodist Church on 24 July 1912 he married Gladys Mary Davies. After serving as lodge secretary of the Collie River District Miners' Union of Workers, he returned to New South Wales where he held offices in the Australasian Coal and Shale Employees' Federation, and represented the northern district on the central council.

In 1928 James was elected to the House of Representatives as the Australian Labor Party candidate for the seat of Hunter; he succeeded Matthew Charlton [q.v.7] and was to hold the seat until 1958. During the protracted lock-out of miners in northern New South Wales in 1929-30, he criticized in turn the conservative government of S. M. (Viscount) Bruce and the Labor administration of J. H. Scullin [qq.v.7,11] for failing to prosecute the mine-owners. *Smith's Weekly* accused him of inciting mob violence, and, in a further effort to discredit him, published his record of convictions for offences that ranged from drunkenness to assaulting police.

Miners and their families dominated James's electorate; their burdens were his constant concern.

As the Depression deepened, he supported J. T. Lang's [q.v.9] controversial proposal that the State should default on its interest repayments to British bond-holders. In March 1931 James joined J. A. Beasley's [q.v.13] 'Lang Labor Party', comprising seven New South Wales members of Federal parliament. The factional bitterness was intense. James repeated in the House allegations that relief-work was being used to win support for Federal Labor. Beasley's group voted with the Opposition in November to defeat the Scullin government. At the ensuing elections the A.L.P. lost heavily; Lang Labor won only four seats.

In 1936 James was readmitted to the A.L.P. A member (1940-46) and chairman (from 1943) of the parliamentary standing committee on public works, he also led the Australian delegation at the first session of the International Labour Organization's coal-mining committee, held in London in 1945. Next year he went on a special overseas mission to inquire into coal-mining. While acting as liaison officer (1943-49) between the government and the local industry, he faced moves to expel him from the Miners' Federation for supporting Prime Minister J. B. Chifley's [q.v.13] tough stand on the 1949 coal strike.

'Big, gruff, yet amiable', 'Old Rowley' was a man who disliked convention and who identified with his inward-looking electorate. After being briefly held by H. V. Evatt [q.v.] in 1958-60, James's seat was won by his son Albert who retained it until 1980—exemplifying the tendency of Newcastle and the Hunter to keep Labor seats in the family. James died on 4 July 1962 at Ashfield, Sydney, and was cremated; his wife, daughter and three of his five sons survived him.

G. Freudenberg, *Cause for Power* (Syd, 1991); *PD* (Cwlth), 14 Mar 1929, p 1257, 25 Nov 1931, p 1904; *Newcastle Morning Herald*, 7 Jan 1950, 5 July 1962.   L. E. FREDMAN

JAMES, THOMAS SHADRACH (1859-1946), schoolteacher, and SHADRACH LIVINGSTONE (1890-1956), Aboriginal activist, were father and son. Thomas was born on 1 September 1859 at Moka, Mauritius, son of Samson Peersahib, an Indian interpreter, and his wife Miriam Esther, née Thomas (d.1876). Named Shadrach James Peersahib, he received his early education at a private school in Port Louis. When his mother died and his father remarried, he boarded a boat for Australia.

Soon after he arrived, Shadrach contracted typhoid fever. He was befriended by Aboriginal people who treated him with a traditional herbal medicine (old man weed). Having recovered, he dropped the surname Peersahib in favour of James and adopted the Christian name Thomas in memory of his mother. In 1881 he met Daniel Matthews [q.v.5], a Cornish missionary who was conducting a revival meeting on the beach at Brighton, Melbourne. James responded to his request for a volunteer teacher at the Maloga Aboriginal School, New South Wales, where he worked for the next two years without payment. On 1 October 1883 he was appointed head teacher by the Department of Public Instruction. He married Ada Bethel Cooper on 14 May 1885 at Maloga with Presbyterian forms.

When the Maloga residents were shifted in 1888 to the government reserve, Cumeroogunga, James reopened his school there and educated a number of Aborigines who were to become active in the early political movement: they included his wife, brother-in-law William Cooper [q.v.8], and later Jack Patten [q.v.11], James's nephew (Sir) Douglas Nicholls, and Eric and William Onus [q.v.], founders (1933) of the Australian Aborigines' League. James also served as a Methodist lay preacher. He conducted a dispensary on Cumeroogunga mission and assisted visiting doctors to perform minor operations.

After his retirement from teaching in 1922, James moved to Barmah, Victoria, and then to Melbourne. He set up a visiting herbal and masseur business from his North Fitzroy home and specialized in the treatment of arthritis. While in Melbourne he published a book on Aboriginal culture, *Heritage in Stone*. Survived by his two sons and four daughters, he died on 9 January 1946 at Shepparton and was buried in Cumeroogunga cemetery with the forms of the Churches of Christ.

Thomas's and Ada's third child and eldest son, Shadrach, was born on 15 May 1890 at Cumeroogunga. He received his early education at his father's school before passing the teachers' examination and working under him as his assistant. At Christ Church, Echuca, Victoria, on 15 December 1909 he married Maggie Campbell with Anglican rites. In their North Fitzroy home, Shadrach and his father gathered together a small pioneering group of politically minded Aboriginal people. On behalf of the group, Shadrach addressed various organizations and lobbied for improvements to the conditions under which Aborigines lived and worked.

In 1928 Shadrach moved with his family to Mooroopna, in the Goulburn Valley, to obtain employment in the fruit-picking and canning industry. He took a position at the Ardmona Fruit Products Co-operative Co. Ltd. Because of his education and capacity for public speaking, he was elected secretary of the local branch of the Food Preservers' Union and vice-president of the Goulburn district council. To the local Aboriginal people he became spokesman, lobbyist, legal adviser and representative, organizer of functions and letter writer.

As honorary secretary (1928-55) of the Aboriginal Progressive Association of Victoria, James persisted with his appeals, in copperplate handwriting. He asked for full education standards for Aborigines and the teaching of technical subjects, for land and the facilities to develop it, and for employment of Aborigines in the public service. He also advocated Federal rather than State responsibility for Aborigines, Aboriginal representation in parliament, and equal rights and citizenship for all Aborigines in the Commonwealth. He recommended payment of the maternity allowance to Aboriginal women, recognition of tribal law in the Northern Territory, and the appointment of educated Aborigines to the Department of Native Affairs. His requests were dismissed by government officials, one of whom minuted: 'S. L. James is not an Aboriginal ... His father is an Indian and his mother is a half-caste Aboriginal'. James died of myocardial infarction on 7 August 1956 at Geelong and was buried with Presbyterian forms in Mooroopna cemetery; his wife, three sons and two of his four daughters survived him.

N. Cato, *Mister Maloga* (Brisb, 1976); Hist Soc of Mooroopna, *Mooroopna to 1988* (Shepparton, Vic, 1989); *Aboriginal and Islander Identity*, 3, Jan 1979; *Aust Hist Studies*, 25, no 101, Oct 1993; James letters, 1926-56, A431/1 item 49/686, and A659/1 item 45/1/4924 (AA, Canb); information from Mrs P. Mackray, Mrs R. Near, Mrs L. Grant and Mrs E. Sinclair, Mooroopna, Mrs H. McLennan, Kyabram, Vic, Mr R. James, St Albans, Melb, Miss P. Thomas, Rosehill, Mauritius, and Mrs J. Danforth, Colombo.   GEORGE E. NELSON

JAMES, WILLIAM GARNET (1892-1977), composer, pianist and director of music, was born on 28 August 1892 at Ballarat, Victoria, son of native-born parents Andrew James, compositor, and his wife Louisa, née Chapman, a pianist. In 1909 Billy entered the University Conservatorium of Music, Melbourne (Dip.Mus., 1912), where he was awarded honours for playing the pianoforte. From 1913 he studied in London and in Brussels with Arthur de Greef, a Belgian pianist who had been a pupil of Franz Liszt. Rejected for active service, James worked in London for the British Red Cross Society. Following his public début (during an air raid) with the Queen's Hall Orchestra in 1915, he appeared in promenade concerts under Sir Henry Wood and at the Royal Albert Hall with (Sir) Landon Ronald, as well as in the provinces. James's

ballet score, *By Candlelight*, was played in a concert at the Savoy Theatre in 1916. He also published a number of compositions, including *Six Australian Bush Songs* which he dedicated to Dame Nellie Melba [q.v.10], and held a contract with the Milan publishing house, Giulio Ricordi & Co. At St Luke's parish church, St Marylebone, London, on 14 September 1921 he married Saffo Buchanan, née Drageva (d.1955), an opera singer from Russia who was known as Saffo 'Arnav'.

Having toured Australasia (1923) with Stella Power [q.v.], James remained in Melbourne and from 1925 taught piano at the university conservatorium under Professor (Sir) Bernard Heinze. In 1926-28 he again toured extensively, with Toti dal Monte and John Brownlee [q.v.7], before accepting a full-time position with the Australian Broadcasting Co. as director of programmes (largely comprising music from gramophone records and live studio performances) for its radio stations, 3LO and 3AR.

When the company was superseded in 1932, James continued with the new Australian Broadcasting Commission as controller of programmes in Victoria. In 1935 he became its federal controller of music, based in Sydney. Emulating the British Broadcasting Corporation, music constituted more than one-half of the total A.B.C. time on air. James recalled: 'I used to audition artists, engage them, give piano recitals and talks on music myself, and conduct the opera and operetta broadcasts. It was very personal and pleasant'.

Under his guidance, the number of musicians in the A.B.C. orchestras increased. By 1936 there were forty-five in Sydney, thirty-five in Melbourne, seventeen respectively in Brisbane, Adelaide and Perth, and eleven in Hobart; the orchestras were augmented by casual players for symphony concerts. Enthusiastically supported by the chairman W. J. Cleary [q.v.8], general manager (Sir) Charles Moses and Heinze, James made numerous trips abroad to hear, interview, recommend and engage nearly all the 'Celebrity' artists brought to Australia by the A.B.C. Sir Hamilton Harty came in 1934 as the first of the famous guest conductors and was rapidly followed by other conductors, singers, pianists, violinists, the Budapest String Quartet (1935) and Marcel Dupré, the French organist (1939).

The procession of celebrities ceased during World War II. Their places were filled by Australians. To ensure the same standard, James adjudicated at all competitions held by the A.B.C. throughout the Commonwealth to discover new talent. From 1942 (Sir) Neville Cardus [q.v.13] conducted a weekly session of expert musical commentary; his place was taken in 1948 by A. E. Floyd [q.v.8]. After the war, air travel made it easier for James to persuade celebrities to visit Australia. By the time he retired in 1957, the nation's musical appreciation had been enriched and transformed, largely 'by his own world-mindedness, his acute distaste for the second rate' and 'his ability to recognise star talent . . . on the way up'.

A modest and retiring man, James was 'short and slim, with a sharply triangular face, and . . . heavy-lidded eyes'. He played golf and tennis, and never willingly missed an important cricket match. In 1960 he was appointed O.B.E. At St Mark's Anglican Church, Darling Point, on 25 June that year he married a widow Caroline Mary Dally-Watkins, née Skewes; they were to be divorced in 1967. He continued writing songs in his retirement. Survived by the son and daughter of his first marriage, he died on 10 March 1977 at St Vincent's Hospital, Darlinghurst, and was cremated. As a composer James is best known for his three books of Australian Christmas carols (words by John Wheeler); he also wrote *Sea Shanties* (1934), some piano pieces and a one-act operetta, *The Golden Girl* (1920).

I. Moresby, *Australia Makes Music* (Melb, 1948); R. Covell, *Australia's Music* (Melb, 1967); K. S. Inglis, *This is the ABC* (Melb, 1983); *Aust Musical News*, 31 July 1913, p 195, 1 Mar 1917, p 277, 1 Jan 1918, p 185, 1 Sept 1922, p 926, 1 May 1923, p i, 1 Sept 1924, p 59, 2 Feb 1925, pp 31, 39, 1 Jan 1927, p 21, 1 Apr 1931, p 27; *Listener In*, 17 June 1933, p 13, 14 Oct 1933, p 11; *ABC Weekly*, 3 Feb 1940, p 25, 21 Dec 1946, p 4, 10 July 1954, p 10, 28 Aug 1957, p 4; *Table Talk* (Melb), 4 Oct 1928, p 19; *SMH*, 9 July, 27 Aug 1957, 11 June 1960, 11 Mar 1977.   HAROLD HORT

JAMIESON, KENNETH GRANT (1925-1976), neurosurgeon, was born on 2 January 1925 at Hawthorn, Melbourne, second child of Victorian-born parents Aubrey Carlyle Jamieson, machinery merchant, and his wife Christina, née Grant. Educated (on a scholarship) at Scotch College, Ken excelled academically and as a rower. He won further scholarships to Ormond [q.v.5] College and the University of Melbourne (M.B., B.S., 1948; M.S., 1954). At the Frank Paton [q.v.11] Memorial Church, Deepdene, on 26 March 1949 he married with Presbyterian forms Margaret Irene MacKinlay. In December 1948 Jamieson had joined the Royal Melbourne Hospital where he developed a fascination for neurosurgery. In 1953-54, while completing his masterate, he was a half-time research scholar at the Baker [q.v.7] Medical Research Institute, Alfred Hospital, and held teaching positions in surgery and pathology at the University of Melbourne.

Following a brief term as a locum tenens in Perth and a study-trip to Europe and North America, Jamieson was appointed to the (Royal) Brisbane Hospital in 1956. He established a neurosurgical unit (1960) which became the department of neurology and neurosurgery (1962). A man of prodigious energy, he fostered a team-management approach to patients, involving the participation of medical, nursing and ancillary personnel. Jamieson was also noted for his clinical acumen and dexterous surgery, and pioneered techniques to reach previously inaccessible regions in the treatment of pineal tumours and arterial aneurysms. Particularly interested in head injuries, mostly due to motor vehicle accidents, he was appalled by the lack of safety precautions which had contributed to them. He led scientific research into these injuries and their treatment through the traffic injury committee of the National Health and Medical Research Council (1961), the road trauma committee of the Royal Australian College of Surgeons and the interim committee of the Australian Resuscitation Council (1976). Largely due to his lobbying, the State parliament introduced legislation imposing limits to drivers' blood-alcohol level (1968), and governing the wearing of crash-helmets by motorcyclists (1970) and seat belts in motor vehicles (1972).

In addition to his commitments at R.B.H., Jamieson provided advice and practical assistance for country doctors faced with emergency treatment of head injuries. With little time to develop a private practice, he shared an operating list one evening each week at St Andrew's War Memorial Hospital. He maintained a keen interest in surgical teaching and administration: he was a member (from 1971) of the council of the R.A.C.S. and was elected to the court of examiners in neurosurgery in 1974. President (1971-73) of the Neurosurgical Society of Australasia, he wrote *A First Notebook of Head Injury* (1965), seven monographs and over fifty scientific papers. In 1973 he delivered the Joseph Bancroft [q.v.3] oration to the Queensland branch of the Australian Medical Association. A fellow of the R.A.C.S. (1963) and of the American College of Surgeons (1970), he was awarded a doctorate of medicine by the University of Melbourne in 1967 and a doctorate of surgery by the University of Queensland in 1975.

Of deep religious conviction, Jamieson was a regular worshipper at St Andrew's Presbyterian Church, Brisbane. He was a councillor of the Presbyterian/Methodist Schools' Association and member of the board of governors of St Andrew's War Memorial Hospital, where he also chaired the planning committee. Survived by his wife, son and five daughters, he died of myocardial infarction on 28 January 1976 in R.B.H. and was cremated. In October the neurosurgical unit he had founded at the hospital was named after him.

He was posthumously awarded the R.A.C.S. medal and the 1976 meeting of the Queensland committee of the R.A.C.S. was dedicated to his memory.

M. D. Cobcroft, 'More than anybody', in J. Pearn (ed), *Milestones of Australian Medicine* (Brisb, 1994); *Scotch Collegian*, 1942, 1943; *MJA*, 26 June 1976, p 1017; *Courier-Mail*, 29 Jan 1976; Roy A'sian College of Surgeons Archives, Melb.

M. D. COBCROFT

JAMIESON, LOMA KYLE; *see* LAUTOUR

JAMIESON, STEWART WOLFE (1903-1975), diplomat, was born on 4 January 1903 in Sydney, only son and elder child of London-born Sydney Jamieson, medical practitioner, and his wife Roslyn Athol, née Stewart, who was born in New South Wales. Educated at Hayfield preparatory school, Carlingford, and The King's School, Parramatta, Stewart gained recognition as a rower and budding writer. He entered the University of Sydney (B.A., 1924) and in 1924-26 studied law at Balliol College, Oxford (B.A., 1938).

Back in Sydney, he became an associate to (Sir) Alexander Gordon [q.v.9 M. J. Gordon] before assisting (Sir) Colin Davidson [q.v.8] with the 1929-30 royal commission on the coal industry. Jamieson was admitted to the Bar on 29 August 1930 but also worked as a freelance journalist. He wrote articles for the *Evening News*, contributed book reviews to the *Sydney Morning Herald*, and reviewed films and produced a series of plays on famous trials for the Australian Broadcasting Commission. On 23 December 1937 at St Mark's Anglican Church, Darling Point, he married Katherine Mary Garvan, grand-daughter of J. P. Garvan [q.v.4]. The Jamiesons sailed for Europe where he reported for the *Sydney Morning Herald*; he continued part time with that newspaper after returning to Australia in 1938. Next year he was appointed to the New South Wales Theatres and Films Commission. In the 1930s he had edited the *Australian and New Zealand Ski Year Book*.

On 1 July 1940 Jamieson was commissioned in the Royal Australian Air Force. He served as an intelligence officer in Papua in 1942-43; after recovering from malaria, he was mostly based in the Northern Territory until his demobilization on 21 December 1945 with the rank of acting wing commander.

In July 1946 Jamieson joined the Department of External Affairs as head of the legal and consular division. He was official secretary at the Australian High Commission, Ottawa, in 1947-50, officer-in-charge of the information and defence liaison branches, Canberra, in 1950-52, and consul-general in San Francisco, United States of America, from 1952. Moving to New York as acting consul-general in 1955, he accepted the post of chargé d'affaires in Dublin in 1956. Appointed Australia's first high commissioner to Ghana in 1958, Jamieson travelled widely and alerted the Federal government to the political and economic significance of Africa's emerging nations. In 1960 he was posted as ambassador to Brazil: on his tours of South America, he explained Australia's stand on such issues as trade, Antarctica, and the Territory of Papua and New Guinea. He arrived in the Soviet Union as ambassador in 1962 and also served (from 1964) as ambassador to Sweden. Appointed C.B.E. in June, he left Moscow for Canberra in October. He retired in 1965.

During his career Jamieson had visited thirty-six countries, often travelling from the cities to the backblocks. His unflagging interest in people and his enthusiasm for his work reflected his view of diplomatic life as 'a privilege'. In 1966 he became a director of Canberra Television Ltd and president of the local branch of the Australian-American Association. He was an official Australian observer at the elections in the Republic of Vietnam (South Vietnam) in September 1967. Survived by his wife and two daughters, he died on 4 May 1975 in Canberra and was cremated with Presbyterian forms.

SMH, 27 Jan 1925, 28 Jan 1939; S. Jamieson, Oral Hist Project, TRC 121/26 (NL); Jamieson file (John Fairfax Group Pty Ltd Archives, Syd); A1068/1 T47/145, A1838/1 1515/2/2/1, A1838/272 168/10/6 part 1, A1838/1 852/9/17/1, A1838/274 69/1/3/5 part 5 and A1838/281 3014/2/4/5 (AA, Canb).   KATHLEEN DERMODY

JARDINE, FITZROY (1896-1964), schoolteacher and scientist, was born on 3 March 1896 at Rockhampton, Queensland, seventh child of Robert Jardine, a railway stationmaster from England, and his native-born wife Mary Ann, née Pearce. Named Fitzroy after the river in flood at the time of his birth, he attended North Rockhampton Primary School. In 1910 he won a scholarship to Rockhampton Grammar School where he excelled academically, and represented the school in rowing, athletics, football, cricket and shooting. The headmaster Henry Kellow [q.v.9] selected Jardine in his senior year to become a junior assistant teacher and sportsmaster. In 1915 he was appointed to the permanent staff. Sailing to England in 1917, he qualified as a pilot in the Royal Naval Air Service and on 20 October was appointed temporary flight sub lieutenant. In April 1918 he transferred to the Royal Air Force and was sent to France where he served as an acting flight commander and flight navigating officer with No.243 Squadron. He was mentioned in dispatches and demobilized in 1919.

On his return to Australia, Jardine entered the University of Sydney (B.A., 1924; M.Sc., 1929) on a repatriation scholarship. He graduated with first-class honours and was awarded university medals in geology and geography. A science research scholarship allowed him to complete a thesis on the geology and physiography of Queensland's wetlands, for which he was awarded the university medal for geology in 1929. The results of his investigations of the Fitzroy basin, Broadsound, Ayr, Townsville, Cairns and Torres Strait were published in eight booklets, reprints from the reports of the Great Barrier Reef Committee. While in New South Wales, he also worked with T. G. Taylor [q.v.12] on a survey of the Kosciusko Tableland and collaborated with him on a study of the Kamilaroi tribe. Jardine declined an offer to undertake research in the Sepik region of Papua. The responsibility of caring for his parents and two unmarried sisters induced him to accept the post of science master at Rockhampton Grammar in 1928. Following Kellow's death, Jardine was appointed headmaster in 1936. At her parents' Rockhampton home on 29 December 1945 he married with Methodist forms Adah Kathleen Williams, a 27-year-old schoolteacher.

As the school's longest-serving headmaster, Jardine had a significant influence on education in Central Queensland. He led Rockhampton Grammar through a period of growth and change, and welcomed the broadening of educational opportunities in Queensland. Although favouring a bias towards science in secondary education, he recognized the dangers of premature specialization. Some of his innovations included the establishment of a hobby-room and the introduction of chess as a school activity. The 'Bomber's' large, powerful build and booming voice were in themselves an incentive to his pupils to develop the self-discipline—as opposed to imposed discipline—that he advocated. Compelled by financial circumstances to forgo a scientific career and follow teaching, Jardine brought to it a brilliant mind, integrity, sportsmanship and a concern for the individual.

After his return to Queensland, Jardine had pursued his interest in ethnography. Over two-thirds of his important ethnographic collection originated in the Rockhampton and Fitzroy region, but it also contained items from the Torres Strait Islands, the North Queensland rainforests, Central Australia, the Territory of Papua and New Guinea, and the Pacific Islands. The collection is held by the Dreamtime Cultural Centre, Rockhampton. Jardine had also continued flying. In 1932

he became an honorary examining officer of local pilot-licence applicants for the Department of Civil Aviation. Only months before his contemplated retirement he died of a coronary occlusion on 3 August 1964 at Rockhampton Grammar School and was cremated with Christadelphian forms. His wife, son and daughter survived him.

L. McDonald, *Rockhampton* (Brisb, 1981); T. A. Clinch, *The History of the Rockhampton Grammar School, Centenary 1881-1980* (Rockhampton, Qld, 1982); P. K. Lauer, *Assessment and Identification of the F. Jardine Ethnographic Collection* (Brisb, 1988); Rockhampton Grammar School, *Capricornus*, 1964, p 5; *Courier-Mail*, 4 Aug 1964; K. C. Gillam, A Brief Review of the Rockhampton Grammar School's 100 Years (1881-1981) (ts, held by Rockhampton and District Historical Society, 1981).

CAROL GISTITIN

JARDINE, WALTER LACY (1884-1970), commercial artist, was born on 6 May 1884 at Macdonaldtown, Sydney, tenth (and seventh surviving) child of Alfred Henry Jardine, carter, and his wife Amy Mary, née Lacy, both from London. Educated locally, Walter showed an aptitude for drawing. About the age of 12 he was apprenticed to J. H. Leonard, newspaper artist, and also studied design, colour and drawing at J. S. Watkins's commercial-art classes. He joined the *Australian Star* as an illustrator and was soon asked to handle advertisements as well. For the next twenty years he worked on and off for the *Star* (*Sun* from 1910), achieving widespread recognition for his full-page, black-and-white illustrations.

From 1905 to 1917 he was in partnership with J. B. Jones in an advertising company. About 1908 Jardine visited England, Europe and the United States of America to study methods of advertising and illustration; he paid for the trip by working freelance in the U.S.A. In Sydney, Jones & Jardine (J. & J. Ltd, 1916-17) employed a staff of twenty artists and apprentices. At St Michael's Anglican Church, Rose Bay, on 1 June 1918 Jardine married Mary Kathleen Sylvia Prior, a 27-year-old hairdresser. Attracted by the high fees that American commercial artists could command, Jardine settled in New York in 1923. Almost instantly successful, he illustrated for such magazines as *Cosmopolitan, Good Housekeeping, Motor* and the *American Legion Magazine*, and drew up advertisements for well-known companies, among them Durant Motors Inc., General Motors Corporation and the Packard Motor Car Co., E. R. Squibb & Sons (toothpaste) and York Manufacturing Co. (refrigerators). His knowledge of typography and layout enabled him to extend his activities to include the design of booklets and campaign posters.

Returning to Sydney in May 1928, Jardine opened a studio in Margaret Street. As a free-lance artist he numbered among his clients Stephen Keir [q.v.] (Akubra hats), William Arnott [q.v.3] Ltd (biscuits), the Orient Steam Navigation Co., Stamina Clothing Co. (menswear), Toohey Ltd and Tooth [qq.v.6] & Co. Ltd (beer), the Department of Defence and the Royal Agricultural Society of New South Wales. Magazines, newspapers, pamphlets, posters and handbills featured his work. About 1933 he published *The Art of Walter Jardine*. During the 1950s and 1960s he taught by correspondence for the Art Training Institute, Melbourne. In partnership (1945-59) with W. F. Paterson, he formed the company, Walter Jardine Advertising Service (later Jardine, Paterson & Co.).

Jardine's reputation as a leading commercial artist in Australia was based on his dexterity and versatility. He was a master of line and brush work—half-tone, colour, pen-and-ink and dry brush. In retirement he continued to work and, at the age of 80, designed a set of postage stamps commemorating George Bass and Matthew Flinders [qq.v.1]. 'A somewhat cadaverous, big-nosed, straight-backed man', Jardine had an austere manner and a gentle nature. He enjoyed golf and gardening. Survived by his wife and two daughters, he died on 24 February 1970 at his Killara home and was cremated.

G. Caban, *A Fine Line* (Syd, 1983); *Art Student* (Melb), 1, no 2, 1932; Art Training Inst (Melb), prospectus, 1950; *People*, 13 Aug 1952; *SMH*, 21 May 1928, 26 Oct 1940, 5 Feb 1964.

ANNE-MARIE GAUDRY

JARMAN, CHARLES ARTHUR (1882-1968), organist and composer, was born on 7 April 1882 at Macdonaldtown, Sydney, sixth child of John Shapley Jarman, a commercial traveller from England, and his native-born wife Elizabeth, née Biddles. Charles learned the piano in childhood, composed his first anthem for full choir at the age of 14, and qualified as an associate and licentiate in music. As a young man he was interim city organist at Sydney Town Hall. On 1 August 1906 he married Linda Pearl Dumbrell at the Methodist Church, Bulli.

Living at Bathurst by 1909, Jarman was organist and choirmaster at All Saints Anglican Cathedral. He also taught music at his studio in Howick Street and was associated with cathedral music at Goulburn. In 1912 he founded the Bathurst Philharmonic Choir which gained second place that year in the South Street competitions at Ballarat, Victoria. Among his compositions was a setting of *In Exitu Israel* (Psalm CXIV) for chorus and orchestra, and for which he is said to have

been awarded a doctorate of music by 'the English senate of the Intercollegiate University' in 1918. He often composed at the piano during the night and had the disconcerting habit of rousing family members from their beds to hear his latest inspiration.

In 1919 Jarman moved to Singleton to take the post of organist and choirmaster at All Saints Anglican Church. Its organ 'gave him more pleasure to play than any other'. From 1922 he held similar appointments in Sydney churches, at St Clement's, Marrickville, and St Peter's, Neutral Bay. While in England in 1924-25 and 1926-27, he is reported to have given recitals in London at the Crystal Palace and Queen's Hall, and to have performed in the presence of Queen Mary at the parish church of St Dunstan-in-the-West.

Back in Australia, Jarman was city organist at Launceston, Tasmania, for five years before returning to Sydney in 1933. He remained there (except for 1938-40 when he was at Armidale), worked at St Stephen's, Willoughby, St Mark's, Darling Point, and other suburban churches, and trained a public-service choir. In the mid-1940s he again went to Singleton. Extending his influence farther up the Hunter Valley, in 1945-53 he made weekly visits to St Luke's Anglican Church, Scone, to train the parish choir and teach the organ. Wherever he went, his pupils admired him and he brought out the best in them. He left for Sale, Victoria, in the mid-1950s and was then in Sydney before going to his beloved Singleton a third time in 1961.

In 1909 Jarman had been made a life member and honorary fellow of the Guild of Church Musicians, England. He was chief adjudicator at Ballarat's South Street contests in 1931; by 1964 he estimated that he had judged at seventeen eisteddfods in Australia, New Zealand and Britain. That year he retired to Dapto where he made his skills available to the local parish. Survived by his wife and three daughters, he died on 5 June 1968 at Hammondville Nursing Home and was cremated with Anglican rites.

G. Wilson, *Official History of the Municipal Jubilee of Bathurst, 1812-1912* (Syd, 1913); *Sun News-Pictorial*, 16 Apr 1931; *SMH*, 29 Sept 1964; *Singleton Argus*, 7 June 1968; *Scone Advocate*, 11 June 1968; information from Mrs J. Newman, Scone, and Mrs L. van Deinsen, Winmalee, NSW.

DAVID R. COLE

JEFFERY, GILBERT KELLY (1875-1954), horse-handler, was born on 23 October 1875 at Omeo, Victoria, ninth child of English-born parents Edward Jeffery, store-keeper, and his wife Selina, née Tonkin. Kell was sent to school in Melbourne. At the age of 12, for reasons of health, he spent a year in the country where he had his first contact with horses. After some years he was forced by illness to abandon plans to study law at the University of Melbourne and convalesced on an uncle's property near Guyra, New South Wales. Although he knew nothing of horse-handling, he successfully befriended an un-broken mare and rode her by the end of the first day. Intuition had led him to the basis of his subsequent 'method'—kindness and con-trol—which he developed and refined over the next sixty years.

While employed as a journalist at Charle-ville, Queensland, Jeffery married 19-year-old Alice Brown on 3 May 1900 at Roma with Methodist forms. For a time they lived at Cowra, New South Wales, where he owned the *Local News*. In 1914 an action against the rival *Cowra Guardian* for £400 damages was settled out of court; the *News* folded during World War I after a fire on the premises. Styl-ing himself 'Kell B. Jeffery', he began to give public demonstrations of horse-handling.

The key to his method was the 'magic hold' exerted by a 22-ft (6.7 m) bullock-hide lasso (with a metal ring on one end) placed around the horse's neck. Split-second holds (pulls) and releases were then applied to control the horse and to allow the handler to advance and retreat so as, in time, to stroke and mount it. The emphasis was on persuasion, not sub-mission. The headstall bridle and saddle were then introduced. Jeffery deplored the cruelty of the usual station method of breaking-in (a term he avoided) and of special tackle for mouthing. He conceded that some old-time, skilful breakers, like L. A. Skuthorp [q.v.11], had unwittingly applied the 'magic hold', but failed to appreciate its fundamental role.

Jeffery demonstrated his 'revolutionary' method all over Australia, claiming to have finally perfected it at the Cheriton Stud, Western Australia, in 1949. His method was widely popularized by H. J. Geddes, officer-in-charge of the University of Sydney's McGarvie Smith [q.v.11] Animal Husbandry Farm at Badgerys Creek, where in 1950 Jef-fery made a 15-minute film, *New Deal For Horses*, sponsored by the Rural Bank of New South Wales. That year the wiry and slightly built Jeffery summed up his technique: 'I talk to the horse and play with it gently. After a while it realizes I'm not such a bad guy, and I can do anything with it'. He had, however, his share of recalcitrant horses, for he added, 'I've had practically every bone in my body broken'. In 1952, when he published a four-part account of his method in the *Pastoral Review*, he claimed that, although he was 'stiff and slow' and had double-vision, he could still handle 'a six-year-old lively blood colt, with-out the slightest concern, let alone apprehen-sion'.

Survived by his wife and two sons, Jeffery died on 18 February 1954 at Kurri Kurri and was buried in the local cemetery. After his death Maurice Wright devised a modified form of the Jeffery method which is now widely used.

M. Wright, *The Jeffery Method of Horse Handling* (Armidale, NSW, 1973); G. Walsh, *Pioneering Days* (Syd, 1993); *Pastoral Review*, June, July, Aug, Sept 1952, Mar, Apr, June, Aug 1953, Mar 1954; *Cowra Free Press*, 18 Apr, 26 Aug 1914, 9 Oct 1920; *SMH*, 16 Feb 1926, 14, 23 Jan 1953; *Herald* (Melb), 6 May 1950.   G. P. WALSH

JEFFREY, MARGARET LILIAN (1896-1977), policewoman, was born on 14 July 1896 at Bundanoon, New South Wales, sec-ond child of Bundanoon-born parents Thomas Hines, farmer, and his wife Susan, née Brody. At St Saviour's Anglican Cathedral, Goul-burn, on 19 April 1919 Maggie married Walter George Baden Jeffrey (d.1931), an 18-year-old labourer. When George joined the New South Wales Police Force they settled in Sydney. Although she was too old to join the force at the age of 35, the commissioner of police William MacKay [q.v.10] accepted her application on 1 March 1932 because of her status as a policeman's widow with four children to support.

Like all policewomen at that time, Jeffrey was appointed a special constable and oper-ated in plain clothes. Her first post was at Clarence Street Police Station. She was transferred to the Criminal Investigation Branch on 26 June 1935 where her duties included inquiries into serious offences. On 24 October 1941 she was complimented by MacKay for good teamwork with other police in the case against Valda Stone and Mervyn Garvey, two criminals charged with at-tempted rape who were sentenced to seven years imprisonment. She was further com-mended by MacKay on 17 February 1942 for the capable and tactful manner with which she had treated a woman who was assaulted on the North Coast mail train in the previous September.

On 1 April 1943 Jeffrey was promoted special constable (1st class). After spending eleven years at the C.I.B., she was trans-ferred to Burwood (October 1946) and to Campsie (August 1947) police stations as officer-in-charge. She returned to the C.I.B. on 14 December 1949 and on 1 August 1950 became a special sergeant (3rd class). On 8 June 1952 she was again specially com-mended by the commissioner for excellent work performed in association with other policewomen in connexion with the arrest and successful prosecution of Thomas Edwin Ju-nor on a large number of charges relating to sex offences. Sergeant Jeffrey was officer-in-charge of women police in New South Wales from 25 January 1954 until she retired on 24 December 1956 with the rank of sergeant (2nd class).

A convert to Catholicism, Jeffrey was fondly remembered by her colleagues as a kind and maternal person who was helpful to new women police recruits and 'uncontrollable' girls. While undertaking all aspects of police work, except attending motor-vehicle accidents on the roads, she was expected to concentrate her attention on the needs of women and children. She was required to take statements from female witnesses in cases of indecent assault, carnal knowledge, rape, incest, abortion, child murder, concealment of birth and bigamy. In addition, she gave advice on domestic troubles and checked truancy.

After her retirement Mrs Jeffrey bought a small poultry farm and orchard near Jervis Bay. Late in life she returned to Sydney to live with one of her daughters. She died on 24 June 1977 at Marrickville hospital and was buried in Rookwood cemetery; her son and three daughters survived her.

A Centenary History of the New South Wales Police Force, 1862-1962 (Syd, 1963); *Advance! Australia* (Syd), Apr 1929, p 50; *Sun* (Syd), 6 Dec 1956; service record of M. Jeffrey (NSW Police Dept, Syd); information from Inspector L. Hoban, Bellevue Hill, Syd.   ALISON HOLLAND

JEFFRIES, SIR SHIRLEY WILLIAMS (1886-1963), lawyer and politician, was born on 28 February 1886 at Crompton, Lancashire, England, son of William Jeffries, Wesleyan minister, and his wife Mercy, née Wibmer. The family emigrated to Queensland in 1890, moving to South Australia eight years later. William held major appointments in the Methodist Church and was president (1904) of the South Australian Methodist Conference. Shirley was sent to schools at Toowoomba, Queensland, and Kadina, South Australia; he attended (1900-04) Prince Alfred College, Adelaide, like his elder brother Lewis [q.v.9], and was later president of Prince Alfred Old Collegians' Association. Proceeding to the University of Adelaide (LL.B., 1909), he competed in tennis and Australian Rules football at intervarsity level, and also played football for Norwood and Sturt in the State's senior league.

Jeffries served his articles with Bakewell, Stow [q.v.6] & Piper [q.v.11] and was admitted to the Bar on 23 April 1910. He practised in Adelaide, eventually as senior partner in Fisher, Jeffries, Brebner & Taylor. At the Methodist Church, Kent Town, on 15 April 1914 he married Catherine Emma Padman

(d.1933); their only child, a son, died at the age of 16. On 21 May 1935 at the Methodist Church, Rosefield, Jeffries married 25-year-old Berta Marion Saint. He served on the boards of several companies and colleges, and in 1939 became the first president of the National Fitness Council of South Australia.

His parliamentary career had begun in 1927 with his election to the House of Assembly as the Liberal Federation member for North Adelaide. Defeated in 1930, he was returned for the same seat in 1933; he won Torrens in 1938, lost it in 1944 and held it again in 1947-53. From 18 April 1933 to 6 May 1944 Jeffries was attorney-general, minister of education, and minister of industry and employment. He was passed over as leader of the party in favour of (Sir) Thomas Playford in 1938. During much of Jeffries' early period in cabinet, the State had been suffering from the effects of the Depression. Economies, especially in the field of education, were necessary but unpopular. Jeffries advocated religious instruction in state schools, a measure which was enacted in 1940; he also introduced area schools to replace scattered, small primary schools, a reform with educational and financial benefits. Acting on (Sir) Archibald Price's [q.v.] report, he introduced legislation to create separate boards for the Public Library, Museum and Art Gallery of South Australia.

On social issues, such as restrictions on the sale of liquor and facilities for gambling, Jeffries could be relied upon to support the campaigns of the Protestant churches. He was respected for his moral rectitude, even by those who were not sympathetic to the causes he espoused. During his last term in parliament he was stricken with cancer of the vocal cords. After surgery, he taught himself to speak again in a husky whisper and resumed public life. The courage and persistence with which he triumphed over his affliction won him added respect. He was knighted in 1953 and retired from parliament that year.

Sir Shirley often spoke warmly of the debt that he owed to his father and remained committed to the Methodist Church, both at the State and national levels. He was the most influential Methodist layman of his generation in South Australia and sat on numerous boards, councils and committees of the Church. Two new institutions established by the Methodists owed much to his support: Lincoln College (1952) at the University of Adelaide and Westminster School (1961) at Marion. Having been elected to the General Conference of the Methodist Church at the age of 31, Jeffries continued to be a representative until 1960. He was also a trustee of the Savings Bank of South Australia and a member (from 1934) of the Adelaide Club.

Tall and good-looking, Jeffries was an impressive debater, both in parliament and at the Methodist Conference. Some found him austere, but those closely associated with him knew his many acts of kindness to the needy. Survived by his wife and their son and daughter, he died of a coronary occlusion on 13 September 1963 at his Leabrook home and was cremated; his ashes were placed in his parents' grave at Payneham cemetery. The chapel at Westminster School commemorates him.

A. D. Hunt, *This Side of Heaven* (Adel, 1985); S. Cockburn, *Playford* (Adel, 1991); *PD* (SA), 1 Oct 1963; Methodist Church of A'sia (SA), *Minutes of Conference*, 1963; *Advertiser* (Adel), 16 Sept 1963; *SA Methodist*, 27 Sept 1963; information from Lady Jeffries, Leabrook, Adel.   ARNOLD D. HUNT

JENKINS, CHARLES ALFRED (1869-1955), Methodist minister, was born on 3 September 1869 at Maldon, Victoria, son of James Jenkins, miner, and his wife Cathrine, née Jeffrey, both from Cornwall. After completing his secondary schooling, Charles became a lay preacher and was accepted as a candidate for the Methodist ministry in 1893. The rapid expansion of Western Australia's population during the 1890s gold rushes prompted an appeal to the Victorian and Tasmanian Methodist conference for additional clergy, to which Jenkins responded in 1896. At Wesley Church, Perth, on 9 April 1902 he married 20-year-old Nellie Bertha Ida Thomas. Ordained that year, he held circuit appointments in turn at Northam, Coolgardie and West Perth, and subsequently ministered at Fremantle and Claremont.

In 1911 Jenkins was commissioned as chaplain in the Citizen Military Forces. He was twice appointed to the Australian Imperial Force in World War I, serving in troop-ships in 1915 and in England in 1917-19. While continuing in the Militia, he ministered at Subiaco and was superintendent (1923-28) of the Central Methodist Mission, Fremantle. In 1929 he was promoted to superintend the Perth Central Mission, at which he was based until his retirement in 1938. He published *A Century of Methodism in Western Australia, 1830-1930* (1930).

The combination of Evangelical fervour, a dignified presence and a warm disposition ensured that Jenkins attracted large and loyal congregations to his inner-city missions. He preached with authority, and, as chairman of Wesley College council, lent strong support to the cause of education. Survived by his son and daughter, he died on 4 December 1955 at Claremont and was cremated.

Two of his nephews served in the Method-

ist Church. SYDNEY JOHN (1903-1983) was born on 20 October 1903 at Kanowna, near Kalgoorlie, eldest child of Victorian-born parents Sydney Arthur Jenkins, goldminer, and his wife Ethel Lucy Ellinor, née Holt. Following his father's death, Sydney left school at the age of 13 to help provide an income for his mother, and was variously employed as a bootmaker, farm labourer and French polisher. In seeking ordination to the Methodist ministry in 1926, he was sent to Wesley College, South Perth, for a special course. After stints as a home missioner in four parishes, he was ordained in March 1930. On 7 August that year he married Elsie Hamlyn Davies (d.1949) at Wesley Church, Perth; his uncle Charles officiated.

A chaplain in the C.M.F. from 1938, Jenkins was mobilized for full-time duty in 1942 and transferred to the A.I.F. that year. He performed staff and regimental duties in Western Australia and Victoria. After the war he remained in the C.M.F. and was senior chaplain (Methodist) at headquarters, Western Command, in 1948-52. In 1945-64 he directed the Home Mission department in Western Australia. At Wesley Church, Perth, on 6 September 1950 he married Gladys Mary Thurza Bales, a civil servant. He was chairman of Wesley College council in 1967-78 and appointed A.M. in 1980. He died on 1 November 1983 in Royal Perth Hospital and was cremated with the forms of the Uniting Church; his wife survived him, as did the son and two daughters of his first marriage.

His brother GEORGE ARTHUR (1907-1981) was born on 4 July 1907 at Kalgoorlie. He attended Fremantle Boys' School, but left at 13 to work in a tailor's and menswear shop. At the age of 18, he formed a preaching group which took regular Church services throughout Perth. Entering the Methodist ministry in 1932, he was ordained in 1935 and later studied at the University of Western Australia (B.A., 1944). At Wesley Church, Perth, on 17 October 1935 he had married Ethel Henrietta Brooks, a clerk.

Jenkins filled several parish appointments—some in the central and eastern wheatbelt—before becoming superintendent of the Central Methodist Mission, Fremantle, in 1958 and chaplain to Fremantle Prison. He served as president of the State's Methodist Conference in 1961 and retired from the ministry in 1968. Chairman (1963-77) of the Kingswood College Council and a former president of the Prisoners' Aid Association, he was appointed A.O. in 1978. Survived by his wife, son and two daughters, he died on 31 August 1981 at Wollongong, New South Wales, and was cremated.

Western Methodist (Perth), Jan 1956, p 5; *Western Impact*, 3, no 16, Oct 1981, p 4, 3, no 37, Dec

1983, p 5; *West Australian*, 3 June 1978, 8 Dec 1955; Uniting Church Archives, Synod of WA (Perth); information from Messrs S. A. and D. Jenkins, Mt Yokine, WA.   PETER BOYCE

JENSEN, SIR JOHN KLUNDER (1884-1970), public servant, was born on 20 March 1884 at Sandhurst (Bendigo), Victoria, eldest child of native-born parents Thomas Peter Henry Jensen, draper and later publican, and his wife Margaret, née McNamara. John attended several state schools for broken periods and St Kilian's Catholic school, Bendigo, until the age of 11. He helped to support the family by taking odd jobs before joining the Post Office and Telegraph Department in 1898 as a messenger-boy. In 1900 he was transferred to Melbourne as a junior messenger in the Defence Department's ordnance stores branch, Victoria Barracks, at a time when it was dispatching equipment for the South African War. Next year he was appointed clerk in the same branch of the new Commonwealth Department of Defence. Jensen, who throughout his life was assiduously self-educated, attended classes in mathematics, engineering and chemistry at the Working Men's College and was promoted clerk (central administration) in December 1908.

In February 1911 he was appointed accountant and chief clerk of the Small Arms Factory, Lithgow, New South Wales, having been sent in the previous year to the United States of America for management training. Responsible for organizing the accounts and general administration of four factories, Jensen, an instinctive bureaucrat, pioneered 'scientific management' and made cost accounting his forte. On 27 September 1911 at the Church of Our Lady of the Sacred Heart, Randwick, Sydney, he married Maria Ruby Gordon; they were to have two sons and three daughters. Recalled to Melbourne in 1914 as a senior clerk, Jensen was promoted chief clerk. The administration of the department laboured under severe wartime pressures and, while managing the central registry, he initiated a new system of classifying and distributing inwards correspondence; he was also responsible for handling industrial disputes. In 1918 he was sent to Britain, by way of the U.S.A., to assist A. E. Leighton [q.v.10] at the British Ministry of Munitions. Jensen investigated the ways in which Britain had mobilized for munitions production in World War I.

Despite the international disarmament movement, the Australian government was committed to national self-sufficiency in munitions production. As a result of an agreement negotiated by the minister for defence (Sir) George Pearce [q.v.11], Jensen returned to Melbourne in 1921 with a bargain collection of surplus British plant. He had been one of the advocates of a scheme to build an arsenal at Tuggeranong, Federal Capital Territory, but the plan was abandoned, and in 1921 the Department of Defence established the Munitions Supply Board to install the newly acquired machinery and organize production. Jensen was the M.S.B.'s foundation secretary (1921) and controller (1937-39). In addition, he was chairman (1923-39) of the Defence Contract Board. The functions of these offices were transferred to the new Department of Supply and Development in 1939. As assistant-secretary (factory production), Jensen introduced a filing system based on cards instead of cumbersome book-registers.

Following the creation of a separate Department of Munitions in 1940, Jensen was its assistant-secretary and secretary (1942-48). A compulsive worker, he presided from his office, flanked by a 'tin hat', Bren-gun and portable typewriter. Tall, spare, and somewhat cadaverous, he was identified in the press as the 'human nerve centre of munitions manufacture in Australia'. In April 1948 he returned to the Department of Supply and Development as secretary. From 1943 he had been foundation chairman of the Secondary Industries Planning Commission in the Department of Post-War Reconstruction: the dubious procedures by which he encouraged General Motors-Holden [q.v.9] Ltd to begin manufacturing motor vehicles in Australia have been criticized. He retired on 31 July 1949. Three months later he joined the Commonwealth Immigration Planning Council, Department of Immigration. A fellow (1929) and life member (1949) of the Australasian Institute of Cost Accountants, he became a director of several companies. He had been appointed O.B.E. in 1938 and was knighted in 1950.

An adroit administrator, Sir John showed shrewdness in discovering ways and means, and his 'stubborn but subtle will' was no secret to colleagues. Energetic but withdrawn, he could appear 'grim and humourless' in pursuit of his duties, but privately harboured romantic and sentimental notions. Jensen numbered 'wandering in the bush' among his recreations and claimed a presence 'somewhat athletic in appearance'. He was an avid reader and writer, in his enthusiasm offering literary advice to Miles Franklin [q.v.8]. In December 1969 the Victorian headquarters of the Department of Supply was named Jensen House. Survived by a son and two daughters, Jensen died on 17 February 1970 at Hawthorn, Melbourne, and was buried in Box Hill cemetery.

S. J. Butlin, *War Economy 1939-1942* (Canb, 1955); L. J. Hartnett, *Big Wheels and Little Wheels* (Melb, 1964); S. J. Butlin and C. B. Schedvin, *War Economy 1942-1945* (Canb, 1977); *Melb Walker*, 38, 1967, 46, 1975; *Herald* (Melb), 7 Jan 1942, 26 Nov 1943, 31 Dec 1941; *Argus*, 18 Nov 1944, 9 Apr 1948; *Age* (Melb), 10 Dec 1969; *Australian* and *SMH*, 19 Feb 1970; *Nation* (Syd), 11 Oct 1958; A. T. Ross, The Arming of Australia: the Politics and Administration of Australia's Self Containment Strategy for Munitions Supply 1901-1945 (Ph.D. thesis, 1986, ADFA); J. L. Knight, Explosives in Australia (ms, ANUABL); Jensen papers, 1918-69 (AA, Melb); Miles Franklin papers (ML).

MARGARET STEVEN

JENSEN, LEO EJNER (1912-1978), wrestler and physiotherapist, was born on 18 February 1912 at Svendborg, on the island of Fyn, Denmark, son of Johan Christoffer Jensen, ship's carpenter, and his wife Juditte Vilhelmine, née Madsen. The family was poor and at 14 Leo went to sea as cabin-boy, jumping ship at Seattle, United States of America. Speaking little English, he worked as a builder's labourer before returning to Denmark at the age of 17. In April 1930 he emigrated to Canada.

At school Leo had enjoyed gymnastics. He began boxing and wrestling in the timber camps of British Columbia where he worked as a lumberjack. Having turned professional about 1933, he wrestled in Canada and Oregon, U.S.A., went to South Africa in 1935, and then to France, England, Germany and Denmark. Based in New York in 1936-37, he toured New Zealand in 1938 and in June came to Sydney, wrestling there, at Broken Hill and in other eastern States. Jensen was persuaded to settle at Newcastle by the owner of the city's new stadium. As the local hero, he took on Australian champions and visiting Americans such as 'Pat O'Shocker' and 'Rudi la Ditzi'. In 1940 he was naturalized.

Jensen began full-time duty with the Militia on 27 January 1942 at the 102nd Australian General Hospital, Tamworth. Transferred to the camp staff at Newcastle in May 1942, he was discharged medically unfit in the following year. He married a teacher and secretary Gladys May Pierre on 7 April 1943 at the Brown Street Congregational Church. In September 1944 he opened a gymnasium in Hunter Street; at first a masseur and bodybuilder, he studied hard and on 9 May 1947 was registered as a physiotherapist. He returned to wrestling in 1949. Short for a matman (5 ft 8 ins, 173 cm), muscular and well proportioned, he weighed 16 st. 4 lb. (103 kg) at his peak, compensating for lack of bulk by speed and craftiness. Jensen was a keen competitor and always a showman who recognized the element of entertainment in his sport, but scorned the later degeneration to outright vaudeville. Noted for his 'mule kick' and wristlock short-arm scissors technique, he was a 'good guy' when matched against the 'villains'. Jensen defeated 'Bonnie' Muir [q.v.] for the Australian heavyweight title at Leichhardt Stadium in December 1952. Thereafter he wrestled part time, sometimes teaming with 'Chief Little Wolf'.

With clean-cut, suntanned features, dark hair, a 20-inch (51 cm) neck, and a slight American accent, Jensen was a popular and colourful Newcastle identity who greeted people as 'pal'. He liberally distributed signed photographs. Footballers and police, as well as skinny kids and polio victims, trained at his academy which moved to the corner of King and Union streets in 1958. He taught physical culture in schools and was always available for charity exhibitions. Swimming all year round was his great enthusiasm. One of the sights at local beaches, he demonstrated his remarkable ability to walk on his hands there (and once on a ledge at The Gap, Watsons Bay, Sydney). He was a good family man and an authoritarian father, and liked to play the mouth organ and piano accordion, but worked long hours. A Freemason, he belonged to the Newcastle chapter of the Royal Arch Masons.

In 1958 Jensen suffered a heart attack. He rehabilitated himself, only to suffer a stroke in 1971. Survived by his wife, daughter and two sons, he died of myocardial infarction on 14 July 1978 at his Adamstown Heights home and was cremated. His widow and sons carried on his physiotherapy practice.

Sports Novels, Feb 1950, June 1953; *A.M.*, 25 Aug 1951; *Sun-Herald*, sporting section, 7 Dec 1952; *Newcastle Morning Herald*, 15 July 1975; information from Messrs L. and B. Jensen, and Mrs G. Jensen, Newcastle, NSW. CHRIS CUNNEEN

JENYNS, EBENEZER RANDOLPHUS (1865-1958) and SARAH ANN (1865-1952), surgical instrument makers and corset manufacturers, were husband and wife. Ebenezer was born on 27 July 1865 at Fortitude Valley, Brisbane, fourth son of English-born parents Joshua Jenyns, grocer, and his wife Betsy, née Willis. As a young man he was employed by Guyatt & Co., surgical instrument makers, Sydney. Sarah was born on 1 March 1865 at Largs, New South Wales, fifth child of Charles Thompson, a builder from Scotland, and his native-born wife Mary, née Bluford. Ebenezer and Sarah were married with Baptist forms on 5 October 1887 at the Burton Street Tabernacle, Woolloomooloo; they moved to Brisbane about 1896 and were to have eight children.

The family was poor, at the start. In 1905

Jenyns worked as a cutler, but by 1907 was also calling himself a surgical instrument maker. With his wife assisting, the business prospered, operating in 1909 from two addresses in Brisbane, one at 321 George Street. Yet the marriage and business partnership was shaky. From 1911 Sarah independently conducted her own business in George Street, making surgical instruments, corsets and belts. In 1910-12 she patented a series of corsets and 'improved' abdominal belts, and travelled abroad to expand her business. In England she contracted to have her corsets manufactured under licence by Symington & Co. of Market Harborough, Leicestershire. She also went to Canada, the United States of America and Germany, seeking to sell her products under licence. By 1915, although still running separate businesses, Sarah and Ebenezer formed the Jenyns Patent Corset Pty Co. to market her reducing, surgical and fashion corsets, accredited by the London Institute of Hygiene. In 1922 the firm (also called The House of Jenyns) was registered as a limited company.

Family relations became extremely acrimonious in the 1920s and remained so. Ebenezer continued to direct his own business, extended his field to include surgical corsets and lodged a patent for 'A Combination Surgical Substitute Corset' on 24 April 1923. That year his son John acquired Ebenezer's business: he traded as Jenyns Truss & Patent Pty Co. at 355 George Street, still using the trade mark of E. R. Jenyns. The split heralded long-term divisions in the family and its businesses.

Ebenezer reactivated his manufacturing in 1925 as the Improved Patent Corset Syndicate. He continued to advertise as a supplier of surgical goods and as a corset-maker in the 1930s and 1940s, though he was not a success in business. An active worker for the Young Women's Christian Association and widely known as an open-air preacher, he was a veritable 'bookworm' and a formidable debater. He eventually retired to Kuraby.

In 1916, having recovered from a stroke, Sarah had built three-storey premises at 327 George Street which remained the core of her business. Her son Herbert, who trained as a surgical instrument maker under Ebenezer during World War I, joined her about 1920. The business was sound and employed fifteen women. She took control of the Jenyns Patent Corset Co. Pty Ltd and in 1925 bought into another building, probably at 309-315 George Street. Sarah continued to patent improvements to her surgical corsets. In 1928 Herbert, by then the manager, branched into the manufacture of foundation garments and underclothing. The firm continued to grow, despite competition in the 1920s from Berlei

[qq.v.13 Burley] Ltd (their main rivals), the Gossard Co. and Symington.

Jenyns prospered as a protected industry in World War II, receiving large contracts to supply garments to the army and navy. In 1946 Herbert became managing director of a new Jenyns company. Sarah lapsed into senility and was placed under a protection order in 1948. Three years later, in the Supreme Court, it was alleged that Herbert had unduly influenced his mother to transfer 13 655 shares in the company to him. She died on 29 February 1952 at Huntingtower, her home at Annerley, and was buried with Presbyterian forms in South Brisbane cemetery. Her estate was sworn for probate at £51 001. Survived by five of his six sons and by one of his two daughters, Ebenezer died on 13 July 1958 at Rocklea and was buried in Toowong cemetery with the forms of the Churches of Christ. Herbert continued to manage the company which expanded extensively in the 1960s; he became a millionaire and a noted yachtsman.

Courier-Mail, 15 Mar 1951, 15 July 1958; *Herald* (Melb), 15, 20 Mar 1951, 24 June 1967; Cwlth Patent and Trade Marks records (Australian Industrial Property Organization, Canb); information from Mr H. C. Jenyns, Brisb.

MARGARET MAYNARD

JEROME, JERRY (1874-1943), stockman and boxer, was born on 24 May 1874 at Jimbour Station, 10 miles (16 km) north of Dalby, Queensland, son of Wollon Charlie, an Aboriginal labourer, and his wife Guli. Jerry was of Yiman descent and won local renown as a horseman, athlete and show boxer. About 1906 he married Alice Davis at Dalby. He entered the ring officially in 1908—at an age when most fighters are 'washed-up'. Competing at the Olympic Stadium, Albert Street, Brisbane, in August 1912 he defeated 'Black Paddy', the noted Aboriginal middleweight from Western Australia, over sixteen rounds before a large crowd and the newfangled camera. Jerome's career of 63 fights for 39 wins included knocking out fellow contender Charlie Godfrey in four rounds on 7 September 1912 in Brisbane to claim the vacant Australian middleweight crown. He became the first of many Aboriginal titleholders.

Standing 5 ft 8½ ins (174 cm) tall, and fighting at weights between 11 st. 2 lb. (70.8 kg) and 12 st. 1 lb. (76.7 kg), Jerome was neither a trained nor a scientific boxer. He confused his opponents with his unorthodox southpaw stance, his dancing and weaving tactics (which greatly amused the crowds) and his dazzling bursts of hurricane-like speed punching. He had a quick right lead, could punch effectively at long range or close quarters, and his left (somewhat 'agricultural') swing was his most dangerous blow. Thirty-two of his wins were by a knockout or by the retirement of his opponent through exhaustion. He had memorable fights against highly rated light-heavyweights, losing twice to Dave Smith and four times to Les O'Donnell, 'the cleverest boxer in the country'. Jerome first lost to O'Donnell on 2 November 1912, after claiming a low blow in the fourteenth round (a view the referee did not share) and refusing to continue. On 14 December that year he suffered a universally unpopular points decision over twenty rounds against the same opponent. In November 1913 he fought himself to exhaustion before losing to O'Donnell on a technical knockout. Jerome also experienced exhaustion at times when he fought with too much weight. Not only did he have a reputation for dodging roadwork, but his age worked against maintaining his fighting-weight. R. L. 'Snowy' Baker [q.v.7] once remarked that, if Jerome could keep fit, 'he would be the greatest middleweight fighter in the world'. Commentators were adamant that he never abused alcohol.

While managed by George Lawrence in 1913, Jerome fought fourteen times (a total of 161 rounds) in nine months against top, sometimes heavier and imported boxers. He defeated the French champion Ercole de Balzac twice in early 1913, earning ovations from the Sydney crowd. On 20 December, at the end of this hectic period, he lost his title to Arthur Evenden, on points over twenty rounds. He was next trained by Peter Felix, a West Indian who was a former Australian heavyweight champion. In 1914 Jerome had only four bouts, three against visiting boxers, losing twice to the Frenchman Jules Dubourg and once to the American Eddie McGoorty after Jerome's arm was broken in the fifth round. He fought nine times in 1915, then retired from a ring career that had reaped £5000. A quarter of his earnings was placed in trust, always notoriously difficult for Aborigines to access.

Jerome fought on in boxing tents before retiring penniless to Cherbourg Aboriginal Settlement where he coached youngsters. He maintained his independent and fighting ways: the Chief Protector of Aborigines J. W. Bleakley [q.v.7] claimed that he sought to 'obstruct discipline and defy authority'. Survived by his three sons and one of his two daughters, Jerome died on 27 September 1943 at Cherbourg and was buried in Murgon cemetery, among his people, whom he never denied in the White world of boxing.

P. Corris, *Lords of the Ring* (Syd, 1980); C. Tatz, *Aborigines in Sport* (Adel, 1987) and *Obstacle Race* (Syd, 1995); *Courier-Mail*, 9 Sept, 16 Dec 1912, 24 Feb 1913, 10 Oct 1942; *Sporting Judge*, 19 Apr 1913, 19 Dec 1914; *Sporting Globe*, 6 Oct 1943; *Smith's Weekly*, 23 Oct 1943; *Herald* (Melb), 2 Aug 1958.
RICHARD BROOME

JERREMS, CAROL JOYCE (1949-1980), photographer, was born on 14 March 1949 at Ivanhoe, Melbourne, third child of Victorian-born parents Eric Alfred Jerrems, clerk to a stock-and-station agent, and his wife Joyce Mary, née Jacobs. Carol studied photography at Prahran Technical School in 1967-70, graduating with a diploma of art and design. An outstanding student, she won the Walter Lindrum [q.v.10] scholarship (1968), the Institute of Australian Photographers award (1970) and first prize in the Kodak Students Photographic Competition (1971). After obtaining a certificate (1971) from the Technical Teachers' College, Hawthorn, she taught part time in Melbourne (Coburg and Heidelberg technical schools), Sydney (Hornsby and Meadowbank technical colleges) and Hobart (Tasmanian School of Art) until 1979.

From the outset, Jerrems was interested in the expressive possibilities of the photographic medium, declaring that she was 'an artist whose tool of expression is the camera'. She concentrated on photographing people; her subjects included her students, and her friends and acquaintances. Her first photographs were documentary in style, but by the mid-1970s the scenes she photographed were often contrived. She used a non-exploitative approach, based on the consent of her subjects. For Jerrems, photography had a crucial social role: 'the society is sick and I must help change it'. Her photographs were a means of 'bringing people together' and offered affirmative views of certain aspects of contemporary life. With Virginia Fraser, she published *A Book About Australian Women* (Melbourne, 1974), to which she contributed the photographs.

One-person exhibitions of her work were held at the National Gallery of Victoria (1973), the Arts Council Gallery, Sydney (1974), and the Australian Centre for Photography, Sydney (1976 and 1978). She also participated in numerous group exhibitions. They included 'Erotica' (with Henry Talbot) at Brummels Gallery of Photography, Melbourne (1972), 'Womanvision' at the Sydney Filmakers Co-op (1973), and 'Heroes and Anti-Heroes' (with Rennie Ellis) and 'Four Australian Women', both at the Photographers Gallery, Melbourne, in 1975 and 1978 respectively. Macquarie University, Sydney, commissioned her in 1977 to produce a folio of photographs that expressed 'the spirit of the university'.

In 1975 Jerrems was awarded an overseas travel grant from the Visual Arts Board of the Australia Council and an experimental film grant from the Australian Film Commission. Her 16-mm black-and-white film, *Hangin' About,* was completed in 1978. She also produced the publicity and production stills for *In Search of Anna* (1979), directed by Esben Storm.

For some years Jerrems practised yoga, which she also taught. The photographs she took in 1978 at the Satyananda Ashram, Mangrove Mountain, New South Wales, were among the last she exhibited. In 1979 she fell ill with Budd-Chiari syndrome. She died on 21 February 1980 at Prahran and was cremated. Her archive of photographs was donated to the National Gallery of Australia, Canberra.

Although one critic regarded her work as uneven—'she took a casual approach'—Jerrems's talents as a photographer were widely recognized. With her camera 'firmly pointed at the heart of things', she produced a body of photographs that symbolized the hopes and aspirations of the counter-culture in Australia in the 1970s. The retrospective exhibition, 'Living in the 70s: Photographs by Carol Jerrems', mounted by the N.G.A., toured Australia in 1990-91.

B. Jenyns and H. Ennis (comp), *Living in the 70s: Photographs by Carol Jerrems,* Aust National Gallery travelling exhibition, cat (Hob, 1990); G. Newton, *Shades of Light* (Canb, 1988); A-M. Willis, *Picturing Australia* (Syd, 1988); C. Moore, *Indecent Exposures* (Syd, 1991); *Sunday Observer Mag,* 14 July 1974; *Sun News-Pictorial,* 12 July 1980; *Age* (Melb), 27 Aug 1991; National Gallery of Aust (Canb) files; information from Mr K. Jerrems, Heidelberg, Melb.   HELEN ENNIS

JESSOP, JOHN CECIL (1892-1968), chairman of the Melbourne and Metropolitan Board of Works, was born on 29 March 1892 at North Carlton, Melbourne, second child of Victorian-born parents John Coote Jessop, telegraphist, and his wife Louise Esther, née Portway. The eldest son of a large family, Cecil began work at 14 as a telegraph-boy to supplement the family income. He described himself as a Baptist minister when he enlisted in the Australian Imperial Force, with which he served from July 1915 to June 1919: he saw action on the Western Front with the 8th Battalion and Australian Corps headquarters as a stretcher-bearer. In her parents' home at Clifton Hill, Melbourne, on 13 September 1919 he married with Baptist forms Catherine Rose Robinson (d.1966); their only child died in 1923. Working as an accountant, Jessop made his way up to become manager of the mortgage and investment department of the Trustees, Executors & Agency Co. Ltd; he was later a director of a home-building and finance company.

His long career of public service began in 1930 when he was elected to the Heidelberg City Council. He was mayor in 1935 and a councillor until 1940. In 1934 he had been chosen as commissioner for Heidelberg on the M.M.B.W. where he rose to be vice-chairman (1937) of the finance committee. In 1940 he was appointed chairman.

Jessop took over the powerful M.M.B.W. at a difficult time. Public dissatisfaction was widespread, relations with other government agencies were poor and staff morale was low. Wartime restrictions on manpower and finance delayed overdue extensions to the water supply and sewerage systems, but Jessop's frank, open style and wide-ranging consultation soon smoothed relations on all sides. His concern for the well-being of workers and his firmly applied set of 'ideals' produced harmonious industrial relations within the board. In the M.M.B.W.'s dealings with constituent metropolitan councils Jessop was fortunate that parliament finally approved reforms to the board's structure in 1944 which gave better representation to newer suburbs and took account of population shifts.

Careful financial management during the years of World War II had produced a healthy reserve fund and lower rates, but the reserve proved inadequate to meet the needs of Melbourne's postwar boom. The delay in constructing the Upper Yarra Dam (which did not begin to fill until 1957) condemned Melbourne to years of inadequate water pressure and summer restrictions. Jessop skilfully guided the M.M.B.W. through a period of massive growth and modernization, indicated by the increase in the number of new houses connected with water from 145 in 1942-43 to almost 15 000 in 1955-56. In the same period capital expenditure rose from £100 000 to £6.5 million, while the number of board employees barely doubled. In a 'city of outgrown services' and 'heartbreak streets' it was a tribute to Jessop's leadership and his encouragement of an ideal of service that the M.M.B.W. continued to be held in generally high regard by both the public and government.

Largely due to Jessop's initiative, the board's powers to shape and direct Melbourne's development were greatly increased in 1949 when it was given authority to prepare a planning scheme for the city. The 'Master Plan', released with a fanfare of publicity in 1954, was a crucial first step towards improving the quality of urban life and marked the end of totally uncontrolled and uncoordinated growth. Jessop retired in February 1956, optimistic that the Board's 'blueprint' for future growth would alleviate some of the most pressing problems, at least in regard to the supply of essential services.

An unpretentious man who often took his cut lunch into the canteen to eat with the board staff, Jessop was firm in decision-making and enjoyed the confidence of those who worked closely with him. His private life was largely given over to the expression of his 'abounding Christian charity' from which many of his ideals of management also stemmed. He was a tireless supporter of community and philanthropic projects, an active advocate of Moral Rearmament in the late 1940s, and a keen gardener and surf fisherman. For many years treasurer of the Sutherland Homes for Children, in 1958 he published a book on the life and work of their founder Sulina Sutherland [q.v.6]. In retirement he built a cottage in the grounds of the Diamond Creek homes where he lived as manager until ill health obliged him to enter the Diamond Valley Community Hospital, Greensborough, which he had helped to found. He died there on 15 March 1968 and was cremated.

T. Dingle and C. Rasmussen, *Vital Connections* (Melb, 1991); *MMBW Officers' J*, Jan 1956; *Argus*, 14 Feb 1940; *East Yarra News*, 20 Mar 1968; information from MMBW and from a retired member of the Sutherland Homes Cte.

CAROLYN RASMUSSEN

JEWELL, WILLIAM RALPH (1894-1975), chemist and public servant, was born on 15 July 1894 at Geelong, Victoria, son of James Thomas Jewell, watchmaker, and his wife Emma, née Williams, both Victorian born. Educated at Geelong College (dux 1912), Bill won a scholarship to Ormond [q.v.5] College, University of Melbourne (B.Sc., 1916; M.Sc., 1922). During World War I he was sent with a select group of young Australian scientists to Britain where he worked with the Ministry of Munitions. Jewell was elected an associate (1917), fellow (1923) and life member (1959) of the Royal Institute of Chemistry. When the war ended, he studied at the University of Sheffield (B.Met., 1919). Returning to Melbourne, he was appointed senior chemist (metallurgy) at the Munitions Supply Laboratories, Maribyrnong. At St James's Anglican Church, Sydney, on 17 October 1921 he married Vera Ironsides Dent; they were to have a son and a daughter.

In 1926 Jewell joined the Victorian Public Service as agricultural research chemist. Six years later he was also given control of the chemical laboratories of the health and mines departments; he continued to administer the combined State laboratories until his retirement in 1959. Meantime, he was appointed chief chemist of the Department of Agriculture in 1948. Due to his skills as a scientist

and as an administrator, he was placed on numerous committees and frequently consulted by government and industry. He took a leading role in reorganizing the beet-sugar industry at Maffra, and advised the Federal government on the feasibility of producing power alcohol from cereals. In association with the Commonwealth Department of Primary Industry, he was involved in the introduction of specifications and standard methods of analysis for foods used by the Australian and allied armed forces. In addition, he was active on the food additives committee of the National Health and Medical Research Council and on the food standards committee of the Victorian Department of Health. In his retirement he wrote *Food Additive Control in Australia* (1961).

Apart from the widespread influence Jewell exercised in his formal duties, he was prominent in the work of the Standards Association of Australia, and in the inception and development of the National Association of Testing Authorities. A founding member (1946) of the council of N.A.T.A., he was Victorian representative, executive-member (1954-62) and chairman (1958-61). Jewell devoted considerable time to the Royal Australian Chemical Institute, first as an office-bearer in the Victorian branch, then as general secretary (1933-43) and finally as president (1945-46); he had become an associate of the institute in 1919 and a fellow in 1924. He was also made a fellow (1958) of the Pharmaceutical Society of Victoria.

Described by a colleague as somewhat shy, sharp of mind, hard working, down-to-earth, honest and humorous, Jewell 'enjoyed a barnyard joke, Thursday-night-with-his-mates at the Kelvin Club and reefing money from the poker machines, whenever he was in Sydney'. He died on 28 January 1975 at Glen Iris and was cremated; his wife and son survived him.

Roy Aust Chemical Inst, *Procs*, Apr 1975; *Herald* (Melb), 22 May 1926; *Sun News-Pictorial*, 16 July 1959; *Weekly Times* (Melb), 22 July 1959.

E. J. O'BRIEN

JOHN, ERIC DANIEL BEVAN (1902-1968), radio producer, was born on 30 August 1902 at Bathurst, New South Wales, son of Bedlington Ernest John, a railway engineer from Tasmania, and his New Zealand-born wife Evelyn Mary, née Hargreaves. Educated at Miss Hamilton's and Trinity Hill State schools, Hobart, Eric spent some time in South Africa. He was employed by the Public Library of Tasmania on a part-time basis (from 1926) and as full-time assistant-librarian on £160 a year from 1929.

Described as 'a well-read and well-educated man', he carried out 'responsible and technical work'.

In his spare time John freelanced as a journalist and reviewed books for the *Mercury*. He was cubmaster (from 1927) and scoutmaster (1933-37) of the 3rd Hobart (The Hutchins School) Scout Group. Rejected for military service in World War II on medical grounds, he supported organizations concerned with soldiers' welfare. In the 1940s he trod the boards with the Hobart Repertory Theatre Society, wrote an audience-participation session entitled *Charades* and co-produced *Richard of Bordeaux* for the Hobart Theatre Guild. His interests also included biography and the history of music, and he collected records that ranged from classics to swing.

Convinced of the educational value of radio, from 1935 John had assisted the Australian Broadcasting Commission's 'Children's Session' and contributed scripts to the series, 'Historic Tasmania', for which he drew on his knowledge of early Australian history. By the time he joined the A.B.C. in May 1942 as a presentation officer, he was considered to have a good radio technique, as well as a flair for writing and arranging material. A prolific worker, he devised and produced features, musical comedy, quizzes and dance-band shows.

John was transferred to Sydney in July 1950 as a producer in the drama and features department. He gathered scripts for 'Quality Street', 'No Mean Company' and 'Poet's Corner'. Affable and charming, he was especially good at casting and encouraging young actors, among them Rod Taylor and Rosemary Hills. In 1952 he took over the production of Gwen Meredith's long-running serial, 'Blue Hills'. Enjoying her complete confidence, for the next sixteen years he worked tirelessly to maintain the highest standards. The programme expressed contemporary Australian attitudes and values, and was immensely popular with both country and city listeners.

Serious and sensitive, he understood human nature and its frailties. Neil Hutchison believed that John waged an unrelenting war 'to keep in subjugation the rebellious heart of which he was always conscious'. Christopher Koch based the character, Martin Gadsby, in *The Doubleman* (London, 1985) on him and remembered the many soirées John held in his Potts Point flat, often holding court in bed. Towards the end of his life, he became cranky, cynical and unhappy. He smoked cigarettes, dressed well and wore a polka-dot bow-tie. Because of high blood pressure, he was never made a permanent member of the A.B.C.'s staff; his salary remained modest, obliging him to live sparingly. He died of cerebral vascular disease on 5 August 1968 in St Vincent's Hospital and was cremated with Methodist forms.

K. S. Inglis, *This is the ABC* (Melb, 1983); *Radio Active*, Sept 1968; *SMH*, 7 Aug 1968; ABC Document *and* Radio Archives, Syd; Hal Porter papers (ML).
                                                    MARION CONSANDINE

JOHNSON, GERTRUDE EMILY (1894-1973), coloratura soprano and theatre administrator, was born on 13 September 1894 at Prahran, Melbourne, second child of George James Johnson (d.1953), professor of music, and his wife Emily Gertrude, née Pridham, both Victorian born. Educated at Presentation Convent, Windsor, at the age of 17 Gertrude enrolled—on (Dame) Nellie Melba's [q.v.10] advice—as a student of Anne Williams at the University Conservatorium of Music. In 1915, when Melba founded a women's singing school at the Albert Street Conservatorium, East Melbourne (later the Melba Memorial Conservatorium), Williams transferred there, taking Johnson with her. Melba accepted Johnson into her classes, eventually endowing her with her own personal cadenzas, a valuable professional asset. Fritz Hart [q.v.9], director at Albert Street, had a particular interest in Mozartian opera and introduced Johnson to what was to be the core of her repertoire throughout her career.

Through Melba, in 1917 she met Guido Cacialli, the leading bass of the wartime-stranded Gonsalez Opera Company. Johnson subsequently toured twice with remnants of the company: to outback Queensland and New South Wales as part of Count Ercole Filippini's troupe, and in 1919 to Melbourne, Sydney, Adelaide and New Zealand with the Rigo Grand Opera Company. In February 1921 she sailed for London where she was engaged for coloratura roles by the British National Opera Company. Her long broadcasting career began on 8 January 1923 when she sang the Queen of the Night in *The Magic Flute* for the first broadcast and operatic programme transmitted from Covent Garden by the British Broadcasting Corporation. She recorded extensively thereafter on the Columbia Gramophone Co.'s dark blue label, notably popular arias in English.

A tall, regal woman, classically handsome rather than beautiful, fair skinned, dark haired and dark eyed, Johnson toured Britain as a concert singer several times, appearing at music festivals and in large-scale oratorio events. Noted for her Mozart interpretations and her ability to sing his roles in the original keys, she performed at the Royal Albert Hall, Queen's Hall and Covent Garden. Her appearances with the B.N.O. at Covent Garden were as Micaela in *Carmen* (1922), Marguerite in *Faust* (1923) and the Princess in Holst's *The Perfect Fool* (1924), but she also sang from the standard bel canto repertoire with that company, which was primarily a touring one. On 7 December 1926 she sang Musetta to Melba's final London appearance as Mimi at the Old Vic Theatre.

Although she became engaged to Dr Pullar Strecker in 1929, Johnson was never to marry. She returned to Australia in 1935 and abandoned her singing career. By then she was of independent means and set about establishing a national theatre movement— modelled on the Old Vic and Sadler's Wells —to provide training and employment at home for Australian performing artists who were being lost to the larger European and American markets. She had in mind a national body which she would co-ordinate, but which would leave the States autonomous. There was support for the proposition in four States; it encountered opposition in Western Australia and New South Wales. The goodwill of a Victorian pressure group, which included (Sir) Errol Knox and James Hume Cook [qq.v.9,8] (the first chairman of the board), determined a Victorian base for her venture. They won her State government support and the directorship of the Australian National Theatre Movement, a position she retained for life. Her wealth, her forceful personality and her social connexions were significant elements in the success of the drama, ballet and opera performances she then staged. In a period of economic depression, when the theatrical life of the country had dimmed, the results were grasped as heralding a new and nationally focussed era for locally made versions of the performing arts.

The A.N.T.M. was inaugurated on 4 December 1935. The first production, a Christmas pageant, was staged in December 1936 at the Princess Theatre. *As You Like It* and *The Barretts of Wimpole Street* followed in 1937. Two years later the first opera productions, *The Flying Dutchman* and *The Marriage of Figaro*, were produced by the owner of the Princess Theatre, Garnet Carroll [q.v.13]. While drama and ballet were to remain major concerns, the A.N.T.M.'s real success was in opera. An opera school was founded in 1938 and a ballet school in 1939.

With the outbreak of World War II and, consequently, no imported competition, the A.N.T.M.'s activities escalated. Fifteen operas—most of them conducted by the octogenarian Gustave Slapoffski [q.v.11]—were produced during the war years. The musical director was the composer Edith Harrhy [q.v.], later replaced by another composer James Penberthy. In 1948 a seven-week season of opera at the Princess Theatre,

given by a company consisting of 45 principal singers, a chorus of 110, 45 dancers, and an orchestra on loan from the Australian Broadcasting Commission, drew 73 000 patrons and the subscription list stood at 2000. Further successful seasons followed in 1949-51, as part of a Three Arts Festival, which also included a ballet season and a season of drama, and which received a Victorian government subsidy of £10 000 in addition to an increased annual grant of £8000.

After these three successful years, the A.N.T.M. collaborated with Clarice Lorenz's recently formed New South Wales National Opera Company to create the basis for a national opera company. In its first season it played at the Tivoli Theatre in Melbourne during Johnson's 1951 A.N.T.M. Arts Festival. The highly successful joint-season of 1952 was staged in Melbourne, Sydney and Brisbane, with John Brownlee [q.v.7] returning home for the Don and Scarpia, and Marie Collier [q.v.13] making a sensational début as Santuzza. At the end of the season the Lorenz group renamed itself the National Opera of Australia. Since Johnson had been appointed O.B.E. in 1948 for her work with the National Theatre Opera Company she was offended; she refused further joint ventures and mounted an ambitious interstate tour instead. In 1954, having outrun her rival, Johnson's company was chosen to present the royal command performance of opera during the visit of Queen Elizabeth II.

The success of the eight-week 1954 season and that of the combined Johnson-Lorenz seasons led to the formation of the Australian Elizabethan Theatre Trust, but Johnson kept her group apart. With the loss of personnel to the Trust (later reorganized as the Australian Opera) which offered better financial rewards and a more professional future, the A.N.T.M. seasons began to dwindle in quantity and quality. An attempt to stem the tide by launching a building fund in 1956 for a National Theatre subsequently failed. A series of fires in premises used by the group sapped initiative and morale. The investment of the remaining building fund, however, permitted the National Theatre to open in 1974 in a renovated cinema at St Kilda, though only the schools remained, with Ballet Victoria and the Victorian Opera Company as the performing bodies. Gertrude Johnson died on 28 March 1973 at Malvern and was cremated. Her estate, sworn for probate at $117 034, provided scholarships for students of the A.N.T.M.

Under Johnson's leadership the Australian National Theatre Movement had provided the basis for later national ballet and opera companies, and acted as a training-ground for the artists who stocked such groups and who ultimately fostered the talents of a younger generation.

B. and F. Mackenzie, *Singers of Australia* (Melb, 1967); J. Cargher, *Opera and Ballet in Australia* (Syd, 1977); A. Gyger, *Opera for the Antipodes* (Syd, 1990); F. Van Straten, *National Treasure* (Melb, 1994); *Age* (Melb), 24 July 1957, 4, 6 Feb, 5 July 1960, 30 Mar 1973; *Herald* (Melb), 6 Jan 1930, 27 June 1935, 3 May 1951, 1, 5 July 1967, 29 Mar 1973; G. Johnson papers *and* National Theatre Movement papers (Performing Arts Museum Archives, Vic Arts Centre, Melb); Melba Memorial Conservatorium Archives, Univ Melb; D. Munro papers (LaTL); H. Schilderberger papers, Aust Jewish Hist Soc collection (LaTL); T. Radic, taped interview with Johnson, 1972; information from the late Mr J. Truscott and Ms I. Mitchell.

MAUREEN THÉSÈSE RADIC

JOHNSON, HERBERT VICTOR (1889-1962), trade unionist and politician, was born on 25 October 1889 at Northampton, Western Australia, son of Arthur Johnson, an ex-convict farmer and miner, and his wife Catherine, née Hartigan. Vic attended the local convent school, then worked as a shearer in the Murchison, Gascoyne and north-western districts of the State. When the Australian Workers' Union organized the shearers in Western Australia in 1908, he took the No.1 membership ticket and was to retain it until the end of his life. On 29 January 1913 at the Catholic Church, Geraldton, he married Ethel May Lucas. Tall and broad shouldered, he reputedly 'sheared 3761 sheep in 17½ days in 1914—a world record at that time'.

In his early years as a unionist Johnson was prominent in opposing the use of Asian and unpaid Aboriginal shearers. He was one of the leaders in the agitation for better living-quarters which led to the Shearers' Accommodation Act (1912). In 1916 he became organizing secretary of the pastoral division of the Western Australian branch of the A.W.U. Energetic and straightforward, he won widespread respect during the difficult times of the 1920s and 1930s by upholding standards and conditions for pastoral workers. He also secured a 44-hour week for the lead miners of Northampton and Ajana. His secretaryship (1920-34) of the Geraldton branch of the Australian Labor Party brought him close to the local member J. C. Willcock [q.v.12], premier in 1936-45.

Having withstood several offers to contest pre-selection for parliamentary seats, Johnson was elected State secretary of the A.W.U. in 1936 and moved from Geraldton to Highgate, an inner suburb of Perth. He was a director of the Labor newspaper, *Westralian Worker*, and of 6KY, the party's radio station (established 1941). But he retained his links with Geraldton, which formed part of Australia's largest Federal constituency, Kalgoorlie. When the sitting member A. E.

Green [q.v.9] died in 1940, Johnson easily secured endorsement for the by-election in November and held the seat without difficulty until his retirement in 1958. In Canberra he spoke sparingly and sensibly; one of his favourite themes was the need to diversify Western Australia's narrow industrial base.

On John Curtin's [q.v.13] death in July 1945, Johnson became the senior Western Australian Labor member and was elected by caucus to the vacant place in cabinet. In the Chifley [q.v.13] administration of 1945-49, Johnson was appointed minister for the interior, partly in recognition of his enthusiasm for northern development. He was also assistant-minister for works and housing (1945-46). Although he proved a loyal and competent member of the team, he was responsible for few striking initiatives. His political opponents criticized him for retaining the federal general presidency (1943-47) of the A.W.U. while a member of cabinet. As chairman (1945-49) of the Australian War Memorial's board of management, he gained government approval to enlarge the premises to take account of World War II.

After Labor was defeated in 1949 and Chifley died in 1951, Johnson grew increasingly unhappy about the direction taken by the party under H. V. Evatt [q.v.]. Johnson remained in the A.L.P. following the 1955 split, but in 1957 was one of a handful of party veterans who publicly voiced their concerns. He deplored Evatt's 'raising of the sectarian issue' and lamented Labor's 'lack of humanity' and loss of idealism under his leadership. The State executive responded by voting to withhold Johnson's re-endorsement in future elections, knowing that he had already decided to retire. Survived by his wife, two of his three sons and three of his four daughters, he died on 10 July 1962 at Royal Perth Hospital. He was accorded a state funeral and was buried in Karrakatta cemetery. Respected by most of his opponents and colleagues alike, Vic Johnson was a sterling example of a Labor tradition now virtually extinct.

Westralian Worker, 25 Oct 1940; *West Australian*, 11 July 1962; C. Menagh, *Westralian Worker* and the A.W.U. (ms, BL).

G. C. BOLTON

JOHNSON, JACK ('MOOLBONG') (c.1868-1943), Aboriginal 'clever man' and song-maker, was born about 1868 and was a Kaliyarrkiyalung—a Wiradjuri man 'from the Lachlan River' in western New South Wales. Jack was removed from his family and sent to Moolbong and was also named after that pastoral station in the Willandra region. He became a skilled stockman, but was lamed by a fall from a horse. Living among and respected by the Ngiyampaa people whose country was to the north of Willandra Creek, he was nicknamed Kiitya. In 1926 the Aborigines Protection Board assembled the Ngiyampaa at Carowra Tank Aboriginal Station, near Ivanhoe, before moving them in 1933 to a new station at Menindee. Moolbong spoke Ngiyampaa (the Wangaaypuwan variety) and Paakantji, as well as Wiradjuri. He spent his last years in Wiradjuri territory, based with his son's family at 'the Bend', the 'mission' near Condobolin.

When the anthropologists Ronald and Catherine Berndt visited Menindee in September-October 1943, Fred Biggs [q.v.13] and Jack King spoke of the late Moolbong as one of the *wirringan* or 'clever' men. These individuals, 'of remarkable character and personality', possessed and controlled the secret knowledge of their people and also practised medicine. Among other 'magical powers', they were believed to be able to read minds, to determine the cause of a person's death and to make rain. They were 'of immense social significance, the psychological health of the group depending on faith in their powers'. Ronald Berndt mistakenly assumed that Biggs, King and other Ngiyampaa were Wiradjuri, like Moolbong. From those he interviewed, Berndt learned that Moolbong was the last man 'who could have brought about a revival of the old "laws"'. He had died on 24 June 1943 at the mission, Condobolin, survived by his son John and daughter Leila. His wife Mary had predeceased him. He was buried with Catholic rites in Condobolin cemetery.

Stories of Moolbong's power still circulate. He 'was greatly feared by the Wembawemba [whose country traversed the Murray River south-east of Swan Hill] as he was reputed to have "sung" his brother-in-law, Ned Briley, a Wembawemba man'. Moolbong and Biggs were the most prolific song-makers among the 'Carowra Tank mob' when some of the last songs 'in language' were composed. Their words were often chastening. 'You might do something wrong, they'd make a song out of you straight away!' There are stories of Moolbong curing snake-bite and making rain, disappearing without warning and appearing in other forms. His enduring memorial is the handful of witty and allusive songs in his own language, tape-recorded by later singers and held by the sound archives of the Australian Institute of Aboriginal and Torres Strait Islander Studies. In one song, Moolbong teased a White weather forecaster for his ineptitude and offered help; in another, his best known, he encouraged recruits departing for service in World War I 'to tear the Germans to pieces', while he limped behind.

A. P. Elkin, *Aboriginal Men of High Degree* (Syd, 1946); L. Barwick et al (eds), *The Essence of Singing and the Substance of Song* (Syd, 1995); T. Donaldson, 'Kids that got lost' in J. C. Kassler and J. Stubington (eds), *Problems and Solutions* (Syd, 1984); L. A. Hercus, *Wembawemba Dictionary* (Canb, 1992); E. Morgan, *The Calling of the Spirits* (Canb, 1994), pp 78-79; *Oceania*, 17, no 4, 1947-48, p 327; information from Mrs M. Knight, Condobolin, and Mrs E. Kennedy, Albury, NSW.

TAMSIN DONALDSON

JOHNSTON, CHARMIAN; see CLIFT

JOHNSTON, GEORGE HENRY (1912-1970), journalist and author, was born on 20 July 1912 at Caulfield, Melbourne, fourth child of native-born parents John George Johnston, tram repairer, and his wife Minnie Riverina, née Wright. George attended Brighton Technical School from 1922 and gained the Intermediate certificate before being apprenticed to a lithographer with the art printers, Troedel [q.v.6] & Cooper Pty Ltd. He took art classes at the National Gallery schools, and spent much time on his boyhood hobby of drawing, painting and reading about classic sailing ships. At the age of 16 he had an article on local shipwrecks accepted by the *Argus*. In 1933 he was taken onto that paper as a cadet reporter, with responsibility for the shipping round. At St Mary's Anglican Church, Caulfield, on 19 March 1938 he married Elsie Esme Taylor, a cashier; they had a daughter Gae (b.1941).

In 1941 Johnston was accredited No.1 Australian war correspondent. He worked in New Guinea (1942), Britain and the United States of America (1943), India, China and Burma (1944), Italy (1944) and in Burma once more (1945); he also witnessed the Japanese surrender on board U.S.S. *Missouri* in Tokyo Bay in 1945. In a popular, racy style, he published in Sydney several quasi-documentary books on the war, including *Grey Gladiator* (1941), *Battle of the Seaways* (1941), *Australia at War* (1942), *New Guinea Diary* (1943) and *Pacific Partner* (New York, 1944). He chronicled his service in *Journey Through Tomorrow* (Melbourne, 1947). Johnston returned in October 1945 to find himself famous and favoured, especially by the *Argus's* managing director (Sir) Errol Knox [q.v.9] who nicknamed him 'golden boy' and appointed him first editor of the *Australasian Post*.

A scandal over Johnston's relationship with Charmian Clift [q.v.13], also employed on the paper, caused him to resign in 1946, after which he and Clift moved to Sydney together, and began writing fiction. Johnston published *Death Takes Small Bites* (London, 1948) and *Moon at Perigee* (1948), and began to write in collaboration with Clift. He was divorced in 1947 and married Charmian on 7 August that year at the court-house, Manly. They were to have three children, Martin (1947-1990), Shane (1949-1973) and Jason (b.1956). Their first joint novel, *High Valley* (1949), won the *Sydney Morning Herald* prize. Early in 1948 Johnston was given a feature-writing role on the *Sun*.

As a couple in these years, Johnston and Clift had the world at their feet: they had fame, good looks and youth, and a burning ambition to make their names in the literary world, especially abroad. Their chance came in 1951 when Johnston was appointed to head the London office of Associated Newspapers Services. They wrote another joint novel, *The Big Chariot* (1953); following a Mediterranean holiday, Johnston wrote *The Cyprian Woman* (1955). The strain of two careers began to tell on his health, and, when Associated Newspapers Ltd was taken over by the Fairfax [qq.v.4,8] family in 1953, he started to consider writing full time. In November 1954 he resigned from newspaper work and moved with his family to the Greek islands, first to Kálimnos, and a year later to Hydra. There his plan was to establish himself as a writer of international repute.

During the nine years he spent in Greece, Johnston worked hard, completing another joint novel with Clift, *The Sponge Divers* (London, 1956). He also wrote a series of five detective books under the pseudonym 'Shane Martin', the novels *The Darkness Outside* (London, 1959), *Closer to the Sun* (London, 1960) and *The Far Road* (London, 1962), as well as numerous short stories for international magazines, published posthumously in an anthology, *Strong Man From Piraeus* (Melbourne, 1984). Although some of this work attracted modest critical acclaim and occasional popular success, it too often suffered from cliché in both language and characterization, and good material and ideas were poorly handled, mainly through too much haste. Essentially, he had not yet found his true subject matter.

Moreover, life on Hydra was not proving to be the idyll that he and Clift had expected. They allowed themselves to get caught up in the constant flow of expatriate 'drop-ins', and the routine binges of talk, cigarettes and alcohol. This, together with the relentless worry over income, had an effect on Johnston's health and on his marriage. In 1959 he developed tuberculosis of the lung, and suffered alarming weight loss. At the same time, he was concerned that Clift was drifting away from him into relationships with other men. They attempted to solve their problems in 1961 by returning with the children to England, where Johnston tried unsuccessfully to go back to journalism. After six months they

gave up and returned to Hydra. There they learned of the unexpected financial success in the United States of America of Johnston's novel, *Closer to the Sun*. But their reprieve was short, and by 1962 the old worries were overwhelming them.

Yet, it was all this suffering and struggle that led to Johnston's breakthrough from literary mediocrity to widespread acclaim. In near desperation to get the mistakes of his life into focus, he began in 1962 to write his first directly autobiographical novel, *My Brother Jack* (London, 1964). It took him seven months, a long time by his speedy standards, with Clift prompting his memory and encouraging him all the way. *My Brother Jack* was immediately hailed as an Australian novel of rare distinction, and has been a great favourite with two generations of Australian readers. In it, David Meredith conducts a search not merely for his own 'mistakes', but for his whole past, to map it, to explain it, and to find meaning in it, much in the mode of contemporary existentialist fiction. Beginning with his childhood, Meredith sees himself as an oversensitive, duplicitous child of artistic temperament, developing in contrast to his more manly and honest brother, Jack. In presenting two figures, the novel thoughtfully explored two Australian myths—success and mateship. It also gave a richly detailed picture of Melbourne between the wars, and a telling contrast between its working-class and middle-class lifestyles.

Johnston returned alone to Australia in February 1964, to a warm and admiring reception. He established himself in Sydney, and later that year Clift and the children joined him. *My Brother Jack* was produced as a television serial, and Johnston set to work on *Clean Straw for Nothing* (London, 1969), the second volume in what was to be a Meredith trilogy. Continual smoking and drinking dogged his health and his relationship with Clift, who was herself under considerable strain writing a regular column for the *Sydney Morning Herald*. Johnston had lung surgery in 1966 and again in 1968. In July 1969, a month before the publication of *Clean Straw for Nothing*, he was devastated by Clift's suicide. She had been afraid of the way in which he might have portrayed her in that novel, which dealt with the painful period of their life on Hydra and the disintegration of their romantic aspirations. The tragic irony was that Cressida in the novel emerged as a figure of generosity and integrity, quite in contrast to the self-pitying David Meredith. Like its predecessor, this novel won the Miles Franklin [q.v.8] award. In January 1970 Johnston was appointed O.B.E.

Although ill, he worked on the final volume of the trilogy, *A Cartload of Clay* (London, 1971). This novel continued Meredith's life-journey, setting itself the specific task 'to plot the arabesque that linked everything together'. It was incomplete when he died of pulmonary tuberculosis on 22 July 1970 at his Mosman home; survived by his children, he was cremated with Methodist forms. His portrait by Ray Crooke won the 1969 Archibald [q.v.3] prize and was bought by the Art Gallery of New South Wales; a study for the portrait is held by the National Library of Australia.

As a novelist, Johnston belongs in the tradition of journalistic realism. However, the autobiographical element in his best work gives it uncommon power and honesty, and in its blend of 'truth' and the fictive, a modernistic narrative sometimes paradoxically results, as in the case of *Clean Straw for Nothing*. Characteristically, Johnston's narrative voice is that of an educated Australian male, better at dealing with material detail than with expressions of emotion.

Johnston bore the marks of his time and background: he was from the working classes, had only basic formal education, experienced the Depression and the war, joined the expatriate exodus to postwar Europe, and returned to participate in, and benefit from, the increased sophistication of Australian culture in the 1960s. The psychological legacy of all this was a deep insecurity about his own talent and, indeed, his right to fame; the chief victims of the legacy were his own health and his marriage. He wrote about this with strength, honesty and descriptive brilliance in the Meredith trilogy, which, through the personal odyssey of its central character, managed to express a varied and crucial era of Australian life.

G. Kinnane, *George Johnston* (Melb, 1986) and for bibliog; *SMH*, 1 Jan 1970; Johnston estate papers (NL); information from Harry Ransom Humanities Research Center, Austin, Texas, US; information from Lilly L, Indiana Univ, Pennsylvania, US.

GARRY KINNANE

JOHNSTON, GRAHAME KEVIN WILSON (1929-1976), university teacher, was born on 11 April 1929 at Marton, near Palmerston North, New Zealand, elder son of Frank Johnston, a journalist from Scotland, and his New Zealand-born wife Kathleen Augusta, née Wilson. Schooled at St Patrick's High, Palmerston North, and St Patrick's College, Wellington, Grahame studied English at Victoria University College (M.A., N.Z., 1951) and taught for two years at Auckland University College before proceeding to Merton College, Oxford (B.A., 1954). He returned to the Antipodes to lecture in English at the University of Queensland (1954-56). At St Thomas Aquinas Church, St Lucia, on

23 May 1955 he married with Catholic rites Eva Rosenbaum, a schoolteacher; they were to have one son and were divorced in 1964.

Moving to Canberra University College (later the School of General Studies, Australian National University), Johnston was promoted associate-professor in 1962 and was a visiting scholar (1963) at the Dublin Institute for Advanced Studies. He held the (Sir) Robert Wallace [q.v.12] chair of English at the University of Melbourne in 1963-65, then accepted a readership at the A.N.U. In 1968 he became professor of English in the Faculty of Military Studies, Duntroon campus, University of New South Wales. He was appointed deputy-director of the Humanities Research Centre, A.N.U., in 1976.

By training and choice, Johnston was primarily a medievalist, but in young departments with small staffs he displayed considerable versatility, teaching and publishing in the fields of American and Australian literature particularly. His approach to teaching was that of a rigorously trained scholar rather than an inspirational critic. He saw his foremost responsibility as being to make texts available to students who were sufficiently independent in their critical judgement to be able to take his exposition as the first step and to develop interpretations of their own.

As a consequence Johnston's publications have a distinctly utilitarian quality: they are necessary tools which facilitate understanding and exploration, and the intellectual quality which informs them is best judged by their range and integrity. His first three books also showed an unusual diversity. *Australian Literary Criticism* (Melbourne, 1962) was a pioneering collection that drew together essays which contributed to the definition of an Australian canon as well as validating an embryonic school of Australian criticism. *An Outline of Middle English Grammar* (Oxford, 1963) was a translation of a work of proven quality by Karl Brunner. Johnston was joint author and editor of the first two editions of the Australian government's *Style Manual* (Canberra, 1966, 1972), one of those enduringly useful books on which people unthinkingly depend.

He developed a close working relationship with Frank Eyre of Oxford University Press, Australia, and was influential in developing Oxford's considerable role in Australian studies. Johnston was appointed general editor of the press's three series—Australian Writers and their Work, Australian Bibliographies, and Selected Essays on Australian Writers. In 1970 he published *Annals of Australian Literature* (Melbourne). The most accessible of his cultural tools was to be his last. His *Australian Pocket Oxford Dictionary*

(Melbourne, 1976) was the first major dictionary aimed specifically at an Australian market. Survived by his son, he died of cirrhosis of the liver on 21 December 1976 in Woden Valley Hospital and was buried in Canberra cemetery.

G. K. W. Johnston, curriculum vitae, 8 Apr 1976, ANU (copy held in ADB file); information from Prof S. Johnston, Lower Hutt, NZ; personal information.
                                W. S. RAMSON

JOHNSTON, Sir WILLIAM WALLACE STEWART (1887-1962), physician and army medical officer, was born on 21 December 1887 at South Yarra, Melbourne, second son of William Edward Johnston, a barrister from Scotland who became a county court judge, and his Victorian-born wife Clara Jane, née Wallace. J. S. Johnston [q.v.4] was his grandfather. Young Bill was educated at Melbourne Church of England Grammar School and Trinity College, University of Melbourne (M.B., B.S., 1914; M.D., 1921). He was a resident medical officer at the (Royal) Melbourne Hospital when World War I broke out.

On 14 July 1915 Johnston was appointed captain, Australian Army Medical Corps, Australian Imperial Force. Posted to the hospital ship, *Karoola*, he sailed for the Middle East in December and was transferred to the 3rd Field Ambulance in Egypt in February 1916. Next month he was sent to the Western Front where he later joined the 12th Battalion as regimental medical officer. In August, at Mouquet Farm, near Pozières, France, he braved an intense barrage to treat the wounded and was awarded the Military Cross. Promoted major in August 1917, he was mentioned in dispatches. At Hooge, east of Ypres, Belgium, he went out in the open in September to attend the wounded where they lay and continued working until he was severely injured by shell-fire. He was recommended for the Victoria Cross but received the Distinguished Service Order. After recovering in England, he rejoined the battalion in February 1918.

Probably the best, and best-loved, R.M.O. in the A.I.F., Johnston returned to Australia in 1919; his appointment terminated on 27 January 1920. While practising as a consultant, he was one of the honorary medical staff at his old hospital. On 3 December 1923 at Scots Church, Melbourne, he married with Presbyterian forms his cousin Jessie Mary Clark, a niece of Alister Clark [q.v.8]. Johnston maintained his interest in military medicine, serving in the Militia as commander of the 2nd Field Ambulance in 1928-34 and then as assistant-director of medical services at Army Headquarters. Promoted temporary colonel in 1938, he was called up for full-time duty in October 1939 as assistant director-general of medical services.

Almost concurrently, Johnston was seconded to the A.I.F. and placed in command of the 2nd/2nd Australian General Hospital which he took to Palestine in April 1940. As deputy-director of medical services, I Corps, from 25 January 1941, he was initially responsible for the care of Australian troops in Palestine and Libya. By March he was based in Greece, co-ordinating the medical matters of the 6th Australian Division with those of British and New Zealand formations. When the Germans overran the country in April, he was evacuated via Crete to Egypt. He was appointed C.B.E. (1941) for his part in the campaign.

Johnston had overall command of medical arrangements for the operations against the Vichy French in Syria in June-July. Promoted temporary brigadier in August, he returned home in February 1942. Six months later he was in Port Moresby as D.D.M.S., New Guinea Force. In the fighting along the Kokoda Track and beyond, the terrain posed severe problems in evacuating sick and wounded men, and in transporting medical supplies to the front. Strict anti-malaria precautions had to be enforced. Largely due to Johnston's efforts, the difficulties were finally overcome and he was again mentioned in dispatches. Although he had retained his health, he was not robust and he was sent to Australia in December 'for a spell from the tropics'. Between February and May 1943 he served in North Queensland as D.D.M.S., II Corps. He was placed on the Reserve of Officers on 20 July.

Resuming both his practice and his honorary post at the R.M.H., Johnston was director (1947-56) and chairman (1956-62) of the Melbourne Medical Post-Graduate Committee. In 1947 he was appointed a knight of the Order of St John; in 1957 he became chief commissioner to the St John Ambulance Brigade in Australia. He was a member (1945-52) and medical director (1943-44) of the national council of the Australian Red Cross Society, and vice-president (1958-60) of the Royal Australasian College of Physicians. In 1960 he was knighted. President (1959-61) of the Graduate Union and a council-member (from 1961) of the University of Melbourne, in 1962 he was awarded an honorary LL.D. He had been elected president of the Melbourne Club in 1945.

Sir William was regarded with respect and affection. His reputation was not due to any outstanding ability as a physician. He was able, hard working and conscientious, but not more so than many of his contemporaries. The true measure of the man lay in his nature and character. His grave and quiet manner, whimsical humour, kindness and humility disguised a spirit of service and a determination to do what he considered fair and just. 'He never did right that he might be seen to do right, but because he could not do otherwise.' Despite the number and the variety of the positions he held, there was never 'one whisper of criticism'. Few have possessed his qualities of 'courage, integrity, humility, faith and kindness'. He taught and inspired others by personal example.

Johnston was tall and distinguished in appearance, and bore a striking physical resemblance to his wife. He died on 21 August 1962 in East Melbourne and was cremated; Jessie and their two sons survived him. Rex Bramleigh's portrait of Johnston is held by the Museum of Medical History, University of Melbourne.

A. G. Butler (ed), *Official History of the Australian Army Medical Services in the War of 1914-1918*, 1-3 (Melb, 1938, Canb, 1940, 1943); A. S. Walker, *Middle East and Far East* (Canb, 1953) and *The Island Campaigns* (Canb, 1957); T. R. Garnett, *Man of Roses* (Syd, 1990); *MJA*, 19 Oct 1963, p 677; information from Dr S. Johnston, Mornington, and Mr D. Johnston, Point Lonsdale, Vic; personal information.   JOHN V. HURLEY

JOHNSTONE, GEORGINA; *see* McCREADY

JOHNSTONE, JOHN EDWARD (1892-1976), deep-sea diver, was born on 25 September 1892 at Kirkdale, Liverpool, England, son of James Johnstone, a drysalter's warehouseman, and his wife Margaret Lee, née Rugbie (d.1910). Enthralled by his maternal grandfather's tales of deep-sea exploits, young John yearned to be a diver. His widowed mother initially insisted on office employment, but compromised and apprenticed him to shipwrights at Birkenhead.

In 1910 Johnstone signed on as a carpenter's mate aboard a cargo steamer destined for Australia. He completed his apprenticeship in a shipyard at Taree, New South Wales, returned to England and enlisted in the King's Liverpool Regiment in 1915. After volunteering for service in naval dockyards, he was attached to a diver's gang before being sent to Invergordon, Scotland, to train for work with the salvage section of the Royal Navy. In 1919 he sailed back to Australia with his wife Edith (née Gill) and their baby daughter. He had married Edith on 26 July 1917 at the parish church of St John the Evangelist, Walton-on-the-Hill, Lancashire. She died on 4 August 1922 following childbirth. At Newport, Melbourne, on 4 April 1925 Johnstone married with Methodist forms Edith Emily Smith, a 31-year-old teacher.

Dissuaded by wiser heads from seeking an illusory fortune as a pearl-diver in northern Australia, Johnstone had settled in Melbourne, at first as a shipwright. He established his reputation as a 'dress-suit' diver in 1922 in the recovery of 454 tons of blister copper from the *Karitane*, beached off Deal Island, Bass Strait. Among much routine surveying of jetties and repairing of dams, notable assignments over the next fifteen years included an unsuccessful attempt in 1934 to salvage the *Joseph Sims*, sunk off one of the Furneaux islands. The reconstruction of the Eildon Weir gave Johnstone an opportunity to use and advise on modifications to a new cutting torch developed by Commonwealth Industrial Gases Ltd. In 1938 French interests called on his expertise with oxyhydrogen underwater burners to remove the coral-encrusted wreck of the *Joliette* from Thio harbour, New Caledonia.

That year Johnstone had won fame by walking along the bed of Bass Strait for 27 miles (43 km) to find a fault in a telephone cable. This feat was overshadowed in 1941 by his role—as chief diver for United Salvage Pty Ltd—in bringing up 555 gold ingots valued at £2 379 000 from the *Niagara*, sunk in 438 feet (134 m) of water in the Hauraki Gulf, near Whangarei, New Zealand. Johnstone and his brother William, a shipwright warrant officer in the Royal Australian Navy on loan to the syndicate led by Captain (Sir) John Williams, directed the recovery of 94 per cent of the bullion from a specially constructed observation diving-bell. A world diving record was claimed.

Johnstone's own 'romantic story of sunken treasure retrieved from record ocean depths', *Niagara Gold* (Wellington, N.Z., 1942), was retold in a succession of collaboratively written memoirs that brought Johnno renown as a man prepared to go to 'Any Depth, Anywhere'. Appointed chief diver and shipwright surveyor to the Commonwealth Salvage Board, he was sent to the United States of America in 1942 to supervise the completion of salvage ships and tugs for Australia. While in the U.S.A. he tested the new artificial lung and qualified in submarine rescue techniques.

From 1943 Johnstone undertook a series of missions in Port Phillip Bay, Victoria, on the Great Barrier Reef and in Moreton Bay, Queensland, and in Papua and New Guinea at Milne Bay, Oro Bay, Finschhafen, Madang and Port Moresby. With Captain Williams, Johnstone went on loan to the Indian government in 1945 to try to raise the troop-ship, *Santhia*, overturned in mud in Calcutta harbour. He put to good use what he had learned from observing the innovative American effort to refloat the liner, *Normandie*, at the mouth of the Hudson River, but was invalided home with amoebic dysentery before the task was finished.

The highlight of an anti-climactic postwar career was the refloating of the *Wanganella* in Wellington harbour in 1947. Periodically announced 'retirements' were interspersed with negotiations to mount a search for the last of the *Niagara* gold. Scorning rumours that he had deliberately left a small hoard for subsequent retrieval, in 1953 he advised a British group which found thirty of the remaining thirty-five bars. His knowledge of Pacific wrecks was valuable to Japanese enterprises in the 1950s until the demand for scrap steel collapsed.

A wiry 5 ft 10 ins (178 cm) in his prime, Johnstone displayed extraordinary endurance and courage throughout a long diving life. Although he was acutely 'sensitive to praise, misunderstanding, or adverse criticism', he was a gifted self-publicist, if a nervous speaker and broadcaster. In 1968 he was appointed O.B.E. He died on 27 October 1976 in East Melbourne and was cremated. The son and two daughters of his first marriage survived him, as did the son of his second.

P. Dawlish, *Johnno the Deep-Sea Diver* (Lond, 1960); J. Williams, *So Ends This Day* (Melb, 1981); C. W. N. Ingram, *New Zealand Shipwrecks 1795-1982* (Wellington, NZ, 1984).

CAMERON HAZLEHURST

JOHNSTONE, WILLIAM RAPHAEL (1905-1964), jockey, was born on 13 April 1905 at New Lambton, New South Wales, son of native-born parents Robert James Johnstone, coalminer, and his wife Elizabeth, née Harney. After his parents separated, Rae lived with his mother in Sydney and attended Marist Brothers' High School, Darlinghurst. Apprenticed at 14 to the Newcastle trainer Jack Phoenix, the diminutive Johnstone rode his first winner, Grey Arrow, at Rosehill in June 1920. He rode over one hundred winners in the 1920-21 season, but began betting, fell foul of the stewards and endured several suspensions. In 1925 Johnstone was banned from riding in Sydney for several months because he had gained access to his earnings (protected while an apprentice) and married Ruby Isabel Hornery-Ford on 20 June at the district registrar's office, Randwick. At Armidale in November 1927 he conspired to lose a race and was banned for two years. Beset by financial problems and a collapsing marriage, he resumed racing in 1930.

Riding with renewed zest in India in 1931 for expatriate trainer Alec Higgins, Johnstone was offered engagements in England by Sir Victor Sassoon's racing manager. He arrived there in 1932, but found better prospects riding for Pierre Wertheimer in France. Life in Paris appealed to him, and he became romantically involved with Marie Marcelle Augustine Goubé ('Gui'), a dancer at the Folies-Bergère. Johnstone was the leading jockey in France three times in the 1930s. His first classic wins were in England in 1934, for the Cardiff shipowner, Lord Glanely. High living, casinos and what Johnstone called 'a certain hypnotic fascination for the limelight' ensured that he retained little of his large earnings.

He was equally cavalier about World War II. Rejected for military service, he rode in India in 1939-40, but returned to Paris where, on 12 March 1940, he married Marie (whom he called Mary). They made their way to Monte Carlo. Johnstone contrived to ride at meetings at Lyon, Vichy and Marseilles until late 1942 before being interned by the Italians. He claimed that he escaped from a German-bound train in 1944 and was helped to cross the military lines to liberated Paris. By mid-December that year he was back in the saddle.

Embarking upon what was to be a celebrated decade, Johnstone won the 1945 Prix de l'Arc de Triomphe. He rode for some of the wealthiest owners in Europe, including the Aga Khan and Leon Volterra. On their horse, My Love, in 1948 Johnstone became the first Australian jockey to win the (English) Derby. Within three weeks he had added the French and Irish Derbys. He lost the 1949 (English) Derby in a photo finish, but was acclaimed for his daring victory next year on Galcador, at a time when he was retained (for three years) by Marcel Boussac's stables in France and England. Their partnership netted seven classic winners in 1950. Johnstone achieved his third (English) Derby, on Lavandin in 1956. He won thirty classic races in England, Ireland and France, and rode in eleven countries. Few Australians witnessed his mature riding skills and how he spared the whip. Jack Pollard, who saw him ride in France and England, described him as 'a bobby-dazzler, daring, crafty, able to spot an opening before his rivals, and a masterly judge of pace'.

Johnstone had become a European celebrity. Following his last ride, in June 1957 at Longchamp, he trained horses in France and published his memoirs, *The Rae Johnstone Story* (London, 1958). He attributed his 'oriental look' to his mixed descent (Irish-German and Portuguese-Welsh) and was offended by being nicknamed 'Togo' (after the Japanese admiral). To the French, he was 'Le Crocodile' who came 'from behind to gobble up the field'. Johnstone died on 29 April 1964 at Chantilly. He divided his estate between his wife and his mistress, Margo Winnick.

J. Pollard, *Australian Horse Racing* (Syd, 1988); *People* (Syd), 28 Mar 1951; *Sports Illustrated* (Chicago, US), 22 July 1957, p 43; *Turf Mthly*, Mar 1978; *SMH*, 8 Nov, 14 Dec 1927, 17, 23 May 1934; *Argus*, 29 Sept 1933; *Age* (Melb), 20 July 1957; *Herald* (Melb), 15 Nov 1965.

ANDREW LEMON

JONES, ARTHUR (1892-1976), trade unionist and politician, was born on 12 June 1892 at Lower Barnes, near Kidderminster, Worcestershire, England, son of Thomas Jones, farm labourer, and his wife Mary Jane, née Nutting. Educated (1897-1904) at an elementary school at Wolverley, Arthur worked as a farm labourer. In 1911 he emigrated to New South Wales. He became a 'gun' shearer in the Hunter Valley and demonstrated shearing at the British Empire Exhibition, Wembley, England, in 1924-25. A trade unionist from the age of 15, he was active in the Australian Workers' Union. By 1923 he was one of its organizers and in 1926 Western District secretary, based at Longreach, Queensland. He married 23-year-old Margaret Fanny Bennett on 18 December 1926 at St Alban's Anglican Church, Belmore, Sydney.

At a by-election on 2 November 1929 Jones stood as the Australian Labor Party's candidate and won the seat of Burke in the Legislative Assembly. After the seat was abolished in 1932, he was appointed an investigation officer, Department of Labour and Industry, Brisbane. In May 1939 he successfully contested Charters Towers, retaining it until his retirement in 1960. During World War II he was secretary for mines (9 February to 16 September 1942) and for public instruction (9 February 1942 to 27 April 1944). A competent minister, he won respect for his administrative ability and grasp of detail in confronting wartime problems due to the high rate of enlistment and the evacuation of families from northern areas. On 27 April 1944 he was appointed secretary for public lands; his outback experience helped him to promote valuable amendments to legislation affecting stock and rural land. From May 1947 to May 1950, as minister for health and home affairs, he was also responsible for the sub-departments of police, native affairs and wards of the state. He subsequently held the portfolio of labour and industry (10 May 1950 to 12 August 1957). In November 1953 he introduced important amendments to the Industrial Conciliation and Arbitration Act (1932) to expand the jurisdiction of the Industrial Court, to extend long-service leave to all employees and to allow for seven weeks accumulated sick leave in place of two.

A prolonged strike in the pastoral industry in 1956 led to a deterioration in the government's relationship with the A.W.U. under R. J. J. Bukowski [q.v.13]. As a senior minister with responsibility for industrial relations, Jones was closely identified with Premier Vince Gair [q.v.] who was expelled from the Australian Labor Party on 24 April 1957. Two days later Jones, with most of his ministerial colleagues, joined Gair's newly created Queensland Labor Party. Although Jones thus left the A.L.P. by his own choice, he was deeply distressed when he was expelled by the A.W.U. Yet his speeches, following the government's defeat on 3 August 1957, lacked the bitterness displayed by many of his colleagues; courteous and quietly spoken, he reflected the charm and wit of his Welsh ancestry. A 'masterly raconteur of jest, anecdote and witty retort', he had a salty sense of humour and was admired by political friend and foe alike. He was an avid reader, and a keen gardener and lawn bowler. Survived by his wife and two daughters, he died on 30 June 1976 in his home at Coorparoo, Brisbane, and was cremated.

C. Lack (comp), *Three Decades of Queensland Political History, 1929-1960* (Brisb, 1962); *PD* (Qld), 25 Aug 1976; *Telegraph* (Brisb), 1 May 1939; information from Mrs P. Clark, Victoria Point, Brisb.

MANFRED CROSS

JONES, SIR DAVID FLETCHER (1895-1977), businessman, was born on 14 August 1895 at Bendigo, Victoria, fifth (third surviving) child of Samuel Henry Jones, a blacksmith from Cornwall, and his Victorian-born wife Mahala, née Johns. After Mahala died in 1897, Samuel remarried and had four more children. The families blended happily, and Fletcher recalled his childhood fondly: 'the greatest inheritance is to have been born into a struggling Christian household'.

The Jones family was Labor in politics, Methodist in religion and improving working class in its social aspirations. This background, together with the camaraderie of Cornish mining families and the fellowship of the Methodist congregation at Golden Square, fostered in Fletcher both a desire for individual improvement and the moral imperative to leave the world better off.

In 1908 he left Golden Square State School; he worked for two years in a Bendigo auction-room and then spent three years establishing for his father a tomato-farm on scrubland at Kangaroo Flat. He read omnivorously, and aloud, in an attempt to overcome a bad stammer. Fascinated by tailors' workrooms, he often walked from Kangaroo Flat to Pall Mall, Bendigo, to gaze in their windows.

Enlisting in the Australian Imperial Force on 15 July 1915, Jones sailed to Egypt and in March 1916 was sent to France with the 57th

Battalion. He saw action in the battle of Fromelles before being evacuated to England in August with trench fever. Repatriated in 1917, he was discharged medically unfit on 8 February 1918. His stammer had returned, worse than before, but repatriation doctors warned that he would have to 'speak or starve'. Rejecting a war pension, he became a door-to-door salesman in Melbourne's inner suburbs, where poverty and hopelessness prejudiced him for ever against cities. He turned his thoughts to hawking in rural Victoria, of which he and his army cobber Stan Clapton had dreamed in the trenches in France.

In 1918 Jones took a loan from the Repatriation Department, bought a hawker's wagon, stocked the outfit with Manchester from Flinders Lane and mapped a circuit in the Western District from Skipton to Terang. Clapton & Jones soon worked up a good trade among shearers, farmers' wives and friendly townsfolk. Offering quality and value, they quickly learned that 'the customer was always right'. When the partnership was dissolved, Jones bought a commercial traveller's drag and initially worked alone, moving into the Otway Ranges and westward into South Australia. Gathering about him a small and loyal staff, he married the flair of the showman to the business of commercial travelling. He bought trucks and trailers, hired shops for three-monthly sales, erected marquees on vacant land, and expanded into tailoring and dressmaking.

On 23 September 1922 at the Methodist Church, Golden Square, Jones married Rena Ellen Jones (d.1970), a friend from childhood, and soon decided to settle down. In 1924 he purchased on credit a menswear and tailoring business at Warrnambool. The poorly chosen site, the town's social conservatism and his rivals' suspicion saw his dignity bruised when he was forced to come to an arrangement with his creditors. Jones was a dedicated reader of American periodicals on modern merchandising techniques. His responses to his precarious business position—daily 'specials', spot sales and competitions—were simple and inexpensive, but attracted the desired attention and custom. Jones's exuberant showmanship spilled over into community activities. He organized Warrnambool's winning entry in the *Sun News-Pictorial*'s 1927 Ideal Town contest, collected and distributed Toc H support for the unemployed during the Depression and ran the highly popular community singing. Above all, he proved astute in business, managing his credit on a knife-edge, buying goods in small quantities and initiating group-buying by tender. He also recruited ambitious salesmen, and skilled tailors discharged by other firms. By 1939 his tailors' room was one of the largest in provincial

Victoria and he had repaid his Melbourne creditors in full.

The year 1941, when he decided to make nothing but trousers, marked a turning-point. The Commonwealth Department of Supply awarded him a contract for army pants and Fletcher Jones rapidly made a reputation for hard-wearing, 'coverdine' work trousers, particularly among men on the land. By 1945 his Warrnambool rooms were supplying 123 retailers in four States. Offended by their indifference to the principle of fractional sizes, he decided to sell directly, to insist on personal fittings and to accept cash only. The response, from Australians chafing from continuing austerity, was astonishing. Customers besieged his first shop when it opened in Collins Street, Melbourne, on 23 June 1946. Queues stretched for blocks under signs proclaiming 'Fletcher Jones of Warrnambool—nothing but trousers. 72 scientific sizes. No man is hard to fit'.

Jones had long been fascinated by American industrial efficiency. A subscriber (from 1922) to Herbert Casson's *Efficiency Magazine*, he was acquainted with the ideas of Henry Ford, Andrew Carnegie, Frederick Taylor and Lillian Gilbreth. The traditional methods which dominated tailoring left him frustrated, not only with the time-wasting but with the depressed nature of the craft and worker exploitation. Yet, he distrusted schemes which encouraged a spurious identification between worker and business, and which seemed designed merely to extract more labour without increasing job satisfaction. Spiritual growth, he believed, was achieved through productive and satisfying work, and the object of business should be social advance rather than individual profit.

Wondering during the depths of the Depression 'why the rich were getting richer and the poor poorer', he read (with self-confessed difficulty) analyses of capitalism by Victor Gollancz, Harold Laski, J. B. S. Haldane and the Webbs, and studied the history of the co-operative movement. Fabian socialism, being eclectic and pragmatic, appealed to him. He became acquainted, too, with the work and writings of the Japanese Christian pacifist and socialist Toyohiko Kagawa, who succoured the homeless of Tokyo's slums and pioneered consumers' and farmers' co-operatives and student credit-unions. Jones arranged for Kagawa to speak at Warrnambool during his 1935 Australian visit; in 1936 he visited Kagawa's Japanese co-operatives. He was influenced by Kagawa's *Brotherhood Economics* (1937) and that year issued his own statement, 'Co-op Pie'. Supported by his wife, he began from the late 1940s to turn his business into a co-operative, the name Fletcher Jones & Staff Pty Ltd first being used in 1947 for a company to replace the

Man's Shop of Fletcher Jones Trousers Pty Ltd in Melbourne. The basic objectives included commitments to raising the quality of Australian-made clothing, to bringing made-to-measure garments within the reach of the ordinary man, and to revolutionizing the firm's management and ownership in line with consultative and co-operative principles.

In 1947 Jones visited England and the United States of America to inspect the latest production methods. What he saw of repetitious operations reinforced his earlier reading and convictions about efficiency. Within a year the firm began a major expansion, buying—as the new factory site on the outskirts of Warrnambool—a rubbish dump in a former quarry, and determining to transform it from an eyesore into a showplace. Disparaged at the outset as a 'shanty town' collection, the factory in a landscaped garden-setting at Pleasant Hill became a tourist mecca by the 1950s.

The 1950s and 1960s saw an expanding range of Fletcher Jones services and products, notably an extension of the range of garment fabrics, the provision of an after-sales cleaning and repair service on a non-profit basis, and the decision in 1956 to make women's skirts and slacks, the last a result of winning the contract to outfit the Australian Olympic team. The company remained at the cutting-edge of industrial innovation, introducing methods-engineering practices (1954), the Australian clothing industry's first textile testing laboratory (1964) and computerized tailoring systems (1974). When in 1966 the company decided to make suits, it found that it had exhausted Warrnambool's supply of skilled labour and had to open in the Melbourne suburb of Brunswick. But Warrnambool remained the administrative centre, production base and social heart of the 'FJ Family'. The original plan for the co-operative envisaged the Jones family retaining a two-thirds interest and the staff one-third, but Fletcher surrendered his interest so readily that the staff held 53 per cent of the shares by the early 1950s and over 70 per cent by the 1970s. At Scots Memorial Church, Surfers Paradise, Queensland, on 5 October 1971 he married with Presbyterian forms Aida Margaret Wells, née Pettigrove, a 66-year-old widow.

Jones was widely admired. In manner he was gregarious and affable, and given to aphorisms; in appearance, he was a trim and neat 5 ft 9 ins (175 cm), impeccably groomed, a non-smoker and teetotaller. His other business activities included chairmanships of Warrnambool Woollen Mill Ltd (1943-58) and of Hanro Ltd (1959-63), and membership of the Victorian Promotion Committee (1962-75). He lived simply, in a two-bedroom bunga-low near Pleasant Hill, and drove a 1962 Rover 2000. Warrnambool named him citizen of the year in 1958. He was appointed O.B.E. in 1959, and knighted in 1974 for services to decentralization and the community, an honour long delayed by the Liberal era, it was thought, because of his clear Labor sympathies and his alternative business practices. Reports of the Whitlams' agnosticism, however, caused him publicly to renounce his political allegiance.

Sir Fletcher remained chairman of Fletcher Jones & Staff Pty Ltd and governing director of the holding company, Fletcher Jones Organizations Pty Ltd, until 1975 when failing health forced some reduction of his direct responsibilities. Reviewing his career in 1974, he said, 'I had no vision or grand dream. Trading was in my blood and I wanted to be good at it . . . that was all'. His memoir, *Not By Myself* (1976), bound in imitation coverdine, acknowledged the vital contribution from friends and well-wishers, some of them total strangers, whose goodwill had sustained his confidence, strengthened his Christian faith and confirmed his belief that religion could be expressed in business life. Symbols of an affluent and self-confident postwar nation, the man and his firm were celebrated for their material success, but in fact embodied a genuine and challenging expression of an Australian egalitarianism informed by Christian teachings.

Survived by his wife, and by the daughter and two sons of his first marriage, Jones died on 22 February 1977 at Warrnambool and was buried in the local cemetery. His estate was sworn for probate at $326 795. At that time his enterprise was one of the largest clothing manufacturers in the world, with almost three thousand employed in four factories and in thirty-three stores through every Australian capital city. Arguably, no single person or firm had done more to transform and, for a time, homogenize Australian dress standards, particularly among men, than Fletcher Jones and his staff.

New Idea, 20 Sept 1990; *Sun News-Pictorial*, 6 May 1953, 1 Jan 1974, 24 Feb 1977; *Herald* (Melb), 23 Feb 1977, 1 May 1978; *Australian*, 23 Feb 1985; personal and business papers held by Mr D. F. Jones, Port Fairy, Vic.   JOHN LACK

JONES, NORMAN EDWARD THOMAS (1904-1972), businessman, was born on 2 August 1904 at Petersham, Sydney, son of Edward Jacob Jones, commercial traveller, and his wife Eliza Esther, née Swain, both Australian born. Following Edward's death in 1906, the family moved to Newcastle, New South Wales. Educated at Hamilton and Cooks Hill high schools, Norman studied part time at Newcastle Technical College (Dip.Chem., 1925) where he won a bronze medal for the highest academic results in chemistry in the State's technical colleges. At St Andrew's Presbyterian Church, Newcastle, on 17 November 1928 he married Mabel Elizabeth Swainson.

In February 1920 Jones had joined the Broken Hill Proprietary Co. Ltd as an office-boy at its Newcastle steelworks. Next year he moved to the chemical laboratory as a junior chemist and in 1926 was sent to the open hearth department to learn steelmaking. In 1933 he was promoted to the manager's office at the steelworks as assistant to the production superintendent. He was transferred back to the open hearth department in 1934 as assistant-superintendent, and in the following year studied steelmaking in Europe and the United States of America. From 1936, as a special cadet, he gained eighteen months general experience working throughout Australia in a range of areas in B.H.P. Two years later he was appointed technical assistant to the general manager Leslie Bradford [q.v.13] at the company's head office in Melbourne. With Bradford, he played a key role in the management of B.H.P. during World War II and was appointed assistant general manager in 1943.

After A. S. Hoskins retired in 1949, Jones became a director of B.H.P.'s subsidiary, Australian Iron & Steel Ltd. In February 1950 he was appointed that company's managing director. In the same month, when Essington Lewis [q.v.10] stepped down, Jones replaced him as chief general manager of B.H.P. He was appointed managing director and joined the B.H.P. board in January 1952. He also joined the board's finance committee on its establishment in 1959. Lewis's retirement as chief general manager and the death of the company's chairman Harold Darling [q.v.8] in the same year had marked the beginning of a new era in B.H.P. Lewis had been the company's chief executive-officer since 1921 and Darling its chairman from 1922. Both men had formidable personalities and Lewis's reputation for ruling the company with a rod of iron was legendary.

Described as humble, quietly spoken, self-effacing and unpretentious, Jones could not have been more different. He had a wiry and athletic figure, and none of the imposing physical characteristics of his predecessor. He hated being photographed and pictures of him taken in later life show his face hidden behind heavy spectacle frames. He was the only managing director of B.H.P. in modern times not to have had his portrait painted for the company's collection.

To add to the challenge of succeeding Lewis, Jones inherited a company whose performance after the end of World War II had been weak. Labour and coal shortages, industrial problems and management's fear that there would be another depression, combined to frustrate growth. As the monopoly producer of steel in Australia, B.H.P. adopted a policy of underproduction and did not equal its pre-war output of steel until 1953. It soon found, however, that consumption of steel, spurred by demand generated by the new immigrant population, outstripped production. Between 1950 and 1952 Australia's steel imports increased by almost 50 per cent. B.H.P. soon lost its competitive edge in pricing (from 1932 it had produced the world's cheapest steel) and by 1955 the company had lost almost all the export markets it had gained before the war.

Jones had a tough job to turn the firm's performance around. Major expansion and modernization programmes were first undertaken at the steelworks at Newcastle and soon after at Port Kembla where a flat products plant, incorporating a hot strip mill, plate mill and tinplate mill, was installed. In 1952 B.H.P. reached agreement with the Western Australian government to build a fence-post plant and steel rolling-mill at Kwinana in exchange for iron-ore leases in that State. A subsequent agreement in 1960, which saw B.H.P. establish a blast furnace at Kwinana in 1968 and agree to build a fully integrated steelworks in Western Australia by the end of the 1970s, secured additional iron-ore reserves for the company. Jones's discussions with the Western Australian and Federal governments were critical in securing approval to mine iron ore for export. This permission would later assist B.H.P. and its co-venturers to develop the massive Mount Whaleback deposits in Western Australia.

At Whyalla the company negotiated successfully with the South Australian government over the security of iron-ore leases and upgraded its operations by the addition of a fully integrated steel plant which opened in 1965. B.H.P.'s commitment to research and development was boosted by the establishment of laboratories at Newcastle and later in Melbourne, and the company began to invest in some innovative technologies, notably basic oxygen steelmaking. As a result of these and other initiatives, B.H.P. profits trebled, steel output more than doubled, and the company's equity base more than trebled in the ten years to 1965.

To support the growth in its steel business, B.H.P. opened a ferro-alloy plant in Tasmania in 1962, established new iron-ore mines in Western Australia and South Australia, and in 1964 secured leases over manganese deposits on Groote Eylandt off the Northern Territory coast. At its yard in Whyalla the firm built seven ships for its fleet in the decade after 1955. In response to the widening scope of operations during these years, B.H.P.'s management structure was reorganized in 1959 and ten general managers, including three at the steelworks, were appointed.

Jones had joined B.H.P. only five years after the company had expanded its business into steel production. He headed the organization in 1960 when it made its next critical decision to diversify, this time into oil and gas exploration. Titles were taken up in Bass Strait in 1960. In partnership with Esso Standard Oil (Aust) Ltd, B.H.P. discovered commercial reserves of natural gas in 1965 and oil in 1967. Sensing the new opportunities presented by oil and gas and minerals, Jones urged the board to commission a comprehensive review and restructure the company's management. The chairman Sir Colin Syme subsequently noted: 'We felt our organisation wasn't as good as it should have been. We were inbred and couldn't see the wood for the trees'.

The review was conducted by the American management consultants, Cresap, McCormick & Paget, during 1966 and resulted in the most thorough overhaul of B.H.P. in its history. The key recommendation of the review was to reorganize the company along product lines—steel, oil and gas, and minerals—and to give each division a degree of responsibility and accountability for its business performance and profits.

In his capacity as managing director of B.H.P., Jones played a significant role in the establishment of the Australian Administrative Staff College at Mount Eliza, Victoria. 'Some of us felt it was vital and necessary to train middle and top management', he said. The college was incorporated as a private company in 1955; a college company of senior executives from prominent Australian businesses acted as guarantors, but with limited liability. Jones was a councillor (1955-72), a member of the college company and signatory to the college's first articles of association.

Having earlier indicated his wish to retire as managing director—as at least one commentator noted, he 'often seemed uncomfortable in the . . . role'—Jones stepped down on 31 January 1967. He had worked with the firm for forty-six years, and been its chief executive for sixteen, during a period of significant growth and change. Later he remarked, 'my time with B.H.P. was not work for me, it captivated me'. In March 1967 he was reappointed to the B.H.P. board as a non-executive director, a position he held until his death.

As a senior executive with B.H.P., Jones had been invited to join the governing bodies of many prominent organizations. In 1947 he had become a councillor of the Victorian Chamber of Manufactures (vice-president 1948-72); the auditorium at its head office was named in his honour. In 1951-71 he was a council-member of the University of Melbourne, and for fifteen of those years chairman of the university finance committee. From 1958 until 1972 he sat on the board of management of the Alfred Hospital (vice-president from 1967). He joined the Institute of Public Affairs as a councillor in 1961, was elected to its board in 1965 and was treasurer (1965-72). In 1960 he had been appointed to the Dafydd Lewis [q.v.10] Trust and in 1961 he joined Sir Leslie Martin's committee, established to inquire into the future of tertiary education in Australia.

In Melbourne the family lived at Toorak. They also had a small property at Kallista in the Dandenong Ranges, where Norman indulged his enthusiasm for gardening. He listed his other interests as golf and tennis. He was a member of the Melbourne, Australian and Athenaeum clubs (Melbourne), the Union Club (Sydney), the Newcastle Club, the Weld Club (Perth) and the Adelaide Club. Following his retirement, in 1967-72 Jones was a director of the National Bank of Australasia Ltd, Australian Paper Manufacturers, and the Colonial Mutual Life Assurance Society Ltd.

A member of the Australasian Institute of Mining and Metallurgy, the Australian Institute of Metals and the Institute of Australian Foundrymen, Jones received international recognition for his contribution to the steel industry. He was a member of the American Institute of Mining and Metallurgical Engineers and in 1962 was made a member of the American Iron and Steel Institute, New York. In 1967-68 he was president of the Iron and Steel Institute, London. He was awarded honorary doctorates of science by the New South Wales University of Technology (1955) and the University of Newcastle (1966). In 1969 he was appointed C.M.G. Like Lewis, he reputedly declined a knighthood.

Survived by his wife and son, Jones died of a ruptured abdominal aortic aneurysm on 10 August 1972 at Prahran and was cremated. His estate was sworn for probate at $385 831. During an association which lasted almost fifty-two years, this man—who once said that he never imagined leading the company and that his ambition was 'simply to be a good chemist'—had seen B.H.P. grow from a young Australian steelmaker into a more diversified business poised for success in international resources and energy markets. His contribution to the company's development was distinguished by absolute loyalty, a fine sense of judgement and outstanding ability in management.

H. Ivurson (comp and ed), *The Leaders of Commerce and Industry in Australia* (Melb, 1963);

A. Trengove, *What's Good for Australia ...!* (Syd, 1975); D. Sawer, *Australians in Company* (Melb, 1985); *BHP Review*, 11, no 1, Dec 1933, 27, no 1, Dec 1949, 27, no 2, Mar 1950, 29, no 2, Mar 1952, 39, no 4, June 1962, 48, no 3, Sept 1972; BHP Co Ltd, *Annual Report*, 1950-1972; *BHP J*, Spring 1971; Univ Melb *Gazette*, Dec 1972; Minutes of Meetings of Directors, BHP Co Ltd, 1950-72, *and* Chairman's Addresses to Shareholders, 1950-72, *and* Jones papers, 1941-69, *and* C. Y. Syme papers, 1945-72, *and* information files, 6E—Jones (BHP Co Ltd Archives, Port Melb); correspondence held by author (BHP archivist).   NARELLE CRUX

JONES, RALPH (1900-1944), labourer, quarry-hand and soldier, was born on 26 September 1900 at Gorleston, Norfolk, England, youngest of fourteen children of Henry William Jones, journeyman wheelwright, and his wife Eliza, née Chapman. Ralph left school at Church Road, Gorleston, at the age of 14; he was later described by a classmate Victor Wright as having been shy, withdrawn and far from robust. Employed as a motor engineering apprentice by the Great Yarmouth Port and Haven commissioners, Jones entered the British Army towards the end of World War I. He served for one year with the Army of Occupation on the Rhine, Germany, until invalided from the force with tuberculosis in April 1920. After a period of recuperation, he took seasonal jobs, but was unable to secure regular employment in Britain.

Emigrating to Australia about 1926, Jones became a labourer in Sydney. When the Depression rendered him jobless, he moved around the bush, finding casual work where he could. In the 1930s he settled at Tuena, lodging with a farmworker Tom Cook and his wife Madelaine. On 15 January 1942 Jones was mobilized as a private in the Citizen Military Forces; he nominated no next of kin, but later named Madelaine Cook with the designation 'friend'. In February he was posted to the 22nd Garrison Battalion at No.12 Prisoner of War Group, Cowra. Apart from a short spell with a P.O.W. labour detachment and another in hospital, he remained at the camp.

No.12 P.O.W. camp contained nearly 1100 Japanese privates and non-commissioned officers in one crowded compound, as well as Italians, Japanese officers, Koreans and Formosans in three other compounds. At about 2 a.m. on 5 August 1944 the Japanese privates and N.C.O.s, angered at news that they were about to be separated, staged a mass breakout. Wielding knives, baseball bats and other makeshift weapons, they stormed across the barbed-wire perimeter of their enclosure. One group headed for a Vickers machine-gun manned by Jones and Benjamin Hardy [q.v.] who had sprinted to take their positions at the gun as shots signalled an escape bid. They fired into the attacking hordes until overcome and bashed to death.

Jones was buried in the war graves section of Cowra general cemetery and posthumously awarded the George Cross. The citation recorded that he had displayed 'outstanding gallantry and devotion to duty' against Japanese 'who were worked up to a state of frenzy with the objective of either wiping out the garrison or getting wiped out themselves'. Four Australians and 231 Japanese died in the fighting; 334 prisoners who managed to escape from the camp were either recaptured or suicided. Details of the episode were kept secret because the authorities feared that disclosure of the extent of casualties among the prisoners could lead to reprisals against Australian captives in Japanese camps. Strangely, the secrecy continued for long after the war. The awards to Jones and Hardy were not announced until September 1950. Jones's G.C. was presented to his brother Walter by King George VI. It is now held by Cowra Shire Council.

L. Wigmore (ed), *They Dared Mightily* (Canb, 1963); H. Gordon, *Die Like the Carp!* (Syd, 1978) and *Voyage from Shame* (Brisb, 1994); Seikei High School (Tokyo), *Cowra-Seikei* (Tokyo, 1992); *Daily Telegraph* (Syd) and *Argus*, 1 Sept 1950; *Eastern Daily Press* (Norwich, UK), 6, 7 June 1991; *Great Yarmouth Mercury* (UK), 14 June 1991; family papers (held by Mrs M. Starr, Cowra, NSW).
                                        HARRY GORDON

JONES, REGINALD STUART (1902-1961), medical practitioner and playboy, was born on 5 September 1902 at Enfield, Middlesex, England, son of Stanley Abel Jones, grocer's assistant, and his wife Selina Rose, née Ingram. About 1912 he followed the family to New South Wales and lived at Woolgoolga, where Stanley was a timber merchant. Educated at Grafton High School, Reginald won a scholarship in 1921 to Wesley College, University of Sydney (M.B., Ch.M., 1926); he was a prominent athlete, cricketer, footballer and rifle-shooter.

After serving his residency (1926-27) at Royal Prince Alfred Hospital, in 1927 Jones sailed for London as ship's doctor in the *Raranga*. He worked as a medical officer (1928) at Queen Mary's Hospital for the East End and as chief medical officer (1929-30) at Australia House, and qualified as a fellow (1929) of the Royal College of Surgeons, Edinburgh. At the parish church, Grange, on 4 November 1929 he married 19-year-old Shena Reid with the forms of the Church of Scotland; they were to have one son before being divorced in 1936. While in Britain, Jones began his enduring passions for betting on racehorses and spending big. Back in Sydney in 1930, he practised at Canterbury and was a specialist in gynaecology (from 1935) in Macquarie Street. He was president (1933) of the New South Wales National Coursing Association, had a string of eighteen greyhounds and raced ponies.

It was not long before Jones established his reputation as a prominent and flamboyant figure in Sydney's underworld. He associated with the notorious Phil 'the Jew' Jeffs, Clifford Thompson, 'Scotty' Jowett, Frederick 'Chow' Hayes and Richard Reilly. Part-owner of a number of nightclubs, in 1936 Jones opened the Four Hundred Club, complete with band and a floor show headed by Roy Rene [q.v.11] and Jim Gerald [q.v.]; in the following year he lost his share of the club after a violent dispute with Jeffs. During World War II Jones allegedly plied drugs and black-market liquor to American servicemen from his yacht, *Sirocco*, which was also used for parties, famous in underworld and nightclub circles.

From the 1940s it was rumoured that Jones ran a profitable abortion practice—in partnership with Ivan Markovics—from his Macquarie Street surgery. Despite his varied activities, he was rarely charged with any offence. In 1944 he was tried for performing an illegal operation on a woman, but she refused to testify. Next year he was acquitted of having an unlicensed revolver in his possession. The only successful charge against Jones was that of driving under the influence of alcohol in 1949. Istov Molnar was arrested in Jones's surgery in 1959 for unlawfully using an instrument to procure an abortion.

At Cronulla on 6 January 1944 Jones had married with Presbyterian forms Mary Kathleen Ryan, a 24-year-old telephone operator. Later that year he was kidnapped by Jowett and Thompson (his wife's lover), and shot at point-blank range while in the back of Thompson's car. Instead of dumping his body as planned, the abductors left Jones at a private hospital. He recovered, his underworld reputation was enhanced, and Jowett and Thompson were convicted of attempted murder in 1945.

On the proceeds of his activities, Jones ran a string of racehorses and built a quasi-Moroccan mansion, Casa Clavel, equipped with its own shooting-gallery, at Bellevue Hill. Divorced in May 1950, he claimed to be aged 39 when he married a 23-year-old beauty queen and typiste Adeline Claudia Morick at St Stephen's Lutheran Church, Adelaide, on 17 June that year; they were to have three daughters. He was involved in some notable betting plunges in the 1950s. In 1958 he was disqualified by the Queensland Turf Club for involvement in a horse-doping scandal, but his appeal was upheld.

A large, round-faced man and a flash dresser, Jones was renowned for his pro-digious appetite for drink and gambling, and was rumoured to carry a pistol which he fired into the ceilings or floors of pubs and bars. In December 1960 he lodged an objection to an assessment of £136 000—for evaded income tax and penalties—on the grounds that the disputed money was race winnings. Survived by his wife and two of their daughters, and by the son of his first marriage, he died suddenly of coronary thrombosis on 10 June 1961 at his Coogee home and was buried with Anglican rites in Waverley cemetery. His estate was sworn for probate at £91 273, with debts totalling £154 565.

D. Hickie, *The Prince and the Premier* (Syd, 1985); *People* (Syd), 29 Aug 1951; *SMH*, 2 Nov 1944, 12 Jan, 28-29 Mar 1945, 5 Apr 1952, 11 Dec 1959, 9 Dec 1960, 14 Aug 1962, 13 Oct 1966; *Truth* (Syd), 27 Mar-5 Apr 1945; *Sun Herald*, 27 Apr, 4, 10 May 1958, 20 Jan 1985; *Truth* (Melb), 24 June 1961; *Mirror* (Syd), 19 Aug 1962.

STEPHEN GARTON

JONES, THOMAS GILBERT HENRY (1895-1970), professor of chemistry, was born on 14 July 1895 at Owens Gap, New South Wales, fourth child of native-born parents Thomas Jones, schoolteacher, and his wife Margaret Sarah, née Bell. Educated at the local public school, Newcastle High School (dux 1911) and the University of Sydney (B.Sc., 1915; D.Sc., 1926), Gilbert graduated with first-class honours; he won university medals in chemistry and mathematics, and was awarded a State government research scholarship. In August 1915 he accepted a post as assistant-lecturer and demonstrator in the department of chemistry, University of Queensland, and was given responsibility for teaching organic chemistry. During World War I Jones was employed (from November 1916) in the production of munitions and explosives at H.M. Factory, Gretna, Scotland; he initially worked on the manufacture of nitroglycerine and was later appointed senior chemist in charge of solvent recovery. It was at Gretna that he became a Freemason.

On 1 April 1920 Jones returned to the University of Queensland where he was promoted to lecturer in May 1921. At St John's Anglican Church, Gympie, on 21 August 1923 he married Vera Haines, a dispensing chemist. The thesis he submitted for his doctorate at the University of Sydney was supported by six publications. He was awarded the H. G. Smith [q.v.11] medal by the (Royal) Australian Chemical Institute in 1930 and was invited to give the Archibald Liversidge [q.v.5] lectures at the University of Sydney in 1934. President (1932-33) of the Royal Society of Queensland, he was a fellow of the

R.A.C.I., president (1938-39) of its Queensland branch and national president (1938-39). On 12 April 1940 he was appointed to the chair of chemistry at the University of Queensland. 'T.G.H.' gave unstinting service to the university in various capacities. A member (1944-68) of the senate, dean (1942-49 and 1960-61) of the faculty of science and president (1951-56) of the professorial board, he served on every senior committee, being especially proud of his work as chairman of the library committee for twelve years.

Wearing a short, white, starched barber's coat, Professor Jones gave stimulating lectures to the very large Chemistry I classes; he also took third-year and honours programmes with great skill, incorporating material recently published in major international journals. He was somewhat shy, but warm and generous, humble and honest. Of swarthy complexion, with a firm mouth and upright bearing, he best indicated his pleasure with a magnificent grin and a glint in his steely eyes.

He was a stalwart defender of the best traditions associated with universities. On 8 April 1957, as acting-president of the professorial board, he led a public meeting in the City Hall, Brisbane, attended by 2400 citizens protesting against the University of Queensland Acts Amendment bill, introduced by the Gair [q.v.] Labor government, which threatened the university's autonomy in making appointments. Ever forceful, Jones opened with 'It is time to stop this insidious nonsense' and closed with a quietly passionate 'Lord forgive them, for they know not what they do'. In spite of massive university agitation, the bill was passed in April 1957, but never implemented as a result of a change of government in August. Jones was appointed C.B.E. in 1960. He retired on 14 July 1965. The University of Queensland conferred an honorary LL.D. on him in 1960 and he received an honorary D.Sc. from the University of Newcastle in 1966. Barry Chiswell's 'A Diamond Period' lists Jones's professional publications, some forty in total. Continuing his interest in Freemasonry, Jones was active in the establishment of the University of Queensland Lodge, of which he became a foundation member in 1955. He was assistant grand master (1950-51), deputy grand master (1951-54) and grand master (1954-57) of the Grand Lodge of Queensland, and received his fifty-year service jewel in 1968.

Survived by his wife, son and daughter, Jones died on 11 August 1970 at St Andrew's Hospital, Brisbane, and was cremated with Presbyterian forms. The University of Queensland commemorated him with a Helidon sandstone grotesque, sculpted by Rhyl Hinwood, set in the south-west wall of the Forgan Smith [q.v.11] building.

Notable Men of Queensland (Brisb, 1950); H. Gregory, *Vivant Professores* (Brisb, 1987); K. Henderson, *The Masonic Grand Masters of Australia* (Melb, 1988); *Courier-Mail*, 12 Aug 1970; *Newcastle Morning Herald*, 13 Aug 1970; B. Chiswell, 'A Diamond Period' (ms, 1986, held by its author, Chemistry Dept, Univ Qld); Univ Qld Archives.

BURT ZERNER

JONES, THOMAS HENRY (1921-1965), poet and literary critic, was born on 21 December 1921 at Cwm Crogau, near Llanfihangel Bryn Pabuan, Brecknockshire, Wales, only son and eldest of five children of Llewelyn Morgan Jones, road-mender, and his wife Ruth, née Teideman. Although his father spoke Welsh, Harri and his siblings adopted their mother's language, English. The bare hills and hard weather of the isolated region where he was raised were to provide the imagery for many of his poems. He attended (from 1932) the county school at nearby Builth Wells, wrote proficiently, was adept at languages and poetry, and won a scholarship in 1939 to the University College of Wales, Aberystwyth (B.A., 1945; M.A., 1947).

Suspending his studies, in 1941 Jones joined the Royal Navy. He served in the Mediterranean and experienced the horrors of the Malta convoys—which he recorded in later poems—before being demobilized in 1946 as a leading wireless telegraphist. On 14 December that year at the register office, Camberwell, London, he married Fanny Christina Madeleine Scott, an art student who became a potter. From 1951 he taught English at the Portsmouth Dockyard School (later Technical College). His poetry first appeared in the *Welsh Review* in 1946. Over the next ten years he was remarkably productive. (Sir) Rupert Hart-Davis unhesitatingly published *The Enemy in the Heart* (London, 1957) and the three volumes which followed: *Songs of a Mad Prince* (1960), *The Beast at the Door* (1963) and, after Jones's death, *The Colour of Cockcrowing* (1966).

In 1959 Jones was appointed a lecturer (senior lecturer from 1962) in English at Newcastle University College and emigrated to New South Wales. Participating enthusiastically in the local literary community, he published verse and reviews in *Quadrant* and *Meanjin*. A number of the poems he wrote in Australia dealt with his sense of exile and his resentment at having to live abroad due to the lack of opportunities in Wales. There are, however, poems which show his delight in his new home and the enjoyment of friends and children. The monograph, *Dylan Thomas* (Edinburgh, 1963), established his claims as a critic. He accidentally drowned in the waters of the Bogey Hole, Newcastle, on 29 January

1965; survived by his wife and three daughters, he was cremated with Anglican rites and his ashes were buried at Llanfihangel Bryn Pabuan.

Jones's early poetry was highly formal and mannered. His writings later assumed a more muscular and individual voice, though the rhetorical cadences of Milton and the Bible can still be heard. Much of his work was concerned with the temptations of sensuality and with the puritan traditions of the Nonconformist Welsh churches. Australia became the hedonist antithesis of the Spartan theology and life of Wales. At the time of his death, his work had developed an authority and fluency which enhanced his reputation in Wales as one of the best Anglo-Welsh poets of the 1950s and 1960s. His Australian poems are fine records of the postwar immigration experience and have often been included in anthologies. *The Collected Poems of T. Harri Jones* (Llandysul, Wales, 1977) depicts a form of his name he never used.

J. Croft, *T. H. Jones* (Cardiff, Wales, 1976), and for bibliog; P. Power, *T. Harri Jones* (Cardiff, Wales, 1987).
JULIAN CROFT

JORGENSEN, JUSTUS (1893-1975), artist, was born on 12 May 1893 at East Brighton, Melbourne, third of six children of Simon Jorgensen, a master mariner from Norway, and his Victorian-born wife Nora, née Schreiber. Sent to a convent kindergarten and a local school, Justus was articled to his uncle, the architect Robert Schreiber, and qualified as a draughtsman. After working briefly in a government office, he learned painting at the National Gallery schools in 1915-17. He later joined Max Meldrum [q.v.10] and soon became his assistant.

On 1 May 1924 at St Francis's Catholic Church, Melbourne, Jorgensen married Lilya Smith, a medical student. They lived in France and England in 1924-28. While in London, Lily completed her degree and took work as an anaesthetist to support her husband. On their return to Australia in March 1928, they bought a house at Brighton and Jorgensen taught in a studio that he built in the grounds. In 1932, having broken with Meldrum, he took a city studio in Queen Street. Although he painted throughout his life, and taught for many years, he exhibited only three times: in 1929, 1930, then jointly with Colin Colahan in 1934. Jorgensen detested the commercialism of exhibitions, mistrusted the judgement of critics and the public, and was reluctant to relinquish his canvases to buyers.

In 1935 Lily bought land at Eltham and, with the assistance of friends and students, Jorgensen built a studio, students' quarters and a three-storey Great Hall. These buildings formed the nucleus of an artists' colony. The Great Hall, which Jorgensen described as 'gothic', was built of local mudstone; fittings such as carved stone windows, hammer beams, gargoyles and huge stone fireplaces were supplied by 'Whelan [q.v.12] the Wrecker'. Over the years the hillside on which the hall stood was covered by a series of lesser buildings, often mud-brick or stone, which reflected the influence of French provincial architecture. He named the settlement Montsalvat.

There, Jorgensen gathered around him a group of friends and followers. He gave them the opportunity to learn to paint and to master the crafts connected with his building—carpentry, sculpture, metalwork, tiling and slating. He also offered them the chance of a freer, more meaningful life—a measure of heightened self-knowledge and the possibility of happiness, including sexual fulfilment. About the time of the birth of his and Lily's son Max, Jorgensen had begun an affair with one of his followers Helen Skipper. This relationship lasted for the rest of his life, produced two sons, Sebastian and Sigmund, and occasioned some notoriety in suburbia and the press.

Jorgensen's fame rested less upon his paintings than upon the creation of Montsalvat, its colony of painters and craft-workers, the philosophy of art and life which he expounded there and the influence which he exercised upon many who called at Eltham. In provincial, postwar Melbourne a visit to his city studio, or his room at the Mitre Tavern, or—for the elect—an invitation to dinner at Eltham were stimulating ventures for inquiring minds. In his company a gamut of ideas was discussed, ranging from psychoanalysis, philosophy and theories of art to views on love and marriage. Many Melburnians tarried and moved on, but were profoundly affected by his contrast between 'the bourgeois world' and a life free of materialism, oppression and prurience.

The social structure at Montsalvat was feudal; Jorgensen dominated as the master. A number of his followers tired of his autocratic rule and left. In the face of soaring costs, Montsalvat was opened to the public in 1963. Justus himself became increasingly private, concentrating upon self-portraits, shown only to a few. In 1971 Sigmund staged an exhibition of his father's works in the Great Hall. Survived by his wife and his sons, Justus Jorgensen died on 15 May 1975 at Upper Fern Tree Gully and was buried in Eltham cemetery. His estate was sworn for probate at $149 101. In accordance with the provisions of his will, Montsalvat was administered by a trust and continued as an artists' colony and function centre.

A. Marshall, *Pioneers & Painters* (Melb, 1971); J. Teichman, *Jorgensen: Conversations and Memoir* (priv pub, Cambridge, Eng, 1976); K. Dunstan, *Ratbags* (Melb, 1980); B. Roland, *The Eye of the Beholder* (Syd, 1984); *People*, 19 July 1950; *Quadrant*, June 1985, p 26; *Age* (Melb), 11 Apr 1931, 16, 24 May 1975, 23 May 1977, 6 Oct 1984; *Bulletin*, 8 May 1971; Michael Jorgensen, Montsalvat (ms, Melb, 1991, held by its author, Carlton, Melb).

MAX TEICHMANN

JORIS, JOANNES JULIUS ALPHONSUS (1888-1963), diamondcutter and merchant, was born on 27 February 1888 at Broechem in the province of Antwerp, Belgium, second of five sons of Joannes Alphonsus Joris, diamondcutter, and his wife Maria Dorothea, née Luyckx. His forebears had been farmers in the region since the twelfth century, but closer generations had entered the diamond trade. Alphonsus Joris trained all his sons as diamondcutters. Jules found employment with several diamond merchants at Antwerp. There, on 10 June 1911, he married Maria Henrica Francisca Dekkers (1889-1959) in a civil ceremony at the town hall.

Early in World War I Joris was seconded from the Belgian Army and sent to Birmingham, England, where he supervised the manufacture of diamond tools at the factories of Kynock Ltd and Birmingham Small Arms Co. Ltd. When the war ended he returned to Antwerp and the gemstone trade, but continued to work with industrial diamonds and was associated with Fabrique Nationale, Liège. Within a decade he was employing forty workmen to cut and facet diamonds.

About 1929 Joris decided to emigrate to South Africa. A chance meeting with an Australian family led him to change his destination. With his wife and children, Albert and Elza, he reached Sydney in the *Oder* on 4 March 1930. They settled at Bondi, before shifting to Wahroonga. Jules started business in George Street in the city, but soon moved to the Bank of New South Wales building in Pitt Street where he was assisted by his son and daughter. His experience with industrial diamonds was quickly recognized.

Following the outbreak of World War II, the Ministry of Munitions prohibited the cutting and polishing of diamonds for jewellery, allowing them to be used only for precision industrial tools. Joris acquired larger premises above the Commercial Bank of Australia, Pitt Street. His was the first and only business in the country that was able to comply with the full extent of the Federal government's wartime requirements. Helped by Albert, he made machines, projectors and jigs previously unprocurable in Australia and eventually an accurate diamond-piercing machine to produce dies for very fine wires.

The firm drew on diamond fields at Copeton in northern New South Wales, but its supplies were largely from South Africa, even in wartime. Joris had long recognized the possibilities of diamond-producing areas of Australia and revealed his fascination with their history and potential in his contribution to I. L. Idriess's [q.v.9] *Stone of Destiny* (1948). Joris gave samples of Australian diamonds to the Mining and Geological Museum, Sydney. After the war he and his son formed a company, Diamond and Boart Products (Australia) Pty Ltd. Jules handled the gemstone trade, and Albert the manufacture and design of diamond tools and industrial machines.

A well-developed and fit man who was capable of dealing with intruders, Jules Joris was a keen gymnast and fond of surfing. As a young man he was an amateur wrestler and boxer. He possessed a good sense of humour and was an artist of some proficiency. Survived by his son and daughter, he died on 13 August 1963 in a railway train near Chatswood station and was buried in the Catholic section of Northern Suburbs cemetery. Arthur Fleischmann's statue of Joris is in the family's possession.

D. P. Mellor, *The Role of Science and Industry* (Canb, 1958); I. L. Idriess, *The Diamond* (Syd, 1969); A. Joris, *A Destiny in Diamonds* (Brisb, 1986); K. A. Lodewycks, *The Belgians in Australia* (Brisb, 1988); *People* (Syd), 31 Jan 1951; *Cwlth Jeweller and Watchmaker*, 10 Mar 1959, 19 Oct 1963; naturalization file A659/1, item 40/1/415 (AA, Canb); information from Mr A. Joris, Vaucluse, Syd.

KEVIN FAHY

JOSE, SIR IVAN BEDE (1893-1969), surgeon, was born on 13 February 1893 at Ningpo, China, eldest of three sons of George Herbert Jose, an Anglican missionary from England, and his wife Clara Ellen, née Sturt, from South Australia. In 1899 George took his family to England where he studied at the University of Oxford before returning to Adelaide in 1903. Ivan was educated at the Queen's School, North Adelaide, the Collegiate School of St Peter (1905-10) and the University of Adelaide (M.B., B.S., 1915; M.S., 1923). He enlisted in the Australian Imperial Force on 27 November 1914, but was discharged in March to complete his degree.

In November 1915 Jose sailed for the Middle East as captain, Australian Army Medical Corps. From June 1916 he served with the 14th Field Ambulance mainly on the Western Front. Near Ypres, Belgium, in September-October 1917 he supervised the evacuation of casualties while under fire, for which he was awarded the Military Cross. He was promoted major in 1918 and his A.I.F. appointment terminated in Australia on 10 December that year. At Christ Church, North Adelaide, on 20 May 1919 he married with Anglican rites Imogen Mervyn ('Jean') Hawkes. Having undertaken postgraduate studies in Britain, he qualified as a fellow of the Royal colleges of Surgeons, England (1922), and Edinburgh (1922), and of Australasia (1929).

Appointed medical and surgical registrar at the (Royal) Adelaide Hospital in 1923, Jose proved an enthusiastic teacher, displaying verve and a systematic approach in his presentations. Honorary assistant-surgeon (from 1924), honorary surgeon (1930-50) and foundation director (1936) of surgical studies, by the age of 40 he was the hospital's senior surgeon. He restructured surgical teaching and became dean of medicine in 1948. Adelaide's busiest surgeon, with a special interest in urology, he was almost always late, yet he expected everything and everybody to be ready when he arrived. Many 'Saturday morning' ward rounds commenced after midday and he was nicknamed 'the late Mr Jose'. Cramming fourteen working hours a day into twelve, he patronizingly substituted a wide smile for an apology for keeping people waiting.

He had served in the A.A.M.C. Reserve from 1921. Transferring to the Royal Australian Air Force Medical Branch in 1940, he worked as a part-time specialist and rose to the rank of group captain. Jose gave a great deal of his time to the South Australian division of the Australian Red Cross Society: he chaired its blood transfusion service, and was a member (1945-65) of the divisional committee and chairman (1966-68). After retiring in 1950, he practised privately, developed a grazing property and continued to belong to the Adelaide Club. He was a member (1953-65) of the council of the University of Adelaide and deputy-chairman of the university's postgraduate committee in medicine. A councillor (1946-58) and president (1955-57) of the Royal Australasian College of Surgeons, he was also president (1955-57) of the South Australian branch of the British Medical Association. In 1963 he was knighted. Survived by his wife, daughter and two sons, Sir Ivan died on 23 November 1969 in his North Adelaide home and was buried in North Road cemetery. The R.A.C.S., Melbourne, holds (Sir) Ivor Hele's portrait of Jose, and a visiting professorship in anaesthesia at the University of Adelaide commemorates him.

J. E. Hughes, *A History of the Royal Adelaide Hospital* (Adel, 1967); V. A. Edgeloe, *The Medical School of the University of Adelaide* (Adel, 1991); *MJA*, 2 May 1970, p 912; *Advertiser* (Adel), 24 Nov 1969; D6878 (Mort L).   RONALD HUNTER

JOSHUA, ROBERT (1906-1970), politician, soldier, bank officer and stockbroker, was born on 6 June 1906 at Prahran, Melbourne, fourth child of Edward Cecil Joshua, a distiller from Mauritius, and his Victorian-born wife Mary Inglis, née Drummond. Educated at Caulfield State School and Wesley College, Robert was briefly employed as a motor mechanic before becoming a teller with the Bank of Australasia. He was to work in Melbourne, and at branches at Leongatha, Korumburra and Ballarat. At St Roch's Catholic Church, Glen Iris, on 27 November 1929 he married Alma Agnes Watson, a schoolteacher. After studying through Hemingway & Robertson's correspondence school, he was admitted as an associate of the Federal Institute of Accountants.

In 1924-30 and 1936-40 Joshua served in the Citizen Military Forces and rose to captain. He joined the Australian Imperial Force on 15 May 1940 and was posted to the 2nd/32nd Battalion in the Middle East. During the defence of Tobruk, Libya, he led a successful raid on an enemy strong-point on the night of 13/14 September 1941 and was awarded the Military Cross. Back in Australia, in July 1943 he was promoted from major (1942) to lieutenant colonel and placed in command of the 2nd/43rd Battalion. From September the unit fought around Lae and Finschhafen, New Guinea. Joshua held command and training posts in Australia from February 1944 and was transferred to the Reserve of Officers on 2 February 1946. 'Jungle Bob' had been thrice wounded in action. Described as 'a man completely without personal fear', he seemed to revel in combat.

War service brought about a considerable change in Joshua's outlook. He was restless on his return to civilian life and considered joining the British Army in India where the rates of pay were far higher than his wages as a bank clerk. Whereas he had been politically conservative, he began to acquire new views. G. D. H. Cole and Raymond Postgate's *The Common People* (London, 1938) and L. F. Giblin's [q.v.8] *The Growth of a Central Bank* (Melbourne, 1951) influenced his thinking, as did discussions with Australian Labor Party supporters; his readings in Russian history made him a firm anti-communist. He obtained, by correspondence, a diploma in commerce (1954) from the University of Queensland. From 1946 he lived at Ballarat. He was president of the local branch of the A.L.P. Despite his background in private banking, he had joined the party because he supported bank nationalization.

At the 1951 Federal elections Joshua won the seat of Ballarat. Another candidate had gained pre-selection, but the result was overturned and Joshua was chosen by the

Victorian central executive. While campaigning, he made a point of distancing himself from unwanted communist backing. In his maiden speech in parliament he attacked the 'capitalistic price doctrine' of supply and demand, and argued that the Commonwealth should have the power to fix prices. He spoke often on economic matters and closely watched the activities of the Tariff Board, insisting that 'Australia's manufacturing industries must be protected and never allowed to fail'. He frequently returned to the theme of price control and was anxious to see an extension of the credit-control powers of that 'great institution', the Commonwealth Bank of Australia. He also expressed concern for the well-being of ex-servicemen and war widows, praised the C.M.F. as the 'backbone' of the A.I.F. and opposed the treaty of peace (Japan) bill of 1952, asserting that the Japanese were 'quite unbalanced in their mental outlook'. Later, he was to modify his views on Japan.

In April 1955 Joshua was one of seven members of Federal parliament who were expelled from the A.L.P. and formed the Anti-Communist Labor Party (Democratic Labor Party from 1957). He regarded H. V. Evatt [q.v.] as 'not fit to lead' the A.L.P. and said that the 'hallmark' of Evatt's activities was 'assistance for and sympathy with Communist ideas . . . That is why I thoroughly distrust him'. Joshua was the only non-Catholic in the new party, a factor which was seen to be crucial in his unexpected election as leader. He 'experienced continual sneers against the authenticity of his leadership' and strenuously denied any connexion with B. A. Santamaria. E. G. Whitlam later noted that Joshua managed to 'hold himself aloof from the extremes of bitterness and vituperation which characterised these tempestuous times'. Joshua's religious background and beliefs resist easy classification. His father was a non-practising Jew, his mother a Nonconformist. At Wesley College his religious affiliation was described as 'Theist'. Although influenced by his wife's faith, he was unable to accept key elements of Catholicism. Instead, he became a devout Anglican, serving as a lay reader and vestryman.

Described as 'solemn' and 'unprepossessing', Joshua was a capable politician, but was overshadowed by other more obviously talented members of his party, such as S. M. Keon, W. M. Bourke and J. M. Mullens. Solidly built, balding and of middle height, with a round face and a moustache, Joshua attracted the nickname 'King Farouk'. His increased weight was a consequence of his war injuries, as was his slight deafness; the latter condition reduced his ability to respond to interjections and increased the impression he gave of plodding, distant earnestness. Nevertheless,

when the House debated the commitment of Australian troops to Malaya in 1955, Joshua's 'curious style of deadpan pugnacity' was effective in marking out a distinct foreign and defence policy for his party.

Joshua expected his defeat at the 1955 elections. He had declined an offer from Prime Minister (Sir) Robert Menzies [q.v.] not to run a Liberal candidate for Ballarat. The seat was a marginal one and Menzies' proposal might have secured his return. Always suspicious of 'big business', Joshua preferred to avoid any obligation to the Liberals. After losing his seat, he established his own accountancy and stockbroking firm at Ballarat. He was federal president of the D.L.P. from its formation and continued to contest Ballarat until 1969.

Survived by his wife, son and five daughters, Joshua died of cancer on 2 June 1970 at Ballarat and was buried with Anglican rites in the Catholic section of Eganstown cemetery. He had continued to work until a few days before his death when he called in his doctors and said, 'I'm dying—what are you going to do about it?'

R. Murray, *The Split* (Melb, 1970); S. Trigellis-Smith, *Britain to Borneo* (Syd, 1993); *Daily Telegraph* (Syd), 20-21 Apr 1955; *Herald* (Melb), 20, 28 Apr 1955; *Courier* (Ballarat), 3 June 1970; information from Dr P. Tenni, Box Hill, Melb.

GEOFF BROWNE

JOSKE, ENID (1890-1973), college principal, was born on 7 September 1890 at Prahran, Melbourne, eldest child of Alexander Sydney Joske, a surgeon from Sydney, and his English-born wife Louisa, née Isaacs. The parents were not wealthy, but their son became a doctor and the three of their four daughters who remained unmarried were educationally equipped to follow a profession —two as teachers and one as a nurse.

Educated at the Church of England Girls' Grammar School, Melbourne, Enid won the Florence Stanbridge scholarship which enabled her to be a resident student (from 1909) in the women's hostel attached to Trinity College, University of Melbourne (B.A. Hons, 1912; Dip.Ed., 1913). She was employed as a teacher, first at her old school and then at Lauriston Girls' School, Malvern (1917-27). While at Lauriston, she helped to found the pioneering Children's Free Lending Library at Prahran. Returning from leave spent in Siam, Japan and New Zealand, she was invited in 1927 to apply for the principalship of her old college, renamed Janet Clarke [q.v.3] Hall. She had not been first choice, and later discovered that she had been expected to stay only three months. Miss Joske remained there for twenty-five years. She did not forget

Lauriston, and, after the school was incorporated, served (1948-52) on its foundation council, but J.C.H. became her life.

The Joske régime (1928-52) was steady, placid and wise. She inherited an institution which lacked physical cohesion, had only recently recovered from a serious dispute over discipline, and encountered the consistent hostility of (Sir) John Behan [q.v.7], the warden of Trinity. She dealt with these problems in her own unobtrusive way. Small and quiet, Miss Joske was also ubiquitous, a characteristic resented by some students until they discovered a care for their concerns which more than atoned for her occasional mistakes. Her main personal handicap, serious deafness, became almost an asset, as legends proliferated about her judiciously selective use of her hearing-aid. Unlike Behan, she never faced a crisis over student discipline. Although the basic boundaries of conventional decorum changed little between 1928 and 1952, Joske enforced her rules with humour and discretion. She met no agitation in J.C.H. for a move towards the much freer style of University Women's College. Miss Joske's college reflected the accepted mores of its time—but without rigidity.

Over the building programme, which finally brought the college under one roof and gradually enlarged it, she resolutely pressed the J.C.H. interest, with the creation of the gardens as a contribution from her own expertise. The subsequent naming of the Enid Joske Wing (1956) acknowledged her efforts, sustained in the face of the warden's lack of sympathy for all J.C.H. concerns. Behan's antagonism had an impact in ways he did not foresee. The underlying point of difficulty was that Miss Joske's position as principal was anomalous. Independently run, J.C.H. remained a Trinity possession, which the warden had the right to criticize and control. Although it was the oldest and largest of the women's colleges, Miss Joske had no place on the heads of colleges' committee. Yet neither was J.C.H. integrated into the Trinity fabric, nor were the claims of the women considered with those of the men. For Behan, J.C.H. was at best an unwanted appendage, at worst the source of dangerous distractions for the Trinity men whose interests he saw as paramount. The resultant frictions drove J.C.H. in upon itself, and fostered a sense of distinctive identity.

Miss Joske's attitude to Behan was tactful and generous. If she saw separation from Trinity as inevitable, she never pushed for it, and she was fully aware of the Trinity case against it. But from 1946 she gladly accepted the greater autonomy offered by Behan's successor R. W. T. Cowan [q.v.13]. While she was principal, she tacitly strengthened the case for independence by consolidating a happy and confident institution, academically sound, with loyal domestic staff and some distinguished tutors. She also widened student horizons by the quality of the visitors to high table. Her college had grown and prospered. Nine years after her retirement in 1952, independence was achieved.

When she withdrew to Harfra, her cottage at Harkaway, there was concern lest she feel lonely and bereft. The concern was misplaced. She made another garden, and for twenty years entertained a stream of visiting ex-students. She died on 17 October 1973 at Harkaway and was cremated with Anglican rites.

L. Gardiner, *Janet Clarke Hall 1886-1986* (Melb, 1986); *Univ Melb Gazette*, Aug 1956, Mar 1974; Lauriston Girls' School Archives; Janet Clarke Hall Archives; J. C. V. Behan diaries (Univ Melb Archives); personal information.

ALISON PATRICK

JOYCE, ANTHONY WALTER (1946-1980), journalist, was born on 9 August 1946 at Lambeth, London, son of Walter Henry Joyce, custodian of enemy property and later branch-manager of an insurance company, and his wife Winifred Maud, née Warboys. Educated at Haberdashers' Aske's School (which moved from Hampstead to Elstree, Hertfordshire), Tony studied modern history at Magdalen College, Oxford (B.A., M.A., 1980). He emigrated to Australia in 1968, performed administrative work on a sorghum project in the Northern Territory and became a production-assistant with a number of film companies. In March 1969 the Australian Broadcasting Commission appointed him a specialist trainee in the talks department, Sydney, where he gained experience in radio with the current-affairs programmes, 'A.M.' and 'P.M.'.

At St John the Baptist Church, Harbord, on 8 November 1969 Joyce married with Catholic rites Monica Eileen Mooney, a production assistant. In 1970 he was sent to Rockhampton, Queensland, for some months as talks officer, and in 1971 to Brisbane to work on the television current-affairs programme, 'This Day Tonight'. He joined the reporting staff of 'T.D.T.' in Sydney in September. His duties included presenting, producing, interviewing and directing; he was promoted senior reporter in May 1972.

The A.B.C. sent Joyce to Singapore as an overseas correspondent in 1975. He flew to Saigon in April and was one of the last reporters to leave before the city fell on the 30th to forces of the Democratic Republic of (North) Vietnam. Travelling extensively in South and South East Asia, he covered the state of emergency in India (1975-77) and military *coups d'état* in Thailand (October

1976 and October 1977), and filed stories on the Vietnamese boat people. In 1978 he was one of the first Australian journalists allowed back into Vietnam. While there, he made a television documentary.

In March 1979 Joyce was posted to London. His 'beat' included Africa, and on 21 November he arrived in Lusaka to report on the escalating conflict between Zambia and Zimbabwe-Rhodesia. With his cameraman Derek McKendry, he travelled some 35 miles (57 km) to film Chongwe Bridge which had been destroyed by Rhodesian commandos. Zambian soldiers arrested the two of them and placed them in a police car. A man, thought to be a political officer with the militia, raised his pistol and shot Joyce in the head. Joyce was flown to London, but never regained consciousness. Survived by his wife and son, he died on 3 February 1980 in St Bartholomew's Hospital and was cremated with the rites of the Church of England. He was posthumously awarded a Media Peace Prize (1980) by the United Nations Association of Australia.

Joyce was a talented and accomplished journalist, admired by his peers for his integrity and high professional standards, and loved for his considerable wit and humour. A thoughtful and compassionate observer of the human condition, including its misery, deprivation, cruelty and hopelessness, he was a humanist and a humanitarian. His experiences made him a realist and a fatalist. His death was an instance of a journalist whose luck ran out while he was engaged in work for which he cared passionately.

SMH, 5 Feb 1980; *Age*(Melb), 7 Nov 1981; ABC Document Archives, Syd; information from Mrs M. Joyce, Chatswood, Syd; personal information.

PAUL MURPHY

JOYCE, DONOVAN MAXWELL (1910-1980), radio producer and writer, was born on 31 October 1910 at Hawthorn, Melbourne, fifth child of Edward James Joyce, clerk, and his wife Edith Elizabeth, née Conder, both Victorian born. Educated at Scotch College, Hawthorn, Donovan probably belonged to the school's wireless club before he left Scotch at the age of 15. He was employed by Broken Hill Proprietary Co. Ltd. Finding himself temperamentally unsuited to that work, he performed in amateur theatricals in Melbourne and was stage manager for several productions of the Little Theatre Company.

In 1932 Joyce entered commercial radio, working with stations at Broken Hill, New South Wales, Mildura, Victoria, and Adelaide. Returning to Victoria, he joined 3HS Horsham as manager and announcer. In 1934 he transferred to 3KZ in Melbourne, produced 'Spelling Bee' and 'Radio Cinema', then moved to 3AW in 1939. At All Saints Church, St Kilda, on 31 July 1937 he had married with Anglican rites Nance Lillian Collins, a milliner. Unable to enlist during World War II because a childhood injury had left the tendons in his right hand severely damaged, he served as an air-raid warden, and wrote a regular and sometimes controversial column in *Radio Times* under the pseudonym, 'Slapper'.

Following a court case over the terms of his employment, Joyce resigned as production manager at 3AW in 1944 and next year formed Donovan Joyce Productions. He wrote and commissioned dramas and documentaries, many of which he exported, particularly to South Africa, where he also advised on local radio production. At one stage his work was broadcast in sixteen countries. He formed a partnership with his elder brother Jim to bring leading actors, such as Lyndall Barbour and Dinah Shearing, from Sydney to perform in radio serials which included 'The Devil's Duchess' and 'The Lillian Dale Affair'. 'The Passing Parade', a half-hour documentary series, ran for over 150 episodes, many scripted by Joyce. One episode, 'The Old School Tie', received much publicity when four actors walked out of a recording session because they felt that the play was a slur on the English class system. His fifty-episode series, 'T-Men', about tax evasion, caught the attention of taxation officials who investigated a suspected 'leak' of inside information. From 1956 Joyce increasingly resented 'being cut off in my prime' by the 'monstrous television screen'; although he wrote the script for one of Crawford Productions' episodes of 'Homicide' in 1966, he never adapted to the new medium.

In 1964 Joyce had travelled to Israel to investigate a scroll allegedly written by Christ, but was thwarted in his efforts to visit archaeological digs at Masada. After a brief return to 3AW, he published *The Jesus Scroll* (Sydney, 1972; London, 1973), an unorthodox story of the life of Christ which became a best-seller and led to death threats and continuing controversy. Survived by his wife and son, he died of hypertensive heart disease on 16 October 1980 at Prahran and was cremated. Over six feet (183 cm) tall, he was a big, bearded man, with a fierce but controlled temper, whose demand for excellence and talent for inventiveness were central to his life.

R. Lane, *The Golden Age of Australian Radio Drama* (Melb, 1994); *NZ Listener*, 28 June 1957; *Age* (Melb), 18 May 1977; Joyce file (Performing Arts Museum, Vic Arts Centre, Melb); information from Mr C. Joyce, Oakleigh, Melb.

DEIRDRE MORRIS

JUAN, JOHN (1901-1979), adagio dancer, radio announcer and compere, was born on 1 May 1901 at Hawker, South Australia, and registered as John Kappen Fox, son of John Henry Fox, solicitor, and his wife Adelaide Kappen, née Porter, a pianist. His father died before John was age 2 and his mother brought him to Adelaide. She took him to England when he was 7 and to Perth when he was 12. In 1915 he entered Scotch College. At 17 he left for England as an able seaman in the merchant ship, *Australplane*; while the ship was strikebound in New York, he haunted Broadway. Back in Perth in 1920, he danced a prologue to the silent film, *Whirl of Life*, and began a theatrical career as an adagio dancer. Five ft 10½ ins (179 cm) tall, lithe, dark and suave, he changed his surname to the more romantic Juan (legalized later). At St George's Anglican Cathedral, Perth, on 22 April 1925 he married Zelda Anne Coleen Bailey, an actress from New Zealand. They went on tour, treading the boards as an underdressed couple in cabaret performances in England, Europe and Australia, and reputedly took top billing at the Palladium and Palace Royal theatres, London.

In the mid-1930s Juan sold dry-cleaning machines in Ireland; a similar venture in Sydney left him insolvent. In 1938 a chance audition in Perth gave him entry to the emerging world of radio as an announcer on the Australian Broadcasting Commission's station, 6WF. For thirty-five years his natural gift for the medium endeared him to thousands of Western Australians who warmed to his sentimental signature tunes, *There'll be a Silver Lining, We'll Meet Again* and *Up with the Curtain*. Listeners liked his breezy presentation, robust humour and endless variety of jokes. Juan's personal life was disciplined: a strict diet, early to bed and up before dawn; on the way to work he noted cloud formations and the direction of the Swan Brewery flag as he formulated his daily weather forecasts. He divorced his wife in 1941. On 10 December that year at Trinity Church, Perth, he married with Congregational forms Thelma Rose Ridley, a 26-year-old hairdresser; their chief relaxation was sailing his 22-ft (6.7 m) yacht, *Victoria*, on the Swan River and around Rottnest Island. His most popular programmes were 'The Breakfast Session', 'The Hospital Hour' and 'I'll Pay That One'. The last-mentioned show was launched on the national network after he had completed full-time military service (1942-46) in Western Australian units of the Volunteer Defence Corps and risen to temporary captain.

Away from radio, Juan was a favourite compere at town hall concerts, Government House balls and other special functions. He made his television début in 1962, compering an A.B.C. variety show. In accordance with Commonwealth regulations, he retired in 1966, but there was such a 'hoo-ha' that, within a month and perhaps with questionable wisdom, the A.B.C. reinstated him in a part-time capacity. For services to radio, he was appointed M.B.E. in 1969. Juan's relationship with his employers, however, soured as he grew testy, due to failing health and several operations. Acrimony finally erupted during his last session in 1974 when he vented his scorn on the A.B.C. Survived by his wife and their son and daughter, he died on 24 February 1979 at Kelmscott and was cremated with the forms of the Uniting Church.

West Australian, 4 May 1966, 1 Jan, 23 Apr 1969, 26 Feb 1979; *Weekend Mag* (Perth), 1 Feb 1969; *Daily News* (Perth), 24 Dec 1973; *Living Today* (Perth), 27 Feb 1975.　　WENDY BIRMAN

JULIUS, MAX NORDAU (1916-1963), barrister and communist, was born on 9 March 1916 in South Brisbane, seventh and youngest child of Julius Isack (known as Isack Julius), a tailor from Hungary, and his Rumanian-born wife Ernestina, née Lang. Max was raised in a non-orthodox Jewish family which ultimately produced six members of the Communist Party of Australia. After attending Leichhardt Street State School, he won a scholarship (1929) to Brisbane Grammar School where he was described in its register as 'able but sometimes rather sluggish'. In 1934 he entered the University of Queensland (B.A., 1938; LL.B., 1940) and successfully combined study with energetic involvement in undergraduate activities. A member (1937) of the Debating Club's intervarsity team, he was secretary (1937-38) of the Radical Club and active in the Law Students' Society. As editor (1938) of the Student Union's weekly paper, *Semper Floreat*, he became well used to the fracas typical of student politics. While forging an enduring friendship with Ted Bacon (later secretary of the Queensland branch of the C.P.A.) and becoming 'well-red' in Marxist literature, he joined the C.P.A. in 1936.

In the late 1930s Julius's involvement with the party became more intense. He had participated in some of the Unity Theatre's socialist productions, performing in *Waiting for Lefty* in 1938, and in 1940 he and another member of the C.P.A., Connie Healy, formed the Queensland branch of the Eureka Youth League. His continued ill health precluded active military service. Next year his application to join the Queensland Bar was blocked on the ground that he was a communist. He took the matter to court, with F. W. Paterson [q.v.], himself a communist, as his able counsel. The judge's decision, which provoked much publicity, found the evidence insufficient to prove that the applicant was 'not of good fame' and Julius was admitted to the Bar on 29 June 1941. Discrimination continued over the next two decades and he received comparatively few briefs from Brisbane's legal fraternity. His only income was earned from cases referred to him by a friendly solicitor Cyril Murphy, but Julius was kept busy by an endless procession of impecunious clients, keen to exploit his generosity and solicit his services for a token fee. At the general registry office, Brisbane, on 22 October 1943 he married Kate Doreen Gillham, a nurse; they were to remain childless and to be divorced in 1962.

Following his involvement in the infamous St Patrick's Day march held during the 1948 railway strike, Julius was sentenced to three months imprisonment for the non-payment of fines totalling £107 11s. 0d. imposed on him under the Industrial Law (Anti-picketing) Amendment Act (1948). With fellow communists Michael Healy and E., C. Englart, he was released after two weeks when their predicament began to attract widespread sympathy from the community and their fines were mysteriously paid by an anonymous donor—widely believed to be the Hanlon [q.v.] Labor government.

Julius's standing within the C.P.A. was assured by his public exposure, formidable intelligence, good humour and legal skill, and he became one of the most respected members of the Queensland branch. In fulfilling his commitment to the party he stood for election to the House of Representatives in 1946, 1954, 1955, 1958 and 1961. On the last occasion his preferences were essential to the Liberal candidate, (Sir) James Killen, winning Moreton, thus securing the return of the Menzies [q.v.] government. Julius also unsuccessfully contested the Senate in 1949, 1951 and 1953, the Queensland Legislative Assembly in 1947 and 1950, and was a mayoral candidate for Brisbane in 1949, 1952 and 1955.

While Australians became increasingly preoccupied with 'the communist spectre', Julius appeared as a counsel for the defence at the royal commission into the C.P.A. in Victoria in 1950. He provided legal support for the challenge to the Communist Party dissolution bill before the High Court of Australia in 1950-51. During the Commonwealth's royal commission on espionage (1954-55), he cross-examined the Petrovs, ably represented Frederick Rose and assisted others. Involved in numerous campaigns, he supported the Aboriginal cause and was an executive-member of the Queensland Peace Committee. Having endured twenty years of economic hardship, on 16 February 1960 he had his name removed from the roll of barris-

ters and was admitted as a solicitor, entering into partnership with Murphy. Julius's new-found prosperity was short-lived. He died of myocardial infarction on 27 February 1963 in Princess Alexandra Hospital, South Brisbane, and was cremated.

Univ Qld Students, *Semper Floreat*, 7, no 23, Oct 1938, p 1; Communist Party of Aust, *Guardian* (Melb), 4, no 8, 5 Mar 1963, p 3; Qld State Reports, 1941; *Courier-Mail*, 3, 11, 12, 16 June, 30 July 1941, 18 Mar, 4, 5, 20, 21 Aug, 16, 17 Sept, 10 Dec 1948, 28 Feb 1963; *Telegraph* (Brisb), 17 Mar, 3-5, 19 Aug 1948; JUS/35, Letters and associated papers re the imprisonment of Communists Max Julius, E. C. Englart and M. Healy, 1948 (QA).

JOHN MCGUIRE

JURY, CHARLES RISCHBIETH (1893-1958), poet and professor of English, was born on 13 September 1893 at Glenelg, Adelaide, eldest of five children of South Australian-born parents George Arthur Jury, merchant, and his second wife Elizabeth Susan, née Rischbieth. Charles was educated at Glenelg Grammar School and at the Collegiate School of St Peter (1909-13) where he was head prefect. His father arranged for Charles's first book of poems, *Spring is Coming*, to be published when the boy was 12 years old; his second publication, *Perseus and Erythia*, appeared in 1912. Next year he entered Magdalen College, Oxford (B.A. Hons, 1918; M.A., 1923). Commissioned temporary lieutenant (1914) in the Oxfordshire and Buckinghamshire Light Infantry, he was badly wounded at Ypres, Belgium, in 1915 and ended his service in March 1916. He lost numerous friends in the war and wrote this epitaph:

> You who shall come, exalt these childless dead
> To be your fathers, from whose life you are bred.
> The dead beget you now: for now they give
> Their hope of sons that you their sons may live.

Graduating from Oxford with a first in English language and literature, Jury returned to Adelaide. His father made him financially independent and he determined to devote his life to the writing of poetry. With (Sir) Edward Morgan [q.v.] and Vernon Knowles, he published *Lamps and Vine Leaves* (Melbourne, 1919); Jury's contribution contained early versions of some of his best poems. From 1919 to 1938 he lived mostly in Europe, but often came back to Australia. *Love and the Virgins* (1929), a poetic drama, was published in London. In 1932 he was tutor in English and senior resident at St Mark's College, Adelaide, and in 1933 relieving lecturer in

English at the University of Adelaide. Much of his time was spent in Italy (especially at Taormina, Sicily) and in Greece, countries whose literature and landscape, together with the landscape of his own country, nourished his poetry.

Late in 1938 Jury settled into a flat at North Terrace, Adelaide. In 1939 he published *Galahad, Selenemia and Poems*, and in 1941 the first version of his poetic tragedy, *Icarius*, a courageous treatment of the 'dreadful and agonizing' subject of homosexuality. Enlisting in the Citizen Military Forces in May 1941 and commissioned next month, he performed intelligence duties at Loveday and in Brisbane before transferring to the Retired List in August 1945 as a captain. In 1946-49 he held the Jury chair of English language and literature (endowed by his mother in 1921 in memory of her husband) at the University of Adelaide. In his last years he wrote three verse plays—later published as *The Sun in Servitude and Other Plays* (Melbourne, 1961) —two of which had successful productions. He also composed a number of short poems, prepared definitive editions of *Icarius* (1955) and *Love and the Virgins* (1958), and wrote a treatise on quantity and quasi-quantity in English verse, *Well Measur'd Song* (Melbourne, 1968). His essays in the Saturday *Advertiser* in 1954-55 brought him to the notice of a wider public.

Jury had a genius for friendship and influenced Adelaide's cultural life by conveying his love of the arts in compelling fashion. His deep understanding of Shakespeare led him to become textual adviser for Colin Ballantyne's theatrical productions. Jury encouraged—often with financial aid—poets, playwrights, actors, scholars and teachers. He assisted *Angry Penguins*, both before and after the magazine's encounter with the law. He bought paintings, gave lectures and radio talks, and initiated poetry-reading circles. He taught more than one generation of South Australians to comprehend urbanity in mind and manners. His gentleness, courtesy, kindness and sense of humour made him loved; his self-awareness, reasonableness and toughness of mind made him respected, even revered. But it was as a poet that he wished to be remembered. His passionate love of Greek culture and the strength of his feeling for form and music in poetry made his strictly organized verse seem out of touch with the times. Yet it is rich, fine and powerful poetry, polished over many years.

Jury died of cancer on 22 August 1958 in his North Adelaide home and was cremated; his estate was sworn for probate at £110 838. A limited edition of his selected poetry and prose, *A Dweller on Delos*, was published in 1993, the centenary of his birth. William Salmon's portrait of Jury is held by Elspeth Ballantyne in Melbourne.

B. Wall and D. Muecke (eds), *The Emperor's Doorkeeper* (Adel, 1988); B. Wall, 'Charles Rischbieth Jury: Poet of Adelaide', *South Australiana*, 5, no 2, Sept 1966, p 79; *Adel Review*, 118, Sept 1993, pp 3, 32; Jury papers (Mort L).

BARBARA WALL

K

KABERRY, PHYLLIS MARY (1910-1977), anthropologist, was born on 17 September 1910 at San Francisco, United States of America, eldest of three children of English-born parents Lewis Kaberry, architect, and his wife Hettie Emily, née Coggins. Lewis had expected to find work at San Francisco following the 1906 earthquake. About 1913 the family moved to New Zealand, thence to Newcastle, New South Wales, and finally in 1914 to Sydney, settling at Manly. From an early age Phyllis proved intelligent and adventurous, spending her childhood exploring Middle Harbour in a boat she and her two younger brothers had fashioned from corrugated iron. She attended Fort Street Girls' High School and the University of Sydney (B.A., 1933; M.A., 1935), winning the Wentworth [q.v.9] medal in 1934 and gaining first-class honours for her master's thesis on 'Culture contact in Melanesia'. At university she and her comrade Margot Hentze [q.v.9] joined Professor John Anderson's [q.v.7] Freethought Society.

In 1934-35 Kaberry spent eighteen months (on grants) following the daily activities of Aborigines living along the Forrest and Lyne rivers in the Kimberley district of Western Australia; while in the area she made enduring friendships with (Dame) Mary and Elizabeth Durack. Kaberry's findings were published in Oceania (1934-36). From September 1936 she worked in Professor Bronislaw Malinowski's department at the London School of Economics (Ph.D., 1938). Her thesis, published as *Aboriginal Woman* (1939), strove to portray 'Aboriginal woman as she really is'—an integral part of Aboriginal culture, interesting in her own right. In a period when native women were generally depicted as either 'domesticated cows' or erotic objects her approach was rare.

With the support of an Australian National Research Council grant, Dr Kaberry carried out field-work (1939-40) in the Sepik district of the mandated Territory of New Guinea. World War II forced her to return to Sydney. She spent 1940-41 writing up field-reports—two of which were published in Oceania (1941-42)—and working for the university's department of anthropology as an honorary assistant-lecturer. While successively holding Sterling and Carnegie fellowships (1941-43) at Yale University, U.S.A., she gave lectures and edited *The Dynamics of Culture Change* (New Haven, 1945), a posthumous collection of Malinowski's unpublished papers. In England, she was a research associate (1943-44) at the Royal Institute of International Affairs.

Invited by the Colonial Social Science Research Council to investigate the cause of malnutrition in the British Cameroons, Kaberry arrived in West Africa in January 1945. The years (1945-46, 1947-48, 1958, 1960, 1963) she spent there were possibly the happiest of her career. The African women she met were not shy and liked to swap gossip with her. Her friendship with them led her to complain on their behalf about the conduct of neighbouring tribesmen whose cattle were destroying the women's farms. Although she later claimed to have done very little, she was credited with having driven the cattle from Nso land and became something of a legend among the women. They honoured her by making her a 'Queen Mother'. Of the many accolades that she received, this was the one she most prized. The results of her research were published in *Women of the Grassfields* (London, 1952).

In January 1949 Kaberry had joined the staff of University College, London, and was reader in anthropology from 1950 until September 1977. She was a council-member (1951-54, 1953-59, 1960-63) and vice-president (1965-68) of the Royal Anthropological Institute of Great Britain and Ireland, and was awarded its Rivers (1957) and Wellcome (shared, 1959) medals. A pretty, vivacious woman, with shoulder-length brown hair which she usually wore tied in a bun, she loved music and English literature. In 1944 she took to Africa Shakespeare's plays, some poetry in compact editions, a recent translation of Jacob Burckhardt's *Die Kultur der Renaissance in Italien*, Lewis Carroll's *Alice in Wonderland* and Jane Austen's novels in omnibus form. She often sent poems inspired by her field-work experiences to her friends. Possessing a dry sense of humour, she liked to regale her male colleagues with the derogatory remarks African women made about their men and their lazy habits. Former students found her kind, helpful and comforting after other teachers had torn strips off them. Phyllis Kaberry died of acute alcohol poisoning by misadventure on 31 October 1977 in her Camden flat and was cremated.

S. Ardener (ed), *Persons and Powers of Women in Diverse Cultures* (NY, 1992); J. Marcus (ed), *First in their Field* (Melb, 1993); *Africa*, 48, no 3, 1978, p 296; *Oceania*, 48, no 4, June 1978, p 301; *SMH*, 20 Dec 1944; *The Times*, 18 Nov 1977; P. M. Kaberry, Australian Field-notes (Aust Inst of Aboriginal and Torres Strait Islander Studies, Canb); Elkin papers, box 8 (Univ Syd Archives); family information.

CHRISTINE CHEATER

KABU, TOMMY (c.1922-1969), political leader, was born about 1922 at Urika, Papua, into the I'ai group of the Purari people of the Gulf of Papua, and named Koivi Au'a. He briefly attended the mission primary school at Urika before he ran away from home in 1935 and a few years later joined the Royal Papuan Constabulary at Samarai.

In 1942 Kabu and some Australians sailed in a small motor vessel to Cooktown, Queensland, fleeing from an anticipated Japanese invasion. At Cairns he was employed as an orderly by N. S. Pixley, an officer of the Royal Australian Navy, and served in H.M.A.S. *Bundaberg* in 1943-44, although he never formally enlisted in the Navy. After his repatriation in 1945, Kabu initiated a programme for economic and social change among the Purari. He collected money to facilitate a co-operative venture which involved production, transport and marketing.

In 1946 the Purari Sago Trading Co. was formed and a settlement, Rabia Camp, established in Port Moresby. Major socio-cultural changes were made in the Purari delta: villages were relocated in disregard of tribal enmities and boundaries; *ravi* (ceremonial houses) were destroyed and European-style houses built in their place; the power and status of chiefs were reduced; and other visible signs of the past were eradicated. Christianity was to be the members' religion and *hiri motu*, the *lingua franca* of Papua, their language.

By 1950 the company had collapsed. Its vessel, bought for £2000, was accidentally gutted and never sailed. The firm's licence to trade in sago was cancelled because it had failed to pay many of the suppliers. Kabu and ninety Purari living in Port Moresby then started another venture which sold sago brought from the delta, and operated a trading store, bakery, tea-house and laundry. The enterprise lasted only six years due to irregular supplies of sago, the unreliability of transport, overstaffing at the Port Moresby depot, faulty costing and unfamiliarity with commercial procedures. Management of the small and uncomplicated business was beyond the means of the handful of semi-literate Purari and their illiterate supporters. They subsequently sought advice and help from the government. Senior officials encouraged what became known as the 'Tommy Kabu Movement', but it encountered opposition from some junior officials in the field who perceived it as usurping their authority. In any case, the government lacked sufficient staff to provide the assistance needed and the missionaries did not like Kabu's influence.

Although Kabu was occasionally accused of being a cargo cultist or a trickster, he genuinely sought to bring about the material progress of his people. Three factors under-

pinned his leadership—his experience during World War II, his charisma and his programme. The movement expressed new ambitions and values which had come gradually from the previous decades of contact with European culture, but it took its specific form from the ideas of relatively young men returning from the areas of war. Kabu's long-term aim was to expand the movement to gain political power throughout Papua. He was an unsuccessful candidate for the House of Assembly in the 1968 elections. Kabu married twice. Survived by his wife, who came from the Central District of Papua, and by numerous children, he died in October 1969. Many Papua New Guineans regard him as a proto-nationalist.

SPC Social Development Notes (Noumea, New Caledonia), no 7, 1951; *Oceania*, 29, no 2, 1958, p 75; *New Guinea Research Bulletin*, no 14, 1967; *Pacific Studies*, 14, no 2, 1991, p 29; *Canb Anthropology*, 15, no 2, 1992, p 89; *Times of PNG*, 5 Sept 1986.
HARRY H. JACKMAN

KAPIU, GAGAI; see GAGAI

KARLOAN (KALONI), ALBERT (1864-1943), Aboriginal doctor (putari), was born in July 1864 on the shore of Lake Albert, near Point McLeay (Raukkan) mission, South Australia, son of Taramindjeri (d.1894), 'spirit-man' and council-member of the Manangki clan, Yaraldi tribe, Ngarrindjeri people, and Paleliwal (Nelly Muldugine), of the Muldjong-gurindjeri clan, Tanggani tribe. Milerum [q.v.10] was his cousin. Kaloni's mother abandoned him as a baby, but he was nurtured by his aunt, a noted sorceress, who showed him her paraphernalia and taught him her techniques. Djinbatinyeri was his child name and rekali, the water rat, his totem. He attended the mission school when George Taplin [q.v.6] was superintendent; by the age of 6, Karloan was raising stones and burning lime to build the church and cottages. The most significant figure in his life was his father. Taramindjeri had a comprehensive knowledge of traditional rules and practices; his healing combined magic with medicinal treatments. In 1882 Karloan was one of the last three youths to undergo full initiation rites in the lower River Murray region. Four years later he began an apprenticeship to his father.

At the mission church, Port McLeay, on 13 March 1884 Karloan had married with Congregational forms Flora Kropinyeri (d.1926), a servant; they were to have two sons and six daughters—five of whom died in infancy. A small, nuggety man, he played for the local football team. In 1888 he was ill with phthisis.

He worked as a shearer, fisherman and mechanic. On 19 March 1889 he was one of a delegation of Ngarrindjeri churchmen who visited Adelaide and petitioned the Aborigines' Friends' Association to remove Frederick Taplin as mission superintendent because of alleged sexual misconduct. In 1894 Karloan and other mission Aborigines constructed their first European boat, a 15-ft (4.5 m) pram, clinker built, ribbed and fastened with copper rivets. Next year they won a government contract to build seven more; the contract was renewed in 1898. Karloan had sung with the mission's Glee Club at Government House, Adelaide, in December 1895 to welcome the governor Sir Thomas Buxton [q.v.7], a member of the British and Foreign Aborigines Protection Society.

The 1911 Act for the protection and control of the State's Aborigines allowed land, stock and implements to be allotted to them for farming. Superintendent David Roper thought that Karloan 'would make a successful settler', but his application of 16 March 1912 received no reply from the chief protector's office. Again backed by the superintendent, in 1916 Karloan requested £150 to buy a cinematograph 'to travel . . . with my Son Clement giving entertainments of illustrated Songs and Recitation by Slide pictures as well as Film'. Chief Protector W. G. South rejected his 'ridiculous request'. When Karloan later asked South for extra rations for his sick wife, this request was also refused. Following Flora's death, Karloan married a widow, Eva Dat, a Wutaltinyeri. In 1930 he moved to Wellington East.

From the time of his father's death, Karloan had determined to preserve the culture of his people. He did so in a period when Aborigines were being actively discouraged from identifying with their Aboriginal past and urged to behave like European-Australians. Later, his curiosity and memory proved invaluable to many anthropologists, including Norman Tindale. At the South Australian Museum, Ronald Berndt recorded Karloan's recollections in 1939-40; with Catherine Berndt, he continued the interviews in 1942-43. His descriptions covered incidents, beliefs and customs, together with other territorial, linguistic and clan matters, as well as the interaction between Aborigines of the lower Murray River and lakes region, and he illustrated his information with numerous pencil sketches.

Karloan declared that only death would part him from his home, a neat shack of hessian and flattened kerosene tins, located near the river at Murray Bridge. Part of a small Aboriginal community, it was situated on land owned by the Hume [q.v.9] Pipe Co. In 1942 he learned that the area was to be 'cleared' of Aborigines. Despite the Berndts' intervention, he and his neighbours received eviction notices. He came to Adelaide and unsuccessfully endeavoured to have the order overturned before returning in despair. Survived by one of his sons, he died on 2 February 1943 at Murray Bridge and was buried in the paupers' section of the local cemetery. The Manangki dialect died with him. The Berndts fulfilled their promise to him and the Ngarrindjeri by publishing *A World That Was* (Melbourne, 1993).

G. Jenkin, *Conquest of the Ngarrindjeri* (Adel, 1979); C. Mattingley and K. Hampton (eds), *Survival in Our Own Land* (Syd, 1992); G. Taplin, Journal/diary, 5 vols (ts, SRSA).

CATHERINE BERNDT*

KATER, NORMAN MURCHISON ('MICK') (1904-1979), grazier, medical practitioner and air force officer, and SIR GREGORY BLAXLAND (1912-1978), businessman and army officer, were born on 26 March 1904 at Sutton Forest, New South Wales, and on 15 May 1912 at Cheeseman's Creek, second and sixth children of native-born parents (Sir) Norman Kater [q.v.9], medical practitioner, pastoralist and politician, and his wife Jean Gaerloch, née Mackenzie. 'Mick' was educated at Tudor House, Moss Vale, The Armidale School and Sydney Church of England Grammar School (Shore). He jackerooed on Tubbo station, Darlington Point, joined his eldest brother Henry at Gummin Gummin, Warrumbungle, in the mid-1920s, and owned Gillinghall (1927-32), Wellington, and Colmlee (1934-37), Moree. As a young man he rode unbroken horses and enjoyed boxing. He was a licensed civil pilot by 1928 and soon acquired his own aeroplane —a Gypsy Moth, followed by a Hornet Moth and a Tiger Moth (the last mentioned was bought from army disposals for £100).

Gregory was educated at Tudor House and The King's School, Parramatta. On 3 November 1930 both brothers matriculated at St John's College, Cambridge. Greg passed the mechanical sciences tripos in electrical engineering (B.A., 1933; M.A., 1937). After reading economics for only one term, Mick spent several years at Egelabra, his father's merino stud at Warren, New South Wales. In 1932 he went on the first of three big-game hunting expeditions in East Africa. Later he became an expert fly-fisherman. At St Peter's Anglican Church, Glenelg, Adelaide, on 15 May 1934 he married Margot Milne; in 1938 they bought a house at Point Piper.

That year Mick entered the University of Sydney (M.B., B.S., 1943). He enlisted in the Royal Australian Air Force on 31 March 1941, but was sent back to university to complete his degree. Following training at Laverton, Victoria, he was commissioned flight lieutenant on 14 November 1944 and served with No.2 Operational Training Unit. As medical officer (from February 1945) of No.75 Squadron, he took part in the invasion of Tarakan, Borneo, in May and was loaned to the 2nd/48th Battalion, Australian Imperial Force. Kater twice carried out major surgery while under heavy fire; on another occasion he silenced a machine-gun post with a hand grenade, rescued a wounded soldier and captured two Japanese prisoners. For these deeds he was awarded the Military Cross.

Transferred to No.77 Squadron in September 1945, Kater served (1946-47) with the British Commonwealth Occupation Force, Japan, and was promoted acting wing commander in October 1947. Back in Sydney, he commanded (from February 1948) No.3 R.A.A.F. Hospital, Concord, before serving with No.77 Squadron in Korea where he helped to develop a system for transporting the wounded to hospital by air. His appointment terminated on 3 March 1952. Dark haired, small and swarthy, he invariably returned from war looking like a bandit, draped in the weapons he had souvenired for his gun collection.

From about 1954 Kater managed Egelabra and ran the stud in an autocratic way. He also practised medicine at Warren and supported the local hospital. Charming and kind, he was loved and respected by his patients, mainly Aborigines whom he treated for nothing. In the absence of a veterinary surgeon he often 'doctored' animals and in 1953 had helped to perform a caesarean operation on a lioness at Taronga Zoological Park. Blind in one eye and unable to walk properly after he and his horse had been knocked over by a bull in 1964, he sold his share of Egelabra to his brothers. He purchased nearby Normandoon and in 1966 bought into Wrenford Mathews's [q.v.] Wahroonga merino stud at Nevertire, forming Mathews, Kater & Co. (half of Wahroonga later became Chatswood). Mick was a member of the Early Birds Association of Australia, patron (1978) of No.77 Squadron and—like Gregory—belonged to the Australian, Union and Royal Sydney Golf clubs. Survived by his wife, son and daughter, Mick Kater died on 27 December 1979 at Grovedale, Victoria, and was cremated.

In the 1930s Gregory had gained practical experience with A. Reyrolle & Co. Ltd, Hebburn, England, and the General Electric Co., Schenectady, New York. On 3 April 1937 he married Catherine Mary Ferris-Scott at the parish church of St George, Hanover Square, London. In Sydney, he bought a house at Bellevue Hill and joined Alan Crook Electrical Co. Pty Ltd. Kater enlisted in the A.I.F. on 12 October 1939 and was commissioned lieuten-

ant on 27 December. Reaching Scotland in June 1940, he was promoted captain and sent to the 44th Light Aid Detachment. He was wounded in action at Tobruk, Libya, in June 1941, then served at the 25th Infantry Brigade's headquarters. Back in Australia, he was promoted major in December 1942 and performed engineering duties. In December 1943 he was posted to headquarters, New Guinea Force, and in April 1944 became chief engineer, mechanical equipment, Lae Base Sub-Area. He returned home in November and transferred to the Reserve of Officers on 4 April 1945.

A founder (1950) and chairman (from 1955) of Electrical Equipment of Australia Ltd, Kater moved the company from agency distribution into manufacturing telephone equipment, transmission-line materials, electric motors, clocks and hot-water systems. He took the firm into solar power by forming a joint company with the Solarex Corporation of the United States of America. Believing 'passionately that oil exploration in Australia would succeed . . . years before practical results silenced the sceptics', he was a director and chairman of Oil Search Ltd for twenty-four years. Kater had succeeded his father and grandfather as a director of the Colonial Sugar Refining Co. Ltd (chairman 1976-78) and the Commercial Banking Co. of Sydney (chairman 1966-78). He also sat on the boards of numerous public companies, and of the family's pastoral holdings—H. E. Kater [q.v.5] & Son Pty Ltd and Egelabra Pty Ltd. Although 'he had a reputation for being conservative in financial matters, he was willing to back innovative developments' and supported C.S.R.'s entry into aluminium and iron-ore production.

Tall and thickset, Kater rarely smiled in public. Over many years he built a huge, model electric-railway with his children. He was a member of the Overseas Telecommunications Commission (1966-75) and of the State advisory board of the Salvation Army, a vice-president of the New South Wales Society for Crippled Children and of the local Institute of Public Affairs, a liveryman of the Worshipful Company of Broderers and a freeman of the City of London. In 1974 he was knighted. Sir Gregory died of gastrointestinal bleeding on 9 July 1978 in Royal Prince Alfred Hospital and was cremated; his wife, daughter and two sons survived him.

A. S. Walker, *Medical Services of the R.A.N. and R.A.A.F.* (Canb, 1961); D. S. Macmillan, *The Kater Family, 1750-1965* (Syd, 1966); *Pastoral Review*, 19 Apr 1967, p 301; *Wings*, 32, Mar 1980, p 24; *SMH*, 18 Aug 1932, 31 Oct 1934, 20 Jan 1938, 5 Jan 1951, 11 July 1978; *Aust Financial Review*, 24 May 1960, 11 July 1978; information from Dr R. Kater, Point Piper, Syd.   MARTHA RUTLEDGE

KAVANAGH, JOHN PATRICK MARCUS (1879-1964), political activist, was born on 12 July 1879, probably in Ireland, son of Thomas Kavanagh and his wife Ellen, née Quinn. His childhood was marked by disruption and loss. The family moved to Liverpool, England, and Thomas later worked as a foreman in a Cornish copper refinery. Jack's father died when he was 8 and his mother when he was 11; he was left to the care of an elder brother. Given a rudimentary Catholic education, Jack subsequently regarded organized religion as a danger to the working class. After several unskilled jobs around Liverpool, he enlisted in the King's Royal Rifle Corps in 1898. He served in Ireland, fought in South Africa in 1900-02, was invalided home with a shrapnel wound and was discharged as a corporal in 1906.

Emigrating to Canada in 1907, Kavanagh settled at Vancouver and learned tile-laying. The Socialist Party of Canada introduced him to Marxist theory. He held office in trades and labour organizations, and from 1917 worked on the wharves. In 1921 he helped to found the underground Communist Party of Canada. He had a daughter by his first wife Hilda and another by his second wife Louise (d.1919). In 1925 he and his companion Mrs Edna Louise Hungerford (née Hay) sailed for Australia, accompanied by Jack's elder daughter and Edna's son; they travelled under the surname Kavanagh and arrived in Sydney on May Day.

The police were soon informed that Kavanagh's 'oratory and knowledge of Marxist principles' had overwhelmed the small and poorly organized Communist Party of Australia. Within three months he was its chairman and editor of the *Workers' Weekly*. In line with the 'united front' policy promoted by the Communist International, he founded the Militant Minority Movement which sought to work within the trade union movement while maintaining the separate identity of the Communist Party. The success of this strategy was evident in his election (1928) to the Labor Council of New South Wales, a position of influence which he would find difficult to surrender when the Comintern changed its policy.

At the end of the 1920s the Comintern directed that all links with the 'social fascists' in trade unions and national labour parties were to be severed. Kavanagh responded by advocating 'exceptionalism', denying the relevance of the new policy to Australia. At the party's conference in December 1929 he was condemned as a 'glaring example of right deviation' and voted from the central committee, but it took time to eradicate his influence from the Sydney and State committees. He stood unsuccessfully for Newtown in the Legislative Assembly elections of 1930 and 1932 (receiving less than 1.5 per cent of the vote), and led the local branch of the Unemployed Workers' Movement. In 1934 he was finally expelled from the C.P.A. for alleged Trotskyism.

Kavanagh's influence on Australian communism was greater than his period in office would suggest. Using the motto 'understand capitalism to abolish it', he had attempted to steer the Australian working class towards Marxism through education. As a result, he was accused of pursuing theory and proletarian enlightenment at the expense of revolutionary practice. He had schooled the cadre who toppled him from power and, in Stalinist fashion, they suppressed his contribution to party history. Moving closer to Trotskyite groups, he helped to form an anti-war committee in 1935 and remained involved in left-wing activity during World War II.

In old age Kavanagh was 'still a communist' and a leader of the pensioners' movement. Edna's marriage had been dissolved in 1927 and Jack married her on 18 January 1946 at the district registrar's office, Randwick. Survived by his wife and daughters, he died on 6 July 1964 in his home at Loftus; his body was bequeathed to the University of Sydney and later cremated.

A. Davidson, *The Communist Party of Australia* (Stanford, California, US, 1969); F. Farrell, *International Socialism and Australian Labour* (Syd, 1981); *Labour/Le Travail* (St John's, Newfoundland, Canada), 30, Fall 1992, p 9; Kavanagh papers *and* J. N. Rawling papers (ANUABL).

MARGARET SAMPSON
DAVID AKERS

KAVANAUGH, ROBERT MURRAY (1906-1976), dentist, was born on 18 December 1906 at Wingham, New South Wales, son of native-born parents Herbert Leo Kavanaugh, dentist, and his wife Alice Rose, née Flood. The family moved to Sydney about 1917. Robert was educated at Waverley and Burwood public schools, and privately by a Russian tutor. At the age of 15 he was apprenticed to his father, undertaking study through the Dental Board of New South Wales. Five ft 10 ins (178 cm) tall, with dark auburn hair and hazel eyes, he played Rugby Union for Eastern Suburbs District Football Club, and belonged to the Sydney Rowing Club and the Kensington Amateur Athletic Association.

At dusk on 12 January 1929 Kavanaugh was swimming at Bondi Beach when he went to aid 14-year-old Colin James Stewart who was attacked by a 10-ft (3 m) shark and dragged underwater. Kavanaugh grabbed Stewart some 50 yards (46 m) from the beach and pulled him to shore, where the boy was assisted by others while Kavanaugh slipped away. Stewart died in hospital. The coroner referred to Kavanaugh's bravery, stating that he merited 'the highest honour that can be given for such a heroic act . . . his parents . . . have a son of whom they can be justly proud'. Kavanaugh later said of the rescue: 'I guess that's part of one's upbringing, but you'd find it hard to live with yourself if you didn't do what I did. Wouldn't you?' He received the Surf Life Saving Association of Australia's meritorious award in silver (1929) and the Albert Medal (gazetted 17 October 1930).

In June 1930 Kavanaugh was registered as a dental surgeon and by 1933 had set up a practice at Narromine. At the Sacred Heart Church, Darlinghurst, Sydney, on 22 April 1933 he married with Catholic rites Mary Sylvia Potter, a stenographer; they were to have four children. Kavanaugh held a flying-licence when he joined the Royal Australian Air Force on 7 October 1940. Disappointed at being commissioned as a flight lieutenant in the Medical Branch (Dental) rather than as a pilot, he was promoted squadron leader in October 1942 and served at bases in Australia. He transferred to the reserve on 9 June 1945 and next year entered the University of Sydney (B.D.S., 1950); he won the Percy A. Ash (1948) and the Annie Praed [q.v.11] (1949) prizes. Kavanaugh practised in Sydney until the late 1950s before buying Karalinga, a run-down sheep-station on the Wollondilly River. In semi-retirement he spent half the year at Karalinga and the other half working as a locum tenens.

In 1972 Kavanaugh flew to London where Queen Elizabeth II invested him with the George Cross in place of the Albert Medal, which was perceived to have been devalued by a higher award for heroism by civilians. At Narromine, Kavanaugh had participated in the local musical and drama societies with the enthusiasm that characterized his life. Survived by his son and three daughters, he died of cardiac failure on 12 September 1976 in the Repatriation General Hospital, Concord, and was buried in the Field of Mars cemetery.

L. Wigmore (ed), *They Dared Mightily*, second ed revised and condensed by J. Williams and A. Staunton (Canb, 1986); Surf Life Saving Assn of Aust (NSW), *Annual Report*, 1928-29; *London Gazette*, 17 Oct 1930, p 6316; *Parade*, 28 Sept 1975, p 28; *SMH*, 14, 22 Jan 1929; *Australasian*, 19, 26 Jan 1929; *Australian*, 8 July 1972; family information.
GERARD OAKES

KAY, MARGARET (c.1904-1967), keeper of Aboriginal relics, was born about 1904 at Broadwater, Richmond River, New South Wales, daughter of Jack Kay, butcher, and his wife Alice King, a Minjungbal woman of the Bundjalung people. When Margaret was aged 10 she was sent with her brother Jimmy to a welfare home at Parramatta under the powers of the Aborigines Protection Act (1909). By 1918 she had become nursemaid to the family of James Lennox Arthur who employed her first at Summer Hill and then at Centennial Park, Sydney. Called Peggy by the Arthurs, about 1930 she moved with the family to Quambetook, a Queensland station near Julia Creek, where she worked as maid and companion. Although she was a keen church-goer, she maintained links with her own people. Bequeathed £50 when Mrs Arthur died in 1948, she retired in the late 1950s to a modest house at Tweed Heads. She had many friends on Palm Island whom she regularly visited.

Kay loved to paint and draw, and her correspondence was often decorated with unusual letterheads and borders. She created delicate sand paintings in bottles, using up to ten different coloured layers. Her creative flair was also expressed in sewing and crocheting. Proud of her Aboriginal descent, she joined the local historical society and was determined to preserve her culture. As her reputation spread, she turned the front part of her house into an Aboriginal museum—a mixture of the old and the new, the authentic and the replica, the commercial and the pragmatic.

From her brother, Kay took over responsibility for maintaining the nearby bora ground, previously used for initiation ceremonies. She had apparently been shown the site by her relations who had visited it with their people in the late nineteenth century. Finding that trees and shrubs dotted the ring, and that the encircling mounds had been worn down by the passage of years and lack of upkeep, she restored the area. In 1961 she obtained approval from the Tweed Shire Council for its preservation as a historic site, at a time when the conservation of places of Aboriginal cultural significance was uncommon. She became caretaker of the bora ground.

In her latter years at Tweed Heads, Kay was a notable local identity, often invited to state and church functions. At the opening of the Opal Hostel for Aborigines in Brisbane, she presented Governor Sir Henry Abel Smith with an official gift. Suffering from hypertension and diabetes towards the end of her life, she died of infectious hepatitis on 5 November 1967 in hospital at Murwillumbah and was buried with Anglican rites in South Tweed Heads cemetery. She had never married. The Lower Tweed River Historical Society stored her collection. In 1980 the National Parks and Wildlife Service took over management of the bora ground and surrounding bushland. Samples of Margaret Kay's work are preserved in the Minjungbal

Resource Museum and Study Centre, Tweed Heads, which opened in 1984 and mounted an exhibition based on photographs and items from her original museum.

J. Nayutah and G. Finlay, *Minjungbal* (Lismore, NSW, 1988); NSW Aborigines Welfare Bd, *Dawn*, 7 Aug 1962, p 10, 17, Nov 1968, p 4.

JOLANDA NAYUTAH

KAYLOCK, SUSIE OLIVE (1892-1959), local government official and community worker, was born on 8 June 1892 at Tintenbar, New South Wales, eldest of four daughters of Henry Harden, a farmer from Ireland, and his native-born wife Miriam Ada, née Everingham, a former schoolteacher. Susie attended school at Tintenbar until 1906 when the family moved to Lower Bucca Creek, near Nana Glen. Miriam supervised Susie's education which was supplemented by piano and singing lessons. At the age of 16 she went to Sydney for 'finishing', continued her musical studies and learned dressmaking. On her return to Nana Glen she taught the piano.

Susie was a vivacious and charming young woman. She met Reginald Burdett Rudder 'who courted her by crossing the range from his banana farm at Woolgoolga'. They were married on 8 October 1915 at St Peter's Anglican Church, Nana Glen. Reg enlisted in the Australian Imperial Force and was killed in action at Bullecourt, France, on 3 May 1917, five weeks after the birth of their son. Mrs Rudder let the banana farm and returned to her parents' home.

Resourceful and determined to make her own way, she studied (by correspondence) shorthand, typing and book-keeping, and began a career in local government. Her commitment and intelligence led to her promotion from clerk to positions of responsibility, including deputy shire clerk (c.1919-22) with the Dorrigo Shire Council, based at Coramba where she bought a house with a loan from the War Service Homes Commission. She was assistant town clerk (c.1926, Coonamble), assistant shire clerk (c.1928, Weddin, based at Grenfell) and deputy town clerk (c.1932, Mudgee). Highly regarded in local government circles, she resigned to marry John George Kaylock—a health inspector with the Mudgee Municipal Council—on 7 December 1932 at St Philip's, Church Hill, Sydney.

Throughout her married life Mrs Kaylock was committed to improving the living conditions of rural women and to establishing baby health centres. She was treasurer (1935-36) and president (1940) of the Kempsey branch of the Country Women's Association of New South Wales. Following a move to South Grafton, she served as the North Coast group's representative on the State executive (1945-47), as the group's secretary (1948-50) and as a delegate to numerous conferences in Sydney. In 1952-54 she was president of the South Grafton branch and in 1956 its treasurer. When the family moved to Bourke next year, she managed to continue her work with the C.W.A. despite failing health.

For many years Kaylock had been involved in the Girl Guides' Association and in training marching girls. In addition, she gave informal classes on public speaking and on the conduct of meetings to help equip women for public life. In her spare time she enjoyed playing bridge and golf. She died of cancer on 18 August 1959 at the district hospital, Bourke, and was cremated; her husband survived her, as did the son of her first marriage who had served with the Royal Australian Air Force in World War II.

P. D. and G. L. Gray, *A History of Coramba Public School, 1888-1988* (Coramba, NSW, 1988); *Country Woman*, 3, Feb 1960, p 39; Country Women's Assn of NSW Archives, Syd; information from Crouchley family papers (provided by Mrs B. Crouchley, Stradbroke Island, Qld).

AUDREY TATE

KEANE, FRANCIS CHARLES PATRICK (1901-1971), public servant and magistrate, was born on 26 October 1901 in Sydney, son of native-born parents Francis Patrick Keane, public servant, and his wife Katie Mary Sarah, née Nolan. Educated at St Aloysius' College, Milsons Point, Frank gained his Leaving certificate in 1918 and was awarded a public exhibition. He was appointed a junior clerk in the New South Wales Department of Public Works on 28 January 1919 and was given leave that year to study at the University of Sydney (B.Ec., 1923); after completing his degree, he resumed work with the department, then moved to the petty sessions branch of the Department of the Attorney-General and of Justice.

At St Anne's Anglican Church, Ryde, on 22 January 1927 Keane married 19-year-old Daphne Elizabeth Fanny Whitmore. Following their honeymoon in Canberra, Frank accepted a post with the Federal Capital Commission. Transferring to the Commonwealth Attorney-General's Department, in 1930 he was appointed clerk of the Federal Capital Territory's new Court of Petty Sessions; from 1931 he was also registrar of companies. He lectured part time in accountancy (1930-32) and public administration (1931) at Canberra University College. In 1933 he was designated the Territory's registrar (titles and courts) and in 1939 his position became clerk of courts and registrar of the courts and titles office. From 1949 he was resident magistrate and coroner in the Australian Capital Territory.

For some twelve years Keane was the sole stipendiary magistrate in the A.C.T., sitting almost daily at the court-house in North-bourne Avenue, or at Jervis Bay during his monthly visits there. Members of the legal profession and the police found him competent and just. He was unfailingly courteous, and particularly considerate to immigrants and children. Slightly built and about 5 ft 11 ins (180 cm) tall, he was a quiet, intelligent man, friendly and warm hearted, with a sense of humour and a sound knowledge of the law. Court business increased as the capital grew, but Keane was, perhaps, a trifle bored towards the end of his career: he loved his cigarettes and coffee, and managed to spend long recesses with other court officers in Leo's Café. In the 1960s he helped to draft a new code of criminal law for the A.C.T.

Keane had enjoyed jujitsu and boxing in his youth; in later life he preferred reading, painting (mainly landscapes and seascapes) and holidaying with his family at their beach home at Rosedale, near Batemans Bay, New South Wales. An associate of the Chartered Institute of Secretaries, a member of the Artists Society of Canberra (president 1962-63) and a Rotarian, he had been president (1946-48) of the A.C.T. division of the Australian Red Cross Society and served on its national council. He retired on 25 October 1966 and was officially farewelled at a ceremony in the Court of Petty Sessions. Survived by his wife and son, he died of a coronary occlusion on 25 April 1971 at Braddon and was buried in Canberra cemetery with Catholic rites.

Canb Times, 25, 26 Oct 1966, 26 Apr, 3, 11 Aug 1971; Artists Soc of Canb papers, 1961-69 (NL); information from Messrs F. W. Keane, Mogo, NSW, R. G. Bailey, Yarralumla, and E. Richards, Ainslie, Canb.   SHEILA TILSE

KEANE, RICHARD VALENTINE (1881-1946), politician and trade union official, was born on 14 February 1881 at Beechworth, Victoria, fourth child of Irish-born parents Timothy Keane, police constable, and his wife Hanorah, née O'Sullivan. After his father was transferred to Melbourne, Dick was educated at Christian Brothers' College, St Kilda. In November 1897 he was employed as a clerk in the accountant's branch of the Victorian Railways. At St James's Catholic Church, Elsternwick, on 9 June 1909 he married Ruby Thorne (d.1923), a milliner; they were to have a son and two daughters. From 1918 Keane held office in the Victorian Railways Union which federated with similar bodies in other States to form (1920) the Australian

Railways Union. He was its general (national) secretary in 1925-29.

In the 1920s the A.R.U. was the largest union in Victoria with about 20 000 members. During times of crisis for the railways, the union criticized E. J. Hogan's [q.v.9] minority Labor governments (1927-28 and 1929-32) for failing to protect the workers. As national secretary, Keane largely isolated himself from this hostile relationship and concentrated on gaining Federal awards for his union. He was a vice-president (1928) and president (1930 and 1937-38) of the Victorian central executive of the Australian Labor Party. In 1925 he had unsuccessfully stood for the Senate, and for the province of Melbourne South in the Legislative Council. Having lobbied against Prime Minister S. M. (Viscount) Bruce's [q.v.7] attempt to dismantle the Federal industrial arbitration system in 1929, in October that year Keane won the seat of Bendigo in the House of Representatives.

He was not prominent in the hectic life of the Scullin [q.v.11] government, but—while the prime minister was in Britain in 1930—helped to secure the passage of the Gold Bounty Act. Keane had no chance of surviving the massive swing against Labor in December 1931, and obtained only 41 per cent of the vote. He resumed his involvement with the A.R.U. and was among those re-elected to the A.L.P.'s Victorian executive to ensure that Hogan's government refused to extend the deflationary Premiers' Plan in 1932. Keane again contested Bendigo in 1934 and was defeated, though this time he gained 48 per cent of the vote. Elected to the Senate in 1937, he was deputy-leader of the Opposition (1938-41) and, from 1943, leader of the government in the Senate. On 29 April 1940 at St Mary's Cathedral, Sydney, he had married Millicent Dunn, a 37-year-old typist.

When the Curtin [q.v.13] government came to office in October 1941, Keane was appointed minister for trade and customs. His department administered wartime rationing and price controls. Restrictions on the consumption of newsprint involved him in controversy, especially on the eve of the 1943 elections. He had a longstanding antipathy to 'the Murdoch press' and was quoted as saying, and repeating, that Sir Keith Murdoch [q.v.10] was 'a damn scoundrel'. In other respects Keane's ministerial career was arduous but not particularly noteworthy. He visited North America in 1944, principally to obtain a commitment from the United States of America to continue to support Australia during 'Stage II' of the Lend-Lease scheme—the period between the expected defeat of Germany and that of Japan. In 1946 he returned to the U.S.A. to terminate the Lend-Lease arrangements.

Keane was six feet (183 cm) tall and weighed some twenty stone (127 kg). He died suddenly on 26 April 1946 in Washington. Accorded a state funeral, he was buried in Brighton cemetery, Melbourne; his wife, their daughter and the children of his first marriage survived him. In November 1946 goods valued at £1230 and shipped from the U.S.A. to his wife, who had been travelling with him, were seized by customs officers in Melbourne. Keane's friend Joseph Goldberg claimed to have bought the articles at his request; Goldberg was fined for importing prohibited goods, but later won an appeal against the conviction.

Apart from the conflict over newsprint rationing, Keane had been a genial figure and generally popular. (Sir) Robert Menzies [q.v.] described him as 'clear headed [and] always fair to an opponent'. Keane was representative of the Labor politicians of his day: he had pursued a successful career by prudently using an important trade union position to secure parliamentary and ultimately ministerial office.

S. J. Butlin and C. B. Schedvin, *War Economy 1942-1945* (Canb, 1977); *Aust Women's Weekly*, 17 Oct 1942; *Age* (Melb), 9 Jan 1930, 8 Dec 1944, 29 Apr, 27 May 1946; *Herald* (Melb), 16 Aug 1943, 27 Apr, 8, 13 Nov 1946, 1 May 1947; *Sun News-Pictorial*, 17 Aug 1943.   Don Rawson

KEAST, ASDRUEBAL JAMES (1892-1980), mining engineer, was born on 21 June 1892 at Dimboola, Victoria, son of James Keast, a Cornish-born farmer, and his wife Rose, née Oldfield, from South Australia. Because the family moved to South Australia, Western Australia and Queensland before settling in 1907 in New South Wales at Broken Hill, young Keast's schooling was meagre and interrupted. On obtaining work as an assayer with the Zinc Corporation Ltd's mine, he began night-classes at Broken Hill Technical College.

On 15 May 1915 Keast enlisted in the Australian Imperial Force. Posted to the 7th Field Ambulance, he embarked for the Middle East. He served at Gallipoli and in France (from March 1916) where he was promoted lance sergeant. At Pozières in July, although wounded and blown off his feet by shells, he organized bearers and continued to carry stretchers, for which he was awarded the Military Medal. Evacuated to England, he was discharged from the A.I.F. on 2 January 1917. He was commissioned in the Royal Engineers next day and sent to Mesopotamia where he worked on water-supply.

Through a British postwar training scheme, Keast travelled to the United States of America and studied at the Michigan School of Mines, graduating top of his year as a mining engineer in 1923. For the next twelve years he was employed at mines in Canada and gained a reputation as a fine planner and manager. On 29 January 1925 at San Francisco, California, he married with Catholic rites Marie Adele Burton, an Australian-born typiste.

In 1936 W. S. Robinson [q.v.11] recruited Keast to manage the Zinc Corporation's mine at Broken Hill. His main task, to reconstruct the entire operation, was completed in three years. Aware of the depressing living conditions at Broken Hill and supported by his metallurgist (Sir) Maurice Mawby [q.v.], he backed the ideas of Albert Morris [q.v.10], an assayer and amateur botanist, on regenerating native flora in the dust bowl surrounding the city.

By 1946, when Keast left Broken Hill for Melbourne, he had become chief general manager (mines and works) of both the Zinc Corporation and New Broken Hill Consolidated Ltd. In October that year he accepted the post of general manager of Broken Hill Associated Smelters Pty Ltd, at Port Pirie, South Australia, which he visited regularly from Melbourne, again instituting improvements to the plant and the town. Late in 1950 he was placed in charge of the construction of an aluminium smelter at Bell Bay, Tasmania, as general manager of the Australian Aluminium Production Commission.

During this period Keast was also a director of Australian Oil Exploration Co. Ltd. His next assignment, beginning late in 1955, was to develop the Mary Kathleen uranium deposit in North Queensland for the English-based Rio Tinto Co. Ltd. There he created one of the best-planned and most successful mining operations in Australia's history. He was appointed managing director of Mary Kathleen Uranium Ltd in 1958, a director of Rio Tinto Mining Co. of Australia Ltd in 1959 and a director of Conzinc Riotinto of Australia Ltd in 1962. He retired from M.K.U. and resigned from all boards in 1963, but remained a consultant for C.R.A. Ltd until 1969.

A member (from 1939), councillor and president (1946) of the Australasian Institute of Mining and Metallurgy, Keast was awarded its medal in 1963. He also belonged to similar institutes in Canada and the U.S.A. In 1957 he was appointed C.B.E. He received an honorary doctorate of engineering (1956) from Michigan College of Mining and Technology and of science (1957) from the University of Ottawa; he was awarded the Kernot [q.v.5] medal by the University of Melbourne in 1962 and made a distinguished alumnus of Michigan Technological University in 1970.

'A.J.' kept fit through diet and exercise, and was virtually a teetotaller. In photographs he carried his head high; his gaze was clear and fearless, and his stance challenging. He was a keen Freemason and his hobbies were tree-planting and painting. In 1974 he privately published his autobiography, *Straws in the Wind*. Robinson described him as 'one of the most notable figures' with whom he had been associated: 'he had determination, courage, imagination and a capacity for hard work rarely equalled but never excelled, though, as he himself fully admitted, he did not always get on well with his staff'. Keast's energetic, impatient and aggressive nature did not suit him for managing people in situations of static production. Survived by his wife and two daughters, he died on 17 March 1980 at Kew, Melbourne, and was cremated.

W. S. Robinson, *If I Remember Rightly*, G. Blainey ed (Melb, 1967); B. Carroll, *Australian Made* (Melb, 1987); R. H. Harding, *Wholeheartedly and at Once* (Melb, 1992); J. Dew, *Mining People* (Melb, 1993); A'sian Inst of Mining and Metallurgy, *Procs*, no 274, June 1980; Univ Melb Archives.

D. F. FAIRWEATHER

KEATING, ADELINE MAY (1885-1957), businesswoman, was born on 8 January 1885 at Sandhurst (Bendigo), Victoria, seventh surviving child of William Keating, a Melbourne-born sharebroker, and his wife Ann Jobling, née Todd, from England. Will resented a seventh child; while Addie secretly admired her father, she grew to fear and hate him. At their school for young ladies, the Misses Berges nurtured her musical talents and encouraged her dramatic ability. By the age of 19 she was acclaimed for her rendition of Romeo and applauded as the new star of the Bendigo Operatic Society. When Will died bankrupt in 1908, Addie moved with her mother to Melbourne and for ten years survived illness and poverty. She abandoned hope of a career in the theatre. In 1914 Sidney Myer [q.v.10] opened his new emporium in Bourke Street, Melbourne. Addie, who had met him through his drapery store at Bendigo, walked miles to the city to join the spectators and found employment in the basement of the Myer Emporium Ltd.

World War I occasioned shortages of male staff and commodities at Myer's. The manager Lee Neil [q.v.10] had faith in Keating's ability, but thought her audacious. She challenged Sidney Myer to let her become a buyer. Placed on a salary of £3 per week, in 1919 she sailed for Japan, commissioned to purchase toys. The language and the mysteries of merchandising in Japan gave her constant worry. She heard of a freight war and dared to exceed her buying power before returning to Melbourne in trepidation. Her male colleagues taunted her with overstock-

ing her department with toys and she hoped that the Christmas season would show a big profit. From the United State of America, Myer cabled her to sail again for Japan and buy for the whole store, there being little available in Europe. Back in Melbourne, she encountered resentment from staff and received scant praise from Myer. That treatment became the pattern of her career, which evolved into travelling for nine months each year.

Keating was one of the earliest female buyers at the Leipzig Fair, Germany, in 1923. Visits to other European countries followed, before her journeys took her to Britain and the U.S.A. In 1927 she was sent to live in Paris, as a full-time buyer of toys in Europe. Every year she came back to Myer's to present a special Christmas attraction for children: in 1928 she created an animated toy zoo on the third floor. Overwork and her volatile nature later caused a debacle which brought her home from Europe in disgrace. She resumed buying in Japan, and began in China. Two more trips to Europe ensued, and then a mental collapse.

Following her resignation in 1932, Keating opened a small factory to produce wooden toys of her own design. It became the A. M. K. Manufacturing Co. and branched out into buttons, buckles and novelties. Affected by the Depression, the company closed in 1939. Miss Keating survived a crippling stroke in 1945. She died on 7 March 1957 in her Brighton flat and was buried with Anglican rites in Cheltenham cemetery.

J. Hellegers, *Against the Current* (Melb, 1987); *Herald* (Melb), 4 Sept 1926, 6 Jan 1927, 4 July, 17 Nov 1928; *Sun News-Pictorial*, 14 Dec 1949; Keating papers (held by Ms J. Hellegers, Brighton, Melb); information from Coles Myer Archives, Tooronga, Melb; personal information.

JOAN HELLEGERS

KEBLE, ALEXANDER ROBERT (1884-1963), geologist and palaeontologist, was born on 19 March 1884 at Hawthorn, Melbourne, third of seven children of George Samuel Keable, a clerk from London, and his Victorian-born wife Janet, née Falconer. Educated at Camberwell State School, Robert entered the law firm of Blake & Riggall as a clerk, but soon left to study classics with a view to entering the Church. At this time he changed his surname by deed poll to Keble after the Oxford divine and poet, John Keble. He took an active part in the life of St John's Church, Camberwell, becoming honorary secretary of its naturalists' club, founded in 1905 under the leadership of the vicar, Rev. A. W. Cresswell.

On Cresswell's recommendation, Keble joined the Department of Mines on 1 December 1910 as a temporary junior clerk in the geological survey branch; he helped Frederick Chapman [q.v.7] in working up the faunas of the Sorrento and Mallee bores and T. S. Hall [q.v.9] in his research on graptolites. At St Alban's Anglican Church, Armadale, on 27 February 1915 Keble married Daisy Julia Major. Appointed permanently as assistant field geologist on 16 April, he undertook graptolite determinations following Hall's death that year. His initial major undertaking continued Hall's zoning of the Bendigo goldfield, the first such attempt at using graptolites for structural purposes. Structural maps containing Keble's zonation were issued and he was to incorporate elements of this work in major papers (published in 1920 and 1932). Returning from Bendigo, Keble carried out minor investigations in central Victoria and set about determining graptolites for other goldfield surveys. In 1919 he worked in the Geological Survey Museum. He was sent to survey the Mornington Peninsula in 1921, a project which occupied him through the 1920s with occasional work in other places.

In 1927 Keble was transferred to the Glenelg River area to conduct geological surveys for oil exploration. Later that year, when Chapman was negotiating to commence palaeontological work for the Federal government, he suggested that Keble be appointed to replace him as palaeontologist at the National Museum of Victoria. Keble agreed, subject to his being able to continue to undertake field-work. The appointment was delayed by William Baragwanath [q.v.7], the director of geological survey, who, like the oil exploration syndicates, wanted Keble to be retained in the Department of Mines, and by museum authorities who were unwilling to have him as a part-time officer. When representations were made by Prime Minister S. M. (Viscount) Bruce [q.v.7], Keble's appointment was confirmed on 5 March 1928, with the right to one month field-work per year.

During his time at the museum Keble embarked on very little curatorial work or specimen collecting. On leave without pay, he conducted field-work for Oil Search Ltd in Queensland in January 1929 and in the Mount Gambier district of South Australia in July 1930, and undertook palaeontological work for Bendigo Mines Ltd for six months in 1934.

In 1931 Keble had joined Professor W. N. Benson's expedition to the south-west of the South Island of New Zealand to ascertain the extent of the Ordovician rocks. This survey, together with material sent to him from other areas, enabled him to publish the second of two papers with Benson (1929 and 1935)

establishing a zonation for the New Zealand Ordovician and correlating it with the Victorian sequence. He was elected a vice-president of the geology section of the Australian and New Zealand Association for the Advancement of Science's meeting at Auckland, New Zealand, in 1937.

Building on Hall's work—first with W. J. Harris and later with D. E. Thomas [q.v.]— Keble established the zonation of the Ordovician and Silurian rocks of central Victoria. His work on graptolites finished in 1939 with a major bibliography co-authored with Benson; thereafter his research centred on quaternary studies, of which he was an early pioneer. On 19 April 1948 Keble transferred to the Department of Mines and was promoted to senior field geologist. He completed his unfinished work on the Mornington Peninsula survey and a monograph on Victorian clay and shale deposits which were published in 1950 and 1952 respectively.

A kindly man with a love of music, particularly that of Gilbert and Sullivan, Keble was also a keen golfer. Following his retirement in 1949, he moved to Walwa and continued his interest in physiography by studying the drainage slopes of the Upper Murray area, the subject of his last paper published in 1954. He died on 18 December 1963 at East Malvern and was cremated; his wife and daughter survived him.

St John's Q, 8, no 3, July 1903, 10, no 3, July 1905-12, no 2, Apr 1908; *Mining and Geological J*, 6, no 5, 1965, p 29; Dept of Mines (Vic), *Annual Report*, 1911-22; Public Lib, Museums and National Gallery of Vic, *Annual Report*, 1928-48; *Age* (Melb), 19 Dec 1963; Keble papers (Museum of Vic, Natural Hist Division).

THOMAS A. DARRAGH

KEIGHLEY, ERNA LAURA (1891-1955), women's leader, was born on 25 June 1891 at Manningham, Bradford, England, one of seven children of Gustav Salomon, shipping merchant, and his wife Josephine Maria, née Jussen. Erna was educated at Belle Vue girls' school, Bradford. On 8 January 1918 at the parish church, Shipley, Yorkshire, she married Albert William Keighley (d.1948). With his brother Frank, Albert established Bradford Cotton Mills Ltd at Camperdown, Sydney, in 1925; he was also a director of Westminster Carpets Pty Ltd, and had interests in other manufacturing and mining companies.

In April 1930 Erna brought their two children to join him in Sydney. She was soon active in conservative organizations and was president (1936-38) of the women's branch of the Sane Democracy League of Australia. In addition, she became involved with women's issues and, while a member of the United Associations of Women, developed a lasting friendship with Jessie Street [q.v.]. From 1934 Mrs Keighley represented the Clifton Gardens group at council meetings of the U.A.W., of which she was elected a vice-president in March 1936. At Cambridge, England, she was a delegate (1938) to the conference of the Open Door International which aimed to protect the rights of female workers.

During World War II Keighley was president (1941-42) of the women's auxiliary of the National Defence League of Australia. Her followers drilled, made camouflage netting, studied military-related subjects such as mechanics, map-reading, signalling and convoy-driving, and formed a comforts group which she headed. In March 1942 she was elected president of the U.A.W. She mounted public campaigns for repatriation and pension benefits to be extended to members of the Women's Auxiliary Australian Air Force and for women to be allowed to serve on juries. By February 1943 she was in England, acting as liaison officer for the U.A.W. and the women's auxiliary of the N.D.L.

Keighley returned to Australia in 1946. Apart from belonging to the ladies' auxiliary of the Royal Empire Society, she virtually retired from public life, although in 1947 she was involved in the Australian Women's Movement against Socialization. She lived at Clifton Gardens and had a second house, Bellevue, at Bowral, known for its garden. Every two or three years she visited England where she enjoyed hunting and country pursuits. Survived by her daughter Sylvia and son Geoffrey, she died of hypertensive cerebrovascular disease on 16 July 1955 at Clifton Gardens; her body was bequeathed to the medical school, University of Sydney, and later cremated; her estate was sworn for probate at £32 244. Sylvia had married (1941) the tennis player Adrian Quist; Geoffrey was a businessman, grazier, sportsman and member (1965-78) of the Legislative Council.

SMH, 3 Nov 1948, 18 July 1955; United Assns of Women papers (ML); information from Mr K. Quist, Mosman, Syd.   MELANIE OPPENHEIMER

KEIR, STEPHEN (1879-1957), hatter and company director, was born on 14 October 1879 at Audenshaw, Lancashire, England, son of Robert Keir, hatter, and his wife Elizabeth, née Baldwin. Stephen was educated locally and apprenticed to his father's trade. In 1902 he emigrated to Sydney and worked for two years for the hatmakers C. Anderson & Co. Ltd. He then joined Benjamin Dunker-ley, an English-born hatter with a small business in Crown Street, who had invented a revolutionary machine for trimming rabbit-fur. On 28 December 1905 at the Methodist Church, Paddington, Keir married Ada Harriet, Dunkerley's daughter and a 'former' of felt hats. Soon after, he was made general manager of the firm which had nineteen employees in 1911 when it became Dunkerley Hat Mills Ltd.

At that time the business operated in partnership with a wholesale merchant Arthur Pringle Stewart (d.1925). In promoting their product, Stewart registered the trade-name of Akubra (an Aboriginal word for head-covering) in August 1912. During World War I Dunkerley's captured the profitable contract for military slouch hats. After the death of his father-in-law in 1918, Keir took up the managing directorship at a newly built factory in Bourke Street, Waterloo. Small, compact and personable, he faced his daily responsibilities sporting a boutonnière fashioned every morning by Ada. He was a pillar (and trustee) of Burwood Methodist Church who delighted in extending his strong, sound voice in hymn-singing and ran his business according to his Christian principles. Following World War I, young (Sir) Garfield Barwick grew up in the Keir household when his own family was dispersed.

By the 1920s there were hundreds of employees in the paternally run Dunkerley's. Its Akubra cricket team (established 1926) had an enthusiastic following. In addition to an annual picnic, a dinner for employees was held every year at Sargents [q.v.11] Ltd—always a notably informal affair where a band accompanied the singing and dancing. More practically, a provident society made generous allowance for employees' sickness benefits. In the Depression Keir's proposal (democratically endorsed) of a 10 per cent wage cut staved off any staff reductions, although many of his competitors folded. He was awarded King George VI's coronation medal in 1937. Business revival was ensured by the outbreak of World War II: most of Dunkerley's production was again directed to making slouch hats. Staff who enlisted had their military pay augmented by the firm to preserve their normal wage level. Keir retired in 1952 in favour of his eldest son.

Keir died on 11 November 1957 at his Burwood home and was cremated; his wife, daughter and three sons survived him. An enterprising hatter, he had kept abreast of international trends, but over the years developed a type of fur-felt headgear so appropriate to its market that Akubra became a familiar element of national life. It endeared itself for flexibility ('water your dog, fan the fire'), for taking the punishment of rugged use, and for a certain insouciance:

... it has an air of Aussie
Of 'come and have a drink?'
The good and easy style that leads
To glory or the clink.

J. Bowen, *The Akubra Hat* (Syd, 1988); G. Turner, *Akubra is Australian for Hat* (Syd, 1988); *Land* (Syd), 8 Sept 1988.   MARGARET STEVEN

KELDIE, AILEEN MARGARET (1936-1961), air hostess, was born on 16 September 1936 at Merewether, Newcastle, New South Wales, younger child and only daughter of native-born parents David Keldie, government valuer, and his wife Aileen Ethel Maude, née Hill. The family moved to Sydney in 1938. Educated at Mosman Public School and Sydney Church of England Grammar School for Girls (Redlands), Cremorne, Aileen proved an excellent student. She obtained employment with the O'Connell Street branch of the Bank of New South Wales where she worked as a machiniste on statements and ledgers.

In 1957 Miss Keldie joined Ansett-ANA as an air hostess. Her initial ground-training took place in Melbourne and she was then based in Sydney where she was promoted to trainer hostess. She was a pleasant woman, quiet, calm and capable. Interested in and committed to her job, she was regarded as conscientious and reliable. As a trainer, she was patient and considerate towards her charges; they liked and admired her.

On 30 November 1961 Keldie was rostered with her trainee Elizabeth Hardy (who had been flying for only three weeks) on Flight 325, due to leave Sydney for Canberra at 7.10 p.m. Throughout a blustery, turbulent day, the weather steadily deteriorated, bringing heavy rain, strong wind, lightning and severe thunderstorms. The aircraft, a Viscount 720, registration VH-TVC, departed at 7.17 p.m., with eleven passengers (ten men and one woman) and four crew members on board. Although its pilots twice communicated with the Sydney control tower immediately after take-off, they failed to respond to radio transmissions from 7.25 p.m. The aeroplane's estimated arrival time in Canberra was 8.05 that night. When the Viscount had not arrived by 8.50, it was posted as missing and 'the Distress Phase of Search and Rescue' was initiated in Sydney.

A full search mounted at dawn on 1 December established that the aircraft had crashed in Botany Bay. Over the next five days divers recovered much of the wreckage and a number of bodies. Investigations showed that the Viscount's starboard outer wing and starboard tailplane had separated from the aircraft in flight and fallen into the sea. The rest of the airliner had virtually disintegrated when it hit the water at some 350 miles (560 km) per hour, about 7.26 p.m. Lacking precise evidence as to what had caused VH-TVC to break up in the air, investigators concluded that the aircraft was subjected to extraordinary levels of stress occasioned by severe turbulence that arose from the abnormally violent weather conditions.

Following a funeral service at Scots Kirk, Mosman, Keldie was cremated with Presbyterian forms; her family was devastated by her death. A board of inquiry into the accident handed down its findings in 1962. All Australian airliners were required to be fitted with weather radar by 1 June 1963.

M. Job, *Air Crash*, 2 (Canb, 1992); *PP* (Cwlth), 1962-63, 5, p 557; *Advertiser* (Adel) and *SMH*, 1, 2 Dec 1961; *Sun-Herald*, 3 Dec 1961; information from Mrs K. Gore, Strathmore, Melb; family information.   MARGARET ROBINSON

KELLEHER, JAMES MICHAEL (1909-1964), newspaper editor, was born on 30 September 1909 at Maryborough, Queensland, son of Irish-born parents Cornelius Kelleher, labourer, and his wife Margaret, née Walsh. Educated locally by the Christian Brothers, James was employed as a journalist on the Maryborough *Chronicle* before moving to the Rockhampton *Morning Bulletin*. In 1932-36 he was based in Asia where he became chief sub-editor on the Hong Kong *South China Morning Post* and gained an appreciation of Asian affairs rare among Australian journalists of his generation.

Returning to his native land, Kelleher obtained the chief sub-editorship of the Sydney *Sunday Sun and Guardian*. On 9 April 1940 at St Vincent's Catholic Church, Ashfield, he married Irene Sadie Maria Malone, a telephonist. Archbishop (Cardinal Sir) Norman Gilroy [q.v.] merged the *Catholic Press* and the *Freeman's Journal* into the *Catholic Weekly* in 1942 and appointed Kelleher editor. Working closely with Gilroy, he provided a channel for the Church's communications. He gave the newspaper an attractive format and, as circulation grew, expanded the range of contributors and features.

Kelleher brought to the *Catholic Weekly* 'a wide journalistic experience, an agile mind and a sense of dedication'. He wrote the popular feature, 'Front Lines', 'one of those personal columns of comment which people seem to enjoy when the opinions expressed coincide with their own'. In 1960 Pope John XXIII appointed him a knight commander of the Order of St Gregory the Great. Kelleher wrote *Roman Fever* (Sydney, 1962), 'a history of the Catholic campaign for justice in educational matters' and a polemic against liberalism.

Inaugurated in an era of comparatively unquestioned faith in Church and hierarchy, the *Catholic Weekly* had suffered from the political tensions of the 1950s and the pressures for Church reform eventually manifested in Vatican Council II (1962-65). In 1956, when the *Weekly* expressed the Sydney bishops' view that there was no need for a split in the Australian Labor Party in New South Wales, clergy and lay people sympathetic to the Anti-Communist (later Democratic) Labor Party roundly attacked the newspaper. On religious matters, the *Weekly* reflected the hierarchy's conservative position. New magazines sprang up to cater for readers who were impatient with the official Church press. Although it survived after rival newspapers had folded, the *Weekly* never regained its peak circulation of 63 000 in the 1960s.

Gilroy and a predominantly clerical board dictated editorial policy for the *Catholic Weekly*, often against Kelleher's journalistic judgement. The cardinal examined proofs of articles and frequently made changes. It was an editorial issue that led to Kelleher's third heart attack. Colleagues saw him leave his office in July 1964 for St Mary's Cathedral to argue against a change which Gilroy wanted made to a report. Kelleher never returned. He died of a myocardial infarction on 9 August at Lewisham General Hospital and was buried in Woronora cemetery. His wife, daughter and two of his three sons survived him.

P. Ormonde, *The Movement* (Melb, 1972); P. O'Farrell, *The Catholic Church and Community in Australia* (Melb, 1977); E. Campion, *Rockchoppers* (Syd, 1982); *Catholic Weekly* (Syd), 13 Aug 1964; K. Hilferty, 'The Formation of a Diocesan Editor or the Education of Young Kevin', *A'sian Catholic Record*, 65, no 3, July 1988, p 303.

KEVIN HILFERTY

KELLEY, RALPH BODKIN (1890-1970), veterinary scientist, was born on 15 December 1890 at Preston, Melbourne, second son of Alfred Aldridge Kelley, a Victorian-born clerk, and his wife Margaret Jane, née Charles, from Ireland. Ralph attended Caulfield Grammar School and went jackerooing before entering the University of Melbourne (L.V.Sc., 1914; B.V.Sc., 1930; D.V.Sc., 1937). He won (1914) the Australian Veterinary Association's [J. A.] Gilruth [q.v.9] prize and the medal of the Royal Agricultural Society of Victoria.

On 30 January 1915 Kelley was appointed captain in the Australian Army Veterinary Corps. That year he took three shiploads of horses to Egypt and was the veterinary member on a remount purchase board, an experience which taught him that horse-trading was 'a very specialised game of catch-as-catch-can'. Transferring to the Australian Imperial Force in March 1916, he served in the Middle East, mainly with the 12th Light Horse Regiment and as officer in command of the 9th Mobile Veterinary Station. His appointment terminated in Australia on 21 June 1919.

Kelley then took a post with a firm that sold livestock; for two and a half years he took shiploads of thoroughbred horses to Asia. In 1922, in Melbourne, he joined the Department of Lands, teaching the care and management of farm animals to 'rookie' soldier settlers. He described their hardships as 'a repetition of the pioneering days ... only those who had lots of guts ... came through'. Three years later he became a soldier settler and veterinarian on a dairy-farm at Tatura. On 5 March 1927 at Camberwell, Melbourne, Kelley married Edith Eileen Malcolm with Presbyterian forms. Lacking sufficient capital, he was forced to sell his farm. In 1928 he was appointed livestock foreman at the Melbourne and Metropolitan Board of Works' sewage farm, Werribee, which ran 30 000 sheep and 12 500 cattle. In January 1931 he joined the division of animal health and production, Council for Scientific and Industrial Research (Commonwealth Scientific and Industrial Research Organization from 1949), as animal geneticist. Asked by Gilruth to investigate the cross-breeding of Zebu (Brahman) cattle in the United States of America, Kelley also undertook refresher courses in animal breeding and genetics in that country and in Britain. On his return in 1933, he was stationed at the Oonoonbah Laboratory, near Townsville, Queensland.

During his American visit he had selected Zebu cattle for a syndicate of Queensland pastoralists. He played a leading role in experiments to cross that stock with British breeds in the hope of producing beef-cattle able to withstand tropical conditions and resist tick infestation. Despite positive findings, the programme remained controversial with many cattlemen until the 1950s. In 1935 Kelley was transferred to Sydney to investigate fertility in merino sheep. He developed the F. D. McMaster [q.v.10] field-station at Badgerys Creek and was its officer-in-charge (1938-53). While planning genetic work at the National Sheep Breeding Research Station, Gilruth Plains, Queensland, Kelley remained committed to the cross-breeding of Zebu cattle. By 1952, when C.S.I.R.O. and the Australian Meat Board established the National Cattle Breeding Station at Belmont, near Rockhampton, some cattlemen had been 'converted'.

In that year Kelley and R. S. Wilson selected Brahman and Africander cattle in the U.S.A. for Belmont, but Kelley's request to organize the research programme was refused and he was appointed assistant-chief, division of animal health and production. Suspecting a 'kick upstairs', he resigned early in 1954 to become a director and part-owner of Tropical Cattle Pty Ltd, North Queensland. He was appointed O.B.E. in 1954. At the Federal government's invitation, he visited Burma, Singapore and Malaya to encourage support for the Colombo Plan. Returning to Singapore as a research specialist, he obtained leave in 1958-59 to fulfil an assignment in Pakistan. Kelley was subsequently foundation professor of animal science at the University of Malaya, Kuala Lumpur. About 1967 he retired to Nambour, Queensland. He contributed numerous papers to scientific journals and wrote several monographs, among them *Principles and Methods of Animal Breeding* (Sydney, 1946), *Native and Adapted Cattle* (Sydney, 1959) and *Sheep Dogs, their breeding, maintenance and training* (Sydney, 1947).

Survived by his wife and son, Kelley died on 13 February 1970 at Nambour and was cremated. His portrait by Norman Carter [q.v.7], entitled 'The Squatter' (1939), is held by the State Library of New South Wales. By the 1980s almost all of Queensland's northern herds of beef-cattle were either fixed hybrid breeds or pure Brahman.

C. B. Schedvin, *Shaping Science and Industry* (Syd, 1987); L. McDonald, *Cattle Country* (Brisb, 1988); R. A. J. Neville, *Faces of Australia* (Syd, 1992); *Aust Veterinary J*, 46, Mar 1970, p 113; *Courier-Mail* and *Morning Bulletin* (Rockhampton), 14 Feb 1970; *Qld Country Life*, 19 Feb 1970; R. B. Kelley, Reminiscences (ms, nd, held by Mr B. Kelley, North Rockhampton, Qld); Minutes, TCRAC/QAIC, 1932-52 (CSIRO Archives, Canb); information from Mr B. Kelley and Mr H. G. Turner, Rockhampton, Qld.

LORNA McDONALD

KELLIHER, RICHARD (1910-1963), soldier and gardener, was born on 1 September 1910 at Ballybranagh, near Tralee, County Kerry, Ireland, son of Michael Kelliher, labourer, and his wife Mary Anne, née Talbot. Dick attended technical college at Tralee and worked as a mechanic in his brother's garage. In 1929 he emigrated to Brisbane with his 15-year-old sister Norah. She later said that, although he was good natured and 'not a very big fellow', he 'wouldn't take it if anyone were nasty'. During the Depression he worked at a variety of jobs: he was sacristan at St Stephen's Cathedral before moving to the country where he was employed as a farmhand. Sickness dogged him, and he contracted typhoid and meningitis.

Enlisting in the Australian Imperial Force on 21 February 1941, Kelliher sailed for the Middle East and was assigned to the 2nd/25th Battalion in October. He performed garrison duties in Syria and returned to Australia in March 1942. Six months later he was with his unit in Papua, helping to drive the Japanese from Ioribaiwa to Gona. Back home from January 1943, he was admitted to hospital with malaria in June. He was again sent to Papua in August. Next month he was based at Nadzab, New Guinea, whence the 2nd/25th advanced towards Lae.

On 13 September, near Heath's plantation, Kelliher's platoon came under heavy fire from a concealed Japanese machine-gun post. Five men were killed and three wounded, among them the section leader Corporal Billy Richards. On his own initiative, Kelliher dashed towards the post, hurled two grenades at the enemy and killed some of them, but was forced back to his own lines. Seizing a Bren-gun, he ran to within 30 yards (27 m) of the machine-gun nest and silenced it with accurate shooting. He then crawled out under enemy rifle-fire and dragged Richards to safety, probably saving his life. Kelliher was awarded the Victoria Cross.

After further spells in hospital with malaria, he was sent to Brisbane in November and posted to the 11th Australian Advanced Workshop next month. He took part in his old battalion's march through the city on 8 August 1944 and was discharged from the A.I.F. on 20 August 1945. In 1946 he was selected in the Australian contingent for the victory parade in London. King George VI presented him with his V.C.; the Kelliher family from County Kerry attended the investiture. Kelliher returned to London in 1953 for the coronation of Queen Elizabeth II and in 1956 for the V.C. centenary celebrations. On each occasion he visited Tralee.

At Epworth Lodge, Bowen Hills, Brisbane, on 30 August 1949 Kelliher had married with Methodist forms Olive Margaret Hearn, a 19-year-old machinist. They moved to Melbourne where he worked as a gardener. He died of cerebral thrombosis on 28 January 1963 in the Repatriation General Hospital, Heidelberg, and was buried in Springvale cemetery with Catholic rites and military honours; his wife, son and two daughters survived him. Olive remarried. In 1966 she sold Kelliher's V.C. and campaign medals to his battalion association which donated them to the Australian War Memorial, Canberra.

L. Wigmore (ed), *They Dared Mightily* (Canb, 1963); *Aust Women's Weekly*, 15 Jan 1944; *Herald* (Melb), 31 Jan 1963; *Canb Times*, 10 Sept 1966; War diary, 2/25th Battalion (AWM); information from Mr G. O'Leary, Kerry Archaeological and Hist Soc, Tralee, Ireland.   RICHARD E. REID

KELLWAY, CEDRIC VERNON (1892-1963), diplomat, was born on 2 July 1892 at Condah, Victoria, son of native-born parents Robert Kellway, stationmaster, and his wife Ellen, née Desmond. Educated in Melbourne by the Christian Brothers, Ced joined the Commonwealth Public Service on 17 December 1908 and worked as a clerk in the Treasury, save for 1910-12 when he was with the Department of External Affairs. On 31 July 1915 he enlisted in the Australian Imperial Force. Commissioned and posted to the 37th Battalion, he served (from November 1916) on the Western Front where he was wounded in action in June 1917 and gassed in September 1918.

At St Mary's Catholic Church, Hawthorn, Melbourne, on 28 April 1920 Kellway married Eileen Mary Hannan; she moved with him to Canberra when his department was transferred there in 1927. He was promoted to budget officer in 1933. Two years later he became senior clerk and accountant (later assistant Australian trade commissioner) in the office of the commissioner-general for Australia, New York. In November 1939 he was financial adviser on the Australian delegation to the conference in Ottawa which led to the establishment of the Empire Air Training Scheme. Next month he returned to Australia to take up the duties of finance member of the Air Board. In 1942 he was sent back to New York as deputy director-general of Australian war supplies procurement.

On 1 September 1945 H. V. Evatt [q.v.] announced Kellway's appointment as Australian consul-general, New York. Using his negotiating skills and experience in managing co-operative ventures between Australia and America, Kellway endeavoured to extend trade links between the two countries and to encourage American investment in projects such as the Snowy Mountains scheme. He also helped distressed Australian citizens, spending a deal of his time on the 'sorry and difficult' task of assisting unhappy war brides. In 1946-47 he was Australian alternate delegate, and in 1949 delegate, to the United Nations General Assembly.

When Australia and Italy agreed to exchange diplomatic representatives in late 1949, Kellway was sent to Rome as minister. One of his major duties was to accelerate emigration from war-ravaged Italy to Australia. He was a careful and penetrating observer of political and diplomatic developments, and adept at analysing events. Forming connexions that allowed him to cut through red tape, he facilitated meetings between Italian officials and visiting Australian dignitaries. His excellent relations with the Vatican enabled him to organize Papal audiences for his countrymen. In 1954 he was appointed minister to Brazil. After that country's

political upheavals in 1954-55, he established a rapport with President Juscelino Kubitschek.

Kellway had gentle features, was quick-witted and possessed a dry sense of humour. While he regretted causing friends and colleagues any inconvenience, he stood firm on matters of justice and international relations. In 1957 he retired to Dublin and subsequently moved to Bath, England, where he died of cancer on 14 June 1963. His wife, daughter and two sons survived him.

J. McCarthy, *A Last Call to Empire* (Canb, 1988); *Herald* (Melb), 20 Aug, 11 Sept 1935, 30 Dec 1939, 19 Nov 1948, 19 Oct 1949; *NY Times*, 2 Nov 1939, 14 Sept 1949; *Age* (Melb), 26 Feb 1954; *SMH*, 12 Nov 1955, 13 Sept 1957; *Canb Times*, 17 June 1963; Series A1, item 1912/16212, Series A1067, item A46/2/11/2 (AA, Canb); papers held by and information from Mrs A. M. Webb, Lond.

JENNY NEWELL

KELLY, AUSTIN MICHAEL (1891-1978), Jesuit provincial and missionary, was born 20 September 1891 at Blackrock, County Dublin, Ireland, fifth child of Edward Kelly, commission agent, and his wife Teresa, née Burke. Educated at Belvedere College, Dublin (1903-08), and at the National University of Ireland (B.A., 1911), Austin entered the novitiate of the Society of Jesus on 29 February 1912 at Tullabeg and took his first vows on 1 March 1914. Following a short juniorate at Rathfarnham, he was sent in September 1914 to study philosophy at Stonyhurst College, Lancashire, England. He returned to Dublin and taught (1917-21) at Mungret College. In 1921-25 he studied theology at Louvain, Belgium, and was ordained priest on 31 July 1923.

After serving his tertianship at Tullabeg, Kelly was posted to Australia in 1926 as prefect of discipline and sportsmaster at Xavier College, Melbourne. On 15 August 1929 he took his final vows. He was minister (1928-30) and rector (1931-37) of St Aloysius' College, Milson's Point, Sydney, and founding rector (1938-47) of St Louis School, Claremont, Perth, the first Jesuit establishment in Western Australia. Cultured, deeply pious and meticulous, he was an outstanding headmaster, ever on the alert to encourage the initiatives of the young teachers he was training, even when he would not himself have done the things they were doing, or done them the way they did. He soon became one of the most prominent and influential churchmen in Perth, and a trusted adviser to ecclesiastical and secular leaders.

In October 1947 Fr Kelly was appointed by Rome to head the Australian vice-province of the order, which, from his base in Melbourne, he steered towards final autonomy from the Irish Jesuits. In 1950-56 he had charge of the newly created Australian and New Zealand province. He judged that the increased membership of the order—which was growing towards its maximum of three hundred and fifty—justified expansion of its works, and he seized the initiative by undertaking the management of new schools, parishes and university colleges in Hobart, Adelaide and Brisbane. Businesslike and energetic, Kelly exerted to the full the organizing ability that his long experience in office had honed. His determination, rhetorical skill and wide circle of influence ensured that the works of the order, and with their success its morale, would flourish.

Some considered his standards impossibly high and his manner unduly autocratic. When he accepted, on behalf of the Australian Jesuits, the challenge of maintaining a foreign mission in Bihar, India, and when the first group of six were sent to Ranchi in 1951, a few critics warned that resources would be overstretched. In this enterprise, however, as in many of his projects, Kelly's thinking was far ahead of his time. He long held that the considerable achievements of the Australians in the Hazaribagh-Palamau region ranked among the most visionary and generous national gestures of the period. On the conclusion of his provincialate in Australia he was appointed superior of the Hazaribagh Mission, and set off in September 1956 on a new phase of what had, in many respects, always been a missionary career.

In Bihar, Kelly was in some ways ill-attuned to the national style which the Australian Jesuits had adapted to India, and his health had become impaired. But he doggedly saw out six years of administration, planning, exhortation and visitation; and he enlarged the foundations of the mission by liaison with an expanding number and variety of religious and secular 'co-missionaries'. In 1962 he returned to reside at the Jesuit Church of the Immaculate Conception at Hawthorn, Melbourne, where he was based (except for the year 1964 which he spent at Lavender Bay, Sydney) until he went in 1974 to Caritas Christi hospice, Kew. He died there on 11 October 1978 and was buried in Boroondara cemetery.

Impressively able, distinguished in appearance, urbane, energetic and imaginative, Kelly was a remarkable 'lace-curtain' Irishman who had become an enthusiastic and loyal patriot in his adopted country. He was impatient of the mediocre, a practical leader rather than a natural scholar, and he remained a staunchly private man, despite his wholehearted pursuit of public goals and cultivation of a wide circle of prominent friends. Very dedicated to the educational and spiri-tual projects of his Church and order, he was ecumenical in outlook and sustained a lifetime cultivation of books, fine arts, music and theatre.

U. M. L. Bygott, *With Pen and Tongue* (Melb, 1980); *Sun News-Pictorial*, 2 Oct 1947; *SMH*, 12 Sept 1966; *West Australian*, 21 Oct 1978; Society of Jesus, Aust Province Archives, Hawthorn, Melb.

J. EDDY

KELLY, JOSEPH LAWRENCE ANDREW (1907-1970), army officer, was born on 10 March 1907 at Cowra, New South Wales, third child of native-born parents Joseph Patrick Kelly, general labourer, and his wife Sarah Mary, née Hennessy. Young Joe's early years were difficult: his father died some three months after his birth and his schooldays ended when he was about 12. He moved to Sydney where he became a builder's labourer. During the Depression he knew the misery of unemployment, often walking from Bondi to the city when he could not afford the tram fare. An active member of North Bondi Surf Life-Saving Club, he also played Rugby League for Eastern Suburbs.

In 1926-29 Kelly served in the 1st Field Squadron, Royal Australian Engineers, under the compulsory training scheme. His service, and the worsening Depression, led him to enlist in the Permanent Military Forces on 29 October 1931. He was posted as a gunner and spent two years in Darwin before returning to Sydney. At St Mary's Catholic Cathedral on 20 April 1935 he married Sybil McKenzie, a milliner. In August 1936 Sergeant Kelly was sent to the Australian Instructional Corps Training Cadre. He was promoted staff sergeant major, third class, in June 1937 and allotted to the infantry in the 1st Division. After the outbreak of World War II he was made temporary quartermaster and honorary lieutenant. This grudging promotion was followed in May 1940 by his elevation to captain, Australian Imperial Force. Posted to the 2nd/13th Battalion, he sailed for the Middle East in October and was given the key appointment of adjutant in November.

Kelly quickly established himself in this young battalion during its first campaign which culminated in the defence of Tobruk, Libya, from April 1941. By September he was at 20th Brigade headquarters as staff captain and by October 1942 at 9th Division headquarters in Egypt. On 29 October, at the height of the battle of El Alamein, G. E. Colvin [q.v.13], the commander of the 2nd/13th, was injured. Kelly was immediately promoted major and sent to take command. 'To the dazed and battered troops, it was like a shot in the arm to see Major Joe back in the fold.' He scraped together men from his Headquarter Company and elsewhere to reinforce his shattered rifle companies and led the battalion until the end of the battle.

Returning to Australia in February 1943, Kelly was dispatched to Papua in July as second-in-command of the battalion. Two months later he took part in the assault on Lae, New Guinea. In the fighting for Finschhafen in September-October he commanded Kelforce, which included two companies of his own unit. After being admitted to hospital in Australia with otitis and post-malarial debility in February-March and May-June 1944, he was promoted temporary lieutenant colonel in November and appointed commander of the 31st-51st Battalion. On Bougainville, from December 1944 to March 1945, he and his Queenslanders knew that their operations made no difference to the outcome of the war, but they fought skilfully and resolutely, as in the three-day struggle for Tsimba Ridge on 6-9 February. For his leadership, Kelly was awarded the Distinguished Service Order. In World War II he was thrice mentioned in dispatches and was probably the only member of the A.I.C. to command an infantry battalion in action.

In 1946-47 Kelly was director of general stores and clothing at Army Headquarters, Melbourne. He then commanded (1948) the Recruit Training Brigade at Greta, New South Wales. While in charge (1949-51) of the 1st Battalion, Royal Australian Regiment, he led Norforce which maintained coal production around Muswellbrook during the 1949 miners' strike. He commanded the 11th National Service Training Battalion (1951-53) in Brisbane, and was chief instructor at the School of Infantry (1953-54), Singleton, New South Wales, and at the Jungle Warfare Wing, Jungle Warfare Centre (1954-55), Canungra, Queensland. His last appointment was staff officer cadets and commander, 2nd Cadet Brigade, based in Sydney.

Transferring to the Retired List as honorary colonel on 11 March 1957, Kelly had charge of the State government's stationery office until 1958 when he was appointed general manager of Craig & Aitken Pty Ltd, a wholesale company in Sydney. He died on 9 September 1970 at Royal North Shore Hospital from injuries received in a motorcar accident and was buried in Northern Suburbs cemetery; his wife and son survived him.

Kelly was a tall, strong man who had found his *métier* in the regular army and the A.I.F., moving easily between staff and command. Calm, considerate and careful in his planning, he counselled junior leaders: 'Remember it is the man that counts NOT the machine, be firm ... and above all study the human factor'. He enjoyed life, whether gardening, extending his home, or watching cricket and

Rugby League. His three loves were 'his wife, his son and the Australian army'.

D. Dexter, *The New Guinea Offensives* (Canb, 1961); G. Long, *The Final Campaigns* (Canb, 1963); B. Maughan, *Tobruk and El Alamein* (Canb, 1966); *Smith's Weekly* (Syd), 2 Sept 1950; information from Mr P. Kelly, Syd, and Lt Col A. Newton, Canb.   A. J. HILL

KELLY, MARY LILY MAY; *see* QUIRK

KELLY, MICHAEL (1905-1967), rheumatologist, was born on 16 April 1905 at Mintaro, South Australia, son of Michael Kelly, farmer, and his wife Rose, née McManus. The seventh of ten children, Michael received his early education from his parents. He won scholarships to Christian Brothers' College, Wakefield Street, Adelaide (dux 1921), and to the University of Adelaide (M.B., B.S., 1928) where he was influenced by the professor of anatomy Frederic Wood Jones [q.v.9].

After hospital residencies in Adelaide, Kelly was a general practitioner (1931-41) at Bunbury, Western Australia. At St Mary's Catholic Cathedral, Perth, on 20 January 1932 he married Olive Marjorie Woolcock. He served as a captain in the Australian Army Medical Corps, and was based in Perth (1941-44) and Melbourne (1945-46). In 1946-47 he spent a year in the department of anatomy, University of Melbourne, working with Professor (Sir) Sydney Sunderland, then entered private practice, initially with clinical-assistant appointments at the Royal Melbourne and St Vincent's hospitals. He took great interest in the physical aspects of treatment and in the pastoral care of his patients at a time when it was generally held that nothing much could be done for arthritis. His practice, clinical and medico-legal, became very busy.

Kelly wrote extensively on a wide range of medical, political, historical, ethical and literary matters. His best work concerned the care of inflamed joints and the neurological aspects of pain and inflammation. He was awarded an M.D. (University of Adelaide) in 1945 for his thesis on 'Interstitial Neuritis and the Pressure Theory of Pain'; and his study, 'The Prevention and Treatment of Polyarthritis by Continuous and Active Immobilization of Joints', won the Geigy prize in 1958. His view of the nature of fibrositis, on which his international reputation rests, appeared in the British Medical Association's *Annals of the Rheumatic Diseases* in 1945-46. 'The Pathology and Treatment of Fibrositis' was awarded the 1946 Buckston Browne prize by the Harveian Society of London. Kelly brought the experimental observation of J. H. Kellgren and Sir Thomas Lewis into the clinical area, proposing a neurological model of fibrositis.

In 1951 Kelly presented this data to the European Congress of Rheumatology, held at Barcelona, Spain. He spoke on the use of phenylbutazone in the treatment of arthritis at the Eighth World Congress of Rheumatology, in Geneva in 1953, and on the disadvantages of corticosteroid therapy at the Tenth International Congress of the International League Against Rheumatism, in Rome in 1961. In the following year he became a member of the New York Academy of Sciences.

A foundation federal delegate (1956) of the Australian Rheumatism Association, Kelly was elected treasurer at the inaugural meeting of the Victorian branch in 1957, but held no further office. Although well known internationally, he always felt that he was not accepted locally. He offended many people by the vigour of his crusade (in which he was mostly correct) against the inappropriate use of the newly introduced drug, cortisone, and by his unqualified advocacy of phenylbutazone. He raised the eyebrows of the medical establishment by calling his rooms in East Melbourne the 'Institute of Rheumatology'. He wrote repeatedly (and sometimes publicly) to State and Federal ministers and to medical authorities, harassing them on medico-political issues, and he frequently expressed extreme religious and social views. These actions, however, should be seen as symptomatic of his manic-depressive illness.

In his last decade Kelly changed from being stimulatingly provocative to being merely disputatious and quarrelsome. He still worked hard, read widely, wrote much, and retained his membership of the Savage Club, but his manner formed a sad contrast to the heady days at Bunbury when he had also played tennis, golf and bowls, and was an important and admired member of society. Throughout his life he never lost his religious conviction and attended Mass each day, even in his final years. Survived by his wife, four sons and two of his four daughters, he died of myocardial degeneration on 5 April 1967 in his home at Kew and was buried in Boroondara cemetery.

R. Travers, 'Michael Kelly, MD (Adel.): Pioneer Australian Rheumatologist', in H. Attwood and G. Kenny (eds), *Reflections on Medical History and Health in Australia* (Melb, 1987); *MJA*, 9 Sept 1967; *Nation* (Syd), 7 Mar 1964; Aust Medical Assn (Vic Branch) Archives, Melb.

RICHARD TRAVERS

KELLY, ORRY GEORGE (1897-1964), dress designer, was born on 31 December 1897 at Kiama, New South Wales, son of William Kelly, a tailor from the Isle of Man, and his Sydney-born wife Florence Evaleen, née Purdue. Orry attended Kiama Public and Wollongong District schools. His distinctive first name (later hyphenated with his surname for professional use) was derived from a variety of carnation in his mother's garden and from that of an ancient Manx king. After working briefly in a Sydney bank, Kelly was attracted to the stage. He studied art, acting, dancing and voice, and became a protégé of Eleanor Weston. Moving to New York in 1921, he found employment first as a tailor's assistant, then as a painter of murals for nightclubs and department stores. He also formed a friendship with a young Englishman Archibald Leach, later known as Cary Grant, sharing living quarters with him and another Australian expatriate Charles ('Spangles') Phelps, a former ship's steward.

Kelly's murals soon led to employment as a title designer for silent films for the Fox Film Corporation, and to designing stage sets and costumes for players like Katharine Hepburn, Ethel Barrymore and Jeanette MacDonald. In 1931 he moved to Hollywood where Grant helped him to gain entry into First National Pictures Inc. Between 1932 and 1944 Orry-Kelly was chief costume designer at Warner Bros, working on hundreds of films and forming—with 'Adrian' at Metro-Goldwyn-Mayer and Travis Banton at Paramount Pictures Inc.—a triumvirate of the leading men in his profession. Kelly dressed many major stars, but his most distinguished work was done for Bette Davis, whose 'red' ball gown in the black-and-white film, *Jezebel* (1938), was probably his best-known single creation.

An uneasy relationship with studio chief Jack L. Warner, caused chiefly by Kelly's alcoholism, came to a head in 1944 when Warner discharged him. Orry-Kelly subsequently secured a three-year contract with Twentieth Century-Fox Film Corporation to dress Betty Grable. From 1950 he freelanced with several studios and established private workrooms. Despite declining health and mounting personal problems, he maintained his professional status, designing for Rosalind Russell, Leslie Caron, Kay Kendall, Shirley MacLaine and Natalie Wood among others. The Academy of Motion Picture Arts and Sciences awarded him three Oscars for best costume design for *An American in Paris* (1951, shared with two others), *Les Girls* (1957) and *Some Like It Hot* (1959).

A quarrelsome, hot-tempered man of slightly less than middle height, with brown hair and large blue eyes, Kelly was brilliant but difficult, a versatile perfectionist who used only the finest hand-finished fabrics. His period costumes were noted for their richness and authenticity; those he designed for

Davis helped to define her strongly individualized screen characters. His style was marked by its felicitous balance of realism and artifice, and achieved glamour without vulgarity. A talented amateur oil-painter, he also designed ties, cushions and shawls. He enjoyed contract bridge and watching prize-fights. Witty, popular and gregarious when not affected by alcohol, Kelly was known to his intimates as 'Jack'. He never married. Leaving an unfinished memoir, 'Women I've Undressed', he died of cancer on 26 February 1964 at Los Angeles and was cremated.

Filmlexicon degli Autori e dell Opere (Rome, 1962); W. Stine, *Mother Goddam* (NY, 1974) and *I'd Love to Kiss You* (NY, 1990); C. Higham, *Bette* (Lond, 1981) and *Cary Grant* (NY, 1989); W. R. LaVine, *In a Glamorous Fashion* (Lond, 1981); J. Finler, *The Hollywood Story* (Lond, 1989); S. Cook (ed), *International Dictionary of Films and Filmmakers*, 4 (Detroit, US, 1993); *Vogue Australia*, Jan 1994, p 162; *SMH*, 5 July 1934, 29 June, 1, 11 July 1939, 6, 21 May 1952; *New York Times*, 27 Feb 1964.   JOEL GREENBERG

KELLY, RAYMOND WILLIAM (1906-1977), detective, was born on 3 February 1906 at Wellington, New South Wales, eldest of six children of native-born parents Hugh Nicholas Kelly, a labourer who became a brewer, and his wife Agnes Constance, née Lynch. After leaving Wellington District School at the age of 15, Ray 'toughened up' in the Broken Hill mines. From there, he drifted through northern New South Wales and Queensland, working on various cattle properties. In Sydney on 3 July 1929 he fulfilled a childhood ambition by joining the New South Wales Police Force. A fit, solid man, almost six feet (183 cm) tall and weighing 12 st. 4 lb. (78 kg), he began probationary duties on foot patrol in the metropolitan area.

Five months later, while on bicycle patrol at Newtown, Kelly identified and chased a stolen car. The driver turned into a dead end, reversed, knocked Kelly off his bicycle and through a plate-glass window, and then attempted to run him down. Kelly managed to fire five shots at the car, killing one man and injuring the other two. His bravery earned him the first of eight commendations and the nickname, 'The Gunner'. In 1931 he again made headlines when, as part of the riot squad, he stormed a barricaded house at Newtown under a volley of gunfire during an eviction siege. In the ensuing mêlée his skull was fractured with an iron bar and he spent several weeks in hospital.

At St Mary's Catholic Cathedral, Sydney, on 8 April 1933 Kelly married Mary Philomena Agatha Barnes, a salesgirl. Promoted to constable (first class) in 1938, he was made a detective in 1941 and remained in plain clothes for the rest of his career. He was mainly based at the Criminal Investigation Branch and developed a reputation as a tough policeman who was cool under pressure. Priding himself on his extensive contacts among criminals, he believed that a detective was only as good as his informants. The nature of some of those contacts, however, as well as his later financial position, led to rumours and allegations of corruption, particularly after his death.

Even as a detective, Kelly cut a glamorous figure; he sported fine suits, wore spectacles and combed his slick, black hair back on his head. He was variously respected, admired, envied and hated. In February 1950 he arrested the armed robbers Darcy Dugan and William Mears for shooting a bank manager after breaking out of gaol. Dugan became notorious as an escapee and Kelly was to recapture him three more times. A number of criminals accused Kelly of obtaining confessions by verbal intimidation: Frederick 'Chow' Hayes (arrested by Kelly in 1952 for killing a former boxer Bobby Lee) yelled from the dock, 'I hope to live for the day when Kelly dies of cancer of the tongue'. Years later Hayes admitted committing the murder. In March 1953 Kelly, then head of the safe-breaking squad, encountered a bank robber Lloyd Day and two associates driving through Drummoyne. In the ensuing chase the police car was rammed and Kelly shot and killed the armed bandit. Kelly served in Queen Elizabeth II's bodyguard on her 1954 tour of Australia.

On occasions his persuasive manner made a gun unnecessary. In 1955 he boarded a cruise ship off Sydney Heads for a 'chat' with Billy Hill, an English gangster who had hoped to emigrate to New South Wales. Following their brief meeting, Hill remained on board and returned to England. Next year Kelly won the Peter Mitchell award for outstanding performance. In 1959 he led the successful hunt for two dangerous escapees Kevin Simmonds [q.v.] and Leslie Newcombe who had beaten a prison warder to death.

Promoted to inspector in 1960, Kelly continued to direct his network of informants with considerable effect, culminating in January 1966 in the recapture of two infamous Melbourne criminals wanted for murder, Ronald Ryan [q.v.] and Peter Walker. Less than a month later Kelly retired. More than eight hundred people—including politicians, judges, publicans, bookmakers, criminals and police—gave him a standing ovation when he addressed his farewell dinner. The premier (Sir) Robert Askin commented: 'no fictional detective could hold a candle to Ray Kelly'.

In retirement Kelly pursued real-estate interests and enjoyed playing golf. He also advised large commercial organizations on robbery prevention and designed a car alarm. In January 1975 he was appointed M.B.E. Survived by his wife and son, he died on 11 August 1977 at his Fairlight home and was cremated.

D. Hickie, *The Prince and the Premier* (Syd, 1985) and *Chow Hayes* (Syd, 1990); R. Hay, *Catch Me If You Can* (Syd, 1992); B. Jenkings, *As Crime Goes By* (Syd, 1992); Police Dept of NSW, *Report*, 1951, 1956, 1960, 1966, 1978; *SMH*, 20 Oct 1953, 25 Oct, 21 Nov 1959, 7, 9 Jan, 30 Sept 1966, 2 Jan 1975, 12 Aug 1977; *Daily Telegraph* (Syd), 19 Jan 1958, 4 Feb 1966, 12 Aug 1977; *Sunday Telegraph* (Syd), 25 Oct 1959; *Sun* (Syd), 16 Nov 1959, 7, 11-12 Jan 1966; *Mirror* (Syd), 18 Feb 1961, 4 Feb, 16 May 1966, 2 Jan 1975, 12, 15, 17 Aug 1977, 11 Mar 1980; *Sun-Herald* (Syd), 9 Jan 1966; Kelly police service record (NSW Police Media Unit, Syd); information from Mr R. Blissett, Five Dock, Mr B. Jenkings, Coogee, and Mrs F. Sedevic, Mona Vale, Syd.   SANDRA HARVEY

KELLY, SIR WILLIAM RAYMOND (1898-1956), industrial court judge, was born on 2 December 1898 at Calcutta, India, son of William Alfred Kelly, assistant-comptroller of the post office, and his wife Ethel Marian, née Johnston. Educated at St Xavier's College, Calcutta, and in Adelaide at the Christian Brothers' College (dux 1916), Ray entered the University of Adelaide (LL.B., 1920) where he won numerous prizes. He was admitted to the Bar on 20 April 1921 and practised at Yorketown (from 1922). In December 1924 he was elected mayor of the town. Appointed magistrate for the Port Augusta District in 1926, in the following year he became a special magistrate for South Australia. At St Ignatius' Catholic Church, Norwood, Adelaide, on 7 June 1928 he married Judith Nesbit.

In March 1930 Kelly was appointed deputy-president of the South Australian Industrial Court; on 18 September he was elevated to the presidency of the court and of the Board of Industry. As royal commissioner, he inquired into industrial problems on the Port Adelaide wharves (1930) and into a 'strike' by students at the Roseworthy Agricultural College (1932). He was appointed a judge of the Commonwealth Court of Conciliation and Arbitration in August 1941. Moving to Melbourne, he was a member of the committee (chaired by B. A. Santamaria) which published *Pattern for Peace* (1943), a plan for postwar reconstruction endorsed by the Catholic Church.

Appointed chief judge on 30 June 1949, Kelly frequently provoked controversy. He repudiated the use of back-room deals with the parties, maintaining that the court's decisions should be based not on expediency, but on an interpretation of the law and the evidence submitted. In contrast to his position that the court had 'no right to assume the role of reformer' and that 'theories and policies should play no part in its deliberations', in 1951-52 he advocated an incomes policy that aimed to curb inflation and redirect resources to rural production. His influence was largely responsible for the court's decision in 1953 to end automatic, quarterly, cost-of-living adjustments to the basic wage. By 1954 the minister for labour and national service Harold Holt [q.v.] was criticizing the 'rigidity' of the conciliation and arbitration system under Kelly's leadership.

Kelly had an independent mind, and was cultured and well read. Enjoying a variety of interests, he chaired (1936-41) the South Australian National Football League tribunal and wrote *A Primer of Australia's National Game* (1944). Contemporaries described him as scholarly and gentle, a person more suited to the relative peace and quiet of university life than the hurly-burly of industrial relations. While he was ostensibly friendly and told a good joke, he was enigmatic and often seemed apart—if not aloof—from those surrounding him. His breadth of knowledge and self-confidence gave the appearance of pompous superiority. In 1952 he was appointed K.B.E. Sir Raymond heard few cases after 1954 due to poor health. Survived by his wife and two sons, he died of acute hypertensive heart failure on 26 July 1956 in East Melbourne and was buried in Boroondara cemetery, Kew.

B. Dabscheck, *Arbitrator at Work* (Syd, 1983) and for sources; C. Larmour, *Labor Judge* (Syd, 1985).   BRAHAM DABSCHECK

3

CORRIGENDA
to accompany volume 14

Australian Dictionary of Biography

This list includes only corrigenda discovered since volume 13 was published in 1993. In making these corrections it is assumed that previous corrigenda have been noted. (The Index volume, published in 1991, includes consolidated corrigenda for volumes 1-12).

Only corrections are shown; additional information is not included; nor is any reinterpretation attempted. The exception to this procedure occurs when new details about parents, births, marriages and deaths become available.

Documented corrections are welcome from readers. Additional information, with sources, is also invited and will be placed in the appropriate files for future use.

1996

Volume 1: 1788-1850 A-H

21a   ANSTEY
line 20 *for* G. *read* John

27a   ARMYTAGE
line 14 *before* Thomas *insert* a former convict

32b   ARTHUR, G.
lines 3-4 *delete* Norley House,
line 5 *after* Arthur *insert* of Duck's Lane

33a   lines 1-2 *delete* On . . . Plymouth.
(amending consolidated corrigenda issued with Index)

37b   line 7 *for* 1844 *read* March 1846
line 9 *delete* in 1846

61b   BARRALLIER
line 1 *for* LUIS *read* LOUIS
line 33 *for* off *read* in
line 46 for *Royal* read *King*

62a   lines 52-53 *for* discovery *read* hearing
lines 61-62 *for* returned . . . and *read* left Sydney in May, having

62b   line 13 *for* at *read* in 1809, participated in the invasion of
line 21 *for* 1818 *read* 1817
line 26 *after* 1846. *insert* On 31 July 1819 he had married Isobel Skyrme at St Mary's, Lambeth, Surrey.

94a   BERRY
line 28 *for* tural *read* cultural
line 39 *for* were *read* was

122b   BLOSSEVILLE
line 7 *for* inque *read* ingue

140b   BOYD, B.
line 1 *for* 1803? *read* 1801
line 2 *after* born *insert* on 21 August 1801

151b   BRISBANE
line 26 *for* 1814 *read* 1815
line 32 *after* K.C.H. *insert* (G.C.H., 1831).

157b   BROOKS
line 5 *for* son *read* sons Richard and
(amending consolidated corrigenda issued with Index)
lines 6-7 *delete* , and . . . Blomfield,
line 8 *after* ; *insert* his daughter Christiana married Thomas Valentine Blomfield;

187b   BUSBY
line 44 *for* of *read* for

217a   CHAPMAN, I.
line 40 *after* 1829 *insert* , within a month of his wife's death,

225b   CLARK, R.
line 1 *for* d. *read* 1762-
lines 2-3 *for* , the year unrecorded *read* 1762 in Edinburgh, son of George Clark, gentleman's servant, and his wife Ann, née Man

226b   lines 24-25 *for* in the same . . . killed *read* on 30 June, in the same ship in which his father had died twelve days earlier

235b   COLLIE
line 37 *for* Kamschatka *read* Kamchatka

247b   CORY
lines 8-9 *for* a . . . captain *read* his father
line 12 *for* brother *read* father
lines 15-16 *for* the brothers *read* they

285b   DARLING
line 56 *for* Tory's *read* Tories'

314b   DOUGLASS
line 5 *delete* which . . . found,

328a   DRUMMOND
line 7 *for* Angus *read* Angas

349a   EARLE
lines 44-45 *for* 'the frank licentiousness of his manners' *read* 'his open licentiousness',

409a   FOVEAUX
line 57 *for* In 1815 *read* On 17 November 1814
lines 60-61 *for* Judging . . . children. *read* His daughter Ann predeceased him.

416b   FRAZER
line 4 *for* served *read* enlisted
line 5 *delete* in . . . Indies

451a   GIPPS
line 64 *after* for *insert* dividing

524a   HAWDON
line 2 *for* baptized on 15 December 1813 *read* born on 14 November 1813
(amending corrigenda published with volume 13)
line 58 *for* 1854 *read* 1853

550a   HOLT
lines 5-6 *for* another *read* a
line 9 *after* . *insert* About 1797 he joined the United Irishmen.
line 13 *delete* and . . . Irishmen
line 14 *for* Inactive *read* Active
line 15 *delete* emerged . . . June,
line 31 *for* family *read* wife and son

line 3 *before* 1858 *insert* 9 December

209a BATES
line 13 *for* 1930 *read* 1932

371b BOYD, A. M.
line 11 *for* early 1880s *read* mid 1870s

439a BROWN, H. Y. L.
line 2 *for* 1844 *read* 1843
line 3 *for* 1844 *read* 1843 *and after* Sydney *insert* Mines
line 7 *for* taught . . . matriculating *read* matriculated

439b line 1 *for* 1859 *read* 1862

542a CAMPBELL, Allan
line 7 *delete* homoeopathic
line 8 *delete* &

542b line 33 *for* treatment *read* diagnosis

Volume 8: 1891-1939 Cl-Gib

83b CONACHER
line 62 *for* main *read* man

198a DALLEY-SCARLETT
line 19 *for* 21st *read* 20th

198b line 45 *for* Pier *read* Peir

368a DUNCAN
line 34 *delete* [q.v.]

431a ELLIOTT, J.
line 13 *for* implements *read* instruments

459a FAIRBAIRN, S.
line 8 *for* Grammer *read* Grammar

470a FARRELL
line 25 *for* Mackade *read* Macknade

493a FIDLER
line 59 *for* Studies *read* Study

585a FREEMAN
line 40 *for* Sergeev *read* Sergeyev

588a FRENCH
line 46 *for* it *read* its

592a FROST
line 20 *for* 1817 *read* 1917

Volume 9: 1891-1939 Gil-Las

18b GILRUTH
line 8 *for* J. D. J. *read* D. J. D.

31b GLYNN
line 59 *delete* three

371a HOSKINS
line 4 *for* April *read* March
line 5 *for* third *read* second

372a line 54 *for* built a *read* produced *and delete* furnace

372b line 9 *for* in an *read* after an
line 19 *for* £12 108 *read* £12 018
line 33 *for* Gwynne *read* Gwynn
line 36 *for* 1872 *read* 1892

392a HUGHES, G.
line 21 *for* Australian *read* Australia

427a IFOULD
line 9 *for* Eugene *read* Eugenie
line 10 *for* 1969 *read* 1955

650b LAMBERT
line 50 *after* and *insert* one of
line 51 *for* self-portrait *read* self-portraits

Volume 10: 1891-1939 Lat-Ner

69b LEIGHTON
line 40 *for* Meteorological Laboratory *read* metrology section of the Munitions Supply Laboratories

70a bibliog. line 2 *delete* British

484b MENNELL
line 50 *for* Wilfred *read* Wilfrid

Volume 11: 1891-1939 Nes-Smi

143b PARKINSON
line 46 *for* A. *read* M.

539a SCHULER
lines 1-2 *for* FREDERICH HENRY (1854 *read* (FREDERICK) HEINRICH (1853
line 3 *for* 24 February 1854 in *read* 23 February 1853 at Heimerdingen,
line 4 *for* Johann Frederich *read* Jacob Friderich
line 5 *for* Catherine Christiana, née Fry. Fred *read* Christine Catharine, née Frey. He

539b line 1 *for* aged 2 *read* about 1860
line 12 *before* Schuler *insert* Frederick

561b SEE
line 55 *for* Waverley *read* Randwick

580b SHARP, G.
line 2 *for* bishop *read* archbishop

598b SHIERS
line 2 *for* Australian Flying *read* Air Force

665a SMITH
line 52 *for* J. C. *read* J. E.

Volume 3: 1851-1890 A-C

212a BOYCE
line 11 *for* G. W. *read* George

248a BROOME
lines 29-30 *for* poems ... setting *read* verse

470b COUVREUR
line 17 *for* 1874 *read* 1873
line 18 *for* them *read* her mother

471a line 5 *for* sisters *read* sister
(amending consolidated corrigenda issued with Index)

Volume 4: 1851-1890 D-J

75b DIXON
line 1 *for* 1832 *read* 1836
line 2 *after* born *insert* on 9 August 1836 at Meanwood,

82a DODERY
bibliog. line 3 *for* 28 *read* 27

176a FITZGERALD
line 2 *after* , *insert* merchant and politician,

191a FLOOD
line 51 *for* four *read* three

243b GIBLIN
line 16 *for* Emily *read* Emmely

299b GRIBBLE
line 46 *for* 1869 *read* 1868

310b GUTHRIE
line 48 *for* 1918 *read* 1916

315b HAINES
line 11 *delete* about 1841

385b HERLITZ
line 16 *for* as *read* at

386a HERZ
lines 2-3 *for* Mecklenberg-Schwerin *read* Mecklenburg, Schwerin

446a HUNT
lines 2-3 *for* born ... in *read* baptized at Brighton, Sussex,
line 4 *after* wife *insert* Mary Ann

Volume 5: 1851-1890 K-Q

105a LOUREIRO
line 3 *for* Academie des Beaux Arts *read* Ecole des Beaux-Arts

137b McCRAE
line 55 *after* by *insert* four of

282a MOORHOUSE
line 31 *for* detatch *read* detach

303a MOSMAN
line 2 *for* April *read* February

378a OSBURN
line 7 *for* 1880 *read* 1881

392a PALMER
line 50 *for* 19 *read* 20 *and for* Eastern *read* Easton
line 51 *for* Grey *read* Gray

Volume 6: 1851-1890 R-Z

17b REID
lines 13-14 *for* its ... 1832 *read* 1834

95a SCOTT, E.
line 1 *for* MONTAGUE *read* MONTAGU

146b SMITH, James (1827-1897)
line 3 *for* at *read* near
line 4 *for* eldest child *read* second of three children
line 5 *delete* Mary

222b SUTHERLAND
line 14 *after* returned *insert* from Dromana
line 23 *for* September 1901 *read* February 1902

438b WOOLNER
line 16 *for* modelled *relievo read* cast reliefs

441b WRIGHT
line 11 *delete* briefly

Volume 7: 1891-1939 A-Ch

13b ADCOCK
line 32 *for* resulting *read* which, he claimed, resulted
lines 39-40 *for* and his brother and Brown were *read* was

32b ALEXANDER
line 2 *for* physiotherapist *read* founder of the Alexander technique
line 17 *for* the early *read* some months in 1894

33a line 1 *delete* 1890s
line 2 *for* but in 1894 *read* then

112b ASHTON, Sir J.
line 18 *for* des Artists *read* de la Société des Artistes

124b AUSTRAL
line 1 *for* 1894 *read* 1892
line 2 *for* 1894 *read* 1892
line 25 *for* 25 *read* 27

149b BAKER
line 6 *for* Belisarious *read* Belisarius

176a BARLOW, C.
line 2 *for* in *read* on

550b line 50 *for* Dunleer *read* Dunleary
line 54 *for* John *read* Joshua
lines 54-55 *delete* and . . . 1799)
line 56 *after* descendants *insert* , and
Joseph Harrison (b.1799)

556a HOVELL
line 3 *after* Yarmouth, *insert* Norfolk,

560a HOWE
lines 2-3 *for* at Redbourne . . .
Howe. *read* probably at Redbourn,
Hertfordshire, England, son of John
How and his wife Mary, née
Roberts.

578a HUXLEY
line 2 *for* Port Essington *read* Cape
York

Volume 2: 1788-1850 I-Z

23a JONES
line 14 *after* died. *insert* On 10 September 1822 he married Elizabeth
Williams (d.1826).

24a line 1 *for* second *read* third

90b LA TROBE
line 38 *for* in 1844 *read* in 1844-
49

121a LOANE
line 62 *for* this house *read* another
house, also named Belle Vue,

140b LYCETT
lines 31-33 *delete* travelled . . .
also

216b MATHER
lines 9-10 *for* 1834 . . . became
members *read* 1837 Mather became a member

216b MAUM
line 1 *delete* (MAUGHAM)
line 2 *for* 1778 *read* 1780
line 3 *before* arrived *insert* was born
on 6 January 1780. He
lines 13-14 *delete* It . . . New

217a lines 1-7 *delete* South . . . 1803.
lines 31-32 *delete* , accompanied . . .
children
lines 53-60 *delete* may . . . he
lines 62-64 *delete* In . . . Diemen's

217b lines 1-2 *delete* Land . . . Plains.
lines 6-7 *for* second . . . Bignell,
read wife Mary (b.1789)
bibliog. line 2 *delete* , 20 Nov
1819

238a MITCHELL, T.
line 3 *for* Craigend *read* Grange-
mouth

269a MURDOCH, J.
bibliog. line 3 *for* 3885 *read* 3994

340a POLDING
line 3 *for* October *read* November

353b PROUT
line 1 *for* 1806 *read* 1805
line 2 *for* probably *read* on 19 December 1805
line 3 *delete* , of Nonconformist
parents
lines 7-10 *for* About . . . 1831. *read*
On 19 June 1828 Prout married
Maria Heathilla Marsh at Colaton
Raleigh, Devon.

354b line 3 *delete* second

394a ROSE, T.
line 2 *for* 1854 *read* 1754
(amending corrigenda published
with volume 13)

402a ROUSE
line 10 *for* the second boy *read* one
of the first boys

458a SOLOMON, J.
line 2 *after* merchant *insert* , son of
Abraham Solomon,
line 4 *for* in London *read* at Sheer-
ness, England,

502b TALBOT
line 60 *for* Robdard *read* Rodbard

527a THOMSON
line 6 *for* premier *read* colonial secretary

530b THROSBY
line 49 *for* south-west *read* south-
east

536b TOWNSON
line 1 *for* 1760 *read* 1759?
lines 2-3 *for* came . . . was *read* was
probably baptized on 4 November
1759 at Clapham, Yorkshire, England. He was the son of John Townson, merchant, and

537b TOWNSON, R.
line 1 *for* 1763 *read* 1762?
lines 2-5 *for* came from . . . His *read*
was probably baptized on 4 April
1762 at Richmond, Surrey, England, son of John Townson, merchant. Robert's
line 16 *delete* (D.C.L., 1795)

576a WEDGE
line 31 *for* in . . . year *read* (1885).
In 1836

583b WENTWORTH
line 17 *for* Raratonga *read* Raro-
tonga

Volume 12: 1891-1939 Smy-Z

5b   SMYTHE
line 8 *for* Elva *read* Elsa

22a   SOUTHERN
line 1 *for* 1862 *read* 1860
line 2 *for* 23 July 1862 *read* 3 October 1860
lines 3-5 *for* eighth ... Northumberland, *read* third surviving child of John Southern, farmer, and his wife Jane, née Elliott, both from

29a   SPENCE, J.
line 6 *for* 11 *read* 8
line 7 *before* sent *read* later
line 25 *for* 20 *read* 26

130b   STUART
line 18 *delete* from 1891

131b   line 8 *for* 1913 *read* 1914

177a   TAYLOR, G.
line 3 *for* Balgonie *read* Balgownie

259b   TRENWITH
line 59 *for* Peacock [q.v.11] *read* Turner [q.v.]
line 60 *after* 1901-02 *insert* under (Sir) Alexander Peacock [q.v.11]

274a   TUCK
line 21 *delete* Étables,

322b   VERNON
bibliog. line 17 *for* 1889 *read* 1899

408b   WATSON
line 41 *delete* A.I.F. reinforcements and

437b   WEINGARTH
line 2 *for* Kenny *read* Canny
line 47 *for* J. *read* John
line 49 *delete* Royal

Index

144a   PLACES OF BIRTH
line 50 *delete* Müller, Frederick, 10

145a   PLACES OF BIRTH
after line 6 *insert* Müller, Frederick, 10

170a   OCCUPATIONS
after line 8 *insert* Sharp, Gerald, 11

175a   OCCUPATIONS
line 62 *delete* Sharp, Gerald, 11

Volume 13: 1940-1980 A-De

28b   ALLAN, N.
line 31 *for* Thorn *read* Thorne

33a   ALLEN, W.
line 11 *for* New ... Wales *read* on the New South Wales border

36a   ALLNUTT
line 14 *for* Denholm *read* Denham

55a   ANDERSON
bibliog. line 10 *delete* Aust
bibliog. line 11 *for* SLV *read* LaTL

63a   ANTON
line 45 *after* October *insert* 1960

78a   ASHKANASY
line 32 *for* After *read* Before

140b   BEASLEY, F.
line 33 *for* daughter, *read* son,

170b   BENSON
line 52 *for* 1940 *read* 1946

172b   BERRICK
line 1 *for* 1905 *read* 1904
line 3 *for* 1905 *read* 1904

192b   BLACKBURN
lines 9-10 *for* Aborigine *read* Aborigines

194b   BLAIR
line 43 *for* Aboriginal *read* Aborigines

253a   BRENNAN
line 40 *for* Service *read* Flying

258b   BRIGGS
bibliog. line 2 *for* . *read* (New Jersey)

273b   BROWN, G.
line 35 *for* Labour *read* Labor

283a   BROWNELL
line 15 *for* personal *read* personnel

291a   BUKOWSKI
line 11 *after* his *insert* alleged

297a   BUNNING
line 28 *for* 1939 *read* 1940
line 29 *after* councillor *insert* ,
line 30 *for* 1939-42 *read* New South Wales chapter, 1940-44
line 32 *for* Bunnning *read* Bunning

304a   BURKE, J.
line 33 *after* Vinton *delete* ,

309a   BURNE
line 34 *after* built *insert* or extended
line 35 *before* Melbourne *insert* Royal

311b   BURNELL
line 21 *after* wife, *insert* and the children of his first marriage,

436b   CLARK, J. (1885-1956)
line 23 *for* Burnett *read* Burnet

474b   COLMAN
bibliog. line 6 *for* R. D. *read* R. S.